ARIADNE'S THREAD

A volume in the series

MYTH AND POETICS

edited by GREGORY NAGY

A full list of titles in the series appears at the end of the book.

WILLIAM HANSEN

ARIADNE'S THREAD

A GUIDE TO INTERNATIONAL TALES

FOUND IN CLASSICAL LITERATURE

CORNELL UNIVERSITY PRESS

ITHACA AND LONDON

First published 2002 by Cornell University Press

Printed in the United States of America

LIBRARY OF CONGRESS CATALOGING-IN-PUBLICATION DATA

Hansen, William F., 1941–
 Ariadne's thread : a guide to international tales found in classical literature / by William Hansen.
 p. cm. — (Myth and poetics)
 Includes bibliographical references and index.
 ISBN 0–8014–3670–2 (cloth : alk. paper)
 1. Tales—Classification. 2. Folk literature—Classification. 3. Folk literature—Classical influences. 4. Folk literature—History and criticism. 5. Classical literature—History and criticism. I. Title. II. Series.
 GR74.6 .H35 2002
 398.2'01'2—dc21 2001002434

Cornell University Press strives to use environmentally responsible suppliers and materials to the fullest extent possible in the publishing of its books. Such materials include vegetable-based, low-VOC inks and acid-free papers that are recycled, totally chlorine-free, or partly composed of nonwood fibers. Books that bear the logo of the FSC (Forest Stewardship Council) use paper taken from forests that have been inspected and certified as meeting the highest standards for environmental and social responsibility. For further information, visit our website at www.cornellpress.cornell.edu.

Cloth printing 10 9 8 7 6 5 4 3 2 1

CONTENTS

Foreword *by Gregory Nagy* ix

Preface xi

Abbreviations xiii

Introduction 1

 The Comparative Study of the Folktale 1

 The Study of Greek and Roman Folk Narratives 6

 Oral Narratives and Oral Narration in Classical Antiquity 12

 The Present Work 19

The Tales

Apprentice and Ghost ✺ Eukrates and the Automaton 35

Asking the Large Fish ✺ Philoxenos the Poet 38

Attentive Donkey 40

Axe Falls into the Stream ✺ Hermes and the Woodcutter 42

Battles of the Pygmies and the Cranes 45

Best Friend, Worst Enemy ✺ Aesop and the Dog 49

Boastful Deer Slayer ✺ Agamemnon 54

Bride Won in a Tournament ✺ Pelops and Hippodameia 56

Brother Chosen Rather Than Husband ✺ Intaphrenes' Wife 62

Carrying Part of the Load ✺ Dionysos and Xanthias 66

Carrying Water in a Sieve 🦢 Danaides 69

Catch-Tale 🦢 Demades the Orator 75

Children Play at Hog Killing 🦢 Makareus the Priest 79

Cinderella 🦢 Rhodopis the Courtesan 85

Cranes of Ibykos 89

Dead Child's Friendly Return 🦢 The Dead Ask the Living to
 Cease Grieving 92

Death's Messengers 95

Devil to Count Stars 🦢 Counting Sand, Stars, Waves 97

Disenchanted Husband 🦢 Cupid and Psyche 100

Dog on the Bridge 🦢 Alexander and the Donkey Driver 114

Dragging Old Man Only to Threshold 117

Dragon Slayer 🦢 Perseus 119

Fairies Send a Message 🦢 Death of Pan 131

Foolish Fugitives 136

Foolish Man Builds Aircastles 🦢 Gripus 138

Fortune in Salt 🦢 Fortune in Water 142

Frog King 🦢 Roman Proverb 145

Frozen Words 146

Gifts of the Little People 🦢 Pandaros and Echedoros 147

Girl as Helper 🦢 Jason and Medeia 151

God and the Emperor of Rome 🦢 Zeus and Tantalos 167

Golden Ram 🦢 Trojan Horse 169

Great Animal or Object 176

Groom Teaches His Horse to Live without Food 187

Hatch-Penny 🦢 Pases' Penny 188

Hearing-Impaired Persons 190

Holding Up the Rock 🦢 Holding Up the Sky 197

Homecoming Husband 🦢 Odysseus 201

Hospitality Rewarded 🦢 Mercury and the Stingy Women 211

House Burned Down to Rid It of Insects 🦢 Shirt Burnt to Rid It
 of Lice 223

Husband's One Good Eye Covered ❧ Husband's Attention Diverted 225

Judgment of Solomon 227

Keep Your Seats! ❧ Prince the Flutist 233

Labor Contract ❧ Aesop and Xanthos 234

Learn to Swim 240

Loading the Wood ❧ Sorites 241

Local Moon 242

Lord's Prayer ❧ Sisyphos and Thanatos 243

Magic Object and the Trolls ❧ Perseus 246

Maiden's Honor ❧ Maiden's Sense 251

Maids Must Rise Even Earlier 255

Making a Rope of Sand 256

Man Does Not Recognize His Own Reflection 257

Man Swallowed by Fish ❧ Lucian 261

Marrying a Man of Forty ❧ Returning a Donkey 264

Matron of Ephesus 266

Money in the Stick 279

Mother Dies of Fright ❧ Secundus the Philosopher 284

Nothing to Cook ❧ Nothing to Eat 287

Ogre Blinded ❧ Odysseus and Polyphemos 289

Ogre Kills His Own Children ❧ Aedon 301

Ogre Steals the Thunder's Instruments ❧ Typhon and Zeus 305

Old Man and Death 314

Our Lady's Child ❧ Gyges and Kroisos 316

Person Does Not Know Himself 327

Peter Stung by Bees ❧ Man Bitten by Ants 329

Planting for the Next Generation 331

Potiphar's Wife ❧ Hippolytos and Phaidra 332

Quest for a Vanished Princess ❧ Apollo of the Vultures 352

Rhampsinitos 357

Sailor and the Oar ❧ Odysseus 371

Schlaraffenland 🍃 Glutton's Paradise 378

Service in Hell 🍃 Philinnion and Machates 392

Seven Sleepers 🍃 Epimenides of Crete 397

Shepherd Who Cried "Wolf!" 402

Slaughter of the Ox 404

Smith and the Devil 🍃 Sisyphos and Thanatos 405

Son of the King and of the Smith 🍃 Kyros 408

Sowing of Salt 🍃 Odysseus 414

Stronger and Strongest 415

Sunlight Carried in a Bag 🍃 Perdikkes 424

Three Brothers 🍃 Roman Proverb 426

Three Joint Depositors 🍃 Demosthenes 427

Three Lazy Ones 🍃 Lazy Debtor and Creditor 429

Threefold Death 🍃 The Hermaphrodite 431

To Sacrifice a Giant Candle 🍃 To Sacrifice a Hecatomb 435

Topsy-Turvy Land 🍃 Mundus Inversus 439

Tree Trunks Laid Crosswise 🍃 Beam Carried Crosswise 445

Trespasser's Defense 🍃 The Lokrians' Oath 447

Twins or Blood Brothers 🍃 Menaechmi 450

Underground Passage to Paramour's House 🍃 Miles Gloriosus 453

Unfinished Tale 🍃 "And Then I Woke Up" 460

White Serpent's Flesh 🍃 Melampous the Seer 462

Wisdom of Hidden Old Man Saves Kingdom 469

Wishing Contest 475

Wooden Doll 🍃 Homo 478

Youth Who Bathed Himself in Blood 🍃 Achilleus's Heel 481

Bibliography 491
Index of Ancient Sources 533
Index of Tale Types and Motifs 539
General Index 543

FOREWORD

GREGORY NAGY

Ariadne's Thread, by William Hansen, combines two distinct humanistic points of interest, classics and folklore. The author himself is both a classicist and a folklorist. Such a combination is relatively rare in the history of scholarship partly because the field of classics tends to be associated with "high art," which invites contrast with "low art" as studied in the newer field of folkloristics. Even the terms *folklore*, *folklorist*, and *folkloristics* evoke an uneasy sense of incompatibility with standard notions associated with the classics, such as artistic perfectionism, literary learnedness, even literacy itself. Whereas the field of classics centers on feats of creativity that strike us as extraordinary or even unique, folklore exemplifies processes of production that may at first seem ordinary by contrast. But the contrast is not so much between the extraordinary and the ordinary, the unique and the nonunique. Rather, it is between what tends toward the singular and what is inherently multiple. Moreover, the multiplicity of folkloristic evidence is precisely what makes it so valuable to classicists. The study of multiple versions, as perfected within the discipline of folkloristics, leads to an understanding of eventually unified choices in form and content. The labyrinthine multiformity of varying directions in folklore leads to the singular directedness of classical models.

The inherent variety of form and content in folklore makes folkloristics particularly suited to the study of variants and of variation itself as a cultural phenomenon. Despite the uneasiness of many humanists with *folklore* and its derivatives to refer to the discipline, no better word has replaced it. In fact, the legacy of multiformity in the use of the word folklore guarantees its survival as the most telling expression of the true sense of the discipline.

The point of departure for *Ariadne's Thread* is the comparison of narratives or tales that may or may not be historically related. The techniques of comparison resemble those of descriptive linguistics, in which the comparison of historically unrelated linguistic phenomena is termed a typology. Typological comparisons between systems yield insights into the inner workings of each system

under examination. In *Ariadne's Thread*, the insights we gain center on the multiform world of ancient Greek and Roman tales, and they are enhanced by comparison with tales from myriad other worlds both familiar and unfamiliar to the classical legacy.

PREFACE

Traditional stories—folktales, legends, and myths—are works of verbal art that human beings deploy in different social and literary situations for a variety of purposes such as entertainment, sensation, instruction, persuasion, consolation, justification, clarification, edification, and the exploration of feelings and beliefs. In the repertory of a storytelling community, which is to say probably in every human community, two kinds of narrative are found, local stories that circulate in the immediate region and migratory stories that are told also in neighboring communities and sometimes in distant lands as well. Some migratory narratives have been in existence for centuries or even millennia and in light of their longevity must rank among the world's most successful artistic creations, springing from host to host like elegantly adapted microorganisms. Since such stories tend not to be fixed in form, each text manifests variations in detail that reflect in interesting ways the culture and time and occasion in which it finds itself, the particular narrator who hosts and transmits it, and the audience that hears or reads it.

This book deals with international narratives that are attested in ancient Greek and Latin literature, including writings penned in these languages by Egyptians, Jews, and others. Although some of these texts are conveniently gathered together in collections of myths, legends, jokes, fables, anecdotes, and the like made by ancient authors, most of them lurk in less obvious places such as in epics, tragedies, comedies, lyric poems, philosophic works, histories, travelers' reports, essays, biographies, novels, religious works, and testimonial inscriptions. The present work contains nearly a hundred essays, or entries, each devoted to a single story type (or cluster of related types) or on a few occasions to a single motif, in which I characterize the international tradition in general, describe its ancient realizations in particular, and explore the nature and relationship of the ancient and modern traditions.

I have benefited at times from the help, encouragement, or friendship of Pack Carnes, Linda Dégh, Hasan El-Shamy, Henry Glassie, Mary Beth Hannah-

Hansen, the late Bengt Holbek, Gregory Nagy, Gregory Schrempp, the late Alex Scobie, Josep Sobrer, Hans-Jörg Uther, and my occasional research assistants Moira Smith and Byron Stayskal. I thank Indiana University for several grants and fellowships that were given in support of this project, the American Council of Learned Societies for the award of fellowships on two occasions (1977–78, 1992), the staff of the *Enzyklopädie des Märchens* and that of the Danish Folklore Archives for help in locating certain texts, and the Indiana University Institute for Advanced Study for my tenure as a fellow.

I gratefully dedicate this book to my teachers, especially to three of them, the late mythologist Joseph Fontenrose, the folklorist Alan Dundes, and the philologist George Koniaris.

WILLIAM HANSEN

Bloomington, Indiana

ABBREVIATIONS

AASH	*Acta Antiqua Academiae Scientiarum Hungaricae.*
AJP	*American Journal of Philology.*
ANET	*Ancient Near Eastern Texts Relating to the Old Testament.* Edited by James B. Pritchard. 2d ed. Princeton: Princeton University Press, 1955.
ARW	*Archiv für Religionswissenschaft.*
Ashliman	D. L. Ashliman. *A Guide to Folktales in the English Language. Based on the Aarne-Thompson Classification System.* New York: Greenwood, 1987.
AT	Antti Aarne and Stith Thompson. *The Types of the Folktale: A Classification and Bibliography.* 2d rev. FFC 184. Helsinki: Academia Scientiarum Fennica, 1961.
BP	Johannes Bolte and Georg Polívka. *Anmerkungen zu den Kinder- und Hausmärchen der Brüder Grimm.* 5 vols. Leipzig: Dieterich'sche Verlagsbuchhandlung, 1913–32.
C & M	*Classica et Mediaevalia.*
CJ	*Classical Journal.*
CPG	*Corpus Paroemiographorum Graecorum.* Edited by E. L. Leutsch and F. G. Schneidewin. 2 vols. Göttingen: Vandenhoeck & Ruprecht, 1839–51. Reprint: Hildesheim: Georg Olms Verlag, 1958.
CPh	*Classical Philology.*
CQ	*Classical Quarterly.*
CR	*Classical Review.*
CW	*Classical World.*
Dvořák	Karel Dvořák. *Soupis Staročeských Exempel. Index Exemplorum Paleobohemicorum. Acta Universitatis Carolinae, Philosophica et Historica Monographia,* no. 72. Prague: Univerzita Karlova, 1978.
EM	*Enzyklopädie des Märchens: Handwörterbuch zur historischen und vergleichenden Erzählforschung.* Edited by Kurt Ranke et al. Berlin: Walter de Gruyter, 1977–.

FFC *Folklore Fellows Communications.*

FGH *Die Fragmente der griechischen Historiker.* Edited by Felix Jacoby. Berlin: Weidmannsche Buchhandlung; Leiden: E. J. Brill, 1923–58.

G & R *Greece and Rome.*

GRBS *Greek, Roman, and Byzantine Studies.*

Grimm Individual tales cited by number in standard editions of the *Kinder- und Hausmärchen* of the Brothers Grimm.

HDM *Handwörterbuch des deutschen Märchens.* Edited by Johannes Bolte and Lutz Mackensen. 2 vols. Berlin: Walter de Gruyter, 1930–40.

HSCP *Harvard Studies in Classical Philology.*

Hsr *Corpus Fabularum Aesopicarum.* Edited by August Hausrath. Vol. 1, fasc. 1–2. 2d ed. Edited by Herbert Hunger. Leipzig: B. G. Teubner, 1959–70.

IG *Inscriptiones Graecae.*

JAF *Journal of American Folklore.*

JFI *Journal of the Folklore Institute.*

JFR *Journal of Folklore Research.*

JHS *Journal of Hellenic Studies.*

K.-A. *Poetae Comici Graeci.* Edited by R. Kassel and C. Austin. Berlin: Walter de Gruyter, 1983–.

LIMC *Lexicon Iconographicum Mythologiae Classicae.* Edited by Hans Christoph Ackermann and Jean-Robert Gisler. 8 vols. Zurich: Artemis, 1981–97.

LSJ Henry George Liddell and Robert Scott. *A Greek-English Lexicon.* 9th ed. Oxford: Clarendon, 1940.

MCSN *Materiali e Contributi per la Storia della Narrativa Greco-Latina.*

ML Reidar Christiansen. *The Migratory Legends: A Proposed List of Types with a Systematic Catalogue of the Norwegian Variants.* FFC 175. Helsinki: Academia Scientiarum Fennica.

Motif Stith Thompson. *A Motif-Index of Folk-Literature: A Classification of Narrative Elements in Folktales, Ballads, Myths, Fables, Mediaeval Romances, Exempla, Fabliaux, Jest-Books and Local Legends.* Rev. ed. 6 vols. Bloomington: Indiana University Press, 1955–58.

Nauck Augustus Nauck, ed. *Tragicorum Graecorum Fragmenta.* 2d ed. 2 vols. Leipzig: B. G. Teubner, 1889.

Perry Ben E. Perry. *Aesopica: A Series of Texts Relating to Aesop or Ascribed to Him or Closely Connected with the Literary Tradition That Bears His Name.* Urbana: University of Illinois Press, 1952.

PMG *Poetae Melici Graeci.* Edited by D. L. Page. Oxford: Clarendon, 1962.

PMLA *Publications of the Modern Language Association.*

RE *Real-Enzyklopädie der classischen Altertumswissenschaft.* Edited by A. Pauly, G. Wissowa, et al. Stuttgart: J. B. Metzler, 1893–.

REG *Revue des Études Grecques.*

RhM *Rheinisches Museum für Philologie.*

Roscher *Ausführliches Lexikon der griechischen und römischen Mythologie.* Edited by W. H. Roscher. 7 vols. Leipzig: B. G. Teubner, 1884–37.

RTP	*Revue des Traditions Populaires.*
SAV	*Schweizerisches Archiv für Volkskunde.*
Schol.	scholiast, scholium.
TAPA	*Transactions of the American Philological Association.*
TGF	*Tragicorum Graecorum Fragmenta.* Edited by R. Kannicht, S. Radt, and B. Snell. Göttingen: Vandenhoeck & Ruprecht, 1971–86.
WF	*Western Folklore.*
WS	*Wiener Studien.*
ZVV	*Zeitschrift des Vereins für Volkskunde.*

Ariadne's Thread

INTRODUCTION

The scholarly world discovered the folktale in the nineteenth century. Before that time there was little serious interest in the phenomenon of oral tales, which were generally viewed by learned persons as a form of amusement proper to simple or uneducated persons, or to children, none of whom had much to teach the rest of us. Accordingly no one thought long about the nature of such stories, no one wondered about how old they were or where they came from, no one asked what they meant to their tellers and listeners.

But in the early nineteenth century, scholars driven by a romantic interest in the folk began to collect and publish folktales and to compare the tales of different places and times, whereupon they made surprising discoveries about the geographical breadth and the historical depth of many folktales. First, oral narrators who were separated by great distances and spoke different languages often told folktales that resembled each other so much that some kind of genetic relationship between the tales had to be assumed. Second, living folktales were often so similar in structure and content to narratives appearing in written sources of the Renaissance, Middle Ages, and even classical antiquity, as well as in the great literary collections of tales originating in the Orient, that it was necessary to suppose a genetic relationship between some of the oral tales of the present day and those of earlier times. In sum, many oral stories were international in their distribution and of such antiquity as to rank among the oldest known narratives in the world. The discovery of this astonishing extension in a phenomenon apparently so humble and familiar as the folktale was unexpected and revolutionary, and no obvious explanation was at hand.

The Comparative Study of the Folktale

The comparative study of the international oral tale began in the early years of the nineteenth century when the brothers Jacob and Wilhelm Grimm published a collection of folktales in two volumes, *Kinder-und Hausmärchen* (1812–15). In the preface and notes to their work they addressed many issues

that have engaged students of folk narrative ever since. These included the methodology of collecting and publishing oral texts and of documenting their relationship to the larger tradition, the question of how old and widespread the telling of folktales is, the question of oral genres, and the problem of the presence of similar stories among different peoples present and past, along with the related problems of continuity and change in oral narrative.

The Grimms said that all their folktales, with a few exceptions, were collected from oral tradition; that they tried to keep the tales as pure as possible by not adding or embellishing or changing anything; and that no such collection existed at that time in Germany, since it was almost always the case that authors, viewing oral tales only as raw material for literary treatment, freely enlarged and modified the originals.[1] The Grimms distinguished folktales (*Märchen*) from local legends (*locale Volkssagen*), characterizing the former as migratory narratives that traveled from place to place and changed in the telling, and the latter as stories that were bound to real localities or attached to historical heroes; moreover, legends were more serious and more historical than folktales. In the preface to the collection of German legends that they published a few years later, they aphoristically described the folktale as more poetic, the legend as more historical.[2]

The Grimms observed that, while tales were constantly renewed in the telling, their base must be very old, for some tales were attested in the same locale for three centuries and were doubtless much older, though a lack of records made a direct proof of the matter impossible. Of the antiquity and general popularity of the telling of tales to children, the brothers claimed that the folktale lay near to the early and simple life of human beings, for which reason the West Africans tell tales to their children as did also the ancient Greeks. In the comparative notes to their tales, the Grimms cited divergent German texts as well as occasional parallels found in the published works of other nations and ages such as in Basile's *Pentamerone* (1634–36) and in classical literature. And in the preface to their second volume (1815), they argued that their folktales cast valuable light upon the ancient heroic legends of the Germanic peoples, an illumination for which they believed there was no comparable source.

The Grimms elaborated these ideas in successive editions of their work. On the presence of similar oral tales circulating among peoples widely separated from one another in space or time, their position, as articulated by Wilhelm Grimm, developed into the following two stances. First, to distinguish the monogenesis of tales from polygenesis, or independent invention, they appealed to the principles of complexity and arbitrariness. They acknowledged that some narrative situations were so simple and natural that tales embodying them could arise in different places and times independently of one another, like nearly identical words in unrelated languages that were formed in imitation of natural sounds. They pointed out, however, that most tales did not fit this description but rather showed traits of an unusual and arbitrary nature such as were unlikely to develop by chance agreement. For example, it was one thing to find in different texts the performance of tasks as a prerequisite to a reward, but it was another thing to find that the particular tasks were identical and unusual.

Second, the Grimms asked how one could explain the fact that a story in a mountain village in Hesse might resemble one in India, Greece, or Serbia. They granted that stories sometimes diffused from nation to nation, as happened, for

example, in the North in the case of the legend of Siegfried. But they also argued that the further one went back in time, the greater was the mythical element in traditional fiction, and that the geographical area in which the bulk of shared stories occurred was coterminus with that occupied by speakers of the Indo-European family of languages. The Grimms concluded from this that German folktales descended ultimately from myths and that the presence of a similar body of tales among ancient and modern Indo-European peoples must be the result of inheritance, like the Indo-European languages themselves. They explained the occasional presence of the same stories among neighboring, non-Indo-European peoples as the result of diffusion.[3]

The Grimms' notion of the Indo-European heritage of folktales and of the devolution of genres became one of the classic theories of the origin, nature, and migration of folktales. Their idea of the devolution of genres was similar to an idea of Walter Scott's found among his comments to his *Lady of the Lake*, published in 1810 and quoted in excerpt by the Grimms.[4] Scott says that one could compile a work of considerable interest on the origins of "popular fiction" as well as on the transmission of similar tales from one age to another and from one country to another. "The mythology of one period would then appear to pass into the romance of the next century, and that into the nursery-tale of the subsequent ages." Scott thus explained similarities in the traditional narratives of different nations and ages as the consequence of diffusion, both horizontal (through space) and vertical (through time), and set forth a devolutionary scheme of narrative genres such that over time oral stories that originally belonged to mythology became in time romances and finally ended up as humble folktales with which adults amused children.

After the Grimms' *Kinder- und Hausmärchen* the most influential book on the folktale published during the century was Theodor Benfey's *Pantschatantra* (1859), in which the author put forth a different theory of the origin of international tales. In his introduction Benfey took up the issue of widely diffused tales and forcefully argued that most animal fables originated in the Occident, being largely transformations of Aesopic fables, while märchen and most other oral narratives came originally from India. At first this dissemination took place exclusively by means of oral transmission, but with Muslim conquests in India in the tenth century many narrative compilations were translated into Persian and Arabic and soon became known throughout the Muslim world, whence they passed to the Christian West. In the East, moreover, oral tales often found expression in Buddhist compositions and consequently followed the spread of Buddhism from India to China, Tibet, and Mongolia, whereafter for nearly two centuries the Mongols held sway in Europe.[5] Benfey's book caused considerable excitement among researchers, motivating many scholars to investigate the history of individual tales in an attempt to confirm or disconfirm his grand thesis.

Clearly Benfey's views were irreconcilable with those of the Grimms. Did folktales come from myths, or have folktales always been folktales? Do most European stories descend from a common Indo-European inheritance, having been brought to Europe by the immigrating Indo-Europeans themselves, in which case the tales themselves must predate the diaspora of the Indo-European peoples, or did they reach the West much later, carried from the East by Muslims and Buddhists via literary works and oral storytelling?

In addition to these two positions, each with its adherents, there was a third

important approach, the Anthropological School, whose leading spirit was An-
drew Lang. Since all human cultures evolved through the same stages, as the
members of the school held, the same motifs and even the same tales might
arise in different societies independently. Consequently, the Anthropological
School traced the fantastic motifs of folktales to their supposed origins in vari-
ous stages of human cultural development.[6]

The esteem for oral stories, which accompanied a new regard for myths and
ballads and other traditional forms of popular expression, led to the energetic
gathering and publication of living stories from oral informants in many lands,
creating an ever expanding base for the study and comparison of international
oral tales.[7] Since the sheer volume of materials prohibited the publication of all
the texts, many were filed in newly founded national folklore archives. Draw-
ing upon the steady flow of published collections of tales and continuing the
practice initiated by the Grimms in the notes to their tales, eclectic scholars
such as Felix Liebrecht published comparative notes on oral tales, Reinhold
Köhler composed detailed annotations of the major collections of European
folktales as they appeared in print, and Emmanuel Cosquin wrote comparative
notes for the tales he published.[8]

Many researchers produced studies on the history of individual international
tales. Since scholars reached different conclusions about the origins of the tales
they studied, their findings tended to support neither the Indo-Europeanist the-
ory of the Grimms nor the pan-Indianist thesis of Benfey nor the Anthropologi-
cal School of Lang in their extreme forms.[9] Taken together, however, the studies
suggested that individual folk narratives came into being at different places and
at different times, although some nations and some periods of history appeared
to be more productive of tales than others. The studies confirmed that many of
the same tales were found among peoples living in an area stretching from Ire-
land to India, which Stith Thompson therefore labeled a "tradition area."[10] Most
investigators agreed that tales diffuse horizontally from narrators in one region
to narrators in other regions as well as vertically from older narrators to younger
ones, that in time tales can develop local variations, and that traditional tales also
disseminate via literary channels.[11] As Thompson observed, "It is always easier
to borrow a myth or a tale than it is to construct one."[12] Accordingly, the theory of
the polygenesis of tales retained few supporters, and most of the discussion cen-
tered rather upon the relative importance of inheritance as opposed to diffusion
and of oral as opposed to literary transmission. The traditional narratives told in
a community are typically a mix of migratory tales, which are also told in neigh-
boring regions or countries, and local stories, which are not found elsewhere.

In the 1930s the Swedish folklorist Carl von Sydow clarified the operation of
horizontal diffusion.[13] He pointed out that in no society are all traditions
known equally to all members; rather, hunting traditions are known to hunters
and by and large not to others, agricultural traditions to farmers, and so on.
Among bearers of a tradition, moreover, there are found both *active bearers*, that
is, persons who know a tradition well and transmit it to others, and also *passive
bearers*, persons who have heard a particular tradition and, if asked, may be
able to recollect it in part but do not keep it alive and ordinarily do not spread
it to others. Active bearers of folktales, especially of the more complex tales
such as magic tales (that is, fairy tales) always make up a very small percentage

of the members in a community.[14] When a tale spreads from one community to another, it does not of course migrate on its own, nor do members of one community collectively pass it on to the members of neighboring communities, for most members of a society are only passive bearers of traditional narratives; rather, an active bearer from one place transmits the tale to an active bearer from another locality, or an active bearer moves from one place to another, bringing the narrative along. That is why a tale sometimes is found in two disparate localities and not in between. In time a tale forms local peculiarities, which von Sydow, borrowing from biology, labeled *ecotypes*.[15]

The efforts of a century of folktale scholarship were eventually brought together in the monumental five-volume work of Johannes Bolte and Georg Polívka, *Anmerkungen zu den Kinder- und Hausmärchen der Brüder Grimm* (1913–32), consisting of extensive comparative notes on the Grimms' tales together with a history of research on the folktale.[16] Responding moreover to the need for a common system of reference for international narratives, a number of scholars in different fields ventured to make lists of recurrent tales.[17] The first to gain wide acceptance was the *Verzeichnis der Märchentypen* (1910) compiled by the Finnish scholar Antti Aarne. Each text of a traditional tale was seen as a reflex of a *type*, that is, a traditional narrative pattern of considerable stability.[18] A type, or tale type, was an abstraction derived by observation of a number of texts that from their similarity were presumed to be genetically related. Aarne's index was translated and twice revised by the American folklorist Stith Thompson, most recently in 1961, with the title *The Types of the Folktale*. Scholars of folk narrative have adopted as standard the practical system of classification and reference devised by Aarne and Thompson for the geographical area that falls within the scope of their index, so that folktales published in scholarly books and periodicals are routinely described, when appropriate, by reference to the conventional number and name assigned them in Aarne-Thompson, abbreviated AT (or AaTh) for this purpose. For example, tales of the marriage of a maiden to a supernatural husband, the loss of the husband following her breaking a taboo, and her successful quest to regain him, are labeled AT 425, *The Search for the Lost Husband*.

The goal of folk-narrative research, as nearly all scholars saw it until around the middle of the twentieth century, was to discover the origin, nature, and dissemination of individual tales.[19] Understanding a tale meant having historical knowledge of it. A typical monographic treatment of an individual folktale involved the researcher's assembling literary and oral texts of a tale type, comparing their content, and from the evidence inferring their mutual relationships and archetypal form. Carried to its logical extreme, this approach became formalized in the 1920s as the *historic-geographic method*, known also as the *Finnish method* because of the major role that Finnish folklorists had in formulating it.[20] The Finnish School held that each tale, equipped with its own unique set of motifs, was invented by a narrator as a logical and coherent whole at a particular time and place, after which, like rings in a pond of water, it spread out from nation to nation, forming regional subtypes. An investigator doing a historic-geographic study of an oral tale located the early literary texts of the tale and assembled as many texts from oral tradition as were available. He or she arranged the former chronologically and the latter geographically (whence the label historic-geographic), analyzed the texts into episodes and motifs, and

by applying certain rules attempted to discern the original form of the tale, its time and place of origin, and its paths of dissemination. Because nineteenth-century folklorists had usually been trained as philologists, it was natural for them to apply the principles of textual criticism to folktales, as though folktale texts were so many little manuscripts. Many studies of this kind were produced, although the procedure never lacked its detractors.

Eventually the historic-geographic method fell out of fashion, partly because of the criticisms leveled against it but mostly because of a gradual shift of interest among folklorists to other aspects of the folktale, indications of which were already appearing in the 1920s.[21] Diachronic issues gave way to questions about the processes of storytelling, drawing scholarly attention to narrators and audiences, narrative situations, and cultural contexts; to questions about the morphology and structure of narratives; and to questions about the interpretation of tales. Since the early 1970s performance studies have dominated folkloristic approaches to narrative.[22]

Not only the historic-geographic method but also its principal object of study, the magic tale, fell on hard times. The classic genre of folktale scholars became less available for direct study by European and North American researchers because the more complex genres of oral story vanished from living tradition in many places in the Western world in the course of the twentieth century. In many lands, especially industrialized lands, the magic tale followed the old mythological genres of myth and heroic legend into oral oblivion, eventually to be known only from the written records that chanced to have been made. Because of the difficulty of locating narrators of magic tales and because of the increased interest in other genres for their own qualities, some scholars of oral narrative turned their attention more and more to the legend, the personal-experience narrative, the anecdote, the joke, and the other structurally simpler forms that do continue to thrive among Western peoples.

The shift of scholarly interest from historical reconstruction to an understanding of processes created a bifurcation of folk-narrative texts into historic and living, in which the high esteem previously enjoyed by older texts passed to newer texts. Some researchers even regarded texts from the past, whether found in early literary works, in folkloric publications, or in folklore archives, as being ill suited for study with modern methods because of the relative poverty of contextual data that attended them, since most of the early collectors of folktales, viewing oral narrators as mere reproducers of inherited tradition, showed little interest in the environment of narration and so recorded little contextual information.[23] Nevertheless, some archival texts and some narratives found in early written sources do contain contextual data, and some scholars have devised ways of applying the newer methods to older materials.[24]

The Study of Greek and Roman Folk Narratives

From the first the Grimms suggested that the stuff of folktales and the telling of folktales could be traced back to classical antiquity, citing the Greek geographer Strabo on the use of protreptic and apotreptic tales in the rearing of children. Strabo says that people tell pleasant tales to children in order to spur

them on, and frightening tales of Lamia and Gorgo and other ogresses in order to deter them.[25] The Grimms represented folktales as something told by adults to children and so cited Strabo rather than, for example, one of the many ancient authors who address an Aesopic fable to an adult, or the fictional old woman in Apuleius's novel who relates the tale of Cupid and Psyche to a young bride. Educated persons, for whom folktales are only a pleasant memory from childhood, typically regard them as a kind of story intended exclusively for children rather than as an art form for adult listeners. But, historically speaking, folktales have not been primarily a kind of oral literature for children, for in communities that cultivate the telling of traditional tales, most raconteurs are adults, and the audiences for their tales consist usually of adults, though it can happen that children are present, and of course there are also particular tales that adult tellers relate only to children, just as there are others that children tell one another.[26] Accordingly, for an understanding of the telling of tales in antiquity we must look primarily at tales told by adults to other adults.

Part of the continuing confusion concerning the traditional audience for folktales springs from an ambiguity in the use of the term "folktale," or *Märchen*, which is employed broadly to refer to any kind of traditional oral tale that is regarded as essentially fictional such as magic tales, novelle, animal tales, tall tales, and jokes, but is also employed more narrowly to mean only magic tales. To make matters more complicated, in the past many scholars including Stith Thompson used "folktale" not as a term for a particular oral genre but as an umbrella term for all genres of folk narrative.[27] In his study *The Legend of Perseus* Edwin Sidney Hartland writes: "The classical myth of Perseus belongs to a group of folktales ranking among the foremost in interest for the student of the evolution of human thought and human institutions."[28] Hartland labels the Perseus story a "legend" in the title of the work and a "myth" in the text, and he treats myth as a variety of "folktale." So for Hartland the story of Perseus is at once a myth, legend, and folktale. The scholarly terms for different kinds of oral story have been developing slowly from vernacular terms during the last two centuries.

Just as the Grimms inaugurated the comparative study of the international folktale, so also were they the first to explore the evidence for folktales among the ancient Greeks and Romans. In his preface to a translation of the *Pentamerone* published in 1846, Jacob Grimm observed that there must have been innumerable old women's tales (γραώδεις μῦθοι, *fabulae aniles*) in classical antiquity, citing the tale of Cupid and Psyche and other evidence for the deep roots of the folktale and in particular for *Kindermärchen* in ancient Greece.[29] Eleven years later the first important study of an international folktale together with its ancient counterpart was made by Jacob's brother, Wilhelm, in an essay on the story of Odysseus and Polyphemus and its analogues, which he read before the Royal Academy of Sciences in Berlin and published in the same year.[30]

Several topics and issues addressed by Wilhelm Grimm in this study recur in subsequent comparative studies of ancient and modern stories. First, Grimm identified the ancient text in question as being a traditional oral narrative after comparing it with other texts whose status as oral texts was known or at least likely. For it is not always apparent whether a particular ancient story is traditional, and, even when it is apparent, it is not obvious whether the story is also

international. Indeed, without comparative texts it may not even be obvious whether a particular text reflects a story.[31]

Second, Grimm considered the problem of the genetic, or historical, relationship of the ancient and later texts. Arguing from probability he concluded that the texts in question were different expressions of a single, extensive tradition, that none of them derived from or (with the possible exception of one text) was influenced by any other, and that the early written texts of the story, including Homer's, were each treatments of texts from oral tradition just as were the later texts whose pedigrees were known. And, third, after distinguishing what was constant and what was variable in the tradition, Grimm drew upon the variables and the constants in order to address other questions, which for him were the original form of the tale and the original meaning of the tale.

Although it is intuitively appealing and certainly simpler to imagine that the earliest attestation of a traditional tale is the source of all later texts, folk-narrative scholars have repeatedly observed that this is rarely the case.[32] A chronologically early text does not even necessarily reflect a developmentally early form of a narrative because narrative change is a function not of time but of particular narrators on particular occasions; consequently, it is possible for a recent text to represent a relatively conservative line of tradition and for an older text to represent a more innovative line. Indeed, it would be wildly improbable in the case of a traditional oral story if the first published text should also chance to be the urtext, the very prototype of the tale. Inasmuch as the widespread collection of oral traditions was not undertaken before the nineteenth century and even so has been carried on unevenly in different lands and at different times, the records of folk narration that we have are unrepresentative of the international oral tradition of every single period. Being a small sampling of the whole, each record must stand for hundreds or thousands of unrecorded tellings in the career of an oral tale. In any assemblage of narrations of the same tale type, whether recent or old or both, it is therefore safest to assume that the texts are independent realizations of the tradition, unless particular relationships can actually be demonstrated to be otherwise.

A feature of the texts that Grimm noticed but did not discuss was that most of them were told as folktales, whereas the story of Odysseus and Polyphemos in the *Odyssey* was told as a legend; that is, it was represented as having a claim to historicity. Although individual oral stories tend to be genre-specific, it can happen that a story is encountered at one place and time in one genre and at another place and time in a different genre, indicating that in the course of its transmission a shift of genre has taken place in one line of the tradition.[33] This phenomenon, in which a story is told by one narrator as a folktale and by another as a legend or myth, can be termed *genre variance*.[34] The phenomenon of genre variance probably helped to suggest the notion of the devolution of genres, an idea that the Grimms elaborated into a theory of the Indo-European origin of the folktale.[35]

An appreciation of genre variance is important for an understanding of the relationship of ancient and modern tales. For one thing, many stories that in modern times are attested as folktales are found in ancient societies as legends. This correlation is extensively demonstrated in the present work. I shall return to the topic later, but for the moment I observe that a consequence of this difference is that the modern tales generally take place in anonymous localities,

are set in the indefinite past ("once upon a time"), and feature generic characters who are nameless or bear conventional folktale names such as Jack, Hans, and Cinderella, whereas ancient Greek stories typically are situated in real places in the Greek world, are located at a definite point in the flow of time, and are peopled by allegedly historical characters equipped with sometimes extensive genealogies. Simply put, the difference is between narratives treated as fictional and narratives treated as historical. The generic frame not only conditions how narrators and audiences understand and respond to a narrative but also affects the structure and content of a narrative. In allegedly historical traditions fabulous elements are often tempered and events may be constrained by geographical and genealogical considerations of which folktales are mostly free.

Modern scholarly surveys of the folktale in classical antiquity are usually unsatisfactory because they ignore differences in genre or treat the differences in a vague or confused manner.[36] For example, in his well-known *Handbook of Greek Mythology* H. J. Rose begins well by distinguishing märchen from other genres, observing that other kinds of story were intended to command belief or something approximating it, whereas "the Märchen aims rather at amusement. It accounts for the cause of nothing; it records no historical or semihistorical event; it need not fit the hearers' notions of probability. It is a story pure and simple, and makes no pretense to being anything else."[37] When however Rose actually cites supposed märchen in ancient Greece and Italy, what he offers are not märchen at all but rather traditional stories that with few exceptions were treated in antiquity as accounts of historical events.[38] They do not therefore qualify as folktales according to Rose's own definition. For instance, Rose reports a tradition related by Pausanias about the town of Ophiteia. A certain man of Phokis, seeing a serpent near his infant son and thinking the serpent intended to attack the child, threw his javelin, killing both the animal and the baby. When later he perceived that the serpent had actually been guarding the child from a wolf, he buried the two together in gratitude. The town of Ophiteia was named after this very serpent.[39] This story, connected with the name of a Greek settlement that signifies Snaketown, obviously conflicts with Rose's own definition of folktale, since the Greek story does in fact claim to record a historical event and does venture to account for the odd name of the town. Tellings of this legend in antiquity were surely prompted, not by an urge to recount a tale pure and simple, but by someone's commenting on the strange name of the place, which was probably how the traveler Pausanias himself came to hear it. The only claim that the story has to the label of folktale is that essentially the same story is found in modern international tradition where it is sometimes recounted as a folktale, for which reason it is included by Aarne and Thompson in *The Types of the Folktale*.[40] But the story reported by Pausanias was not told by the people of Ophiteia as a folktale. Genre variance between ancient and modern stories misleads Rose into labeling as folktales ancient legends that correspond in their plots to narratives that in our day are found as folktales.

Classical philologists presently joined in the quest for ancient folktales and for ancient analogues of modern folktales, two categories of story that, as we have seen, have not always been clearly distinguished. Ludwig Friedländer's

comparison of the tale of Cupid and Psyche with similar folktales (1860) appeared only three years after Grimm's lecture on the Polyphemos story, and Friedländer followed it with a pioneering essay on the tale of Cupid and Psyche and other traces of the folktale in classical antiquity, one of the appendices to his social history of Rome.[41] Meanwhile, folklore scholars continued to investigate individual tales, some of them having ancient analogues, and occasionally considered evidence for the folktale in Greco-Roman antiquity.[42] Most scholarly scrutiny of the folktale in ancient societies was directed at Greek and Roman literature because it was much better known to scholars than were other ancient literatures and because, in comparison with the literary remains of other ancient nations, so much of it had survived; but other traditions were not neglected, especially the rich storytelling literature of India that played so important a role in discussions of the origin and dissemination of international tales. The *Märchenjäger* also sought and found evidence for the folktale and analogues of modern folktales in the literary remains of ancient Israel, Egypt, and Mesopotamia.[43]

The chief aim of the early investigators was the identification of analogues to modern folk narratives, especially folktales, in different ancient literatures, regardless of the genres to which individual ancient texts belonged, in order to cast light upon particular passages in ancient authors, to discover the extent to which international migratory tales suffused the ancient repertory, and to uncover the role they played in it. In addition, the converted wished to convert the unbelievers, for some classical scholars continued to doubt that such apparently puerile forms of expression had really existed among the Greeks and Romans. Friedrich Welcker happily explained: "Childishness was foreign to the Hellenic spirit, that childishness which constitutes the essence of the German and Slavic and Persian märchen, in which the bright world of nature and of human society seems to be reflected as in the eyes of children, and which renounces the deliberations of reason and the experience of the sophisticated observer."[44] However, as Friedländer retorted, before the German romantics turned their attention to the folk, no one knew that Germans had märchen either.[45] James George Frazer probably spoke for most folktale investigators when he wrote: "It seems not improbable that the element of folktale bulks larger in Greek tradition than has commonly been suspected. When the study of folk-lore is more complete and exact than at present, it may be possible to trace to their sources many rivulets of popular fiction which contributed to swell the broad and stately tide of ancient literature."[46]

Early scholars of the ancient folktale frequently treated tales, incidents, and motifs indiscriminately, failing to distinguish between tales and parts of tales, a confusion that led scholars into many muddy discussions and unfounded conclusions. Naturally, it was difficult to compare properly when scholars were unclear what the units of comparison should be. Their problem sprang in part from a conceptual vagueness and in part from the lack of standard systems of reference for the international tale. The same vagueness characterized all early folk-narrative scholarship, but with the advent and use of tale-type indices it gradually disappeared among folklorists. Whereas nowadays a folk-narrative scholar can identify the class to which a particular text belongs simply by citing the conventional number and catchword in Aarne-Thompson or another register, the early comparativists were obliged either to refer to published col-

lections in which comparable tales and motifs were found (e.g., "Grimm No. 14") or to employ ad hoc catchwords, which often suffered from being either too vague ("the dragon slayer"), too idiosyncratic ("tales of the Abhorred Marriage class, particularly in those of the Unnatural Father type"), or too specific to the traditions of a particular nation ("Catskin") to be useful for international scholarship.[47]

In the first phase of the comparative study of the classical folktale, beginning with the brothers Grimm, philologists-turned-folklorists initiated the study of the international tale, pointing out that parallels to some living folktales and motifs could be found in classical authors. In the second phase, beginning with Friedländer in the 1860s and culminating in the productive decade of the 1920s, classical scholars tapped into the interdisciplinary study of the folktale, collecting the evidence for folktales, folktale-like narratives, and oral storytelling in classical times in an effort to document the presence of these features and to gain a perspective on the phenomenon as a whole. William Halliday's discussion of folktales in his *Greek and Roman Folklore* (1927), Rose's chapter on märchen in his *Handbook of Greek Mythology* (1928), and Wolf Aly's article on *"Märchen"* for Pauly-Wissowa (1928) were the last major surveys of the subject produced by classical scholars. The overview of classical tales by the folklorist Joseph Bédier in *Les Fabliaux*, forming part of an anti-Benfeyist argument (that is to say, an anti-orientalist argument), and the characteristically sound survey of Bolte and Polívka appeared around the same time.[48]

The nineteenth-century discovery of the international migratory tale should have led to a revolution in the understanding of ancient oral story and storytelling, especially in the study of classical mythology. The idea should have become common that, whatever else Greek mythology *might* be (deliberate allegory, confused history, a complement to rituals, imaginative fiction, propaganda, etc.), a large part of it *certainly* consisted of regional adaptations of international narratives creatively fitted to Greek ways and intricately woven together into labyrinthine genealogical and geographical legends that knotted together successive generations as well as neighboring and disparate regions. It should have become clear that in addition to the relatively few migratory myths appropriated by the Greeks from the international tradition such as the Succession Myth, the Combat Myth, and the Flood Myth, many nonmythic narratives in international circulation were borrowed by the Greeks and Romans and made their own.[49] Every major study of, say, the Theseus legend should have included at least an acknowledgment of the international folktale to which the core of the story corresponds (see "Girl as Helper"). It did not happen. Instead, in the third phase of comparative studies, in the 1930s and following, classical scholars became decreasingly familiar with the scholarly literature on folk narratives, a state of affairs that folklore scholars matched in their turn as their studies developed into an independent and specialized academic discipline with its own language and scholarly literature.[50] Trained now in folklore rather than in philology, folklorists moved not so handily amidst Greek and Latin texts as had their classically trained forebears, while classicists for their part found it more difficult to make unguided excursions into folkloric scholarship than had their late-nineteenth-century and early-twentieth-century predecessors. Typical investigations by classicists during this third phase have

been comparative studies of single tales and their analogues with the aim, not of identifying an ancient narrative as an international story as such or of contributing to the larger picture of the international folktale in Greek and Roman culture, but of applying what may be learned to an immediate problem of classical literature, mythology, or history.

Oral Narratives and Oral Narration in Classical Antiquity

In addition to general words for "story" or "narrative," the Greek and Latin vocabulary included terms for certain forms of the traditional fictional tale such as the fable and the joke.[51] In certain periods, at least, the closest word in ancient Greek to "folktale" or "märchen" was *mythos* (μῦθος), which, however, could also refer to other kinds of narrative, especially stories containing elements that were unrealistic by the standards of ordinary life. It could therefore encompass stories ranging from myths of the gods to legends of the heroes to Aesopic fables about animals or plants. For the geographer Strabo in the first century B.C., therefore, the whole apparatus of the Homeric gods with their thunderbolts, aegis, trident, and other divine weapons, were "myths"; so were hero legends such as the labors of Herakles or Theseus; and so were the tales that adults recounted to children, both those told to encourage them and those told to frighten them, such as tales about Lamia, Gorgo, Ephialtes, and Mormolyke.[52] By the time of Julian the Apostate in the fourth century A.D., if not before, a *mythos* is simply an entertaining narrative for children.[53] The Latin equivalents of *mythos* were *fabula* and its diminutive *fabella*. According to the author of a rhetorical handbook of the first century B.C., a *fabula* is a story containing matter that is neither true nor probable.[54]

Classical authors represent both men and women as narrators of *mythoi*, and both adults and children as listeners, although most of the references to tellers are to nurses and old women, whence the expressions "old women's (nurses') tales," which male writers use contemptuously.[55] The ancient terms are parallel in etymology but not quite in meaning to our expression "old wives' tales" ("wife" originally = "woman"), since among us the expression commonly refers not to folk narratives but to folk beliefs. Since ancient nurses (that is, nannies) were usually foreign slaves, the role of the nurse in the international transmission of oral tales in antiquity may in fact have been considerable. Foreign-born nurses probably introduced many stories into Greece and Rome, and Greek nurses brought Greek tales to Italy. Because of their low status as women, slaves, and foreigners, educated males held their artistic expressions in low esteem. But certainly tellers of oral tales were not exclusively old women. Rather, men and women probably had specialized audiences, male narrators telling stories mostly to other men, and females telling stories to mixed groups and to children, with a positive correlation between age and storytelling and with additional differences reflecting such factors as education, social standing, and community.[56]

Ancient sources illustrate different functions of tale-telling. Among them are education and manipulation (to inform, to illustrate or emphasize a point, to encourage or discourage a certain behavior), management of emotions (to calm down children, to console, etc.), pleasure (to entertain, to amuse), pastime (to

divert time during communal work such as spinning), and soporific (to help children or adults fall asleep).[57] Among the times favored for storytelling was after meals, which seems to have been the usual time for conversation or entertainment, at least for men, and during the winter at fireside.[58] The telling of tales was customary during the Athenian festival of Oschophoria, commemorating those Athenian mothers who, according to tradition, had heartened and encouraged their sons and daughters with tales when they were being sent as tribute to King Minos.[59] In addition to amateur narrators there were also professional storytellers who earned money by performing in public.[60]

We know something of conventional introductions to folktales, corresponding to our "once upon a time" and similar formulas in other languages.[61] In Aristophanes' *Wasps* the old man Philokleon starts to tell a folktale: "So once there was a mouse and a weasel," and the scholiast comments that this was the customary way to begin a tale, citing "So there was an old man and an old woman."[62] The woman who relates the tale of Cupid and Psyche in Apuleius's Latin novel begins her narration with a similarly simple and indefinite statement: "In a certain city there were a king and queen . . ."[63] There were also closing formulas, as in the English formula for magic tales: "And they lived happily ever after." A Greek closing formula for tales told to children was "The tale (*mythos*) has been saved."[64] Subgenres such as the fable had their own formulas.[65] Sometimes one can perceive features of an oral style in written compositions, as for example in a preference for paratactic constructions and a liberal use of the connective "and."[66]

Among the many narratives that have come down to us from antiquity, several closely resemble the complex *magic tales* found in modern oral tradition: (1) The closest resemblance occurs in Apuleius's narrative of Cupid and Psyche, which is a reflex of an international tale, although somewhat allegorized and mythologized (see "Disenchanted Husband"). (2) An ancient story that resembles a modern magic tale of simpler structure is Hermes and the Woodcutter, in which a supernatural being tests first an honest woodcutter and then a dishonest woodcutter (see "Axe Falls into the Stream"). Other motifs found scattered in different authors have struck scholars as possible reminiscences of ancient wonder tales, such as the magic table that provides a banquet whenever its possessor utters the command "Table, set yourself!" mentioned in a fragment of a lost Greek comedy.[67] So also the magic ring of Gyges, which, when Gyges turns it a certain way, makes him invisible; and the imaginary magic rings with various powers wished for by a character in a dialogue of Lucian.[68] And motifs appearing in an extravagant prayer uttered by an old woman for an infant boy in one of Persius's satires: "May a king and queen wish him for a son-in-law, may girls chase after him, may whatever he steps upon become a rose."[69] So also the line spoken by a character in Petronius's *Satyrica*, reminiscent of the magic tale of the enchanted frog who was really a prince: "So your friend who once was a frog is now a king" (see "Frog King"). And there are other suggestive passages that may possibly be vestiges of ancient magic tales.

If we find very few magic tales as such in classical authors, we do find many ancient *legends* that closely parallel modern magic tales in their basic program of action. (3) The legend of the Argive hero Perseus and the Ethiopian princess Andromeda, for example, corresponds in all important respects to the modern folktale of the youth who rescues a princess by slaying the dragon to whom she

is being sacrificed, disposes of another claimant, and weds her (see "Dragon Slayer"). (4) Similarly, the legend of the Iolkan hero Jason and the Colchian princess Medeia parallels the magic tale of the youth who goes to the dwelling of an ogre, accomplishes seemingly impossible tasks with the help of the ogre's daughter, flees with her, and eventually deserts her (see "Girl as Helper"); (5) the legend of the Athenian hero Theseus and the Cretan princess Ariadne is another form of the same story. (6) According to a report inscribed on a tablet displayed at the healing temple of Asklepios at Epidauros, the god miraculously removes certain tattoos from the forehead of Pandaros the Thessalian and transfers them to the head of a dishonest man named Echedoros, a story that in modern times is usually told of a hunchback who encounters the fairies (see "Gifts of the Little People"). (7) The legend of the hero Pelops and princess Hippodameia has a later counterpart in the tale of the knight who, helped by the grateful ghost of a dead man whom he has piously buried, wins the hand of a princess in a tournament (see "Bride Won in a Tournament"). (8) The Argonauts who sail with Jason in search of the Golden Fleece are mirrored by a group of similarly gifted helpers in a modern magic tale.[70] (9) The legend of the seer Polyidos and the child Glaukos parallels the central episode of a magic tale in which the protagonist, buried alive with his wife and observing how a snake revives a dead snake, resuscitates his own wife.[71] (10) The legend of the labors of Herakles closely resembles the modern tale of the astonishingly strong youth to whom a hostile master assigns a number of physical tasks.[72] (11) The legend of Achilleus's heel corresponds to the modern tale of the youth who has been made invulnerable except in one place (see "Youth Who Bathed Himself in Blood"). (12) The legend of the seer Melampous is parallel in its main points to the magic tale of the man who, having learned the speech of animals, overhears animals saying that a certain house is about to collapse (see "White Serpent's Flesh"). (13) Lastly, the ancient legend recounting how Polykrates miraculously recovers the ring he has discarded is a reflex of an international story that over the years has been told of many different persons.[73] In sum, although very few international magic tales are attested in ancient tradition as *magic tales*, many are found in the form of *legends*. To express it more precisely, numerous ancient Greek legends correspond in action but not in genre to modern magic tales.

Among international *novelle*—or realistic tales set in the familiar world and focusing largely upon romance, intrigue, or wisdom—recounted by the ancients are (1) the tale of the father who tells his sons that he has buried a treasure somewhere in their fields, inducing them to work the soil,[74] (2) the tale of the father who uses a bundle of twigs to teach his sons a lesson about strength in unity,[75] (3) the tale of the wily Aesop who demonstrates to his master that his most devoted supporter is not his wife but his dog (see "Best Friend, Worst Enemy"), (4) the tale that recounts how Aesop is falsely accused to his master and later reinstated,[76] (5) the tale of the old man who, when asked why he is planting trees, says he is planting them for the gods (see "Planting for the Next Generation"), (6) the tale of the boy who, it is prophesied, will meet his death from a crow, and does so in an unexpected way, despite all efforts to prevent it,[77] (7) the tale of the boy whose father dreams he will perish by a lion and who, despite his father's efforts, meets his death from a picture of a lion (another

form of the preceding tale),[78] and (8) the tale of the boy who, it is foretold, will meet three different deaths and actually does so (see "Threefold Death"). Among modern international novelle that ancient authors narrate as legends rather than as novelle are (9) the legend of the love of Phaidra for her stepson Hippolytos (see "Potiphar's Wife"), (10) the legend of Alcestis, who sacrifices her life for that of her husband,[79] (11) the legend of Kyros (Cyrus), who as a child is king of his playmates (see "Son of the King"), (12) the legend of Oedipus, who kills his father and weds his mother,[80] (13) the legend of the clever Egyptian thief who helps himself to the treasure of Pharaoh Rhampsinitos (see "Rhampsinitos"), (14) the legend of how the murderers of the poet Ibykos are discovered (see "Cranes of Ibykos"), (15) the legend of the return of Odysseus after a long absence just as suitors are pressing his wife to remarry (see "Homecoming Husband"), and (16) the legend of Intaphrenes' wife, who unexpectedly chooses the life of her brother over that of her husband (see "Brother Chosen"). So a sampling of modern international novelle with ancient narratives of essentially the same plot reveals that about half of the ancient stories are presented as novelle in agreement with later tradition, and about half are presented as legends.[81]

Consider briefly other subforms of the folktale. The *lying tale*, or tall tale, is a brief narrative of comic exaggeration such as Lucian's account of being swallowed, ship and all, by a giant fish, within which he lives for a long time (see "Man Swallowed by Fish"). With a few exceptions, the ancient analogues of modern international tall tales are likewise tall tales, whose narrator may playfully present them as true accounts of events that he himself has experienced, just as tellers of tall tales in our day often do. The correspondence between the ancient and modern *numskull tale* is similar, such as that of the unhappy man whose donkey dies just when he has managed to train it not to eat (see "Groom Teaches Horse"), and also the ancient and modern *animal tale* such as that of the country mouse and the city mouse.[82] Greek and Roman authors regularly present these tales as amusing fictions, not as historical reports.

Although this sample is incomplete, it shows how the ancient parallels to modern international folktales sometimes agree and sometimes disagree with regard to the genre in which they are expressed. At the simpler end of the narrative continuum, when international tall tales, numskull tales, and animal tales are found in ancient sources, they are nearly always presented in the same genre as we find them today, being recounted in antiquity respectively as tall tales, numskull tales, and animal tales. The case is different with ancient analogues to international novelle, in which about half of the ancient parallels are recounted as fictional and half as historical; that is, half are presented as novelle and the rest as legends. And the relationship is turned completely around in the case of international magic tales, which lie at the more complex end of the narrative continuum. The ancient analogues to these tales nearly always appear as legends.

What precisely is the historical relationship of international folktales to ancient legends (and sometimes myths) that display more or less the same plot? Do the Greek hero legends derive from old, international folktales? Or have the old hero legends turned into the folktales of today, as the theory of genre devolution has it?[83] Close comparisons of ancient and modern variants of the same story lead me

regularly to the conclusion that when a Greek legend and an international folktale share a similar plot, the legend derives from the folktale rather than the other way around, for it is almost invariably easier to understand how an individual Greek legend might have developed as a special adaptation of a more general story than to understand how the folktale might have developed from the particularized and highly adapted story that a legend is. A folktale, owing little allegiance to geography, history, or genealogy, is generally freer than a legend to be its own story, whereas an ostensibly historical tradition is more likely to have undergone creative distortion in the course of its adaptation to a real locality, a particular slot in traditional history, and a cast of supposedly historical characters. In short, legends are more dedicated than folktales are. The likeliest explanation for the striking parallelism of many ancient legends and modern folktales is that the legends are special adaptations of international tales, branches off the main stalk of the tradition.

Many stories may have coexisted in Greece and Italy both as folktale and as legend, as traditional fiction and as traditional history, since the appearance of the same plot in different oral genres is not an unusual phenomenon.[84] Indeed, we know that some ancient stories did circulate simultaneously in more than one genre, so that genre variance is attested for the ancient repertory. For example, (1) the story of the aggressively lustful matron, the chaste youth who declines her advances, and the woman's subsequent accusation that he made improper advances to her is told of characters both in ancient Greek legend and also in literary fiction (see "Potiphar's Wife"). (2) The story of the widow who remains in her deceased husband's tomb, prepared to follow him in death, but presently is seduced by a soldier to whom she hands over her husband's corpse, is found both as a pure novella among the fables of Phaedrus, where the narrative lacks all qualifications of place, time, and person, and as a quasi-legend in the novel of Petronius, where it is represented, though not very insistently, as a true event that took place in Ephesos in the recent past (see "Matron of Ephesus"). (3) The tale of the man who removes a thorn from the paw of a lion, and whose kindness is later repaid by the lion, is told both as a general folktale without any definite setting and also as an astonishing historical event that occurred in Rome.[85] (4) The comic tale of the customer who, when asked by a talkative barber how he would like him to cut his hair, replies, "In silence," is recounted as a joke about an anonymous patron but also as a historical anecdote about King Archelaos of Macedon.[86]

Although some persons surely noticed that certain stories were very similar to one another, they were not likely to have been any more disturbed by this observation than persons are in our own day when they notice parallelisms of the same sort. For some narrators in Greece today the legend of the Sailor and the Oar is about the prophet Elijah whereas for others it is about St. Nikolaos (see "Sailor and the Oar"), but the improbability of both saints having had the same unusual experience does not deter Greek narrators of the present day from transmitting the story. In a fragment of papyrus dating to the second century B.C., an unknown Greek author declares that a statement made on one occasion by one person has sometimes been credited later to another person. For example, the author says, two women were laying claim to a child, each alleging that she herself had given birth to it, and a certain arbiter ordered the child to be cut in two and one half given to each woman; the arbiter's solution was

originally attributed to a certain man but subsequently has been told also of another man (see "Judgment of Solomon"). The unknown Greek writer accepts the fact that tales migrate and are told of different sets of persons.

Were the ancient oral narratives from which Greek hero legends apparently developed truly magic tales in the modern sense?[87] That they corresponded closely to modern magic tales in their sequence of action is clear enough, but whether they also corresponded in atmosphere, in "semantic qualities," and in other attributes is less certain.[88] Modern European magic tales are typically set in the timeless past and in a wondrous world of small, anonymous kingdoms. Their protagonists are either nameless, bear very common names (Hans, Jack, Jean) or have ad hoc names that are unique to particular folktales (Snow White, Little Red Riding Hood), and the tales feature certain kinds of ogres (witches, giants, trolls, dragons, etc.) and certain kinds of helpers (e.g., an old woman possessing supernatural objects). Although none of the fairytale-like narratives from antiquity matches this description exactly, Apuleius in his narration of Cupid and Psyche does create essentially the same atmosphere of wondrous unreality that often suffuses magic tales found in later times.[89] If one such tale is attested in ancient sources, it is likely that there were others. But the ancient wonder tales probably differed from their later counterparts in some other ways such as in assigning to deities certain roles that later magic tales assign to lower supernatural beings or to other characters. Thus we find Olympian and chthonian deities in the tale of Cupid and Psyche, Hermes as donor in the tale of Hermes and the Woodcutter, and the gods Bata and Anubis in the Egyptian tale of Two Brothers. A fitting role for the god of the unexpected find, Hermes may often have played the role of donor, as he already does in Homer's *Odyssey* when he provides Odysseus with a magic plant to assure the hero's success in his forthcoming dealings with Kirke.[90] Several of Athena's actions in the same epic on behalf of Telemachos and Odysseus—she suddenly appears when the hero is in need and facilitates his immediate task, sometimes after playfully testing him—are also reminiscent of folktale donors. Jason's divine fosterer Hera plays a similar role in the Jason legend. Disguised as an old woman in order to test men, she is kindly carried across a flooding river by Jason as he makes his way toward Iolkos and his eventual task.[91] So the pagan gods may have been characters in ancient magic tales. If so, they did not survive the conversion of oral narrators and their audiences to the universalistic religions.

The magic tale was a nonhistorical genre, and no fictional genre of traditional story is well represented in ancient literature for its own sake, since ancient authors as a rule did not regard purely fictional narratives as meriting literary treatment, whether traditional or original. That is presumably why we find so little direct evidence for the magic tale in ancient authors. As a genre, moreover, the magic tale may have been especially popular among the poor and uncultured, expressing the fantasies of the relatively powerless, as we know it has done in certain later times and places.[92] If so, few ancient authors would have regarded such tales as meriting their attention. Certainly this is the attitude toward the wonder tale that characterized nearly all European authors during the ensuing two millennia.[93] When Apuleius composes his novel's centerpiece, the tale of Cupid and Psyche, he does not record it for its own sake as a lovely tale of fantasy but places it in the mouth of a lowly character, an old

slave woman who is drunken and a little crazy.[94] Apuleius himself does not take responsibility for narrating the tale.

Among ancient tales intended specifically for children is one to which in the second century Aristeides and Tertullian each allude. Aristeides says that in order to lull children asleep nurses tell them about a certain sea that is sweet, a sea that flows into a river, river horses, and other such soporifics, and Tertullian compares the cosmological views of a certain author to the nonsense of children according to which fishes grow on trees and apples are produced at sea (see "Topsy-Turvy Land"). Another familiar story represented as a tale for children is related by one of the sages in Plutarch's *Dinner of the Seven Sages*.[95] Kleoboulos, describing his tale as one that his daughter told her brother, says that Selene ("Moon") asked her mother to weave her a chiton fitted to her measurements. But her mother asked how she could do so, since sometimes Selene is full, sometimes crescent-shaped, and sometimes gibbous. Kleoboulos applies the tale metaphorically to the current topic of adult discussion, arguing that some things cannot really be measured because they change. We are probably intended to imagine that Kleoboulos had overheard his daughter recounting the tale to her younger brother. If that is so, the tale could be told either to amuse or to illustrate a point. Featuring as it does female characters and women's work, it was likely to have been transmitted mostly by females.

Authors also allude to *Kindermärchen* that are unknown to us, or at least not certainly known, as when Horace mentions a child's being removed alive from the belly of a Lamia who had just dined on it, an incident that is reminiscent of the conclusion of the Grimms' version of Little Red Riding Hood, in which the heroine is rescued from the belly of the wolf.[96] The Lamia appears as an ogress in both adult and children's narratives, and in the latter she resembles the witches in the magic tales of later times. Intriguingly, Tertullian alludes to "the towers of Lamia and the combs of the sun" as the sort of tale a nurse might tell a child who is having difficulty falling asleep, images that faintly resemble the wonder tale in which a maiden, imprisoned by a witch in a tower, lets her hair hang out of the tower, a scene familiar to us from the tale of Rapunzel.[97]

Some authors, especially in later antiquity, mention as tales for children stories that other persons, at least in earlier times, regarded as historical traditions concerning the gods and heroes of old. For Cicero the legend of Castor and Pollux engaging in battle is an instance of a *fabella anilis*, or old woman's tale.[98] And in the third century of our era Philostratos writes: "You have perhaps heard from a nurse how Theseus mistreated Ariadne by deserting her on the island of Dia as she slept. Nurses are skilled at such things and shed tears over them at will."[99] Similarly, Libanios in the fourth century A.D. refers to the story of Apollo and Daphne as a children's tale.[100] While this state of affairs reflects the decline in credence and esteem accorded the old myths and legends especially by educated persons and by Christians, it may also be the case that some myths and legends had always been regarded as suitable for children as well as for adults, with different emphases given to the telling depending upon the audience and the occasion, just as in the different uses to which Kleoboulos's daughter and Kleoboulos himself each put the tale of the Moon's request for clothes. Indeed, Paul's exhortation to Timothy to avoid "the vile tales of old women" makes more sense if their repertories included not only light tales but

also mythological narratives, and one may speculate that the presence of strong women in Greek mythology is owed in part to the fact that such stories were transmitted by women of little power.[101] The manner in which male authors, especially after the Hellenistic period, often distance themselves from mythological traditions indicates that in the realm of myth and hero legend the learned and popular cultures were increasingly diverging.

The Present Work

This book deals with international oral narratives in ancient Greek and Latin literature, narratives that in light of their longevity must rank among the world's most successful stories.

For the present purposes, ancient Greek and Latin literature includes documents written in Greek and Latin from the beginning of Greek literature in the eighth century B.C. until the closing of the pagan temples and the last celebration of the Olympic Games around A.D. 400, including of course the usual Byzantine scholars who preserve earlier material. Writings in these two languages reflect more ethnic diversity than is commonly thought by nonspecialists in the field, for many Greek authors did not come from Greece, nor did all Latin authors come from Italy. The first language of Lucian, for example, was probably Aramaic, Augustine was born in what is now Algeria, the Senecas came from Spain, Pompeius Trogus was a Gaul, Phaedrus was a Thracian who wrote in Latin, Babrios was evidently a Hellenized Roman who wrote in Greek, and so on. This book includes within its scope all ancient works in Greek and Latin, regardless of the national origin of their authors and regardless of whether the compositions are originals or translations such as the Hebrew Bible, which by the second century B.C. Jewish scholars had translated into Greek for the convenience of Greek-speaking Jews.[102] Indeed in many Jewish compositions it is difficult to discern whether a work was composed originally in Greek or translated from an earlier Semitic text that no longer survives. Some of the ancient narratives treated in this book, therefore, probably never circulated orally among Greeks or Romans, but not even truly Greek and Roman stories were distributed throughout the classical world with perfect consistency, since it is not the nature of oral story to do. Rather, some will have circulated among Greeks but not Romans, some only among inhabitants of a particular region, some primarily among females, some among older persons, and others among the practitioners of a particular occupation such as soldiering.[103] However, our evidence for conduits of transmission of individual ancient oral stories is usually scanty.

No one knows how many international tales are found in Greek and Roman literature, for no exhaustive catalogue of international stories exists, and the published indices of the oral tales of different geographic regions make only rare and inconsistent reference to ancient texts.[104] In any case the aim of the present work is to be representative rather than exhaustive. Included here are about one hundred essays on tales and motifs from the international repertory for which there are clear or suggestive analogues in classical literature. They reflect the variety of ancient oral narrative (folktale, including the magic tale, novella, tall tale, numskull tale, joke, fable, and so on; legend, including the

hero legend and other kinds of legend as well as the anecdote; and myth) as well as the different genres of written expression in which ancient authors employ them (epic, drama, history, philosophy, novel, essay, handbook, scientific treatise, etc.). I select mostly whole stories for treatment, although some entries deal only with a particular episode (for example, "Cinderella") or motif (for example, "Carrying Water in a Sieve") when the interest that the material holds for the ancient repertory justifies their inclusion. I do not select only stories in which the parallelism between the ancient and the modern texts is obvious but include also some whose parallelism must be demonstrated. I arrange the entries alphabetically, employing as titles more or less the catchwords devised by Aarne-Thompson for their catalogue of international folktales, but omitting the initial article and adding in most cases a reference to a corresponding ancient story such as "Homecoming Husband ≋ Odysseus." For the few stories and motifs discussed here that are not found in Aarne-Thompson, I borrow titles from Christiansen's *Migratory Legends* or Thompson's *Motif-Index of Folk Literature* or I supply them myself.

Since Aarne-Thompson's *Types of the Folktale* plays an important role in the present work, providing referential and bibliographic information on individual tales, it will be helpful for the reader to understand the scope, nature, and conventions of the index as well as some of its shortcomings. Designed for the professional folk-narrative scholar rather than for the casual browser, the work is not particularly user-friendly, especially in its most recent edition, in which Thompson assumes that his readers are acquainted with the successive editions of the index. So it is best approached historically.[105]

Antti Aarne compiled his *Verzeichnis der Märchentypen* at a time when the enthusiastic collecting of oral narratives was causing folklore archives in different European lands to teem with unpublished texts. Although comparative studies were the order of the day, it was difficult for comparativists to locate tales of a particular type in unpublished collections, since every archive had its own system of arrangement and nomenclature, as did every scholar. An international scholarly organization, FF (Folklore Fellows, Fédération des Folkloristes, Folkloristischer Forscherbund), had recently been founded, and among its principal aims was to make folkloric materials from different lands more easily available to scholars and to publish catalogues of collections. Aarne's original index, issued in 1910 as FF Communications, no. 3, was intended to serve both as a practical listing of living folktales and also, if the index should be generally adopted, as a system of arrangement that would facilitate the retrieval of texts for comparative study. Aarne catalogued around 550 types but numbered them from 1 to 1960 in order to leave numbers open for subsequent expansion, for he acknowledged that his index was not complete, being based upon the Finnish collections, the Danish collections, and the tales of the Brothers Grimm, thus being limited mostly to types that were found in northern and eastern European collections.

Aarne treated two kinds of tale in special ways. First, he differentiated subtypes by the addition of letters. For example, Type 313 was distinguished as Type 313A (standard form), Type 313B (standard form plus a particular introductory episode), and Type 313C (standard form plus a particular concluding

episode). Second, although each of Aarne's types was a complete narrative, he found that one kind of tale—later termed a *conglomerate* by Carl von Sydow— did not lend itself well to this kind of cataloguing.[106] A conglomerate is a narrative containing a string of brief tales that can appear in different combinations. An example is the folktale commonly known as the Anger Bargain, in which a youth enters the service of a cruel farmer with the understanding that whichever of them first becomes angry shall be whipped or suffer some other punishment. The ogrous farmer assigns the youth a series of tasks, but the boy accomplishes each of them in such a way as to destroy some part of his master's property or family until finally the man bursts into anger, thereby losing the bargain. Within this frame, narrators relate different tasks in different sequences. Aarne chose to list each incident of a conglomerate as a separate type. Thus the tale of the Labor Contract, or Anger Bargain, became Types 1000–1029 (see "Labor Contract").

For the purpose of classification Aarne divided folktales into three broad groups: animal tales (*Tiermärchen*), folktales proper (*eigentliche Märchen*), and humorous tales (*Schwänke*). He classified the animal tales according to which animal played the leading role in the tale (e.g., fox), and he divided humorous tales into numskull tales (*Schildbürgergeschichten*), tales featuring a married couple, tales featuring a woman or girl, tales featuring a man or boy, and lying tales (*Lügenmärchen*). The centerpiece of the arrangement was his second group, folktales proper, which Aarne grouped into magic, or wonder, tales (*Zaubermärchen* or *Wundermärchen*), religious tales (*legendenartige Märchen*), novelle (*novellenartige Märchen*), and tales of the stupid ogre (*Märchen vom dummen Teufel/Riesen*). Magic tales and religious tales featured supernatural elements, whereas novelle eschewed the supernatural. Magic tales were in turn divided into subgroups according to the nature of the supernatural element: supernatural adversaries, supernatural spouses, and so on. Aarne found tales of the stupid ogre hard to classify, since they were at once wonder tales and humorous tales, so that he placed them on the border of the two groups. Although he acknowledged that some tales might be listed in more than one place, Aarne was confident that the index would serve scholars well as a practical tool, which in retrospect one can say it has done.

Presently various scholars began issuing detailed surveys of the oral folktales found in individual countries, cataloguing tales according to Aarne's index but also calling attention to tale types that Aarne had not listed. In addition, Bolte's and Polívka's monumental commentary on the Grimms' tales began appearing in 1913, bringing together great amounts of information concerning the international folktale and clarifying the relationship of many types to one another. Aarne's index soon needed updating, and it fell to the American folklorist Stith Thompson to translate and revise it in 1928. He expanded the brief descriptions of the tales that Aarne had provided, which were adequate only for experienced folklorists, and added bibliographical glosses on individual tale types.[107]

After the publication of still more regional surveys of folktales, Thompson revised the index a second time (1961), reportedly listing approximately three thousand types and subtypes.[108] This revision featured two innovations, one practical and one conceptual. As a practical matter, Thompson integrated into

the index many tales that had been collected only rarely or only in a single country, setting them off from regular types by the addition of an asterisk (e.g., Type 870C*) and giving them provisional status as international tale types. Conceptually, Thompson described for the first time the ultimate scope of the index. First, it was intended as a listing of folktales, not of legends, though the index admittedly included some narratives that were not folktales, and of course some stories vary in their genre. Second, it included only tales that had been encountered in the field, thereby excluding inter alia narratives found in the great literary collections of traditional tales such as the compilations of Aesopic fables and the *Thousand and One Nights*, except of course when these tales had also been recorded from the lips of oral narrators in modern times. And, third, its geographical range was now defined as including the lands stretching from Ireland to India, a region in which many of the same tales were found, sometimes throughout the entire area. Indeed, according to Thompson the index could be called "The Types of the Folktale of Europe, West Asia, and the Lands Settled by These Peoples." It was not intended to be a listing of the world's folktales, to cover which (Thompson said) it would be necessary to devise other indices on other principles.

Entries now took the following form:

> **1137** *The Ogre Blinded (Polyphemus)*. Escape under the ram's belly. Cf. Type 1135.
>
> Motifs: G100. Giant ogre. Polyphemus. K1011. Eye-remedy. Under pretence of curing eyesight the trickster blinds the dupe. (Often with a glowing mass thrust into the eye.) K521.1. Escape by dressing in animal (bird, human) skin. K602. "Noman." K603. Escape under ram's belly.
>
> **Hackman *Die Polyphemsage in der Volksüberlieferung* (Helsinfors, 1904); *BP III 375 ff., incidents A[1], B[1], (Grimm No. 191 a); Coffin *1*; Anderson on Wesselski 46 n.; Delarue: unpublished study.—Finnish *25*; Finnish-Swedish *1*; Estonian *5*; . . . ; Greek *9*, Dawkins *More Greek Folktales* No. 4; Turkish: Eberhard-Boratov No. 146 *5*; India *1*.

This entry means that the narrative is classified as Type 1137, which locates it among tales of the stupid ogre. The authors employ *The Ogre Blinded* as a generic title, while acknowledging in parentheses that it is commonly known by the name of Polyphemus because of the famous version of the story in Homer's *Odyssey*. There follows a very economic description of the tale, consisting of an allusion to the ruse by means of which the hero escapes from the ogre's lair and a list of the principal motifs of the tale, taken from Thompson's own *Motif-Index of Folk-Literature*.[109] The rest of the entry is made up of bibliographic information. First comes a list of scholarly treatments, in which a double asterisk signals a monograph devoted to the type and a single asterisk denotes a lesser treatment of some importance. These items are followed by an indication of the geographic distribution and popularity of the oral tale based upon the numbers of texts cited in published surveys and held in archives. I reproduce only the beginning and the end of this list, which altogether amounts to about twelve lines. The information on texts is necessarily approximate,

since collecting and surveying have taken place unevenly throughout the tradition area and because collecting did not cease with the publication of the index.

Although the usefulness of the Aarne-Thompson index is obvious enough, it is nonetheless not a perfect instrument, and some of its drawbacks should be mentioned.[110] First, it does not give a complete listing of international stories, partly because it selects only for folktales, partly because it relies on incomplete data (it cannot list tales that collectors have failed to collect or that are not available in publications and archives), partly because it does not include all known tales that fall within its scope (for example, obscene narratives are underrepresented), and partly because it excludes as a matter of policy oral stories that did not survive into the nineteenth century.[111] Second, it provisionally includes a small number of tale types that are attested only in one country and therefore may not prove to be international. Third, its citation of illustrative texts is sporadic and unreliable. Fourth, the inclusion and the description of some types are due to accidental factors such as the chance prominence of the tales published by the Grimms.[112] Some of these drawbacks are faults of the sort that are likely to characterize a complex typology or ambitious index of any kind, whereas others are serious defects. Although the work is not a perfect instrument, it has no real competitor, and as a practical listing of international tales found in oral tradition it is a welcome, if sometimes also an exasperating, aid to the scholar.

The first aim of the articles in the present work is to connect particular international oral narratives to particular classical stories.[113] The identification of such tales in ancient literature is a more difficult enterprise than it may appear to be. Naturally, it requires of the investigator a familiarity with both classical literature and international tales. Unlike tales collected in the field or found in published compilations, however, most story texts from antiquity do not appear straightforwardly in collections as such (although we do possess some ancient collections of myths, legends, anecdotes, fables, jokes, and the like) but are found scattered throughout literature of every kind including epic, tragedy, comedy, lyric poetry, philosophy, theology, history, travelers' reports, geography, essays, biography, oratory, romance, and inscriptions.[114] Stories in ancient literature are not always readily identifiable as stories, let alone as traditional stories or international stories, since the texts are found in works intended for a variety of purposes, none of them having to do with the study of oral stories. In some cases the entire evidence for a story rests on a casual allusion or on a proverb, implying that the story was familiar despite the very slight trace it has left in surviving literature.

Another challenge for the researcher is the fact that resemblances between ancient and modern stories of the same narrative type are not always obvious. There are, of course, certain kinds of narrative change that are likely to be observed in any collection of tales of the same type, changes that narrators make deliberately or inadvertently in the course of retelling stories. They have been described by researchers.[115] In addition, differences between the ancient and modern texts can reflect such variables as culture, genre, medium of expression, and occasion of transmission.

Most instances of correspondence between ancient and modern texts fall into one of six categories. (1) *Overall*. The ancient texts and the international texts are generally similar to each other throughout in structure and content. Although close correspondence of this kind is more often found in the case of shorter narratives, there are examples as well among more complex stories such as that of Odysseus and Polyphemos (see "Ogre Blinded"). (2) *Partial*. An ancient story corresponds to an *episode* appearing in a modern tale but not to a whole tale. For example, the entire legend of Rhodopis parallels the final portion of the folktale of Cinderella, namely, the shoe test and the marriage of the heroine to the prince (see "Cinderella"), but contains nothing corresponding to the earlier part of the tale. (3) *Intermittent*. The ancient texts show considerable but inconsistent parallelism, some elements corresponding in both content and function, some corresponding in function but not in content, and others showing no apparent connection at all. An example is the legend of the Mermnad dynasty of Lydia (see "Our Lady's Child"). (4) *Structural*. The ancient text and the international tradition resemble each other structurally in that they display a similar sequence of action, although they are dissimilar on the surface. The legend of the capture of Sardis illustrates this phenomenon (see "Youth Who Bathed Himself in Blood"). (5) *Allusive or fragmentary*. An ancient statement, proverb, or fragment implies an acquaintance with the international tale, which is known to us fully only from later sources. Thus the Greek proverb, "The man carrying the beam," appears to refer to a particular numskull tale (see "Tree-Trunks Laid Crosswise"). (6) *Nascent*. The ancient narrative shows a remote or somewhat simple resemblance to a familiar oral tale and may be a developmentally early form of the type. For example, ancient representations of the dead urging the living not to weep for them are reminiscent of later, more complex narratives on this theme (see "Dead Child's Friendly Return").[116] When the parallelism between a particular text and a particular tale type is partial, intermittent, or otherwise uncertain, folklorists indicate the weak correspondence by enclosing the classification in parentheses, such as (AT 830a, *The Boastful Deer Slayer*). I employ this convention in the present work, as in the conclusion of the entry "Boastful Deer Slayer."

When the correspondences between ancient and later traditions of a story are not obvious, or when the story is complex, I list their shared features in order to make the parallelism explicit. Lists of this sort that are found here and there in the scholarly literature are frequently unsystematic and inconsistent in that they may abstract only the most obvious correspondences, which is an underuse of the comparative method, or may compare different orders of things, which is an abuse of the comparative method. In contrast I give extensive comparisons of narrative action, usually ordered according to the sequence in which the action appears in the narratives. The object is to make the clearest possible case on which to base inferences concerning the historical relationships of narratives. In addition, I hope to demonstrate that typology possesses more value for the understanding of classical mythology than is generally recognized, for it enables researchers to reach conclusions about certain aspects of traditional narratives with something approaching objectivity, whereas the conventional approaches often involve the piling of guesswork upon guess-

work. So this book is inter alia an argument for a greater use of comparative and typological techniques.[117]

The second aim of the essays is to characterize the narrative traditions to which the tale types belong in order to compare the ancient stories with the larger tradition with regard to features such as structure, content, and genre. For some tale types the primary and secondary literature is abundant, whereas for other types no studies exist or so few texts are available that all generalizations must be regarded as tentative. The scholarly literature, especially the older literature, has often concerned itself principally with reconstructing the history of individual stories in oral tradition, a subject about which many conclusions but little certainty has been reached over the years, while it has paid less attention to the texts themselves as stories. Reversing this emphasis, I treat the narratives first and foremost as stories, and I conjecture little about the country and period in which the different stories may have arisen, their presumed paths of dissemination among nations, or the succession of changes in content they have undergone in the course of their journeys through space and time; for what I hope to get at is not the chimerical origins of stories but the stories themselves as we have them, their structure and content, their presence in ancient societies as cultural artifacts, their availability to ancient authors as works of verbal art that invited deployment in different oral and literary contexts, and, when it is the case, their Hellenization and Romanization. The juxtaposition of narratives belonging to the same family is in itself a cognitively and aesthetically pleasurable experience for the investigator, revealing creative surprises that emerge when clusters of similar narrative ideas are shaped in unpredictable ways by different narrators in different societies and times, each text lending insight into a neighboring formulation.[118]

1. Despite their claims, the Grimms produced quite unscientific folktale texts, since they took many tales from literary sources, combined different versions of a tale in order to make a more satisfactory text, and rewrote tales to give them what they regarded as an appropriately folktale style (BP 4:419–487; Cocchiara 1981:225–229; Bottigheimer 1990). See further *EM* 6:171–195; McGlathery 1991; Kamenetsky 1992. Richard Dorson (1957:55) points out that over the years folktale collectors have had to choose from among money, art, and truth. Most collectors have modified the texts they published in order to make them more readable and commercially acceptable, or they have used them as raw material for literary treatment. But what the texts may gain in art, they lose in truth. See further Fine 1984.

2. Grimm 1956:7. Although Holbek (1983:146) sees in the Grimms' preface to their *Deutsche Sagen* the first scholarly attempt at genre analysis, the distinction already appears, if somewhat casually, in the preface to the first edition of their folktales; moreover, J. G. Herder, following C. G. Heyne, had previously divided the stories of Greek mythology analytically into three classes, corresponding approximately to myth, legend, and folktale (Chase 1969:36). On the tripartite system of genres—myth, legend, folktale—commonly in use among folk-narrative scholars, see Bascom 1965; for finer distinctions, Sydow 1948:60–88 and Dégh 1996; and, more generally, *EM* 5:744–769. For European and American folklorists the principal genre discrimination for oral narratives encountered in the field has been a bipartite distinction between straightforwardly fictional traditional tales recounted for the purpose of entertainment or illustrating a moral point (that is, what in English we have come to term folktales) and traditional stories about allegedly historical events of the

human past (that is, legends); see, for example, Lüthi 1961. To these is added, as a third genre of traditional oral story, traditional accounts of the formation and establishment of the cosmos and other stories of the doings of the gods in the remote past (that is, myths), a kind of narrative known from older literature and collected by ethnographers among certain traditional peoples in our day but almost never encountered in the field today as living oral stories in Europe or in North America, except among Native Americans.

3. Thompson 1946:368–370, citing *Kinder- und Hausmärchen* (Leipzig: Reklam, 1856) 3: 427 ff. and Margaret Hunt, *Grimm's Household Tales* (London 1884) 2:575 ff. Cf. BP 5:239–249.

4. Grimm (1986) 1:xxiii–xxiv.

5. Benfey (1859) 1:xxi–xxvii. On Benfey and the Indianist theory see further *EM* 2:102–109, 7:151–157.

6. For example, Lang 1873; Hartland 1900.

7. On the collection and study of folktales and other oral narratives in Greece see Megas 1962; Herzfeld 1982; Beaton 1986; *EM* 6:143–161; and Meraklis 1993. For the same in Italy see Simeone 1961; Bronzini 1993; *EM* 7:336–370.

8. Liebrecht 1879; Köhler 1894, 1898–1900; Cosquin 1886–87. Among other scholars who might be mentioned is the prolific Italian folklorist Giuseppe Pitrè, who probably contributed the extensive comparative notes to Afanas'ev's *Russian Secret Tales;* see Dundes 1998.

9. See, for example, Krohn 1931.

10. Thompson 1961:7.

11. On the oral and literary transmission of ballads see, for example, Richmond 1954. A minority tradition of skepticism about oral tradition and the oral transmission of tales extends from Benfey through Albert Wesselski (1931) to the classical scholar Detlev Fehling (1977, 1984) and others; for the principal battlegrounds see the entries "Disenchanted Husband," "Ogre Blinded," and "Rhampsinitos." Fehling (1984:82–83) complains about a lack of true evidence for the oral transmission of narratives from antiquity to the present. Although he grants that certainty in the matter would be nearly impossible to attain, he should nevertheless like to see two conditions met that he acknowledges are almost mutually contradictory: an old document showing that the story in question already existed at a particular time, and proof that no one in the meantime has read the document, since a later reader could have reintroduced the old story into oral circulation. Perfect instances of these conditions are surely not plentiful, but instances that approximate them are not unusual and do illustrate in principle that narratives can be transmitted orally over long periods of time. For the case of a story in current oral circulation that was published in the twentieth century and subsequently discovered on Mesopotamian cuneiform tablets dating to the eighth and seventh centuries B.C. see Gurney 1972; Ellis 1974; and Jason and Kempinski 1981:4–5. For a less dramatic instance see Roberts 1966a:43–44. For a different kind of evidence, a comparative study of an oral story that controls for dissemination via written sources, see Stith Thompson's monograph on the North American Indian story of the Star Husband (Thompson 1953), on which see further Lévi-Strauss 1978:226–273; Young 1970; and Rich 1971. In my view the case for long-term oral transmission is most convincingly made not by the dramatic evidence of old documents but by the thousands of instances of similar stories collected from oral narrators at different places and times. On the questions of the antiquity of folktales and of the continuity of transmission see further Levin 1966; Bausinger and Brückner 1969; Jason and Kempinski 1981; Dalley 1991; Rosenberg 1991; Bottigheimer 1993; *EM* 1:407–419, 8:237–245.

12. Thompson 1958:175–76. Similar observations have been made by other investigators including Franz Boas (Eggan 1958:108); Gudmund Hatt 1949:106; and Christine Goldberg 1986:168.

13. Sydow 1948:11–59.

14. Folktales of the sort commonly known in English as "fairy tales" are often referred to in the scholarly literature as "magic tales" (German *Zaubermärchen*) or "wonder tales" (German *Wundermärchen*, French *contes merveilleux*), since this kind of tale regularly features supernatural elements but rarely fairies. Types 300–749 in Aarne-Thompson's index are magic tales. Some scholars reserve the term fairy tale for the literary magic tale, that is, literary tales composed in imitation of magic tales.

15. On the concept of the ecotype (also spelled *oikotype* or *oicotype* by Anglophone folklorists), see Sydow 1948:11–59; Thompson 1946:440–441; Bødker 1965:220; Cochrane 1987; *EM* 10:258–263.

16. Accounts of the study of the folktale can be found in BP 4–5, especially 5:239–264; Thompson 1932, 1946:367–405, and 1960; Sydow 1935, 1948:189–219; Taylor 1940; Kiefer 1947; Leyen 1958; Lüthi 1964:53–70; Honko 1979–80; Bausinger 1980:11–69; Cocchiara 1981;

Holbek 1983, 1992a, 1992b; Simonsen 1984:29–82; and Dundes (in Bascom 1992:vii–xx). See also note 20, below, on the historic-geographic method. The *Enzyklopädie des Märchens* (1977–), the major work of synthesis on the folktale and folk-narrative scholarship in our own day (see Uther 1986), also features many articles touching upon the history of folktale scholarship.

17. See BP 4:466–467; Georges 1983; Azzolina 1987 (and the review by Uther 1989); Uther 1996, 1997; Jason 2000. *Journal of Folklore Research* 34, no. 3 (1997), is devoted entirely to essays on type and motif indices.

18. Holbek 1990:482.

19. For a sense of the thinking at mid-century see Thompson 1953b; Swahn 1955; and Röhrich 1955, 1956, 1957; Roberts, Dorson, and Halpert 1957.

20. On the historic-geographic method see Aarne 1913; Krohn 1926; Taylor 1927–28; Thompson 1953b:267–286; Jason 1970; Korompay 1978; Goldberg 1984, 1986; Honko 1985a, 1985b; Georges 1986; Apo 1986; and *EM* 5:1012–1030.

21. For example, Asadovskij 1926; Propp 1968.

22. Interpretation of tales: Honko 1979–80, 1984; Simonsen 1984:51–82; Stahl 1989:29–49; Siikala 1990; Holbek 1992a, 1992b; *EM* 7:216–229. Performance: Georges 1969; Ben-Amos 1971; Abrahams 1972; Paredes and Bauman 1972; Ben-Amos and Goldstein 1975; Bauman 1977, 1986; Fine 1984; *EM* 4:315–342; Limón and Young 1986; Fine and Speer 1992; Dégh 1995a; cf. Martin 1989:4–8. Narrators: Wehse 1986.

23. On the texts of the past being unsuited for study with modern methods: Honko 1979–80.

24. For example, Hansen 1976, 1977b, 1990; Holbek 1981, 1987; Herranen 1981; Apo 1986; Lindahl 1987; Stitt 1992.

25. Grimm (1986) 1:22. Strabo 1.2.8.

26. Dégh 1989.

27. For example, Bascom 1965:3.

28. Hartland (1894) 1:v.

29. Aly 1928:254.

30. Grimm 1857.

31. For an example see Hansen 1977b.

32. For example, von Sydow 1948:47–48; Gurney 1972:157; cf. Fontenrose 1981:3–4.

33. Lüthi 1961; Bascom 1965:7–8; Jauhiainen 1998:26.

34. Hansen 1997a:445.

35. Other prominent proponents of the notion of genre devolution were J. G. von Hahn, an influential collector and annotator of Greek folktales ([1864] 1:5), and George Lawrence Gomme (1908:129). The idea is still frequently found (e.g., Lord 1965:175). The Indo-Europeanist theory was revived in a more sophisticated form in the 1920s by von Sydow, who held that the geographical distribution of the magic tale coincides largely with the areas of settlement of Indo-European speakers and their immediate neighbors (Taylor 1931). For a different view see Jason 1978; Jason and Kempinski 1981.

36. Hansen 1983b.

37. Rose 1928:14.

38. Rose 1928:286–304.

39. Rose 1928:294, citing Pausanias 10.33.9–10.

40. AT 178A, *Llewellyn and His Dog*.

41. *Darstellungen aus der Sittengeschichte Roms*. The first edition of this work appeared in 1862–64; the tenth and last appeared in 1921, edited after the author's death by Georg Wissowa. Friedländer's essay "Das Märchen von Amor und Psyche und andere Volksmärchen im Altertum" was printed as an appendix at least as early as the edition of 1871. An English translation of the essay as it is found in the sixth edition appears in Friedländer 1913. Otto Weinreich revised the essay for the last edition of the work.

42. Most extensive are the surveys by Friedländer 1910; Joseph Bédier 1925:90–121; Wolf Aly 1928; Rose 1928; Bolte and Polívka (1930) 4:41–47, 108–126; Röhrich 1984; Καλλέργης 1995.

43. The pioneering survey of folktales in the Old Testament is that of Hermann Gunkel (1987), a founder of form criticism, who argues that the Old Testament contains many narratives of a legendary nature that closely parallel the folktales of today. On Gunkel see Eissfeldt 1962; Rogerson 1979:66–85, as well as his essay in Gunkel 1987:13–18; and *EM* 6:299–302. On the evidence for folktales in ancient Israel see further BP 4:105–108; Goebel 1932; Baumgartner 1959; *EM* 1:419–441, 628–647; and more generally Kirkpatrick 1987; Yassif 2000. On folktales in ancient Egypt see BP 4:95–101; Brunner-Traut 1959, 1965; *EM* 1:175–214; and Hollis 1990. On ancient Mesopotamia see BP 4:102–105; Williams 1956; Perry

1965:xxviii–xxxiv; *EM* 4:494–499; and for the Ancient Near East generally, Jason and Kempinski 1981. Nor has Norse mythology, for which the principal sources are mediaeval, been neglected in this respect. Pioneering studies are those by Olrik 1892 and Leyen 1899; see also the surveys of Sveinsson 1929:xiv–xvi; Bødker 1959; and Schier (*EM* 3:993–995) on folktale analogues in Old Icelandic literature.

44. Welcker (1857) 1:110, cited by Petersmann 1981:43.

45. Friedländer 1910:527.

46. Frazer (1921) 1:xxxii. The same thought has often been stated by other researchers: Nilsson 1925:47–49; Perry 1960:444; Forbes Irving 1990:172.

47. Comments by non-folklorists can still take the unhelpful form of a vague statement that a particular legend is *märchenhaft* or contains elements of folktale, an observation that the writer may not support in any useful way such as by reference either to a type or motif index or to oral texts, as though the author's intuition in these matters were sufficient. So Geoffrey Kirk: "Oedipus himself has a bizarre name redolent of folktale, if indeed it means 'swollen-foot'; his exposure by his parents, his rescue by a shepherd, his winning the kingship of Thebes by solving the Sphinx's riddle–all these, too, are folktale elements" (1974:164–165). But in what sense are they "folktale elements"? What particular folktales do they occur in? What does the assertion mean–that the legend is a transformed folktale? that the legend has borrowed a few motifs from an unrelated tale type or from Folktale as an abstract notion that has no avatars in the particular? And if the motifs can also occur in legend, as here, are they not equally legend elements?

48. Bédier 1925:90–121; BP 4:108–126 (coauthor Georg Polívka was a classical scholar).

49. Succession Myth: West 1966. Combat Myth: Fontenrose 1959. Deluge Myth: Frazer (1918) 1:104–361; Fontenrose 1945; Dundes 1988.

50. For a withdrawal of classical scholars also from hermeneutics and anthropology at about the same time, see Peradotto 1990:3–31.

51. Perry 1952:234–236; Hansen 1988; Dijk 1997:79–111. Story/narrative: *historia, apologos*. Fable: *ainos, Aisopeios mythos, Aisopeios logos*. Joke: *geloion, asteion, iocus, facetia*.

52. Strabo 1.2.8. The meanings of *mythos* shifted in the thousand or so years during which ancient Greek literature was produced; see Lincoln 1999.

53. *Oratio* 7 = *Opera* 1:268.9 Hertlein, cited by BP 4:44. Julian says that an *ainos*, or fable, differs from a *mythos* in its being fashioned not for children but for men, and in its providing not only entertainment but also an exhortation of some kind.

54. *Rhet. Her.* 1.8.13: "fabula est, quae neque veras neque veri similes continet res, ut eae sunt quae tragoediis traditae sunt."

55. γραῶν (τιτθῶν) μῦθοι, γραώδεις μῦθοι, γέροια, *fabulae (fabellae) aniles*, etc. Otto 1890:28, no. 121; BP 4:41–47; Massaro 1977; Scobie 1983:11–30.

56. Cf. Holbek 1987:171. Aristotle says it is unseemly for persons who are not advanced in years to tell certain kinds of tales or to use maxims (*Rhet.* 2.21.9).

57. The Modern Greek term for folktale, παραμύθι (< παραμύθιον), implies a view of folktales as providing consolation and comfort.

58. Hesiod fr. 274 Merkelbach & West. Xenophanes fr. 22 Diels-Kranz.

59. Plutarch *Theseus* 23; Parke 1977:78.

60. Salles 1981; Scobie 1983:10–16.

61. BP 4:13–20, 41–42; Fehling 1977:79–88; Kenney 1990:116. On the Greek "Hear, then, the tale," which serves to introduce the telling of a tale, see Crusius 1879:135 n. 1. On the use of the adverb οὕτως "so," corresponding somewhat to our "once upon a time," to begin the telling of a tale, see Henderson 1987:170 (on *Lysistrata* 784). On introductory formulas in folktales in general see *EM* 3:1227–1244.

62. *Wasps* 1182: οὕτω ποτ' ἦν μῦς καὶ γαλῆ. Scholiast: ἦν οὕτω γέρων καὶ γραῦς.

63. Apuleius *Met.* 4.28.1: "Erant in quadam civitate rex et regina." But cf. Fehling 1977:79–88.

64. Photios *Lex.* s.v. μῦθος ἐσώθη: ἐπίρρημά ἐστι λεγόμενον ἐπ' ἐσχάτῳ τοῖς λεγομένοις μύθοις τοῖς παιδίοις. The contrary apparently was "The tale has been lost" (ὁ μῦθος ἀπώλετο), though the scholiasts explain it variously as indicating that the tale treats unreal matters (schol. Plato *Resp.* 621b), that it has not reached its conclusion (schol. *Theaet.* 164d), or that the listeners are not paying attention (schol. *Phileb.* 14a). In Plato's *Republic* (*Resp.* 10.621b) Socrates, after recounting the Myth of Er, uses both expressions with literal force ("And so, Glaukon, the tale has been saved and not lost . . ."), referring to the fact that Er was able to give to the living an account of the death realm because he had returned from the dead and because he had been excused from drinking from the stream

of oblivion. Petsch's study of closing formulas in folktales (Petsch 1900), which does not examine any material earlier than the mediaeval period, illustrates no formula comparable to "The tale has been saved" from another nation or time. Closest in spirit perhaps is the statement that the narrator has recounted the tale just as he/she heard it, assuring the listener that it has been transmitted faithfully on the present occasion. See further Kratinos fr. 63 K.-A.; Krates fr. 25 K.-A.; Plato *Theaet.* 164d, *Laws* 645b, *Phileb.* 14a; LSJ s.v. *mythos* II.1.

65. Karadagli 1981:97–139.

66. Ruiz Montero 1982; Henderson 1987:170.

67. Krates *Theria* fr. 16 K.-A. = Athenaios 6.267e: παρατίθου, τράπεζα· αὐτὴ παρακεύαζε σαυτήν. Motif D1472.1.7, *Magic table supplies food and drink*, is found in several folktales such as AT 563, *The Table, the Ass, and the Stick*. See further "Schlaraffenland."

68. Gyges: Plato *Resp.* 359d–360c; BP 4:42; EM 6:331–333 (see "Our Lady's Child"). Other magic rings: Lucian *Navigium* 42 (see "Wishing Contest"); cf. also the international tale AT 560, *The Magic Ring*.

69. Persius 2.37–38; Friedländer 1910:539; BP 4:45.

70. AT 513, *The Extraordinary Companions*.

71. AT 612, *The Three Snake-Leaves*.

72. AT 650A, *Strong John*.

73. AT 736A, *The Ring of Polycrates*.

74. Perry 42, Hsr 42. AT 910E, *Father's Counsel: Where Treasure Is*.

75. For example, Babrios 47; Perry 53, Hsr 53. AT 910F, *The Quarreling Sons and the Bundle of Twigs*; EM 3:1256–1261.

76. Vita Aesopi 101–123. AT 922A, *Achikar*; EM 1:53–59.

77. Perry 162, Hsr 171. AT 934A, *Predestined Death*.

78. Babrius 136; Perry 363, Hsr 279. AT 934A, *Predestined Death*, or AT 934B, *The Youth to Die on His Wedding Day*.

79. AT 899, *Alcestis*; EM 1:315–319.

80. AT 931, *Oedipus*; Edmunds 1985.

81. AT 850–999 are international novelle. See further EM 10:120–129.

82. Lying tales are catalogued as AT 1875–1999. Tales of foolish persons are found at AT 1200–1349 (Numskull Stories) and AT 1675–1720 (The Stupid Man). Tales in which the principal actors are animals are AT 1–299, among them AT 112, *Country Mouse Visits Town Mouse*.

83. These seem to me to be the two likeliest stances, but many variations of them have been put forth as well as other explanations such as that old legends and international folktales are unrelated, or at least not immediately related, and run on separate tracks. Parallelisms between mythological narratives on the one hand and international folktales on the other hand are not peculiar to Greek tradition but are found also, for example, in Old Germanic literature. See Welcker (1857) 1:107–114; Hartland 1900; Honti 1931; Vries 1954; Kirk 1974:30–37; West 1985:137–139; Holbek 1987:604–606; Stitt 1992:206–207; Goldberg 1992:51–53; Clunies Ross (1994) 1:31.

84. Lüthi 1961:49–56.

85. Aelian *NA* 7.48; PhS (Perry 563); Aulus Gellius *Attic Nights* 5.14 (Perry 563a), citing Apion's *Aigyptiaka*; cf. Pliny *NH* 8.21. AT 156, *Thorn Removed from Lion's Paw (Androkles and the Lion)*; EM 1:501–508.

86. Joke: *Philogelos* 148. Anecdote: Plutarch *Mor.* 177a.

87. Aarne 1913:18; EM 1:407–419; Holbek 1987:254–257.

88. Jason and Kempinski 1981:6. On the other hand, it is difficult accurately to assess the style and atmosphere, or the styles and atmospheres, of the modern traditional magic tale from published collections, since nearly all published texts have been edited and rewritten. See further Lüthi 1984, 1986.

89. A similar atmosphere pervades the mythological narration of Ovid's *Metamorphoses*. Since it is not otherwise characteristic of classical mythology, I conjecture that Ovid imports it into his narration, recounting many of his myths and legends as though they were wonder tales, mixing higher and lower mythology, as it were.

90. Homer *Od.* 10.275–309. See further Propp 1968:39–50; Petersmann 1981:64–68; Hansen 1997a:458–459.

91. Apollonios of Rhodes 3.66–75.

92. On the folktale as the oral literature of the lowly in nineteenth-century Denmark see Holbek 1987.

93. Perry 1960.

94. *delira et temulenta illa.*

95. *Mor.* 157 = Perry 468. See further BP 4:43, no. 8; Sieber 1957; Karadagli 1981:66–67.

96. Horace *Ars* 340 (*neu pransae Lamiae vivum puerum extrahat alvo*); Friedländer 1910:531. Little Red Riding Hood = Grimm 26, which is a version of AT 333, *The Glutton (Red Riding Hood);* see further Dundes 1989; Zipes 1993.

97. Tertullian *Adv. Valentianos* 2 (*Lamiae turres et pectines solis*); see further BP 4:46, no. 27. Rapunzel = Grimm 12, which is a telling of AT 310, *The Maiden in the Tower.*

98. Cicero *On the Nature of the Gods* 3.12.

99. *Imagines* 1.15, cited by BP 4:44, no. 12.

100. *Oratio* 31.43, cited by BP 4:44, no. 14. See also the comments of another fourth-century figure, the church father Joannes Chrysostomos, against the telling of tales to children, in his essay "On Vanity and the Education of Children."

101. 1. *Tim.* 4:7: τοὺς δὲ βεβήλους καὶ γραώδεις μύθους παραιτοῦ. Cf. also Plato *Resp.* 377.

102. Schürer (1986) 3:476–477.

103. See Dégh and Vázsonyi 1975; *EM* 3:124–126.

104. I conjecture that there may be around four hundred international stories with Greek and Roman parallels. I count over two hundred parallels and partial parallels in Aarne-Thompson's *The Types of the Folktale,* others in Christiansen's *The Migratory Legends* and in other indices, and others that have escaped the notice of the cataloguers.

105. See especially Aarne 1910:i–x; Aarne and Thompson 1928:3–6, 1961:5–9.

106. Sydow 1948:72.

107. A typical example is Aarne's entry on the international tale that underlies Homer's narrative of Odysseus and Polyphemos: "1137. Riese geblendet (Polyphemsage): Flucht unter dem Bauche des Widders."

108. At the 1998 meeting of the International Society for Folk-Narrative Research, a committee of folk-narrative scholars under the leadership of Hans-Jörg Uther was established to undertake a third revision of the index, which is in progress.

109. Stith Thompson's *Motif-Index of Folk-Literature* (1955–58, a revision of the original edition of 1932–36) in six volumes must be clearly distinguished from Antti Aarne's and Stith Thompson's *Types of the Folktale* (1961). The latter classifies whole tales from a limited geographical area and a limited range of time, whereas the former classifies the small narrative ideas that in combination make up whole stories, and includes material from all folk-narrative genres from all parts of the world and from all periods of history, whether it is attested in oral tradition or not. Indices also exist for other culture areas and for other narrative genres (see note 17, above), but they concern us only occasionally in the present work. On motif indices see further Azzolina 1987; Uther 1996; *EM* 9:957–968.

110. Sydow 1958:11–43, 60–88, 127–145; Honti 1931; Schwarzbaum 1963; Holbek 1962–63, 1965, 1987:157–161, 1990; Roberts 1965; Jason 1970:287–288; 1972; Tenèze 1979; Lundell 1983, 1986; Dundes 1997.

111. Although Aarne-Thompson's index proclaims itself to be a catalogue of folktales, it does include some stories that are better classified as myths or legends, such as the legendary AT 751A, *The Peasant Woman is Changed into a Woodpecker* (see Roberts 1964:62–64), and the mythic AT 1148, *The Ogre Steals the Thunder's Instruments* (see "Ogre Steals the Thunder's Instruments"). And some of the tales it lists are known almost exclusively from the literary tradition so that their status as oral tales is questionable, at least in recent times.

112. Jason 1972.

113. According to Alan Dundes, the two basic steps involved in the study of folklore in literature and culture are identification and interpretation. Identification is an objective and empirical operation in which the investigator shows how an item resembles known items of folklore, while interpretation is a subjective and speculative operation in which the investigator shows how and, if possible, why the item differs from other known instances (Dundes 1965). The present work is a contribution to the former operation with some attention also to the latter.

114. So Ben Perry (1960:444): "A motif-index of the folktales used, told, or referred to throughout Greek and Roman literature, if keyed to Thompson's *Index,* would show that many narrative themes, which are commonly known or cited only from mediaeval sources, have their counterparts in ancient lore. In their ancient setting these story-patterns are often overlooked or unrecognized by folklorists, because they are not presented outright as stories, but as parts of or implicit in other literary forms, such as drama, myths, or local legends, and because the texts in which they are found are so widely scattered and often obscure."

115. Propp 1972; Thompson 1946:435–436; Fontenrose 1959:7–9, 1981:2–3; Dundes 1962a; Young 1979; Honko 1986:119–120; Hansen 2001.

116. One could perhaps add a seventh category, *Motific*, in which a motif that is central to an international tale is found in antiquity, although the tale itself is not attested and probably arose later. See for example "Carrying Water in a Sieve" and "Loading the Wood."

117. See further Hansen 1997b.

118. Cf. Schrempp 1992:5–6.

The Tales

Apprentice and Ghost 🍃 Eukrates and the Automaton

A sorcerer's apprentice (servant) reads a verse aloud from the forbidden book belonging to his master and thereby evokes a ghost (devil, etc.), which he is unable to make disappear again. When finally the sorcerer comes and utters the proper formula, the troublesome spirit disappears.

This little story of near disaster is AT 325*, *Apprentice and Ghost*, which Aarne-Thompson classify among tales of supernatural adversaries.

In a narrative evidently from Yorkshire, there once was a learned man living in the north country who knew all the languages of the world and all the mysteries of the universe. He possessed a book bound in black calf that he kept locked with an iron key, and this book contained the secrets of the spiritual world. The master had a foolish boy as his servant, who was not allowed to look into the black book. One day the master was gone, and the curious servant went into his chamber. The master had forgotten to lock his book, so that the boy opened it, put his finger on a line, and read it aloud. Suddenly the room became darkened, there was a clap of thunder, and the Evil One stood before him, saying: "Set me a task!" The boy gave him the only task he could think of, which was to water a pot of geraniums. The spirit instantly left the room and returned with a barrel of water, which he poured over the pot. This he did repeatedly, so that the floor of the room was filling up with water. The boy said that was enough, but the spirit paid no attention. The water had now reached his chest, and all Yorkshire would have drowned if the master had not suddenly remembered that he had neglected to lock his book, returned home, and uttered the words that cast Beelzebub back to where he had come from.[1]

In a tale from Devonshire first published in 1850, the vicar of a certain parish was a student of sorcery and possessed many books on the subject. One day while he was away conducting a service in another village, one of his servants found a book lying open in the vicar's study and began reading it aloud. The sky darkened, a storm arose, and the door opened. In walked a black hen and a

black chicken, who presently began to increase in size, becoming as large as a bullock. At this moment, the vicar abruptly broke off his sermon and rushed home. When he arrived he found the hen to be as tall as the ceiling. He cast down some rice to distract the creatures and then reversed the spell.[2]

The basic course of events in *Apprentice and Ghost* is attested elsewhere in both tale and legend. In his index of migratory legends, Reidar Christiansen lists a story commonly told in Norway in which a certain person owns the Black Book, which he keeps hidden. Once, however, he is away and sends his servant to fetch it. The inexperienced person, looking into the book, happens to summon the devil and, since he must give him a task, assigns him a difficult or impossible job, such as to braid a rope out of sand.[3] Presently the owner of the book returns and exorcises the devil, though sometimes traces of the devil's activities can still be seen in the region. Christiansen labels the legend *Inexperienced Use of the Black Book*.[4]

The tale of *The Magic Mill* (AT 565) features a magic pot or mill instead of a supernatural being, but otherwise the principal events are essentially those of *Apprentice and Ghost* and *Inexperienced Use of the Black Book*. In this tale a magic pot comes into the possession of a woman inexperienced in magic who commands the pot to produce porridge, but since she does not know how to command it to stop, the pot fills the house with porridge until finally the owner of the pot returns and stops it. Or the magic object is a mill that grinds meal or salt endlessly until commanded to stop. Thus, in a folktale collected by the brothers Grimm from Dortchen Wild in 1813, a poor girl and her mother lived alone and had nothing to eat. The girl met an old woman in the forest who gave her a pot. All she had to do was to say, "Pot, cook," and the pot would produce millet porridge, and when she said, "Pot, stop," it would stop cooking. The girl brought the pot home with her, and thereafter she and her mother had all the porridge they wanted. One day when the girl was away, the mother said, "Pot, cook." After she had her meal of porridge, she wanted the pot to stop producing porridge, but since she did not know the correct command it continued to cook, filling the house with porridge, and soon nearly every house in the town was filled with porridge. At that moment the girl returned, uttered the proper command, and it stopped. But people had to eat their way back into town.[5]

Eukrates and the Automaton

The earliest attestation of this story, as Grimm perceived,[6] is in Lucian's *The Lover of Lies*, a dialogue about the telling of incredible stories. A certain Eukrates says he will relate an incident from his own experience, not something he has merely heard. In his youth his father sent him to Egypt as part of his education. Once he was sailing up to Koptos to see a certain sight when he made the acquaintance of a fellow passenger, a temple scribe from Memphis named Pankrates, a man of amazing wisdom and learning in things Egyptian. People said he had spent twenty-three years underground in a sanctuary where he was instructed in magic by Isis. Pankrates performed all sorts of wonders whenever the boat was at anchor, such as riding upon crocodiles and swimming with wild animals, which fawned upon him. Eukrates recognized that Pankrates was a holy man, after a while they became companions, and Pankrates shared some se-

crets with Eukrates. Eventually the holy man persuaded Eukrates to leave his servants in Memphis and travel alone with him, assuring Eukrates that they would not lack persons to wait upon them. And indeed whenever they passed the night at an inn, Pankrates would take a door-bar, a broom, or even a pestle, put clothes on it, and say a spell over it, after which it walked and appeared in every way to be a human being, drawing water for them, buying provisions, preparing meals, and in general waiting upon them. When Pankrates was finished with his servant, he would say another spell, and it would become a broom or a pestle again.

Since Pankrates would not share this one secret with him, however, Eukrates concealed himself in a dark place and overheard Pankrates utter the three-syllable spell, changing a pestle into a servant. The following day when Pankrates was out, Eukrates took the pestle, dressed it in clothes, uttered the syllables, and told it to carry water. After it had filled an amphora with water, Eukrates told it to stop carrying water and become a pestle again, but it kept on carrying in more water, filling the house with it, so that Eukrates became desperate. He cut the pestle into two with an axe, but the result was that now there were two servants carrying water. Presently Pankrates returned, perceived what had happened, turned the creatures into wood again, and departed forever, leaving Eukrates behind.[7]

Lucian's narrative brings together a young Greek student on an educational trip in an ancient and exotic land and an accomplished Egyptian sorcerer steeped in occult learning. As in later texts, complete power over a certain thing resides in the knowledge of two magic formulas, one to initiate supernatural action, and the other to terminate it, of which the Greek tyro acquires only the former.[8] The supernatural actant in Lucian's story—the pestle that becomes a humanoid servant—resembles both branches of the modern story: *The Magic Mill* in that the actant is an ordinary object like a pot or a mill, and *Apprentice and Ghost* and *Inexperienced Use of the Black Book* in that it also is a supernatural being like a ghost or devil. The problem encountered by the sorcerer's apprentice in the Greek story is exactly that of the sorcerer's servant in the Yorkshire tale, the production of a water carrier who bears water endlessly and cannot be stopped, a simple service that is useful in moderation but becomes nightmarish in excess, like the ceaseless production of porridge.

In all these texts, regardless of type or genre, (1) a magic object or magic formula (2) comes into the hands of an inexperienced person, (3) who wittingly or unwittingly utters a command for a particular supernatural action to begin. (4) Once the action has begun, (5) the hapless person is at a loss to stop it. At the last moment, however, (6) the magician who owns the item returns and (7) by uttering the proper formula puts a stop to the action. The modern story is well attested in oral tradition, and Lucian's narrative of Eukrates must draw upon the oral story in one of its ancient forms. There is no need to wonder, as does Bompaire, whether the story of the sorcerer's apprentice is the product of Lucian's imagination.[9]

As in some modern texts it is the protagonist's excessive curiosity about forbidden matters that leads to a crisis beyond his competence to solve. In this respect the hero resembles the would-be magician Lucius in a story known from two ancient novels, Pseudo-Lucian's *Lucius, or the Ass* and Apuleius's *Metamorphoses*. After secretly watching a Thessalian witch turn herself into a bird, Lu-

cius was eager to experience the same transformation, but mistakenly applying the wrong magical ointment to his body he was transformed, not into a bird, but into an ass. In the story of the ass the problem is not the protagonist's lack of knowledge concerning the means of disenchantment, and therefore the solution is not a timely arrival of the witch (the antidote, as his accomplice informs him immediately, is merely to eat some roses); rather, the hero's problem is how to put this knowledge into practice, for one obstacle after another delays his gaining access to roses and so bringing about the desired retransformation.[10]

Lucian puts the story of the young Eukrates into the mouth of Eukrates himself, who presents the story as something that actually happened to him in his youth; that is, the story is framed as a personal-experience narrative. Eukrates is now an old man in the company of other, mostly credulous old men. His story concluded, Eukrates is asked by Deinomachos whether he still knows how to turn a pestle into a human being, and Eukrates replies that he does, though he still cannot change a water carrier back into a pestle again. The thoroughly skeptical Tychiades rebukes both men for spinning such tales and filling the minds of the young with them.[11]

Lit. AT 325*, *Apprentice and Ghost*. BP 2:438–440. ML 3020, *Inexperienced Use of the Black Book*. Cf. Liungman 1961:167–171. Ashliman, type 325*. Hayes 1997:59–73.

1. Briggs (1970–71) A1:411–412.
2. Briggs (1970–71) B2:622.
3. For activities that frequently serve in different tales as difficult or impossible tasks to keep unwelcome spirits occupied, see "Carrying Water in a Sieve," "Devil to Count Stars," and "Making a Rope of Sand."
4. Christiansen 1958:28–35 = ML 3020, *Inexperienced Use of the Black Book*. For a study of British and American versions of the legend see Hayes 1997:59–73.
5. Grimm 103.
6. BP 2:438.
7. Lucian *Lover of Lies* 34–36.
8. As Reitzenstein (1963:5 n. 3) points out, Pankrates' magic corresponds in some respects to that found in Greco-Egyptian magical papyri in which the magician obtains a supernatural helper. A manual of the fourth or fifth century A.D. instructs the magician how to summon the familiar, how to put him to work, and how to dismiss him. "Whenever you want him to do something, just say his name into the air and say, 'Come,' and you will see him; indeed, he will be standing nearby. Say to him, 'Do this task,' and he will do it immediately. When he has done it he will say to you, 'Do you want anything else? For I am in a hurry to the sky.' If you do not have an immediate task for him, say to him, 'Go, sir,' and he will depart" (Preisendanz 1:10–13, no. 1.180–186).
9. 1958:695.
10. On the affinity of this story to international tales of magic and transformation see Scobie 1983.
11. Lucian *Lover of Lies* 36–37.

Asking the Large Fish ≈ Philoxenos the Poet

At a meal the host serves the small fish to the guest but reserves the large fish for himself (herself), either secretly or openly. Perceiving this, the guest puts one of the small fish to his ear and, when asked what he is doing, explains that

he asked the fish a question but that the fish replied it was too young to possess the requisite information, saying that the guest should rather ask the large fish. Thereupon the host gives the guest the large fish.

This comic tale of trickery is AT 1567C, *Asking the Large Fish*.

In an anecdote about the legendary Muslim cleric, Hodja Nasreddin, the hodja's mother one day was cooking large and small fish, and the hodja observed her through a hole in the door. The mother proposed to the father that they hide the big fishes under the bed and place the small ones on the table for their meal; after their son had departed they would fetch the big ones and eat them. So the little fish were served. During the meal the hodja picked one up and held it to his ear. His father asked him what he was doing. He said he was questioning it. "About what?" asked the father. "I wanted to learn from it what kind of fish it was that swallowed Jonah, but it answered: 'I don't know. Under the bed there are larger fish. You'll have to ask them.' "[1]

More commonly the opposing characters in the tale are defined, not as parents and son, but as the master of a house and an unrelated but relatively humble person such as a beggar. Generally all the fish are on the table in full view of everyone, so that the clever protagonist triumphs not by revealing his awareness of the existence of the larger fish but by embarrassing or amusing his host, and so inducing the man actually to give him the larger fish. Thus, in a French narrative a farmer in Morvan named Gaspard went to his landlord's house to pay his rent. The landlord, who at the time was entertaining several friends, invited Gaspard in with the intent of subtly mocking him in front of his companions. But Gaspard soon extracted from the landlord an invitation to join in their meal. When fish was brought in, the landlord served his tenant the smallest fish. The farmer picked them up one after another, held them to his ear, put them down, and shook his head. The landlord asked why he was putting the fish to his ear, the farmer replied that he was asking them for news of his uncle, who had drowned three years previously, but the fish said they were too young and had not been born yet. Thereupon the landlord, asking Gaspard if he wanted to consult the big fish, handed him a carp. The tale concludes with the farmer outwitting his landlord one more time before departing with the landlord's ham. After he had gone, the landlord's guests laughed, not at Gaspard, but at their host.[2] In this text, *Asking the Large Fish* appears as the central incident in an implicit match of wits between a landlord and a tenant, in which the clever underling gets the better of his master.

The Poet Philoxenos as Guest

In the course of a discussion on prominent gourmands, the Greek author Athenaeus records an anecdote, taken from the peripatetic philosopher Phainias, about the poet Philoxenos, who had a passion for fish. Philoxenos was dining at the court of Dionysios I of Syracuse, and seeing that a large mullet had been set before Dionysios and a small one before himself, he took the little fish in his hands and held it to his ear. When Dionysios asked him why he was doing that, Philoxenos replied that he was composing a poem on Galateia and wanted to ask the mullet some things about Nereus; the mullet (he said) had answered that it had been caught too young to join Nereus's company but the fish lying be-

fore Dionysios, which was older, knew absolutely everything Philoxenos wished to learn. Dionysios laughed and sent over his own fish to Philoxenos.[3]

This text is the earliest attestation of the tale and represents its only occurrence in ancient literature. Athenaeus (ca. A.D. 200) gives as his source for the anecdote the philosopher Phainias of Eresos (fl. 320 B.C.), a pupil of Aristotle, which indicates that the story must have been current at least by the fourth century B.C. The reputation of Philoxenos of Kythera (436–380 B.C.) for being fond of fish as well as his actually having composed a poem featuring the sea nymph Galateia evidently helped to attract the tale to him. Reflecting a bias for narratives of ostensibly historical rather than fictional content, the ancients more commonly framed witty narratives as anecdotes attached to prominent persons than as jokes told of anonymous types.

There was also some irony in telling this tale of Philoxenos if, as Athenaeus also reports, the poet was caught trying to seduce Dionysios's mistress, Galateia. Dionysios had him thrown into the quarries, where Philoxenos retaliated by composing *Kyklops*, a poem *à clef* in which he represented his experience metaphorically, Dionysios being the Kyklops, the flute-girl Galateia being the sea nymph Galateia, and himself being Odysseus.[4] Galateia appears as the name of a Nereid, or daughter of Nereus and Doris, as early as Hesiod and in later mythology attracts the amorous interest of the cyclops Polyphemos, whose love she rejects.[5]

Lit. AT 1567C, *Asking the Large Fish.* Wesselski 1911 1:247–248, no. 158. Pauli 1924 2:407–408, no. 700. Avanzin 1954:133–135. *EM* 4:1218–1221.

1. Wesselski (1911) 1:82–83, no. 158; similarly, Başgöz and Boratav 1998:113.
2. Ranke 1972:72–73, no. 98, citing A. Millien and P. Delarue, *Contes du Nivernais et du Morvan* (Paris 1953), pp. 215–218.
3. Athenaeus 1.6e–f = Phainias fr. 13 Wehrli.
4. Athenaeus 1.6f–7a.
5. Hesiod *Th.* 250; Theocritus 11; Ovid *Met.* 13.738–897.

Attentive Donkey

"The villager believes that the donkey who is moving his ears listens to what he tells him." Aarne-Thompson so describe the content of a little tale that they classify as AT 1213*, *The Attentive Donkey.* Since they cite only one text of this tale, the narrative is possibly not international, as the asterisk indicates; nevertheless, the modern text they cite is Greek, so that it has likely enjoyed a continuous life in Greece from ancient to modern times.

A Greek Proverb

In his compilation of Greek proverbs, made in the second century of our era, Zenobios includes the following proverb: "Someone was telling a story to a donkey, and it was wiggling its ears."[1] Zenobios explains that the proverb is applied to persons who display a want of perception or feeling and thereby resemble a donkey, a sluggish animal that (he says) wiggles its

ears as though it has already heard on a previous occasion everything the person says. The same proverb is found in the paroemiological collection of Zenobios's contemporary Diogeneianos, and the *Suda* lists "A donkey wiggling its ears."[2]

The form of this narrative is that of the fable-proverb, or short fable. When a fable is extremely short, it is indistinguishable from a proverb that is structured as a narration of a past event, a form of proverb that is found in Greece and Western Asia in ancient and mediaeval times.[3] An anglophone example of this form of proverb is "Curiosity killed the cat." The most familiar classical instance of a fable-proverb is that of the mountain in labor. Diogeneianos gives it in his collection of proverbs as "A mountain was in labor and then gave birth to a mouse," explaining that it refers to disappointed expectations.[4] Phaedrus, stretching the minuscule story to two and a half lines, includes it in his collection of Aesopic fables.[5] So Diogeneianos classifies the mountain in labor as a proverb, while Phaedrus identifies the same material as a fable.

The fable-proverb of the donkey that wiggles its ears when it is addressed seems to have been well known in the second century when Zenobios and Diogeneianos compiled their collections, for we find apparent allusions to it in other works of the time. In his book *On the Natural Faculties*, Galen explains that persons who care greatly about learning must really work at it, and that it is for such persons that he hopes his own book will be useful. "They will only be few in number. For other people my treatise will be superfluous, like a person telling a tale to a donkey."[6] The allusion, which cites only the tale teller and not the donkey, emphasizes the futility of giving information to those who cannot understand it rather than the incompetency of the audience. Galen alludes to the tale once again in another passage, this time focusing instead upon the listener. Several men were engaged in a discussion about defining words, and each time that one discussant offered a definition, the narrator called attention to other meanings of the word that the proffered definition did not take into account. Finally, the narrator asked what a dog was. When one of the discussants replied that it was an animal with four legs that barked, the speaker asked whether dog in the sense of sea-dog (that is, shark) was also an animal with four legs that barked, whether dog in the sense of the dog-star was, and whether dog in the sense of the facial ailment (unilateral facial paralysis) was. "At these words the old man wiggled his ears like a donkey."[7] Here Galen emphasizes the plight of the listener, who, though baffled, presumably looked on gravely as though he fully appreciated the problem.

Lucian illustrates an interesting biform of the fable-proverb when he says of an ignorant collector of books, "You hold a book in your hand and you are always reading, but you understand nothing of what you read. You are a donkey listening to a lyre and wiggling your ears."[8]

The only hint that the fable-proverb of the donkey was known to the Romans appears in a poem of Horace in which the poet imagines how the philosopher Demokritos, if he were alive in Horace's day, would respond to the experience of being present at the noisy Roman theater. So far as concerns the din of the theater, Horace remarks that Demokritos would think that the authors were telling their tale to a deaf donkey ("*scriptores autem narrare putaret asello/fabellam surdo*"), a locution that appears to mix the fable in its allusive form of "tell a tale

to a donkey" with the Roman proverbial expression "tell a tale to a deaf (person)" (*surdo fabellam narrare*).[9] The result is somewhat strange logically (if the listener is deaf, what difference does it make if he is also a donkey?), but poetically it probably suggests that the audience cannot hear because of the noise but would not understand even if it could hear.

Lit. AT 1213*, *The Attentive Donkey.*

1. Zenobios 5.42: ὄνῳ τις ἔλεγε μῦθον, ὁ δὲ τὰ ὦτα ἐκίνει.
2. Diogeneianos 7.30; *Suda* s.v. ὄνος τὰ ὦτα κινῶν.
3. Perry 1965:xx–xxxiv.
4. Diogeneianos 8.75.
5. Phaedrus 4.24. See further Horace *Epist.* 2.3.139; Plutarch *Agesilaus* 36; Lucian *Hist. Conscr.* 23; Schwarzbaum 1979:530–533.
6. Galen *Nat. Fac.* 3.10.
7. Galen *De Puls. Diff.* 2.3 (8:573 Kuehn).
8. Lucian *Adversus Indoctum* 4; cf. Diogeneianos 7.33 and the note of Leutsch and Schneidewin (*CPG* 1:291–292). On donkeys and musical instruments see further Adolf 1950; *EM* 4:426–428.
9. *Epist.* 2.1.199–200. Otto 1890:335, no. 1715.

Axe Falls into the Stream 🪓 Hermes and the Woodcutter

A woodcutter's axe falls into a stream or pond. While he laments its loss, a supernatural being fetches him a golden axe, which he refuses, saying it is not his. The scene is repeated with a silver axe. Finally, the creature brings him his original axe, which the man accepts. Because of his honesty he is given also the two other axes. Learning of the woodcutter's experience, another man deliberately drops his axe into the same water. When the supernatural being offers him first a gold and then a silver axe, the man identifies them as his own. Consequently, the supernatural being neither gives him the precious axes nor fetches his original axe.

This little tale, AT 729, *The Axe Falls into the Stream*, is found mostly in European oral tradition.[1]

A French text of the tale was recorded in 1952 from Onias Ferron, a nineteen-year-old illiterate French-Canadian fisherman from New Brunswick, according to whom an old man was once cutting wood near a river. At noon he became thirsty and went to drink from the river. While drinking he dropped his axe in the river and began to bawl. A mermaid who heard him asked him what was causing him to bawl. He explained that he had an axe, which he lost in the water and could not find. She plunged into the water, returned with a silver axe, and asked if this was it. The man said it was not his axe. She descended again and showed him a golden axe. No, that was not his either. She went down again and showed him his axe, and when he saw it he said that that one was his. She said that since he was an honest man, she would give him the three axes.

That evening the woodcutter encountered another woodcutter, who asked him where he came from with these three axes, and the first man explained that

he had lost his axe in the water while drinking and that a mermaid had given him the three axes. The next morning the second woodcutter took a fine axe, went to the woods, threw it into the water, and began to bawl. The mermaid asked him why he was crying, and he said that he had lost his axe in the water. She descended and then showed him a silver axe. When he saw it, he said, yes, that was his axe. But she said: "You are a liar. This isn't your axe. It's mine. Since you're a liar, if you want to have your axe, go down and look for it yourself."[2]

Hermes and the Woodcutter

The earliest texts of this story, and its only attestations in classical antiquity, appear in the anonymous collections of Aesopic fables in Greek prose. The earliest of these collections, the *Collectio Augustana*, also called Recension I, was composed probably in the latter half of the first century A.D. or in the second century. The different recensions of the fable vary little in content.

According to the author of Recension I, a man who was cutting wood beside a river accidentally dropped his axe in the stream, which carried it away. The man sat on the bank and lamented its loss. Pitying him, Hermes came, learned the cause of his grief, and, going down into the stream and bringing up a golden axe, asked the man if this was his. When the man said it was not, Hermes brought up a silver axe. When the man again said it was not his, Hermes brought up the man's own axe, which the man acknowledged as his own. Because of his honesty, Hermes gave him all three axes. Having left with the axes, the man related the incident to his companions.

One of his companions, wishing to have the same experience, went to the same river to chop wood, purposely dropped his axe into the river, and then sat down and wept. When Hermes came and asked what had happened, the man said he had lost his axe. The god brought up a golden axe and asked him if it was his. The man greedily said it was, but Hermes neither gave him the golden axe nor returned to him his own axe.[3]

Interestingly, the French-Canadian narrator prefers to introduce the false axes in a climactic order of ascending value, first the silver and then, even more temptingly, the gold axe, whereas the classical narrator arranges them in a descending order of value: gold, silver, and, finally, the man's own axe, which presumably is of iron. The value of an axe of silver or gold is of course intrinsic rather than practical; gold and silver are the favorite metals of the folktale.[4]

Neither narrator chooses to draw out the episode of the second woodcutter. As soon as the mendacious woodcutter reveals his dishonesty, which he does immediately upon seeing the first valuable axe that the supernatural being brings up, the test is over. He gets no second chance.

It may seem odd in the Greek tale that Hermes appears to be connected closely with water, as though he were a water deity, but the connection is only apparent. Hermes is rather the deity of lucky finds (*hermaia*), regarded as gifts of the god, and of unexpected good fortune in general; moreover, he is, like Pan, a rustic deity, a frequenter of the countryside. The woodsman's recovery of his lost axe is a gift of Hermes, which in the tale is expressed concretely by having Hermes himself return it to its owner; it merely chances that the object

in question is lost in water. The apparent connection of the god and the river misleads the author of Recension II (fourth or fifth century A.D.), who adds by way of explanation that Hermes is "the god of the river."

Structurally the tale is comprised of two episodes, one in which a character is successful and one in which a second character, attempting the same action, fails. On this level the tale is identical to the many other stories constructed upon the idea of *unsuccessful repetition*. The device is common in oral narrative, both for whole tales and for episodes within tales.[5] See for example "Gifts of the Little People," which like the present tale portrays an encounter between the natural and the supernatural worlds.

The evident function of the tale is to recommend honesty and discourage dishonesty by presenting a simple drama in which honesty is rewarded and dishonesty is punished. The consequences of this behavior are external rather than internal, largely because oral narrative prefers the concrete, and it is of course easier to represent material well-being than, for example, spiritual well-being. Since the ancient texts appear only in collections, we possess little information from antiquity about the actual employment of the tale in social situations. Each of the texts is, however, accompanied by an epimythium, that is, an ideal application of the tale from the viewpoint of the fabulist, and these epimythia are in agreement: "divine providence (*to theion*) helps honest persons as much as it opposes dishonest persons." So the fabulists themselves view the tale as illustrating divine benevolence toward the honest person and divine hostility toward the dishonest person.

More information about the story is provided by the Byzantine paroemiologists Makarios Chrysokephalos and Michael Apostolios, who include in their collections the proverb "A river does not always bring axes."[6] Evidently the tale of the woodcutter was familiar enough to generate a proverb. Since both men explain that the proverb applies to a person who does not always present the same things (meaning, I believe, that a person does not always behave the way that he or she has done in the past), it appears that the tale and the proverb were not applied in the same ways.

An incident in the life of the Old Testament prophet Elisha shows an interesting, if remote, similarity to our tale. Some men were cutting wood by the River Jordan when one man lost his axe-head in the river. He exclaimed in distress. The man of god asked him where it fell in, and the other man showed him. Elisha threw a piece of wood in, the iron axe-head floated to the top, and the prophet told the man to lift the axe-head out, which he did.[7]

Lit. AT 729, *The Axe Falls into the Stream*. BP 2:227; 3:192. Holbek (1962) 2:187, no. 149. Schwarzbaum 1979:xlv–xlvi, note 76. *EM* 1:1109–1110. Ashliman, type 729.

1. *EM* 1:1109.
2. Barbeau 1954:210–211.
3. Perry 173, Hsr 183.
4. Lüthi 1986:27.
5. See, for example, Dundes 1962b; *EM* 7:92–100.
6. Makarios 6.68 (*CPG* 2:197), Apostolios 13.67a (*CPG* 2:593–594): *Ouk aei potamos aksinas pherei*.
7. 2 Kings 6.4–7 = *Septuagint* 4 Kings 6.4–7.

Bargain Not to Become Angry. *See* Labor Contract

Battles of the Pygmies and the Cranes

A traveler comes to a land of dwarves, who suffer periodically from attacks by cranes (storks, geese, or other animals). The traveler fights on their behalf or shows them how to combat the large birds (animals) by striking them with clubs (by twisting off their necks, etc.). The grateful dwarves reward their helper or arrange for his return home.

This story is not registered in any type index, but Thompson lists the Greco-Roman tradition of the conflict of the Pygmies and the cranes in his *Motif-Index* as F535.5.1, *War of pygmies and cranes*.

The lore of many peoples tell of the periodic attacks of cranes or other large birds upon a community of dwarves, although the tradition may receive little or no narrative expression beyond the quasi-ethnographic report of regular attacks by large birds upon a particular community of small persons. So in his *History of Northern Peoples* the sixteenth-century Swedish author Olaus Magnus says that dwarves in Greenland wage war against cranes, a conflict that he compares to the classical tradition of the battles of Pygmies and cranes.[1] Such an inversion of the usual relationship of predator and prey is also a common motif in tales of topsy-turvydom (see "Topsy-Turvy Land").[2]

In other cases a story tells how one or several human beings come upon the land of the dwarves by chance, learn of their sufferings, and show them how to defend themselves, winning thereby the gratitude of the locals. The events are recounted from the viewpoint of the visitors, for whom the dwarves are exotic persons in a faraway land, like a nation of Tom Thumbs or, since the dwarves are helpless before their enemies the birds, like a nation of children in need of adult help.[3] The Arab author Mūsā Ud-Damīrī, who composed his Hayāt ul-Hayawān in the second half of the fourteenth century, tells how during a voyage a man of the Rūmīyah came to an island inhabited by people around three feet tall and for the most part one-eyed. He was taken prisoner and brought before the king, who had him placed in a cage. One day he saw the men preparing for battle, and asked them about it. He was told that they had an enemy that usually attacked them around this time. Presently a flock of storks set upon them, and it emerged that the dwarves who lacked an eye did so because the storks had pecked it out. The visitor attacked the birds furiously with a club, causing them to fly away, and as a result the dwarves held the man in high esteem.[4]

In a Central Asiatic story told by the Turkish Karagass, a man came to the edge of the world where he found a folk that rode hares. They were dwarves, who suffered from attacks by their enemies the sables, which killed them. The visitor killed a sable, thereby winning the friendship of the dwarves.[5]

According to a Cherokee story, some Cherokee youths once traveled south until they reached a tribe of very small people, about the height of a man's knees, called Tsundige/wǐ. Being weak and puny they could not fight and

lived in terror of the wild geese and other birds that came in flocks from the south to make war on them. At the time of the travelers' arrival the little men were fearful because the wind from the south blew white feathers in their direction, indicating that their enemies were on their way. When the Cherokee asked them why they made no defense, they explained that they did not know how. Since the time was insufficient for making bows and arrows, the youths told them to use sticks as clubs, striking the birds on their necks to kill them. Several days later the birds arrived in great numbers, and the men hid in their homes in the sand, from which the birds attempted to pull them out with their bills and eat them. But the little men attacked the birds on their necks, killing so many that the rest departed. The little men gratefully hosted the Cherokee youths with the best they had until the youths left to visit other tribes. The youths heard that the little men succeeded in driving off the birds several more times by means of their clubs but were eventually killed by sandhill cranes, which were so tall that the men were unable to reach up to their necks to strike them.[6]

In a story told by the Comox tribe, several brothers chanced to be towed across the ocean where, after some adventures, they came to a village. When they stole a halibut from a dwarf who was fishing, the man captured them and took them to the village of the dwarves. The chief instructed the newcomers to help them in their war against the Birds, which shot the dwarves with their feathers. The brothers helped them by clubbing the Birds, and one of the brothers thereafter removed the feathers from the bodies of dead dwarves, after which they revived. The grateful chief sent the men back to their home across the ocean.[7]

As is apparent, this narrative is found in both the Old and the New Worlds, and since the New World texts display no features suggesting that the Amerindian story has been borrowed recently from abroad, and since it is perhaps hard to imagine that so unusual a narrative has been invented more than once, the story was possibly brought from Asia to North America in pre-Columbian times, as apparently several other traditional tales were.[8] But if its oddness has suggested to some scholars the probability of prehistoric diffusion, its simplicity has suggested to others the likelihood that it arose in different places independently.[9] Although the story has been studied only piecemeal, it is uncertain that a systematic study of the known texts could clarify its prehistory.

The Pygmies and the Cranes in Antiquity

The best-known tradition of warfare between dwarves and large birds is of course the Greek, and later also Roman, lore of the battles of the Pygmies and the cranes. Obviously the idea was already known to Homer and his audience in the eighth century B.C., since the poet alludes to it familiarly in a simile in which he likens the martial behavior of Trojan warriors on a particular occasion to that of migrating cranes who attack Pygmies:

> But after each contingent of men had arranged itself together with its leaders,
> The Trojans went with screaming and shouting, like birds,

> Just as the screaming of the cranes takes place beneath the sky,
> Who, when they flee winter and boundless rain,
> Fly with screams to the streams of Ocean,
> Bringing death and fate to Pygmy men,
> And through the air they offer evil strife.
> But the Achaeans, breathing might, went in silence,
> Eager in their hearts to defend one another.[10]

For Homer, it appears, cranes migrate south for the winter, going as far as the River Ocean at the edge of the earth, where they aggressively attack the Pygmies, who must be thought as dwelling there. The Greek word "pygmy," meaning "dwarf," derives from *pygmê*, which signifies "fist" and also is a unit of measurement, a cubit, the distance from the elbow to the clenched fist. The word could be used generically ("pygmies") to refer to dwarves generally or as an ethnic label ("Pygmies") to refer to the particular community of dwarves who battled against cranes. Although in ancient art Pygmies are often given negroid features, their skin color is rarely mentioned by ancient authors, who were interested more in their size than in their race.

With one variation or another the hostility of the Pygmies and the cranes is found in many authors after Homer. In his *History of Animals* Aristotle mentions that cranes migrate from the Scythian plains to the marshes of upper Egypt, whence the Nile flows and where the Pygmies live. He adds that the tradition is no myth (*mythos*): they are in reality small in stature, as people say, as also are their horses, and they live in caves.[11] A symposiast in Athenaeus quotes from the *History of India* by the historian Basilis, who declares that certain dwarves in India are at war with the cranes and employ partridges as steeds.[12] The poet Kallimachos refers to the crane that, delighting in the blood of Pygmies, flies from Egypt to Thrace.[13] In one of his fables Babrius recounts how certain cranes, driven from a farmer's wheat field, decide to flee to the land of the Pygmies.[14] Aelian tells a story of the origin of cranes and of their hostility toward Pygmies. Gerana, a queen of the Pygmies who was overly proud of her beauty, was changed into an ugly crane by angry goddesses and thereafter waged war on her former people, blaming her excessive pride on their excessive adulation.[15] According to Pliny the Pygmies live beyond India and are a little over two feet in height; in the spring they ride rams and goats to the seashore, where they eat the eggs and chicks of the cranes, for otherwise they would not be able to withstand the flocks of cranes that would result; they build their houses out of mud, feathers, and eggshells.[16] Juvenal describes a Pygmy warrior rushing into battle armed with tiny weapons, only to be snatched up by the fierce talons of a Thracian crane and borne away.[17] Representations of Pygmies in ancient art agree in showing Pygmies armed with diminutive clubs, spears, or swords and engaged in combat with cranes, men and birds being around the same size.[18] And so on. The core of the tradition is obviously that there is ongoing hostility between Pygmies and cranes, in which the birds attack the men. Beyond that core we hear that the origin of their conflict has to do with the origin of cranes as a species, that the Pygmies employ weapons against their enemies, that they are not strong, that they ride small animals as steeds, that they live somewhere far away (at the edge of the world, in

upper Egypt, etc.), that they live in unusual dwellings of one type or another, that they harvest the eggs and the chicks of the cranes in the absence of the parents, etc.

What one does not find in any classical author, however, is the international story illustrated above, according to which travelers arrived at a distant land of dwarves, who like innocent children were unable to fend off the large birds that regularly attacked them, until the traveler showed them how to do so or helped them himself, winning their affection and gratitude. Rather, the classical Pygmies and cranes battle on with no resolution, armed Pygmies against cranes with a taste for Pygmy blood, a bizarre, recurrent event in a land so far away that the familiar rules do not apply.[19] The nearest approach that any ancient narrative makes to the international story is a legend reported by Herodotos, which he says he heard from some men of Cyrene, who in turn learned it in conversation with the king of the Ammonians, Etearchos, who had gotten it from certain Nasamonians, an African people. According to Herodotos, five adventurous Nasamonian youths once set out to penetrate further into the Libyan desert than anyone ever had done before. After traveling for many days through desert they came upon some fruit trees. As they picked fruit, small men who were shorter than men of middle stature attacked them, captured them, and took them to a town of similarly short, black men. Neither the Nasamonian youths nor the locals could understand each others' speech. Herodotos's Cyrenaean informants told him that the youths returned home safely and that the inhabitants of the land they visited were magicians.[20] This narrative certainly resembles the frame of the story of the dwarves and birds, in which travelers go to some faraway country where they come upon a nation of dwarves, who may take them captive and may later arrange for their return; but there is no hint here of the central features of the attacks by large birds and of the help provided by the visitors, nor are the natives labeled Pygmies, nor is the story Greek. If the international narrative type of the visitors to the land of the dwarves circulated in antiquity, the Greeks borrowed from it only the basic conflict, the geranomachy, which they subsequently elaborated in different ways.

What is unusual in the case of the Greco-Roman tradition, however, is that there really did, and does, exist biological communities of black persons of very short stature in Central Africa, to whom Europeans have given the old Greek name, Pygmies.[21] They are not visited by migrating cranes, at least in their present homes, which are in the forest, though they may have lived elsewhere in antiquity. Nor are cranes aggressive birds that attack human beings. So the classical tradition of the conflict of Pygmies and cranes rests upon little or no fact except for the actual existence of human groups of very small stature in Central Africa. The fact that the story of the dwarves and the birds is told also in regions in which ethnic dwarves are not found indicates that the story does not depend upon the actual existence of such communities, just as the Old World myth of a world flood did not depend for its existence upon the occurrence of an actual cosmic deluge.[22]

Lit. Motif F535.5.1, *War of pygmies and cranes*. Halliday 1921. Dangel 1931. Toivonen 1937. Vajda 1953. Roberts 1966b:164–166. Scobie 1975, 1977a. Ballabriga 1981.

1. *Historia de Gentibus Septentrionalibus* 11.11, cited by Toivonen 1937:89–90. An illustration shows the dwarves armed with spears; one dwarf is mounted on a goat.

2. Dangel 1931:134.

3. Cf. AT 700, *Tom Thumb*, and indeed Thompson locates motif F535.5.1, *War of pygmies and cranes*, among motifs of thumblings.

4. Scobie 1975:125, citing A. S. G. Jayakar, *Ad-Damîrî's Hayât al-Hayawân*, vol. 2, pt. 1 (Bombay 1908), p. 450.

5. Dangel 1931:133. The Finns also have a tradition according to which a traveler went to the land of dwarves and helped them inter alia in their war against the cranes or other large birds; see Toivonen 1937:90–94.

6. Scobie 1975:126, citing James Mooney, "Myths of the Cherokee," *Annual Report of the Bureau of American Ethnology* 19 (1900):325. The first classical scholar to call attention to this text was Halliday (1921).

7. Scobie 1975:127, citing Franz Boas, *Annual Report of the Bureau of American Ethnology* 31 (1916):867. Boas gives two similar texts, one from the Nass and the other from the Nisqually; all three peoples are located in the northwest coast of the United States and Canada. For additional Amerindian texts see Dangel 1931.

8. For example, Roberts (1966:164–165) raises the question.

9. Thus, Dangel 1931 argues for monogenesis, Vajda (1953:256) favors polygenesis, and various other scholars incline to the one position or the other or acknowledge the difficulty of attaining certainty in such a problem (e.g., Scobie 1975, 1977a).

10. Homer *Il.* 3.1–9.

11. Aristotle *HA* 8.12, p. 597a, 4–9. He does not explicitly allude to the conflict of the dwarves and birds, which is marginal to his topic.

12. Athenaeus *Deipnosophistae* 9.390b. Basilis was a Greek historian of the third and second centuries B.C. whose work survives only in fragments. Basilis calls the Indian dwarves *hoi mikroi* "the small folk," however, not *hoi Pygmaioi.*

13. Kallimachos *Aitia* 13–14. Ovid similarly alludes to "the bird that delights in Pygmy blood" (*Fasti* 6.176).

14. Babrius 26.

15. Aelian *NA* 15.29; for other versions of the story see Ballabriga 1981:64–66; Forbes Irving 1990:21–23.

16. Pliny *NH* 7.26–27.

17. Juvenal *Sat.* 13.167–170. Ancient authors agree however that the Pygmies are feeble (e.g., Hesiod fr. 150.18 MW; Oppian *Hal.* 1.620–625) rather than great warriors.

18. See Dasen (1993), plates 58–70; *LIMC* 7.1:594–601 and accompanying plates.

19. Therefore there is no reason to suppose, with Scobie (1975:125), that a Greco-Roman *story* of a geranomachy spread from the West to the Middle East and Far East, since we have no evidence for such a story. The simple nonnarrative tradition of ongoing hostilities between dwarves and cranes was, however, borrowed by the Chinese from the Greeks (Scobie 1975:123–124).

20. Herodotos 2.32–33.

21. See further Roscher (1902–9) 3:3283–3317; Hennig 1932; *RE* (1959) 23:2064–2074; Dasen 1993:175–188 and passim.

22. Cf. Dangel 1931:129.

Best Friend, Worst Enemy ✒ Aesop and the Dog

A man is instructed to bring along his best friend and his worst enemy. Taking his dog and his wife he demonstrates how the former is his best friend and the latter is his worst enemy.

This is the core of AT 921B, *Best Friend, Worst Enemy,* which consists essentially of one character's posing a task and another character's cleverly solving it. These two events are elaborated or augmented in various ways. Often the reason why a task is posed at all or why this particular set of problems is posed is not made

very clear, but this difficulty, if it is a difficulty, is soon forgotten as the narrative quickly turns its attention to the protagonist's response to the challenge. The hero may merely present his dog and his wife respectively as his best friend and worst enemy, or he may strike each of them in order to display their dissimilar reactions (his dog loyally returns to him when called, whereas his wife rages and/or betrays him), which he interprets as perfectly illustrating their respective characters. In some texts the man must also bring his most faithful servant (he brings his donkey) or his best jester (he brings his infant child) or both, for a total of three or four problems, but only the first two problems are invariably present since they form a contrastive pair and are more closely connected to the larger plot.

Best Friend, Worst Enemy is usually found as an episode within some larger tale, into which it is integrated. When it appears in *Wisdom of Hidden Old Man Saves Kingdom*, its principal function is to exemplify the cleverness of the old man, who advises his son how to accomplish the tricky task. According to a text collected in 1930 from a narrator in Jalisco, Mexico, a king once decreed that all old persons should be shot, but one son hid his old father underground and brought him food daily. When finally the son's money ran out, he asked his father what they should do. The old man told him to go to a certain rich man named Miguel and ask for a loan of a hundred pesos. When the son asked Don Miguel for the loan, Miguel asked about the purpose of the loan. He answered that it was for his field. Miguel asked: "And your father, where is he?" He replied that they killed him in accordance with the decree. But Miguel decided to pose a difficult problem, and if the young man could solve the problem, it would show that his father was alive. So Miguel said: "I'll give you the loan, but on the condition that you bring me your friend and your enemy." The son agreed, went away, and told his father, who told him to bring his wife and his dog, to strike each one of them in Miguel's presence, and then to call his dog. The son did so, and his dog came to him again, but when he called his wife, she told Miguel not to lend her husband any money, saying he has kept his father hidden underground. Miguel admitted that this was what he wanted to know. He gave the son five hundred pesos to take to his father, revealed that there was a plot to overthrow the king, and asked the son to be governor. In time the king was overthrown, the young man became governor, and when he came to power he issued all kinds of guarantees to all the old people, and they all lived very happily.[1]

The articulation here between *Best Friend, Worst Enemy* and the host tale is typically casual. Why does Miguel suspect that the youth's father may still be alive? Why does he believe that this strange task is likely to bring out the truth of the matter?

Whether the husband hits his wife, as here, or merely presents her as his worst enemy, the tale holds the spouses to somewhat different standards, largely passing over the husband's unkind treatment of his wife but condemning the wife's ready disloyalty toward her husband. So in a mediaeval text, after the man merely labels his wife as his worst enemy, the angry wife yells at him for his thanklessness, inasmuch as she has shown so much compassion for his father whom he has not executed but rather keeps hidden underground; then the youth points out to the king how true his characterization of his wife has been, since for

the sake of a mere word she has revealed his secret and thereby condemned him to death. On this host tale see "Wisdom of Hidden Old Man Save Kingdom."

Best Friend, Worst Enemy can play a role in another international tale in which the wife reveals her husband's secret, although in this case the secret is fictive.[2] In a tale in the *Gesta Romanorum* (124), after a knight had offended a king the knight's friends obtained a pardon for him on the condition that he come before the monarch both walking and riding (*pedester et equester pariter*) and that he bring with him his most devoted friend, his best jester, and his worst enemy (*amicum fidelissimum et joculatorem optimum et inimicum perfidissimum*). In the meantime the knight and his wife played host in their home to a pilgrim, and when the man suggested to her that they kill their guest and take his money, she agreed to the idea. During the night the husband sent the traveler on his way and slaughtered a calf, placing its remains in a sack. He showed his wife the sack, saying that he had buried the man's body in their stable. On the day of his appearance before the king he took his dog in his right hand and his wife and infant baby on his left side. As he approached the castle he continued to walk with his left leg and placed his right leg over the dog as though he were riding, and so entered as both pedestrian and equestrian.[3] The king observed his cleverness, and asked where his most devoted friend was. The man wounded his dog with his sword so that it ran away howling, then he called it, and the dog came back to him, whereupon the knight called it his most faithful friend. The king, accepting this, asked about his jester, and the man pointed to his infant, explaining how much pleasure the child's play gave him. When finally the king asked him about his worst enemy, the man turned to his wife and struck her, accusing her of looking seductively at the king. The woman was enraged at the injustice of her husband's treatment, asking him why he hit her and asking him if he had forgotten the murder he had committed at their house. The knight struck her again, chiding her for disgracing their child, whereupon she angrily led the party to the supposed remains of the pilgrim. But as they found only the remains of a calf, the nobles admired the cleverness of the man and the king held him thereafter in honor.

According to a text collected from a black Portuguese emigrant from the Cape Verde Islands to Massachusetts, two *compadres* in San Vincente were good friends, one being married and the other a bachelor. One day the bachelor asked the married man who his best friend was, and the man answered that his wife was. The bachelor told him he was mistaken. To demonstrate his point, he told the married man to put a pig in a sack and take it that evening to his wife, explaining that he had killed a man and needed to bury him secretly. The man did so, and his wife quickly helped him. The next day the bachelor instructed the married man to move the furniture around in his house and tell his wife that she was not taking proper care of it. The man did so, and when his wife became angry he slapped her. She cried out, people came, and she said her husband wanted to kill her, just as he had done to a man on the previous night. They arrested the husband but, upon investigation, found only a dead pig, so that they released the man. Finally the bachelor instructed the married man to beat his dog and then snap his fingers, after which the dog would come to him.

That would prove that a man's best friend was his dog, not his wife, for women are interested only in themselves.[4]

Aesop and the Dog

Although *Best Friend, Worst Enemy* does not occur as such in ancient sources, an episode in the so-called *Aesop Romance* contains essentially the same elements and is so reminiscent of it that it must be a literary reworking of the oral tale.

The philosopher Xanthos, attended by his slave Aesop, went to a dinner at the house of one of his students. During the dinner Xanthos handed a portion of the meal to Aesop and told him: "Take this to her who likes me." Aesop took the basket of food home and, wishing to repay his master's mistress for her earlier maltreatment of him, showed her the food, asking her to observe that nothing was missing. She confirmed as much and asked whether the food had been sent for her. Aesop replied that it had not, having been sent rather to her who liked her master. Then he called his master's pet, a bitch, and gave her the food to eat, after which Aesop returned to the dinner party. Xanthos asked Aesop whether he had given her the food, whether she had eaten it, and whether she had enjoyed it, to each of which Aesop replied affirmatively. Xanthos asked what she had said, and Aesop answered that she did not say anything but had expressed her gratitude internally. Xanthos was angry at this. Meanwhile, at home Xanthos's wife announced to her maids that she could no longer live with Xanthos, since he preferred his dog to her. After the party Xanthos returned home. When he showed affection to his wife, she told him not to come near her, called him a dog lover, and said that she wanted her dowry back. Xanthos, inferring that this trouble was caused by Aesop, summoned him and asked him to whom he had given the food. Aesop asked Xanthos to whom he was supposed to give the food. Xanthos said he was to give it to her who liked him. Aesop then called Xanthos's dog, saying that the dog liked him and that Xanthos's wife said she liked him but really did not. The proof of this (Aesop continued) was that his wife wanted her dowry back and wanted to leave her husband for the sake of a trifling amount of food, whereas his dog could be beaten and knocked down and would still return to her master wagging her tail. So if Xanthos had wanted Aesop to deliver the food to his wife, he should have said so and should not have told him to deliver it to her who liked him.[5]

An interesting difference in the composition of the literary episode and the oral tale is that the protagonist, instead of defining "friend" and "enemy" in relation to himself, defines them in relation to someone else. That is because the present tale is conditioned by certain prior events that motivate Aesop to punish his master and his master's wife, so that the episode is shaped as one of a series of episodes in which Aesop torments Xanthos by playing the literal fool, following his instructions with exasperating precision, while at the same time Aesop now sees an opportunity to avenge himself on his mistress. Xanthos is accordingly cast in the role of the task giver, though somewhat unwittingly in this case since he does not really intend for the task to be a difficult or subtle one at all, and Aesop plays the correlative role of the problem solver, deciding to devise a clever solution for the task despite the fact that it does not require one. Wishing to embarrass his master and mistress individually and to sow dissension be-

tween them, Aesop compares, not his own wife unfavorably with a dog as in the folktale, but the wife of his master. Consequently the injured feelings are those of his mistress, and it is his master who bears the brunt of her displeasure.

Consider these similarities and differences between the literary treatment and the ordinary oral tale. (1) In the folktale the protagonist's task is to present his own best friend and worst enemy, that is, to determine and reveal who they are. The Greek text accomplishes the same end by a less direct route, for in this case the hero's task is to bring something to a special friend, which Aesop perversely chooses to interpret as a task to determine and signify who the special friend actually is and who it is not. (2) Whereas the hero of the oral tale identifies his dog as his best friend and his wife as his worst enemy, angering his wife, the romancer makes a significant shift to his master's family, making the hero identify the master's dog as the master's good friend and the master's wife as no friend at all, with the same effect on the wife. (3) The offended wife now responds by entirely withdrawing her loyalty from her husband, in the oral tale by betraying his secret, and in the ancient romance (in which there is no conspiratorial secret) by deciding to leave him. This gesture in turn sets up (4) the resolution, in which the folktale hero and Aesop each justify their identification of dog as friend and wife as unfriend by contrasting the dog's loyalty with the wife's disloyalty. Whereas the folktale hero may actually strike each of them in turn in order to provoke a reaction, the ever verbal Aesop *describes* how the dog would respond if its master should strike it.[6] The folktale protagonist sometimes points out how the wife is ready to betray her husband for the sake of a mere *word*, as in the mediaeval text cited above; in exactly the same way, Aesop points out how the wife is ready to leave her husband for a trifling amount of *food*.

The literary episode and the international folktale are clearly forms of the same tale, and it is certainly easier to suppose that the Greek text is a literary adaptation of the folktale to the fictional life of Aesop, creatively distorted to suit the author's purposes, than it is to suppose that the oral tale arose from this episode in the ancient romance. Since the *Aesop Romance* appears to have been composed in Egypt in the first century A.D. by a Greek resident or a Greek-speaking Egyptian, the author presumably drew upon a telling of *Best Friend, Worst Enemy* in oral circulation in Egypt.

Lit. (AT 921B, *Best Friend, Worst Enemy*.) Pauli (1924) 2:355–356, no. 423. BP 2:364–367. Wesselski 1925:237. Vries 1928:223–230. *EM* 5:275–282.

1. Wheeler 1943:6–7, no. 3.
2. See AT 1381C, *The Buried Sheep's Head* (not attested in antiquity); *EM* 5:276–277; Ashliman, type 1381C.
3. A common motif in several folktales, the injunction to come both walking and riding or to satisfy some other set of apparently contradictory conditions is often part of the protagonist's task in the present tale. I do not explore it further since it does not appear in the ancient text to be considered presently. Notice, however, that the motif itself is ancient, since riddles constructed upon this idea are found in the ancient repertory: "A man who was not a man killed a bird that was not a bird sitting on wood that was not wood with a stone that was not a stone," the solution being eunuch, bat, fennel, pumice (Athenaeus 10.452c; cf. BP 2:365 n. 1).
4. Parsons (1923) 1:202–203, no. 68.
5. *Vita Aesopi* 44–50.
6. The romance presents Aesop as one who expresses himself through words more than

action, so that it is in character for him to make this point verbally and hypothetically rather than by acting it out; moreover, as a slave who must always fear a beating, Aesop is perhaps hesitant to inflict this punishment on another helpless creature.

Boastful Deer Slayer ☙ Agamemnon

A lazy man complains that he is hungry or that god never gives him anything. An old man urges him to hunt (fish). When the man catches a deer (some fish), the old man returns and reminds him to thank god for the catch, but the man declares that it was he, not god, who caught the game. Thereupon the slain deer revives and runs back into the woods (the cleaned fish revive and leap back into the stream). Often the story concludes with an aetiological coda.

AT 830A, *The Boastful Deer Slayer*, is manifestly a moralistic or cautionary tale illustrating how a person may be punished if he denies due credit to god, for that which god gives god can also withdraw. The narrative has been collected in modern times in Estonia and Latvia.

Thus, an Estonian legend recounts how a lazy man spent his days at the hut he had inherited from his father, either sunning himself or lying in bed complaining to god that he was poor and hungry. One day an old man came out of the woods and called his attention to the wild game that he could easily capture. So the man set out a net and caught a stag. He killed the animal with a knife and had just stuck the knife in the stag's rear leg to begin eviscerating the animal when the old man returned, calling his attention to god's kindness and urging him to give his thanks. But the man replied arrogantly that everything was the result of his own effort and skill. Thereupon the stag leapt up and darted into the woods. As a sign of the man's ingratitude god let the knife remain, so that all stags have a bone that resembles a knife.[1]

Agamemnon as Hunter

The earliest evidence for the legend of Agamemnon as an arrogant deer hunter is found in the *Kypria*, a poem of the epic cycle that was composed around 700 B.C. Though the epic itself has not survived, we learn from a summary of it made by the Byzantine scholar Proklos that when the Greek forces gathered in Aulis for a second time with the intention of sailing to Troy, Agamemnon went hunting, shot a deer, and declared that he had surpassed even Artemis.[2] The enraged goddess prevented the Greeks from sailing by sending a storm. The seer Kalchas disclosed the goddess's anger and bade them sacrifice Iphigeneia to Artemis. They sent for her on the pretense of a marriage to Achilleus, and attempted to sacrifice her, but Artemis carried her away to the Taurians, made her immortal, and substituted a deer for her at the altar.[3]

Other accounts give the story with some differences in detail. According to the mythographer Apollodorus, Agamemnon, having shot a deer, said: "Not even Artemis." For this reason and because previously Agamemnon's father

Atreus had not sacrificed to Artemis a golden lamb that he had vowed to her, the Greek fleet setting out from Aulis for Troy had no wind for sailing.[4] The seer Kalchas declared that the fleet could not sail unless the most beautiful of Agamemnon's daughters should be brought forth as a sacrifice to the goddess. So Agamemnon sent for his daughter Iphigeneia on the pretense of marrying her to Achilleus. Agamemnon was preparing to sacrifice her at the altar when Artemis carried the girl off, putting a deer in her place and making her a priestess among the Taurians. Some authors say that Artemis made her immortal.[5]

Agamemnon's boast is given in full by a scholiast on Homer. He says that while the Greek fleet was assembled in Aulis in Boiotia and unable to sail, the seer Kalchas declared that they would not be able to proceed to Ilios unless Agamemnon should sacrifice his daughter Iphigeneia to Artemis, because he had slain the sacred doe that was being reared in her grove and moreover had boasted that not even Artemis could have shot like that. So Agamemnon was forced to bring Iphigeneia to the altar, but the goddess took pity on her and substituted a deer for the maiden, whom she relocated in her temple among the Taurians in Scythia.[6]

Impious boasters, both male and female, are a common sight on the Greek mythological landscape, offending one or another deity by claiming to be the deity's equal or superior and then suffering the deity's wrath. In this story Agamemnon takes one of Artemis's deer—one of her special children, as it were—and to make it worse claims to be a better hunter than the goddess. So Artemis, protectress of wild creatures and of the young, takes in exchange one of his children, his most beautiful daughter, a child for a child. The equivalence is manifested again, though in reverse order, when Artemis substitutes a deer for Iphigeneia at the sacrificial altar: deer = Iphigeneia = deer.

The ancient and the modern legends agree in their most basic features. (1) A hunter kills a deer and (2) makes a sacrilegious boast, saying that god did not give him the deer (or god could not have shot as well). As a result, (3) god punishes him (the stag revives and escapes, or he must sacrifice his own daughter to the deity). The narratives are nearly identical in their first two features, the protagonist being a deer hunter and an impious boaster who asserts his superiority to god. But the third feature is the most interesting because it is similar in function in each tradition though dissimilar in content; or rather it is unobviously similar in content, for even here the corresponding events show some resonance. The two deer that appear serially in the Greek legend—one is slain, after which another materializes alive—are reminiscent of the single deer in the modern legend that first is slain and then revives. Or, to pursue instead the equivalence of Artemis's deer and Agamemnon's daughter, the legend concludes with Iphigeneia's escape from death, thanks to the intervention of Artemis, while the folktale concludes with a deer's escape from death, thanks to the intervention of god. A historical connection between the ancient and the modern stories certainly seems possible.

Differences in the ancient and modern traditions are also telling. The sin of the Christian hunter is his unwillingness to give due acknowledgment to the role of the divine in human activity, though he has no thought of really competing with god, let alone vaunting his own superiority. Agamemnon's offense, on the other hand, is precisely to see himself as a rival of the deity, and in the deity's own divine province. His audacity is graver and more typically

Greek, like that of such mythological impious boasters as Niobe, Kassiepeia, Arachne, the Pierides, and Haimon and Rhodope. Just as Agamemnon's offense is the more outrageous, so also are its consequences the more terrible, and these are developed to such an extent in the Greek legend that the pathos of Iphigeneia—her betrayal by her own father, the false promise of marriage, her sacrifice to further the ambitions of men, her dramatic rescue—dominates the interest of the Greek story, relegating the hybristic hunter to the background.

Lit. (AT 830A, *The Boastful Deer Slayer.*) *EM* 6:12–16.

1. Dähnhardt 3:15.
2. ὑπερβάλλειν ἔφησε καὶ τὴν Ἄρτεμιν.
3. *Chrestomathia* 5:104 Allen.
4. Atreus promised to sacrifice to Artemis the most beautiful of his sheep, but when a golden lamb appeared he neglected his vow (Apollodorus *Epit.* 2.10–11). See "To Sacrifice a Giant Candle."
5. Apollodorus *Epit.* 3.21–22.
6. Schol. Homer *Il.*1.1.108: οὐδὲ ἡ Ἄρτεμις οὕτως ἂν ἐτόξευσε. Other authorities for the story include Sophocles *Electra* 563–576, who mentions that Agamemnon came upon the deer in a grove of Artemis; Euripides Iphigenia in Tauris 1–41; Callimachus *Artemis* 3.260–263; schol. Euripides *Orestes* 658; Tzetzes *Schol. on Lycophron* 183; and Hyginus *Fab.* 98. On the legend and its sources see Roscher 1:93; Frazer 2:190–193; Platnauer 1938:vii–xiii; Fraenkel 2:97–98; Gantz 1993:582–588; cf. also Brelich 1977:16–17. According to some authors Iphigeneia was actually sacrificed (e.g., Pindar *Pyth.* 11.17–25; Aeschylus *Agamemnon*). The substitution of an animal for a human being in sacrificial ritual is a familiar motif in stories, as in the Hebrew legend of Abraham and Isaak and in the story of Alexander and the donkey driver (see "Dog on the Bridge"). See also *LIMC* 1.1:262

Bride Won in a Tournament 🔗 Pelops and Hippodameia

The hero learns that a king has promised the hand of his daughter to the man who wins a tournament that the king has established. On his way to the tournament the hero comes upon a corpse that has been refused burial. He arranges for the proper burial of the corpse, sometimes at so great expense to himself that he scarcely has the resources to proceed to the tournament or to compete in it (he may give up all his resources, including his weapons and horse). Presently however he encounters a man (knight, merchant, etc.) who furnishes him with a fine steed (and equipment or weapons, as necessary), usually on the condition that the hero share half of whatever he may win. After the hero is victorious, winning the princess and the kingdom (or half the kingdom), his benefactor reappears to ask for his share. He may demand the bride or the possessions, or he may demand to share the bride. For his part the hero may offer his possessions in order that he may keep his bride, or he may offer his bride in order that she not be harmed. When the hero thus signals his willingness to keep their bargain, the benefactor declines his share, explaining that he is the man whom the hero once buried. Then the ghost, or revenant, disappears.[1]

This tale is AT 508, *The Bride Won in a Tournament*, one of a number of traditional tales featuring a supernatural helper known to folk-narrative scholars as

the Grateful Dead Man.[2] Popular in the Middle Ages, this tale is particularly well attested in mediaeval romantic literature.

So in *Richars*, a French romance dating to the end of the twelfth century, the impoverished knight Richars heard that the king of Montorgueil had promised his daughter to the victor in a tournament, and because of the generosity of a provost he was able to set out with a horse, several attendants, and an amount of money. On the way he stayed at a house in which the corpse of a man lay exposed, and he learned that it was the body of a knight who had died owing the owner money. Richars gave all he had in order to secure the release and burial of the man, and proceeded alone with a poor borrowed horse to the tournament. On the way a White Knight joined him, offered him help in the contest, and gave Richars his fine steed. After winning the tournament and the princess, Richars offered the White Knight his choice of the lady or the property, but the stranger declined, explaining that he was the ghost of the knight whom the man had buried, and disappeared.[3]

In *Rittertriuwe*, a Middle High German poem also from the twelfth century, Graf Willekin von Montabour learned that a rich and beautiful maiden had established a tournament, promising her hand to the knight who should win it. He went there and found lodging at the house of a man who would receive him only if he should pay the debts of a dead man whose body lay in the dung. Moved by the story, Willekin used almost all his money to ransom and bury the corpse. For the tourney itself he borrowed a horse from a knight he did not know, on the condition that they would divide everything he won. Willekin won and married the maiden. A couple days later the stranger came to his room and demanded a share in his marital rights. When the stranger refused Willekin's offer of all his possessions instead, Willekin yielded the bed to him. But then the stranger explained that he was the ghost of the dead man, and disappeared.[4]

For the mediaeval romancer, and perhaps for the mediaeval raconteur as well, it was natural to cast the hero as a knight, to fashion the contest as a tourney, and to present the narrative stuff as a quasi-true adventure.

In a folktale in Straparola's *Pleasant Nights*, composed in the sixteenth century, a man died, leaving a bequest to his son Bertuccio, who was something of simpleton. Setting out on his travels with a third of his inheritance, Bertuccio came upon a thief who had just killed a merchant on the public highway. Bertuccio pitied the dead man, whose corpse he purchased from the highwayman and carried to a nearby church, where he arranged for an honorable burial, leaving the rest of his ducats to be spent for masses for the dead man's soul. Since he now had no money, Bertuccio returned home, where his mother reproached him for his folly. Taking his remaining ducats he came upon some soldiers with a maiden they had captured, and ransomed the girl with his money, not knowing that she was Tarquinia, daughter of King Crisippo of Navarre. Bertuccio took her home to his mother. The king sought his lost daughter and soon located her in the house of Bertuccio. Before departing she instructed him that if her father should give her in marriage, Bertuccio should come to Navarre and signal her in a certain way, for she wished to wed no other man but him. Presently the king proclaimed that he wished to find a husband for her. Hearing this, Bertuccio set out on an old mare, and on the way he encountered a noble cavalier, who bade him exchange clothes and horse with him, making one condition, that when Bertuccio returned, he

should give the cavalier back his clothes and horse together with half of whatever he might have won. Bertuccio agreed, and then he rode to court, gave the agreed sign, was recognized by the princess, and wed her. As Bertuccio was conducting his bride home he met his benefactor again. The youth gave up the horse, the clothing, and half of the gifts given him by the king, but the cavalier pointed out that he had not yet divided his wife. When Bertuccio asked how they could possibly divide her, the cavalier replied that they could cut her in half, whereupon the youth told the cavalier to take her. When the cavalier saw how simple and kindly Bertuccio was, he gave Bertuccio everything he had. He explained that he himself was the spirit of the man to whom Bertuccio had given honorable burial, the man for whose soul Bertuccio had arranged for many masses to be said. Then the spirit vanished. Rejoicing, Bertuccio returned home with Tarquinia.[5]

Pelops and Hippodameia

The ancient Greek legend of Pelops and Hippodameia tells essentially the same story as *The Bride Won in a Tournament*.[6] King Oinomaos offered the hand of his daughter Hippodameia to the man who could beat him in a chariot race from Pisa (= Olympia) to Corinth. The young Pelops went to Pisa to compete against Oinomaos, and with the aid of a grateful dead man, of supernaturally swift horses, of his opponent's charioteer, or of some combination of these, was victorious, winning the hand of the princess and the kingdom. Some versions tell of a pact to share the princess.

That Pelops has the help of a grateful dead man when he wins Hippodameia is related by the fourth-century historian Theopompos.[7] After Pelops got horses and a chariot from Poseidon he set out for Pisa in the Peloponnesos to win Hippodameia, eager to compete against her father Oinomaos. While he was on his way to Pisa, his charioteer Killos died. The dead Killos appeared to Pelops in a dream, grieving over his death and asking for a funeral. Pelops cremated him, buried the ashes, heaped a mound over him, and constructed a sanctuary to Killaion Apollo in commemoration of Killos's sudden death. He even founded a city named Killa after him. After his death Killos helped Pelops overcome Oinomaos in the race.

Like the heroes in the international tale, Pelops treats the dead man grandly. In this case the deceased is known to him, a situation that is less common but not unparalleled in texts of the Grateful Dead Man.[8] Unfortunately this intriguing text is so summary that it does not explain how the ghost of Killos helped Pelops win his race against Oinomaos, merely saying that he did so.

That Pelops won the race with borrowed horses and equipment is related by Pindar and other authors. As a youth Pelops had been a lover of the god Poseidon. When now Pelops wished to race against King Oinomaos for the hand of his daughter Hippodameia, he asked Poseidon to help him succeed, if Pelops's love for him had been pleasing. Poseidon lent Pelops his golden chariot and winged horses, with which Pelops was victorious, acquiring Oinomaos's daughter and kingdom.[9] This version is probably implied in all texts and illustrations in which Pelops is equipped with winged horses or a winged chariot. The earliest such de-

piction is found on the sixth-century chest of Kypselos, which Pausanias describes thus: "Oinomaos is chasing Pelops, who has Hippodameia. Each man has a pair of horses, and those of Pelops have wings growing from them."[10]

And a pact to share the princess or the kingdom is attested by several authors in a third version of the legend, in which Oinomaos's charioteer Myrtilos helps Pelops. This is the form of the story most commonly mentioned by ancient authors. Collating these sources, we get the following composite account. Because Oinomaos received an oracle that he would be slain by his eventual son-in-law, or because he was in love with his own daughter, he was unwilling simply to give Hippodameia away in marriage. Instead he established a contest for her hand. A suitor had to take the girl in his chariot and race from Pisa to the Isthmus of Corinth. Oinomaos would pursue him in his own chariot and kill the youth if he should catch him. In this way the king slew a dozen or so suitors. When Pelops arrived, he persuaded Myrtilos to betray Oinomaos, promising him one night with Hippodameia or promising him half the kingdom; or, alternatively, Hippodameia fell in love with Pelops and induced Myrtilos to help him, promising Myrtilos first sexual rights to her. Myrtilos sabotaged Oinomaos's chariot by not inserting the linchpins or by inserting linchpins of wax, so that during the race a wheel rolled off and Oinomaos perished. Pelops thereby won Hippodameia and her father's kingdom. As Pelops, Hippodameia, and Myrtilos were returning, Myrtilos kissed Hippodameia or tried to rape her or reminded Pelops of his oath to share her or reminded Hippodameia of her oath to sleep with him. Pelops cast him into the sea, where he drowned.[11]

In the different versions of the Greek story, then, three different characters are said to help Pelops win the race, each one answering in one or more ways to the grateful supernatural helper of the folktale. In the Killos version there is the deceased Killos, who in gratitude for Pelops's generous treatment of his corpse helps Pelops in an unspecified way to win the race. In the Poseidon version there is Poseidon, who in gratitude for a previous favor lends the youth his wondrous horses and chariot, with which Pelops wins the race. And in the Myrtilos version there is Myrtilos, who makes a pact with Pelops or Hippodameia for a share of Hippodameia or the kingdom. Each helper reflects an aspect of the benefactor in *The Bride Won in a Tournament*. Killos, as a helpful dead man, corresponds to the actual person of the Grateful Dead Man. Poseidon's loan of wondrous horses and equipment is formally identical with the fine steed and sometimes also equipment that the supernatural helper lends the hero in the international story. And the pact that Myrtilos makes with the hero (or Hippodameia), according to which he will get a share of the winnings, is reminiscent of the usual pact between the dead man and the hero. So the person and actions of the helper in the international story—a grateful dead man who makes a pact with the hero to help him in exchange for half of his winnings (which prove to be a princess and a kingdom) and whose help consists in his providing the hero with a fine horse— are distributed over three characters in the different Greek texts: Killos the grateful dead man, Poseidon the provider of horses, and Myrtilos the pact-maker. Ultimately these helpers must be separate developments of the same character, the grateful dead man. Notice that two of the helpers are charioteers: as soon as Pelops buries one charioteer, another emerges to help him, as though Killos re-

layed the role to Myrtilos. And the other, Poseidon, provides the protagonist with a chariot.

The theme of the covenant between the helper and the hero takes an interesting form in the legend. Instead of an abstract bargain in which the hero agrees to share half of his winnings, which in the folktale always prove to be the princess and usually wealth or a portion of the kingdom, the bargain in the Pelops legend takes the concrete form of sharing the princess or dividing the kingdom. These traditions are really two forms of the same thing, one stated as an abstract principle, the other as its application. When the helper in *The Bride Won in a Tournament* demands his share, the hero learns that the helper wants to divide or share not only the hero's wealth but also the princess, by which the helper usually means a physical division of the bride, although a sexual sharing is found in a few texts, as in the story of Graf Willekin summarized above.[12] In no text ancient or modern does the helper actually get the bride. In the international tale, once the hero acknowledges the helper's claim, the revenant identifies himself as the dead man, voluntarily gives up his share, and disappears. In the legend of Pelops, the hero's ignoble helper Myrtilos makes his claim, but Pelops with equal ignobleness denies it and kills him.

So *The Bride Won in a Tournament* and the legend of Pelops and Hippodameia share the following important features (the form a feature takes in the Pelops legend is occasionally added in parentheses for the sake of clarity or when it deviates somewhat from the norm of the international tale). (1) A king offers the hand of his daughter in marriage to the man who wins a tournament he has established. (2) Learning this, the noble hero sets out to compete in the contest. (3) On the way he arranges for the burial of a dead man with unusually great liberality. (4) The hero subsequently meets a man who agrees to be his helper in exchange for a share of his winnings (a night in bed with Hippodameia; half of the kingdom). (5) The helper helps him win the contest, usually by furnishing a fine horse (the grateful dead man Killos helps Pelops win the contest in an unspecified way; the grateful Poseidon provides him with wondrous horses; Myrtilos helps him by sabotaging Oinomaos's chariot), so that (6) he wins the princess and the kingdom. (7) Sometime thereafter the helper asks for his share of the hero's winnings (Myrtilos wants to share Hippodameia's bed; Myrtilos wants half the kingdom); however, (8) he yields his claim (Pelops denies his claim). (9) The helper disappears, returning to death (Pelops drowns Myrtilos).

The Greek story corresponds so closely to *The Bride Won in a Tournament* as we know it from mediaeval and modern tellings that we can conclude that both must be forms of the same story. That the legend of Pelops is a form of the international story does not of course mean that it was normative, representing *the form* the story took in antiquity. As with several other Greek heroic legends it is easier to imagine the Greek legend developing from the international story as we know it than the latter developing from the Greek legend. The Greek story appears to be a special development of a more general story.

Pelops shows the usual traits of the hero of stories in the cycle of the grateful dead man. He is adventurous, going abroad to win a bride and competing

against a deadly opponent. He gives liberally: he shares his body with Poseidon, expends his wealth on behalf of the deceased Killos, and even negotiates to share his future bride and kingdom, though in the end he reneges on his promise. At the same time, the story abounds in a lusty sexuality that is not matched in later texts: Pelops goes after a wife with horses and chariot provided by his former lover Poseidon; Hippodameia's father is in love with her and does not want to give her up; Myrtilos is also in love with Hippodameia and betrays Oinomaos. Indeed, almost everyone is in love with Hippodameia. The Greek story is also quite violent, from Oinomaos's slaying his daughter's suitors and displaying their heads on his house, to his own violent death, and finally Pelops's murder of Myrtilos.

The traditions associated with Pelops had deep roots and blossomed long. Homer mentions both Pelops and "sacred Killa," the town Pelops founds on his way to compete for Hippodameia's hand.[13] Strabo reports that the town of Killa, on the mainland opposite Lesbos, still existed in his day. There was in it a temple of Killaion Apollo, and next to it the tomb of Killos in the form of a large barrow.[14] Pindar weaves parts of the legend into his first Olympian Ode, composed in 476 B.C. Both Sophocles and Euripides wrote tragedies, now lost, on the story. Almost a thousand years after Homer, the Greek traveler Pausanias visited the mound of earth that was believed to be the mass grave of the suitors of Hippodameia, and in Arkadia he saw the grave of Myrtilos.[15]

Simonides

The motif of the grateful dead man as the hero's helper is found elsewhere in Greek tradition in a story told of the poet Simonides (ca. 556–468 B.C.). When Simonides' ship came to land at Tarentum on its way to Sicily, the poet saw the corpse of an unknown dead man and had it buried. Warned by the dead man in a dream not to embark the next day lest he perish in a shipwreck, Simonides remained ashore, whereas those who sailed perished in a storm.[16] A poem purporting to have been composed by Simonides as an epitaph for the dead man and referring to his experience is preserved in the Greek Anthology.[17] The anecdote contains familiar features of the theme of the helpful dead man, but in a simple form: the hero kindly buries the neglected corpse of a stranger, whereupon the ghost of the dead man appears to the hero and helps him. If nothing else, it illustrates that the idea of the grateful ghost was current in ancient oral narrative.[18]

Lit. AT 508, *The Bride Won in a Tournament.* Hippe 1888. Marx 1889:114–115. Gerould 1908:33–40. Collison-Morley 1912:58–59. Liljeblad 1927:58–63 and passim. Röhrich (1967) 2:156–212, 438–446. *EM* 3:306–322. Scherf (1995) 2:915–917, 993–995. Hansen 2000b.

 1. Gerould 1907:33–40; Liljeblad 1927:58–63.
 2. See AT 505–508, *The Grateful Dead.*
 3. Gerould 1908:33–34; BP 3:507–508.
 4. Gerould 1908:36; BP 3:508–509; *EM* 3:309–310.
 5. *Le Piacevoli Notti,* eleventh night, second tale. On Straparola's tale see Scherf (1995) 2:915–917; for an English rendering see Straparola (1906) 2:273–283.

6. Hansen 2000b.

7. We have only a scholiast's summary of Theopompos's text: *FGH* 115 F 350 = schol. A on Homer *Il.* 1.38.

8. See Gerould 1908:48–49.

9. Pindar *Ol.* 1.23–89.

10. Pausanias 5.17.7.

11. Pherekydes (*FGH* 3 F 37a + 37b); Apollodoros *Epit.* 2.3–2.9; Pausanias 8.14.10–12; schol. Euripides *Or.* 990; Hyginus *Fab.* 84; Servius ad Verg. *Georg.* 3.7. Pausanias tells of Pelops's oath to share Hippodameia for one night, Hyginus recounts his promise to Myrtilos of half the kingdom, and Servius tells of Hippodameia's own promise to Myrtilos of a night with her in return for his help. On the sources for the legend in general see Frazer (1921) 2:156–163; Gantz 1993:540–545; *LIMC* 5.1:434–440, 6.1:47, 693–696, 7.1:19–23, 282–287.

12. In a modern Greek folktale, when the helper insists on dividing the bride, the protagonist angrily asks whether he has in mind that each of them should have the woman alternately for five days at a time (Dawkins 1953:225). Notice also Abraham's otherwise puzzling sharing of his wife Sarah with other men, which appears to be a reflex of the same theme of the sharing of the princess, in another story belonging to the Grateful Dead Man cluster (see Hansen 1995b and note 18 below). This form of the theme may have been more common in antiquity than it is in recent texts, in which physical dividing is the rule and sexual sharing is the exception.

13. Homer *Il.* 2.104–105; 1.38.

14. 13.1.62–63.

15. 6.21.6–11; 8.14.10.

16. Cicero *De Divinatione* 1.27; Valerius Maximus 1.7 *ext.* 3; Libanios 4.1101.

17. *Anth. Pal.* 7.516, 7.77 = Simonides (Page, *Epigrammata Graeca* lxxxiv–lxxxv).

18. There is evidence that other recognizable tale types belonging to the Grateful Dead Man cluster were known in the ancient Near East, suggesting that the tradition has a very long history. For AT 506, *The Rescued Princess*, see Hippe 1888; Gerould 1908:76–118; Liljeblad 1927; Huet 1917:150–151; Delarue and Tenèze 2:235–244; Ashliman, type 506; and, for its underlying kinship with the Hebrew legend of Abraham and Isaak, Hansen 1995b. For the relationship of AT 507B, *The Monster in the Bridal Chamber*, to the Jewish book of *Tobit* see Simrock 1856:131–132; Hippe 1888; Groome 1898; Plath 1901; BP 3:490–517; Schmidt 1907:66–67; Gerould 1908:44–75; Charles 1913:174–199, esp. 188; Huet 1915; Gunkel 1921:90–93; Liljeblad 1927; Wesselski 1925:200–202; Goebel 1932:38–41; Zimmermann 1958:5–12; Dvořák, no. 4891*; Ashliman, type 507B; Lüthi 1969:85–100; *EM* 3:306–322; Soll 1988; Wills 1995:73–76; Moore 1996:11–14.

Brother Chosen Rather Than Husband ⚘ Intaphrenes' Wife

A woman is granted the life of one of her family members, whomever she chooses; the others shall die. She surprises everyone by selecting neither her husband nor her child but her brother, which she justifies by saying that she can get another husband or other children, but since her parents are dead, she can never get another brother.

This story is AT 985, *Brother Chosen Rather Than Husband or Son*.

It was pointed out over a century ago that the story of the woman who preferred her brother's life to that of her husband or child is attested both in Greece and in India, so that the tale, wherever its origin may lie, is an international one.[1] Since then scholars have pointed out other literary treatments among other peoples, and fieldworkers have recorded texts from oral informants.

In *Jataka* 67, written in Pali, a woman went to the king of Kosala and begged for the lives of her brother, her husband, and her son, who had been arrested as thieves. When the king agreed to spare one of the three, the woman chose her brother. Asked why she did so, she explained to the king that if she

should live, she could get a husband and a son, but inasmuch as her parents were dead she could not get another brother. The king thereupon spared all three.[2] The same reasoning appears in a modern Greek ballad. A bird informs three comrades, Kostas, Yannis, and Vlachopoulo, that robbers have taken Kostas's children, Yannis's wife, and Vlachopoulo's sister. Kostas can have other children, and Yannis another wife, but Vlachopoulo cannot have another sister. So whereas Kostas and Yannis do nothing, Vlachopoulo rescues his sister.[3] In the Sanskrit epic *Ramayana* the hero Rama, believing that his favorite brother and companion Laksmana was dead, lamented that he could get a wife, a son, and all other kinsmen anywhere, but he did not see where he might get a brother.[4]

While the *Jataka* tale is more reflective of the norm, the other texts show some of the interesting variations found in the tradition. In the ballad of Vlachopoulo the gender roles are reversed, the person making the choice being a man (or more precisely three men) and the person regarded as irreplaceable being a sister. It also illustrates how the protagonist's choice can be expressed not only verbally and in the solemnity of a monarch's court but also in the form of physical action in the external world. And the story of Rama is one in which the protagonist does not actually have to choose who will live and who therefore must die, but only comments after the fact of the death (or apparent death) of a loved one on the special value that person has for the speaker within a hierarchy of valued persons.

Intaphrenes' Wife

The well-known story of Intaphrenes' wife is first told by Herodotos in the fifth century, ostensibly after Persian tradition.[5] According to the Greek historian, King Darius of Persia arrested Intaphrenes, his children, and his relatives, since he believed that they were plotting a revolt against him. He imprisoned them with the intention of executing them. Intaphrenes' wife came to the palace and wept incessantly. Taking pity on her, Darius sent a messenger to her saying that he was willing to spare one of her imprisoned kinsmen, whichever one she wished. She chose her brother. Surprised at her choice, the king had his messenger ask her why she chose her brother rather than her husband or children, seeing that her brother was not so near to her as her own children and not so dear as her husband. She replied that, god willing, she could get another husband and other children, if she should lose these; but since her parents were no longer alive, there was no way that she might get another brother. Pleased with her reasoning, Darius spared her brother and also her eldest son but had the others killed.

The idea that spouses and children are replaceable is expressed with cynical humor in another Eastern tradition recounted by Herodotos, who tells of an Egyptian garrison that had been on duty for three years without relief. The men finally decided to desert to the Ethiopians. Learning this, King Psammetichos tried to induce them to stay, urging them not to leave their children and wives. But one of the deserters pointed to his genitals, saying that wherever these were, there would be both wives and children.[6]

Antigone

The same reasoning as that of Intaphrenes' wife appears in another fifth-century Greek work, Sophocles' *Antigone*. The heroine, having shown honor to her brother's corpse against the will of King Kreon, has been condemned to die. Reflecting upon her actions and her fate, Antigone explains that she would not have so acted had she been a mother or a wife and the corpse been that of her child or husband, for she could have gotten another husband or borne another child. But since her parents were both deceased she could never have another brother, so that she honored her brother.[7]

It is impossible to know whether Sophocles borrowed this argument from Herodotos or was familiar with the tale independently, since, for one thing, we do not know whether the tale was in actual oral circulation among Greeks or was only learned by Herodotos in the course of his foreign travels. (There is no good reason to suppose, as some scholars have, that these verses were composed by someone else and subsequently interpolated into Sophocles' text.) It is, however, worth noticing that Herodotos's narrative and the Buddhist story, one set in the Persian court and the other associated with the court at Kosala, are very close parallels: (a) a king arrests the members of a woman's family; (b) when he agrees to spare the life of one of them, whichever the woman chooses, (c) she picks her brother; (d) the king asks her to explain her choice, and (e) she says that, since her parents are dead, her brother is irreplaceable whereas she could get another husband or child; (f) as a result the king spares not only her brother but also one or more others as well. In contrast to these narratives, which are truly stories, the musing of Antigone in the Sophoclean passage is only a commentary upon the value to her of a person already dead, and in this respect it corresponds quite closely to the lamentation of Rama, which is a commentary upon the value to him of a person he supposes to be dead. In short, the Herodotean and the Sophoclean passages appear to belong to different branches of the tradition, one being a story in itself, the other being a commentary set within a story.

Abauchas

In a revealing Greek variation of the type, the protagonist—in this case a man rather than a woman—selects not his brother but a devoted friend. In his dialogue on friendship Lucian has one of the discussants tell of a certain Abauchas, who had just moved with his beloved wife and his two children to the city of the Borysthenites. He was also accompanied by his dear friend Gyndanes, who was suffering from a wound inflicted by highwaymen. That night, as they all slept in the upper part of the house, a fire broke out, and Abauchas, urging his wife and children to fend for themselves, carried his friend safely from the house. His wife and daughter barely managed to escape alive, but his son perished in the flames. When subsequently someone reproached Abauchas for his action, he explained that he could easily beget other children, and it was uncertain whether his present children would turn out well, but he would not find another devoted friend like Gyndanes in a long time.[8]

Spouses do not fare well in either female or male forms of this story. Female pro-

tagonists do not save their husbands, and husbands do not give their wives preference. Indeed, in another story recounted by Lucian, King Seleukos declares that it is a greater misfortune to lose a son than to lose a wife.[9] Nevertheless, it is surprising that in the present story Abauchas does not even mention his wife. It is perhaps all but inevitable that in a variation in which the beneficiary is a friend rather than a sibling, the protagonist and the friend are both males. In Greek legend, at least, there are many accounts of close friendship between two males (Achilleus and Patroklos, Damon and Phinthias, etc.) but few or none between females.

Although Kakridis argues that in Greek tradition the devotedness of siblings has long contended for the top rank with the devotedness of spouses,[10] and Trenkner remarks that "in the ideology of many peoples a brother has the highest place in the scheme of human relations,"[11] the choice that the woman or man makes in these stories is certainly intended to strike the listener or reader as surprising rather as obvious and inevitable. Whether the underlying values are acknowledged and even shared by the larger community or not, the protagonist's choice itself is wonderfully unexpected, and it is this quality that makes the story interesting and memorable. Darius is startled at the decision of Intaphrenes' wife and craves an explanation, and similarly Abauchas must explain his action to a person who has reproached him for it. In his *Rhetoric* Aristotle cites Antigone's preference for her brother over her husband or children as an instance of something incredible and therefore requiring an explanation, which he says she gives. Earlier in the same work he mentions the cynical reply of the Egyptian deserter as an example of the sort of statement that a speaker ought to attribute to his opponent in order to illustrate the latter's wickedness.[12] The protagonist's choice is not the culturally expected one. The peculiar feel of the woman's reasoning springs from her functionalist perspective. The woman does not see "a man she has lived with nor children she has borne and raised but rather the 'offices' of husband and children, which admit of being filled by other individuals."[13]

The dilemma of Intaphrenes' wife is similar to that of Paris in the legend of the Judgment of Paris. In each case a person must judge which of three desirable things is the most desirable of all, and having chosen that must forego the other two. Intaphrenes' wife has to choose between brother, husband, and child. Paris must choose between Hera with her promise of political prowess, Athene with her offer of military prowess, and Aphrodite with her offer of sexual prowess. The narrative poses a problem, a virtual riddle: which of three excellent options is the best? There is no easy or correct answer, but the protagonist must give an answer anyway and live with the consequences. Paris, choosing Aphrodite, is gifted in love but is forever without talent in the civic and military spheres of his life. The bereft woman chooses her brother, not necessarily because she rates brothers higher than husbands or children, but because husbands and children are more replaceable. Paris is self-indulgent, since he may increase his family's renown and benefit his community by means of his talents as a ruler or warrior but not by means of his sexual talent. The woman might be expected to favor her husband or at least to plead emotionally that the choice she has been given is an impossible one; instead, she makes her selection quickly and with a strangely cool efficiency,

treating spouse, child, and sibling as so many generic slots to be filled and replaced rather than as particular living persons with whom she has a history and a relationship.

Lit. AT 985, *Brother Chosen Rather Than Husband or Son*. Tawney 1883:121. Pischel 1893:465–468. Nöldeke 1894:155–156. Aly 1969:65–66, 109. Gabrieli 1937:111–113. Kakridis 1949:152–164. Trenkner 1958:75. *EM* 2:861–864. Beekes 1986:225–233. Murnaghan 1986. Hardy 1996.

1. Tawney 1883:121. The question of where the story arose interested the earliest commentators, of course, but as usual it shall not trouble us since, for one thing, it is surely unanswerable and, for another, it makes no difference in the present discussion, inasmuch as the oldest attested texts are doubtless many steps away from the original.
2. Pischel 1893:466–468.
3. Kakridis 1949:155–156.
4. Pischel 465–466, citing *Ramayana* 6.24.7 ff.
5. Herodotos 3.119.
6. Herodotos 2.30.
7. 897–915.
8. *Toxaris* 61. For this story in the context of Lucian's *Toxaris* see Pervo 1997.
9. *De Syria Dea* 18.
10. Kakridis 1949:152–164.
11. Trenkner 1958:75.
12. 3.16.9; 3.16.5.
13. Hardy 1996:107; see also Murnaghan 1986.

Carrying Part of the Load 🕸 Dionysos and Xanthias

A foolish man takes a load (or part of a load) on himself in the belief that he thereby unburdens the donkey (horse, ox) that carries (or draws) him.

This tale of the kind-hearted fool is AT 1242A, *Carrying Part of the Load*.

The earliest known text is found in Poggio's *Facetiae*, dating from the fifteenth century. According to Poggio, a farmer plowed his field with two oxen and then set out for home on his donkey, on which he also loaded his plow. When he saw that the animal was suffering under its burden, he got off, placed the plow on his shoulder, and got back on the animal, saying: "Now you must run along nicely, since you are no longer carrying the plow."[1]

In a nineteenth-century Danish tale told of the foolish people of Mols, a certain Hans rode to the mill to buy some malt. As he was leaving, the miller remarked: "Your old horse looks a bit worn out. It's a shame for her to have to carry so much—why don't you carry the malt yourself and let her go unburdened?" Hans replied that he could do that, so that he put the malt over his neck and mounted. In this way the old horse got out of carrying the malt, since of course Hans was carrying it himself on his back.[2]

In a modern Greek tale from Chios, a man went to Chora to make some purchases. He bought sixty *okades* of merchandise, loaded his donkey with it, and mounted the donkey again. Later he bought twenty-five *okades* of wheat, which he placed on his own shoulder as he remounted his donkey. When the

animal would not move, the villagers asked him how he could put so much weight on the donkey and then also sit on it. He replied: "Are you so blind that you can't see that I'm carrying twenty-five *okades* on my own shoulder?"[3]

The tale is told also in the Middle East and India.

Dionysos, Xanthias, and the Donkey

Although no ancient text of the tale as such has come down to us, the basic idea of the tale appears in a dialogue in Aristophanes' *Frogs*, produced in 405 B.C. In the opening scene, Dionysos is traveling with his slave Xanthias, who is carrying a load on his shoulder and riding a donkey. I paraphrase the relevant portion of their dialogue (vv. 19–32).

> Xanthias: The weight is pressing down on my shoulders.
> Dionysos: Now that shows outrageous softness, since I, Dionysos, am walking and toiling while I let him ride in order that he not have to bear a load and be miserable.
> X: You mean I'm not carrying anything?
> D: How can you carry something when you're being carried?
> X: Well, by carrying this load here.
> D: Isn't the donkey carrying the load that you're carrying?
> X: No, not the load that I'm carrying.
> D: How can you be carrying anything, since you yourself are being carried by another?
> X: I don't know, but my shoulder here is under a lot of pressure.
> D: Well, then, since you say that the donkey is not helping you, take a turn and carry the donkey.

Like the Chian defending himself against the onlookers in the modern Greek tale, Xanthias defends his belief that the load he bears on his shoulders is a burden only to himself and not to the donkey he is riding.

Now, Aristophanes seems actually to interweave portions of two thematically similar but otherwise unrelated tales of foolish persons here: *Carrying Part of the Load* and *The Miller, His Son, and the Ass*. Both tales ordinarily deal with one or two foolish men and a donkey (or other beast of burden), and both tales feature comic absurdities concerning lifting.

The Miller, His Son, and the Ass

The latter tale recounts the experiences of a father and his son (daughter, wife) who are traveling with their donkey. As they walk, passersby blame them for not letting the donkey carry them. When the father then walks and lets his son ride, passersby criticize him for letting the youth, rather than himself, ride. When he rides and has his son walk, they criticize him for making the boy walk. When both ride, they are blamed for overloading the poor animal. When finally in exasperation the two of them carry the donkey, people laugh at their folly. Sometimes they dispose of the donkey, or it perishes accidentally.

So in AT 1215, *The Miller, His Son, and the Ass: Trying to Please Everyone*, a fool-

ish person responds to the reproaches of a succession of other wayfarers, adopting one solution after another until he seems to exhaust all the possibilities, trying without success to please everyone. Although some texts employ some possibilities not listed here (the father is reproached for seating his son behind him and at another time for seating his son in front of him), the texts typically include only a few of the possible combinations. These are presented in a varying but more or less climactic sequence. In different versions the son may be a fool whom the father is teaching a lesson about life, or the father may be the fool, or the two characters may be little differentiated. The tale often concludes with the father or the narrator (or both) pointing out the moral, and indeed narrators often refer to the tale as a fable. The narrative is, or can be, comic or didactic. I have seen texts in different European languages and in Arabic, and the story is also known in Turkey and India. Despite its geographical spread, it has rarely been collected in oral tradition, which suggests that the oral texts may be dependent largely on the literary tradition.[4]

In the narration of the fourteenth-century monk Ulrich Boner, who recounts the tale in his collection *Der Edelstein*, a man was taking his son and his donkey to market. He was riding, and his son was walking. People said: "Look how the man is riding and lets his son walk. He would do better to walk alongside and let the boy ride." When the old man heard this, he dismounted and let his son ride. Then people said: "The old man must be a fool, since he lets his son ride." So the old man joined his son on the donkey. Then people said: "They're going to kill the donkey: the old man should ride and the youth walk alongside." The father said: "We are both going to walk. The donkey should also have a little rest." So they walked alongside the animal. Then people said: "Look how foolish they are for letting the donkey walk without a load." To which the father said: "We'll carry the donkey and see what the people say." So they hung the donkey from a pole with its feet bound, and carried it. Then people said: "Two men are carrying a donkey that ought to be carrying them. They're obviously fools." Then the old man said: "No matter what we do, we are called foolish. My advice to you is just to do what is right; a man who does what is right is a happy man." To which Boner adds his own moral, declaring in effect that it is scarcely possible for a person to live without reproach, so that each person must decide for himself what to do.[5]

Although the earliest reported texts of this folktale date to the thirteenth century, the scene in Aristophanes' comedy has seemed to some classical scholars to presuppose a familiarity with the tale.[6] As in the oral tale, two foolish men (father and son, or master and slave) travel with a donkey. Dionysos complains about having to go on foot while his servant rides, and he suggests more or less that since the present arrangement is not working out, the donkey should be carried. The idea is carried no further, giving way instead to other witticisms, but this latter thought in particular may refer to the memorable climactic scene of the folktale in which the two foolish men actually end up carrying their donkey. If so, the comic tale must have been in oral circulation in Aristophanes' day.

In *Carrying Part of the Load* the foolish hero decides to relieve his beast of burden of the weight it bears by placing the load on himself, although he in

turn is supported or pulled by the animal. In *The Miller, His Son, and the Ass* the two protagonists, stung by the criticisms of various persons they pass on the road, try various combinations of using and not using their donkey (one walks and the other rides, they exchange places, both walk, both ride) until, in exasperation at their inability to please everyone, they resolve to carry their beast of burden. In both tales the silly humans exchange roles with their animals by adopting the role of beasts of burden themselves. It is perhaps this similarity in illogic together with the virtually identical situations of men and a donkey in the two tales that may have prompted Aristophanes to draw upon both narratives in creating the scene, framing the central idea of *Carrying Part of the Load* with motifs suggestive of *The Miller, His Son, and the Ass*.

Lit. (AT 1242A, *Carrying Part of the Load.*) Wesselski (1911) 2:163–164, 229–230, no. 490. Clouston 1888:19–20. *EM* 4:18–21. Ashliman, type 1242A.
(AT 1215, *The Miller, His Son, and the Ass: Trying to Please Everyone.*) Gödeke 1862:531–560. Gildemeister 1862:733–734. Wesselski (1911) 2:244, no. 541. Herbert (1910) 3:420–421. Pauli (1924) 2:384–385, no. 577. Radermacher 1913:194–195; 1921:147. Trenkner 1958:85–6. Holbek 1964:32–53. *EM* 1:867–873. Ashliman, type 1215.

1. *Facetiae* 56.
2. Christensen 1939, no. 88.
3. Megas 1970, no. 59.
4. Holbek 1964:50.
5. Gödeke 1862:535–536.
6. Radermacher 1913:194–195; Trenkner 1958:85–86.

Carrying Water in a Sieve ❧ Danaides

The task of carrying water in a sieve (riddle, colander, cracked dish, etc.) can function as an impossible task for an ogre. So in a Scottish tale a young woman on a journey lost her way and sought shelter for the night. A little dog joined her. After a while Kelpie (a kind of water spirit) appeared, telling her to make her bed and he would lie with her for the night. She did not know how to keep Kelpie away. At the dog's suggestion she said she had nothing to make a bed with, but Kelpie presently reappeared with bedding and repeated his order. On the dog's advice the girl said she was thirsty and asked him to fetch her a drink in a sieve and a cracked dish. The spirit went off to fetch the water but soon returned complaining that the sieve and dish would not hold it. When he was instructed to stop up the holes and the crack with fog, he set out to gather fog. Though he toiled hard, the water still escaped, and since the day had dawned when he returned, the girl was free.[1] Similarly, in a cycle of stories about the devil and a man named Davies, the devil is always bested by Davies. Once when the devil asked Davies to give him an impossible task, Davies bade him carry water in a riddle, which the devil tried but failed to do.[2]

At other times, especially in more complex tales, the task serves as a difficult, though ultimately solvable, problem for a heroine. Thus, at the beginning of an

English tale, a hateful woman gave her stepdaughter a sieve and told her to fill it with water at the well of the World's End. When the maiden found the well but was unable to fill her sieve, a helpful frog told her to stop it with moss and daub it with clay.[3] In some pious legends the protagonist is so pure or holy that he or she is able to carry water in a sieve.[4]

The motif of carrying water in a leaky vessel is also found as one of several strange activities carried on by persons in the other world. In a vision of, or a visit to, heaven a man sees men carrying a beam sideways, another man drawing water from a well with a bottomless bucket, and other men hitching horses backwards to a cart, or the like.[5]

Although carrying water in a sieve is not known from ancient sources as a task to distract or frustrate a stupid ogre, the idea of carrying water in a sieve or other leaky vessel was current in different ways in both Greek and Roman tradition.

Ancient Water Carriers

Although we now automatically think of the mythological water carriers in the Greek realm of the dead as being the Danaides, in early Greek tradition the water carriers seem to be nameless. They may be male or female or a mixed group of males and females, and their number is not fixed. They are described simply as unjust persons or uninitiated persons, or they are not characterized at all. They toil in Hades' realm, in the neighborhood of other active ghosts such as Sisyphos and Oknos, where they endlessly carry water in a sieve or pour water into a perforated *pithos* (a large storage jar) or both.

Evidence of the ancient water carriers is found first on an Attic black-figure amphora dating from the end of the sixth century B.C. that shows four figures emptying water pots into a *pithos*. The figures are winged, indicating that they are souls of the dead. Though the water pots are not broken and only the upper half of the *pithos* is visible, not showing us a hole at the bottom, the image was evidently familiar enough or unambiguous enough that it did not require this detail to be understood.[6] In exactly the same way one could abbreviate the Greek proverbial expression "to pour water into a perforated *pithos*" by saying simply "to pour water into a *pithos*" (see below).[7]

In the fifth century Polygnotos executed a painting of the realm of the dead for the Knidian Lesche at Delphi, which the traveler Pausanias describes in detail.[8] In part of the painting two women, one old and one beautiful, are carrying water in broken pots; they are labeled as women who have not been initiated into the mysteries. In another place there are an old man, a old woman, a boy, and a young woman, most of them carrying water to a *pithos*, and the old woman's pot is perhaps broken.

The earliest literary allusions to the water carriers are found in Plato. In the *Republic* we learn that in Hades' realm unholy and unjust persons are forced to carry water in a sieve.[9] In the *Gorgias*, in a more elaborate image, Socrates says that some clever man has compared the part of our soul in which appetites are found to a *pithos*, more specifically, to a perforated *pithos*, because of its insatiableness. He mentions how the most miserable denizens of Hades' realm, the foolish or uninitiated, carry water in perforated sieves to a perforated *pithos*. Furthermore, the souls of the foolish are like sieves, for they are not watertight

but leaky with disbelief and forgetfulness.[10] Xenophon, Plato's contemporary, remarks that he finds pitiable those persons who, according to tradition, pour water into a perforated *pithos*, since they labor in vain.[11]

Danaides

By the first century B.C., if not earlier, the anonymous water carriers in Hades' realm became identified with the Danaides, the legendary daughters of Danaos.[12] According to Horace the daughters of Danaos draw water and pour it into a storage jar (*dolium*) from which the water runs out at the bottom.[13] In the pseudo-Platonic *Axiochos*, the date of which is uncertain, the author speaks of the "never-ending water-buckets" of the Danaides.[14] When a reason is given for their endless toil, it is that they murdered their husbands. Since the Danaides brought about the death of their cousins, Ovid says, they seek again and again the waters they lose.[15] According to the usual story, the fifty daughters of Danaos were betrothed—against their will or that of their father—to their cousins, the fifty sons of Aigyptos. On their wedding night, they killed their husbands. Or, rather, all but Hypermnestra did, who spared her husband Lynkeus. Subsequently, either the other forty-nine Danaides were purified of their crime and remarried, or Lynkeus slew them to avenge the death of his brothers. In either case, upon their own death they toiled in Hades' realm, carrying water ceaselessly in or to leaky containers.

Proverbial Expressions

A number of Greek proverbs also employ the image of the sieve or *pithos*. In a collection of proverbs attributed to Plutarch, the author lists as metaphors for impossibility "You're pouring water into a *pithos*" and "You're pouring water into a perforated *pithos*."[16] The former is obviously an abbreviated form of the latter, suggesting that the expression was a common one. In "You're pouring water with a sieve" and "You're carrying water with a sieve," we have a second pair of variant expressions.[17] The first group refers to a leaky storage jar, the second group to leaky vessels of transport. Plautus speaks of "pouring words into a perforated *dolium*," obviously a play on the usual Greek expression, but he also says, "You're pouring rainwater into a sieve," which may have been proverbial among the Romans.[18]

Zenobios, a compiler of proverbs who was contemporary with Pausanias, explains the expression *aplestos pithos*, or "unfillable storage jar," as meaning a glutton. He identifies the unfillable storage jar with the *pithos* into which the daughters of Danaos pour water and which is never filled. The souls of the uninitiated gather about it, and the Danaides, filling broken vessels with water, carry it to a perforated *pithos*. He explains that the fifty daughters of Danaos were betrothed to the fifty sons of Aigyptos, and that on their wedding night all the Danaides except for Hypermnestra killed their husbands; because of their crime they were condemned to pour water into a perforated *pithos*. The expression, Zenobios adds, can also refer to Hades' realm, since it is never filled regardless of how many people die.[19]

So Zenobios knows two significations of *aplestos pithos*: insatiable appetite, a meaning that we find in Plato and a few other authors,[20] and Hades' realm, an-

other great container that is never filled. It is certainly possible, if not probable, that the traditional expression *aplestos pithos* was an old, humorous metaphor for a glutton and became the source for, rather than a derivation of, the image Plato elaborates in the *Gorgias*, in which the part of the soul concerned with appetites is likened to a perforated *pithos*. Whether the notion of the *aplestos pithos* really was borrowed ultimately from the perforated *pithos* of the other world or was an independent though similar image, Zenobios believes it derives from the *pithos* of the water carriers, who in his day were the Danaides.

The proverbial expressions and the mythological tradition run parallel, both usually conveying the notion of fruitless or unending toil when the focus is upon the water carriers, as it usually is, and of insatiable appetite when the focus is upon the receptacle.

In the Realm of the Dead

It is unclear why the Greek death realm is peopled with strange persons who carry on repetitive or continuing tasks that resemble those of living persons, except that they are fruitless: Sisyphos pushing uphill a stone that always rolls down again, Oknos braiding a rope that his donkey eats as soon as it is completed, the Danaides carrying water in leaky vessels to a leaky container.[21] The Greeks imagined crimes for which these fruitless activities might be thought fitting punishments, but the purported offenses vary and the causal connections are unconvincing. According to Pherekydes, Hades made Sisyphos roll a stone up a hill in order that he might not run away again (see further "Lord's Prayer"), a connection that makes no sense at all in connection with Sisyphos's task. During his life Oknos was not even a criminal but rather a hardworking man with a spendthrift wife,[22] and now in Hades' realm he metaphorically reenacts his unhappy domestic relationship, though it is not clear why he should do so. In the case of the water carriers, as we have seen, they do what they do because they are unjust or because they are uninitiated or because they murdered their husbands. The otherworldly behavior is constant, while the cause is variable or uncertain. Keuls suggests that they are sinners who are somehow trapped in time, unlike the souls of the good.[23]

In mediaeval and modern Switzerland and Germany a number of humorous traditions assign impossible or unending tasks as punishments to unwed persons after their death, especially to old maids.[24] Since their lives were seen as useless, having failed to achieve their true goal, so also their souls were condemned to unedifying and useless tasks that accomplished nothing. Old maids had to measure the cold ground of a certain bog with their fingers or polish a certain tower or sweep a certain place with the beards of old bachelors. In a tradition reminiscent of the Danaides, who, if they are not exactly unwed, do at least reject living their lives in a marital state, deceased bachelors had to carry sand in perforated baskets from the Rhone to a mountain.[25]

We find a group of such fools in the humorous folktale, *Master Pfriem*, in which the protagonist, a man given to criticizing and complaining, sees in heaven three or so instances of such apparent folly that he has great difficulty not criticizing; for example, two men trying to carry a beam sideways through a doorway, a man drawing water from a well with a bottomless or leaky pail, a man already overburdened with wood adding even more wood to the load he

attempts to carry, and a man hitching horses backward to a wagon. Sometimes the protagonist learns that the apparently foolish behavior he witnesses actually means something quite different from that which he initially infers. This vision of strange and apparently foolish otherworldly activities is found as early as A.D. 800 in the Greek legend of St. Arsenios, who similarly saw in a vision a man carrying a heavy load of wood and always adding more to it, a man carrying water in a sieve, and two horsemen who were trying to pass through a doorway while holding a beam crosswise. Each man, he learned, represented a different kind of sinner.[26] Again, the set of fools is nearly constant, whereas the interpretations vary. In the Arsenios legend, Arsenios learned that the man carrying water in a sieve was a man who did good works but his sins exceeded them so that his good deeds were lost. But in the Grimms' version of *Master Pfriem*, Pfriem saw in his dream two angels drawing water from a well into a vat that had holes throughout, so that the water ran out everywhere; in truth, the angels were soaking the earth with rain.[27]

The idea of a cluster of otherworldly fools is therefore many centuries old, and the idea may well be many centuries older even than Arsenios. It is conceivable that it underlies the puzzling cluster of characters in Greek tradition who in time became the Danaides, Sisyphos, and Oknos. If so, these classic figures did not enter Greek tradition individually but instead came as a group, as a set of fools belonging to the otherworld, each one performing a different unending task. One fool repeatedly tries to push a stone to the top of a hill, but inasmuch as the stone is too heavy for him it always rolls back before he reaches the top; another braids a rope that, unknown to him, his own donkey eats as fast as he braids it; and another carries water in leaky vessels to a leaky vat. On this hypothesis, the familiar Greek names and the different interpretations come later, and the latter are never entirely standardized because they have no inherent and necessary connection with the enigmatic behaviors to which they are attached.

Tuccia

According to a popular Roman tradition an unnamed man falsely accused a Vestal Virgin named Tuccia of having violated her sacred vow of chastity. When Tuccia was told to make her defense, she said only that she would do so by her actions. Having then called upon Vesta to be her guide and with the permission of the pontiffs, she led the way to the Tiber, escorted by the population of the city. "They say she came to the river," reports Dionysios of Halicarnassus, "and undertook the task that proverbially is in the first rank of impossibilities. She drew water from the river in a sieve, carried it as far as the Forum, and poured it out at the feet of the pontiffs." After Tuccia's vindication, a search was made for her accuser, who could not be found.[28]

Tuccia's ordeal could not be more different from the ritualistic rites of the Greek otherworldly tradition with their almost autistic repetition and lack of consequence, as though the performers of the tasks, not yet having discovered solutions for them, were condemned to repeat them until they should do so. In contrast, the Roman legend is set in the world of the living, the task is attempted once only, and, being executed successfully, it is not repeated. Its point moreover is clear, having been announced in advance. The Roman story attrib-

utes the task of carrying water in a sieve to a pure and pious priestess, just as in later pious legends the apparently impossible task is accomplished by a saintly male or female of extraordinary purity or holiness.[29]

See also "Devil to Count Stars" and "Making a Rope of Sand." For other denizens of the death realm, see "God and the Emperor of Rome" and "Lord's Prayer."

Lit. Motifs H1023.2, *Task: carrying water in a sieve.* H1023.2.1, *Task: carrying water in a leaky vessel.* F171.6.2, *People in otherworld pour water into tub full of holes.* Q512.1, *Punishment: filling leaky vessels with water from a bottomless jar.* Preller (1894) 1:824. Roscher 1:950. Waser 1898. Frazer (1898) 5:388–391. Bonner 1902:164–173. Radermacher 1908. Rohde 1925:586–588. Megas 1933:425–426. Cook (1940) 3:338–451. Keuls 1974. *EM* 1:963–964, 3:267–270. Ashliman, type 1180. Sissa 1990:127–177.

1. Briggs (1970) A1:561–562.
2. Briggs (1971) B1:66. These two tales exemplify AT 1180, *Catching Water in a Sieve*, which is not attested in antiquity.
3. Briggs (1970) A1:563–564. See for example Roberts (1958:86) on AT 480, *The Spinning-Women by the Spring*, and Ting (1974:11) on Chinese tales. A functionally similar problem is that which the hero faces when he is told to drain a body of water with an inadequate tool such as a bucket. But the solution can be different, for in this case his supernatural helper may simply execute the task by magical means. So in a French tale the devil gave a boy a skimmer with which to empty a pond in a single day, but in the end the devil's daughter emptied it instantly by means of her magic wand (Massignon 1968:23). Although this task can occur in versions of AT 313, *The Girl as Helper in the Hero's Flight* (see "Girl as Helper," and Knopp 1933:213), it does not appear in the ancient variants of the type that we have.
4. BP 3:476–477.
5. See AT 801, *Master Pfriem*, which is not attested in antiquity; Grimm 178; Clouston 1888:117–118; and BP 3:297–305. For fools carrying a beam sideways, see also "Tree Trunks Laid Crosswise."
6. Roscher 1:949–950; Keuls 1974:34.
7. *Pithoi* (large storage jars) were used to store wine, oil, and grain but apparently not water: Sissa 1990:136.
8. 10.31.9–11.
9. 363d.
10. *Gorgias* 493a–c.
11. *Oeconomicus* 7.40.
12. See briefly Gantz 1993:207 and for ancient illustration *LIMC* (1986) 3.1:337–341. It is not obvious why the Danaides were drafted to be the water carriers of the death realm, but the question goes beyond the scope of this article. The widely accepted suggestion made by Rohde (1925:586–588), that the Danaides, since they died unmarried and therefore symbolically uninitiated, try without success to bring the water for their ritual bridal bath, has been challenged by various scholars, most recently by Keuls (1974), who argues that the Danaides' water carrying reflects the rite of purification that they underwent after the murder of their husbands, and by Sissa (1990:127–177), who points out that they had in fact married and rather were trapped in an intermediate state between virginity and motherhood, representing "the utmost possible incompleteness of the female body" (171), opened vessels that would never be filled. A clue that has perhaps been given too little weight is the fact that in Argos the Danaides were closely connected with water, having been credited with introducing the art of digging wells and of having discovered a number of springs (see Keuls 1974:49–50).
13. *Carm.* 3.11.22–27.
14. 371e.
15. *Met.* 4.462–463.
16. *Ekloge* 4 (*CPG* 1:343). *Ekloge* 46.
17. *Ekloge* 8. *Ekloge* 50.
18. *Pseud.* 369. *Pseud.* 100–102; see further Otto 1890:98, no. 466.

19. Zenobios 2.6. Cf. Diogeneianos 7.27.
20. Keuls 1974:51, 106 n. 2.
21. Keuls 1974:13–23.
22. Pausanias 10.29.1–2.
23. Keuls 1974:22.
24. Waser 1898; Zingerle 1898:134–135; Bonner 1902:169–171; Megas 1933:426.
25. Waser 1898:58.
26. BP 3:302–303, citing *Acta Sanctorum* Julii 4, 626 E (cap. 3.19). Bolte and Polívka remark that the woodcarrier is reminiscent of Sisyphos and the Danaides. On Arsenios see further *EM* 1:827–828.
27. Grimm 178.
28. Dionysios of Halicarnassus 2.69; other sources include Livy *Epitome* 20; Valerius Maximus 8.1.5; and Pliny *NH* 28.12. See further *RE* 7 A I:768–770; Sissa 1990:127–134.
29. For persons so pure or saintly that they can carry liquid in a sieve or the like, see BP 3:476–477.

Catch-Tale ≫ Demades the Orator

A catch-tale is a structurally defined narrative in which at a certain point the listener is induced to ask a particular question, for which the narrator has a ready answer that makes the listener appear foolish. Or at a certain point the narrator himself (herself) pauses to ask the listener a question about the tale, but when the listener offers the obvious answer the narrator rejects the answer as being incorrect, providing instead a prepared answer that is unobvious and usually silly.

AT 2200, *Catch-Tales*, is the general classification for tales of this sort, in addition to which several traditional catch-tales are assigned type numbers of their own. Such question-and-answer tales, which in modern tradition appear to be confined to children's lore, have not been recorded with much consistency by collectors, probably because collectors have not regarded them highly.[1] An example of a catch-tale is the following.

> Narrator: A king had two sons, of whom one was clever and one was stupid. To one he bequeathed his kingdom, to the other three *Schrummel*.
> Listener: What's that?
> Narrator: That's what the stupid son asked, too.[2]

A Danish catch-tale recorded from an informant in Jutland by the author and amateur folklorist Jeppe Aakjær goes as follows.

> "Now I'm gonna tell you a story. There once was a man, and he insisted on beginning to plow. But he had no idea how to begin. At last he drove over the field behind the house and started to tackle it. When he reached the one end, he said, 'Turn!' and when he reached the other end, he said the Lord's Prayer. Say, maybe you know it?"
> "No."
> "Don't you know the Lord's Prayer? Ha, ha, ha."[3]

The listener is tricked into taking the query to be about a knowledge of plowing, whereupon the narrator pretends rather that he was asking about an ac-

quaintance with the Lord's Prayer. Although the collector does not record his informant's age or gender, the content of the story suggests that the narrator was probably an adult male.

In a British text a young man who was loved by two girls threw two rings into the sea, promising to marry the one who could bring a ring back to him. Both girls went to the sea daily, but neither of the rings ever washed up. Years later, when one of the girls was preparing to cook a fish, she cut it up to remove the guts, and what do you think she found?–(the listener is expected to reply, "One of the rings," or the like)–the guts![4]

Demades

That this rhetorical structure has not always been confined to children's storytelling is shown by an ancient Greek anecdote concerning the orator Demades that is found in the anonymous collections of Aesopic fables in Greek prose. The orator Demades was once addressing the Athenians, who were not paying close attention to him. He then asked if he might tell them an Aesopic fable. When they assented, he said that Demeter, a swallow, and an eel were traveling together; when they came to a river, the swallow took to the air and the eel entered the water. Saying this he fell silent. The Athenians asked: "And Demeter, what did she do?" Demades said: "She is angry at you for neglecting the affairs of the city while listening to Aesopic fables."[5]

Catch-tales, like dilemma tales (see "Wooden Doll") and some unfinished tales (see "Unfinished Tale"), entail the active participation of the listener, so that in written texts they are best represented dramatically in order to capture the interaction of teller and hearer. So here the tale is incorporated into a supposed dialogue between Demades, an Athenian politician of the fourth century B.C., and his audience of Athenian men. In the classic fashion of the catch-tale, Demades begins narrating a tale into which he introduces an element of interest or suspense (the three characters in the tale encountered an obstacle, at which point one flew and one swam) and abruptly stops, inducing his listeners to ask a particular question (what did the third character do?), which in turn sets up his answer, a reply that is meant to make them look foolish.

Among children the telling of a catch-tale seems to be primarily a form of playful behavior in which the teller gains a laugh by tricking his or her listener into looking foolish. In the story about Demades it is probably all this too, but in addition the orator also has the non-playful purpose of chiding his audience for not paying closer attention to important matters. Since an Aesopic fable did not purport to be an account of a historical event, it ordinarily had little claim in and of itself to the attention of a serious-minded person Greek or Roman, and when a narrator told a fable for its own sake as an amusing tale rather than subordinately for the purpose of illustrating a general point, it had no such claim at all. There is some irony in the fact that the anecdote that provides a frame for the fable is in turn classified as an Aesopic fable by the unknown Greek compiler who includes it in his collection of Aesopic fables. But Demades' fable-within-a-fable is not a fragment of a real fable. Like other incomplete tales (see "Unfinished Tale"), this tale exists

only as the beginning of a story, as a fragment of an adventure. There is no correct answer to the Athenians' question other than that which Demades gives.

Demosthenes

A similar anecdote was also told of the Athenian orator Demosthenes. Demades and Demosthenes were contemporaries, though they were not allies, and it was in fact Demades who procured a decree for the death of Demosthenes, which led to the latter's suicide.

According to this tale, which is recounted in an anecdotal biography of Demosthenes, when the orator was once being prevented (evidently by the shouts of the Athenians) from speaking in the assembly, he said he wished to address them briefly, and they became silent. "A young man," Demosthenes said, "hired a donkey one summer to go from Athens to Megara. When it was noontime and the sun was burning down, both the youth and the owner of the donkey wanted to rest in its shadow. Each man prevented the other from doing so, the owner saying that the young man had hired the donkey only and not its shadow, the young man saying that he had hired the animal and so had all rights to it." Saying this, Demosthenes began to depart. But the Athenians held him back and asked him to finish the story. Demosthenes said: "You are willing to listen to me speak about a donkey's shadow, but you are not willing to listen to me speak about serious matters."[6]

Instead of tricking his listeners into asking a particular question, Demosthenes induces them to ask him to finish his tale, but the outcome is the same, for the audience's response sets up the speaker's reply, the effect of which is to make the audience appear foolish.

The unknown author of the biography does not dwell upon the anecdote, which is merely one tale among many that the author relates in quick succession and without further comment. Essentially the same story is told by the paroemiologist Zenobios, where Demosthenes is defending a man accused of a capital offense; by the Byzantine lexicographer Photios, who mentions also that the listeners were initially very noisy; and in the *Suda*.[7] These sources all relate the anecdote in the course of glossing the proverbial phrase "a donkey's shadow" or "concerning a donkey's shadow." The expression is a metaphor for worthlessness (*Suda*) and is applied to persons who wrangle over something of no value (Zenobios). It circulated in oral tradition independently of the anecdote about the orator and is attested before the time of Demosthenes.

Whether the proverb gave rise to the tale of the men wrangling over the right to the donkey's shadow or the reverse is not the sort of question that I address here, but it is worth noticing, as van Thiel observes, that Greeks would have been able to catch the sense of the proverb without the aid of the tale. "Shadow" was a familiar metaphor for something fleeting or worthless, as in *eidolon skias* "image of a shadow" and *skias onar anthropos* "a human being is a dream of a shadow."[8] The form / genitive + shadow / appears also in other Greek proverbs such as *kantharou skia* "a dungbeetle's shadow."[9] As for the donkey, the animal was metaphorical for something humble and of little value, as in the proverb *aph' hippon eis onous* "from horses to donkeys," referring to a descent in dignity or esteem.[10] By itself, then, "a donkey's shadow" indicated something of no value.

Demosthenes' tale of the two men wrangling over a donkey's shadow is also an unfinished tale, like Demades' narrative of Demeter, the swallow, and the eel. Both Demades and Demosthenes tell all there is to tell. Although the tale-within-the-tale, so far as it goes, is an entertaining fable or fable-like tale in both cases, each narrative conveys its message in a different way. In the former anecdote the boundary between the frame and the fable is broken when Demades, declaring that Demeter is angry with his listeners, brings a character out of the fable and into the frame itself in order to reprimand the audience that has inquired about her.[11] In the latter anecdote Demosthenes illustrates how his listeners misuse their energies not only in his capturing their attention by relating to them a frivolous tale, demonstrating how they prefer such entertainment to more important matters, but also in his selecting a tale that is itself about men who waste their time over trifles, so that the men who waste their time wrangling over the rights to a donkey's shadow are a metaphor for Demosthenes' listeners.

Diogenes

Essentially the same point is made in a less elaborate Greek anecdote concerning the famous Cynic philosopher Diogenes of Sinope that is found in an anecdotal biography of the philosopher. Once when Diogenes was discoursing in public on a serious topic and no one gathered around him to listen, he started whistling. When people now collected about, he reproached them for coming earnestly to listen to nonsense and for coming slowly to listen to earnest matters.[12]

The tradition of the public speaker who relates a catch-tale or the like to an inattentive audience is also found in ancient Jewish literature, where it is attached to different rabbis. Unlike the classical anecdotes, which usually close with the orator's admonition, leaving us to wonder whether he resumes his address or not, the Jewish anecdotes clearly relate how the speaker, once he has gained the attention of his audience, resumes or launches into his sermon; indeed, he gains their attention by presenting, not an imported tale, but an element of his sermon in an intriguing form. Thus, when Rabbi Judah Ha-Nasi, who lived in the second and third centuries A.D., was delivering a sermon to a drowsy audience and wished to attract their attention, he started to relate a story about a certain Egyptian woman who gave birth to six hundred thousand infants at the same time. Then he stopped speaking, and one of his disciples asked him who that marvelous woman was. The Rabbi replied that she was the mother of Moses, who was equal to six hundred thousand Israelites.[13]

The last trace of the tradition of the clever orator may be an anecdote told by the mediaeval author Caesarius of Heisterbach, who reports that Abbot Gevardus was preaching on the occasion of a high holiday when he noticed that many members of his audience, especially the newly converted, were sleeping, some of them even snoring. Then he called out: "Listen, brothers, listen. I want to tell you a splendid new story. Once upon a time there was a king called Artus . . ." He did not continue but said instead: "You see your need, brothers. When I spoke of god, you slept, and now that I have inserted frivolous matter you are all awake with ears alert in order to hear me." Caesarius writes that he himself was present at the sermon.[14]

Lit. AT 2200, *Catch-Tales*. Wesselski 1909:222–223. Freeman 1945:36. Thiel 1971:105–106. Schwarzbaum 1979:xi–xiii. Ashliman, types 2202 and 2204. *EM* 5:29–30.

1. *EM* 5:29.
2. *EM* 5:29.
3. Aakjær 1966:135, no. 597. I am grateful to Bente Høilund, who kindly helped me to translate this text, which is in the Jutish dialect.
4. Briggs (1970) A2:338. The tale is AT 2204, *The Dog's Cigar*.
5. Perry 63, Hsr 63.
6. Pseudo-Plutarch *Vit. Dec. Orat.* 848a = Perry 460. The tale of the donkey's shadow is also found independently as a joke without the frame of the orator and his audience, in which case it is recounted as a complete tale. "A certain man hired a donkey. When the day became hot, he got down in its shadow. But the other man quarreled with him, saying: 'It was the donkey I let out to you, not its shadow' " (Diogeneianos 7.1 = *CPG* 1:287).
7. Zenobios 6.28 (*CPG* 1:170); Photios s.v. *onou skia*; *Suda* s.v. *onou skia*.
8. Aeschylus *Agamemnon* 839; Pindar *Pyth.* 8.95.
9. Diogeneianos 5.88.
10. Zenobios 2.33. Thiel 1971:106; Freeman 1945 (my examples come from among those cited by van Thiel and Freeman). On the anecdotes featuring Demades and Demosthenes see further Karadagli 1981:49–52 and Dijk 1997:296–305.
11. Dijk (1997:303–304) suggests that there is a play upon the similarity of the names Demades and Demeter so that the rebuke of the audience by Demeter should be understood as a rebuke by Demades.
12. Diogenes Laertius 6.27.
13. Schwarzbaum 1979:xi, citing *Midrash Shir-Ha-Shirim Rabbah* 1.64.
14. Wesselski 1909:74, no. 64, citing Caesarius of Heisterbach 4.36. Wesselski (222–223) also mentions a similar anecdote told of Abbot Cassianus in the *Vitae Patrum*.

Children Play at Hog Killing 🔊 Makareus the Priest

Several children play butcher, sometimes after watching an adult slaughter an animal. The boy playing the butcher slits the throat of the boy playing the pig. The implications of this initial situation are developed in several different ways.

AT 2401, *The Children Play at Hog-Killing*, is often presented not as a folktale but as a report of actual events that took place recently in this or that town. The story is found first in antiquity and thereafter in fourteenth-century Arabic literature, in German works beginning in the sixteenth century, and in the literature of other lands. After making an appearance in the first edition of the Grimm brothers' *Kinder- und Hausmärchen* (1812), the Grimms dropped the grisly legend in their 1819 edition as being unsuitable for children.[1] Since the tale develops variously after the initial situation, I summarize several texts here.

The sixteenth-century *Zimmern Chronicle* reports that around 1520 in a little town near the city of Bremen the sons of a butcher saw their father slaughter pigs at Shrovetide. The children imitated him, one child killing the other. Their mother rushed to the scene, letting her infant drown in the bath. In despair she hanged herself. When the butcher returned he died of grief. Three days later the bodies were found in the locked house. The bishop promised to award the best benefice to the cleric who could explain the enigmatic deaths. The village sexton called upon the Evil One, who said the sexton should be able to elucidate the matter by means of the following distich:

A ram and some boys, one boy, a wife, a husband
Perish by means of a knife, water, rope, grief.[2]

In a German text from 1600, a man slaughtered a pig as his children looked on. Later when the children were playing, one child said to the other: "You be the little pig and I'll be the butcher." He took a knife and cut the throat of his little brother. The mother, who was bathing her youngest child upstairs, heard the screaming of her other little child, ran down, took the knife from the throat of her child and angrily drove it in the heart of the child who had played the butcher. Then she ran back to check on her child in the bath, who in the meantime had drowned. The woman hanged herself. The father returned from the fields, and when he saw the scene he was so afflicted that he died shortly thereafter. Now the pope, being an accomplished poet, tried to capture these events in a distich but was unable to do so. So he established a prize for the man who could. A poor student wished to win it but eventually gave up and cast away his quill shouting: "If I can't do it, then the devil may do it." The latter appeared immediately, took the quill, and wrote:

A pig, two boys, one boy, a wife, a husband
Perish by knife, water, rope, grief.[3]

An Arabic text dating to the early fourteenth century tells how an Arab slaughtered a sheep and invited Mohammed to dine with him. One of the host's two small children had witnessed the slaughtering of the animal and, wishing to show his little brother what happened, cut off his brother's head. As his mother rushed to the scene, the boy ran away in fear, falling into the bake-oven where he perished.[4]

In a German text describing an event that allegedly took place in 1540, two children watched an animal being slaughtered in the farmyard, reenacted the scene with their younger siblings, and fled from their father by going into the bake-oven, in which their unsuspecting mother built a fire. As a result the mother cast herself into a well, and the father hanged himself.[5]

Although the children in the Sicilian folk ballad "La Donna di Calatafimi" are not said to be making a game of an adult activity, the ballad is certainly a reflex of the present story. After kneading dough a mother dressed herself for church. She instructed her young son to watch over his little brother in the cradle, but after she left the foolish older brother took a knife and slit the infant's throat. When blood gushed out the frightened boy hid himself in a bake-oven, where he fell asleep. The mother came home, quickly placed some brushwood in the oven, and made a fire. Presently she found one child dead in the cradle, the other burned in the oven. The father, thinking his wife had killed the children, grabbed the knife and killed her.[6]

A German account from 1557 relates how in Franicker, a town in West Friesland, some children five and six years of age were playing together. They made one boy play a butcher, another a cook, and a third a pig; of the girls, one was to be a cook and another was to be her assistant, catching the blood of the pig in a vessel in order to make sausage. The butcher pulled down the boy who was playing the pig, and cut his throat with a little knife as the assistant cook caught his blood in a vessel. A town councilman who was passing by at this

time took the young butcher and brought him to the proper official, who immediately convened the town council. The councilmen did not know what to do, since the killing had happened in a children's game. One of them, a wise old man, suggested that the judge should take in one hand a red apple and in the other a gold coin, summon the child, and give him his choice. If he chose the apple, he should be acquitted, but if he chose the coin, he should be put to death. This advice was followed. The child laughingly took the apple and so was let go.[7]

The *Zimmern Chronicle* reports an event that took place in Hechingen. After slaughtering a calf in front of his house a butcher went on to Mass. While he was gone his children played at butchering, and one child killed the other. Their mother ran to them, forgetting the infant that she was bathing, which then drowned. When the butcher came home from church, he saw the miserable scene and killed himself with a bread knife. The wife was prevented from killing herself. The boy who had killed his brother was tried and acquitted when, offered the choice between an apple and a gold coin, he chose the apple.[8]

The considerable variation in action in these texts renders it difficult to abstract a standard form for purposes of discussion. Nevertheless, the gist of a number of the texts is that the children imitate their father in their play. One child takes the role of a butcher, another of a pig, and the butcher slits the throat of the pig. The young slayer then suffers one of several fates, which one might characterize as summary execution, negligent execution, or acquittal. In what I shall call Subtype A his mother rushes to the gory scene and impetuously kills him for killing his brother, sometimes leaving an infant child that she has been bathing, which drowns in her absence. In Subtype B, after slaying his brother, the boy hides in a bake-oven, which his mother subsequently fires up, unknowingly roasting him. In either subtype she then kills herself from despair, or her husband, blaming her for the deaths of his children, kills her in anger, and he himself dies soon thereafter. In Subtype C the slayer is tried and acquitted on the grounds that he acted as a child, not as an adult.

These alternatives taken together form a kind of meditation on guilt and innocence, with which the entire story is concerned in one way or another. Often the children are said to imitate in their play the slaughtering of an animal that they have just witnessed their father perform. The guilt of one or the other parent is suggested in those texts in which the father slaughters an animal just before going to Mass or the mother kneads bread just before going to Mass. After all, the mother would not have made a fire in the bake-oven if she had not been making bread that day. This behavior, which perhaps is imagined to transpire on a Sunday, seems somehow to trigger the cosmos quietly to effect the horrible punishment that ensues, suggesting that the misfortune the parent suffers is partly deserved. In two forms of the story (A and B) the mother now kills the slayer, either impetuously, using the first weapon she comes upon, or negligently, roasting him in her bake-oven. And while she impetuously stabs one son, she may also negligently allow a third child to drown. With equal impetuosity the woman may then take her own life, or her husband, no more given to deliberation than she, may stab her, blaming her just as she earlier blamed her son. In short, one thoughtless act leads quickly to another. One

might suppose that an ancient Greek tragedy had been married to a modern urban legend.[9]

The texts of Subtype A continue with a coda that narrates how the strange chain of deaths leads to the composition of a poem that economically sums up the events.[10] The bishop cannot explain the enigmatic deaths, or the pope understands them but cannot capture them in a distich. So he offers a prize to the person who can. When a particular sexton or student is unable to do so and calls upon the Devil for help, the latter immediately composes a Latin elegiac distich that neatly elucidates or summarizes the tragedy. The Devil does well for himself in this story, for not only is it a splendid day for unchristian behavior and untimely deaths, but the Church even resorts to the Evil One for help. The verses themselves belongs to a class of poem, for which there are specimens from antiquity onward, called variously *versus paralleli* or *correlativi*, *versus rapportati*, and *Spaltverse*.[11]

The Discrimination Test

The judicial subtype, C, takes up the issue of the guilt or innocence of the boy who has slain his brother. What sort of responsibility ought a child bear who has committed an adult crime? The judges decide that only a child who is mentally an adult must be held responsible. The determination of the child's mental age is accomplished by a remarkable test in which the child is given a choice between two attractive objects, the less valuable object symbolizing a child's interests, the more valuable object an adult's interests. The child is released after choosing the former, which promises immediate and obvious gratification, as opposed to the other, whose function is unknown to the child or perhaps whose promise of gratification is more remote.

The test of the child is a traditional one.[12] According to an interesting tradition, a somewhat similar test was employed by Tibetan monks in 1936 after the death of the thirteenth Dalai Lama in their effort to identify his new incarnation. Signs and an oracle pointed to a peasant boy living in a remote village. Among the tests administered to him by the delegation of disguised monks was giving the boy a choice of three possessions of the previous Dalai Lama mixed with near duplicates of them: two rosaries, two walking sticks, and two ritual drums. The drum that had belonged to the deceased Dalai Lama was plain, whereas the other was brightly ornamented. Making all the right choices, the two-year-old boy eventually became the fourteenth (and present) Dalai Lama, the Buddhist monk Tenzin Gyatso.[13]

A similar test is also found independently in Greek tradition, where as in the Tibetan legend it establishes the maturity rather than the immaturity of the child. According to the orator Hyperides, the young son of the priestess of Artemis at Brauron took a drachma that was among the offerings to the goddess. As a test of his intellect, both the one-drachma and a four-drachma coin were placed before him. He chose the latter, showing that he could make discriminations of value.[14] In what appears to be another version of the same legend, a boy picked up a gold leaf that had fallen from the garland of a statue of Artemis. Judges then placed toys, dice, and the gold leaf in front of the boy.

Since he went for the gold leaf, they put him to death for sacrilege, not forgiving him on account of his age.[15]

Makareus the Priest

That *The Children Play at Hog Killing* also circulated in classical oral tradition is shown by its retelling by Aelian, who, like most of the narrators of the more recent texts, relates it as a legend, as an actual event that occurred, in this case in the Greek city of Mitylene.

According to Aelian, Makareus was a priest of Dionysos in Mitylene. Though he appeared to be an upright man, he was in reality the most unholy of men. A stranger once came and deposited some gold with Makareus, who buried it in the temple. Later when the man returned and asked for his gold back, Makareus brought him inside as if to return the gold, and killed him. He then dug up the gold and buried the stranger in its place. He supposed that his deed escaped the notice both of men and gods. Some time later the time came round for the triennial festival of the god. Makareus performed sacrifices on a grand scale. While he was taken up with the Bacchic rites, his two children were left in the building. There they went to the altar, where the burnt sacrifices were still smoldering, and began imitating their father's sacrificial rites. The younger boy offered his neck, and the older boy, finding a sacrificial knife lying around, killed his brother as though he were a sacrificial victim. When people saw this they screamed. The boys' mother came running, and when she saw one child dead and the other holding a bloody knife, she took a piece of wood from the altar and killed her son with it. News of these events now reached Makareus, who left the rites and rushed into the building; there he killed his wife with the thyrsus he was carrying. Makareus was arrested and under torture confessed his original crime; he died in the course of punishment. The man who had been illegally butchered received public honors and was reburied. So Makareus experienced poetic justice, having been punished with the loss of his own life together with those of his wife and children.[16]

In the Greek story the father is a priest, a sort of religious butcher, who by performing sacrifices of animal victims provides a model for his sons' play. The story is a form of Subtype A, for the mother impetuously slays the slayer, and the father presently returns and, as in the Sicilian ballad, kills her with similar impetuosity.

But Makareus is more than merely the model for his children's game. Like the impious parents who perhaps treat Sunday as an ordinary workday, the Bacchic priest is an impious man who cheats a depositor of his money and his life, making Makareus a prime candidate for divine retribution or cosmic rebalancing. Another Greek story of a cheated depositor is found in Herodotos, narrated by the Spartan Leutychides to the Athenians after they had declined to surrender their hostages. A Spartan named Glaukos (said Leutychides) had a reputation for outstanding honesty. Trusting this, a man from Miletos deposited half of his money with him for safekeeping. Years later when the sons of the Milesian came to Glaukos and requested the re-

turn of the money, he denied any recollection of it but promised to give it some thought. Glaukos consulted the oracle at Delphi, asking whether he should perjure himself, but the priestess replied that the descendants of a perjurer would be destroyed, and that even to ask permission to commit a crime was the same as actually committing it. So Glaukos returned the money. But today (Leutychides concludes) Glaukos has no living descendants whatsoever; everything connected with him has vanished entirely.[17] Like Glaukos, Makareus cheats a depositor and as a consequence is cheated of his family. The two ideas are linked in the Greek word *tokos*, which has the double sense of "offspring" and "interest," that is, the offspring of lent money.

From Aelian's narration it is unclear why Makareus's action leads to his arrest and torture. Perhaps in Aelian's source Makareus is overheard remarking how his earlier crimes are now causing him grief, making the bystanders suspicious, as in the legend of the murder of the poet Ibykos (see "Cranes of Ibykos"). In any case, the story ends with the revelation of Makareus's secret, the solving of a problem, a feature that is suggestive of the later variants of Subtype A that also conclude with an enigma (what terrible thing happened in the locked house?) or a problem (how can these events be summed up poetically?), which is solved in a poem. Since the ancient narrative appears in a collection of stories, it comes with little contextual information other than the narrator's concluding remark that in the end Makareus experiences poetic justice.

Lit. AT 2401, *The Children Play at Hog-Killing.* BP 1:202–4. Schönberger 1967. Oinas (1978) 2:576–583. Richter 1986. *EM* 7:1264–1267.

1. Grimm 22: *Wie die Kinder Schlachtens miteinander gespielt haben.* BP number it as 22a in their commentary. For an interesting discussion of the circumstances leading to the excision of the story, see Richter 1986. The story fell victim to the growing conception of märchen as tales that ought to be suitable for children. Although the story was dropped in order to protect children from the violence of the butchering, Wilhelm Grimm himself reported that he had heard the story from his mother in his youth, and it had had the effect of making him careful and timid in play (Richter 1986:7).

2. "Vervex et pueri, puer unus, nupta, maritus/Cultello, nimpha, fune, dolore cadunt." Schönberger 1967:413, citing *Zimmerische Chronik*, urkundlich berichtet von Graf Froben Christof von Zimmern, *1567, und seinem Schreiber Johannes Müller, *1600, nach der von Karl Barrack besorgten zweiten Ausgabe neu herausgegeben von P. Hermann (Meersburg 1932) 2:175. Schönberger's summary implies but does not explicitly state that the mother kills her son. *Vervex* "ram" refers of course to the slaughtered animal, which however the narrative represents as pigs rather than sheep.

3. "Sus, pueri bini, puer unus, nupta, maritus/Cultello, lympha, fune, dolore cadunt." BP 1:203–204, citing Martin Zeiler, *Miscellanea* (Nürnberg, 1661), p. 388, who took it from Johannes Wolf, *Lectiones Memorabiles* (Lauingen, 1600).

4. Wesselski 1930:430–431.

5. Brückner 1961:233–234, citing Jobus Fincelius, *Wunderzeichen* (1559).

6. Gesemann 1972:134–135 n. 466 and Schenda 1970:382–383, who summarize Giuseppe Pitrè, *Canti popolari siciliani* (Palermo, 1891), 2:204–207.

7. Georg Wickram, *Rollwagenbüchlein*, no. 74 = *Georg Wickrams Werke*, ed. Johannes Bolte (Tübingen: Gedruckt für den Litterarischen Verein in Stuttgart, 1903), 3:97. See further Bolte's annotations in 3:383–384 and 8:346 of his edition of Wickram.

8. Schönberger 1967:413, citing *Zimmerische Chronik*, 2:174 ff.

9. Fine discussions of modern urban legends with ancient analogues are found in Ellis (1983), Mayor (1992, 1995), and Lassen (1995). For an interesting consideration of whether the legends of the past and the legends of the present day really belong to the same genre, see Klintberg 1990.

10. BP 1:204; Schönberger 1967.

11. Schönberger 1967:410–411.

12. Motif H256, *Test of innocence: apple and gold offered*. See further note 7 above, and *EM* 1:626–628.

13. Hicks and Chogyam 1990:17–23.

14. Hyperides fr. 199 Kenyon = Pollux 9.74.

15. Aelian *VH* 5.16.

16. *VH* 13.2.

17. Herodotos 6.86, noticed by Schönberger 1967:411. See further Fontenrose 1978: 118–119 and "Money in the Stick."

Cinderella ◈ Rhodopis the Courtesan

Cinderella has been found in the oral tradition of many nations and is probably the best known folktale in the world. The most familiar texts in the storybooks of the West derive from Perrault and the Grimms. In his *Histoires ou contes du temps passé* (1697) Perrault recounts the tale of Cendrillon, which, translated or retold in English, is the version of the tale that is most often found in anglophone countries.[1] The Grimms' tale of Aschenputtel, no. 21 in their *Kinder- und Hausmärchen* (1812), is somewhat less familiar.

Aarne-Thompson list it as AT 510A, *Cinderella*.

In the second half of the tale a prince (king, etc.) holds a party which the heroine's stepmother and stepsister(s) attend, while hindering the heroine from attending. The heroine manages to go anyway, dressed in splendid clothes that she has acquired magically, and the prince falls in love with her. As she leaves the festivities, often on the third of three nights, she loses one of her shoes (or, less commonly, another object such as a ring). The prince seeks the mysterious owner of the shoe in the populace by means of a shoe test, and when he locates her he marries her. In this form of the tale, which is characteristic of Western texts, the prince falls in love with the beautiful heroine, who is more or less in disguise, so that her shoe is only the means by which he is able to distinguish her from other women. In another form of the tale, which is more characteristic of Eastern texts, the future husband first encounters the heroine's lost shoe and conceives a passion for its unknown owner, after which the tale proceeds in the usual way with the shoe test and the marriage.[2] In this case, the shoe serves both to prompt love in the prince for the heroine, whom he has never seen, and also to identify her.[3]

Cinderella is sometimes told as a legend; in fact, it is as a legend that the story is first attested in its entirety, in a Chinese work of the ninth century.[4] In the second half of this text, the heroine Sheh Hsein went to a cave festival accoutered in fine clothes that she had obtained supernaturally, including a pair of golden shoes. When her stepmother and stepsister seemed to recognize her, she hurried away, leaving behind one of her shoes. It came into the hands of one of the local people, who in turn sold it in the nearby kingdom of T'o Huan where eventually it came

to the attention of the king. He asked all his subjects to try on the shoe, but it did not fit anyone. It was as light as a hair and made no noise in walking. Finally, the king put the shoe at the roadside, sent people to search every house, and eventually found another shoe of the same pattern at Sheh Hsien's house. The king searched the house, found Sheh Hsien, and asked her to put on the shoe. She dressed up, put on the shoes, and came to the king looking as beautiful as a goddess. The king married her. The heroine's stepmother and stepsister presently perished; the local people pitied them, buried them in a stone pit, named it the Tomb of Regretful Women, and prayed to them as goddesses of marriage.

Rhodopis

The resemblance between the Greco-Egyptian legend of Rhodopis and the Pharaoh and the international tale of *Cinderella* has often been noticed. The ancient legend corresponds to the final episodes of the oral tale, when the prince seeks the owner of the shoe and then weds her.

While discussing the pyramids of Egypt, the Greek geographer Strabo tells of a small pyramid that was constructed at great expense, its lower half having been made of black stone brought from Ethiopia. It is called the Tomb of the Courtesan and was built by this woman's lovers. The poetess Sappho, he says, calls her Doricha, the lover of Sappho's brother Charaxos, who transported wine from Lesbos to Naukratis for sale, but others call her Rhodopis. They tell a fabulous story (*mytheuousi*) about her. Once when she was bathing, an eagle snatched one of her sandals from her maid and carried it to Memphis, where the king was administering justice in the open air. When the eagle was above the king's head it flung the sandal into his lap. The king, moved both by the form of the sandal and by the strangeness of the event, dispatched men throughout the land to search for the woman who wore it. Found in the city of Naukratis, she was brought to the king and became his wife. When she died she acquired the tomb mentioned above.[5]

The same story is told by Aelian in his miscellany of legends, anecdotes, and the like. Aelian says that according to the stories of the Egyptians a very beautiful courtesan, Rhodopis, once was bathing when an eagle flew down, snatched one of her sandals from the maids who were watching her clothes, and flew off. The bird carried it to Memphis, where Psammetichos was judging cases, and dropped the sandal onto his lap. Psammetichos, marveling at the shape of the sandal, the charm of its workmanship, and the action of the eagle, ordered that a search be made throughout Egypt for the woman to whom the sandal belonged. When he found her he made her his wife.[6]

The association of Rhodopis with the Third Pyramid at Giza was current as early as the fifth century, when Herodotos attempts to discredit it. Herodotos relates that the Egyptian king Mykerinos (that is, Menkaure, a pharaoh of the Fourth Dynasty) was entombed in this pyramid but that some Greeks say the pyramid belongs rather to the courtesan Rhodopis. This attribution is quite impossible (he continues), first, because the construction of such a pyramid would have cost a vast amount of money, and, second, because Rhodopis lived much later than the period of the kings who build the pyramids. She was a Thracian by birth and a fellow slave of Aesop the fabulist. Xantheus of Samos

had brought her to Egypt, where Charaxos of Mytilene, brother of Sappho the poetess, bought her freedom. She remained in Egypt and because of her loveliness amassed a fortune, but certainly not enough to build a pyramid.[7] Diodorus Siculus, writing four centuries after Herodotos, reports that some persons say that this pyramid is the tomb of the courtesan Rhodopis. She had among her lovers some of the nomarchs, or provincial governors of Egypt, who because of their passion for her carried out the construction of the building.[8] Not long after Diodorus, Strabo gives both the tradition that the tomb was constructed in her memory by her former lovers and also the tradition that she eventually married the ruler of Egypt—two traditions which, one might think, would have been difficult to reconcile, for it is not easy to imagine that the pharaoh's wife might be placed in a tomb constructed for her by her former lovers. Strabo's saying that Sappho calls the woman Doricha whereas others call her Rhodopis suggests that her given name was Doricha but her nickname as a courtesan was Rhodopis, or "Rosy Face." Stories about Rhodopis evidently circulated in the Greek communities of Egypt where she once had plied her trade: as a fabulously wealthy courtesan she built the Third Pyramid as a tomb for herself, or her admiring lovers built it for her, or her husband the pharaoh built it for her. There was undoubtedly a delicious irony to be seen in the lavish Tomb of the Courtesan.[9] Whether the little island off the Phoenician city of Tyre that, according to Achilles Tatius, was called Rhodope's Tomb had any connection with the Greco-Egyptian tradition of Rhodopis's tomb, I cannot say.[10]

The Greco-Egyptian legend agrees with *Cinderella* in that (1) a lowly heroine (courtesan, cindergirl) loses a shoe (sandal, slipper), (2) which comes into the possession of a prince (king, etc.). (3) The prince, who is already in love with the girl or whose interest in her is prompted by the shoe, orders that a search be made throughout the kingdom for the owner of the shoe. (4) His agents locate her, and (5) he marries her. The motif complex shared by the ancient legend and the international folktale implies a genetic connection of some sort between the two. It indicates as well that the motifs form an interrelated cluster, a group of coherent narrative ideas that belonged together rather than an odd assemblage that grew piece by piece around the name of Rhodopis: the lost shoe entails the figure of a love-struck king, who calls for the shoe test, which leads to a marriage with the owner of the shoe. Classical scholars have tended to see the motifs individually rather than as parts of a cluster.[11]

The Chinese legend of Sheh Hsein and the Greco-Egyptian legend of Rhodopis have a number of features in common. In both versions the king is first moved to love by the sight of her shoe rather than by the sight of her, both narratives are cast as legends rather than as tales, and both legends were attached to a local tomb that was believed to be the burial place of the heroine or of her stepfamily.[12] Indeed, the story frequently circulates as a legend in the East, and monuments sometimes commemorate the event.[13] Of special interest is the fact that Chinese and Indo-Chinese texts often have the motif of the eagle (or crow) that snatches up one of the heroine's shoes and carries it to a prominent man, who then vows to marry the shoe's owner.[14] For example, in the latter half of a Miao tale from Western Hunan a humble girl, Yang Lang, made herself a new pair of shoes from certain roots after her old shoes wore out. One

day when these pretty shoes got wet, she took them off to dry in the sun. A pass-ing eagle, dazzled by the shoes, picked one up in its beak, flew away with it, and dropped it into the rice yard of a handsome young man, Pa Kuo. The youth was delighted with the shoe and wondered what skillful girl had made it. Cer-tain that he would lead a blissful life if he could marry her, he set out to find her. He finally succeeded at a Beef-Eating Festival, where Yang Lang passed the shoe test, easily slipping on the shoe that she herself had once made for her-self.[15] In short, the legend of Rhodopis belongs to the Eastern form of the *Cin-derella* tradition.

Venus and Mercury

The story attached to Rhodopis and the Pharaoh was also told as a ribald myth. According to Hyginus, in a passage in which he surveys different mythological accounts of the origin of the constellation called *Aquila*, or the Eagle, some people say that Mercury fell in love with Venus because of her beauty. When he was unable to gain access to her, he was dispirited. But Jove felt compassion for him, and, while Venus was bathing herself in the River Achelous, he sent an eagle to carry away her slipper (*soccum eius*) to Amythao-nia in Egypt and give it to Mercury. Venus followed the eagle and came to Mercury. After he had obtained Venus, he placed the eagle in the heavens in gratitude.[16]

Recounting the myth in Latin, Hyginus employs the Roman names for the deities, but like the legend of Rhodopis this myth seems really to belong to Egyptian Greeks, taking place as it does in Greece and Egypt and displaying a kind of Alexandrian sweetness. It is the only ancient text that assigns a motive to the actions of the eagle.[17]

Lit. AT 510A, *Cinderella*: episodes 4, *Proof of Identity*, and 5, *Marriage with the Prince*. Cf. AT 516B, *The Abducted Princess* (Love through Sight of Floating Hair): episode 1, *A Hero Wins a Princess*. Marx 1889:42–50. Cox 1893. Sartori 1894:160–161. BP 1:187. Hall 1904. Aly 1969:69. Waley 1947. Sydow 1948:209–210. Rooth 1951. Bourboulis 1953:40–52. Liungman 1961:125–135. Ting 1974. Lloyd 2:84–85. Scobie 1977b:17–18. *EM* 3:39–57, 4:1021–1025. Dundes 1983. Scherf 1982:9–13. Ashliman, type 510A. Pre-ston 1994. Stramaglia 2000:267–270.

1. Opie 1974:117–127.
2. Rooth 1951:75–76.
3. The pioneering study of *Cinderella* is that of Cox 1893, who compiled 345 texts of this and related stories. Among recent works are those of Rooth 1951:69–75; Ting 1974; *EM* 3:39–57; and the anthology compiled by Dundes 1983. For the device of erotic footwear and/or *Fernliebe* more generally, see Sartori 1894:160–161; Bourboulis 1953:45–50; Rohde 1960:49 n. 4; Ting 1974:37, 39; and *EM* 4:1021–1025.
4. Jameson 1932:47–85, reprinted in Dundes 1983:71–97; Waley 1947; Ting 1974; Scobie 1977b:17–18.
5. 17.1.33 (808).
6. *VH* 13.33.
7. 2.124–135.
8. 1.64.14.
9. Consequently we do not need the palaephatistic explanation of Hall (1904:210), ac-

cording to whom the association of Rhodopis and the pyramid was the result of the Greeks' calling the red-faced Sphinx *rhodopis* and then subsequently making the erroneous inference that this Rhodopis was actually a representation of the famous courtesan of the same name. On the name Rhodopis see Jacob Grimm 1865:388–389; Stramaglia 2000:269–270.

10. Achilles Tatius 2.17.

11. For example, Aly 1969:69; Lloyd 1988:84.

12. The association of the Third Pyramid at Giza with a beautiful woman continued in popular tradition in later times. According to Hall (1904:210), "The Arab historian al-Murtadi mentions a story current in his day to the effect that the pyramids were haunted, and that the spirit of the Third Pyramid was a beautiful naked woman, who appeared to men with a wonderful smile upon her face, which so infatuated all who saw her that they immediately followed her and wandered in the desert bereft of their reason."

13. Ting 1974:39.

14. Ting 1974:26, 28.

15. Ting 1974:53–60, no. 3.

16. *Astron.* 2.16.

17. Cf. Marx 1889:46–50.

Cranes of Ibykos

Assaulted by his traveling companion (escort, robbers) for his money, a man begs in vain for his life. Seeing no other human beings to whom to appeal for help, he calls upon passing cranes (pigeons, partridges, wild geese, etc.) to bear witness to his murder (or to avenge him). The man is killed. Sometime later the sight of such birds causes the murderer to comment to himself about the birds acting as witnesses (or to laugh to himself), prompting an inquiry into the fate of the murdered man (or into the cause of the laughter). The man acknowledges his deed, or the truth presently comes to light in another way.[1]

Often told as a true occurrence, this story is known from Europe to India. It is classified as AT 960A, *The Cranes of Ibycus.*

According to a tale collected in the nineteenth century from an Italian, a poor man traveling on a lonely road encountered a second man, who was in search of work. The latter, convinced that the former must have some money, attacked him with the intention of killing him. Although the poor man begged for his life and swore that he had no money, the attacker replied that he would die in either case. As the man lay near death, he spotted a pigeon flying past and called out: "Pigeon, no one is here to see me. Since you alone are passing by, be my witness." Paying no attention to these words, the murderer continued on his way and came to a nearby place where he entered service in a household as a cook. One day the master brought him a pigeon to prepare. As he plucked it, he shook his head laughing. The daughters of the master noticed his laughter and asked him the reason. He asked them in turn whether the pigeon was able to serve as a witness. They pressed him to explain himself, and the man, confident that he was beyond punishment, recounted what had happened. The girls summoned their father and made the cook repeat his story, after which the father secretly sent for the police. The cook was jailed, the family testified against him, and he paid for the murder with his own life.[2]

In a text collected from an eighty-year-old English shepherd in 1903, there was a shepherd who managed a small farm on the Black Mountain above Longton, and nearby there lived two brothers who were jealous of him. One day when the brothers found him alone they decided to murder him, saying that no one was around and the deed would never be known. The victim replied that if they killed him, the very crows would cry out and speak of it. Nevertheless, they murdered him, and no one found evidence to indicate who the murderers were. Soon the crows came to where the brothers were and wheeled around their heads crying: "Crawk, crawk, crawk." The brothers could hardly stand it, and finally one asked the other whether he remembered that when they killed the shepherd on the mountain, the shepherd said the very crows would cry out against them. A man in a nearby field overheard these words, the matter was investigated, and the brothers were hanged for murder.[3]

The Cranes of Ibykos

The tale type is best known in the form which it came to have in connection with the Greek lyric poet Ibykos of Rhegion, who lived in the sixth century B.C.[4] From ancient authors we have allusions to and partial tellings of the legend. The earliest surviving mention is in an epigram composed in the second century B.C. by Antipatros of Sidon. According to the epigram, robbers set upon Ibykos after he disembarked from a ship and came ashore at a lonely place. But before he was murdered he cried out to a "cloud of cranes," who came to witness his miserable death. Ibykos's summons was not in vain, for on account of the cry of the cranes a Fury avenged his murder in Corinth.[5]

In his essay "On Talkativeness" Plutarch calls attention to the fact that the murderers of Ibykos were detected because of their loose tongue. After recounting how a certain robbery was solved as a consequence of the robber's own talkativeness, Plutarch recalls how the murderers of Ibykos were discovered in a similar way. They were sitting in a theater, and when some cranes came into view the men laughingly whispered to one another that the cranes of Ibykos had come. Persons sitting nearby overheard them, and since Ibykos had been missing for a long time, the remark was reported to the authorities. Convicted of the crime, the men were taken away, not punished by the cranes but induced by their own talkativeness to confess the murder, just as if a Fury or other spirit had compelled them to do so. Plutarch draws the lesson that babblers should employ reason to check their tongues.[6]

The paroemiographer Zenobios, writing in the second century of our era, includes "the cranes of Ibykos" in his compilation of Greek proverbs, saying that it is used of persons who are punished unexpectedly by those whom they wronged. He explains that when Ibykos was being killed by robbers, he saw some cranes flying overhead and called them to witness the deed. Later the robbers, as they sat in a theater, observed some cranes flying and said to one another: "The cranes of Ibykos." As a result of this they were detected and punished.[7]

According to an entry in a Byzantine lexicon of the tenth century A.D., when Ibykos was attacked in a desolate place by robbers, he said that the very cranes

that were flying overhead would be his avengers. He was killed, and a while later when one of the robbers was in the city he saw some cranes and said: "Look, the avengers of Ibykos." Someone overheard this and inquired into it, the deed was admitted, and the robbers were punished. From this event there arose the proverbial phase "the cranes of Ibykos."[8]

Roman authors also allude to the legend. In a catalogue of poets, for example, Statius refers to *uolucrumque precator Ibycus*, that is, "Ibykos, who prayed to birds."[9] In the early sixteenth century Erasmus of Rotterdam, drawing upon classical authors, includes "the cranes of Ibycus" in his compilation of proverbs and once more recounts the legend in explanation of the proverb, and his retelling the Ibykos legend passed into different collections of proverbs, exempla, and other literature.[10] So the story was well known in classical antiquity, familiar enough indeed to inspire a proverb.

It is not possible to say when the story first became part of the traditional biography of Ibykos, but once established the legend of Ibykos's death appears to have varied little. His murderers are always robbers, not companions or escorts; his witnesses are always cranes; and the site of the murderers' conviction, when it is mentioned, is always Corinth. The Ibykos legend corresponds to the form of the international story in which the murderers give themselves away by making a significant comment about the birds they see; but a hint of the other form of revelation, in which they give themselves away by means of their enigmatic laughter, can probably be seen in Plutarch's version, where the murderers laugh as they whisper to one another.

Similar Legends

Several other ancient stories are reminiscent of *The Cranes of Ibykos*. In his essay "On Divine Vengeance," Plutarch tells the story of a certain Bessos, who had killed his father. He was undetected for a long time, until one day when he went to dine at a certain house he deliberately pierced a swallows' nest with his spear, knocked it down, and killed the nestlings. The people present asked him why he behaved so strangely. "Why, have they not been accusing me for a long time and crying out that I killed my father?" he asked. The astonished company reported the matter to the king, the case was investigated, and Bessos was punished.[11] And elsewhere, while discussing remarkable dogs in his essay "On the Cleverness of Animals," Plutarch reports that while on a journey King Pyrrhos came upon a dog guarding the body of a murdered man. The king, learning that the animal had remained beside the body for three days without food, ordered that the corpse be buried and the dog cared for and brought along. A few days later the king was inspecting his soldiers, who passed by in review. The dog sat beside the king quietly until the murderers of its master were passing by, at which point it ran toward them and barked vehemently, causing Pyrrhos and everyone else to be suspicious of the men. Arrested and interrogated, the men confessed and were punished.[12] But with this narrative we stray far from the basic vision of the international tale, in which it is characteristic not so much that the animal points out the murderer as that the murderer gives himself away at the sight of the animal.

Lit. AT 960A, *The Cranes of Ibycus*. Marx 1889:78–82. Amalfi 1896. Zachariae 1899. BP 2:532–535. Aly 1928:266. Dvořák, no. 2799. Ashliman, type 960A. *EM* 8: 331–334.

1. Amalfi 1896.
2. Amalfi 1896:115–116. The story was collected by Amalfi himself from an illiterate man in Tegiano in the province of Salerno.
3. Briggs (1971) B2:577–578.
4. For the life and works of Ibykos see *RE* 9:816–818, and for the story of Ibykos and the cranes see Welcker 1883. According to an anonymous epigram (*AP* 7.714), the poet's grave was in Rhegion.
5. *AP* 7.745.
6. *Mor.* 509F–510A.
7. Zenobios 1.37. Similarly other paroemiographers: Diogeneianos 1.35; and Makarios 1.50, who locates the theater in Corinth.
8. *Suda*, s.v. *Ibykos*.
9. *Silvae* 5.3.152–153.
10. *Adagia* 1.9.22; see *EM* 8:332.
11. *Mor.* 553e–f.
12. *Mor.* 969c–d. See further Aelian *NA* 7.10; Pliny *NH.* 8.142; Marx 1889:78–82. The motif of animal as witness and avenger is also found in the Aesopic fable of the hare pursued by an eagle. Since there was none that might come to his aid, the hare supplicated a dung beetle. The latter warned the eagle not to carry away his supplicant, but the eagle, scorning the small size of the beetle, devoured the hare. Thereafter the beetle tormented the eagle by destroying its eggs (Aristophanes *Wasps* 1446–1449; *Vita Aesopi* 139; Perry 3).

Dead Child's Friendly Return ⚘ The Dead Ask the Living to Cease Grieving

When a child (husband, lover, mother, brother, etc.) dies, the mother (wife, lover, daughter, sister, etc.) weeps incessantly. At length the ghost of the deceased person appears to the mourner and begs her (him) to cease weeping, explaining that the weeper's tears actually harm the deceased (they keep his shroud wet and heavy or wet and chilly, they burn like fire, they pierce him, they cause a flood, they must be carried around by him in a pitcher, they disturb his rest, etc.). Sometimes it is said that the mourner ceases her weeping and that the lot of the deceased improves.

This sad story, which circulates as both prose narrative and ballad as well as both tale and legend, is AT 769, *Dead Child's Friendly Return to Parents*.

In a common form of the tale, a mother mourns the loss of a dear child. The father is not mentioned at all. A Danish legend collected from a woman in Jutland in the nineteenth century tells how a woman had a little child who died, after which the woman grieved constantly. Once she dreamed that she saw many small children walking past, each carrying a green branch, and her own child trailed far behind. When she asked her child why he did not come sooner, the child replied that it was her fault, for all the tears that she cried for him fell upon his body, making it so wet and heavy that he could scarcely move. The woman awoke and understood that the dream was a sign to cease her crying.[1]

According to a Scottish story, also from the nineteenth century, an only sister lost an only brother, after which she wept incessantly and called his name. Fi-

nally the brother appeared to her, dressed in his wet shroud and shivering. He reproached her for the extravagance of her sorrow, which he called a "rebellion against the decrees of Providence," and explained that until she should be penitent, every tear she should shed would fall upon his shroud without drying and would chill and encumber him.[2]

In an English ballad, "The Unquiet Grave," sung by a girl in Sussex and published in 1868, a youth sits and mourns at the grave of his beloved for a twelvemonth and a day. When the time is up, the dead girl speaks to him, asking why he sits weeping on her grave and does not let her sleep. He answers that he craves one kiss of her cold lips. She explains that if he has a kiss of her lips, his own time will not be long. She points out that the flowers in the garden where they used to walk are now withered, just as their own hearts will decay, and urges him to make himself content until god calls him away.[3]

This story gives expression to the widespread belief, attested in Europe from antiquity to the present, in ancient Persia, in India, and elsewhere, that excessive grieving for the dead disturbs their rest, causes them pain, or confounds their normal activities.[4] In the oral story the belief is acted out, the survivor grieving extravagantly and the dead person objecting. The mourner is instructed that tears actually harm the deceased. The point is simply that eventually all-consuming grief should cease. After an appropriate period of time, unbounded grief at the loss of a loved one becomes self-indulgence and even a form of rebellion against the divine plan or the nature of things, which the mourner must learn to accept. The story conveys the message that grief should be bounded, that eventually one must let go of the dead and continue with life, and narrators have doubtless employed the story in order to communicate this idea memorably and persuasively.

Excessive Expressions of Grief in Greece and Rome

By and large what we find in ancient authors is not the developed narrative itself but stronger or weaker hints of the narrative situation in which the cultural value against excessive grieving is acted out in a little drama between the living and the dead, the living grieving and the dead objecting in some way. Thus Homer portrays the protracted grief and rage of Achilleus at the loss of his companion Patroklos and at his own responsibility in the matter. Finally the ghost of Patroklos appeared to Achilleus as he slept and told his companion to cremate and bury him as soon as possible in order that his soul might cease its wandering and join the other souls in Hades' realm, and Achilleus promised to do so. When Achilleus tried to embrace his friend for the last time, Patroklos's ghost disappeared into the earth. Achilleus presently buried him.[5]

Achilleus delays Patroklos's entering the proper home of the dead, causing his companion's ghost to remain against its wishes in limbo. The idea is similar to that in the Danish text in which the mother's constant weeping weighs down her dead child, preventing him from joining the society of deceased children. In both stories, the behavior of the mourner eventually impedes normal cosmic progress, causing distress to the deceased person, who desires only to move on to the next stage of things. Similarly, Achilleus's desire to embrace Patrokos, that is, to treat him as a living, palpable person, resembles the desire of the youth in the English ballad who, likewise denying the full reality of his

beloved's death, desires a last kiss from her. Like Patroklos, she flees from the idea, explaining in this case that he would not long survive a kiss from her cold lips.

On the other hand, the Homeric and the modern narratives differ in the use or avoidance of fantastic images that are more at home in folktales than in narrative genres such as epic. Thus, in the international tale the tears of the mourner literally burden or burn the deceased, whereas in Homer protracted grieving delays attending to the funeral rites. And in the ballad the youth learns that it would be fatal to kiss the cold lips of the deceased, whereas Achilleus learns merely that it is futile to embrace the dead.

Later representations in classical literature of the dead communicating with the living show less resemblance to the modern story. In a dialogue of Lucian, a speaker imagines that if the ruler of the dead should allow a deceased son to address his grieving father, the boy would ask his father why the man is causing him trouble, crying out and tearing out his hair and scratching his skin and saying that the boy is unfortunate, when in fact death is superior in some ways to life, since, for example, the dead do not age, and they are not subject to appetites.[6] And an elegy of Propertius begins with the verse "Cease, Paullus, burdening my grave with your tears." The deceased woman explains that her husband's weeping is in vain, for no tears or prayers can bring back the dead.[7]

In the former work the father's grieving for his son's lot bothers the dead youth, not because it causes physical distress or the like, but because it is misplaced. In the latter work the dead woman addresses her living husband, not really to complain of distress caused by the survivor's grieving, but to urge her husband to accept the reality of her death, explaining that his grieving will not change things. In both passages, great or extensive grieving brings perhaps mild distress to the dead, but the authors emphasize rather that the grief is wasted.[8]

It is noteworthy that the postclassical tradition commonly represents women as the excessive grievers, whereas in the Greco-Roman passages cited here the mourners are all men. The ancients evidently deemed men to be the more interesting studies in this context, not merely because men were expected to be less extravagant in their mourning (for this expectation has been generally characteristic of postclassical societies in the West as well), but perhaps because men's struggles were regarded as more important than women's. While the evidence does not suggest that AT 769 existed in antiquity as a developed story, it does attest to the same cultural attitude toward excessive grieving as that which underlies the later international story, and it does show artistic experimentation with the idea of representing the dead (rather than, say, the mourner's friends or relations) as actively discouraging prolonged or extravagant grief in the living.

Lit. (AT 769, *Dead Child's Friendly Return to Parents.*) Schenkl 1866:451–452. BP 2:485–490. Rohde 1925:190 n. 49. Child (1956) 2:234–238, no. 78.

1. Kvideland and Sehmsdorf 1988:59–60, no. 6.3.
2. Child (1956) 2:235.
3. Child (1956) 2:236.
4. Rohde 1925:190 Child (1956) 2:234–237; BP 2:488–490.
5. *Il.* 23.62–107.

6. *De Luctu* 16.

7. 4.11.

8. Compare the passage in Plato in which a speaker says that if we must die young, we beseech our parents not to spend the rest of their days lamenting our death, for if the dead have any consciousness of the living, they will be less gratified by heavy mourning than by lightheartedness (*Menexenus* 248b–c). Similarly, Cicero *Fam.* 4.5.6.

Deaf Man and the Proud Nobleman. *See* Hearing-Impaired Persons

Death's Messengers

Death promises a man to send several messengers before he himself comes. In time, the man experiences various symptoms of old age or weakness (gray hair, bowed back, sickness), which he ignores or explains away. When finally Death comes for him, the man objects that Death promised not to come before sending several messengers. Death explains that the symptoms the man ignored were his messengers, and he takes the man away.

This melancholy, moralistic tale is AT 335, *Death's Messengers*. It has not been collected frequently in oral tradition in modern times.[1]

According to a Latin text in the fourteenth-century *Summa Praedicantium* composed by the English Dominican John of Bromyard, a man concluded a pact with Death in which the latter agreed not to take him away before he had sent him some three or four messengers. Sometime later the man fell ill. The doctor came and warned him to take thought for his soul, since his pulse and urine showed the symptoms of death. The man himself said that he had lost his appetite. Shortly thereafter Death came and summoned him. The man said he would not come, for Death had not sent the messengers he had promised. But Death replied that on the contrary he had sent them all just as he had promised. One messenger was a fever that had beset the man; another was when the doctor had warned him of the symptoms in his pulse and urine; and the third was his loss of appetite. So Death said the man's complaint was unjust, and ordered him to rise and come along.[2]

The notion of Death's messengers is also found in nonnarrative contexts. Christian authors from the Middle Ages onward frequently admonish their readers to heed Death's messengers, mentioning phenomena such as gray hair, diminished eyesight, loss of memory, mental rigidity, illness, old age, coughing, and facial wrinkles.[3] The same ideas, if not precisely the same tale, are found as far east as India.

Death's Messengers in Greece

Although *Death's Messengers* is not attested as a tale in classical literature, Lucian employs the principal motif of the tale, from which we can infer that at least the metaphor was already established in ancient Greece or perhaps in Syria, the author's homeland. The work in question takes the form of a dia-

logue between Hermes and Charon in which the ferryman of the dead takes a break from his duties in order to learn something of the life that the dead leave behind.

Hermes explains that the lives of all persons hang by threads, some shorter and some longer, but all of them slender, with the result that many persons perish unexpectedly in the midst of their ambitions and hopes, snatched away by Death. His messengers and servants are many in number: chills, fevers, consumption, inflammations of the lungs, swords, pirates, hemlock, judges, tyrants. So long as a person fares well, he gives no thought to them, but when he is in difficulty, he moans and exclaims. If from the beginning a person had considered that he was mortal, had only a brief time to live, and would have to take leave of everything that is on the surface of the earth, he might live more prudently and be less miserable in death. But since he expects to retain possession forever of what he now has, he is very upset when the servant of Death comes to his bed, summons him, and takes him away, fettered in fever or consumption; for he has never really expected to be separated from his property. The ambitions and dreams of many persons are vain, for, unknown to them, the above-mentioned messengers and servants will summon them before they have the opportunity to enjoy what they expect someday to enjoy.[4]

Formally, Hermes' metaphor differs in a couple ways from the later narrative tradition. First, he speaks both of Death's "messengers" and of his "servants."[5] Second, his examples include not only physical symptoms such as fevers but also external agents of death such as swords and tyrants. One might distinguish symptoms as being Death's messengers and agents as being his servants, although Lucian himself does not appear to make such a distinction. But Lucian's apparently indifferent use of messengers and servants in this context is probably not significant. In a Maltese text of *Death's Messengers* published in 1906, the narrator prefers to speak of Death's "servants" (six times) but refers synonymously also to Death's "messengers" (twice) and once even to his "people."[6]

Interestingly, the tradition drawn upon by Lucian consists not only of the metaphor but also of the accessory notion that people generally disregard Death and his messengers until the final hour. This idea is regularly present in the folktale. Death sends messages to persons, forewarns them, in order that they not be unprepared when finally he comes for them, but they fail to perceive the messengers for what they are, and consequently are surprised at Death's eventual arrival. Unwilling to recognize Death's messengers, people are indignant when he himself shows up without, as they think, a forewarning. Though Lucian's use of this theme shows that the basic idea upon which *Death's Messengers* is built was in circulation by at least the second century A.D., we cannot be certain whether Lucian borrows the theme from a tale like that known to us from later, mostly religious sources or only draws upon a popular notion that was subsequently used to construct *Death's Messengers* as a narrative. But the presence in Lucian's dialogue both of the basic metaphor and also of the accessory notion of human disregard for the messengers of Death suggests that probably the whole tale was already in circulation. The parodist borrowed as much of it as was useful for his composition.

Lit. (AT 335, *Death's Messengers.*) Morris 1889. BP 3:293–297. Schwarzbaum 1957:63–67. Röhrich (1962) 1:80–92, 258–262. *EM* 2:636–639. Ashliman, type 335.

1. Röhrich (1962) 1:261.
2. BP 3:293.
3. Morris 1889:188–189; BP 3:295–296.
4. *Contemplantes* 17.
5. ἄγγελοι δὲ καὶ ὑπηρέται αὐτοῦ.
6. Röhrich (1962) 1:91–92.

Devil to Count Stars 🦢 Counting Sand, Stars, Waves

A man sells his soul to the devil in exchange for the latter's services, and then saves it by imposing on the devil a counting task (or several such tasks) that he cannot accomplish.

This is the plot of AT 1172*, *Devil to Count Stars*.

In a Walloon text cited by Aarne and Thompson the devil was to count the stars, the blades of grass, and the sands of the sea.[1] That is, he had to count units of particular natural phenomena that were so numerous as to be virtually uncountable. An English text recounts how a man trying to lay the devil might assign him up to three tasks. He told him to count the raindrops on a certain hedge, to count the ears of corn in a particular field, and to twist a rope of sand and wash it in the river without losing a grain, an assignment that combines counting and noncounting tasks. In another English narrative the tasks were to count the blades of grass in a certain locality, the grains of sand in a place, and the letters in the bible belonging to the parish church. In both texts the devil was able to perform the first two seemingly impossible tasks but not the third, and so departed.[2]

The Motif of Impossible Counting in Antiquity

No analogue of this tale as such is attested in ancient sources, but the basic motifs of counting the stars, the sands, and waves were already well known in antiquity as impossible tasks.[3]

Many ancient authors speak of counting or measuring the sands. A hint of the thought appears in Homer's *Iliad*, when Achilleus passionately refuses Agamemnon's gifts and offer of reconciliation, saying that even if Agamemnon should offer as many gifts as the sands and the dust, he still would not persuade Achilleus's heart.[4] Earlier in the poem, as the Achaean forces march against Troy, the goddess Iris links sand and leaves as uncountables when she tells Hektor: "I have never seen so great a host before,/for much like leaves or the sands/they proceed across the plain to fight against the city."[5] In a late Greek novel, the so-called *Alexander Romance*, King Darius of Persia claims to have so many troops that, like the grains of sand, they are beyond counting.[6]

Indeed the impossibility of measuring the sands was proverbial, and the idea

is found in Greek collections of proverbs and proverbial expressions; for example, Zenobios lists "to count sand," which he glosses as an expression applied to something impossible and unattainable.[7] The idea was also familiar to Latin authors.[8] And in Hebrew tradition god tells Abram that he will make his seed like the sand of the earth, and if anyone can count the sand of the earth he will be able to count the seed of Abram.[9] That is, Abram's offspring will be too numerous to be tallied.

In this context one can appreciate the outrageousness of the claim made by the Greek mathematician Archimedes in his essay "The Sand-Reckoner," where he not only denies that the sands of the world are infinite or inexpressible by a number but even says he will provide a number that exceeds the number of grains of sand not just in his own town of Syracuse or in all of Sicily, nor just the amount of sand that it would take to fill up the world, but rather the amount that would be required to fill the entire cosmos.[10] By his reckoning the number of grains of sand that a sphere the size of the cosmos would contain would not exceed 10^{63}.

The association of the sands and the stars as uncountables was also common in ancient discourse. A speaker in Plato's *Euthydemos* asks his interlocutors if they know how many stars there are and how much sand there is.[11] The poet Catullus, when Lesbia asks him how many kisses are enough, replies that as many as are the sands in Libya and the stars in the sky.[12] In Genesis an angel similarly links stars and sand, though he does not speak of actually numbering them, when he tells Abraham that his seed will be as numerous as the stars in the sky and as the sand beside the sea.[13]

Similarly, counting the waves was proverbial among the Greeks as an impossible and therefore useless activity.[14] The poet Theokritos says that one may as well stand on the shore and count the waves driven landward by the wind as to try to win over with words a man infected with a love of gain.[15] Plutarch lists as signifying impossibility the proverbial expression "You're counting waves."[16] And the paroemiologists Zenobios and Diogeneianos both have the proverbial expression "More silly than Koroibos," which they explain as referring to a moron named Koroibos who spent his time trying to count the waves.[17] According to an Aesopic fable told by Lucian, a man who was sitting on the shore counting the waves lost count of them and as a result became very upset. Thereupon Profit appeared and asked him why he was upset about those that were gone; he ought to forget about them and start counting from here.[18] In this tale however the emphasis is not upon the folly of counting waves but upon the folly of dwelling uselessly upon what is past and therefore beyond one's control.

Interestingly, the tasks that are impossible for mere mortals and usually impossible for the Christian devil are within the powers of the ancient gods. Cheiron says that Apollo knows how many leaves the earth produces in spring and how many sands there are in the sea and in the rivers; and Apollo's mouthpiece the Pythia says in an oracle that she knows the numbers of the sands and the measures of the sea.[19] When the Hebrew deity declares that the number of Abram's descendants will resemble the number of grains of sand on the earth and that if anyone can count the sands he will be able to count Abram's offspring, he implies that he himself knows their numbers.

Although a developed tale corresponding to *Devil to Count Stars* is not

known to be ancient, most of the counting tasks that the international tale employs as impossible chores for the ogre were proverbially impossible activities already in antiquity. Moreover, the underlying structure of *Devil to Count Stars*, in which one party to an agreement assigns an impossible task to the other party in order to void the agreement, can also be found in ancient tradition. An episode in the *Aesop Romance* recounts how the philosopher Xanthos bet his students that he could drink the sea dry, and each party to the bet deposited a ring with a stakeholder. At the seashore on the following day Xanthos pointed out that he promised to drink dry only the sea, not the waters of the rivers that were flowing into it, and he bade the other party as a countertask first stop up the mouths of the streams. Since they were unable to do so, the bet was voided.[20] In this tale the first party, himself facing an impossible task, assigns an impossible task as a precondition to the second party, and since the second party is unable to execute it, the contract between them is dissolved. In short the protagonist escapes from an agreement by assigning to the antagonist a task he cannot perform, and this, abstractly stated, is the plot of *Devil to Count Stars*.

For other traditional tales in which a person eludes an ogre by giving him impossible tasks, see "Making a Rope of Sand" and "Carrying Water in a Sieve."

Lit. (AT 1172*, *Devil to Count Stars*.) Motif H1144.2, *Task: counting the waves.* EM 1:968.

1. Aarne and Thompson 1961:369.
2. Briggs (1971) B1:134–136.
3. Canter 1930:37–38.
4. 9.385–386.
5. 2.799–801. In modern Greek folksongs stars and leaves continue to represent virtual uncountables; see Sifakis 1998:178.
6. 1.36.
7. 1.80 (*CPG* 1:27): ἄμμον μετρεῖν. So also Diogeneianos 2.27 (*CPG* 1:199).
8. Otto 1890:159, no. 786.
9. For example, Gen. 13:14–16. Not only will it be beyond the powers of a mortal to enumerate the offspring of Abram, he will not be permitted even to attempt it. Thus King David incurs divine displeasure for taking a census of the people; see Frazer (1919) 2:555–563.
10. Dijksterhuis 1987:360–373.
11. 294b.
12. Catullus 7. For other instances in classical authors of counting the stars, see Otto 1890:342, no. 1643.
13. Gen. 22:15–17.
14. See further Marcovich 1976.
15. 16.60–63. See further Gow 1931.
16. *Ekloge* 17 (*CPG* 1:345): κύματα μετρεῖς.
17. Zenobios 4.58 (*CPG* 1:101); Diogeneianos 5.56 (*CPG* 1:262). Another silly counter of waves is Koikylion, mentioned by Aelian *VH* 13.15 in a brief catalogue of fools.
18. Lucian *Hermotimus* 84 = Perry 429.
19. For Cheiron see Pindar *Pythian* 9.46–47; to my knowledge, no classical author mentions counting the blades of grass as a task, a motif found in *Devil to Count Stars*, but Pindar's representing Apollo as knowing how many leaves the earth produces in spring amounts to the same thing, and counting all the leaves of the trees appears explicitly as an impossible task in the *Anacreontea* (14.1–2). For the Pythia see Herodotos 1.47.3; cf. Fontenrose 1978:113.
20. *Vita Aesopi* 69–73. The same tale is recounted of other characters by Plutarch in his *Symposium of the Seven Sages* (*Mor.* 151).

Disenchanted Husband 🌿 Cupid and Psyche

A father agrees to give his daughter in marriage to an animal (or the heroine agrees to such a marriage on her own). Frequently the youngest and most beautiful of three daughters, the girl joins the creature as his mate. Sometimes they live luxuriously in his palace, and in any case she becomes fond of him. The mysterious husband forbids his wife to look upon him by light at night (to reveal to anyone that he is a handsome youth at night, to ask or to reveal his name, to burn his animal skin, etc.), for, having been enchanted, he is an animal by day and a man at night. Induced by her sisters (mother, father), however, she breaks the taboo, upon which her husband immediately departs.

She sets out to look for him, and after an arduous quest, in the course of which she may be helped by various beings (old women, winds, stars, etc.), she reaches the house of the witch who has enchanted her husband. One or more of three events follow: (a) The witch engages the heroine as a servant or quasi-servant and assigns her a number of seemingly impossible tasks (carrying water in a sieve, sorting a large amount of grain), which her husband, whom she may not recognize, assists her in performing. (b) The witch sends her to her sister, who is also a witch, to fetch a particular item (jewelry, box, music, letter). During her journey the heroine may encounter persons (animals, objects) that she must treat in a particular way (for example, she must feed certain ones) in order not to be harmed during her return. The second witch may give her food to eat, which she, having been warned, conceals and only pretends to consume. Eventually the witch gives her the desired item, forbidding her to open it, but on her way back she does so, with the result that the contents (e.g., musicians, snakes) escape. (c) The heroine must hold the candles (or torches) at the wedding of her husband to her rival (the witch or the witch's daughter). But the task leads to the destruction (demise) of her rival.

The heroine regains her husband and disenchants him (makes him recognize her, induces him to choose her over her rival). If the heroine is pregnant, the witch is tricked into permitting her to give birth. If the heroine's evil sisters have not yet been punished, they are dealt with. Finally the husband and wife punish the witch (rival), or they escape from the witch by means of a magic flight.[1]

This complex tale is AT 425B, *The Disenchanted Husband: the Witch's Tasks*. The latter part of its title refers to one of its defining features, the heroine's entering into the service of a witch, who assigns her apparently impossible tasks. AT 425B is a subtype of AT 425, *The Search for the Lost Husband*, a cluster of similar and presumably related tales recounting how a human girl enters into a marriagelike relationship with an enchanted being, whom she loses after the breaking of a taboo but eventually wins back.[2] Each subtype of this popular and prolific plot has its own characteristic features.

The subtypes tend to show a stable sequence of basic action, which may be summarized as (1) the heroine's marriage is set up, (2) the heroine weds an enchanted husband, (3) the husband establishes a taboo, (4) the heroine violates the taboo, (5) as a result, the husband departs, (6) the wife searches for her lost husband, coming finally to the house of the witch who is responsible for his plight, (7) the witch assigns impossible or dangerous tasks to the heroine, who accomplishes them, and finally (8) the husband and wife are reunited. These

slots are filled variously in accordance with factors such as subtype, local culture, and storyteller. Frequently a particular text elaborates a feature of the basic sequence such as the heroine's trials, or it economizes a feature, such as omitting the taboo or cutting short the heroine's quest for her lost husband.[3] The basic framework can accommodate different narrative strategies. For example, a text may initially dwell upon the supernatural being's family rather than upon the heroine's family, emphasizing *his* early history over *hers*, as if toying with the idea of making the youth the central figure of the tale, rather than the maiden. I summarize four texts in illustration of the tale.

A colorfully recounted Gypsy text collected in Bulgaria tells of a king who had four daughters and a horse that was the son of an ogress. Discovering that the horse was enamored of his eldest daughter, he gave her to the animal, placing her in the stable. As the girl wondered how the horse would couple with her, the horse cast its skin, became a beautiful youth, and mated with her. He informed her that on the morrow he would dress in green and ride a green horse; however, she should not reveal that he was her husband, for if she did, she would have to make iron shoes and find him in a distant land. She followed his instructions. On the following day the youth informed her that on the morrow he would dress in white and ride a white horse. But when her sisters mocked her for having a horse as a husband, she revealed that the youth in white clothes was in fact her husband. That evening he rebuked her and told her that she must make shoes and a staff of iron and seek him in a certain distant land. Then the horse, whose name was Batim, flew away to his mother. The wife fashioned shoes and a staff of iron and sought her husband for ten years before she found him. Fearing that his ogress mother would eat her, Batim turned his wife into a needle and pinned her to his chest. When Batim's mother came, she perceived the presence of edible flesh. After exacting an oath from his mother not to attack his bride, he turned her back into human form. Presently the mother gave the girl a task, telling her to fill a certain tank with her tears, or else the mother would eat her. The girl tried in vain to cry enough to fill the tank with her tears, but failed. Batim came and filled it with water mixed with salt. When the ogress saw that the girl had filled it, she was angry and set a second task: she was to fill forty-one rooms with feathers. Again, Batim showed her how to summon birds and induce them to drop their feathers. Angry that the girl accomplished this task as well, the old mother said she was going to celebrate a wedding feast, and instructed the girl to invite the mother's sister, also an ogress. Batim informed her how to manage the feat. When the girl returned, the mother told her to invite the mother's brothers to the feast, and she accomplished this task as well. The next day the girl and Batim fled. Unable to catch them, the ogress gave them her blessing.[4]

The elements of the basic sequence are easily seen. (1) The father arranges his daughter's marriage (2) to an enchanted horse. The horse (3) forbids her to reveal that he is really a human being, but (4) mockery by her sisters induces the heroine to reveal his secret, whereupon (5) he flies away. (6) Wearing iron shoes and bearing an iron staff she searches for him for ten years. Finding him, (7) she moves into the house of his mother, who assigns her tasks: to fill a tank with tears, to fill rooms with feathers, to invite her ogrous sister and brothers to a wedding, all of which she accomplishes with her husband's help. Finally (8) the two flee together.

According to a tale collected in India, there once was a Rajah named Bunsi Lall, whom a witch had enchanted, turning him into a snake and causing him to live underground. Desiring to see the world, the snake made a dwelling aboveground, where he encountered a girl gathering sticks in the forest. Struck by the beauty of this girl, whose name was Sukkia, the snake asked her to marry him. But she was afraid to wed a snake, not knowing that he was a snake only by day and at night had his human form of Rajah Bunsi Lall. But she told her cruel stepmother of the offer, and the woman, who had no concern for the girl, gave her consent if the snake would fill the house with silver. The snake met the condition so that Sukkia became his bride and went to live with him, where she was happy. Some time later the stepmother went to see if the girl was still alive, and to her surprise she found that Sukkia was prosperous and happy. Now, the stepmother knew of the enchantment of Bunsi Lall and knew furthermore that if he revealed his name he would have to return to his underground home. So she advised Sukkia to pester him until he should tell her his name. Sukkia asked him what his name was, and though he begged her not to persist, saying it would bring her bad luck, she kept asking, until finally he declared that his name was Rajah Bunsi Lall. Then he disappeared. For days she sought him in the bazaars and streets. Meanwhile arrangements for his marriage to another girl were being made in his own country. Sukkia learned of these plans from his servants, who came for water from the well. She implored them to take her ring to their master, which they did, and the ring put Bunsi Lall in mind of his wife's suffering, so that he went back to the world to find her and bring her to his country. But when the snake's mother learned of the daughter-in-law, she intended to kill her. The mother housed Sukkia in a room full of scorpions, but Rajah Bunsi Lall rid the room of its creatures. The mother then tested her, saying that the girl would die if she did not give proof of her cleverness: she strewed the floor with mustard seed, telling the girl to divide it into equal lots. The girl only cried, but the snake came and summoned some birds, who divided the mustard seed. Finally the mother ordered Sukkia to follow the snake's wedding procession, carrying the torches in such a way that, when the wind blew in her direction, she would be burnt to death. But as she cried out from burning, Rajah Bunsi Lall came to her rescue. The two ran away together, escaped to the upper world, and lived happily thereafter.[5]

In the Indian narration (1) the girl arranges her own marriage (2) to an enchanted snake, (3) who tells her not to ask his name. (4) She does so anyway, and when he utters it, (5) he disappears. (6) She searches for him for days, and finally (7) he brings her to his mother's house, where the ogress gives her tasks: to divide mustard seed into equal lots and to bear a dangerous wedding torch, both of which she manages with the help of her husband. Then (8) they flee together.

A retelling published in 1634 by the Neapolitan author Giambattista Basile tells of a poor man who had three daughters. One day the youngest, Parmetella, chanced to discover in the woods an opening in the ground with a staircase of porphyry. The girl, whose curiosity knew no bounds, descended the stairway, coming eventually to a plain on which stood a magnificent palace surrounded by gold and silver. Inside she found a table set with food and drink and, being hungry, sat down to enjoy herself. A handsome, black slave appeared, announcing that he wished her to stay and become his wife. Although

frightened, Parmetella agreed, whereupon the slave presented her with a diamond coach drawn by winged horses and a troop of monkeys attired in gold as her personal attendants. That night the slave told her that she must extinguish the candle as soon as she lay down in bed. After she did so, the slave changed into a white youth and made love to her, but before dawn he leapt out of bed and resumed the form of a black slave. The second night began the same way, but after the bridegroom fell asleep, the bride lit a candle, lifted the coverings, and saw a lovely youth with ivory skin. As she gazed, he awoke and swore at her, saying that because of her curiosity he must bear his accursed penitence for another seven years. After telling her to be off, he disappeared. Parmetella made her way back to the upper world, where a fairy gave her seven spindles, seven figs, a jar of honey, and seven pairs of iron shoes that she was to wear until she wore them out, and advised her how to avoid the dangers that lay ahead. After she had worn out the iron shoes, she would see seven women spinning from the balcony of a house down to the ground, winding their thread about the bones of dead men. Parmetella must then stand still, replace the bone with a spindle smeared with honey, placing a fig on the spindle tip. Pleased by the sweetness the women would ask her to show herself, which she must not do until they should swear a particular oath not to eat her. After walking for seven years, Parmetella wore out the iron shoes and came to a large house with a balcony, where she followed the fairy's instructions. The women angrily reproached her for being the cause of their brother's misery, but they also warned her against their ogress mother, explaining how to deal with her in order not to be eaten. The girl followed their instructions and so escaped being eaten, but thereafter the ogress sought an opportunity to feast upon Parmetella. One day she took twelve sacks of mixed vegetable seeds, telling her that if she did not finish sorting them by the evening she would be eaten. While she wept in despair, her husband, Thunder-and-Lightning, having completed the term of the curse, appeared, and arranged for an army of ants to sort the seeds, which the girl then placed in separate sacks. The angry ogress assigned her another task, to fill twelve mattresses with feathers by nightfall. Again Thunder-and-Lightning saved the day, telling her to call out that the King of the Birds was dead, whereupon birds came, beat their wings in grief, and dropped enough feathers in an hour to fill the mattresses. Next the mother sent her to the house of her sister to fetch musical instruments for Thunder-and-Lightning's wedding to an ogress, but at the same time she secretly sent word to her sister to kill the girl and cook her. Her husband advised Parmetella what to do: she was to take a loaf, a bundle of hay, and a stone. First she would come upon his aunt's furious dog, to whom she should give the bread; and then a runaway horse, to whom she should give the hay; and finally a banging door, which she should stop with the stone. Then she should grab the box in which the musical instruments were kept, and leave. Finally he warned her not to open the box. She did as she was told, and when the sister perceived that the girl had slipped away, she told the door to crush the girl, but it refused, saying that the girl had propped it open; then she ordered the horse to trample her and the dog to bite her, but they each refused because of the food the girl had given them. But as she returned Parmetella opened the box so that the instruments escaped. Thunder-and-Lightning appeared, reproaching her again for her curiosity and

putting the instruments back into the box. During the wedding Parmetella had to hold a torch in each hand and sit beside a well, so that if she fell asleep she would fall in. The groom asked for a kiss from Parmetella, who declined, whereupon the bride reproached her, saying that she herself let a shepherd kiss her for two chestnuts. The enraged Thunder-and-Lightning killed his ogress bride, embraced Parmetella, and they retired to bed together. The next day the mother killed herself from despair, but Thunder-and-Lightning made peace between his wife and his sisters.[6]

In Basile's tale (1) the girl arranges her own marriage (2) to an enchanted black slave, (3) who requires that she extinguish the candle as soon as she goes to bed. But (4) one night she lights it again, so that (5) he disappears. (6) Wearing iron shoes she finds him after a search of seven years. (7) Moving into her mother-in-law's residence, she is assigned tasks: to sort seeds, to fill mattresses with feathers, to fetch musicians from an ogress and bring them back in a box, having treated certain beings or objects in a certain way, and to hold two torches during her husband's wedding, all which she does, mostly with the help of her husband. After the ogress bride is killed, (8) the hero and heroine are reunited.

Finally, a Danish folktale published in 1854 recounts how there was once a farmer who promised to buy his daughter some bands of red silk in town. But he drank up his money, so that he left town heavy at heart because he lacked the means to purchase the bands his daughter wanted. On his way home a little white dog came running up and asked the farmer what was the matter. When the farmer explained his problem, the dog immediately produced silk bands, in return for which the farmer was to give him the first thing that should meet him when he came home. The farmer agreed, feeling certain that it would be his dog, but as it turned out, his daughter was the first to greet him in her eagerness for the silk bands. The father gave her the bands and said nothing. That evening there was a knock on the door, and there was the little white dog demanding the farmer's daughter. The farmer explained the matter to his daughter, who agreed to go with the dog. The animal took her to a dark forest, where they sank down into the earth, and then they were in a delightful castle. The dog explained that he would be gone during the days but would come to her each night, but he forbade her ever to light a candle. They lived there a long time in wealth and finery, the dog coming each evening and leaving each morning. He was not really a dog, but she never saw his true form because there was never light in the castle. Three years passed, during which time she bore three sons. She began to miss her father and asked the dog if she might visit him. The dog brought her to him, warning her again that no candle must be lit in their dwelling. She told her father that the dog was good to her and that they lived happily. Her father said that he was doubtless a prince, and that she should light a candle at home in order to learn the truth. The girl let herself be persuaded, and that evening at home she gently arose, lit a candle, and in the light saw the loveliest prince lying in the bed. But as she bent over him, three drops of tallow fell on his breast, so that he woke up. He said that they must now be separated for a long time; she was to leave the castle and children and take service in the household of the old witch who lived at the edge of the woods. She did so. One day the witch announced that she was going to have a

wedding, for which purpose she wanted the girl to go to her sister in Hell to fetch musicians; she gave her a box to put them in. The girl was at a loss concerning how to proceed and wished for the help of the little white dog, who suddenly appeared and instructed her. She was to go until she reached a bridge, where she should repair a loose plank, and passing over the bridge she would come to a gate hanging on one hinge, which she should fix, and passing through the gate she would come to Hell, where she would see a dog growling at an upside-down butter-form, which she should turn right side up; finally, the witch would give her cake and wine, which she should not consume. She followed the instructions, came to her mistress's sister, who also was a witch, and requested the musicians. The girl pretended to consume the cake and wine, got the musicians, and departed with the box, which the witch told her not to open. Despite the witch's orders, the dog, gate, and plank refused to hinder her, each remembering her act of kindness. But as she returned she opened the box to see if it really held musicians, and the musicians all escaped. The frightened girl wished for the little white dog, who appeared and whistled the musicians back into the box. After she had delivered the box, the woman told her that she must wash some clothing white for the wedding. She was able to do so with the dog's help. When the witch saw all this, she perceived that her own power was gone and that there would be no wedding for herself and the little white dog. From sheer vexation she burst into a thousand pieces. The little white dog had changed into a lovely prince, and they both lived happily and long.[7]

In this narration (1) the father inadvertently agrees to a marriage between his daughter (2) and a dog, (3) who forbids any illumination in his castle at night. But (4) the girl lights a candle anyway, obliging them (5) to separate for a long time. (7) She enters into the service of a witch, who assigns her tasks: to go to Hell to fetch musicians for a wedding from the witch's sister and bring them back in a box, having treated certain objects and beings in a certain way, and to wash certain clothing white, all of which she accomplishes with her husband's aid. When the witch, who is also the intended bride, perishes, (8) the hero and heroine are reunited. This version omits the element of the girl's search (6).

In these four illustrative texts, ranging geographically from Europe to India and temporally from the seventeenth century to the early twentieth century, we find considerable agreement in the basic sequence of events coupled with variety in their surface expression. For the purpose of the tale it appears not to be very important how the girl enters into her relationship with her unusual husband.[8] The particular kind of being that she weds varies greatly: horse, snake, dog, some other animal (in texts not illustrated here), or a groom who is not an animal at all but a black slave. What these enchanted husbands initially have in common is their apparent undesirability as a mate. The narrators handle this impossible marital relationship with charming restraint, as when the bride's sisters in the Gypsy tale mock her after their father marries her to a horse, but only as they might mock her if he had married her to a beggar; however bizarre her marriage is, they nevertheless treat it as a possible one.[9] The husband immediately forbids his wife to do something, which she presently does anyway, thereby losing him and initiating her suffering and heroism. The taboo can be one of speech or one of sight, information that she has but must not share, or information that

she does not have and must not acquire. The reason for his strange prohibition, if and when it is ever explained, is that the limitation is necessary for his eventual disenchantment, but details of the back story–why the man was placed under a magic spell, who did it, what must happen in order for him to be free of it–may not be given, leaving parts of the larger story intriguingly mysterious. The cause of her violating the prohibition may be her excessive curiosity, as it is in the Italian tale, in which she seeks information that she lacks, but it may have other causes, and in the Gypsy tale, in which she possesses information that she must keep to herself, her fault if anything is her pride. Because of her disobedience she now suffers trials, first in the form of a sometimes long and arduous quest for her lost husband and subsequently in the form of brief, difficult tasks assigned by the hostile ogress in whose house she dwells and who usually is her mother-in-law. The girl may adopt an attitude of helplessness at the prospect of each undertaking or she may not, but generally her husband or another helper appears and tells her what to do or sometimes simply does it himself.[10] In any case she perseveres, and in the end she frees her husband and wins him back.

The Disenchanted Husband has aptly been described as a feminine folktale in the sense that for most of the tale the heroine is the more active of the two principal characters and serves ultimately as the agent of her husband's liberation, whereas the hero is somewhat limited by his enchantment.[11] It is he who needs to be rescued, not she. A female is the principal character in only about one-third of magic tales.[12] Although the evidence is not abundant, it appears that female narrators are also more important than male narrators in the transmission of this folktale, in which case it is a feminine tale also in terms of repertory.[13]

Cupid and Psyche

Already around the mid-nineteenth century scholars had pointed out impressive parallels between AT 425, *The Search for the Lost Husband*, and the ancient tale of Cupid and Psyche, the most fairytale-like of all ancient stories.[14] The text appears in the *Metamorphoses*, also known as *The Golden Ass*, by Apuleius, a Roman novelist of the second century A.D. Within the novel the events are narrated by a certain Lucius, whose fascination with magic leads to his unintended transformation into a donkey, in which form he has many adventures until he manages to effect a re-transformation back to his original shape. In the course of the action, which takes place in Greece, Lucius recounts how a band of robbers returned to their cave with Charite, a beautiful girl from a wealthy family, whom they had snatched from home on her wedding day and were holding for ransom.[15] Although the robbers assured her they would not harm her, she cried uncontrollably. Leaving her in the charge of an old slave woman they departed. The miserable girl spoke of killing herself, and in an effort to console her the old woman said she would tell her a tale or two: "But right now I'll divert you with some amusing tales of the sort that old women tell."[16] In a very leisurely manner she then told her the following tale.

A king and a queen had three beautiful daughters. The youngest, Psyche, was so beautiful that people honored her as they would a goddess, neglecting the cult of Venus. Angered at her rival, Venus summoned her son and asked him to cause Psyche to fall in love with some poor wretch. Psyche herself was

miserable, since everyone marveled at her beauty from a distance. Her older sisters had already married kings. Her father, seeking a husband for Psyche and fearing that the gods might be angry, consulted the oracle of Apollo at Miletus. Apollo responded: "You must attire your daughter for a deadly marriage and place her on the cliff of a mountain. You should expect, not a mortal son-in-law, but one who is fierce, wild, and viperous, one who flies through the air and with fire and sword makes all things weary and weak, one whom both the gods and the Stygian realm dread." The unhappy king told his wife of the oracle, and they wept. In due time the sad wedding procession led Psyche to the cliff and left her there trembling and weeping. But the West Wind gently lifted the girl up and placed her in a flowery valley below. From there she walked to a woods in which she came upon a royal palace of divine craftsmanship, full of treasure, and without lock or guard. A invisible maid addressed her, explaining that these treasures were all hers and suggesting that she rest awhile in her bedroom, take a bath, and proceed to the banquet. When eventually she went to the table, invisible maids served her food and drink, and invisible musicians entertained her until she retired. In the middle of the night her unknown husband joined her in bed and made her his wife but left again before sunrise, and invisible servants took care of her in the morning. This routine continued for some time, and Psyche came to enjoy it.

Meanwhile her parents grieved incessantly, and her older sisters, learning the news about her, rushed to their parents' side. That night Psyche's husband warned her that she was in mortal danger, saying that her sisters would presently be looking for her: she must not make contact with them, for to do so would mean grief for her husband and ruin for her. Psyche promised to do what her husband wanted, but later she cried and pleaded with her husband until he agreed that she might see her sisters in order to comfort them and might even present them with jewelry, but he warned her lest her sisters persuade her to try to discover what he looked like, for such curiosity would be the end of her good fortune and her husband. Psyche persuaded her husband to have the West Wind bring her sisters down to her. Psyche's sisters went to the cliff where she had been left, and wept. But Psyche, hearing them, called out to them, and soon the West Wind gently brought them below. After they embraced, Psyche showed them her riches and her invisible servants, which made the two sisters envious. They pressed her to tell them of her husband. Psyche invented an account of him and then hurriedly loaded her sisters with jewelry and had the West Wind bring them back. The two jealous sisters agreed to keep secret what they had learned of Psyche, and to plot her downfall. They hid their presents and told their grieving parents that they had found no trace of Psyche.

Once again Psyche's husband warned her of the danger threatening them from her sisters: they will urge her to look at his face, but if she does, she will lose him; she should not even talk to them, but if she does so, she must answer no questions about him. He added that Psyche would bear a child who would be a god if she kept her husband's secret, but mortal if she did not. Psyche's sisters visited again. They pretended to be delighted that she was pregnant. They asked about her husband once again, and Psyche naively invented a different account of him from the one she had given before. Psyche's sisters

then concluded that she probably had not seen her husband's face; if so, he was probably a god and she would bear a god. They deceitfully told Psyche that her husband was in fact a huge serpent, reminding her that the oracle had declared she would marry a beast, and claiming that people in the neighborhood had seen the serpent and believed it would devour her when she was close to giving birth. Frightened, Psyche acknowledged that she had never seen her husband's face, and agreed that he probably was some kind of animal. They urged her to conceal a sharp knife and an oil lamp in the bedroom, and, when her husband was well asleep, to take the knife and lamp and cut off her husband's head.

That evening, when her husband had fallen asleep, Psyche approached him with lamp and knife only to discover in the light that he was that most gentle and sweet beast, Cupid himself. She dropped the knife. Seeing his bow and arrows at the foot of the bed, Psyche picked up an arrow from curiosity but accidentally pricked her thumb with its point, which caused her to fall in love with Love. Meanwhile a drop of hot oil fell upon the god from the lamp which Psyche still held, so that he leapt up from the bed. He bemoaned what she had done, saying that although his mother Venus had instructed him to cause Psyche to marry a miserable wretch, he had married her himself, and although he had warned Psyche about her sisters, she had tried to cut off his head. The two sisters would get their punishment, he said, but Psyche's punishment would be his flight. Saying that, he flew away.

Psyche cast herself into a river, but the river, honoring the god, placed her on its banks. The god Pan chanced to be nearby and said that since she was manifestly a woman in love, she should cease trying to kill herself and rather approach Cupid with prayers. Psyche went on and came to a city in which one of her sisters lived. When she was admitted to her sister's presence, Psyche told her that, following her advice, she had attempted to kill her husband and discovered that he was Cupid himself, who then divorced her and said he would marry her sister instead. The sister rushed off to her parents' city and to the cliff, from which she jumped in the expectation of being gently conveyed by Zephyr and of becoming Cupid's wife; but she perished in the descent. Psyche proceeded to the city of her other sister, who met her end in the same way.

Cupid lay in his mother's house suffering from the oil which had burned him. A bird informed Venus of the relationship of Cupid and Psyche, and she went to her son and angrily complained that instead of his arranging a disgraceful love for Psyche he had himself married her.

Psyche wandered through country after country in search of Cupid, hoping that by her charms or her prayers she might bring him to set aside his anger. She came upon a temple and went inside in the hope that her husband might be there. When she found things in disarray in the temple, she reverently began to arrange them. Ceres, to whom the temple belonged, appeared and informed her that Venus was angry at her and was searching the world for her. So Psyche went on her way, and coming to a temple of Juno she prayed to the goddess to come to her aid. Juno appeared but said that she could not help Psyche. So Psyche gave up her hope of escape and surrendered to Venus.

The angry goddess abused her verbally and physically. Then Venus mixed

many different kinds of seeds and grains into a single heap and told Psyche that she was to separate them into separate piles before nightfall. Psyche herself did not attempt the huge task, but an army of ants took pity on her and sorted out the items for her. The next day Venus gave Psyche a second task. From some golden sheep which pastured in a grove next to a nearby stream, Psyche was to bring a flock of wool to Venus. Psyche was about to cast herself in the river and end her life, when a reed revealed to her how to gather the wool. She was not to approach the sheep at that time of day, when the sun made them dangerously violent, but later in the day when they were calm she should gather golden wool from the plants on which it was caught. Psyche did so. Then Venus assigned a third task. She was to fill a little urn with Stygian water that flowed out of a steep precipice halfway up a mountain and which was guarded by sleepless dragons. Jove's eagle, remembering an occasion when Cupid had helped him, took the urn and fetched the water for her.

But Venus's anger was still unassuaged, and the goddess assigned her a final task. She was to take a box and proceed to the realm of the dead, where she was to ask Proserpina for a small amount of her beauty and bring it to Venus that same day. Since Psyche saw that she was being sent to her death anyway, she climbed a tall tower and was about to leap off, thinking that this would be a good route to the dead. But the tower itself addressed her, explaining that although this method would indeed bring her to Tartarus, she would not be able to return; rather, she should enter via an airhole located at Taenarum near Lacedaemon; by this channel she would reach Orcus's kingdom; she should also bring with her bread in her hands and coins in her mouth; on the way she would encounter a lame ass loaded with sticks and a lame driver who would ask her to hand him some of the sticks which had fallen, but she was to pass him by in silence; when she reached the river of the dead, she should cross it on Charon's ferry, allowing him to take his fee himself from her mouth; as she crossed the stream, she would see in the water a dead old man raising his putrid hands and begging her to take him onto the boat, but she was not to respond; on the shore three weaver-women would ask her for help, but she was not to touch their cloth; all these figures were traps set by Venus to induce Psyche to give up one of the pieces of bread, without which she would not be able to return; Psyche should give one of the pieces of bread to Cerberus and thereby enter the presence of Proserpina, who would offer her a seat and fine meal, but Psyche should instead sit on the ground and ask only for a piece of ordinary bread; then she should make her request, take what would be given, give Cerberus the remaining piece of bread and Charon the remaining coin, and return by the same route to the upper world, taking special care not to open the box. Psyche did exactly as she had been instructed, except that after she had returned to the surface of the earth she opened the box, overcome by curiosity. Inside it she saw neither beauty nor anything else, but a Stygian sleep came out of it and overcame her so that she lay like a corpse.

But Cupid had now recovered and, unable to bear his separation from Psyche any longer, flew to her, returned the sleep to its box, roused Psyche, and sent her on her way to Venus. Then he himself flew to Jupiter and pleaded his case. Jupiter decreed that Psyche should be Cupid's wife and also made her immortal in order that Venus not be offended by her son's marrying a woman

who was not his equal. A wedding banquet was held, and in time Psyche gave birth to a daughter, Voluptas.[17]

The old woman finished her tale. Lucius, standing nearby in the form of a donkey, remarks that this was the pretty tale that the crazy, drunken old slave woman told, and he regretted not having the means to write it down.[18]

Apuleius's tale shows the basic sequence of events as well as many smaller features of *The Disenchanted Husband*.[19] The major points of agreement are as follows. (1) A marriage is arranged for the heroine, (2) who weds an enchanted husband. (3) He establishes a taboo, (4) which the heroine violates, and (5) as a result he abruptly departs. (6) The wife searches for her lost husband, coming finally to the house of the witch (goddess) who is responsible for his plight. (7) The witch (goddess) assigns the heroine a series of impossible or dangerous tasks, but (8) she accomplishes all of them with the aid of different helpers, after which (9) she and her husband are reunited.

In Apuleius's narrative the husband's residence is a palace filled with wealth and servants, as it is in some other texts such as Basile's, and once she is there, Psyche's daily routine is the same as Parmetella's and the heroine of the Danish tale: she has the days to herself, and in the evenings her mysterious husband joins her in bed but departs in the morning. While he is present, he forbids her to look upon him lest she discover his true identity. Denied such basic information about her spouse, however, she is easily tempted to acquire it, as also the heroines in the Indian, Italian, and Danish tales are. Family members serve as tempters: the jealous sisters (Apuleius), the evil stepmother (India), the unwise father (Denmark). Psyche violates her husband's prohibition in the same way as her Italian and Danish sisters do, by holding a light to his face as he sleeps. But he awakens, in some cases from drops of oil or tallow that fall upon him, and departs in anger. Of the three initial tasks given Psyche by her abusive mother-in-law, that of sorting seeds is found in other tales, and with the same solution (India, Italy); the task of gathering wool is somewhat similar to that of gathering feathers (Gypsy, Italy); and the task of fetching water is perhaps like that of producing tears (Gypsy).[20] Psyche's final and more complex task, going to Venus's sister Proserpina in the realm of the dead and bringing something back in a box without opening it, a prohibition that she violates on her return journey, is closely paralleled in two texts (Italy, Denmark), in which the task is similarly complicated by a series of persons or things that the heroine encounters during her task and that, as her adviser carefully instructs her, she must treat in a particular way in order to return successfully. Thus in the Italian version Parmetella is to prop open a door, feed hay to a horse, and give bread to a dog, and for this purpose she is to take along a loaf of bread, a bundle of hay, and a stone, while in Apuleius's text Psyche is to give the ferryman Charon a coin for passage in each direction and the dog Cerberus a piece of bread upon her arrival and at her departure, for which purpose she is to take coins and bread with her. Interestingly Psyche is to ignore other needy persons whom she will see in the course of her journey, for they are traps set by Venus, a negative form of the usual motifs in which the heroine helps others.[21] In the same spirit—that is, temptations to be resisted—Psyche is to decline the meal that Proserpina will offer her while she is in the death realm, requesting instead ordinary bread, just as the Danish heroine is instructed to avoid eating the cake and wine that she will be offered in Hell.

It is surely impossible to explain this impressive correspondence in basic

events and in details between Apuleius's tale and later texts of *The Disenchanted Husband* otherwise than as a consequence of their belonging to the same narrative tradition, and the simplest assumption about Apuleius's relationship to the tradition is that he drew upon it for his narrative. It was common practice among ancient authors at all periods to rework traditional stories, and in his novel Apuleius even frames the narrative as an oral tale recounted by an old woman, who herself labels it as an old women's tale. After more than a century of scholarly comparisons of the Apuleian tale and the international folktale, this is the conclusion that most scholars have reached, although not without an occasional reservation.[22]

That there are some differences between the ancient text and the international tale is also true. The most obvious one is the pervasive mythological coloring of the former, most importantly the assignment of the role of the supernatural husband to Cupid, so that the husband is not an enchanted human but a god, and it is this secret that he wishes to conceal from Psyche; in effect, Apuleius supplies a detailed back story. The text contains hints of a more traditional version in which the husband has the form of a snake or dragon by day and that of a human by night, for the oracle received by Psyche's father describes his future son-in-law as "fierce, wild, and viperous" and as having wings, and Psyche's sisters later suggest to her that her husband is a serpent and that people in the neighborhood have actually seen it.[23] Apuleius evidently replaced the enchanted snake of the oral tale with a god. Cupid, or Amor, is a Latin rendering of Greek Eros, and since Eros ("Love") and Psyche ("Soul") were traditional lovers in Greek iconographic tradition, Cupid as husband entails Psyche as wife, and since Eros was a son of Aphrodite, Cupid as son also entails Venus as mother, so that the goddess assumes the role of the wicked mother-in-law.[24] The principal characters in the narrative became Psyche together with her family of humans and Cupid along with his family of gods. By assigning the folktale lovers the names Cupid and Psyche, Apuleius (if it was he who was responsible) could play allegorically with Platonic philosophy in the passion of Psyche (*psyche* or "soul") for the divine, specifically for Cupid (*eros* or "love"), as described in Plato's *Phaedrus* and *Symposium*.[25]

Since Apuleius's narrative sources were largely Greek, the question has inevitably been asked whether the folktale that served as the source for his tale of Cupid and Psyche was also Greek. The only other ancient author to recount the story of Cupid and Psyche is Fulgentius, a Christian allegorist of around 500 A.D., who retells it very briefly from Apuleius but mentions that the tale was told at great length also by Aristophantes of Athens in his *Dysarestia* (Distress).[26] Unfortunately nothing at all is known of this author or his work. Approaching the problem a different way, the regional distribution of the subtypes of AT 425 in modern oral tradition, Georgios Megas argues that Apuleius's source was more likely to have been Greek than Italian.[27]

Some scholars construct the parallels between Apuleius and the international folktale differently. The champion of the opposition is Detlev Fehling, who treats all claims for the oral transmission of folktales and for the viability of oral tradition in general as greatly exaggerated.[28] His own thesis is that Apuleius invented the tale himself in order to explain the representations of Eros and Psyche in ancient art, providing the different scenes with a narrative, for which purpose he borrowed motifs here and there from Greek mythology; and that the entire international folktale arose in mediaeval times as a mix of

elements from Apuleius and mediaeval sources.[29] Fehling's skepticism regarding oral tradition is so extensive that he scarcely allows even for the existence of international folktales, believing as he does that human memory is so limited that oral narrators must be constantly fed by written texts, which along with iconography constitute the only reliable means of transmitting information. This vision seems to me a caricature of the philological model, in which all knowledge is transmitted via written documents, which derive in turn from other written documents. It does not jibe with the experience of fieldworkers who have collected oral texts from illiterate narrators and from semiliterate narrators with little access to books, nor with the fact that good storytellers may recount tales that they heard decades earlier. In 1950 folklorist Linda Dégh collected a text of AT 425A, *The Monster as Bridegroom*, from a talented seventy-year-old Hungarian peasant woman, Zsuzsanna Palkó. The narrator, who never learned to read or write, had heard the tale when she was fourteen years old from an older woman, Anna Petres.[30]

Certainly Apuleius's choice of the tale of *The Disenchanted Husband* as the centerpiece of his novel was thoughtfully made and executed, resonating both with its immediate environment and with the larger story of Lucius. In its situational context the tale is recounted by an old woman to a despairing girl to divert her and to encourage her to persevere, for the tale tells of a girl who loses her husband and considers putting an end to her own life, as the listener Charite does, but who by persevering through difficult trials regains her lover and her happiness. Of course the biographical details of Charite's life were devised by Apuleius in such a way that the tale of Cupid and Psyche might be an appropriate consolation for her. In gender and age the old woman fits the ancient stereotype of folktale narrators, and she even calls her story an old women's tale; moreover, the slight modern evidence suggests that the folktale of *The Disenchanted Husband* may be a woman's story in the sense that women may play a more important role than men in transmitting it.[31] In its larger context Psyche also parallels the protagonist of the novel, Lucius, a man who gets into trouble as a result of naivete and curiosity but perseveres and eventually finds happiness.[32] Lucius's magical transformation into an animal and his return to human form also resonate thematically with the experience of the husband in the folktale (though not in Apuleius), who is transformed into an animal and then back to human form.

For a related story see "Service in Hell."

Lit. AT 425B, *The Disenchanted Husband: the Witch's Tasks.* Meyer (1885) 1:195–207. Clouston (1887) 1:205–214, 469–470. Friedländer (1888) 1:522–564. Carnoy 1889a. Dietze 1900. Schaller 1901. Roscher (1884–93) 3:3237–3256. Schröeder 1916. BP 2:229–273, 3:37–43, 4:125–126. Tegethoff 1922. *HDM* 1:63–66. Weinreich 1930. Boberg 1938. Meyer 1938. Dermenghem 1945. Köchlin 1945. Thompson 1946:97–102, 281–282. Swahn 1955, 1984. Anderson 1955. Liungman 1961:91–97. Arnott 1962. Grimal 1963. Woeller 1963. Kagan 1965. Binder and Merkelbach 1968. Mantero 1970. Walsh 1970:190–223. Wright 1971. Megas 1971. Schlam 1976; 1992:82–98; 1993. *EM* 1:464–472. Fehling 1977, 1984. Scherf 1982:289–291. Kenny 1990. Dégh 1990. Scherf (1995) 2:1122–1127.

1. Swahn 1955. For a discussion of the motif cluster of the magic flight, which occurs in different tale types, see "Girl as Helper."

2. The fourteen subtypes of AT 425 that appear in Aarne-Thompson derive from the analysis of the international tradition made in 1955 by Swahn, who distinguishes different forms of the tale mostly according to the form of the heroine's quest for her departed husband. Accordingly, scholarly studies of the tale type published before 1955 may analyze subtypes differently from the way that they are sorted out in the latest edition of Aarne-Thompson (1961). Although Aarne-Thompson adopt Swahn's scheme in most respects, they confusingly convert his subtype 425A, with which the ancient tale of Cupid and Psyche most closely agrees, into AT 425B in their own index and then incorrectly tag AT 425A as *The Monster (Animal) as Bridegroom* (Cupid and Psyche).

The principal studies of the folktale are Friedländer (1888) 1:522–564; Tegethoff 1922; Boberg 1938; Swahn 1955 (the standard study); and Megas 1971 (the Greek versions).

3. For an instance of a text that lacks an explicit taboo see Dawkins 1950:213–222, no. 17.

4. Gilliat-Smith 1911–12. The author collected the tale in Romani in 1909 from a male who had just learnt it from an eighty-year-old man. The text ends with a form of the magic flight known as a transformation flight, in which the escapees successively transform themselves into different objects, whose true identity their pursuer does not immediately recognize.

5. Dracott 1906:15–19. The narrator was a village woman "belonging to the agricultural class of Hindus in the Simla district."

6. Basile (1932) 2:120–128 (5th day, 4th tale).

7. Grundtvig (1854) 1:100–105, no. 107. Collected from a female narrator.

8. The tales take no interest in distinguishing between relationships that are formalized by marriage and those that are not.

9. Similarly when the little white dog asks the farmer what is the matter, the farmer responds only to the question and not at all to the amazing phenomenon of a talking dog, which he treats as nothing surprising. As Lüthi (1986:4–10) puts it, magic tales lack a "sense of the numinous," the characters responding to supernatural phenomena no differently from the way they respond to natural phenomena.

10. The situation is very similar to that in *The Girl as Helper in the Hero's Flight* (see "Girl as Helper"), in which the nominal hero often is assigned tasks that he cannot accomplish unaided, so that the heroine must execute them for him or instruct him what to do: without Medea's help, Jason could not accomplish the tasks set by Aietes.

11. Cf. Berendsohn 1921:39; Nikiforov 1975:160.

12. *EM* 9:226, citing K. Stone, "Romantic Heroines in Anglo-American Folk and Popular Literature" (PhD. diss., Indiana University, Bloomington, 1975), p. x.

13. Swahn 1955:437–438; Holbek 1987:164; Dégh 1990.

14. To my knowledge the first comparative study of Apuleius's tale of Cupid and Psyche is that by Ludwig Friedländer, *Dissertatio, qua fabula Apulejana de Psyche et Cupidine cum fabulis cognatis comparatur* (Progr. Königsberg 1–2, 1860), which I have been unable to see. His classic essay, "Das Märchen von Amor und Psyche und andere Volksmärchen im Altertum," was printed as an appendix in his *Darstellungen aus der Sittengeschichte Roms* at least as early as the edition of 1871. But as long ago as 1695 Charles Perrault observed in passing that Apuleius's tale was a folktale (Arnott 1962:242–243 n. 29).

15. We should therefore imagine her to be around fourteen years old, the average age of girls at menarche and at marriage in Greece and Rome. See Friedländer (1913) 4:123–131; Amundsen and Diers 1969.

16. "sed ego te narrationibus lepidis anilibusque fabulis protinus avocabo" (*Met.* 4.27).

17. Apuleius *Met.* 4.28–6.24.

18. "Sic captivae puellae delira et temulenta illa narrabat anicula; sed astans ego non procul dolebam mehercules, quod pugillares et stilum non habebam, qui tam bellam fabellam praenotarem" (*Met.* 6.25).

19. See Swahn 1955:374–380; Wright 1971.

20. Psyche's first three tasks are inspired by ordinary domestic chores (sorting produce, gathering feathers or wool, fetching water), just as Herakles' labor of cleaning the Augean Stables and Jason's Colchian tasks of yoking fire-breathing bulls and sowing a field with dragon's teeth are nightmarish forms of ordinary farm chores (see "Girl as Helper").

21. Swahn 1955:375; Wright 1971:279–280.

22. See, for example, Schlam 1993. A succession of scholars (e.g., Reitzenstein 1912; Wesselski 1931:57–58; Merkelbach 1958) derives Apuleius's tale from ancient myth instead, but the parallels between Apuleius's tale and *The Disenchanted Husband* are far more pervasive than those between it and any single myth.

23. "saevum atque ferum vipereumque malum" (*Met.* 4:33). The suggestion is at least as old as Friedländer (1910) 1:546–547.

24. On the iconographic tradition of Cupid and Psyche see Schlam 1976; *LIMC* 3.1:850–1049, 4.1:1–12, and 7.1:569–585. Cueva (1999) interprets an illustration on a vase of the fourth century B.C. as a representation of the four tasks of Psyche; if he is correct, the names Eros and Psyche must have been associated with the tale before Apuleius's day.

25. See Grimal 1963:12–14; Schlam 1992:94–96; Sandy 1999.

26. *Mitologiae* 3.6. "sed quia haec saturantius et Apuleius pene duorum continentia librorum tantam falsitatum congeriem enarrauit et Aristofontes Atheneus in libris qui disarestia nuncupantur, hanc fabulam inormi verborum circuitu discere cupientibus prodidit, ob hanc rem superuacuum duximus ab aliis digesta nostris libris inserere, ne nostra opera aut a propriis exularemus officiis aut alienis addiceremust negotiis." On Fulgentius see further Moreschini 1999.

27. Megas 1971; *EM* 1:464–472.

28. Fehling 1977:99 and passim. Some scholars of Apuleius (e.g., Sandy 1999:132–133) seem to be torn between the two positions, citing with approval both the tradition of folktale scholarship and also Fehling. But the two positions exclude each other.

29. Fehling 1977:11–28; 1984. For a reply to Fehling see Swahn 1984; for a critique of Fehling see Holbek 1987:250–257.

30. Dégh 1990; 1995b:77–92, no. 7: "The Serpent Prince."

31. See note 13 above.

32. Tatum 1969:508–514; Kenney 1990:13–17; Sandy 1999.

Dog on the Bridge 🦮 Alexander and the Donkey Driver

A person makes a bargain with the devil according to which the devil agrees to build a certain bridge (or complete a bridge that is under construction) on the condition that he obtain the first one to cross it. But when the bridge is finished, the person tricks the devil by arranging for an animal (dog, cat, rooster, pig, goat, etc.) to cross first.

This comic story of the outwitting of the stupid ogre by the clever trickster is AT 1191, *The Dog on the Bridge*. It usually is told as a historical event, though the published texts give little indication of how much credence narrators and audiences actually accord the story.

A nineteenth-century French text relates how Guillaume, duke of Toulouse, wanted to construct a bridge on the Hérault, but each night the devil overturned what the duke had built during the day. Finally Guillaume made a pact with the devil according to which the first to pass over the bridge would belong to the devil. But the duke, who was more wily than Satan, informed all his friends of the bargain in order to preserve them from harm, and then let loose a cat. Since it was the first creature to cross the bridge, the demon had to content himself with it.[1]

In a British legend told of the Devil's Bridge at Kirkby Lonsdale, a poor woman, unable to cross a river to retrieve her cow, made an agreement with the devil, who had appeared in human form. He promised to build a bridge on condition that he should get the first living thing that passed over it. The woman, worrying that she or her husband had been singled out as the victim that was to "propitiate the building of the bridge," returned at the appointed hour with her dog and a morsel of food, and threw the morsel across the

bridge. The dog ran after it, and the devil, seeing that he had been outwitted, gave a terrific howl.[2]

Alexander and the Donkey Driver

It is difficult to imagine what form a tale type of this kind might take in Greco-Roman antiquity, where the devil and Jesus do not compete for souls. True, Thanatos may come to fetch a person whose time has come, as he does for Alkestis, and the House of Hades always has room for more tenants, but for the most part the Lord of the Dead is content to remain in his kingdom rather than to roam the earth using his wits to add to the number of souls in his realm, for in the end he will get them all anyway.[3] Nor is Death a builder of bridges, a supernatural mason with whom one might make a deal. What form, then, might this story have taken before the Christian devil assumed the role of antagonist in it?

One answer is given in the *Facta et Dicta Memorabilia* compiled by the Roman historian Valerius Maximus in the first century A.D., a collection of Greek and Roman exempla. One of his Greek stories relates how Alexander, king of Macedon, was once advised by an oracle to kill the first being he met after he went out of the door. This happened to be a donkey driver, whom Alexander ordered to be taken away and executed. When the donkey driver asked him why he was putting an innocent man to death, Alexander reported the oracle to him. "In that case," the man said, "the oracle has designated another for death, since the donkey that I was driving in front of me was the first to meet you." Alexander was delighted both because of the man's clever argument and because he himself had been saved from error, and took the opportunity to perform an expiatory sacrifice (*occasionem . . . expiandae religionis rapuit*) by means of a meaner beast. Valerius, who appears to accept the story as a historical incident, remarks that the narrative illustrates the clemency of Alexander and the cleverness of the donkey driver.[4]

Valerius's story features not the ruler of Hell contending for a soul but the ruler of Macedon who plans to take a life. Alexander the Great assumes the role here of the dangerous antagonist, and the donkey driver takes the role of the clever protagonist who saves his life by means of his wit.

When narrators envision the final scene, they imagine the two characters standing on opposite ends of the new bridge, the devil on one end waiting for the first being to cross over, the human on the other end. In a British text the "bridge was thrown across the ravine, and the Evil One stood beyond bowing and beckoning to the old woman to come over and try it."[5] Similarly, in an Austrian story in which the mayor of a town lacked money to build a needed church, the devil gave him the money in return for the souls of the first three visitors to the church. After the church was built, the devil waited inside the church, and the mayor released a rooster, a goat, and a cat into the building.[6] The first creature to cross over the bridge or to enter the church and the first creature the devil meets are therefore the same. In all forms of the story, ancient and modern, the victim is simply the first creature whom the antagonist meets. Crossing over the bridge or entering the church are only particular realizations of this idea.

The Greek legend and *The Dog on the Bridge* thus share the following features. (1) Relying upon an oracle or pact, (2) the antagonist intends to claim the first being to meet him, which he expects to be a human being; however, (3) the clever protagonist points out (or sees to it) that the first creature to have met him is an animal, so that (4) the antagonist is obliged to take the animal victim instead, and (4) the trickster escapes. The essential plot, then, in which the clever protagonist tricks a powerful antagonist into taking a substitute victim, an animal in place of a human, is found already in the ancient legend attached to Alexander, which evidently is a precursor or biform of the later, Christianized story in which the devil plays the role of the antagonist and the site of the encounter is usually a bridge.

The idea lies near at hand that in *The Dog on the Bridge* the devil has replaced some ancient divinity to whom a sacrifice was formerly made at the completion of a new bridge, and that the sacrifice of various animals was a substitution for the original immolation of a human being. Accordingly, the animals are a memory of the time in which such sacrifices actually took place, and with the passing of the custom the only trace of the rite that has remained is the present legend, which preserves the idea in a weakened form.[7] The single ancient text that we possess does not, however, lend support to this hypothesis, inasmuch as the role of the claimant is played not by an ancient deity but by a human being. Nor is there any reason, other than the romantic appeal of such interpretations, to understand this story as a historical allegory that portrays a change from human to animal sacrifice. A similar interpretation has often been applied to the episode of Abraham's near sacrifice of Isaak, namely, that the story preserves a memory of the practice of child sacrifice, which in later times was replaced by the sacrifice of animals.[8] But there is as little reason to accept this construction as there is the other. Indeed, it is doubtful that there ever was such a change at all. Consider the tradition found in Africa and elsewhere that in former times kings used to be put to death when they showed signs of physical weakness. When were these former times? The same claim was being made back in the sixteenth century, and before that it was made in antiquity, when Diodoros of Sicily reports that the killing of the king *used to be* practiced in Africa.[9] No matter how far back one goes, regicide is always represented as something that the community used to do sometime in the past. So the tradition is a way of characterizing the present by contrasting it with a past that has been constructed for this purpose, rather than its being an accurate memory of actual historical practice.

For another story of Death as the stupid ogre, see "Smith Outwits the Devil."

Lit. (AT 1191, *The Dog on the Bridge*.) Motif J1169.4, *The ass beheaded*. Sébillot 1891. Pineau 1891. Wünsche 1905:25–33. *EM* 2:838–842. Ashliman, type 1191.

1. Sébillot 1891:281–282.
2. Briggs (1971) B1:88–89.
3. For Alcestis and Thanatos ("Death") see Fontenrose (1959:323–327); the legend is the Greek form of an international story (AT 899, *Alcestis*). For an ancient tale in which a man summons Thanatos to him, see "Old Man and Death."

4. 7.3. Ext. 1.
5. Briggs (1971) B1:87.
6. Branky 1891:185–186.
7. Sébillot 1891:286–287.
8. Gunkel 1921:119–120.
9. Diodorus Siculus 3.5–7. See further Fontenrose 1966:10–11.

Dragging Old Man Only to Threshold

As a man drags his father to the door of his house, intending to put him out, the old man bids his son not drag him past the threshold, since he dragged his own father only that far when he had in mind to put him out of his house.

This little tale is AT 980C, *Dragging Old Man Only to Threshold*, attested in various European countries and among Spanish speakers in the New World.

The sixteenth-century Spanish author Juan Timoneda recounts it as the fourth tale of his *Buen aviso y Portacuentos*, relating how a son who wished to put his father out of the house was dragging him across the room by the arm. When they reached the doorpost, the father said to his son: "Son, for the love of God let go of me here, since I dragged my own father only up to this point and no further."[1]

According to a modern French text, a rich farmer used to handle his aged father roughly if the old man forgot something or was clumsy. He would strike him and, if he was angry enough, drag him by his white hair out of the house onto the courtyard. Thirty or forty years passed, and when the son in turn grew old, his son would do the same to him, throwing him down and dragging him by his hair out of the house. The old man finally realized that it was God's will and that he was only receiving his due. One day when the son was particularly angry, he dragged his aged father by his hair past the courtyard, through the gate, and out onto the road. At that point the old man revolted, saying his son had gone too far: "I never dragged my father by his hair beyond the courtyard gate!"[2]

The near ejection of the old man can be represented as a unique event as in Timoneda's telling, the onetime act of a man who decides in anger or ingratitude to discard his old father, or as a recurrent event as in the French text, the abusive behavior of a grown son who habitually gives in to anger and cruelty. The scene is strikingly visual: the ungrateful or abusive son acts out his feelings by dragging his father to the door of the house rather than, say, ordering him to leave the house. From the father's protest that the son should haul him no further than he himself hauled his father before him, it suddenly becomes clear why the present son is doing what he is doing: he learned it from his father, who had previously abused his own father in the same way. The sons and fathers of this family are linked together by a chain of abuse that goes back for generations. The naivete of the father's argument is particularly revealing. This man views abuse as normal and unobjectionable in itself but holds it unjust for his son to exceed the limits that he himself observed. The effect of the remark is at once comic and sad because of its indignant shortsightedness and because of

the history of behavior that it implies. With this appeal the scene freezes, since the particular response of the son is beside the point.

This tale of the abusive son and the old father is one of several similar moral tales (AT 980A–D) in which a grown son treats his aged father to one or another indignity, with a variety of outcomes. In one tale, known from Europe to the Far East, a man gives his aged father only half a blanket to keep him warm. When the man's little son asks for the other half, explaining that he will save it until his own father grows old, the man changes his mind. This is AT 980A, *The Half-Carpet*. In a parallel tale a man, disgusted at the way his aged father eats or drinks, makes him eat or drink by himself from a wooden bowl. But when the man's little son prepares to make a wooden bowl for his father's eventual old age, the man relents. This tale is AT 980B, *Wooden Drinking Cup for Old Man*.[3] In these two stories the man's little son innocently reveals that he is learning from the present mean example how eventually to treat his own father when he himself grows up. The naive comment or action of the child corresponds to the naive utterance of the old man in *Dragging Old Man Only to Threshold*. When a man treats his aged father with indignity, a character (old man/young son) makes a naive comment upon the action that places it in a new perspective (there is, or is about to be, a chain of abuse in this family). In the tales of *The Half-Carpet* and *The Wooden Drinking Cup* the remark is prospective in that the man is made to see how his present mean action will begin a chain of events that eventually will affect him in the same way, but there is still time for him to change his mind, and he does so. In contrast, in the tale of *Dragging Old Man Only to the Threshold* the remark is retrospective, and now it is too late to relent. In a fourth tale, the son's bad behavior leads directly to a grotesque punishment. Not wishing to share a roasted chicken with his old father, a man hides the cooked bird when his old father comes by for a visit. When the father departs and the son reaches for the hidden fowl, it is changed into a toad or the like and lodges permanently upon his face. In this odd story, AT 980D, *Meat Springs as a Toad on the Face of an Ungrateful Son*, the mean son is given no opportunity to learn and relent, his ugliness of spirit having been reified immediately as physical repulsiveness.[4]

Aristotle on Anger

Aristotle knew the tale of *Dragging Old Man* and relates it in his *Nichomachean Ethics* in support of his proposition that it is more excusable for a person to follow an impulse that is natural than one that is not, and that anger and ill-temperedness are more natural than are various kinds of excessive desires. Thus, a man was on trial for beating his father. In his defense he said: "My father here used to beat his father, and he used to beat his before him. And (pointing now to his son) when he grows up, he will beat me. It's inborn in us." Another man, as he was being dragged by his son, used to tell him to stop at the door. "For I myself," he said, "only dragged my father that far." Aristotle goes on to distinguish between overt and covert action, the former being more just and the latter less just. He points out that anger is manifest whereas erotic desire is crafty, Aphrodite being called a "weaver of wiles," so that lack of restraint in the expression of anger is more acceptable than it is in the expression of desire.[5]

Both comic tales that the ethicist cites involve a son's hot-tempered mistreatment of his old father; both portray the misbehavior as being passed down from father to son, and both present it as being more or less acceptable behavior, even though it might land one in court. Beating one's aged father obviously runs in one family, just as dragging one's old father to the door runs in the other family. For Aristotle the tales serve to illustrate that angry behavior is common, natural, and overt, and that such behavior is more just and excusable than a comparable lack of restraint in erotic matters, which is a way of saying that male excesses are culturally more acceptable than female excesses, since physical violence is a male vice, as the exempla illustrate, whereas lust and deviousness are thought of as female vices, as the ready allusion to Aphrodite indicates.[6]

Aristotle employs the two tales, not for their manifest point or structural message, but for incidental information that they happen to contain or imply about the expression of anger, a common use of stories for intellectual purposes.[7] His brevity suggests that the stories were familiar ones, though it is hardly remarkable for Aristotle to be terse. As is generally the case in other texts of *Dragging Old Man*, the characters are generic: the father and son are not given names, nor is the tale localized.

Lit. AT 980C, *Dragging Old Man Only to Threshold*. Cf. BP 2:135–140; 3:167–169. Ashliman, type 980C.

1. Chevalier 1983:134, no. 78.
2. Pourrat 1954:163–164.
3. On the two tales see Clouston (1887) 2:372–378; BP 2:135–140, 4:172 n. 14.
4. See further BP 3:167–169; Dähnhardt 4:262–265. This story is also told of female characters.
5. *EN* 7.6.2–3 = 1149b.4–20. The defendant in the former case was acquitted, Aristotle says elsewhere (*Magna Moralia* 2.6.20 = 1202a.25–29), for the judges concluded that in light of his family history his fault was congenital (*physikên*) rather than an individual illness. Aristotle does not give the verdict in the second case, probably because there was none; it is a migratory legend masquerading as a true report.
6. For another tale type that illustrates the supposed lustfulness of women see "Potiphar's Wife."
7. See Hansen 1982.

Dragon Slayer ☙ Perseus

A youth obtains a helpful dog (horse) and/or a magic sword (stick). He comes to a certain land that is suffering from the depredations of a monster (dragon, sea monster, troll, giant, etc.), where a king has been obliged to give up his daughter to the monster. The monarch offers her in marriage to any man who should rescue her. The girl is exposed, and the hero goes to meet the monster. When it arrives, the hero slays it with the help of his dog (horse) or weapon, cuts out its tongue (teeth, eyeballs, etc.), and withdraws. Subsequently an impostor cuts off the dragon's head and claims to be the slayer. When the impostor is about to wed the princess, the hero arrives and by means of the tongue (teeth, etc.) establishes his identity as the dragon slayer. He weds the princess, and the false hero is punished.

This extremely popular folktale, known over much of the world, is AT 300, *The Dragon Slayer*. It appears both as an independent tale and also as an episode in other folktales. Its core is a combat between a human hero and a nonhuman opponent, in which typically the latter is presented as monstrous in habits and form, and the former is enhanced by a special helper or weapon. There are two elaborations on this core. One is a romantic or erotic element. The monster demands the sacrifice of a maiden, whom the hero hopes to rescue and win for himself. The other is a complication of the plot. An impostor identifies himself as the monster slayer and claims the reward. When this theme occurs, the hero acquires a token early in the story by means of which he is later able to prove he is the true dragon slayer. Not all texts show all these features; on the other hand, certain features may be multiplied: the hero has several helpers, the dragon has many heads, the combat takes several days, etc.

In a Spanish tale first published in 1942 there was a cavern where a huge serpent called Dragon hid. Since the serpent had been devouring many people, the local inhabitants made a pact with him according to which they would provide him with a girl each year, provided that he left everyone else alone. So each year the heads of families drew lots, and this year the lot fell to the princess. Thereupon the king announced that whoever could free his daughter from the dragon might wed her and inherit the throne. On the appointed day, the princess was tied to a tree. A shepherd came along with his dog, inquired of the maiden what she was doing, and learned of the dragon. When the dragon suddenly appeared with a roar, the shepherd set his dog on him, and the dog tore the gigantic creature to pieces. The shepherd untied the girl and cut out the tongues from the dragon's seven heads. The king's servants, who had been watching from nearby trees, rushed over. One of them cut off the heads of the dragon. The king held a banquet in honor of his daughter and her fiancé, the man with the dragon's heads. The shepherd had not been invited, but he and his dog came anyway, whereupon the princess recognized the dog. Claiming that his dog had killed the monster, the shepherd declared that he should wed the princess. When the fiancé presented the dragon's heads as proof of his deed, the shepherd pointed out that something was missing from the heads, and produced the tongues. He wed the princess and became the king's heir.[1]

According to a Japanese narrative, an itinerant priest once went to a mountain village and found a house in which everyone was crying. When he entered and inquired the reason, the head of the household explained that on a nearby mountain there stood a shrine to a deity whose name was no longer remembered; however, every year at harvest time the village had to offer it a young girl, or else a great storm would destroy all their fields. This year it was the turn of the present family. They were mourning the loss of their only daughter, whom they had to give up in seven days. The priest offered to go in the girl's place. Proceeding to the shrine, he hid nearby, and at midnight a horde of creatures gathered and sang a song, the gist of which was that no one should inform Shippei Taro. The priest set out in search of the man named Shippei Taro, who proved to be not a man at all but a dog as big as a calf. Just as the villagers were carrying the chest containing the girl up the mountain, the priest and Shippei Taro arrived. Substituting the priest and the dog for the girl, the villagers deposited the chest at the shrine and ran away. At midnight

the ogres came and took the lid off the chest, whereupon the dog and the priest leapt out and attacked them. The next day the villagers, expecting the priest to have been eaten by the deity, climbed the mountain and saw only dead monkeys everywhere. After that there was no need for human sacrifices.[2] This text lacks the complication of the false hero, nor does the hero marry the maiden.

One of the best-known realizations of the type is the mediaeval legend of St. George and the dragon, one of several adventures told of the saint. The story is known from prose narratives, ballads, and mummers' plays. Born in Cappadocia, the Christian warrior encountered a dragon in Cappadocia, Palestine, or Libya. The multiheaded beast, which lived in a lake and devoured men and animals, had been sent by the Lord to plague a community because its monarch and people were pagans who persecuted Christians. To avoid his depredations the townspeople gave him two sheep daily, and when they had exhausted their sheep they offered their sons and daughters on a daily or annual basis. Now the lot had fallen to the princess, who was sent forth to the dragon. The Lord sent George to the region in order that he might kill the dragon and thereby convert the king and the citizens. Armed and mounted on his horse, George either dispatched the monster at once or caused the dragon to be submissive by means of the sign of the cross and a prayer, after which the creature followed him like a tame dog into town where George cut off his head. Thousands of persons were converted. A shrine to St. George was built and an annual festival in his name was established.[3] Except in a few märchen-like texts,[4] the complication of the false hero does not appear. The saint, like the Japanese priest, foregoes the maiden as prize.

Lit. AT 300, *The Dragon Slayer*. Clouston (1887) 1:155–167. Hartland (1896) 3:1–65. BP 1:547–556. Ranke 1934:186–260, 307–341. Schmidt 1957. Liungman 1961:38–43. Lüthi 1976:47–57. *EM* 3:787–820. Ἀλεξιάδης 1982. Scherf 1982:61–64. Ashliman, type 300.

The classical tradition contains numerous accounts of combats between mortals and dragons or dragonlike monsters. Like the folktale of *The Dragon Slayer* these accounts appear sometimes independently and sometimes as a component of larger stories. Some of these stories closely resemble the international tale, and although none of the ancient legends contains all the elements of the scheme given above, virtually all the motifs found in the modern oral tale appear in one or another of the ancient sources.

Generically the ancient narratives of which we have knowledge are cast as legends rather than as folktales, so that more fantastic elements characteristic of the folktale tradition appear in a somewhat modulated form. I take up the legends individually in the survey that follows.

In addition to legendary combats between a human protagonist and a dragon, Greeks and Hebrews also told of mythic combats between a god and a dragon, such as that between Zeus and Typhon, Apollo and Python, Yahweh and Leviathan.[5] Since these myths feature neither the exposed maiden nor the false hero, they show little resemblance to the international folktale beyond the combat itself, and so will not be discussed here. Divine combats tend to clear the way for the establishment of cosmic order (or, on a smaller scale, of local order in the form of the founding of a city or cult). In the nature of things cosmic there is no local king and hence no endangered maiden, nothing to moti-

vate an impostor; and in any case the cosmic concerns of the gods are too grand to be driven by the prospect of a human maiden as bride or to be trifled with by human competitors. Even some hero legends are of this sort, such as the combat between Kadmos and the dragon that clears the way for the foundation of Thebes. In later times something of the divine and the heroic traditions mix in the combat of St. George and the dragon that results in the rescue of a maiden and also in mass conversions of pagans to the new religion and in the establishment of a shrine and festival for the dragon slayer. But the legends more typically emphasize heroism, romance, intrigue, and treachery than the establishment of a new order.

Perseus

The classical story most often mentioned in connection with *The Dragon Slayer* is the legend of Perseus, slayer of a monster sometimes called Ketos (*ketos* = sea monster).

According to the account given by Apollodoros, which he appears to have taken from the mythographer Pherekydes, Perseus was returning from his encounter with the Gorgons, carrying the head of Medusa in a pouch, when he came to Aithopia, ruled by King Kepheus. There he saw the king's daughter Andromeda exposed to a sea monster. For Kepheus's wife Kassiepeia had boasted that she herself was more beautiful than the Nereids, and this vaunt had angered both the Nereids and Poseidon, as the result of which the god had sent a flood and a sea monster against the land. When the god Ammon said that the Aithopians would be delivered from their calamity if Kassiepeia's daughter should be set out as food for the monster, the people forced Kepheus to bind his daughter to a rock. Perseus fell in love with her when he saw her, and promised Kepheus that he would slay the monster if Kepheus would give him the princess as his wife. They swore oaths to this effect, after which Perseus confronted and killed the monster and released Andromeda. But Andromeda had originally been betrothed to Kepheus's brother Phineus, who now plotted against Perseus, but when Perseus learned of it, he showed the Gorgon's head to Phineus and his fellow conspirators, turning them into stone.[6]

Differences in details in the ancient authorities for the legend are not of much importance here. According to several authors, the scene of the combat was not Aithiopia but Joppa in Palestine, where Andromeda's fetters were still pointed out in later times.[7] Lucian describes how Perseus sensibly dispatches the sea creature with double weaponry, striking it with the sickle and petrifying it by means of the Gorgon's head, whereas more commonly he is imagined to use only his curved sword, more in the manner of a hero.[8] Lykophron alludes obscurely to a version in which Perseus kills the monster from inside (see "Man Swallowed by Fish"). According to the mythographer Hyginus, Andromeda's fiancé was Agenor, not Phineus, but like Phineus he plotted against Perseus's life and was even aided by Kepheus.[9]

As in the modern folktale, (1) the hero is enhanced with special weapons (Perseus possesses a sickle; the Cap of Hades, which makes the wearer invisible; winged sandals, which allow the wearer to fly; and the Gorgon's head, with

which he can petrify adversaries). (2) He comes to a land where a monster is plaguing the community, so that (3) the local king is obliged to sacrifice his daughter to satisfy the creature. The youth falls in love with the maiden, and (4) when the king agrees to give her in marriage to the man who can save her, (5) he determines to meet the monster. (6) Slaying it in combat, (7) he rescues the girl.

All the principal elements of the oral folktale can be seen in the Perseus legend except for the incident of the false hero. But a trace of this unpleasant character can be discerned in the person of Phineus, who emerges as a rival of the hero for the hand of Andromeda after the slaying of the monster, as though he were claiming to be the rescuer of the princess.[10] Indeed, Phineus appears at the same point in the narrative as does the impostor of the folktale, and like him he boldly claims the prize that the hero has earned, ultimately fails, and is punished for his effrontery. The two characters really differ only in the basis of their claim, the folktale rival alleging he has killed the monster, whose head he possesses as apparent proof of his deed, and Phineus alleging prior betrothal.[11] In both cases the rival is cowardly and sneaky. Though not courageous enough to fight the monster, he removes the creature's head when no one is looking, or he plots secretly against the hero. Hyginus's version, in which the rival has the support of the king, is reminiscent of the support of the king that the false hero temporarily enjoys in the folktale.

For other episodes of the Perseus legend, see "Magic Object and the Trolls."

Lit. AT 300, *The Dragon Slayer.* Carnoy 1889:353–355. Hartland 1894–96. BP 1:556. Krappe 1933a.

Herakles

The encounter of Herakles and a giant sea creature is part of a larger story according to which Poseidon and Apollo constructed the walls of Troy for King Laomedon, who then cheated the gods of their promised wages. The deities responded angrily, Apollo sending a plague against the Trojans, Poseidon sending a sea monster that even made sallies against persons on land. An oracle revealed that the people would be free of these calamities if King Laomedon should sacrifice his daughter Hesione as food for the monster. So the king bound her to rocks bordering on the sea. Seeing her, Herakles promised to save the princess in return for the immortal horses that Laomedon had once received from Zeus, but after Herakles had killed the sea creature and saved Hesione, Laomedon cheated him, refusing to give him the promised compensation. Herakles later returned, attacked Troy, and killed Laomedon. He gave Hesione to his comrade Telamon.[12] According to some authors (Diodoros, Hyginus), Herakles was to receive Hesione, but in the end the king refused to hand her over.

The legend of Herakles and the sea monster is basically the same story as that of Perseus and the sea monster. Together they constitute a subtype of the tradition: a royal family offends Poseidon (Kassiepeia boasts/Laomedon reneges), who angrily sends a *ketos* against the city; an oracle informs the citizens that to avoid further depredations the king (Kepheus/Laomedon) must sacrifice his daughter (Andromeda/Hesione) to the monster; exposed on the seashore, the princess is spotted by the passing hero (Perseus/Herakles); the king agrees to give him the princess (or other rewards) if he should slay the creature; the hero succeeds, res-

cuing the princess; he then experiences an obstacle to his obtaining the princess (Phineus/Laomedon). Laomedon's unwillingness to hand Hesione over to Herakles is possibly a weakened form of the incident of the false hero, for also in the folktale the hero is initially ignored by the king, who prepares to give his daughter in marriage to another man. Finally, there was also a version in which Herakles, like Perseus, killed the monster from within (see "Man Swallowed by Fish").

Lit. AT 300, *The Dragon Slayer.*

Alkathous

Among the monuments Pausanias viewed in the Megarid was one dedicated to Apollo and Artemis. People said that Alkathous had it made after he had slain the Kithaironian lion, which had killed many men including a son of King Megareus, Euhippos. Megareus had promised that if any man should kill the lion, he could have the king's daughter in marriage and succeed him on the throne. Alkathous, son of Pelops, managed to kill the beast and, when he became ruler, built the sanctuary for Artemis and Apollo. Though Pausanias goes on to criticize the veracity of some elements of Megarian tradition, he expresses his confidence in the story that the lion was killed on Kithairon by Alkathous.[13]

According to the fourth-century Megarian historian Dieukhidas, Pelops's son Alkathous was banished because of a murder he had committed. As he was departing for another city he happened to cross paths with the lion that was ravaging Megara and against which the king of Megara had dispatched various men. Alkathous slew the beast, cut out its tongue, placed it in his pouch, and returned to Megara. When the men who had been sent against the lion reported that they were its slayers, he produced his pouch and disproved them. After sacrificing to the gods, the king placed the tongue on the altar, and from that time onward this has been the custom among the Megarians.[14]

As it happens, neither of these reports is concerned primarily with Alkathous. The traveler Pausanias characterizes the man who was responsible for a monument he visited in Megara, and the historian Dieukhidas gives the etiology of a Megarian custom. Accordingly, both accounts are sparing in details about the adventures of Alkathous, but taking the notices such as they are and combining them, we get an idea of his story, which parallels *The Dragon Slayer.* (1) A beast (Kithaironian lion) is plaguing a community (Megara), killing persons. (2) The king (Megareus) offers the hand of his daughter in marriage to the man who kills the creature, and (3) a youth (Alkathous), who is passing by, encounters the animal and (4) slays it. (5) He cuts out its tongue, puts it in his pouch, and departs. (6) He proceeds to the dwelling of the king, where (7) another man claims to be the slayer, but (8) by means of the tongue the protagonist proves that he himself is the victor. (9) He weds the princess and succeeds to the throne.

The legend of Alkathous is especially interesting because it contains, explicitly or by implication, all the elements of the incident of the false hero. The hero slays the creature that is plaguing the community, cuts out its tongue, and departs. In the meantime, other men find the slain beast, cut off its head—so we

must infer, for if they did not, the subsequent proof offered by the hero (the animal tongues) would make no sense—and show it to the king. Since the king has offered the hand of his daughter to the slayer, one of the men must declare himself to be the slayer (so again we must infer, for otherwise the hero's counterproof would have no point) and claim the princess. At this point the hero displays his superior proof and wins the princess. The impostors are presumably punished.

This story differs from the texts we have encountered so far in showing a natural beast rather than a fabulous monster. The destructive animal has been assimilated to a favorite theme of Greek mythology, the powerful and dangerous lion, boar, sow, fox, serpent, or the like that roams a region causing death and damage; indeed, one of Alkathous's sons later perishes while hunting such an animal, the Kalydonian boar.[15] One does not ordinarily sacrifice maidens to such a creature, since it is simply a wild animal, not a supernatural being.[16] Whether the presence of the lion was in origin a natural disaster or a divine punishment for an offense against a god, as in the legends of Perseus and Herakles, we do not know from our meager sources. But King Megareus treats the Kithaironian lion as seriously as other monarchs do their sea monsters, offering the hand of his daughter and the succession to his throne to the slayer of the animal, even though the life of his daughter is not immediately in danger. In this story, then, the prior loss of a son Euhippos to the beast functions in the same way as the possible future loss of a daughter, motivating the father to take action against the animal.

Lit. AT 300, *The Dragon Slayer*. Roscher (1884–93) 1:231–232. Frazer (1898) 2:528–529. Schmidt 1963:41–47.

Peleus

According to Apollodorus, Peleus accidentally killed a man so that he fled to King Akastos of Iolkos to be purified. There the king's wife Astydameia fell in love with Peleus and propositioned him, but he rejected her, after which she falsely accused him to her husband, saying that he had propositioned her (for this episode see "Potiphar's Wife"). Unwilling to kill the man he himself had purified, Akastos took him on a hunt on Mt. Pelion. During a competition in hunting, Peleus killed a number of animals, cut out their tongues, and placed them in his pouch. Subsequently, when Akastos and his men took his game and mocked him as if he had gotten nothing, he produced the tongues and said he had slain as many animals as he had tongues. When Peleus fell asleep on Pelion, Akastos hid his sword in some cow dung and returned home. After the youth awoke and was looking for his sword, he was captured by the centaurs and was about to perish when Kheiron rescued him. Kheiron also found his sword and returned it to him.[17] Peleus's sword, it turns out, was no ordinary weapon. According to the paroemiographer Zenobios, the gods rewarded Peleus for his chastity with a sword made by Hephaistos, a wondrous weapon with which Peleus was always successful in battle and in the hunt.[18] The mention of chastity must be a reference to the hero's virtuously refusing the sexual proposition of his hostess Astydameia.

The episode begins when Akastos, believing his wife's false accusations against Peleus, angrily decided to do away with the youth. Averse to killing him outright, he intended that the youth should perish in the wilds. He established a competition in hunting, presumably as a pretext for escorting Peleus into the countryside, where he planned to desert him unarmed. According to a scholiast on Aristophanes, Akastos, unwilling to kill the man he had purified, sent Peleus out to Mt. Pelion in order that he might be devoured by wild animals, but the gods gave Peleus as a reward for his chastity a sword in order that he might defend himself against the animals. Or Akastos, learning of his wife's accusation, took Peleus into the wild, deprived him of his weapons, left him there, and departed, saying that if Peleus was innocent, he would be saved; and when Peleus was about to be killed by wild animals, the gods had Hermes give him a sword made by Hephaistos, whereby he escaped the danger.[19] But according Hesiod, Akastos decided to hide the sword of Peleus that had been made for him by Hephaistos, for Akastos thought that while Peleus was looking for his sword he would quickly be overcome by wild centaurs.[20] This is the incident to which Apollodorus refers, saying that Akastos hid the sword in the cow dung while Peleus slept, and that the kindly centaur Kheiron intervened in a timely way, saving Peleus from the other centaurs and locating his sword.

It appears that we are dealing with doublets here. In one version, Akastos disarms Peleus on Mt. Pelion in order that he may be devoured by wild animals, but the gods provide him with a wondrous sword in time for him to defend himself. In another version, Akastos disarms Peleus on Mt. Pelion while he sleeps, in order that he may be overcome by wild centaurs, but Kheiron comes to the rescue, saving the youth from the centaurs and returning to him his stolen sword. Different authors give one version or the other, and perhaps some narrators give both, one after the other, as two successive attempts on the hero's life.

Mannhardt long ago argued that this legend is a reflex of an international *märchen*, in proof of which he cited texts from various lands, including versions of *The Dragon Slayer*.[21] Among other features he points to the hunt on Mt. Pelion (he sees it as a weakened form of the combat, analogous to such hunts as that for the Kithaironian lion), the hero's magic sword, the hero's cutting out of the tongues, and the hero's sleep (the folktale hero sometimes falls asleep just before or just after he confronts the monster) as elements shared by the Greek legend and the international tale. Indeed, it seems an inescapable conclusion that *The Dragon Slayer* has influenced this episode in the biography of Peleus, for the legend really lacks only a clear expression of the theme of the monster. In the folktale the incursions of a fabulous monster cause the king to expose his daughter and to offer her to the man who slays the beast; in short, he institutes a kind of competition in hunting for her hand in marriage. In the present legend the king simply institutes a competition in hunting. Thanks no doubt to his wonder-sword, Peleus bags the most game, removing the tongues of the animals and storing them away. In the meantime his competitors presumably steal the heads of the game he killed, claiming the kills as their own, but Peleus unexpectedly shows up their fraud by means of the tongues he possesses. If there is a prize for the winner, we do not hear of it.

This adventure of Peleus is quite similar to that of Alkathous, which together probably represent another ancient Greek subtype of *The Dragon Slayer*. In both

legends the initial element of the fabulous monster has been weakened and, consequently, the element of the exposed princess does not appear, while the narrator emphasizes the presentation of the tongue evidence and the false hero. It is the inverse of the stories of Perseus and Herakles, both of which foreground the depredations of the monster and the exposure of the maiden, and weaken the incident of the tongues and the false hero.

Lit. (AT 300, *The Dragon Slayer*.) Mannhardt (1877) 2:49–60.

Euthymos

When Pausanias describes a statue of the Olympic boxer Euthymos, he pauses to recount another famous victory of the athlete. At the Greek city of Temesa in Italy, there was a revenant that prowled about, killing persons of every age. He was the ghost of one of Odysseus's companions who perished there while Odysseus was making his way home from Troy. The man had gotten drunk, raped a girl, and as a consequence was stoned to death by the local people. Odysseus sailed away, but the spirit of the murdered man continued to wreak havoc among the Temesans. Finally, the folk wanted to abandon Temesa, but the Pythia (that is, the Delphic oracle) would not permit them, instructing them instead to placate the Heros (that is, the powerful ghost, used here as a proper name) by constructing a sanctuary for him and offering him annually the most beautiful maiden in Temesa as a wife. They did so, after which the Heros caused them no other harm. Now, one year it happened that the boxer Euthymos came to Temesa at the time of the ritual, and when he learned of the situation he went to the temple to see the maiden. Euthymos fell in love with her, and she swore to marry him if he saved her, so that he awaited the spirit. When it arrived, Euthymos fought it and won, driving it into the sea. Then the youth and the girl were married.[22]

According to the *Diegesis*, or narrative, accompanying the fragments of Kallimachos's poem, it was the Heros himself who instituted the tribute, according to which the inhabitants should bring him a bed and a maiden, and then depart without looking back; in the morning when the parents came to take her away, they would find her no longer a maiden but a woman. The practice continued until the boxer Euthymos did away with it. So the passion of the Heros in death, as in life, was for sex.

Except that it lacks the feature of the rival hero, the legend of Euthymos corresponds closely to the international tale type: (1) When a maiden is exposed as tribute to a monster, (2) the hero, passing by, notices her and inquires about the situation. (3) He falls in love with her and (4) agrees to kill the monster (5) in return for the maiden in marriage. (6) Awaiting the arrival of the monster he slays it, after which (7) he weds the maiden.

As in the legends of Perseus and Herakles, the city is plagued by the monster because of an earlier offense, in this case, the stoning of a drunk sailor who had raped a local girl. No matter that the man deserved to be executed: revenants are not moral creatures. This supernatural monster evidences the usual taste of monsters for maidens, but for sexual intercourse rather than as food. As in many texts of *The Dragon Slayer* a periodic tribute to the ogre is established,

and, as usually happens, the hero just chances to come by at the crucial time. Being an Olympic boxer, Euthymos's special weapons are his fists, so that no other weapons or helpers are mentioned. Euthymos is a historical person, an athlete of the early fifth century, a three-time Olympic victor in boxing.

Lit. AT 300, *The Dragon Slayer.*

Eurybatos

According to a legend recounted by Nikander, there was a immense ogress named Sybaris who lived in a large cave near Delphi. Every day she sallied out to seize humans and young animals. Finally, the Delphians decided to move elsewhere and asked Apollo's oracle where they should go, but the god replied that they would be free of the ogress if they should sacrifice to her a Delphic youth. The lot fell to a handsome boy, Alkyoneus. As the priests prepared him, an Aetolian hero Eurybatos saw Alkyoneus, fell in love with him, and determined to rescue him. Dressing as the victim, he went to the ogress's cave, seized her, and cast her over a cliff. Her body disappeared, and in its place there appeared the spring called Sybaris.[23]

As Fontenrose points out, this story is the same as that of Euthymos, except that the monster and the victim have exchanged sexes: a murderous demon terrorizes a city, leading the people to consider moving elsewhere, but the Delphic oracle instructs them rather to sacrifice a youth or maiden to the demon; as they prepare to do so, the hero passes by, falls in love with the beautiful victim, goes to meet the demon, and overcomes the creature, who disappears into water.[24]

This is a rare instance of a variant in which the monster is female and the victim male, for in the other ancient texts discussed here and certainly in most of the modern texts the monster (if its gender is known) is male, the victim is a youthful female, and the rescuer is a youthful male. As a rule the active roles, that of the monster and that of the rescuer, are assigned to male characters, while the passive role of intended victim and prize is given to a female. Actually, the gender of the victim appears to be influenced by the gender of the monster, regardless of whether the monster's preferred activity is eating or sexual intercourse. The monster is usually male and the victim therefore female, and the Teumessian fox, who is female (at least grammatically: the noun "fox" is feminine in Greek), receives a tribute of boys, just as here the ogress Sybaris receives a sacrifice of a youth.[25] The gender of the rescuer is influenced in turn by that of the victim, for the hero frequently is motivated by his amorous attraction to the victim. Since the victim is regularly female, her rescuer is regularly male; homosexual versions such as the present one are infrequent. In general, males cause the problems, and females motivate males to solve them.

It is striking that the six legends discussed above fall clearly into three groups, characterized by similarity of theme and plot, of two stories each. In the first group—let us call it the *ketos subtype*—an offended god sends a sea monster against a country, leading to the exposure of a princess whom the princely hero (Perseus, Herakles) saves by slaying the monster in combat. Oddly, there is also

a version in which each of these heroes enters the creature and slays it from within. The false hero appears in a weakened form. This pair of rather fabulous stories is attached to exotic, coastal communities. In the second group, the *hunter subtype*, the hero (Alkathous, Peleus) wins a hunting competition featuring natural rather than fabulous animals, for which, in one legend at least, a princess is the prize. There is a false hero. This group of fairly realistic stories is localized on the Greek mainland. In the third group of stories, the *demon subtype*, an anthropoid ogre or ogress plagues the people of a community, who are on the verge of abandoning the site when an oracle instructs them to sacrifice a maiden or youth to the demon. A lad (Euthymos, Eurybatos) falls in love with the intended victim and outwrestles the demon, saving the victim. There is no false hero.

It is an old question whether the Perseus legend is indebted to the international tale or the tale developed from the legend.[26] Assuming that the question is correctly posed, we must answer that it is always improbable to derive a widespread tradition from any particular instance of it, regardless of how early or familiar the example may be. That being the case, we are on much safer ground if we suppose that the Perseus legend, or rather the episode of Perseus's combat with the sea monster, is a particular elaboration of international narrative material that has been adapted to the traditional biography of Perseus, rather than concluding that the entire international tradition derives from this Greek story. On this view, Phineus/Agenor is a rationalized form of the false hero, which does seem more likely than the reverse.

But there really are two questions here. Is the Perseus adventure a local adaptation of an international story, and, if so, was that story a folktale? To the first question the evidence indicates an affirmative answer. Indeed, the foregoing analysis indicates that the question is too narrow, for the Perseus adventure is a member of a family of six such adventures in Greek tradition, which, taken individually, show considerable correspondence to the international folktale and, taken collectively, show all the important features of the folktale, sometimes strengthening and sometimes weakening particular features of the type. Accordingly, it would be arbitrary to label the Perseus episode (or any of the other ancient stories) as the fount of the international tradition, even of the ancient Greek tradition. It is simplest to explain the three subtypes with their individual legends as different realizations of *The Dragon Slayer*. As to genre, the old international story may have circulated as a folktale, as a legend, as something in between like the Egyptian tale of Two Brothers, or as all of these.[27] For all we know, the plot may have been a thousand years old in the time of Hesiod, or even ten thousand, and have entered Greece many times. On the basis of our evidence it is safer to make inferences about plot than about genre and age.

Lit. AT 300, *The Dragon Slayer*.

 1. Bødker, Hole, and D'Aronco 1963:174–175.
 2. Seki 1963:33–36, no. 15.
 3. See further Baring-Gould 1967:266–316; Hartland (1896) 3:38–47; Dawkins 1955:123–128; Briggs A1:474–476; Briggs B2:442–443; Fontenrose 1959:515–521; and *EM* 5:1030–1039.
 4. For example, Dawkins 1955:123–128.

5. Fontenrose 1959.

6. *Bibl.* 2.4.3. In addition to Apollodoros, see especially Lucian *Dialogi Marini* 14; Ovid *Met.* 4.663–5.235; and Hyginus *Fab.* 64. The hero, but not the adventure, is mentioned as early as Homer (*Il.*14.319–320) and Hesiod (*Th.* 280, *Scutum* 216–231). See further Roscher 3:1986–2060; Schmidt 1907:12–22; Frazer (1921) 1:158–161; Halliday 1933:113–142; Woodward 1937; Brommer 1955; Fontenrose 1959:275–306; Gantz 1993:307–309; *LIMC* 7.1:332–348; Jameson 1990. On the sickle as a weapon see Schmidt 1963:41–47 and Jameson 1990:217–218.

7. For example, Pausanias 4.35.9; Josephus *Bellum Judaicum* 3.9.3.

8. *Dialogi Marini* 14.

9. *Fab.* 64.

10. Hartland (1896) 3:152.

11. Ovid *Met.* 5.220.

12. Apollodoros *Bibl.* 2.5.9, 2.6.4. See further Homer *Il.* 5.638–651, 7.452–453, 20.145–148, 21.441–457; Hellanikos (*FGH* 4 F 26b) *apud* Schol. AB on Homer *Il.* 20.146; Diodorus Siculus 4.32, 4.42; Lycophron *Alex.* 31–37, 468–478; Tzetzes *Schol. on Lycophron* 34; Ovid *Met.* 11.199–217; Valerius Flaccus *Arg.* 2.451–578; Hyginus *Fab.* 89; Servius on Verg. *Aen.* 1.550, 5.30, 8.157; *LIMC* 5.1:1–262. An illustration on a Greek vase shows Herakles poised to cut out the tongue of the sea monster, who is, however, still very much a living adversary; consequently, it is unclear whether the hero is clearing a path into the creature's belly, answering to the version in which he leaps inside the fish and kills it from within (see "Man Swallowed By Fish") or, like the folktale hero, is gathering proof of his deed, which the vase painter chooses to show proleptically. On the legend of Herakles and the sea monster see Schmidt 1907:3–12; Frazer (1921) 1:206–209; Weinreich 1942:17–22; Fontenrose 1959:347–350; Schmidt 1963:41–47; Lesky 1967; Gantz 1993:400–402; *LIMC* 8.1:624; Mayor 2000a.

13. 1.41.4–1.41.5.

14. *FGH* 485 F 10 *apud* Schol. on Apollonios of Rhodes 1.516. See further *LIMC* 1.1:531–533.

15. Pausanias 1.42.7.

16. The only exception known to me is that of the Teumessian fox, to which the Thebans offered a youth every month in order that the fox not kill a large number of citizens (Apollodoros *Bibl.* 2.4.6–7).

17. Apollodoros *Bibl.* 3.13.3. Other sources for the story are Hesiod fr. 209 M & W *apud* Schol. Pindar *Nemian* 4.95; Pindar *Nemian* 4.54–72; Zenobios 5.20; schol. Aristophanes *Clouds* 1063; and schol. Apollonios of Rhodes 1.224. See also Mannhardt (1877) 2:49–51; Roscher 3:1831–1833; Frazer (1921) 2:62–65; Gantz 1993:225–226; *LIMC* 7.1:251–269, esp. nos. 7–10.

18. 5.20. "Peleus' sword" was a proverbial expression, taking several forms (Zenobios 5.20 = *CPG* 1:123 and note; *Appendix Prov.* 4.57 = *CPG* 1:446), which suggests that the incident was well known.

19. Schol. Aristophanes *Clouds* 1063.

20. Fr. 209 M & W.

21. Mannhardt (1877) 2:52–60. His argument is approved by Lesky 1967:4–5.

22. Pausanias 6.6.7–10. Other sources for the legend are Kallimachos *Aitia* fr. 98–99 Pfeiffer; Strabo 6.1.5, p. 255; and Aelian *VH* 8.18. See further Frazer (1898) 4:23–24; Rohde 1925:153–154 nn. 115, 116; Fontenrose 1959:101–103, 119–120; and Fontenrose 1968:79–83.

23. Nikander *apud* Antoninus Liberalis 8.

24. Fontenrose 1959:102–103. On the story see further Fontenrose 1959:100–104, 119–120; 1968:81–83. Similar is the Boeotian legend of Menestratos. A serpent was once plaguing the Thespians, and Zeus told them they must choose a youth every year by lot and give him to the monster. One year when the lot fell to Kleostratos, his lover Menestratos fashioned armor made of bronze and fishhooks, donned it, and took the place of the intended victim, sacrificing his own life while also killing the serpent (Pausanias 9.26.7). See Frazer (1898) 5:143–145, who regards the story as a version of *The Dragon Slayer*. This story is unusual in that the monster and the intended victim are of the same gender.

25. For the Teumessian fox see note 16, above.

26. Krappe 1933a:229; Liljeblad 1935:31–32; Vries 1954; Liungman 1961:41.

27. On the genre of the Egyptian story see Hollis 1990.

Esdras Chain. *See* Stronger and Strongest

Fairies Send a Message ◈ Death of Pan

When a traveler passes a supernatural dwelling (a hill, a grave mound), an inhabitant calls out to him, bidding him report, when he comes home, that so-and-so is dead. Although the traveler scarcely understands the message, he mentions this news at home, and immediately a lament arises from somewhere in the house. Sometimes someone or something disappears out of the door.

This narrative, which is regularly recounted as a true event, is known in varying forms throughout northern Europe, especially in Denmark and Germany but also in Norway, Sweden, Finland, Estonia, France, the Netherlands, Belgium, and elsewhere. Christiansen lists it as ML 6070A, *Fairies Send a Message*, in his index of migratory legends.

A Danish text told around 1863 recounts how a certain Christian Østberg, the fourth man to live where Søren Madsen now lives, was coming from Nibe one evening with some herring, and when he reached Tisted Field a little fellow came to him and asked if he would tell Atis that Vatis was dead. After the man had come home, sat down to table, and gotten something to eat, he recounted how when he came to Hessel Hill, there was a little fellow who told him to say to Atis that Vatis was dead. Then lamentation and weeping arose in the room, along with the cry: "Oh, Vatis is dead, Vatis is dead!" The people could not see anything. The creatures lived under the oven.[1]

According to another text from the same country, collected in 1868, as a man from Agerskov was driving past Rind Hill a voice called to him from the earth: "Greet Bildser, saying that Baldser is dead." When the man came home, he recounted to the members of the household what he had heard, and scarcely had he uttered these words when a voice under the stove said: "Oh, is old Baldser now dead!"[2] A third text, collected around 1877, tells how some elves (*nissefolk*) lived on a certain farm located at Udbreds-Agre. The man was returning one day from Randers when some of the little people from the hill came and asked if he was the man from that farm. When he said he was, they asked if he would not greet Hikke, saying that Hakke was dead. When the man reached home and had something to eat, he recounted the event. Then weeping was heard within the oven.[3] According to a German text published in 1859, while a certain man was plowing his farm on the Dettersberg a dwarf came asking him to tell Hübel that Habel was dead. As the farmer later recounted this strange event at home during his midday meal, a woman appeared in a corner of the room and rushed out of the house and up the mountain loudly lamenting. He had never seen her before and never saw her again.[4]

In these narratives, told as actual events that happened to certain persons in particular places on particular occasions, an elf or fairy or the like who dwells in a hill outside of town asks a passerby to relay a certain message, giving the name of the intended receiver of the message and the name of the deceased.

The two names are odd but similar in a singsong way. Not really understanding the message or for whom it is intended, the man mentions it casually to his wife or other members of the household, sometimes as part of the evening's conversation after supper, whereupon they suddenly hear unseen beings in the house grieving. As the sender of the message evidently intended, these beings overheard the message as it was relayed from husband to wife. In some texts the mysterious receiver of the message, having learned that so-and-so is dead, returns home or goes to the funeral. Sometimes also the human inhabitants of the house express surprise or fear upon learning that their house is home to unseen creatures of whose presence they were previously unaware. The narrator often says that the event actually happened to his or her grandfather or grandmother or other relation, the characteristic "friend-of-a friend," or two degrees of removal from the narrator, that is typical of legendry.[5]

The different redactions of the legend vary mostly in how the household, the nonhuman creatures, or both respond to the man's message, the variation usually resulting, as it appears, from the combination of the legend with another traditional story that is also found independently. In the most common such conflation, found in Germany and Scandinavia, the basic legend is combined with traditions of little folk who poach beer or milk or bread from the household. So a certain Rasmus Andersen was driving past Drage Hill when a voice from within the hill called out: "Oh, tell Ade that Dade is dead." When he reached Hill Farm, he related what he had heard, and then heard a cry up in the main room of the house: "Oh, is Dade dead!" They ran up there and saw a little troll, who leapt from the room, forgetting a large brass kettle that he was about fill with ale from a barrel that lay ready for guests.[6] Frequently such kettles remained on display in the house or farm as a prized possession of the family. In this form of the story, of course, the creature who responds to the news is not an unseen resident of the house but an intruder.

When W. B. Yeats reportedly said to his sister upon learning of the death of Swinburne, "Now I am king of the cats," he was alluding to a different form of the present story, related as a folktale, in which the nonhuman roles are taken by cats.[7] Aarne-Thompson list it among the animal tales as AT 113A, *King of the Cats is Dead*. In this tale a cat, sometimes one of several cats celebrating a funeral, asks a passing man to go home and tell so-and-so that so-and-so is dead. When the man does so, the family cat immediately departs for good, often with a word of explanation that he must go, that the deceased is a relative, or that now he is king of the cats. For example, in a tale from Lancashire, a man was sitting at home reading when a cat came down the chimney and called out: "Tell Dildrum, Doldrum's dead!" Sometime later the man's wife returned with the family cat, and the man related to his wife what had transpired, whereupon their cat exclaimed, "Is Doldrum dead?" and then rushed up the chimney and was never seen again. It was generally assumed by people that Dildrum had succeeded Doldrum as king of the cats.[8]

The cat redaction is an old one, attested from the sixteenth century onward.[9] Like the nonhuman creatures of the legend, the cats are represented as being supernatural creatures who can speak and have their own society, which is organized along the lines of human society and includes such familiar institu-

tions as royalty and funerals. So there is really not much difference here between elves, trolls, fairies, cats, and the like, and indeed in a text of the story from northern England the narrator explains that fairies often take the form of cats.[10] A more significant divergence in the tradition perhaps is the particular emotion that the news calls forth in its supernatural receiver, which in the legend is commonly grief, but in the folktale joy. In some lands such as in Scandinavia and France both forms of the story—the legend featuring anthropomorphic creatures and the folktale featuring cats—circulate simultaneously, but Britain knows only *King of the Cats is Dead.*[11]

The Death of Pan

In antiquity a story very much like that of the simple legend is recounted by a character in a dialogue by Plutarch, *On the Obsolescence of Oracles.*[12] Philip, responding to the question of whether demigods were mortal or immortal, said that he had heard it from a reliable man, the orator Aemilianus, whose father was Epitherses, a fellow citizen of Philip's and a teacher of grammar. Epitherses said that once he was sailing on a ship with freight and many passengers from Greece to Italy. It was evening, the wind died down near the Echinades Islands, and the ship was carried near the islands of Paxos.[13] Suddenly from the islands they heard a voice of someone calling for Thamous, which astonished them. Now, Thamous was an Egyptian pilot who was not known by name to many on board. Twice Thamous was called and made no reply, but the third time he responded to the caller. Straining his voice the caller said: "When you come opposite Palodes, report that the great Pan is dead."[14] Everyone, said Epitherses, was amazed at hearing this. As the others discussed whether it was preferable to carry out the instruction or to avoid meddling in the affairs of others, Epitherses himself decided that if there was a wind, he would sail past saying nothing, but if it was windless and the sea about the place was calm, he would report what he had heard. When he was near Palodes, there was neither wind nor wave, so that Epitherses stood at the stern, looked toward land, and said: "The great Pan is dead." Before he even finished speaking, there arose a great moaning mixed with amazement, not of one but of many beings. Inasmuch as many persons had been present, the report spread quickly in Rome and Epitherses was sent for by Tiberius Caesar. Tiberius was so convinced of the story that he made inquiries about this Pan. The emperor's scholars conjectured that he was the Pan who was born of Hermes and Penelope. Philip had as witnesses among those present at the discussion several persons who had heard the aged Aemilianus (that is, heard from him his father's remarkable story).

The parallelism of Philip's narrative and the modern tradition, in particular the legend in its simple form, is striking. Specifically they agree that (1) someone calls out to a traveler making his way past a certain place, (2) asking him, when he comes to a particular site (Palodes/home), to report that so-and-so is dead. (3) Although the man does not really understand the message, (4) he does report it at the specified place, (5) whereupon a lamentation made by unseen beings is suddenly heard. These are certainly forms of the same story.

In the ancient narrative, which perhaps circulated in western Greece where the events were localized, the role of the creature of lower mythology (elf, troll,

fairy, etc.) is assigned to the god or demigod Pan, offspring of a divine father and a mortal mother.[15] Although the text is unique in treating Pan as mortal, the question of the immortality or mortality of supernatural beings, especially those of a lower order, is precisely the topic of conversation in Plutarch's dialogue at the moment when Philip contributes this particular story, which is intended to cast light on the question. As in some modern texts, the speaker of the original death-message in Plutarch's version is unseen, merely a mysterious voice heard from somewhere, and the text seems to feature a pair of proper names with similar phonemes, Palodes and Pan, answering to Atis and Vatis, Dildrum and Doldrum, and the like, although the ancient names do not manifest the oddness that the modern ones do, and the first of the pair, Palodes, is attached not to the receiver of the message but to the receiver's habitat.[16] In Plutarch's account the traveler delivers the message at a location along his way, so that the mysterious event is given a public setting, and the ship with its many passengers provides disinterested witnesses, including at least one educated man, the teacher Epitherses, who can subsequently attest that it all really happened.[17] Indeed the ancient narrator takes considerable pains to establish the credentials of his story: the internal narrator Philip has personal ties to the prominent person who experienced it, Epitherses, as well as to Epitherses's well-known son, Aemilianus, a trustworthy person with no reason to deceive and known personally to some of the interlocutors; the particular sites of the event, which are carefully specified, are all real places in western Greece; many chance witnesses are present; and finally the investigation by so important a person as the Emperor Tiberius, whose reign (14–37 A.D.) gives the dramatic date of the events, vouches for the credibility of the report.[18] The text even shows the two degrees of separation between the narrator and the person who allegedly experienced the event that is so frequently found in the transmission of legends: Philip ← Aemilianus ← Epitherses.

The Greek story of the death of Pan has enjoyed a long history of learned explanation, popular speculation, and artistic allusion from early Christian times to the twentieth century. That the death of a pagan god should be announced precisely during the time of Jesus' ministry inevitably attracted comment linking the two events, beginning with the church father Eusebios, who sees the report of Pan's death as an instance of Christ's beginning to rid the world of evil spirits. Later interpreters along these lines sometimes take the being more specifically as the devil or more generally as a representation of dying paganism at a time of nascent Christianity. Somewhat surprisingly some Christian commentators identify Pan with Christ, taking Pan to signify "all" (the proper name "Pan" and the Greek adjective for "all" are nearly identical) and understanding the story therefore to refer to the Christian savior, from whom everything derives and who is everything to the world.[19] But there is no sound reason for seeing Christian allusions or allegory in a non-Christian author at this period in Greece.[20]

Proponents of a ritual interpretation however confidently see in Pan's death and in the lamentation that ensues two elements that are typical of ancient cults of dying gods: the myth of the deity's death and the ritual of the worshipers' lamentation. They identify the Pan of the story variously with Egyptian Pan, with Mesopotamian Tammuz (whose name resembles that of the pilot Thamous in

Plutarch's story), with Pan in a supposed vegetation cult in Epirus, or with another such spirit. But these explanations are all forced and raise more problems than they solve.[21] A third, quite different explanation was proposed by Archer Taylor, who argues that the narrative tradition arose from auditory hallucinations.[22]

Just what these explanations are trying to account for is to a large extent a function of the time in which they are offered. The Christian interpretations take Plutarch's narrative either as a true event or as an allegory, reflecting two approaches to mythological narrative that were important before the modern period. The dying-god and the hallucinatory explanations each seek to understand the tradition by discovering its origin, the main concern of philologists and folklorists in the nineteenth and early twentieth centuries. If none of these interpretations seems very satisfying now, it is perhaps because none of them looks to the narrative itself, asking what kind of appeal such an artifact might have for narrators and audiences to induce them to host it and transmit it to others. Philip and his fellow interlocutors in Plutarch's dialogue are doubtless atypical of the tradition, since their interest in the story is mostly an intellectual one. For most persons the pleasures of the story have probably included the enjoyable mystery inherent in encounters with the supernatural and in particular the idea that there are supernatural beings who, unknown to us and unseen by us, live in societies very much like our own. The plot is moreover cunningly and artfully constructed in that it has a supernatural being employ a human being as a messenger, a role that neither the human messenger nor the audience of the story fathoms until the messenger hears the sudden and strange reaction of the being for whom the message is intended.

Lit. ML 6070A, *Fairies Send a Message.* Cf. AT 113A, *The King of the Cats is Dead.* Gerhard 1915a, 1915b, 1916. Taylor 1922a, 1922b. Boberg 1934. Loorits 1937:7–11. Hudson 1953.

1. Boberg 1934:18.
2. Boberg 1934:26.
3. Boberg 1934:30.
4. Taylor 1922b:24.
5. Cf. Boberg 1934:8. The newsletter of the International Society for Contemporary Legend Research is appropriately named *FoafTale News*, that is, "Friend-of-a-Friend Tale News."
6. Boberg 1934:32–33.
7. Yeats anecdote: Dupee 1984:38.
8. Briggs (1971) B1:206, citing Harland and Wilkinson, *Lancashire Legends, Traditions, Pageants, Sports, etc.* (London, 1873), p. 12. See further Taylor 1922b; Boberg 1934:142–150; Hudson 1953. For Germanic traditions of elf and fairy sovereigns and expressions of grief at their death see Grimm (1966) 2:453 and note.
9. Boberg 1934:11–12.
10. Briggs (1971) B1:309.
11. Inger Boberg, who has made the most extensive and detailed study of the whole tradition, sees a pattern according to which the creature ecotype, or legend, corresponds to settlements of Germanic peoples and the cat ecotype, or folktale, to Celtic peoples (Boberg 1934:136, 151–157).
12. Plutarch *de defectu oraculorum* 17 (*Moralia* 3.419b–e).
13. That is, Paxos and Propaxos (Gerhard 1915a:4 n. 1), of which the latter appears to have been used mostly by shepherds and fishermen and so was a likely site for a cult of Pan (Roscher 1892:465 n. 1).
14. Palodes was the harbor of the city of Bouthroton in Epirus (Strabo 7.7.5). Since the region was renowned for its cattle and sheep, it was, like Paxos and Propaxos, a likely site for the worship of Pan (Roscher 1892:465 n. 3).

15. Pan as the son of Hermes and Penelope was one of the traditional genealogies; see Herodotos 2.145 and Frazer (1921) 2:305. But according to the *Homeric Hymn to Pan* (33–37) he was the son of Hermes and the nymph Dryope. The Penelope in question may be a nymph in the minds of some authors (in which case she is still a mortal, just a longer-living one), but for others she is Odysseus's wife Penelope.

16. Boberg 1934:16. There is also some similarity in the names Pan and the initial element of Thamous: Pan and Tham-; the names are less dissimilar when they are inflected in the oblique cases.

17. Reinach 1907:12. The relayer of the message is made to be the pilot of the boat perhaps only because he is in control of its course.

18. Cf. Gerhard 1915b:346. For the Roman emperor as a repository and investigator of marvels see, for example, the preface of Dictys of Crete's *Trojan War;* Hansen 1996b:142.

19. Eusebios *Praep. Evang.* 5.17. The tradition is surveyed in detail by Gerhard in several articles (1915a, 1915b, 1916); see also Weinreich 1910 and Merivale 1969:12–16, 103–118.

20. Roscher 1892:466–467.

21. See Roscher 1892; Reinach 1907; Gerhard 1915a; Haakh 1958. These scholars (and others) champion the dying-god view, which arose in the mid-nineteenth century. Although some investigators draw upon texts of *Fairies Send a Message,* they wrote before the availability of extensive studies of the entire legend tradition, published by Taylor (1922b) and Boberg (1934), who criticize earlier investigators' skewed use of the legend materials (Taylor 1922b:60, 95–100; Boberg 1934:8–9, 59). See also Boberg 1940.

22. Taylor 1922b:10–11. This odd explanation is approved by Boberg (1934:151; 1940) and Loorits (1937:10).

Father, Son, and Donkey. *See* Carrying Part of the Load

Foolish Fugitives

Several numskulls hide themselves from invading soldiers (hunters). One of them foolishly speaks out and so is captured (killed). A second numskull may similarly speak out, giving himself away. Perceiving this, the last fool declares out loud that he will not say anything; as a result he too is discovered.

This numskull tale is classified in the Greek Folklore Archives as *1298, *The Foolish Fugitives.*[1]

In a Turkish text from the fifteenth century, evidently drawn in turn from a thirteenth-century Arabic work, the fugitives are *nesnas,* humanoid animals having half a body and no brains. Some men hunting *nesnas* came upon three of them. The hunters killed one, and the other two *nesnas* hid among the trees. When a hunter remarked how fat and ruddy the slain *nesna* was, one of the hidden *nesnas* called out by way of explanation that of course he was, since he had been eating pistachio nuts. Since his voice gave him away, the hunters found him and killed him, saying that if the *nesna* had not spoken, no one would have known he was there. Then the third *nesna* said, "All right, I'm not speaking," whereupon he too was caught and killed.[2]

A modern Greek text from Chios relates that when the Turks conquered the island in 1822, they massacred the three thousand inhabitants of the village of Vrontado except for three men, one of whom who hid in a tree, the second on a rooftop, and the third behind a wall. As the janissaries were marching by, they

did not see the hidden men. But when a soldier at the rear paused to knock the ashes out of his pipe on the tree, the man in the tree mistook the pipe for a sword and, thinking the janissary was about to cut down the tree, called out and climbed down, whereupon the soldier slew him, exclaiming how black the blood of the Christian dog was. The villager hidden on the rooftop then explained that the first man ate olives, though he himself had advised him not to; the janissary then told him to come down, and killed him. When the villager behind the wall now declared, "I'm better off for saying nothing," the soldier slew him as well.[3]

This Chiote tale, first published in 1913, lampoons the inhabitants of the village of Vrontado. But the foolish folk of Chios do no better during the Second World War, when similar behavior is attributed to them. In a Greek joke collected in the 1970s, the Germans invaded Chios during World War II, and after capturing the major villages they combed the countryside for men in hiding. Their procedure was simply to pause every kilometer and call out, asking if there was anyone they had not yet captured, and the stupid Chiotes would reply, "Only me!" after which the Germans would grab them. Finally, however, the Germans encountered a smart Chiote, who, when he heard the Germans calling, replied: "I who have brains will not speak." But of course, having spoken, he too was captured.[4]

Here, as often in numskull tales, the problem facing the numskulls is finally solved, as it were, by the most clever of the numskulls.

An Ancient Greek Joke

The earliest attestation of this international joke is in the ancient Greek jokebook, *Philogelos*.[5] In this version, two cowardly fools hid themselves, one in a well and the other among some reeds. As soldiers let a helmet down into the well in order to draw water, the man below thought a soldier was coming down for him. He begged the man not to harm him, and so was captured. The soldiers then remarked that if he had remained silent, they would have passed him by. So the man hidden in the reeds said, "Then pass me by, since I am remaining silent."

The first coward in *Philogelos* gives himself up after naively misinterpreting the sight or sound of a helmet being lowered into the well as that of a soldier being lowered into the well. His folly is of the same sort, though with different imagery, as that of the first Chiote, who gives himself up after misinterpreting the knocking of a pipe against the tree as the sound of a sword striking a tree. But the ancient joke has no incident corresponding to that found in the Turkish and Chiote jokes in which the hunter (janissary) comments upon the color of the body (blood) of a fugitive he has killed, inducing a second fugitive naively to volunteer an explanation for the color, thereby giving himself away.

Lit. Greek Folklore Archives *1298, *The Foolish Fugitives*. Mundy 1965. Marzolph 1987:210–211.

1. Megas 1970:244.
2. Mundy 1965:326.
3. Megas 1970:178, no. 61; Ranke 1972:49, no. 51.
4. Orso 1979:82, no. 124. Orso classifies this Chiote text as AT 1341B*, *Escaped Slave's Talka-*

tiveness, a tale otherwise attested only in Cuba. In the Cuban tale a talkative slave repeatedly escaped, and the master, familiar with the slave's usual hiding place, went to the place and shouted out an obvious inaccuracy about goats. The slave, unable to resist an urge to speak, replied that the statement was a lie. And so the master recaptured him. (For the Cuban tale see further Hansen 1957:153, type **1709A.) In the Cuban text, as in the Chiote, the seeker or seekers are aware of the fugitive(s), actively search for him (them), and by calling out induce him (them) to give himself (themselves) away, and in these respects these texts differ from the norm of *The Foolish Fugitives*. But the Chiote joke, like texts of *The Foolish Fugitives*, also features the capture of several foolish fugitives, culminating in the capture of a fugitive who is discovered when he says aloud that he will not speak. So ideally, if not historically, the Chiote text is a mix of these somewhat similar tales about foolish fugitives who give themselves away by speaking.

5. *Phil.* 96. Although the numskulls are described as cowards (δειλοί), this trait explains only why they hide themselves; otherwise, the joke is about their simplemindedness, so that the joke is not grouped together with jokes that focus upon cowardice, *Phil.* 206–210 (Thierfelder 1968:231).

Foolish Man Builds Aircastles ≈ Gripus

A man (youth, maiden) happens upon a wild animal (fox, hare, etc.) or acquires a modest amount of food (a pail of milk, a pot of honey, etc.). He imagines how he will sell the item and thereby make his fortune. Lost in his daydream he works out the details of his opulent future. At the height of his imagined fortunes, however, he inadvertently loses the lucky find or destroys the container of food, so that he ends up with nothing.[1]

The tale is AT 1681*, *Foolish Man Builds Aircastles*.

The dreamer can be either a man or a woman. When a man, he usually stores his pot on a shelf above his head but accidentally knocks it down with a stick as he imagines reprimanding his future wife or children for some minor form of misbehavior. When a woman, she is most often a milkmaid carrying milk to market, when she makes a quick gesture (e.g., she tosses her head back in scorn for her future suitors, she strikes her head for joy, she kicks her feet like the colt she someday will have), spilling all her milk. Since the ancient texts that we have all feature men, I illustrate the type with male versions.

In a twelfth-century Indian text appearing in the *Panchatantra*, a Brahman who lived in a certain town got an amount of barley meal by begging. He ate some, and the rest he placed in a jar that he hung on a peg above his cot. Gazing at the jar one night, he imagined that if there should be a famine, he could get a hundred rupees for the jar of meal, and with the money he would buy two she-goats, who would bear other she-goats every six months. From goats he would move on to cows, buffaloes, and finally mares. From the sale of his horses he would get much gold, with which he would buy a great mansion. A wealthy man would then offer him his daughter with a dowry, and she would bear him a son. One day the boy would go too near to the horses, and he himself would be angry with his wife, telling her to take the boy, but she would be busy with her chores and pay no attention to him, so that he would get up and kick her. And he gave such a kick that he smashed the jar, covering himself and the ground with barley-meal.[2]

According to a Russian tale collected in the nineteenth century, a poor peas-

ant came upon a hare under a bush. Overjoyed at his luck, he said that he would catch the hare, kill it, and sell it for twelve kopeks. With the money he would buy a sow that would bear twelve piglets, and each of the piglets would in turn bear twelve more piglets, so that when he slaughtered them he would have a barnful of meat. Having sold the meat, he would acquire a house and a wife, who would bear him two children, Vaska and Vanka. He himself would sit and give the orders, while the children plowed the field. And he would yell at them since, never having known poverty, they would overwork the hired laborers. At this point the peasant shouted out the reprimand he imagined he would make to his children, and the hare ran away, and with it he lost his riches, his house, his wife, and his children.[3]

These tales illustrate the dashed hopes of the poor man, suggesting that because of character or fate he is destined to continue as he is at present. Just when the dreamer becomes fully in charge of his dreamworld, reprimanding his future spouse or children from his commanding position as head of the family, he destroys the meager reality that supports his extravagant fantasy. As in the motif of the three foolish wishes, the fantast who comes so close to having everything ends up instead with nothing (see "Hospitality Rewarded").

The summaries of the texts given here are misleading to the extent that in the originals the musings of the protagonist, which make up nearly all the tale, are monologues delivered in the first person. For this reason, perhaps, the tale has recommended itself to writers of comic drama.

An Ancient Aircastle?

Some fragments of a play by Epicharmos called *The Pots* seem to refer to our tale.[4] Epicharmos was a Sicilian composer of comedies who was active around the beginning of the fifth century B.C. His language was Sicilian Doric. Some three or four lines of verse from *The Pots* are quoted by the grammarian Julius Pollux in illustration of an unusual word for "coin" in Sicilian Greek.[5] In one fragment (136), a character says that fine, fat lambs will fetch him ten coins when he sells them. In another fragment (137), he instructs a messenger to go quickly and buy him a fine female calf for ten coins. Evidently these lines come from the middle of a character's reverie, when his imagined earnings will have grown from something modest to a ewe, who in turn will produce fat lambs, which he imagines selling for cash, with which he will purchase a calf—at which point our brief glimpse into the play breaks off.

Crusius compares the Greek proverb κεραμέως πλοῦτος, "a potter's fortune," which according to paroemiographer Diogeneianos was applied to things unsound, unsure, or breakable.[6] Crusius supposes that the proverb goes back to Epicharmos, whose play *The Pots* he believes featured a potter who constructs aircastles upon the pots he possesses, and accidentally destroys his stock of pots. Scenes of this sort are in fact found in some Eastern narrative texts. In the tale of Alnaschar, or En-Nashshar, from the *Thousand and One Nights*, the protagonist used a hundred pieces of silver to buy many articles of glass. He put his stock on a large tray in order to offer it for sale, and leaned back against a wall. His fantasies carried him to the point at which he was

treating his future wife with disdain, spurning her with his foot, when in reality he kicked his tray of glassware, which fell and broke.[7] In an Indian tale from the *Hitopadesa* a Brahman obtained a dish of flour and, since the day was very hot, lay down in a potter's shed that was filled with pots. Guarding his dish of flour with a staff, he soon became lost in daydreams of future opulence, culminating in his thrashing his several jealous wives with a stick, at which point he threw his real stick, breaking his dish of flour as well as many of the potter's pots, causing the angry potter to turn him out.[8]

Gripus

Foolish Man Builds Aircastles seems to have been adapted again in the following century by Diphilos. A comedy by Diphilos, now lost, was the original of Plautus's *Rudens*, or *The Rope*, which features a scene in which a slave named Gripus, having discovered a trunk in the sea, is dragging it home in his fishing net. Perceiving that its contents are heavy and believing the trunk contains gold, he sees the find as his opportunity to become a free man. He forms a plan. He will cleverly approach his master and buy his freedom as cheaply as possible. Then, when he is free, he will acquire farmland, a house, and slaves, and he will become a merchant with big ships and be esteemed a king among kings. Later, to amuse himself, he will have a yacht built for himself and sail to different towns as Stratonicus does, and when he is at the height of his fame he will build a big fortified city and name it Gripsby after himself, as a monument to his renown and accomplishments, and he will establish a great kingdom there.[9] Slowly emerging from his reverie, Gripus begins to turn his attention to hiding the trunk, while still fantasizing about what kind of food it will please King Gripus to dine upon. At this point, unfortunately, another slave abruptly happens upon the scene, leading to a dispute over the ownership of the trunk.[10]

While the imagery of Gripus's fantasy is mostly different from that of the aircastle builders in Epicharmos's comedy and in the texts we have from oral tradition, the basic ideas are the same. A poor man makes a lucky find and, before securing it, loses himself in an extravagant fantasy of his future opulence. Like the Brahman beggar and the Russian peasant, he will acquire a mansion or large farm, and so forth. The fantasy suddenly ends when he loses control of the quarry upon which it depends, in this case a chest.

The main difference between the Plautine passage and the oral folktale is that Gripus, who believes he has found a treasure, imagines himself straightaway as a wealthy man, whereas the folktale protagonist pictures himself becoming monied as his wealth happily increases geometrically from the small initial investment he now has to the eventual grand wealth he expects to acquire. A progressive quality is also found in Gripus's daydream, but instead of growing from a jar of honey to a family living in a grand mansion, Gripus's ambition begins with a chest imagined to be full of gold, proceeds quickly to a country estate, and culminates in a kingdom of which he will be the monarch.

Adeimantos

The folktale of the daydreamer who builds grand aircastles has also been adapted to nondramatic literature, being found in a narrative in Lucian's dialogue, *The Ship, or the Wishes.*[11]

The fantasy is framed as a report of an experience recounted by Adeimantos to his friends. Having learned that a huge grain ship from Egypt, the Isis, was moored in the Piraeus, Adeimantos and several friends went to see it. As it happened, Adeimantos and friends became separated, and when the others later spotted Adeimantos they hailed him. Adeimantos acknowledged that he had been lost in his thoughts, in fact had been daydreaming about wealth, and that his companions had come upon him at the height of his luxury and fortune. They pressed him to reveal his daydream, and, though he was afraid they would think it childish, he did so. When he had been separated from the others and had been examining the ship, he had asked one of the sailors how much annual income the ship brought its owner, and the man had said it brought in at least twelve Attic talents a year. Adeimantos went ashore again and began imagining that if some god should suddenly put him in possession of that ship, what a happy life he would lead, benefiting his friends, going to sea himself sometimes and sending his slaves at other times. With the twelve talents he had already built a house near the Painted Stoa and purchased slaves, clothes, horses, and chariots. And then he was sailing at sea, envied by all the passengers, respected by the crew, and deemed a virtual king, but just as he was managing his ship and was scouting the harbor in the distance, his companion Lykinos showed up, sinking his wealth and capsizing his ship, which had been sailing so nicely, propelled by the tailwind of his wishing.[12]

The parallelism of content shared by Lucian's narrative and the Gripus passage in Plautus's (Diphilos's) comedy is striking. (a) Each fantast is a poor man (Gripus is a slave/Adeimantos is a self-proclaimed poor man),[13] (b) who acquires a large amount of money from the sea (he fishes a trunk full of gold from the sea/he gets an annual income of twelve talents from his merchant ship), with which (c) he purchases a fine house and slaves. Then (d) he sails around on a merchant vessel or on a pleasure yacht and (e) is esteemed as a king.[14] But (f) just as he is dealing with the enjoyable details of the grand world he commands, another person unexpectedly comes upon the scene, interrupting and destroying his fantasy.

The kind of correspondence shown by the two versions suggests that Lucian's story does not derive immediately from Diphilos but that Diphilos in the fourth century B.C. and Lucian in the second century A.D. each adapt for their own purposes a form of the oral tale that circulated in their own day. Evidently the comic tale was fairly stable in Greek oral tradition, reflecting an ancient Greek ecotype.

Lit. AT 1681*, *Foolish Man Builds Aircastles*. Cf. AT 1430, *The Man and his Wife Build Aircastles*, for information that is pertinent also to this tale. Joly 1877:91–113. Müller 1881. Clouston (1887) 2:432–443. Crusius 1891–1893:293–294. BP 3:261–267, 275–276. Kristensen 1949. Trenkner 1958:126–127. Liungman 1961:296–297. Cf. Ashliman, type 1430. Braid 1993. *EM* 8:1260–1265.

1. For an amusing essay on the art of building aircastles, see Polle (1896:17–30). For a performance study of several tellings of the aircastle tale "The Traveller and the Hare" by the Scots storyteller Duncan Williamson, see Braid 1993.

2. Clouston (1887) 2:438–439; BP 3:263; *Panchatantra* 1956:453–454.

3. Afanas'ev 1975:161.

4. Crusius 1891–93:293–294.

5. Pollux 9.79 = Epicharmos fr. 136–137 Kaibel.

6. Crusius 1891–93:294. Diogeneianos 5.97 = *CPG* 1:269.

7. Clouston (1887) 2:440–441.

8. Clouston (1887) 2:439–440.

9. Stratonicus was a famous musician who lived at the time of Alexander the Great. Since the allusion is Greek rather than Roman and fits the time of Diphilos better than that of Plautus, the present scene with its building of aircastles presumably goes back to Diphilos (Marx 1959:172–173).

10. *Rudens* 926–937.

11. Clouston (1887) 2:443.

12. Lucian *Navigium* 11–15.

13. *Navigium* 22.

14. *apud reges rex perhibebor* (*Rudens* 931); μονονουχὶ βασιλεὺς νομιζόμενος (*Navigium* 13).

Fortune in Salt ☙ Fortune in Water

A youthful merchant sells a shipload of salt in a saltless land, earns a fortune, and marries a princess.

This tale, AT 1651A, *Fortune in Salt*, belongs to a cluster of tales in which the principal idea is that a character who possesses something rather ordinary finds himself haply in a place where the item, because of its usefulness and unfamiliarity, is extremely valuable. In anglophone countries the most familiar tale of this sort is AT 1651, *Whittington's Cat*, in which a poor youth inherits or otherwise acquires a cat, takes it to a mice-plagued country in which cats are unknown, and sells it for a fortune. The story is found as early as the thirteenth century but became attached particularly to Richard Whittington, a mayor of London who died in 1423.[1] *A Fortune in Salt* has been collected in several European lands and as far east as India.

In a nineteenth-century Russian folktale, a merchant had three sons, of whom the youngest was Ivan the Fool. The father loaded two ships with precious cargo and sent them to foreign lands in the charge of his two elder sons. When Ivan begged to be sent abroad and earn money, his father dispatched him on a ship with a load of the cheapest possible merchandise, wood. Ivan came to an island with a mountain containing pure Russian salt, so that he cast the wood overboard and took on a cargo of salt. Then he sailed to a wealthy city where, as it happened, salt was unknown, demonstrated to the king the wonderful savor of salt, and sold his load of salt for an equal amount of gold and silver. After a number of other adventures he returned home and married a princess.[2]

In a nineteenth-century Sicilian folktale retold by Italo Calvino, a man and a woman once had a child, and they were very devoted to St. Michael the Archangel, observing his feast-day every year. The man died, and eventually the woman was so poor that she sold her son to the king. So the boy, whose

name was Peppi, grew up in the palace with the king's daughter, who was the same age, and in time they fell in love. The king's counselors, attempting to head off a marriage between the two, advised the king to dispatch Peppi as a merchant on an old, rundown ship and leave him alone in the middle of the sea to drown. The king liked the idea and informed Peppi that he must sail as a merchant and had three days to load his ship. Since the youth had no idea what kind of cargo to take on, he called upon St. Michael, who instructed him to load his ship with salt. So Peppi sailed out to sea, where the captain deserted him, and Peppi's boat began to sink. He called upon St. Michael, who brought Peppi and his boat safely to a port. The local king invited Peppi and his companion to dine with him. St. Michael informed Peppi that the people of that land were unacquainted with salt, so Peppi brought some along in a little sack. He found that the local dishes were as bland as straw, so he added an amount of salt to them and thereby won over the king, who purchased his entire load of salt for its weight in gold. Peppi returned home, and after several more adventures of the same sort, he wed the princess.[3]

Aphrodite of Dexikreon

An ancient Greek legend told by the inhabitants of Samos is constructed upon the same idea as the sale of salt except that the cargo is water. The story is known only from Plutarch's *Greek Questions*, a work in which the author poses a series of questions about puzzling features of Greek culture and suggests one or more answers to each question. In the present case he asks what is the reason why people on Samos invoke "Aphrodite of Dexikreon." Plutarch offers two possible explanations, of which only the second will concern us.

Is it because (Plutarch asks) a shipowner named Dexikreon sailed to Cyprus on business and, when he was going to load his ship, Aphrodite instructed him to load it only with water and to set sail immediately? He did so, loading the ship with a great amount of water and sailing off. When the sea became calm and windless and the other merchants and shipowners were thirsty, he sold them his water and amassed much money. So he had an image of the goddess made, which he named "Aphrodite of Dexikreon." If this is the true reason (concludes Plutarch), Aphrodite evidently wished not so much to enrich one man as to save the lives of many through one man.[4]

The merchant takes on a cargo of something ordinary and inexpensive, in this case water, and sells it for a fortune to persons who have a great need or desire for it. As in the Italian tale, a supernatural helper (Aphrodite/St. Michael) instructs the hero to take on the unusual cargo and advises him in general. The Greek legend, at least as Plutarch relates it for his present purpose, is quite simple compared to the Russian and Sicilian stories. There is no father, no older brother or ill-disposed counselor, no princess as bride. No event precedes the instructions of the supernatural helper to the hero to take on a particular cargo. From the viewpoint of the modern texts summarized above, it is a slice cut from the middle of the story. Perhaps it is a developmentally early form of the type that we know, or perhaps it is a special development of the type.

In any case, for the Samians it was a religious legend that related a miracle attributed to Aphrodite and provided an aition for a particular image of the

goddess.[5] For Plutarch the story illustrates the goddess's compassion for persons whose lives are threatened. Dexikreon acted only as her agent in this matter, and his becoming wealthy from the sale of water was merely a byproduct of her scheme to save the lives of stranded seamen. A concern for sailors lay within the divine sphere of Aphrodite, since she was a goddess not only of the erotic but also of seafaring.

An idea remotely similar to a monopoly on salt or water lies behind the well-known anecdote of Thales and the olive presses. Since the philosopher Thales himself was poor, people taunted him, saying that philosophy was useless. So the philosopher, deducing from his knowledge of astronomy that there would be a large crop of olives, placed deposits on all the olive presses in Miletos and Chios, using a small amount of money. When demand for them became great, he leased them out at his own price and made much money, showing that philosophers could easily become wealthy if they should choose to do so.[6]

Sarapis and Syrion

A fragment of a Greek papyrus from Egypt dating from the second century of our era contains a narrative of a miracle (*aretê*) of the god Helios-Zeus-Sarapis, which bears the title "The Miracle of Zeus-Helios, great Sarapis, concerning Syrion the pilot."[7] Apart from the title, only the conclusion of the story is preserved:

> He said, "Thanks to you (*dia se*) I will bestow the water upon the people of Pharos." And having waved goodbye he sailed away, gave the water to the people of Pharos, and received from them in compensation one hundred drachmas of silver.
> This miracle is registered in the libraries of Mercurium. Let those who are present say: "There is one Zeus Sarapis."

Evidently the god provides the mariner Syrion with water, thanks to which Syrion is able to supply the inhabitants of Pharos with water, for which he is paid handsomely. Something in the events must be wondrous, or it would not have been recorded as a miracle of the god. The editors of the papyrus speculate that the water probably had healing properties or some other miraculous quality, but the water may simply be fresh water.[8] If the story of the sailor Syrion was more or less parallel to that of the sailor Dexikreon, then *A Fortune in Water* (as we may call it) must have been a migratory story in the area of the ancient Aegean, a religious legend in which a deity arranges for a sailor to take on a load of water and sell it at great profit to persons in need of it on a particular occasion, after which the mariner piously honors the deity.

Lit. (AT 1651A, *Fortune in Salt*.) Halliday 1928:204–205. Ashliman, type 1651A.

1. BP 2:69–76; Liungman 1961:325–326; Ashliman, type 1651.
2. Afanas'ev 1975:40–44 = Thompson 1974:420–423.

3. Calvino (1979) 2:719–723, no. 173.
4. *Moralia* 303A = Perry 433.
5. Compare the Ephesian legend of a miracle attributed to Apollo and attached to an altar for Apollo of the Vultures; see "Quest For a Vanished Princess."
6. Aristotle *Politics* 1259a9; Diogenes Laertius 1.26; Cicero *De Divinatione* 1.49.111.
7. *Oxyrhynchus Papyrus* 1382.
8. Halliday 1928: 205.

Frog King ⚘ Roman Proverb

A frog in a well allows a princess to draw water (or the like) in exchange for her promise to take him as her companion (or husband). Presently the frog appears at her home and holds her to her promise. She complies, willingly or unwillingly, taking the frog to her bedroom and thereby disenchanting the creature, who in reality is a prince. (The story may continue with additional adventures.)

This tale is AT 440, *The Frog King, or Iron Henry*. The tale of the frog who is really an enchanted prince is especially well known to readers today, in part because it stands as the first tale in the classic collection of the Grimms and in part because it lends itself to so well to parody.[1]

A Roman Proverb

Although the story of *The Frog King* is not attested in ancient literature, several scholars have seen a possible allusion to it in an utterance made by a character in Petronius's *Satyrica*. The parvenu Trimalchio says, referring to himself: "Sic amicus vester, qui fuit rana, nunc est rex" (So your friend who once was a frog is now a king). "Qui fuit rana, nunc est rex" (He who once was a frog is now a king), with its alliteration of *rana* and *rex*, was probably a proverbial expression.[2] The proverb may allude to *The Frog King* or to a similar tale among the Romans, but if it does we know no more of it. The evidence allows no certain conclusion.[3]

There are also other proverbial expressions in Petronius that may allude to recognizable folktales: "If you were anywhere else, you'd say that there were baked pigs walking around here" (see "Schlaraffenland"), and "He could trim the claws of a kite in flight" (see "Three Brothers").

Lit. (AT 440, *The Frog King or Iron Henry.*) Otto 1890:294, no. 1505. Crusius 1889:46. Friedländer 1910:534. BP 1:1–9. Liungman 1961:102–103. Opie and Opie 1974: 183–187. Röhrich 1979. Scherf 1982:133–138. *EM* 5:410–424. Ashliman, type 440.

1. Legman 1971:443; Röhrich 1979.
2. Petronius *Sat.* 77.6. Otto 1890:294.
3. Nineteenth-century scholars often assumed that the presence of a characteristic motif implied the existence of a whole tale, whereas later scholars have been more conservative in this regard; cf. Taylor 1940:22.

Frozen Words

The weather is so cold that words freeze immediately upon utterance and are not heard until a fire melts them or until they thaw naturally in the warm air of a new season.

This tall tale, which is also told of animal sounds, music, and other phenomena, is classified as AT 1889F, *Frozen Words (Music) Thaw*. The basic idea can be realized in numerous ways.

In the fifth chapter of *The Adventures of Baron Münchhausen*, first published in 1785, the baron relates that, while traveling by carriage in Russia, he bade his postilion give a horn signal in order that other travelers might not block a narrow passage. The man blew with all his might, but he could not make the horn sound. Later, when the party arrived at an inn, the postilion hung his horn on a peg near the kitchen fire, and presently the horn began to sound, for the tunes had been frozen inside. The company thus were entertained by several melodies from the horn without the postilion's putting his mouth to it.[1]

A Spanish narrator similarly tells of being in a country in which the winter was so cold that words froze as they left people's mouths, so that people had to stand by the fire in order to understand one another.[2] A black male from Philadelphia boasted that he had "seen it so cold that a nigger talked and it took him two weeks to thaw out the words."[3] In a Canadian tale a farmer called to his pigs from his back door on a cold winter morning, but it was so cold that his words froze in the air. In the spring when the words thawed out, the pigs heard them and came home.[4]

Antiphanes' Tall Tale

The tall tale of the frozen words is first found in Plutarch's essay *Progress in Virtue*, where it is credited to a certain Antiphanes: "Antiphanes said jokingly that there was a certain city in which, because of the cold, all the words froze as soon as they were uttered, and then later as the words thawed in the summer the people heard what they had conversed about during the winter."[5]

The saying attributed to Antiphanes, at least in the form in which Plutarch reports it, is not strictly a story, since it describes a recurrent phenomenon rather than a particular event. But Antiphanes' original words probably did take the form of a story; indeed, if he adopted the pose that many tellers of tall tales employ, he narrated the event in the first person with apparent seriousness as being a true occurrence that he himself had witnessed and could vouch for.[6] We do not have the context of Antiphanes' original narration. Our own source, Plutarch, gives the utterance a double frame. In the immediate frame, Plutarch reports that one of Plato's companions cited Antiphanes' witticism about frozen words, saying that the same thing was true of the doctrines that Plato taught his youthful listeners, for only much later when they were old men, if even then, did they perceive the point of what Plato had said. In the larger frame, Plutarch employs the witticism and the Platonist's metaphoric use of it in order to emphasize his point about differences between mature philosophers and beginners in the study of philosophy.

The Antiphanes mentioned by Plutarch is likely to be Antiphanes of Berge, who seems to have lived in the fourth century, rather than the fourth-century comic poet Antiphanes.[7] Antiphanes of Berge became in fact a byword for the telling of lies. Strabo refers to him, together with Pytheas and Euhemeros, as liars by trade, and there was even an adjective *bergaios* "fanciful, having the attributes of a tall tale" and a verb *bergaizein*, that is, "to bergize," meaning "to say nothing truthful," derived from Antiphanes' birthplace Berge, a town in Thrace on the Strymon.[8] If this was the same man as the Antiphanes whom Antonios Diogenes drew upon for his novel *The Wonders beyond Thule*,[9] then Antiphanes of Berge probably wrote a fabulous account of a journey to the North, earning for himself a reputation as a great liar. Like Baron Münchhausen's travels in Russia, this sort of work would provide the kind of context in which one might expect to find the tale of the frozen words.[10]

There is no reason to assume that Antiphanes' tall tale was original with him, since it is unwarranted to identify the earliest attestation of a traditional tale as the archetype simply because it is the first published text we happen to have. It is similarly unwarranted to assume with McCartney and others that all subsequently published tellings of the tale go back directly or indirectly to Antiphanes, although some of them obviously do, since a few writers cite Antiphanes or Plutarch or a variation on Plutarch's inner frame, such as that men do not hear good advice when they are young since they are indifferent, but only when they are mature.[11]

Lit. AT 1889F, *Frozen Words (Music) Thaw*. BP 4:119. Weinreich 1942. McCartney 1953a. Vidossi 1955:7–8. Bond 1971:227–228. Ben-Amos 1976:40–41 n. 3. Ashliman, type 1889F. *EM* 5:846–849.

1. Raspe 1971:40–42.
2. Chevalier 1983:419.
3. Abrahams 1970:253.
4. McCartney 1953a:171, citing H. Halpert, "Tall Tales and Other Yarns from Calgary, Alberta," *California Folklore Quarterly* 4 (1945): 43. A somewhat similar tale relates how a person cheerfully revives after being inadvertently frozen by his forgetful friends, or even how old persons are deliberately frozen for the winter in order to save on scarce food, and then thawed out in the spring (Randolph 1993:107–109, 206–207).
5. Plutarch *Moralia* 79A.
6. For ego-narration and/or the tall tale see further Perry 1967:325–329; Thomas 1977:12–13; Brown 1987:17–22; *EM* 7:10–15; Brown and Rosenberg 1998:643–645.
7. Weinreich 1942:6–30.
8. Strabo 2.3.5; Stephanos of Byzantium, s.v. *Berge*.
9. The original novel is lost, but its contents are summarized by Photios in his *Bibliotheca* (166).
10. Weinreich 1942:12.
11. McCartney 1953:171–172. Weinreich (1942) traces the literary history of the tale in detail.

Gifts of the Little People ≋ Pandaros and Echedoros

A handicapped man (usually hunchbacked) traveling at night comes upon a group of supernatural beings (fairies, elves, dwarves, witches) who are singing and dancing, and he good-naturedly joins them (or they ask to cut his hair and shave him, and he complacently lets them). In return for his good company (or

the like) they cure his handicap (e.g., remove his hump). Learning of this, a similarly handicapped man tries to repeat the experience, joining the same supernatural beings, who are engaged in the same activity as before. Because of his greed (discourtesy, poor musical performance, etc.), however, they are displeased and add to his handicap (e.g., give him the first man's hump). Sometimes the supernatural beings give the first man gold, and the second man coal.

This story, told sometimes as a folktale and sometimes as a legend, is AT 503, *The Gifts of the Little People*.

According to a Spanish tale, a hunchbacked man heard some small voices singing: "Lunes y martes y miércoles, tres" (Monday and Tuesday and Wednesday, three), which he continued by singing: "Jueves y viernes y sábado, seis" (Thursday and Friday and Saturday, six). The fairies were so pleased with this that they removed his hump and sent him away with honor. Learning of this, another hunchback, who was a stupid fellow, joined the fairies in the same way, but when they were singing their song he added: "Y domingo, siete" (And Sunday, seven). The indignant fairies, presumably angry at the breach of rhythm and rhyme, gave him a shower of blows and sent him away after having added the first man's hump to the one he already had. Whence "Y domingo, siete" is a Spanish proverbial expression for inappropriate speech or action.[1]

In a nineteenth-century German tale from Halle, a tailor and a goldsmith were journeying together one evening when they heard distant music, which proved to be a group of little men and women singing and dancing merrily. Their leader invited the two men to join them, and they did so. At one point the leader took a sharp knife, whereupon the two men became frightened, although they had little time to reflect, and then he quickly cut off the two men's hair and beard, after which he treated them in a friendly way as if to say that the two men had done well in not resisting. Finally, the leader indicated that the men might fill their pockets with coal, if they wished. After doing so, the men continued their journey and found lodging for the rest of the night. In the morning they awoke to find that their pockets were full of gold rather than coal and that their hair and beards had been restored. But the greedy goldsmith, who was a hunchback, wanted more, whereas the mild-mannered tailor was satisfied with what he had. Taking along extra pouches, the goldsmith sought out the wee folk again that night, had the same experience, and filled his pouches with gold. But the next morning he found that the coal was only coal, and when he checked the previous night's treasure he found that it too was coal. Moreover, his hair had not grown back so that he was bald-headed and beardless, and in addition to the hump on his back he now had a second one on his chest. He recognized that he had been punished for his greed. The kind tailor shared some of his wealth with the goldsmith, but the latter had to live with his bald head and twin humps.[2]

In a tale from Japan, there were two old men who each had a cyst the size of a fist on their foreheads. Unhappy at being so unsightly, they went to a mountain shrine to ask the deities to remove the cysts. They prayed every night, and one night they heard the sound of music approaching the shrine. Five or six mischievous ogres (*tengu*) entered the shrine, making music but soon becoming bored since they knew no dances. When the *tengu* saw the humans, they

urged them to dance. Though frightened, one of the men danced merrily to the music and improvised a song. Delighted with his dancing, the *tengu* removed the ugly wen from his forehead. Then they made the other man dance, but he was so frightened that he scarcely could dance and he sang out of tune, until finally he fell down crying. The *tengu* were angry at his timidity so that they gave him the cyst they had removed from the first man, slapping it onto the top of his nose just below the one he already had. Now he was so ugly that no one ever wanted to look at him again.[3]

The oral story has two episodes, one in which a character is successful and one in which a second character, usually attempting the same action in order to gain the same reward, is not only unsuccessful but ends up in a worse condition than when he started. On an abstract level the story is identical with other stories built upon the notion of unsuccessful repetition, which is a common structural device in traditional narratives.[4] Since such stories are attested in antiquity, the device is a old one. For example, in the Greek fable of Hermes and the Woodcutter (see "Axe Falls into the Stream"), as also in *The Gifts of the Little People*, there are two successive encounters between mortal men and the supernatural, in which, as is often the case, the first man does not seek out the experience but happens upon it, whereas the second man seeks it out. Narratives of unsuccessful repetition vary in the ways in which they differentiate the two protagonists, ranging from a moral contrast between good and evil, as in the good-naturedness of the first man and the calculated greed of the second in the German tale and in the fable of Hermes and the Woodcutter, to a contrast of abilities, as in the talented and trusting man and the man with little rhythm or courage in the Spanish and Japanese texts. In the latter group the spirits, acting like amoral children, reward and punish mortals not for their moral qualities or their good intentions but purely for having added to or detracted from the festivities.

Pandaros and Echedoros

An ancient Greek version of *The Gifts of the Little People* is recorded on a stone tablet found in the ruins of an incubation sanctuary of the healing god Asklepios, near Epidauros.[5] There was a colonnade that served as a dormitory where persons seeking relief might sleep and hope to receive a therapeutic dream.[6] The stone is one of several inscribed tablets at the site that have survived into recent times, one of many that once were displayed in the sanctuary. They recorded cases of marvelous healing credited to the god, some set up by individual men and women who had been healed, and others, including a collection of testimonies, set up probably by the priests.

One of the tablets, dated to the late fourth or the third century B.C. and bearing the heading "Cures of Apollo and Asklepios," relates several miracles, including the following story, which it presents in two parts as two successive cases, each with its own title.[7]

> *Pandaros the Thessalian, who had marks on his forehead.* When Pandaros slept in the sanctuary he saw a vision. It seemed to him that Asklepios tied a headband onto him, covering the tattoos on his forehead, and told him to remove

it once he was outside the dormitory and to dedicate it as an offering in the temple. At daybreak Pandaros removed the headband, and his forehead had been cleared of its tattoos. He dedicated the headband, which bore the letters from his face, as an offering in the temple.

Echedoros, who got tattoos in addition to those he already had. Echedoros received from Pandaros an amount of money to dedicate to the god in Epidauros on Pandaros's behalf. But he did not render the money, and as he slept in the sanctuary he saw a vision. It seemed to him that the god stood above him and asked if he had any money from Pandaros as an offering for the temple. Echedoros said he had received no such thing from Pandaros, but if the god healed him he himself would dedicate a painted image of the god. Then Asklepios tied Pandaros's headband around the marks of Echedoros, telling him to remove the headband once he was outside the dormitory, wash his face in the fountain, and look at his reflection in the water. At daybreak Echedoros went outside and took off the headband, which no longer bore any letters. Looking at the water he saw that his face had gotten the tattoos of Pandaros in addition to the ones he already had.

As in *The Gifts of the Little People*, the ancient testimony tells of dealings between handicapped persons and the supernatural, structured as a mirror story of unsuccessful repetition. In both the ancient text and the modern story (1) a handicapped man encounters one or more supernatural beings at night and (2) wins their favor, so that (3) they grant him as a boon the removal of his handicap. Subsequently (4) a second man who is similarly handicapped seeks out the same spirits, but (5) he displeases them so that (6) rather than removing his handicap the beings give him also the first man's handicap.

A number of elements that are explicit in the oral texts are implicit in the terse Greek testimony. Presumably Pandaros resorts to Asklepios in the hope of ridding himself of the "marks" (στίγματα) on his forehead, probably certain words tattooed on him indicating his former status as a slave.[8] We may assume from the outcome that he wins the favor of the god, in part simply because he is an honest man, unlike Echedoros, who has the temerity to steal from the god at the same time as he seeks a favor from him.[9] The difference between Pandaros and Echedoros is therefore a moral one. Other testimonies represent Asklepios as powerful, as working his cures in a variety of ways (by dreams, by means of his sacred dogs, etc.), and as helping even skeptics; accordingly, we can conclude that he cures Pandaros, not as a reward for Pandaros's trust in him, but simply because the patient has come to him with honest intent.

The ancient text differs from almost all other texts of the type in not representing the otherworldly power as a group of dancing or singing beings, perhaps because it is told here of the healer Asklepios and not, say, of carefree nymphs, or perhaps because the tale type had not yet developed this feature. The ancient story agrees with the modern tradition in the detail that the encounter and transformation take place at night, which in the case of the ancient testimony agrees well with the custom of incubation practiced at the sanctuaries of the healing god. It is remarkable that of all the modern texts it is the geographically distant Japanese story that most closely resembles the Greek, since in both texts the protagonist suffers from marks or growths on his forehead rather than the almost universal motif of the hump of the hunchback, and he piously makes his way to the temple of a god in order to seek a cure rather than

coming by chance upon supernatural beings. Possibly this represents a very ancient form of the story.

The coal that turns out to be gold or the gold that turns out to be coal does not figure in the ancient story, although the money that Pandaros asked Echedoros to give to the god, and that, when asked by Asklepios, Echedoros denies having, may be connected with this motif. Gold or treasure that turns out to be coal was a proverbial notion among Greeks and Romans. The Greeks said, "Our treasure has turned out to be coals," and the Romans, "We have found coal instead of treasure," both expressions referring to disappointed expectations.[10]

Lit. AT 503, *The Gifts of the Little People.* Clouston (1887) 1:352–372. BP 3:324–329. Wesselski 1925:207–208. Dawkins 1950:265–269, no. 25. Greverus 1958. Liungman 1961:120. *EM* 5:637–642. Ashliman, type 503.

1. Clouston (1887) 1:363–364.
2. Grimm 182.
3. Seki 1963:126–128, no. 36.
4. Cf. Greverus 1958:278; Dundes 1962b; *EM* 7:92–100. Tales of unsuccessful repetition are in turn a form of mirror construction, in which an episode reflects elements in the preceding episode (Greverus 1958:269).
5. Wesselski 1925:207–208.
6. On the site see Pausanias 2.26–28; Frazer (1898) 3:236–251, 5:570–579; LiDonnici 1995.
7. *IG* IV², 1, No. 121–122 (VI–VII); Edelstein and Edelstein (1945) 1:223, no. 423 (VI–VII); LiDonnici 1995:88–91, no. A6–A7.
8. For a full discussion see Perdrizet 1911; cf. LiDonnici 1995:91 n. 15.
9. As Perdrizet (1911:92) observes, the man's name is significant and appropriate: Echedorus = Gift-Keeper.
10. Zenobios 2.1; Diogeneianos 1.90. Phaedrus 5.6; Otto 1890:76, no. 350.

Girl as Helper 🪶 Jason and Medeia

A youth comes into the power of an ogre, who gives him a number of seemingly impossible tasks. But the ogre's daughter falls in love with the hero and helps him accomplish the tasks, after which youth and maiden flee. Pursued by the ogre, the lovers escape by throwing into the pursuer's path ordinary objects that become great natural obstacles ("obstacle flight") or by transforming themselves into various persons or things in order to deceive the ogre ("transformation flight"). After breaking a taboo, the youth magically loses his memory of his bride, but she causes it to be restored.

This folktale is AT 313C, *The Girl as Helper in the Hero's Flight.*[1] Paul Delarue has called it one of the longest, best composed, and most beloved of Indo-European tales, and because of its extreme popularity, its worldwide distribution, and its apparent antiquity, it has been the subject of considerable scholarly interest.[2] Grace Knopp studied over two hundred texts of the folktale (six literary versions from the eleventh to the seventeenth centuries, and 226 oral texts collected in the nineteenth and twentieth centuries) in connection with the ancient Greek legend of Jason and Medeia, so that much is known about the content, form, and distribution of the international oral tale.[3]

The narrative regularly begins by bringing the hero to the abode of an ogre

or ogress (giant, devil, witch, evil king, troll, etc.), who usually possesses supernatural powers. The hero's arrival is set up in quite different ways, such as a pact made by the youth or by his parents with the ogre (for example, a parent promises his child to an unknown being in return for a boon that he has received) or the hero's coming more or less by chance to the ogre's abode (he loses his way while hunting, he is out searching for adventure, etc.). The ogre now assigns the hero several tasks of superhuman difficulty, typically one a day for three days. Among the most common are to plow a field, plant a crop, and harvest it in a single day; subdue and ride (or drive) certain wild or fierce animals, which are usually the ogre and his family in disguise; fetch an object from a virtually inaccessible place such as the depths of a body of water or the top of a tower or tree; fell a forest in one day with inadequate tools (e.g., wooden tools); erect a certain kind of edifice overnight or from unlikely materials (e.g., feathers); empty a pond, sometimes with an inadequate vessel (e.g., a thimble or a sieve); move or level a mountain; clean a large stable that has not been cleaned for years.[4] Some narrators do not make it entirely clear why the ogre is entitled to assign tasks and why the hero is obliged to perform them, but this vagueness can also add an enjoyable atmosphere of mystery to the narrative. In any case, the ogre's daughter (or younger daughter, if he has several) becomes enamored of the hero and, endowed with magic powers of her own, she advises him each day on how to accomplish the forthcoming task, or she simply performs it herself. Upon the completion of the tasks, the ogre's daughter urges that they flee, sometimes explaining that her father intends to kill the hero in any case. Her father (and/or mother) pursues them, but the heroine effects transformations by means of her magic arts (for example, the fugitives become a lake with a boat on it) or creates obstacles (for example, she casts behind them a comb that becomes a forest) or, less often, diversions (for example, she casts berries that the pursuer pauses to gather) that delay her father and enable the couple to escape. The ogre gives up his pursuit or perishes. Arriving home and disobeying his bride's warning (e.g., not to kiss someone, not to eat something), often unwittingly, the youth instantly loses all memory of her. But the forgotten fiancee succeeds in regaining access to him and reawakening his memory of her (for example, she kisses him, she trains animals to recount the events of their courtship and flight), sometimes just as he is about to wed another, so that the two lovers are reunited.

Focusing as it does upon the crises of transition that in reality a young man and woman typically make in late adolescence, the story can be experienced in part as a metaphor for these common events. At some time a youth must leave his childhood home and find his own way in the world, deal with unkind masters and potential fathers-in-law in a manly way, and usually take a bride away from her parents' house. For her part a maiden ordinarily must transfer her primary loyalty from her parents to her husband, leave her childhood home to accompany him, and mediate between him and her possibly jealous or hostile parents, while the youth too must transfer his loyalty and thoughts from his family of origin to his new wife. In the oral tale, these features appear as extremes. The world outside the home is exotic and full of very dangerous and of very kindly persons. The maiden's parents are deceitful, inordinately hostile, and supernaturally powerful, wishing to destroy the young man openly or

cunningly, while the youth's own household is seductively domestic, happy to lull him into a forgetfulness of the bride he himself has chosen in his new independence. Dawkins points out that the mother's kiss as a cause of forgetfulness is a common feature in Greek folktales of this type, and suggests that it aptly symbolizes the youth's feeling for his early home life and for his parents which now must yield to a new set of relations with his wife.[5]

A striking feature of the folktale is the powerful role played by the maiden, whose resources are essential to the youth's success in dealing with and escaping from her parents, for the youth, however capable he may be, is no match for the ogre. Once the maiden decides to help the lad, she directs their partnership; indeed, in Scandinavian texts she is often called Mastermaid (*Mestermø*).[6] Although the hero is adventurous, the heroine has extraordinary powers waiting to be tapped for the right cause, which proves to be love.

A Mexican text will illustrate the type.[7] In a version collected in 1963 in Indiana from a mestizo who had learned it in his native Mexico, a magician named Don Juan and a clever cardplayer named Don Pedro met in a casino where Don Pedro lost everything to Don Juan, including his life. Thereupon the magician gave Don Pedro a horse that magically brought him to Don Juan's house. Don Juan ordered his daughter Blancaflor to prepare Don Pedro's bedchamber so that he would be in condition to undertake his first task on the following day. When Blancaflor saw that Don Pedro was handsome and agreeable, she felt sorry for him and warned him that her father would try to kill him. She gave him some powder to take when breakfast should be brought to him, so that he would not be burnt by it.

The next day Don Juan said that the first task he was giving Don Pedro in order for him to regain his liberty and life was to retrieve a certain ring at the bottom of the sea. When Don Pedro told Blancaflor of the seemingly impossible task, she turned into a mermaid and retrieved the ring.

The second day, after Don Pedro survived his second hot breakfast, his taskmaster told him he must construct a palace for Don Juan in twenty-four hours. When again Don Pedro informed Blancaflor of the task, she gave him a magic wand and instructions for its use. By dawn the palace was finished.

On the next day, after a third hot breakfast, Don Juan assigned the last task, after which Don Pedro might return home. When the youth informed Blancaflor that he was to tame a certain wild stallion, she explained that the stallion would be her father, the saddle her mother, other equipment her sisters, and she herself the bridle, and she instructed him how to use his spurs and whip in order to break the horse, which he did.

Don Juan then left word that Don Pedro was free to choose a horse and depart. On Blancaflor's advice he chose the least-promising horse, and the two fled in the dead of night. When Blancaflor's father discovered that they had left, he pursued them in the form of a bird. Seeing this, Blancaflor turned herself and the horse into a church and Don Pedro into a bell-ringer. The father reached the church and asked the bell-ringer if he had seen the youth and the maiden, but he received a useless answer so that he gave up the pursuit and returned home. When the man told his wife what had happened, she explained that the church and the bell-ringer were really the youth and the maiden.

So she herself turned into a heron and went after them, but Blancaflor threw

down her hairbrush, which turned into mountains. When the heron at last passed through the mountains, Blancaflor threw down her mirror, causing Don Pedro and the horse to become a lake and herself a fish.

The mother, unable to catch her daughter, uttered a curse to the effect that if the youth should allow any of his relatives to embrace him upon his return to his homeland, he would forget Blancaflor for at least seven years. When they reached Don Pedro's native city, he went ahead to prepare for her arrival. Although he told his family not to embrace him, one of his female relatives did so after he fell asleep, as a result of which he completely forgot about the girl. Having magical powers the maiden understood what had happened. She told her story to two pigeons, and years later, when the unknown girl was invited to the youth's house for a social occasion and was asked about her past, she had the two birds narrate her story. Reminded of their adventures, Don Pedro regained his memory of Blancaflor, and they were reunited.

Jason and Medeia

There are many similarities between *The Girl as Helper* and the ancient Greek legend of Jason and Medeia. According to the mythographer Apollodoros, King Pelias of Iolkos once ordered Jason, son of Aison and Polymede, to bring him the Golden Fleece, which was hanging from an oak tree in the Grove of Ares in Kolchis where it was guarded by a dragon that never slept. Jason had a ship constructed, the Argo, and embarked in the company of many other heroes; after a number of adventures the Argonauts reached Kolchis.

Jason explained his mission to King Aietes of Kolchis and asked him for the fleece, and Aietes promised to give it to him if he could single-handedly yoke two huge brazen-footed, fire-breathing bulls and with them sow a field with dragon's teeth. Jason was at a loss how he might yoke the bulls, but Aietes' daughter Medeia, who was a witch, became enamored of Jason and, fearing that the bulls might destroy him, promised to help him yoke the bulls and to hand over the fleece to him if he swore to marry her and take her back to Greece with him. When Jason so swore, Medeia gave him a substance that she instructed him to rub on his body and weapons, telling him that for one day thereafter neither fire nor iron could harm him. She explained, moreover, that after he had sown the teeth, armed men would spring up from the earth; when he saw them grouped together he should throw stones into their midst from a distance, and when they began to fight each other he should kill them. So Jason anointed himself with the drug, yoked the bulls, and sowed the teeth, whereupon armed men arose from the ground. Unnoticed he threw stones at them, and while they then fought with one another, he killed them. Nevertheless Aietes did not give Jason the fleece, for he wished to burn the Argo and kill its crew.

That night Medeia took Jason to the fleece, put the dragon to sleep with her drugs, took the fleece, and went to the Argo. She brought along her brother Apsyrtos. Aietes set out in pursuit of the ship, but Medeia killed her brother, cut him up limb from limb, and cast the pieces into the sea. Aietes gathered up the pieces, fell behind, and gave up the chase. But he dispatched other Kolchians to search for the Argo and bring Medeia back to him. Some of them eventually

found the Argo among the Phaiakians, whose ruler Alkinoos agreed to return Medeia to her father if she had not yet slept with Jason, but to give her to Jason if she had. But Alkinoos's wife Arete joined Medeia and Jason before this test, so that Medeia remained with Jason. Four months after they had set out, the Argonauts returned to Iolkos.

Upon their return, they found that Pelias had caused Jason's father Aison to take his own life, after which Jason's mother had also killed herself. Jason now gave Pelias the fleece and awaited an opportunity to get revenge. He asked Medeia to devise a plan. Medeia went to Pelias's palace, where she urged his daughters to cut up their father and boil the pieces, promising that she would make him young again by means of her drugs. To gain their confidence she cut up and boiled a ram, making it into a lamb. Believing her, the daughters cut up their father and boiled him, so that he perished at their hands. The inhabitants of Iolkos buried Pelias and expelled Jason and Medeia.

The couple went to Corinth, where they lived for ten years. King Kreon of Corinth betrothed his daughter Glauke to Jason, who set aside Medeia and married her. Medeia responded by sending the bride a magic robe that consumed her with fire and killed King Kreon as well when he tried to help her. Medeia herself fled.[8]

The story of Jason and Medeia is alluded to as early as Homer and Hesiod.[9] By the fifth century B.C. we possess accounts of or allusions to all the main features of the story, which seems to be essentially the same story as that known at least as early as Hesiod, so that the legend in more or less its familiar form was probably in circulation by 700 B.C., and likely long before that.[10]

From the nineteenth century onward scholars have commented upon correspondences (and differences) between *The Girl as Helper* and the Greek legend of Jason and Medeia. The agreement is especially impressive in the episodes of the Tasks, the Flight, and the Forgotten Bride. Most scholars have concluded that the Greek story is a form of the folktale that has been modified to accord with Greek thought and the genre of heroic legend.[11]

Like the folktale hero, Jason comes into the power of an ogre, in his case that of the wizard Aietes, son of the Sun, brother of the witch Kirke, and father of the witch Medeia. Aietes is a powerful, devious, and evil being who possesses monstrous creatures: terrifying bulls with which to plow his fields and a huge dragon that guards his treasure, the Golden Fleece. The tasks that Aietes gives Jason are reminiscent of tasks that are assigned the hero in many versions of the folktale. (1) Jason's yoking of Aietes' dangerous bulls is suggestive of the folktale hero's taming of one or more wild animals, which are sometimes the ogre himself and his family in disguise. Medeia helps him accomplish the task by providing him with a magic ointment that protects him from the flames, just as in the folktale the ogre's daughter reveals a particular trick or provides the hero with a whip or stick that subdues the wild animals.[12] (2) Jason's plowing Aietes' field, sowing dragon's teeth, and instantly producing a crop of armed men is the same as the folktale hero's task of plowing a field, planting it, and harvesting the crop all in one day.[13] Medeia helps Jason by warning him of the forthcoming crop of armed men and revealing how to overcome them, just as the ogre's daughter also helps her lover to perform his task. Though the task of raising a crop in one day is essentially identical in both legend and tale, the em-

phasis differs, for in the tale the point is the impossibility of planting and harvesting a crop in a single day, whereas in the legend the emphasis is upon the danger inherent in the plowing and in the deadly crop that results.[14]

In view of the fact that two of Jason's tasks are parallel to tasks commonly given to the hero of the folktale, (3) his third and principal mission of obtaining the Golden Fleece may be connected with another common task of the folktale hero, namely, to fetch an object from a certain lofty place such as a tower or a tree, for the Golden Fleece hangs from a tree in the Grove of Ares. The Greek legend, however, represents the difficulty for Jason as being the sleepless and powerful guardian of the Fleece, not the height at which the prize resides.[15]

Another motif of the legend may have a connection with one of the tasks commonly appearing in the oral tale. When the folktale hero's task is to fetch an object from the bottom of a body of water, the usual and rather bizarre solution is for the girl to instruct the youth to cut her into bits and throw the pieces into the body of water, from which she emerges whole with the desired object. The dismemberment of the maiden, casting the pieces of her into the water, and her return to life and reemergence with the object in hand have possibly been displaced to a later episode in the Jason legend and reinterpreted, becoming instead the dismemberment of Aison, casting the pieces of him into the cauldron, and his return to life as a young man.[16] For there was a tradition, attested as early as the *Nostoi*, according to which Medeia rejuvenated Aison in her cauldron, presumably after cutting him up and doubtless in order to illustrate the wondrous process for the benefit of Pelias's daughters so that they might be persuaded to subject their father to the same treatment, as in the (to us) more familiar version in which she first rejuvenated a ram; and there was a similar tradition, attested in literature and art, in which she cut up and rejuvenated Jason.[17] If the sequence has been displaced, the objective of the submersion has been reinterpreted from capturing something external to oneself to recapturing a part of oneself, one's youth. Part of the sequence can also be seen in the episode of the dismemberment of Apsyrtos, who is cut into pieces and cast into the sea but, like the dismembered Pelias, does not return to life. The gory motif of dismemberment reappears several times in different episodes and versions of the legend, evidently displaced from its usual site in the international tale and assigned a different function in the legend.

In the folktale the episode of the flight is usually but not always a magic flight. The most common device is for the girl magically to transform herself and her lover temporarily into something else in order to disguise themselves, or to cast behind them ordinary objects that magically become great obstacles, or to effect a mixture of transformation and obstacle. Less commonly, the heroine resorts to other devices such as to cast behind objects that merely arouse the pursuer's interest or cupidity ("diversion flight"): while the pursuer pauses to examine or gather them, the lovers make their escape.[18] The objects themselves can be virtually anything, such as food, tools, stones, even live animals. This is Medeia's strategy when she cuts up her brother Apsyrtos and scatters his limbs in the water before her pursuing father, causing him to pause in order to pick up the pieces of his son. Since the diversion flight is attested in the tradition of *The Girl as Helper*, it is not necessary to regard its appearance in the Greek legend as a rationalized form of the similar and more usual obstacle flight.[19] While Medeia's scattering the members of her brother in the water

serves functionally as a diversion to delay her pursuers, the unusual form that the diversion takes—pieces of a dismembered body—is probably inspired by the folktale task that entails the dismemberment of a character and the casting of her bodily parts into water.

Finally, Jason forsakes Medeia for another bride. Though his action occurs years after the lovers' escape from Aietes, it answers to the behavior of the folktale hero, who magically forgets his bride.[20] The most interesting difference between the legend and the folktale in this episode is, not how much time passes before the hero deserts his helper, but the nature of the forgetting or desertion. The folktale hero forgets his bride literally; the legend hero, metaphorically. For whereas the former magically loses his memory of his lover and prepares to wed another bride, the latter behaves *as though* he has lost his memory of Medeia when he sets her aside without cause and prepares to wed Glauke. In *The Girl as Helper* the girl eventually disenchants the youth, reminding him of their ties and preventing his remarriage, so that the tale ends happily. But in the Greek story (in Euripides' *Medeia*, for example), where there is no magic spell to break, Medeia can only remind Jason of their ties as though he has suddenly and unaccountably forgotten them, and when this action proves ineffective she magically destroys the new bride, so that the legend ends tragically for all concerned. So the hero's forgetfulness appears in a rationalized, or disguised, form in the Greek story, but it is nonetheless present.

Lit. AT 313C, *The Girl as Helper in the Hero's Flight*, followed by the episode of *The Forgotten Fiancée*. Lang 1970:87–102. Cosquin (1887) 2:9–28. Friedländer (1910) 1:539; (1913) 4:198. Meuli 1921:5. Krappe 1925. Christiansen 1927. Aarne 1930. Knopp 1933. Liljeblad 1935. Sydow 1948:192, 210–212, 216–217, 232–240. Vries 1954:84–98. *HDM* 1:311–314. Swahn 1959. BP 4:113. Delarue (1957) 1:234–241. Longo 1984. *EM* 1:963–972; 3:655–657; 9:13–19. Scherf 1982:138–141. Ashliman, type 313. Goldberg 1989:329–336; 1992. Moreau 1994:255–256.

Theseus and Ariadne

Whereas many investigators have perceived that the story of Jason and Medeia is a form of *The Girl as Helper*, few have seen that the same is true for the story of Theseus and Ariadne.[21] Its course of action, however, essentially parallels that of the Jason legend: (1) a youth goes to the land of a hostile king, (2) who intends to do away with him; (3) the king's daughter becomes enamored of the youth, (4) helps him to perform a superhuman task, and (5) flees with him; (6) the youth abruptly abandons her.

The earliest continuous narratives of the story of Theseus and Ariadne are found in the history of Diodorus Siculus, Plutarch's *Life of Theseus*, and the mythological handbook of Apollodoros, though the story is alluded to as early as Homer, who mentions the attempted flight of Theseus and Ariadne from Crete to Athens.[22] Apollodoros's account goes as follows.[23]

Theseus, son of Aigeus and Aithra, journeyed to Athens where his father, King Aigeus, recognized him as his son. In those days Athens was obliged to send seven youths and seven maidens to King Minos of Crete to be food for the Minotaur, which lived confined in a labyrinth. Theseus either volunteered

or was chosen to be among the youths making up the current year's tribute. Before he departed, Aigeus told him that if he should return alive he should change the black sails of the ship to white. When he reached Crete, Minos's daughter Ariadne became enamored of him and offered to help him if he agreed to marry her and take her back with him to Athens. Theseus swore to do so. Ariadne then asked the builder of the labyrinth, Daidalos, to reveal to her the way out. At Daidalos's suggestion she gave Theseus a clew of thread as he entered the labyrinth. Theseus fastened one end of it to the door and drew the rest along after him. Encountering the Minotaur in the innermost part of the labyrinth he killed him with his fists and then found his way out again by means of the thread. That night Theseus, Ariadne, and the others fled by ship to Naxos. There, however, Dionysos fell in love with Ariadne, took her away, and begot children with her. Because of his grief at the loss of Ariadne, Theseus forgot to change the sails to white. From the acropolis Aigeus saw the black sails of the ship and, supposing Theseus to have perished, threw himself down from the heights. Theseus succeeded his father as king of Athens.

Like Jason, Theseus comes into the power of an ogrous monarch, in this case King Minos of Crete, who like his counterpart in the Jason legend is a master of monsters. Happily, the ogre's daughter Ariadne falls in love with Theseus and promises her help, which proves to be essential to Theseus's survival, just as Medeia's help is crucial to Jason's success. In Apollodoros's telling, Theseus's task is only implicit: if he should overcome the Minotaur and escape from the labyrinth, he might survive. Of course, one would then expect Minos simply to put him and his companions to death in another way, and in any case the hated subjection of Athens to Crete with its periodic tribute of human food for the Minotaur would continue as before. But there was also a tradition according to which Theseus's task, like Jason's, was explicit. The fifth-century logographer Hellanikos reports that Minos came personally to Athens to select the victims and chose Theseus first of all; the victims were to carry no weapons, and if the Minotaur should be slain the tribute would cease.[24] In this case, then, Minos explicitly assigns Theseus a task with stated conditions, a task that appears to be impossible but could conceivably be accomplished.

Theseus's escape from the labyrinth is managed by Ariadne. Just as her father is no wizard she herself is no witch, so that the solution to the problem of the labyrinth is one of cleverness rather than of magic. She gives Theseus a ball of thread that he is to tie to the door as he enters, unraveling it as he proceeds inside and rewinding it as he retraces his steps. Theseus's task is not reminiscent of any task that is typical of *The Girl as Helper*, although it is familiar from other folk-narrative contexts.[25]

Just what is the "labyrinth" that houses the monster and threatens to imprison Theseus? The Greek word referred either to a large building of intricate or confusing design or to a maze in the strict sense. The former signification is the earlier attested.[26] Different etymologies have been suggested for the word, the best-known being that which derives *labyrinthos* from *labrys* "double axe" + locative suffix *-inthos,* in which case the word originally signified Place of the Double Axe, a doubly apt designation for Minos's palace at Knossos, since the palace was a religious center in a culture in which the double axe was an important cultic artifact and since the palace itself was rambling and huge—over

10,000 square meters.[27] The labyrinthine palace at Knossos evidently became a metaphor for any structure whose complexity or unclear structure might be confusing, and then by a further extension the word came to be the term for a formal maze. Legend seems to have followed philology here, for the labyrinthine palace at Knossos becomes in the Theseus tradition a true maze. In the classical period Knossos issued coins showing a maze on one side, and the legend was frequently illustrated in Roman times and later by means of a maze featuring Theseus and the Minotaur in the center. Formal mazes are attested in Greece as early as around 1200 B.C.[28] Oddly, however, Greek mazes were unicursal, having only one route. The passage from the entrance to the center and back again was winding and lengthy and might reverse directions, but for the traveler there were no multiple choices, no false solutions, no dead-ends. While one might lose heart, one could not really get lost in such a maze, since if one proceeded in one direction one would inevitably reach the center, and if in the other direction, the exit. In the context of ancient Greece the motif of Ariadne's thread makes better sense if Minos's labyrinth is a labyrinthine building that offers many confusing options for a person making his way in or out, rather than a unicursal maze, for which a person would require no clew of thread.[29]

We hear nothing of King Minos pursing the fugitives, and certainly of no diversion flight as in the Jason legend, only that Theseus cut holes in the bottom of the Cretan ships in order to prevent their pursuing him.[30] But of the episode of the Forgotten Fiancee we have more than ample indication, for nearly all the ancient authorities report that Theseus abruptly separates from Ariadne, though the authors do not agree on the details. In his *Life of Theseus* Plutarch assembles a host of versions of the event, remarking on their inconsistency with one another: Theseus deserted Ariadne after which she hanged herself; or sailors brought her to Naxos where she wed a priest of Dionysos; or, according to Hesiod, Theseus left Ariadne after falling in love with Aigle; or Theseus had two sons by Ariadne; or Theseus set the pregnant Ariadne ashore at Cyprus, after which he himself was driven back to sea by a storm and the deserted Ariadne died in childbirth; or there were two Ariadnes, one wed Dionysos on Naxos and the other retired to Naxos after Theseus carried her off and then deserted her.[31] He does not mention the version alluded to by Homer, according to which Artemis, acting upon the indictment of Dionysos, slew Ariadne on the island of Dia while Theseus and Ariadne were on their way from Crete to Athens.[32] Theokritos says that Theseus forgot Ariadne, and the scholiast on the passage explains that it was Dionysos's will that Theseus forget her and that the event took place on Dia, now called Naxos.[33] Diodorus Siculus, also identifying Dia with Naxos, says that when Theseus and Ariadne put in at the island, Dionysos took her for his own wife because of her beauty, which greatly distressed Theseus; elsewhere he says that Dionysos appeared in a dream to Theseus on Naxos, threatening him if he should not abandon Ariadne; the youth sailed off in fear, and the god led the maiden away that night.[34] According to Ovid, Theseus cruelly abandoned her on the shore of Dia, after which Bacchus came and embraced the weeping maiden.[35] And so on. Nearly every source agrees that, voluntarily or involuntarily, Theseus suddenly abandons Ariadne or Ariadne suddenly leaves him. The explanations vary, but the ancient sources insist upon the fact of an abrupt separation.

In this thicket of variation we need only observe that Theseus deserts Ariadne as abruptly as Jason leaves Medeia, each youth acting *as though* he has suddenly forgotten the ties that should bind him to his helper. This sudden (and sometimes poorly motivated) separation of the hero and heroine seems best understood as a rationalization of the magical loss of memory of the heroine that the folktale hero experiences after the breaking of the tabu. Close traces of this feature are evident in the Theseus tradition. The poet Theokritos states outright that Theseus forgot Ariadne, and his commentator explains that the loss of memory was of supernatural origin (the god Dionysos caused it). And several authors (for example, Apollodoros, Diodorus Siculus, Pausanias) inform us that Theseus in his distress at losing Ariadne *forgot* to change the sails of the tribute ship from black to white. Here the hero's forgetfulness appears to be displaced from being the cause of the desertion to being its consequence.[36]

In sum, the evidence points to both the legend of Jason and Medeia and the legend of Theseus and Ariadne being early reflexes of *The Girl as Helper*, with which they share the same overall plot. Of the two legends, the content of the story of Jason and Medeia is closer to that of the folktale as we know it, notably in the episodes of the Tasks and the Flight, and for this reason it attracted the notice of folktale scholars already in the nineteenth century. Nevertheless, the legend of Theseus and Ariadne is closer to the folktale in several other respects, especially in the motif of the hero's abrupt loss of memory in connection with the episode of the Forgotten Fiancée.

Each Greek variant has developed in its own direction. The Iolkan legend displays a sharper contrast between Greeks and ogres: the Colchian royal family is remote, treacherous, capable of magic, and given to unusual violence. In contrast, in the Athenian legend the Greeks and the Cretans are essentially the same sort of people, though the Cretan royal house has its own style, being inclined to sexual perversity (resulting in the hybrid Minotaur) and intellectualism (the labyrinth). Both legends are biographical, tracing each hero from birth to death, and altogether they bring together a number of stories in a rather loose, episodic structure. The legend of Jason and Medeia is especially drawn out, since the voyage to Colchis is intertwined with the story of the Argonauts, essentially an independent story that has little to do with the events at Colchis;[37] and Jason's abandonment of Medeia is so postponed that it takes place years after the couple's escape. Both of the ancient narratives are legends set in the Greek heroic past rather than folktales set in a vague and timeless past; accordingly, they are connected with particular traditional characters and specific geographic places, employ magic sparingly, and conclude tragically rather than happily for the hero and heroine.

Lit. AT 313C, *The Girl as Helper in the Hero's Flight*, followed by the episode of *The Forgotten Fiancée*. Lang 1910.

Herakles Cleans the Augean Stables

One of the best-known stories attached to Herakles tells how in one day he removed the dung from King Augeias's cattle yard, which had not been cleaned in years. The task of cleaning in only one day stables that have not been cleaned for many years or that house a great number of animals is a traditional

idea in oral narrative. It is among the tasks sometimes assigned to the hero in *The Girl as Helper*.[38]

Thus, in a Scottish text of the folktale the hero, called Nicht Nought Nothing, came into the power of a giant, who announced that he had work for Nicht Nought Nothing on the following day. There was a stable seven miles long and seven miles broad, and it had not been cleaned for seven years. He must clean it tomorrow, or the giant would have him for his supper. The next day the lad tried to clean the stable, but as he cleaned a bit out, it fell in again. The giant's daughter, saying she would help him, cried to the beasts of the field and the fowl of the air, and in a minute they cleared away everything in the stable.[39] In another Scottish text the hero was given three tasks, the last of which was to clear a stable where two hundred horses had stood for two hundred years, and to find in it a golden needle that the ogre's grandmother had lost there a thousand years before. The ogre's daughter possessed a box containing thousands of fairies, by means of which she helped the youth perform the tasks.[40]

In a Norwegian text of AT 313 collected in the 1840s, the young hero came to the manor of a troll and entered the troll's service. As his task for the first day the troll ordered him to shovel out the stable. The young man thought that work would be easy enough. But the troll's daughter revealed to him that if he should shovel the way people usually do, ten shovelfuls would come in for every one the youth threw out. She showed him that the way to do it was to turn the dung fork upside-down and shovel with the handle, after which the dung would fly out by itself. The lad followed the girl's advice, and presently the stable was as clean as if he had scrubbed it.[41]

In a text of the same type collected from a Hungarian gypsy in 1948, the hero, Handsome András, was ordered to curry three filthy horses in the stable and clear away their dung. His heart sank when he learnt that he was assigned such work, but he went at it. Taking a shovel he began mucking out the stable, working so hard that the sweat trickled down his body in seventy-seven streams. But the faster he shoveled, the more muck there was. Finally he sat down and began to weep in despair. How could he stop the three horses from their endless defecating? Then one of the horses spoke to him, telling him to prop the shovel and the broom against the wall upside-down, and when he turned around he would find the horses' coats gleaming and the stable well cleaned out. And so it happened.[42]

The motif of cleaning out the stables in one day is therefore a traditional "impossible task." The special difficulty may be expressed quantitatively by the great number of the animals, the immense size of the stables, and the many years since the place was last cleaned, or it may appear to be a simple task until the hero discovers that the more dung he shovels the more is produced. In short, an ordinary agricultural task is exaggerated into a stableboy's nightmare. The solutions vary. In the present texts the hero's helper calls upon the aid of a myriad animals or fairies to do the job on behalf of the hero, or instructs him simply to turn the shovel or broom upside-down, which by a kind of ironic magic brings about the desired result, a stableboy's dream.

The story of Herakles and King Augeias's stables or cattle yard is the earliest attested example of this impossible task in traditional narrative. I consider the versions of the historian Diodorus Siculus, the traveler Pausanias, and the mythographer Apollodoros, which are the earliest full accounts.[43]

According to Diodorus, Eurystheus gave Herakles as his Sixth Labor the task of cleaning the cattle yard of Augeias without the help of anyone else. The yard contained dung that had accumulated for many years. Eurystheus's motive in assigning the hero this kind of work was to insult him, but Herakles, rejecting the indignity of carrying dung on his shoulders, avoided the intended insult by directing the Alpheios to the yard. So he cleaned it by means of the stream, completing the job in one day. Herakles subsequently took up arms against Augeias because the latter had refused him his reward for the removal of the dung. Herakles was eventually successful in slaying Augeias and capturing his city, whereupon he recalled Augeias's son Phyleus from exile and handed the kingdom over to him. Phyleus had previously acted as an arbitrator between his father and Herakles, had decided for Herakles, and as a result had been exiled by his father.[44]

According to Pausanias, in his chapter on Elis, King Augeias was so wealthy in cattle and goats that most of his land lay idle from the dung produced by these animals. He persuaded Herakles, either for a portion of his kingdom or for some other reward, to cleanse his territory of the dung. Herakles then directed the stream of the Menios toward the dung. But Augeias refused to give him his payment on the ground that Herakles employed cleverness more than hard work. When Augeias's eldest son Phyleus disagreed with his father, saying that he was treating his benefactor unjustly, Augeias sent him into exile. But Herakles later captured Elis, looted it, and turned it over to Phyleus.[45]

According to Apollodoros, Eurystheus commanded Herakles as his Fifth Labor to carry out by himself and in a single day the dung of the cattle of Augeias. King Augeias of Elis was said variously to be the son of Helios or Poseidon or Phorbas. He had many herds of cattle. Herakles approached King Augeias and, without mentioning Eurystheus's command, offered to carry out the dung in one day if Augeias would give him a tenth of his cattle. Incredulous, Augeias agreed to do so. Having taken Augeias's son Phyleus as witness of the pact, Herakles made an opening in the cattle yard as well as an exit, and then diverted the nearby streams of the Alpheios and the Peneios into the yard. But when Augeias learned that Herakles had performed this task at the command of Eurystheus, he not only refused to give Herakles his payment but even denied that he had promised to do so, saying that he was prepared to submit the matter to arbitration. In the presence of the arbitrators Herakles summoned Phyleus, who testified against his father, declaring that Augeas had indeed agreed to pay him. Before the arbitrators voted, Augeias angrily ordered both Phyleus and Herakles out of Elis. Phyleus settled in Doulikhion. Herakles later captured Elis, killed Augeias, restored Phyleus, and gave him the kingdom.[46]

In the Greek legend, then, Herakles and King Augeias make a private agreement according to which Herakles will clean Augeias's cattle yard and Augeias will give him a certain payment. Herakles may also be performing the task on the orders of Eurystheus, as one of his prescribed Labors (Diodorus, Apollodoros), an obligation that he does not mention to Augeias, since he wishes to exact payment from him. Special conditions may be attached: Herakles is to have no help (Diodorus), and he must complete the task in a single day (Apollodoros; this condition was probably known also to Diodorus, since he records

that Herakles completes the task in one day).[47] The task is difficult because the dung has accumulated for many years (Diodorus) or because Augeias has many herds of cattle (Pausanias, Apollodoros). The Greek narrators, recounting the story as a legend rather than as a folktale, avoid the rounded or formulaic numbers that some of the folktale narrators employ. But Pausanias pushes the content almost to the limit of realism when he says that the problem is a matter not of neglected cattle yards but of an entire country that is so rich in herds that the accumulated dung has rendered the land useless! And in a poem of Theokritos that features Herakles visiting Augeias and conversing with Augeias's son Phyleus, the scene becomes virtually mythic. The poet emphasizes the thousands and thousands of cattle owned by Augeias, cattle beyond numbering, more herds than ten men wealthier than kings might be expected to possess. Helios granted to his son to be wealthy in cattle beyond all other men.[48]

The Greek hero solves the problem of removing the dung by himself and within one day by diverting one or two streams through the cattle yard. Interestingly, for Diodorus this is a trickster narrative: Herakles' cleverness in outwitting his taskmaster is more important than his physical feat of diverting a stream. Diodorus emphasizes that the task of removing dung is menial work, the sort of job that is proper more to stableboys than to heroes, and indeed Handsome András in the Hungarian text expresses the same attitude. For Diodorus the story neatly illustrates how Herakles fulfills his obligation while maintaining heroic dignity. The episode is illustrated on an imperfectly preserved metope from the Temple of Zeus at Olympia, but it is unclear whether the metope reflects a different version or merely represents the artist's solution to the difficulty of illustrating the present version, wherein the ancient written accounts are unanimous in having Herakles accomplish the task by diverting a stream through Augeias's property.[49] The fragmentary metope shows Herakles shoveling or employing a crowbar to the walls of the stable (the implement that he once held has not survived), while Athene looks on. In this version Athene may have acted as the hero's adviser, and the solution may possibly have been, as in some modern tales, the reversal of the implement.[50]

In any case Herakles succeeds, Augeias refuses payment for one reason or another, Augeias's son Phyleus testifies for Herakles and thereby incurs the anger of his father, who sends him away, and Herakles eventually avenges himself. The aftermath of the immediate episode is of interest for the present inquiry because Homer alludes to it in the Catalogue of Ships, saying that Phyleus once moved to Doulikhion because of a quarrel with his father, and Pindar also mentions it, describing the revenge that Herakles took on Augeias for denying him due payment.[51] So the tradition of the quarrel of Augeias with his son is at least as old as the *Iliad*, and if the cause of the quarrel was the same as we know it from later sources, namely, Augeias's refusal to pay Herakles the reward he agreed to pay for cleaning the cattle yard, then the narrative motif is equally old.

Is Herakles' cleaning of the cattle yard an isolated use of a traditional motif, or is it related to the larger tradition of *The Girl as Helper*? There are a few hints that it may be part of a larger narrative constellation. Apollodoros lists Augeias's daughter Epikaste is one of the wives or lovers of Herakles, so that it is possible that in a story now lost to us Epikaste played the role of the ogre's daughter who falls in love with the hero and helps him in his tasks.[52] Additional support for

this possibility may be seen in the existence of a curious genealogical connection that links the ogre's family in this story with the ogre's family in the stories of Jason and Medeia and of Theseus and Ariadne. The ogres' families are all related to one another, for the sun god Helios is the father of King Augeias, King Aietes, and King Minos's wife, Pasiphae.[53] Altogether the evidence for the existence of a third variant of *The Girl as Helper* in Greek mythology, one featuring Herakles and Epikaste as hero and heroine and Augeias as ogre, is intriguing but not compelling. In any case the story of the cattle yard is a traditional narrative sequence that has been attached to Herakles and become part of his cycle of adventures.

Lit. AT 313, *The Girl as Helper in the Hero's Flight*, Episode 2b: *The Ogre's Tasks* (Motif
 H1102: *Task: cleaning Augean stable*). Köhler (1898) 1:170–171. Radermacher 1911:177.
 Preller (1921) 2:453–456, at 454 n. 4. Schweitzer 1922:146–149. Weinreich
 1924:827–829. Aarne 1930:108. Knopp 1933:214. *EM* 1:1014–1015.

1. Aarne-Thompson's title, *The Girl as Helper in the Hero's Flight*, is odd for the folktale as a whole. For one thing, the heroine helps the hero as much in the performance of his tasks as in their eventual flight; for the same reason the tale's other common name among scholars, *The Magic Flight*, is no better. So I shorten it here to *The Girl as Helper*. For another thing, one may ask whether the maiden is not as much the hero of the tale as the youth, if not more than he.

The tale is classified in general as AT 313, and three common variations of it are further distinguished as AT 313A, AT 313B, and AT 313C. This last, AT 313C, refers to texts in which the escape of the hero and heroine is followed by the episode of *The Forgotten Fiancee*, in which the youth magically loses his memory of his bride for a time.

2. Delarue (1957) 1:234–241. For example, Christiansen 1927; Aarne 1930; Knopp 1933; Liljeblad 1935; von Sydow 1948:192 and passim. On the worldwide distribution of the motif of the magic flight, see Hatt 1949:92–94.

3. Knopp 1933:148–363.

4. For the apparently impossible task of carrying water in leaky containers, which in Greek mythology is associated especially with the Danaides, see "Carrying Water in a Sieve." For the apparently impossible task of cleaning in one day a stable that has not been cleaned for a long time, which Greek mythology associates with Herakles, see the section "Herakles Cleans the Augean Stables" below.

5. 1953:333. For some scholars however the basic meaning of the story lies rather in the relationship of the Realm of the Living and the Realm of the Dead (Aarne 1930:154–155); for earlier views, see Lang 1970:96–102.

6. Asbjørnsen and Moe (1965) 3:189–207; Holbek 1989b:51.

7. Paredes 1970:78–88, no. 30.

8. Apollodoros *Bibl.*1.9.16–28.

9. Homer *Od.* 12.70–72; Hesiod *Th.* 956–962, 992–1002.

10. Notable surviving treatments of the story in whole or in part by Greek authors, in addition to those already mentioned, include the *Argonautika* of Apollonios of Rhodes; Diodorus Siculus 4.40–52; Zenobios 4.92; schol. on Pindar *Pyth.* 4; and Tzetzes *Schol. on Lycophron* 1.175. Treatments by Latin authors include Ovid *Met.* 7.1–403, *Tristia* 3.9, *Heroides* 6, 12; Valerius Flaccus *Argonautica*; Hyginus *Fab.* 12–25; Seneca *Medea*; Servius on Vergil *Ecl.* 4.34; and Lactantius Placidus on Statius *Theb.* 3.516. The sources give somewhat differing accounts of the fate of the dragon (Jason killed it, or Medeia killed it, or Medeia magically caused it to sleep), the fate of Apsyrtos (he was dismembered by Medeia to delay the pursuers, he was murdered in the Kolchian palace, or he was ambushed during the pursuit), and various details that are not important for the present discussion. On the ancient sources see further Roscher 2:63–88, 2482–2515; Frazer (1921) 1:92–125; Knopp 1933:2–7; Radermacher 1968:157–237; Moreau 1994; Zinserling-Paul 1979; *LIMC* 5.1:629–638 and 6.1:386–398; Gantz 1993:340–373.

11. Knopp 1933:13–14. See in particular Lang 1970:87–102; Cosquin (1887) 2:28; Alfred Nutt (McInnis 1890:439–440); Friedländer (1910) 1:539 (= [1913] 4:198); Meuli 1921:5; Nilsson 1952:48–60; Rose 1928:292; BP 4:113; Knopp 1933:7–14 and passim; Liljeblad 1935; Delarue (1957) 1:234–241; Moreau 1994:255–256. On the other hand, Aarne 1930:151–152 and

Halliday 1963:93–94 are somewhat skeptical, and Vries 1954:91–94 quite so. Many commentators upon the legend, being unaware of the folktale parallels, take no position.

12. Knopp 1933:202–203.

13. Knopp 1933:201.

14. The hero's sowing dragon's teeth and growing a crop of armed men is found also in the Theban legend of Kadmos, which most commentators view as the source of the motif in the present story (e.g., Radermacher 1968:202). The Greek hero flings stones at the armed men, whereupon they blame one another, fight among themselves, and either kill one another or are finished off by the hero; or they simply fight one another unprovoked. But it is unnecessary to suppose a borrowing from the Kadmos legend since this motif can occur in *The Girl as Helper* (see Briggs [1970] A1:160, "The Black Cloak") and so is likely to have belonged to the narrative tradition from which the Jason legend developed. The protagonist's duping stupid ogres into fighting among themselves by casting stones at them is a well-known strategy in modern folk tradition (Motif K1082.1 *Missile thrown among enemies causes them to fight one another*).

15. See Knopp 1933:205. The precise nature of the quest object, the Golden Fleece, is unclear or at least has occasioned much speculation from antiquity onwards. The quality of golden I take literally as referring to fleece made of gold; this is after all heroic legend. But many commentators take it merely as a color term and rationalize the feature in one way or another (see Ryder 1991; Smith and Smith 1992). The term "fleece" itself is strictly misleading; it would be more accurate to say "wooled skin" (Ryder 1991:57), since the referent is not an amount of sheared wool but the unshorn skin of a flayed ram, as the ancient literary and visual sources show (e.g., Apollodoros *Bibl.* 1.9.1: Phrixos sacrificed the golden-fleeced ram and *gave the skin to Aietes*, who nailed it to an oak tree in a grove of Ares). But the object is remarkable for its wool, not its skin, so that I retain the traditional terminology.

16. So Friedländer (1910) 1:539; cf. Knopp 1933:206–208.

17. *Nostoi* fr. 6 Allen. See further Frazer (1921) 1:121–122; Gantz 1993:367.

18. Knopp 1933:225–226. A diversion flight also appears in the legend of Atalanta and Melanion (or Hippomenes): wishing to outrace the swift maiden, Melanion cast in her path several golden apples, which Atalanta paused to gather, thereby losing the race (Ovid *Met.* 10.560–680; Apollodoros *Bibl.* 3.9.2; Hyginus *Fab.* 185). A transformation flight appears in the myth of Zeus and Aigina: fleeing from Aigina's father, Zeus turned her into an island and himself into a stone (schol. Homer *Il.* 1.180). I know of no instance of an obstacle flight in classical storytelling.

19. The suggestion that the dismemberment of Apsyrtos is a rationalized obstacle flight is made by Nilsson 1949:52.

20. Pointed out, for example, by Rose 1928:292; BP 4:113.

21. When Andrew Lang (1910:139–146) declares that the legend is an Attic adaptation of a worldwide märchen, he probably has in mind a form of AT 313. Meuli (1921:5) certainly does when he briefly compares Theseus and Ariadne with Jason and Medeia and with folktales in which a princess without her parents' knowledge helps her suitor perform his tasks.

22. Diodorus Siculus 4.61.1–8, 5.51.4; Homer *Od.* 11.321–325. Other useful sources in Greek include Theokritos 2.44–46; Pausanias 1.22.5; Eustathios on Homer *Od.* 11.320, p. 1688; schol. on Homer *Od.* 11.322; schol. on Plato *Minos* 321A; schol. on Apollonios of Rhodes *Argon.* 3.997; schol. on Theokritos 2.45. Useful Latin authors include Vergil *Aen.* 6.20–30; Catullus 64; Ovid *Met.* 8.152–182, *Heroides* 10, *Ars Amat.* 1.527–564; Hyginus *Fab.* 41–43; Servius on Verg. *Aen.* 3.74, 6.14, and on *Georg.* 1.222; Lactantius Placidus on Statius *Achill.* 192, *Theb.* 12.676. On the legend itself see Preller (1921) 2:679–696; Roscher 5:678–760; Frazer (1921) 2:112–139; Webster 1966; Radermacher 1968:241–303; Ward et al. 1970; Eisner 1977; *LIMC* 3.1:1050–1077, 6.1:574–581, and 7.1:922–955; Calame 1990; Tiemann 1992; Gantz 1993:249–298; Walker 1994.

23. *Bibl.* 3.15.6–*Epit.* 1.11.

24. Hellanikos *FGH* 4 F 164 = Plutarch *Theseus* 17.

25. The motif of Ariadne's clew (R121.5 *Ariadne-thread*) appears occasionally in other narratives. In a modern Rumanian text a king promised his son to the maiden who could find her way through the thousand rooms of his palace, which a poor but clever maiden did by unreeling a spool of thread (AT 874* *Ariadne-Thread Wins the Prince*). The maiden's strategy is basically the same as that devised by Hansel and Gretel (AT 327 *The Children and the Ogre*) who, when their parents took them into the woods with the intention of abandoning them, dropped pebbles or breadcrumbs as they proceeded in order to find their way back home again. See further Radermacher 1909; Brassloff 1914:87–89; Radermacher 1918:52–60; Wünsch 1906:114; *EM* 1:773–774.

The motif recurs in Cretan legend, for Daidalos, who suggested the idea of the clew of thread to Ariadne, actually employs it himself on a later occasion. After he had escaped from Crete, Daidalos was sought by Minos, who promised a reward to the man who could pass a thread through a spiral sea shell. Minos hoped thereby to discover the whereabouts of Daidalos, who he judged was the only man clever enough to solve the problem. As it happened, Daidalos did so by boring a hole in the spiral shell and introducing into it an ant to which he had fastened a thread; the ant traversed the windings of the spiral shell (Apollodoros *Epit.* 1.14–15). Curiously, the Greeks called such a shell a "labyrinth" (LSJ s.v. *labyrinthos* II; cf. Elderkin 1924:199–205).

26. First in Herodotos 2.148 of a building in Egypt. Before him the word seems to appear in the phrase "One amphora of honey for the mistress of the labyrinth" on a clay tablet from Knossos dating to around the fifteenth century B.C. (Chadwick 1973:310, no. 205; Tiemann 1992:20), but if so it is uncertain what the word "labyrinth" means here.

27. According to Kern (1982:17), however, the derivation from *labrys* is linguistically untenable. On the etymology of *labyrinthos* see further Tiemann 1992:4–6 and Guidi 1990–91. Elderkin (1924:199–205) long ago connected it with a root **labyr* "coil, curve," an etymology that would harmonize well with ancient circular labyrinths as well as Hesychios's definition of a labyrinth as a place resembling a spiral snail shell. On the palace see, for example, Ward 1970:114–117.

28. Tiemann 1992:117.

29. On mazes, including ancient mazes, see Pliny *NH* 36.19; Matthews 1922; Elderkin 1924:199–205; Cook (1964–65) 1:472–490, 3:1086–1087; Borgeaud 1974; Doob 1990; Tiemann 1992:115–120.

30. Pherecydes *FGH* 3 F 150 = Plutarch *Theseus* 19.

31. *Theseus* 20. Hesiod fr. 298 MW.

32. *Od.* 11.321–325.

33. 2.42–46; schol. Theokritos 2.42–46.

34. 4.61.5–6; 5.51.4.

35. *Met.* 8.174–179.

36. One can possibly see a trace of the reunion of Theseus and Ariadne in Theseus's subsequent marriage to Phaidra, Ariadne's sister.

37. The legend of the Argonauts corresponds in many respects to another international folktale, AT 513, *The Extraordinary Companions;* see further *EM* 1:767–773. The combination of AT 313 and AT 513 is found not only in Greek mythology but also in other folk-narrative traditions; see Liljeblad 1935:39. See further "Three Brothers."

38. Radermacher 1911:177; Preller (1921) 2:453–456; Schweitzer 1922:146–149; Weinreich 1924:827–829; Aarne 1930:108; Knopp 1933:214. The task appears in twenty-four of the 232 texts surveyed by Knopp.

39. Briggs (1970) A1:425.

40. Briggs (1970) A1:297.

41. Christiansen 1964:213–216.

42. Dégh 1965:36–37.

43. On the legend and its sources see Preller (1921) 2:453–456; Frazer (1921) 1:194–197; Brommer 1986:29–30; *LIMC* 5.1:1–262, nos. 2284–2305; Gantz 1993:392–393.

44. 4.13.3, 4.33.1–4.

45. 5.1.9–10, 5.3.1.

46. *Bibl.* 2.5.5, 2.7.2. For other accounts in Greek see Tzetzes *Schol. on Lycophron* 41, *Chiliades* 2.278–290 (seems to follow Apollodoros); schol. Homer *Il.* 2.629; schol. Apollonios of Rhodes *Argon.* 1.172–173; in Latin see Hyginus *Fab.* 30; Servius on Verg. *Aen.* 8.299–300.

47. In a brief account of the episode, Hyginus (*Fab.* 30) declares that Hercules had help: (sc. Hercules) "Augeae regis stercus bobile uno die purgavit, maiorem partem Ioue adiutore; flumine ammisso totum stercus abluit." Jove as helper is possibly an error for Iolaus (Rose 1963:34), but the mention of any helper at all is puzzling.

48. 25.85–137.

49. For an illustration of the metope see, for example, Carpenter 1991, fig. 173 and 188.

50. Preller (1921) 2:454 n. 4; Weinreich 1924:827–829.

51. Homer *Il.* 2.628–629; Pindar *Ol.* 10.24–42.

52. *Bibl.* 2.7.8; Radermacher 1911:177; *EM* 1:1015.

53. For Augeias as a son of Helios see Theokritos 25.54; Apollonios of Rhodes 1.172–173, 3.362–363; Pausanias 5.1.9; Apollodoros *Bibl.* 2.5.5.

God and the Emperor of Rome ◁ Zeus and Tantalos

"It is permitted to the Emperor of Rome to enjoy the companionship of God. Once when the Emperor conceals his wife that she may listen, God ceases coming to him."[1] This tale is AT 775*, *God and the Emperor of Rome*, known from three unpublished Estonian texts. Aarne-Thompson include it as an international tale (provisionally, as the asterisk indicates), classifying it among religious stories.

Tantalos

Although an exact counterpart to the modern tale is not found in classical antiquity, the Greek legend of Tantalos's enjoying and then losing the favor of Zeus and the other gods is structurally and to an extent also thematically similar. Probably the difference is no greater than that which might be reasonably expected in a story among different peoples at an interval of over two millennia, although that is not to say that the legend of Tantalos and the tale of the emperor of Rome are necessarily cognates.

According to nearly all ancient authorities, Tantalos offends the gods and in consequence is punished in one way or another. In many authors his offense is specifically an abuse of the gods' trust, and it is this important branch of the tradition that interests us here.[2] Although Tantalos was held in high esteem by the Olympian gods and dined with them, sharing in their secret counsels or in their nectar and ambrosia, he incurred Zeus's anger when he shared with his mortal companions the plans or food and drink of the gods. As a punishment he had to endure a rock that always hovered above his head, like the sword of Damocles, threatening to fall upon him at any time.[3] Or he was immersed in a pool of water within reach of fruit-laden branches; whenever he tried to quench his thirst the water sunk, and whenever he tried to satisfy his hunger the wind wafted the fruit beyond his grasp. Or he was simultaneously oppressed by the rock and tantalized by the food and drink. This is a legend not just of the abuse of hospitality but of the abuse of hospitality in which the host is god, as in the modern folktale.

Tantalos's perpetual tantalization is first recounted by Homer as a sight witnessed by Odysseus during his extraordinary visit to the realm of the dead, though Homer does not explain why Tantalos was thus tormented.[4] The earliest mention of an offense is in an ode of Pindar composed in 476 B.C., according to which Tantalos used to dine together with the gods, who held him in high regard, sharing with him their nectar and ambrosia and thereby making him immortal, but he brought ruin upon himself by secretly sharing the gods' nectar and ambrosia with his mortal drinking companions. When the gods discovered his breach of trust, Zeus punished him by placing a great rock over his head.[5] Tantalos's garrulity is mentioned in the same century, by Euripides.[6] I shall not pursue here the various branches and intertwinings of the traditions about Tantalos's offense and punishment or speculate about which are older or younger, contenting myself with pointing out that the basic plot is necessarily at least as old as Pindar, who gives both an offense against the gods and a resulting punishment, and that, among later authorities, some authors give as his

offense his sharing the secrets of the gods with mortals, whereas others cite his sharing their special food and drink, and some represent his punishment as the threatening rock, whereas others describe the elusive nourishment, and still others list both.[7] Thus the mythographer Apollodoros includes all four motifs when he reports that Tantalos is punished in Hades' realm by having a rock threatening him from above; he is in a lake with fruit trees growing on both sides of him, and when he wishes to drink, the water dries up, and when he wishes to eat, the wind lifts the fruit up to the clouds. The reason for his punishment is that he babbled to humans about the mysteries of the gods, or he shared ambrosia with his companions.[8]

Like a man who slips a piece of silverware into his pocket while dining at the house of a rich man, Tantalos abuses the gods' hospitality and trust by making off with food or information. His two offenses are so similar that they may be regarded as forms of the same misdemeanor. And in some cases little difference can be seen in his punishments. In one version of the story Tantalos went to the gods and, obtaining from Zeus the privilege of making any wish, asked to live the same way as the gods. Though angry at the wish Zeus was obliged to fulfill it. In order that Tantalos not enjoy himself but live in continual anxiety, however, Zeus placed a rock above his head that prevented him from obtaining any of the delights set on the table before him.[9] In this case the torment of the rock differs only in emphasis from the torment of the pool and fruit, each being a means of teasing Tantalos with food and drink while preventing him from satisfying his hunger and thirst.

In both the Estonian tale and the Greek legend (1) a mortal is privileged to enjoy the companionship of god or the gods, but (2) he abuses their trust by covertly sharing their private conversation with another mortal (he smuggles in an eavesdropper, or he smuggles out the gods' secrets, sharing them with his friends); as a result, (3) he is deprived of divine privileges. In both stories the protagonist is not an ordinary man but a monarch, the hero of the modern tale being the emperor of Rome, the hero of the ancient story being the king of Lydia or Phrygia. In both there is a relationship between offense and punishment, for at least some of Tantalos's punishments are related to the nature of his crimes, a deprivation of food and drink answering to his misuse of privileged food and drink, and a deprivation of the gods' company (in those versions in which Tantalos is placed in Hades' realm) answering, as in the folktale, to his misuse of privileged conversation. The imagery of Tantalos's punishment, both the deprivation of food and drink and also the rock hanging over the head, probably are inspired by the punishment of the food-stealing giant in the Caucasian myth of the bound giant.[10]

The Estonian tale of the emperor of Rome and the Greek story of Tantalos are so similar in plot and theme that it is certainly conceivable that both traditions are realizations of an old migratory story type, but so little is known of the modern tradition, even whether it is an international tale, that the question of a genetic connection between the two traditions must remain open, subject to further investigation of the modern tradition.

For other inhabitants of the Greek death realm, see "Carrying Water in a Sieve" and "Lord's Prayer."

Lit. (AT 775*, *God and the Emperor of Rome*.)

1. Aarne and Thompson 1961:268, which is Thompson's translation of Aarne 1918:49.

2. Among the chief authorities for the story are Homer *Od.* 11.582–592; *Nostoi* fr. 10 Allen; Pindar *Ol.* 1.54–66; Euripides *Orestes* 4–10; schol. on Euripides *Orestes* 7; Apollodoros *Epit.* 2.1; and Hyginus *Fab.* 82. On the legend see Comparetti 1873; Roscher 5:75–86; Radermacher 1908; Frazer (1921) 2:154–155; Scodel 1984; Gantz 1993:531–536; *LIMC* (1994) 7.1:839–843.

3. The best known account of the sword of Damocles is that of Cicero *Tusc.* 5.61–62: Damocles, one of the flatterers of the tyrant Dionysios, spoke of the tyrant's wealth and declared that no one had ever been happier than he. Dionysios asked him if he would like to experience such fortune. When Damocles assented, the tyrant placed Damocles on a luxurious couch, assigned attractive servants to wait upon him, surrounded him with fine food and perfume, and finally above the man's head hung a sword that was attached to the ceiling by a horsehair. Damocles did not reach for anything on the table and in general found himself unable to enjoy any of the fine things before him. Indeed he asked Dionysios to release him, as he no longer wished to be happy.

4. Homer *Od.* 11.582–592.

5. Pindar *Ol.* 1.54–66, on which see Comparetti 1873. It is unclear in Pindar's version where Tantalos suffers his torment. I believe, with Comparetti, that he continues at the gods' table on Olympos, forever tantalized by the nectar and ambrosia but not daring to partake of any food or drink for fear that his movement would cause the rock to fall upon him. It makes no sense for Tantalos, who has been made deathless by the gods' nectar and ambrosia and therefore cannot die, to reside in the realm of the dead, where moreover he cannot be tormented by the sight of divine food and drink.

6. Euripides *Orestes* 4–10, on which see Scodel 1984.

7. Other offenses and punishments are also associated with Tantalos, for which see Roscher 5:78–80. Reckless speech runs in the family, since Tantalos's daughter Niobe comes to her own unhappy end as the result of imprudent speech that offends the goddess Leto (e.g., Homer *Il.* 24.603–617). Her eventual metamorphosis into a rock is perhaps reminiscent of the rock that in the end overhangs Tantalos.

8. Apollodoros *Epit.* 2.1.

9. Athenaeus 7.281B–C = *Nostoi* fr. 10 Allen; see further Roscher 5:79 and Radermacher 1908.

10. See Olrik 1922:264–265; cf. West 1966:315.

Golden Ram ⚜ Trojan Horse

In this tale of cleverness and seduction a man gains access to a princess by concealing himself in a hollow, artificial animal. Two forms of the tale, redactions A and B, have been distinguished.[1]

In redaction A, a man (often a soldier) writes in a public place "Money is all-powerful" or a similar statement about the power of money or gold. The king, who reads the declaration with indignation, decides to put the matter to the test. The man is free to take as much money as he wishes from the royal treasury, but after a stated period of time he must have seduced the king's daughter; if he fails to do so, he will be executed. The king's daughter is then confined to a tower (underground chamber, etc.). On his own or upon the advice of a helpful person, the hero has a craftsman construct a figure of a ram (stag, horse, bird, etc.) out of gold (silver, copper, bronze) or less commonly out of wood, which is hollow in order that he may conceal himself inside. The animal may be outfitted with wheels and/or an apparatus to make music. Hiding within it, the man has the animal drawn to the palace, where the king purchases the wondrous artifact and places it in his daughter's room to amuse her during her confinement. The hero exits from the hollow animal at night and enjoys himself

with the princess, who for her part is receptive to his company. The hero arranges for the animal figure, within which he himself again is concealed, to be taken outside the palace. In the meantime the king discovers that the princess is sleeping with the hero (is pregnant, has given birth), and is obliged to arrange for the marriage of his daughter to the hero.[2]

In redaction B, a king proclaims that the man who can find his daughter, whom he has hidden, may have her to wife. Or three brothers (princes) set out into the world and come one after the other to the king's city, where the king tells each one that if he is able to find the princess he may marry her but, if not, will lose his life; and the first two try and fail. The hero has a golden animal constructed, as above, and by concealing himself in it manages to reach the hiding place of the princess. Again, the hollow animal is removed from the palace together with the hidden suitor. By describing the route or by showing a token that he has obtained from the princess, the hero proves to the king that he has discovered where she is hidden.[3] Redaction B intensifies prominent motifs found in redaction A, matching the clever hero with a clever king and balancing the concealed hero with a concealed princess.

The tale, reported from Europe, Turkey, India, and the Americas, and attested since the fourteenth century, is AT 854, *The Golden Ram*.

In a nineteenth-century Danish text, a soldier on guard duty wrote on the wall of a house, "Money can accomplish everything good." The words came to the ears of the king, who asked the soldier if he stood by what he wrote, and the man said he did. The king then told the soldier that he would have a chance to test his claim. He could take all the money he wanted from the king's treasury, but in two years' time he must either seduce the king's daughter, in which case the king would give her to him as his wife, or he must lose his life. The king had a large stone tower constructed, in which the princess was to sit until two years had passed. No one had access to her except for the king, who had the key to the tower.

The soldier had no idea of how to accomplish the goal, and set out traveling. He spent one evening at the house of an old woman in a woods, to whom he described his problem. She advised him to have a craftsman built a golden stag that was large enough for him to sit in, and when it was finished, he should crawl inside, having hired someone to draw it around. The soldier returned immediately to the city and arranged for a goldsmith to fashion such an animal. The craftsman made it so well that no one could see the hatch that gave access to the interior of the animal. The hired helper led the animal away, and the soldier, who was a good musician, made music from inside. Wherever they went, people gathered to see and hear the wonder. In time they reached the palace, where the king greatly enjoyed the golden stag that could make music. The princess, who had now been confined to her tower for a year, also saw and heard the golden stag, and persuaded her father to buy it for her, which he did. In the evening after the king had retired to his own quarters, the soldier opened the hatch and crawled out. He calmed down the frightened princess, convincing her that he meant her no harm and that on the contrary he would entertain her. She liked the idea and even shared her meal with him. In the meantime the king, desiring the see and hear the golden stag once more before going to sleep, returned to the tower. The soldier jumped into bed with the

princess just as the king entered, and the king was forced to acknowledge that the soldier had won.[4]

In a tale collected from a Chilean woman in 1962, a rich gentleman built a house as large as a block and wrote on it, "He who has money does what he likes." The king, summoning him, said that he had a daughter locked by seven keys and guarded by seven guards; if the man could do with his money whatever he wished, he must get the king's daughter pregnant within nine months. The man did not know what to do, but a poor old woman advised him to use his money to have a wagon made and a gold turkey with a secret door in it; the turkey was to be placed on the wagon, and the man was to hide inside the turkey; the old woman would pull it along the street. So the gentleman had a waggoner make a wagon and a jeweler make a golden turkey in which he could sit down. The old crone pulled the turkey down the street, charging people fifty pesos to visit with it. When she reached the palace, the king rented the turkey for the entire night, thinking it would please the lonely princess. At night the wealthy gentleman opened the door and exited from the turkey. He chatted with the princess, slept with her that night, and in the morning returned to the turkey. After three days the old woman took away the animal, despite the pleas of the princess. Nine months later the king discovered that the princess had given birth to a child, and learned moreover that the rich gentleman was the father. The king sent for him, and the wedding was arranged.[5]

The dispute about a general proposition such as "Money is all-powerful" is a familiar device in different stories for framing the central events. Two characters adopt different stances regarding the validity of a proposition, introducing an interesting tension into the narrative at the start—which of them will prove to be correct?—and giving special meaning to the subsequent actions. Thus a Jewish tale begins with a general proposition about women, "All women are frivolous," the truth of which is tested in the action that follows.[6]

The hero and the king are adversaries in a contest in which the princess is the prize, the hero gambling his life, the king his daughter. The principal difference between the two forms of the oral tale lies in the events that frame the central ruse. In redaction A, the hero must show that, given unlimited material resources, he could seduce the princess, which he does; in redaction B, he must use his wits to discover the whereabouts of the hidden princess, which he does. The strategy the hero employs is essentially the same in each redaction: he gains access to the confined (hidden) princess by concealing himself in a hollow animal.

The Capture of Joppa

Close in spirit to *The Golden Ram* is the ancient Egyptian legend of the capture of Joppa. An Egyptian manuscript from around 1300 B.C. tells how the Egyptian general Thoth (or Thuti) was besieging the port of Joppa (present-day Jaffa) in Palestine. The beginning of the papyrus is lost, but when the text begins the Egyptian general is conferring with the Prince of Joppa. Thoth had evidently offered to capitulate, but his offer was a sham, for Thoth presently assaulted the prince and placed him in fetters. Thoth then had two hundred baskets (or sacks) brought, into which he placed two hundred soldiers, and he

instructed five hundred soldiers to carry them into the city, where they were to release them and place the inhabitants of the city in bonds. The Egyptians, representing themselves as speaking for the prince, now told the prince's charioteer to inform his wife that the god Seth was handing over to them Thoth, his wife, his children, and an amount of tribute, including the two hundred baskets. The charioteer went ahead to bring his mistress the good news that Thoth had been captured. So the inhabitants opened the gates of the city, and the soldiers entered, released their companions, placed the inhabitants in bonds, and thereby captured the city.[7]

General Thoth's ruse for entering his enemy's city has much in common with the folktale soldier's ruse for entering his opponent's palace. Each man creates a hollow package of apparent value to his opponent (sacks of alleged tribute, an artificial animal that allegedly produces music) in which a man is concealed. His opponent joyously brings the deceptive package inside the city or palace, unwittingly giving the hero precisely the access he desires.[8]

Nevertheless, the Egyptian general wants to capture a city, whereas the hero of *The Golden Ram* wants to capture a woman. To my knowledge the only ancient story that combines the ruse of the hollow animal with the idea of a confined woman is the legend of the Trojan War. Although many scholars have remarked on the similarity between the taking of Troy and the taking of Joppa, few have mentioned the parallels between the Trojan Horse of Greek legend and the hollow animal of the international folktale.[9] The wooden horse is a ruse to capture a city, but only secondarily so, for the primary goal of the campaign is to retrieve a woman, Helen; entering Troy means gaining access to Helen.

The Trojan Horse

According to the mythographer Apollodoros, Alexander (= Paris) carried Helen off to Troy. In order to retrieve his wife King Menelaos of Sparta asked his brother Agamemnon to muster an army against Troy. He did so, and the Greek forces sailed to Troy. Menelaos and Odysseus demanded that the Trojans return Helen, but they refused; indeed, they almost put the two envoys to death. For nine years the Greeks fought the Trojans and were unable to take the city. In the tenth year Odysseus conceived the trick of the wooden horse, which the architect Epeios constructed. It was hollow inside and had an opening on each side. Led by Odysseus the best of the Greeks entered the horse, which bore this inscription: "The Greeks dedicate to Athene this thank-offering for their return home." The rest of the Greeks burnt their tents and sailed away at night, waiting off the island of Tenedos. The next day the Trojans, seeing that the Greek camp was deserted, thought that the enemy had departed. They joyously drew the wooden horse inside the city and placed it next to Priam's palace while they deliberated what to do with it. That night, when the Greeks in the horse judged that the Trojans were sleeping, they exited from the horse and opened the gates for their comrades, who in the meantime had sailed back from Tenedos. They slew the sleeping Trojans in their houses. Menelaos killed Deiphobos (whom Helen had married upon the death of Alexander) and led Helen away to his ships.[10]

The principal plot elements that sustain *The Golden Ram* and the Trojan leg-

end are essentially the same. (1) A princess (queen) is confined to a room (city). (2) A soldier consults the king about obtaining her. (3) At the suggestion of a clever adviser, a hollow artificial animal is constructed, within which (4) the soldier (with his supporters) conceals himself. (5) The hollow animal is brought to the palace (city) where the woman is confined. (6) The king of the palace (the inhabitants of the city) happily bring the artificial animal inside. (7) At night while the residents sleep the soldier (the soldier and his supporters) exits from the hollow animal and (9) gets the woman, (10) who becomes (resumes her role as) his wife. So the folktale and the legend have much in common, significantly more than merely their central ruse, for both begin with the confinement of the woman within the royal compound and the hero's contemplating how to get to her, which lead in turn to the unusual ruse, and both conclude with the hero's success and his making the woman his wife. The Greek legend is particularly close to the branch of the international folktale represented by redaction A, since Helen is confined rather than hidden, and Menelaos's object is to gain access to her rather than merely to discover her whereabouts. It seems probable that these stories are related and go back ultimately to the same tradition.[11]

Of course, the differences between the Greek legend and the modern folktale are also many. First of all, the story of Menelaos and Helen is part of great patchwork of narratives about Troy that have been stitched next to one another, within one another, and so on. As a story, it was so popular and so frequently narrated in classical antiquity that different versions of virtually every detail developed, and the details themselves are often greatly elaborated. Among the more obvious differences is that the Greek story is told on a grand scale. The events take not a month or a year but ten years, and the cast of characters is enormous. Yet these differences of scale have little direct effect on the central story of Menelaos and Helen, for Helen is confined and remains so until the trick of the wooden horse allows Menelaos to liberate her. Equally important is the difference in genre between folktale and heroic legend. There is little place in a story of heroic endeavor for such playful motifs as the hero's asserting that money can accomplish anything or his discovering the hiding place of a princess, however old these motifs may be.

The tradition of the Trojan Horse was current among the earliest Greek poets of whom we have knowledge. Homer's *Iliad* is set during the confinement of Helen at Troy. In the *Odyssey* Helen, now back home with Menelaos after the war, relates how at Troy she regretted the infatuation that Aphrodite had given her, causing her to leave her homeland, her daughter, and her husband.[12] And Menelaos describes for Telemachos what it was like when he and other were inside the wooden horse.[13] In the Eighth Book, Odysseus asks the Phaiakian bard Demodokos to sing of the wooden horse that Epeios constructed with the help of Athene, a piece of trickery that Odysseus filled with men and brought into Troy. Demodokos sings how most of the Achaians burnt their huts and sailed away, while Odysseus and the men with him sat concealed in the horse in the midst of the Trojans. The Trojans drew it into the citadel and deliberated what they should do with it. Later, as the Achaians exited from their hollow hiding place and destroyed the city, Odysseus and Menelaos proceeded to the house of Deiphobos.[14]

If Homer relates much of the story in allusion, the composers of the cyclic epics *Little Iliad* and *Iliou Persis* (Destruction of Ilios) narrate many of the events

directly. The poet of the *Little Iliad* mentions the marriage of Helen to Deiphobos after the death of Alexander, and tells how Epeios constructed the wooden horse, how the bravest of the Greeks entered it while the others burnt their tents and pretended to sail away, and how the Trojans believed that their sufferings were at an end, brought the wooden horse into the city, and celebrated their victory. The *Iliou Persis* treats inter alia the decision of the Trojans to dedicate the wooden horse as an offering to Athene, the return of the men who had pretended to sail home, the exit of the men concealed in the horse, the capture of the city, Menelaos's finding Helen and bringing her back to his ships after slaying Deiphobos, and the departure of the Greeks.[15] And of course the story of the Trojan Horse is treated by many other poets and prose authors, both Greek and Roman.[16]

What Was the Trojan Horse?

A few scholars appear to accept the tradition of the wooden horse as history.[17] Much more commonly scholars interpret the tradition as distorted history. Denys Page distinguishes, as an indication of their historicity, elements in Homeric epic that are "typical" from those that are "individual." If an element is individual, it is probably historical; if it is a typical motif, it is probably an elaboration on history, a fiction. Page applies this distinction to the question of whether the episode of the wooden horse is founded on historical fact or not. Since (he says) the wooden horse does not appear to belong to the storyteller's stock-in-trade, it is likely to be historical, probably (in the words of H. J. Rose) "a confused remembrance of some Oriental siege-engine."[18] But as we have seen, Page's premise is wrong, since the device of the hollow animal is in fact the central motif of an international folktale. If we should employ Page's yardstick for measuring historicity, we must declare the episode nonhistorical.

Many other scholars have drawn a conclusion similar to Page's; indeed, the idea that the Trojan Horse is a confused memory of a battering ram or the like is as old as the ancient rationalists. Pausanias, describing a bronze model of the wooden horse that he saw on the acropolis at Athens, declares that, unless one regards the Phrygians (that is, the Trojans) as wholly simpleminded, one understands that the wooden horse constructed by Epeios really was a device to break down the walls of Troy.[19] Pliny, in his list of the inventors of different weapons of war, credits Epeios with the invention of the "horse," which is now called the "ram," by which Pliny means the battering ram.[20] Servius, commenting on Vergil's *Aeneid*, similarly explains the wooden horse as an engine of war, like the "ram" and "tortoise."[21]

There are however serious difficulties with this interpretation. One problem is historical. So far as we know, battering rams and moveable towers were not in use in the Late Bronze Age, for they are first attested in Assyria in the ninth century B.C. Mycenaean warriors trying to take a walled town might climb the walls with ladders or tear apart the defenses with picks and crowbars; they might starve the inhabitants; or they might trick them into surrendering or into opening their gates, as in the Egyptian siege of Joppa. But no one had yet devised the battering ram as a weapon of war. A second and more serious problem has to do with the nature of oral tradition. This is the assumption, codified in antiquity in the work of Palaiphatos, that one can work back from legends to

the historical incidents that inspired them. Of course, if one possesses independent evidence for the historical events, one can describe the ways in which oral narrators have transformed these events in the course of time. But if we have only the oral stories, we cannot reliably imagine the tradition back into the history from which it arose. The transformation is irreversible.[22] The suggestion has been made that the wooden horse is a mythologized battering ram that entered the Trojan legend centuries *after* the fall of Troy, in the age of the battering ram.[23] This solution escapes the first objection but not the second.

Fritz Schachermeyr similarly works back from the episode of the wooden horse to the historical kernel that he believes lurks behind it, but he arrives at different results. For him, Troy was overcome by an earthquake rather than by military conquest; consequently, he identifies the Troy of tradition, not with Troy VIIa, but with Troy VI, which according to the excavators was destroyed by an earthquake. Since Poseidon, god of earthquakes, was sometimes represented in the form of a horse, the folk expressed the catastrophe by saying that Troy was destroyed by the horse-formed earthshaker Poseidon, and this statement developed by stages into the image and stratagem of the wooden horse.[24] But Schachermeyr's transformation of legend back into history is, like that of other rationalists, essentially arbitrary. Like Palaiphatos, he simply discards the fabulous elements in the tradition or explains them away as simpleminded distortions of historic events.[25]

These approaches have in common a denial that the wooden horse is what it appears to be—a memorable episode in a memorable story, a clever stratagem for smuggling men into a closed city. The interpretations share an insistence that the ruse must be bad history for something else, either an engine of war or a natural disaster. But it is the Greek representation of the taking of Troy, not Trojan history itself, that has captured the Western imagination for over two millennia. If the Trojan Horse is bad history, it is certainly good legendry. Faraone observes that different explanations of the Trojan Horse fall into one or the other of two classes, being either military (the horse is a poetized or mythologized machine of war) or religious-mythological (the horse represents a theophany or ritual of some sort).[26] In both cases, the horse is explained away as a representation of something else. The present thesis, which explains the motif of the hollow animal by reference to traditional oral narrative, falls into neither of these classes of explanation and has the advantage of accepting the motif precisely as it is rather than taking it as a distortion of something else, the existence of which one must hypothesize.[27] The hollow, artificial animal of international folktale is essentially a stratagem whereby a hero tricks a king into introducing the hero into the king's fortress, where a woman is being kept from the hero. The ploy belongs to the imagination, not to history. As a military stratagem it would be conceivable, but as a narrative motif it is exciting and memorable because it is bold, unusual, and unlikely. Its improbability should not be explained away but cherished.

Lit. (AT 854, *The Golden Ram.*) Crooke 1908:187–188. *BP* 1:446 n. 2. Krappe 1927:12 n. 41. Hepding 1954. *EM* 2:561–565.

 1. Kurt Ranke, in *EM* 2:561–563.
 2. Hepding 1954; *EM* 2:561–562.
 3. Hepding 1954; *EM* 2:562–563.

4. Grundtvig 1958:151–157.

5. Pino-Saavedra 1967:168–170, no. 33.

6. Schwarzbaum 1979:410–413 n. 21. See further "Matron of Ephesus," redaction B.

7. Pritchard 1955:22–23; Brünner-Traut 1965:147–149 (no. 26), 286–287.

8. Notice also a story in the Indian *Katha Sarit Sagara* 2.12, in which a king fills an artificial elephant with his bravest men and succeeds thereby in taking an enemy king captive. See Müller (1881) 4:149–150; Halliday 1933:48 n. 1; Scobie 1983:237 with n. 17.

9. On Joppa and Troy: Crooke 1908:187–188; Aly 1928:272; Fehling 1991:50.

10. Apollodoros *Epit*. 3.1–5.22. The mythographer also records many variations on the legend that I do not reproduce here.

11. One cannot easily treat the folktale simply as a derivative of the Trojan legend, whose basic plot recedes into the background because of the greatly elaborated element of the siege and the numerous stories that the central events have attracted into their orbit.

12. *Od*. 4.260–264.

13. *Od*. 4.271–289. In book 11, Odysseus describes to the ghost of Achilleus how frightened most of the men inside the horse were (11.523–532).

14. *Od*. 8.492–520.

15. Proklos *Chrestomathia* 5:106–108 Allen.

16. See the fragmentary *Iliou Persis* of Stesichoros; Diktys of Crete *Bellum Troianum* 5.9–12; Tryphiodoros *Halosis Iliou*; Quintus Smyrnaeus *Posthomerica* 12–13; Tzetzes *Posthomerica* 629–723; Tzetzes *Schol. on Lycophron* 930; Vergil *Aeneid* 2; Hyginus *Fab*.108. On the sources of the story, see Roscher 5:1232–1261; Preller (1921) 3:969–1289; Frazer (1921) 2:170–237; Fehling 1991; Gantz 1993:646–657.

17. Gilbert Murray (1934:33), though not arguing the historicity of the stratagem of the Trojan Horse, declares that it has "a special air of verisimilitude"!

18. Page 1959:296 n. 119, citing Rose 1928:252 n. 50.

19. Pausanias 1.23.8.

20. *NH* 7.202.

21. 2.15.

22. The observation has frequently been made; for example, Carpenter 1946:60.

23. Anderson 1970; Gallucci 1996.

24. Schachermeyr 1950:189–203.

25. For other interpretations of the wooden horse, see Leaf 1915:31; Knight 1930, 1931; Nilsson 1972:256; Austin 1959:23–24; Jones 1970; Burkert 1983:158–161; Andersen 1972:16 n. 1; Bremmer 1972; Nagler 1987:448; Hölscher 1988:61–63; Fehling 1991; Faraone 1992:94–112; Garvie 1994:334; Gallucci 1996. See more generally Davies 1984 and Hainsworth 1984. For similar rationalizations of the Golden Fleece in the legend of Jason and the Argonauts, see Ryder 1991; Smith and Smith 1992.

26. 1992:94–95.

27. Hölscher (1988:61–63) also sees the origin of the Trojan Horse in traditional tales, but for him it is a rationalization of a wonder horse found in various folktales, an animal that has the ability to leap walls and serves the hero generally as a helper. Hölscher's folktale analogues are more remote than the tale of *The Golden Ram*, and once again the Trojan Horse becomes merely a rationalization of something else.

"Good Day"—"A Woodchopper." *See* Hearing-Impaired Persons

Great Animal or Object

This is a group of lying tales in which the size of different things is greatly exaggerated. The general reference is AT 1960, *The Great Animal or Great Object*, each tale being distinguished as a subtype depending upon its subject, such as AT 1960A, *The Great Ox*.

For the most part these texts are not stories in the usual sense of the term, for they do not necessarily show any action, let alone a conventional pattern of action.[1] Great magnitude may be conveyed by description or illustrative incident or both. Thus, in AT 1960E, *The Great Farmhouse*, narrators often claim that a cow stall is so large that a cow that is brought to one end of the stall gives birth to a calf before she can return to the other end. In a Norwegian tale recorded in 1959, Ola describes how the ship he sailed in reached the English Channel but was too big to pass through, so that the skipper had to pour soap between the sides of the ship and the land. A hundred horseloads were required, but they did the trick. The first time Ola ever climbed up the mast he nearly fell overboard, but he was saved by the man who had been painting the mast ever since the ship had been built.[2] This is AT 1960H, *The Great Ship*.

Mass or number greatly out of proportion to normal, whether great or small, numerous or few, is wondrous.[3] The notion of an object such as an enormous ship is wondrous to imagine, as is its opposite, something unnaturally small such as a person the size of a thumb, and as is an enormous number, such as a catch of fish that takes a year to haul in, and its opposite, something that is extremely rare.[4] While some folktales exploit the motifs of extraordinary smallness or rarity, *The Great Animal or Great Object* exploits extraordinarily great size or quantity. The wit of the narrator and narrative in demonstrating great size or number by means of concrete illustration—a cow would go through her entire cycle of gestation just traveling from one end of such a great cow stall to the other—is, when well done, a source of logical and aesthetic pleasure for the listener.

The tellers of lying tales, who are almost exclusively males, often report the matter with false seriousness and in the first person as something they themselves observed or experienced. The tone may be dry or cheerfully naive. The adventures of Baron Münchhausen, written in the eighteenth century, are among the best-known literary adaptations of lying tales in modern times, just as Lucian's *True Stories* furnishes the best example from antiquity.

Here follows, not an exhaustive catalogue, but an illustrative sampling from ancient sources.

Lit. AT 1960, *The Great Animal or Great Object*. BP 2:515–516. Bødker 1954. Liungman 1961:344. Henningsen 1963, 1965. Alstrup 1967. Rooth 1983:34–45. *EM* 6:239–249.

The Great Animal

A German tale collected in 1813 begins with a farmer who was plowing with a pair of oxen. The horns of the oxen grew so much as he worked that when he was ready to return home the animals could not pass back through the gate. The narrative continues paratactically with similar absurdities on various topics in quick succession.[5] Many tales claim that for a bird to fly from one horn of a particular ox to the other requires a full day or some other long period of time.[6] These are examples of AT 1960A, *The Great Ox*, a subtype that includes tales about huge horses, sheep, pigs, snakes, etc.

Herodotos says that India, which he regards as the easternmost country of the inhabited world, has four-footed animals and birds that are far larger than

those of the other regions of the inhabited world. Closer to home the historian says that in Arabia there are found sheep with such long tails that shepherds construct little carts to support their tails in order that they not drag along the ground and develop sores.[7] Other authors describe other huge creatures in distant India. Of these we get considerable detail about the giant worm that Ktesias says lives in the River Ganges. This snakelike beast is around six cubits in length and lies in the mud of the river during the day. At night it comes out onto land, and if it encounters a cow or a camel or the like, it drags the victim to the river by means of its two teeth and consumes it all except for the belly. The local inhabitants hunt this worm with a huge hook baited with a kid or a lamb, and they extract a strange oil from it.[8] The truth, the innocent distortion, and the deliberate lie cannot easily be distinguished in these reports on the basis of content alone. For example, modern commentators from Marco Polo onward assure us that Barbary sheep can grow tails weighing over seventy pounds, which shepherds sometimes support on wheeled contrivances.[9]

The best-known instances of abnormally large animals in the classical tradition are the huge beasts that gods and heroes confront in Greek mythology. So, for example, Apollo slays Python, and Kadmos slays the Theban dragon, son of Ares; both monsters are huge snakes, as the Greek *drakon* signifies. We find in addition to snakes other exaggerations of natural animals such as giant boars as well as composite mythological creatures of enormous size such as the partly anthropomorphic and partly serpentine Typhon, who was so tall that his head often touched the stars.[10] But there is no playful lying in the telling of these stories, until educated persons ceased taking them very seriously.

Perhaps the closest approximation to the whimsically enormous animal of the lying tale is found in a work of the philosopher Aristotle, who adduces the idea of an animal a thousand miles long in order to illustrate a point about aesthetics. For an object to be beautiful, Aristotle says, it must be of an appropriate size. If it is extremely small, our perception of it will not be clear, and if it is extremely large, we cannot take it in all at once and so will be unable to perceive its unity and wholeness: for example, if there were an animal a thousand miles long.[11]

Lit. (AT 1960A, *The Great Ox.*) BP 2:515. Ashliman, type 1960A. *EM* 6:241–242.

The Great Fish

In a Russian tale from the nineteenth century a pike with long teeth was born in the Sheksna River on the night before St. John's, agitating the waters and almost overturning a ferryboat. Other fish marveled at the wonder, which grew an inch a day and was soon catching the shad and perch with his long teeth. The smaller fish held an assembly and decided to move to smaller rivers.[12]

According to a tale collected in West Virginia a strong man named Oto was told of a great fish in another land that no one had been able to catch. So he went there. He bought a cable an inch thick, sharpened an anchor for a hook, and placed two twenty-pound turkeys on it. Trying to throw the hook into the river, he at first threw it too hard so that it landed on the far bank, where two pigs got caught on it. As Oto was pulling the hook back across the river, the

giant fish grabbed it, and Oto and the fish fought for a week. When the fish leaped out of the water, Oto jumped on its back and rode it like a wild stallion. Finally the fish leaped so high that both fish and man froze to death. The villagers hauled them north so that they would not spoil. They set up Oto as a statue, and they built a cannery inside the fish. They found there a ton of hooks with which earlier fishermen had tried unsuccessfully to land the fish. They sold the scales for sailboats, and they have been canning the meat, of which more than half is still left.[13]

The foregoing two texts illustrate AT 1960B, *The Great Fish*.

Reports of wondrously large fish in antiquity fall into several groups. Some are simply descriptions. Thus, Pliny asserts that the largest animals are found in the Indian Sea, among them whales 4 *iugera* in size (about 3 acres), *pristes* 200 cubits in length (about 300 feet), lobsters 4 cubits in length, and eels in the Ganges River that are 300 feet long.[14] On the authority of a work written by Juba, Pliny reports that *ceti*, that is, whales or other large sea creatures, measuring 600 feet in length by 360 feet in width have entered a river in Arabia.[15] Other enormous fishes mentioned by the Roman author are giant tunny, one of which weighed fifteen talents and had a tail over three feet wide, and the *attilus*, a slothful fish found in the Po River that grows so fat it sometimes reaches a thousand pounds, so that when it is caught with a hook and chain it is drawn out of the water by teams of oxen, somewhat like the method for catching the giant worm of the Ganges described by Ktesias.[16] Though Pliny's account of fishing for the fat and slothful *attilus* by means of a hook and chain and teams of oxen certainly has the flavor of a lying tale, he reports this and other exaggerations with apparent earnestness, as does Herodotos about the great size of animals in India.

Not so Lucian in his *True Stories*, however, who cheerfully admits he is lying when he tells of traveling to the moon and of incredible battles between giants who sail on islands instead of ships and whose weapons are oysters the size of wagons and sponges a hundred feet in diameter. Indeed Lucian says he is parodying the descriptions of exotic places that various writers have published, such as what Ktesias says about India and what Iamboulos says about the Atlantic Ocean. Lucian calls them lies, but enjoyable ones, declaring that the man who started this nonsense was Homer's Odysseus in his apologue to the Phaiakians.[17] The parodist declares that his own story is a big lie but differs from that of all others in that he acknowledges that it contains no truth.[18]

Somewhere in between the ethnographic seriousness of a Herodotos and a Pliny and the acknowledged lies of a Lucian is the pose of the Jewish author of *Tobit*, who mentions a great fish in his novelized folktale, which he presents as a wondrous but true occurrence. He recounts how a fish leaps out of the River Tigris in its eagerness to seize the foot of the youth Tobias.[19] The creature is presumably large, but there can be no doubt about the great magnitude of the fish cast by the water upon the land in a tale in the *Babylonian Talmud* attributed to Rabbah bar Bar Hana. Sixty towns were thereby destroyed, sixty towns ate from the fish, sixty towns salted the remainder, and from one of its eyeballs three hundred kegs of oil were extracted. When the narrator returned a year later, he saw that people were cutting rafters from the skeleton and rebuilding the towns.[20]

A second group of traditions about giant fish is comprised of texts of the international tale of the fish-island.[21] Mariners put in at an island and begin cooking their meal. But the island turns out to be the back of a huge fish or turtle, and the creature, becoming hot from the fire, plunges into the depths of the sea.

According to the ancient Greek bestiary *Physiologos*, which perhaps came into being in Alexandria around A.D. 200 and was presently translated into Ethiopic, Syrian, Armenian, and Latin, there is a large sea creature called a shield-turtle (*aspidokhelone*). It is huge, like an island. Mariners ignorantly tie their boats to it as they would to an island, and drop anchor. Disembarking they build a fire on the creature in order to boil some food for themselves, but when the creature becomes hot it plunges into the depths, sinking their boats. The entry concludes with a Christian allegory: "Similarly, if you depend on the hope of the devil, he will take you with him down into the Gehenna of fire. So Physiologos spoke well of the shield-turtle."[22]

Another Greek account appears in a counterfeit letter purportedly written by Alexander the Great to his former teacher Aristotle, wherein the adventurer relates an amazing experience he had in faraway India. As Alexander and his men sailed near the capital of India, they spotted a promontory on which he and a few of his men disembarked. The dwellers were human beings who had female form and ate fish. Alexander tried to converse with some of them but found that they were barbarian in speech (that is, they did not speak Greek). As he inquired about the place, they pointed out an island, which Alexander and his men had noticed lying in the middle of the sea, and said that it was the tomb of a very ancient king in which a large amount of gold had been consecrated. The text is troubled at this point, but it seems that Alexander made known his desire to visit the island. When the text resumes, we learn that the natives disappeared, leaving their small boats behind, and that several of Alexander's companions forbade him to cross over to the island. His closest friend Pheidon then declared his wish to go in Alexander's place, promising to send a boat back for Alexander if there should be no danger. He argued that if he, Pheidon, perished, Alexander would find other friends, but if Alexander perished it would be a misfortune for the world. Persuaded, Alexander let him cross over, but after an hour the beast suddenly submerged. Alexander and his men cried out as the beast disappeared and Pheidon and his comrades met a miserable death. Very upset, Alexander searched for the natives but could not find them.[23]

In *Physiologos* the huge sea creature is a kind of turtle, as the appellation *aspidokhelone* indicates, whereas in the letter of Alexander the nature of the beast is unclear. The bestiary presents the phenomenon as a recurrent danger of the sea, while the latter presents it as a story, that is, as a particular misfortune that befell a particular group of sailors on a particular occasion. Although the setting in the epistle is richer than that of the spare entry in *Physiologos*, it dwells mostly on the events leading up to the encounter with the sea creature, saying little about the beast itself. No cooking fire is mentioned, and the transition from island to beast occurs with no explanation, as though the reader should already know that the apparent island is really a great creature of the sea. Later treatments of the story are typically more elaborate than those of the two ancient texts. Frequently they describe the apparent island and in general exploit

the drama of the disembarked sailors cooking their meal, the sudden realization that the island is alive, the rush back to the ship, and so on.

Early accounts of the fish-island are also found in the *Babylonian Talmud* and in a hymn of the *Zend Avesta*. In the former, the narrator says that once when he was on a boat he saw a fish upon which sand had accumulated and grass was growing. He and the others, thinking it was an island, disembarked and cooked upon it. But when the back of the fish grew hot, the fish turned over, and they would have drowned had their ship not been nearby.[24] The Persian hymn alludes briefly and somewhat obscurely to an adventure of the hero Keresâspa, who at noontime was cooking meat in a kettle on top of a horned monster. As the creature grew hot he rushed forth from under the kettle, upsetting it, and Keresâspa fled in terror.[25] Scholars disagree whether the horned monster is a creature of the land or, as in all the other texts, the sea.[26] Among later literary treatments the best known are that in the First Voyage of Sindbad the Sailor in the *Thousand and One Nights* and that in the *Navigatio Sancti Brandani*, or *Voyage of Saint Brendan*.[27]

For a third group of ancient narratives concerning great fish, see "Man Swallowed by Fish."

Lit. AT 1960B, *The Great Fish*. Runeberg 1902. Coulter 1926. Schenda 1965. Ashliman, type 1960B. *EM* 6:242.

The Great Vegetable

The teller describes the great size of a particular vegetable, problems caused by it, or the like. This is AT 1960D, *The Great Vegetable*.

In an Irish tale collected from Hugh Nolan in 1972, the narrator relates how John Brodison once had a field of potatoes. As he dug one day he found a potato of great width and depth, requiring much effort and digging to uncover. When finally John got it out of the ground, it started to roll, and he was too tired from digging to pursue it. Then he heard a bang. The potato had rolled onto the road and collided with a cart, knocking it over, so that there were sacks of meal lying everywhere.[28] A English narrator tells how Jack Thorkel raised big parsnips. A man asked him if he would dig them up, since their roots were coming through the roadway so that the ponies could not get past.[29] According to a Spanish tale, in a conversation between an Andalusian and a Galician, the former said that on his land there was a cabbage occupying an area of two square miles. Then the Galician said that on his land they were constructing a cauldron so large that a hundred coppersmiths were working on it, and they did not hear the sound of one another's hammers. The Andalusian asked why they were making such a big cauldron. The reply: "To cook your cabbage in."[30]

As for reports of great vegetables in antiquity, in his *True Stories* Lucian mentions several kinds of absurdly large vegetables in fantastic contexts. The lineup before a battle between extraterrestrials included slingers called Air Dancers (*Aerokordakes*), who slung giant radishes instead of stones, and if a man was hit his wound was malodorous. Beside them in battle were arrayed the Stalk Mushrooms (*Kaulomyketes*), a folk so named because they used

mushrooms for shields and asparagus stalks for spears. And next to them were the Dog Acorns (*Kynobalanoi*), dog-faced men who fought mounted upon winged acorns.[31] Later he speaks of pumpkins sixty cubits in length and giant nutshells that were fifteen fathoms in diameter, that is, about ninety feet.[32] Both were so big that boats were made from them (see The Great Ship, below). Giant vegetables are also found in the *Alexander Romance*, which mentions apples and nuts as big as melons, and truffles weighing twenty-five pounds.[33]

Lit. AT 1960D, *The Great Vegetable*. BP 2:515–516, 3:169–193. Ashliman, type 1960D. *EM* 6:243–244.

The Great Tree

A tree grew so high that it reached the sky, or the trunk of a pine tree was so large that eighty men could dance the polka on it, or three hundred bears had their winter holes under its roots.[34] These are examples of AT 1960G, *The Great Tree*.

Pliny reports that not only do the biggest animals grow in India, but also the trees there are said to be so tall that one could not shoot an arrow over them. If you can believe it (Pliny continues, suggesting that his own credulity is now being strained), an entire squadron of cavalry can be sheltered beneath a single Indian fig tree. And reeds grow so high there that one can sometimes make a three-man boat from a section of reed between two knots.[35]

Lit. AT 1960G, *The Great Tree*. BP 2:511–513. Ashliman, type 1960G. *EM* 6:245–246.

The Great Ship

A ship is so long that it takes three days to travel from one end to the other.[36] In a Norwegian text a ship was so large it got stuck in the English Channel, and its masts were so tall that the old man painting them had begun the job as a youth.[37]

In his *True Stories* Lucian describes a number of ships that are fantastic with regard both to their enormity and also to the material of which they consist. The narrator reports seeing men of giant stature who employed large islands as ships. Each island was around a hundred stades in circumference (about twelve and a half miles) and was manned by 120 giants using large cypress trees as oars. The pilot of the ship stood on a lofty hill holding a tiller five stadia (three thousand feet) long. The forest on the island served as sails. The giants used large octopuses in place of grappling hooks and hurled at the enemy hundred-foot sponges and oysters the size of wagons.[38] Elsewhere the narrator tells of the Pumpkin Pirates (*Kolokynthopeiratai*), islanders who fashioned boats from enormous pumpkins that were sixty cubits long. They dried and hollowed out the pumpkins, and for masts and sails they used reeds and pumpkin leaves. On the other hand, their enemies the Nut Sailors (*Karyonautai*) sailed around in the halves of giant, hollowed-out nutshells that were ninety feet in diameter.[39]

The ships in the modern tall tales are unrealistic in their absurdly great size,

whereas the ships in Lucian's narrative are unrealistic both in their size and in their material. Lucian is more interested in the material, for whereas the modern raconteur employs different images to convey the idea of enormity, Lucian offers different natural objects—islands, pumpkins, nuts—that share some property with ships, however remote it may be, to convey the idea of shipness, though in every case the fantastic ship is also of great size.

Lit. AT 1960H, *The Great Ship*. BP 2:516. Henningsen 1963. Henningsen 1965:198–200. Ashliman, type 1960H. *EM* 6:246.

The Great Bird

A bird is so large that it takes several days for it to pass by, or the great size of the bird is implied by the great size of its nest.[40] One of its feathers can be used as the mast of a ship.[41] This subtype is AT 1960J, *The Great Bird*.

In his *True Stories* Lucian describes a number of giant birds. When a whirlwind once brought his ship to the moon, the first beings he encountered were the Horse Vultures (*Hippogypoi*), who arrested him and his companions. The Horse Vultures were men who rode large, tricephalic vultures, using them as horses. You could judge the size of the birds from the fact that each of their feathers was longer and thicker than the mast of a large merchant ship.[42] Among their allies were the Vegetable Wings (*Lakhanopteroi*), who rode upon huge, shaggy birds that had plumage consisting of vegetation and had something resembling leaves of lettuce for wings, and the Horse Cranes (*Hippogeranoi*), who originated in the stars above Cappadocia and whose nature Lucian says he hesitates to describe inasmuch as he did not have the opportunity to see them himself, though he heard some amazing things said about them.[43] Lucian's reticence is, of course, absurd in the context of his other fantastic statements. We may suppose that, if Lucian had been willing to describe them, he would have said that the Horse Cranes used giant cranes as horses.

In a later context Lucian reports that the ship he and his party were sailing in ran aground on the enormous nest of a kingfisher. It was sixty stades in circumference (about seven and a half miles). The female kingfisher was in the nest sitting on her eggs, and she was only slightly smaller than the nest, which was built of large trees and sailed on the sea like a raft. It contained five hundred eggs, each larger than a Chian wine jar. The travelers cut open one of the eggs, finding a chick that was bigger than twenty vultures.[44] In this passage, as in some modern texts, the narrator conveys the great size of the bird by describing the enormity of its nest.

We hear also elsewhere of persons riding upon birds. In Aristophanes' *Lysistrata* a woman desiring the company of a man plans to fly down from the Acropolis upon a sparrow.[45] Since sparrows are in reality a small but common bird, the choice of bird is probably determined by the fact that *strouthos* "sparrow" is also slang for "phallos."[46] In the *Aesop Romance* the clever Aesop had fowlers catch four eagles and rear them, teaching them all the while to carry boys in the air, so that eventually the boys were able to mount the eagles and fly. What sets these eagles apart from other eagles, however, is not their size but their training.[47]

Lit. AT 1960J, *The Great Bird*. Ashliman, type 1960J. *EM* 6:246–247.

The Great Piece of Food

Lies concerning great loaves of bread, great cakes, and other baked goods, and whole cheeses of great size are classed as AT 1960K, *The Great Loaf of Bread, the Great Cake, etc.* I shall include also immense drinkables.

Once again Lucian provides an ancient text. He and his companions sailed into a sea consisting of milk rather than of water. In it there was a white island full of grapevines. They later discovered that the island, which was twenty-five stades in circumference (over three miles), was made of cheese and that the abundant grapes produced milk, so that the earth supplied their bread and meat, and the vines supplied their drink. A temple on the island was consecrated to Galatea the Nereid, and the queen of the place was Tyro, daughter of Salmoneus.[48] Lucian chooses these characters from Greek mythology since their names suggest the words "milk" (*gala*) and "cheese" (*tyros*).

Lit. AT 1960K, *The Great Loaf of Bread, the Great Cake, etc. EM* 6:247.

The Great Egg

Accounts of a great egg are found in descriptions of a great bird as well as in other connections. This is AT 1960L, *The Great Egg.*

As mentioned above, Lucian describes coming upon the nest of a giant kingfisher. The huge nest contained five hundred eggs, each one larger than a Chian *pithos*, or wine-jar.[49]

Lit. AT 1960L, *The Great Egg. EM* 6:247.

The Great Insect

Mosquitos carry human beings or animals. A mosquito is so large that a man makes a fence from the bones of one. Tall tales about insects and insectlike creatures are classified as AT 1960M, *The Great Insect.*

Herodotos reports that in a desert of India huge ants are found that are smaller than dogs but larger than foxes. A number of them, having been captured, are in the possession of the king of Persia. When the ants burrow into the ground, they throw up large amounts of sand mixed with gold, and Indians make expeditions into the desert with their camels to obtain this gold.[50] Giant ants are also mentioned by other authors. Thus giant ants and fleas as big as frogs are found in the *Alexander Romance.*[51] And Lucian tells of giant ants that served to convey the Horse Ants (*Hippomyrmekes*), who were the cavalry of Phaethon, ruler of the sun. These winged ants were very large—one of them reached a length of two hundred feet—but otherwise looked like Greek ants.[52] Other warriors in the battle between the forces of the sun and of the moon described by Lucian include the Flea Archers (*Psyllotoksotai*), who rode on great fleas, each of which was the size of twelve elephants; giant spiders, each one much larger than the Cycladic Islands; and the Sky Mosquitoes (*Aerokonopes*), archers who rode on large mosquitoes.[53]

At least one giant insect appears in an ancient comedy. In Aristophanes' *Peace* Trygaios rears a giant dung beetle, upon which he ascends to Zeus's house in

the heavens. The creature is called a horse dung beetle (*hippokantharos*).[54] The immediate inspiration for Aristophanes' great dung beetle is not a lying tale but the mythological Bellerophon, who flew heavenward on his winged horse Pegasos, and in particular Euripides' drama *Bellerophontes*, which the comic writer parodies in more than one play.[55] More distant inspirations may be the Aesopic fable of the dung beetle that flew up to Zeus, a tall tale featuring a giant insect, or perhaps even a international fairy tale such as *The Louse-Skin*, in which a princess rears and fattens a louse until it is as large as a calf.[56]

Lit. AT 1960M, *The Great Insect*. Ashliman, type 1960M. *EM* 6:247.

The Great Object

AT 1960Z, *Other Stories of Great Objects and the Like*, serves as the bin for lying tales about great objects that are not classified in the preceding subtypes. So in an English tale about a great wind, a locally famed liar named Tommy Boots once had a dog that one day was carried upward by a whirlwind and never seen again.[57]

Many other exaggerations of size are found in classical sources. There are, for example, scattered descriptions, mostly whimsical, of huge body parts. Thus a poetic fragment attributed to Sappho mentions a doorman with immense feet wearing shoes fashioned by ten cobblers from five oxhides.[58] Among the enormities mentioned by Lucian is a community of men who sailed around on their backs, being at the same time sailors and ships; they used their large phalluses as masts, on which they had spread sails, and held the sheets in their hands.[59] Immense phalluses are found in Greek and Roman art in association with Priapus, satyrs, and others. Some of them are virtual narratives; for example, an amusing fresco in the House of the Vettii, Pompeii, shows Priapus (or a man) weighing his huge phallus with a scales.[60] And Martial derides a certain man's nose, saying it is so huge that Atlas would be unwilling to bear it.[61]

Motifs in which familiar kinds of animals and objects possess enormous size are found in different genres of ancient literature and art. In written works there is little that distinguishes lying tales from many quasi-scientific statements about exotic lands other than that the former may be presented as pleasurable untruths whereas the latter are put forth as ethnographic realities, either because the travel reports are really collections of lying tales framed as descriptions of distant lands or because their authors have uncritically accepted wondrous tales as true information and pass them on to their readers. Lucian's great web of lying tales, *True Stories*, is, as the author says, a parody of unreliable ethnographies and travel reports. Some of the same motifs of enormity are found in mythology, but the atmosphere of myths and hero legends is quite different from those of tall tales.

There is not much correspondence between the ancient and the modern lying narratives with regard to patterns of action and particular motifs for expressing bigness; of course there are exceptions, such as the episode of the fish island and the device of expressing the magnitude of a great bird indirectly by describing the enormity of its nest. What the old and the new texts do have in common is the basic idea of the absurd exaggeration in size of certain familiar animals or objects such as birds and ships, which is conveyed sometimes simply by statis-

tics such as an island of cheese that is twenty-five stades in circumference, or by a simple but striking comparison with an ordinary referent such as giant ants that are smaller than dogs but bigger than foxes, or birds eggs that are bigger than Chian wine jars, or, most enjoyably, by a more complex image or incident such as fish so heavy that it requires oxen to drag them from the water or trees that are too high to shoot an arrow over. The modern texts taken as a class of story similarly display a mixture of traditional themes and unique expressions.

Lit. AT 1960Z, *Other Stories of Great Objects and the Like.* Ashliman, type 1960Z. *EM* 6:248.

1. Henningsen 1963:203.
2. Henningsen 1965:199.
3. See further Hansen 1996b.
4. See AT 700, *Tom Thumb*, and AT 1960C, *The Great Catch of Fish.*
5. Grimm 112.
6. *EM* 6:241.
7. 3.113.
8. Ktesias *FGH* 688 F 45r; Henry 1947:82–83; and Aelian *NA* 5.3. The literary history of Ktesias's worm is traced by Kitchell 1993:352–356.
9. How and Wells 1:292.
10. Apollodoros *Bibl.* 1.6.3. For a discussion of these monsters see Fontenrose 1959.
11. *Poetics* 7.1451A.
12. Afanas'ev 1975:54–55.
13. Musick 1970:260–261, 296–297, no. 75. Musick collected the tale in 1959 from a male raconteur, whose grandmother had told him the tale in Hungarian.
14. *NH* 9.2.4.
15. *NH* 32.4.10.
16. *NH* 9.17.44.
17. *Od.* 9–12.
18. *True Stories* 1.1–53.
19. *Tobit* 6.1–5. See further Moore 1996:198–200.
20. *Baba Bathra* 73b, cited by Ben-Amos 1976:26.
21. Runeberg 1902; Coulter 1926; Motif J1761.1, *Whale thought to be island.*
22. *Physiologus Graecus* 17. The narrative is not strictly a story, since it is recounted as being a recurrent phenomenon.
23. *Alexander Romance* 3.17. The author elsewhere (2.38) mentions giant fishes and crabs.
24. *Baba Bathra* 73b. See Runeberg 1902:356; Coulter 1926:34–35.
25. *Yasna* 9.10–11. See Runeberg 1902:361–362; Coulter 1926:35–36.
26. Runeberg 1902:388–389.
27. Sindbad: Runeberg 1902:349–351; Coulter 1926:37. Brendan: Runeberg 1902:352; Coulter 1926:44–47.
28. Glassie 1985:104–105, no. 36.
29. Briggs (1970) A2:104.
30. Ranke 1972:81–82, no. 114.
31. *True Stories* 1.16.
32. 2.37–38.
33. 2.32; 3.21; 2.37.
34. *EM* 6:246.
35. *NH* 7.2.21. Similarly, in a Danish narrative collected in 1854 from Maren Mathisdatter the teller claimed that her father had a head of cabbage so big that the king with his entire armed forces could find decent shelter under a single leaf (Bødker 1954:112, 116).
36. *EM* 6:246.
37. Henningsen 1965:199.
38. *True Stories* 1.40–42.
39. 2.37–38.
40. *EM* 6:247.
41. Bødker 1954:115.
42. *True Stories* 1.11.

43. 1.13.

44. 2.40.

45. Vv. 723–725. Greek vases illustrate birds serving as flying steeds. For example, Aphrodite rides a large goose or other bird (see *LIMC* [1984] 2.1:96–98, no. 903–946); women and satyrs ride upon phallos-birds, that is, surreal birds with a neck in the form of a penis (Dover 1978:133).

46. Henderson 1975:129.

47. *Vita Aesopi* 111, 116.

48. *True Stories* 2.3.

49. *True Stories* 2.40. An egg, presumably huge in size, is frequently an element in mythic cosmogonies, both in Greece (e.g., Kirk and Raven 1957:41–48) and elsewhere.

50. 3.102.

51. 2.24–33.

52. *True Stories* 1.12, 16.

53. 1.13–16.

54. *Peace* 181.

55. Platnauer 1964:74.

56. Fable: Hsr 3; Perry 3. Folktale: AT 621, *The Louse-Skin*, not attested in antiquity.

57. Briggs (1970) A2:110.

58. Sappho fr. 29 LP.

59. *True Stories* 2.45.

60. Photograph in Grant 1982:53.

61. Martial 13.2.

Groom Teaches His Horse to Live without Food

In this little tale, a foolish man trains his horse to live on little or no food. It dies.

An English tale relates how a man was training his horse to live on one straw per day, when it suddenly died.[1] According to a tale from Austria, people in Timelkam, Upper Austria, wanted to get a certain white horse out of the habit of eating. So each day they cut down its feed by a handful of hay, but just when it had almost gotten out of the habit it died. The people quickly gave it a handful of hay so that it could not be said that the horse died of hunger.[2] This is AT 1682, *The Groom Teaches His Horse to Live without Food*.

A Greek Joke

The witticism is found in *Philogelos*, a Greek jokebook dating from around the fourth century of our era.[3] In this text, a fool wanting to train his donkey not to eat stopped giving it any food. When the animal died from starvation, the man said: "What a loss! Just when it had learned not to eat, it died."

The trainer in the present tale is foolish because of poor reasoning rather than, for example, inexperience of the world. He thinks that since one can train donkeys or horses to do many things with good results, one can train them to do all things with good results, including not to eat. Similarly he reasons that if a little dieting is beneficial, a lot of dieting must be even better. He is possibly the kind of fool who is all the more foolish for thinking he is clever, for his crowning folly is that when the animal dies of starvation, he fails to see the il-logic of his strategy and instead bemoans the loss of an animal whose training he has just completed. Faintly reminiscent of the present tale is a humorous re-

mark quoted by Cicero from a farce: "The silly man, just when he began to be a man of substance, died."[4]

The protagonist of this and many other jokes in the collection is a *scholastikos*, that is, a student or a professor, but in *Philogelos* the word signifies little more than "numskull," perhaps having developed from an intermediate sense of "learned fool."[5]

Lit. AT 1682, *The Groom Teaches His Horse to Live without Food.* McCartney 1931:197. Ashliman, type 1682. Marzolph 1987:198–199.

1. Clouston 1888:2.
2. Ranke 1972:44, no. 40.
3. *Phil.* 9. The manuscripts present the joke in two nearly identical versions, one told of a donkey and the other of a horse.
4. *De Orat.* 2.67.274: "Homo fatuus/Postquam rem habere coepit est emortuus."
5. Cf. Thierfelder 1968:17–18.

Hatch-Penny ✺ Pases' Penny

Hatch-penny, a magic coin that always returns to its original owner, figures in a number of more or less similar tales. The original owner may acquire the coin in a supernatural fashion, and it may bring bad luck to anyone who acquires it wrongfully, but in any case the coin always returns to the possession of its owner.[1]

This story is AT 745, *Hatch-Penny.*

In an Arabic legend recorded in the seventh or eighth century, an early ruler of Egypt named Hûgîb made a dirham (a kind of coin) out of certain marvelous things. This coin always brought its owner the advantage in buying and weighing, and it was passed down from one generation to the next. A special property of the dirham was that whenever one bought something, paying for it with the coin, and said the words, "O dirham, remember the old agreement you made," he would find the coin in its usual place upon his return home, and the seller would find in its place only a leaf.[2]

Different traditions tell how to acquire a hatch-penny. In the ones I have seen, a person must perform a particular ritual outside the church in order to acquire the coin, usually from the devil. According to a nineteenth-century Danish informant, for example, you must put a cat in a sack on Christmas morning and walk around the church three times before sunrise, whistling through the keyhole each time you pass it. Then a fellow will come and ask what you want. You offer to sell him the cat for a dollar, and he will accept. You must take care to tie the sack with many knots in order to get away safely before he manages to open the bag, or things will go wrong. With that dollar you can purchase all you want, and you will have it back again before the evening.[3] The aspirant whistles in the keyhole of the church door because the keyhole was commonly regarded as a place to communicate with the devil, in this case to summon him.[4]

Another Danish informant says that you must go to the church and take a piece of lead from the church windows. You read something over it and then

lay it in your coin purse. After that you can give a dollar away a hundred times a day and it will return. "It's called a hatch-penny (*vekseldaler*), and Jens Smed in Hasseris had such a one. I saw him use it three times in a tavern, and he stood and shook his coin-purse and had no other money in it."[5]

Other objects can show the hatch-penny's property of returning to its owner. A Hungarian folktale recounts how a cartman, János, acquired a fine whip from a man in a saloon in exchange for a mere quarter cup of brandy. He gradually perceived that there was some magic in the whip, for once he possessed it his previously sluggish horses became very high-spirited. He sold it several times for more than he had paid for it, but each time found it hanging in its place on its hook when he returned home. János rid himself of the whip only when he sold it for the same modest amount of brandy as he had paid for it.[6]

Pases' Penny

The Greeks had a proverbial expression, "Pases' penny" (τὸ Πάσητος ἡμιωβέλιον, literally "Pases' half-obol"), which the ancient commentators explain as referring to a certain Pases, who excelled all men in magic. By means of his spells he could make a lavish meal together with servants appear and disappear again. In particular, he had a half-obol coin that always returned to him.[7] The sources say something about the making of his magic coin, but unfortunately the texts are unsound at this point: "He also had a half-obol made by (or for) him from a . . . , which he gave to sellers from whom he wished to buy something, and it was found again on his person whenever he wanted."[8]

A Roman Hatch-Penny?

The idea may also have been familiar to the Romans as well, for in his satire on wives Juvenal mentions magic coins that may be hatch-pennies, although it is unclear whether the magic coins return to their owner or multiply of themselves. Illustrating his proposition that women, in addition to being poor managers of money, are given to extravagance, the satirist remarks that they spend their funds thoughtlessly "as though the coin would renew itself in their empty coffer and the pile from which it is taken would always be full."[9] Juvenal's magically inexhaustible money box is doubtless an allusion to Roman folk belief and possibly also to a well-known story in which such a money box served as a motif. Inexhaustible purses are found in modern folk belief.[10]

Mestra the Shape-Changer

In Greek mythology Erysichthon has a magician daughter who behaves rather like a hatch-penny. Erysichthon incurred the anger of Demeter when he cut down a grove sacred to her, and as a result she caused him to feel an insatiable hunger. He had a daughter Mestra, who, being a magician, had the power to metamorphose into any kind of animal. To support his appetite for food Erysichthon sold her daily, and she changed form again and returned to her father.[11] According to the version of the story recounted by Ovid, Erysichthon

sold his daughter Mestra as a slave after he had exhausted his funds. She prayed to Neptune, asking the god, who earlier had taken her virginity, to save her now from slavery. Neptune changed her into a man, allowing her to escape her new master, and then restored her shape. When Erysichthon learned that his daughter had the power to change her form, he sold her repeatedly, and she escaped each time by taking the form of a mare, bird, cow, stag, or the like, and thereby earned provisions dishonestly for her greedy father until he died.[12]

In sum the motif of the hatch-penny, both in the strict sense of a magic coin that returns to its owner each time it has been used, and in the loose sense of any other thing that returns magically to its owner after it has been sold, is well established in ancient oral story.[13] Too little is known of the story of Pases' coin–if indeed there was a story–for us to assess how similar it was to later tales of hatch-pennies.

Lit. AT 745, *Hatch-Penny.* Liebrecht 1879:89. Roscher 1:1379; 3:1664. Crusius 1889:40–41; 1895:55–57, no. 50. Otto 1890:185, no. 908. Friedländer 1910:532. Feilberg (1886–1914) 4:1031. Siebs 1930–31. Liungman 1961:209. *EM* 6:640–645.

1. *EM* 6:640.
2. Wüstenfeld 1862:332, cited by Leibrecht 1879:89.
3. Kristensen (1886) 8:290, no. 498.
4. Similarly a Scandinavian who wished to make a written contract with the devil placed his or her signed contract in the church keyhole, which served as the devil's mailbox. Several such contracts have survived; see Kvideland and Sehmsdorf 1988:282–283.
5. Kristensen (1900) 6:235, no. 695.
6. Dégh 1965:240–243, no. 51. The ultimate, if not immediate, source of János's whip must be the devil; similarly, hatch-pennies are often gotten from the devil (Siebs 1930–31:1620).
7. Diogeneianos 8.40 (τὸ Πάσητος ἡμιωβόλιον); Plutarch *Prov. Alex.* 50 (*CPG, Supplementum,* IIIa); *Suda* s.vv. Πάσης and Ἡμιωβόλιον; Apostolios 17.6. He was mentioned by the first-century grammarian Apion in a lost work Περὶ μάγου (*FGH* 616 F 23). On the story and its sources and analogues see Crusius 1895:55–57.
8. The entries in Plutarch and the *Suda* (s.v. Πάσης) are essentially identical. The *Suda* gives: εἶχε δὲ καὶ ἡμιωβέλιον ἐκ μιᾶς αὐτῷ πεποιημένον, ὃ διαδιδόμενον ὑπ' αὐτοῦ τοῖς πιπράσκουσι, παρ' ὧν ἤθελεν ὠνεῖσθαι, εἰ ἠβούλετο, πάλιν παρ' αὐτῷ ηὑρίσκετο (the sources vary between the forms *hemiobolion* and *hemiobelion*). Among the emendations that have been suggested are "made by/for him from *a mina*" (ἐκ μνᾶς) and "by *magic*" (ἐκ μαγείας).
9. *Sat.* 6.363–364: "ac velut exhausta redivivus pullulet arca/nummus et e pleno tollatur semper acervo."
10. Feilberg (1910–14) 4:1031.
11. Hesiod fr. 43(b) MW = schol. Lykophron 1393.
12. *Met.* 8.738–878. Cf. Antoninus Lib. 17.
13. The legend of the Samian tyrant Polykrates, according to which Polykrates cast into the sea a gold ring that was presently found in a fish he was served (Herodotos 3.40–43), is another international tale with some resemblance to tales of hatch-pennies. See further AT 736A, *The Ring of Polycrates.*

Hearing-Impaired Persons

Hearing-impaired persons often carry on as though they heard well, trying to conceal their impairment. Such persons may act as though they understand a question or a statement when in fact they understand only a part of it or nothing at all. Their behavior can have humorous results when they mistake a

poorly heard word for a different word of similar sound or when the answer they give is unrelated to the question posed.[1]

International narratives about hearing-impaired persons fall into two broad classes, those in which all the interacting characters are hearing-impaired, and those which bring together a hearing person and a hearing-impaired person. In both kinds of story the principal idea is that the deaf person gives a reply that does not match the question he has been asked, a reply that is amusing because of its inappropriateness or ironic appropriateness.[2] The texts do not always distinguish sharply between characters who are entirely deaf and characters who are hard-of-hearing, so that my own terminology is also approximate. Similar tales can be told of characters who are not hearing-impaired but behave somewhat as if they were: for example, persons who do not understand a particular language.[3] This entry discusses four comic tale types whose humor has to do with to hearing impairment.

1. Search for the Lost Animal

In this tale, in which all the characters are hearing-impaired, a deaf man (A) in search of his strayed animals approaches another deaf man (B) who is engaged in his own activity. A asks B about the animals, but B does not understand him. When B make a gesture with his hand for some other purpose, A believes that he is pointing out the location of the animals. A goes there, by chance actually finds them, returns to B, and offers him as a reward for his help one of the animals, which sometimes is slightly injured in some way. B, not understanding what A says, thinks that A is demanding something of him (e.g., compensation for harm done to the animal), and defends himself. After arguing a while they refer the matter to a judge (C). Because of his own deafness C entirely misunderstands what the two men say, so that the judgment he gives (the content of which varies considerably) has no connection with the issues before him.

This tale, classified as AT 1698A, *Search for the Lost Animal*, is known in oral tradition from Europe to India. Texts are also found in which more characters appear, drawing out the tale; but whether the tale features three persons or more, it regularly begins with the encounter of the two deaf men and ends with the inappropriate settlement decreed by the deaf judge.[4]

Thus, in a modern Greek tale featuring five characters, a deaf shepherd who had lost his sheep asked a deaf farmer if he had seen them. The latter replied: "God bless you," and urged on his oxen with his goad, which the first man took as a sign that he should look in that direction. When he actually found his sheep there, he selected the fattest and brought it to the farmer as a reward. The farmer replied: "I have no sheep. Why do you want payment for the use of pasture?" They argued and decided to go to court. On the way they met a third man, who was riding a mule. They brought their argument to him, but the third man, who also was deaf, replied: "You want to buy the mule? It belongs to another man." The three men now met a deaf woman, to whom they brought their request, but she answered, "My daughter-in-law has sent you to reconcile me to her, but I'll never do it." All four now reached the Turkish judge, who also was deaf. As the woman listened and raised her hand to the

sky in protest, the judge said, "What, it's the new moon? Bring me the lamb so that I can celebrate Bairam." So he took the lamb, and the other four departed.[5]

An Epigram by Nikarchos

Although *Search for the Lost Animal* is not found in its entirety in ancient literature, an epigram by the poet Nikarchos seems to imply an acquaintance with it or with a tale very much like it.[6] Nikarchos was an epigrammatist of the first century A.D., many of whose brief poems are preserved in the Greek Anthology. Here is a prose rendering of the poem.

> A hard-of-hearing man went to court with another hard-of-hearing man,
> and the judge was deafer than the two of them.
> One contended the other owed him five months' rent, and the other said the first
> man had milled during the night.
> Looking at them the judge said: "Why are you quarreling?
> She's your mother. Both of you must take care of her."

A composer of verse epigrams cannot recount a folktale such as *Search for the Lost Animal* from beginning to end. If he deems it suitable for epigrammatic treatment, he must rather capture some aspect of it, something comic or striking that can stand by itself. Each of Nikarchos's three couplets makes one point. The first summarizes the situation, the second lists the unrelated complaints of the two disputants, and the third gives the irrelevant decree of the judge. The poem catches the absurdity of two hearing-impaired litigants in court, each of whom raises a different issue, presumably in the belief that the other man is defending himself against it rather than, as the case actually is, making an unrelated charge of his own, and of the deaf judge whose fervent and confident verdict has nothing to do with either charge. If Nikarchos was inspired by a form of the international tale, he has reduced the narrative to its final, climactic episode.

Lit. (AT 1698A, *Search for the Lost Animal.*) Aarne 1914:16–28. Weinreich 1954:692–704.

2. Misunderstood Words

This tale belongs to the second class of narrative about hearing-impaired persons, those that portray a conversation between a hearing person and a hard-of-hearing person. In this tale a person of normal hearing speaks with a person who, because of a hearing impairment or other reason, consistently misunderstands the key words that the hearing person tries to impart. AT 1698G, *Misunderstood Words Lead to Comic Results*, refers not so much to a particular sequence of action as to a particular situation.

An example is found in a collection published in 1670, the *Fasciculus Facetiarum Novissimarum*. An aristocratic man who had to go on a journey sent his wife ahead in a carriage. In the woods he encountered a peasant and asked him if he had seen a carriage with a woman's compartment (*Frauenzimmer*) go past.

"No, I haven't seen any carpenters (*Zimmerleute*)," replied the peasant. As the conversation proceeded, the traveler said to the peasant: "You are rather rude (*grob*)," which the peasant understood as "big" (*groß*) and answered: "Yes, sir, but my brother is even bigger," and so on.[7] In a Danish oral tale published in 1885 a man went to a house and asked a woman who was hard of hearing for fire (*fyr*) for his pipe. "We don't have a bull (*tyr*)," she replied, "though there's one at the parsonage." "I asked for fire (*ild*)," the man repeated. "Yes, it's too bad (*ill*) that it's so far from here and the road is poor," was the answer. "Are you crazy (*gal*)?" he asked. "If you think I'm well (*daal*) dressed, you should see me in my Sunday clothes," etc.[8]

In these dialogues a passer-by (A) makes an inquiry of a local person (B). Every time A speaks, B mistakes an important word in his speech for a similar word of different significance and so misinterprets the speaker's intent. The exasperated passer-by eventually departs. There is little or no similarity in the content of the conversation from one narrative to the other since the puns and other misunderstandings are dependent upon the particular language in which the story is related.

Nikarchos Again

Another epigram by Nikarchos concerning hearing impairment has come down to us. In this one the poet complains to an acquaintance about an old slave woman who is hard of hearing. He urges Onesimos to send the woman away, since she causes the poet so many problems. If they tell her to bring some cheeses (*tyrous*), she comes with wheat (*pyrous*). Yesterday, the speaker complains, he had a headache and asked her for rue (*pêganon*), but she brought him a frying pan (*têganon*). If he asks for juice (*opon*), she brings in a beam of wood (*dokon*). If he says: "Bring me some greens (*lachanon*)," she rushes back with a chamber pot (*lasanon*). If he asks for vinegar (*oxos*), she brings a bow (*toxon*); if a bow, then vinegar. Whatever he says, she never gets it right. The old woman is turning him into a herald.[9]

As in the modern texts, the epigram portrays the conversation of a hearing person and a person who is (or behaves as if) hearing-impaired, except that in the epigram the portrayal takes the nontraditional format of a report by the narrator to an addressee. Of the six elegiac couplets, the first introduces the situation, the next four comically illustrate instances of miscommunication between the poet and the old woman, and the concluding verses express the speaker's exasperation. The modern texts show a somewhat more complex and orderly progression in the dialogue, one topic leading logically to the next, whereas the ancient poem has an additive structure, one topic proceeding to the next in a more or less random order. In the Greek poem, as also in the German text (and perhaps in the Danish tale), the hearing person (poet, aristocrat) belongs to a refined set, whereas the hearing-impaired other (slave woman, peasant) is a member of a lower stratum of society.

Lit. AT 1698G, *Misunderstood Words Lead to Comic Results*. Aarne 1914:40–41, 76–77. Weinreich 1954:704–718.

3. The Deaf Man and the Proud Nobleman

Another tale featuring a conversation of a hearing man and a person who is hard of hearing takes a less kindly view of the arrogant aristocrat. A nobleman who is taking a walk with his friends decides to amuse them by engaging in conversation a man whom they encounter. He asks the man several leading questions that are intended to mock him, and, as he presumably expects, the second man, being hard of hearing, misses the mockery. But the latter's innocent replies unintentionally have the effect of mocking the mocker. In the end the nobleman says: "I wish you many thousands of gallows and ropes around your neck," to which the man, believing the nobleman has wished him a good evening, replies: "Sir, I wish you twice as many," and goes his way.[10]

This tale is AT 1698F, *The Deaf Man and the Proud Nobleman*.

Theophrastos's Inattentive Man

A possible reminiscence of the final exchange in this tale is found in an unlikely source, Theophrastos's *Characters*, a work in which the philosopher defines and describes a number of character types. In his fourteenth chapter he takes up *anaisthesia*, literally "insensibility," which he defines as "mental slowness in speech and action." The *anaisthetos*, Theophrastos says, is the sort of man who will do a problem in arithmetic, write down the answer, and then ask the person next to him what the answer is. Or the sort of person who, when he is a defendant in an action and the court date is imminent, will forget it and take an excursion to the country. To judge from these and other examples of behavior that Theophrastos lists as typical for this type of character, the *anaisthetos* does not focus appropriately on the present occasion but behaves distractedly, as though his mind were elsewhere. Theophrastos gives the following exchange as typical of the *anaisthetos*. "If someone asks him, 'How many corpses do you think have been carried out through the Sacred Gate?' he replies: 'I wish you and I had so many.'" Theophrastos's inattentive man seems to think the conversation is about money or goods or children, and gives an answer that would be appropriate to that topic. Some of the instances of behavior that Theophrastos attributes to his different types are paralleled in anecdotes, jokes, and fables, and he must have taken some of his examples from humorous tales that circulated orally in his day and whose subjects were generic types such as misers, cowards, fools, and the like.[11] The exemplary conversation of the *anaisthetos* and his interlocutor resembles the final exchange in *The Deaf Man and the Proud Nobleman*, where the mocking nobleman wishes the hearing-impaired man a thousand gallows (or the like), and the other man, only half hearing him, wishes the first man twice as many. Although the exchange in Theophrastos does not feature an insult, it may have been from a tale such as *The Deaf Man and the Proud Nobleman* that the philosopher borrowed the idea of the exchange, adapting it to his own purposes.

Similar gaffes are found elsewhere in ancient literature. In Apuleius's *Metamorphoses* a certain Thelyphron was hired to spend a night with a cadaver in order to guard it against witches. In the morning the mistress of the house, after examining the corpse and finding it unharmed, paid Thelyphron hand-

somely for his services and thanked him, saying that she would henceforth regard him as a member of the household. Exhilarated by the gold coins in his hand, Thelyphron replied: "On the contrary, madam, consider me one of your servants and feel free to call upon my services as often as you have need." The moment he uttered these ominous words the whole household set upon him angrily and threw him out of the house.[12] And a joke in a Greek jokebook tells how a numskull at a wedding celebration expresses a wish that "all these celebrations of yours be happy ones," a sentiment that is suitable to an event such as a birthday, which one hopes will be celebrated repeatedly, but not to a wedding celebration.[13]

Lit. (AT 1698F, *The Deaf Man and the Proud Nobleman.*) Aarne 1914:39–40. BP 3:149. Trenkner 1958:152.

4. *"Good Day"—"A Woodchopper"*

In another tale involving a conversation between a man who hears and a man who is hard of hearing, A is a traveler (official, neighbor, etc.) and B is a local. Usually neither is acquainted with the other, so that the traveler is unaware that the local man is hard of hearing. The local is occupied in some activity, commonly the carving of an axe haft. Seeing a man approaching, he rehearses to himself four or so questions that he expects the other to ask and the answers that he himself will give. For example: "First, he will ask what I am making, to which I'll say it's an axe haft. Then, he'll want to rent my boat to cross the river, and I'll say it's broken. Then he'll ask to borrow a horse, but I'll explain she is indisposed. Since he cannot secure transportation from me, he'll ask how to continue his journey, and I'll point out the way between the two trees." The traveler arrives and greets the local: "Good day," to which the man replies (for example): "An axe haft." The stranger continues: "Where is your wife?" The local replies: "Broken." The traveler: "How about your daughter?" The local: "She just foaled." The traveler, now angry: "You ought to be hanged!" to which the local answers: "Over there between the two trees."

This narrative is AT 1698J, *"Good Day,"—"A Woodchopper,"* a European tale that is especially popular in Scandinavia.[14] It is one of several comic tales in which a deaf man carefully plans out a conversation in advance.

A Norwegian text tells of a deaf ferryman, who was expecting a visit from an official from a nearby town and was considering what the official would ask about and what he himself would say. He decided to occupy himself with an activity, namely, carving an axe haft, so that the man would ask what it was going to be, and he could say: "An axe haft." Then the official would ask how long it was going to be, and he would reply: "Up to this twig." Then the man would ask where the ferry was, and the ferryman would say: "I've got to tar her. She's lying down on the beach with cracks in both ends." Then the man would ask: "Where is your gray mare?" and he would say: "She's in the stall about to foal." Then the official would ask: "Where are your herds and summer cowhouse?" and he would say: "Not far away. When you get to the top of the hill, you're almost there." When the official arrived, he said: "Good day." "An

axe haft," replied the ferryman. "Well . . . ," said the official, "How far is it to the inn?" "Up to this twig," he replied, pointing a little way up the material he was carving. The official shook his head and asked: "Where is your wife?" The ferryman answered: "I've got to tar her. She's lying on the beach with cracks in both ends." "Where is your daughter?" "She's in the stall ready to foal." The deaf man thought he had done pretty well for himself, but the official said: "Oh, go to the devil!" "Yes, it's not far away. When you get to the top of the hill, you're almost there."[15]

A Scene in Heliodoros

Writing in the third or fourth century of our era, the novelist Heliodoros describes how a certain Kalasiris disembarked at the island of Zakynthos and set out to look for lodging among the local inhabitants. Presently he approached an old fisherman who was sitting at the door of his house and mending his net.

> "Greetings, sir, can you tell me where one might find lodging?" he asked.
> "Near the headland," he replied. "It got caught on a sunken rock yesterday and was torn."
> "That's not what I asked you," said Kalasiris. "Would you be so kind as to inform me either if you could take us in or if you could lead me to someone else who might do so?"
> "I didn't actually sail with them myself," he said. "No, I hope I never get so old that I'd make such a mistake. It's the fault of the young boys, who don't know what they're doing yet, dropping their nets where they shouldn't."

Finally, Kalasiris perceived that the fisherman was hard of hearing. So he yelled his greeting and inquiry to the old man, who then invited Kalasiris and his party to lodge with him.[16]

In this passage, as in the oral tale, (1) a traveler comes upon a local man (2) who is engaged in some ordinary craft (carving a haft, mending a net). (3) The traveler greets him and asks for his help. The local man, who (4) is hard of hearing and (5) mistakenly assumes that the stranger is inquiring about his present activity, (6) explains instead what he is doing. (7) The confused traveler persists in his inquiry, and (8) the local man gives another answer that is irrelevant to the question that was asked. Folktale and fiction now diverge, for in the oral tale the traveler keeps making fruitless attempts at communication and then angrily departs, whereas in the novel the traveler now realizes that the fisherman is hearing-impaired, and deals with him appropriately and successfully. Underlying the passage in Heliodoros is probably an early form of the present tale type that the author has adapted to his own purposes.

The oral narrator of this folktale exploits the misunderstandings for comic effect in several ways: by drawing the conversation out; by arranging most of the questions and answers in such a way that the deaf man's rehearsed utterances can be understood comically as almost appropriate responses to the traveler's queries; and by having it end in exasperation, abuse, and a final, unintentionally funny remark. In contrast, Heliodoros fashions a scene that is more realistic, more urbane, and only gently humorous.[17] Since the novelist presents the

episode from the point of view of the traveler rather than that of the local, he does not say whether the fisherman works out his comments in advance or simply improvises, and indeed the reader does not know in advance that the old man is hard of hearing.

Lit. (AT 1698J, *"Good Day"*—*"A Woodchopper.")* Aarne 1914:51–60 and passim. Weinreich 1954:718–721.

1. Aarne 1914:3.
2. Aarne 1914:80.
3. Aarne 1914:80–81.
4. Aarne 1914:16–23.
5. Weinreich 1954:692, citing Paul Kretschmer, *Neugriechischen Märchen* (1917), pp. 58 ff., no. 17.
6. *AP* 11.251.
7. Aarne 1914:40–41.
8. Aarne 1914:76.
9. *AP* 11.74.
10. Aarne 1914:39–40.
11. Trenkner 1958:149–154.
12. *Met.* 2:26. See Trenkner 1958:152.
13. *Philogelos* 72. Compare also the comic folktale, AT 1696, *"What Should I Have Said (Done)?"*
14. Aarne 1914:51–60.
15. Asbjørnsen and Moe (1965) 2:332–334: "God dag, mann!"—"Økseskaft."
16. *Aethiopica* 5.18.
17. Cf. Weinreich 1954:720.

Holding Up the Rock ≈ Holding Up the Sky

At the approach of another character a trickster positions his shoulder under a large rock (wall, tree, etc.) and pretends to be holding it up; then he induces the second character to take his place. Or the trickster tells another character that a ceiling (rock) is about to fall, and he induces the second character to hold it up. Often the trickster promises to go after a prop or food. In any case he departs, taking advantage of the dupe's immobility in order to eat the dupe's food (take his goods, make his escape). The dupe remains behind holding up the rock for hours (days, indefinitely).

This little tale of trickery, told of humans or more frequently of animals, is AT 1530, *Holding Up the Rock*. Although it is found in Europe, it is especially popular in Africa and the Americas. It is sometimes told as an independent tale, but more usually it is one of a series of short episodes recounted of a trickster and a dupe.

A tale collected in 1968 from a Mexican-American woman in Texas features one trick after another played by a rabbit on a coyote. At one point in the cycle, the coyote, angry at having been duped by the rabbit, caught up with him and was about to capture him. Then the rabbit said that he was holding up a big rock and that people were going to bring him a big meal there. The coyote said that he did not believe the rabbit, since he was a big

liar. But the rabbit insisted he was telling the truth, saying that the coyote should take his place and he would see. So the coyote took the rabbit's place. A while later a fox came by, and the coyote asked the fox to help him hold up the rock. The fox asked who left the coyote there, and when the coyote said the rabbit had, the fox said that the coyote was there and should stay there, after which he himself ran off.[1] In this text the logical connection between holding up a rock and being served dinner, presumably as a reward for doing so, is rather weak, since the task of holding up the rock is not presented as benefiting anyone who might wish to repay the holder by bringing him dinner. But precisely the same situation can also be found in other texts.[2]

In another cycle of tales, collected in the United States in 1916–17 from Portuguese Negro immigrants from the Cape Verde Islands, the dupe and the trickster are, respectively, the animal companions Lob ("wolf") and Subrinh ("nephew"), also called Pedr. A male raconteur relates how Uncle Lob and Nephew Pedr stole a pig, took it to a cave, put it in a pot, and started cooking it. When the food was nearly ready, Pedr threw a little stone at the roof of the cave, and as it fell down he said that the roof of the cave was coming down and that Uncle Lob should stand up and hold it up. Uncle Lob did so, and Pedr took the pot, ate all the food, and departed. Uncle Lob held the roof for three days before jumping aside and splitting open his head. He was so angry at Pedr he wanted to kill him. Or, in a variant ending, the narrator comments that he went by the cave yesterday and saw Uncle Lob still holding it up.[3]

In these animal texts the interest turns on food. In the former tale, the rabbit and the coyote are in a relationship of prey and predator. The prey induces the predator to hold up the rock by promising that he will receive food, and the result is that the predator is cheated both of his original prey and of the promised substitute. In the latter tale Pedr dupes his dull-witted companion in order to have all of their stolen food, or—since the principal characters are animals— prey, for himself.

In many texts the trickster claims that the world will fall if he does not continue to hold up the rock (or tree or the like) that is supporting it. Thus, in a Hitchiti Indian text collected in Oklahoma and published in 1929, a man saw Rabbit eating peas from his garden and chased after him. When Rabbit saw him he knelt beside a tree, pretending to brace himself against it. The man threatened to kill Rabbit, but Rabbit said that if the man killed him they both would die, for this tree was bracing up the earth and was going to fall down; if it did, then the earth, sky, and everything else would be destroyed. Rabbit said he had already dispatched others to help him brace the tree. When the man looked, it did appear that the tree was touching the sky and was about to fall. So he ran off, after which Rabbit also ran off.[4]

Finally, a Puerto Rican tale relates how Pedro de Urdemalis promised to kill Juan el Astuto. Juan placed a large stone on his head, and when they met he explained that he was tired but that if he let the stone fall the world would come to an end. Pedro offered to keep the world from coming to an end in exchange for twenty pesetas. So Juan told Pedro to hold the stone and not let it fall, while he himself went to look for the money. Pedro took the stone, but Juan did not

come back. When Pedro became very tired he threw away the stone, but the world did not come to an end. He vowed to avenge himself on Juan.[5]

The Eleventh Labor of Herakles

According to the mythographer Apollodoros, Eurystheus assigned to Herakles as his Eleventh Labor the task of bringing golden apples from the Hesperides. These apples, which Earth had given to Zeus upon his marriage to Hera, were "on Atlas among the Hyperboreans" and were guarded by a certain dragon and by the Hesperides. On the way Herakles slew the eagle that tormented Prometheus, and freed him from his bondage. Returning the favor, Prometheus acted as Herakles' adviser in his quest, instructing him not to go after the apples himself but instead to relieve Atlas of the support of the sky and send him after the apples. Herakles reached the Hyperboreans and did so. When, however, Atlas got three apples from the Hesperides and came back to Herakles, he informed Herakles that he did not want to hold up the sky anymore, and bade Herakles hold it up in his stead, saying that he himself would convey the apples to Eurystheus. On the advice of Prometheus, Herakles promised to do so but asked Atlas to take back the sky just until Herakles should place a pad on his head. So Atlas put the apples on the ground and took the sky from him, but Herakles then departed with the apples and gave them to Eurystheus. Presently they were returned, since it was improper for the apples to be anywhere else.[6] The legend of the duping of Atlas is really only one of two solutions to this task, for according to a different story Herakles simply killed the dragon and picked the apples from the tree himself.[7]

The parallels between the Heraklean legend and the modern international tradition can be summed up as follows. (1) The trickster assumes—in reality or in pretense—the support of a great object, (2) which he asks the dupe to hold just long enough for him to perform a certain chore. (3) The credulous dupe relieves the trickster of the burden, after which (4) the trickster takes the dupe's goods and (5) departs, while (6) the dupe remains behind for a long time, holding up the real or supposed burden.

In ancient Greek tradition, then, *Holding Up the Rock* appears to have been incorporated into a comic legend featuring two strongmen of tradition, the hero Herakles and the god Atlas. On the other hand, Kurt Ranke thinks it probable that this narrative situation has been invented more than once by oral narrators.[8] Of course, it is impossible to prove or disprove either possibility or for that matter the more remote possibility that the ancient legend has given rise to the international folktale. But the close parallelism between the legend and tale with respect to their basic action, in addition to their agreements in small detail—the trickster's alleged burden often being the sky or world, the trickster's having designs upon the dupe's food–strongly suggests that we are dealing with genetically related versions rather than independently invented stories. And the ancient legend's peculiar complexity (first Atlas supports the sky, then Herakles, and then Atlas again, with Prometheus acting as Herakles' adviser) and obscurity (why does Herakles initially send Atlas after the apples?) make it an unlikely model and source for the international tale. It is easier to imagine

that the simpler international tale has been integrated into an established mythological system.

When the present tale was attached to Herakles and Atlas, it was necessarily constrained by mythological details that were already in place. The dupe had to be Atlas, since everyone knew that Atlas, not Herakles, was the bearer of the sky; even his name Atlas "Bearer" (formed from **tlaô* "carry, bear") said as much. And since it was already established how Atlas had become the sky bearer (Zeus had assigned him the task as a punishment), a new narrative would have both to begin and to end with Atlas as sky bearer. Moreover, the basic trait of both Atlas and Herakles was extraordinary strength, not cunning, so that Herakles was coupled with the trickster Prometheus, presumably in order to be supplied temporarily with cleverness. Finally, since in Greek thought, as commonly in nonscientific cosmologies, the sky was conceived of as being something heavy and solid that had to be supported, rather like a roof over the earth, the Greek mythological sky corresponded closely to the rock or roof or world or sky that the trickster in the folktale claims he is holding up. The significant difference between the ancient and many modern versions of the tale in this respect lies not in the kind of burden the trickster holds up, since many modern texts also speak of his holding up the world, but in the fact that he really does sustain a burden rather than only pretending to do so.

But Prometheus's first piece of advice to Herakles is puzzling. Why must he take the sky from Atlas and send him for the apples? Why should the hero not just fetch the apples himself? Perhaps it is because Apollodoros imagines that the apple trees grow upon Atlas, whom he conceives of both as a mountain and as an anthropomorphic deity. Or perhaps because it is natural for Atlas, represented by some mythographers as father of the Hesperides, to fetch the fruit from his own daughters, who are described sometimes as guardians of the apples.[9] But probably the most important reason lurks backstage, having to do with the mechanics of the story. The narrator's problem is to get Herakles, who will be assigned the role of trickster, into proper position for the action of *Holding Up the Rock*. Getting the characters into position is also the backstage function of Atlas's announcement that he does not care after all to take the sky back just now and will deliver the goods to Eurystheus in person, although at least in this case the motivation is clear enough, since the job of supporting the sky is not a voluntary one nor an honor but a punishment inflicted on Atlas by Zeus.[10] One could suppose, if only whimsically, that Atlas might enjoy occasional relief from his tiring and monotonous task, but in any case we need not imagine that he acts from cunning. When he is suddenly and unexpectedly free of his burden, the happy thought simply comes to him that he really need not resume it, at least not immediately.

The result of this exchange is that the two principal characters are now in the initial position for the story of *Holding Up the Rock*. Acting upon the advice of his trickster ally, Herakles deceives Atlas into taking the sky upon his own shoulders. Herakles' false promise that he will take the burden back as soon as he has placed a pad on his shoulders corresponds to the false promise made by the trickster in many modern texts, most commonly the avowal that he will return with a prop for the rock. The same affected casualness as that shown by Herakles, who asks Atlas to hold the sky briefly while he gets a pad for himself, is found in the Puerto Rican tale, in which Juan el Astuto asks Pedro de Urdemalis

to hold the stone while he goes home to fetch Pedro's wages. As soon as Atlas relieves Herakles of the load, Herakles absconds with the goods, leaving Atlas holding up the burden. In nearly all the texts food is an issue between the two principal characters, and the Greek story with its golden apples is no exception.

Several folklorists maintain that *Holding Up the Rock* is an African tale.[11] It may well be that it has diffused in recent times from Africa, but the presence of the story in fifth-century Greece shows how problematic are speculations about the origin of a traditional tale or declarations about the essential ethnicity of an international tale. A story that is popular with Africans in recent times may have been popular with Middle Easterners or Europeans previously and again with Africans before that and so on, in grand cycles that have left few traces because of the perishable medium by means of which the tales are transmitted.

Lit. AT 1530, *Holding Up the Rock. EM* 1:954–956. Ashliman, type 1530. Bascom 1992:114–136.

1. Paredes 1970:56, no. 26.
2. For example, Bascom 1992:124, no. 45; 127, no. 59.
3. Parsons 1917:237; (1923) 1:59. In a somewhat similar Baltic tale, a fox pretends to hold up a rock or a roof, ostensibly in order that it not fall on the bear's head but in reality in order to avoid having to join in the threshing. This tale is AT 9A, *In the Stable the Bear Threshes.* In *Holding up the Roof* the trickster's strategy is to persuade the victim to stay in a certain place in order that the trickster may thereby take advantage of him, whereas in the Baltic tale it is the trickster himself who stays in one place, pretending to be helpful in order to escape having to join in the common work.
4. Bascom 1992:126, no. 54.
5. Bascom 1992:131–132, no. 87.
6. Apollodoros *Bibl.* 2.5.11, supplemented by the scholiast on Apollonios of Rhodes *Argon.* 4.1396, who gives as his authority Pherekydes (*FGH* 3 F 17). The accounts of Apollodoros and of the scholiast are in essential agreement, except that the scholiast localizes the events in the distant west or southwest, the conventional residence of Atlas and the Hesperides, whereas Apollodoros locates the events among the Hyperboreans, a fabulous people of the far north. By the way, Thompson's motif index is incorrect in describing Atlas as supporting the earth rather than the sky (A842, *Atlas.* A man supports the earth on his shoulders.); Greek mythology has no earth supporter.
 On the ancient sources for Herakles' Eleventh Labor, including illustrations, which date to the sixth century B.C., see Sellers 1892:9–12 and plate 3; Frazer (1898) 3:523–525; Schweitzer 1922:135–141; Murley 1924; Brommer 1986:49–54; Carpenter 1991:129 and fig. 173, 209; Gantz 1993:410–413; *LIMC* 3.1:2–16 and 5.1:1–262, esp. nos. 2676–2787.
7. Euripides *Herakles* 394–407; Eratosthenes *Catasterisms* 3–4; Diodorus Sic. 4.26.4; Apollodoros *Bibl.* 2.5.11; Hyginus *Fab.* 30, *Astron.* 2.3.
8. *EM* 1:955.
9. Diodorus Sic. 4.27.2; Hyginus *Astron.* 2.3.
10. Hesiod *Th.* 507–520.
11. For example, Haring 1982:484; Bascom 1992:114–116.

Homecoming Husband 🐚 Odysseus

The story of the man who returns home after a long absence just as his wife is about to remarry is known to many peoples, sometimes as a folktale, often as a legend attached to an allegedly historical character. The story frequently takes the form of a ballad or epic song rather than a prose narrative.

Aarne-Thompson classify it as AT 974, *The Homecoming Husband*, cataloguing it among the novelle, or realistic romantic tales. It is found as a legend as well, and Christiansen includes it in his index of migratory legends as ML 8005.

In the oral story, a man leaves his wife shortly after their marriage to make a journey to a distant land (to travel, to go to war, to make a pilgrimage, etc.). Sometimes he instructs his wife to wait a certain number of years for his return, after which she is free to remarry; or he says that he will return at such and such a time; or he simply goes. He is absent (at war, in prison, etc.) for a long time, commonly seven or nine years. Finally, his wife decides to choose a new husband because the stated period of time has passed, because she is being forced to do so (by her kinsmen, by her suitor, etc.), because she has received a false report of her husband's death, or because she is unfaithful. The hero is mindful that the period of time that he has asked his wife to wait is nearly up; or he unexpectedly learns of his wife's imminent wedding. If the wedding is several days away, he manages on his own to return home before the event; if it is the next day, he returns with wondrous speed (a supernatural helper magically transports him home in one night as he sleeps, or his horse travels many miles with each leap). Or he just happens to return at this critical time. Back home the hero is unrecognizable (because of changes due to time and climate, because of years in prison, or because he is disguised). He encounters a local person who informs him of the wedding plans, and he may speak with other persons at various times, testing their loyalty. Although his kinsmen and former acquaintances remain unaware of his true identity, one of his animals (dog, horse, camel) may recognize him. With his humble appearance as a traveler (beggar, minstrel) he gains admittance to the house in which the wedding is being or about to be celebrated. Eventually he himself is recognized, usually by means of a token (his wedding ring, or half a ring that matches his wife's half) or a song that he sings, less often by means of a mark (birthmark, scar, etc.) or a feat that he accomplishes; or he may simply declare who he is. If his wife is loyal, they are reunited; if not, he punishes her. Similarly, if her suitor is innocent of misconduct, he is reconciled with the hero, but if not, he flees or is slain.[1]

A Christian legend recounted by Caesarius of Heisterbach in the early thirteenth century illustrates a prose text of the type. There lived in the town of Hollenbach a man named Gerhard whose descendants (says Caesarius) were still living in his own day, and the miracle concerning Gerhard was known to everyone in Hollenbach. Gerhard was an ardent devotee of St. Thomas. One day God permitted the devil in the guise of a traveler to come to Gerhard's door and ask for hospitality in the name of St. Thomas. Gerhard admitted him immediately and, since the devil feigned being cold, Gerhard gave him a cloak to keep him warm for the night. In the morning both the stranger and the cloak were gone. A short time later Gerhard conceived a desire to go to the tomb of St. Thomas. As he was setting out he took a gold ring and divided it in half in front of his wife, giving half to her and keeping the other half. He told her to trust it as a token, and asked her to wait five years for his return after which she might marry whom she would; and she so promised. Gerhard's journey was long and difficult, but finally he reached the city of St. Thomas, where he prayed, commending himself, his wife, and all his possessions to St. Thomas. Recalling that the fifth year would be over that very day, he lamented that his

wife soon would marry another man. But God had deliberately prolonged his journey because of what would follow. Gerhard saw the aforementioned demon walking around wearing his cloak. The demon explained that it was he who had asked hospitality in the name of St. Thomas and had taken his cloak. He explained that he was the devil, that Gerhard's wife was marrying another man, and that he himself had been ordered to bring Gerhard back to his home before the couple should consummate the marriage. Then he conveyed him from India to Germany and deposited him unharmed in his own land at dusk. The man entered his house looking utterly unkempt, saw his wife dining next to the groom, and gave her the half-ring. She recognized him as her husband and acknowledged him immediately. Gerhard dealt amicably with the groom, whom he deemed an honorable man.[2]

In a French folktale published in the nineteenth century, a brave, devout nobleman and his beautiful, upright wife were childless, so that the nobleman vowed to the Virgin to go to the Holy Land for seven years to fight the enemies of the Lord if his wife should give him a child. When his wife gave birth to a boy nine months later, the man said he had sworn to fight in the Holy Land for seven years. He warned her that men would tell her he had perished there and would ask for her hand in marriage; she should not believe them. Since she might not recognize him upon his return, he cut their marriage contract in two and gave half to each of them; when he should produce it upon his return, she would know that it was he. He departed, fought for a year, and was captured and imprisoned, after which no one heard any news of him. So three wicked brothers went to the nobleman's wife, declared that he was dead, and said she must wed one of them. She refused, since there was no proof of his death, but the brothers moved into her chateau anyway and treated it as their own, feasting there and gambling with the money from the harvest. When the husband had been gone for five years, the brothers again pressed the woman to marry, and she said she would wear black and be in mourning for a year, after which she would choose one of them as husband. The devil, hidden in the room, went to the imprisoned husband, informed him of the events, and offered to convey him home in return for a drop of his blood; but the man refused. At the end of the sixth year, the brothers again pressed the woman, who said she needed a year to sew her wedding dress. The devil offered once more to convey the nobleman home for a price, but the man declined. When only three months remained until the wedding, the devil again made his offer of conveyance in exchange for a portion of the first meal taken by the man and his wife, to which the man agreed. The devil flew for three days with the man and deposited him near his chateau. At nightfall, the unkempt man, looking like a beggar, knocked at the door and was informed that the mistress of the house was to be married on the morrow. He dashed upstairs, saying he had come from the Holy Land, and challenged the three good-for-nothings to fight. After he had killed them, he asked the mistress for his payment, and she offered him half of the property. He said she must marry him, but she refused. Then he produced the marriage contract, proving that he was her husband, and they embraced. After they had dined, the devil came for his due. The nobleman gave him the carcasses of the three dead man as well as the empty walnut shells from his meal. Since the devil found no meat in the shells, he had no power over the man and left with

the carcasses. The nobleman and his family lived happily ever after, and when they died they went to paradise.[3]

Epic forms of *The Homecoming Husband* are found in the tradition of several peoples. The story forms the second half of the Central Asian epic of the hero Alpamysh, who left his wife Barchin to do battle in another land. He was captured and spent seven years in a dungeon before he escaped. In the meantime, his half-brother usurped power over the tribe, persecuted Alpamysh's kin, and made preparations for Barchin to wed him, despite her refusals. Alpamysh learned of these affairs as he returned home. In his homeland an old camel recognized him. Disguised as a beggar, he went to the wedding feast, where he saw his parents and servants, noting who was loyal to him and who was not. One of the wedding games was an archery contest, in which he alone was able to draw Alpamysh's old bronze bow. He convinced himself that his wife was true to him. Eventually he and his friends fell upon the usurper and his followers, and slew them. The tribe was reunified under Alpamysh's rule.[4]

In Muslim Serbo-Croatian epics of this type, which have about a dozen different heroes, the husband is called to war on his wedding night, but he is captured and languishes in jail for many years.[5] One day he learns from a new prisoner that he has been presumed dead and that his wife will remarry in a certain number of days. The hero now shouts continuously until the banica intervenes with the ban, who in turn agrees to release him on the condition that he later return with ransom. The man sets out for home in disguise. He is unrecognized except by his horse. He tells deceptive stories to various persons but eventually reveals his identity to his mother (who dies from shock or joy), his wife, and others. Finally, he deals with the groom and with his wife according to their merits, which can be good or bad. Then, as promised, he returns to prison, after which the matter is settled peacefully or violently, and the hero returns home.[6]

In the modern heroic epic texts, as in the *Odyssey*, the pace of the narration is more leisurely and the detail much richer than in the prose and ballad texts. The end of the story is also more prolonged than in the non-epic texts because the situation at home is more often hostile and dangerous, giving the hero reason for cautious observation and testing rather than for immediately identifying himself. The atmosphere of the narrative is also more charged, since the societies portrayed in the epics are warrior societies, and the principal characters are members of the ruling families and their champions, who are typically persons of considerable ambition, courage, and honor. Probably because of the more serious tone of the epics, certain otherwise common motifs such as the term of years that the wife should wait and the husband's unnaturally swift return, are less commonly found in them.

The Return of Odysseus

Already in the nineteenth century some scholars perceived that the main tale of the *Odyssey* was a form of this international oral story.[7] The observation that the *Odyssey* is a kind of *Märchenepos* has been made many times, and indeed the poem does teem with migratory oral narratives.[8]

Since the legendary Trojan War lasts ten years, all the Greek participants who

survive the campaign are away from home for a decade or more. This feature of the Trojan cycle makes a nice fit with the events of *The Homecoming Husband*, in which the husband is required to be absent for a long time, and perhaps this condition facilitated the attachment of this international story to one of the Greek warriors who fought at Troy. The conclusion of *The Homecoming Husband*, at least in its epic form in which the absent warrior returns in deceptive disguise to an uncertain reception, requires a hero capable of cunning. That the plot of *The Homecoming Husband* became attached specifically to Odysseus is probably a consequence of his being a trickster or tricksterlike. Odysseus's long absence at war and his cunning nature, then, match two of the salient characteristics of the hero of the international story.

In Homer's story, Odysseus left his young bride Penelope with their infant son at her breast when he joined the other Argives to go to Ilios.[9] Before leaving he told his wife that if he should not have returned by the time that their son had a beard, then she should marry whomever she wished and leave their home.[10] After the war at Troy, which lasted ten years, Odysseus set out for home and after various adventures came to the isle of the nymph Kalypso.[11] For seven years she forced him to remain with her.[12] He spent his days on the shore, looking out at the sea, longing for his homeland, weeping and groaning, wishing to die.[13] Finally, after Athena complained to Zeus of Odysseus's confinement, Athena went to Ithaca to send Odysseus's son Telemachos to the mainland after news of his father's homecoming, while Hermes was dispatched to Kalypso to order Odysseus's release. Odysseus reached the land of the Phaiakians, who in turn conveyed him to Ithaca overnight in a supernaturally swift ship while he slept, twenty years after he had departed for Troy.[14] Athena informed him that for three years suitors had been enjoying themselves in his palace, consuming his livelihood and wooing his wife, who for her part encouraged each man, although she really grieved for her husband's return. The two considered how to destroy the suitors. Athena transformed Odysseus's appearance into that of an old vagabond in order to make him unrecognizable, and instructed him to proceed to the lodging of his faithful swineherd Eumaios. Odysseus went to the hut of Eumaios, who, not recognizing him, informed him about local events. Odysseus's son Telemachos came to Eumaios's hut, where Odysseus revealed his true identity to him, and they discussed how to destroy the suitors and whether to test the loyalty of the men and the women. Soon Odysseus went to town where, outside the palace, his old dog Argos recognized him and died.[15] Inside the palace the suitors abused him. Penelope put in an appearance, revealing that Odysseus, upon departing twenty years ago, told her that he might not survive the war and she should remarry when Telemachos was bearded; and she saw that all this was now happening.[16] That evening Penelope interviewed the vagabond privately. She told him how the suitors had been pressing her to marry, how she had deceived them for a time but now was unable to avoid a marriage. When she asked the stranger who he was, Odysseus told her a deceptive story. Then Penelope had Odysseus's old nurse Eurykleia wash the vagabond's feet, and as she did so the nurse recognized him by an old scar, but Odysseus told her to say nothing. Penelope revealed to Odysseus her intention of holding a contest: she would leave her home and go with that man who should most easily string the bow

and shoot through twelve axes standing in a row, as Odysseus used to do. The next day Odysseus tested the loyalty of the swineherd Eumaios and the cowherd Philoitios, revealing his true identity to them. After each of the suitors had failed to string the bow, the disguised Odysseus asked to be allowed to try. He easily strung the bow, shot an arrow through all twelve axes, and announced to them that he was Odysseus. In the battle that ensued Odysseus and his supporters slew all the suitors. Eurykleia summoned Penelope, informing her that the old beggar was actually her husband, but Penelope tested his identity by ordering Eurykleia to make up a bed for him, taking the bed out of the bedroom. Odysseus exclaimed that it would be hard to move that bed, for he had built both the bed and the bedroom by himself, constructing the bedroom around an old olive tree that was growing on the spot, and fashioning the olive tree into one of the bedposts for the bed. Penelope thereupon acknowledged that he was her husband, saying that he had declared tokens that no other mortal had seen. They retired together to their bed. The next day he made himself known to his father.

How does the *Odyssey* agree with the international type? Here are the major parallels. (1) The hero leaves his wife (2) in order to go to war, on a pilgrimage, or the like. (3) Before his departure he instructs his wife to await his return for a certain amount of time, after which she is free to remarry. (4) After the husband has been absent for a long time, (5) his wife is about to remarry. Meanwhile, (6) the hero returns overnight by wondrous means, (7) returning by chance, it seems, at the critical time. (8) There he is unrecognizable or disguises himself, and (9) a local person informs him of the situation at home. (10) An old animal recognizes him unaided. (11) The hero gains admittance to his house in the guise of a beggar, minstrel, or the like, and (12) tests the loyalty of his wife and others. (13) He is finally recognized. (14) After he punishes the misbehaving suitor and his supporters, (15) he is reunited with his wife.

In addition to the usual features of the international oral story, there are certain motifs that appear to be peculiar to the Greek and Serbo-Croatian epic traditions. One is that the shock of the hero's return causes a death—that of his dog in the Greek version, his mother in the Serbo-Croatian.[17] In both traditions the disguised hero is also fond of telling certain kinds of elaborate deceptive tales, though deceptive tales also appear in other traditions.[18] A third feature is that Homer and many of the South Slavic singers begin their narration of the story in medias res, and at the same critical point—the absent hero is held captive far away and believed dead by those at home, while his wife is being pressed to remarry. The period of seven years that Odysseus spends as the prisoner of Kalypso ("Concealer"), at the end of which Homer begins his narration, corresponds to the many years the Slavic hero spends imprisoned in the ban's dungeon, the point at which the Serbo-Croatian singers usually begin their Return Songs. Indeed, Athena's intervention with Zeus, who instructs Kalypso to release the weeping Odysseus, is strikingly similar to the banica's intervention with the ban, who thereupon permits the release of his shouting prisoner. These shared features seem to indicate a particularly close relationship between the two epic traditions.

The plot of *The Homecoming Husband* plays itself out on two sites—home and abroad. It would be possible for the narrator to remain at the home front,

telling the story from the viewpoint of the wife, or to follow the husband abroad and narrate the events from his viewpoint. In practice narrators regularly take the second route, relating the story from the point of view of the husband throughout, defining the events as a chronicle of his problems rather than of hers, making a man's story out of a plight that could be either a man's or a woman's story. In this respect Homer's *Odyssey* is not typical, for it divides its attention more or less equally between the two sites, dwelling first upon the wife and son at the home front, then upon the absent husband, and then, after the protagonist's return, upon all three at home.

While most scholars agree that the story of Odysseus's return is derived from the international story of *The Homecoming Husband*, they disagree about the genre of the tale from which the Greek story comes. For Kaspar Schnorf, writing in the heyday of the nature mythologists, and Albert Lord, reviving nature mythology in the present day, it derives from myth, in particular the myth of the vegetation god who dies, causing a crisis, and later returns to life.[19] There is, however, only a very general similarity between such a myth as this and *The Homecoming Husband*, certainly nothing that requires us to posit a historical connection between them. And even if there were one, there would be no reason for us to conclude, with Lord, that mythic significance still somehow clings to texts of *The Homecoming Husband*. The contention of Tolstoi and Zhirmunsky that the story of Odysseus's return derives from a folktale is better supported by the evidence, inasmuch as we sometimes find the international story in this form, although not as often as in the form of a legend.[20] But the question, like many other questions of origin, is really unanswerable, and we should content ourselves with the conclusion that the Greek legend of Odysseus's return is an epic development of an international story found both as a legend and as a folktale, both in song and in prose.

Three Linked Motifs

When they are present in a given version, there is a chain of three motifs that are closely linked to one another by the logic of the events: *the establishment of a term* after which the husband releases his wife to remarry; *the husband's concern* that the term is now nearly over, so that his wife soon may remarry (though the wives do not necessarily prepare to remarry immediately upon the expiration of the agreed time); and *his miraculous return*, by which the husband is magically conveyed home from afar in one day or night in the hope of preventing the remarriage. The first motif defines the rules of the game; the second expresses the pressing problem in which the hero finds himself as a result of the rules; and the third is his solution to this problem. These motifs, to the extent that they are present in the *Odyssey*, are somewhat atypical of the tradition.

First, the period for which the protagonist of *The Homecoming Husband* expects to be gone varies in the different texts (e.g., a year, a month, and a day; five years; seven years; nine years). Although Odysseus does establish a term, it is of different in kind: Penelope is free to remarry once their son has grown a beard. This condition has two drawbacks. First, the length of time required for a boy to grow a beard is not entirely predictable. Second, it is a less useful standard for Odysseus than for Penelope, for while she, being home, will be able to

observe the signs of Telemachos's progress into manhood, her absent husband will not. Consequently, the term cannot be more than an approximate guide for Odysseus, who can never be sure exactly when the condition will be met. In fact, the form of Odysseus's term indicates that his interest in time is not so much absolute as functional. He wants Penelope to wait until their son reaches his majority, when control of Odysseus's property will pass to Telemachos's authority; after that, Penelope is free to leave the house and remarry.[21] Odysseus's emphasis is on the control of his material possessions rather than on his marriage to Penelope.

Second, in *The Homecoming Husband* the man becomes concerned that the agreed time is presently coming to an end. In the Greek epic, however, Odysseus longs in general for Ithaca and his wife while he lives as Kalypso's prisoner, but nothing suggests a concern that Penelope may remarry, and indeed his longing for his homeland is mentioned more than his longing for his wife. Nor does he unexpectedly learn from another person or by some other means, as many other heroes do, that his wife is about to remarry, thereby motivating an urgent return at this time.[22] Homer mentions no concern at all in Odysseus's mind for the condition he established twenty years earlier for Penelope's remarriage. Rather, he is represented simply as returning home as soon as he is able to do so, acting upon a general longing to be home. So the motif of the husband's anxiety is totally absent from the *Odyssey*.[23]

Third, in *The Returning Husband* the man's return is miraculously swift.[24] Usually a supernatural being transports the hero in one evening from a foreign land to his home while he sleeps. In Homer the Phaiakians transport Odysseus in one night, as he sleeps, from their country to Ithaca on one of their ships. The Phaiakian sailors seem to be regular human beings, but their ships are as swift as a bird or as thought, travel without pilots or rudders, know men's thoughts, are acquainted with all cities and lands, and are wrapped in mist, that is, are invisible; in particular, the ship carrying Odysseus home moves more swiftly than a falcon, swiftest of birds.[25] So in Homer it is the ships rather than the beings that are supernatural, although the result is the same, so far as the transport of Odysseus is concerned. What is different is the motive for the magically swift conveyance, which in the case of the *Odyssey* is lacking.[26] Although the motif of supernatural speed is present, the familiar reason for its presence is not.

When the three motifs are present, their connection is ordinarily foregrounded, giving the story a clear, somewhat mechanical structure but also adding tension and wonder. In the *Odyssey* this structure has been deliberately weakened. The first motif, the term, is not mentioned at all at the beginning of the narrative, since Homer begins his presentation in medias res, and in fact the poet buries this information in the middle of the poem, in book 18, when Penelope is made to mention it in a conversation. The term is therefore not on the audience's mind throughout the epic, as it is when it appears in the international tale. Moreover, the form the motif takes in the *Odyssey* is such that there is no point in Odysseus's absence at which he, like Caesarius's Gerhard, can know when the term will be over. Consequently, the second motif, the husband's concern for the imminent remarriage of his wife, is simply absent from the poem. But without it, the third motif, the miraculously swift return, has no particular motivation, for there is no urgent problem for which this is the unex-

pected, magical solution. Homer, then, or the Greek epic tradition, has de-emphasized this chain of motifs so that they lack the prominence and importance that they have in other texts of the international story, resulting in a looser, more realistic narrative.[27]

The Identity Test

The curious identity test that Penelope administers to Odysseus is reminiscent of a kind of test found in certain popular ballads that are similar to *The Homecoming Husband* to the extent that they also tell of the return of a husband after a long absence.[28] The returning husband comes to the door of his house and asks his wife to let him in (or he sees her at a fountain where he is watering his horse), but she for her part is unsure of his identity and so makes him prove it by his knowledge of certain domestic matters. Thus, in a Russian song the husband first says that in her yard there is a nut tree; to this the wife replies that a neighbor could have told him that. Then the husband says that in her room there is a bed of brown ebony; the wife replies that the nurse could have told him that. Finally he says that she has a mark between her breasts; she opens the door.

Some 280 texts of this ballad have been collected in Greece, the song reportedly being one of the best-known ballads in modern Greece and little known elsewhere. In one Greek text the doubting wife asks the man to describe the landmarks of their dwelling. He: There is an apple tree by the door, a grapevine in the yard, and a lemon tree that I planted myself. She: A neighbor could have told you that. He: You have a mark on your breast, a mark on your neck, and in the middle of your chest you wear a picture of your husband. She: Yes, you are my husband, you are my beloved. In another Greek text, when the woman asks for signs, the man first mentions the apple tree by the door and the grapevine in the courtyard (she: you saw these as you passed by), then a golden lamp in the bedroom (she: a wicked neighbor told you that), and finally a dark spot on her chest, another on her armpit, and her husband's amulet between her breasts (she: you are my husband).

So the returned husband in these ballads must provide progressively more intimate knowledge, from yard to bedroom to body, each instance of which his suspicious wife dismisses as inconclusive until the last, very intimate piece of knowledge, which she accepts. For the wife to doubt at this point would be an acknowledgment on her part that more men than her husband have had intimate knowledge of her.

The intimacy test administered by Penelope in the *Odyssey* is the same sort of test with some of the same motifs (notably a knowledge of the couple's bedroom) in the same sort of situation, and so doubtless belongs to the same tradition as that underlying the ballad. The differences are also instructive. Whereas the wife in the ballad tests openly, Penelope tries to entrap the man who claims to be her husband. She is cagey, and Odysseus responds with exasperation since he does not know that she is testing him. Penelope's test, moreover, avoids the progressive, climactic structure of the ballad and instead goes directly to the decisive test, which in this case concerns the couple's bedroom. This token, corresponding to the second level of intimacy in the ballad rather than to the third, is in harmony with the decorum of Greek epic, in which a dis-

cussion of Penelope's body would be inappropriately undignified. The other two tokens do appear but not until Odysseus's recognition scene with his father Laertes on the following day, and Kakridis cleverly conjectures that Homer has redistributed the traditional three tokens of the husband-wife recognition scene over these two recognition scenes.[29] In the later scene Odysseus establishes his identity by displaying his scar (level three) and by giving an exact description of the pear trees, apple trees, fig trees, and vines that he owns (level one). The poet's dismantling of the progressive, climactic structure that we find in the recognition scene in the modern ballad, like his weakening the causal linkage of the three motifs discussed earlier, reduces the narrative formularity of the epic, giving it a more realistic quality.

Lit. AT 974, *The Homecoming Husband* = ML 8005, *Heim til konens bryllup*. Rajna 1877. Schnorf 1879:27–32. Splettstösser 1899. Huet 1911. Finsler (1914) 1:37–38. Radermacher 1915. Huet 1917. Tolstoi 1934. Wüst, in *RE* 17:1952–1953, 1988. Seemann 1951. McCartney 1953. Parry and Lord 1954, vol. 1, nos. 4, 20, 28, 32; 1974, vol. 3. Kretzenbacher 1957. Trenkner 1958:61. Marót 1958. Lord 1965; 1962; 1969; 1972. Seemann 1965. Zhirmunsky 1966. Kakridis 1971:151–163. Fochi 1972:201–333. Coote 1978:280, n. 23. Gresseth 1979. Clark 1980. Coote 1981. Foley 1986. Beekes 1986:236–237. Hölscher 1988. Tubach, no. 3792. Dvořák, no. 1580. Ashliman, type 974. *EM* 6:702–707. Foley 1990:359–387. Lord 1991:211–244. Edmunds 1993:23–25, 81–86. Hansen 1997a:446–449.

1. Huet 1917; Tolstoi 1934; Lord 1965:121, 242–259; Zhirmunsky 1967:275–276; Fochi 1972. The relative sequence of the events can differ especially toward the end of the story, when, for example, a number of testings and recognitions may take place. In addition, the content of the story varies not only with nationality (e.g., Rumanian ballads differ somewhat as a group from Greek ballads) but also with medium (prose narrative, ballad, epic). There are moreover other ballads and prose tales that relate how the husband arrives home *after* the remarriage of his wife; these stories are resolved in various ways, but not with the reunion of the original married couple (Splettstösser 1899:8–30; Clark 1980). Thus in ancient Greek tradition Agamemnon returned from a long absence at war after Klytaimnestra had taken Aigisthos as her virtual husband, and was murdered. On the other hand, it is the returning husband who is the murderer in an imaginary case described by the rhetorician Quintilian (*Declamationes* 347). A wife heard a report of the death of her husband, who had been gone on a journey. Using the house as her dowry, she remarried, but her first husband came home one night and, taking his wife and her second husband for adulterers, killed them both. Quintilian composes a speech for the imaginary defendant.

2. *Dialogus Miraculorum* 8.59.

3. Edmunds 1993:81–84, citing Bladé (1885) 1:43–53.

4. Zhirmunsky 1967; Paksoy 1989, esp. 119–157; Lord 1991:211–244.

5. In at least one song, he tells his wife she should wait seven or eight years but may marry in the ninth (Lord 1960:243).

6. Lord 1960:121, 242–259; Fochi 1972:277–306; Foley 1990:359–387. The oldest Slavic text of a Return Song belongs to a collection that was made around 1720 (Seemann 1951:177–178). Lord (1969) analyzes the story-pattern of the Return Songs into five themes (Absence, Devastation, Return, Retribution, and Wedding), but as these units correspond approximately to episodes rather than to individual actions, they are too large to serve as units of comparison here. Related to Return Songs are Return-Rescue Songs, for which see Lord 1960:121–122, 260–265.

7. For example, Schnorf 1879:27–32.

8. See Radermacher 1915; Calhoun 1939; Page 1973; Petersmann 1981; Bertolini 1989; Hölscher 1988; Hansen 1997a. Our most important source of information for the story of Odysseus's return is Homer's *Odyssey*. For other ancient sources see Roscher 3:602–681; *LIMC* 6.1:943–983; Gantz 1993:703–713 and passim.

9. Homer *Od*. 11.447–449.

10. 18.250–270.

11. The war lasted ten years: 5.105–108.

12. 1.55; 5.13–15; 7.259–266.

13. Or Poseidon, angry at Odysseus for blinding his son Polyphemos, kept Odysseus from reaching his homeland: 1.74–75.

14. 13.70–125; 17.327.

15. 17.301, 326–327.

16. Telemachos was now bearded: 18.175–176.

17. Lord 1972:315–316.

18. Coote 1981.

19. Schnorf 1879; Lord 1960, 1972.

20. Tolstoi 1934; Zhirmunsky 1967:281.

21. Cf. *Od*. 19.530–534; Tolstoi 267. In late antiquity, if not also earlier, there were laws specifying how long a married woman had to await a husband absent at war before she was permitted to remarry. Constantine the Great decreed four years of waiting; Justinian enlarged the term to ten but later decreed that the woman should wait indefinitely (Fochi 1972:303–304).

22. He is, however, informed years earlier by Teiresias that if and when he should return home he would encounter suitors in his house (11.115–117).

23. Tolstoi 1934:267–268.

24. Huet 1917. Since the protagonist's marvelous return is a feature of the international story, it requires no special explanation here, such as that it reflects an acquaintance with shamanism.

25. 7.36; 8.557–562; 13.86–87.

26. Tolstoi 269.

27. It is moreover easier to understand the Homeric treatment of these motifs as a deliberate attenuation of the motifs as we find them in the international narrative than it is to imagine that the three linked motifs of the international story were inspired by and somehow derive from the narrative in its Homeric form.

28. Splettstösser 1899:59–61; Kakridis 1971:151–163; Fochi 1972:314–316.

29. *Od*. 24.327–344. Kakridis 1971:151–163.

Hospitality Rewarded 🐚 Mercury and the Stingy Women

One or more supernatural beings (gods, angels, fairies, saints, etc.) in the guise of mortals visit a household where, being hospitably received, they reward their hosts or, being inhospitably received, they punish the inhabitants.

The testing of a human being, whether planned or not, is aptly expressed in terms of hospitality and inhospitality because travelers' and beggars' asking for food or lodging at the houses of private persons was formerly quite common and because it is a situation in which a person's essential kindness or unkindness is clearly revealed, inasmuch as the host of a passing traveler can ordinarily have little expectation of repayment.

This is the basic idea of the three closely related subtypes AT 750A, *The Wishes*, AT 750B, *Hospitality Rewarded*, and AT 750*, *Hospitality Blessed*, which include a variety of similar stories. In *The Wishes* the supernatural visitor grants the fulfillment of one or more wishes, which may turn out well or ill, while in *Hospitality Rewarded* the visitor resuscitates the animal that was slaughtered to feed him or performs some other food miracle. *Hospitality Blessed* is a provisional classification that appears to be designed for similar tales of reward and punishment that do not fit comfortably into the established categories. Since

these tales overlap to some extent and cannot always be neatly distinguished, it is convenient to treat them together here.[1]

Deities Traveling in Disguise

The basic presuppositions of all these stories, that supernatural beings sometimes walk the earth in disguise and that they may reward good persons and punish bad persons, were familiar notions in the classical and Semitic worlds. When in Homer's *Odyssey* the arrogant suitor Antinoos, dining in Odysseus's palace, treats a beggar abusively by throwing a footstool at him and threatening him verbally, the other suitors are indignant and say to one another: "Antinoos, it was not a good thing that you struck a poor beggar, but a dangerous thing, in case he may be a heavenly god. For the gods in the likeness of strangers of all kinds visit cities and observe the insolence and the respectfulness of hu-mankind."[2] The beggar is really Odysseus, whose coming in the guise of a beggar to his own house and punishing those who treat him inhospitably shows some resemblances to stories of theoxenies, or the hosting of a god.[3] The penchant of the gods for taking on a human aspect is well illustrated in Homer, where an apparent human being is often a deity in disguise. The idea of gods disguised as humans is found throughout classical literature, although such deities mingle with humans for a variety of reasons, only one of which is to observe and test mortals, for they also impart information, help their favorites, harm those they dislike, seduce or rape those they find attractive, and so on.

If a god walking the earth can be taken for a human being, a human being can also be taken for a god. When the apostles Paul and Barnabas were preaching the gospel at Lystra in Asia Minor and Paul healed a crippled man, the local people assumed that gods, taking human form, had come down among them. They inferred that Paul was Zeus and that Barnabas, since he acted as spokesman, was Hermes.[4] The successors of Zeus and Hermes in Christian popular tradition are Christ and St. Peter, who travel the earth together in many stories. Also in Jewish tradition divine beings can take the guise of men, as the angel Raphael does in the apocryphal book of *Tobit*.

The Wishes

According to a nineteenth-century German tale, in olden times God walked the earth among men, and as evening came on he found himself before two houses, one opulent and one modest. He decided to pass the night with the rich man, since he would be no burden to the man, but when he knocked and asked for lodging the rich man, seeing that the traveler wore simple clothes, turned him away. When God applied at the other house, the poor man welcomed him, and his wife boiled potatoes and milked their goat in order to offer the wanderer something to eat and drink. They also gave him their bed for the night. After breakfast in the morning God offered to fulfill three wishes for them. The poor man wished for eternal salvation, good health and sufficient bread for the two of them, and, when prodded by his guest, a new house. God fulfilled their wishes. When the rich man saw his neighbor's new house, he sent to wife to enquire about it, and she learned that the poor couple had hosted a wanderer

who had granted them three wishes. Thereupon the rich man jumped on his horse and caught up with God, to whom he offered various excuses for not having taken him in the previous night, inviting him to stay on a future occasion. He also asked whether he might have three wishes. God said he might do so but that they would not turn out well. As the rich man was returning home, he became angry with his horse and said he wished it would break its neck. This inadvertent wish was immediately accomplished, so that the man had to continue on his way on foot, carrying the saddle. It angered him that, while he struggled with the saddle, his wife sat comfortably at home, so he thoughtlessly wished that the saddle were home and she were stuck on it, which happened. When he reached home, he had to use his third wish to free his wife from the saddle.[5]

This is a classic text of AT 750A, *The Wishes*. As the narrative illustrates, the hospitable man employs his wishes wisely, and the inhospitable man unwisely. The usual pattern for the three foolish wishes is that the first wish is wasted on something trivial and the second on a silly curse or other foolish idea that the third must undo, bringing the unwise wisher more or less back to where he started, his big chance for fortune or royal rank having thus eluded him.[6] So in a Scotts tale collected from an eleven-year-old boy, a little man came to a little house on a rainy day asking for supper. His hosts gave him soup and bread, and when he departed he gave them an object that would give them three wishes. In the morning the man of the house, seeing that he was being served soup again, thoughtlessly wished for pudding, which he immediately got. His wife, angry that he had wasted a wish, wished the pudding on his head. He used the third wish to get the pudding off his head.[7] Narrators sometimes dwell upon the dilemma faced by the man who has one wish remaining: it is still within his power to become a king, but to do so he must resign himself forever to the results of the second wish, such as a sausage growing from his wife's nose.

The granting of three wishes is one of several forms that the supernatural boon can take in the present tale. Another is for the visitor to grant that the person continue doing all day that which she first does that day. The hospitable woman starts the day with an activity such as pulling linen from a container and so ends up with an abundant supply of cloth, whereas the inhospitable person begins the day with an activity such as urinating and so must continue urinating all day.[8]

Other forms are illustrated in a Japanese tale. There was a rich landowner named Agari, who lived in a mansion, and nearby a poor man named Iri, who had no money or children. Since it was late December, Iri and his wife yearned for some proper food to celebrate the end of the year, but deciding that it would be a waste of time to try to borrow anything from their wealthy neighbor they resigned themselves to a small amount of millet that they had. At this time the Sun deity decided to come down from the sky to see what was in people's hearts. Taking the form of a poor itinerant priest he went to the house of Agari and asked for lodging, but Agari rudely sent him off. When he went to Iri's house, the man and wife invited him in and offered to share their millet gruel with him. The priest, however, instructed the woman to place a kettle containing water and three green leaves on the fire; presently the kettle was full of rel-

ishes. And when he had her put on the fire a kettle of water, into which he had dropped three grains of rice, the kettle became full of cooked rice. So the three of them enjoyed a year-end celebration. When they had finished their meal, the priest asked the old couple whether they would like to receive a treasure or to regain their youth. They chose to regain their youth. The priest had them fill a kettle with hot water, into which he sprinkled some yellow powder, and had the couple enter the kettle of water simultaneously. They became young people again. When Agari learned how the traveling priest had given the poor old couple their youth again, he asked the priest to visit him. The priest said Agari had no need of money but that he could make him young again. He instructed Agari and his family to enter a kettle of water into which he had sprinkled some red powder, but the man and his wife became monkeys and their children became dogs. The disguised god then turned Agari's estate over to the poor couple.[9]

This story resembles tales featuring wishes in that the hospitable couple is granted their choice of treasure or youth, but it differs from them in that the disguised god also grants them a number of boons without consulting their desires, namely, magically produced food and a new house. A distinction between wishes and other boons can be overly fine, as this tale shows, for the narrator makes clear at the beginning of the tale that the poor couple greatly desires appropriate food to celebrate the year-end. The granting of open wishes, the choice from a range of wishes, the satisfaction of an preexisting desire, and the unexpected boon lie on a continuum. How the boon is determined usually makes little difference to the structure of the story. Indeed, the German and the Japanese tales share a common structure. In both, (a) a supernatural visitor seeks hospitality at a wealthy household (b) from which he is turned away, (c) whereupon he applies at a poor household and (d) is received hospitably. (e) He rewards his hosts (with wishes, food, a new house, etc.). On the following day (f) when the members of the wealthy household learn of this boon, they greedily offer hospitality to the wanderer in the hope of being rewarded similarly, but instead (g) they are punished or gain nothing.

Mercury and the Stingy Women

An ancient tale that belongs to this tradition was given literary treatment by the fabulist Phaedrus, who relates it in Latin verse. According to Phaedrus, Mercury was once entertained in a stingy fashion (*hospitio . . . inliberali et sordido*) by two women, one of them a mother with a baby son, the other a prostitute. In order to repay their hospitality as he was departing, he revealed that he was a god and said he would grant each of them a wish. The mother asked to see her son with a beard as soon as possible, and the whore asked that whatever she touched follow her. The god flew away, and when the women went back inside they saw that the baby had a beard. The prostitute laughed so hard that her nose became clogged and, wishing to clean her nose with her hand, she drew it all the way to the ground, so that she was laughed at in turn.[10]

Since this fable can stand by itself as a story, we cannot know whether it was

an independent whole tale or only a fable-sized episode extracted from a larger tale in which hospitable and inhospitable hosts were contrasted. In either case, the tale as we have it features only an inconsiderate household, but it agrees with later texts of *The Wishes* in that it shows (a) a supernatural being traveling on earth in disguise, (b) his being treated inhospitably at a certain household, (c) his granting the inhabitants wishes, and (d) their using the wishes foolishly.

Mercury, corresponding to the Greek Hermes, the messenger of the Olympians and patron deity of travelers, is by his nature a frequent traveler among mortals. His granting of wishes to his unhostly hosts is an ironic boon, since the granter must know that the wishes will be misused, as the deity does in the German text above. The narrator does not explain whether the wishes are used foolishly because of the inherent wrongheadedness of the hosts or because the deity so wills it, for the emphasis is simply upon the humorous details of the hosts' getting their deserts. As the tale shows, the association of inhospitality and the divine granting of a number of wishes used foolishly is ancient and exists independently of the specific motif of the three foolish wishes.

Theseus's Three Wishes

The motif of three wishes granted by a god also appears in the legend of Theseus, but they are not the three foolish wishes of the comic folktale. According to ancient tradition, Poseidon promised to fulfill three prayers for his son Theseus. Theseus used one of them to ask Poseidon to bring about the death of his own son Hippolytos, who he mistakenly believed had made sexual advances to his stepmother, Theseus's wife. After Poseidon had fulfilled his prayer, Theseus learned the truth and regretted his wish.[11] For the story, see "Potiphar's Wife."

Like the first and second unwise wishes of the comic tale, Theseus's wish is rash and foolish, and he quickly regrets he made it; but it is not comic. The ancient authorities differ on whether this fatal wish is Theseus's first (so apparently Euripides) or last (so at least a scholiast). If the last, it would be the more foolish and poignant for being irreversible.

The motif is puzzling. No ancient author clearly explains why or under what circumstances Poseidon granted Theseus the three wishes. Evidently the boon is simply a gift in virtue of the fact that Theseus was Poseidon's son.[12] The only advantage of a guaranteed wish for the present episode is that Poseidon is bound to honor it whether it is wise or foolish, and presumably this is its chief raison d'être. How are the other two wishes used? According to the scholiast on Euripides, Theseus employs his first prayer to escape from Hades' realm and the second to escape from the Cretan labyrinth. But no ancient source for these adventures mentions a prayer to Poseidon in the course of relating these happenings, and in those episodes a prayer seems otiose.[13] So Theseus's having been granted three wishes by his divine sire seems to be the same as if he had been granted one wish and used it foolishly, just as Phaethon misused the single wish granted him by his divine father, Helios, and just as Semele used unwisely the one wish granted her by her divine lover, Zeus.

Resuscitation of a Slaughtered Animal

In another group of stories, the supernatural boon takes the form of the re-vivification of the animal that the poor but generous host slaughters and cooks in honor of his guest. Thus, a Welsh legend of the ninth century relates how St. Germanus wished to pay a visit to a certain cruel king of Britain in order to acquaint him with Christianity. When Germanus and his followers reached the town and requested an audience, the king swore that even if they stood there till the new year they would not gain entrance into the town. Evening came on while Germanus waited for his answer, and he did not know where to go. Then one of the king's servants came out of the town, bowed before the saint, gave him the king's message, and invited the saint to his own house, where the saint and his men were well received. The only animals their host owned were a cow and its calf, which latter the man slaughtered and served to his guests. Germanus instructed his followers not to break any of the bones. The next day they found the calf healthy and unharmed next to its mother. When the saint and his men were again denied admission, fire came down from heaven and burnt up the town together with the inhospitable king and his men. St. Germanus baptized the hospitable man, his family, and the rest of the people, and installed the hospitable man as king.[14]

In a German legend, Jesus and St. Peter once came to the dwelling of a poor man and asked for food. He butchered his only sheep for them. Jesus told him to pick up all the bones and place them on the hide. When the poor man awoke the next day, he found the slaughtered sheep alive together with a large herd of sheep. When he later went to town and reported how he acquired all his sheep, his rich but stingy neighbor slaughtered all his own sheep and gave them to the poor, but his sheep did not return to life.[15]

These texts illustrate AT 750B, *Hospitality Rewarded*. Narrators sometimes describe how the supernatural visitor spreads the bones upon the hide of the slaughtered animal and performs a ritual such as a prayer in order to quicken the animal. Thus in the well-known Norse myth Thor and Loki were traveling together and came one evening to a farmhouse, where they lodged. Thor slaughtered his two goats, cooked them, and shared the meal with his hosts. He spread out the goat skins, intructing the diners to throw the bones onto the skins. The next day Thor raised his hammer Mjöllnir over the skins and consecrated them, and the goats stood up.[16]

In an Indian text collected in 1971 from an elderly Brahman housewife, a poor Brahman and his wife had seven daughters but no son. One day a beggar came to the house seeking alms, and the Brahman showed him generous hospitality. The visitor asked if there was anything he could do for them. They told him how they longed for a son, and the saintly beggar said they would have a son but only on the condition that they return him when he was twelve years old. Saying this, the holy man mysteriously disappeared. Nine months later the Brahman's wife gave birth to a son. He was much loved by his family, but when he reached the age of twelve the saintly beggar showed up again and claimed him. The beggar then took a knife, cut off the boy's head, and dismembered him. The women were all wailing. He had the boy's mother cook the

pieces, and they all had to sit down to eat. Finally, the stranger told them to call their son. When he was called he suddenly appeared, and as his family embraced him the saintly beggar and the cooked food disappeared.[17] According to the editors, this tale is popular among both Moslems and Hindus and is found in both classical and folk drama.

For the present investigation, what is especially interesting about the Indian story is that a son plays the role in it that an animal plays in the European texts: the son/animal is slaughtered, cooked, served as food, and then magically resuscitated. Putting the Eastern and Western traditions together, we have the equivalence: animal = son. The principal structural difference between the two traditions is that the Indian story necessarily takes place in two parts rather than one.[18] In the first, the holy beggar grants the boon of a son; in the second, he claims the son, treats him as food, and replaces him.

Hyrieus

These stories lead us to one of the most curious stories to have come down to us from ancient Greece, the Boiotian legend of the birth of the hero Orion.

The gods Zeus, Poseidon, and Hermes came in the guise of mortal travelers to the house of Hyrieus in Tanagra or Hyria. Hyrieus was a king or, according to Ovid, a poor farmer. After he entertained the deities in a hospitable and kindly fashion, they revealed their divinity and offered to grant him any wish. A childless widower, Hyrieus desired to have a son. So the gods took the hide of the ox that Hyrieus had slaughtered for their meal (according to Ovid, it had been Hyrieus's only ox), spread it out on the ground, and ejaculated or urinated into it, telling Hyrieus to bury it in the ground for ten months and then take it up again. When the time had passed, a son was born. Called Ourion, after the gods' urinating, his name was later altered to Orion. He grew to be immense.[19]

The ancient sources differ about whether the visiting deities masturbated or urinated on the hide. But the idea of urination must be a reinterpretation of the story that was inspired by a folk etymology connecting the name of the hero Orion with the Greek noun *ouron* "urine," to which in fact it is unrelated, and by the similarity of ejaculation and urination. Before the folk etymology, the idea was simply that the gods impregnated the Earth with their semen, an idea for which there is a parallel in the myth of the begetting of Erichthonios. Trying to rape Athene, Hephaistos ejaculated onto her. In disgust she wiped the sperm off and threw the cloth on the ground, and from the semen that fell upon the earth Erichthonios was eventually born.[20] The mother of each hero was Earth. Pausanias calls Erichthonios a son of Hephaistos and Earth, just as Apollodoros calls Orion earth-born.[21]

The story of Hyrieus perfectly mediates the European and Indian stories of resuscitation, for in the ancient Greek narrative the slaughtered animal *is transformed* into a son. As in the usual Western story of *Hospitality Rewarded*, supernatural guests come in mortal guise to the door of a poor man, who receives them hospitably, slaughtering perhaps his only animal for them. When, as in the Eastern story, the visitor offers to grant a boon, the host's dearest wish is for

a son. Following the Western tradition, the guests spread out the hide of the slaughtered animal, perform a rite over it, and then, as in the Eastern tradition, a son is conceived and born in due time. The story exactly illustrates the animal-son equivalence.

Abraham and Sarah

The legend of Hyrieus has been compared with the story in Genesis in which Abraham and Sarah very hospitably receive three supernatural visitors who come in the guise of men, after which one of the visitors announces the unexpected boon of a son for their hosts in their old age.[22]

According to the *Septuagint*, god appeared to Abraham as he sat at the doorway of his tent at midday. Looking up, Abraham saw three men standing. He ran to meet them, prostrated himself on the ground, and said: "Lord, if I have found favor with you, do not pass by your servant, but let him get water for you and let him wash your feet. Refresh yourself beneath the tree. I'll get bread for you to eat, and afterwards continue your journey." They agreed. So Abraham hurried to Sarah in the tent, instructing her quickly to bake some bread, and then ran to his cattle, where he selected a fine calf, giving it to a servant who hurredly prepared it. He fed the men these and other foods, and stood by as they ate beneath the tree. One of them asked Abraham where his wife Sarah was, and Abraham said she was in the tent. He said he would return in a year, and Sarah would have a son. Sarah overheard these words from the door of the tent. Abraham and Sarah were quite advanced in age, and Sarah was past menopause. So Sarah laughed, saying to herself that she had not yet had a son, and her husband was older than she. At their departure Abraham escorted them for a while. The Lord did as he said. Sarah conceived and bore a son to Abraham in old age, and Abraham called him Isaak.[23]

The narrator treats the supernatural visitors somewhat vaguely. While they represent an epiphany of god to Abraham, it is unclear whether three angels in the guise of men are agents of god or whether god appears as one man accompanied by two angels also in the guise of men. But the distinction is unimportant for an understanding of the events, for what is significant is that Abraham sees them as men whereas we know that the visitors are somehow divine. The visitors reveal that they are more than mere men when they enquire about Sarah without having asked her name and when they foretell the future. They do not offer to fulfill an open wish for their generous hosts but instead gratify the long-standing desire of Abraham and Sarah to have a son. So great is this wish that, as we learn earlier, the barren Sarah even encouraged Abraham to beget a son with Sarah's Egyptian maid Hagar; but they still have no son of their own.[24] The granting of a son for Abraham and Sarah, as for Hyrieus, is a double boon, first, because it is the gift of a son, and, second, because it is beyond all expectation, since in the one case the couple is well past the age of producing children (Abraham is a hundred years old and Sarah is ninety when their son is born) and in the other case the man is a widower. The inclusion of the detail of Sarah's laughing is inspired by the name Isaak, which derives from the Hebrew word for "laugh." Indeed, the authors of Genesis knew three different incidents that serve to account for the name: either, as here, Sarah

laughs at the prospect of bearing a child in her old age, or Abraham laughs when he is told by god that he and his wife will have a son in their old age, or god makes Sarah a laughingstock for bearing a child at her age.[25]

The Canaanite legend of Aqhat is somewhat similar to that of Abraham and Sarah. According to an Ugaritic text from the fourteenth century B.C., the childless Daniel hosted gods liberally for a week, after which the god Baal asked El to grant Daniel a son. El granted the request, saying that when Daniel should lie with his wife, she would conceive. She bore a son, Aqhat.[26] It is unclear from the narration whether the gods visit Daniel as themselves or in the guise of mortals.

If these stories are historically connected to one another, as they appear to be, it seems that the Eastern tradition favors the granting of a son, and the Western tradition favors the resuscitation of an animal, and that the traditions meet in the legend of Hyrieus.

The Deluge

In a third group of similar stories, the supernatural traveler causes a flood to overwhelm an entire village of inhospitable folk but spares a single hospitable household.

Thus according to an English legend there was long ago a village called Simmerdale in the North Riding of Yorkshire. One day a witch came to the village and asked at each house for food and drink, but she was refused at every house until she came to the house of the Quaker woman, who gave her bread, meat, and beer on her porch. When the visitor was finished eating, she waved an ash twig over the village and uttered a curse to the effect that Simmerdale should sink except for the house of the woman who gave her something to drink. Thereupon the water rose in the valley and covered the entire village except for the house of the old Quaker woman. Nowadays Simmer Water is a lake, at the bottom of which people fancy they can see the ruins of the old village.[27] In a French legend Jesus and Peter in the guise of beggars were refused hospitality at every house until finally a poor old couple took them in. The visitors departed during the night, instructing the old couple to accompany them. Where the village was, there now was a body of water, which was called Llers after the village. Only the hut of the old couple was spared.[28]

In this story the supernatural visitor determines the reward of the good and the punishment of the bad, without consulting the kindly hosts at all. The punishment of the unhostly is to be overwhelmed with water, and the reward of the kindly host is to escape this fate. The water may remain to this day covering the village of old, in which case the legend provides an aition for an actual body of water. But sometimes the inhospitable folk are destroyed by catastrophes other than water. Their households sink into the earth, or fire rains down on them from the sky, as in the Welsh legend of St. Germanus related above, or sand and earth rains down upon them.[29]

Although the deluge story is not recognized in Aarne-Thompson as a subtype of AT 750, it is similar in structure and theme to *The Wishes* and *Hospitality Rewarded*, in that supernatural visitors in the guise of ordinary human beings punish inhospitable persons and reward hospitable persons. Since the story is

attested both in antiquity and in modern times, and since the story of Phile-mon and Baucis, to be considered next, is regularly cited as an early instance of disguised gods seeking hospitality, I include here the type of the flood—or, more generally, catastrophe—story. There can be no doubt that the familiarity of the classical legend of Philemon and Baucis and of the biblical legend of Lot has had some influence on later folk legends of catastrophes, but I see no rea-son to conclude that the latter are merely a reintroduction of the former into oral tradition.[30]

Philemon and Baucis

The ancient Phrygian legend of Philemon and Baucis is known from Ovid's *Metamorphoses*, where it is put into the mouth of an old man, Lelex, who relates the story in response to a member of the company who scoffs at stories of the power of the gods. The narrator declares that he himself has seen the very place where the events took place, a sanctuary in Phrygia containing two trees side by side, an oak and a linden. A marsh or lake now, it had been habitable land. Once Jupiter and Mercury in the guise of mortals came there and asked for lodging at a thousand households, all of which refused them. Only Philemon and Baucis, a pious old couple living in a humble house, took them in and shared generously of their food and furnishings. When the old couple noticed that as often as they drew off wine from the mixing bowl it refilled itself mirac-ulously, they grew frightened, prayed indulgence from their divine guests for their modest fare, and prepared to slaughter their only goose. Jupiter and Mer-cury now revealed themselves as gods, told them to spare the goose, and said that the impious neighborhood, except for Philemon and Baucis, would be punished. The gods instructed the old couple to accompany them on foot up a nearby mountain. When Philemon and Baucis looked back down from the mountain, they saw that all the houses of the village except for their own were covered with water and that their tiny thatched cottage had been transformed into a marble temple with a golden roof. The gods then asked them to make any wish, and the couple asked to serve the gods as priest and priestess of their temple and, when the time should come, to die at the same time. So they took charge of the temple until one day they were transformed simultaneously into two trees, which the Bithynian inhabitants still point out.[31]

The story tells of the wanderings of Jupiter and his son Mercury, correspond-ing to the Greek Zeus and Hermes, and being set somewhere in Phrygia the site of the events cannot be far from Lystra, where the wonder-working travelers Paul and Barnabas were themselves taken by the natives for Zeus and Hermes. These deities, or their local equivalents, must have figured as wandering gods in native lore. The pious couple Philemon and Baucis enjoyed several boons in addition to being spared the flood that drowned their neighbors. The gods caused the container of wine to be inexhaustible, and they replaced their cot-tage with an opulent temple. We have met similar motifs in other texts of AT 750, where the supernatural visitor magically creates food for the meal or re-places the kindly hosts' modest house with a new one. Philemon and Baucis were also granted open wishes, to serve as priest and priestess in the temple and not to outlive one another.

To summarize the shared features in the English, French, and Phrygian texts, (a) one or two supernatural persons in the guise of ordinary mortals ask for hospitality at many—probably all—houses in a community, but (b) everyone turns them away (c) except for the kind inhabitant or inhabitants of one cottage, who are sometimes described as old and poor. (d) After enjoying this single instance of hospitality (e) the supernatural beings destroy the entire community (f) in a deluge of water, (g) sparing only the hut of the kindly folk who entertained them. (h) The watery place is still pointed out today by the local people as the site of these events.[32]

Lot

The Phrygian story has a counterpart in Hebrew tradition in the legend of Lot. Two angels came to Sodom in the evening where Lot, sitting at the gate of the city, hospitably insisted that they lodge with him and continue on their way in the morning. The two angels accepted his invitation, and he prepared a meal for them. Before they lay down to sleep, all the men of Sodom, from young to old, surrounded his house and called out to Lot to bring out to them the two men who were visiting him, in order that the men of Sodom might lie with them. Lot went outside his door and told the men not to behave wickedly, offering the crowd his two virginal daughters to do with as they pleased but denying them access to the two men to whom he had given shelter. But as the men then threatened to do violence to Lot, who was a resident alien, and to break through his door, the two men inside drew him back indoors, closed the door, and struck the Sodomites near the door with blindness. The men warned Lot to flee with his family from Sodom, and not to look behind them or to stop, for the outcry against the city had reached the Lord, who had sent them to destroy the place. Lot, his wife, and daughters fled, eventually if not immediately to a mountain, and the Lord rained fire and sulphur down upon Sodom and the surrounding region, destroying it and everyone in it. But Lot's wife looked behind her and was changed into a pillar of salt.[33]

In accordance with the tradition of catastrophe legends, the story of Lot focuses not upon one household or two contrasting households, but upon an entire community. As usual, all the inhabitants of the community are inhospitable except for a single household, which generously admits the traveling strangers. But whereas the other three narratives cited here are content to allude to the inhospitality of the villagers in a sentence or two before focusing in detail upon the kindness of one household, the Hebrew narrator dwells at length both upon the generosity of Lot and also upon the inhospitality shown by the other men of Sodom (the narrator ignores the women of Sodom), who here give a new meaning to the notion of inhospitality. For unlike other inhospitable folk they do not turn men away from their doors but rather seek them out, the Sodomites being portrayed as aggressive homosexuals, exiting from their houses in the evening in their eagerness to rape any hapless stranger who finds himself in their town at night, a caricature of inhospitality more suited to a village of vampires than to one of mortal men. The agent of punishment in the legend of Lot is a downpour not of water but of fire and sulphur, which like an excess of water brings about the utter destruction of the community, or, more

precisely, of the cities of the plain, for whose destruction the present story provides an aition. Not even the house of the pious hero is spared.

The Phrygian legend of Philemon and Baucis and the Hebrew legend of Lot are genetically related to the Old World myth of the Great Deluge that is attested among the Mesopotamians, Hebrews, Greeks, Romans, and a few other peoples.[34] The stories of Philemon and Baucis and of Lot attest to the existence of an offshoot of the usual story that differs in several respects from the main stock of the tradition, notably in its introductory episode, which depicts human evil and piety in terms of the inhospitable and hospitable treatment of divine beings in disguise; in its subsequently representing the pious couple as walking rather than sailing to safety, for which reason we could dub it the Pedestrian Redaction; and in its representing the event as a local catastrophe set in the historical period rather than as world catastrophe set in the primordial past (that is, the story is a legend, not a myth), which has left its mark on the local landscape.[35]

Lit. (AT 750A, *The Wishes.* AT 750B, *Hospitality Rewarded.* AT 750*, *Hospitality Blessed.*) Landau 1900–1901. Dähnhardt 1909:123–153. Sydow 1910. Gunkel 1910:199–201, 214–217. BP 2:210–229. Gunkel 1921:77–82. Krohn 1922:207–215. Baumgartner 1959:154–155. Fontenrose 1945. Liungman 1961:210–211. Bertolotti 1979. Ashliman, types 750A, 750B. Chesnutt 1989.

1. For a history of the somewhat confusing typology see Chesnutt 1989:318–320.
2. Homer *Od.* 17.481–487; cf. *Od.* 7.201–206.
3. Kearns 1982.
4. Acts 14.8–18.
5. Grimm 87.
6. On the motif/tale of the three foolish wishes, see Bédier 1925:212–228; BP 2:210–229; Motif J2071, *Three foolish wishes;* Röhrich (1962) 1:62–79, 253–258; Opie 1974:151–155; Wieringa 1997.
7. Briggs (1970) A1:522.
8. See Dähnhardt (1909) 2:140–153; Schwarzbaum 1968:241–245.
9. Seki 1963:142–145, no. 41.
10. Phaedrus *App.* 4 Perry = Perry 534. The mother's unwise wish that her baby get a beard is also found in modern oral tradition (e.g., Pino-Saavedra 1967:88–89). For the elongated nose, see motif J2072.3, *Short-sighted wish: all he pulls on will follow.* Immense noses also figure in Greek invective literature (Brecht 1930:93–94).
11. For Theseus's three wishes or prayers see Euripides *Hippolytus* 43–46, 887–890, 1315–1324; schol. Euripides *Hippolytus* 46, 887, 1348; Asklepiades of Tragilos (*FGH* 12 F 28); Plutarch *Parall. min.* 34 (*Mor.* 314b); Cicero *On the Nature of the Gods* 3.31, *De Off.* 1.32; Seneca *Phaedra* 943–949.
12. Kakridis 1928:22. Euripides (*Hippolytus* 45) says only that Poseidon granted Theseus the fulfillment of three prayers "as a *geras*," a gift of honor or privilege.
13. On Euripides' employment of this *märchenhaft* motif, see further Kakridis 1928 and 1929:26–45; Barrett 1964:39–40; Segal 1972:172–177.
14. Sydow 1910:91–92, citing Nennius *Historia Britonum*, ed. San Marte 48, ed. Gunn 63.
15. Sydow 1910:95.
16. The story is alluded to in the *Hymiskvidha* in the *Elder Edda* and is related in full by Snorri in his *Gylfaginning*, part of his *Prose Edda.* The myth of Thor and his goats represents, however, a different subtype of the story of the resuscitated animal, one in which the supernatural visitor slaughters his own animal, his host breaks one of the bones in order to get at the marrow, and the animal therefore proves to be lame when its owner resuscitates it. For a discussion see Sydow 1910:96–97; Chesnutt 1989:324–330.

In a third branch of the story reminiscent of the Greek legend of Pelops, a girl is cut into pieces, cooked, and eaten. When her companions collect her bones in order to resuscitate

her, one bone is missing. They fashion a substitute for the bone out of wood and bring her back to life (Sydow 1910:80–83; Schmidt 1963:145–155). In the ancient legend Tantalos dismembered his son Pelops, cooked his limbs, and served them to the gods at a banquet; after Demeter ate the shoulder, it was replaced by one of ivory before the boy was resuscitated. For the Greek story see Frazer (1921) 2:156–157; Gantz 1993:532.

17. Beck, Claus, and Handoo 1987:81–85, no. 24.

18. For a striking mono-episodic text from Bangladesh, however, see Glassie 1997:108–115.

19. Palaiphatos 5; Euphorion 101 Powell; Nonnos *Dionysiaca* 13.96–103; schol. on Homer *Odyssey* 5.121; schol. on Nicander *Theriaca* 15; Tzetzes *Schol. on Lycophron* 328; Ovid *Fasti* 5.493–544; Hyginus *Fab.* 195; Lactantius Placidus *Theb.* 3.27, 7.255–257; Servius on Verg. *Aen.* 1.535, 10.763. On the story of Hyrieus see Roscher 3:1030–1031; Fontenrose 1981:6–7 and notes; Gantz 1963:273. For another story involving Hyrieus, see "Rhampsinitos."

20. For example, Apollodoros *Bibl.* 3.16.6; Frazer (1921) 2:90–91; Fowler 1949.

21. Pausanias 1.2.6; Apollodoros *Bibl.* 1.4.3.

22. For example, Gunkel 1910:200; Rad 1972:205.

23. Gen. 18:1–16, 21:1–4.

24. Gen. 16 (Abraham and Hagar).

25. Gen. 17:17, 21:6.

26. Cf. Fontenrose 1981:218–219; for a translation, *ANET* 1955:149–151.

27. Briggs (1971) B2:349.

28. Dähnhardt (1909) 2:135.

29. Dähnhardt (1909) 2:139 (sinking into the earth); Gunkel 1910:214 (downpour of sand and soil).

30. Dähnhardt (1909) 2:133–134; Chesnutt 1989:325–326.

31. Ovid *Metamorphoses* 8.616–725. On the story in general see Calder 1922; Malten 1939; Hollis 1970:106–128; Bömer (1977) 4:190–232.

32. Notice also a myth of Demeter reported by Pausanias (2.35.4), according to which Demeter once came to the Argolid. Athera and Mysios showed the goddess hospitality, whereas Kolontas neither received her in his home nor showed her any other honor. His behavior was, however, contrary to the wishes of his daughter Chthonia. In consequence, they said, Kolontas was incinerated in his own house and Chthonia was brought by Demeter to the city of Hermion where she built a temple of Demeter for the inhabitants. In a story recounted by Ovid (*Met.* 5.446–461) the wandering Demeter elsewhere encountered a similar mix of hospitality and inhospitality within a single household, in this case a kindly old woman and a rude boy; Demeter punished the boy.

33. Gen. 19:1–26.

34. Fontenrose 1945.

35. Fontenrose 1945:97. Similarly, in the apocryphal *Acts of Andrew and Matthias in the City of the Cannibals* a punishing flood is called upon the cannibalistic inhabitants of Myrmidonia by the apostle Andrew, who, like his predecessor Matthias, was treated inhospitably by the locals; see MacDonald 1990.

House Burned Down to Rid It of Insects ◎ Shirt Burnt to Rid It of Lice

In order to rid his house (barn) of flies (fleas, rats, mice, etc.), a fool burns it down.

This simple numskull tale, AT 1282, *House Burned Down to Rid It of Insects*, featuring a foolish overreaction to a problem, is attested from Europe to India.

In one of his Latin exempla Jacques de Vitry employs it as a cautionary tale: "Some persons are so timid that they yield immediately to the blows of the Enemy, preferring to sin and to be destroyed rather than to suffer temptation. They are like the fool who, when he had an infestation of flies, burned up his own house in order to burn up the flies at the same time. Thus many persons, when they do not wish to put up with flies, let themselves be destroyed and burnt with the fire of luxury."[1]

A Tyrolian anecdote published in the early twentieth century recounts how a violinist named Zängerle from Unterramsach had a house full of rats. None of the means he employed to be rid of them worked until finally he had a good idea: he simply set his house on fire. Then he took his violin under his arm, went outside, and played and sang a certain song while his house burned. According to a slightly different version, Zängerle's house was infested with bedbugs, lice, and cockroaches. He set it on fire, took his violin under his arm and his Black Forest clock from the wall, and went outside, and as his house burned he sang and played on the violin in time with the ticking of the clock.[2]

An Ancient Cautionary Tale

A tale about destroying the entire site of a pest only to be rid of the pest is put into the mouth of Sulla by Appian, an Alexandrian Greek who lived in Rome and wrote a Roman history in the second century of our era.

By way of illustrating the frightful anger of Sulla, the historian relates how Sulla arranged for the murder of Quintus Lucretius Ofella in the middle of the forum. Sulla then gathered the people together and addressed them: "Listen, citizens, and hear it from me in person. I have had Lucretius killed because he did not obey me." Then Sulla added the following. "Some lice were nibbling at a farmer while he was plowing his field. Two times he left off plowing and cleaned his shirt of lice, but since he continued to be bitten, he burnt his shirt in order to avoid any further interruption. I warn those who have been overcome by me twice not to require fire the third time." After terrifying his hearers with these words, Sulla ruled as he wished.[3]

Although the ancient tale features an infested article of clothing whereas other texts feature an infested building, the problem is identical and the remedy adopted by the protagonist is the same: to destroy the host along with the pests.

Whereas the main character in the international tale is clearly a fool, the farmer in the fable is seemingly an ordinary rational man who loses his patience with the vermin who are bothering him. This is how the immediate narrator of the fable, Sulla, understands the farmer, for in his epimythium, or application of his tale, he draws a parallel between the farmer and himself as men who will be patient with their opponents only up to a certain point. And yet, however sensible the farmer in the fable may be, he overreacts when he sacrifices his shirt merely in order to destroy the vermin in it. Is he exasperated at his own inability to rid his shirt of lice? Or, to interpret the fable back from Sulla's application of it, does he believe that twice he patiently gives his enemies notice to desist, and when they nevertheless persist in their activities he coolly exterminates them, dwelling and all? In the former case the farmer is a ordinary man who in his exasperation responds somewhat irrationally, but in the latter case he is a fool through and through, thinking lice can be party to a truce, and destroying his own goods in order to prosecute their transgression. But surely that is not the intent of the narrator here (whether Appian or Sulla), which is rather to communicate in a colorful and memorable fashion the fact that, like the farmer, Sulla is a man not to be trifled with: if his enemies persist

in their activities despite having been decently warned, he will destroy them without hesitation and at any cost, as though they were mere vermin. An international numskull tale has been put to rhetorical use as a fable, and whereas in the usual telling of the tale the behavior of the protagonist in dealing with bothersome pests is comic because of its wastefulness due to his foolish overreaction, it is represented here as being intelligently calculated in its ruthlessness. This fable is one of several instances in ancient storytelling in which a normally comic tale has been adapted to noncomic use.[4]

Lit. (AT 1282, *House Burned Down to Rid it of Insects.*) Achelis 1917. BP 3:288. Wesselski (1911) 1:72–73, 244–245, no. 137. Christensen 1939:220. Tubach 1969:212, no. 2697. Ashliman, type 1282. *EM* 7:1123–1124.

1. Crane 1890:128, no. 306.
2. Dörler 1906:286, no. 7.
3. *Civil War* 1.101 = Perry 471.
4. See Hansen 1997c.

Husband Cannot Recognize Himself. *See* Underground Passage to Paramour's House

Husband's One Good Eye Covered ⚘ Husband's Attention Diverted

A clever wife distracts her husband's vision after he returns home unexpectedly, allowing her lover to escape.

This ribald tale has two principal forms, depending upon which of two ruses the woman improvises.[1] AT 1419C, *The Husband's One Good Eye Covered (Treated)*, takes its name from the so-called Oculus, or "Eye," subtype. I have seen texts from Europe, the Middle East, and India.

In the folktale a wife hears her husband returning home unexpectedly while she is entertaining her lover. She barely has time to conceal the man in a closet (under the bed, behind a curtain, or the like). When her husband enters, she cleverly diverts his attention in such a way that her lover is able to make his escape out the door. In the Oculus subtype the returning husband is one-eyed, and his wife straightaway covers his one good eye with her hand, making some excuse such as that she dreamed that he now could see out of both eyes. Or she pretends to treat his good eye with medicine in order to preserve its health. In the Linteus, or "Linen," subtype the woman, often aided by her mother, immediately spreads out piece of cloth such as a sheet that was recently completed, in order to draw away the man's attention, and as he examines it the hidden lover escapes. Or she throws the cloth over his head and holds it there while conversing with him (for example, she says in a joking manner that she has a lover who is now escaping from the room), with the same result.[2]

Only the Linteus subtype, in which the woman pulls the wool over the

man's eyes, so to speak, will concern us here. According to the *Disciplina Clericalis* of Petrus Alphonsi, a woman, her mother, and her lover were enjoying a meal together when her husband, who had been absent on a long journey, suddenly knocked at the door. The lover was hidden, and the husband asked for his bed to be prepared. As the wife stood in confusion, the mother said that they must show her husband the linen cloth they had just sewed. They spread it out, each holding one corner, and the lover escaped. The cloth was placed on the bed, and the husband marveled that his wife had been able to make such an object.[3]

Similarly in a modern Greek joke a girl from a well-to-do family married the poor boy she loved rather than the rich man her mother wanted her to marry. Their life together was hard, so the girl's mother found a rich man who would sleep with the girl and give her money. The mother brought the rich old man over one day, and he and the daughter had just gone to bed when the husband unexpectedly came home. The rich man hid under the bed. The girl's mother told the husband that his wife was upset because the new blanket the mother had made for the bed was too short. The wife was in bed crying. The girl's mother suggested he get into bed with her in order that they might see if the blanket was big enough. After he got into bed, his mother-in-law pulled the blanket over his head, which allowed the rich man to leave the house. The mother-in-law asked the husband if he liked the blanket, and he said he did. The woman replied that she has been making blankets like that for *her* husband for years, and he has always liked them.[4]

An Aristophanic Allusion

That the Linteus form of the tale was known in Aristophanes' day is shown by an allusion to it that one of the characters makes in his comedy *Thesmophoriazusae*, which was produced in 411 B.C.: "Euripides hasn't mentioned this one yet: how a woman held up a garment to the light for her husband to see, and so managed to let her lover, who had been hiding, escape."[5] In the comedy, women have gathered to celebrate the Thesmophoria, a women's festival. There they discuss the many uncomplimentary things that the tragedian Euripides has presented about women in his plays, which have had the effect of discouraging husbands from trusting their wives. But Mnesilochos, a man who has joined the celebrants disguised as a woman, declares that for all the female misbehavior featured in the plays of Euripides there are in reality many more instances that Euripides has not even mentioned. He proceeds to relate four instances of adultery and other deceptions practiced by wives on their husbands, among them the present ruse. The women respond to Mnesilochos's catalogue of female treachery with indignation.

The comic poet treats the tale as one that is already familiar to his audience, since he is content merely to allude to it, whereas he relates the other ruses at length. The present context of transmission, though an extremely improbable one, suggests nevertheless how Greek men might have told the story to other men or perhaps even to women as an example of the lustfulness and treachery of wives. One can only speculate whether Greek women, in the privacy of their own conversations, might also have told the tale and enjoyed it for the successful ruse improvised by the clever but immoral wife.

Lit. AT 1419C, *The Husband's One Good Eye Covered (Treated)*. Rohde 1876:66 n. 1. Clouston (1887) 1:53–55. Söderhjelm 1912:57–67. Bédier 1925:119. Sedgwick 1947:288–289. Trenkner 1958:80–81. Holbek (1962) 2:196–197, nos. 195–196. Tubach 1969, no. 4319. *EM* 3:1082–1084. Ashliman, type 1419C.

1. Söderhjelm 1912.
2. Söderhjelm 1912; *EM* 3:1082–1084.
3. Söderhjelm 1912:58.
4. Orso 1979:143–144, no. 208.
5. vv. 498–501.

Judgment of Solomon

Two women dispute over the possession of a baby, each claiming to be its mother. A clever king (or judge or both) orders that the infant be cut in half, whereupon the true mother gives up the child in order that it may live. Or he orders that the women both pull on the baby, who will be awarded to the stronger woman, and presently the true mother lets go in order not to harm the child. Or another test is employed. The judge recognizes the true mother by the maternal concern she shows for the welfare of the child, and awards the child to her.[1]

AT 926, *Judgment of Solomon*, is found in oral tradition and in orally inspired literature from southern Europe to China.

In a Jaina text from India, a merchant had two wives. Of the women, one had a son and the other was childless. While they journeyed in a foreign land, the man died, and both the wives claimed the child. They brought the dispute to a court of justice, where the minister of justice ordered his men to divide the property and then to saw the child in half, giving one half to each woman. But the true mother cried out that she wished to give up the child to the other woman, saying that money was of no use to her; the other woman said nothing. The magistrate, seeing the distress of the one woman, declared that the baby belonged to her. He made her the mistress of the house and rebuked the other woman.[2]

In another Indian story, a man had two wives, each of whom gave birth at the same time to similar children. Once when they were sleeping in a forest on their way to a festival, a wolf came and dragged away the child of the younger wife. She awoke, found the remains of her child in the forest, buried them, and took for herself the child of the older wife. When the latter awoke, she recognized her child in the arms of the younger wife and tried to take him away. The noise awakened the husband, who was unable to resolve the dispute. They went from town to town until they found a judge who could decide the case. The judge ordered the child to be cut into equal parts and each wife to be given one half. At this point the older wife renounced her claim, asking only that the child be allowed to live. The judge then recognized in her the true mother and forced the younger wife to confess. The judge's wisdom was praised.[3]

A Tibetan tale employing a different test relates how a villager wed a woman of his own class but remained childless. So he took a concubine, who bore him a child. The concubine, reasoning that the worst of enmities was that between a

wife and a concubine and that the wife would certainly seek to kill her child, gave her child over to the wife. Soon thereafter the husband died, and a dispute arose between the women for the possession of the child. They went to the king, who was unable to decide which of the women the child belonged to. But a shrewd woman advised him to inform the women that, inasmuch as the officials were unable to learn which of the women the child belonged to, the stronger of the two could have the child, for when each of the women should pull the infant by the hand and the child should begin to cry from pain, the true mother would be overcome with pity and would release the child, knowing that if the child was alive she would be able to see it again, whereas the other woman, who would have no affection for it, would not let go. Then the king should strike the latter with a rod and she would acknowledge the truth. This, the shrewd woman concluded, was the true way to put the two women to the test.[4]

To judge from the texts at my disposal, the Eastern narratives typically present the dispute as being one between co-wives, and prefer the tug-of-war as the means of discerning the true mother, although several other kinds of test are also found, including the proposed division of the child. In Western texts the disputants are usually members of different families, and the preferred method of testing is the proposed division of the infant. In both cases, the clever judge employs an emotional test to solve an apparently logical problem, an unexpected twist that gives the story much of its appeal. He announces a procedure that is logical in a perverse way (viz., each claimant may have half of the baby, or the claimants may each pull on the baby in a tug-of-war, since the true mother will surely pull harder), but in truth his procedure is a covert test that forces each woman to weigh how much she loves the child against how much she wants to win.[5] So the story moves through three dramatic moments: the seemingly impossible problem of discovering which is the true claimant; the judge's strange solution; and finally the revelation that the judge's apparent solution is really a covert test, the aim of which is to induce the claimants to reveal their true feelings and motives.

Indian texts of the *Judgment of Solomon* have been known to Western scholars since the mid-nineteenth century, and the burning issue, especially for the early scholars, has been where the story originated and whether it migrated east or west. Some interpreters have held that the Indian narratives are better motivated than the Biblical legend, which suggests to them an origin in India, while others see an origin in the Occident.[6] But for all we know, a story is as likely to improve as to degenerate in the course of its retellings, so that we really have no way of answering this question, on which speculation continues.[7]

King Solomon

According to a story in the *Septuagint*, two prostitutes came before King Solomon. The first said that the two of them shared the same house, that she herself gave birth to a baby, and that three days later the other woman did likewise. However (she continued), during the night the other woman's baby died, and while she herself slept the other woman switched the two babies. When she awoke she perceived that the child with her was not the child she had borne. The other woman denied this, saying that the living child was her own

whereas the dead child belonged to the other woman. While they thus disputed, Solomon called for a sword and ordered the child to be cut into two, one half to be given to each woman. Then the mother of the child, moved by her concern for it, told the king not to kill the child but to give it to the other woman. But the other woman urged that the child be cut in two and that neither of them have it. Then Solomon judged that the child should be given to the first woman, for she was its mother. When the people of Israel heard of this judgment, they stood in awe of Solomon's wisdom.[8]

In ancient Jewish literature the anonymous compiler of *Kings* relates this traditional story of a clever judge in his account of King Solomon's reign as an illustration of the monarch's wisdom.[9] He explains that God gave Solomon such profound wisdom that he was wiser than any other man of his time, a quality that made him famous in surrounding nations.[10] *Kings* was composed probably in the sixth century B.C., and it was translated into Greek by the second century B.C.[11]

In *Kings* the two women live together as prostitutes sharing the same house. As prostitutes they have less at stake in their dispute than do the co-wives of Eastern texts, for whom the issue is not only the possession of the child but also the inheritance of the deceased husband's goods, since a childless co-wife has no claim on her husband's estate. In the Hebrew legend, as in the second text summarized above, both women give birth at about the same time, and when the child of one woman unexpectedly perishes as the two mothers sleep, the woman who loses her child steals the other's child and represents it as her own. In one interesting respect the story in *Kings* differs from other texts in its strategy of presentation. Texts typically begin with an objective narration of the domestic events leading up to the dispute, and end in court with the judgment of the clever king, who finds a way to discover what we ourselves are privileged already to know. But the Hebrew text begins immediately with the court scene, in the course of which the disputants give their versions of the antecedent events. At this point we know no more than the king does concerning which woman is the true mother and which is the false. Although the Hebrew text provides our earliest attestation of this international story, that is of course no reason to conclude that it must be the source of the international tradition.

The Philiskos Fragment

A recently discovered fragment of papyrus shows that the story of the clever judge and the two women was also known to the Greeks of the classical period. Neither the author of the work represented by the fragment nor the date of its original composition is known. The copy itself dates to the early second century A.D., but the writer cites as an authority for the story a certain Philiskos of Miletos, who wrote in the early fourth century B.C.[12]

Speaking of a certain man whose name does not appear in the fragment as we have it, the author declares that several utterances or judicial decisions have been transferred to him that seem originally to have been made on earlier occasions by other persons. By way of illustration the author says:

"Philiskos of Miletos has written that in the case of the two women who were laying claim to a child, both of them alleging they had given birth to it, he ordered that the child should be cut in two and one half given to each of the women."[13]

Brief though this fragment be, containing only the last part of one sentence and the first part of the following sentence, it informs us, first, that a fourth-century Greek, Philiskos of Miletos, was acquainted with the story of the two women and the clever judge; second, that migratory anecdotes were readily attached to the person who was the subject of Philiskos's essay, so that he became the protagonist in a cycle of tales in which he presumably played the role of a clever judge; and, third, that the story of the two women and the clever judge was one of these. That is, the international story was in circulation in Greece, where in time persons attributed it to a figure who was traditionally famous for his cleverness and wisdom, as elsewhere Jews did in the case of Solomon and Buddhists in the case of the Buddha.

Ascyltos, Encolpius, and Giton

That the story was also known to the Romans is implied by an incident recounted by Petronius in his *Satirica*.[14] According to the Roman novelist, Encolpius one evening made love with his lover Giton. After he had fallen asleep and drunkenly relaxed his grip on Giton, Ascyltos took the boy away to his own bed, so that Encolpius woke up to find his bed empty. Thereupon he told Ascyltos to take his belongings and leave, since he had violated their friendship. After they had divided their possessions, Ascyltos said that they should also divide the boy; and he drew his sword, saying that Encolpius would no longer enjoy the boy alone, since he, Ascyltos, wanted his share. Encolpius drew his own sword, but the boy begged them not to fight. Ascyltos then proposed that Giton be allowed to go with whichever of the two he preferred. Encolpius confidently agreed, but the boy chose Ascyltos. Encolpius fell upon his bed, and Ascyltos left with his prize.[15]

In this passage two companions room together in an inn, and as in the Hebrew story they are a pair of lowlifes—prostitutes there, homosexual rogues here. Just as in the folktale, one of them steals a child belonging to the other during the night while the other sleeps, transferring the child from one bed to the other, except that here the principals are adult male friends and the contested child is a lover rather than an infant son. Upon awakening in the morning the victim notices the theft and complains about the other's misdeed. In the folktale the two claimants lay their case before a judge, who orders the child to be cut into half and shared equally between the claimants, but in Petronius's narrative one of the claimants—the untrue friend Ascyltos, corresponding to the false mother—now proposes to divide the boy between them by cutting him in half. The other claimant, Encolpius, draws his sword to fight, presumably to defend Giton against being physically divided, wherein Encolpius corresponds in an odd way to the true mother, whose overriding concern is for the welfare of the child. As in the oral tale the resolution of the dispute is nonviolent, for the claimants put their swords away and appoint the boy himself to be judge (as Encolpius says: "commisique iudici litem"). After this point the direc-

tion of Petronius's story diverges from that of the folktale, for Giton ironically selects the false friend Ascyltos and departs with him, leaving Encolpius alone and in despair.

The novelist preserves most of the events of the folktale and also their usual sequence (the theft of child during the night, the accusation of thievery in the morning, the agreement by the untrue claimant that the child should be divided in half, the objection by the true claimant that the child should not be harmed, the judge's awarding the child to one of the claimants), but there are also interesting innovations, which presumably are his own. The dispute is set among male claimants (though male claimants are not unparalleled in oral tradition), and the contested child is a male lover.[16] Since no legal theft occurs, the disputants do not refer the matter to formal adjudication, but the characters thereupon pick up parts of the judge's usual role, Ascyltos proposing that they divide the child in two, Giton deciding to whom the child is to be awarded.

Although this adaptation of the tale gives us our only trace of the story in Roman literature, the story itself must have been familiar, for it is also found in Roman illustration. A remarkable wall painting found at Pompeii in 1882 quickly acquired the nickname the Judgment of Solomon (see figure).[17] The painting shows, on the right, a tribunal upon which there are seated three judges, or one judge flanked by two subordinates. Several soldiers stand nearby as guards. Before the tribunal a soldier and a woman hold a naked infant down on a butcher block, and the soldier, holding a meat cleaver in an uplifted arm, is about to cleave the child. Immediately before the tribunal another woman, on her knees with arms uplifted and anguish on her face, is

Detail of a wall painting discovered at Pompeii in 1882. Reproduced from Jules Martha, *Manuel d'Archéologique Étrusque et Romaine* (Paris: A. Quantin, 1885), p. 260.

imploring the judge. On the left, a number of spectators look on. The fresco certainly depicts the story of the two women and the clever judge, wherein the judge's test is taking the form of a proposed division of the infant. The painting necessarily predates the eruption of Mt. Vesuvius, which destroyed Pompeii in A.D. 79.

Now, the characters in the fresco are depicted as Pygmies. Accordingly, it would hardly have been commissioned by a Jew and in any case is unlikely to portray the Hebrew story. Since hippopotamuses and ibises appear in other paintings in the same house, the scene of the judgment must be Africa or Egypt. If this is the case, the painting may illustrate a famous episode in the life of King Bokchoris of Egypt, whom classical authors in the first centuries of our era mention as a man of great wisdom and whose judicial decisions were still current in their day.[18] Several other Roman paintings have also been interpreted as being illustrations of this story.[19]

Although there is ample evidence then that AT 926 was current as an oral story in the classical lands, no Greek or Roman author seems to have given it memorable treatment, and it is attested in surviving literature only in allusion. As a result, in the West the narrative is best known from its appearance in the Hebrew bible as an instance of the wisdom of Solomon.

Lit. AT 926, *Judgment of Solomon.* Motif J1171.1, *Solomon's judgment: the divided child.* Pitrè 1883:133–134. Lumbroso 1883. Gaidoz 1889:313–316, 337–341, 366–367, 385–387, 414, 446, 457–460. Köhler (1898) 1:531–533. Lucas 1903. Engelmann 1904. Roscher 3:3309–3311. Zachariae 1906:133–138. Frazer (1918) 2:570–571. Gunkel 1921:143–146. Goebel 1932:21–34. Turner 1973:8–14. Ashliman, type 926.

1. Gaidoz 1889; Zachariae 1906:133–138; Frazer (1918) 2:570–571.
2. Frazer (1918) 2:570–571, citing L. P. Tessitori, "Two Jaina Versions of the Story of Solomon's Judgment," *The Indian Antiquary* 42 (1913): 149.
3. Zachariae 1906:136–137.
4. Gaidoz 1889:366.
5. For another disguised test see Homer *Od.* 23.177–230, where Penelope slyly bids Eurykleia, in the hearing of Odysseus, take the bed out of the bedroom and prepare it for the man claiming to be Odysseus; however, as only Odysseus and Penelope know, a tree serves as one bedpost for the bed, so that the bed cannot be moved from the bedroom. The claimant protests that it would be impossible to move the bed, proving thereby that he must be Odysseus. If Penelope's test were straightforward, she would challenge the claimant to describe the bed. See further "Homecoming Husband."
6. For example, Köhler (1898) 1:533.
7. For example, Turner 1973:13. See more generally Dundes 1969.
8. 3 Kings 3:16–28.
9. 1 Kings 3:16–28.
10. 4:29–34.
11. Schürer (1986) 3:476–477.
12. Turner 1973:9.
13. *P. Oxy.* 2944; Turner 1973:8–14.
14. Lucas 1903:257.
15. *Sat.* 79–80.
16. For a version with male claimants, see Lumbroso 1883:573–574.
17. Pitrè 1883; Lumbroso 1883; Gaidoz 1889:314–316; Engelmann 1904; Roscher 3: 3309–3311.
18. Diodorus Sic.1.94.5; Plutarch *Demetrios* 27; Aelian *VH* 12.63; Zenobios 2.60. See further Lumbroso 1883; Lucas 1903:261–262; cf. Rohde 1960:370 n. 1.
19. Lucas 1903; Goebel 1932.

Keep Your Seats! 🖎 Prince the Flutist

A proud woman enters church just as the congregation is rising. Assuming that they are rising for her she bids them be seated.

This comic tale, which pokes fun at the foolish pride of the lowly, has been collected in northern and central Europe. It is AT 1861*, *Keep Your Seats!*

In its modern form the tale is probably first attested in the collection of comic tales made by Heinrich Bebel and published in the early 1500s. When a certain man became mayor of a village, he purchased a new sheepskin coat for his wife. Haughty in part because of her new garment and in part because of her husband's elevation in the county, the woman entered church on Sunday with a proudly uplifted head. The gospel had just been read and the congregation had stood up, which she interpreted as a gesture of honor for herself. Thinking of her previous status she said: "Do sit. I am mindful of how I too was poor."[1]

According to a Tyrolian text published in the early twentieth century, one Sunday a woman from outside the community entered the little church of a certain village. The sermon was just ended, and the devout arose from their seats. When the woman saw that everyone stood up as she entered, she said: "Oh, stay seated. I'm not that noble."[2]

In some variants the action is given an academic setting. A student who has been summoned to appear before the academic council (*das akademische Konsistorium*) sees the professors standing and calls out to them that they should remain seated, since there is room enough for him at the door.[3]

A Roman Anecdote

It has gone unnoticed that the modern story has an ancient counterpart in an anecdote recounted as a fable in Latin verse by the fabulist Phaedrus in the first century A.D. The church or university setting of recent texts is answered by a theatrical setting in the ancient narrative.

A flute player named Princeps ("Prince"), who provided music for the stage, once fell and broke his shin. Some months passed, and the spectators missed him. When Prince began to walk with a crutch, he was induced to put in an appearance at a show. The chorus was singing a song that was new to him since he had been away from the theater for a time, and it contained this line: "Rejoice! Rome is secure, since (the) Prince is safe"[4] The audience stood up to applaud, and the flute player, thinking that his fans were congratulating him, threw kisses to them. Part of the audience, seeing his foolish mistake, laughingly called for an encore. The chorus repeated the song, and Prince now took a full bow. At first the audience thought that he was taking a bow on behalf of the chorus, but when they perceived that he was proudly taking the honor being paid to the emperor, they threw him out headlong.[5]

Phaedrus introduces his fable with an apt promythium to the effect that when an empty mind has received some small encouragement and comes to exaggerate its own importance, it is easily brought into ridicule. Similarly, in his motif index Thompson places the central idea of the Phaedrian tale among instances of what he calls the self-deception of the lowly, a common theme in

Aesopic fables.[6] The empty mind in this case apparently belonged to the flutist Cassius Princeps, a historical person known from inscriptions, the event that evidently gave rise to the anecdote having taken place in A.D. 9.[7]

In both the ancient and modern tales (1) the lone protagonist joins an assembly of people (at the theater/at church), and (2) when for one reason or another the crowd stands, (3) the person foolishly imagines that he (she) is being honored, and (4) acknowledges the supposed honor (throws kisses and bows/bids them be seated). The stories are parallel in their main features, but since they are also rather simple, I see no way to discern whether an ancient event or anecdote has been influenced by *Keep Your Seats!* as an established story pattern in oral tradition, or whether the parallelism is the result of independent invention.

The protagonist of the modern tale is marked as being exceptional in some way: the wife of a locally important man, an outsider who is visiting the little village, or a student in a context of professors. In the ancient tale the protagonist is exceptional in several ways, being at once an entertainer with the marginal and ambiguous status of servant and celebrity and also a person who has been absent from the theater for some time because of an accident. Thus he is simultaneously a person of low status (like the student), a person of high status (like the major's wife), and a stranger (like the woman from outside the village). Moreover, whereas the protagonist of *Keep Your Seats!* characteristically makes one mistake, misinterpreting the standing of the assembled persons, Prince makes two, for after foolishly misunderstanding the chorus's honorific reference to the Prince (that is, the emperor or his named successor) as being to himself, he goes on to misinterpret the audience's rising to applaud the chorus as also being for his own benefit. Finally, whereas the joke normally concludes abruptly with the main character's foolish mistake, the ancient tale continues with the audience's deliberately inducing the protagonist to repeat his folly and then ejecting him from the place for his presumption. In short, the comic fable is worked out more elaborately than the modern joke.

Lit. AT 1861*, *Keep Your Seats!* EM 2:1039–1040.

1. Bebel (1907) 2:53, no. 119.
2. Dörler 1906:294, no. 81.
3. *EM* 2:1039.
4. Phaedrus 5.7.27: "laetare! incolumis Roma salvo principe." The misunderstanding is less natural in English than in Latin, which lacks definite articles.
5. Phaedrus 5.7 = Perry 529.
6. Motif J953.3, *Flute-player thinks song meant for the prince is sung to him.*
7. Perry 1965:lxxiv.

Labor Contract ☙ Aesop and Xanthos

A youth is hired by a farmer, who agrees to pay him an amount of money in return for his services for a period of time. The master also proposes that they enter into a bargain according to which the first one to become angry shall re-

ceive so many blows (forfeit an amount of money, have his nose or ears cut off, lose his life, etc.), and the youth agrees. In each of the episodes that follow, the cruel master assigns the youth a chore of some kind. Some tasks are intended to frustrate the youth so that he will become angry, but others are simply tasks, usually of an agricultural or pastoral nature. For his part, the clever youth responds to each assignment in such a way that he either escapes the intended frustration or causes major damage to his master's property or family or both. In the end the youth triumphs when his master bursts into anger, thereby losing the bargain, or desperately agrees to buy off the youth so that he will quit the place.

This humorous and very popular tale is AT 1000–1029, *Labor Contract (Anger Bargain)*. Often the protagonist is the youngest of three brothers. The first brother enters the service of an ogrous master and fails miserably, and then the second brother does so with the same outcome. But the clever third brother succeeds, for he turns against the unkind master the ploys that the master used in order to enrage the first and second brothers. As usual in tales of three brothers, the first two serve merely as foils for the third, whose adventures are the focus of the tale, although the initial episodes also serve to illustrate the master's cruelty and the customary success of his tactics, preparing us to enjoy the well-deserved reversal of his fortunes that the third brother presently brings about.

The core of the tale is the series of individual tasks that are framed by the labor contract and in particular by the anger bargain between the master and the hero. Although the central episodes are traditional in content, they have no fixed number and no fixed order, except that they tend to appear in a more or less climactic sequence so that the damage caused by the hireling and the exasperation felt by the master increases. This kind of folktale, a frame enclosing a variable number of smaller tales in variable sequence, has been called a *conglomerate*.[1]

According to an Irish tale recounted in the 1920s by an elderly farmer, Thomas Moran, a certain widow had three sons. Each spring one of the boys went to the hiring fair in Newcastle West where he was hired by a farmer offering double wages for the spring work—the job to last until they heard the first cuckoo—but with the strange bargain that if either of them should become vexed with the other, he would receive twelve lashes with a whip. The first and second brothers each quickly lost the bargain. In the third spring the youngest brother was hired. One day the farmer hid his calves and then ordered the youth to look high and low for them, saying he would get nothing to eat until he had found them. The boy leveled the hay barn, explaining that he was looking high and low for the calves. He asked the farmer if he was vexed with him, but the man said he was not. The next day the farmer told the youth to drive the calves across the river, taking care not to get their feet wet. The boy dragged the creatures across the water upside down, drowning the calves but keeping their feet dry. When the boy asked the farmer if he was vexed, he replied he was not. The next day the farmer's wife told the boy to keep an eye on every head of cabbage in her garden, lest she be robbed. So the boy killed all their chickens, ducks, geese, and sheep, placing one eye on each head of cabbage. Again, the farmer denied he was vexed. Finally, the farmer's wife, having con-

spired with her husband, hid under a hedge and imitated the sound of a cuckoo, the sign that the youth's term of work was over. The plan was to induce the youth to leave them and go home. But the youth remarked that it was early for a cuckoo, and threw a stone at the hedge, nearly killing the woman. This time when the youth asked the farmer if he was vexed with him, the farmer said he had never been so vexed in his life. So the boy got his wages, and the farmer got his lashes.[2]

Since the central episodes are potentially complete little tales that can often be found elsewhere as independent narratives, Aarne-Thompson classify each episode as an independent tale. Thus the Irish text can be described typologically as AT 1000, *Bargain Not to Become Angry* + AT 1002, *Dissipation of the Ogre's Property* + AT 1006, *Casting Eyes* + AT 1029, *The Woman as Cuckoo in the Tree*.

According to a Danish tale collected in 1887, a poor man had three sons, Povl, Per, and Esben. Setting out into the world, Povl hired on with a farmer who agreed to pay him a bushel of money at the end of a year if he did everything he was asked, but the first one of them to lose his temper was to have a piece cut out of his belly and his backside. Povl failed, and so did Per, and now Esben set out and was hired by the same man. That evening the family sat down to eat, and when no one invited Esben to join them, he sat down at the table, took a spoon from his pocket, and helped himself. The same thing happened at breakfast in the morning. The farmer then ordered Esben to plow the field, telling him he could return home when the master's dog came home. But long after all the neighbors had gone home, the dog remained lying down in the field, so that Esben struck it with a plow handle. It ran home whining, after which Esben cut loose the horses and rode home on one of them. He asked the master if he was angry. He said he wasn't. One day the master told Esben to take care of his pigs, watching out that they not run into the mudhole. Esben cut off their tails, drove the pigs home to his father's house, planted the tails in the mud, and shouted to his master that all the pigs had run into the mudhole. The master tried pulling one of them out, but its tail apparently broke off so that the man fell into the mud. Esben asked his master if he was angry, and the man said he was not. On another occasion the master's wife asked the youth to wash her child inside and out. So Esben took him to a brook, stripped him, scrubbed him, hung him up to dry, and returned home. By the time the woman checked on her child, he had frozen to death. Another day the master told Esben that he and his wife were going to a party. Among other things Esben was to come to the party and cast an eye in the direction of his master now and then, and to arrange for some light for the walk home. He admonished the youth to do exactly as he had told him. Esben killed his master's four sheep and set fire to the barn. At the party he threw a sheep's eye in the direction of his master whenever he had a chance. When the master asked Esben about a lantern for the walk home, Esben explained that he had set the barn afire. In the hope of getting rid of the hired boy, the master tried to kill Esben in bed but was foiled. In desperation the man told Esben he could leave now with his full wages for the year, but Esben declined. Finally, the man offered him all the money that a team of two horses could carry. So Esben was driven home with a large amount of money.[3]

The central episodes of the folktale typically have the following form: assignment, execution, confrontation, and evaluation. Thus, the master (or mistress) assigns the youth a task; the youth goes to work, escaping the intended frustration or causing damage to the farmer; with feigned naivete the youth gives the farmer an account of his performance; and the farmer, asked if he is angry, says he is not, or simply holds his peace. Usually the hero deliberately accomplishes the assigned task in a reckless and injurious way, such as when he conveys the farmer's calves across the stream upside down and so drowns them, and when he sets the barn on fire in order to provide light. Often he plays the literal fool, as when he pretends to understand literally the farmer's instructions to "look high and low" and when he takes literally the instruction to "cast an eye" in the direction of his master.

Aesop and Xanthos

Although no straightforward text of the Anger Bargain as such is known from ancient literature, a cluster of episodes in the *Aesop Romance* gives the impression of having been created from the same template as the tale type.[4] The *Aesop Romance*, a humorous Greek novel purporting to be a biography of the fabulist Aesop, was composed for a popular readership by an unknown author, probably in Egypt in the first century A.D.[5] The composer drew his material from a variety of sources, mostly traditional narratives of various kinds.[6]

The novel relates how Aesop, a Phrygian slave, was sold by his master to an itinerant slave dealer, who took the slave to the island of Samos where he sold him to the philosopher Xanthos. The outspoken Aesop soon clashed with Xanthos and his wife. Unfortunately, there is a lacuna in the text at this point, but from subsequent allusions it is clear that in the missing page Xanthos, not wishing Aesop to cause him any more trouble, instructed his slave not to do *anything* more or less than he has been told to do; otherwise, he would receive a beating.[7] Xanthos now told him to pick up the oil flask and towels and accompany his master to the bath. Aesop vowed to himself to teach his master a lesson in giving orders. At the bath when Xanthos asked for the flask and found it empty, he asked Aesop where the oil was. Aesop replied that it was at home, for Xanthos had said to bring the flask and towels but had said nothing of the oil. Aesop explained that he was following his master's instructions not to do any more than he had been told to do, so as not to get a beating.

Next, seeing some of his friends at the bath, Xanthos told Aesop to go home and prepare lentil. He gave meticulous instructions, telling Aesop to put it in a pot, add water, place the pot on the hearth, put wood under it, and light it; and if the fire died down, he was to blow on it. Aesop went home and cooked one lentil seed. Presently Xanthos invited his friends home for a lentil dinner. When they arrived, Xanthos told Aesop to bring something to drink for men right from the bath. So Aesop filled a container of bath water and served it. When Xanthos asked what it was, Aesop said it was something to drink right from the bath. Xanthos became sullen and told Aesop to bring his footbath. Aesop brought it and merely stood there. Xanthos asked about this, and Aesop explained that Xanthos had asked for his footbath; he had not said to put water in

it or to wash Xanthos's feet. Xanthos asked Aesop to let him see if the lentil was cooked yet. So Aesop brought him the lentil seed, and Xanthos ate it and told him the meal was ready to be served. Aesop served everyone lentil water. When Xanthos asked where the lentil was, Aesop said that Xanthos had eaten it. When the philosopher asked whether he had cooked only one lentil seed, he explained that Xanthos had told him to cook lentil, which was singular, and not lentils, which was plural.

Xanthos then instructed Aesop to cook the four pigs feet he had bought. Looking however for a pretext to give Aesop a beating, Xanthos sent his slave on a brief errand, and while Aesop was gone, Xanthos took one of the feet from the kettle and hid it. Upon his return Aesop guessed that Xanthos had hidden one of the feet in order to have a pretext to beat him. So he went out in the yard and cut a foot off of a pig that Xanthos was saving for his wife's birthday, and added it to the kettle. In the meantime it occurred to Xanthos that Aesop might run away if he did not find the missing foot, so that Xanthos secretly returned it to the pot. When Aesop presently served five pigs feet, Xanthos turned pale and asked how many feet that pig had. Aesop replied that the sum was correct, since there were five feet there and three on the pig outside. Xanthos complained to his guests that Aesop would soon drive him crazy, but Aesop commented that if Xanthos had not formulated so strict a policy toward him, Aesop would have been a proper servant. Xanthos said nothing, since he had no pretext for whipping Aesop.

On another occasion Xanthos was dining at the home of one of his students. He took some portions of the food and gave them to Aesop, telling him to take it to her who felt kindly toward him. Aesop took the food to Xanthos's house, where he gave it, not to Xanthos's wife, but to the family dog. He explained to Xanthos that his dog felt more kindly toward him than his wife did.[8] Xanthos assured his angry wife that he would find an excuse to whip Aesop.

The next day Xanthos invited some of his students to dinner and instructed Aesop to cook something that was good. Aesop served tongue for every course, ending with tongue broth. Xanthos's guests all became sick. Aesop explained to Xanthos that he had only followed orders, preparing something that was good, for what was more useful in life than a tongue? Apologizing to his students, Xanthos invited them for dinner again. This time he instructed Aesop, in front of his students, to buy something that was no good. Aesop went out and bought more tongues, which he cooked for dinner. When again all the courses again proved to be tongue, Xanthos angrily asked why he had bought tongue. Aesop, pointing out the terrible things in life that result from the use of the tongue, asked whether anything was worse than a tongue. When one of the students criticized Aesop as a troublemaker, Aesop called him a busybody for trying to encourage his master's anger.

Then Xanthos, still seeking a pretext to whip Aesop, challenged Aesop to find a person who was not a busybody, and to invite him to dinner the next day. If the man meddled in another's business three times, Aesop would receive a beating. Aesop invited a man who appeared to mind his own business, but Xanthos thrice managed to induce him to meddle, so that Xanthos had Aesop whipped. Moreover, Xanthos threatened to inflict worse torture upon

Aesop if he did not succeed in finding a wholly unmeddlesome person. So Aesop found a man who so entirely minded his own affairs that Xanthos was unable to exact a single meddlesome comment from him. Even when Xanthos, conspiring with his wife, feigned anger at her for a minor oversight and had a pyre built right in the room in order (he said) to burn her alive, the guest did not protest at all and even offered to add his own wife to the pyre. At this point Xanthos acknowledged that Aesop had defeated him. He asked Aesop to set aside his chicanery, and Aesop agreed to serve him well from then on.[9]

The nature of the bargain between master and servant in the *Aesop Romance* differs somewhat from that in the folktale, for the one who will receive a beating is not he who is first to become angry, but the servant if he fails in an instruction. Nonetheless the characters in the novel and the folktale behave in essentially the same way throughout, for in both the master tries to force the servant to fail, the servant gives the appearance of following instructions while in reality sabotaging the task, and the resultant frustration felt by the master builds until he can no longer tolerate it. The ancient work of fiction and the international folktale display the same episodic structure, and the episodes tend to show the same form: assignment, execution, confrontation, and evaluation. So the slight difference in the terms of the bargain has little or no effect on the nature of the narratives.

The principal features shared by the folktale and the novel are the following. (1) The protagonist goes (is taken) out into the world, where (2) he is hired (purchased) by a new master. (3) The master makes a rule that whichever of them first becomes angry shall receive a beating (or that if the servant does not follow orders exactly, he shall receive a beating). (4) The master now gives the servant a series of tasks, (5) which he performs, though in a deliberately reckless manner or playing the literal fool, (6) causing harm to his master. Each time (7) he justifies his actions to his master, (8) who restrains his anger. (9) As the master's frustration grows, his desire to induce the servant to become angry (to execute an order inexactly) increases, but in the end (10) the frustrated master acknowledges that his servant has defeated him.

The comparison shows that the folktale and the Aesopic story share the same general story-idea and pattern of realization, suggesting that they are probably forms of the same tale. Since none of the specific tasks assigned by the master are actually common to both the oral tale and the novel, their similarities are primarily structural; nevertheless, they are not entirely different in content. Xanthos's deliberately hiding one of the pigs feet is quite similar to the Irish farmer's deliberately hiding the calves; Aesop's cutting off the leg of his master's pig is reminiscent of the folktale episode in which the hero cuts off the tails of his master's pigs (AT 1004, *Hogs in the Mud*); and the failed conspiracy of Xanthos and his wife in the final episode of the story is like the failed conspiracy of the Irish master and his wife (AT 1029, *The Woman as Cuckoo in the Tree*), both of which, being desperate in nature, also occur at the end of their tales. The structural parallelism and these unusual correspondences in substance constitute together a strong case for a historical connection of some kind. Most likely the novelist has adapted a version of the Anger Bargain to his fictional biography of Aesop.

Unlike the hireling in the folktale, Aesop is a slave, and his lowly status necessarily affects the narrative in some ways. Unlike the folktale hero, Aesop cannot set out from home to seek employment; instead, he is sold by a slave dealer to a new master. For the same reason he cannot be the youngest of three brothers who in succession work for the same master. And unlike the symmetrical bargain between the hero and his master in the folktale in which either party may receive a beating, the rule between Aesop and Xanthos must be asymmetrical, for it would be inconceivable for the slave to whip his master. The folktale moreover is regularly set in a world of farmers, whereas the Aesopic tale has an urban locale; accordingly, the tasks in the former are mostly agricultural chores, while the tasks in the latter have to do with house and town. This raises the interesting possibility that the folktale may once have circulated in an urban redaction, but we cannot know whether the urban setting of the Aesopic narrative derives from an ancient urban version of the oral tale or is part of the author's adaptation.

Lit. (AT 1000–1029, *Labor Contract (Anger Bargain)*.) BP 2:293–294. Köhler (1898) 1:326–329. Liungman 1961:253–256. Holbek (1962) 2:33. Ashliman, types 1000–1029.

1. Sydow 1948:72.
2. Danaher 1967:28–32, no. 7.
3. Bødker, Hole, and D'Aronco 1963:78–86; cf. Thompson 1974:369–376, no. 85. The summary, wherein I omit a few episodes in the interest of brevity, contains AT 1000, *Bargain Not to Become Angry* + AT 1003, *Plowing* + AT 1004, *Hogs in the Mud* + AT 1012, *Cleaning the Child* + AT 1006, *Casting Eyes* + AT 1008, *Lighting the Road* + AT 1115, *Attempted Murder with Hatchet* + AT 1153, *Wages: As Much as He Can Carry*.
4. Holbek (1962) 2:33.
5. Perry 1952:5.
6. Notably, the author transfers to Aesop (ch. 101–123) the international story of the wise Achikar, for which see AT 922A, *Achikar*. See more generally Zeitz 1936; Perry 1981:1–70, 1952:1–241; Holbek (1962) 2:21–38; Hansen 1998:106–111.
7. On the lacuna see Perry 1981:4–7.
8. See further "Best Friend, Worst Enemy."
9. *Vita Aesopi* 11–64 (*Vita* G). Somewhat illogically, Aesop returns briefly to playing the literal fool and generally to causing his master problems in several episodes that follow, before he drops this behavior for good. Perry (1981:37) suggests that these incidents belong together with the story summarized above but became detached from it during the composition or transmission of the work so that they are now logically out of place.

Learn to Swim

Aarne-Thompson summarize this comic tale as follows: "The fool almost drowns when swimming. The others blame him: 'Learn to swim on dry ground before you go into the water.' "

They classify the joke as AT 1293*, *Learn to Swim*, among the numskull tales, and give its provenance as Eastern Europe, citing a text from Estonia and indicating that the tale is known also in Russia. The same joke is told of skiers: "To a novice whose first attempt at skiing ended with his nose furrowing the snow a companion shouted: 'You jumped too late, Joe!' 'Naw'—from the smother below—'I jumped too soon. Should have learned more about the game first.' "[1]

A Greek Joke

> The witticism is found in *Philogelos*, a Greek jokebook from late antiquity.[2] "A numskull almost drowned while swimming. So he swore not to go into the water until he had learned how to swim well." In the ancient joke the silly idea of postponing engaging in the sport until the sportsman has learned how to do it is attributed to the swimmer, whereas in modern texts it is voiced sometimes by the sportsman and sometimes by the bystanders. The effect is more or less the same.

Lit. AT 1293*, *Learn to Swim*. McCartney 1931:197. Marzolph 1987:197–198.

 1. McCartney 1931:197, citing *Everybody's*, June 1922, 186.
 2. *Phil.* 2.

Loading the Wood ✎ Sorites

A fool loading his horse (oxen) keeps adding more stones (wood, etc.) to the load, saying that if his horse can draw or carry one stone, it can carry another. He so overloads the horse that it cannot move (or collapses), whereupon, using the same logic, he completely unloads the horse.

This tale is AT 1242, *Loading the Wood*.

So in a Danish narrative written down by the informant himself in 1884, a man from the island of Fyn was hauling stone. After loading the horse sufficiently, he stayed another hour throwing stones into the wagon, since every time he threw in a stone he said: "If it can pull those, it can also pull this one." When the man was ready to go, the horse could not pull the load, so that the man had to unload the stones. For every stone he tossed from the wagon, he said: "If it can't pull those, then it can't pull this one either." And so he continued till the wagon was empty.[1]

Sorites

> The tale of the foolish drayman is not attested in ancient sources, but the logical problem of the heap was familiar to learned persons in antiquity, among whom it was known as *sorites* (from Greek *soros* "heap") or *he sorike aporia* "the problem of the heap."[2] Does one grain of wheat make a heap? If not, when you add another, do you now have a heap? As you add more one at a time, with which grain of wheat do they become a heap? As you remove one grain at a time from a heap, does the departure of any single grain cause it to cease being a heap?[3] No individual unit seems to have a decisive effect on the whole.[4]
>
> Sorites was one of several problems propounded by Euboulides of Miletos, a contemporary of Aristotle, and ancient authors frequently refer to it.[5] Horace alludes to sorites in one of his *Epistles*, saying that, since the oldest writers are regarded as the best, how old must a writer be to be accounted good? Is a hundred years enough? If so, what of a writer who died a month or a year short of

a hundred years ago? It is, he says, like plucking hairs from a horse's tail one at a time or like the diminishing heap (*ratione ruentis acervi*), suggesting that the attempt to make such discriminations is folly.[6]

Although *Loading the Wood* is not itself known to be an ancient tale, the calculation illustrated by the fool was recognized and described by ancient thinkers, who saw that no single item in a series of increments or decrements is the determining factor in the constitution of a pile.

Lit. (AT 1242, *Loading the Wood*.) Christensen 1939:223–224. *EM* 1:827–828, 6:1203–1205.

1. Christensen 1939:163, no. 86.
2. Christensen 1939:224.
3. Lalande 1968:1011–1012.
4. Cf. Cicero *Academica* 2.16.
5. Diogenes Laertios 2.108 (on Euboulides). Ancient allusions to sorites include Cicero *De Div.* 2.4.11, *Academica* 2.16.49, 2.48.147; Persius 6.79–80; Lucian *Symposium* 23; Sextus Empiricus *Adv. Math.* 1.68, 80, *Pyrr.* 2.253, 3.80.
6. *Epist.* 2.1.47. Horace's mention of the tail of a horse must be an allusion to a similar puzzle that asked how many hairs make a horse's tail. It is presumably the same as *phalakros* "the bald man," which Euboulides is also said to have propounded (Diogenes Laertios 2.108).

Local Moon

Seeing a moon above a town that he is visiting for the first time, a numskull naively infers that (or wonders whether) each town has its own moon, or concludes that the moon he sees belongs to his own town, etc.

This little numskull tale, AT 1334, *The Local Moon*, is known in Europe, the Middle East, and India.

According to a Spanish joke current in the sixteenth and seventeenth centuries, students often went to Salamanca under the pretext of studying but in reality passed their time sleeping, whoring, and gambling, so that when they returned home they were even more stupid than before. One such student, returning to his hometown and seeing the moon there, asked his father whether this moon and the one in Salamanca were one and the same, observing:

> "The moon of Salamanca
> Is round and white like this one."

The silly ass did not know whether this moon was the same as that one![1]

In a tale heard by Katharine Briggs from W. S. Hannam, a Yorkshire solicitor, in 1915, two Yorkshiremen from Slaidburn had gone to work in Leeds. After a number of overcast nights, the sky finally cleared and a full moon shone. Gazing in amazement, one of the men commented to the other that, aye, there was their Slaidburn moon.[2]

Some Greek Numskulls

In his essay *On Exile* Plutarch says that persons who have moved from one region to another may display either provincial or cosmopolitan attitudes, and mentions that "we laugh at the silliness of the man who declares that there is a better moon in Athens than in Corinth."[3] Plutarch merely alludes to the joke here. The full tale may have recounted how an Athenian numskull, visiting Corinth and observing the moon one evening, commented that the Athenian moon was superior to the Corinthian moon. For example, he may have said that the Athenian moon was fuller; for there are modern texts in which a traveler, confronted with only a half-moon, deems himself fortunate that back home they have a full moon.[4]

A different form of the little tale appears in two versions in the manuscripts of the ancient Greek jokebook *Philogelos*. In one, a fool seeing the moon asked his father if there were such moons in other towns as well. In the other, a fool who saw the moon while he was in town asked his father if other towns also had such moons.[5] The first version gives no hint of what prompts the question, but in the second version we may suppose that the youthful speaker accompanies his father from their village into a town or city and, being surprised that the town possesses a moon like that in his village, wonders whether all towns have their own moon.[6] Here, as in the Spanish tale, the interlocutors are a naive boy and his father, whereas in Plutarch's tale the self-satisfied numskull appears to be an adult.

Lit. AT 1334, *The Local Moon*. Thierfelder 1968:217. Marzolph 1987:195. Ashliman, type 1334. *EM* 9:802–805.

1. "La luna de Salamanca / así es redonda y blanca." Chevalier 1983:170–171, no. 101.
2. Briggs (1970) A2:278.
3. Plutarch *Mor.* 601C.
4. *EM* 9:802.
5. *Phil.* 49.
6. Thierfelder 1968:217.

Lord's Prayer ⚘ Sisyphos and Thanatos

The devil (Death, etc.) agrees not to take a man until he has said a certain prayer for the last time. So the man avoids saying the prayer, thereby preserving his life.

This tale is AT 1199, *The Lord's Prayer*.[1]

In a humorous narrative collected in Israel from a Moroccan-born Jew, there was a town whose inhabitants were very pious. Among the inhabitants was a watchman named Meir, who had an evil wife. Not trusting in God, she wanted to put money aside for their old age, whereas Meir told her he trusted in God so that they should not be afraid. God, seeing all this, instructed the Angel of Death to fetch the soul of Meir, because he no longer trusted in God. When the

Angel of Death revealed himself to Meir, the latter pleaded to him not to take away his soul until he should have prayed the *Shema* prayer. The angel agreed, saying: "I shall be damned if I take your soul before you have prayed this prayer." Then Meir began the prayer, stopped, and said: "I shall be damned if I ever complete this prayer."[2]

Sisyphos and Thanatos

The ancient Greek trickster Sisyphos plays a similar though more complicated trick on Death. Indeed, he outwits Death twice in succession.

According to the mythographer Pherekydes, Sisyphos once incurred the anger of Zeus, who thereupon sent Thanatos (Death) for him. But Sisyphos perceived the approach of Thanatos and bound him in strong bonds, whereupon human beings ceased to die. Eventually Ares released Thanatos and handed Sisyphos over to him. Before he died, however, Sisyphos instructed his wife, Merope, not to make the customary funeral offerings upon his death. When some time had passed and Merope still had not performed the rites, Hades asked Sisyphos about it and let him go in order that he might reproach his wife. But when Sisyphos reached Corinth he did not return until he had died of old age. After he died, Hades made him roll a stone so that he might not run away again.[3]

Our only narrative source for Sisyphos's deception is Pherekydes, and of his account we possess only a summary by a scholiast, who relates the two stories of Sisyphos's trickery in explanation of Homer's calling Sisyphos "the craftiest of men."[4] In the second story, which concerns us here, the cunning Sisyphos has the foresight secretly to instruct Merope not to perform the customary offerings to him upon his death.[5] So after Thanatos has taken Sisyphos to Hades' realm and his wife has puzzlingly failed to perform the usual rites, Hades allows Sisyphos to return to the world of the living only long enough to instruct his wife to do her duty. Once he is home, however, he does no such thing, living there happily until he dies a natural death.

The poet Theognis apparently mentions a variant form of the legend when he compares different desirable possessions that a man might have—wealth, wisdom, cunning, persuasive speech, and swiftness of foot–and as an example of cunning cites Sisyphos, who (Theognis says) used his cunning to return from Hades' realm, something that no other person has contrived to do, having persuaded Persephone with clever words.[6] In this version Sisyphos evidently persuades Persephone rather than Hades/Thanatos to allow him to return to the world above. A character in a Sophoclean tragedy also alludes to the story when he speaks of a certain person's dying and returning from Hades' realm, just as Odysseus's father did.[7] He means Sisyphos, having in mind the tradition according to which Odysseus's biological father was not Laertes but Sisyphos, who had seduced Odysseus's mother Antikleia.

The Sisyphos legend is similar in structure and spirit to modern tales of a respite from death, especially *The Lord's Prayer*. In both the ancient legend and the modern tale (1) the trickster gains from Death (god, etc.) a respite from death until (2) he will have performed a final religious rite (he will have in-

structed his wife to do so). (3) Death agrees. (4) The trickster avoids performing the rite (avoids instructing his wife to perform the rite), and thereby (5) prolongs his life.

The Lord's Prayer is one of a number of tales in which a human being or animal gains a respite from death and thereby postpones or entirely escapes his fate. Thus when it is learned that a certain person will live only until a particular candle burns itself out, someone extinguishes the candle, postponing the first person's death indefinitely.[8] Or a man who is to belong to the devil when his work is finished chooses never to finish it.[9] The same idea appears in stories in which a creditor agrees not to collect a debt until the debtor's beard is completely shaven off, or a certain man is not to be killed until he has completely drained his cup.[10] Animal tales constructed on the theme of a respite from death are also found. The captive persuades his captor not to devour him until after a particular, apparently innocent condition is met, the predator agrees, and the victim escapes, as in the Aesopic fable in which a dog persuaded a wolf to eat him not then and there but later when he would be fatter, but when the wolf returned he found the dog lying on the roof of the house, out of his reach.[11]

The legend of Sisyphos and Thanatos shows that later Christian tales in which a trickster and the devil contend for the soul, or life, of the trickster draw upon pre-Christian models. But although the Greek spirit of death, whether he is called Hades or Thanatos or something else, is happy to win more souls for his realm, he is not a spirit of Evil competing against a spirit of Good for the acquisition of souls; he is simply the spirit of death, and in the end he will get all the souls anyway. When the pagan stories were Christianized, the role of Death was assumed by the devil, for in Christian dualism it would have been illogical for a mortal to contend with Jesus for the possession of his or her soul.

Lit. (AT 1199, *The Lord's Prayer*.) Meyer 1885:242–276. Ashliman, type 1199. *EM* 5:801–803.

1. The motif of a respite from death until a prayer is concluded occurs also in AT 322, *Godfather Death*. See Meyer 1885:242–276; Christiansen 1915:78; Goebel 1932:148–153. When Death comes for the aged hero, the latter asks Death to wait until he has said the Lord's Prayer, and Death agrees. The man starts the prayer but then declines to finish it, and Death, acknowledging that he has been tricked, departs. The trickster finally dies when, having lived as long as he wishes, he deliberately completes the prayer, or, when tricked in turn by Death, the man unthinkingly utters the entire prayer.

2. Noy 1963:17–18, no. 8. The narration appears to be illogical here. Although Meir is unwavering in his trust in God, the Angel of Death comes for him anyway. In the continuation of the tale, the trickster is eventually duped when the Angel of Death pretends to be a dying man, Meir is induced to say the prayer over him, and the disguised Angel jumps out of bed and takes Meir's soul.

3. *FGH* 3 F 119 = schol. Homer *Il.* 6.153. See further Wilamowitz-Moellendorff 1884:201–202; Roscher 4:961; Gantz 1993:174.

4. Homer *Il.* 6.158.

5. For a discussion of the first story, in which Sisyphos binds Thanatos, see "Smith and the Devil."

6. 699–718.

7. *Philoctetes* 622–625.

8. AT 1187, *Meleager*; see further Hansen 1997a:452–453; *EM* 9:547–551.

 9. AT 1187*, *Unfinished Work.*
10. BP 1:381 n. 1.
11. Perry 134, Hsr 137. This international tale is AT 122F, *"Wait till I am Fat Enough."*

Magic Object and the Trolls ☙ Perseus

Two brothers are born and immediately set out wandering, each in his own direction. The first brother encounters three old women (men) who share one eye, which he steals and then returns in exchange for three magic objects or items of knowledge: a magic sword (stick) with which he can kill anything, a ship that travels on both land and water, and a recipe for brewing an immense amount of beer at one time (a prayer that no one can withstand). Going on, he comes to a land where a princess is being sacrificed to three trolls. The youth confronts the three ogres in succession, killing them and cutting out their tongues, which he stores away. An impostor claims to have killed the trolls and is about to wed the princess, but the hero, producing the tongues, proves himself to have been the slayer, so that the impostor is executed. The hero now voyages on his magic ship to a place in the sea where a troll is about to wed a captive princess. The hero kills the troll and the entire ogrous wedding party by brewing them beer of great strength, and rescues the princess. Bringing her back to the previous kingdom, he summons his brother, whereupon he himself weds the first princess, his brother the second.

Found in northern Europe, this tale is AT 581, *The Magic Object and the Trolls.*

The tale is typically made up of several parts: (1) an introduction that takes the story from the birth of two brothers till their departure and separation, (2) one brother's acquisition of wondrous objects through his encounter with one-eyed persons, (3) his rescue of a princess, (4) his rescue of a second princess, and (5) the outcome, in which the brothers reunite, the hero marrying the first rescued princess, his brother the second. We shall not be equally interested in all parts of this tale; I dwell on the two episodes (2 and 3) for which there are ancient analogues.

In a German text from Schleswig-Holstein, a man had a son who set out to seek his fortune. He reached a forest, and presently there came along three persons who had only one eye between them, such that whoever possessed the eye had to see on behalf of the other two and to lead them. After the youth scampered up a tree, the three persons sat beneath it. The three thought they heard something in the tree, so they took turns using the eye and climbing the tree to look around, but the first two saw nothing. As the second man was passing the eye to the third, the youth grabbed it, so that the men could no longer see. Each man now offered the hero a wondrous object in exchange for the eye: a prayer that no one could refuse, a land-and-water ship, and a stick that would kill whomever it struck. They made the exchange. The youth went on, came to a king's palace, and hired on as a cook's helper. Now, a giant came to ask for the king's daughter in marriage, threatening to cause havoc in the kingdom if he should be refused. A certain Rinroth offered to do combat with the giant in exchange for the king's daughter, and the king agreed. But the hero

sailed in his magic ship to the land of the giant, engaged him in battle, and killed him with his magic stick. After cutting out the giant's tongue he sailed back home, reporting that nothing had happened. When Rinroth found the giant dead, he cut off his head, told the king he had slain the giant, and claimed the princess. These events are repeated with the slain giant's brother and then with the father of the two, with few differences other than that Rinroth increases his demands and the hero employs his magic prayer. When the king, pressed by Rinroth to give him his daughter, observed that the three giant heads had no tongues, Rinroth explained that giants had no tongues. The cook's helper produced the tongues and was declared the true slayer of the giants. The youth wed the princess and became the king's successor, whereas Rinroth was hanged.[1] This version of the tale features only one hero, so that there is no rescue of a second princess and no double marriage.

In a Norwegian text, two sons born to a poor couple immediately set out to seek their fortunes. One called himself Lillekort, the other, King Lauring. They parted ways, and Lillekort presently encountered an old hag with a single eye. Lillekort grabbed it, and the old hag gave him a magic sword in return for her eye. Soon he met a second old hag, stole her eye also, and exchanged it for a magic ship. The same transpired with a third old hag, from whom he obtained a recipe for brewing a great amount of beer at one time. Sailing then in his magic ship, he arrived at a king's palace where he became a cook's helper. But the palace was in mourning, as it turned out, since the king's daughter had been promised to three trolls, of which the first would come shortly to fetch her, although Knight Red had promised to rescue her. When the day came, Knight Red escorted the princess to the shore to await the troll but did not himself stay to confront the troll. Meanwhile, Lillekort showed up and fought the five-headed troll, killing him with his magic sword, took the troll's treasure, and returned home, after which Knight Red reappeared, cut out the troll's lung and tongue, and forced the princess to say that Knight Red slew the ogre. The episode is repeated with the second and third troll. In the eventual confrontation of the hero and Knight Red, each produced his trophies, the former the treasure, the latter the lungs and tongues. The king found Lillekort's tokens the more convincing, so that he got the princess and half the kingdom, while Knight Red was thrown into a snake pit. The tale continues with the rescue of a second princess, the reunion of the brothers, and a double marriage.[2] In this text the group of three persons with a single eye become three individual persons, each possessing one eye. Oddly, the hero takes the treasure of the slain trolls and the false hero cuts out their tongues and lungs, whereas normally the hero cuts out their tongues, after which the false hero cuts off their heads.

The hero's tricking a group of persons who share a single eye—let us call it the Graiai motif after the corresponding characters in Greek mythology—is an episode found in several different folktales.[3] It appears in the tale known as *A Boy Guards the King's Garden*, in which a boy steals the eye of three women or three giants who have only one eye among them, as well as in many texts of *The Princess on the Glass Mountain*.[4] The motif is found sporadically in other tales, such as in an Italian folktale from Tuscany published in 1885 that shows a remarkable resemblance throughout to the Perseus legend. The hero was told to go to a palace in which dwelled two women who had only one eye between

them. He went there, took the eye as one woman was handing it to the other, and returned it in exchange for a mirror. While looking into the mirror he killed a certain witch, for if he had looked at her directly, he would have become a statue.[5]

The odd owners of the single eye, despite their ophthalmic handicap, are well endowed with magical objects or useful knowledge. The protagonist steals their eye as it is being passed from one to another, and returns it in exchange for wondrous objects or information, an act that the narratives present as being clever rather than immoral. The Graiai motif not only serves to provide the hero with the wondrous tools he will require in order to accomplish the tasks ahead, it also offers a wonderfully fanciful and grotesque image, a curious mixture of vulnerability (only one of the eye sharers can see at a time) and powerfulness (they possess magic objects), shrouded in one-dimensional mystery, since they have no history and no future, and neither their handicap nor their ownership of wondrous objects is explained.

Another adventure in *The Magic Object and the Trolls* that can also be found in other traditional narratives is the hero's rescue of a princess who is being sacrificed to a monster; indeed, unlike the Graiai motif, which is not a common narrative idea, the rescue of a princess from a monster is one of the most popular of all international oral tales, recounted sometimes as an independent tale and sometimes, as here, as a component of a larger folktale (see "Dragon Slayer"). The gist of its plot is that the hero, who usually possesses wondrous helpers or weapons, comes to a land where a monster is plaguing the community. To placate the monster the king is obliged to give it his daughter, but the hero undertakes to fight the monster in return for the hand of the princess, and the king agrees. The hero overcomes the demon, cuts out its tongue(s), and withdraws, after which a cowardly impostor cuts off the head(s) of the monster, claims to be its slayer, and prepares to marry the princess. The hero returns, proves by means of the tongues that he is the slayer, and weds the princess. The false hero is punished.

Perseus

Scholars have long remarked on the similarity of *The Magic Objects and the Trolls* and the ancient legend of Perseus, for the Greek hero, like the hero of the modern folktale, steals the eye of three old women, acquires thereby various wonderful objects, and goes on to rescue and wed a princess.[6]

In the corresponding episodes of the Perseus legend, King Polydektes ordered Perseus to bring him the head of the Gorgon Medusa. Advised by Hermes and Athena, Perseus went first to the daughters of Phorkos and Keto, namely, Enyo, Pephredo, and Deino. They were sisters of the Gorgons and old women from birth, having only one eye and one tooth among them that they passed to one another in turn. Perseus took their eye and their tooth, and when they asked for them back, he said he would return them if they would show him the way to the nymphs who possessed winged sandals, the *kibisis* (pouch), and the Cap of Hades, which made its wearer invisible. When the Graiai showed him the way, he returned to them their tooth and eye. Perseus put on the pouch, sandals, and helmet, and taking a sickle provided him by Hermes

flew off to the Gorgons. After he obtained Medusa's head and was returning to King Polydektes, he passed by Aithiopia, where he saw Andromeda set out to be devoured by a sea monster. She was the daughter of the rulers of the land, Kepheus and Kassiepeia. Kassiepeia had boasted that her own beauty exceeded that of the nymphs, as a result of which Poseidon angrily sent a sea monster (*ketos*) against the land, and the god Ammon had revealed in an oracle that the people might escape from the calamity if Kassiepeia should sacrifice her daughter Andromeda to the monster. Forced by the Aithiopians, Kepheus bound his daughter to a rock. Seeing her and falling in love with her, Perseus promised the king he would kill the monster if Kepheus would give him Andromeda to wife, which the king swore to do. The hero overcame the monster and rescued the princess, but a certain Phineus, to whom Andromeda had been betrothed, now plotted against Perseus. The hero discovered the plot and petrified Phineus and his supporters by showing them the Gorgon's head. Returning to King Polydektes, he did the same to that treacherous monarch and his men, after which he handed over the sandals, pouch, and cap to Hermes, who returned them to the nymphs; and he gave the Gorgon's head to Athena, who placed it in the center of her shield.[7]

The ancient legend and the modern tale agree in featuring the two sequences discussed above (the hero's encounter with the monocular folk and his rescue of the princess), presenting them in the same sequence, and employing them in a generally similar way. Broadly speaking, each story is biographical in structure, with certain differences associated with the genre in which each is expressed. The modern folktale concludes with the hero's marriage to the princess, while the ancient story, recounted as a biographic legend, continues after the hero's marriage until his eventual death. In both narratives, the encounter with the one-eyed folk (= Graiai motif) is the hero's first adventure, providing him with the equipment he needs for the combats with monsters that will follow, the high points of his heroic career; and relying upon these tools, he rescues a princess from a monster and weds her (= dragon slayer tale). The characters in successive episodes of the folktale are unrelated to one another (except of course for the hero and his brother, when he has one): the eye sharers have no connection with the giants or trolls in the episodes that follow, each existing only in their own adventures. But the Greek legend tends to soften the episodic structure of the story by linking characters appearing in different episodes. Thus the Graiai and the Gorgons are sisters, and the sea monster (*ketos*) whom the hero slays brings to mind Keto, the mother of the Graiai and the Gorgons. These characters belong to the time and space and families of the Greek mythological universe, unlike the anonymity and historical flatness of the folktale world.

Each story tradition contains episodes that are not found in the other. For example, Perseus confronts the Gorgons, and the folktale hero confronts another set of ogres. In the ancient legend, the additional combat precedes the rescue of his future wife, whereas in the modern tale, it follows it. Thus:

Legend	*Folktale*
Graiai	Eye sharers
Gorgons	———

Andromeda	Princess 1
————	Princess 2

Other than that the additional episodes concern combats with monsters, the noncorresponding episodes do not particularly resemble each other.

To sum up the points of agreement, (1) the hero, setting out on his first adventure, (2) encounters three persons with a single eye, (3) steals their eye as they pass it, and (4) returns it in exchange for three wondrous objects or pieces of information (or information that leads to the acquisition of three wondrous objects). Subsequently (5) he comes to a land in which a king is obliged to sacrifice his daughter to a monster. (6) The king agrees to give his daughter to the man who saves her, whereupon (7) the hero slays the monster, (8) thereby rescuing the princess. (9) A false hero claims the hand of the princess, but (10) the hero prevails by proving he is the true rescuer or by overcoming the aggressor in combat. (11) The rival perishes, and (12) the hero weds the princess.

The impressive correspondence suggests that there is a connection of some kind between the two traditions, but it throws no light on the nature of the relationship. The obvious options are that (a) the Perseus legend and the modern tale are independent branches of an old oral narrative, (b) the modern tale is a direct oral descendent of the Greek Perseus legend, or (c) the folktale has been influenced by literary texts of the Perseus legend.

Since I discuss Perseus's rescue of Andromeda in detail elsewhere (see "Dragon Slayer"), it remains to say something here of the one-eyed Graiai (Old Women), or Phorkides (daughters of Phorkys).[8] They are first mentioned by the poet Hesiod in his *Theogony*: "Keto bore to Phorkys fair-cheeked old women, / white-haired from birth, and the immortal gods and humans who tread the earth call them the Graiai, / beautifully robed Pemphredo and saffron-robed Enyo."[9] For Hesiod the Phorkides are two in number rather than three, and although they are born with white hair, earning them the name Old Women, they are evidently attractive maidens, for they are fair-cheeked and attractively attired, and there is no mention of the grotesque feature of their single eye and single tooth, features that could also earn them a name such as Graiai.[10] Nevertheless, Hesiod implies that they are monstrous in some way, since his genealogy situates them in a family of monsters, and their names Pemphredo and Enyo, which might be rendered Wasp Maiden and Battle Maiden, certainly suggest aggression. Their mother is Keto (formed from *ketos* "sea monster"), and among their siblings are the Gorgons and Echidna. Hesiod does not mention the Graiai's shared eye and tooth, but since the poet does not mention Perseus here either, this detail is perhaps irrelevant to the present context, although his representing them as sisters of the Gorgons suggests that he does associate the Graiai with the Perseus story. In most authors, including Aeschylus and Pherekydes, the Graiai are three in number (the third is named Deino, or Frightful Maiden) and share either a single eye or a single eye plus a single tooth. Aeschylus alludes to other, somewhat puzzling features, saying that the three aged maidens were swan shaped (*kyknomorphoi*) and were not seen by the sun or moon, the latter presumably meaning that they lived in a cave or underground.

The mythological job of the Graiai is to be born, dwell as monstrous oddities

in the distant mythological landscape,[11] and on one important occasion be Perseus's unwilling helpers, providing him with information that leads to the death of one of their sisters (the Gorgon Medusa) and subsequently of a sea monster (*ketos*), whose name is reminiscent of that of their mother Keto. The only story in which they play an actual role is that of Perseus. According to a variant tradition found in Aeschylus's lost tragedy *Phorkides*, the Graiai were guards of their sisters the Gorgons. Perseus stealthily got hold of their single eye and cast it away, effectively blinding them, after which he was able to come upon the Gorgons as they were sleeping and to decapitate Medusa.[12] Aeschylus's Graiai are more closely linked to the Gorgons than in the usual tradition, being connected not only genealogically but also in their function as guards, and to this extent they are less like the eye sharers of the folktale.

Lit. (AT 581, *The Magic Object and the Trolls*). BP 1:536, n. 1; 4:112 n. 5. Ranke 1934:365–367. Ranke (1958) 2:326–330. *EM* 6:82–85. Ashliman, type 581.

1. Ranke (1958) 2:227–230.
2. Asbjørnsen and Moe (1965) 3:323–337 = Dasent 1970:131–149.
3. Motif F512.1.2, *Three women have but one eye among them. Pass it around; EM* 6:82–85.
4. AT 328*, *A Boy Guards the King's Garden;* AT 530, *The Princess on the Glass Mountain; EM* 6:84.
5. Hartland (1894) 1:11–14, citing Giuseppe Pitrè, *Novelle Popolari Toscane* (Firenze, 1885), 1; Hartland (1896) 3:164. Compare the similar narrative idea of the two giants who, possessing only one axe between them, throw it back and forth to each other (motif G151, *Two giants with one axe*).
6. Hartland 1894:31–34, 1896:164; BP 1:536 n. 1; Ranke 1934:367; Ranke (1958) 2:326–327; *EM* 6:82–85.
7. Apollodoros *Bibl.* 2.4.2–3.
8. On the Graiai see Pherekydes (*FGH* 3 F 11); Aeschylus *Prometheus* 792–800; Palaiphatos 31; Eratosthenes *Catasterisms* 22; Ovid *Met.* 4.772–781; Hyginus *Astron.* 2.12. See further Roscher 1:1729–1738; Rohde 1960:196; Herzog-Hauser 1933; *EM* 6:82–85; Gantz 1993:19–20, 305–306.
9. *Th.* 270–273.
10. Or it may have been inspired by monsters like Lamia, who can remove their eyes. See Rohde 1960:196 n; Fontenrose 1959:285.
11. Aeschylus situates them on "the Gorgoneian plains of Kisthene," a place of uncertain location, at least to us (Fontenrose 1959:280–281).
12. See especially Aeschylus *Phorkides* fr. 262 Nauck; Palaiphatos 31; Eratosthenes *Catasterisms* 22.

Maiden's Honor 🕮 Maiden's Sense

"The mother tells the girl to guard her honor. The tailor promises to sew up her 'Honor.' "[1]

So runs Aarne-Thompson's economical description of the ribald comic tale, AT 1542**, *The Maiden's Honor*, which is told in a number of European lands, especially in eastern Europe.

In a Finnish joke a girl who often went to dances was warned by her mother to take care not to lose her honor. One day when she came home she informed her mother that she had met a man at the dance who had told her that she would not lose her honor if it was nailed down, and that he had nailed it down

for her. The girl's mother replied: "You poor girl, you are ruined." The girl asked what was the good of honor that was so near one's backside.[2]

Structurally similar to this is another comic tale of seduction, AT 1425, *Putting the Devil into Hell*, which is found in oral tradition as well as in French and Italian novelle. In this tale a holy man seduces a naive girl by explaining the sexual act as having a particular spiritual benefit, for example, putting the devil (= penis) back into hell (= vagina). Subsequently she naively describes the event in these terms to someone else, who like the mother in *The Maiden's Honor*, perceives their true sense.

The best-known treatment of this tale is that by Boccaccio in his *Decameron*. It is there recounted by Dioneo, who introduces his tale by musing whether his companions have heard how to put the devil back into hell. Alibech, the pretty, fourteen-year-old daughter of a rich man in Capsa, Barbary, wished to acquaint herself with the Christian faith and was told that the best way to serve God was to flee the things of the world, as the desert hermits do. The girl set out secretly and alone in search of such a place, and finally reached the hovel of a holy man. Asked what she was seeking, she replied that she sought someone to show her how best to serve God. The pious man, fearing that he might fall into temptation if she stayed, sent her further to another holy man, and the second holy man for the same reason sent her to a third. Reaching finally the cell of a young hermit named Rustico, she stated her quest, and he invited her to stay with him. Soon, however, he was tempted by her and began to devise how he might enjoy her. Since she was very innocent, he decided that the best way was to convince her that she was doing it in God's service. First, he explained to her what a terrible enemy of God the devil was, and then he instructed her that the way she could most please God was to put the devil back into the hell to which God had condemned him. She asked how to do that, and he told her to disrobe, as he himself did; seeing her beauty, Rustico got an erection, which he explained to her was the devil, which was giving him trouble; furthermore, although she did not have such a devil, she had in its place hell itself, and she could do the Lord a service by allowing Rustico to put the devil back into hell whenever he caused trouble. They put the devil back in hell six times that night before the devil was willing to remain in peace, and they tamed him often on later occasions. Alibech began to like the game, commenting that this must be what the men of Capsa meant when they said that it was delightful to serve God, and soon she was taking the initiative such that Rustico with his diet of mere roots and water could not keep pace with her desire to calm the fury of her own hell. Eventually a young man from Capsa sought her out, found her, and brought her back to Capsa in order to marry her. When the women of Capsa asked her how she served God in the desert, she showed them how she put the devil back into hell. The women got a good laugh from that, and they joke about it to this day.[3]

A lively North American text of the same tale collected in 1950 from an Arkansan, Bob Wyrick, is cast as a "preacher story." A Holy Roller preacher who was walking through the woods saw a pretty girl and asked her if she was saved. She said yes, she was a Christian, and what a blessing it was. The preacher asked if she had seen the glory-pole. When she said she had not, he pulled out his penis, saying that was the glory-pole, "the axis of the world and the fount of all creation." He asked if he might ease it into her and bring salva-

tion to her soul. He did so, and in time she yelled "Praise God!" She went on to the meeting with pine-straw clinging to her back, got the Holy Spirit, and cried out:

> "Whoo-ee, he stuck the glory-pole up my piss-hole,
> and squirted salvation all over my ass-hole!"

The preacher was flabbergasted, but soon she was drowned out by the folk yelling "Amen!" Some folks do not know what they are saying when they get the Power, and other people act as though they did not hear anything.[4]

These two tale types confront a sexually naive girl and a lustful man. The man misrepresents sexual intercourse as conferring some desirable, nonsexual benefit (fixing her honor in place/serving God/bringing salvation to herself), and proposes sexual intercourse. The simple girl accepts the man's misrepresentation, and they have sexual relations. In *The Maiden's Honor* she is enthusiastic about the supposed benefit she has received; and in *Putting the Devil into Hell* she enthuses about the sexual experience itself. When the girl presently alludes happily to the sexual activity, naively employing the imagery supplied by the man, the bystanders (her mother/women of Capsa/preacher) understand the truth of the matter and respond in some way (resignation/amusement/surprise).

The humor springs from several sources: the representation of holy men as being hypocritical and lustful, the colorful imagery for sexual intercourse employed by the seducer,[5] the simplemindedness of the girl with regard to sexuality and the consequent ease of her seduction, the innocent enthusiasm of the girl herself resulting from the sexual encounter, and finally the irony of her naive allusion to the experience before sophisticated listeners. Since humor based upon the easy seduction of a naive maiden by a man doubtless appeals less to women than it does to men, it is hardly surprising that Boccaccio's internal narrator is a man, the Ozark tale was collected by a man from a male raconteur, and the ancient tale to be considered presently is represented as being told by a man.[6]

A Tale Recounted by Aesop

In a fable told by Aesop in the so-called *Aesop Romance*, a woman had a daughter who was simpleminded, and the girl often heard her mother praying to the gods that she get some sense. One day mother and daughter journeyed to the country, and the girl, leaving her mother outside of a farmyard, saw a man having sex with a donkey. She asked him what he was doing, and he said he was putting some sense into her. The simple girl, recalling her mother's prayer, bade him put some sense into her, too. At first the man refused but after being pressed by the girl, who said her mother would reward him since she had prayed for her daughter to get some sense, complied with her request, deflowering her. The overjoyed girl ran back to her mother, saying: "Mother, I have some sense." "And how did you get sense, child?" The girl explained that a man put a long, red, sinewy thing in and out of her. When the mother heard her daughter's explanation she said: "Daughter, you have lost what sense you had."[7]

The ancient Greek story shows considerable similarity to the modern tale traditions discussed here. In the Aesopic tale, as in *The Maiden's Honor* and *Putting the Devil into Hell*, (a) a naive maiden encounters a man who misrepresents sexual intercourse colorfully as conferring some desirable benefit, and (b) they have sexual relations; when (c) the girl subsequently refers enthusiastically to the encounter in the terms supplied by the man, (d) her interlocutor perceives the true nature of the encounter. The Greek fable shares several features with *The Maiden's Honor* in particular, notably its framing the central sexual encounter as discourse between the mother and daughter. Before the encounter the mother prays to the gods that her daughter will get some sense (Greek fable), or she warns her daughter to take care not to lose her honor (Finnish tale). And afterward the girl informs her mother that she has acquired some sense, whereupon her mother comments that she has lost what sense she had (Greek fable); or she informs her mother that she learned that she would not lose her honor if it should be fixed in place, and when she describes what happened, her mother comments that the poor girl is ruined (Finnish tale). The emphasis here is upon the girl's naive belief that she has found a solution to her mother's concern, rather than upon the unexpected pleasure that she herself derives from the sexual encounter, as in *Putting the Devil into Hell*.

Anton Wiechers argues that the original Greek tale featured a play on words in the Ionic dialect that has been lost in the course of transmission, so that the joke has been deprived of its comic point. He believes that the man, when asked what he was doing, originally said he was "putting a donkey (*onon*) in," and the foolish girl, confusing the word "donkey" with the word "sense," replied, "Put some sense (*noon*) in me, too."[8] But Wiechers's supposition seems to me unnecessary and, if the ancient and modern tales belong to the same narrative tradition, improbable as well, for in both *The Maiden's Honor* and *Putting the Devil into Hell*, just as in Aesop's tale, the lustful man misrepresents the sexual act in a colorful way as conferring some nonsexual benefit, the naive maid accepts his representation, and subsequently she characterizes it in this same way to another person.

The employment of the tale in the *Aesop Romance* is unusual for an Aesopic fable. Aesop, in jail in Delphi on a trumped-up charge, is visited by a sympathetic friend who asks him why he chose to insult the Delphians and so incur their anger. Why is it, the man asks Aesop, that you who have advised whole cities are witless in your own cause? In reply Aesop recounts the tale of the naive girl, concluding with the exclamation of the girl's mother: "You have lost what sense you had." Aesop adds as an epimythium: "The same thing has happened to me, friend. When I came to Delphi I lost what sense I had." So the fable is told by Aesop about himself. For another tale recounted by the fabulist on this occasion, see "Matron of Ephesus."

Lit. AT 1542**, *The Maiden's Honor*. Cf. AT 1425, *Putting the Devil into Hell*, and Ashliman, type 1425.

1. Aarne-Thompson 1961:445.
2. Ranke 1972:112, no. 174.
3. Boccaccio *Decameron*, day 3, tale 10. See further Lee 1972 (1909):108–109.
4. Randolph 1977:185–186, no. 76.
5. Especially in texts of *Putting the Devil into Hell*. In addition to the expressions that ap-

pear here, I find "putting the Pope in Rome," "putting the key to heaven in the lock," and "unlocking the Golden Gate" (Hoffmann *apud* Randolph 1977:186; Baker 1986:161, no. 278). See also Legman (1971:417) for a related limerick.

6. The colorful seduction of the outrageously naive Queen Olympias by the Egyptian prophet Nektanebo, related in detail in the first book of the *Alexander Romance*, seems to me to have the same spirit. On the tradition of this story see Weinreich 1911.

7. *Vita Aesopi* 131 = Perry 386, Hsr 305. İlhan Başgöz points out that in peasant communities in the Middle East and Asia, nearly every family owns a donkey; since the boys spend much time alone with the animals and since premarital sex for girls is strongly prohibited, bestiality between young boys and donkeys is common and tolerated by adults (Başgöz and Boratav 1998:31–32). Presumably the circumstances of the present tale, set in rural Greece, were not much different.

8. Wiechers 1961:9 n. 5. So also Nagy 1979:283 n. 1; Holzberg 1993:13–14; and Stramaglia 2000:314 n. 6.

Maids Must Rise Even Earlier

Maids (daughters) kill the rooster whose crowing awakens them (their mistress, their mother) each morning. They think thereby to avoid rising so early, but instead they are made to rise even earlier.

This little tale is AT 1566A*, *Maids Must Rise Even Earlier*. Aarne-Thompson's placement of the tale, which concerns foolish women, is odd, for it is classified with tales about a clever man or boy. It is attested in Finland, Russia, Poland, and perhaps elsewhere.

According to a Swedish-speaking narrator in Finland, an old woman had three lazy daughters whom she woke every morning when the rooster crowed. The girls, who did not like this routine, killed the bird. So the old woman, who did not sleep well, woke them even earlier than she did before.[1]

An Aesopic Fable

In an Aesopic fable in the Augustana recension, a compilation of Greek prose fables made in the first or second century A.D., a hardworking widow had the habit of rousing her maids to begin their work at cockcrow, when it was still dark. The exhausted maids decided to kill the rooster, thinking that it was responsible for their troubles, inasmuch as it was the rooster who roused their mistress during the night. But when they did so, their troubles only worsened, for the mistress, not knowing when it was cockcrow, roused them even earlier.[2]

The ancient and modern texts appear to be essentially the same. The anonymous Greek fabulist gives as the epimythium, or application, of the ancient fable the generalization that for many persons the source of their miseries is their own plans.

Lit. AT 1566A*, *Maids Must Rise Even Earlier*. Schwarzbaum 1979:1 n. 107.

1. Ranke 1972:48, no. 48.
2. Perry 55; Hsr 55.

Making a Rope of Sand

A man makes a contract with the devil, according to which the devil will perform tasks for the man in exchange for the man's soul. In order to escape from the contract, the man assigns the devil the task of making a rope out of sand, which the devil is unable to do.

The impossible task of making a rope of sand appears as the motif of central interest in AT 1174, *Making a Rope of Sand*, and more marginally in other stories.[1]

So in a German legend collected in 1921 from an elderly master mason, a peasant named Hansjörg made a bargain with the devil. The peasant sold the devil his soul, but if the man had enough work for the devil to do, he would be free; after thirty years, either the peasant or the devil would win. The devil performed all sorts of tasks on the peasant's farm, and the man was running out of jobs for him. Then the peasant's clever wife told Hansjörg to heat some sand in the oven until it was very dry, and order the devil to make a rope with it. The devil departed, saying he wanted nothing to do with a woman's cunning.[2]

In a somewhat different story, a man opens a book of magic and is confronted suddenly by the devil; to keep him busy he orders him to make ropes of sand. Thus in a Norwegian legend, also collected in 1921, the minister Nils Dorph possessed the Black Book. One day a farmhand came upon it, started reading it, and happened to conjure up the devil. The devil asked what to do, for the devil must be given a task to perform. So the boy sent him to the fjord to make a rope of sand. From a distance the curate noticed the sand flying high in the air, came home immediately, and bound the devil before he did any harm.[3]

An Ancient Proverbial Expression

Although no analogues to these legends as such are found in ancient authors, the task of making a rope out of sand was a traditional *adynaton*, or impossibility, among the ancient Greeks. The proverbial expression "You're (he's) braiding a cord out of sand" (i.e., "That's impossible") is employed by several Greek prose authors and is included by the Byzantine paroemiographers in their collections.[4] Roman authors in turn adopted the expression from the Greeks.[5]

Lit. (AT 1174, *Making a Rope of Sand*). (ML 3020, *Inexperienced Use of the Black Book. Ropes of Sand.*) Motif H1021.1, *Task: making a rope of sand.* Feilberg (1886–1914) 3:25b, s.v. reb. Zachariae 1907:172–186. Vries 1928:155 n. 1. BP 2:513. Liungman 1961:271–273. *EM* 1:968. Ashliman, type 1174.

1. For example, Knopp 1933:221; see further motif H1021.1, *Task: making a rope of sand.* For other narrative types in which a person eludes an ogre by giving him impossible tasks, see "Carrying Water in a Sieve" and "Devil to Count Stars."
2. Ranke 1966:172–174, no. 70.
3. Christiansen 1964:32, no. 15. The Reverend Nils Dorph lived in the eighteenth century. See also "Apprentice and Ghost."
4. The Greek expression was ἐξ ἄμμου σχοινίον πλέκεις. See *CPG* 2:114 n. 46; Gregorios Kyprios (Cod. Mosq. 3.46 = *CPG* 2.114); Makarios 3.97 (*CPG* 2:165); *Proverbs of Aesop* 10 (*CPG* 2:229 = Perry 1952:290); Apostolios 7.50 (*CPG* 2:407).

5. Otto 1890:160, no. 790, citing for example Columella 10, praef. 4: eadem tam exigua sunt, ut, quod aiunt Graeci, ex incomprehensibili parvitate harenae funis effici non possit.

Man Does Not Recognize His Own Reflection

A person does not understand the principle of reflection so that, upon seeing his or her own reflection for the first time, he or she draws a comically erroneous conclusion. A second person does the same.

This is the basic narrative idea underlying AT 1336A, *Man Does Not Recognize His Own Reflection in the Water (Mirror)*.

A Spanish story tells how at harvest time some peasants had a jug of water resting among the reeds. A boy came up to it and, seeing his face in the water, told the other harvesters that there was a boy inside the jug. Astonished, they left their work to see the boy. The first one to reach it, seeing himself in the water, said: "By God, and he even has a beard!"[1] Similarly, in an Arabic joke a boy once looked in a well and saw his own face. He ran to his mother, saying that in the well there was a thief. She came, looked in the well, and said: "Yes, by God, and next to him is an ugly old woman."[2] In a different form of the type, a farmer acquires a mirror and thinks it is a picture of his father (or grandfather or the like). Subsequently his wife comes upon the mirror in her husband's belongings and, seeing her own reflection for the first time, believes it is a picture of her husband's lover (or the like). She takes satisfaction in seeing that the woman is quite ugly.[3]

The tale develops in a somewhat different way, depending upon whether the reflective surface is water or a mirror. In Subtype A (as I shall call it) a naive person mistakes his own reflection in water for the actual presence of another person, after which a second naive person does the same. In Subtype B a naive man seeing a mirror for the first time mistakes his own reflection for a picture of a kinsman, and later his wife similarly mistakes her own reflection in the same mirror for a picture of her husband's lover, commenting with unwitting irony on the woman's ugliness. In both forms the tale has two moments: one person misinterprets his reflection, followed by another person who does the same thing, usually making a comment that extends the error comically.

The Man in the Well

In an ancient Greek joke about a boy and his father, the boy was playing with a ball, which fell into a well. Leaning over the edge of the well and seeing his own reflection, he asked for his ball back. When he complained to his father that he had not gotten it back, the father leaned over the well, saw his own reflection, and said: "Sir, give the boy back his ball!"[4]

This tale is a reflex of Subtype A and, like the Spanish and Arabic tales described above, derives its humor mostly from the fact that the second character, rather than correcting the first character, naively repeats and builds upon his error. The tale is found in *Philogelos*, a compilation of Greek jokes dating from

late antiquity. As usual in *Philogelos* the characters are simply fools. Their naivete is not explained by their being rustics, as in the modern tales cited above.

Several other narratives centering upon a misunderstanding of a reflection in water or a mirror are worth noticing.

Akko

There is first of all silly Akko, one of several proverbial Greek fools.[5] The name Akko was a synonym for a foolish person, and there was even a verb connected with her name: *akkizesthai* "be foolish, feign simplemindedness, coyly dissemble." She is mentioned by paroemiologists and other ancient commentators, who typically offer one or two brief instances of her folly, most commonly that she wore a cloak that she had only half-finished weaving and that she chatted with her reflection in the mirror as though to another woman.[6] Akko appears as a character in at least two Greek comedies, Hermippos's *Athenas Gonai*, or *Offspring of Athena*, perhaps an ironic collective term for a number of characters who were represented as being hopelessly incompetent in domestic matters, and Amphis's *Akko*.[7] Akko belonged to folk tradition, whether the comedies drew their material from Greek folklore or the lore concerning Akko arose from the comedies, or both. According to Plutarch, women employed Akko's name to rouse little children from idleness, by which Plutarch evidently means that mothers and nurses cautioned idle children against becoming as foolish and lazy as Akko.[8] Since Akko is said to be from Samos, she may have sprung from Samian tradition.

Akko's folly is like that of the characters in Subtype A, who believe their reflection is another person, rather than like that of the characters in Subtype B, who think that their reflection is a picture of another person. But it is much simpler than Subtype A, first of all because in form it is not strictly a tale at all, a narrative of a unique sequence of events, but rather a description of recurrent behavior; and, second, because the tradition does not feature the additional fool who confirms and extends the mistake of the first fool.

Another Greek fool who does not fully understand the use of a mirror is the man who, wanting to see if he looked good in his sleep, looked in a mirror with his eyes closed.[9] This error is of a different kind from Akko's. She does not understand that the reflection in her mirror is (a) not a real person and (b) an image of herself rather than of someone else, whereas the fool in the present joke understands reflections well enough but conflates the action of posing with his eyes closed with the action of seeing with his eyes open.

Narcissus

The best-known character of ancient story who misunderstands the nature of reflections is not a comic fool at all but rather the legendary, semidivine Narcissus, a handsome and overly proud adolescent who, cursed by one of his rejected lovers, fell in love with his own beautiful reflection in a pool of water.[10] Narcissus does not understand that the image he sees is only a reflection of himself and so, like Akko, treats it as though it had substance and were actually someone else.

Narcissus's puerile behavior troubles the Greek traveler Pausanias, who visited the traditional site of Narcissus's spring on the crest of Mount Helikon. People say, he reports, that Narcissus looked into the water and, not understanding that he was seeing his own reflection, fell in love with himself without realizing who it was, and perished from love at the spring. Pausanias remarks that the tradition is extremely naive, since it relates that the boy was old enough to fall in love but could not tell the difference between a human being and a reflection of a human being. In place of this account Pausanias offers what he says is a little-known version according to which Narcissus had a twin sister who looked exactly like him. He was in love with her, but she died. Narcissus used to look at his reflection in the spring, knowing it was his own image but telling himself that it was his sister's because it consoled him somewhat to do so.[11] But the rationalized version preferred by Pausanias is hardly more credible than the usual version.

Narcissus becomes like Akko, responding to his reflection as to another person. She converses with hers; he loves his. The tale of Akko and the legend of Narcissus are striking instances of precisely the same folly being comic in one narrative and noncomic in another, or perhaps tragicomic in the other, since there is also something comic in Narcissus's ignorantly falling in love with his own image, in his being transformed into an Akko and acting out his narcissism so concretely and naively. In any event the Narcissus legend manifests the development of a traditionally comic motif in a predominantly nonhumorous way.[12]

Akko's folly is of the sort that betrays a faulty understanding of a phenomenon of everyday life, like the simpleminded person who thinks that every town has its own moon, that Black persons are unwashed White persons, and so on.[13] It is the sort of mistake that a child may make upon the first encounter with the unfamiliar but does not make upon the second encounter. It can actually happen to an inexperienced adult. Folklorist Linda Dégh relates how Zsuzsanna Palkó, an intelligent Hungarian peasant woman, staying in a hotel in a city for the first time in her life and encountering a full-length mirror for the first time, mistook the image of herself for her aunt.[14] It is an amusing error, but understandable. Akko is silly because she makes several errors of inexperience or incompetence, and she keeps making them, just as (we are sure) the fool and his son will never figure out who the mean-spirited fellow dwelling at the bottom of their well is, and that they will similarly make many other errors about ordinary reality.

A Foolish Dog

The error of mistaking a reflection for the actual presence of another being also appears in the well-known Aesopic fable of the dog that was crossing a river with a piece of meat in its mouth. Seeing its reflection in the water and thinking it was another dog with a bigger piece of meat, it dropped the piece it had in order to go after the bigger piece, with the result that it lost what it already had.[15] But it is the dog's greed rather than its folly that is emphasized in the fable, and of course the misinterpretation of one's own reflection has more comic force when it is attributed to a human than to an animal, in whom such behavior is less surprising.

All ancient Greek characters, human and animal, who misunderstand the

nature of their reflection in water or in a mirror mistake it for an actual being, not a picture of a being, and in this respect they resemble Subtype A rather than Subtype B. One comic tale, the joke about the man in the well, shows the characteristic structure of AT 1336A, in which one fool interprets his reflection as another being, provoking a second fool, looking upon the same water or in the same mirror, to do the same. But other Greek tales that exploit the idea of misunderstood reflection employ the idea more simply or in a different way.

The Moabites

The motif is also found in Hebrew legend. The Moabites once heard that the kings of Israel, Judah, and Edom were coming to wage war against them, so that the men armed themselves and stationed themselves at the border. When the sun arose the next morning, the men saw the nearby waters red like blood, and they said, "This is blood from the sword. The kings have fought, each man striking his neighbor. Now to the plunder, Moabites!" When they reached the Israelite camp, however, the Israelites sallied out and thoroughly vanquished them.[16]

In this story the Moabites naively misunderstand the reflection of the rising sun upon the water, as though they had never seen the sun or moon reflected upon water before, taking the red color of the water to be blood, which they interpret as the blood of their enemies, whom they assume to have quarreled among themselves. So they advance against them in the belief that they will enjoy an easy victory, but instead are utterly defeated. Gunkel suggests that this strange incident rests upon an old fool's tale, and indeed there is an international folktale in which a fool mistakes the reflection of the moon upon the water for cheese or gold and dives in after it.[17]

Lit. AT 1336A, *Man Does Not Recognize His Own Reflection in the Water (Mirror)*. Friedländer 1910:531–2. Wesselski (1911) 1:177, 276–277, no. 311. Wesselski 1935. Ashliman, type 1336A. Marzolph 1987:202–203.

1. Chevalier 1983:173, no. 103.
2. Marzolph 1987:202–203.
3. For example, Seki 1963:189–189, no. 55; Briggs and Tongue 1965:134–135, no. 77; Glassie 1985:89–90. Somewhat similar is an anonymous blonde joke that I received from Karen Bouchard, Switzerland (September 2000): Two blondes are walking down the street. One notices a compact on the sidewalk and leans down to pick it up. She opens it, looks in the mirror, and says, "Hmm, this person looks familiar." The second blonde says, "Here, let me see!" So the first blonde hands her the compact. The second one looks in the mirror and says, "You dummy, it's me!"
4. *Philogelos* 33.
5. Crusius, "Akko," in *RE* 1 (1893) 1171–1173; Winkler 1982.
6. Plutarch *Proverbia* 65 (*CPG* 1:331); Suetonius *Peri Blasphemion* 194 Taillardat; Zenobios 1.53 (*CPG* 1:21); Diogeneianos 2.4 (*CPG* 1:197); schol. Plato *Gorg.* 497a; *Etymologicon Magnum* p. 49 Gaisford.
7. Hermippos fr. 6 K.-A; Amphis (2:214 K.-A.). See Winkler 1982.
8. Plut. *Moralia* 1040b; cf. Hesychios s.v. *akkos;* Winkler 1982.
9. *Philogelos* 11; Marzolph 1987:194.
10. Ovid *Met.* 3.339–510; see also Konon 24. On the story see Roscher 3:10–21; Pellizer 1988; Forbes Irving 1990:282; Zimmerman 1994:1–23; *LIMC* 6.1:703–711; *EM* 9:1218–1221. On mirrors in ancient thought and literature generally, see Meslin 1980 and McCarty 1989.
11. Paus. 9.31.7.
12. Cf. Hansen 1997c.

13. For the first, see "Local Moon." For the second, the ancient tale of a man who purchased an Aethiopian (that is, a dark-skinned) slave and tried to wash away his color under the mistaken impression that it was the result of the previous owner's neglect, see Themistios *Or.* 32.359c (Hsr 2:135); Aphthonios 6 (Perry 393, Hsr 2:135), cf. 40 (Perry 398, Hsr 329); cf. schol. on Persius 5.116. The ancient tale, which also circulated as a proverbial expression, is a form of AT 1312*, *Trying to Wash Black Animal White*, for which see further Roberts 1958:86; Perry 1962:310–311; Snowden 1970:5, 197–198, and notes; *EM* 1:968.

14. Personal communication; cf. Dégh 1995b:vii. The American country-music singer Loretta Lynn recounts a similar anecdote in illustration of how backward people are in the part of eastern Kentucky where she grew up. A patient in a hospital was standing in front of an elevator with a look of confusion on his face. When a doctor inquired what the matter was, the patient said he had seen a nurse get into a closet, but she was gone when the door opened again. The patient, who had lived all his life in a hollow, or valley, had never before seen an elevator (Lynn 1977:22).

15. Perry 133, Hsr 136. For other texts see Phaedrus 1.4; Babrius 79; Lucian *Hermotimus* 79; Irenaeus *Against Heresies* 2.11; Ps.-Dositheus 40 no. 11 (Hsr 2:126); Epiphanios *Panarion* 41.1; Aphthonios 35 (Hsr 2:149). See further AT 34A, *Dog Drops His Meat for the Reflection*.

16. 4 Kings 3:21–25 in the *Septuagint* (otherwise, 2 Kings 3:21–25).

17. Gunkel 1921:134–135. A less persuasive explanation is that the red seen by the Moabites is red sandstone, said to be common in the area (Suggs, Sakenfeld, and Mueller 1992:377). For if the Moabites merely see red stone, what is the point of the narrator's mentioning the rising sun and the waters? Even if the Moabites correctly understand that the red color upon the water is the reflection of the morning sun but incorrectly interpret the color as signifying the blood of their enemies, the incident may nevertheless spring from a numskull tale in which the numskulls do take the red water to be blood. The folktale in which a person mistakes the reflection of the moon for something such as cheese is AT 1336, *Diving for Cheese*.

Man Swallowed by Fish 🐟 Lucian

A man is swallowed by a great fish, inside of which he sometimes finds other living people, cultural objects, and the like. Eventually he devises an escape or is rescued.

This lying tale is AT 1889G, *Man Swallowed by Fish*.

In the eighth chapter of *The Adventures of Baron Münchhausen* the hero reports how he was bathing in the Mediterranean Sea near Marseilles one summer afternoon when he spotted a very large fish approaching him quickly with extended jaws. The baron doubled himself up and passed into the fish's stomach, where it was dark and comfortably warm. In order to encourage the fish to dislodge him, the baron tried various tactics, but nothing worked so well as when he danced a hornpipe. The fish roared and stood almost straight up in the water, whereupon persons in a passing Italian trading ship harpooned it. After they had brought the fish on board and cut open its belly, the baron called out. They were astonished to see a naked man emerge from the fish, and they broke out in laughter. The baron refreshed himself, returned to the sea, and found his clothes where he had left them.[1]

As in children's tales in which the swallowed child is later delivered alive from the belly of the devourer,[2] the hero happily exits from the great fish and resumes his activities, as though no great thing has occurred. There is at least one case on record in which a man actually did survive the experience of being swallowed by a sperm whale. In 1891 James Bartley, a member of a whaling crew operating near the Falkland Islands, was thrown overboard by the lash-

ing of a whale's tail and, as it turned out, was swallowed by the creature. After the whale was killed and dissected, the missing sailor was found in its stomach. He was doubled up and unconscious, and although he soon revived, the whale's gastric juices had bleached his face, neck, and hands, which never regained their color. Unlike the happy-go-lucky Baron Münchhausen, James Bartley was a "raving lunatic" for two weeks following his rescue, but at the end of three weeks he had recovered entirely and returned to his duties.[3] Remarkable as this account is, we should resist drawing the conclusion that lying tales recounting the swallowing of persons by a great fish must have been inspired by actual experiences, for surely the creativity of raconteurs is not so meager that they must find everything precisely modeled to scale in nature.

Lucian

The earliest comic allusion to a person's being swallowed by a great fish may be in Aristophanes, who refers to "the old woman whom the sea monster (*ketos*) swallowed," referring to a comedy by Phrynichos that was a burlesque of the Perseus and Andromeda legend.[4] In the second century of our era the geographer Dionysios attests to the existence of sea creatures in the vicinity of Taprobane that swallow ships and men.[5] Such ideas had doubtless been part of Mediterranean folk belief for centuries.

The first actual narration of a tale in the spirit of *Man Swallowed by a Fish* is given by Lucian in a string of lying tales, which like many other lying tales are recounted in the first person.[6] According to Lucian, as he and his companions sailed upon the sea they saw many large sea creatures, among them a fish that was 1,500 stades long (that is, over 150 miles). It came at them with mouth open and teeth showing. The mariners all bade one another farewell, and in a moment the creature swallowed them, ship and all. They passed by its teeth and entered its insides, where it was dark. When the creature opened its mouth, they saw a cavity large enough for a populous city as well as much else—fish, animals, parts of ships, human bones, soil with hills on it, trees of all sorts, and birds. Presently they made fire by rubbing sticks together and fixed themselves a meal. Exploring the woods they found a temple of Poseidon, a number of graves, a spring of fresh water, and a farmhouse where an old man and a youth were working their garden. They were Cypriotes who had been swallowed by the creature twenty-seven years earlier. The farmer told them of various warring tribes that dwelled in the fish, and Lucian and his party went on to defeat them all, after which they led a life of luxury in their prison. After a year and eight months, however, Lucian found the life there unendurable and sought a means of escape. At first they tried to dig their way out, but after digging into the right side of the animal for some five stades (that is, over half a mile), they gave up. Next they started a forest fire. It raged for days without affecting the fish, but by the twelfth day the creature was all but dead. They propped open its mouth so that they would not become trapped inside after it expired, and made ready their ship. The following day, when the creature was dead, they dragged their vessel out through its mouth and into the sea.[7]

The idea of a person's being swallowed by a great fish is found not only in lying tales but also in noncomic narratives of various kinds.

Greek Heroes

The Greek hero Perseus battled with a great sea creature off the coast of Africa or Palestine in the course of his rescue of Andromeda. According to the usual version Perseus cut off its head, but the poet Lycophron, in his customary dark manner, alludes to a version in which Perseus slew the creature from within, saying that the creature snatched Perseus in its jaws but the hero destroyed it by attacking its liver.[8] The hero Herakles had a similar experience. The gods Poseidon and Apollo once constructed walls for the city of Troy, but when the walls were completed, the treacherous King Laomedon cheated the gods of their promised wages. The deities responded angrily, Apollo sending a plague against the Trojans, Poseidon dispatching a sea monster that even made sallies against persons on land. An oracle revealed that the people would be free of these calamities if Laomedon should sacrifice his daughter Hesione to the *ketos*. So the king bound her to rocks bordering on the sea. Seeing her, Herakles offered to save the princess in return for a certain reward, to which Laomedon agreed, but after Herakles killed the sea creature and thus saved Hesione, Laomedon cheated him also, refusing to give him the promised compensation.[9] Concerning the battle itself, we learn that the hero, who was helped somehow by Athene, leapt through the mouth into the belly of the monster as it came at him with its mouth gaping, and spent three days inside hacking at its flank or liver before he emerged again. An odd feature of the story is that Herakles' hair fell out because of the internal heat of the creature.[10]

An apparently similar episode in which Jason is swallowed by a great serpent may be mentioned, although the beast is a creature of the land rather than of the sea. A fifth-century Attic vase shows a helpless man labeled Jason hanging partly out of the jaws of a huge serpent; in the background the object of his quest, the Golden Fleece, hangs from a tree; facing the monster is Athena. Inasmuch as the version of the Jason legend that is implied by these events is not known from written sources, we can only guess what has transpired. Presumably Jason tried without the aid of Medeia's magic to steal the Golden Fleece guarded by the Colchian dragon. Perhaps the dragon even held the fleece in its jaws, as Pindar seems to say.[11] In any case, the monster must have swallowed Jason as he attempted to take the fleece, and Athena or Medeia presumably had to rescue him.[12] If so, the story diverges from the pattern of the legends of Perseus and Herakles, in which the heroes save themselves by killing the creature, hacking at its organs from inside.

Jonah

Finally, there is the Hebrew prophet Jonah, who was swallowed by a great sea creature and spent three days in its belly before being spewed up by the huge fish onto dry land.[13] In the Jonah legend, however, the animal comes to Jonah's rescue, whereas the creatures mentioned earlier are hostile adversaries of the human hero; indeed, Jonah's fish acts on the Lord's orders.[14] And yet there is also an ambivalence in Jonah's rescue, for while the fish saves the prophet from drowning, it only replaces one problem with another, for how is Jonah now to escape from the inside of the fish? The answer is that, whereas Lucian burns his way out, Herakles and Perseus fight their way out, and the

unconscious Jason appears to be rescued by a female with supernatural powers, Jonah prays his way out.

The swallowing of a hero or a prophet by a great sea creature in Greek and Hebrew legendry shows that the motif of the swallowing of a man by a giant fish is also employed for noncomic effect, even when quite fantastically the man is represented as living within the creature for several days, as Herakles and Jonah each do. Whether the protagonist is an ordinary person, a heroic warrior, or a prophet, he always survives and the fish usually does not. What most distinguishes the treatment of the theme in folktale and in legend is not the sequence of events, which may be more or less identical (fish swallows man, man kills fish, man emerges safe from fish), but the whimsical atmosphere and unbounded fantasy of the folktale in contrast to the serious tone and relative restraint of the legend.

For other instances of giant creatures of the sea, see "Great Animal or Object."

Lit. AT 1889G, *Man Swallowed by Fish*. Radermacher 1906. Coulter 1926:40–50. Baumgartner 1959:156–157. Schenda 1965. Henningsen 1965:202–204. Ashliman, type 1889G.

1. Raspe 1971:55–56.
2. BP 1:40.
3. Wilson 1927:635–636.
4. Aristophanes *Clouds* 555–556.
5. Dionysios *Descriptio Graeciae* 603–604.
6. See Perry 1967:325–329; Henningsen 1965:213–218; Röhrich 1991:199–201; *EM* 7:10–15.
7. *True Stories* 1.30–2.2.
8. Lycophron *Alexandra* 834–841. On the story see Schmidt 1907:12–22; Fontenrose 1959:298–299; Gantz 1993:359–360.
9. See, for example, Homer *Il.* 7.452–453, 21.441–457; Apollodoros *Bibl.* 2.5.9; Diodorus Siculus 4.42; Hyginus *Fab.* 89; Valerius Flaccus *Argonautica* 2.451–549; Gantz 1993:400–402. On the international character of the story, see Fontenrose 1983.
10. Hellanikos *FGH* 4 F 26b; Lycophron *Alexandra* 31–37, 468–478; Tztetzes *Schol. on Lycophron* 34. On the legend of Herakles and the sea monster generally see Schmidt 1907:3–12; Frazer (1921) 1:206–209; Weinreich 1942:17–22; Fontenrose 1959:347–350; and Lesky 1967. The idea of baldness as the result of being swallowed is found among many peoples; see motif F921, *Swallowed person becomes bald*. For the combats of Herakles and Perseus with a sea monster, see further "Dragon Slayer."
11. *Pythian* 4:244.
12. See further Schmidt 1907:22–24; Radermacher 1968:204–205.
13. The story is recounted in the Old Testamental book of Jonah, called *Ionas* in the Septuagint. On the fish episode in the Jonah legend see Clouston (1887) 1:403–411; Schmidt 1907; Frazer (1919) 3:82–83; Gunkel 1921:133–134; Schenda 1965:438–440; Duval (1973) 2:14–16. On the events that lead up to it (AT 973, *Placating the Storm*) see Hardy 1896; Child (1956) 1:244–247, 2:13–16, 4:452–453, 462–463, 5:220, 288, 292; Röhrich 1963; Ashliman, type 973; and *EM* 7:625–628, 9:191–195.
14. Schmidt 1907:96. *Ionas* 2.

Marrying a Man of Forty ※ Returning a Donkey

"A husband on his deathbed advises his wife to marry a man of forty. She prefers two of twenty each. It all comes to the same."[1]

This comic tale is AT 1362B*, *Marrying Man of Forty*.

In the Romanian texts known to Aarne-Thompson a dying man advises his wife to remarry a forty-year-old man. Appearing to follow his advice by honoring his numbers, the lusty widow in fact subverts it by converting into two youthful lovers the middle-aged mate her late husband envisioned for her. The humor of the tale lies partly in the lustiness of the woman but mostly in the fact that with a neat mix of logic and illogic she slyly treats things that can be quantified as though their numerical aspect were the only relevant factor, so that two twenty-year-old men equal one forty-year-old man, just as in the realm of pure numbers $20 + 20 = 40$.

There is also a male form of the tale in which a male protagonist similarly selects two young females. Thus in a joke found in a sixteenth-century French collection, *Nouvelles Récréations et Joyeux Devis*, a bishop forbade a priest to have housemaids who were not at least fifty years old; so the priest hired one who was twenty years old and another who was thirty.[2] A twentieth-century German or American version of the tale reformulates it as a sort of comic brag. A man says that his idea of a wife at forty is that he should be able to take her to the bank and trade her for two twenties.[3]

The basic idea can be found today in jokes and newspaper comic strips. A "blond joke" transmitted by a female acquaintance asks "How blond was she?" and replies to its own question with a series of answers, each one an instance of extreme stupidity; one of them reads: "when she missed the 44 bus, she took the 22 bus twice instead."[4] In the first panel of a "Nancy" strip, Aunt Fritzi is shown painting a fence and asking Nancy to bring her a six-foot ladder. In the second panel Nancy returns with a ladder in each hand, commenting that she couldn't find it but brought two three-foot ladders.[5] In a "Frank and Ernest" strip, Frank or Ernest turns in a completed intelligence test to the tester while explaining that he didn't have a number 2 pencil so that he used two number 1's.[6] Either the humorists have come up with the same basic idea independently or they have adapted a familiar idea to new situations.

Regardless of their content, all texts agree that character A specifies a single unit (spouse, maid, ladder, pencil) with a quality (age, length, softness) that is designated by a number, whereupon character B substitutes two units whose sum equals it.

A Greek Joke

The same mathematical joke occurs in the ancient Greek jokebook *Philogelos*. An Abderite owed a man a donkey but did not have one. So he asked if he might give the man two mules instead.[7]

Abderites, citizens of the city of Abdera in Thrace, were a community of fools in Greek tradition, like the silly men of Gotham in English lore, the Schildbürger among the Germans, and the inhabitants of Mols in Denmark.[8] The logic of this Abderite's folly is less obvious in English than in Greek, for Greek "mule" (ἡμίονος) means literally a "semi-donkey" (donkey = ὄνος). Rendering the witticism etymologically we can say that a fool owed a man an ass but, not having one, asked to pay with two half-asses. Like the lusty widow or priest of the international joke, he substitutes (or proposes to substitute) two creatures

for one, treating a single quantifiable aspect of the creatures as if it were the only pertinent factor, and using it to form an equation.

An Inversion

Philogelos contains a second variant of essentially the same joke. A fool who was going on a trip was asked by a friend to buy him two slaves, each fifteen years old. The fool replied that he would do so, but if he should not find two fifteen-year-olds, he would buy him one thirty-year-old.[9]

The slave joke is unusual in that character B proposes to substitute a single larger quantity for two smaller ones rather than the reverse. The joke shows that, at least when the joke has to do with age, character B can be represented either as trading up or as trading down. In the former case character B emerges as cleverly exploiting the mathematical fallacy for personal gain; in the latter, character B is a fool who fails to perceive the fallacy. Most such texts of *Marrying a Man of Forty*, including all the modern ones, represent the lusty acquirer as trading up, roguishly treating two youthful persons as the equivalent of one older person, whereas the Greek joke about the slaves represents the acquirer as trading down, naively supposing that one older person is equal to two youthful ones.

Lit. AT 1362B*, *Marrying Man of Forty*. Legman 1971:615–616. Marzolph 1987:194.

1. Aarne and Thompson 1961:405, citing two Romanian texts.
2. Des Périers 1980:153, no. 34; motif J2212.1.1, *Priest to have maid at least fifty years old*.
3. Legman 1971:615.
4. Sent to me by Susan Jones (Bloomington, Indiana), February 1, 2000.
5. "Nancy" (September 4, 1999), drawn by Gus and Brad Gilchrist and distributed by United Feature Syndicate.
6. "Frank and Ernest" (October 12, 1999), drawn by Bob Thaves and distributed by NEA, Inc.
7. *Philogelos* 127.
8. *Philogelos* 110–127 are jokes about Abderites, on whom see further Thierfelder 1968:16–17; *EM* 1:10–11.
9. *Philogelos* 12. For other mathematical jokes, see also *Philogelos* 175 and 222.

Matron of Ephesus

A man dies (or seems to die), and initially his widow clings to his memory. But soon she gives her love to a second man, and when she must choose between honoring her late husband and furthering the welfare of her new love, she readily sacrifices the former for the latter. In some texts she mutilates the cadaver of her husband for the sake of her lover.

This misogynic novella is AT 1510, *The Matron of Ephesus*, also known as *Vidua* among scholars of *The Seven Sages of Rome*, a mediaeval composition that contains the present tale. *The Matron of Ephesus* comically highlights two immoderate attitudes that the protagonist displays in short succession toward her dead husband, extreme reverence and extreme irreverence; at worst it mocks the grieving of widows as hypocritical and the sexuality of women as incon-

stant and treacherous.[1] Known in both the East and West, the tale has been the subject of numerous literary treatments from antiquity to the present and has been called one of the world's most popular novelle, which perhaps it is. Much less attention has been paid to the oral tale than to its literary realizations.[2]

The Matron of Ephesus shows, it seems, two principal branches, which I shall call redactions A and B. Because the best-known texts of redaction A are European and the most-discussed text of redaction B is Chinese, the former tradition is sometimes referred to as the Occidental branch and the latter as the Oriental branch, but in fact neither form is limited to the Orient or the Occident. I focus upon redaction A because the ancient texts belong to this branch and also because the precise relationship of the two redactions to each other is uncertain.

Redaction A: The Dead Husband

An extremely popular collection of mostly traditional tales, *The Seven Sages of Rome* is a complex frame-story in which an unfaithful queen recounts seven tales to her husband that are intended to put a bad light upon her stepson, whom she accuses of attempting to seduce her. Alternating with her, each of seven sages recounts a tale that puts women in a bad light, the tale of the faithless widow being one of them. And in the end the stepson himself speaks, exonerating himself. This literary work reached the West from the Orient around the ninth century A.D., after which in the course of time it developed over forty distinct versions that are preserved in more than two hundred manuscripts. Some Western elaborator added the tale of the inconstant widow to the collection early in the course of its European career, for the Eastern editions do not contain it.[3]

To illustrate: according to a text from a Middle English version of *The Seven Sages of Rome* a knight who was very fond of his wife died of grief one day after accidentally causing her a minor wound. The inconsolable widow stayed beside his grave, weeping and refusing to depart. Her friends built a shelter for her next to her husband's grave and provided her with a fire and nourishment, but she declined to eat or drink. Nearby a knight was guarding through the night the bodies of three thieves hanging from a gallows, to make sure that their friends not make off with the corpses. Chilled by the frost and attracted by the widow's fire he approached her shelter. He soothed and encouraged the young and attractive woman with his words. When the knight returned to the gallows, he found that one of the bodies was missing. Going back to the widow, he explained that as a result of the loss he would lose his lands. But she cheered him, proposing this solution: if he should agree to marry her, he could replace the missing cadaver with that of her husband. They agreed, removed the corpse from its grave, and placed it upon the knight's horse. The knight said that she would have to hang the body, since it would be dishonorable for a knight to hang a knight. She agreed, placing a rope around his neck. When the knight pointed out that the thief had had a wound on his head, she said that the knight should wound her husband's head in a similar fashion; and when he declined, saying that it was not right for him to strike a dead knight, she herself took his sword and made the wound. Perceiving now the woman's unkind character, the knight mentioned that the thief also was missing his front teeth,

and when the widow proposed that he strike out her husband's teeth, he declined on the grounds that it would be villainous for a knight thus to strike a knight; whereupon the widow straightaway took a stone and knocked out her husband's front teeth. "Sir," she said, "now shall thou wed me." But the knight replied that he would never marry her, since she would hang him with a rope just as she has done her lord; indeed, she had shown him such sorrow that he would never trust women again.[4]

The widow and her lover enter into a contract according to which she will help him by supplying her husband's cadaver and he in turn will marry her. Connected with this arrangement is mutilation, the widow's surprising willingness to mutilate her late husband's cadaver in order to benefit her new lover, a gruesome theme that is found sporadically in both occidental and oriental tellings of the tale, the specific mutilations varying somewhat from text to text. Her wounding him and her knocking out his front teeth are typical, to which some versions add her pulling out his hair or cutting off his ears or even his testicles.[5] The widow's sudden change of heart is usually not well motivated in *The Seven Sages* or elsewhere: one moment she is ready to waste away on her deceased husband's grave, and the next moment she is prepared to give herself to a stranger.[6]

According to an Arabic text collected in Tunis from an illiterate male in the 1880s, two married brothers dwelled in the same house, one brother having a daughter and the other a son. When the children grew up, their parents married them to each other. In time the parents died, and their offspring continued in true love. Once the young man proposed to his wife that they make a promise to each other, that after one of them died the other would not remarry; and they both so promised. Sometime later the man died and was buried. The woman wept, had a tent set up over his grave, and declared that she would remain there until death united them. Now at that time the city was plagued by a thief who stole from everyone, including the sultan. The exasperated sultan told his vizier that if the vizier did not bring the robber, living or dead, to him by the next day, the sultan would have the vizier executed. The unhappy vizier, wondering how he might capture a man whom the guards and troops had been unable to catch, rode his horse out of the city and happened to spot the widow's tent. He dismounted and peered in, and she invited him to sit. Noticing that he was upset, she asked him what was the matter, and he explained his plight, saying that he expected to die on the morrow. Straightaway the woman asked him if he would wed her in return for some advice. The vizier agreed. Then she explained that her husband lay in this grave, dead a half-month. They should dig him up and cut off his head, which the vizier should present to the sultan as being that of the robber, since the sultan was himself not acquainted with the thief. After the body was exhumed, the vizier said that the thief had only one eye, whereupon the widow tore out one of the cadaver's eyes. The vizier brought the head to the sultan, identifying it as that of the robber, and on the following day the woman reminded the vizier that he now must marry her. But the man replied that if there were any good in her, she would not have been capable of digging up her husband and robbing him of his head and eye. Since her husband had experienced no good from her, how could he expect otherwise for himself? She should look for someone else.[7]

Again, the woman's change of heart is instantaneous and the themes of marriage and mutilation form a linked pair.

In an oral narration from mid-ninteenth-century Russia, a woman who had just buried her husband was inconsolable. She refused to leave his grave, saying that she wished to be left alone to grieve until death. So she dwelled upon the grave without eating or drinking for one, two, three days. Not far away there was a gallows where a corpse was being watched over. The guard, a soldier, heard the widow's wailing and declared he would heal her. Taking a bottle of wine and something to eat, he went to the grave and began speaking to her to get her to leave off crying. After he engaged her in a conversation on one topic or another, the woman became cheerful. He told her that wine was good for grief, and they drank a glass of wine and then several, and ate a bit. She became more cheerful, gradually changed completely, and lay with the soldier. While they passed the night together, the corpse was stolen. What was the soldier to do? He was terrified. The woman said to him: "Why are you frightened, love? Come, let's dig up my husband and put him in place of the stolen man. Who will notice it? No one." Said and done. No one learned of it. That's the way women are![8]

In this narrative the aggressor is the man rather than the woman, and the widow's change of heart is portrayed as being gradual, although it still contrasts sharply with her earlier attitude. The themes of marriage and mutilation do not occur.

The sixteenth-century story of Wooden John illustrates a jocular realization of the type. According to a tale recounted in an anonymous English jestbook, a man named John died, leaving a wife who had loved him so much that upon his death she had a wooden image of him made, which each night she had her maid wrap in a sheet and lay in her bed. She called it Old John. She also had an apprentice named John, who would gladly have wedded the rich widow for her money. Wherefore he bribed the maid to wrap him in a sheet and lay him in the widow's bed one night instead of the statue. It was the widow's habit to kiss the image before and after sleeping, and this night she kissed the young man, thinking he was the statue. Suddenly he took her in his arms and pleased her so well that she was content to lie through the night with Young John and completely forgot about Old John. In the morning the widow, wishing to please Young John, told her maid to prepare some meat for breakfast. After a while the maid informed her mistress that she could find no dry wood with which to cook the meat, except for the image of Old John that lay under the bed. The woman instructed her to lay Old John on the fire, for she saw that he would never do her any better service than serving as firewood, regardless of how long she should keep him. So the maid made a fire with the image and therewith cooked breakfast, so that Old John was cast out and Young John now occupied his place. The tale (says the text) illustrates that there is no wisdom in a person's long keeping or cherishing that which provides no pleasure or service.[9]

In this narrative the widow's exceptional reverence for her deceased husband takes the form of taking him to bed each night in the form of a wooden statue that she continues to kiss and sleep with more or less as though he were still alive, and her eventual gesture of disrespect for him takes the form of disposing of the statue by employing it as firewood merely to facilitate her new

lover's breakfast. The relative satisfaction given her in bed by Old John and Young John serves as the turning point for the widow, bringing her to the conclusion that Young John would serve her better as a bedfellow.

These texts exemplify the range of variation found in redaction A. The following traits can be seen in most or all of the summarized texts. (1) After a certain man dies, (2) his wife displays remarkable faithfulness to him (she remains at his grave/she takes an image of him to bed with her nightly). Presently (3) another man joins her (he comes to the tomb/he joins her in bed), and in time (4) they become lovers (they become engaged/they sleep together). When (5) the widow is informed of a problem in connection with her lover (the body guarded by him has been stolen/he despairs of capturing a certain thief/there is no firewood for his breakfast), (6) without hesitating she contributes the remains of her late husband to allay the crisis (she offers her husband's cadaver as a substitute corpse/she offers her husband's image as substitute firewood).

Redaction B: The Apparently Dead Husband

Before turning to the ancient treatments, I give an example of a set of stories that appear to constitute a different branch of the tale. A legend in the *Jingu qiguan*, or *Strange Stories from Contemporary and Ancient Times*, a Chinese work said to date to the fifteenth and sixteenth centuries but containing earlier material, tells of Zhuangzi, a Taoist holy man who possessed supernatural powers as a result of his spiritual progress. Once Zhuangzi saw a woman swinging a fan over a fresh grave. When he asked her about it, she explained that inasmuch as her late husband had asked her not to remarry before the earth on his grave was dry, she was fanning it to speed up its drying. The holy man magically dried out the earth for her, and the grateful widow gave him her fan in remembrance of his deed. At home he reported the event to his wife, Tian shi, who became enraged and declared that, whereas all men were alike, there were few women like the widow; and as for herself, if her husband should die she would never remarry. When Zhuangzi said it was impossible to say, she tore up the fan. Presently Zhuangzi became sick and died, and his wife grieved greatly. Many persons paid visits of condolence, among them a young and handsome prince, who said he had been on his way there in the hope of being instructed by Zhuangzi and was sorry to have arrived too late. Donning clothes of mourning, he paid his respects to the corpse and also begged to see Tian shi. Somewhat reluctantly she agreed, but when she saw him she was struck by his looks and fell in love with him. He stayed on for some days to take charge of the funeral, and whenever he lamented the deceased she did also, in order to have an opportunity to converse with him. Two weeks after her husband's death she proposed marriage to the prince through his servant. The prince was willing but regretfully declined because of three obstacles, but the widow energetically found ways to remove them. For example, when he objected that it would be ill-omened to begin a marriage in the midst of a funeral, she bade her husband's coffin be transferred from the house to a dilapidated hut behind the house. Having answered his objections, she proposed that they wed that very evening. The prince agreed, and they changed from mourning to festive attire, celebrated their wedding ceremony, and were pro-

ceeding to the bridal chamber when the bridegroom became convulsed and fell to the floor unconscious. His servant explained that there was only one cure for his master's fit: the marrow of a living man's brain, cooked in wine; when pressed, he said the brain of a man dead fewer than forty-nine days would do. The woman offered the brain of her late husband, who had been dead only twenty days. She took an hatchet, went to the hut, and after some thirty blows managed to force the coffin open. But then she heard the body sigh, and suddenly Zhuangzi sat up and exited from the coffin. She cunningly tried to put a good face upon her actions, saying that she had opened his coffin in the hope that he had returned to life, but he in turn asked her why she was not wearing mourning clothes and why his coffin had been tossed into a ruined hut, and in general he expressed his mistrust of her loyalty toward him, so that she felt ashamed. Then Zhuangzi, employing the art of dividing himself into shadow and being, magically caused the prince and his servant to appear and then to disappear again. Tian shi hanged herself with her belt, and Zhuangzi burnt down his house and roamed westward, never remarrying.[10]

The saintly Zhuangzi, equipped as he is with special powers, feigns his death and creates during his inactivity a handsome prince and servant to test his wife's declaration of lifelong fidelity to him; at the proper time he has the prince fall ill and the servant inform Tian shi of the prerequisite for his recovery, after which the hero allows himself to return from his pretended death and permits the phantom prince and servant to reappear briefly in order to convict his wife. In short, the protagonist sets his wife up, and when she fails the test he reappears to point out that her vaunted constancy is a lie.

The Chinese text is atypical of redaction B in featuring a supernatural protagonist, but the essential events are the same as in other texts of the branch. In redaction A the husband is dead and passive throughout the core of the tale, and the wife's constancy chances to be tried by a man whose life happens at the time to intersect with hers, whereas in redaction B the husband remains a living, active character who deliberately feigns his death and arranges for a confederate to test his wife's constancy, whereupon the husband reappears to convict her.

A telling feature in the Chinese novella is how far the wife is willing to go in order to secure her marriage to the second man. Tian shi's actions correspond to redaction A in two ways, *functionally* to the motif of the substitute cadaver and *formally* to the motif of mutilation. Functionally, the need for brains in redaction B is the same as the need for a cadaver in redaction A: the woman is informed of a crisis in connection with her lover (in B, he can be revived only by means of the brain of a human being), and without hesitation she contributes the body of her husband to allay the crisis (in B, she goes immediately to fetch his brain). Formally, the mutilation required to extract the husband's brains in redaction B is of the same order of indignity as the mutilation required to force the husband's cadaver to match the appearance of the criminal's cadaver in redaction A, and it is driven by the same motivation, which is to facilitate the widow's new marriage. Again the theme of mutilation is linked with the theme of remarriage.

Some scholars have expressed skepticism about the genetic relationship of redactions A and B, holding that these two narrative traditions developed in-

dependently of each other.[11] But much does argue for their being different branches of a single stock. First, their plots correspond in basic ways: (1) the death (or apparent death) of the husband, (2) the remarkable constancy of the widow, (3) the appearance on the scene of a second man, who woos the widow, (4) his winning of the widow, and (5) the widow's ready sacrifice of her husband's physical dignity for the benefit of her lover. Second, there is the wife's readiness to mutilate her husband's cadaver as a condition of marriage to her fiancee, a theme that occurs in each redaction, although not in every text.

The apparently broad geographical distribution of *The Matron of Ephesus* attests to its appeal, and the variety of its realizations implies a vigorous life in oral tradition. Because the novella has been so frequently anthologized it has probably reentered oral tradition sporadically from literary sources, so that the tale has been transmitted both orally and literarily.

The Inconstant Widow in Rome

Among the fables recounted in Latin verse by the Greek freedman Phaedrus, writing in the first century A.D., is that of the widow and the soldier. A certain woman lost the husband she had loved, had his body preserved in a sepulcher, and spent all her time there mourning him, for which she won renown as a chaste wife. In the meantime some men who had plundered a temple of Jove were crucified for sacrilege, and, adjacent to the monument in which the widow grieved, soldiers were stationed to see that their bodies should not be removed. In the middle of the night one of the soldiers became thirsty, peered through the door of the monument just as the widow was going to bed, and asked the woman's maidservant for some water. The extraordinary beauty of the widow filled him with desire for her, and thereafter he found a thousand pretexts for visiting her. Daily association gradually made her complaisant, and presently she felt there was a close bond between them. While the guard thus passed his nights with the widow, a body was removed from one of the crosses. Very upset, the soldier explained the matter to the woman. Replying that there was no reason for him to fear, she handed over to him her husband's body to be attached to the cross in order that the soldier not be punished for his neglect. Thus was virtue besieged by vice.[12]

The details of Phaedrus's fable are recounted generically, as is usually the case in fables, for the authority of the narrative derives from its offering not a historical precedent but a convincing analogy to real-life situations. An apparently illogical feature of Phaedrus's narrative is the mention of a number of soldiers rather than one soldier. Probably we should imagine that the several guards function not as a group but in shifts consisting of one man on duty at a time, so that the other or others may eat and sleep. The soldier in question leaves his post during his shift in order to quench his thirst and eventually to pass time with the widow.[13]

In the course of the *Satirica* (traditionally known as the *Satiricon*), a novel authored by Phaedrus's contemporary Petronius, a character relates the story of the Matron of Ephesus to a group of persons, and it is from this famous, lively, and complex telling that the international tale type takes its name. According to Petronius some men and women aboard a ship fell to fighting and in time

made peace. After a while Eumolpus, who had authored the reconciliation and did not wish the merriment to lapse into silence without a few tales, began to make some gibes about the fickleness of women—how easily they fell in love, how quickly they forgot even their children, how no woman is so chaste that she cannot feel madly passionate about a stranger. He did not have in mind (he said) characters in the tragedies of old or other famous persons but rather an event of their own time, which he would relate if they should care to hear it. Everyone turned his way, and he began his narration.

A married woman of Ephesus (he began) was so famous for her fidelity that women from neighboring communities used to come just to view her. When her husband died she followed his corpse to his underground vault and remained there mourning. No one was able to induce her to leave, although in time she had not eaten for five days, and everyone agreed that she was the one true example of fidelity and love. Meanwhile the governor of the province ordered some thieves to be crucified near the place where the tomb was, and a soldier was stationed there to prevent the thieves' bodies from being removed for burial. The soldier saw a light burning among the tombs and heard moaning, so that he went down into the vault to investigate, and there he found the extremely beautiful woman grieving for her dead husband. He offered her some of his food. At first she refused, but in time her maid accepted some of the food and drink and then persuaded her mistress to do so as well. Then the soldier, having persuaded the woman to live, turned his attention to her virtue. The woman found him attractive and, encouraged by her maid, she lay with the soldier. Each of the next three nights he brought his meal down into the vault, closed the door of the tomb, and passed the night with the widow. But the family of one of the crucified men, noticing that the guarding was not strict, removed a body by night and gave it burial. When the soldier saw one of the crosses without a corpse, he decided not to wait for his punishment but rather to kill himself there in the widow's vault. But the woman said that she did not want to see at the same time the corpses of the two men she had loved, adding that she would rather expend a corpse than kill a live man. So she had the soldier take her husband's corpse from its coffin and affix it to the vacant cross, and the next day people wondered how the dead man had managed to ascend the cross.

The sailors broke out laughing; a lecherous woman named Tryphaena blushed and hid her face; and a certain man, Lichas, shook his head and exclaimed angrily that the governor should have replaced the husband's body in its tomb and affixed the woman to the cross in its place.[14]

The tales of Phaedrus and Petronius are parallel in their essential action. (1) A woman loses her husband and (2) mourns him day and night at his sepulcher, winning renown for her devotion to him. (3) A nearby soldier who is guarding the corpses of crucified criminals goes to the tomb (to ask for water/to investigate a light he sees) and finds a beautiful widow and her maidservant there. (4) He turns his attention to the widow, and soon (5) he is passing his nights with her at the tomb. Meanwhile (6) one of the corpses he is supposed to be guarding is stolen. When (7) the upset soldier explains the matter to the widow, (8) she reassures him, giving him the body of her late husband to attach to the vacant cross in place of the criminal.

Most scholars suppose that the two authors drew upon a common literary source—a Hellenistic work such as Aristides' *Milesiaka* (Milesian Tales) or Sisenna's Latin translation of it—while some scholars claim that Phaedrus borrowed the tale from Petronius.[15] In fact we do not know where they learned their stories. Scholarly speculation has focused on literary sources for no apparent reason other than that the scholars are philologists, for it certainly is just as possible that one or both authors drew upon an oral tale.

There are reasons for supposing that the novella reached Rome from Greece. Phaedrus, although retelling his fable in Latin, is himself of Greek extraction. Petronius is not, but the Greek color in his narrative and the setting of the story in the Greek city of Ephesus argue for the Roman borrowing of a Greek tale; moreover, Eumolpus describes the repository of the husband's remains as being an underground sepulcher "in the Greek manner" rather than their being cremated.[16] Although the observation "in the Greek manner" is somewhat illogical in the mouth of the internal Greek narrator Eumolpus, it is nonetheless understandable as a comment added by the Roman author by way of explanation.[17] And of course Petronius represents the participants in the storytelling session as being Greeks. However it was transmitted, the tale must have become fashionable in Rome during the first century of our era, for in the palace of the Emperor Nero, who reigned in the years A.D. 54–68, there is said to have been a bas relief, now lost, depicting the story.[18]

The Latin texts obviously belong to redaction A, which tells of the actual death of the husband and the trying of the widow's fidelity by chance, as it were, rather than by design. Except perhaps for the wonderfully eccentric development represented by the tale of Wooden John, texts of the redaction from all periods are easily recognized as being variations on the same plot. Differing cultural practices reflected in the texts, such as the execution of criminals by crucifixion or by hanging, affect only the surface of the tale, not its basic action. Some of the later texts begin the story at an earlier point than the Roman texts do, narrating something of the life of the husband and wife and of the cause of the husband's untimely death, but the principal difference between the Roman texts and apparently the bulk of the non-Roman texts is that the ancient narratives portray the fickle widow more kindly. Although all texts chronicle her quick change from extreme devotion toward her late husband to extreme disrespect, the Roman texts do not take the extra misogynic step found in many later texts. In Phaedrus and Petronius the amorous aggressor is the soldier, not the widow, and her change of loyalty does not occur instantaneously. The woman does not trade her help in return for a promise of marriage, nor does she coolly mutilate her husband's cadaver. We do not know whether the more misogynic tradition is a later, mediaeval development, as is usually (and reasonably) supposed, or an old feature of the type that did not appeal to the Greeks and Romans.

Phaedrus relates his Milesian novella as an Aesopic tale, including it in his collection of versified fables. Like most fables, it is a generic rather than a particularized tale, not naming the characters, not situating them in a labeled locale or in a particular period of time, and like most literary fables it concludes with an epimythium, a coda giving a generic application for the tale.

In contrast, Petronius presents his story as a legend. His internal narrator al-

leges that the traditional story is a true occurrence, a historical event located in time and space, the events being contemporary with Eumolpus and his audience (*rem sua memoria factam*) and taking place in Ephesus, a city with more than its share of unfaithful wives, according to ancient stereotype.[19] The alleged veracity of the account adds weight to the narrative, but Eumolpus does not push his assertion of historicity, making his claim with a measure of playfulness in the hope of reviving the merry mood of the group. Nor is the issue of historicity of much interest to Eumolpus's hearers, who do not debate it. The angry comments upon the widow's treacherous behavior uttered by Lichas, a man who evidently was cuckolded by his wife, imply that he takes Eumolpus's narration as a true report. Like Phaedrus, Eumolpus states the point of his narrative (namely, that women are fickle), and, as oral narrators often do, he announces it first, like a promythium, before he relates his story.

When the primary narrator employs a secondary narrator to relate a story, as Petronius does, the narrative operates on two levels. Mimicking an oral performance, the second-order narration suggests what sort of person might know and relate this tale, what circumstances might prompt him/her to do so, and how listeners might respond to it. In the present case the ribald narrative belongs (appropriately enough, one feels) to the repertoire of a lowlife male, and the participants in the storytelling event are a mixed group of males and females, a party in which, at the moment of Eumolpus's intervention, the convivial mood is beginning to flag. As a tale teller Eumolpus has a good sense of timing, since everyone accepts his offer of a story by giving him their attention. Not surprisingly, their response in the end is mixed, varying mostly with gender, for most of the males guffaw and one of the females blushes; more exactly, there is glee (the sailors), anger (Lichas), and embarrassment (Tryphaena) at this new proof of female fickleness.[20] Eumolpus's intent is to amuse and tease, at which he succeeds, beginning and concluding his narration with a straightforwardly comic remark. He says that there was at Ephesus a matron who was so faithful to her husband that women came from miles around just to look at her, implying that a faithful wife is such a rarity that she would be a tourist attraction. This parodies the familiar *incipit* of ancient narratives telling of a maiden of such beauty that suitors come from far away to woo her.[21] Similarly, rather than ending his story with a serious epimythium referring to the levity of women, the narrator says: "on the following day the people wondered how the dead man had ascended the cross."[22] Never mind the moral implications of their act, the lovers' ruse does not even *fool* the local citizenry, for the good-natured folk of Ephesus with their casual morality merely marvel how a corpse has managed to clamber up a cross! Eumolpus's narrative strategy is reminiscent of that of the Homeric bard Demodokos, who sings the comic and ribald story of the love affair of Ares and Aphrodite to a party of males, to dissolve the tension that arises among the high-strung heroes.[23]

On the level of first-order narration the story of the Matron of Ephesus resonates also with other events in the novel, notably with the ensuing amorous situation in which the characters Tryphaena and Giton engage in erotic play, mirroring the roles of the widow and the soldier in the novella, and exclude Eumolpus, whose part now becomes that of the dead husband. Just as when a Homeric character uses a myth it has a meaning beyond that intended by the

character,[24] so also in the present passage the narrative significance of Eumolpus's legend is greater than its immediate role as teasing entertainment.

A Greek Fable

According to a tale recounted by Aesop in an anonymous fictional biography of the fabulist, the *Aesop Romance*, a work that probably is contemporary with Petronius, a certain woman buried her husband and remained sitting beside his grave weeping without cease. When a ploughman saw her and desired to lie with her, he left his oxen standing in the field, went over to her, and pretended to weep. She became silent and asked why he was crying, to which the ploughman replied that he had buried his wife, a wise and good woman, and that when he cried it relieved his grief. She explained that she too had lost a good husband, and crying lightened her grief. The man said that inasmuch as they had both suffered the same misfortune, why did they not become acquainted with each other? He would love her as he had loved his wife, and she should love him as she did her husband. With this thought he won the woman over. While they lay together someone unhitched his oxen and drove them away, and when the ploughman returned and did not find his oxen he wept and cried out in earnest. The woman asked why he was weeping, and he said: "Now I've got a *reason* to mourn."[25]

The tale is framed by a friend's visiting Aesop in jail and asking him how things are going, prompting Aesop to tell the present fable, which he concludes by asking: "You see the predicament I'm in, and still you ask me *why* I'm upset?" In this case the internal tale, one of many in the work, seems not to play off themes of the larger narrative, perhaps because of the large number of boxed tales and the very episodic composition of the romance.

Up to a certain point Aesop's comic and ribald tale closely parallels the Roman story of the matron and the soldier. To wit, (1) a woman who has just lost her husband mourns ceaselessly at his grave and (2) comes to the attention of a ploughman (soldier) who happens to be working nearby. (3) Erotically attracted to her, the man deserts his own work in order to keep her company and (4) in time seduces her. (5) When he returns to his work he discovers that someone, taking advantage of his absence, has stolen his oxen (cadaver). And (6) after he responds with grief (fear) for his loss, (7) the widow expresses her concern for him.

The tale appears to belong to the tradition of *The Matron of Ephesus* but as an odd branch off the main stalk, like the sixteenth-century joke about Wooden John. And, indeed, concluding as it does with a punch line, it is best understood as a joke that has been pressed into service here as a fable, for Aesop recounts it more for the parallel it offers to the situation in which he finds himself than for its inherent humor as an entertaining tale.

This last tale is notably devoid of the misogyny that otherwise characterizes this tale type. The mediaeval widow volunteers her husband's corpse and also proceeds to mutilate it, the Roman widow offers her husband's corpse and does no more, but the Greek widow does not dishonor her husband in any way. If the Greek tale puts anyone in a bad light, it is rather the dishonest lover who misrepresents his own feelings in order to exploit the woman's. This man

is the true center of interest, and it is his grief that is revealed as false. As Gerlinde Huber observes, this tale stops just at the point at which the events and the figure of the widow in the usual story captivate us.[26]

Concerning the Origin of the Tale

Some scholars speculate that Petronius based his tale upon an actual event.[27] Although there is no way to confirm or disconfirm this hypothesis, there is always of course a possibility that the tale is an aesthetic reshaping of a historical incident, and the belief that the tale arose in this or that land is not inconsistent with the notion that some real-life event gave rise to the narrative.

The main contenders for the honor of having given the world this fine tale are India and Greece. Benfey voiced his suspicion that the tale originated in India and spread therefrom to the Occident, and he was followed by Eduard Grisebach in his study of the tale, after which the opinion that the tale arose in India sometimes appears to be an established fact rather than the pure conjecture that it is.[28] Grisebach's book, which some investigators treat as the standard study of the international tale, draws almost exclusively upon the literary monuments and is driven by a pan-Indianist bias. It was harshly criticized for its illogic and orientalist mania by Joseph Bédier, and an earlier version of the book published in 1877 drew a scathing and mocking review from Rohde.[29]

On the other hand, Abel de Rémusat supposed that the tale traveled from Greece to India.[30] And the classical scholar Ben Perry, followed by folklorist Haim Schwarzbaum, pinpointed the origin of the tale in the Aesopic fable of the widow and the ploughman, which Perry believed the author of the *Aesop Romance* took from the pioneering collection of fables made by Demetrios of Phaleron in the late fourth and early third centuries B.C.[31] For Perry the Roman story represents a retelling and expansion of the Greek tale in which simple irony is replaced by cynicism. But since nothing certain is known concerning where and when the tale came into being or even whether the two apparent redactions really are forms of the same tale, all these views rest upon nothing more solid than conjecture.

For another tale of female faithlessness that also became a part of *The Seven Sages* see "Underground Passage to Paramour's House," and for another misogynic tale with some similarity to the present tradition see "Mother Dies of Fright."

Lit. AT 1510, *The Matron of Ephesus (Vidua)*. Dacier 1780. Benfey (1859) 1:460. Rohde 1877b. Clouston (1887) 1:29–34. Grisebach 1889. Campbell 1907:ci–cviii. Weber 1913. Rank 1913. BP 1:364, 4:330 no. 6; 4:340 no. 80. Herrmann 1927. Weinreich 1931:53–75. Espinosa 1934. Espinosa (1947) 2:355–367. Ranke 1953. Ure 1956. Liungman 1961:300. Cabaniss 1961. Perry 1962:329–330. Holbek 2:172, no. 82, 2:298. Scheiber 1963:149–152. Brandon 1965. Lacy 1967. Legman 1971/1968:647–650. Rastier 1971. Pecere 1975. Colton 1975. Small 1976:193 note 44. Scobie 1977b:15–17. Runte 1978. Schwarzbaum 1979:394–417. Müller 1980. Massaro 1981. Parca 1981. Pepe 1981. Dvořák, no. 5262. Schwarzbaum 1982. Boerma 1982. Bömer 1986. Sega 1986. Cicu 1986. Ashliman, type 1510. Boldrini 1989. Huber 1990. Runte 1994.

1. Legman 1971:649.

2. Literary histories of *The Matron of Ephesus* began appearing as early as the late eighteenth century; see Dacier 1780; Grisebach 1889; Campbell 1907:ci–cviii; and other works cited in the scholarly literature appended below. Of particular interest to classical scholars are Pecere's detailed commentary on Petronius's story (Pecere 1975) and Huber's survey (1990) of literary treatments of the tale in Latin from antiquity through the Middle Ages. Although no extensive study of the tale type has been made by a scholar of oral tales, there are good discussions by Espinosa (1947) 2:355–367; Brandon 1965; and Schwarzbaum 1979:394–417.

3. On the tale of the fickle widow in *The Seven Sages of Rome* see Runte 1978, 1994; Huber 1990:153–176. On *The Seven Sages of Rome* in general see Campbell 1907 and Niedzielski, Runte, and Hendrickson 1978.

4. Campbell 1907:96–104, Twelfth Story, verses 2811–3044.

5. For a modern folktale telling of a man's disgust at a widow's physical maltreatment of her husband's corpse, with the result that he departs, see AT 1352*, *The Woman's Coarse Act*.

6. Runte 1978:112.

7. Stumme (1893) 2:79–80, no. 5, one of a pair of balanced tales, this one featuring an immoral woman and the second featuring a moral woman, both boxed within an elaborate frame-tale, a structure that is similar to that of *The Seven Sages*. Schwarzbaum (1979:415 n. 53) cites a similar tale in the Israeli Folktale Archives (IFA 6445) collected in the twentieth century from a Libyan Jew.

8. Lerch (1864:373–374) gives a literal German rendering of a text of a tale that he says was recorded in Russian from oral tradition and published in Moscow in 1860.

9. Zall (1963:149–150, no. 100), reprinted from *A C. Mery Talys* (= *A Hundred Merry Tales*), dated 1526; also printed in Ranke (1953:92–93) and Briggs (1970) A2:207–208. A slightly different version of this lively tale appears in Kirchhof's *Wendunmuth*, a collection of jokes from written and oral sources that appeared in Germany later in the same century. This tale, recounted to Kirchhof by a male informant, Martin Schirmer, tells how a widow so greatly loved her husband that upon his death she had a wooden statue of him made to size and painted with colors. She called it "den hölzteren Johannes." It was her custom to keep this Wooden Johannes next to the stove during the day and next to her in bed at night. One day the woman's maid conceived the idea of substituting her handsome young brother for the statue. This Johannes warmed the woman so well that she kept him with her all night, whereas she was wont to put the other Johannes aside once he lost his warmth. In the morning the maid reported that there was no dry wood with which to cook the fish the woman wanted. "Oh," she said, "then take the Wooden Johannes, who is dry enough, cut him into pieces, and cook with him as long as he lasts." The maid's brother became a wealthy man, for the widow married him (Kirchhof [1980] 1:388–389, no. 348). Among the interesting details of this text is the emphasis upon warmth rather than sex, nicely rounded off by Wooden Johannes's final flash as firewood. Notice also the hint of mutilation in the widow's instructions to cut him up (*den zerhauw*), followed by her marriage to his rival. This tale has been attested only in England, Germany, and the Netherlands. Ranke (1953) sees it as a West European redaction of AT 1510.

10. [Birch] 1843 gives the story in translation from the Chinese. In the Wade-Giles system, the title of the Chinese work would be rendered *Chin-ku ch'i-kuan*, and the husband and wife would be respectively Chuang-tze and T'ien-shih (I owe the *pinyin* and Wade-Giles transliterations of the Chinese to the kindness of Dr. Liangyan Ge).

According to Grisebach, the story is known in China in two versions: a ballad still sung in the streets of Shanghai, and a prose tale found in the great collection of novelle, the *Jingu qiguan*. Novelle from this collection were made known in European publications from the eighteenth century onward, and by the beginning of the nineteenth century the Chinese tale of the unfaithful wife had been compared by Western scholars to Petronius's novella. The consideration that the protagonist of the Chinese story was a Taoist saint of the fourth century B.C. leads Grisebach (1889:26) to infer that the legend must have been attached to him within or shortly after his lifetime, but this conclusion is unwarranted, for the tale itself, however old it may be as a story type, could have been fitted to Zhuangzi any time between his lifetime and the composition of the *Jingu qiguan*, a stretch of almost two millenia; the period in which the protagonist actually lived tells us nothing one way or the other about the age of the narrative in China. For a rather similar Jewish legend, told of Rabbi Meir and his wife, Beruriah, see Grisebach (1889:26–29) and Schwarzbaum (1979:410–413 n.

21), and for a recent oral text from Afghanistan see Schwarzbaum (1982:601); see further "Mother Dies of Fright."

11. Lacy 1967:17–20; Runte 1978:110; Schwarzbaum 1982:594 n. 9.

12. *App.* 15 = Perry 543.

13. Müller 1980:119–120; Massaro 1981:224–225.

14. Petronius 110.6–113.9.

15. For a survey of some opinions see Huber 1990:69–70. Neither Aristides' collection of Milesian tales nor Sisenna's Latin rendering has survived.

16. 111.2: positumque in hypogaeo Graeco more corpus.

17. Boerma 1982:97.

18. Dacier (1780:524–525) mentions the remains of a bas-relief on which the story of the matron and the soldier is recognizable, found among the ruins of Nero's palace in Rome. He gives a description of it from an engraving in a work entitled *Costume des Grecs & des Romains*. Grisebach (1889:37–38) mentions the same bas-relief, citing a facsimile in Dandre Bardon's *Costume des anciens peuples* (Paris, 1772), vol. 1, part 8, plate 12, and adding that he was unable to locate the piece during a stay in Rome. See further Herrmann 1927:55.

19. Trenkner 1958:8, 170–171; Cicu 1986:256.

20. From a literary viewpoint, one can say that Petronius authorizes multiple interpretations of the tale (Slater 1990:108–111). Huber similarly observes that in Petronius's polysemous narrative none of the hearers becomes the authorized judge of the story, so that the reader is free to choose his or her own viewpoint; moreover, the contrary is true in most Latin literary texts of the tale, which avoid plurality in favor of a single, unmistakable meaning (Huber 1990:53–56). See also Galand 1989.

21. Pecere 1975:42–47.

22. posteroque die populus miratus est qua ratione mortuus isset in crucem.

23. Homer *Od.* 8.266–366.

24. Edmunds 1993:35–39.

25. *Vita Aesopi* 129 = Perry 388; cf. Hsr 299.

26. Huber 1990:94–95 n. 2.

27. Dacier 1780:523–525; Herrmann 1927:51–57. Cabaniss (1961) supposes that Phaedrus either invented the tale or versified an actual event; from the accounts of Phaedrus and Petronius the tale passed into world literature and into folklore.

28. Benfey (1859) 1:460; Grisebach 1889. Indian origin as established fact: for example, Liungman 1961:300; Scheiber 1963:149.

29. Bédier 1925:462. Rohde 1877b.

30. Grisebach 1889:36, citing Abel de Rémusat, *Contes chinois* (Paris, 1827), p. ix.

31. Perry 1962:329–330; Schwarzbaum 1979:407–408.

Miller, His Son, and the Ass. *See* Carrying Part of the Load

Misunderstood Words. *See* Hearing-Impaired Persons

Money in the Stick

One man, A, deposits an amount of money with another man, B (or, in more recent versions, he lends money to B). Later when A attempts to collect the money, B declares that he has already returned (or repaid) it. A brings B to court, where he will be obliged to swear an oath that he has returned the money. Before going, B melts down an amount of gold equal to the disputed

money and pours it into a hollow stick. When they meet in court, B enters employing the stick as a walking stick and asks A to hold it for him while he gives his oath. When B then swears that he has returned the money to A, the latter in anger throws down the stick, which breaks, revealing the gold and making B's deception manifest (or the stick is broken in some other way, or the judge perceives the deception). A retrieves his money, and B usually suffers in some way.

AT 961B, *Money in the Stick*, is found as a folktale and legend in Europe and the Orient.[1]

A German text from the early decades of the twentieth century tells how a certain local man once swore that he had returned an amount of money that he had borrowed from another man. He gave the lender his staff to hold while he swore. As he was making his way home, a horse-drawn vehicle struck him and ran over his stick, breaking it into pieces. The money rolled out of the stick onto the street. The man had hidden it in the stick.[2]

According to a West Prussian folktale recounted in the late twentieth century by Hildegard Blaser, there lived in a certain place a very rich man who had inherited his wealth. Living a life of splendor and pleasure, he soon wasted away his entire fortune, whereupon he borrowed an amount of money from an old friend, promising to repay it in one year. When the year had passed and the lender had not gotten his money yet, he demanded it from the borrower, but the latter declared that he had long ago returned it. The lender now sued the borrower, who made the same declaration at city hall. When the borrower was obliged to swear an oath, his walking stick was in the way, and he handed it to the lender, saying once again that the money was in the hands of the lender. Since the borrower had now executed his oath, the judge supposed that all was in order and sent the two men home. The borrower departed in joy because of course he did not have to repay the guilders, but the lender was unhappy since his money had not been restored. As the two men were going down the high steps of the city hall, the borrower tripped on his walking stick and fell down the steps. The stick was broken in two and the guilders fell down the steps, as many guilders as the lender was to have gotten from the borrower. The lender gathered up the guilders and thereby got his money.[3]

The tale has frequently received literary treatment. There is a fine episode in Cervantes' *Don Quixote de la Mancha*, published in 1605, in which Sancho Panza plays the role of the clever judge who sees through the borrower's ruse.[4] An early story that has been overlooked in discussions of *Money in the Stick* is the mediaeval legend of Hamlet, most fully told around A.D. 1200 by Saxo Grammaticus in his *Gesta Danorum*, or *History of the Danes*. One of Hamlet's adventures shows the influence of the folktale. According to Saxo, Amleth was sent by his uncle to the king of Britain accompanied by two of his uncle's men, who secretly bore a letter requesting the monarch to put the youth to death. But Amleth rewrote the letter his companions were carrying and instructed the king rather to execute the youth's two escorts. When the king complied, Amleth pretended to be offended by the executions and exacted from the British king his companions' worth in gold, which he melted down and poured into two hollow sticks. Upon his return to Denmark, his uncle's men asked him where his companions were, whereupon Amleth held up the sticks saying: "Here they

are, both of them." As usual Amleth responded to a query in such a way as to tell the truth and yet not be properly understood, in this case by holding up the wergeld as though it were the men themselves so that most of the onlookers thought his answer was senseless.[5]

In Saxo's story the slain men and the wergeld are identified (escorts = gold), as though Amleth had been entrusted with a deposit or loan that he subsequently must repay. The Danish story and the international tale are therefore quite parallel. The king gives Amleth two escorts (a man deposits gold with another man); Amleth converts the men into wergeld, which he melts down and places inside two sticks (the receiver melts down the gold and places it inside a stick); when the king's men then ask Amleth where the escorts are, Amleth produces the sticks filled with gold, declaring that they are the missing men (when the depositor asks for the return of his gold, the receiver hands him the gold-filled stick, swearing that he has repaid the deposit). The principal elements of the plot are all present except for the exposure of the fraud and the consequent punishment of the debtor with which the folktale often concludes. In the adaptation of the tale to Danish legend the role of the deceitful debtor has been assigned to the protagonist rather than to the antagonist and the ruse has been transvalued from a piece of despicable villainy to a clever trick.

The Milesian Depositor

The earliest text of *Money in the Stick* is found in the *Narrations* of Konon, a Greek mythographer of the late first century B.C. and early first century A.D. His work, consisting of fifty prose retellings of Greek legends, does not survive directly, but we possess a summary of its contents made in the ninth century by the Byzantine scholar Photios.

Konon's thirty-eighth narrative, as summarized by Photios, relates how a man of Miletos, seeing that his homeland was threatened by the Persians, voyaged to Tauromenion in Sicily, deposited his gold with a friend who was a banker, and sailed back home. Subsequently Miletos was in fact made subject to the Persian king but otherwise suffered little, so that the Milesian went back to Tauromenion to recover his deposit. Although the man who had received the money acknowledged its receipt, he maintained that he had already returned it. They argued for a while, and the Milesian summoned the wrongdoer to swear an oath in court. The banker now devised the following trick. Hollowing out a stalk of fennel like a flute, he melted down the deposit and poured it into the stalk. Then he proceeded to court, using the stalk as a walking stick and supporting himself with it on the pretext of being weak in the legs. As he was about to swear his oath he handed the stalk to the Milesian as if asking the man to hold it for him briefly, and then he lifted his hands and swore that he had returned the deposit to the depositor. Greatly distressed and decrying the faithless of men, the Milesian threw down the stalk, which broke, and the sight of the gold therein revealed the ruse of the banker. The man from Miletos got his gold, but the perjurer hanged himself from shame at the reproaches of his fellow citizens.[6]

Archetimos of Erythraie

Another ancient author who narrates *Money in the Stick* is Stobaios, a Greek anthologist of the early fifth century A.D. whose materials are organized by theme. In a chapter on perjury, he remarks on the necessity for good faith among men and on the certainty that perjurers are punished eventually if not immediately. By way of illustration Stobaios tells how a certain Archetimos of the Ionian city of Erythraie was in Tenedos, where he had a hospitable relationship with a man named Kydies. Archetimos had accumulated a large amount of gold that he deposited with Kydies for security, relying on their close friendship. But greed worked an evil plan into the mind of Kydies, and when he was asked to return the money, he refused. The men fell to arguing and finally decided to confirm their positions by oath. Arranging to put off the swearing for several days, Kydies went home and devised a trick. Hollowing out a stalk of fennel he poured all the gold into it. On the appointed day he used the stalk as a support. When he reached the temple Kydies gave Archetimos the stalk to hold until he should complete his oath, and then, lifting his hands, he swore that he had received a deposit from Archetimos and had returned it. Grieved by the words Archetimos threw the stalk on the floor, and the stalk broke, exposing its contents. Archetimos got his gold thanks to the forethought of the gods, while Kydies lost his life. Seeing this, concludes Stobaios, people ought to treat oaths respectfully.[7]

Konon and Stobaios tell essentially the same story. In each case a depositor living in an Ionian city in Asia Minor leaves gold for safekeeping with an islander. When the depositor comes to reclaim his money, the money holder declares that he has already returned it, and when he is obliged to swear an oath to that effect, he attempts to have it both ways—to swear a truthful oath but also to retain the gold for himself, for although the man is manifestly cynical he is not wholly unmindful of divine power. In both legends the perjurer (for so the narrators regard him despite his care to be literally truthful) conceals the gold in a *narthex*, or stalk of giant fennel, precisely as Prometheus does in Greek myth when he smuggled fire out of Olympos to give to mankind.[8] Although the story exemplifies for Stobaios how, with the help of the gods, perjurers inevitably come to a bad end, neither narrator dwells long upon the principal characters after the revelation of the fraud. The principal interest of the story for them, and for us, lies in the dishonest money holder's deception and its surprising exposure.

Lucius Junius Brutus

The device of the gold-filled stick is sometimes found as an independent motif in a traditional story without any connection to the international story of *Money in the Stick*. It is so employed in an interesting way in the Roman legend of Brutus, who according to tradition overthrew the last king of Rome and founded the republic in 509 B.C. Lucius Tarquinius, called Superbus or the Arrogant, had killed the ruler of Rome and made himself king; he also murdered other men including the father of a certain kinsman Lucius Junius Brutus. Fearing for his own life, Brutus played the fool. On one occasion the king dispatched his sons Titus and Arruns to Delphi to consult the oracle of Apollo about a certain matter and sent Brutus along with them for their amusement.

As an offering for Apollo Brutus brought a stick that he had covertly filled with gold. According to some authors, Titus and Arruns laughed at Brutus for offering the god a mere stick that had no value so far as anyone could see; according to other authors, the stick symbolized Brutus's mind, whose dull exterior concealed a splendid interior.[9] Their official business finished, Titus and Arruns concluded by inquiring of the oracle which of them would be the next king of Rome, and the god replied that he who should be the first to kiss his mother would hold supreme authority in Rome. The king's sons drew lots to determine who should be the first to kiss his mother, or agreed to kiss her simultaneously, but Brutus, who alone perceived the god's true meaning, pretended to trip and kissed the earth, mother of all creatures.

In the Roman legend, then, Brutus presents the god with a valuable votive offering that he has disguised as a thing of no value because it is too dangerous for him to venerate the deity openly, or he delivers to the god a metaphoric message (gold-filled stick = Brutus), revealing that within his outer self is an inner self of great value. Evidently pleased by the offering and understanding the message, Apollo responds with a metaphor of his own (mother = earth), revealing in a fashion that only a clever mind can apprehend the precondition that the next ruler of Rome must satisfy.[10] Here the gold-filled stick functions as a secret offering or secret message or both, and it calls forth a secret message in response (Apollo's metaphor) and perhaps a secret offering as well (the rulership of Rome).

The use of the motif of the gold-filled stick in the Brutus legend differs from that in the international tale type of *Money in the Stick* in certain ways that happen to agree with the Amleth legend. In both the Brutus and Amleth legends, the stick is wielded by the protagonist rather than the antagonist. Both heroes employ their gold-filled sticks covertly as metaphors for human beings, Brutus for himself (gold-filled stick = Brutus), Amleth for others (gold-filled sticks = escorts).[11] In both stories the deception is unpunished since it plays the positive role of illustrating the inventiveness of the hero under duress.

The reason for this agreement is that the legends of Brutus and Amleth are themselves genetically related stories, both being developments of a traditional story for which I have suggested the name *The Hero as Fool*, an old migratory legend featuring the murder of the hero's father by the king (or future king) of the land; the hero's stratagem of playing the fool in his own defense; the king's sending the hero and two companions on a mission to a foreign land, the episode in which the motif of the gold-filled stick appears (Brutus and the king's two sons to Delphi/Amleth and the king's two henchmen to Britain); one or more sexually charged episodes involving the confrontation of the hero and a woman (the Lucretia episode in the Brutus legend/the prototypes of the Ophelia and Gertrude episodes in the Amleth legend); and finally the hero's overthrowing the king and his own acclamation as ruler.[12] Since there is no good reason to believe that either legend story borrowed directly from the other, the motif of the gold-filled stick was evidently a feature of the parent story that the Roman and Scandinavian traditions developed somewhat differently.

For another tale involving a deceptive oath see "Trespasser's Defense," and for another tale of a depositor cheated of his money see "Children Play at Hog Killing."

Lit. AT 961B, *Money in the Stick.* Rohde 1876:67. Gaster 1880. Wünsche 1897:48–59. Zachariae 1923–24:78–80. Lewy 1928:83–84. *HDM* 2:478–480. Tubach (1969), no. 3469. Fontenrose 1978:118–119 and response Q92. *EM* 5:963–970.

1. *EM* 5:963–970.
2. Zender 1966:177–178, no. 520.
3. Cammann 1980:67.
4. *Don Quixote* 2.45.
5. *Gesta Danorum* 3.6.16–22 (1:81–83 Olrik & Ræder). See Hansen 1983a:139 and note.
6. *FGH* 26 F 1 (38).
7. 3.28.21.
8. Hesiod *Th.* 567, *WD* 52; Lewy 1928:84 n. 5.
9. The principal sources for the story are the Roman historian Livy, for whom the gold-filled stick is a symbol of Brutus's mind (1.56), and the Greek historian Dionysios of Halicarnassus (4.69.3), for whom it is a secretly valuable offering. Other ancient authorities generally agree with one or the other of these interpretations; see Hansen 1983a:168 n. 16.
10. Hansen 1983a:169 n. 17.
11. Detter 1892:2.
12. For a full discussion see Hansen 1983a:25–35.

Mother Dies of Fright ✍ Secundus the Philosopher

Responding to an assertion that all women are faithless or that his own spouse is exceptionally virtuous, a man decides to test his wife (mother). He arranges for an accomplice to try to seduce her, and when she yields, she is convicted in the presence of her husband (son), which confirms for him the truth of the statement that women are ultimately faithless or at least that his own wife (mother) is no exception to the rule. The woman kills herself or dies from shame, and the man (or his accomplice) is profoundly changed by the experience.

This misogynic story is classified by Aarne-Thompson as AT 823A*, *Mother Dies of Fright When She Learns That She Was About to Commit Incest with Her Son*, the asterisk indicating the provisional status of the type as an international tale.

So in a Jewish legend recounted around A.D. 1000 by Rashi in his commentary on a Talmudic treatise, the wife of Rabbi Meir, Beruriah, once scoffed at the rabbinical saying "Women are fickle," prompting her husband to respond that she herself might someday illustrate the truth of the adage. In order to test her virtue the rabbi instructed one of his students to attempt to seduce her, and after much effort he succeeded. Beruriah committed suicide from shame, and Rabbi Meir fled from his home.[1] According to another version of the legend, recorded in the sixteenth century by Rabbi Gedaliah Ibn Yahya, Beruriah derided the rabbinical saying about the fickleness of women, claiming that she herself was an exception to the rule. Rabbi Meir then asked one of his pupils to test her faithfulness. The disciple urged her to have an affair with him, and she yielded to his overtures. But Rabbi Meir disguised himself and took the place of his student in bed. After he revealed to her his true identity the next morning, Beruriah hanged herself from shame, and Meir himself, overcome with remorse, fled to Babylon.[2]

In a similar legend found in a Turkish text, the first king of the Achaemenian dynasty in Persia, Kay-Qubād, had a wife who was so modest that she could

not tolerate even the mention of men, whom she described as being unclean. Angered by her hypocrisy, her husband wished to test her virtue. So he asked a young and handsome slave to seduce the queen, which the youth succeeded in doing. Having observed their lovemaking from a place of hiding, the king came forth and mockingly rebuked her as a "modest whore." The queen was thus shamed.[3]

Further east, an Indian legend in one of the *Jatakas* tells how the Bodhisattva once was reborn as a learned man into a certain Brahman family. A woman in Benares sent her son to him to learn wisdom, but when the boy returned home without having learned of the vicious character of women, his mother sent him back for additional training. His teacher then instructed the youth to flatter the teacher's mother, an old crone of 120 years, and to report the results back to the teacher. The boy was so successful that the old woman was willing to go to bed with him. When he expressed to her his fear of his master, the old woman urged the boy to kill him, and when the youth said he was unwilling to do so, she said she would do it herself. The boy informed his teacher. The Bodhisattva carved a wooden statue and told the boy to give the old woman an axe, and the old woman, who was blind with age, struck the statue that she thought was her son. From the sound of the wood she perceived that she had been tricked, and when she heard her son asking her what she was doing, she died on the spot from shame. The pupil himself was so affected by the experience that he chose to renounce the world and become a hermit.[4]

Secundus the Silent Philosopher

According to an ancient Greek work of popular philosophy, *The Life of Secundus the Philosopher*, in his boyhood Secundus was sent away to school by his parents, and during this time his father died. The youth often heard it said that every woman was a whore. When he grew up he adopted the habit of a Cynic philosopher, wearing few clothes and letting his hair and beard grow. He returned to his mother's house in Athens and took an apartment, unrecognized by his mother and her servants. In his wish to test the truth of the statement he had heard about women, he bribed one of the maidservants to arrange a meeting with his mother, pretending to be in love with her. The maid persuaded her mistress on his behalf with a promise of fifty pieces of gold. So the philosopher dined with his mother that evening, and after dinner when she expected to have sexual intercourse with him, he merely embraced her as a son might embrace his mother, and went to sleep. At dawn as he was about to depart, she asked him if he had acted thus in order to condemn her, and Secundus, revealing that he was her son, declared that it was wrong for him to defile that part of her from which he was born. His mother could not bear the shame and hanged herself. Secundus, blaming his mother's death on his own words, resolved never again to speak, and abstained from speech until his death. When therefore the Emperor Hadrian came to Athens and wished to converse with the philosopher, Secundus wrote out his own part of the discussion on a tablet.

The main points of contact between the international tale and the Greek story are as follows. (1) Women are said to be fickle or vicious (Secundus hears that all women are whores). (2) The protagonist decides to test the virtue of his own

wife or mother. (3) He has one of his students attempt the seduction of his wife or mother (the disguised Secundus attempts the seduction of his own mother), and (4) the woman proves to be agreeable to his advances. (5) The protagonist thereupon confronts her with her shameful behavior. As a result (6) the mortified woman takes her own life, and (7) the protagonist too is profoundly changed. The story of Secundus clearly reflects the main features of the type.

The Life of Secundus the Philosopher was composed in Greek by an unknown author around in the latter half of the second century A.D.[5] It is therefore the earliest attestation of the tale. The composition was highly esteemed in the Near East and in mediaeval Europe, certainly more than it was in antiquity itself. Versions of the work are found in Syriac, Armenian, Arabic, and Ethiopian. A Latin translation from the Greek was made in the twelfth century, and from it derive many translations into different European vernaculars.

The texts of *Mother Dies of Fright* surveyed here generally agree in presenting, on the male side, a master and a subordinate (usually a teacher and his disciple, but a king and his young slave in the Turkish text), and the variants agree in making the underling the actual seducer. They vary, however, in foregrounding sometimes the master and sometimes the subordinate as the protagonist, so that a shift of emphasis must have occurred in some developments of the narrative. Thus the Jewish legend features a rabbi and a student of whom the rabbi is the focus of interest, the Turkish story features a king and his slave of whom the king is the protagonist, the Indian version features a teacher and his student of whom the student is the more important character, if only marginally, and in the Greek story the person of the teacher is merely implied by the school attended by Secundus, who of course has the role of the student and is the protagonist of his story. From the viewpoint of the international story the Secundus narrative has maximized the role of the student at the expense of that of the teacher.

The fact that the principal male characters in the story are typically a teacher and student makes a good fit with the misogynic proposition, set forth toward the beginning of the narrative and stimulating the protagonist to act, that women are whores (Greek) or fickle (Jewish) or vicious (Indian). The device of introducing a general proposition whose truth a character is provoked to test is found also in other traditional tales. In a Chinese legend from around the sixteenth century a man describes to his wife the extreme eagerness of a recent widow to remarry, prompting the man's wife to declare that few women in fact are like the widow and, in her own case, she would never remarry if her husband should die; her husband presently feigns his own death in order to test her resolve.[6] In the international tale known as *The Golden Ram* a man scrawls in a public place the statement that money is all-powerful, which prompts the local king to test whether the statement is true or not.[7] The Turkish text, however, begins its action with the claim that a particular woman is exceptional in virtue, and the Jewish legend begins with both the misogynic proposition and also the claim that a particular woman is an exception to the rule. But the two devices amount to the same thing, for the assertion that women are not virtuous implies that a genuinely virtuous woman would be exceptional, and the assertion that there is found a woman of true virtue implies that as a rule women cannot be so characterized. What is crucial is the extremity of the claim, which suggests to another character the idea of testing a particular woman of

supposed virtue, a wife or a mother. The intensity of the shock and shame that result from the test is expressed by the extreme reaction of the principals, each of whom generally withdraws from life, the woman via her own death, the man by some form of rejection of normative domestic life: he flees his house and country (Jewish), he becomes a hermit (Indian), he renounces speech (Greek). Secundus's adopting the habit of a Cynic philosopher before he comes to his mother's house appears to be proleptic, anticipating the motif of the protagonist's rejection of the world following the virtue test, although in Secundus's case it is also necessary for the sake of the test that his mother not recognize him.

Of the present texts, the Greek is the mildest and most intellectual, and the Indian certainly the liveliest. The Greek version focuses upon the horror of near incest, while the Indian composition, in which the woman and the seducer are not mother and son, emphasizes the treachery and lustfulness of women in general, which it illustrates comically and grotesquely by the unseemly eagerness of the Bodhisattva's 120-year-old mother to kill her own son in order to have sex with a young man.[8] In contrast to the attention paid in every version to the failings of the mother or wife who is put to the test, little condemnation is accorded the behavior of the son or husband who is willing to use his mother or spouse as an unwitting subject in a test of wontonness.[9] Only Secundus condemns himself for his own role in the test, sentencing himself to a life of silence.

For another notably misogynic tale see "Matron of Ephesus."

Lit. AT 823A*, *Mother Dies of Fright When She Learns That She Was About to Commit Incest with Her Son.* Krappe 1927:181–190. Gaster 1928:108–109. Perry 1964. Schwarzbaum 1982:595–597. Tubach 1969:215, no. 2733.

1. *Avodah Zara* 18b, cited by Gaster 1928:108–109 and Schwarzbaum 1979:410–413 n. 21, 1982:593–595.
2. *Shalshelet Ha-Qabbalah* (Jerusalem, 1962), p. 71, cited by Schwarzbaum 1979:411–412 n. 21, 1982:594 n. 9. Grisebach (1889:26–29) gives a composite account of the two versions of the legend.
3. The Ninth Vezir's story, in *The History of the Forty Vezirs*, trans. by E. J. W. Gibb (London, 1886), p. 390, cited by Schwarzbaum 1979:411 n. 21, 1982:594 n. 9.
4. Krappe 1927:185–186.
5. Perry 1964:1.
6. For the story and its sources see "Matron of Ephesus," redaction B; this misogynic story is so similar to the present tale that the two may be historically related.
7. See "Golden Ram."
8. Krappe 1927:186–187.
9. Hansen 1998:67.

Nothing to Cook ◎ Nothing To Eat

"The bride says she cannot cook. The groom: it doesn't matter since I have nothing to cook."[1]

Aarne-Thompson classify this comic tale provisionally as AT 1464D*, *Nothing to Cook*, citing texts from Finland, upon which they have based their summary, reproduced above. According to Legman, however, the Finnish material

has been expurgated, and behind it lies a slightly risqué joke that is attested in French and Scots literary sources from the sixteenth century onward.[2] If Legman is correct, a more accurate summary of the tale would be the following: "When a man asks his wife whether they should dine or engage in sex, she replies that they should do as he pleases, but their food is not ready." The humor lies in the wife's succinctly dry and lusty reply, offering her husband his choice of food or sex, while pointing out that actually their only option is sex. Although the principals are sometimes presented as newlyweds, they need not be, as in an anonymous ballad found in Robert Burns's collection from around 1800, *The Merry Muses of Caledonia*, under the title "Supper is Na Ready."[3]

> Rosebery to his lady says,
> "My hinnie [honey] and my succour [sugar],
> "O shall we do the thing you ken,
> Or shall we take our supper?"
> *Fal lal, &c.*

> Wi' modest face, sae fu' o' grace,
> Replied the bonny lady:
> "My noble lord, do as ye please,
> "But supper is na ready."
> *Fal lal, &c.*

A Greek Joke

The earliest text of the joke appears in *Philogelos*, a Greek jokebook from late antiquity.[4] "A young man said to his wife, a lusty woman: 'Wife, what should we do, eat or have sex?' She replied: 'Whatever you like. We don't have any bread.' " As in the later French and Scots versions, the punch line is assigned to the wife, but in referring to a lack of food rather than to a meal that is not yet ready to eat, it agrees with the Finnish texts.

Legman points out the similarity between this joke and another ribald joke in *Philogelos*.[5] "A young man, entertaining two old women who were enamored of him, told his servants: 'Serve a drink to whoever wants one, and have sex with whoever wants to.' The old women said: 'We're not thirsty!' " In both jokes the man asks the woman (women) in effect if she would prefer to eat (drink) or engage in sex, and the randy woman (women) expresses with comic indirectness her (their) preference for sex by ruling out food (drink) as an option. The bibulous and/or lusty old crone is an ancient comic stereotype.[6]

Lit. AT 1464D*, *Nothing to Cook*. Legman 1964:219–222; 1971:689–691.

1. Aarne and Thompson 1961:427.
2. Legman 1971:690. Notice the distribution of the roles: the punch line belongs to the groom in the Finnish version but to the bride in the French and Scots versions.
3. Burns 1965:45–46. For the literary history of this joke see Legman 1964:219–222 (= Legman *apud* Burns 1965:171–174), and Legman 1971:689–691.

4. *Phil.* 244.
5. *Phil.* 245. Legman 1964:221.
6. Thierfelder 1968:277.

Ogre Blinded ◎ Odysseus and Polyphemos

Alone (or with a number of companions) a man comes to the dwelling of an ogre, usually a giant. The ogre keeps him (them) in his lair (and eats some of the men). In self-defense the hero, sometimes pretending to be able to cure the ogre's faulty eyesight, destroys the ogre's eyes (his only eye, his one good eye) by means of a spit (boiling liquid, etc.).

Subsequently the hero covers himself (and his companions) with a sheepskin (sheepskins), joins the ogre's sheep, and crawls out of the lair (or they cling or tie themselves to live sheep).

Having escaped from the ogre's dwelling, the hero sometimes mocks the ogre, provoking him to retaliate in some fashion, such as by casting something harmful at the hero or by tossing to the hero a magic ring (or other magic object) that, when the hero puts it on his finger, repeatedly yells "Here I am," thereby guiding the blinded ogre to him; since the ring cannot be removed, the man is obliged to cut (bite) off his finger, after which he escapes, sometimes taking with him the ogre's sheep.

This complex tale of the clever man and the stupid ogre is AT 1137, *The Ogre Blinded (Polyphemos)*, attested in Europe, the Middle East, Northern Africa, and further afield. As usual, most of the oral texts are found in collections made in the nineteenth century since it was in that century that scholarly enthusiasm for the collection of folktales arose, but a scattering of texts embedded in earlier European and Middle Eastern literature is also known.[1] Thus the story appears in Icelandic sagas of various dates and in the mediaeval Turkish romance *Dede Korkut*.[2] Before these, the French Cistercian monk Johannes de Alta Silva (Jean d'Haute-Seille) relates a version in his *Dolopathos*, a collection of tales in Latin prose composed around 1185.[3] Earlier still, *The Arabian Nights* contains two texts of the folktale, one of them forming part of the Third Voyage of Sindbad and so dating perhaps to the ninth century A.D.[4] And earliest of all, of course, Homer recounts the story of Odysseus and Polyphemos in the ninth book of his *Odyssey*, composed around 700 B.C.

According to the tale in *Dolopathos sive de Rege et Septem Sapientibus*, some robbers once learned that a solitary giant, dwelling some twenty miles away from human habitation, possessed a great amount of gold and silver. So they went, a hundred in number, to his dwelling and, since the giant was not at home, carried off as much of his treasure as they could. As they proceeded homeward, however, the giant and nine of his companions came upon them and captured them. The captors divided up the prey, and the hero of the tale and nine other robbers fell to the lot of the giant whom they just had robbed. Their hands were tied behind their backs, and they were driven to his cave. The men offered to ransom themselves, but the giant only mocked them, saying the

only ransom he wanted was human flesh, whereupon he took the plumpest of the robbers, slit his throat, tore him apart, and tossed him into a pot to cook. So it continued until at last it came to the turn of the hero. To save his own life, the robber pretended to be a doctor, promising to heal the giant's eyes if the giant would spare him, for the giant's eyes ached terribly. The giant agreed. So the robber heated on the fire a potion consisting of oil, sulphur, arsenic, and other harmful ingredients, and when it was boiling he poured it on his patient's head. The result was that the giant lost his sight and was considerably injured. The giant cried out and groped around for the robber. Since the only exit was a door that was secured with iron bolts, the robber climbed a ladder to the roof where he clung to a beam for a day and a night, but eventually he came down and meditated escape. The giant had a thousand sheep that he counted each day, keeping one back for himself and letting the rest graze. The robber took the fleece of a slaughtered ram, placed it upon himself, and in the guise of a ram proceeded to exit with the sheep. Seven times the giant tried to keep back that very ram with the intention of eating it, but seven times the hero slipped away, until finally the enraged giant drove the would-be ram out of his cave with a curse. When the hero was safely outside he mocked the giant. Thereupon the giant tossed a gold ring to him as a gift, but when the robber placed it upon his finger, he could not help but shout repeatedly: "Here I am!" As the blind giant now made his way to the robber, the latter, unable to remove the ring, bit off his finger and threw it at the giant.[5]

An Irish narrative collected in the late nineteenth century relates how Finn and his dog Bran came in the course of their adventures to a large cave in which there were a herd of goats and a smoldering fire. They entered and rested themselves, and after a while a one-eyed giant came, bringing a salmon. He instructed Finn to cook it, warning him that if he raised a single blister on the fish the giant would cut off Finn's head. So while the giant slept Finn roasted the salmon on the fire. But when there arose a blister on the salmon, Finn pressed it with his thumb in order to conceal it, and in so doing burnt his thumb, whereupon he put his thumb in his mouth and chewed it, and from that he acquired a knowledge of all things. Acting upon this knowledge he drove the hot spit into the eye of the sleeping giant, blinding him. The giant leapt up and positioned himself at the entrance of the cave, planting one foot on each side of the passageway and roaring out that the man would not leave the place alive. So Finn killed and skinned the largest of the goats, placed the skin on himself, and drove the goats toward the giant, where they exited in single file between his legs. When Finn's goat reached him, the giant took hold of it by its horns, but Finn slipped out of the skin and ran outside. The giant acknowledged that the man had escaped, but said he wished to make him a present. Finn declined to approach him, telling him to place the present on the ground and withdraw, whereupon the giant put a ring on the ground. When Finn placed the ring onto his little finger, it clung too tightly to be removed. And when the giant asked the ring where it was, it cried out: "On Finn's finger." The giant kept asking, and when the ring answered, the giant would spring at Finn, almost catching him. Bran suggested to Finn that he chew on his thumb again. When Finn did so, he knew what to do. Taking the knife with which he had skinned the goat, he cut off his finger and cast it, ring and all, into

a deep bog, so that the giant, pursuing the voice of the ring, leapt into the bog. Then Finn and Bran continued on their way.[6]

Odysseus and Polyphemos

In 1857 Wilhelm Grimm published a modest but pioneering study of Homer's story of Odysseus and Polyphemos and its international analogues, the first of many investigations by folklorists and classicists of this tale. Among the works of Grimm's successors that deserve special mention are Kristoffer Nyrop's discussion, Oskar Hackman's study of well over a hundred texts of the folktale, Frazer's convenient summary of the content of three dozen texts, Denys Page's influential discussion of Homer's storytelling against the background of the folktale tradition, and the systematic comparisons of Homer and folktale by the folklorist Lutz Röhrich and the classicist Justin Glenn.[7]

The Homeric narrative forms part of Odysseus's apologue, his detailed account of the fabulous adventures he has been having in the course of his voyage home from Troy, a string of narratives that he relates to his hosts the Phaiakians, filling books 9–12 of the *Odyssey*. According to Odysseus, he and his companions visited the land of the Kyklopes (Cyclopes), a people who planted no crops, simply harvesting those which happened to grow. Without laws or assemblies they lived in mountain caves, each man ruling his own wife and children and being indifferent to the others. As Odysseus and his companions neared this land in their ship they saw a cave near the sea with a pen for sheep and goats. A giant lived there, alone and lawless. When they reached land, Odysseus took twelve of his best men and a skin of very strong wine, and proceeded to the cave. Since the giant was not at home, they made a meal and waited for him. In time the giant, named Polyphemos, returned with his flocks, driving some of them into the cave, the entrance of which he closed with a huge stone. When he saw Odysseus and his men he asked them who they were, and Odysseus replied that they were Achaians on their way back from Troy; he asked the giant for hospitality and reminded him that Zeus was the avenger of the suppliant. But the giant said that the Kyklopes were stronger than the gods and were indifferent to them. Then the Kyklops grabbed two of Odysseus's men, crushed their heads against the earth, and ate them limb by limb. The helpless onlookers wept. Odysseus considered stabbing him in a fatal place with his sword, but then he remembered that if he should do so, they would all perish in the cave since he and his men would be unable to move the stone that blocked the doorway.

In the morning the giant ate two more of Odysseus's men and drove his sheep out of the cave, closing up the entrance again with the stone. Odysseus now devised a plan of revenge. He took a piece of wood that was lying the cave, sharpened one end of it, hardened it in the fire, and hid it in the dung. His plan was to drive the stake into the giant's eye while he lay asleep. The Kyklops returned, siezed two more men, and prepared his meal. Odysseus offered him the strong wine he had brought. The Kyklops drank it and asked for more, inquiring after Odysseus's name and promising him a gift. Odysseus gave him more wine and told him that his name was Nobody. The Kyklops replied that Nobody's gift would be to be eaten last of all. When he presently

fell into a drunken sleep, Odysseus and his men heated the stake in the fire and plunged it into his eye. The giant hurled the stake away and cried out for the other Kyklopes who lived in nearby caves. Hearing his cries they came and, standing around his cave, asked him whether someone was stealing his sheep or trying to kill him. Polyphemos that Nobody was trying to kill him. The other Kyklopes said that if no one was assaulting him, then he must be sick, in which case he should pray to his father Poseidon. Then they departed.

Odysseus devised a scheme for the escape of himself and his companions. Tying sheep together in groups of threes, he placed a man under each middle sheep, and he himself took the largest ram and lay beneath its belly. At dawn the animals went out to pasture, and Polyphemos felt their backs as they passed by. When they were all out of the cave, Odysseus untied himself and his companions, whereupon they drove the sheep aboard ship and quickly rowed away. Odysseus taunted the Kyklops, who responded by throwing boulders at the ship. Then Odysseus announced that the man who put out his eye was Odysseus, son of Laertes, of Ithaca. The Kyklops recalled a prophecy that a certain Odysseus would someday blind him, but he had expected a bigger and stronger man; he bade Odysseus come to him in order that he might give Odysseus a guest-gift. But Odysseus only taunted him the more, so that Polyphemos prayed to his father Poseidon to bring harm to Odysseus, and Poseidon heard his prayer.[8]

Although Homer's epic narrative and the folktale tradition each contain a number of features that are rare or lacking in the other, the ancient and the modern stories agree closely in their main lines. (a) The hero comes to the lair of an ogre, often a one-eyed giant, (b) who threatens him in one way or another. In self-defense (c) the hero blinds the ogre, so that the ogre can no longer see his intended victim. (d) The man disguises himself as one of the ogre's sheep or goats and (e) escapes in the company of the flock. All scholars agree that all texts featuring this sequence of events must be genetically related.

The question of the precise relationship of the Homeric text to the folktale tradition was first addressed in detail by Wilhelm Grimm, and has provoked much discussion. After surveying his sample of ten texts, Grimm remarked upon their mix of similarity and variation. Although a single plot obviously went through all the versions, each text differed from the others and gave no sign of being a mere imitation or transcription of another. Taken together, the texts logically implied a parent tale. Grimm concluded that the poetic intuition of each people had preserved the basic story, while at the same time each nation had impressed it with the stamp of its own life. He rejected out of hand the view advanced by H. F. von Dietz, who in 1815 had compared the Homeric version with the mediaeval Turkish version and argued for a Turkish original, opining that Homer had learned an Oghuz legend in its ancient form and adapted it imperfectly to his own purposes. Grimm observed merely that this suggestion would not easily gain adherents, which it has not. On the other hand, Grimm argued, if one simply hypothesized that the Greek text belonged to the beginning of the tradition, and derived all the more recent texts from it, other problems arose. For how could one then explain why the Turkish legend and the French *Dolopathos* recount the liberation of the imprisoned hero from the cave of the giant more fully and coherently than Homer does? At the same time, the Turkish and French texts puzzlingly not only lack the Homeric hero's

use of wine to make the ogre drunk before blinding him, a motif that in Grimm's view was so natural that it was hard to understand why it was not retained by other narrators, but they also lack the famous Nobody ruse by means of which Odysseus deceives the giant. In addition to these internal arguments against the derivation of the international tale from the *Odyssey*, Grimm adduced external arguments. Was Homer really known to the Estonians and the Oghuz? Assuming that the Greek poem had reached them, how did the Turkish narrator come by an acquaintance with the story in *Dolopathos*, or the French monk with the Turkish story, since these texts agreed in important details?[9]

On the question of precedence, then, Grimm states the basic case for regarding both the Homeric and the later texts as essentially independent realizations of an international oral tradition of *The Ogre Blinded*, and in this conclusion he has been followed by Hackman, Frazer, Page, Röhrich, Glenn, and most other scholars. The many texts of the folktale that have become available since Grimm have done nothing to undercut his arguments. The majority position acknowledges that a few oral texts show the literary influence of the *Odyssey*, and perhaps it would be surprising if no text did. Additional internal arguments of the kind made by Grimm can be added to the overall argument, and have been, notably that the folktale hero and his companions usually escape by covering themselves with the skins of slaughtered animals, whereas Odysseus and his companions make their escape from the ogre's lair by riding beneath live animals; and that many texts of the folktale follow the escape with an additional incident, the so-called Ring Episode, which is not found as such in Homer.

In sum, the texts of this unusual story show sufficient similarity to one another to justify the conclusion that they are genetically related, but the younger texts cannot simply derive from the *Odyssey* by means of multiple instances of borrowing, for if they did, they would not show so much agreement as a group in features in which they disagree with the ancient Greek story. Nor, with their considerable geographical distribution and temporal spread, can they plausibly be explained by diffusion via any other literary work.

The skeptics, who include among their number van Gennep, Meuli, and Mundy, have for the most part merely stated without counterargument their skepticism or their belief that the later tale most likely springs from Homer, and the few counterarguments that the earlier skeptics offered, such as that the motif of wine may have dropped out in places where wine was uncommon or forbidden, are clearly inadequate to the task.[10] More recently, a different line of argument has been put forth by Detlev Fehling, who holds that the considerable agreement in content in the post-Homeric texts proves only that they have a common source, not that their source is independent of and ultimately older than Homer. For Fehling, it is more probable that the international tradition is subsequent to Homer, having developed from him over time. In his view the legend of Odysseus and Polyphemos was in origin a uniquely Greek story that descended via literary channels to Byzantine times, when it was developed in the West as the tale we find in *Dolopathos* and in the East as the tale of Sindbad in *The Arabian Nights;* and from these two tales the bulk of the more recent texts have descended.[11] Fehling is very vague about this last step: *somehow* the entire modern tradition derives from *Dolopathos* and *The Arabian Nights*. In short, he shares with earlier skeptics a mistrust in the stability of oral narratives

over time, to which he adds his own all but unlimited faith in the literary tradition and in the dependence of the oral tradition upon it.[12] What the skeptics really balk at is the lacuna of over a thousand years that separates the *Odyssey* from the earliest non-Greek text, during which time they expect that an oral tale would undergo radical change or disappear; at the same time, united in their low estimation of oral tradition and their high estimation of the written tradition, they find it improbable that so celebrated a published work as Homer's *Odyssey* could have had so little influence on international oral storytelling.

The question looms unusually and curiously large, perhaps because the story of Odysseus and the Kyklops is so *märchenhaft*, for there is no corresponding controversy about the relationship of the *Odyssey* as a whole to the traditional story that underlies it, *The Homecoming Husband*, a relatively realistic novella that has not attracted nearly so much scholarly attention. Some scholars are under the false impression that very few narratives are known to both ancient and modern traditions; indeed, Fehling talks as though there were only three, quite exceptional folktales that are attested in classical and also in modern tradition—*The Ogre Blinded, The Treasury of Rhampsinitos*, and *Cupid and Psyche*—whereas in fact there are hundreds.[13]

The epic episode begins with a summary ethnography of the Kyklopes. Putting their trust in the gods, the Kyklopes do not plant or plough, since crops of wheat, barley, and grapes grow of themselves, thanks to Zeus's rain. Nor do the Kyklopes have assemblies or shared laws but rather live individually in mountain caves, where each man establishes the laws for his own family and no one cares about the others. Although a luxuriant island lies offshore, home to numerous goats, the Kyklopes have no ships by means of which to reach it, so that the island is uninhabited by them. In short, their agriculture, social organization, and technology are very simple.[14]

Nevertheless, this simple society that entrusts its welfare to the gods strains with apparently conflicting tendencies, for whereas the happy state of their agriculture (or rather lack of it, since their crops grow automatically with no effort on their part) is a familiar and characteristic feature of Greek paradisal traditions such as that of the Golden Age (see "Schlaraffenland"), the Kyklopes are described as being indifferent to one another and basically arrogant, and the specimen Kyklops we actually meet is a cannibalistic pastoralist who boasts that his fellows as a group do not care about the gods, traits that are strikingly at odds with the typically liesurely, joyous, and reverent inhabitants of traditional Greek utopias. Mondi explains this uneasy picture as a Homeric conflation on the one hand of a tradition of a paradisal home in which Zeus settled his old allies and helpers, the Kyklopes, and on the other hand of an ogrous character appropriate to the particular Kyklops Polyphemos in his role as the monster in the present tale.[15] If he is correct, material properly pertaining to the good Kyklopes, as it were, has been attracted into a narrative of the bad Kyklopes because of their identical names and simple culture, so that the incongruity found in the Homeric tale reflects the incongruous nature of the two unlike sorts of Kyklopes that inhabit Greek mythological tradition, the good smiths who forge the thunderweapon for Zeus and the inhospitable pastoralists whom Odysseus encounters on his way home from Troy. Mondi's idea

must remain a conjecture, however, since the supposition of an ancient tradition of a Kyklopean paradise is entirely hypothetical. In any event the dissonance is not entirely without a parallel in modern tradition. In a folktale from the Caucasus the ogre's homeland sports a stream of honey that flows from the shore to the sea, a pleasantry that is common enough in both earnest and comic utopias (see "Schlaraffenland") but seems out of place in a cannibal's front yard; however, it does serve as a kind of bait for hapless travelers, enticing them into the evil land, where they become prey for the ogre.[16]

Although the appellation "Kyklopes" indicates a connection of some kind between the characters in the present adventure and the three mythic Kyklopes represented as being the offspring of Ouranos and Gaia, the two groups appear not to have much in common apart from their singular appearance.[17] Polyphemos claims Poseidon, not Ouranos, as his father, a somewhat surprising connection in view of the fact that Polyphemos and his fellows have no acquaintance with seafaring.[18] Though it is not obvious which group of Kyklopes, if either, has lent its name and aspect to the other, one may notice that the possession of a single eye is functionally of some importance to the story of *The Ogre Blinded* but of no obvious relevance to the mythic makers of the thunderbolt, which perhaps lends weight to such claims of precedence as the Kyklopes in the present story may care to make.

Oddly, Homer does not explicitly say that the Kyklopes are one-eyed, but his narration implies that Polyphemos is monophthalmic, and Kyklopes in later literature were so, even if ancient visual artists portrayed them variously as having from one to three eyes. The poet's not bothering to call attention to Polyphemos's single eye probably indicates only that tale and ogre were well known to his hearers.[19] Doubtless the one-eyed giant who appears in more than half of the modern folktale texts of *The Ogre Blinded* was a traditional character in the ancient story since he was a convenience for the mechanics of the plot, it being easier for a hero to poke out one eye than two.

The most memorable incidents of the epic narrative that do not usually figure in the international folktale are the inebriation of the giant and the Nobody ruse. The hero of the folktale does not ordinarily ply the unsuspecting giant with wine, nor is the element really necessary to Homer's story, since an ogre need not be intoxicated in order to fall deeply asleep. But Homer employs the wine anyway, probably because its use is amusing and perhaps because the Kyklops is thereby better disposed to accept Odysseus's unlikely claim that his name is Nobody.[20] If so, presumably the intoxicating wine and the false name enter the epic story not separately but as linked themes. Polyphemos himself simply declares that Odysseus blinded him after overcoming his mind with wine.[21]

Very exceptionally does the folktale hero mislead the ogre by giving his name falsely as Nobody or the like; rather, the Nobody ruse is the central feature of a different traditional story, a simple narrative told as a folktale or legend in which a human being encounters a supernatural creature and, when asked, gives out his or her name falsely, usually as "Myself." When the human presently does harm to the supernatural being, and the latter cries out, his fellows ask what is the matter, and, hearing an answer such as that "Myself has harmed me," they ignore him, concluding that he is the source of his own dis-

tress.[22] Thus in a British narrative Jock decided to pass the night in a haunted mill. Eventually there entered a roguish man who was three feet high, looked eighty years old, and acted like eighteen. He asked Jock what his name was, and Jock said he was "Mysel' and mysel'." When the intruder became aggressive, Jock scalded his face with a duck he was roasting. The creature cried out in terror, attracting other similar beings to the place who asked him who did it. "Mysel' and mysel'," he explained. "An' if it was yoursel' and yoursel'," they answered, "who can help that?"[23]

The usual view of scholars is that *Myself* (to give the tale a name) and *The Ogre Blinded* are oral tales that were in independent existence before the *Odyssey* and have continued to exist independently after it. In ancient Greek tradition *Myself* was attracted into *The Ogre Blinded*, forming a single story, which is a common phenomenon in oral storytelling. One reason why the two tales otherwise rarely appear together is doubtless because the ogre of *The Ogre Blinded* is most often a loner, whereas *Myself* requires other creatures in the vicinity who care about the ogre, implying a society of ogres of some sort, and indeed the victim in *Myself* is ordinarily a social being such as a dwarf.[24] Homer cleverly has it both ways, treating Polyphemos and his fellows as loners in a loosely knit society of Kyklopes, each family inhabiting its own cave and caring little for the others, while Polyphemos himself lives entirely alone, and the only role the other Kyklopes play in the story is briefly to respond to his cry for help.

Homer has Odysseus give his false name as Nobody (*Outis*) rather than the usual Myself, perhaps because in Greek "nobody" sounds more like Odysseus than "myself" (*autos*) does and so allows a pun-like play on the hero's name, and because in certain clauses "nobody" takes the form (*mê tis*), which makes a virtual pun on a word meaning "cunning intelligence" (*mêtis*), Odysseus's defining trait.[25] To illustrate the apparent wordplay: Polyphemos tells the other Kyklopes that *Outis* (Nobody/Odysseus) is killing him by deceit or force, and they reply that if *me tis* (nobody/cunning) is employing force against him, he must be sick.[26]

Odysseus and his companions blind the sleeping Kyklops by thrusting a stake into his single eye. Similarly in the folktales a spit, stake, or similar implement is the most common means of blinding the ogre and is particularly apt for a victim who has only one eye or one good eye, though it can be employed also against dupes with two good eyes. The next most common method is for the hero to pour boiling liquid onto the ogre's eye or eyes, sometimes on the pretense of improving his failing eyesight.[27] Austin cleverly suggests that the liquid medicine of the folktale is present latently in Homer's narration, first in the form of the wine that Odysseus gives the Kyklops and later in the simile of the smith who "treats" (*pharmasson*), that is, "tempers," an axe or adze by dipping it in water.[28] The captive Greeks then escape from the giant's cave by exiting with his flock, Odysseus clinging to the underside of a ram, his companions each being tied to the underside of several sheep. In the folktales it is far more usual for the hero simply to cover himself with a sheepskin that he finds in the dwelling or procures for himself by flaying a sheep.[29]

A memorable feature that commonly appears in the folktale texts but not in Homer is the episode of the magic ring by means of which the blinded ogre makes one last attempt to get hold of the hero, though a trace of the ruse can

possibly be discerned in Polyphemos's offer of guest-gifts to the departing Odysseus, an offer that the hero wisely ignores in view of the fact that Polyphemos's previous favor was merely his granting to Odysseus the privilege of being eaten last.[30] The poet perhaps chooses to suppress the Ring Episode in its usual form since a talking ring that obliges the hero to cut off his finger would be incongruous in a Greek heroic epic; moreover, the trick might seem too cunning for a rogue so stupid as to fall for the Nobody ruse, not to mention the fact that the presence of so splendid a ring in Kyklopean society with its rudimentary technology might seem to call for an explanation. Actually, the Ring Episode probably does persist, having been transformed into the ogre's curse, which like the magic ring does the hero some harm but fails to prevent his escape. More appropriate to epic than a magic object, the curse also links the Kyklops adventure with the remainder of Odysseus's return by motivating Poseidon's anger at Odysseus and so requiring the eventual reconciliation of Odysseus and the sea god.[31]

In sum, Greek legend labels the lone ogre of the international tale a Kyklops, outfits him with a genealogy (in order to motivate Poseidon), and situates him in a community (to facilitate the Nobody incident), but it lets him remain a loner (for the sake of the principal plot), a shepherd (to enable the hero's characteristic escape), and one-eyed (to facilitate the blinding). The wit of the cunning Greek hero is enhanced by the addition to the narrative of the use of wine (to intoxicate the ogre) and the ruse of the name (to deflect the ogre's helpers), while the meagerness of the ogre's own wit is suggested positively by the simple culture of his society and by his being repeatedly duped, and negatively by the absence of a good ruse of his own such as that of the magic ring. The result is a heightened contrast between the cleverness of the hero and the simplemindedness of the ogre. Finally, the Homeric telling lends playful credibility to the narration by providing naturalistic detail such as the mini-ethnography of the Kyklopes and describing Polyphemos's orderly pastoralism, while, in contrast to the folktale tradition, it de-emphasizes the supernatural, notably by transforming the Ring Episode.

Unlike most other texts of *The Ogre Blinded*, Homer's story is cast as a legend rather than as a folktale, that is, as an allegedly historical event rather than as only an amusing fiction, but the Greek bard hedges, since he does not relate the present story in his own voice but puts it instead into the mouth of Odysseus, thereby placing the responsibility for the veracity of the adventure on a character within the story. An internal narrator may be reliable or he may be a liar, and in fact Odysseus is each of these at different times in the poem; indeed, even in the present story he oscillates between one and the other (he lies twice to Polyphemos, once about his ship, once about his name). Which of these, then, is Odysseus at the moment when he narrates this adventure in the Phaiakian palace? To his internal audience he appears to be a truthful narrator, for King Alkinoos declares: "You don't give us the impression of being one of those deceivers and imposters that the black earth produces so abundantly, men who tell lies without another man's being able to know it."[32] But his external audience (at least in later times when we hear from them) was less generous in its evaluation, for the "apologue to Alkinoos" (*apologos Alkinoou*) became a proverbial tag for nonsense or for an overly long story.[33] Plato's Sokrates,

preparing to relate an incredible tale of his own, assures his interlocutors that it is no "apologue to Alkinoos."[34] And in the preface to antiquity's greatest collection of tall tales, Lucian's *True Stories*, the author traces the history of outrageous travelogues back to Odysseus's apologue, declaring that Odysseus originated this kind of foolishness when he recounted to Alkinoos and company tales of bagged-up winds, one-eyed beings, cannibals, savages, and the rest.

The Polyphemos story was handled in antiquity also by later authors, often in a comic fashion and probably always with an awareness of the Homeric telling. It figured as well in ancient art, especially in vase painting. Some scholars see in these works features of a popular tradition that was independent of Homer, a story that is less suggestive of Homer's version than of the folktale. Whether such a tradition existed is difficult for us to ascertain, however, because the presence of a feature that is absent in Homer need not indicate that a writer or artist drew upon a non-Homeric source, since the feature may be his own innovation or may have been suggested by the particular medium in which he worked. Mondi points out several details in which Euripides' satyr play, *Kyklops*, more closely resembles the modern folktale than it does Homer's text: (1) the ogre cooks his victims, (2) he is blinded with a spit rather than with a stake, (3) and he is ignorant of wine.[35] Certainly Euripides may have borrowed these motifs from a contemporary oral version of *The Ogre Blinded* that was independent of Homer, but surely they are also ideas that might arise in the mind of any competent storyteller who was not concerned primarily to reproduce a famous text.

Similarly, the Greek vase painters treat the Polyphemos episode differently in some respects from Homer's narration.[36] For example, representations on vases of the blinding of Polyphemos differ in how many men assist Odysseus in driving the stake into the giant's eye (in Homer four men help the hero), and Odysseus himself is sometimes in the vanguard, sometimes in the rear, and sometimes not distinguished from his companions (in Homer he is at the far end). Moreover, Homer represents the stake as being twisted vertically down into the victim, who is lying down, whereas the vase painters regularly represent the stake as being driven horizontally into him as he sits propped up against a wall. The instrument of blinding appears usually to be a stake, as one expects, but on occasion it is possibly a spit or spear. Sometimes the vase painters' Polyphemos holds a kantharos, or cup, of wine in his hand, sometimes he does not, and sometimes he grasps at the stake with his other hand, while sometimes he does not. Furthermore, he may be awake or (as in Homer) asleep, and the painters even differ in how many eyes they give him. Does all this mean that the artists drew upon a popular, non-Homeric tradition, or does it mean only that they did not view their mission to be the precise illustration of Homer's text? The medium itself doubtless encouraged a composition featuring an upright Kyklops and a horizontal stake because this arrangement was easier to represent clearly and simply in the space available to the artist. When an artist portrays Polyphemos with a cup of wine in his hand, we may suppose that he is taking the liberty of synoptically incorporating into the scene an earlier moment of the story, reminding us how the victim was made drunk; and when a painter portrays the Kyklops as grasping the stake, we may

assume that he is giving us a proleptic glimpse of the victim's next action, which is to pull the hurtful weapon out of his eye. Although these and other differences from the Homeric story *may* spring from other sources, they seem to fall within the range of variation that one might expect from painters who saw themselves as representing a famous story but not as picturing a scene from Homer's text with the fidelity of a modern book illustrator, whose viewers will have the written text at hand for comparison.[37]

As a mythological narrative, the Polyphemos adventure has been the subject of a succession of wildly different intepretations from antiquity onward. Explanation began anew with Grimm's mid-nineteenth-century monograph on the tale type in which he interpreted the ogre's single eye as the world-eye, that is, as the sun itself, and the contention of the hero and the giant as an allegory of the struggle between different forces of nature. In addition to the sun, the figure of Polyphemos has been seen by different scholars as having been prompted by an actual person, a volcano, a gorilla, a nature spirit, a nightmare, and so on. The history of these speculations is traced by Glenn, who offers his own psychoanalytic interpretation.[38]

Despite the large number of investigations of this folktale both in itself and in its relationship to Homer's story, certain questions seem rarely to have been asked. We know a lot about the content of the narrative but virtually nothing about its employment: what sorts of person told it? why? to whom? in what manner? on what kinds of occasion? The early collectors of oral tales characteristically recorded little information about their informants or the performance of tales, but no one has surveyed the published texts to glean what contextual information they may contain.[39] So when, for example, scholars casually refer to the story of Polyphemos and the other stories in Odysseus's apologue as old sailors' tales or old sea stories, as they frequently do,[40] they really have no grounds for doing so other than that in Homer's *Odyssey* these adventures occur during the hero's voyage home from Troy, a circumstance that does not qualify them as having been sea stories in the sense of traditional oral stories told primarily by, for, or of mariners. It seems likely that several Odyssean stories and motifs such as the bag of winds, the sea terrors Skylla and Charybdis, and the petrified ship do spring from mariners' narratives, but perhaps the only Odyssean story that has been demonstrated actually to be a mariners' story is *The Sailor and the Oar*, which is transmitted at the present day almost exclusively by seamen and their kin (see "Sailor and the Oar").[41] It is quite unlikely that *The Ogre Blinded* is also such a story: only exceptionally does the folktale protagonist arrive at the ogre's dwelling from the sea, and there is nothing in the tale that should appeal to seafolk more than to anyone else.[42] The hero's occasionally traveling by ship is not significant in this regard, being no more than a convenient narrative device for conveying a character to an exotic place where anything may happen, like the use of a spaceship in science fiction.

Lit. AT 1137, *The Ogre Blinded (Polyphemos)*. Grimm 1857. Nyrop 1880–82. Wiedemann 1894. Polívka 1898a. Köhler (1898) 1:181–184. Peschier 1902. Hackman 1904. Dieterich 1905:380–382. Crooke 1908:172–174. Gennep 1908:155–164. BP 3:374–378.

Nippgen 1914. Radermacher 1915:13–16. Settegast 1917. Meuli 1921:65–80. Frazer (1921) 2:404–455. Cook (1964–65) 2:988–1003. Wesselski 1925:217–218. Jax 1930. Germain 1954:55–129. Dawkins 1955:12–24. Page 1955:1–20. Mundy 1956. Dimitrijevic 1958. Comhaire 1958. Mundy 1961. Liungman 1961:265–266. Röhrich 1962. Σπυρι- δάκης 1963. Walsdorff 1965. Faure 1965. Broholm 1966. Röhrich (1967) 2:213–250, 447–460. Schein 1970. Glenn 1971, 1978. Vajda 1971. Matičetov 1972–73. Fry 1977. Calame 1977a, 1977b, 1995:139–173. Fehling 1977:89–97. Knox 1979. Naumann 1979. Mondi 1983. Austin 1983. Imellos 1984. Beekes 1986:235–236. O'Sullivan 1987, 1990. Ashliman, type 1137. Heubeck et al. (1989) 2:19–42. Bertolini 1989:149–152. Edmunds 1993:29–33. Hansen 1997a:449–451.

1. Glenn 1971:135.
2. Icelandic sagas: Hollander 1912; Naumann 1979. Turkish romance: Mundy 1956.
3. Röhrich 1962; Gilleland 1978.
4. Comhaire 1958; Perry 1959.
5. Frazer (1921) 2:405–410; Gilleland 1977:106–109 (includes the Latin text). Frazer slightly mistranslates *Dolopathos* when he has the robber cut off his finger, for according to the original the robber bites it off ("coactus sum ipsum digitum cum anulo dentibus abscidere").
6. Glassie 1985:239–241, no. 109.
7. Nyrop 1880–82; Hackman 1904; Frazer (1921) 2:404–455; Page 1955:1–20; Röhrich 1962, 1967; Glenn 1971. Rhys Carpenter (1946) imaginatively but unpersuasively connects the Polyphemos tale, not with *The Ogre Blinded*, but with AT 301, *The Three Stolen Princesses*, one of the international tales commonly known as *Bear's Son* because its strong hero is sometimes represented as the son of a bear and a human being. The folktale is related to the legend that underlies the Anglo-Saxon epic poem *Beowulf*. For a hint of the tale of *Bear's Son* in the ancient repertory, see "Quest for a Vanished Princess."
8. Homer *Od.* 9.105–542. The story was also treated by other ancient authors, notably by Euripides in his satyr play *Kyklops* (see Seaford 1988:51–59) and by the mythographers Apollodoros *Ep.* 7.4–9 and Hyginus *Fab.* 125. See also *LIMC* 6.1:943–983, esp. nos. 67–138, and 8.1:1011–1019.
9. Grimm 1857:23–24.
10. Skeptics: Gennep 1908:155–164; Meuli 1921:65–70; Mundy 1956. See Glenn 1971: 135–142.
11. Fehling 1977:89–97; cf. O'Sullivan 1987.
12. Holbek 1987:250–257.
13. Fehling 1977.
14. Cf. Austin 1975:143–149.
15. Mondi 1983:22–23, 37.
16. Frazer (1921) 2:448.
17. Hesiod *Th.* 139–146, 501–506.
18. Meuli 1921:65.
19. Page 1955:14–15.
20. Vajda 1971:253; O'Sullivan 1987:12–13.
21. *Od.* 9.515–516.
22. See further Nyrop (1880–82:246–251); Hackman (1904), Group B; Jax (1930); and motif K602, "*Noman.*" Hackman divides his texts into three groups: A, corresponding to *The Ogre Blinded;* B, the *Myself* tale; and C, a tale that features both the blinding of a creature and the Noman/Myself ruse (see note 23 below). Compare also AT 1700, "*I Don't Know,*" a tale not attested in antiquity, in which a man naively thinks that "I-don't-know" is a person's name; and Jones 1994.
23. Briggs (1971) B1:222–224. Curiously, the deceit is also found in a narrative told only among the Finns and neighboring peoples in which the human protagonist blinds the supernatural being, a tale that in content therefore is halfway between the simple *Myself* tale and more complex tale of *The Ogre Blinded*. This is Hackman's Group C. Thus, in a Finnish story a one-eyed goblin lived on a certain farm to which he brought wealth and luck. One Sunday when the farm folk were in church, the goblin asked a hireling what his name was, and the lad said his name was I-Myself, declaring that he was a foundryman of eyes. Since the goblin wished to have a second eye, he allowed himself to be bound to a table, after which the lad poured molten tin onto his eye. The creature fled to the roof with the table on

his back. When the farmer returned and asked the goblin who did it, the goblin replied: "I-Myself," so that the boy was not punished (Hackman 1904:136–137, no. 178).

24. Nyrop 1880–82:251; Röhrich 1962:68.

25. Marót 1958:331; Bergren 1983:48; Peradotto 1990:147–149.

26. *Od.* 9.408–411.

27. Cf. Glenn 1971:164–166.

28. Austin 1983:34 n. 10. Simile of the smith: *Od.* 9.391–393.

29. Cf. Glenn 1971:167–169.

30. Page 1955:19 n. 15; Glenn 1971:177–179.

31. The Greek legend of Meleager furnishes a similar narrative strategy, the epic tradition substituting there a curse for the magic object found in the international folktale (AT 1187, *Meleager*); see Hansen 1997a:452–453.

32. *Od.* 11.362–366.

33. Diogenianos 2.86 = *CPG* 1:210.

34. Plato *Rep.* 614b2.

35. Mondi 1983:36 n. 64. O'Sullivan (1987:17–18) observes that, although Homer never expressly says that Polyphemos eats his guests raw, interpreters of the poem regularly assume that Polyphemos does so.

36. Röhrich 1962:60–68; Mondi 1983:36 n. 64; Snodgrass 1998:89–100.

37. See further Fellmann 1972 in particular, and Lowenstam 1992 and Snodgrass 1998 in general.

38. Glenn 1978; see also Nyrop 1880–82:252–254.

39. A rare example among collectors of *The Ogre Blinded* is Milko Matičetov (1972–73), who describes collecting this and other tales in 1970 from a Slovene-speaking raconteur, Edda Di Lenardo, who had in turn acquired her repertoire of tales from her maternal aunt.

40. For example, Fellmann 1972:34; cf. Vajda 1971:246–247.

41. Bag of winds: Radermacher 1915:18–21; Strömberg 1950; Page 1973:73–78; Hansen 1997a:454–455. Petrified ship: Radermacher 1915:36; Hansen 1997a:455–456.

42. Approach by sea: Röhrich (1967) 2:452–453; Glenn 1971:146.

Ogre Kills His Own Children ◈ Aedon

An ogre (or ogress) plans to kill certain children while they sleep, either to get rid of them or in preparation for eating them. He arranges for his own children to sleep in a certain place in the bed (to wear clothing of a certain color) in order that they may be recognized in the dim light; or they regularly sleep in that place or manner. Learning of the plan (suspecting the plan), however, the intended victims trade places in bed (exchange clothing) with the ogre's children while the latter sleep. Mistaking his own children for the intended victims, the ogre unwittingly kills them in their sleep and does not perceive the error until the following morning.

This tale of the stupid ogre and his clever opponent, AT 1119, *The Ogre Kills His Own Children*, is popular in Europe and Africa as well as among American Blacks and Native Americans. The murderous or cannibalistic ogre devises a plan of killing certain children in the dark while they sleep, expecting to be able to distinguish them from his own children by a particular sign, usually their clothing (often the nightcaps) or their location in bed. When, however, the clothes of the children are subsequently traded or their respective places in the bed are exchanged, the ogre stupidly mistakes his own children for the intended victims, kills them instead, and goes to bed satisfied with his work.

The plot of this *Schreckmärchen* often appears as part of a larger tale. An

early example is Charles Perrault's *Le petit Poucet*, the eighth tale in his *Histoires ou contes du temps passé, avec des moralités*, published in 1697. In Perrault's telling, a woodcutter and his wife had seven young sons, the youngest of whom had been only about the size of a thumb at his birth. Eventually the parents had so little food and money that they brought the children into the woods and deserted them there. The miserable children made their way to a house, which turned out to be the dwelling of an ogre. Taking pity upon them, the ogre's wife took them in and hid them under the bed, but the ogre discovered them and decided to butcher them for himself and several of his ogrous friends to eat. Having talked her husband into postponing the killings, she put the seven boys to bed. Now, in another bed of the same size lay the ogre's seven ogrous daughters, each wearing a gold crown. The youngest brother, fearing that the ogre might regret not having slit the boys' throats earlier, got up in the middle of the night and exchanged the caps that he and his brothers were wearing with the crowns that the girls were wearing. Just as he had foreseen, the ogre awoke, regretting having put off the slaughter. He groped his way into his daughters' room, went to the boys' bed, and passed his hand over their heads. Feeling the crowns and deducing that he had gone to the wrong bed, he went to the girls' bed, felt the boys' caps there, and slit the throats of the seven sleeping children, after which he returned to bed. When the youngest brother heard the ogre snoring, he awakened his brothers, and they all ran away from the house. In the morning the woman discovered her seven daughters with their throats slit. Donning his magic boots, the ogre pursued the children, but the elder six managed to reach their parents' home, and the youngest brother stole the ogre's magic boots and used them to acquire a great amount of wealth.[1]

In the tale of *Der liebste Roland*, collected by the Grimms in 1812 from eighteen-year-old Dorothea Wild, the identity of the children is signaled instead by their relative position in bed. A witch had two daughters, an ugly and bad girl whom she loved, and a beautiful and good girl whom she hated. The former was her own daughter, the latter a stepdaughter. When once the witch's daughter told her mother how she envied a certain apron belonging to her stepsister, the witch promised her she would have it, saying that she would cut off the girl's head as she slept that night, since the girl deserved to die. The witch instructed her daughter to sleep at the far side of the bed. The stepdaughter happened to overhear the conversation, however, and that night, after the daughter had climbed into bed first in order to sleep at the far side near the wall, and had fallen asleep, the stepdaughter gently changed places with her. During the night the old woman crept up to the bed with an ax, felt around for the girl lying at the front of the bed, and chopped off her head. When the witch left, the stepdaughter arose and roused her lover Roland, and the two fled together. Donning her magic boots, the ogress pursued them. The tale continues, with an eventual happy ending for the lovers.[2]

The story of the parent who, intending to kill another's child, unwittingly slays her own, appears twice in ancient Greek tradition, the role of the ogre being assigned in both instances to a female character. As it happens, each legend employs a different one of the two methods of signaling the identity of the

intended victims that are familiar from modern tradition: location in bed and type of bedclothes.

Aedon

In a passage in Homer's *Odyssey*, Penelope alludes in a simile to the nightingale and its offspring. The nightingale (*aedon*), daughter of Pandareus, sings her song during the spring in grief for her dear son Itylos, Zethos's son, whom in her folly she slew with a sword.[3] Penelope goes on to make a comparison with certain aspects of her own situation.

The scholiasts on the passage, citing the mythographer Pherekydes and other, unnamed authorities, give several accounts of Aedon's crime. Putting these together we get more or less the following story.[4] Zethos wed Aedon, daughter of a Milesian named Pandareus, and Zethos's brother Amphion wed Niobe (or Hippomedousa), daughter of Tantalos. In time, however, Aedon became jealous of her sister-in-law Niobe because of the many children she had borne, beginning with her son Amaleus. Aedon herself had borne either only a son, Itylos (or Itys), or only Itylos and a daughter, Neis. Now, the cousins Itylos and Amaleus were being reared together and slept in the same bed. Aedon secretly instructed her son to take the innermost position in bed in order that during the night she might easily dispatch Amaleus. But when the time came Aedon unwittingly slew her own son with her sword. In the end, overcome with suffering, or because of the anger of Zethos or of Zeus, Aedon prayed to be changed into a bird, whereupon Zeus transformed her into a nightingale, in which form she continually mourns for Itylos.[5]

None of the scholiasts explains exactly how it happened that Aedon unwittingly slew Itylos. According to the comments of the Byzantine commentator Eustathios on the same passage, Itylos "forgot or otherwise did not obey" his mother's instructions, but his explanation is so vague and uncertain that Eustathios probably knew no more about the matter than we do, and has only filled in the lacuna between the plot and the murder in a way that seemed to him likely.[6] If Eustathios actually does relay a genuine tradition to us, we can conjecture that the cousins Itylos and Amaleus may have felt such a bond of affection with each other from their shared rearing that Itylos preferred to die rather than to betray his cousin. But if the commentator is merely guessing, then the ancient tradition is lost to us and our only clue is the modern folktale, in which the intended victim overhears the plot and sabotages it by a change of places in bed.

Although there is nothing inconsistent between the Homeric allusion to the nightingale and the later story that has been extracted from the ancient commentators, it is nevertheless unlikely that this really is the story that Penelope has in mind in the nineteenth book of the *Odyssey* since little in it is comparable to her situation. The ancient commentators cite also a different nightingale legend, that of Philomela and her sister Prokne, who was metamorphosed into a nightingale after killing her son Itys, a story that better parallels the plight of Penelope, since she passes her time in lamentation, describes herself as having a divided heart, and fears that she may endanger her son Telemachos.[7]

Themisto

The course of events is clearer, although no less strange, in the legend of Themisto. Athamas, king of Thessaly, wed Ino and begat two sons by her. When he thought that she had perished, he married Themisto, daughter of a nymph, and begat two (or four) sons by her. Later, learning that Ino had not perished but had gone to Parnassos to celebrate the rites of Dionysos, he brought her back but kept her concealed. Presently Themisto learned that Ino had been found and conceived a desire to kill Ino's sons. Not knowing what Ino looked like, Themisto unwittingly took into her confidence a captive slave woman, who was none other than Ino herself, and instructed her to cover Themisto's sons with white bedclothes and Ino's with black. But Ino did the reverse, and Themisto killed her own sons. When she realized what she had done, she killed herself.[8]

The portrayal of Ino in this story is certainly odd, with her mysterious disappearance to celebrate Bacchic rites and her presumed death, followed by her husband's discovering that she was alive, only to reincorporate her into his household as a maidservant for his present wife. Why does she accept this situation? Without additional detail it is difficult for us to make good sense of the events.

The Greek realizations of the story of *The Ogre Kills His Own Children* correspond fairly closely to the folktale tradition in the abstract sequence of events: (1) the plot to murder certain children, (2) who are to be identified by their position in bed or by the color of their nightclothes, (3) the sabotaging of the plot by the exchange of places or clothing, and consequently (4) the murderer's unwittingly murdering his (her) own children. The murderer's motive, jealousy, is among the motives found in modern tradition, as in the tale that Dorothea Wild recounted to the Grimms.

But in other respects the Greek tradition has its own peculiar character. The families of Amphion and Zethos and of Athamas are prominent in northeastern Greek mythological tradition and are the subject of numerous other stories as well, the two brothers being kings of Thebes, and Athamas being king of Thessaly in our story. Both of the present stories, being traditions about certain families in early times, are generically legends rather than folktales, and as a result there is greater realism in their presentation. Accordingly the households in which the action is set are not those of marginal or fabulous characters such as witches or cannibals but of mainstream persons of high status. The king's wife, who plays the role of ogress in each story, is motivated by her jealousy of another woman and the woman's children—Aedon by her jealousy of her fertile sister-in-law, Themisto by her jealousy of her co-wife Ino and Ino's children, rather like the evil stepmother in the Grimms' tale but not at all like the cannibalistic ogre in Perrault's tale. She plans to reduce the perceived threat posed by her affine by doing away with the latter's children. The role of trickster is played in the folktale by the intended victims, but evidently not in the ancient stories, for in the Aedon legend it is (according to Eustathios) Aedon's own son who foils the plot, and in the Themisto legend it is her co-wife Ino, with whom Themisto makes the fatal error of conspiring. That is, the murderer is betrayed by her very co-conspirator. And whereas the folktale ogres, once they perceive that they have slain their own children, may aggressively and

even magically pursue the tricksters, the women of Greek legend turn inward, overcome with remorse for their horrible deed (or they must face the anger of others), and choose to end their own human existence, Aedon by her transformation into a perpetually mourning bird, Themisto by suicide.

Lit. AT 1119, *The Ogre Kills His Own Children*. Köhler (1898) 1:196, 467, 547. BP 1:124–125, 499–501; 4:113–114. Liungman 1961:66–67, 263–264. *EM* 8:268–270. Scherf 1982:224–228, 258–259. Ashliman, type 1119.

 1. In this text *The Ogre Kills His Own Children* is incorporated into a version of AT 327B, *The Dwarf and the Giant*.
 2. Grimm 56.
 3. *Od.* 19.518–523.
 4. On the legend see Forbes Irving 1990:248–249 and Gantz 1993:239–240. Halliday (1963:96) incorrectly reports that in "the version of the *Aedon* story which was used by Euripides in his *Ino* the nightclothes, in Pherecydes the caps, and in a variant given by the scholiast the positions of the children were changed," and the error is repeated by Kurt Ranke in his article on Aedon in *EM* (1:125–127; cf. *EM* 8:269).
 5. Schol. Homer *Od.* 19.518.
 6. Eustathios *Comm. Od.* p. 1875.20.
 7. Russo *apud* Heubeck (1989) 2:100.
 8. Our main source is the Roman mythographer Hyginus (*Fab.* 1 and 4), together with the late poet Nonnos (*Dion.* 9.302–321). Hyginus (*Fab.* 4) credits the story to Euripides' *Ino* (= *TGF*, ed. Nauck, 2d ed., p. 482). For a discussion of this and related legends see Fontenrose 1948:128 and passim; Gantz 1993:177–180.

Ogre Steals the Thunder's Instruments ⁋ Typhon and Zeus

While the thunder god sleeps, the devil (devil's son) creeps up and steals his thunder-making tool, which is a musical instrument, and conceals it in a secure place (e.g., behind many locks). When the god discovers his loss, he sets out, sometimes accompanied by his son, to retrieve it. In the guise of a youth he enters the service of a fisherman, and the two of them catch the devil (devil's son) stealing fish for a wedding (or other celebration); they release him in return for an invitation to the party (or the disguised thunder god enters the service of the devil himself, goes fishing with him, and proves to be extraordinarily strong; or the disguised god and his servant set out and simply arrive by chance at the devil's dwelling).

At his house the devil boasts of the stolen instrument and is induced to display it. But since the devil himself is unable to play it, the youth is given permission to try. Sometimes one of the ogres suspiciously points out that the youth's eyes (fingers) resemble those of the thunder god, but this suspicion is disregarded.[1] When now the youth plays the instrument, it produces a terrible thunderstorm. Thunder and lightning issue from the instrument, causing the dwelling to explode and overcoming the devil and his ogrous guests, who perish or flee. The thunder god, who has resumed his true form, returns to the sky. It rains for a long time, putting an end to the drought that plagued the earth following the theft of the thunder instrument.

Aarne-Thompson classify this story as AT 1148B, *The Ogre Steals the Thunder's*

Instruments (Pipe, Sack, etc.), placing it among tales of the stupid ogre. With its supernatural actors and cosmic implications the story is more properly labeled a myth than a folktale. Texts were collected from Estonians, Finns, and Sami (or Lapps) in the nineteenth and early twentieth centuries; it probably died out as a living story in the later twentieth century.

The narrative falls into two parts: the stealthy theft of the thunder god's instrument, an act that usually is reported in a mere sentence or two, and the retrieval of the instrument by means of cunning, the principal focus of the story, usually consisting in turn of two episodes, one in which the thunder god works as a hireling and one in which he visits the devil's abode. That the story is intended to be humorous is clear in some texts, and the fact that the thunder deity always regains his weapon by duping the devil guarantees that the narrative contains at least one fundamentally humorous element, since trickery, one might argue, is inherently comic. Unfortunately, the documentation made by collectors in the field is too meager to indicate anything about the tone of the story in its telling or reception. I draw here mostly on Estonian tradition, for it has been the most thoroughly studied and the texts are easily available in German translation.[2]

An Estonian text recorded in 1891 tells how in ancient times Pikne ("Thunder") fell asleep and the Devil stole his thunder tools. The Master of the House then drove Pikne out for being so careless. Pikne wandered about seeking work, coming at last to an old cottager and his wife in the forest, who took pity on the poor youth. Since they had no children, they took him in as if he were their own. Once the father went fishing with his foster son. After they had fished a while, the Devil also came in search of fish. As the father was laying his fish in the boat, he found he had caught the Devil. The latter begged for fish for the baptismal ceremony for his baby son, in return for which he invited the two to the ceremony; and father and son agreed. On Sunday the two found the Devil's house and were hospitably received. The son warned his father against eating anything. After the guests had eaten and drunk, they brought out musical instruments. The Devil's son looked at the fisherman's foster son and said, "Father, that's the thunder lad!" but his father chided him for talking nonsense, saying that he was only the son of the fisherman. Then the Devil told his guests that he had another musical instrument from their grandparents' days; he would fetch it from the bottom of the sea, and then everyone, young and old, could frolic about. When the instrument was brought, the old Devil tried blowing in it, but no sound came out. Everyone else tried with the same result. The fisherman's foster son asked his father to request the instrument and then pass it to him. With some hesitation they gave the instrument to the man, who handed it to his son. The son instructed his father to stand behind him. Then the young man blew once into his thunder trumpet, blowing everything away. The father was left alone in a bog. Everything else had disappeared, including the Devil and Pikne.[3] According to Oskar Loorits, the idea that the Devil hides in the water from thunder is a widespread idea in Estonian tradition, which is why the Devil appears in the sea in this text and why he hides the thunder instrument at the bottom of the sea.[4]

According to another Estonian text, dated 1910, in ancient times the devils stole the thunder instrument from heaven and slit open the rain bag, where-

upon the waters followed the devils to the sea. For seven years the Devil possessed the thunder instrument, and there was a great drought on earth, so that everyone was hungry and thirsty, both humans and animals. Now, there was a beggar on the streets seeking alms, and a youth came to him saying: "Let's go to the christening-feast of the Devil's mother." The beggar was hesitant, but the youth explained that they were playing thunder instruments there, and that he should say: "Give the instruments to my boy here, since he may know how to play them." So they went, and they were well received. There were many devils, and they were beginning to play the thunder instruments. So the beggar asked: "Please let my boy have a try, too, on the chance that he can play." They gave them to him, and he began to play like an apprentice: first softly and then gradually louder and louder. The Devil told him: "Softly, softly, the child's mother is frightened!" But then he gave a great blast, after which there was nothing left of the Devil except for blue dust.[5]

In an Estonian text recorded sometime before 1873, Lightning fell asleep, and during his slumber the evil spirits got hold of the thunder horn with which he thundered. They went happily away to celebrate a wedding, knowing full well that they had no need to fear Lightning's thunder since the thunder horn was in their possession. Then Lightning awoke and straightaway missed his thunder horn. He departed with a companion to go in search of it. Finally he arrived unrecognized at the wedding party of the evil spirits and asked them to show him the horn. One of the celebrants, however, warned the others not to hand over the horn, saying: "That is Lightning himself, for I recognize him by his red eyes." Lightning's companion grabbed the man with the horn and held him fast until Lightning took the horn. Then Lightning blew the horn so frightfully that everyone present, except for his companion, was thundered to dust.[6]

According to different Finnish versions the Devil robbed the thunder god Ukkonen or Jumala ("God") in his sleep, taking his thunder tools, a musical instrument. Recognizing immediately who the thief was, the god disguised himself as a human and went to work for the Devil as a hireling. The two went fishing, where the youth proved to be extraordinarily strong, prompting the Devil to boast that he too once accomplished a great deed, the theft of the thunder instruments. The youth induced him to fetch the thunder tools from their place of security. Since the Devil did not know how to employ them, the youth was allowed to try. He played softly and poorly at first but then louder and better. The Devil asked him to stop, but he continued playing until the Devil's children and cave were destroyed, and the Devil himself was overcome.[7]

The Finnish and Estonian traditions are quite close, the major difference being in the fishing episode that leads to the climactic scene in the ogre's house. In the Estonian texts the god works for a human fisherman, they catch the Devil stealing fish, and in exchange for releasing him they get an invitation to a party at his house, whereas in the Finnish texts the god works for a fisherman who is the Devil himself, and fishing provides an opportunity for the god to display his superhuman strength, prompting the Devil to boast of his own doings, which leads to the scene in the Devil's house.

The Sami version differs from Finno-Estonian tradition in that it is the thunder god himself who is taken. No rain fell while the thunder god Termes was held prisoner in a cave by the mountain giant Jettanas, so that the earth suf-

fered from drought. But once while the giant was asleep, a servant of the thunder god crept into the cave and cut the bonds that held his master, freeing him. The thunder god then rose up to the clouds and for a long time produced thunder, lightning, and rain.[8]

The narrative role of the thunder god in the Sami tradition corresponds to that of the thunder instrument in the Finno-Estonian tradition: the theft and concealment of the thunder god (or his instrument) produces cosmic drought, and the subsequent liberation brings about the resumption of rain. Though both the Finno-Estonian and the Sami traditions feature the ruse of the robbing of a character while he sleeps, the ruse appears in different episodes of the story, being attached in the former tradition to the first episode, in which the victim is the sleeping thunder god, and in the latter tradition to the final episode, in which the victim is the slumbering ogre. All the texts imply, and many of them mention, that the earth experiences a drought while the thunder god lacks his storm equipment. As a theme the cessation of a cosmic function attending the inactivity or absence of a deity is familiar from a number of different mythological stories, including very early texts. In ancient Greek tradition, for example, Sisyphos fettered Thanatos ("Death"), after which humans ceased to die (see "Smith and the Devil"); and when Demeter absented herself from the other Olympians, mourning the loss of her daughter, she caused agriculture to come to a halt.[9] The theme of the absent deity was particularly common in Hittite mythology, and interesting modern examples are found in Finnish, Mordvin, and Belorussian songs.[10]

Thor and Thrym

Already in 1858, upon the first publication of an Estonian text of the present tale type, Jacob Grimm observed that it resembled the well-known Scandinavian myth of the theft and retrieval of Thor's hammer, best known from the þrymskviða in *Elder Edda*.[11] According to this poem, which dates to the ninth century or earlier, Thor awoke one day to find that his hammer Mjöllnir had been stolen. He informed Loki, who borrowed a coat of feathers from Freyja and flew to the home of Thrym, king of the giants. Thrym acknowledged that he had taken the hammer, which was now hidden eight leagues deep within the earth, and said he would return it only if he should be given Freyja as wife. When Freyja angrily rejected the suggestion that she don bridal clothes for Thrym, Thor was dressed as Freyja and Loki as her handmaid, and the two of them proceeded to Thrym's house. The supposed bride ate huge portions of meat and drank a great amount of mead, provoking Thrym to comment that he had never seen a bride eat or drink so much, to which Loki responded that in her longing for Giantland Freyja had been fasting for eight days. When the giant lifted the bride's veil for a kiss, he asked why Freyja's eyes looked so fierce, and Loki responded that in her longing for Giantland Freyja has remained awake for eight days. Then the groom instructed that the hammer Mjöllnir be brought in order to consecrate the bride and that it be placed upon the bride's lap. But as soon as Thor got hold of his hammer, he laid low Thrym and his followers.

The mediaeval Scandinavian text agrees in the following ways with the basic

story of *The Ogre Steals the Thunder's Instruments* as it is found in Finno-Estonian tradition: (a) while the thunder god sleeps, (b) an ogre steals his thunder instrument and hides it away; (c) the god sets out in disguise to retrieve it, (d) regains it by cunning, and (e) immediately employs it, destroying the ogre. Both traditions agree that thunder is produced by a portable instrument belonging to the thunder god, a cosmic version of an ordinary tool in common use among humans, a hammer in mediaeval Scandinavian myth and a musical instrument in Finno-Estonian oral narrative. In addition, the two traditions agree in a number of smaller details: the disguised god is accompanied by a helper, the climactic event at the ogre's house is a wedding party, and a suspicious ogre comments on a physical feature of the disguised god but his observation is explained away.[12] The extensive agreement between the mediaeval and the modern texts clearly indicates that they are variations of the same story. This story must be at least as old as its oldest witness, þrymskviða.[13]

No one has discovered the story in ancient literature; indeed, Waldemar Liungman declares that such thefts from powers of nature are unknown to ancient literature.[14] But in fact the story is found in Greek myth as an event that took place in the early days of the cosmos during the conflict of the thunder god Zeus and his enemy, Typhon or Typhoeus.

Zeus and Typhon

According to a myth recounted in the fifth century A.D. by the Greco-Egyptian poet Nonnos of Panopolis in his epic poem about Dionysos, Zeus hid his thunderbolts in a cave while he went to bed with Plouto. There the thunderbolts gave off smoke and heated the underground waters. The monstrous giant Typhoeus, tipped off by his mother Gaia ("Earth"), stole Zeus's fiery tools and concealed them in a cave of his own. Then he went on a rampage, causing all manner of destruction on earth and the heavens, eventually trying to wield the heavy thunderbolts himself with his own two hundred hands, though without success. Taking Eros and Kadmos as accomplices, Zeus devised a plan for retrieving his weapons, fearing that otherwise the monster would replace him as the lord of the universe. He disguised the mortal Kadmos as a herdsman, outfitting him with appropriate clothes and a reed pipe, a shepherd's hut, and animals contributed by Pan, and told him to play for Typhoeus. As a reward he promised to give him Harmonia to wife. He instructed Eros to shoot the giant with one of his arrows in order to instill in him a passion for Kadmos's music. Then Zeus left. Attracted to the sound of the pipe, Typhoeus left Zeus's weapons in the cave in the care of his mother, Gaia, as he sought out the source of the music. When the monstrous giant came upon the disguised Kadmos, the piper recoiled in fear, but Typhoeus declared that he who had encountered Zeus would hardly pursue a mere mortal, and that he who had carried off lightning would hardly carry off panpipes. The herdsman could keep his pipe, for he himself had an instrument of his own, a self-playing Olympian one. No doubt Zeus could use a shepherd's pipe, since he now sat quietly without thunder or clouds! But he himself had no use for a reed pipe, since he could make thunderous noises among the clouds.

Typhoeus now proposed that he and the herdsman have a friendly match, the

herdsman playing his pipe and Typhoeus crashing his thunderbolts. As payment for his song, Typhoeus promised to take the herdsman with him to Olympos when he replaced Zeus on his throne, and to give him Athena to wife—or any other goddess except Hera, whom he himself claimed, for now that Zeus was weaponless, Typhoeus intended to make a victor's journey to Olympos. The disguised Kadmos, seeing that the giant had been seduced by the sound of his pipe, said he would play a victory hymn to Typhoeus on his lyre if only he could get hold of the sinews he needed for strings. Typhoeus rushed back to his cave, fetched Zeus's sinews (they had fallen to the ground during his battle with Typhoeus), and gave them to Kadmos. Kadmos hid the sinews in a cave and continued to play for the giant on his pipe. As the giant listened entranced, Zeus crept silently into the cave and retrieved his thunderbolts. Kadmos was concealed in a cloud (= made invisible) by Zeus and stopped playing, whereupon Typhoeus rushed furiously back to his cave to look for Zeus's thunder and lightning, which of course were now gone. Typhoeus went on another rampage, prompting the gods, except for Zeus, to flee. The giant challenged Zeus to battle. God and monster joined battle, for which the stake was heaven. After a long and difficult fight, Zeus overcame the giant with his thunderbolts, lightning, and rain, laying him low. Then he lifted the cloud of invisibility from Kadmos, promised to help celebrate his wedding, and, as the other gods returned to Olympos, departed to celebrate his own victory.[15]

The Greek myth agrees with the basic story as it is found in Scandinavian and Finno-Estonian sources: (a) while the thunder god sleeps, (b) an ogre steals his thunder instrument and hides it away; (c) in order to retrieve it, the god disguises himself or an accomplice, (d) gets hold of it by cunning, and immediately (e) employs it to destroy the ogre. In addition, the Greek myth agrees with the later tradition in the god's employment of an accomplice and in the hint of a wedding party at the ogre's house, which can be seen in Typhon's own imminent plans to claim Hera as wife and in his promise to reward Kadmos with a goddess as wife. It is notable moreover that Zeus's potency is virtually identified with a musical instrument as in the Finno-Estonian tradition, a feature to which I shall return presently. These correspondences of structure and content imply that the ancient Greek myth is a realization of the same migratory story as that attested in Scandinavia during the Middle Ages and in parts of Europe in our own century, for it is scarcely imaginable that the several Northern traditions derive somehow from Nonnos's diffuse, exotic, and little-known narrative, while at the same time the myths of the theft of the thunder weapon are too similar in their essential and incidental motifs for us to suppose that they might have arisen independently of one another.

Several elements of Nonnos's narrative are not handled clearly. The intertwined loss and retrieval of both the sinews and the thunderbolts of the god is confusing, especially since Nonnos does not actually narrate the episode in which Zeus loses his sinews to Typhon, mentioning the incident only by way of explanation at the point at which Kadmos manages to effect their return. And for all his lack of sinews Zeus acts in no way disabled, nor is he ever said to restore his sinews to his body after they are retrieved. Probably we have a doublet here, since the loss of either thunderbolts or sinews would be sufficient to render the thunder god impotent. Although Nonnos acknowledges both ver-

sions of the story, he foregrounds the thunderbolt version, detailing its loss and retrieval, and plays down the sinew version, whose loss he merely alludes to and whose restoration to Zeus's body he does not bother to report. In the composite version that Nonnos gives, then, Typhon has gotten Zeus's sinews in an earlier combat and subsequently steals Zeus's thunder weapons by stealth; later Kadmos induces Typhon to hand over the sinews, after which Zeus retrieves his thunderbolts by stealth.

The myth of the loss of Zeus's sinews is also related by the mythographer Apollodoros, who tells how in the early days of the world Ge ("Earth") mated with Tartaros, producing Typhon, an aggressive monster of prodigious size. When the rest of the gods fled in fear to Egypt, Zeus grappled with the monster and wounded him, but Typhon overcame Zeus and severed the sinews of his hands and feet. He placed the disabled god in the Korykian cave in Cilicia, hiding the deity's sinews there in a bearskin and leaving the dragon Delphyne as guard. But Hermes and Aigipan ("Goat-Pan") stole the god's sinews back—the mythographer does not say how—and covertly refitted them to Zeus, whereupon Zeus, having regained his strength, suddenly appeared in the heavens riding a chariot and pelting Typhon with thunderbolts. Typhon fled to Mount Nysa, where the Moirai ("Fates") deceived him into tasting the "ephemeral fruits," telling him falsely that he would thereby be strengthened. Finally Zeus overcame the monster by throwing Mount Aetna on top of him.[16]

In the Greek myth, then, Zeus's potency can reside either in his thunder weapon, as in Finno-Estonian and old Norse tradition, or in his sinews, inasmuch as when he is deprived of either one he is impotent as a thunder god. Apollodoros's text is interesting not only because Typhon takes Zeus's sinews and not his thunderbolt but also because he carries off the thunder god himself, as in the Sami text. Accordingly, both the ancient and the modern tellings vary between the taking of the thunder god or his instrument, either of which brings cosmic thundering to a halt, and the ancient tradition varies additionally between the theft of the god's instrument or his sinews, each of which effectively renders the thunder god powerless.

In his poem *On Fishing* the second-century epic poet Oppian alludes to another version of the myth. Hermes' son, Pan, luring Typhon with a banquet of fish, induced the giant to come from out of his pit to the shore of the sea, where he was then destroyed by thunderbolts and lightning.[17] Functionally the ruse of the fish feast is a variant of the ruse of the ephemeral fruits, each being a kind of deceptive food to which Typhon succumbs when Zeus's allies set him up for Zeus to finish him off. Thematically, however, the fish as bait very much resembles the episode in the modern Estonian narrative in which the Devil is lured out of the sea by a catch of fresh fish that he desires for a feast, coming thereby into the power of the thunder god's ally, a fisherman; and the fish banquet itself as the site of the destruction of Typhon resembles the next episode in the Estonian story, the Devil's fish feast, when the Devil is destroyed.

The mythographers Nonnos and Apollodoros agree that Typhon hides his booty in a cave, entrusting it to the care of a female ally, Gaia or Delphyne, and that the thunder god is aided by helpers of his own, either Kadmos, Eros, and Pan (Nonnos) or Hermes and Goat-Pan (Apollodoros). The two sets of helpers are quite similar in that the goat-god Pan appears in both versions, and Kad-

mos in his disguise as a shepherd and Hermes as the god of shepherds are presumably variants of the same figure. Nonnos explains at length the deception that Kadmos executes (first, he induces the ogre to hand over the god's sinews by the promise of wondrous music, and, second, he diverts the ogre's attention by means of music, allowing the god to steal back his weapons); Apollodoros does not relate the ruse employed in the version known to him, but doubtless the story entailed a similar creeping into the ogre's cave, for that is where the thunder god and his sinews were stored in Apollodoros's version. The mythographer goes on to relate a second deception of the stupid ogre, this one involving the mysterious ephemeral fruits that presumably have the ironic effect of weakening rather than strengthening the eater. This ruse does not appear in Nonnos's version, but the role of Eros there is somewhat comparable in that Eros weakens the ogre by implanting in him an infatuation, or hunger, for music. So Nonnos's and Apollodoros's versions of the myth differ in certain details, their main difference being that the former foregrounds the loss of Zeus's thunderbolts, the latter the loss of his sinews.

Intriguingly, Nonnos associates both the thunderbolts and the sinews with music making. With regard to the former, he has Typhon make an extended comparison between Kadmos's pipes and Zeus's thunderbolts in which the giant denies that he has any design on the shepherd's pipes since he himself possesses thunderbolts, which he calls a "self-playing instrument" (*organon autoboêton*), and suggests sarcastically that the pipes should be given to Zeus, who is incapable of making any noise at all now that he is deprived of his thunder-maker.[18] This speech pointedly compares Zeus's thunderbolts with a shepherd's pipe, treating them as functionally similar tools, both being noisemakers that serve to delight their possessors, except that the thunder tool is the more desirable of the two since it is also a powerful cosmic weapon. And when Typhon proposes to the herdsman that they engage in a friendly match, the shepherd playing his pipe and Typhon sounding his thunderbolts, he is expressly treating the two implements as rival musical instruments. The parallel Finno-Estonian tradition shows that the treatment of the thunder weapon as a musical instrument in Nonnos's poem is not a mere poetic conceit. In the other case, that of the sinews, the identification of the god's sinews with music making is virtually complete. Kadmos turns the topic from wind instrument to string instrument, hinting that he needs sinews for lyre strings in order to play.[19] Typhon promptly fetches Zeus's sinews from his cave and hands them over to the disguised Kadmos in the expectation that he will be able to produce music with them, just as in Finno-Estonian texts of *The Ogre Steals the Thunder's Instruments* the ogre fetches the god's thunder instrument and hands it to the disguised god on the chance that he will be able to play it. In all cases the stupid ogre wants to hear music but lacks competence to play the musical instrument himself, being a rude and simple being who has little understanding of the fine, cosmic instrument he briefly possesses.

The Storm God and Illuyankas

As has long been noticed, a story very similar in its outline to that of the loss of Zeus's sinews is found already in one of the two surviving versions of the

Hittite myth of Illuyankas, which dates to at least the second millennium B.C. The Storm God was defeated by the Serpent, who took his heart and eyes, after which the god was afraid of the Serpent. So the Storm God wed the daughter of a poor man and begot a son, and when the son grew up, he married the Serpent's daughter. Before the youth set out for the house of his bride, the Storm God instructed him to demand his heart and eyes as bride-price. The youth did so, acquired them, and returned them to his father. As soon as the Storm God was whole again, he began to do battle against the Serpent at sea. Seeing this, the Storm God's son told his father not to spare him either, so that the god killed his own son as well as the Serpent.[20] The copies of the Hittite text that we possess date to the New Kingdom (ca. 1500–1190 B.C.), but their archaic language suggests that the narratives themselves go back to the Old Hittite period (ca. 1750–1500), and the stories themselves are thought to have been borrowed from the Hattians, an indigenous people of Central Anatolia.[21]

This brief narrative agrees with the myth of Zeus and Typhon (for simplicity of comparison I combine the versions of Apollodoros and Nonnos) in that (a) a serpentine ogre defeats the thunder god in combat (b) and takes from him some components of his body (heart and eyes/sinews). Temporarily defeated (c) the thunder god dispatches an ally to retrieve his missing body parts, and (d) the ally succeeds in inducing the ogre to hand the missing parts over to him. (e) He in turn gives them back to the thunder god, (f) who promptly attacks the ogre, defeating him. Interestingly, the incidental theme of the wedding at the ogre's house is observable in the marriage of the Storm God's son and the dragon's daughter, when the god's accomplice manages to get his hands on the lost components. And, as in Finno-Estonian tradition at least, the ogre's abode is in the sea. A drought is implied, and indeed the Hittite text is part of a ritual that may have to do with encouraging rainfall. Its most interesting difference from the other texts that we have examined lies in the decision of the thunder god's accomplice to perish with the ogre, into whose family he has married and with which he manifestly feels a bond of kinship.

It is of course tempting to see an evolution from Hittite myth to Greek myth to Scandinavian myth to modern oral story, the primitive theft of the thunder god's organs generating as a variant the theft of his thunder tool, and the organs and the thunder tool developing somehow an association with musical instruments. In such a case, the Greek myth did not borrow from an early form of *The Ogre Steals the Thunder's Instruments* but rather was itself an ancient antecedent. But the texts at our disposal are so few and may well be so unrepresentative of the life history of the type that a developmental reconstruction of the international story should be resisted. The story was probably known to many ancient and mediaeval peoples, in which case it is merely fortuitous that we know something of the content of the Hittite, Greek, and Scandinavian traditions at certain periods of time. In any event the notion of a simple, unilineal development even from Greek myth to Norse myth to Finno-Estonian myth would be difficult to argue, since the ancient and the modern stories show significant features—such as the stolen object conceived of as a musical instrument—that are absent in the hypothetical intermediary as we have it. Nonnos's text stands more or less in the center of the tradition as it is known to us, combining in a single, occasionally confusing narrative the theft of the god's body part (as in

Hittite myth), the theft of his thunder weapon (as in mediaeval and modern myth), and the stolen object as musical instrument (as in modern myth).

Lit. AT 1148B, *The Ogre Steals the Thunder's Instruments (Pipe, Sack, etc.).* Olrik 1905:140–146; 1906. Krohn 1922:202–207; 1931:122–128. Loorits 1932; 1951:22–27. Vries 1933:99–124. Balys 1939:206–209. Anderson 1940. Liungman 1961:267. Rooth 1961:56–59. *EM* 3:763–764. Hansen 1995a.

1. This motif (Z18.1, *What makes your ears so big?*) is otherwise familiar from the formulaic conversation between the heroine and the disguised wolf in the tale of Little Red Riding Hood (AT 333, *The Glutton*), in which the heroine successively exclaims upon the big eyes (mouth, teeth, etc.) of her supposed grandmother and the disguised wolf replies, "The better to see you with" (etc.); see further Dundes 1989.
2. Loorits 1932; Anderson 1940.
3. Loorits 1932:75–76, no. 9.
4. Loorits 1932:100.
5. Loorits 1932:77–78, no. 11A.
6. Loorits 1932:80, no. 13A.
7. Krohn 1931:123; Balys 1939:207.
8. Olrik 1906.
9. *Homeric Hymn to Demeter* 302–313; see further Richardson 1974:258–260.
10. Hittite myth: Hoffner 1990. Modern songs: Oinas 1983, 1993.
11. Loorits 1932:51–52.
12. Further, in both traditions the invitation to the wedding party is part of an exchange. In the modern myth the hero receives an invitation to the ogre's wedding party in return for releasing the ogre from his fishing net, and in the mediaeval myth the hero agrees to go to the ogre's wedding party in return for his stolen property.
13. See also Grundtvig et al. (1853) 1:1–7 for the Danish ballad "Thord af Havsgaard." On the old and widespread conception of thunder and lightning as stones or axes that strike the earth during thunderstorms, see Blinkenberg 1987.
14. Liungman 1961:267.
15. *Dionysiaca* 1.145–2.712. On the Greek myth see Fontenrose 1959:70–93 and passim; Vian 1960; West 1966:391–392; Gantz 1993:50–51. Nonnos's account is the only version of the conflict of Zeus and Typhon in which Zeus's thunderbolts are stolen. Except for a passing reference by Walter Burkert in a review of *EM* (1984:548), classical scholarship makes no mention of the Finno-Estonian myth.
16. Apollodoros *Bibl.* 1.6.3.
17. *Hal.* 15–25.
18. 1.427–438.
19. The use of a defeated opponent's sinews as lyre strings is perhaps an Egyptian motif, for in his essay on Egyptian mythology, Plutarch mentions an Egyptian mythical tradition according to which Hermes (= Thoth) removed Typhon's (= Seth's) sinews and employed them as strings for his lyre (*Mor.* 373). Nonnos himself was an Egyptian or Greco-Egyptian from Panopolis in Egypt.
20. Hoffner 1990:13–14. See further Porzig 1930; Fontenrose 1959:121–125, 162; Vian 1960:28–31; and Burkert 1979:5–10. Fontenrose believes that in the myth of Zeus and Typhon the thunderbolt version is a later development of the sinew version; Vian argues that the myth in this form first came to Greece in the Hellenistic period.
21. Hoffner 1990:9–11.

Old Man and Death

An old man who is weary from carrying a load calls upon Death. But when Death actually appears, asking what he desires, the man asks Death only to help him with his load.

This little tale, illustrating how tenaciously a human being may cling to life, is AT 845, *The Old Man and Death*. Exhausted from his years and the burden he bears, an old man cries out for Death to come, but when the opportunity to die actually presents itself he pretends instead that he has summoned Death merely to help him with the immediate load he is carrying.

In a version known to an elderly couple living in New York and recounted in Yiddish to their son in the 1940s, a very old man was once carrying some faggots home. He was tired, the sun was hot, and his load grew so heavy that he set it down and sat in the shade of a tree to rest. When the time came to resume his journey, he felt too tired—tired of work and tired of life. "O Death, come quickly!" he said. Instantly the Angel of Death stood there, scythe in hand, saying: "You called me. What can I do for you?" The old man stood up nimbly. "Just help me get this bundle of faggots up onto my back, so that I can get on home," he answered.[1] The narrators had learned the tale some sixty years earlier in Minsk, Russia. The collector believed that the tale was of Russian folk origin and speculated that his parents had learned it from a grammar-school text.

He is probably correct about the schoolbook. Although attested in the United States and in an area stretching from Europe to India, the tale has been collected only sporadically from oral narrators, a pattern that suggests, as with most other Aesopic fables, that the tale does not have deep and secure roots in oral storytelling but enters oral tradition here and there mostly from retellings of the ancient fable in printed works such as schoolbooks and popular anthologies and from sermons.[2]

A Greek Tale

The tale is first found in full in Recension I (also called Augustana) and Recension II (also called Vindobonensis) of the anonymous collections of Aesopic fables in Greek prose. Both editions are relatively late, the Augustana dating perhaps to the early second century A.D. and the Vindobonensis perhaps to the fifth century A.D. Differences in the texts of the fable are minor.

According to the Greek fable, an old man once cut some wood and was carrying it a long distance. Because of his weariness he lay down his load and called Death to come. But when Death appeared and asked why the man had called him, the old man said: "To carry my load."[3] According to the epimythium, the tale illustrates how every human being is fond of life, even when he is very unhappy (Recension I) or faces countless dangers (Recension II, somewhat inconsequently, since danger is not the issue).[4]

The tale was in oral circulation as early as the fifth century B.C., for Euripides alludes to it, appropriately enough, in his *Alcestis*. The time came for Admetos to die, and the Fates allowed Admetos to escape death if he should find someone else to die in his place. When each of his aged parents refused to do so, his wife Alcestis agreed to die for him. Now, on the day on which Alcestis was scheduled to be carried off by Death, Admetos's old father paid a visit of condolence to his son, but Admetos angrily rejected him because of the old man's cowardice in clinging to life at any cost. Admetos concluded his speech with this gnomic observation: "It is pointless that old men pray to die, complaining

of old age and the long course of life. Whenever death comes near, no one wishes to die. Their old age is then no longer a burden."[5]

For another story of Death's coming to carry off a human being, see "Smith and the Devil." Compare also "Dog On the Bridge."

Lit. AT 845, *The Old Man and Death.* BP 3:294–295. Dvořák, no. 2563*. *EM* 1:382–383. Ashliman, type 845.

1. Elish 1946:59.
2. Holbek 1987:253–254; *EM* 1:382.
3. Perry 60; Hsr 60.
4. For a discussion of inappropriate epimythia see Hansen 1982.
5. *Alcestis* 669–672. On the Greek passage see further Dale 1961:105.

Our Lady's Child ✂ Gyges and Kroisos

A young girl is given by her parents to a supernatural being (the Virgin Mary, a demonic woman, etc.), who takes her into her house. The woman forbids the heroine to look into a certain room, but the heroine disobeys, opening the door to the room and seeing the forbidden sight (e.g., the Trinity, the demonic woman). Perceiving that the heroine disobeyed her, the woman confronts her, but the heroine denies it. The woman expels the girl from her home and also takes away her power of speech.

The king (prince) of the land comes upon her and, struck by her beauty, weds her in spite of her dumbness and unknown origin and sometimes also in spite of opposition to the marriage on the part of his mother (or the people). When the heroine gives birth to her first child, the woman appears and asks her again whether she looked into the forbidden room, and when the heroine again denies it, the woman takes away the girl's infant and smears the girl's face with blood (or her mother-in-law takes away the infant). Thereupon her mother-in-law (the people, etc.) claims that the girl is an ogress who has eaten her own child and urges that she be put to death. After the girl loses her second and third child in the same way, the king (prince) condemns her to be burnt at the stake. As she is about to perish by fire, the woman reappears, and the heroine, regaining her power of speech, acknowledges her guilt at last (or once again denies it), whereupon the woman rescues her from the flames. The woman restores her children, the vindicated heroine is reunited with her husband, and, when appropriate, the mother-in-law is punished.

This international tale, AT 710, *Our Lady's Child*, has been collected throughout Europe and elsewhere, and is said to be especially popular in Slavic lands.

It is found in two principal subtypes, both widely known, one in which the antagonist is a celestial being, usually the Virgin Mary, and the other in which the antagonist is a mysterious demonic woman, sometimes called the Black Lady or the Black Maiden. Each subtype attributes a different significance—indeed, an opposite significance—to the heroine's persistent silence. In the Celestial Subtype (as I shall call it), the Virgin Mary takes the child to live with her in heaven, the forbidden sight is glorious, the children are taken away by Mary,

and the girl's obstinate refusal to acknowledge her disobedience is defined as misbehavior. But in the Demonic Subtype the demonic woman takes the girl to live with her in her earthly house, the forbidden sight is frightening or enigmatic, the children are taken away by the evil mother-in-law, and the girl's stubborn refusal to acknowledge her disobedience, which brings misery upon her, is defined sometimes as a heroic act that brings about the disenchantment of the demonic woman.[1] When therefore the antagonist is good, the heroine's obstinacy is bad, and when the antagonist is evil, the heroine's obstinacy is virtuous, though the sense of the events in the Demonic Subtype sometimes remains somewhat obscure. So the meaning of the action differs in the two subtypes, although the action itself is almost the same in both cases, with a slight difference in its distribution to the characters, the kidnapper of the children being Mary in the former and the mother-in-law in the latter. Researchers assume that one of these subtypes arose as a modification of the other, and have offered inconclusive arguments for one or the other as the older form, but these arguments need not concern us here.[2] Similarly, the general opinion of scholars is that this magic tale is of recent origin, but nothing at all prevents us from supposing that the tale may have a long history. For all we know, the Celestial and the Demonic Subtypes may both be recent variations on a very old plot.

In a tale taken down by Jacob and Wilhelm Grimm from twenty-year-old Gretchen Wild in 1807, a woodcutter and his wife had a three-year-old daughter for whom they were too poor to provide. One day a beautiful, tall woman appeared to the woodcutter, announced that she was the Virgin Mary, and offered to take the child into her care and be her mother. The man gave the girl to Mary, who took her to Heaven. One day, when the girl was fourteen years old, Mary said she was going on a journey, gave the girl the keys to the thirteen doors of the Kingdom of Heaven, and told her that she might unlock twelve of the doors and marvel at the glories inside but must not unlock the thirteenth door. Promising to obey, the girl unlocked one door each day until she had opened all twelve, finding an apostle sitting in glory in each dwelling. Desiring to know what lay hidden in the thirteenth, however, she finally opened the last door, whereupon she saw the Holy Trinity sitting in glory. When Mary returned, she asked for her keys back and inquired whether the girl had opened the thirteenth door. The girl denied having done so. Mary said that since the girl had disobeyed her and also had lied, she was unworthy of dwelling in Heaven. When the girl next awoke, she found herself in a wilderness on earth, unable to speak. Some years later the king of the country came upon her sitting under a tree, a beautiful girl with long golden hair. When he asked her questions, she made no reply. He brought her back to his palace, dressed her properly, and, despite her inability to speak, married her. A year later the Virgin Mary appeared to her, saying that if she would confess to unlocking the forbidden door, Mary would restore her speech, but if not, Mary would take her newborn child from her. Given the power to reply, the girl denied opening the forbidden door, so that Mary disappeared with the child. Some people believed that the queen had killed her own child, which the queen was unable to deny. When she gave birth to a second child, the same thing happened. At the birth of her third child, Mary took her to Heaven to see her other two children happily playing, and offered to return them if the girl would admit to opening the door.

But again she denied it, so that Mary took away her third child. Now the people were convinced that the queen was a cannibal, and since she could not defend herself, she was condemned to die at the stake. As the fire was burning, the girl thought: "I wish that before I die I could confess to opening the door." Then she regained her power of speech and cried out to Mary that she had done it. Thereupon it suddenly began to rain, and the flames were extinguished. Mary appeared, returning her three children.[3]

According to a Chilean text collected in 1962 from Amelia Quiroz, a poor housemaid turned over her baby girl to the child's godmother to raise, and the godmother reared the child for some years before giving her in turn to the Virgin Mary. One day Mary said that she was going away for a while and that Juanita should take care of the little angels. Mary gave her the keys, telling her that she could open all the doors except for a certain one. But after she wondered for three days what was in that room, she opened the door and saw glory, a beautiful sight. When the Virgin returned, she asked Juanita if she had opened that door, and the girl said she had not. So Mary took her away from heaven, abandoning her. A prince who lived nearby happened upon the lovely girl and asked what she was doing there, and the girl said her mother had abandoned her. The prince took her to the palace and married her. When the girl gave birth to her first child, the Virgin came as she slept, and stole the baby after covering the mother with blood. Her mother-in-law, accusing her of eating the child, thought she should be put to death. After a similar loss of her second and third children, the king ordered that she be burnt on a stack of logs. As the flames roared, the Virgin appeared with Juanita's three children and asked if she had not opened the forbidden door, whereupon Juanita acknowledged she had. Juanita said she had not admitted it earlier because Mary had said she would be angry with her. Mary lifted her from the top of the burning logs, reunited her with her husband and children, and caused the house of the mother-in-law to burn down.[4]

A Finnish folktale recounts how a smith who had drunk away his possessions was about to hang himself when he encountered an old woman riding a black horse. She gave him money in exchange for his daughter. When the girl was fifteen years old, she came to a house in a forest where she was given all the keys and was permitted to open all the rooms except one. The witch largely left the girl alone, looking in on her once in a while. Eventually the girl broke the prohibition, and as she opened the door, a dead man who was bound to the door cried out that she should not admit her guilt. So the heroine lied about opening the door and thereupon was given her choice of becoming deaf, dumb, or blind. She became dumb and was cast naked into the sea. While out hunting, some princes found her, and the king wed her. Three times the witch came to her childbed and, when the girl continued her denial, took her child, leaving some bones near her. Everyone accused the girl of murdering her children, so that she was condemned to be burnt to death. At the stake, when the queen persisted in denying that she had opened the forbidden door, the witch blew out the fire, restored her speech and children, and left her in peace because she had passed the test, not acknowledging her deed.[5]

What exactly the heroine sees in the forbidden room varies considerably. In the Celestial Subtype she sees such sights as Mary with the body of Christ, God

and Christ writing in the Book of Fate, Mary healing the wounds of Christ, Christ on the cross, God and Mary in the heavenly gardens, the Trinity, paradise, a corpse, a blue fire, or a fountain of blood.[6] In a Norwegian version, for example, the heroine opened three forbidden doors. From the first a star escaped; from the second, the moon; from the third, the sun.[7] In the Demonic Subtype she sees such sights as the demonic woman together with black dwarves, the woman as half-fish and half-woman or as a skeleton, the woman playing cards with the devil, the woman sitting on a casket, the woman stretched out dreaming, an ornamented woman lying in bed, or four maidens. Thus in a text featuring three forbidden rooms the first contained bones, the second a skull, and the third the demonic woman.[8] The idea of a forbidden room or forbidden sight is therefore more important for the mechanics of the tale than is the particular content of the room. Of course the sight is generally consonant with the nature of the antagonist, the former instances being mostly light and glorious, the latter dark and evil. But it is noteworthy how often the forbidden sight proves to be a person—in fact, how often it is the woman of the house herself, alone or in company, engaged in some activity.

Gyges and Kroisos

There is no obvious analogue to *Our Lady's Child* in ancient tradition, and no folklorist has ever suggested that the tale might be that old. There is, however, an ancient narrative that is remarkably similar to the international tale at the crucial points of the action, if sometimes in surprising ways. The episode of the rescue of Kroisos from a burning pyre by Apollo is strikingly similar to the episode of the rescue of the heroine from the flames by her supernatural antagonist.[9] Earlier in the Kroisos legend, moreover, we find themes of muteness and the loss of children, and if we pursue the events further back in time, we find a significant episode in which Kroisos's kinsman Gyges saw a beautiful sight in a forbidden room.

That there are major differences as well must also be acknowledged, but most of these do not affect the ensuing argument for a genetic connection since any story can incorporate new motifs and episodes, be adapted to historical characters and events, and so on. Perhaps the most important differences between the legend and the international tale are the way the action is distributed to the characters (the ancient story assigns the role of protagonist and antagonist to one set of characters in the first half of the story and to another set in the second half) and the particular gender of the protagonists (male in the legend, female in the folktale).[10] So far as the question of a genetic connection is concerned, the pertinent consideration is how similar they are in structure and content.

Although there exist many scholarly investigations of the story of Gyges and that of Kroisos, there are few that view the rise and fall of the Mermnadai dynasty as a single story. But the careers of these two Lydian rulers are inextricably linked, for the story of Gyges is the story of the commission of a notable crime, whereas the story of Kroisos is the story of a terrible fall, and the fact is that Kroisos pays by his fall for the crime that Gyges commits. Herodotos himself views the story of Gyges as a preface to the story of Kroisos. The intimate

connection between the two events is made explicit by Apollo when he de-
clares that the clan of the Herakleidai will have their revenge for Gyges' crime
in the fifth generation; that is, Gyges' actions are paid for by his great-great
grandson, Kroisos. The role of the protagonist is distributed over two charac-
ters, the first and the last Mermnadai rulers of Lydia, one relaying it to the next.
Gyges' part—the forbidden room, the royal marriage—corresponds mostly to
the first half of the folktale, and Kroisos's part—the muteness, the loss of chil-
dren, the rescue from the fire—corresponds to the second half, with some over-
lap and doubling of motifs between the two halves.

According to Herodotos, the sovereignty of Lydia passed from the Heraklei-
dai to the family of Kroisos, the Mermnadai, in the following fashion. King
Kandaules of Lydia believed that his wife was the most beautiful of women. He
used to praise her beauty to one of his favorites, Gyges, a member of the royal
bodyguard. Deciding however that Gyges did not believe his praises, Kan-
daules insisted that the man himself must see her naked. Gyges protested that
a man should look only at what belonged to him and begged Kandaules not to
ask him to behave unlawfully. But Kaudaules insisted. He would hide Gyges
behind the bedroom door where Gyges would be able to watch the queen un-
dress; then Gyges should slip out of the room as the queen made her way to
bed. So at bedtime the king brought Gyges to his bedroom, after which the
queen came and undressed, and Gyges slipped out. The queen, however, no-
ticed him but said nothing at the time. She intended to avenge her shame, for
among the Lydians it was very shameful even for a man to be seen naked. The
next day she summoned Gyges to her and gave him two choices. Either Gyges
must kill Kandaules and take her and the Lydian kingdom, or he himself must
die then and there. Since he had no alternative but to choose, Gyges chose to
live. So that night he followed her to her bedroom where she hid him behind
the door and gave him a knife; Gyges killed the king as he slept and thereby got
his wife and kingdom. Although the Lydians were angry at the murder of Kan-
daules, they agreed to let the Delphic oracle decide Gyges' fate. If the oracle de-
clared him king, he should rule; but if not, he should give the kingdom back to
the Herakleidai. The oracle declared him king, so that he ruled. But the Pythia
(Delphic oracle) also said that the Herakleidai would have their revenge in the
fifth generation, a statement to which no one paid any attention until it actually
happened.

Following Gyges the kingdom passed to Ardys, Sadyattes, Alyattes, and fi-
nally the descendent of Gyges in the fifth generation, Kroisos, who subdued
most of the nations west of the Halys River. Since the Lydian capital Sardis was
then at the height of prosperity, many Greek sages of the period visited it,
among them Solon the Athenian. Solon was hosted by Kroisos, who had his
servants show him the royal treasuries and other signs of his prosperity and
grandeur. Then the Lydian king asked the Greek sage who was the happiest
man he had seen, the king supposing that he himself would be named. But
Solon named another man, so that Kroisos asked him who was the second hap-
piest he had seen, expecting this time at least to be that man. But again Solon
named other men. When finally Kroisos asked why Solon so scorned the hap-
piness of Kroisos, Solon answered that he could not declare the king's life
happy until he had learned how it ended. After Solon's departure god pun-

ished Kroisos for supposing that he was the happiest of men. Kroisos had two sons, one who was mute and one who excelled his peers, the latter being named Atys. Kroisos had a dream that Atys would die after being struck by a spear. The king took precautions to avoid this outcome, but despite his efforts the dream came true. After grieving for his son, Kroisos learned that the might of the Persians under Kyros was increasing, and he wondered if he might check their power before it grew great. After sending rich gifts to Delphi, he asked the oracle if he should make war on the Persians, and the oracle replied that if he did so, he would destroy a great empire. Misunderstanding the oracle and expecting to subdue Kyros and the Persian empire, Kroisos began military operations. Kyros responded with an army of his own and in the end overcame the Lydians in their own country. As for Kroisos himself, when one of the Persian soldiers was about to slay him, Kroisos disregarded the threat, not caring whether he lived or died, but the king's mute son broke into speech for the first time, saying: "Fellow, don't kill Kroisos!" So the Persians captured Sardis and Kroisos in accordance with the oracle, Kroisos having destroyed his own great empire. Kyros had Kroisos bound and placed on a pyre. Then Kroisos remembered the wise words of Solon, uttered as though a god had inspired them: not to regard any man happy while he lived. Kroisos broke his long silence, sighing and thrice uttering Solon's name. Hearing this, Kyros had his interpreters ask Kroisos who this was whom he was calling. Kroisos remained silent for a while but finally spoke, saying that Solon was a man who should have spoken with every ruler. He recounted Solon's visit, his disregard for Kroisos's wealth, how it all had ended just as Solon had said, and also how Solon's point applied no more to Kroisos than to all other men. When Kyros was told what Kroisos had said, he meditated on how the point applied to him as well, and changed his mind about burning Kroisos alive, but the fire had already been lit, and the Persians were unable to extinguish it. When Kroisos perceived this, he tearfully called aloud to Apollo to save him, if any of his gifts had pleased the god. And although the weather was clear, a sudden storm broke out and put out the fire. Seeing that Kroisos was a good man and dear to the gods, Kyros had him brought down from the pyre. Kroisos gave Kyros good advice, so that Kyros offered to grant him any wish. Kroisos said he wished to send his fetters to Apollo, asking him if it was his habit to deceive his benefactors. It was so done. The Pythia responded. First of all (she said) not even a god can escape his destiny; Kroisos has expiated the crime of his ancestor Gyges, who murdered his master and took his kingdom; Apollo wanted the fall of Sardis to occur in the lifetime of Kroisos's sons and not in the lifetime of Kroisos himself, but was unable to change what was fated other than to induce the Moirai to postpone the capture of Sardis and Kroisos for three years. Second, the god did save Kroisos on the pyre. And, finally, when the oracle informed Kroisos that if he marched against the Persians he would destroy a great empire, he should have asked whether the god meant his or Kyros's. The Lydians reported her reply to Kroisos, who acknowledged that the fault was his, not the god's.[11]

The folktale consists of two parts, the first in which the heroine lives as an unwed dependent in the house of a powerful mistress, the second in which she dwells in her own palace as the wife of a king and the mother of children. I consider each in turn.

The first part centers upon a great misdemeanor, the violation of a visual taboo. The protagonist comes to dwell in the house of the antagonist, is forbidden to open the door of a certain room, but looks into the forbidden room anyway and sees its contents. The antagonist perceives this and confronts her (or perceives the truth upon confronting her). When the protagonist persistently denies the deed, the antagonist renders her mute and expels her from the house. She goes on to wed a prince or king.

At the onset of Herodotos's narrative, the protagonist (Gyges) dwells or works in the house of the antagonists (Kandaules and his wife). The principal event of the episode, the protagonist's seeing in a forbidden room what he should not see, takes the form of Gyges' hiding in Kandaules' bedroom in order to see his beautiful wife unclothed. Whereas the folktale sets up the misbehavior with a prohibition (the protagonist is forbidden to look into a certain room), the legend sets up the same event with a command (the protagonist is instructed to look into a certain room). Here, as elsewhere in folk narrative, commands and interdictions play the same role.[12] Since an interdiction in folk narrative regularly introduces a violation of the interdiction, as though the interdiction were really an injunction, both the interdiction in the folktale and the command in the Greek legend lead to precisely the same result. Moreover, Gyges' act is at once both the execution of a command and also the violation of a taboo, since his act violates a cultural taboo: Gyges is horrified at Kandaules' plan—the narrator Herodotos comments that among the Lydians it is regarded as very shameful even for a man to be seen naked—and Kandaules' wife considers it absolutely impermissible for anyone other than her husband to see her unclothed; but the best indication of the forbidden nature of Gyges' act is the simple fact that he does it secretly, in the hope that he will not be perceived.

What Gyges actually sees is the Lydian queen in her bedroom undressed. The forbidden sight is therefore similar to that in the folktale. Since Kandaules' wife is described as the most beautiful woman in the world, the naked beauty of the queen is an earthly counterpart to the spiritually glorious sight that the protagonist in the Celestial Subtype glimpses. And since Gyges' forbidden sight is the mistress of the dwelling herself, we are put in mind of the forbidden sight in the Demonic Subtype, in which the centerpiece is usually the enigmatic mistress of the house herself. Indeed, in a couple versions of the oral tale the forbidden sight is identical with that which Gyges sees, a beautiful woman in her bedroom; thus in a Slavic text the protagonist sees the mistress stretched out dreaming, and in an Italian text the protagonist sees the woman adorned and lying in bed.[13]

Like the antagonist in the folktale, Kandaules' wife perceives what the protagonist has done and quickly confronts him. She gives Gyges his choice of two alternatives: he may either kill the king or be killed. Gyges chooses the former, and so it happens. Also in some texts of the folktale, as in the Finnish text summarized above, the antagonist gives the heroine her choice of ills at this point. Since the heroine always chooses to be mute, the result is the same as in texts in which she is not given a choice.[14] Gyges' story concludes with a royal marriage.[15] He weds the queen of the land, but the people, indignant at the murder of the king, are hostile to his becoming king, just as in the folktale the heroine

weds the king of the land, a marriage to which sometimes the people or the king's mother are opposed.

In the second part of the legend the role of protagonist is played by Kroisos and the role of antagonist is played in succession by Solon and Apollo. Of the two forms of the folktale, the Celestial and the Demonic, this part of the legend more closely resembles the Celestial Subtype, Olympian Apollo corresponding to the heavenly Mary. So I focus here upon parallels between the Kroisos legend and the Celestial branch of the folktale, resuming the legend with Gyges' great-great-grandson Kroisos, whose story begins thematically where that of Gyges leaves off: the man becomes ruler of the Lydian Empire.

Just as the first half of *Our Lady's Child* centers upon the violation of a looking taboo, the second half centers upon a moral lesson. In the folktale the two themes are intimately connected since the protagonist remains identical throughout: it is she who violates the taboo and, since she denies it, it is she who requires a lesson. In the legend, however, the connection between the themes is more remote, since it is Gyges who violates the looking taboo but it is his descendent Kroisos who requires a moral lesson.

In the latter part of the folktale the antagonist, determined to impart a lesson, pressures the protagonist with more and more misery, while the protagonist, determined to hold out, endures the increasing misery and relents only when the misery becomes life-threatening, and then only at the last moment. When that happens, the antagonist miraculously rescues the protagonist, and the two are reconciled. The narrative logic of the folktale protagonist's muteness is transparent. Having repeatedly denied the truth, the protagonist is made to lose the ability either to affirm or to deny. Because she has misused speech, she forfeits her right to it. Then she is put into ever worsening situations in which speech—specifically, the ability to deny falsehoods—is crucial, and she cannot employ it.[16]

In the story of Kroisos the moral truth is uttered by Solon, and the pressure on the stubborn protagonist is applied by Apollo. First, there is the confrontation of the protagonist and the antagonist, with the initial denial. Kroisos, the wealthy and powerful ruler of an empire, regards himself as the happiest of men and expects his visitor, Solon the Athenian, to share this view, but Solon counsels him to regard no man's life as happy until after the man has lived his entire life, since life is chancy. As a result the king sends his visitor away in scorn. Here the antagonist insists that the protagonist should not regard himself as the happiest of men, while Kroisos, denying the truth, stubbornly holds that he is. A discourse of insistence and denial is the essential relationship of the protagonist and the antagonist in the folktale. In the folktale its intensity is often conveyed by the antagonist's asking the same question several times and the protagonist's denying it each time. In the legend the intensity takes the form of Kroisos's asking Solon who is the happiest man he has encountered; when the questioner does not get the answer he wants, he asks again, and when he still does not get the answer he wants, he persists in asking. Kroisos will not acknowledge the truth.

Pressure is now applied to the protagonist. Herodotos attributes the ensuing misery of Kroisos to divine indignation: Kroisos's belief that he is the happiest

of men incurs the anger of god, who in this story is Apollo. In the folktale the Virgin Mary pressures the heroine in two ways: muteness and loss of children. Both of these themes can be discerned in the Kroisos legend, but as scattered motifs rather than as related parts of a coherent divine plan for the education of Kroisos.

Kroisos has two biological children, an unnamed son and a son named Atys; in addition, he takes into his household a foreign youth, Adrastos, whom we may regard here as a kind of foster son. Of these three youths, the first has a physical disability, the second perishes in a hunting accident, and the third kills himself. Though the details differ, the overall loss is the same as in the folktale: the protagonist's three children experience unhappy fates.

The theme of speechlessness shows up first in Kroisos's first son, who is mute. The trait has perhaps been transferred from father to son here, but we find traces of it in Kroisos as well. There is a strange hint of muteness in the oracular reply that Kroisos receives when he sends an embassy to Apollo's oracle at Delphi: "I know the number of the sands and the measures of the sea; I understand the mute and hear the voiceless."[17] The Pythia seems to address the inquirer as though he were mute. Later, when the Persians storm Sardis, bringing an end to Kroisos's empire, Kroisos begins actually to behave as though he were dumb. A Persian soldier who does not recognize Kroisos is about to cut him down, and although Kroisos sees the soldier coming at him, he is indifferent to death because of his misery. Kroisos survives only because his own mute son cries out for the first time: "Fellow, don't kill Kroisos!"[18] Kroisos's unnatural silence in this scene is difficult to distinguish from true muteness. He remains oddly quiet during his capture and his placement on the pyre. Finally he breaks his silence to utter Solon's name. When Kyros's men ask him whom he is calling upon, he resumes his silence for a while before answering them.[19] In this climactic scene Kroisos's behavior exactly parallels that of the mute protagonist in the folktale who stubbornly maintains her silence until she is on the pyre.

We reach the climax of the story, the protagonist on the pyre. While the protagonist continues to deny the truth, the antagonist continues to pile on the misery, which culminates in the near execution of the protagonist. In the folktale the heroine's near execution follows economically from the heroine's muteness and from the unexplained disappearances of her children, all engineered by Mary, which result in the heroine's condemnation as an ogress who has eaten her own children. In the legend, the instances of muteness and loss of children are also causes or symptoms of the hero's growing misery, but it is specifically the loss of his empire, engineered by Apollo via an ambiguous oracle, that results in Kroisos's capture by his enemy and in his near execution.

In both the modern and the ancient stories, the king decides to execute the protagonist by fire, so that the protagonist is tied to a stake or placed on a pyre. After the fire is set, the protagonist relents and finally acknowledges her or his particular truth (she admits opening the door/he admits that Solon was right), whereupon the divine antagonist (Mary/Apollo) causes a sudden rainstorm to extinguish the fire or rescues the protagonist in some other way at the last moment. The protagonist has finally learnt the lesson.[20]

The folktale concludes with the reconciliation of the heroine and Mary, including the return of the heroine's children. The legend concludes similarly

with the reconciliation of Kroisos and Apollo, when Kroisos acknowledges that he himself, not the god, is to blame for his misery.[21] The folktale heroine's reunion with her husband perhaps has a parallel of sorts in Kroisos's new relationship with Kyros, who gives Kroisos a seat next to him and holds him in high esteem as a personal counselor.[22]

Since the correspondences between the folktale and the legend are sometimes straightforward and sometimes disguised, sometimes structural and sometimes thematic, I recap the parallels, employing for simplicity of comparison the Celestial Subtype as representative of the folktale. (1) The protagonist dwells in the palace of the antagonist, where (2) the antagonist forbids (commands) the protagonist to look into a certain room. (3) The protagonist secretly looks into the forbidden room and (4) sees its beautiful contents, but (5) the antagonist (Mary/Kandaules' wife) perceives the misdemeanor and (6) confronts the protagonist.[23] (7) The antagonist gives the protagonist a choice of ills, and (8) the protagonist chooses one (muteness/regicide). (9) The protagonist weds a queen (king) and becomes a king (queen). (10) The celestial antagonist (Mary/Apollo) now engineers various kinds of misery for the protagonist, including loss of the faculty of speech and (11) loss of children, (12) leading eventually to the ruler's decision that the protagonist be put to death by burning. (13) When the protagonist is tied to a stake (placed on a pyre) and the fire is lit, (14) the protagonist finally relents, regaining her (his) speech and acknowledging the truth of the antagonist's contention (that she looked in the forbidden room/that no living man should be counted happy). Then (15) the antagonist miraculously extinguishes the fire by a sudden rainstorm, rescuing the protagonist from the flames, and (16) the two are reconciled with each other.

The extensive structural correspondences and occasional detailed agreement on the narrative surface make it inconceivable that the Lydian legend and the international folktale arose independently of each other. They must be realizations of the same, rather complex plot, the roots of which therefore reach deep into antiquity. Although we cannot know exactly what form the international story had in, say, the seventh century B.C., it is certainly easier to imagine the Gyges-Kroisos legend starting from an oral tale like that which we know than to imagine how the folktale might have issued from the legend, which distributes the action over two sets of protagonists and antagonists separated by several generations, and which at least in its Herodotean form is complicated by numerous digressions, which I have not reproduced here, that are unrelated to the story of the Lydian Empire. Moreover, some features of the legend are much better understood in the economy of the folktale than in that of the legend, such as the motif of muteness, whose role in the tale is coherent and essential to the action but whose role in the legend is sporadic and inessential, however dramatically effective. Similarly, as a form of punishment the climactic burning of the protagonist at the stake is unremarkable for a convicted ogress but strange for a fallen monarch, and even Herodotos can only guess why Kyros chooses to burn Kroisos to death without further ado.[24] These features are more readily understood as resulting from a free rehandling of the folktale than as being the fount from which the folktale drew.

It appears, then, that the traditional history of the Mermnad dynasty was cast in the narrative mold of *Our Lady's Child*, the rise and fall of the dynasty being adapted to the rise and fall of the protagonist of the folktale. Narrators

developed the careers of the first and last members of the dynasty individually, each in its own direction, corresponding more or less to the two halves of the folktale. In short, the legend of Gyges and Kroisos is a special development of a more general tale, a branch off the main tree of the international story.

Whose legend was it? Although at one point in his narration Herodotos alludes casually to Lydian informants, this and similar attributions of source in Herodotos must be taken with a grain of salt.[25] The story as we have it has a markedly Greek character, including the many appearances of the Delphic oracle, beginning with Apollo's confirmation of Gyges as king of Lydia and concluding with the god's defense against Kroisos's rebuke, and including the infamous oracle in which Apollo informs Kroisos that if he campaigns against the Persians he will destroy a great kingdom; the beloved Greek confrontation of a powerful monarch and a wise sage, in this case Kroisos and Solon,[26] reformulating the moral lesson of the second half of the old folktale into philosophic statement; and the organization of the story of Kroisos as a kind of Greek tragedy, in which the king moves from prosperity to hybris to recklessness to ruin.[27]

The earliest trace of the Gyges-Kroisos story is on a red-figured amphora of about 500 B.C. that shows Kroisos on the pyre, followed shortly by literary treatments of Gyges or Kroisos or both by Bakchylides, Xanthos, Herodotos, Plato, and others.[28] The relationship of these different ancient treatments to one another is uncertain, but Herodotos's narrative is the closest to the international folktale.

Lit. (AT 710, *Our Lady's Child*.) BP 1:13–21. Aly 1969 (1921):45. Espinosa (1946–47) 2:345–348. Seifert 1952. Liungman 1961:202–205. Scherf 1982:273–276. *EM* 6: 331–333; 9:336–342. Ashliman, type 710. Hansen 1996a.

1. In her historic-geographic study of *Our Lady's Child*, Seifert (1952:7–8) distinguishes four forms of the tale according to the nature of the antagonist: two principal forms in which the antagonist is a demonic woman or Mary, and two minor forms in which the antagonist is an enchanted prince or a male demon.

2. Seifert 1952; Liungman 1961:202–204; Scherf 1982:275.

3. Grimm 3. For Wilhelm Grimm's continuous reworking of the text of *Das Marienkind* between 1808 and 1864, see Bottigheimer 1990.

4. Pino-Saavedra 1967:149–153.

5. Seifert 1952:61, citing Löwis of Menar, *Finnische und estnische Märchen*, no. 33, and Aarne, *Finnische Märchenvarianten* (1911), no. 713.

6. Seifert 1952:27.

7. Asbjørnsen and Moe 3:80–86 = Dasent 1970:188–193.

8. Seifert 1952:27–28, 62, 68–69.

9. Aly 1969:45 notices that two motifs of the Kroisos legend are found in Grimms' tale *Das Marienkind*, namely, muteness suddenly overcome and rescue from a burning pyre by means of divinely sent rain. He does not pursue the correspondence further, and the general opinion of scholars is that no analogue for the stories of Gyges and Kroisos, individually or as a whole, is known to exist.

The episode of the miraculous escape from the burning pyre is not unique to the present stories but is found elsewhere in other international folktales (for example, AT 451, *The Maiden Who Seeks Her Brothers*) and in ancient Greek mythology and fiction. Thus, in Xenophon's *Ephesiaca* (4.2), Habrokomes is placed on a pyre on the Delta, and when it is set afire he utters a prayer, whereupon the Nile arises and puts out the flames. According to Heliodoros's *Aethiopiaca* (8.9.9–15), Charikleia is put on a pyre, but the flames do not harm her because of a magic stone she carries. Similar to the rescue of Kroisos is that of Thekla, who mounts the pyre and makes the sign of the cross. When the fire is lit, the Lord causes rain to fall, dowsing the flames (*Acta Pauli et Theclae* 22). The same story was attached to Alkmene, as we can infer from two vases that illustrate how her husband Amphitryon,

angry at her for sleeping with Zeus during his absence, prepares to burn her on a pyre, but Zeus puts out the fire by means of a rainstorm (Roscher 1:247).

10. On roles as constants in folktales and the characters who perform them as variables, see Propp 1968:19–21 and Dundes 1962a. *Our Lady's Child* is a so-called feminine folktale, in the sense that it features an active heroine (Holbek 1987:161–169). The antagonist in the present tale is also regularly female, although texts featuring a male antagonist are found. The slight evidence at my disposal suggests that AT 710 is popular with female narrators, for in the three cases in which I have information about the oral narrator she is female. Grimms' *Marienkind* was taken down from Gretchen Wild, the Chilean text summarized above was recorded from Amelia Quiroz, and in nineteenth-century Denmark E. T. Kristensen collected a text from a certain Johanne Rasmusdatter (Holbek 1987:130–131). So in its modern form, at least, it is predominantly a women's tale in terms of its principal characters and probably its transmitters. By the same criteria the ancient narrative of the Mermnadai dynasty is a masculine story.

11. Herodotos 1.6–13, 28–91.

12. Propp 1968:27.

13. Seifert 1952:62, 68–69.

14. Cf. Seifert 1952:31.

15. Gyges' new wife shows some of the typical features of the heroine in the folktale just before her marriage, when the king first sees her: she is beautiful, naked, and to some extent even mute (Herodotos reports that when she sees Gyges in her bedroom, the Lydian queen says nothing).

16. The folktale presupposes a peasant world of illiterate persons.

17. Herodotos 1.47.3.

18. 1.85.3–4.

19. 1.86.3–4.

20. For Kroisos see Segal 1971:45–49.

21. 1.91.6.

22. 1.88.1.

23. The motif of denial is lacking in the confrontation of Gyges and Kandaules' wife but appears later in the confrontation of Kroisos and Solon, which restates the confrontation of the protagonist and the antagonist for the second part of the story.

24. 1.86.2.

25. Herodotos 1.87.1. Fehling 1989:152–154.

26. Lefkowitz 1981:40–48; Hansen 1997c.

27. Fontenrose 1978:111–115.

28. Amphora: Segal 1971:41 n. 8. Apart from Herodotos the most important sources for the story are the poet Bacchylides (3), the historian Xanthos the Lydian as preserved in the historian Nikolaos of Damascus (*FGH* 90 F 47, 65, 68), a fragmentary tragedy of unknown authorship and uncertain date concerning Gyges (Page 1951), and Plato *Rep.* 2.359d–360b. The tragic fragment, so far as it goes, agrees with Herodotos, whereas Nikolaos and Plato represent a second and third line of oral or literary tradition. Ironically, the older scholars generally regarded Plato's account of Gyges as probably being close to the supposed folktale source of the story because of its märchen-like features such as a ring of invisibility by means of which Gyges is able to seduce the queen (Liebenau 1900; Smith 1902, 1920; Bickel 1921), although Plato's narrative does not closely resemble any known folktale. Some scholars have also hypothesized that a folktale lies behind Herodotos's story, though no particular tale has ever been proposed. See further Pichler 1986:8–33; *EM* 6:331–333.

Person Does Not Know Himself

A man goes to sleep, and someone cuts off his hair (shaves his beard, blackens him, changes his clothes, etc.), usually as a joke. When he awakens, he concludes that he is someone else.

This numskull tale, AT 1284, *Person Does Not Know Himself*, is known from Europe to the Far East.[1] Altogether four redactions can be distinguished.[2] Illus-

trated here is redaction 1, the most widely known form of the narrative and the only one attested in antiquity.

So in an English tale collected from a certain Reuben Gray in 1914, a bearded Irishman who was staying at an inn asked to be awakened early. During the night some wags shaved off his beard. He was roused late and rushed off but on the road discovered that he had no beard. Concluding that they had wakened the wrong man, he returned to the inn where he instructed them to call the bearded man and tell him to hurry.[3]

Clouston recounts a similar tale of a Highlander "fresh from the heather" who spent the night at an inn at Perth, sharing the room with a black man. Some jokers blackened the Highlander's face during the night, and when he was roused very early the next morning, as he had requested, and saw himself in the mirror, he exclaimed angrily that they had called the wrong man.[4]

Each text features a dupe and a trickster, or tricksters. The dupe may be presented as a simpleton, and the trickster as a jokester or covetous man. In the mechanics of the tale the person for whom the protagonist thinks he has been mistaken—let us call him the *comparandus*—may appear as a third character or not. In the English text the victim anxiously thinks he has been mistaken for someone else, though he has no particular person in mind, but in the Scots text the *comparandus* is a distinct character, the black man. What is amusing in the joke is the earnest but mistaken behavior of the numskull, who rashly concludes from the change in his appearance that he must be someone else.

A Greek Joke

Person Does Not Know Himself is found in the ancient Greek jokebook *Philogelos*, according to which a numskull, a bald man, and a barber were traveling together. Having to pass the night in a desolate place, they agreed that each in turn would stay awake for four hours to watch over their belongings. The first watch fell to the barber. Deciding to play a trick on the numskull, the barber shaved off all his hair before awakening him. Stroking his head as people do when awakening, and finding that he had no hair, the numskull said: "That barber is an idiot. He woke up the bald guy instead of me."[5]

The Greek joke assigns the three roles to three separate characters. The dupe is described as a *scholastikos*, one of several terms for numskull protagonists in *Philogelos*, so that he is represented as a simpleton from the beginning, as the Highlander is in the joke above. The *comparandus* is described simply as a bald man because, like the black man in the Highlander tale, he possesses a single characteristic of importance for the tale. And the trickster is identified as a barber because his only significant act is the cutting of hair. The trickster's motive, as in some of the modern texts, is simple mischief.

An epigram by the Greek poet Lucilius resembles the humorous idea upon which this international joke turns. It is one of several comic epigrams by the poet that make fun of real or imaginary boxers whose faces have become disfigured by their sport. In the present epigram the poet addresses Stratophon, declaring that when Odysseus returned home after an absence of twenty years his dog Argos recognized him by his appearance, but after only four hours of boxing, Stratophon has became unrecognizable to both dogs and the city, and if

he looks at his face in a mirror he himself will swear he is not Stratophon.[6] As in *Person Does Not Know Himself* it is comically assumed that a person decides who he is by the presence or absence of his external characteristics rather than by an internal and continuing sense of self. In this one-character tale the boxer Stratophon plays all the roles, but the crucial one is that of the numskull who, following a change in his appearance, will conclude that he is someone else.

Another comic tale in which a character becomes uncertain of his own identity is *Husband Cannot Recognize Himself*, for which see "Underground Passage to Paramour's House."

Lit. AT 1284, *Person Does Not Know Himself*. Wesselski 1909:193, no. 152. BP 1:340–342. Christensen 1939:221. Sedgwick 1947:290. Marzolph 1987:195, no. 56. Ashliman, type 1284. *EM* 7:20–27, esp. 23–24.

1. *EM* 7:23; for India see Thompson and Roberts 1960:135. Compare also AT 1531A, *Man Shaved and with Hair Cut Does Not Recognize Self;* a similar tale, AT 1383, *The Woman Does Not Know Herself,* is told of a female protagonist.
2. *EM* 7:23–24.
3. Briggs (1970) A2:362.
4. Clouston 1888:6–7.
5. *Phil.* 56. As often in ancient tales, travelers pass the night on the ground rather than in an inn.
6. *AP* 11.77.

Peter Stung by Bees 🐝 Man Bitten by Ants

A man complains about the injustice of God, who destroys many persons for the sake of one unjust man. When the man is thereafter stung by a bee and kills the whole hive, God points out the parallel in the man's behavior.

This religious legend, featuring a human complainer and a divine explainer, is AT 774K, *Peter Stung by Bees*, one of a number of theodicy narratives in which a god reveals the justice of apparently unjust divine acts or at least affirms the divine prerogative to act in certain apparently unjust ways.

After the complainer in the present story reproaches God for indiscriminately destroying innocent persons along with guilty ones, God demonstrates that in fact the complainer metes out precisely the same justice in his turn to relatively lower creatures. Although one might expect the human interlocutor to object that a god should uphold a higher standard, he instead accepts the divine lesson. Thus one message of this odd tale can be that a person must accept the apparent injustice of some divine decisions, inasmuch as it is not the place of humans to judge the ways of God.[1]

According to a Muslim text of *Peter Stung by Bees* found in Damiri's *Hayat al-Hayawan al-Kubra*, an Arabic composition of the fourteenth century, Moses once protested against the injustice of Allah, declaring that God would punish an entire town for its sins even when some righteous persons dwelled in the town. Allah, wanting to teach Moses a lesson in divine justice, made the sun blaze down so that Moses sought refuge from the heat in the shadow of a tree. A city of ants was also located there, and while Moses was sleeping under the tree he

was bitten by an ant, as a result of which he angrily destroyed both the ants and their dwelling. This was the lesson given by Allah to his beloved prophet.[2]

In a Catalan legend collected in 1913 from a woman in Barcelona, Jesus and St. Peter were walking along the seashore one day when they heard passengers on a boat crying out to heaven to save them. When Peter noticed that Jesus was not responding, he asked him whether he heard those poor persons asking for his help. Jesus told him to go his way and not to concern himself about what he, Jesus, did; on that boat there was a man who did not deserve to be saved. Peter objected that the other persons ought not to pay the penalty of this one man. Meanwhile a wasp bit St. Peter, who angrily went to the tree in which the nest was located, knocked it down, and stomped on it with his feet. Jesus asked Peter why it was that because one wasp had bitten him he had destroyed the nest, killing the other wasps who had done nothing to him. He pointed out to Peter that one sees another's fault more readily than one's own. Recognizing the correctness of the master, Peter followed in silence.[3]

A classic exploration of this problem of justice is the negotiation of Yahweh and Abraham about the fate of Sodom and Gomorrah. God revealed to Abraham that he had heard an outcry concerning the sin of these cities and was going to investigate its truth. Abraham asked if he would really sweep away the good and the bad together. Suppose, he said, there were fifty good men in the place: would God pardon the city on their account? God agreed to pardon Sodom if fifty good men should be found in it. In small decrements, after the manner of the logical problem known as *Sorites* (see "Loading the Wood"), Abraham persisted: What if there were only forty-five good men? thirty? twenty? ten? Yahweh agreed not to destroy the city if there should be as few as ten good men in it.[4] As it turned out, there were not, but in any case the deity was prepared to sweep away some good persons along with their evil fellows.

A Greek Fable

According to a fable recounted by Babrius, a man seeing a ship sink with everyone onboard said that the gods made unjust decisions, for many innocent persons died merely because one impious man had boarded the ship. As he was saying this a large number of ants crawled upon him, and one of them bit him, so that he trampled upon the others. Thereupon Hermes appeared, saying: "Will you not let the gods judge you humans the way that you have judged the ants?"[5]

The ancient tale is known only from the collection of fables in Greek verse made by Babrius in the first or second century A.D. No epimythium, or ideal application of the tale, is appended to the narrative. Although one might have expected the role of explainer in the Greek tale to be assigned to Zeus as a deity concerned with justice, it is given to Hermes, not because he has a traditional interest in justice, but probably because he is the deity most likely simply to appear to a human at a crucial time, apparently out of nowhere, as he does to Odysseus when the hero is making his way to the house of the witch Kirke, or as he does to the woodcutters in the fable of the lost axe.[6] In the present tale he mediates between gods and humans, an appropriate role for the herald of the gods.

The relational idea that ants are to humans as humans are to gods seems to have been a commonplace in Greece, just as it doubtless is among different peoples in the present day. A scholiast on Homer observes that whenever the bard wishes to dwell upon the dignity of the gods, he represents them as being unconcerned with mortals, "just as we ourselves are unconcerned with ants."[7]

Lit. AT 774K, *Peter Stung by Bees*. Schwarzbaum 1979:xiii–xiv.

1. The same point with a different emphasis is found in another theodicy tale, AT 759, *God's Justice Vindicated*, in which a divine guide arranges for a human being to witness a series of apparently unjust acts, and then explains why in an unobvious way each of the acts is actually *just*.
2. Schwarzbaum 1979:xiv.
3. Amades 1950:1040, no. 1309. A similar version recorded in Irish is given as follows in English summary: "Peter protests when a ship is sunk because of one sinner aboard. Our Saviour sends him to fetch honey from a hive. Peter crushes all the bees when one stings him" (*Béaloideas* 21 [1951]: 305).
4. Gen. 18.
5. Babrius 117 = Perry 306.
6. See for the former Homer *Od.* 10.275–309 and for the latter "Axe Falls into the Stream."
7. Schol. ABT on Homer *Il.* 9.429.

Planting for the Next Generation

An old man who is planting a tree is told that it will not bear fruit during his lifetime. He replies that he is planting it for the next generation.

In this little novella, AT 928, *Planting for the Next Generation*, the doubter takes the shorter view, expecting men to act only in their own immediate interest, whereas the old farmer takes the longer view, seeing himself as part of a tradition from which he has benefited and to which in his turn he wishes to contribute.

A number of Near Eastern texts relate that when an old man was planting a date palm, the Emperor Maximilian (or another important person) expressed his doubt that the old man would ever taste its fruit. The doubter rewarded the old man's clever answers with gifts and honors.[1]

A Greco-Roman Apothegm

In his essay *On Old Age* Cicero speaks of old men who are intellectually and physically active. In one passage, after remarking that no one is so old that he does not think he can live for another year, Cicero observes that men also devote their labor to projects from which they know they themselves will get no use, quoting a verse from Statius's *Synephebi*: "He plants trees to benefit another generation."[2] Cicero continues: "Nor does the farmer, however old he may be, hesitate to reply to the man who asks him whom he is planting for: 'For the immortal gods, who have wanted me not only to receive these trees from my forebears but also to hand them on to my descendants.' "[3] Cicero then continues with his immediate theme of old men who look ahead to the next generation.

As Cicero informs us, he has his tale from a literary source, a comedy by Caecilius Statius, *Synephebi*, an adaptation of a comedy by the Greek playwright Menander. Neither work has survived. If, as seems likely, the tale of the old man came along with Menander's play, we can follow it back as far as fourth-century Athens, where the popular playwright perhaps heard it and used it in his play.[4]

Cicero casts the tale, perhaps unconsciously, in the form of an apothegm, a kind of anecdote that frequently takes the following form in ancient Greece and Rome: a particular person, when asked by someone about a particular matter, replied such and such.[5] For example: "Aristeides, when asked what justice is, said: 'Not desiring what belongs to other persons.' "[6] Whereas the Near Eastern texts characterize the doubter as an important man who acknowledges the surprising wisdom of a humble interlocutor, as in the classic confrontations of king and philosopher, Cicero's narrative minimizes this contrast between the two, relegating the doubter to the anonymous background and foregrounding the reverent planter.

Lit. AT 928, *Planting for the Next Generation.* Wesselski (1911) 2:235, no. 516. Chauvin (1897) 2:208, no. 75. *EM* 1:1391–1392.

1. *EM* 1:1391.
2. *De Senectute* 24: "Serit arbores, quae alteri saeclo prosint." Cicero quotes the verse also in his *Tusculan Disputations* (1.14.31).
3. *De Senectute* 24–25: "Nec vero dubitat agricola, quamvis sit senex, quaerenti, cui serat, respondere: 'Dis immortalibus, qui me non accipere modo haec a majoribus voluerunt, sed etiam posteris prodere.' "
4. Elisheva Schoenfeld is therefore incorrect when she says that the oldest text of the tale is found in talmudic literature of the first century A.D. (*EM* 1:1391). The tale appears nevertheless to be especially well attested in the Middle East.
5. See further Hock and O'Neil 1986; Skidmore 1996:35–43.
6. Hock and O'Neil 1986:305, no. 8.

Potiphar's Wife 🖎 Hippolytos and Phaidra

A married woman propositions a man, usually a younger man, who virtuously turns down her advances. She then accuses him to her husband, falsely alleging that the youth made advances to her and that she rejected them (or that he raped her). Accepting her account without question, the husband punishes the innocent youth.

This international story, recounted usually as a legend, is classified as motif K2111, *Potiphar's Wife.*[1]

The basic plot is found with numerous variations in ancient oral and literary narrative. Indeed, of ancient plots in the Mediterranean culture area, and more particularly of erotic plots, it is the most productive, being attached to around twenty different sets of characters in classical legend and fiction. The tale has also been very popular in the orally inspired literature of India.[2] Though the story is complete in itself, the encounter of the lustful woman and the virtuous youth almost invariably appears as an episode in a larger narrative.

The tale of *Potiphar's Wife* is essentially a triangle story involving two men and a woman. Usually one man is young and unattached, and the other is married to the woman who finds the young man's youth or looks or virility attractive. The action of the story has a logical, almost mechanical quality. The lustful woman approaches the virtuous youth; he *always* declines her advances; angry or afraid, she *always* slanders him to her husband, who *always* believes his wife. But inasmuch as the different realizations of the plot present different reasons for the presence of the young man and define his relationship to the other two characters differently, each variant attaches its own significance to the woman's advances and to the youth's spurning of them. There is interesting variation both in the cunning employed by the matron, who often reinforces her words with a visual rhetoric in order to persuade her husband that she has been abused, and also in the form of punishment devised by the outraged husband. Many changes are rung on the central narrative ideas.

In an African tale collected from a Dogon informant in 1935, two brothers lived together. The elder was married. One day when he had gone into the bush, his wife asked the younger brother to lie with her, and he refused. Chagrined, the woman made a whitish meal that she poured on her loincloth; then she sat crying. When her husband returned, he asked the reason for her tears, and she showed him her stained loincloth, saying that his brother had taken her by force despite her resistance. The man questioned his brother, who denied it. The following day the woman carried on in the same way, and when her husband came back she reproached him for ignoring her. In the night the elder brother got up, went to find his young brother, and saw him lying on his back without his pants. Taking a knife he cut off his brother's penis. The young man asked why he had done that, but the elder brother made no reply. Early the next day the young man collected his belongings and left. The story continues, ending with the success of the young hero, including his magical acquisition of a new penis. The narrator adds as an interpretive epimythium that one should never pay attention to what women say.[3]

The story of the calumniated youth is first found in the *Story of Two Brothers*, an ancient Egyptian text of the New Kingdom that dates to the thirteenth century B.C., one of the earliest literary treatments of an oral story that we have. In the Egyptian tale, the gods Bata and Anubis were brothers. Anubis was married and had a house, while his younger brother Bata lived with him like a son. Bata was beautiful and strong. One day when the brothers were working in the fields of the farm, Anubis sent Bata to the village to get some seed. As Bata was leaving the house with five sacks of seed, Anubis's wife praised his strength, took hold of him, and proposed that they lie together for an hour. Bata was enraged at the suggestion, and the woman became frightened. He said that she and Anubis were like a mother and father to him. Ordering her not to make the evil suggestion again and promising to tell no one, he returned with his load to the fields. But the wife was afraid because of the proposal she had made, and made herself look beaten and ill. When her husband came home she accused Bata of wishing to lie with her when he had come for seed, saying that when she refused he beat her to dissuade her from telling Anubis. She told her husband that if he should let Bata live, she would die. So Anubis angrily took a spear and lay in ambush in the stable for Bata, who had not yet returned with

the animals. Warned by the farm animals, whose speech he understood, Bata fled and was pursued by his brother. Bata prayed to the sun god, who caused the brothers to be separated by a crocodile-filled river. Bata now gave his brother a true account of the events, reproached Anubis for accepting the word of a whore, and finally cut off his penis and threw it into the water. Anubis returned home, killed his wife, and mourned his brother. The story continues, concluding with Bata's triumph after a succession of deaths and rebirths.[4]

The accessibility of the young man to the lustful woman, which each version of the story must explain in some way, is here justified by Bata's being a younger, unmarried brother who lives in his older brother's household and helps with the farmwork. When he receives the sexual proposition he responds angrily, and since his brother and sister-in-law are virtual parents to him, he suggests that such a relationship would verge on incest. In her turn Anubis's wife modifies her appearance in order to enhance the credibility and emotional impact of her account to her husband. The fraternal relationship of the husband and the youth, and the striking feature of the youth's emasculation during the confrontation of the two brothers are motifs that do not commonly appear in this story; so far as I know, they are found only in the ancient text of Bata and Anubis and in the modern oral tale summarized above, of which texts have been collected in southern Arabia and northern Africa. Such a correspondence in subsidiary features makes it likely that there is a close relationship between the modern Arabo-African tale and the ancient Egyptian story, one of the most impressive instances of apparent oral-narrative continuity—over 3,000 years—of which I am aware.[5]

Scholarly discussion of the ancient Egyptian narrative began in 1852, and investigators quickly noticed parallels between it and other texts including the biblical story of Joseph and Potiphar's wife, which is also set in Egypt. The question naturally arose whether the Egyptian and Hebrew stories were in some way related. It was soon remarked that essentially the same story was told also of characters in ancient Greek mythology and in other traditions, so that the story is an international one that belongs to no single nation.[6] The two literary treatments that we happen to possess from the ancient Near East—the Egyptian and the Hebrew—probably represent thousands of individual oral narrations in that region for which we have no direct records. In any case there is no reason to conclude that either the Egyptian or the Hebrew story is immediately indebted to the other.

Because the tale regularly occurs within complex stories that differ from one another considerably, I do not consider the larger narratives here, which would require too much space. The innocent youth's encounter with the lustful matron is usually one of several youthful trials he endures and survives, after which, like Joseph, he goes on to have other adventures and perhaps to attain a position of power and esteem; in this case the trial serves as a foil to his eventual triumph. But there is no inherent necessity that it should turn out thus, so that the calumniated hero may instead perish as the result of the accusation made against him, in which case his own story is at an end.[7]

For another story of a lustful woman, see "Matron of Ephesus."

Lit. Motif K2111, *Potiphar's Wife*. Clouston (1887) 2:499–502. Roscher 3:2224–2226. BP 4:372–373. Faverty 1931. Schlauch 1934:99–101. Trenkner 1958:64–66, 184 n. 2. Keene

1962. Paulme 1963:5–21. Horálek 1964. Yohannan 1968. Dvořcák 1978, no. 2840. *EM* 1:930–931. Ranelagh 1979:1–16. Hollis 1989; 1990:97–102. Goldman 1995.

Joseph, Potiphar's Wife, and Potiphar

In the West the story is best known in its biblical incarnation, in which it is part of the cycle of stories telling of the trials and triumphs of the Hebrew hero Joseph. In the scholarly literature the entire international tradition takes its name from the lustful woman who takes advantage of Joseph: the story (or motif) of *Potiphar's Wife*. The woman herself, like Anubis's spouse, is not given a personal name in the narrative so that she must be labeled in terms of her husband. The Hebrew legend appears in *Genesis*, which along with the rest of the Pentateuch was translated into Greek by Jews in the third century B.C. for the use of the Hellenized Jews of Alexandria.[8]

According to this account, the Hebrew youth Joseph was sold in Egypt to Petephres (the form of the name in the *Septuagint* corresponding to Potiphar in English renderings from the Hebrew), a eunuch and the Pharaoh's chief cook. Joseph lived in the house of his master and eventually was put in charge of the household. The youth was handsome, and Petephres' wife, noticing this, bade him lie with her. Joseph refused to do anything so wicked. Day after day she asked and he refused. One day when no one else was around she caught him by his cloak, telling him to lie with her, but he ran from the house leaving the cloak in her hands. Summoning the servants in the house she accused him, and when her husband came home she repeated the accusation, saying that the Hebrew slave that he had brought into the household to play games with her had told her he would lie with her, and when she screamed for help he ran off leaving his cloak. Furious, Petephres imprisoned Joseph.[9]

The Hebrew narrative is set in Egypt sometime in the second millennium B.C., and the special tensions of the incident spring from the hero's status as a foreigner and a slave. Joseph, who has already suffered from the jealousy of his own brothers, now must suffer the games of the lustful Egyptian matron in whose household he currently serves as a privileged house-slave. Her lust for Joseph, by the way, should not to be understood merely as a consequence of her husband's being a eunuch, for although eunuchs could not procreate, they were ordinarily quite capable of sexual intercourse.[10] Rather, she is not only lustful but also cunning, for she immediately reports the alleged aggression, claiming that she screamed for help, as Israelite law required an innocent woman to do if she was being sexually assaulted in an urban area, where someone might be expected to come to her aid.[11] As a slave whose master's wife makes a pass at him, Joseph finds himself in a situation in which he cannot win, for whatever he does he is likely to incur the wrath of either Petephres or his wife, and as it turns out he incurs the wrath of them both. A Hebrew among Egyptians, he also endures the ethnic prejudice promoted for her own ends by Petephres' wife, who reproaches her husband for introducing into their home a Hebrew slave to play games with her, implying that Petephres should know better than to expect otherwise from a Hebrew.[12] On the other hand, Joseph's penalty is light, for he is merely imprisoned rather than put to death, as one might have expected.[13]

Its literary career begun in Hebrew literature and broadened in the Greek translation, the episode of Joseph and Potiphar/Petephres' wife was retold and elaborated in later works in Greek and other languages. Philo interprets it allegorically in his *De Josepho*, and Josephos paraphrases it generously in his *Antiquities of the Jews*.[14] An especially interesting treatment is found in the *Testament of Joseph*, part of the *Testaments of the Twelve Patriarchs*, a Greek pseude-pigraphon modeled on the deathbed testaments of Jacob and Moses.[15] In the *Testaments* the patriarchs individually say farewell to their families by re-counting their own life stories in the first person, mixed with predictions, ad-monitions, and exhortations. This popular didactic work perhaps was begun by a Jewish author or authors in the second century B.C. and revised by Chris-tians in the second century A.D. It is uncertain whether the *Testaments* was composed originally in Greek or translated into Greek from Hebrew or Ara-maic.[16] In the *Testament of Joseph* the authors have transformed the terse novella of Joseph and Potiphar/Petephres' wife found in Genesis into a vir-tual romance by expanding it with typical features from classical and Hel-lenistic Greek tradition, including the story of Phaidra and Hippolytos.[17] Most of the composition is devoted to an elaboration of this one episode in Joseph's life.

According to the *Testament of Joseph* the wife of his Egyptian master tried for years to persuade him to lie with her, begging and threatening in turn, but Joseph, rejecting her advances, fasted and prayed. She tried various ap-proaches. Sometimes she came to him at night and pretended to embrace him as a son, having no son of her own, but her maternal embraces became erotic. Then she pretended to want religious instruction. Later she offered to kill her husband in order that Joseph might avoid committing adultery. She tried to en-chant him with drugs. She threatened suicide. Finally, she grabbed his garment in order to force him to lie with her, and when he fled without it, she accused him to her husband, who whipped and imprisoned him. Her passion did not abate, and she sent him messages offering to arrange for his release if he should fulfill her desire. But Joseph only prayed. So one should pray to the Lord and be chaste, and the Lord will rescue one from evils. The *Testament* continues with an account of how the Egyptian matron was attracted to Joseph at first sight and had encouraged her husband to purchase him, with exhortations to pray and to live in accordance with the Lord's commands, with a mention of Joseph's marriage to a daughter of the priest of Heliopolis, with prophecies and instructions, and finally with Joseph's death.[18]

Lit. Motif K2111, *Potiphar's Wife*. Gunkel 1921:125–126. Braun 1934. Braun 1938:44–104. Yohannan 1968:14–17. Redford 1970:91–93. Ranelagh 1979:1–16. Sternberg 1987: 423–427.

Whereas the ancient Near Eastern attestations of *Potiphar's Wife* amount to two stories treated in few texts, in the case of the Greek and Roman realizations we usually possess several or even many texts and allusions, their disagreements reflecting variations in oral storytelling and in literary treatment over many centuries. This abundant material can be dealt with here only very selectively.

Hippolytos, Phaidra, and Theseus

This legend belonged to the local traditions of Athens and Troizen (in the northeastern Peloponnese) and was best known to the Greeks as well as to the Romans with this cast of characters. Pausanias observes that even a barbarian who learned Greek would know the story of Phaidra.[19]

According to the mythographer Apollodoros, Theseus's wife Phaidra fell in love with her stepson Hippolytos and asked him to lie with her. But Hippolytos, who hated all women, shrank from sexual dealings with her. Fearing that he might now accuse her to his father, she broke her bedroom doors, tore her clothes, and falsely charged Hippolytos with assault. Believing her, Theseus prayed to Poseidon that Hippolytos might perish. When Hippolytos was riding on his chariot alongside the sea, Poseidon sent a bull from the sea that terrified the youth's horses, destroying his chariot and entangling him in the reins, in which he was dragged to his death. After her passion became known, Phaidra hanged herself.[20]

Euripides' tragic presentation of the story in his second *Hippolytos*, produced in 428 B.C., differs from this account significantly in its handling of the youth and especially of the matron. First, he makes Hippolytos less appealing by portraying him as a proud and intolerant person, and, second, he ennobles Phaidra somewhat by making her resolve to die, keeping her lovesickness a secret, since she cannot master it and does not wish to dishonor herself and her children by acting upon it. It is the nurse who spoiled Phaidra's plan. Learning her mistress's secret, she approached Hippolytos on Phaidra's behalf but without her knowledge or permission, and the youth of course rejected a liaison with angry horror; moreover, he reproached Phaidra in person. Phaidra now feared that Hippolytos would reveal the matter to Theseus. Wishing to preserve her honor for the sake of her sons, she decided to die, and responding to Hippolytos's contempt for her feelings toward him, she decided also to include him in the disaster. So she anticipated him by hanging herself, holding in her hands a letter in which she accused Hippolytos of improper behavior toward her.

The oral and the literary traditions of Hippolytos and Phaidra are difficult for us to distinguish. When an ancient author living after the fifth century gives a prose retelling of the story, he may be drawing upon one of the lost tragedies on the subject, and in any case he is probably drawing upon a variety of sources. So let us simply take the texts as we find them. In general the feature that most distinguishes the story of Phaidra and Hippolytos from other such stories is the extreme immoderation in love shown by both of the principals. For her part, Phaidra not only is an obsessively passionate woman but also comes from a family of such women. Her mother Pasiphae conceived a passion for a bull, mated with it, and gave birth to the Minotaur; her sister Ariadne instantly fell in love with the foreigner Theseus, who was a prisoner of her father, and helped him kill the Minotaur, her half-brother (see "Girl as Helper"); and now Phaidra herself falls in love with her own stepson. For his part, Hippolytos, whose mother was the Amazon Antiope or Hippolyte, is a devotee of the virgin huntress Artemis, goddess of the Amazons, and like her is a chaste hunter, at least in Euripides' play; consequently, he is averse to a sexual relationship with any woman at all. Expressed in terms of Greek cult, in his devo-

tion to Artemis he entirely neglects Aphrodite. He is as deficient in passion as Phaidra swims in it. Euripides complicates the lustful matron and the innocent youth, rendering the woman more sympathetic and the youth less so.

Lit. Motif K2111, *Potiphar's Wife.* Trenkner 1958:64–66. Keene 1962. Yohannan 1968:20–27. Herter 1975:128–132. Rocca 1976. Donnini 1981:145–60.

Comminius, Gidica, and Comminius Super

Comminius Super of Laurentum and the nymph Egeria had a son, Comminius. Later the father married a woman named Gidica, who fell in love with her stepson Comminius, and when she could not gratify her desire she hanged herself, leaving behind an accusatory letter. Reading the letter and believing its false accusations, the elder Comminius called upon Neptune, who sent a bull as his son was riding in his chariot. The horses dragged the boy to his death.[21]

In his little compilation of Greek stories with Roman parallels, Plutarch matches the legend of Hippolytos and Phaidra with that of Comminius and Gidica, citing as his authority for the latter the third book of Dositheus's *Italika.* But the story, which is otherwise unknown, can hardly be other than a direct transfer of the Greek story of Hippolytos and Phaidra to Italian characters, effected possibly by Dositheus.

Oddly, the nymph Egeria, who is the biological mother of the calumniated youth in this story, is the wife of Hippolytos *redivivus* in Roman tradition. According to Vergil, after Hippolytus's violent death while riding his chariot, the youth was recalled to life by the herbs of Aesculapius and the love of Diana (i.e., Artemis). Angry that a mortal should have been brought back from death, Jove cast Aesculapius himself into the death realm, but the goddess Trivia hid Hippolytus away before he should suffer a like fate, sending him to the nymph Egeria, with whom he thereafter lived under the name of Virbius in Italian woods. Because horses had caused Hippolytus's death, no horses were allowed in Trivia's temple and groves.[22]

Lit. Motif K2111, *Potiphar's Wife.*

Tenes (Tennes), Philonome (Polyboia), and Kyknos

This variation on the theme, which features a stepmother's desire for her stepson, is enlivened by her producing a witness who attests to her false accusation against the youth.

Kyknos's wife, Philonome, fell in love with her stepson Tenes. When she did not win him over she falsely accused him of seducing her, and she produced a flute player Eumolpos as a witness. Believing her, Kyknos put Tenes and his sister Hemithea in a chest that he set adrift in the sea. The chest landed at an island that Tenes called Tenedos after himself. Later when Kyknos learned the truth he stoned the flute player and buried his wife alive.[23]

Lit. Motif K2111, *Potiphar's Wife.* Stramaglia 2000:339–341.

Hebros, Damasippe, and Kasandros

This narrative is an aetiological legend giving the origin of the Hebros, a river in Thrace.

King Kasandros wed Krotonike, who bore him a son, Hebros. Separating from his first wife he wed Damasippe, who conceived a desire for her stepson and sent him a proposal about lying together. But he fled from his stepmother as from an Erinys (= Fury) and spent his time hunting. When the licentious woman failed to obtain her desire she falsely accused the chaste youth to her husband, saying that he had wanted to force her. Carried away with jealousy, Kasander rushed off to the woods, drew his sword, and pursued his son, on the grounds that he was plotting against his father's marriage. When overtaken the son cast himself into the Rhombos River, which was renamed the Hebros after him.

The story, preserved by the author of Pseudo-Plutarch's work *On Rivers*, derives from Timotheos's lost book of the same name.[24] Retold from a work that has not survived, the narrative is found in a compilation of traditions about rivers. The narrator makes no comment about the legend other than to give his source. In Greek tradition a stream or body of water is frequently said to have gotten its name from a human being who had drowned in it.[25] Thus, while Phrixos and Helle pass over water as they ride on the back on a ram, Helle falls off and drowns, after which the water is called the Hellespont, or Helle's Sea, after her. When Ikaros flies too near the sun, the wax that holds together his man-made wings begins to melt, causing him to plunge to his death into the water below, which is thereafter called the Ikarian Sea. Indeed, the aim of Pseudo-Plutarch's compilation *On Rivers* is essentially to explain how different rivers got their names from the heroes who drowned in them. In Thracian tradition the events that lead to Hebros's drowning are drawn from the *Potiphar's Wife* story, and the drowning occasions the naming of the river.

Lit. Motif K2111, *Potiphar's Wife*.

Son, Concubine, and Father

The powerful ghost of a dead man who remained active, sometimes as a revenant, in the region in which his bones lay buried was called by the Greeks a *heros*, or hero. Heroes were typically irascible, and the hero Anagyros in particular had a reputation for ferocity.[26] There was a tradition that a man cut down the hero's sacred grove. Anagyros then caused the man's concubine to desire his son. When she was unable to win over the youth, she accused him of licentiousness to his father. As a result the father maimed and immured his son and then hanged himself, and the concubine threw herself into a well.

The commentators who briefly summarize this story cite as their authority Hieronymos's book *On the Tragic Poets*, which likens the events to those in Euripides' *Phoinix*.[27] This play has not survived, but the story of Phoinix as we know it from other sources agrees with the present legend in that a concubine makes amorous overtures to a man's son, which are rejected, after which she falsely accuses the son of amorous advances; as a result, the father physically maims his son. (For the legend of Phoinix, see below.) It is remarkable that the

hero Anagyros, like the gods themselves, can affect the will and emotions of human beings, for heroes more usually cause trouble by means of physical force, rather like unruly bullies.[28]

According to a slightly different version, a certain farmer in the deme of the Anagyrasioi did violence to a nearby altar. Terrible misfortunes followed. First his wife, the mother of his son, died. Next, after the man remarried, his second wife made a false accusation against his son, and acting upon her word he maimed his son, put him aboard a boat, and left him on a wretched islet. After this he and his wife so suffered from the reproaches of their fellow townspeople that the man locked himself up in his house with all his possessions and set fire to it, burning himself to death, and his wife threw herself down a well. Whence (says the commentator) the expression *Anagyrasios daimon*, or "Anagyrasian spirit," used when terrible misfortunes one after the other befall an entire household.[29] I assume that the mistreated altar was that of the hero Anagyros, varying with the motif of the impious felling of trees in the hero's sacred grove found in the version cited above. Some commentators say more generally that people in the neighborhood tried to desecrate the hero's shrine.[30]

Lit. Motif K2111, *Potiphar's Wife*. RE 1:2027. Rohde 1925:134.

Phrixos, Demodike, Kretheus, and Athamas

In this variation the lustful woman falls not for her husband's son but for his brother's son, with the same results. The youth is not interested in a liaison, she accuses him to her husband, and the husband unhesitatingly arranges for the youth to be punished.

Kretheus was married to Demodike, who fell in love with Phrixos, son of Kretheus's brother Athamas. Though she made herself available to him, she could not obtain her wish. So she began to accuse him to Kretheus, saying that he had almost forced her and other things such as women might say. As befitted one who loved his wife and also was a king, Kretheus was very upset and persuaded his brother Athamas to punish Phrixos. But Phrixos's mother Nephele intervened and saved Phrixos and his sister Helle, placing them on a golden ram and instructing them to flee as far away as possible.[31]

Pindar alludes to the story in his Fourth Pythian Ode, where he describes the aunt's plot against Phrixos metaphorically as "the stepmother's ungodly arrows."[32] Authors call the woman variously Demodike, Gorgopis, Nephele, or Themisto.[33] Happily, Phrixos escapes thanks to a timely escape arranged by his mother. The golden ram on which he flies is the creature whose fleece Jason and the Argonauts later set out to obtain (see "Girl as Helper").

Lit. Motif K2111, *Potiphar's Wife*.

Eunostos, Ochne, and Ochne's Brothers

In his *Greek Questions* Plutarch asks: Who is the hero Eunostos in Tanagra, and why are women forbidden to enter his sacred grove? Eunostos (Plutarch

then explains) was a handsome, chaste, and austere youth who had been raised by the nymph Eunosta, from whom he got his own name. His cousin Ochne fell in love with him and made advances to him, but he rejected them, reproached her, and went off to tell her brothers what she had done. The maiden, however, beat him to it. She accused Eunostos of raping her and incited her three brothers to kill him. They lay in ambush and murdered the youth. Eunostos's father Elieus placed them in bonds. Then Ochne repented of what she had done, and, wishing both to free herself from the pain of her love and feeling pity for her brothers, she revealed the truth to Elieus, who in turn told her father Kolonos. When Kolonos rendered his judgment, his sons were banished and his daughter threw herself down a precipice. Women were forbidden to enter or approach the hero-shrine and grove of Eunostos. The story (Plutarch concludes) was told by the lyric poetess Myrtis.[34]

In this variant the lustful female is a maiden rather than a matron, and the males who take responsibility for her are brothers rather than a husband. Other than this, the narrative follows the usual pattern of the calumniated youth. Upon his death Eunostos becomes a hero, and since a woman is responsible for his undoing, no woman is allowed in his sacred grove. As in the Thracian legend of Hebros, the youth's death provides the aition for a feature of local interest, in that case the name of a river, in this case a hero cult with an unusual taboo. The class of being responsible for the hero's death (e.g., horses, women) is thereafter prohibited from entering the victim's sacred space, a familiar pattern in Greek cult.

Lit. Motif K2111, *Potiphar's Wife*. Rohde 1925:134.

In two traditions the object of the woman's passion is her houseguest.

Bellerophon, Stheneboia (Anteia), and Proitos

The mythographer Apollodoros recounts how Bellerophon accidentally killed a man and came to King Proitos to be purified. There Proitos's wife Stheneboia fell in love with him and sent him a proposal that they lie together. When he refused, she told Proitos that Bellerophon had sent her such a proposal. Believing her, Proitos dispatched Bellerophon to King Iobates bearing a letter in which Iobates was instructed to kill Bellerophon.[35]

Homer, for whom Proitos's wife is Anteia rather than Stheneboia, tells much of the legend in the *Iliad*.[36] The poet also reports that the gods gave Bellerophon beauty and manliness. According to a Roman mythographer, Anteia promised Bellerophon her husband's kingdom if he should accede to her request. When he refused, she was afraid that he would accuse her to her husband, so she told Proitos that Bellerophon wanted to take her by force.[37] The implication of Anteia's offering Bellerophon her husband's kingdom is presumably that she herself would kill her spouse or assist the youth in killing him.

Lit. Motif K2111, *Potiphar's Wife*. Roscher 1:768–770, 4:1509–1512. West 1997:365–367. Hansen 1997a:451–452.

Pelops, Hippodameia, and Myrtilos

A scholiast on Homer reports that Pelops, his new bride Hippodameia, and Myrtilos (the charioteer of Hippodameia's late father) were crossing the Aegean Sea together. When Hippodameia became thirsty and Pelops went in search of water for her, Hippodameia made advances to Myrtilos, urging him to take advantage of the opportunity afforded by Pelops's absence. Myrtilos declined. Upon Pelops's return, she accused Myrtilos of having forced her. So Pelops pushed him from the chariot into the sea, which was afterwards called the Myrtoon Sea after him.[38]

According to the more usual account, however, Myrtilos was the sexual aggressor, having previously been promised sexual favors with Hippodameia in return for helping Pelops win the chariot race against Hippodameia's father (see "Bride Won in a Tournament").

Lit. Motif K2111, *Potiphar's Wife*. *RE* 16:1157.

Peleus, Hippolyte (Astydameia), and Akastos

In this interesting variation not only the matron but also the guest is married. When her overture is rejected, the matron responds more out of hatred rather than from fear of exposure, taking steps to destroy the guest's relationship with both his wife and his host. The story is told or alluded to by a number of authors, beginning with Hesiod.[39]

Having accidentally killed a man, Peleus fled to Iolkos where he was purified by Akastos. Akastos's wife Astydameia fell in love with Peleus and sent him a proposal to lie together. When she was unable to persuade him, she sent word to Peleus's wife that he was about to marry another, and upon hearing this Peleus's wife hanged herself. Astydameia also falsely accused Peleus to her husband, saying that he had tried to seduce her. Akastos, being unwilling to kill the man he had purified, took him hunting, and when Peleus had fallen asleep, Akastos hid his sword and deserted him.[40]

Lit. Motif K2111, *Potiphar's Wife*.

A number of Greek legends closely resemble *Potiphar's Wife* and are sometimes labeled as such in the scholarly literature even though they lack one or more of the features of the basic story. Four such traditions follow.

Phoinix, Phthia (Klytia), and Amyntor

In this legend, the two men are father and son, as in the story of Theseus and Hippolytos, and the accuser is the father's concubine.

Amyntor's concubine Phthia falsely accused Amyntor's son Phoinix of seducing her or of attempting to enter her bed, as the result of which Amyntor blinded his son. He also placed a curse on his son that he would beget no offspring, and the gods accomplished this curse. Achilleus's father, Peleus, brought Phoinix to the centaur Cheiron, who healed him of his blindness and

made him king of the Dolopes, and Phoinix later accompanied Achilleus to Troy.[41]

These authorities do not say whether Phthia first attempted to seduce Phoinix, only that her own accusation was false.

The logic determining the blinding of the son is perhaps that Phoinix, like Oidipous (Oedipus) and also Teiresias, has seen things that it was improper for him to see, as a consequence of which his instrument of sight is removed.[42] The thought underlying Amyntor's curse presumably is that, just as Amyntor has no son, inasmuch as Phoinix has not been a proper son to him, so also Phoinix, being the person Amyntor holds responsible for this condition, should have no son of his own.[43]

Homer tells the story otherwise. Amyntor loved a concubine and neglected Phoinix's mother, who continually begged young Phoinix to lie with the concubine in order that the concubine might lose interest in old Amyntor. Phoinix did as she asked, and when his father found out he cursed his son repeatedly, calling upon the Erinyes (Furies) to bring it about that Phoinix should never beget a child of his own; and the gods effected this curse. Escaping from his father's house, Phoinix fled to Phthie where Peleus took him in and treated him as a son, and he remained there as ruler of the Dolopes.[44] A scholiast on the Homeric passage explains that Amyntor loved a concubine Klytia and detested Phoinix's mother Hippodameia, at whose urging Phoinix lay with Klytia. Fleeing his father's curses, he was taken in by Peleus, who gave him Dolopia and turned over to him the baby Achilleus to rear. This, the scholiast says, is the story as it is found in Homer, which the tragedians modified.[45]

In the form in which Apollodoros reports it the story is strictly not a version of *Potiphar's Wife* since it lacks the first element, wherein a woman attempts to seduce a youth and is rebuffed; and in Homer's day the legend resembled the story of the calumniated youth even less. But if the relative dates of Homer's and Apollodoros's texts reflect the historical development of the story in Greek tradition, then it appears that the legend of Phoinix was being assimilated to the plot of *Potiphar's Wife*.[46]

Lit. (Motif K2111, *Potiphar's Wife*.) Dundes 1962a:102.

Eteokles and Polyneikes, Astymedousa, and Oidipous

According to this somewhat obscure variation on the affairs of Oidipous (Oedipus), the hero divorced Iokaste, who had borne him two sons, Eteokles and Polyneikes. He then married Astymedousa, who accused her stepsons of attempted seduction. As a result, Oidipous placed the curse on them that they should acquire the land by blood, and handed the kingdom over to them, whereupon Eteokles drove his brother Polyneikes into exile on the grounds that Polyneikes was the younger brother.[47]

As in the foregoing story of Phoinix, the story as we have it lacks the feature of attempted seduction by the older woman; moreover, the narrator does not say whether Astymedousa's accusation is true or false.

Lit. (Motif K2111, *Potiphar's Wife*.)

Plexippos and Pandion, Idaia (Eidothea), and Phineus

Phineus's wife Idaia falsely accused her two stepsons Plexippos and Pandion of seducing her. Believing her, Phineus blinded them both.[48]

The mythographer Apollodoros does not make it clear whether Idaia's false accusation follows a sexual rebuff, as in a classic *Potiphar's Wife* plot, or is motivated by something else, such as jealousy toward her stepchildren. Notice that Phineus, like Phoinix, blinds his sons.

This story is told with interesting variations in our sources, apart from the usual disagreements here and there concerning the characters' names. According to a version known to Sophocles, the stepmother herself blinded the youths and confined them in a tomb; but her motive is not given.[49] The mythographer Asklepiades says that Phineus remarried a woman named Eurytia, and because of an accusation against the youths he turned them over to their stepmother to be destroyed.[50] Diodorus Siculus says that the youths were held prisoner in a vault where they were continually whipped, for their stepmother had said they offered her insolent violence in order to gratify their mother.[51] Since no author asserts that Idaia expressed a sexual interest in her stepsons, these variations take the legend no nearer to the plot of *Potiphar's Wife*.

Lit. (Motif K2111, *Potiphar's Wife*.)

Antheus, Kleoboia, and Phobios

Antheus, a youth of royal family from Halikarnassos, lived as a hostage at the house of Phobios, ruler of Miletos. Kleoboia, Phobios's wife, fell in love with him and schemed to win him over, but he rejected her, sometimes saying that he was afraid of being discovered and at other times using as a pretext Zeus, protector of hospitality, and the bond of the table they shared. Finally, Kleoboia grew angry, called him merciless and overbearing, and determined to avenge herself. As time went on she pretended that her love for him had passed. One day she drove her pet partridge down into a deep well and asked Antheus to go down and bring it up for her. Suspecting nothing, he readily descended, whereupon she dropped a rock on him, killing him instantly. Conscious that she had done a terrible deed and still burning with passion for the youth, she hanged herself. For his part Phobios was accursed as a result of this event and gave up his rule. The story, according to Parthenios, is found in the works of Aristotle and the historians of Miletos.[52]

In this variation on the lustful woman's passion for the houseguest, the woman does not accuse the youth to her husband but punishes him directly, with disastrous consequences for all.

Lit. (Motif K2111, *Potiphar's Wife*.)

The *Potiphar's Wife* motif was very productive in Greek and Roman fiction. "Just as colloquial speech provides us with a great store of verbal clichés," Jack

Winkler observes, "so popular narrative is the extensive substratum of plot clichés for literary fiction."[53]

Stepson, Stepmother, and Father/Husband

The Roman composer of mimes, Decimus Laberius, probably adapted the *Potiphar's Wife* plot to his composition, *Belonistria*, of which only a few words survive. For one of the characters, presumably a slave addressing a fellow slave, remarks: "Our mistress is vehemently in love with her stepson."[54]

Lit. (Motif K2111, *Potiphar's Wife*.)

Privignus, Noverca, et Pater/Vir

Apuleius weaves into his *Metamorphoses*, or *Golden Ass*, a novella employing the plot of *Potiphar's Wife*.

The master of a house had an educated and virtuous son. The boy's mother had died, and the father also had a twelve-year-old son from a second marriage. The stepmother, outstanding more for her beauty than for her character, was attracted to her stepson. As love burned within her, she wept and seemed ill, but the physicians could not determine the cause of her symptoms. When she could keep silent no longer, she summoned him to her bedside, and when he asked the cause of her illness, she replied that it was he, revealing her passion for him and asked him to satisfy it, lest she die. Disturbed, he cautiously said he would do so when opportunity permitted. And he left to consult an old tutor for advice. The old man said the best the youth could do was to flee. In the meantime the stepmother had arranged for her husband to leave on a journey and called upon her stepson to fulfill his promise, but the youth, who hated the sight of the woman, put her off with excuses. Finally, the woman perceived that the youth did not return her affection, and her own love turned to hatred. She plotted with a servant to kill the youth. The servant purchased poison and mixed it with wine, but, as it happened, the woman's own son drank the wine and collapsed. She coolly blamed his death on her stepson, saying that her stepson had killed his half-brother because she had refused to lie with him. Believing his wife's charges of murder and attempted incest, the father begged the magistrates to execute his remaining son. At the trial the slave gave false testimony against the youth, who would have been convicted had not an old physician offered testimony at the last moment, declaring that he himself had sold the drug to the servant and that, fearing mischief, he had supplied him with a soporific rather than a poison. So the apparently dead child was revived and the crimes of the servant and the stepmother were revealed. She was exiled and he was hanged.[55]

In this elaborate tale, the stepmother's original plan of revenge is to murder the youth, and only when that unexpectedly fails does she accuse him of licentious behavior toward her.

Lit. Motif K2111, *Potiphar's Wife*. Hammer 1923. Donnini 1981:145–60.

Timasion and His Stepmother and Father

A charming and inventive use of the motif occurs in the novelistic biography of the sage, Apollonios of Tyana, composed around A.D. 200.

Apollonios and his disciples were sailing up the Nile while a certain youth named Timasion was sailing down river. The boy was in the prime of his youth and strength. He had left Naukratis, where his stepmother had fallen in love with him and was pressing him. When he did not respond to her, she set his father against him, not as Phaidra did, but by accusing him of being effeminate and of having male lovers. So he had left Naukratis for Memphis, where he now lived and worked as a boatman on the Nile. Seeing Apollonios and his companions and judging by their clothing and books that they were wise men, he now asked if he might join them. Apollonios said they should accept him since he was a wise and moderate youth, and he recounted the youth's story privately to his companions even before Timasion's boat came alongside. When Apollonios asked the youth if he sacrificed to Aphrodite, he said he did so every day since he believed she had much influence in human and divine affairs. Then Apollonios, who was delighted, said that they should vote a crown for wisdom and moderation for him rather than for Hippolytos, since the latter, insulting Aphrodite, never experienced love in his life but was austere and rigid, whereas Timasion avoided his stepmother precisely out of respect for Aphrodite. Nevertheless, Apollonios nicknamed the youth Hippolytos.[56]

The story nicely illustrates Pausanias's declaration concerning the familiarity of the story of Phaidra, for when Apollonios (or rather Philostratos) wishes to relate the experience of Timasion and his stepmother to a supposed historical precedent, he selects the encounter of Hippolytos and Phaidra as the locus classicus. Apollonios also contrasts the passionless austerity of Hippolytos unfavorably with the moderation of Timasion, who does not reject love out of hand, only inappropriate love.

The episode of Timasion and his stepmother differs from the usual scheme of *Potiphar's Wife* stories also in that the frustrated matron accuses him not of making advances to her but of being an effeminate homosexual, a charge that is intended presumably to disappoint his father and alienate him from the boy. Whether the allegation is true and what if anything the father does we do not hear.

For another story of Apollonios of Tyana, see "White Serpent's Flesh."

Lit. Motif K2111, *Potiphar's Wife*.

Habrokomes, Manto, and Apsyrtos

In Xenophon's novel *An Ephesian Tale*, the strikingly handsome Habrokomes plays the role of the calumniated youth in two different adventures.

The newlywed Habrokomes and Anthia, having been captured by pirates, came into the possession of Apsyrtos, the chief of the pirates, in Tyre. They swore to be faithful to each other, no matter how trying the circumstances in which they should find themselves. While Apsyrtos was away on business, his daughter Manto fell in love with Habrokomes. She sent him a letter confessing her love, offering marriage, and threatening revenge if he should refuse her. But the

servant to whom she entrusted the letter did not deliver it and instead wrote a reply that he represented as being from Habrokomes, to the effect that he would not agree to her proposition. Manto was greatly angered, and at her father's return she messed up her hair and clothes, and declared to him that the slave Habrokomes had tried to take her by force, for which she now demanded revenge. Believing her without further investigation, Apsyrtos had Habrokomes whipped and tortured. Later, however, he chanced upon his daughter's original letter, perceived that Habrokomes was innocent, and freed him.[57]

Habrokomes is in a situation much like that of Joseph in the house of Potiphar/Petephres. He is a handsome, freeborn youth who because of unexpected ill fortune has been sold into slavery and now finds that a member of his master's family—in Joseph's case, his master's wife; in Habrokomes' case, his daughter—has conceived a passion for him. Oddly, Habrokomes himself does not reject the girl's advances, since the courier never delivers the message and, unknown to Habrokomes, replies negatively on his behalf. This incident as well as much of the rest of the novel contrasts the chastity and self-control of the Greek hero and heroine favorably with the excessive passion of the barbarian robber's daughter, which even Manto herself is made to mention unselfconsciously.[58]

Lit. Motif K2111, *Potiphar's Wife*.

Habrokomes, Kyno, and the Townsfolk

Later our same Habrokomes was sold as a slave in Egypt near the Nile Delta, coming into the possession of Araxos, an old soldier, and Kyno, his ugly wife, who immediately fell in love with Habrokomes and wished to satisfy her lust. While Araxos treated the youth kindly, Kyno pressed Habrokomes, offering to kill Araxos and marry him. Finally he agreed, but when she had killed her husband the Greek youth left in disgust, saying he would never lie with such a murderess. The next day she went to town, grieved over her dead husband, and accused the slave of murdering him. As a result Habrokomes was arrested.[59]

In this brief adventure the obsessed woman is willing even to kill her husband, as is Anteia in the legend of Bellerophon. The hapless Habrokomes finally consents to the matron's plan because she will not take no for an answer, but after she murders her husband the youth reaffirms his refusal. Then she, somewhat like the stepmother in Apuleius's tale, improvises an accusation of murder, for there is suddenly a corpse for which someone must be accountable, and the extreme contrast in age and looks between Kyno and Habrokomes would not permit her credibly to charge the youth with sexual aggression. Since Araxos is dead, the townsfolk take over the role of the gullible prosecutor in the tale.

Lit. Motif K2111, *Potiphar's Wife*.

Knemon, Demainete, and Aristippos

Heliodoros's story formally follows the usual pattern of the calumniated youth in all respects except that instead of the stepmother's accusing him of approaching her sexually she accuses him of kicking her pregnant belly.

Knemon recounted how his father, Aristippos, was an Athenian who, after the death of Knemon's mother, took a second wife, Demainete, a cunning and manipulative woman. She showered Knemon with an ambiguous mixture of motherly and amorous affection, and on the day he became an ephebe (that is, turned eighteen years of age) and was dressed in festive clothing she openly expressed her passion for him, calling him her young Hippolytos. Since her husband was away that evening, she tried to join her stepson in bed, but Knemon rebuffed her advances, and eventually she withdrew and began to plot against him. In the morning Demainete remained abed, explaining to her husband that Knemon had learned that she was pregnant, and that on the previous evening when she was advising Knemon not to waste his time drinking and whoring, he had kicked her in the belly. Believing her, Aristippos found his son in the house, beat him with his fists, and then had his slaves whip the youth. Knemon asked the reason for the beating, but his father only yelled at him and departed. In the continuation Demainete, carrying her revenge still further, framed Knemon by means of an elaborate scheme so that he was further alienated from his father and was forced to go into exile, where Demainete continued to pine for him. But Aristippos eventually learned the truth, and Demainete committed suicide.[60]

The matron calls the youth her Hippolytos, once more attesting to the special status of the Hippolytos and Phaidra story among the Greeks as the classic expression of the stepmother's love for her stepson. Apollonios of Tyana similarly gives Timasion the affectionate nickname of Hippolytos.

Lit. Motif K2111, *Potiphar's Wife*. Rocca 1976. Donnini 1981:145–160.

Sostratos, His Mother, and the Proconsul

In a Christian romance the victim is a young Christian, and the sexual aggressor is his own mother, a pagan.

A Christian youth named Sostratos came to the apostle Andrew and revealed that his mother, lusting after his good looks, had repeatedly pestered him to sleep with her, as a result of which he had run away; but now she has gone to the proconsul in order to charge Sostratos with her own wrongdoing. Sostratos said that if he was accused he would not defend himself, since he would rather lose his life than reveal his mother's wrongdoing, and he asked Andrew to pray for him. In the meantime the agents of the proconsul arrested Sostratos, and Andrew followed them.

The young man's mother claimed that she had barely escaped being violated by her own son. The proconsul asked Sostratos whether his mother's charges were true, but the lad made no response. When Andrew spoke up for the youth, the mother told the proconsul that after her son wanted to violate her, he stayed in the company of Andrew. The angry proconsul then ordered the boy to be enclosed in a leather bag, after the manner of parricides, and thrown into the river, and for Andrew to be incarcerated for later execution. But then the apostle prayed, there was an earthquake, and the mother was struck dead by lightning. The proconsul fell at the apostle's feet and begged him as a ser-

vant of God to save them from the earthquake. After the apostle prayed once again, the earthquake stopped. The proconsul and all his household received the word of God and were baptized by Andrew.[61]

The apocryphal *Acts of Andrew* was composed in Greek probably no later than A.D. 200, although this portion of the text is known only from the Latin epitome made by Gregory, bishop of Tours, in the late sixth century. Since Gregory did not himself read Greek, he must have found the *Acts* already translated into Latin, which he then epitomized and to some extent reworked.[62]

Sewing parricides into a leather bag (*culleum*) and throwing them into a river was a peculiarly Roman form of punishment, which the proconsul condemns Sostratos to suffer even though he is not a parricide.[63] The underlying thought is probably that Sostratos's outrageous act is tantamount to that of a parricide, for a son who sexually violates his mother destroys his family as utterly as a son who kills his father. The proconsul assigns the youth the worst possible penalty for the worst imaginable crime.

In this fictional treatment of *Potiphar's Wife* the lustful matron is the youth's biological mother, and since the male to whom she accuses the youth is not her husband but the local magistrate, she should probably be understood to be a widow. The proconsul is as credulous and rash as the husband in such stories tends to be. The Christian author delights in the contrast between the pagan mother, who is not only lustful but perverse, and the innocent Christian lad, who not only is averse to sex with his mother but will not even testify against her publicly. The youth's strategy is essentially passive-aggressive, a characteristically Christian style of behavior, for although he himself will not stand up to his mother he arranges for Andrew to do so.

In the context of the apocryphal *Acts*, this incident is one of many episodes in which the blessed Andrew draws upon the magical powers of the Christian god in order to impress and convert pagans. The story, set in Amasia in Anatolia, is one of a series of adventures Andrew has after he and the other apostles cast lots in Jerusalem in order to determine where each of them should go in order to preach the gospel.

Lit. Motif K2111, *Potiphar's Wife*. MacDonald 1994:117–119.

This survey includes all the many ancient versions of *Potiphar's Wife* known to me. Clearly the plot was extraordinarily popular among Mediterranean peoples, especially the Greeks.

Since the handsome youth may be a brother-in-law, stepson, nephew, cousin, guest, foreigner, slave, Christian, and so on, in relation to the amorous and conniving female, the narrative is capable of many nuances having to do with differences in gender, age, attractiveness, ethnicity, power, passion, self-control, morality, and religion. But the principal contrast across all the texts is that of a scheming woman whose lust is illicit and uncontrollable and a straightforward youth who can and does control his sexuality appropriately. This portrait of male and female sexuality reflects the common view in antiquity that, while

both men and women have sexual impulses, men are more able to subject them to rational control. Or, to place the notion in a more general category: men are stronger and therefore better able to show restraint in this and other areas of life, whereas women are weaker and consequently more self-indulgent.[64] Aristophanes' *Lysistrata* humorously illustrates how Greek women have great difficulty in mustering sufficient will to be sexually continent, though both men and women suffer from the sex strike and though it is a woman who devised the idea of the strike. Lysistrata finds it hard to persuade the women to undertake the strike in the first place, and presently she finds it difficult to restrain the women from deserting, overcome as they are by their desire for sexual intercourse. In Rome, Ovid similarly comments in his *Art of Love* that a man's libido is more moderate and bounded, whereas a woman's rages, and after he gives a catalogue of ten women from mythological tradition who show excessive, misdirected passion, he concludes with the observation that these instances of destructive passion are all prompted by female lust, which has more vehemence and madness than men's.[65] And the Jewish authors of the *Testaments of the Twelve Patriarchs* are fascinated with promiscuity as the worst kind of misbehavior, placing most of the blame for it upon women. In the *Testament of Reuben* the dying Reuben declares that women are evil, and since they lack authority and power over men they attract men to themselves by their looks or, failing this, by deception. Reuben goes on to claim that the angel of God instructed him that women are more overcome by the spirit of promiscuity than are men. They scheme against men in their hearts, and by decking themselves out they lead men's thoughts astray.

1. The story is not recognized by Aarne and Thompson in their *Types of the Folktale*, except as an element of the provisional tale type AT 870C*, *Stepmother Makes Love to Stepson*, for which they cite one text.

2. Bloomfield 1923.

3. Paulme 1963:11–12.

4. Pritchard 1955:23–25; Brunner-Traut 1965:28–40 (no. 5), 258–260; *EM* 1:925–940; Hollis 1990:5–15 and passim. For a text of *Potiphar's Wife* deriving from modern Egyptian tradition and collected from a female narrator, see El-Shamy 1999:215–222, no. 26.

5. Paulme 1963; Horálek 1964; *EM* 1:930–931. For the theme of emasculation see Hillers 1973.

6. Gunkel 1921:125–126; Hollis 1990:16–17.

7. *Pace* John Yohannan (1968:1), Hans Herter (1975:128–129), and Susan Hollis (1990:97–102), for whom the hero must eventually succeed. "In its original form the Potiphar motif demands a happy ending, which the *Märchen* loves," writes Herter (1975:128), who then tries to explain away the exceptions, that is, the versions in which the youth meets an unhappy ending. His error is his identifying the story as a folktale, when (with the possible exception of the ancient Egyptian story, whose oral genre is disputed) all the texts plainly represent either oral legends or literary treatments, such as the popular mediaeval work *The Seven Sages of Rome* (for which see Jaunzems 1978). In any case a happy ending is only one option.

8. Schürer (1986) 3:474–493.

9. Gen. 39:1–20.

10. Penzer n.d.:134–151.

11. Deut. 22:22–27.

12. The Greek is ἐμπαῖξαί μοι: "to play games with me" or "to mock me." Similarly Adam, when asked by God whether he has eaten anything from the forbidden tree, implies that the blame lies with God, who gave him the woman; she in turn blames the serpent (Gen. 3:12–14).

13. Redford 1970:92.

14. Philo *De Josepho* 37–79. Josephos *Antiquitates Judaicae* 2.39–59; see Braun 1934.

15. Gen. 49. Deut. 33.

16. Schürer (1973) 3:767–781; Hollander and de Jonge 1985:1–85.

17. Braun 1938:44–104.

18. For the Greek text see de Jonge 1978:144–166; for a commentary, Hollander and de Jonge 1985:362–410. There is an English rendering by H. C. Kee in Charlesworth (1983) 1:819–825.

19. Paus. 1.22.1.

20. Apollodoros *Epit.* 1.18–19. On the legend and its treatments see further Roscher 1:2681–2687; Frazer (1921) 2:146–147; Barrett 1964:1–45; Herter 1975:119–156; *LIMC* 5.1:445–464; Gantz 1993:285–288. The principal Greek sources, in addition to Euripides and Apollodoros, include Asklepiades of Tragilos (*FGH* 12 F 28 = schol. on Homer *Od.* 11.321); Diodorus Siculus 4.62; Plutarch *Mor.* 314a–b; Pausanias 1.22.1–3, 2.32.1–4; schol. Plato *Laws* 931b; Tzetzes *Schol. on Lycophron* 1329, *Chiliades* 6.504–507. Two important literary treatments have not survived, the earlier of Euripides' two dramatic treatments of the story, both entitled *Hippolytos* (distinguished in modern scholarship as *Hippolytos Kalyptomenos* and *Hippolytos Stephanephoros*, respectively), and Sophocles' *Phaidra*. Among Roman treatments see Ovid *Met.* 15.497–546, *Heroides* 4 (Phaedra); Seneca *Phaedra*; Hyginus *Fab.* 47; Servius on Vergil *Aen.* 6.445, 7.761.

21. Plutarch *Mor.* 314a–b.

22. *Aen.* 7.761–782. Cf. Ovid *Met.* 15.479–551 (the revived Hippolytos tells his tragic story to the nymph Egeria); Pausanias 2.27.4 (when Asklepios brought Hippolytos back to life, the youth refused to forgive his father and went to live in Italy).

23. Apollodoros *Epit.* 3.23–25. Our authorities for the story tell it with little variation. See further Diodoros Siculus 5.83.4; Konon 28; Pausanias 10.14.2–3; schol. Homer *Il.* 1.38; Eustathios on Homer *Il.* 1.38 (p. 33); schol. vet. on Lykophron 232. See further Roscher 5:363–365; Frazer (1921) 2:193; Fontenrose 1948:126–127; Gantz 1993:590–592.

24. Ps.-Plutarch *De Fluviis* 3.1.

25. More rarely, water is named after a human being or demigod whose body, tears, or the like has been transformed into a stream or spring that did not previously exist. See Forbes Irving 1990:299–307; cf. Hansen 2000a.

26. Diogeneianos 3.31 (*CPG* 1:219).

27. *Suda* s.v. *Anagyrasios* = Apostolios 9.79 (*CPG* 2:479).

28. Rohde 1925:134. For example, in Euripides' *Hippolytos* (24–28) the goddess Aphrodite causes Phaidra to fall in love with her stepson.

29. *CPG* 1:219–220, note to Diogeneianos 3.31.

30. Zenobios 2.55; Diogeneianos 1.25.

31. Schol. vet. in Pindar *Pyth.* 4.162 (288); Hyginus *Astron.* 2.20.

32. 4.159–162.

33. Schol. Pindar *Pyth.* 4.288. On the story see further Fontenrose 1948:127; Gantz 1993:176–180.

34. Plutarch *Mor.* 300D–F = *PMG* 716; see further Halliday 1928:173–176. Myrtis, none of whose poetry survives, was a contemporary of Pindar.

35. Apollodoros *Bibl.* 2.3.1–2.

36. Homer *Il.* 6.152–202.

37. Hyginus *Astron.* 2.18. Other sources for the story of Bellerophon and his amorous hostess include Zenobios 2.87; Tzetzes *Schol. on Lycophron* 17; and Hyginus *Fab.* 57. See also Roscher 4:1509–1512; Frazer (1921) 1:151; Hillers 1973; Reckford 1987:86–89; Gantz 1993:313–316.

38. Schol. A Homer *Il.* 2.104. Also, Eustathios on Homer's *Il.* (pp. 183.31–184.9).

39. See Hesiod fr. 208–209 MW; Pindar *Nem.* 4.57–61, 5.25–39 (where the poet says that Peleus spurned the woman's advances out of respect for Zeus, protector of hospitality); schol. Pindar *Nem.* 4.54 (88); schol. Aristophanes *Clouds* 1063 (who calls the wife Astydameia); schol. Apollonios of Rhodes *Argonautica* 1.224. See further Frazer (1921) 2:63–65; Gantz 1993:225–227.

40. Apollodoros *Bibl.* 3.13.2–3.

41. Apollodoros *Bibl.* 3.13.8; schol. Plato *Laws* 931b.

42. Oidipous blinded himself after perceiving that he had had his own mother to wife. According to one version of the blinding of Teiresias, the youth accidently came upon the goddess Athena bathing, as a result of which she tore out his eyes (e.g., Kallimachos *Hymn* 5.75–136; Apollodoros *Bibl.* 3.6.7); see further Hansen 1996b:116.

43. Dundes (1962a:102), however, suggests that both punishments are variations on the idea of castration, as found in the story of Bata and Anubis.

44. Homer *Il.* 9.430–484.

45. Schol. Homer *Il.* 9.448. On the story see Frazer (1921) 2:74–75; Gantz 1993:618.

46. Cf. Trenkner 1958:65 n. 2.

47. Schol. Homer *Il*. 4.376; Eustathios on *Il*. 4.376 (pp. 484.41–48); cf. schol. Euripides *Phoenissae* 53. See further Frazer (1921) 1:349.

48. Apollodoros *Bibl*. 3.15.3. See further Roscher 2:94–95; Frazer (1921) 2:106–107; Fontenrose 1948:144; Gantz 1993:351–353.

49. Sophocles *Antigone* 968–980; schol. Sophocles *Ant*. 981.

50. Schol. Homer *Od*. 12.69.

51. Diodorus Siculus 4.43.3–6. See also schol. Apollonios of Rhodes *Argon*. 2.178; Hyginus *Fab*. 19; Servius on Verg. *Aen*. 3.209; schol. on Ovid *Ibis* 265, 271.

52. Parthenios 14 = Aristotle fr. 556 Rose.

53. Winkler 1980:156.

54. Laberius *Bellonistria* (p. 341 Ribb.³); cf. *fab*. X, p. 363.

55. Apuleius *Met*. 10.2–12.

56. *Vita Apollonii* 6.3.

57. Xenophon of Ephesos *Eph*. 2.2–2.10.

58. 2.5: *orges . . . barbarou*.

59. Xenophon of Ephesos *Eph*. 3.12.

60. Heliodoros *Aethiopica* 1.9–17.

61. *Acts of Andrew* 2.4 (MacDonald 1990:190–194) = Gregory of Tours *Liber de virtutibus sancti Andreae apostoli* 4.

62. MacDonald 1990:1, 59.

63. MacDonald 1990:193–195 n. 7.

64. Dover 1974:98–102; Just 1991:157–165.

65. *Ars Amatoria* 1.281–282 ("Parcior in nobis nec tam furiosa libido: / Legitimum finem flamma virilis habet"), 1.341–342 ("Omnia feminea sunt ista libidine mota; / Acrior est nostra, plusque furoris habet"). Cf. Rocca 1976:31.

Quest for a Vanished Princess 🖎 Apollo of the Vultures

When his three daughters disappear, a king offers a reward for their rescue. Three men (youths) set out to look for them. Eventually, the hero is lowered by his companions by means of a rope into a well (cistern, cave, underworld, etc.) where he finds the three stolen princesses, who are being held captive by three ogres (trolls, dragons, etc.). After overcoming the monsters and rescuing the princesses, the hero has his companions pull up the princesses (and the treasure he has found, if any), but when it is time for the hero himself to come up, his companions treacherously desert him. Eventually the hero manages to reach the upper world again (e.g., with the help of a bird that he feeds, sometimes with his own flesh). Arriving at the palace on the wedding day of the princesses, he is recognized and marries one of the princesses. His companions are punished.

This very popular folktale is AT 301A, *Quest for a Vanished Princess*. I do not give a detailed summary of the whole narrative because the full range of variation does not concern us and in any case parts of this tale have no parallel in ancient tradition.[1] The early French and German investigators dubbed it the tale of the Bear's Son (*Fils d'ours, Bärensohn*) because the hero, who often is represented as being very strong, is sometimes made to be the offspring of a human being and a bear, and this convenient though somewhat misleading label is commonly used in the scholarly literature. In a famous study of the folktale, Panzer pointed out many analogues to the tale in whole or in part, including the Grendel episode of the Old English epic *Beowulf*.[2]

In a Westphalian tale collected at the beginning of the nineteenth century a king had three daughters and also an apple tree of which he was so fond that he put a curse upon anyone who should eat of it. One day his daughters, ignoring the curse, tasted the fruit of the tree, whereupon they sank into the ground and disappeared. The king offered marriage with one of them as a reward to their finder. Among other persons, three huntsmen set out to look for them. From a gnome (*Erdmänneken*) the youngest youth learned that the king's daughters were to be found down in a deep well. The gnome told him what to do and also warned the boy against his two older brothers. The next morning the three brothers went to the well with a basket and a bell. When the two older brothers were afraid to go all the way down the well, the youngest let himself be lowered down in the basket. He found the three princesses and with his hunting knife killed the three dragons that guarded them. Then he put the princesses one by one into the basket and had them pulled up. But when his turn came, he recalled the gnome's words and, instead of himself, put a stone in the basket. When the basket was halfway up, the older brothers cut the rope so that the basket fell to the bottom. Thinking their younger brother was dead, they left with the princesses, forcing them to name the older youths as their rescuers. Meanwhile, the young huntsman down in the well did not know what to do. But, seeing a flute on the wall, he began to play it, and presently many gnomes appeared. When they asked what he wanted, he said he would like to get back to the upper world. So they took hold of him, including every hair of his head, and flew with him up to the surface of the earth. He proceeded to the king's palace, and when the king learned the truth he had the two older huntsmen hanged and married the youngest to the youngest princess.[3]

According to a modern Greek text collected in Thrace, there once were three brothers who heard that there were three girls at the bottom of a well. Deciding in advance that the oldest brother should have the oldest girl to wife, the middle brother the middle girl, and so on, they went to bring them up. Going down into the well by a rope, the oldest brother sent up the two younger sisters, and as he was about to send up the eldest sister she warned him that, since she was the most beautiful of the three sisters, his brothers would want her for their wife and would pull up the rope, leaving him in the well. But since he was unwilling to go up before she did, she gave him two nuts, each containing a marvelous dress, and told him that he would see two sheep; if he succeeded in throwing himself upon the white sheep it would carry him to the Upper World, and if upon the black sheep, to the World Below. As soon as the third girl was hauled up from the well, the two youths above fell in love with her and did not let the rope down into the well again. The middle youth pressed her to marry him, but she put off marrying him until she should have two particular dresses, which were the ones contained in the nuts. Meanwhile the youth in the well waited for the rope to be thrown down, but nothing happened. Then he saw the two sheep. Failing to grip the white sheep, he flung himself upon the black one, which carried him to the World Below. There he saved some chicks from a snake, earning the gratitude of the mother bird. When she asked how she could return the favor, he asked her to carry him to the Upper World. She instructed him to load forty sheep and forty skins of water on her wings, and take a seat,

which he did. She soared. When she cried *kra* he gave her meat to eat, and when she cried *krou* he gave her the water to drink, but eventually the supply of meat was exhausted, and when the bird next cried *kra* he cut a piece from his own hip and fed it to her. Finally the bird reached the Upper World, set the man down outside the town, and replaced the man's flesh in his thigh. The youth gained entrance to the wedding by means of the two dresses, was recognized by the bride, and married her.[4]

Apollo of the Vultures

The fifty stories in the little book compiled by the mythographer Konon are preserved in excerpt by the Byzantine scholar Photios. As we have them they are presented one after the other without commentary.

According to Konon's thirty-fifth narrative, *Apollon Gypaieus*, or *Apollo of the Vultures*, two shepherds were pasturing their flocks at the foot of Mount Lyssos near Ephesos. Noticing a swarm of bees far down in a steep cavern, one of the shepherds got into a basket, and the other, tying a rope to himself, lowered him down. The man in the cavern found not only honey but also a large amount of gold. After sending up three basketloads of gold, the man called out that there was no more, so that it remained only for he himself to be pulled back up, but at that moment a suspicion of treachery entered his mind so that instead of getting into the basket himself he put a stone in it, telling his companion to pull it up. The other man pulled the basket up nearly to the rim of the cavern and then suddenly let go of it in order to kill the man inside. Then he buried the gold and devised a plausible story for persons who inquired about the disappearance of the other shepherd. As for the man in the cavern, who despaired of surviving, Apollo appeared to him in a dream and instructed him to lacerate his body with a sharp rock and lie still. The man did so, after which vultures, taking him for dead, flew down, put their claws into his hair and clothing, carried him unharmed out of the cavern, and deposited him in a hollow at the base of the mountain. The man went to the authorities and told what had happened, and the Ephesians exacted a confession from the treacherous companion, forced him to show where he had buried the gold, and punished him. They declared that half the gold should belong to the victim and half should be dedicated to Artemis and Apollo. The man who had been rescued, having become honored and very rich from the gold, built an altar for Apollo of the Vultures on the top of the mountain in honor of his rescue.[5]

This Ephesian legend provides the aition for a local altar that appeared to have been named for an unusual epiphany of Apollo, one connected with vultures, just as the Samian legend about the merchant Dexikreon provides the aition for a local cult and image with the odd name Aphrodite of Dexikreon (see "Fortune in Salt"). Notice these correspondences between the Greek legend and one or both of the modern folktale texts summarized above. (1) Seeking something (honey, princesses) in a deep hole, (2) the hero is lowered down by means of a rope, while his companion(s) remains above. (3) The hero finds something valuable (gold, princesses), (4) which he sends back up to his companion(s) via the rope, but (5) when it is his turn to come up, his companion(s) treacherously deserts him, (6) keeping the valuables for himself (themselves).

(7) The deserted hero induces a bird (birds) to carry him up to the surface of the earth, feeding it (them) his own flesh, and, once there, (8) makes the events known to the proper authorities, (9) who reward the hero and (10) punish the malfeasants.

In addition to this sequence of actions, there are a number of other interesting correspondences. First, the hero's supernatural adviser. In the ancient story the god Apollo advises the shepherd how to escape from the cavern, just as in the modern Thracian tale the elder princess, whose knowledge and wondrous objects are preternatural, advises the elder brother on how to escape from the well. The corresponding figure in the German text is the gnome, who advises the younger brother earlier in the tale, though he offers him no help while he is down in the well. Then there is the basket by means of which in the ancient Greek and modern German tales the hero is lowered, and the "stone test," in which the suspicious hero substitutes a stone for himself when it is his turn to be drawn up, following which his companion(s) attempt to kill him by drawing the basket part way up and suddenly releasing it. Notice also that the Ephesian shepherd, though seeking honey, incidentally finds a treasure in gold, just as in many folktale texts (though not in those summarized here) the hero, whether seeking princesses or not, incidentally comes upon a treasure in the hole. Finally, each of the rescuers in the modern texts answer to one or more features of the rescuer in the ancient text. The hero is carried by many birds in the ancient text just as he is carried by many gnomes in the German text, and in both cases the creatures take hold of his hair.[6] And in both of the Greek texts the hero's saviors are birds, whom he must entice by offering his own flesh, either lacerating it or cutting a piece out. The ancient text, as far as it goes, shows remarkable parallels to the modern oral tale.

Certain characters that are central to the modern folktale—the princesses and the ogres—are entirely absent from the ancient text. Liebrecht remarks that Konon's story must be connected to the märchen of the Bear's Son, containing as it does the central and final episodes of the tale, though it lacks the fight with the ogre and the freeing of the maidens.[7] Panzer adds that it also lacks the first part of the tale, though this is only a different way of making the same observation, for it is in the initial episodes that the princesses disappear, and it is the ogres who steal them. Panzer views the Ephesian legend as a text of the Bear's Son, but an incomplete one because of what he views as a garbling of the story.[8] But who is to say that this is a garbled text? While the shared features indicate that the narratives are somehow historically related, the lack of full correspondence makes the exact nature of the relationship problematic. Is the ancient text a developmentally earlier form of the folktale? Does it represent a minor tradition that has branched off from the main stock? Or is it an incompetent narration, as Panzer believes, a garbled telling of the familiar tale?

Recently Ting has brought new evidence to the question, showing at least that Konon's story is not an incomplete version of the Bear's Son, or more precisely of *Quest for a Vanished Princess*, but is a reflex of a stable, international tradition in its own right.[9] Thus, in a Chinese text there was a cliff a thousand feet high facing the Yangtze River, and halfway down the cliff there were four large beehives. Though many passersby had desired the honey, none was able to find a way of reaching the hives until two woodcutters devised a plan. One of

them was lowered by a rope connected to a long stake and, reaching the honey, sent it back up. But the man on top, wishing to monopolize the find, cut the rope and so deserted his companion on the side of the cliff. The man below yelled for a while, consumed the rest of the honey, and finally crawled into a dark cave wherein there lay a foul-smelling, python-like creature. One day the python crawled out of the cave, and the man, deciding that the creature offered him his only chance, climbed upon it. The python flew away and eventually deposited the man on the earth, after which the man made an appeal to the local magistrate, who executed the faithless companion.[10]

The Chinese text is astonishingly parallel to the Ephesian legend, even down to the details of the nature of the object sought (honey) and of the number of questers (two rather than three), while the foul-smelling flying serpent in the cave is reminiscent of the evil dragons and foul-smelling trolls that often play the role of the ogre in *Quest for a Vanished Princess*.

A somewhat similar narrative appears in mediaeval Scandinavian literature. In these episodes, the immensely strong hero and his companions decide to break into the howe, or grave mound, of a dead man. They dig a hole in the roof, and the hero is lowered by means of a rope into the barrow, where it is dark and foul-smelling. The hero gathers together the treasure he finds there and in a terrible battle overcomes the horrible revenant who dwells in the mound. In the meantime his companions, thinking he is dead, depart so that he must climb up the rope and remove the treasure on his own.[11]

Ting believes that the tradition represented by Konon's legend and the Chinese legend, which he labels Type 301F, is the progenitor of *Quest for a Vanished Princess*—that is, that the shorter tradition is a developmentally earlier story.[12] Stitt holds rather that legendary narratives such as the Chinese texts are probably branches off the main stock of the folktale rather than precursors.[13] It is hard to see how such historical questions can be answered.

There is no other substantial evidence for *Quest for a Vanished Princess* in classical antiquity. Carpenter argues charmingly for Odysseus as a representative of the Bear's Son tradition, but other than the fact that Odysseus has an ancestor named Arkeisios, or "Bearman," Odysseus's story has little in common with those of the Bear's Son tradition.[14] Actual bear's sons are found in the myth of Polyphonte, who scorned Aphrodite and her works and so became a companion of Artemis. As a result the goddess caused her to conceive a passion for a bear. After Polyphonte mated with a bear, she was rejected by Artemis and fled to the house of her father, where she bore two sons, Agrios and Oreios, who were very large and possessed immense strength. They also proved to be cannibals, which drew the disapproval of the gods, and in the end, after divine negotiations, most of the principal characters were transformed into different kinds of birds. This myth, which appears among the stories of metamorphosis compiled by Antoninus Liberalis, is sometimes cited in connection with the Bear's Son tradition, and the myth of Polyphonte does show a strong resemblance to the beginning of some texts of the Bear's Son, but the resemblance fades quickly thereafter.[15]

Lit. (AT 301A, *Quest for a Vanished Princess*.) Panzer 1910. BP 2:297–318. Liungman 1961:43–47. Ting 1970, 1971. Scherf 1982:105–111. Ashliman, type 301A. Stitt 1992.

1. For a fuller analysis, see the entries in Aarne-Thompson at AT 301 and AT 301A.
2. Panzer 1910.
3. Grimm 5 in the first edition of 1815; Grimm 91 thereafter.
4. Dawkins 1953:140–144, no. 26.
5. Konon 35 = Jacoby *FGH* 26 F 1, no. 35.
6. Konon: "tous onykhas hoi men eis ten khaiten." Grimm: "da fatten se ünne alle an, an jeden Spir (Faden) Haar, wat he up sinen Koppe hadde."
7. Liebrecht, cited by Panzer 1910:230.
8. Panzer 1910:229–230.
9. Ting 1970, 1971.
10. Ting 1970:108.
11. Stitt 1992:131–169. Stitt makes the interesting observation that the motif of abandonment appears in two characteristically different forms in the Bear's Son tradition. There is treacherous abandonment and innocent abandonment. In the märchen texts the hero's companions abandon him treacherously, in order to have the princesses and the treasure for themselves, whereas in the legend and quasi-legend texts—*Beowulf* and the Icelandic sagas—the companions abandon their post because they conclude the hero has perished (1992:27). In the Ephesian and Chinese legends, however, the companions are treacherous.
12. Ting 1970.
13. Stitt 1992:207.
14. Carpenter 1946:136–156. For traditional stories involving Odysseus, see "Homecoming Husband," "Ogre Blinded," "Sailor and the Oar," and "Sowing of Salt."
15. Antoninus Liberalis *Met.* 21. It is cited, for example, in Gaidoz 1886–87:395 and *EM* 1:1234. On Polyphonte see further Forbes Irving 1990:254–255.

Rhampsinitos

Two thieves (two brothers, father and son, uncle and nephew, master and apprentice, etc.) break into the royal treasury and remove some of the valuables, usually on a recurrent basis. The elder thief, who was one of the builders of the treasury, had secretly left one stone loose during the construction of the building so that it could easily be removed and returned, giving him entrance to the treasury (or the thieves enter through the roof or through an underground tunnel or by some other means). When the king perceives that his treasure is diminishing, but sees no sign of forced entry into the treasury, he is puzzled and distressed. He consults a sage old man (often a blind old thief) about what to do, or he simply devises his own plans. First he has a small fire built inside the treasury in order to observe where the smoke exits, whereby he discovers the thieves' secret entrance. Then he sets a trap near the entrance (usually a vat of tar or pitch) or near the valuables. When next the thieves enter, the first thief falls into the trap and is unable to escape. He instructs the second thief to cut off his head in order that, when he is found, he not be identified and his family not be implicated. The second thief does so, and the next day the king is astonished to find a headless corpse in his treasury.

Concluding that the dead thief had an accomplice, the king causes the corpse to be displayed in public, ordering his guards to arrest anyone seen weeping at the sight of it. The hero eludes this trap in one of two ways. Either the king has the corpse dragged through every street, and when it comes to his own street and the woman of the house, who is the mother (or widow) of the dead thief, bursts into tears, he deliberately wounds himself, explaining the woman's weeping as an expression of concern for his injury. Or the king displays the

corpse in a public place, and when the mother or widow of the dead thief wishes to be able to mourn him safely, the hero counsels her to pretend to drop a jar of milk (oil) in the vicinity of the corpse and to explain her weeping as being for the loss of her milk (oil); and she does so.

The king now displays the heavily guarded body in the hopes of catching the surviving thief in the act of retrieving it for burial. The hero succeeds in stealing the corpse in one of several ways. He disguises himself, drives a donkey laden with wine (often said to be drugged with a narcotic) to the place, and devises an excuse to share the wine with the guards, who presently fall into a drunken or drugged sleep, whereupon he inflicts on them some sign of ridicule (cuts their hair, shaves off half their beard, changes their clothing) and makes off with the body. Or the corpse is guarded by two groups of men, one dressed in white and the other in black, and the hero, dressed half in white and half in black, rides between the two groups of guards and, unnoticed by them, steals the body. Or when the king displays the body in a cemetery, the hero approaches the guards in the guise of a supernatural spirit, and when they flee in fear he takes the body. Or pretending to be a member of a religious sect, he makes off unnoticed with the cremated remains of his partner and disposes of them properly.

Various other episodes occur frequently in which the king attempts unsuccessfully to identify or capture the thief, such as one in which the king tries to lure the thief into stealing a certain animal (e.g., a camel) in the hope of catching him. When the thief succeeds, the king dispatches persons to beg at every door for a certain kind of food (e.g., camel fat) in order to learn which household possesses it. When the lady of the house unthinkingly gives the beggar some of the food, the beggar marks the house with it in order that it can be distinguished later. But the hero kills the beggar and/or places similar marks on all the houses of the neighborhood.

Eventually the king employs his daughter as a lure (as a prostitute, in the palace garden, etc.) and/or holds a ball or banquet at the palace. The thief is detected in one way or another (he alone is so bold as to lie with or dance with the princess, he is induced to tell his story, he becomes drunk and speaks unguardedly, he is found to have stolen goods, etc.), but he escapes capture. Either he covertly brings along the arm of a cadaver, treating it as his own, and when the princess tries to grab him she gets the cadaver arm while he himself escapes. Or she secretly marks him in some way (putting a black mark on his forehead, shaving his hair or beard as he sleeps), but he discovers the mark and similarly marks the other men as they sleep, so that he cannot be distinguished from the others. Finally, the king decides to give up trying to capture the thief and offers the man his daughter in marriage. The hero comes forward and identifies himself, or the king employs a child to identify the thief. The hero weds the princess.

This international tale of the master thief, AT 950, *Rhampsinitos*, consists of a series of episodes illustrating a contest of wits between a king and a thief, in which the king cleverly attempts to identify and capture the thief by various stratagems while the thief even more cleverly succeeds in his thievery at the expense of the king. In the end the monarch usually gives up the game as hopeless and, concluding that his opponent is too clever for him, decides to ally

himself with the man by making the thief his son-in-law and successor. In some tellings the thief is already a recognized master of thievery at the onset of the tale, but in most texts he simply follows his father or uncle into the profession and happily chances to be almost preternaturally talented at it. Similarly, the king also chances to be clever or employs a cunning, retired thief as his adviser, pitting trickster against trickster.

Like many other trickster narratives, *Rhampsinitos* is not a moral tale. The hero shows some qualities of conventional morality such as that he is loyal to his family, but beyond that he is fundamentally amoral. He enjoys cleverness for its own sake, caring little whether his actions are legal or illegal, just or unjust, harmless or harmful, being more engaged by the game than by the prize. He is a rogue, a charming sociopath, and we become caught up in his almost childish delight in playing games, in having fun. We want him to win, not because he deserves to win, but because we like him.

The folktale tradition is difficult to summarize because different texts vary in how many episodes they include, in the point at which they bring the tale to a close, and in the content of the episodes. Some divergences in content reflect regional ecotypes. One of the most interesting of these is the episode of the Weeping Test.[1] The European texts regularly present the king's instructing his men to drag the corpse all through the town in the hope that someone will be unable to suppress his or her grief at the sight of it. When in fact this happens, the hero must improvise an excuse on the spot, which he does by deliberating injuring himself and falsely presenting the injury as the cause of the woman's weeping. In the Eastern and modern Greek texts, on the other hand, the woman generally does not burst out into grief but instead creates an opportunity for herself to grieve safely. Since the woman wants to be able to mourn in the presence of the corpse, the hero devises in advance a ploy that will enable her to do so. For the French folklorist Gaston Paris the variation reflects the different ways that East and West envisage mourning: for the European it is a matter of feeling, whereas for the Asiatic form is everything.[2]

The tale is found in many lands. In one of the early studies of the tale, Paris found nineteen texts in fourteen different languages.[3] The earliest texts are found in fifth-century Greece, while in the Orient it is attested as early as the third century A.D., in a Chinese text translated from the Sanskrit.[4] I summarize a number of texts, giving more attention to features that appear also in ancient authors and omitting a few episodes in the interest of economy.

In *Dolopathos*, a work composed in Latin at the end of the twelfth century, there was a king who possessed immense wealth, which he enclosed in a strong tower. The king's treasurer retired, having grown old, but when the extravagances of his elder son all but ruined him, he decided to draw upon the royal treasury. One night, accompanied by his son, he broke through the wall with iron tools, took what he wanted, repaired the breach, and left; and thereafter he and son often repeated this stratagem. One day the king visited his treasury and found it greatly diminished but with no sign of entry. Now, the king had in his palace an old man, once a famous thief, whom the monarch had blinded but then taken care of. When the king posed the puzzle to him, he had some fresh vegetation burnt in the treasury, telling the king to see if any smoke escaped from the tower. The king found that it escaped through the thieves' en-

trance, which they had closed with a single, unmortared stone. On the advice of the old man, the king placed before it a vat of hot tar and pitch. When the thieves returned, suspecting nothing, the father entered first and fell into the vat, sinking to the level of his chin and being unable to move. He told his son to cut off his head in order that he not be recognized and thereby endanger and dishonor his family, and the son, being unable to free his father, decapitated him and returned home with the head. The next morning the king was surprised at the sight in his treasury. His old adviser told him to attach the corpse to a horse and drag it through the streets; soldiers should follow and arrest anyone who wept at the sight of the corpse. When they reached the thief's house, the thief, knowing that he would not be able to hold back his tears, deliberately cut off his thumb. His cries brought his mother and his siblings, who wept and tore their hair. The youth was arrested and brought to the king, but he explained his cries and the weeping of his family by his mutilated hand. When the corpse was dragged past the thief's house a second day, the thief cast his only son into his well. Brought before the king once again, he explained the grieving of his family by the loss of his son. Now the old sage advised the king to suspend the corpse in public, guarded on one side by twenty knights dressed in white and on the other side by twenty knights dressed in black; the thief would surely try to take the corpse and would be captured. But the youth dressed one side of himself and his horse in white and the other side in black, and approached the gallows in the moonlight. The white guards, seeing only his black side, took him for one of the black guards, and vice versa, so that they let him pass. In the morning the guards saw that the body had been removed. When the king was so informed, he gave up trying to catch the thief.

So far the Latin text. But in a translation of the Latin composition into French verse made by Herbert at the beginning of the thirteenth century, the tale continues. The king, at the advice of his counselor, invited all the knights to his palace for a tournament, followed by a banquet in the palace that would include the king's beautiful daughter; the adviser did not doubt that the thief would make his way to her if the gates were left open. And, indeed, the thief slipped into the palace and found his way to the princess's room. She did not resist him but, following her father's orders, placed a black mark on his forehead. When the young man later discovered the mark and found that he could not wash it off, he put a similar mark on the foreheads of all the knights sleeping in the palace as well as on the counselor and the king himself. The king's adviser had only one more plan. All the knights were assembled at the palace, and the old counselor gave a knife to a young child, telling him to hand it to the man who robbed the treasury.[5] But the thief proposed to the child to exchange the knife for a toy, which the child did, enabling the thief to claim that the child's judgment was motivated and therefore invalid. The old thief told the king that, though the youth surely was the thief, he was always clever enough to justify whatever occurred; accordingly, the king should grant the thief clemency and give the man his daughter in marriage, since she would not find a better marriage. The king did so.[6]

This narrative contains, broadly speaking, the Theft (break-in through the wall), the Sage Adviser and Smoke Test, the Trap (vat of pitch) and Decapitation, the Weeping Test (twice, employing improvised injuries), the Theft of the

Corpse (in the form of the black and white guards), the Princess as Lure (with the marking of the hero foiled), the Child as Detector (foiled), and the Marriage of the Hero and the Princess.

According to the *Pecorone* of the Florentine Ser Giovanni, composed in 1378, a certain Bindo of Florence constructed for the duke of Venice a chamber in which the treasure of the republic was stored.[7] The architect, however, deliberately left one stone loose. Subsequently he entered it with his son Ricardo and stole much gold. Upon the advice of one of his men, the duke burnt wet straw in the room and saw that the smoke escaped around the loose stone. He placed a container of boiling pitch beneath the stone, and when Bindo fell into it the father ordered his son to cut off his head. Another counselor advised the duke to drag the corpse through the city and arrest anyone who wept at the sight. When Bindo's widow, who was watching from a window, cried out, she and her son would have been arrested had he not taken his knife and cut a big gash in his hand. The duke then had the corpse hung by its feet in the city square, which caused the mother to reproach her son. So he acquired black outfits, masks, and torches for twelve of his companions, and dressed himself as the devil. At the sight of this infernal procession, the guards fled, and the youth recovered the corpse and gave it burial. Next, the duke forbade the sale of fresh meat in Venice for twenty days, while he offered a calf for sale at an extravagant price, expecting that only the thief could afford it. But Ricardo found a pretext for giving the guards some vine with which he had mixed a soporific, and carried away the calf as they slept. The duke dispatched a hundred beggars to find a house at which they would be given fresh veal and to mark the house. Ricardo's mother gave veal to one of the beggars, but Ricardo invited him in for more meat and then killed him. On the advice of another counselor, the duke invited twenty-five clever youths to the grand hall of the palace, near the room of the duke's daughter, who was instructed to mark, by dipping her finger in ink, anyone who should approach her. She so marked Ricardo, but when he perceived it he placed the same sign on the other sleepers. The next day the duke, admiring the unknown thief, promised him his daughter and a large dowry, whereupon Ricardo made himself known and got both daughter and dowry.[8]

Here we have the Theft (entry by movable stone), the Sage Adviser and Smoke Test, the Trap (vat of pitch) and Decapitation, the Weeping Test (improvised injury), the Theft of the Corpse (infernal procession), the Animal as Lure (guards inebriated) and the Beggar (killed), Princess as Lure (marking of the hero foiled), and the Marriage.

In a Cypriote text published in 1868 an uncle and his nephew broke into a king's treasury by making a hole in the roof. To discover how the thieves entered, the king turned to an old, imprisoned thief, who counseled him to close the windows and doors and see if any light entered the room. Finding thereby the opening in the roof, the king placed a vat of boiling pitch beneath the place. The uncle fell in, and the nephew cut off his head. The old thief told the king to hang the corpse in the bazaar and arrest anyone who came there to mourn. The nephew advised the widow to fill a jar with milk, proceed to the cadaver, let the jar drop, and pretend that she was weeping for her spilled milk. She did so. On another occasion the king loaded a camel with precious goods in the hope that

the thief would not be able to resist stealing it. The youth, disguising himself as a wine merchant, offered his wares to the men escorting the camel. Won over by the excellent bargain, they drank liberally, became drunk, and fell asleep, whereupon the thief shaved their beards and half of their hair and then took the camel to his aunt's house where he slaughtered it. The king dispatched an old woman to beg for camel fat, and when the thief's aunt gave her two pots of it the beggar marked the door with the grease. But upon his return the young man understood what had happened, and marked every house in town. At this point the aged thief informed the king he could not compete with the unknown thief. So the king collected his soldiers and offered rich presents to the thief if he would introduce himself. When the thief, who was disguised as a soldier, said, "It's me," the king cried out, "Arrest him!" So the thief cried out just as the others did and mixed with the soldiers so that he was not recognized. Then the king let it be known that the man who should reveal to the princess the villainy he had done would become the king's son-in-law and heir. So the thief went to the cemetery, cut off the arm of a cadaver, and went to the princess during the night, telling her of all the tricks he had played on her father. She grabbed him and called out for people to come, saying she had the thief by the arm. But when persons came with torches, they found that she had only the arm of a cadaver. Finally, the king really decided to give up his throne to the man who had stolen his treasure, and when the youth introduced himself, the king gave him his daughter and throne.[9]

This text shows the Theft (entry through roof), the Sage Adviser and the Smoke Test (in the form of a light test), the Trap (vat of pitch) and Decapitation, the Weeping Test (solution: the dropped jar), the Animal as Lure (guards inebriated) and the Beggar (all houses marked), False Offer of Clemency, the Princess as Lure (the cadaver arm), and the Marriage.

In a Turkish text, two brothers broke into a king's treasury through the roof. The king consulted an old, onetime thief, who discovered the hole and placed a container of pitch beneath it. The elder brother was caught and decapitated by the younger brother. Then comes the Weeping Test, in the form in which the widow deliberately drops a jug of milk. Then the thief himself went with a wagon loaded with alcohol to the gallows where the corpse of his brother was displayed. After making the guards drunk, he stole the body and buried it. After a couple more unsuccessful attempts to ensnare the thief, the king placed his daughter in the roadway at night with a prohibition against anyone's approaching her, not doubting that the thief would attempt it. It so happened, and she cut off his mustache on the right side in order that he might be recognized the next day, but in the meantime he had cut off half the mustache of a hundred other men, and the next morning the king was astonished to find that a hundred men had passed the night with his daughter. The king determined to try the same trick once more, but this time the girl was to seize the thief by the arm. But the thief cut off the arm of his dead brother and let the princess seize it. The next day the princess was congratulated for holding on so tightly to the thief that she had torn off his arm when he fled, and the king's men searched all over for a one-armed man, but in vain. The tale continues with several more adventures, and in the end the clever thief marries the king's daughter.[10]

The tale contains the Theft (via the roof), the Sage Adviser, the Trap (vat of pitch) and Decapitation, the Weeping Test (jug of milk), the Theft of the Corpse (guards inebriated), the Princess as Lure (twice: first with marking, second with cadaver arm), and the Marriage.

Finally, in a Buddhist tale from Tibet translated from a lost Sanskrit original, the nephew of a weaver learned the trade of thievery from his uncle and presently surpassed him in it. When the master made a hole into a house in order to gain entrance, the apprentice advised him to enter backward. The people in the house grabbed the uncle by his legs so that the nephew cut off his head and left with it. The king, wishing to learn who committed the crime, had the corpse displayed on a gallows, and ordered his guards to arrest anyone who wept or embraced the body. The nephew pretending to be a fool went to the place and, embracing everyone he encountered, was able to embrace also his uncle without exciting suspicion. Wishing now to cremate the corpse, the nephew dressed as a carter, filled his wagon with dry wood and shavings, went to the gallows, pretended to drop his load by mistake, and after unyoking his bullock set fire to it cart and all, thereby cremating the corpse. In order to cast his uncle's bones into the sacred river, the youth now disguised himself as a skull-carrying worshipper of Shiva. Going to the remains of his uncle, he managed to fill the skull with the remains of his uncle and cast it into the Ganges. The king dispatched his daughter alone to a garden near the Ganges, not doubting that the thief would approach her. She was to cry if anyone touched her, and soldiers were posted nearby. The thief managed to enter the garden, threatened to kill her if she made a sound, had sex with her, and departed. She became pregnant and gave birth to a son. The king obliged all men to assemble at a certain place. The princess's son held a garland, and the man to whom he offered it would be regarded as his father. The boy handed it to the thief, who thought himself lost, but the king, admiring his talent, pardoned him and give him his daughter in marriage.[11]

In this narrative we find the Theft (break-in, which is foiled), the Decapitation, the Weeping Test (hero as fool), the Cremation of the Corpse, the Theft of the Corpse (religious disguise), the Princess as Lure, the Child as Detector (successful), and the Marriage.

Rhampsinitos

Herodotos devotes the second book of his *Histories* to an extended account of Egypt, in the course of which he relates the famous legend of the Treasury of Rhampsinitos, the earliest treatment in literature of this international oral tale. The historian represents Rhampsinitos as a monarch who ruled Egypt after Proteus and before Kheops, and he has three things of tell of him: first, his contributions to what Herodotos calls the Temple of Hephaistos; second, the robbery of his treasury; and, third, his descent to and return from the death realm. This figure, whose Greek name "Rhampsinitos" is a rendering of the Egyptian royal name "Rameses" plus the royal epithet signifying "son of (the goddess) Neith," appears to reflect no single pharaoh of Egyptian history but rather to be a traditional composite inspired by the pharaohs of the Nineteenth and Twentieth Dynasties, almost all of whom bore the name Rameses.[12]

The story itself, Herodotos implies, he heard from Egyptian priests at Memphis, from whom he says he acquired much other information about Egypt. Some scholars doubt the reality of this source, but in the case of the present story it seems unreasonable on the basis of internal evidence to declare that the historian cannot have gotten the narrative from them, and if he did not learn this particular story from the priests of Memphis, he surely learnt it from other residents of Egypt, either natives or Greeks.[13] The issue has occasioned much discussion among scholars who wish to credit Herodotos's excellent story either to the genius of the Greeks or to that of the Egyptians.[14] Often it is unclear whether the scholars, in arguing origins, have in mind the actual oral text upon which Herodotos drew (was it Greek? Egyptian? both?) or the urtext of the entire tale tradition (did the tale of the two thieves arise in Greece? Egypt? elsewhere?), since many scholars fail to distinguish clearly between these two kinds of text, simply identifying without further argument the earliest published text with the roots of the oral story. But I leave aside the quest for origins, which has added little to our understanding. In fact no one knows where or when the oral story itself arose, and it could have already been ancient in Herodotos's day.

Its success as a folk narrative is proved by its international circulation and demonstrably long life. The particular version that Herodotos heard in Egypt is—to judge from the content and organization of Herodotos's narrative—a very competent instance of the type, but the fame of the story of Rhampsinitos among educated persons is clearly due in no small part to the charm with which Herodotos, a master raconteur, relates it. We do not have a text of the oral story that was told in ancient Egypt, only a Greek literary retelling that was inspired by it. If the text we possess needs an ethnic label, we can call it Greco-Egyptian. Herodotos's story goes as follows.

King Rhampsinitos of Egypt had so much silver that he had a stone treasury constructed in order to house it. But the man who built the treasury had designs on the silver, so that he made one of the stones of the outside wall such that it could easily be removed by one or two men. When the builder was on his deathbed he summoned his two sons to him and revealed to them the secret of the king's treasury, saying that he had constructed it in this way with them in mind in order that, if they kept the secret, they might have a life of abundance. The man died, and the sons went at night to the treasury, found the removable stone, and took away a considerable amount of money. The next time the king went to his treasury, he was surprised to find some of his valuables gone. He did not know whom to accuse, since the seals and locks were intact. When this happened a second and a third time, the king had traps placed around the vessels in which he stored his money. The thieves came again, and the first man to enter was caught in one of the traps. He summoned his brother, explained what had happened, and told him to enter and cut off his head in order that the one not be recognized and thereby cause the downfall of the other as well. The second brother did so and after replacing the stone went home with his brother's head. The next day the king was surprised to see the headless body of the thief in the trap and the room itself undamaged.

Not knowing what else to do, the king had the thief's body hung from a wall, where he stationed guards with orders to arrest anyone who should weep or grieve. The boys' mother was very upset by the display of the corpse and told

her remaining son that if he did not devise a way of obtaining his brother's body, she would turn him in as the thief. Filling some skins with wine and loading them on some donkeys, he drove the animals to the place where the guards were. There he secretly loosened the openings of some of the skins and, as the wine flowed onto the ground, he cried aloud and beat his head, pretending to be in despair. The guards ran over to collect the flowing wine with their pots, counting it a piece of luck. The thief pretended at first to be angry and then to have calmed down, and presently they all fell in drinking and joking together, with wine provided by the thief. After a time the guards fell asleep, and when it was dark the thief took down his brother's body, put it on the donkeys, and went home, after shaving the right cheek of each of the guards. The angry king, craving to learn who had devised these capers, sent his daughter to a brothel—Herodotos remarks that he himself finds this incredible—with instructions to receive any man who came to her and, before they had sexual intercourse, to compel him to tell her what was the most clever and most unholy thing he had done in his life; and if any man told of the thief, she was to grab him and not let him go. The thief learned of her mission and wanted to outdo the king. Concealing the arm of a corpse under his cloak, he went to the king's daughter and, when he was asked the questions, replied that his unholiest act was to cut off his brother's head in the king's treasury and his cleverest act was to make the guards drunk and steal his brother's body. When she heard this and started to grab him in the dark, he held out the arm of the cadaver, and while she held it he fled out the door. When this was reported to the king, he marveled at the man's inventiveness and daring, and proclaimed throughout Egypt that the thief would be both pardoned and rewarded if he should come before the king. When the thief came, Rhampsinitos gave him his daughter in marriage, saying that the Egyptians were the most intelligent of men but this man was the most intelligent of the Egyptians.[15]

The Greco-Egyptian text includes the Theft (movable stone), the Trap (evidently a kind of animal trap) and the Decapitation, a trace of the Weeping Test, the Theft of the Corpse (guards inebriated), the Princess as Lure (cadaver arm), and the Marriage. Obviously, we have a narrative belonging to the same tradition as that to which the texts summarized above belong, while at the same time the ancient narrative shows some interesting differences from them.[16] There is no Sage Adviser to whom the pharaoh resorts for help, and no Smoke Test or vat of pitch; instead, as occasionally happens in modern texts, a kind of snare is placed in the vicinity of the valuables themselves. The Smoke Test and the vat of pitch are linked features, since the Smoke Test enables the king or his adviser to pinpoint the exact spot at which the thieves enter and thereby indicates precisely where the vat must be placed. A king who places a snare near his treasures does not need to know how the thief enters, only what he is after.

The Weeping Test appears only vestigially, as several investigators have noticed.[17] Herodotos sets the episode up, saying that the king ordered the body displayed in a public place while instructing his guards to arrest anyone who should weep or mourn for it; but the narrator does not follow through, explaining how the trickster solved this problem, and consequently no one at all is mentioned as weeping for the dead youth. Since this preparation for the episode shows that it figured as part of the oral story at that time, it follows that

either Herodotos curtailed the incident or it happened to be curtailed in the version he heard. I observe in passing that the fragmentary condition of this episode militates against the assumption, if anyone should wish to make it, that all subsequent texts somehow derive from Herodotos, for it is easier to imagine that Herodotos's text reflects an omission or confusion in the telling of the tale than that later narrators expanded the hint found in Herodotos into so logical and appropriate an episode as that of the Weeping Test, which is found in almost every text of the tale.[18] If we did not possess the later texts of the tale, we would not have suspected that an entire episode lay concealed behind Herodotos's reference to the king's order to arrest anyone who should mourn the corpse.

We can even say with some confidence what form the remainder of the episode must have taken in the ancient Egyptian story, for it is characteristic of the oriental form of the folktale that the thief's body be displayed in a stationary, public place, forcing any would-be mourner to come to the corpse, which is what we find in Herodotos' account, in which the thief's decapitated corpse is hung from a wall rather than dragged through the streets. Furthermore, as Paris cleverly suggests, we can probably see a trace of the abbreviated episode in the action of the episode that immediately follows, when the hero, loading a donkey with wineskins and driving it to the place where his brother's corpse was displayed, *deliberately unloosed the wineskins as though by accident, crying out as the wine flowed onto the ground*. This is exactly the ploy that the mother or widow, following the advice of the hero, regularly uses in the Eastern texts in order to gain access to the corpse and weep in its presence, except that as a woman she drops milk or oil rather than wine. Since the thieves in Herodotos's story are brothers, the mourner would be their mother. If this inference is correct, we also perceive what has happened in the retelling of the Weeping Test. The narrator does not entirely omit the conclusion of the Weeping Test; rather, he conflates it with the following episode, where it becomes the deliberately spilled wine.[19]

Before he departs from the drunken guards the thief humiliates them by shaving off half of their beards. This act has occasioned some scrutiny by scholars, who point out on the one hand that this form of insult is attested elsewhere in the ancient Near East (II Samuel 10:4–5 recounts how the king of the Ammonites, taking David's envoys for spies, cuts off half their beards as well as the bottom half of their cloaks up to their buttocks) and, on the other hand, that Egyptian soldiers did not ordinarily wear beards.[20] However that may be, the idea is one of several floating motifs, as one might call them, in the tale taken as a whole. It can occur either here, where it is a sign of derision employed by the hero, or later, with a different meaning and a different function, as a sign of identification employed against the hero. In the former slot the shaving is an insult, but the same point can be made in other ways, most often by the hero's dressing the guards in different clothing while they drunkenly sleep. In the latter slot it is part of a plot to capture the hero. The princess shaves the sleeping hero, thereby branding him for later identification, a ploy that also can be done in other ways such as by her placing a mark on his forehead.

Another floating motif in the tale is that of the thief's making the guards drunk or drugged. The ruse may be attached either to the episode in which the guards watch over the corpse of the dead thief or to the episode in which the

guards watch over a valuable animal, an incident that frequently follows the former and rather resembles it. In both cases the guarded object is really a lure to entice the thief to show himself and attempt a theft. In both cases it is only one of several ways that the tale tradition as a whole contrives for the hero to accomplish the theft, for both the corpse and the animal can be stolen in other ways as well.

After the theft of the corpse, Herodotos's story moves to the king's final ploy in which he uses his daughter as a lure. There is no trace in the Greco-Egyptian story of the several other episodes (such as the Animal as Lure) that in various later texts can be found at this juncture in the tale. The Princess as Lure is ordinarily the high point of the tale, the king's most drastic gamble as well as a preliminary encounter between the princess and the thief, thematically preparing for their eventual marriage. In Herodotos's story the lure is so outrageous and unrealistic—the princess as prostitute—that the narrator distances himself from it, declaring that he does not believe it. But it is scarcely unique, for many other texts feature the princess as bait, and in some of them the lure is clearly sexual in nature, as it is in the Greco-Egyptian story, while in others the sexual element is toned down or absent, perhaps reflecting an increasing use of this tale, like other folktales, as entertainment for children.[21] With this episode Rhampsinitos and the thief have become morally alike, for just as the thief decapitated his own brother to gain something, the king has now descended to prostituting his own daughter in order to obtain something for himself. The thief moreover has become more kingly because of his successes, while the king has been humiliated by his failures. Over the course of the story the great differences between them become gradually reduced to insignificance, paving the way for the reconciliation of the two men and for the marriage of the thief to the pharaoh's daughter.[22]

Other elements in this episode are known as well from other texts of *Rhampsinitos* or from other oral-narrative contexts. Thus, the idea of the brothel at which every man must tell of his best and worst deed, though it does not appear in other texts of *Rhampsinitos* that I have seen, is obviously a close kin to the motif, found in other folktales, of the inn in which everyone must relate his life story, which leads to a recognition scene.[23] On the other hand, the trickster's use of an arm from a cadaver to escape from the princess in the brothel is an occasional feature of this folktale and also occurs in other oral stories in which the trickster, as in Herodotos's narrative, leaves it behind with a surprised dupe.[24]

Lit. AT 950, *Rhampsinitos*. Prato 1882. Maspero 1885. Clouston (1887) 2:115–165, 480–488. Mayor 1893. Koehler (1898) 1:198–210. Paris 1907. Campbell 1907:lxxxv–xc. Huet 1908, 1916, 1918a, 1918b. BP 3:395–406. Aly 1969:67–68. Penzer (1926) 5:245–286. Wesselski 1931:146–151. Liungman 1961:244–245. Petropoulos 1965. Brunner-Traut 1965:287–289. Fehling 1977:89–97; 1989:210–211. Matsubara 1978. Lloyd 2:53–54. Dvořák, no. 1996. Ashliman, type 950. Speer 1990. Munson 1993.

Trophonios and Agamedes

If the legend of the thief who weds the pharaoh's daughter is essentially an Egyptian story, the legend of Trophonios and Agamedes is certainly Greek. In it we recognize the first episode of the tale.

From the historian Charax of Pergamon, as reported by a scholiast on Aristophanes, we learn that Agamedes, ruler of Stymphalos in Arkadia, was married to Epikaste, who had a son, Trophonios, out of wedlock. Agamedes and Trophonios surpassed all other men of their day in their craftsmanship, executing for example the temple of Apollo at Delphi. They also built a golden treasury for King Augeias of Elis, leaving in it a stone joint by means of which they—together with Kerkyon, a legitimate son of Agamedes and Epikaste—could enter it at night and rob the king of his money. Augeias did not know what to make of his losses and asked Daidalos, who was staying with him at the time, to track down the thief. Daidalos placed a trap in the treasury, and Agamedes was caught by it and perished. Trophonios cut off his head in order that he not be recognized, and fled together with Kerkyon to Orchomenos, but because of the bloodshed Augeias, on the advice of Daidalos, pursued them, so that Kerkyon fled to Athens while Trophonios fled to Lebadeia in Boiotia. There he constructed an underground dwelling for himself and lived in it. When he died, the place manifested itself to people as an oracle, and they sacrifice to him as a god.[25]

The story was perhaps treated in literature as early as the sixth century B.C., for it was evidently recounted by Eugammon of Kyrene in his epic, *Telegonia*. The poem is lost, but according to a summary of its contents by Proklos, Odysseus after the slaughter of the suitors sailed to Elis where he visited Polyxenos. His host gave him as a gift a mixing bowl on which there was pictured the story of Trophonios, Agamedes, and Augeias.[26]

In Charax's narrative we have the Theft (movable stone), the Sage Adviser, the Trap (a kind of snare), and the Decapitation, followed by the king's continued but unsuccessful pursuit of the robbers. The explicit motive for the decapitation, to efface the identity of the trapped thief, seems inexplicably not to work, since we next hear how the king sets out in pursuit of the thieves, whose identity he must therefore know. But the whole account is abbreviated, and we cannot say what is missing from it. It is uncertain, for example, whether Trophonios reluctantly decapitates Agamedes upon the latter's instruction or does so entirely upon his own initiative in order to protect himself against incrimination. Charax's narrative agrees with that of Herodotos in showing the motif of the movable stone secretly left by the builder of the treasury and the trap that takes the form of a snare set around the goods rather than a vat of pitch placed at the thieves' entrance. These shared features evidently reflect the way the story was told in antiquity, at least in Mediterranean lands, as opposed to the Smoke Test and its associated Trap in the form of a vat of pitch that characterizes many later texts.

Interestingly, in some respects Charax's narrative differs from Herodotos's text and resembles many modern ones. First, the king resorts to a clever adviser to help him catch the thief, in this case Daidalos, who has evidently made his way to Elis after his escape from his imprisonment in the Labyrinth of Minos, for Charax says that Augeias "begged Daidalos, who was staying with him, through Minos to track down the thief."[27] The phrase "through Minos" in this passage is corrupt and probably represents a phrase such as "on his flight from Minos," for according to tradition Daidalos, after his winged escape from the Labyrinth to the Greek mainland, was pursued through many lands by Minos. He finally made his way to Sicily, where Minos found him, but he was murdered before the Cretan king could retrieve him.[28] As a trickster, convicted

murderer, and recent escapee from imprisonment, Daidalos makes a nice parallel to the old imprisoned thief who frequently acts as the king's adviser in the modern texts. A second point of agreement between Charax and later tradition is that it is the older thief who perishes in the trap. For it is the father Agamedes who is caught, just as in later tradition it is regularly the father or uncle or master rather than the son or nephew or apprentice who falls into the trap. These features support the assumption, which we should be justified in making even in their absence, that the legend of Trophonios and Agamedes does not derive from the legend of Rhampsinitos, as many scholars have held; nor should the reverse be assumed.[29]

A slightly different version of the legend is given by Pausanias in his book on Boiotia, according to which Agamedes and Trophonios are not father and son (or rather stepfather and stepson) but brothers. Erginos had two sons, Trophonios and Agamedes, though it was also said (and Pausanias agrees) that Trophonios was really a son of Apollo. The youths became skilled at constructing sanctuaries and palaces, building the temple of Apollo at Delphi and the treasury for Hyrieus. They made one stone in the latter building removable from the outside and regularly helped themselves to the valuables stored in it. For his part, Hyrieus was speechless, seeing that the keys and seals were untouched while his possessions were disappearing. So he placed a snare or some other contrivance above the vessels containing his gold and silver in order to catch the man who was entering and taking them. When Agamedes entered he was caught by the trap, but Trophonios cut off his head in order that on the following day Agamedes not be tortured and he himself revealed as a partner in the crime. Then the earth opened up and received Trophonios at the place in the grove in Lebadeia where there are now found the so-called Pit of Agamedes and the nearby stele.[30]

Pausanias's account agrees with that of Charax in representing Trophonios and Agamedes as great builders and thieves. They are brothers (so Pausanias) or father and son (so Charax), or, more strictly, half-brothers or stepfather and stepson. They build the temple of Apollo at Delphi and the treasury of Hyrieus (Pausanias) or of Augeias (Charax), and they steal from the treasury by means of a stone that they left removable when they constructed the chamber. The king traps Agamedes with a snare, Trophonios cuts off his partner's head and departs, and sometime later, in Lebadeia in Boiotia, the earth swallows Trophonios (Pausanias) or he builds for himself an subterranean chamber where he dwells until he dies (Charax).[31] In both accounts the final reference is to the famous underground oracle of Trophonios in Lebadeia, for which the legend provides an aition.[32]

The scholarship on the ancient and modern texts of *Rhampsinitos* has been dominated by the nineteenth-century passion for origins, the folklorists working with the worldwide tradition, and the classical scholars dealing with the ancient Mediterranean tradition. For the latter the burning question has been: Greece or Egypt? But the question has been too naively posed. Trying to create a stemma for the ancient story, for which we possess a few traces in ancient literature—mere hints of the oral tradition—is as doomed to uncertainty as trying to reconstruct a three-thousand-piece jigsaw puzzle from three pieces. It is even more naive to believe that these three pieces were all there were. Few scholars have adopted so reasonable a view as that of J. A. K. Thomson, who

accepts the Greek and Egyptian traditions simply as different variants of the same story rather than forcing them into a relationship of model and copy.[33]

The prehistory of the international story is unknown and presumably unknowable. At some time in the past, Greeks in Elis or Boiotia attached the initial episode of the story of the two thieves to the masterbuilders Trophonios and Agamedes, creating an aetiological legend for the strange subterranean oracle of the murderer and hero Trophonios. The brief narrative figured in no great poem or prose work, at least none that has survived, and we know it only from a couple of late, cursory tellings. At another unknown time, Egyptians adapted the same migratory story to their own purposes, retaining more of its fullness and humor, and attaching it to one of their legendary kings. It came to the ears of the Greek traveler and writer Herodotos while he was in Egypt, and he retold it liesurely and with charm, making it famous. If any Egyptian ever gave it literary treatment, we know nothing of it. We know of the Greek and the Egyptian stories because they were told of allegedly historical characters of some importance. The story of the two thieves may also have circulated in Greece and Egypt as a simple tale of entertainment that, attached to no curious monument or prominent historical figure, interested no historian.

Lit. AT 950, *Rhampsinitos*, episode 1: *Theft from the Treasury.* Frazer (1898) 5:176–179. Hartmann 1917:65–70. Krappe 1933b. *EM* 1:1014–1015.

1. Paris 1907:276–277; Huet 1918b:257.
2. Paris 1907:277.
3. Paris 1907.
4. BP 3:403–404; Matsubara 1978.
5. The narrator does not explain how the child would know the thief.
6. Köhler (1898) 1:201–202; Paris 1907:160–164; Campbell 1907:lxxxv–lxxxvi; BP 3:397–398.
7. *Pec.* 9.1.
8. Köhler (1898) 1:203–204; Paris 1907:171–172; BP 3:399.
9. Paris 1907:178–180.
10. Paris 1907:183–185.
11. Clouston (1887) 2:145–148; Paris 1907:180–182.
12. How and Wells (1928) 1:224; Lloyd (1988) 3:52.
13. Fehling (1989:71–77), for example, is skeptical.
14. See Hartmann 1917:67–70; BP 3:396; Aly 1969:67; Krappe 1933b:238–241; Penzer (1926) 5:245–286; How and Wells (1928) 1:225; Halliday 1933:48–51; Liungman 1961:245; Petropoulos 1965:344–345; Lloyd (1988) 2:53–54. Gaston Paris (1907:299–311) rejects both Greece and Egypt in favor of Babylonia.
15. Herodotos 2.121.
16. As usual, Fehling (1989:210–211) is skeptical.
17. For example, Frazer (1898) 5:179.
18. So Campbell (1907:lxxxviii) for one simply assumes that the mediaeval texts derive directly or indirectly from Herodotos. But Köhler ([1898] 1:200) unconditionally rejects a similar view expressed by Campbell in an earlier work, where the Scotts scholar derives a West Highlands tale from Herodotos. As Köhler points out, the Scotts tale has much more in common with other oral tales of the type than it does with the text of Herodotos.
19. Paris 1907:278–279.
20. Egyptian soldiers: for example, How and Wells (1928) 1:225; Lloyd (1988) 3:55. Cf. Mayor 1893.
21. Paris 1907:284–285.
22. Munson 1993:40–41.
23. Motif H11.1.1, *Recognition at inn (hospital, etc.) where all must tell their life histories.* Notice also H152.1.1, *Woman entertains every traveler in hope of finding her husband.*

24. For the motif of the cadaver arm see Motif N384.0.1.1, *The cadaver arm;* Brewster and Baughman 1945; and Dorson 1959:259.

25. Schol. Aristophanes *Clouds* 508 = Charax *FGH* 103 F 5.

26. Eugammon *Tel.* (Allen 5:109).

27. Daidalos as clever adviser: Paris 1907:301.

28. Apollodoros *Ep.*1.13–14; cf. Frazer (1921) 2:142–143. According to Zenobios 4.92, Minos perished when his host's daughters poured boiling pitch upon him as he lay in the bathtub, an odd means of death that is reminiscent of the demise of the thief in our tale who falls into a vat of boiling pitch.

29. Wilamowitz-Moellendorff (1884:186) believes that the story of Trophonios and Agamedes was simply the Egyptian story transplanted via Kyrene to the Odysseus legend. Krappe (1933b:239), arguing that Herodotos's text is mutilated but those of Charax and Pausanias are even more so, concludes that the tradition of Trophonios and Agamedes is secondary and derivative, and therefore comes from Egypt. For Brunner-Traut (1959:182) Herodotos's story reached Greece via Eugammon of Kyrene and became the story of Trophonios and Agamedes, and Lloyd ([1988] 3:53–54) is inclined to the same opinion. For additional views, including those of the champions of a Greek origin for the story, see note 14 above.

30. Pausanias 9.37.4–7. For these and other traditions concerning the masterbuilders Trophonios and Agamedes, mostly relating to prominent buildings they were supposed to have constructed or to traditions of how they met their death, see Roscher 1:89–90, 5:1265–1278; and Preller (1920) 2:133–135. And for a possible illustration of the story on a fragment of a bowl from Kyrene see Hartmann 1917:67. The victims Augeias and Hyrieus also figure in other legends that are Greek adaptations of international material. For the well-known task of the Augean stables see "Girl as Helper," and for the kindly host Hyrieus see "Hospitality Rewarded."

31. For an interesting but somewhat remote parallel to the motif of decapitation compare the robbers' strategy in Apuleius *Met.* 4.9–11, in which the robber Lamachus and his companions attempt to break into the house of a rich man, but when the latter manages to nail Lamachus's hand to the door, his companions cut off his arm and flee.

32. See, for example, Frazer (1898) 5:200; Burkert 1985:115. Trophonios died, or was translated into, an underground dwelling where he continued to be active, foretelling people's future or otherwise advising them. The consulters themselves had to go underground into the hero's tomb or dwelling, one of whose names was the Katabasion, or Place of Descent. This feature forges a strange thematic link with the tradition of Pharaoh Rhampsinitos, who according to Herodotos descended alive into the death realm and returned, an action that the Egyptians commemorated with a regular festival in which the descent was reenacted (2.122). That is, both Trophonios and Rhampsinitos, who are connected by their roles in the story of the two thieves, one as thief and one as victim, were also said to have made a descent into the earth, the prototype of ritual reenactments later performed in Greece and Egypt. Of some possible significance is the fact that both figures also have a connection with Demeter, or the Egyptian goddess with whom Herodotos identifies Demeter. For Rhampsinitos played dice with Demeter in the netherworld, and the later ritual is connected with the temple of the goddess, while Demeter Europe is said to have been the nurse of Trophonios (Pausanias 9.39.5).

33. Thomson 1914:111–112.

Sailor and the Oar ⚓ Odysseus

Because of the dangers of the sea (hard labor, etc.) a mariner becomes disgusted with seafaring. Determined to find a community that knows nothing of the sea, he places an oar on his shoulder and starts walking inland. Whenever he meets another person, he asks what it is he is carrying, and so long as the landsman answers, "An oar," the mariner continues walking inland. When finally a man (community) identifies the oar as a stick (piece of lumber, baker's peel, etc.), the mariner plants it in the ground and declares that he intends to remain there.[1]

This story does not appear in any published index of types or motifs.

The classical scholar W. H. D. Rouse, who was proficient in Modern Greek,

reported a conversation he once had with a Greek skipper. Kapetan Giorgis remarked that seafaring was a poor trade, as St. Elias had also found. Prompted by Rouse, Giorgis explained that the prophet Elias was a fisherman, who experienced terrific storms so that he came to fear the sea. Leaving his nets and boat, he put an oar on his shoulder and walked toward the hills. On the way he saw a man and asked him, "What's this, can you tell me?" "That?" says the man, "Why, that's an oar." Elias went on, met another man, and got the same response. Finally he came to the top of a mountain and asked a man, who replied, "Why, that's a stick." Declaring that this was the place for him, Elias planted his oar in the ground. That is why the chapels of St. Elias are all built on hilltops.[2]

Indeed chapels and monasteries dedicated to St. Elias are found on the tops and sides of mountains and hills all over Greece, a phenomenon for which this legend as well as others provide an aition. Elias therefore always finds his ignorant landsman or village on a mountaintop, and the texts usually conclude with a reference to the location of his chapels. According to a version collected in the nineteenth century, St. Elias was a seaman who had lived a dissolute life but came to repent what he had done, or he suffered much at sea, nearly drowning several times. So he became disgusted with voyaging and resolved to go to a place where they did not know what the sea was or what ships were. He put an oar on his shoulder, stepped ashore, and whomever he met he asked what it was he was carrying. So long as the response was "An oar," he kept moving higher and higher inland. Finally he asked the people at the top of a mountain, and they answered, "A stick." Perceiving that they had never before seen an oar, he remained there with them.[3]

In Greece *The Sailor and the Oar* is told as a legend about St. Elias (that is, the prophet Elijah), who otherwise has no connection with the sea, and also about St. Nikolaos, patron of sailors, while outside Greece the story is found as a novella, or realistic tale.

Although it is not necessary in the mariner's final encounter that the landsman mistake the oar for any particular thing, only that he not recognize it for what it is, some versions play elegantly or amusingly with the man's error. So in another Greek version the sailor's oar is mistaken for a baker's peel, a landsman's tool that is isomorphic with the mariner's tool, both being wooden implements consisting of a long handle and a flat blade.[4] The idea is exploited nicely in a version recounted by an American narrator, according to whom an old sailor put in his thirty years, took his retirement option, and walked down the gangplank with a gunnysack over one shoulder and an oar over the other. Proceeding from the east coast, he headed due west inland. On a road somewhere in New Jersey someone waved to him and asked him where he was going with that oar over his shoulder. The old sailor merely nodded and marched on westward. In the middle of Ohio or Indiana, another person greeted him and asked what he was doing with that rower over his shoulder. The sailor kept on walking. Somewhere further along, perhaps in Nebraska, a person along the side of the road asked, "Hey, mister, what on earth are you carrying the piece of lumber over your shoulder for?" A grin broke across his face, he stamped his foot on the ground, and said, "This is where I'm settling down."[5] In this text the familiarity with seafaring displayed by the successive landsmen fades as the sailor proceeds inland. The first man calls the oar an oar;

the second man calls it a rower, which is not quite right and not quite wrong; and the third man takes it for an ordinary piece of wood.

In all three texts the mariner becomes unhappy with the sea for one reason or another, usually because of the dangerous storms he has experienced. Putting an oar on his shoulder one day he walks inland, asking each person he meets what it is he is carrying, or the persons he meets comment upon what he is carrying. Narrators may make the mariner's intention explicit, revealing it from the outset (so the second text, in which the disgusted seaman resolves to go somewhere where people have never heard of the sea), or they may leave it implicit, letting the man's actions more or less speak for themselves (so the first and third texts).

Not surprisingly, persons who work at sea (sailors, fishermen, sea captains) are the primary conduits for the story.[6] In this sense it is a genuine sea story, a narrative about a seaman that circulates among seafolk. The mariner in the story acts out the fantasy that every seaman must sometimes have, the desire simply to walk away from the sea.[7] A typical context for the telling of the story is a conversation in which the topic of seafaring as a desirable or undesirable way of life arises. By recounting the story a discussant gives expression to his negative feelings about seafaring in a symbolic and aesthetically interesting way.[8] When Kapetan Giorgis remarks, "Ah well, 'tis a poor trade this, as the holy Elias found," his musing on seafaring as a miserable profession leads him immediately to think of the fisherman saint who quit the sea.[9] Narrators of the Elias legend may also recount the story to give aetiological meaning to the location of the chapels and monasteries of Elias on countless Greek hilltops, although this intellectual use of the story appears to be less important than its affective one.[10]

In modern British and American tradition the story is often treated humorously. Most frequently it takes the form of a simple, humorous remark in which the narrator declares that someday he himself will take an oar (anchor, binnacle light, etc.) and walk inland until he meets someone who does not know what it is, and there he will settle down. For example, a seaman in the merchant marine remarked on one occasion: "One of these days I'm gonna take an oar out of one of those lifeboats, and I'm gonna start walking inland, and I'm gonna go in until somebody says, 'What's that funny-looking thing you've got over your shoulder?' and then I'm gonna settle down and build a house there."[11] Wits have reworked the idea to fit other conditions of perceived misery, most commonly winter, in which case the narrator, weary of snow, declares that he will travel with a snow shovel until he finds somebody who does not recognize it.[12] I have even encountered a version in which a man said he was going to put a tortilla on the aerial of his pickup truck and drive north until he reached a place where someone asked him what it was, and there he would stay. This narrative circulated among Anglos in a Texan town during a time of cultural tension between Anglos and Chicanos.[13]

More rarely the tale is heard as a ribald joke in which a marriage-minded mariner undertakes a quest for a girl who knows nothing of the sea. In a nineteenth-century Spanish text a sailor who was tired of the sea wanted to find a girl who knew nothing about the sea or sailors. So he set out with an oar over

his shoulder and showed it to a girl in a village, asking her what it was. She replied that it was an oar. He asked the same question in one village after another and got the same answer. When finally he came upon a girl who said it was a stick or beam, he was pleased to have found a girl who knew nothing of the sea, and married her. But on their wedding night she asked whether to get into bed on the port or starboard side.[14]

Odysseus and the Oar

The story of the mariner who walks inland with an oar on his shoulder is first attested in a passage of Homer's *Odyssey*. In the course of his return from Troy to Ithaca, Odysseus visits the realm of the dead, where he consults the soul of the seer Teiresias. Explaining that the god Poseidon is angry with Odysseus, the seer advises Odysseus how to reach home safely and what to do afterward in order to reconcile himself with Poseidon.[15]

> Take a well-shaped oar and go
> until you reach men who do not know of the sea
> and who eat food unmixed with salt:
> they know neither of red-cheeked ships
> nor of well-shaped oars, which are the wings of ships.
> I'll tell you a very clear sign, and you won't miss it:
> when you come across another man on the road
> who says that you have a chaff-wrecker on your shining shoulder,
> then plant the well-shaped oar in the earth
> and perform a fine sacrifice to lord Poseidon—
> a ram, a bull, and a boar, mounter of sows.
> Then return home and sacrifice holy hekatombs
> to the immortal gods, who dwell in the broad sky,
> to all of them in order.

The connection of this little adventure with Teiresias is, as it happens, accidental. From the viewpoint of the poet of the *Odyssey*, the episode is set in the future, and a Greek oral poet who narrates a future event must put it into the mouth of a deity or a seer, the only characters who are privy to what lies ahead. Here it is Teiresias who, in the form of instructions to Odysseus, foretells the action. Since Odysseus's quest takes place after the last events described in the epic, all mention of it could have been omitted from the poem entirely except for the fact that its absence would have left unresolved the tension between Odysseus and Poseidon. Instead, Homer refers to the reconciliation as imminent.

If Homer had an opportunity to recount it in its proper place in the sequence of events, he would naturally have told it as something that took place in the past, as in the case of the other adventures of Odysseus, rather than placing it into the mouth of a seer.[16] So let us convert the passage into the usual narrative past.

> Odysseus took a well-shaped oar and went
> until he reached men who did not know of the sea

and who ate food unmixed with salt:
they knew neither of red-cheeked ships
nor of well-shaped oars, which are the wings of ships.
There was a very clear sign, and he did not miss it:
when he came across another man on the road
 who said that he had a chaff-wrecker on his shining shoulder,
then he planted the well-shaped oar in the earth
and performed a fine sacrifice to lord Poseidon—
a ram, a bull, and a boar, mounter of sows.
Then he returned home and sacrificed holy hekatombs
to the immortal gods, who dwell in the broad sky,
to all of them in order.

If we now put this into informal prose, we get more or less the following story. Odysseus put an oar on his shoulder and walked inland in search of a community that knew nothing of the sea, did not use salt in their food or know what ships or oars were. He asked each person he met what it was he was carrying. Finally he met a man who said he was carrying a chaff-wrecker on his shoulder. Then he planted his oar in the ground and performed a sacrifice to Poseidon, after which he returned to Ithaca and performed additional sacrifices.

Let me comment on these lines.

1. "Odysseus put an oar on his shoulder and walked inland in search of a community that knew nothing of the sea, did not use salt in their food or know what ships or oars were." The mariner's purpose in carrying the oar is to create a simple test for persons he may encounter: a landsman who does not recognize an oar is a landsman who knows nothing of seafaring or the sea.

Odysseus's goal, like that of the mariner in the modern texts, is simply to find any community that is ignorant of the sea, and the oar test is his device for doing so. Ignorance of salt and ships and oars does not distinguish one particular such community from all other such communities but is simply Homer's elaboration of the idea of ignorance of the sea. The sort of place that Odysseus seeks is so removed from the sea that its inhabitants are unacquainted with all the things that Greeks commonly associated with the sea. The same kind of elaboration is found in some modern texts. It is true, as commentators point out, but entirely irrelevant that some communities get their salt from inland mines rather than from the sea.[17]

In modern texts the mariner's motive is most often relief from the dangers of the sea, as in the two Modern Greek texts summarized at the head of this article. This is also Odysseus's motive, in a slightly more complicated way. Though Odysseus's enemy is not the sea but the Lord of the Sea, it amounts to the same thing because as a sea god Poseidon expresses his hostility in the form of storms at sea. Indeed the deity creates a terrible storm just for Odysseus, causing him to spend two days and nights clinging to wreckage before he washes up on the shores of Scheria.[18] In the present epic passage Teiresias informs Odysseus of Poseidon's anger at him and instructs him how to placate the hostile sea god.[19]

2. "He asked each person he met what it was he was carrying." Homer does not explicitly say that Odysseus asks each person he meets, but the logic of the

situation suggests it and it makes a good fit with the statement of the landsman that follows. Illustrative instances of the kind found in modern texts—in which the mariner encounters one or two landsmen who recognize the oar before he finally comes upon a man who does not recognize it—are natural enough in a narrative set in the past but would be awkward in a narrative set in the future, which probably is why they are absent in Teiresias's instructions to Odysseus.

3. "Eventually he encountered a man who said he was carrying a chaff-wrecker on his shoulder." Proceeding inland Odysseus finally meets someone who does not recognize the oar as an oar, indicating that the man and the community to which he belongs are surely unacquainted with seafaring and the sea. The man says, presumably in response to Odysseus's asking what this thing is, "You have a chaff-wrecker on your shoulder." A chaff-wrecker, as the scholiasts explain, is a winnowing shovel.[20] A winnowing shovel is a wooden implement with a long handle and a blade; that is, it looks very much like an oar.[21] So the landsman confuses a common marine tool for a common agricultural tool of similar appearance, like the confusion of oar and baker's peel in a modern version of *The Sailor and the Oar*.

Some scholars deduce from Teiresias's instructions that Odysseus is obliged to wander until he encounters a mysterious man who will call his oar a chaff-wrecker, using precisely these words or making precisely this error and no other.[22] This misunderstanding springs from taking Homer's adaptation of the legend for the *Odyssey*, his putting it in the mouth of Teiresias in the form of instructions, as an intrinsic feature of the legend rather than an accidental one. If you transform the ordinary past statement "He went until he encountered a man who said he carried a chaff-breaker" into the imperative, it becomes "Go until you encounter a man who says you carry a chaff-breaker," which misleadingly sounds as if there were only one acceptable solution to the oar test.

4. "Then he planted his oar in the ground and performed a sacrifice to Poseidon, after which he returned to Ithaka and performed additional sacrifices." Sometimes the mariner in the modern texts also plants his oar in the ground, indicating that he has no further need for it: he has found the kind of place he was seeking. There is no reason to see any deeper significance (e.g., cultic) in the gesture.[23]

As for the identity of the community unacquainted with the sea, ancient commentators mention different places in Epirus or in landlocked Arcadia or else obscure towns like Bounima or Kelkea.[24] The traveler Pausanias visited the remains of a temple for Athena Savior and Poseidon that was believed to have been built by Odysseus after his return from Troy. It stood atop Mount Boreion in Arcadia, very much like the hilltop chapels dedicated to St. Elias that commemorate his quest in Greece today.[25]

At the conclusion of the narrative the Homeric story and the modern story diverge formally though not functionally. The point of the mariner's quest in the modern story is to identify a place far removed from the sea where he might settle down, which he does. Unlike the lone mariner of modern story, however, the Greek hero Odysseus has a kingdom and a family, a whole network of ties that it would be too drastic to sever without a second thought. Narrators could attach the story of *The Sailor and the Oar* to Odysseus, but, as it appears, they had to allow him to return home in the end. Accordingly

Odysseus's enemy takes the form not of the sea but of the Sea, personalized as Poseidon, Lord of the Sea, and the point of Odysseus's quest is to make his peace with Poseidon. As an ancient commentator explains, the best way to honor a god who is already honored in one place is to bring it about that he is honored also elsewhere; accordingly, Odysseus brings knowledge of Poseidon, that is, of his cult, to inland mainlanders who, being unacquainted with the sea, are also unacquainted with its ruler. The story of Odysseus's inland quest is inter alia a foundation legend for one or another inland sanctuary of Poseidon, an aetiological narrative that purports to account for a phenomenon that some persons might find strange: the presence of shrines of Poseidon far removed from the sea.[26] Having made his peace with the sea god, Odysseus himself is free to go, for he has no reason to fear the sea or its ruler thereafter.

The principal difference between the modern and the Odyssean versions lies in whether the mariner seeks to be free of the sea or of the Lord of the Sea. A subtle shift of the mariner's enemy from sea to sea god permitted this story to be integrated into the traditional biography of Odysseus, articulating as it did with Poseidon as Odysseus's persecutor in Homer's *Odyssey* and permitting Odysseus, as a hero in Greek legend with an established biography, to have it both ways: to undertake a quest for a community unacquainted with the sea and then to return home again.

If any legend has been in continuous circulation in Greece from ancient to modern times, it is probably this old mariners' story. Seafaring was and is still dangerous and difficult, so that seafolk have as much reason to tell the story today as their forebears did centuries ago. Even the aetiological element may have a long history, for the temple for Athena and Poseidon founded by Odysseus on top of Mount Boreion appears to be a predecessor of the chapels of St. Elias on the hilltops of present-day Greece.

Lit. Halliday 1914. Hansen 1976, 1977b, 1990, 1997a. Moser 1979.

1. The principal survey of the tradition is Hansen 1990.
2. Rouse 1904 (= Hansen 1990:263–264, no. 15). For St. Nikolaos see, for example, Sanders 1962:35.
3. Πολίτης (1904) 1:116, no. 207 (= Hansen 1990:243, no. 3). He prints a second text at 2:801–802 (= Hansen 1990:243, no. 2).
4. Hansen 1990:253, no. 11.
5. Recorded by the present author in Bloomington, Indiana, in 1975 from Adam Horvath, who had heard the tale while serving in the United States Navy; for the full text see Hansen 1990:244, no. 6. For another folktale version see Reinhardt 1948:505–506 n. 30 (= Hansen 1990:243–244, no. 5).
6. Hansen 1990:265.
7. Hansen 1990:267.
8. Hansen 1990:263–267.
9. Hansen 1990:266–269.
10. Hansen 1990:267–268.
11. Recorded by the present author in Bloomington, Indiana, in 1972 from Professor Philip Appleman, who had heard it in 1948 while serving in the merchant marine; for the full text see Hansen 1976:226.
12. For example, Hansen 1990:261, no. 13.
13. Written down by the present author in Tucson, Arizona, in 1994 from the narration of Ms. Jane Willingham, who had heard it in Texas.
14. Ranke 1972:28, no. 12, citing *Chascarrillos andaluces* (Madrid, 1898). A nineteenth-cen-

tury French version is printed in Clébert 1986:52–54. Richard Dorson (1964:38–39) collected a version in the mid-twentieth century from a lobster fisherman in Maine; see further Hansen 1976, 1997a, and Moser 1979. Cf. also Randolph 1977:132–133, no. 49.

15. Homer *Od*. 11.121–134; cf. also *Od*. 23.248–284. Odysseus recounts his interview with Teiresias to the Phaeacians in the former passage, and to Penelope in the latter, with one or two slight differences in detail. A few illustrations are extant: *LIMC* 6.1:943–983, nos. 221–223.

16. So, for example, Apollodoros *Epit*. 7.34; cf. Frazer (1921) 2:300–301.

17. Hansen 1990:250–251.

18. Homer *Od*. 5.282–493.

19. Homer *Od*. 11.100–103, 121–134.

20. Schol. QBHV on *Od*. 11.128; Hansen 1990:254–255.

21. A winnowing shovel (πτύον) must be distinguished from a winnowing fan (λίκνον), also known as a winnowing basket. Although these implements serve essentially the same purpose—to help separate grain from chaff—they are quite different in form and in the materials from which they are made. No one would mistake an oar for a winnowing fan. For illustrations of these implements see Harrison 1903–1904.

22. See Hansen 1990:254.

23. Hansen 1977b:38–41.

24. Bounima, Kelkea: schol. H Homer *Od*. 11.122. See further Hansen 1977b:33.

25. Pausanias 8.44.4; cf. Frazer (1898) 4:418–419.

26. Schol. V Homer *Od*. 11.121, 130. Hansen 1977b:32.

Schlaraffenland 🥬 Glutton's Paradise

A certain land (or a certain time) is characterized by such features as an absurd abundance of food and drink (e.g., edible houses, fences made of sausages, a mountain of cheese, a lake of milk, rivers of wine or milk or honey, trees bearing prepared foods, cakes raining down from the sky, roasted pigs walking around saying "Eat me," roasted birds flying right to one's mouth), the easy availability of women (men), a fountain of youth, inversions of the familiar (e.g., slothfulness is rewarded and industry punished), and generally nonsensical activities (e.g., a cow puts bread in the oven).

This lying tale, AT 1930, *Schlaraffenland*, describes a land of plenty, ease, or general absurdity.

Most texts classified as *Schlaraffenland* portray a comic utopia, an earthly paradise of the material and the physical rather than the spiritual, a sluggard's fantasy of a world devoid of work (indeed, a world in which work is punished), a carefree land where the feaster need not even fetch his food since it will come to him, asking to be consumed. It is this world that "Schlaraffenland" ordinarily brings to mind, but texts featuring a miscellany of nonsensical sights are sometimes also so classified because the two ideas are often found mixed, though themes of nonsensical activities have their own history. The loose, motific structure of the type is similar to that of narratives of comic inversion (see "Topsy-Turvy Land"), and ideas that belong conceptually to a topsy-turvy world are commonly found here also.

The happy place of food and ease is often described in the first person, as often in lying tales, in which the narrator may present himself as an eyewitness. The narrative can consist of a simple paratactic series of descriptive statements that are not really a story in the ordinary sense, or, taking the form of an ostensible traveler's report, can be framed as an account of how the narrator

once managed to reach the fabled place. Whether the narrative is in prose or done up into verse or song, the tone is usually whimsical, except when it is employed within another tale as a yarn told by a liar, in which case the internal narrator presents his account as though it were truthful. So in Boccaccio's *Decameron*, in a novella related by the character Elisa, a clever rogue named Maso del Saggio played a trick on a simpleminded fellow named Calandrino. Among other lies, Maso told him that certain remarkable stones could be found in a place called Bengodi in the Basque province of Berlinzone. In Bengodi the vines were fastened to their stakes by means of sausages, and a goose cost only a penny, with a duck thrown in for free. There was a mountain consisting of grated Parmesan cheese, and the folk who lived on it spent all day making macaroni and ravioli, which they cooked in broth and rolled down the hillside, so that whoever was the quickest got the biggest share to eat. Nearby flowed a stream of the most delicious wine.[1]

In a dialogue composed in the Siglo de Oro by the Spanish author Barahona de Soto, a speaker mentions a sensual, earthly paradise named Jauja "where they say Fortune lives, and the streets are paved with eggs and candies, and rivers of wine and honey flow, and roasted partridges fly to people's mouths with omelets in their beaks, saying: 'Eat me, eat me.' "[2]

An English folktale recorded in 1909 begins with the following formulaic introduction: "Once upon a time—a very good time it was—when pigs were swine and dogs ate lime, and monkeys chewed tobacco, when houses were thatched with pancakes, streets paved with plum puddings, and roasted pigs ran up and down the streets with knives and forks in their backs, crying, 'Come and eat me!' That was a good time for travellers."[3] After this beginning the narrator relates the tale of Jack the Giant-Killer. Here the comic paradise of food and nonsense, identified as a time in the past rather than a land far away, serves to elaborate the introductory "once upon a time" as a time that never was.

Another English narrative mixes motifs of inversion, nonsense, and comic utopia. A certain Lander Smith used to tell a tale about himself, according to which he fell into an old mine shaft around Derbyshire, and when he landed he found himself in a strange place. He saw a man ploughing a lake, a ship sailing in a park, a donkey riding a man, a roadman breaking up stones with a feather, and a woman fetching water in a colander. When he asked the woman for something to eat, she showed him a tree on which a crop of black puddings was growing, telling him to help himself. Eventually he crossed the sea and reached his own home.[4]

Schlaraffenland (or Schlauraffenland) is the usual name of the comic utopia in German tradition, while variations on the name Cockaigne are found in French, Italian, Spanish, Dutch, English, and elsewhere, referring in some countries to the fabled glutton's paradise and in others to an actual carnivalesque festival. Many other names are also in use. For example, Boccaccio mentions Bengodi (*bene godere*, from *bene gaudere*, that is, Joyland), perhaps a designation of his own devising; the English speak of Lubberland; and in the United States we have songs about the Big Rock Candy Mountain, Oleana, and Doo Wa Ditty.[5] Cockaigne goes back to a presumed *Cucania*, implied by the adjective *Cucaniensis* that is found in one of the *Carmina Burana*, a miscellany of mediaeval Latin songs collected in the thirteenth century, in which a singer de-

clares: "I am the abbot of Cucania, and my council is with the drinkers."⁶ Cucania was formed in turn probably from Germanic *kakan* or *kôkan*, "cake," or from a form of Latin *coquinus* "pertaining to cooking" (e.g., *coquina* "kitchen") so that Cucania, Cockaigne, etc., seem originally to have signified either Cakeland or Kitchenland—in effect, Foodland.⁷ Schlaraffenland was formed from German *Slûraffe* "slumbering ape, slothful fool," and so originally meant Lazyland.⁸ For the sake of simplicity in the present discussion I use Cockaigne generically for the idea of a utopia of food and ease.

The idea of a land or a time of absurd plenty is mentioned by several ancient authors, reappears in literature in the thirteenth century (e.g., in the French *Fabliau de Coquaigne*), and flourished in European tradition in the fifteenth and sixteenth centuries, when Hans Sachs wrote a poem on Schlaraffenland and Pieter Breughel the Elder painted a picture of the place. From the seventeenth century onward the New World was often portrayed in Europe as a Land of Cockaigne, enticing citizens to cross the sea to a life of easy abundance.⁹

The Land of Cockaigne in Classical Antiquity

In Greek and Roman tradition, narratives of impossibly abundant food and drink in a context of easy living are found both in comic and noncomic literature. The humorous texts show a considerable resemblance to later accounts of the Land of Cockaigne and presumably are literary adaptations of a folk-narrative tradition, as Johannes Poeschel pointed out already in the nineteenth century.¹⁰ Since some of the comic literary treatments take the form of parodies of primarily noncomic material, the traditions intermingle to a certain extent.

The earliest evidence for Cockaigne in the proper sense of a comic utopia of ease, absurdly abundant and convenient food, and the like is found mostly in Athenaeus's symposiast dialogue in which one of the banqueters, Demokritos, quotes from a number of Greek comedies, now lost, in illustration of his assertion that the poets of Old Comedy represent life in the early days as being without slaves.¹¹ The excerpts Demokritos quotes do not always appear to be relevant to his thesis, but that is of no importance to us. They are all from plays composed in the latter half of the fifth century B.C. and are given below in the order in which Demokritos cites them, which he says is the order in which they were produced, except for the last two, which were not produced. In most cases we know neither the context of the excerpt nor even the identity of the speaker.

In a passage from the *Ploutoi* of Kratinos, a speaker says that in ancient times when Kronos ruled, men played dice with loaves of bread and used barley cakes to pay their fees in the wrestling schools.¹² That is, during the mythical Golden Age when the god Kronos ruled the cosmos, food was so plentiful that men actually used it in place of dice and money. Demokritos quotes next from Krates' *Theria* (Wild Animals), in which a character asks whether it is true that no man will own slaves any longer but instead must take care of himself, even if he is old. A second character explains that persons will not have to take care of their own needs, for he will render all utensils capable of walking, so that they will come when called. "Table, come here and set yourself! Trough, knead! Ladle, pour! Cup, go wash yourself! Pot, disgorge your beets! Fish, come here!"

"But I'm not yet cooked on the other side." "Okay, then, turn yourself over and baste yourself with oil and salt!" A third character then boasts that he will devise a system of warm baths, whereby water drawn from the sea will flow on its own into each person's bathtub until the person wishes it to stop, and after the bath the perfume bottle, sponge, and sandals will come to the bather automatically.[13] In this exchange automated objects will discharge their tasks upon command, some in the kitchen and others in the bath, relieving human beings of the necessity of possessing slaves.[14] These conveniences will, it seems, ensue from a contemplated revival of the good old days of Kronos.

A character, generally thought to be Amphiktyon, in Telekleides' *Amphiktyones* (Amphictyons), describes the conditions of life that he once provided for mortals: there was peace; the earth bore neither diseases nor anything else to fear, while necessities were produced automatically: every mountain stream flowed with wine, barley cakes and loaves of bread competed with each other for the mouths of persons, begging to be devoured, fishes went to people's houses and cooked themselves and then lay down on the table, a stream of broth with hot meat flowed to people's dining couches, roast thrushes with cakes flew into people's mouths, and boys played dice with bits of food. People were fat and as big as giants in those days.[15] The speaker portrays a world of harmony, health, and foods so abundant that, as in Kratinos's *Ploutoi*, people employ edibles rather than knucklebones for dice. Cooked foods of all kinds—bread, soup, fish, birds—move about, some of them approaching the inhabitants and even asking to be eaten.

In a passage from Pherekrates' *Metalles* (Miners), a female speaker, evidently one of a party of women who for some reason visited the death realm, describes it as a place full of wealth and other good things. There were rivers full of porridge and broth and bits of bread and cheesecakes, and pieces of these things slid automatically down the throats of the dead.[16] Sausages and roast fish in various sauces lay on riverbanks like shells, and roast thrushes asking to be eaten flew around the mouths of their group as they lay among flowers on the ground. Beautiful apples hung above their heads, not growing on anything, and maidens drew wine through a funnel for those who wished to drink. And whenever anyone had eaten or drunk anything, it was immediately replaced by a double quantity of the same.[17] Once again we have a world of plentiful cooked foods, sometimes mobile, and of liquid nourishment in streams, in addition to wealth. It is an idler's paradise, where diners lie in a meadow as various meats present themselves to be eaten, fresh fruit is within reach, and slaves provide ample wine. The scene of these luxuries is the realm of the dead, which to judge from the title of the play the visitors may have reached through a mine shaft, as did Lander Smith in the English text cited above. In popular thought the nether world was the source of water, fertility, and wealth.[18]

In another play attributed to the same author, *Persai* (Persians), a speaker asks rhetorically what use there will be any longer for ploughmen or craftsmen or seeds. For the springs of Ploutos will produce rivers of broth full of cakes, and Zeus will rain down wine from above. On the roofs of houses the gutters will convey cheesecakes and pea soup, and on the mountains the trees will sprout roasted tripe, cuttlefish, and boiled thrushes.[19] The setting of this excerpt, in which a speaker foresees automatic food and drink, is unknown. The

ethnic label "Persians" is probably used metaphorically rather than literally, to refer to persons living a life of gluttony or luxury.[20] In this fantasy, food rains down from the sky above and percolates up from the netherworld below. In addition, various cooked dishes originate on housetops or at least are conveniently conveyed by the gutters, while cooked meat and fish sprout on trees.

A speaker in the *Seirenes* (Sirens) of Nikophon says: "Let it snow barley meal! Let it drizzle loaves of bread! Let it rain pea soup! Let broth roll pieces of meat through the streets, and let a cake give the order: 'Eat me'!"[21] The title of the play suggests that the speaker may be Odysseus or one of the Sirens.[22]

In an excerpt from Metagenes' *Thouriopersai* (Thurio-Persians), a speaker mentions the Krathis River bringing down huge barley cakes that had kneaded themselves, and another river bringing cooked fishes of various kinds, while slices of fish leap into their mouths, other slices leap at their feet, and cakes swim around them in a circle.[23] The setting is the Greek city of Thourion in southern Italy, for whose inhabitants the playwright has perhaps invented the name "Thurio-Persians" in order to satirize their luxury or gluttony. Like *Sirens*, the play was never produced.

A few comic fragments in the same vein preserved in other contexts could also be cited, but the passages above sufficiently characterize the Greek tradition of Cockaigne as it is reflected in the fragments of the Athenian comic poets. Four centuries later we briefly glimpse a Roman Cockaigne in a conversation in Petronius's picaresque novel. When a character utters a string of complaints about the declining quality of life locally, his interlocutor responds: "When you are somewhere else, you will say that the pigs *here* are walking around already cooked."[24] The motif of cooked animals walking around evidently becomes a comic proverbial expression among the Romans for paradise, whether from Roman popular tradition or as a learned borrowing from Greek tradition it is impossible to say.

In the following century Lucian parodies the Kronian Golden Age. In a dialogue between Kronos and Lucian, Kronos explains that he used to rule the universe but abdicated in favor of Zeus. Periodically, however, he takes back the sovereignty for a few days during the festival in his honor, the Kronia, in order to remind human beings of what life used to be like for them when he ruled. Everything grew without sowing or ploughing—not ears of wheat but loaves of bread and prepared meats. Wine flowed in rivers, while honey and milk came from springs, and everyone was good and golden. That is why the celebrants at his festival clap, sing, and play games, and why there is no distinction between slaves and free men, for during his reign there were no slaves.[25] In a letter written by Lucian to Kronos, the author explains that poverty prevents his participation in the god's festival. He has heard the poets saying how in ancient times under Kronos' rule things were different from the way they are now. The earth produced its goods for mankind without sowing and ploughing, everyone had all he could eat ready at hand, and there flowed rivers of wine, milk, and honey. Best of all, the people were of gold so that there was no poverty among them, whereas the folk of Lucian's day would not even be rated as being of lead, most people must earn their food by hard work, and for Lucian and the other poor there is poverty, want, helplessness, and general distress.[26] Lucian joins Kratinos and other comic poets, upon whom he perhaps

is drawing, in portraying the world under the reign of Kronos as a Land of Cockaigne.

Similarly, Lucian's parody of unbelievable travel narratives, *True Stories*, presents the legendary Island of the Blessed and Elysian Field as a Cockaigne. The author reports that soon after coming upon a sea of milk encircling a huge island of cheese, he stumbled onto what proved to be the Island of the Blessed, home of the heroes of old. He and his comrades were taken prisoner, bound with rose garlands (the strongest fetters the inhabitants had), and brought before their ruler, Rhadamanthys, who declared they might stay a while, whereupon their bonds fell off. They were brought to the city, which was of gold, its wall of emerald, its seven gates of pure cinnamon. Its ground was made of ivory, its temples and altars were constructed of semiprecious stones, and a river of the finest myrrh ran around it. The season there was always spring, and the inhabitants never aged. Their grapevines produced twelve vintages a year, while their pomegranate trees, apple trees, and other fruit trees bore thirteen times a year. In the fields there grew loaves of bread, ready to eat, and springs of water, honey, myrrh, milk, and wine flowed nearby. The inhabitants of the island dined on floral couches in a meadow called the Elysian Field where they were served by the winds. When they wanted to drink they plucked cups from nearby trees of glass, and the cups immediately became full of wine. Birds dropped flowers upon them to serve as garlands, and a dew of myrrh drizzled upon them for perfume. At the beginning of the feast they drank from two springs, the Spring of Laughter and the Spring of Pleasure, ensuring that they had a convivial time.[27]

Many motifs employed by the comic poets and by Lucian are recognizable as conventional features of the folk narrative of the glutton's utopia, such as rivers or lakes of wine or honey or milk or soup, a mountain of cheese, cooked food that grows on trees, food that rains down from the sky, roasted birds that fly to one's mouth, cooked food lying around and walking around, talking food that begs to be eaten, food employed as construction material, and idle, gluttonous people enjoying it all. In Greek comedies and parodies Cockaigne is situated variously in the past during the Golden Age, in the future, down below in the realm of Ploutos, on the Islands of the Blessed at the ends of the earth, in the city of Thourion in Italy, and elsewhere. The humorists adapted the folk idea of a comic utopia to whatever time or place suited their purpose.

If Cockaigne had its own conventional name in Greek tradition, it has not come down to us. *Aphannai* may have been such a name, for there was a story that once when the Sybarites prayed for victory in an imminent battle with the Krotonites, one of the Krotonites jokingly remarked: "You'll get that in Aphannai," whence the proverb "(Go) to Aphannai."[28] Various explanations of Aphannai have been offered in ancient and modern times, such as that it was the name of an obscure town, but the anecdote makes best sense if Aphannai was taken as deriving from *aphanes* "unseen" and as signifying an imaginary land, a nonexistent Cockaigne where everyone got what he or she wanted. If so, its meaning changed in time, since this usage was not known to the ancient commentators.

It is not necessary to suppose, as some scholars have done, that Cockaigne arose in the first place as a parody of the mythic Golden Age, since the favorite

motifs do not appear to be comic distortions of motifs of the Golden Age except in a very general way. The Hesiodic myth speaks of predictable and abundant crops, requiring only harvesting, whereas the folktale speaks of rivers of food, showers of food, self-cooking food, talking food, and so on. The myth portrays a farmer's paradise, whereas the folktale represents the idle glutton's paradise. Moreover, the Golden Age was only one of many human paradises in Greek tradition, though to be sure it was the human paradise par excellence because it was the earliest such paradise in the traditional chronology and because it was inclusive of all persons of the time, whereas subsequent utopias were restricted in one way or another. The evidence suggests that the earnest tradition and the lying-tale tradition have lived parallel and sometimes intermingling lives, one serious and one whimsical, one describing a lost past or an inaccessible Shangri-la for which mankind sometimes yearns, the other portraying an outrageous, mostly materialistic fantasy, an Eden and a Cockaigne, each expressing different aspects of the human longing for a life free of cares. It is impossible to say which arose first; all we know is which received literary treatment first.

Mythological Cockaignes

Cockaigne-like narratives and motifs are found in a number of mythological contexts, especially in association with the myth of the primordial paradise, as well as in descriptions of the wondrous conditions obtaining in this or that exotic country. Since some peoples such as the Aithiopians belong both to the mythological tradition and to the quasi-ethnographical tradition, a clear line between the two categories cannot always be drawn. The tone of these narratives is not uniform but ranges from reverence and yearning to lighthearted wonder, verging on the whimsical.

According to Hesiod in his poem on work the gods created a Golden Race of mortals, who lived during the reign of the god Kronos. Like the gods they lived without cares or labor or old age, and they passed their days in feasting. When it was time to die, they died in their sleep. The earth produced its crops for them abundantly and automatically as they went about their work.[29] Hesiod does not imagine a life entirely without work, only without hard work and without the uncertainty of good harvests and bad. As he says earlier in his poem, if the gods had not hidden away man's "livelihood," a man could store up enough from one day's work to live on for a year.[30] This is a farmer's fantasy, not an idler's fantasy. He describes a primordial earthly paradise characterized by youthful inhabitants, feasting, the absence of suffering and hard work, and abundant crops that grew unsown and untended as wild plants do, needing only to be harvested. Plato similarly describes a number of idyllic features of the Kronian era such as that the earth produced generous crops on its own without agriculture.[31]

In the Roman adaptation of this tradition the god Saturn was identified with Kronos. According to Ovid the Golden Age was a time of everlasting spring when the earth produced every crop, streams of milk and nectar flowed, and honey dripped from oak trees. During the Silver Age that followed, when Jupiter succeeded Saturn, spring became only one of several seasons, and men

began to plant and plough for the first time.[32] Vergil mentions the rivers of wine that flowed during the Golden Age.[33]

In Greece this happy time in the earth's early history was commemorated, as some believed, in the Attic-Ionic Kronia, or festival of Kronos, an annual festival during which Kronos reigned again and in which the distinction between free person and slave was suspended temporarily, so that everyone, free and slave, rich and poor, dined and played games together.[34] The festival seemed to reenact some of the conditions that obtained during the reign of Kronos when there was unending feasting and good cheer, and no man was the property of another.[35] Slavery was absent from the Kronian age because it was a period of thorough harmony in which hierarchical, exploitative, and predatory relationships were nonexistent; moreover, from the purely practical perspective, there was so little work for anyone to do that slaves were not really needed by anyone, a point that, as we have seen, the Attic comic poets and the parodist Lucian develop humorously. The Roman festival of Saturn, the Saturnalia, resembled the Greek Kronia in the custom of the dining together of masters and slaves and in its being commonly interpreted as a reenactment or commemoration of the Golden Age.[36]

Some Greek and Latin authors speak of the forthcoming return of a Golden Age or its equivalent.[37] Vergil thus predicts that Saturn will once again reign, a Golden Race will arise again, and every land will bear every crop without ploughing and without pruning, so that traders will no longer sail the seas with wares. Goats will return home of their own accord with full udders, and herds will not fear lions. Even rams will change their fleece into different colors so that the falsification of color from the dyeing of wool will no longer take place. Serpents and poisonous plants will perish.[38] Accordingly, the Roman poet must have in mind that during the original reign of Saturn the land produced every kind of crop on its own, requiring only harvesting; goats tended themselves, needing only milking; sheep came in various colors so that the dyeing of their wool was unnecessary; and there were no predators, poisonous animals, or poisonous plants. The world was a place of ease and plenty without danger or discord or falsity. There is certainly a touch of Cockaigne here.

Similarly the Hebrew prophets portray the last days as a Cockaigne-like Golden Age to come.[39] According to Amos, there will be harvests in astonishingly rapid succession, the mountains will run with sweet wine, and crops will be growing on every hill.[40] Joel says that the mountains will run with sweet wine, the hills will flow with milk, and all the channels will be full of water.[41] Ezekiel describes how every kind of food-bearing tree will spring up and never lack fruit.[42] Isaiah foresees peace among all the animals, predators and prey alike, and between animals and humans, a leveling out of all relationships into complete harmony.[43]

In Greek mythological tradition the Elysian Field and the Isles of the Blessed were special preserves to which certain heroes were translated when their ordinary life reached its end. They were contemporary earthly paradises of a sort, distant places where the Golden Age seemed to persevere for a privileged few.[44] In Homer's *Odyssey*, Menelaos learned from Proteus, the Old Man of the Sea, that because he was a son-in-law of Zeus he would not die; rather, the gods would send him to the Elysian Field at the end of the earth where life was very easy and the weather was always like spring.[45] Hesiod mentions a similar

earthly paradise, the Isles of the Blessed, also located at the ends of the earth beside Okeanos, where thanks to Zeus select heroes live a carefree life, and the soil yields three crops a year.[46] The ruler of the place is Kronos, an explicit link between the Golden Race and the Isles of the Blessed (and also the Elysian Field, for the two were not ordinarily distinguished as separate places). Homer emphasizes the excellent weather of the place, while Hesiod, seeing it with a farmer's eyes, cites the abundant crops. Horace's description is all but identical with Vergil's description of the Golden Age: crops grow without ploughing or pruning, goats return home on their own to be milked, bears do not prey on the sheep, no vipers exist, and the weather is always temperate.[47] Obviously there was some cross-fertilization between the concepts of the early paradisal state and of the distant paradisal preserve for select heroes. Meanwhile, on the fringes of the Greek mythological world, certain peoples enjoy utopian conditions, much like the carefree heroes who inhabit the Islands of the Blessed. In the far north the Hyperboreans pass their days in feasting and music, engaging neither in hard work nor in war.[48] Even the Kyklopes enjoy a primitive paradise in which they simply trust that the gods will provide. Wheat, barley, and grapes grow in their unsown and unploughed fields, watered by the showers of Zeus. They themselves dwell in caves and have no political organization larger than the family.[49]

Similar phenomena on a more modest scale are reported in other mythological contexts. For example, during the revels of the god Dionysos and his followers, wine and milk and honey flow as signs of the god's wondrous power. A Euripidean chorus describes how at an epiphany of the god the ground flowed with milk, wine, and the nectar of bees, and an eyewitness to the activities of the bacchants reports having seen them produce actual springs or streams of water, wine, milk, and honey.[50] This could as well be a portrait of Canaan, the Promised Land, which God describes to Moses as "a land flowing with milk and honey."[51] The imagery suggests a delirious abundance of food.

Hebrew tradition had, of course, its own notion of a primordial paradise. According to the *Septuagint*, the original human couple who dwelled in Eden (called Edem in the Greek) enjoyed a simple and presumably carefree life in a pleasant, well-watered garden (Greek *paradeisos*) free from toil, pain, and death.[52] This agrees with the general Greek conception to the extent of being an early human paradise of abundance and ease, though it expresses these notions differently, since, for example, the two denizens of Eden are an innocent, childlike couple devoid of adult sensuality, whereas the Golden Race is a fully adult society that passes its time in convivial feasting. In Hebrew myth the primordial couple lose their residence in God's garden because of their breaking a rule, the first of many instances in which humans disappoint God, whereas in Greek myth the Golden Race simply dies out.

Ethnographic Cockaignes

Quasi-ethnographic reports of Cockaigne-like conditions among various foreign peoples allegedly rest on the authority of contemporary travelers or the like and so convey the sense of being less remote in time than the Golden Age and less remote in space, though perhaps not by much, than the Islands of the Blessed.

The most curious and complex of these is Herodotos's account of the Aithiopians and their mysterious Table of the Sun. The Persian monarch Kambyses once sent some men of the Ichthyophagoi ("Fish-Eaters") as spies to the Aithiopians to collect information and in particular to learn if the so-called Table of the Sun really existed. The Table of the Sun was said to be a meadow in the outskirts of the city that was full of boiled meat from all kinds of quadrupeds. City officials placed the meat there during the night, and during the day anyone who wished went there and dined; but the local people said that the earth itself sent up the meat each night. The visitors brought the king of the Aithiopians a number of gifts: a purple garment, some gold jewelry, a box of myrrh, and a jar of palm wine. When the visitors explained to him that the garment was colored by means of dyes, the king scorned it as being mendacious. Thinking the gold necklace and bracelet were fetters, he laughed, since the Aithiopians had stronger bonds than these, and when he learned that the myrrh was employed as a perfume for the body he rejected it for being as mendacious as dyed clothing.[53] He liked only the palm wine. When the Aithiopian king asked them what the Persian king ate and how long Persians lived, the visitors, explaining what wheat was, replied that the king ate bread and that the Persians lived to around eighty years of age. The Aithiopian monarch attributed the short life-span of the Persians to their consumption of bread, which he called dung, and said they would not live even that long if it were not for their wine. He explained that most Aithiopians lived to the age of a hundred and twenty and that their diet consisted of milk and boiled meat. When the men expressed surprise at the longevity of the Aithiopians, he showed them the spring in which the Aithiopians bathed. It possessed these properties: it made bathers shiny as though it were oil rather than water, it smelled of violets, and it so lacked density that nothing floated upon it. If this is true (Herodotos muses), their use of this spring must be the cause of their longevity. From there the king took them to a prison in which all the inmates were bound with gold chains, for among the Aithiopians the rarest and most precious metal was not gold but bronze. The visitors also were shown the so-called Table of the Sun before they departed.[54]

The format of Herodotos's account is a familiar one in utopian narratives: outsiders visit a wondrous society, providing an occasion for a local guide to explain the nature of the place, which inevitably is far superior to anything previously known to the visitors. Herodotos's Aithiopians are ideally situated as utopians, for they dwell on the southern coast of Africa at the furthest reaches of the earth; that is, their land lies precisely opposite that of the Hyperboreans and at the other extreme of the world.[55] Although dwelling within the realm of human beings, they are, in the viewpoint of Greeks, all but unreachable. Kambyses himself does not send his own men to them, but intermediaries, some men of the Ichthyophagoi, who know the language.

There the Aithiopians, the tallest and best-looking of all peoples, live a life of abundance and ease.[56] They owe their Cockaigne-like conditions mostly to two marvelous possessions. First, their Table of the Sun provides the fortunate inhabitants with an infinitely renewed supply of meat from every kind of quadruped, sent up automatically by the earth itself every evening while the

inhabitants sleep (the alternate tradition according to which local magistrates secretly replenish the Table at night is clearly an attempt to rationalize this wonder, but not a very good one since deception is out of place in this society), like the automatic crops the earth produced for the Golden Race and still produces thrice a year on the Islands of the Blessed. Not only that, the meat is already cut up and boiled, ready to eat, exactly as in Cockaigne, where the food is not only plentiful but also fully prepared. If Hesiod's Golden Race expresses a farmer's fantasy, this is a pastoralist's dream: abundant meat ready to consume, and milk. And indeed Helios, whose wondrous Table the Aithiopians enjoy, does possess famous herds of cattle and flocks of sheep.[57]

Second, a certain spring used by the Aithiopians has wondrous qualities. Not only does it automatically oil the skin of the bathers, saving them the bother of doing so after their bath, but also, being a Fountain of Youth, it extends the bathers' lifetime by half, so that they generally live, not eighty, but one hundred and twenty years.[58] (Were it not for the Aithiopians' scorn for perfume, I would add that the water must also lend fragrance to the bodies of the bathers.) Another Cockaigne-like feature is the inversion of metallic values. Gold is so common that the natives do not even regard it as precious, using it to make fetters, like the floral fetters described by Lucian.

I shall not dwell long on other quasi-ethnographic instances, for which a couple examples will suffice. For several ancient authors, India was a Land of Cockaigne. In his novelistic biography of the Greek sage Apollonios of Tyana, Philostratos describes a meal at which Apollonios was present while on a visit to India. He saw robots, consisting of tripods below and brazen cupbearers above, move of their own power; he saw the earth spread out soft grass beneath the diners; and he saw different foods—dried fruits, bread, vegetables, and fruits—present themselves more nicely than if cooks had prepared them. Of the robotic cupbearers, two flowed with wine, one with warm water, and one with cold water. The drinking utensils were all made of precious stones of the sort that in Greece were so small that they could be used only for necklaces and rings.[59] In short, he witnesses a household with automatons like those created on Olympos by the god Hephaistos, prepared foods that were mobile, ordinary utensils composed of huge precious stones, and a carpet of grass sent up automatically by the earth.[60] Another portrayal of India as a Land of Cockaigne is found in Dio Chrysostomos.[61]

If Philostratos borrowed his household robots from Homer (Philostratos himself points out the similarity), an anonymous Greek geographer, writing in Antioch or Alexandria in the mid-fourth century A.D. but known only in a Latin translation, drew inspiration from the *Septuagint* and other sources. The Camarini (he writes) are an Eastern people, living in the Eden mentioned by Moses. They are pious and good, devoid of evil. They neither eat ordinary bread or other similar food nor cook with fire but instead eat bread that rains down on them from the sky daily, and drink a beverage of wild honey and pepper.[62] The sun is so hot there, however, that as soon as it rises they must immediately jump into the river in order not to burn up; on the other hand, their clothing never gets dirty because it is cleansed by the sun's fire. There are no fleas, lice, bugs, or any other noxious things to pester them. Their

mountain stream washes down emeralds, pearls (!), sapphires, and other precious stones, which the Camarini collect by simply stretching nets across the narrows. They live in great happiness, doing no work and suffering from no illnesses, and since they all live to the age of one hundred and twenty, it never happens that a parent must mourn a lost child. Each person, moreover, foresees the exact day of his or her death and prepares appropriately.[63] In this pleasant but hot place, then, the lucky Camarini live a carefree existence sustained by food that rains down upon them from the sky in the form of bread, and since they are not obliged to do any work, not even to wash their clothes, they pass the time fishing in their local stream for precious stones. They live to be a hundred and twenty years, the upper limit for human longevity established by god in *Genesis* as well as the norm for Herodotos's Aithopians.[64]

Greek and Roman literature, then, from Homer and Hesiod at the beginning of Greek literature to authors at the end of antiquity, is replete with accounts of special little societies in which the folk enjoy (or used to enjoy) Cockaigne-like conditions of life: the primordial Golden Race or Age, the Elysian Field or Islands of the Blessed, the Hyperboreans in the north, the Aithiopians in the south, India and Eden in the east, and so on. Although these individual traditions are not so similar that they could be labeled as expressions of the same narrative type, and few of them are even stories as such, they do show a general similarity, and they have drawn ideas from one another.

The leitmotif of all the Cockaigne and Cockaigne-like narratives is automation: automatic crops (that grow without ploughing and sowing), automatic goats (that go to pasture and return home on their own for milking), automatic meat (that the earth sends up like a crop ready to eat or that grows on trees or that flows in rivers of broth or that walks and flies around asking to be eaten), automatic bread (that rains down from the sky ready to eat or grows in the fields as a crop), automatic beverages (cascading in streams or raining down from the sky, ready to drink), and automated service (mobile food, mobile utensils, robots, a bath that oils one's skin, a sun that washes one's clothes, etc.). Two conditions are regularly associated with these motifs: ease, which is of course the main point of the automation, and abundance, especially of food (three crops a year, beverages that flow in streams, a daily crop of meat, a daily rain of bread, etc.). Beyond that the individual narratives emphasize different notions of the desirable life in their conceptions of earthly paradises: eternal spring, youth, long life, wealth, harmony, festivity, and so on.

The tradition of such utopias in antiquity is old, extensive, and persistent, and over time they almost converge as the noncomic tradition shrinks in mythic earnestness and grows in utopian detail. Some of the straight narratives could be retold convincingly as lying tales, since many of the motifs are the same, functioning earnestly in one context and whimsically in another, not only the ubiquitous rivers of wine but also the seemingly more bizarre ideas of naturally occurring cooked meats and foods that rain down from the sky.

For other instances of narrative content common both to lying tales and to myths, see "Great Animal Or Object."

Lit. AT 1930, *Schlaraffenland.* Schenkl 1862:193–194. Poeschel 1878. Zielinski 1885. Crusius 1889:36–38. Bonner 1910. BP 3:244–258, 4:118–120. Gunkel 1921:42–49. Lovejoy and Boas 1965. Ackermann 1944. Baldry 1953. Cocchiara 1956:159–187. Tassy 1959. Langerbeck 1963. Howard 1967. Kenner 1970:69–82. Rooth 1983:50–107. Wunderlich 1986. Versnel 1988. Reckford 1987:89–92. Ashliman, type 1930. Rammel 1990.

1. *Dec.* 8.3.
2. Chevalier 1983:425; cf. Poeschel 1878:410–412.
3. Briggs (1970) A1:331.
4. Briggs (1970) A2:63–64.
5. Rammel 1990.
6. Ego sum abbas Cucaniensis, et consilium meum est cum bibulis.
7. Poeschel 1878:404–406.
8. Poeschel 1878:416–419. On different appellations for the glutton's paradise and on their etymologies see further Wunderlich 1986:55–59.
9. Rammel 1990:18–22. My maternal grandmother, Marie Jensen, an immigrant from Denmark, could recite by heart a long Danish poem composed for children in 1830 by Christian Winther, *Flugten til Amerika* ("The Flight to America"), in which two young children plan to run away to America, which they picture as a Land of Cockaigne where children live riotously. A few years after the publication of Winther's poem, Hans Christian Andersen composed a song, "Brothers, Very Far from Here," in which he describes America as a land in which roasted pigeons nest, champagne flows from springs, etc.; the song became popular throughout Scandinavia. In 1853 a Norwegian journalist, inspired by a Norwegian utopian settlement in Pennsylvania, composed "Oleana," which became as popular in America as in Norway. On these songs see Jensen and Koustrup 1976:22–25, 60–62; Wright and Wright 1983:221–231. On one occasion at least there really was a river of wine in the New World. In 1926, after six years of Prohibition, Foppiano Vineyards in California had in their cellars 150,000 gallons of wine that could not be sold and was turning to vinegar. As two federal agents watched, the winemakers dumped it all into a creek beside a highway, whereupon the inhabitants of nearby Healdsburg, equipped with tin cans, quart bottles, gallon jugs, and anything else they could lay their hands on, retrieved as much of it as they could (*The Fresno Bee,* December 5, 1993).
10. Poeschel 1878.
11. *Deipnosophistae* 6.267e–270a.
12. Kratinos fr. 176 K.-A.
13. Krates fr. 16–17 K.-A.
14. The motif of the wonder table that lays out a feast upon command (D1472.1.7, *Magic table supplies food and drink*) is frequently cited as evidence for the presence of the magic tale in antiquity. The motif is found in several different tales in modern times, including AT 511, *One-Eye, Two-Eyes, Three-Eyes,* and AT 563, *The Table, the Ass, and the Stick.*
15. Telekleides fr. 1 K.-A.
16. The soup conveniently brings along its own "spoons" (*mystilai* = pieces of bread scooped out so as to be usable as spoons; see LSJ s.v. μυστίλη, just as in the thirteenth-century *Fabliau de Coquaigne* the river of wine (both red and white!) brings along its own goblets (Poeschel 1878:407).
17. Pherekrates fr. 113 K.-A.
18. Baldry 1953:55.
19. Pherekrates fr. 137 K.-A.
20. Baldry 1953:57.
21. Nikophon fr. 21 K.-A.
22. Hoffmann 1910:23.
23. Metagenes fr. 6 K.-A.
24. *Satirica* 45.4: tu si aliubi fueris, dices hic porcos coctos ambulare = Otto 1890:284, no. 1450.
25. *Saturnalia* 7.
26. *Saturnalia* (*Ep. Sat.* 20).
27. 2.3–16.

28. εἰς Ἀφάννας (Zenobios 3.92; Crusius 1889:37).
29. *WD* 109–120.
30. *WD* 42–44.
31. *Pol.* 272a–b.
32. *Met.* 1.89–124.
33. *Georg.* 1.121–135.
34. In Lucian's day another interpretation of the philanthropic treatment of slaves during the Kronia evidently was that it was done in honor of the bondage that Kronos suffered (*Sat.* 8). Strictly speaking, the free and rich hosted the unfree and poor, so that one could view the feast as an inversion of roles, the masters serving the servants, but the ancient writers place more emphasis on the egalitarianism of the festival than on the inverted hierarchy. The rich hosted the others because only they had the resources to do so. But to the extent that the wealthy were the patrons of the festival, they stood in a relationship to the poor as Kronos and the Titans stood to the Golden Race and as Zeus and the Olympians stood to the heroes dwelling in the Elysian Field or Isles of the Blessed. On the ambiguity of the myths and rites associated with Kronos in ancient Greek tradition see the discussion of Versnel (1988), who argues that both myth and rite say in effect the same thing, namely, that the apparent utopia is really a dystopia that cannot and must not be allowed to exist in ordinary reality. Myth conveys the exceptional character of Kronian conditions by locating them on the distant margins of space and time, and ritual similarly restricts them to a few chaotic hours (1988:146).
35. Lucian *Sat.* 7. Among the games played during the Kronia were dice (*kyboi*), knucklebones (*astragaloi*, a game similar to dice), and a board game resembling checkers (*pessoi*), the sorts of games that Kratinos and Telekleides represent as being played with food. A winner at knucklebones had the right to require the loser to do something silly such as to make an embarrassing statement about himself or to dance naked. Among the prizes mentioned are sausages; among the punishments, dunking in water. See further Lucian's *Saturnalia*.
36. Lovejoy and Boas 1965:65–70; Parke 1977:29–30; cf. West 1966:204–205.
37. Lovejoy and Boas 1965:85–89.
38. *Ecl.* 4.
39. Gunkel 1921:44–49; Childs 1962:65–69.
40. Amos 9:13–15.
41. Joel 3:17–18.
42. Ezek. 47:12.
43. Isa. 11:6–9, 65:25.
44. Compare Lovejoy and Boas 1965:290–303.
45. 4.561–569.
46. *WD* 166–173 West.
47. *Epod.* 16.41–66.
48. Pindar *Pyth.* 10.29–43. See further Lovejoy and Boas 1965:304–314; Romm 1992:60–67.
49. Homer *Od.* 9.107–115; cf. Mondi 1983.
50. *Bacchae* 141, 704–711; cf. Horace *Odes* 2.19.9–12; Bonner 1910.
51. Exod. 3:8.
52. Gen. 2:8–3:24.
53. Regarded as dishonest, dyed textiles imply the desire of one person to deceive and exploit another, and so are absent from the society of the blameless Aithiopians, just as they are absent from Vergil's second Golden Age, when sheep will come in different colors.
54. Herodotos 3.17–25. See further Romm 1992:45–60.
55. 3.17, 3.25.
56. 3.20.
57. Homer *Od.* 12.260–419. On the Aithiopians and the Cattle of the Sun, see Vernant 1972, 1989; Hansen 1972:25–26.
58. This is the first appearance of a Fountain of Youth in Greek literature, *pace* Rohde 1960:207 n. 1, who finds the first such mention in the fourth-century historian Theopompos. Herodotos's and Theopompos's two fountains have somewhat different properties. The former slows down the normal process of aging, whereas the latter, like Medeia's magic brew for the rejuvenation of Pelias, actually reverses it, making the user younger than before. See in general Cocchiara 1956:126–158.
59. *Vita Apoll.* 3.27.
60. Hephaistos: Homer *Il.* 18.375–377; cf. Bruce 1913.
61. *Orat.* 35.
62. Compare Exod. 16:14–36.

63. *Liber Junioris Philosophi in quo continetur Totius Orbis Descriptio* (Müller *Geographi Graeci Minores* 2:513–515).

64. Gen. 6:3. In fact, there are only one or two documented cases in which human beings have lived till their 121st birthday. For some Greek and Roman speculations concerning the maximum life span of human beings see Hansen 1996b:186–187.

Search for the Lost Animal. *See* Hearing-Impaired Persons.

Service in Hell ◎ Philinnion and Machates

A young woman enters service in a household and lodges there. One day she encounters the son of the household, who informs her he died and was damned. He instructs her to lodge in his old room, where he secretly visits her at night, and she bears him a child. One day when she does not arise from bed, the mistress sends a maidservant to check on her. Peeking through the keyhole the servant sees the woman with a baby in her arms and a man sitting at her bedside. She runs to inform her mistress, who recognizes the man as her late son. Pretending that it is necessary to store some things in the lodger's room, the mistress has herself bundled up in some clothing and carried into the room. That night when she sees her son arrive and sit beside the bed, she throws off her disguise and catches hold of him. But the son complains that if his mother had only waited a while longer, she would have had him forever, but as it is he must spend seven years in hell.

The youth's mother and father each offer to go in his place, but they fail because of the heat. When the heroine also volunteers, the youth instructs her not to eat anything there, giving her a ring that will produce food and drink for her. She succeeds in reaching the place and staying the requisite number of years or even longer, carrying away many souls as the wages of her work there. Upon her return many years later the father of her child is about to wed, but by means of the ring she brings about her recognition, and they marry.[1]

AT 425J, *Service in Hell to Release Enchanted Husband*, is well established at the present day only in Irish-Gaelic tradition.[2] The folktale is classified by Aarne-Thompson as one of the many subtypes of AT 425, a grouping of tales that because of their general similarity are presumed to be ultimately related to one another.[3]

An Irish text collected in 1936 tells how a woman named Máire left her heartless husband, taking her widowed mother with her, and traveled until she came to a farmhouse. The farmer said he would pay Máire to stay in a haunted house on the farm. She inquired of one of the ghostly beings there what had damned him, and he explained that when the house was being built, he cheated the men of the money they earned. He now instructed her not to accept money from his father but instead to ask permission to sleep in his old room in the house. She slept there for some time, but one day when she did not get up out of bed, the woman of the house send a servant to peek through the keyhole.

When she did so, she saw Máire holding a baby and a young man sitting at her bedside. She ran to tell her mistress. The woman of the house, declaring that the young man was her son, instructed the servant to tell Máire that they wished to store some things in her room. Máire had no objection, so that they bundled the farmer's wife up in some clothes and carried her into Máire's room. When night came on, she saw her son come and sit down beside the bed with Máire and the child. Losing patience, the mother cast away the clothes that concealed her, and took hold of her son. "May God help us now, mother! If you had waited two more hours, you would have had me for ever. Now, I'll have to spend seven years in Hell because of you!" The mother volunteered to go there in his stead, but she soon returned all scorched. The father also tried and failed. Máire said she would go, provided they took care of her mother until her return. The young man gave her a ring, telling her not to eat any food she got in Hell, giving it instead to the dog lying at the threshold of Hell; the ring would provide her food. So she went to Hell and spent seven years there and then seven more. Since she had not eaten any food there, she got as her wages all the souls she could carry out on her back, and turned them over to the Savior. When she reached her old home, she learned that the widower of fourteen years was getting married again. But she sent him the ring he had once given her, so that he recognized her as his wife. Declaring that she was the only wife he would have, he dismissed the wedding party.[4]

According to another Irish text, Máire left her husband, taking her widowed mother along, and traveled until they reached a fine house. The woman of the house gladly hired her in exchange for room and board. After some months she noticed a handsome man standing by the fence. He asked her a favor, explaining that he would be restored to life and health if she should not tell anyone about him for a year and a day. He was his parents' only child, taken from them by death when he was young, and he has been suffering since he was not a Christian. He instructed Máire to request a change of rooms from the little room she now had to his old room. Then he vanished. The mother reluctantly agreed to Máire's request. She moved into the room, and around midnight the youth entered, visited for a while, and left. After some months it appeared to the woman of the house that Máire was pregnant, and she blamed her husband and became jealous of Máire. One morning everyone was up except for Máire, so that the woman of the house sent another servant girl to see what was wrong with the hussy. When the girl looked through the keyhole, she saw a handsome man sitting at bedside, and Máire in bed nursing a baby. The girl went running to her mistress, crying that Máire was in bed feeding a baby and talking with a man at her bedside. The woman went, looked through the keyhole, and recognized her own son. She said nothing for the time being, but a few days later, when Máire was able to get up, the servant girl told Máire that the mistress wished to hide something in Máire's room. In reality the old lady disguised herself in some clothing and had herself carried into the room. Making no sound, she observed the young man enter at midnight, sit down, and talk with Máire. Then the mother lost patience, tore off her disguise, ran to her son, and embraced him. But he cried: "Oh shame, shame, shame, Mother! That's a hateful thing you have done to me. Had you waited until I had been coming here for a year and a day, I would have been as well as I had ever been.

But now, I must go back to suffer in hell for seven years more." His mother tried to fight off the demons of hell, and failed, and his father did even less well. Máire volunteered to go. Her lover gave her a ring, instructing her to get her food and drink from it but not to touch any nourishment in hell. She went to hell and worked for seven years, providing her own food. When the time was up, she took as her wages the souls that she could carry, whom she turned over to the King of Sunday. Learning that the father of her child had lost hope that Máire would ever return and was about to remarry, she made herself known to him by means of the ring he had given her.[5]

The mysterious atmosphere of these events derives in part from the implied back story of which the narrative gives only tantalizing hints, the story of the dead man and his world, which intertwines with the events seen from the viewpoint of the living. In one text the dead man is said to be enchanted because he let the workers starve to death when they were building the house, and was sent to hell as a punishment; according to another text he was taken by "the good people" (fairies) and has to spend a certain period of time with them.[6] So the youth dies and is damned for one reason or another (his mother inadvertently sold him to the devil, he did something cruel or dishonest in life), or the fairies take him, or something else happens. Although he is dead, he nevertheless is active, which the narrator may explain vaguely as the result of an enchantment or spell, or may not account for at all. The notion of enchantment or spell fits better with the fact that after his failed attempt to regain life the youth must return to hell for a certain term, for if he were simply dead, we should expect him to return to death permanently. But if he is enchanted, we are not told who enchanted him, and if he is only dead, we are not told why he, unlike other dead persons, is permitted an attempt to regain his life. In either case the seemingly arbitrary conditions for his salvation remain unexplained, which seem to be more or less that he enter a relationship with the heroine for a specified period of time undisturbed by anyone else. Enchanted or dead or both, the youth presently rises to the status of an unenchanted, fully alive person when his lover takes his place in hell. Although one could conceivably devise a coherent story for these odd events and conditions, no narrator does so, preferring the pleasure of the elusive to the satisfaction of full disclosure and keeping the revenant in the background as a character of secondary importance.

Philinnion and Machates

The central events of *Service in Hell*—the ghostly lover, the confrontation of mother and child, and the dead child's rebuke—appear strikingly in an ancient Greek story, with a reversal of genders, the lodger being male and the ghost being female.[7] Our knowledge of the story depends precariously upon a document composed probably in the late Hellenistic period, a letter supposedly written by a certain urban official, Hipparchos, to a higher official, Arrhidaios, informing him of an extraordinary event that took place in Amphipolis and offering to send witnesses in case Arrhidaios should wish to write about the matter to the king, Philip II of Macedon. Consequently the events described in the letter are set sometime within the period 356–336 B.C., during the reign of

Philip and after his capture of Amphipolis. The letter itself is spurious, but it was uncritically accepted as genuine in the second century A.D. by the para-doxographer Phlegon of Tralles, who copied the document entire into his compilation *On Marvels*, grouping it with his other accounts of embodied ghosts.[8] Unfortunately the first part of the letter is lost, and the extant text begins at the moment when the maidservant discovers the lovers in the bedroom. The letter was also taken as the real thing by other authors, among them the neoplatonic philosopher Proklos, who summarizes it in a commentary he wrote on Plato. Putting Phlegon and Proklos together, we get the following story.

Philinnion, daughter of the Amphipolitans Demostratos and Charito, married a man named Krateros but died soon afterward and was placed in the family tomb. Around six months later a youth named Machates came to Amphipolis from Pella and lodged with Demostratos and Charito. Philinnion secretly visited him in her parents' house, and the two lovers exchanged rings. On the evening of her second visit—Phlegon's text begins at this point—the maidservant went to the door of the guest room and saw Philinnion sitting beside Machates. She ran to Charito and Demostratos, screaming for them to come to see their daughter, but when the skeptical Charito finally did peer into the room, the occupants were already asleep. Thinking that she recognized her daughter's clothes and features, however, Charito planned to confront the girl or Machates the next morning. But in the morning the girl left unnoticed, so that Charito asked Machates to tell her everything that had been going on. The youth explained that the girl's name was Philinnion and that she visited him because of her desire for him, coming without her parents' knowledge.[9] He showed Charito a ring that Philinnion had given him and a breastband that she had left behind the previous evening. When Charito burst into tears, Machates promised to show her the girl when she came again. That evening Philinnion came at the usual time and sat down on the bed. Machates found it hard to believe that the girl he was consorting with was actually dead, but, as promised, he secretly sent his slaves to notify Demostratos and Charito. They quickly came, cried out, and embraced their daughter, whereupon Philinnion said: "Mother and father, how unfairly you have grudged my being with the guest for three days in my father's house, since I have caused no one any pain. For this reason, on account of your meddling, you shall grieve all over again, and I shall return to the place appointed for me. For it was not without divine will that I came here."[10] Having said this, she collapsed dead upon the bed, and the household began weeping afresh.

Word now reached Hipparchos—the official who allegedly writes the present letter in which the extraordinary event is described—who acted to keep in check the crowd that gathered at the house of Demostratos and Charito. At dawn the people met in assembly and decided to go first to Philinnion's tomb to see if it contained her body or was empty. Opening the family tomb they found it empty except for the ring and wine cup that Machates had given her on the first day. Frightened and astonished they proceeded to the house, where they found the dead girl lying in the guest room. They returned to the place of assembly where a seer advised them to burn her body outside the city boundary and to perform certain purificatory sacrifices, which they did. In the meantime Machates became despondent and killed himself.[11] Hipparchos now writes about the matter to Arrhidaios.

Let us compare the story of Philinnion with *Service in Hell*. (1) A family suffers the loss of a son/daughter, and sometime later (2) a person arrives at the household and lodges in the house. (3) Presently the deceased son/daughter begins secretly visiting the lodger in the guest room at night, and (4) they become lovers. One day (5) a maidservant, peering into the guest room, observes the deceased son/daughter of the household sitting together with the guest, and (6) runs to inform her mistress, (7) who confirms the identification. (8) The mistress conspires with the maidservant (with the guest) to be present in the room (to be summoned to the room) when her son/daughter next returns. (9) That evening, when the son/daughter enters at the usual time, the mother (father, mother and father) suddenly irrupts and embraces her child, whereupon (10) the son/daughter rebukes the parent, saying that if she (he, they) had only waited a little longer and had not thus interfered, the son/daughter would have regained his/her life, but as it is he/she must return to the realm of the dead.

After following so parallel a course up to the point of the rebuke the ancient and modern stories now diverge, and the reason is surely literary. The composer of the fraudulent letter obviously reworks a traditional ghost story, not only presenting the occurrence as a true event that happened in Amphipolis in the fourth century B.C. but also representing the letter as an account of it written by an official who was present as an eyewitness. The official's own involvement begins after the parents' confrontation with the ghost, requiring the narrator to shift the events abruptly from the private setting of the folktale to a public one in order that he may insert himself into the scene as an observer. As a result the author is obliged to take greater liberties with the second part of the story. Even so we glimpse a continued parallelism of sorts, for at this point in the ancient story (11) the people deliberate in assembly about what course of action to take, while in the folktale the family deliberates about what to do; (12) the people next make their way to the tomb, while in the folktale the heroine now makes her way to hell, and subsequently (13) the people return from the tomb to the family home, while the heroine eventually returns from hell to the family home. In short, what the death realm is to the latter part of the folktale, the tomb is to the latter part of the letter. Finally, in a scene of verification, (14) the people verify that Philinnion's corpse is found in her house, or the youth verifies the identity of the long-absent heroine.[12] The stories are so similar up to the point of the rebuke and they are just enough parallel thereafter to suggest that the source reworked by the ancient epistolographer closely resembled the Irish folktale of today, except of course in transitory features such as the pagan or Christian setting.[13]

As a form of AT 425, the story of Philinnion and Machates belongs to the same cluster of narratives as the tale of Cupid and Psyche (see "Disenchanted Husband"). These tales characteristically tell of the arrival of a human being at the house of a supernatural being, their entry into a marriagelike relationship, the breaking of a taboo, the loss of the supernatural lover, the heroic effort made by the human lover to regain the supernatural lover, and their eventual reunion. The story of Philinnion furnishes our earliest literary evidence for tales of this type.[14] The fact that AT 425 had already developed at least two stable subtypes by classical times implies that it had been in existence for a long while.

Lit. (AT 425J, *Service in Hell to Release Enchanted Husband.*) Swahn 1955:329–333. Hansen 1980; 1989; 1996:79–85. Ashliman, type 425J. Radner 1989.

1. Swahn 1955:329–333. For sense of the variety of the texts, see Swahn's summaries of eight different versions.
2. An isolated American text of the tale collected in the Ozarks presumably derives from an Irish storyteller; see Morris 1931:95–96.
3. Aarne-Thompson follow Jan-Öjvind Swahn, who justifies the classification (Swahn 1955:332–333).
4. Bødker, Hole, and D'Aronco 1963:136–142. The tale was collected in Gaelic and is preserved in manuscript in the Irish Folklore Commission.
5. O'Sullivan 1966:151–164, no. 24. The tale was recorded from Peig Sayers in 1944.
6. Swahn 1955:329–331, nos. CI 5, CI 25.
7. Gender reversal is not unusual in tale types; for example, AT 425P is a subtype of AT 425 in which the enchanted person is the woman rather than the man. Despite the inverse assignments of gender to the lovers in the Irish tale and the Greek story, the female (Máire, Philinnion) is the principal character of interest in each, and among the parents it is similarly the mother who carries the action; see Hansen 1996b:83.
8. On the question of whether revenants should be classified as ghosts, see Felton 1999:25–29.
9. At this point Machates shows no understanding that Philinnion is the daughter of his hosts Demostratos and Charito, or that they even had a daughter who died some months earlier. Accordingly he is not a close friend of the family. Philinnion leaves her tomb nightly to visit him, but she evidently represents herself as someone living in town who comes to him at night because of her love for him. See Hansen 1996b:69.
10. Like the Irish folktale, the story of Philinnion drops tantalizing hints of a back story that it never fully discloses.
11. Phlegon of Tralles *De Mir.*1. Proklos *In Platonis Rempublicam Commentarii* 2, p. 116 Kroll. On these texts see Rohde 1877a; Wendland 1911:5–11; Mesk 1925; Hansen 1980, 1989, 1996; Stramaglia 1999:230–257, 2000:167–184.
12. Notice the importance of rings. The youth gives Máire a magic ring, which she brings along with her to hell; Machates gives Philinnion a ring, which she takes with her to her tomb (Hansen 1996b:82); each ring has some importance in later events.
13. Hansen 1996b:81–83. Things end happily in the folktale with the lovers' wedding or reaffirmation, whereas events turn out tragically in the pseudohistorical text, first one lover dying and then the other. The lovers are joined in life or death.
14. Hansen 1980, 1996:83–85.

Seven Sleepers 🥬 Epimenides of Crete

A man falls asleep, often in a cave, and sleeps for a long time, usually many years, without aging. When he awakens, he believes he has slept only a little while. But he presently discovers that his physical environment (fields, town, monastery, etc.) has changed and that he neither recognizes the people nor is recognized. Finally, the truth emerges (he perceives what has happened, or someone recognizes him, finds an old record of his disappearance, etc.). Sometimes he ages quickly and dies shortly thereafter.

The story, AT 766, *The Seven Sleepers*, is found both as a folktale and as a legend.

In a Swiss legend, a certain Prior Evo took a walk one day in the forest, heard a bird that was singing very beautifully, and fell asleep. He awoke after a half hour, as he thought, and returned to his monastery, where neither he nor the gatekeeper recognized each other. Since Evo claimed to be the prior of the monastery, the gatekeeper fetched the current prior, who summoned the stranger as

well as all the monks. No one knew the stranger, and Evo was astonished. Then the prior recalled reading in the chronicle of the monastery that a monk had gotten lost many years ago. Searching in the book, he found that Evo had disappeared in the year 1208. So Evo had slept for 308 years. Hearing this, Evo fell and crumbled into dust.[1]

Essentially the same story is also told of persons who, whether they actually sleep or not, pass a day or two in the company of the supernatural (witch, fairies, marvelous animal, etc.), for they discover upon leaving that much time has passed in the natural world.[2] So a piper was walking in the evening and heard lively music behind him. He turned to see a great castle with lights and music and people dancing. He piped for the fairies a day or two, and they let him go. There he was again in the quiet evening. He went back home in order that his folks should not worry, but he recognized no one in his father's house. He was bewildered, saying he had been gone only a couple days. At that point a gray old man said he had heard as a boy from his father that a piper had gone away one evening, and no trace of him had ever been found. The piper had been with the fairies for a hundred years.[3]

Epimenides of Crete

The earliest known version of this story type is that which is told of Epimenides of Crete, and our earliest source for the story is the historian Theompompos in the fourth century B.C. Theopompos's account of Epimenides appeared in his *Philippika*, part of which was a survey of wondrous events associated with different localities. His work has not survived directly, but his account of Epimenides was retold by a number of authors including the anecdotal biographer Diogenes Laertios in his *Lives of the Philosophers*, the paradoxographer Apollonios in his collection of marvelous events, and Pliny in his encyclopedic *Natural History*.[4]

According to Theopompos, Epimenides was told by his father to go to the farm and bring a sheep back to town. Because of the midday heat (or because night overtook him), he left the road for a cave, where he fell asleep. He slept for fifty-seven years. When he finally awoke he looked for the sheep, thinking that it was the same day as that in which he had fallen asleep, but he failed to find it. Then he went on to the farm, which he discovered had been sold, and all its equipment was different. Puzzled, he went back to town to his own house, whose inhabitants asked him who he was. Finally he found his youngest brother, now an old man, who told him of everything that had transpired since his disappearance. Epimenides now grew old in the same number of days as the number of years he had slept, though he lived for a total of 157 years.[5]

The number of years that Epimenides slept ranges slightly in different authors from a low of forty to a high of sixty.[6] Diogenes Laertios reports that some people do not believe he slept so long, and Pliny—who repeats the information that he slept for fifty-seven years, grew old in the same number of days as the number of years he had slept, and lived to the age of 157—also expresses some skepticism about the whole tradition.[7]

Epimenides is, so far as we know, a historical person who lived in approxi-

mately the sixth century B.C. In addition to sleeping for a half-century and living for a century and a half, he was said to have purified Athens after the slaughter of the associates of Kylon, issued prophecies, composed a number of mystical poems, returned from the dead, and been capable of soul-travel.[8] Other than the fact that he was associated with a variety of wonders, however, it is not obvious why the traditional story of the marvelously long sleep should have become attached to him in particular. According to Maximus of Tyre, the cave in which Epimenides slept was that of Diktaian Zeus, and during his deep sleep various deities including Truth and Justice appeared to him in a dream.[9] Maximus therefore implies that Epimenides obtained his powers by incubation, receiving a divine revelation in a dream while sleeping in a sacred place, but this is surely only Maximus's own attempt at a later time to interpret Epimenides' wondrous sleep in connection with the rest of his unusual life.[10] More likely, Epimenides' fifty-seven-year sleep was seen as a prefiguration in his boyhood of his later ability as an adult for soul-travel–according to the *Suda* his soul was able to leave his body for as long as he wanted and then return to it again—and perhaps also of his later ability to return from death. A man whose soul, like that of a shaman, temporarily leaves his body, or who can die and return to life, is much like a man in a state of supernatural sleep, so that there is a thematic consistency in the three ideas.

In the legend of Epimenides, as in that of Prior Evo, an air of mystery surrounds the protagonist's long sleep. There is no obvious motivation for it, nor is it really explained after the fact. Why did it happen to this person? Why did it happen on this occasion? How did it happen? The ancient narrators, like their modern counterparts, report the exact number of years that the hero has been asleep, giving thereby an air of precision and truth to the wondrous event. Upon awakening, Epimenides is said with touching irony to search for his sheep, lost over fifty years earlier. Unaware of the astonishing experience he has had, the boy naturally gives his attention first to the mundane matters of ordinary life. The narrative dwells upon the confusion and puzzlement he feels as he deals in succession with the lost sheep, the changed farm, and the unfamiliar inhabitants of his house, for the protagonist's experience of sudden enigma is no doubt the most fascinating part of this story. A wonderful and a terrifying fantasy intermingle here. On the positive side, the hero is privileged to travel into the future, but on the nightmarish side, the familiar world becomes suddenly and inexplicably alien, the hero no longer having a family, a home, a place in the network of society. His contemporaries are old or dead. The significant relationships of his life are gone overnight. Catching up with time as though it had somehow overlooked him, Epimenides ages quickly, although, strangely, he also goes on to live a long life.

The Nine Heroes of Sardinia

Unnaturally long sleep is also found in the Sardinian tradition of the Nine Heroes.[11] Aristotle refers to it when he observes that unless people perceive change they do not perceive a lapse of time, "just as happens upon awakening to those persons who, according to legend, sleep next to the heroes in Sar-

dinia."[12] Commenting on this passage, Simplicius explains that the nine heroes are nine sons of Herakles and the daughters of Thestios.[13] They died in Sardinia, where their bodies remain intact and undecayed as though they were only sleeping. The Greek commentator Philoponos says that "sick persons were said to go to the heroes in Sardinia and be healed, and going there they slept for two days in a row, and when they awoke they thought it was the same time as when they had stood by the heroes."[14] So the texts indicate that there was a Greek legend localized in Sardinia according to which nine heroes lay in the earth so preserved in death that they appeared merely to be asleep; that some persons visited them to be healed of a sickness; that the visitors fell asleep next to the heroes and upon awakening found to their surprise that a long period of time had passed.

In modern European traditions heroes such as Charlemagne, Holger Danske, and King Arthur sleep, often in a room in a mountain, awaiting the time when their help will be needed. Many legends tell how persons come upon (or are brought to) the place where the great hero and his men sit sleeping, where strange events take place including an unnoticed passage of time.[15]

Abimelech

More like the experience of Epimenides is that of Abimelech, found in *The Chronicles of Jeremiah*, a composition most likely of Jewish origin with secondary Christian reworking dating to around the second century A.D.[16] It is known in Greek, Ethiopic, Armenian, and Slavonic versions, although it was probably written originally in Hebrew or Aramaic.[17]

According to this work, Jeremiah prayed to the Lord to spare the Ethiopian slave Abimelech from seeing and experiencing the ruin of Jerusalem, since Abimelech had done so much for the people of the city and for Jeremiah in particular. The Lord instructed Jeremiah to send him to the vineyard of Agrippa, where the Lord would take care of him until the people should return to the city. So on the following day Jeremiah sent Abimelech to the vineyard of Agrippa to get some figs to give to the sick. After Abimelech got the figs it was midday, so that he lay in the shade of some trees, and rested his head on his basket. He slept for sixty-six years. When he awoke, he thought he had slept only a little while. The figs were still fresh and dripping with milk. He returned to Jerusalem where he recognized neither the city nor his house. When he asked an old man where Jeremiah the priest, Baruch the Levite, and the other people of the city were, the old man answered that the people were in Babylon, having been captured and taken there by King Nebuchadnezzer sixty-six years earlier, and Jeremiah had gone there to prophesy to them. After Abimelech told the old man his story and showed him the figs, which were fresh out of season, the old man concluded that God wished to spare Abimelech the ruin of the city.[18]

The Seven Sleepers of Ephesus

From the legend of Abimelech it is only a few steps to the famous story of the Seven Sleepers of Ephesos, a Christian legend found in Greek as early as the sixth century and thereafter for many centuries in different authors and lan-

guages. It is perhaps best known today in the thirteenth-century Latin telling of Jacobus a Voragine.

According to Jacobus, when the Emperor Decius was persecuting the Christians in Ephesus, seven Christian men gave away their worldly goods and fled to Mt. Celion to hide. There they fell asleep. Three hundred and sixty years later, during the reign of the Christian emperor Theodosius, there arose a heresy denying the resurrection of the dead. The seven sleepers awoke, feeling as if they had slept only overnight, and resumed their concern about the threat from Decius. One of their number, Malchus, went to the city to buy bread and obtain information, and was astonished to see a cross over the gate and to hear people using the name of Christ. When he bought bread, the baker noticed the old coin with which he paid. Thinking that the stranger had found an old treasure, the baker began whispering to others, which caused Malchus to believe his identity had been discovered. Soon he was summoned before St. Martinus, the bishop, and Antipater, the governor, who questioned him about his family and about the old money. No one recognized the names of his kin. And when Malchus asked about Decius, the bishop explained that he had died long ago. Malchus now led them to the cave, and when they saw the holy youths with glowing faces they fell down and glorified God. The emperor Theodosius was summoned to Ephesus. One of the seven explained that God had resurrected them in order that people might believe in the resurrection of the dead. Then the seven died.[19]

In the story of the Seven Sleepers, as in the Abimelech legend, the supernaturally long sleep acquires a purpose, which becomes apparent to the protagonist and to others. The arbitrariness concerning the person who falls asleep, the occasion on which it occurs, and the means by which it happens in the nonreligious legends is transformed in the Jewish and Christian narratives into meaningfulness, for the mysterious sleep is effected by God, who brings it about in order to protect the protagonist on a certain occasion or to convey a message to persons at a later point in history.

Lit. AT 766, *The Seven Sleepers.* Gibbon (1946) 3:1052–1053. Rohde 1878:209–210 n. 2; 1880; 1882. Meyer (1885) 1:277–286. Demoulin 1901:95–100. Baring-Gould 1967:93–112. Hartland 1891:161–254. Frazer (1898) 2:121–123. Huber 1910. Liungman 1961:215–216. Colker 1963:131–133. Tubach 1969, no. 4440. Lüthi 1976, chap. 2. Ashliman, type 766. *EM* 4:42–58. Karlinger 1986.

1. Lüthi 1976:41–42.
2. Hartland 1891:161–254; Röhrich (1962) 1:124–145, 274–280.
3. Briggs (1971) B1:336.
4. Diogenes Laertios 1.109, 115; Apollonios 1; Pliny *NH* 7.154, 175.
5. *FGH* 115 F 67–69.
6. Forty: Pausanias 1.14.4. Sixty: *Suda* s.v. Epimenides.
7. Diogenes Laertios 1.112. Pliny *NH* 7.175.
8. Demoulin 1901.
9. *Philos.* 16.1.
10. Rohde 1880:161.
11. Rohde 1880, 1882.
12. *Physica* 218b.21–26.
13. Schol. on Aristotle, p. 388a, ed. Brandis.
14. Schol. on Aristotle, p. 388b, 3 ff., ed. Brandis.
15. Rohde 1880:160; Hartland 1891:161–254.
16. *Paraleipomena Jeremiou* 3–6.

17. Huber 1910:407–418, 422–426; Schürer (1986) 3:292–294.

18. Compare Varro's *Sexagesis*, a Menippean satire composed in the first century B.C. that survives only in fragments. It recounts how a ten-year-old boy sleeps for fifty years, returns to Rome, and is shocked to observe the extent to which Romans have declined morally. See further Cèbe (1998) 12:1895–1941.

19. *Legenda Aurea* 96.

Shepherd Who Cried "Wolf!"

A shepherd repeatedly calls out for help against a wolf (or other predator), and the villagers rush to help him, only to find each time that he is lying. When a wolf really comes, nobody believes his cry so that the wolf devours his sheep.

This simple and familiar tale is AT 1333, *The Shepherd Who Cried "Wolf!" Too Often*. It is found in Europe, India, and elsewhere. The many printed texts of the popular Aesopic fable have probably contributed much to the oral tradition.[1]

According to a German text, in which the story is recounted as a legend, on the road from Oberweis to Altenhof there is an old cross with an image of a wolf on it. That is what people say, reports the narrator, but it is really a lamb of God. There was a shepherd with his flock who cried out that a wolf was coming. People ran there to drive the wolf away, but there was no wolf, and the shepherd laughed at them. The shepherd did the same thing again, and a couple persons ran to him. But the third time a wolf really did come. The shepherd could scream all he wanted, but no one came to help him. The wolf tore the shepherd and quite a few sheep to pieces. That is why the cross stands there. The narrator then apologized for telling so familiar a story, one that is also found in schoolbooks. But in Oberweis, the narrator says, it has always been told of the cross.[2]

The Foolish Shepherd in Ancient Fable

The tale is found in two ancient fable collections, the collection composed in Greek verse by the Roman fabulist Babrius in the first or second century A.D. and the so-called Augustana Collection, or Recension I, an anonymous compilation of Aesopic fables in Greek prose composed around the second century A.D. Though Babrius's text of this fable has not survived, we know its contents from a later paraphrase.[3]

According to the Augustana narrative, a shepherd who pastured his flock at a distance from a certain village used to play a joke. He would call to the villagers for help, saying that wolves were attacking his sheep. Two or three times the villagers ran from the village and then departed as the shepherd laughed. Finally it happened that wolves actually did attack the sheep, cutting the shepherd off from his flock. He called for help, but the villagers, supposing that he was joking as usual, paid no attention to him, so that he lost his sheep.[4]

Since the ancient fable is found only in collections, it is accompanied by little contextual information. However, according to the epimythium (that is,

the application or moral) of the fable in the Augustana Collection, the tale illustrates how the reward of liars is that no one believes them even when they are telling the truth. This truism is an international proverbial saying, known also among the Romans.[5] The fable can of course be employed as a cautionary tale illustrating the bad consequences of lying, and since the behavior of the shepherd is essentially infantile, adults have often deemed this tale appropriate for children, placing it from the sixteenth century onward in readers for schoolchildren.[6] Aarne and Thompson classify the tale as a numskull tale, which it really is not, for the shepherd's behavior is not that of a born fool so much as that of an immature person showing poor judgment when, like an irritating child, he serially repeats a joke or prank that enjoyed some success the first time.

The Foolish Hunter

The basic argument of the tale is found with different imagery in other classical contexts. The earliest of these occurs in Xenophon's *Education of Kyros*, composed in the fourth century B.C., in which the Persian prince Kyros is portrayed as being instructed in military science by his father. When Kyros declares that nothing seems to inspire soldiers more than hope, his father counters by saying that this is like a hunter who always summons his dogs with the specific call that signifies he sees their quarry. At first they obey him eagerly, but if he deceives them often, eventually they do not obey him even when he calls them with his eye on the prey. So also (continues the father) with hope: if one person often gives another person false hope, then he is not believed even when he speaks of hope that is well grounded. Accordingly, a general should allow himself to say only that of which he is completely sure.[7] The conversation between the two men that Xenophon invents may illustrate the kind of conversational context that could trigger the telling of the fable of the shepherd, since it makes the same point. One discussant suggests that taking liberties with the truth can be useful, prompting another discussant to counter by citing a hypothetical instance illustrating how a person who lies may not be believed when it is important to be believed. Kyros's father selects the aristocratic example of the hunter and his dogs rather than the humble tale of the shepherd and the villagers, and concludes by giving the moral and its application to the topic of conversation with utmost clarity: a hunter who behaves this way with his dogs loses credence; indeed, any person who behaves this way loses credence; therefore, a military leader in particular should never behave this way.

The Foolish Mistress

The same underlying thought is expressed by Horace. At the end of one of his epistles, the poet compares a constantly grumbling traveling companion to the tricks of a mistress who so often laments this or that piece of lost or stolen jewelry that she is not believed when she suffers an actual loss and really

grieves; similarly, a person who has been tricked once before does not care to help a beggar with a broken leg at a crossroads, though he weep and swear by Osiris that he really is lame.[8]

Lit. AT 1333, *The Shepherd Who Cried "Wolf" Too Often.* Perry 1962:292–293. Holbek (1962) 2:186, no. 146. Scheiber 1969:57 = 1985:253. Bødker 1957:100, no. 1012. Schwarzbaum 1979:xlv n. 76. Ashliman, type 1333. *EM* 6:1083–1086.

1. *EM* 6:1083–1084. For India see Bødker 1957:100, no. 1012.
2. Zender 1966:157, no. 424.
3. BaP 169 = Babrius 169 Crusius.
4. Perry 210; Hsr 226.
5. Cicero *De Divinatione* 2.71, 146; Otto 1890:219; *EM* 6:1083; cf. also Perry 1962:292–293.
6. *EM* 6:1083.
7. *Cyropaedia* 1.6.19.
8. *Epist.* 1.17.52–62.

Slaughter of the Ox

The fool or fools cut off the feet of an ox in the evening in preparation for its slaughter on the following day.

This tale is AT 1261, *The Slaughter of the Ox.* AT cites one Finnish and one Russian text. The protagonists' folly is, of course, that they reverse the proper order of things: first one slaughters the ox, *then* one cuts off its feet.

A Greek Proverbial Expression

The same idea with almost identical imagery is found in the Greek proverbial expression "You're flaying it before you've slaughtered it." The paroemiographer Apostolios, who records the proverb in his collection, includes it in a list of several sayings that (he explains) apply to persons who do the last thing first.[1] Although Apostolios lived in the fifteenth century, many of proverbs in his collection are demonstrably ancient, and since the language of the expression is ancient Greek, it seems likely that it is an ancient proverbial expression. Although we cannot know whether the idea also circulated independently as a comic tale, the proverbial expression itself is a virtual tale, as in our own proverbial expressions "You're counting your chickens before they hatch" or "You're putting the cart before the horse."

For other instances of proverbs that imply the existence of folktales see "Hatch-Penny" and "Tree Trunks Laid Crosswise." But "Pases' penny" and "The man carrying the beam" are more likely to refer to tales outside of themselves than is the expression under discussion, inasmuch as "You're flaying it before you've slaughtered it" makes sense by itself without reference to something external, whereas the former two do not convey a complete meaning by themselves and so presumably allude to independent narratives.

Lit. (AT 1261, *The Slaughter of the Ox.*) Crusius 1889:39.

1. Apostolios 14.75 = *CPG* 2:623: πρὶν ἐσφάχθαι δέρεις.

Smith and the Devil 🍃 Sisyphos and Thanatos

A smith (farmer, etc.) receives Christ and St. Peter hospitably, for which he is granted three wishes. Instead of asking prudently for eternal salvation, he wishes, for example, that whoever sits in his bench (chair) stick to it until the smith should permit him to rise, that whoever climbs his tree be forced to remain in it until the smith should allow him to descend, and that he have the power to will persons or things into his knapsack. When the devil (Death) comes to fetch the smith, the latter employs one of these powers to trap and discomfit him until he relents, agreeing to depart without taking the smith. (The incident is usually repeated with each of the smith's powers.) While the devil (Death) is bound, it is sometimes said that no one on earth dies. In the end the smith proceeds to the gates of Hell, where he is refused admittance, whereupon he goes to the gates of Heaven, where he is likewise rejected. He may then get into Heaven by a trick, or he may go elsewhere.

This comic tale of the clever man and the stupid ogre is AT 330A, *The Smith and the Devil (Death)*.

In the Grimms' tale *De Spielhansl*, or "Gambling Hansel," a gambler nicknamed Gambling Hansel gave lodging one evening to Our Lord and St. Peter, in return for which Our Lord on the following morning offered to grant him three wishes, thinking that the gambler would ask for Heaven. But instead he wished for cards that never lost, dice that never lost, and a fruit tree from which no one could get down once he had climbed it, until Gambling Hansel should bid him. The man now gambled in earnest and was winning so much that in fear St. Peter suggested to Our Lord that since the man might end up winning the whole world they should send Death for him. Death came to the man while he was gambling, and asked him to step outside for a moment, but the man told him to wait until the game was over and in the meantime to go climb the tree and get them something to eat. Death climbed the tree and could not get down again. When he had been there for seven years, during which time no one had died, St. Peter said to Our Lord that no one was dying anymore and that they themselves would have to go down. They went to the place and released Death, who immediately throttled the gambler and went off with him to the netherworld. When the man was rejected first at the gates of Heaven and then at the gates of Purgatory, he went to the gates of Hell, which admitted him. But there he began gambling again, this time winning the devil's minions by means of his unbeatable cards. With the help of these demons he assailed Heaven until they let him in, but he caused so much tumult there that they threw him out again, whereupon his soul shattered and entered into living gamblers.[1]

In a German *Meisterlied* composed in 1551, a peasant was granted three

wishes for having given shelter to St. Peter. He asked to be able to recognize Death, that anyone who blew on his coal fire had to keep blowing, and that whoever sat on his chair would be stuck so long as the peasant wanted. Twice thereafter the man bound Death, who wanted to carry him away. The first time the man asked Death to light him a fire before his departure, and the second time he asked that Death sit long enough for him to make out his will. Thirty years later when the earth had become too full of people, St. Peter returned and persuaded the farmer to release the devil, who had become gaunt and black. In return, the saint promised the man an additional hundred years of life.[2]

According to a narrative collected in India, a clever and skillful carpenter grew old and was concerned that the god of death would take him away. So he hollowed out a tree and constructed a door in it so skillfully that it could not be seen. When the god of death came for him, he invited the god to inspect his handiwork and then imprisoned him in the tree. Meanwhile, people ceased dying, the earth became overcrowded, and crime increased. The relatives of the missing god pressed Bhagwan, the Almighty, to locate the missing deity. Bhagwan invented the first alcoholic beverage, descended to earth, and offered the drink to everyone. The intoxicated drinkers became talkative, among them the carpenter, who thereby gave himself away. The Almighty released the god of death, who was himself half dead, and the carpenter was taken away to the land of death. Bhagwan taught the local people how to make the drink, which has since helped people prepare themselves better for death.[3]

Sisyphos and Thanatos

There is a touch of the mythical in these texts in which the celestial powers express concern when an unstoppable gambler threatens to win the entire world or human beings cease dying because a smith or carpenter has bound Death. But the ancient Greek counterpart of the tale is, as usual, not a myth but a legend. It was attached to Sisyphos and Thanatos (that is, Death). Unfortunately, the narrative has come down to us in only one passage, and it is abbreviated.

According to the mythographer Pherekydes, as summarized by a scholiast, Sisyphos once incurred the anger of Zeus, who thereupon sent Thanatos for him. But Sisyphos perceived the approach of Thanatos and bound him in strong bonds, whereupon human beings ceased to die. Eventually Ares released Thanatos and handed Sisyphos over to him. Before he died, however, Sisyphos instructed his wife, Merope, not to make the customary offerings upon his death. When some time passed and the wife of Sisyphos still had not performed the rites, Hades asked Sisyphos about it and let him go in order that he might reproach his wife. But when Sisyphos reached Corinth he did not go back again until after he died of old age. After he died, Hades made him roll a stone so that he might not run away again.[4] The scholiast cites these exploits of Sisyphos in explanation of Homer's calling him the "most cunning of men."[5]

A similarity between Sisyphos and the clever smith of *The Smith and the Devil* has long been noticed, though the extent of the parallelism between their stories has not been perceived, for despite the condensed nature of the Greek text and, of course, the differences in the societies that shaped the ancient and the modern narratives, they have more in common than at first ap-

pears. (1) A deity, upset at a certain man, (2) dispatches Death to fetch him. (3) But the man recognizes Death and (4) cunningly tricks him by binding him, so that the man escapes being carried away by Death, and (5) in general human beings cease to die. As a result (6) the deity must see to it that Death is released from his bondage, and, (7) once freed, Death seizes the man and carries him off to the death realm. (8) There the man employs his cunning to enter into, or to escape from, this or that cosmic realm (Heaven, Erebos/Hell, earth, etc.). In the ancient as in the modern tradition the tone of the story is comic.

Zeus's anger at Sisyphos, which motivates his dispatching Thanatos for him, corresponds to the point in the Grimms' tale in which Christ and St. Peter are greatly anxious about Gambling Hansel, which motivates their sending Death to fetch him. The scholiast's statement that Sisyphos "perceived the approach of Thanatos" takes on a new meaning when it is read in light of the *Meisterlied* summarized above, in which the hero selects as one of his wishes the ability to recognize Death. The idea is that Death may walk up to his intended victim in the guise of an ordinary man, like an undercover agent, which gives the demon an initial advantage, but if the intended victim can recognize Death in any guise, he has an opportunity to take countermeasures. Perceiving the approach of Death, the trickster renders him ineffectual by binding him. Exactly how Sisyphos accomplished this we are not informed. Perhaps he has a magic chair, as in recent forms of the tale, or perhaps he employs another trick, such as that in *Solomon Binds the Devil in Chains in Hell*, in which the hero asks the ogre to try on the chains intended for the hero, whereupon the ogre finds that he is bound.[6] The Greek text says only that Sisyphos binds Thanatos with strong fetters.

The binding of Death has in turn a cosmic consequence, the cessation of all activity in his sphere of influence; in short, death as a force ceases to exist, a condition that in Grimm and the *Meisterlied* causes consternation in Heaven and prompts divine intervention.[7] Though nothing is said about this in the Greek text, it is likely that Zeus is similarly upset by this threat to cosmic order and so sends an agent to correct matters, for we next hear that Zeus's son Ares comes and releases Thanatos from the fetters with which Sisyphos bound him. Thanatos now executes his original mission, carrying Sisyphos off to the death realm, though not before the cunning man has had a chance to conspire with his wife, just as in the Grimms' tale Death now resumes his original task, carrying Gambling Hansel off to the otherworld.

Although the conclusions of the ancient and the modern stories differ in their content, we also find a range of endings in the modern texts, and they all, ancient and modern, have in common the hero's using his wiles to escape from an undesirable cosmic realm (the death realm or Hell) and/or to enter into a desirable cosmic realm (earth or Heaven).

For a discussion of the final trick by means of which Sisyphos wins a respite from death, see "Lord's Prayer."

Lit. (AT 330A, *The Smith and the Devil (Death).*) Grimm (1966 [1883]) 2:854. Wünsche 1905:88–98. BP 2:163–189. Rohde 1925:53–54 n. 82. Ranke (1955) 1:245–264. Liungman 1961:71. Ashliman, type 330A.

1. Grimm 82.
2. BP 2:177–178.
3. Beck et al. 1987:283–285, no. 94.
4. *FGH* 3 F 119 = schol. Homer *Il.* 6.153. See Gantz 1993:173–174.
5. *Il.* 6.152.
6. AT 803, *Solomon Binds the Devil in Chains in Hell.* Magic chairs that hold one fast are found in Greek, Germanic, and Celtic mythologies (Kittredge 1929:201–202). In Greek tradition the smith Hephaistos fashioned a throne with invisible bands and sent it to his mother, Hera, as a gift; as soon as she sat in it, she was bound and could not rise (Roscher 1:2054). Hephaistos was angry at her for casting him out of Olympos. In the Greek myth, as in *The Smith and the Devil*, the motif of the magic chair is connected ultimately with residence in different cosmic realms.
7. In classical mythology the motif of the bound or absent deity, wherein the deity ceases to exercise his or her normal influence in the world, causing consternation in heaven or on earth, is most familiar from the myth of Demeter, who, distraught at the loss of her daughter, withdraws to her temple and causes the agricultural cycle to cease (*Homeric Hymn to Demeter* 303–333); a similar but less familiar story was also told of Black Demeter (Pausanias 8.42). The idea was frequent in the mythologies of the ancient Near East. In Akkadian myth all sexual intercourse ceases after Ishtar descends to the netherworld (*ANET* 1955:108), and the theme of the absent deity is particularly common in Hittite mythology, where it is attached to a number of different gods (see Hoffner 1990). See further Wesselski 1929b; Burkert 1979:123–142; Oinas 1983, 1993; and "Ogre Steals the Thunder's Instruments."

Son of the King and of the Smith ◎ Kyros

A king (queen) becomes angry at the prince because of an embarrassment the boy has caused (e.g., he makes one of the king's decisions look absurd, as an infant in the womb he comments metaphorically upon his mother's adultery or other misbehavior). He (she) orders a servant to put the boy to death, but the servant compassionately exchanges the prince with the son of a smith (peasant). One way or another, the prince grows up in the house of the smith (peasant) while the smith's (peasant's) son grows up in the house of the king. As a youth the prince is chosen leader of his playmates and manifests his princely qualities. He passes judgment on a misdemeanor committed by one of his playmates and has the boy punished (or while traveling with the king and his supposed son, the hero makes observations of a princely sort whereas the putative son of the king makes observations that reflect his humble birth). The suspicious king now gives the hero (or his supposed father) a number of seemingly impossible tasks, which he successfully accomplishes and in various ways shows his cleverness. Finally, when the hero flees from the angry king and takes service as a shepherd, the king dispatches men to find the youth, whom they recognize by his clever answers to their questions. In the end, he is reunited with his father.[1]

This tale, AT 920, *The Son of the King (Solomon) and of the Smith*, is attested in Eastern Europe and as far east as India and Indonesia.

In several countries the story is told of the youth of King Solomon. Thus, according to a Russian literary treatment going back to the eighteenth century but said to be much older, Solomon as a three-year-old child gave hints to his father of his mother's adulterous behavior. His mother decided to do away with him and instructed a servant to kill him and bring her Solomon's cooked heart to eat. But the boy was rescued and brought up in the household of a

peasant, and the son of the smith was substituted for him in the royal household. The young Solomon showed his cleverness in making a number of perceptive judgments. His father David, noticing that the boy who had been substituted for Solomon was not his own son, dispatched the same servant to find Solomon and bring him back. The youth was recognized by a clever judgment he made, and after a number of other episodes, Solomon returned to his father.[2]

According to an Estonian version the queen of a certain country issued an unjust judgment, whereupon her unborn son exclaimed that the whore dispenses the justice of a whore, which greatly angered the queen, who threatened to get her revenge after the birth of the child. Some weeks later, having delivered a son, she ordered the midwife to take him to the kitchen, cook him, and bring her his heart to eat. But as the woman was about to kill the infant, he begged her to kill a dog instead, bring its heart to his mother, purposely dropping it as she served it so that the queen would decline to eat it, and finally carry him to the smith's barn, where someone would find him. Now, the queen worried about what the king would say when he returned, since he knew that she was pregnant. Having learnt that the smith's wife had recently given birth to a fine son, she went to the smith's house and took the woman's son for herself. But the next morning the smith's maid discovered a small child lying in the straw of the barn. The smith and his wife accepted the child as a gift from God in place of their own son and gave him the name Solomon. The son of the smith and the son of the king, being of the same age, often played together. One day when the king and his son were walking on a plain outside the city, Solomon joined them. The king asked his son what such a field was good for, and the lad answered that if the land should be properly prepared, in ten years it would yield fine harvests. The king then asked the same question of Solomon, who replied that it was a good place for training an army. Pleased with the boy's reply, the king adopted him as a foster son. Solomon grew up to be a fine man. After more displays of Solomon's cleverness, the king lamented that his own son was so foolish whereas his foster son was so outstanding and intelligent. Solomon then revealed to him the truth of his origin. The queen fled the land in order to escape her husband's wrath, and was never located. When the king died, Solomon ascended the throne and enjoyed a long reign until he too died.[3]

In a Turkish text summarized by Eberhard and Boratav, the sultana gave birth to a Negro child in the absence of the sultan and in order to avoid difficulties exchanged it with a gypsy child. As the supposed child of the sultana grew up, he showed the traits of a gypsy. One day when the sultan came by chance to a gypsy camp he saw a Negro child commanding all the gypsies and having everyone work for him. Seeing that the child must be his own, he exchanged the two children again.[4]

The game featured in the episode of the children's kingdom has been reported as a children's game in Asia. The boys assign the roles for their drama and then follow a course of action that is familiar to all before their play begins. The game is said to have been very popular in nineteenth-century Kashmir, where it was called *suhul*. It was usually played by four youngsters, who tossed marked sticks according to certain rules to determine the assignation of roles, which were *pádsháh* (king), *wazír* (vizier), *tsúr* (thief), and *said* (honest man).

When play starts, the vizier brings the thief before the king, hails the king, and presents the thief, telling the king of the thief's crime. The king then announces one or another punishment from a large repertory, such as "to give him Bengali cannon," in which case the vizier kicks the backside of the prisoner.[5]

Sometime in late antiquity *The Son of the King and of the Smith* seems to have been drawn upon for an anonymous literary composition treating the childhood of Jesus, the so-called *Arabic Infancy Gospel*. Probably translated from Syriac, the Arabic work became well known in Muslim lands and influenced the *Koran*.[6] According to this work, in the month Adar the young Jesus gathered around him the other boys as though he were their king, and they spread out their clothes on the ground for him to sit on, placed a garland of flowers upon his head, and stood on either side of him as guards. They forced all passersby to come before Jesus and prostrate themselves before him, after which they might continue their journey. Jesus also wrought a number of miracles.[7]

Since several features of Jesus' biography as related in the canonical gospels make a nice fit with the folktale, it was easy and evidently tempting for later narrators to draw upon the oral tale in order to fill in details of his early life. Like the protagonist of the tale, Jesus was sired by a monarch (= God) but was reared by a humble, putative father (= the carpenter Joseph). This arrangement leads neatly into the second episode of the folktale, in which the princely qualities of the apparently humble protagonist emerge in the simple games of childhood. The subsequent incident of Jesus' learned discussion in the temple in Jerusalem harmonizes with the episodes of the tale in which the youthful hero's cleverness and judgment are illustrated, and at his death Jesus rejoins his father in the "kingdom of heaven." His royal status is expressed by his messianic title of King of the Jews and by his secular title of King of Kings.

The Kyros Legend

There are interesting points of contact between the modern oral story and the ancient legend of Kyros (Cyrus) of Persia, at least as it was known to the Greeks. Herodotos's narrative of the early life of Kyros forms part of his account of the rise of the Persian empire. According to him, Astyages, ruler of the Medes, had a daughter, Mandane. The girl once had a dream that she urinated so much that her urine filled all of Asia. When Astyages learned the interpretation of the dream that the Magi gave, he was afraid; so when the girl was old enough to marry, he married her not to a Mede at all but to a Persian of middle rank named Kambyses. Mandane had a second dream, in which a vine grew from her genitals and spread over all Asia. The Magi interpreted the dream to mean that Mandane's son would rule in place of Astyages. So he sent for his daughter, who was now pregnant. When she gave birth to a son, Kyros, Astyages sent for his most trusted servant, Harpagos, and instructed him to take the child home, kill it, and bury it. But Harpagos gave the baby in turn to Mitradates, one of the king's herdsmen, ordering him to expose the child in some desolate place. And Mitradates, bringing the child home, was informed by his own wife that she had just given birth to a dead child. She persuaded her husband to exchange the children, keeping Mandane's child and raising it as their own, and exposing their own dead child. Mitradates did so, and a couple

days later he went to Harpagos and reported that he was prepared to show him the corpse of the child. Harpagos sent trusted men to view and bury the baby.

When Kyros (who did not yet bear this name) was ten years old, his identity was revealed in the following way. He was playing in the street of the village with some other boys, and they chose him to be their king. He assigned different jobs to different boys, some to build houses, some to be bodyguards, one to be a messenger, etc. But one of the boys, the son of a noble Mede named Artembares, did not carry out his orders, so that Kyros told the other boys to arrest him, which they did, and he whipped him badly. The boy complained to his father, who in turn complained to Astyages that his son had been beaten by the son of a herdsman. The king sent for the herdsman and his son. Astyages asked the boy how he, the son of a herdsman, had dared to outrage the son of a distinguished man. Kyros replied that he had acted justly, for in their game the village boys had made him their king, since he seemed to them the most fit for the role; and whereas the other boys carried out their orders, this boy paid him no attention until he was punished. As Kyros spoke, the king recognized who he was from his looks, his age, and his unservile reply. Astyages dismissed Artembares, saying that he would take care of the matter. Then he extracted the truth first from the herdsman and next from Harpagos. The king dismissed the herdsman but punished Harpagos horribly by cooking and feeding him his only son at a banquet. Concluding, however, that the prophecy had been fulfilled when Kyros was made "king" of his playmates, so that he himself had no more to fear from him, he sent Kyros to his real parents in Persia. Later, at the instigation of Harpagos, Kyros began to foment revolt among the Persians. Astyages dispatched a messenger to him, summoning him, but Kyros answered only that he would come before Astyages wished it. He overcame Astyages in battle and became ruler in his stead, ending the supremacy of the Medes over the Persians and establishing Persian domination. But he did no other harm to Astyages, keeping him with him until he died.[8]

The international folktale and the Herodotean legend have in common that (1) a monarch is upset by a metaphoric message (2) issuing from (or concerning) his son (grandson). (3) Determining to have the infant done away with, (4) he orders a trusted servant to kill the child, but (5) the compassionate executioner (or his agent) allows the child to live and (6) substitutes for it the newborn child of a humble family. The hero, grown to be a child or youth, shows his royal qualities when (7) his playmates choose him as king in their games. (8) When one of his "subjects" commits an offense, (9) the boy has him punished. (10) The disciplined child complains that a child of humble birth has maltreated a child of high birth, (11) attracting the attention of the king, (12) who perceives the truth. (13) The king turns his attention to the supposed parents of the youth, after which (14) the youth flees (or is sent away). (15) When the king sends a messenger after him, (16) he discomfits the messenger with his answer(s). Eventually (17) he is reconciled, after a fashion, with the king.

The first episode takes the story from the source of the hostility felt by the parent toward the infant prince, through the effort to do away with him, to the exchange of the prince for a pauper. These parallels are sometimes easier to perceive than to describe. First of all, the ancient legend introduces an additional generation, presenting the hostility as originating in the child's grandfa-

ther rather than in his father or mother, so that the child's grandfather plays the role that in the folktale is played by one of the child's parents. But a shift from father to uncle or grandfather is a common kind of variation in oral narrative. Second, the folktale texts often dramatize the threat posed by the infant, and the consequent hostility felt by the parent, by having the unborn prince embarrass his mother by uttering some private truth about her while he still resides in her womb, a truth that he often expresses metaphorically such as by using a proverbial expression. For example, when the queen gossips with the wife of a smith, he says: "One bitch yaps to another." In another text he observes: "See, a thief behaves like a thief, a whore like a whore."[9] There is certainly a connection between this odd event, in which metaphors issue *from* a son in a womb, and the dreams that Mandane has, which the Magi interpret as metaphors *about* the son in her womb. And the consequences are the same, in that the metaphors provoke anger or fear, and ultimately hostility, in the monarch toward the unborn child, leading to a decision to do away with the baby. The attempt on the child's life is unsuccessful, and, since the monarch delegated it to another, the monarch is now unaware of the true status of his (her) child. Again the Greek narrative is slightly more complicated here, having Astyages delegate the job of executioner to a trusted kinsman, Harpagos, who in turn delegates the task to a herdsman, Mitradates, with the result that now neither Astyages nor Harpagos knows the true status of Kyros. The ancient legend, like *The Son of the King and of the Smith*, features an exchange of the royal infant and the humble infant as well as the subsequent rearing of the royal infant in the household of the humble family, but the royal family does not correspondingly rear the humble infant, who dies in childbirth.

The next episode shows how the prince's noble qualities of intelligence and leadership, which the tale treats as inborn rather than acquired, naturally express themselves in a form appropriate to the activities of his age, indicating that the boy was born to rule, not to be ruled, and that the punished child, who sometimes is the supposed child of the king, was born to be ruled, not to rule. There is an implicit suggestion that one cannot successfully tamper with destiny, which being part of the inherent order of things will win out in the end. The naturalness and inevitability of the prince's role as leader foreshadow his later role as king, and in the Greek story they also follow up the prophecies made at the beginning of the story, according to which the boy would someday rule.

In the final episodes the correspondences between the tale and the legend seem thinner. We hear much about the hero's movements and little about his wit, whereas this part of the folktale contains many meaty instances of cleverness: the accomplishment of seemingly impossible tasks that the king assigns the hero or his supposed father, and the hero's displays of keen judgment or the like. In the legend there are traces of something similar in the events that follow, rather than precede, Kyros's departure for Persia. One piece of cunning is attributed there to Harpagos, another piece to Kyros. Harpagos, wishing to send a letter to Kyros in Persia but being unable to do so because of the roads' being guarded, slit open the stomach of a hare, inserted a letter, sewed it up again, and dispatched a servant dressed as a huntsman to deliver the hare personally to Kyros, with instructions to Kyros to cut it open himself while alone. The ruse worked, and Harpagos thereby implanted in Kyros the idea of revolt-

ing against the Medes. In the second case, Kyros, wishing now to persuade his fellow Persians to make war on the Medes, assigned every man in the Persian army a day of hard physical labor followed by a day of feasting at Kyros's expense. Then he asked them which they preferred: misery or pleasure; by which he meant Median or Persian supremacy. This plan also worked, for the Persians appreciated the point of the lesson and chose to follow Kyros.[10] One could characterize Harpagos's ploy as a solution to an apparently impossible task, while Kyros's demonstration, which illustrates the relative desirability of two different conditions, shows clever judgment.

A possible connection between *The Son of the King and of the Smith* and Herodotos's account of Kyros was pointed out by Wolf Aly in the first edition of his book on folk narratives in Herodotos.[11] Since Aly knew the tale only from the brief description of it given by Aarne in his *Verzeichnis der Märchentypen* in its initial edition of 1910, he was unable to compare the stories in any detail (and indeed I too have found it difficult to locate texts of the tale). In his study of folktales that involve riddling, de Vries devotes a short chapter to a survey of eastern European texts of the tale, following up a Russian study published by Wesselofky in 1872, but he makes no mention of the Kyros legend and is content to follow Wesselofsky in his conclusion that the folk narrative of the present day developed out of apocryphal legends concerning Solomon.[12] A year later Wesselski restudied some of the same material but included the Kyros legend in his discussion, concluding that the legend of Solomon as king of his playmates went back to the legend of Kyros.[13] Like other scholars of their day, de Vries and Wesselski were interested primarily in discovering the origin of traditional stories and motifs and in tracing their diffusion in the oral and literary traditions. Their investigations typically show an unwarranted confidence in the ability of scholars to deduce such information from the collections of folktales recently made in the field and from the sporadic literary evidence that antedates the collections. De Vries concludes that the story arose in connection with Solomon because the Solomon tradition seems to him to be the most ancient, whereas for Wesselski, who shows that the Solomonic stories of a boy-king do not have deep roots, the tradition goes back to Kyros because Herodotos's narrative is the oldest text with which he is acquainted. In truth we have no way of knowing how old the oral story itself is, only that it must predate the earliest written texts of it that we happen to have and that it is arbitrary to identify the earliest published versions with the original story, since for the most part it is essentially chance that this or that oral text was committed to writing and survives to our day as an artifact of the past.

Lit. AT 920, *The Son of the King (Solomon) and of the Smith*, especially episodes 1–2. Aly 1969:50. Vries 1928:320–335, 432–435. Wesselski 1929a. *EM* 8:23–25, 692–694.

1. Vries 1928:322–324; Thompson 1946:159.
2. Vries 1928:320–321.
3. Loorits 1959:166–171, no. 152. The text continues with additional adventures of Solomon in Hell, which I omit here, since they are not relevant to the present discussion.
4. Eberhard and Boratav 1953:342, type 302.
5. Knowles 1893:464–465.
6. Oscar Cullmann, in Schneemelcher (1991) 1:456–457.
7. For a discussion of the text of the gospel and a French translation, see Peeters 1914;

for an English translation, see Platt (n.d.:38–59), where the work is entitled "The First Gospel of the Infancy of Jesus Christ." The episode of Jesus as king of his playmates is found at Peeters (1914:50, chap. 41); Platt (1926:55, chap. 18). On the different infancy gospels generally, see Cullmann, in Schneemelcher (1991) 1:414–469 and, for the *Arabic Infancy Gospel* in particular, 1:456–457. Vries (1928:329–331) and Wesselski (1929a:7–8) discuss the relationship of the infancy gospel and *The Son of the King and of the Smith*.

 8. Herodotos 1.107–130. On the legend see also Justin 1.4–6.
 9. Vries 1928:326.
 10. Herodotos 1.123–126.
 11. Aly 1969:50 (the first edition appeared in 1921).
 12. Vries 1928:334–335.
 13. Wesselski 1929a:10–11.

Sowing of Salt ☙ Odysseus

A fool sows salt in the hope of growing a crop of salt (or plants something else equally absurd).

This tale is AT 1200, *The Sowing of Salt*. It is known throughout Europe and Asia.

A Danish tale about the foolish folk of Mols, the Molboer, relates that once when salt was costly a certain man of Mols had the idea of buying a ton of salt, plowing a field, and sowing the salt, so that no one would ever lack salt again. The other Molboer were taken with the idea, and a general decision was made to follow this good advice. They did so, and around harvesttime one of them went out to see how the salt was doing. He found the field overgrown with nettles bearing white flowers, which he thought must be salt.[1]

Similarly in a German version, when salt was once scarce the silly people of Schwarzenborn conceived the idea of sowing their remaining salt in order to produce their own crop of salt. They did so, but the only thing that came up were stinging nettles.[2]

Other numskulls sow other inappropriate things, such as cheese to bring forth a cow, a hog to bring forth pigs, tails or bones to grow young animals, and grain that has already been cooked, such as the fool from India who sowed roasted sesame seeds.[3] In a modern joke a clever man, feigning naiveté, says he intends to plant cooked beans.[4]

Odysseus Sows Salt

In classical tradition the sowing of salt is attached not to a fool as such but to the clever Odysseus, who only pretends to be a fool. The episode of Odysseus's feigned folly is first mentioned in the *Kypria*, an epic composed in the seventh or sixth century B.C. and now known only in summary.[5] The episode was the subject of a lost tragedy by Sophokles, *Odysseus Mainomenos*, or "The Mad Odysseus." Odysseus's feigned madness is next mentioned by Lycophron, Apollodoros, and Lucian, as well as by the Latin authors Cicero, Pliny, Hyginus, Servius, and Lactantius Placidus.[6] From these sources we learn that Odysseus, pretending to be a fool in order to avoid military service, put on a fool's cap, yoked together two different kinds of animal to his plough (either an ox and a horse or an ox and a donkey), and sowed salt; and that Palamedes

demonstrated Odysseus's madness to be feigned. Palamedes did so either by placing Odysseus's infant son Telemachos on the ground in front of Odysseus's moving plough so that when Odysseus stopped ploughing, he thereby acknowledged his rationality; or, less cleverly, by threatening to kill Telemachos with his sword, whereupon Odysseus in fear granted that his madness was only a pretense. In short, Odysseus pretended he was mentally incompetent, notably by yoking two different kinds of animal to his plough and then sowing his field with salt, in order to avoid conscription into the forces that were being assembled for the purpose of going to Troy to retrieve Helen.

The detail of sowing salt is mentioned explicitly only by Servius (ca. A.D. 400) in the course of a mythological comment on Vergil, who is followed almost word for word by Lactantius Placidus.[7] How old the tradition really was and whether the incident was found in Greek epic and tragedy, or even in Greek oral tradition at all, is of course impossible to say. In any case this instance of Odysseus's cunning folly is doubtless an adaptation to the Odyssean legend of the widespread oral tale of the simpleminded farmer who plants salt in the happy expectation of a crop of salt, a tale that must therefore already have been in oral circulation in antiquity, if only in late antiquity. The first straightforward attestation of *The Sowing of Salt* is found in the German *Lalebuch*, published in 1598.

The appropriation of numskull tales by tricksters who only pretend to be simpletons is well attested. In the ancient *Life of Aesop* the clever slave Aesop exasperates his master by playing the literal fool, intentionally interpreting his master's words with excessive literalness, as when his master orders Aesop to prepare lentil for himself and his dinner-guests, and Aesop cooks one lentil.[8] In Roman tradition the clever hero Lucius Junius Brutus plays the fool in order to allay the suspicions of the king, as does Brutus's cunning cognate in Northern legend, Hamlet.[9]

Lit. (AT 1200, *The Sowing of Salt*.) Wesselski (1911) 2:96–98, 209–210, no. 423. Christensen 1939:143–144, no. 57. Ashliman, type 1200.

1. Christensen 1939:143–144, no. 57.
2. Ranke 1966:177.
3. Christensen 1939:29.
4. Ranke 1972:97.
5. Proklos *Chrestomathia*, p. 103 Allen.
6. Lycophron *Alexandra* 815–819; Apollodoros *Epit.* 3.7; and Lucian *De Domo* 30; Cicero *On Duty* 3.26.97; Pliny *NH* 35.129; Hyginus *Fab.* 95; Servius's commentary on Vergil *Aeneid* 2.81; and Lactantius Placidus on Statius *Achilleis* 1.93. See also Gantz 1993:580.
7. Servius: "cum enim ille iunctis dissimilis naturae animalibus salem sereret, filium ei Palamedes opposuit, quo viso Vlixes aratra suspendit."
8. *Vita Aesopi* 39–41. See "Labor Contract."
9. Hansen 1983a.

Stronger and Strongest

In certain tales an important structural feature is a chain of items, thematically linked and appearing in succession. Among these are tales in which a character seeks the strongest thing (being) there is; however, for each item considered,

there proves to be another thing (being) that is even stronger, until for one reason or another the series of successively stronger things comes to an end.

These tales belong to AT 2031, *Stronger and Strongest*, for which several subtypes are distinguished, differing from one another in their narrative situations and in the content of their chains. The tradition is known from Europe to the Far East.

In some tellings of *Stronger and Strongest* the principal character blames someone for an injury. Thus, in a Mexican text collected from an elderly woman in 1948, an ant once broke her leg in the snow and brought suit against the snow. But the snow told the judge that the sun was mightier, since he melts the snow. The sun in turn said the cloud was mightier, since she hides the sun. According to the cloud, the wind was mightier, since he pushes the cloud. The wall was mightier yet, because she stops the wind. But a mouse was mightier than the wall, because it gnaws the wall. The mouse said the cat was mightier, inasmuch as it eats mice. The cat yielded to the dog, which chases cats; the dog to the stick, which beats dogs; the stick to fire, which burns sticks; fire to water, which puts fires out; water to the cow, which drinks it; the cow to the knife, which kills cows; the knife to the blacksmith, who forged it; and the blacksmith to God, who made the blacksmith. There the judge had to stop, because he could not interrogate God.[1]

Here we have the chain: snow, sun, cloud, wind, wall, mouse, cat, dog, stick, fire, water, cow, knife, blacksmith, God.

In a Chilean variant of the same tale collected from a male informant in 1962, a thrush looking for food in the cold broke one of her claws. She blamed the frost, but the frost said the sun was worse, since he melts her. So she flew to the sun, who said the clouds were worse, since they covered the sun. (The chain continues with wind, wall, rat, cat, dog, club, fire, water, ox, knife, and blacksmith.) But when the thrush accused the smith, he said: "Why is this ill-omened bird pestering me?" and killed her.[2]

Chains with similar elements are sometimes found cast not in narrative situations such as this, but simply as factual statements. These statements have something both of the proverb and of the riddle in them, since they mix general truths with an enigma. For although each statement can be true comparatively, only one statement can be true superlatively, since of course many things can be stronger than other things but only one thing can be the strongest of them all. They differ from an ordinary riddle—Motif H631, *Riddle: what is the strongest?*—in that there is not simply a correct answer or a best answer but rather a chain of answers that in the telling of the story appear in a fixed order and have a relationship of strong and stronger: Motif Z42, *Stronger and strongest*.

Thus in a Jewish story, Rabbi Jehuda said that there were fourteen things of which one was stronger than the other and of which one was strongest of all. Strong is the abyss, for only the earth rises above it; strong is the earth, but the mountains rise mightily above it. The chain continues with iron, fire, water, clouds, wind, wall, mankind, sufferings, wine, sleep, sickness, the Angel of Death, and finally an evil wife.[3] Here, as often, the last item in the chain—the solution, as it were—is comically ironic. Stiefel points out that Rabbi Jehuda's chain actually includes sixteen items rather than the promised fourteen, but the

rabbi seems not to have counted the Angel of Death and the wife as part of the total. This text is a story only in the sense that the statements are attributed to a character who utters them on a particular occasion; but in some cases even this minimal frame is absent.[4]

A Greek Chain

That stories of this sort circulated among the ancient Greeks can be seen from a fragment of a lost play composed by Diphilos, a poet of New Comedy. A scene from the poet's *Theseus* is described by Athenaeus in the course of a discussion of riddles.[5] Diphilos represented three Samian girls drinking and riddling during the Adonia, or festival of Adonis. The riddle was propounded: "What is the strongest of all things?" One of the girls said it was iron, adducing as proof the fact that men dig and cut everything with iron and in general use it against all other substances. The second girl declared, however, that a smith was much stronger, since he works the iron, bending it and softening it and making whatever he wants out of it. But the third girl proved that a penis was the strongest of all things, pointing out that the rump of the groaning smith is pierced with it.[6]

Diphilos's tripartite chain is iron, smith, penis. The sequence of iron followed by smith (or fire) is a traditional sequence within chains, as can be seen both from other texts and from the texts summarized above, in which we find (1) knife (that is, a tool exemplifying metal), smith, god; (2) knife, smith; and (3) iron, fire (really a variant of smith, since the smith masters iron by means of fire). The third item in the Greek chain, penis, concludes the chain with witty and ribald irony, just as the Jewish chain concludes with an unexpectedly domestic element: an evil wife. The chain iron, fire, water may have been a familiar one in Greek riddling, for it appears to underlie an ancient allegorical interpretation of the Homeric myth of Ares and Aphrodite. According to Herakleitos in his book of Homeric allegories, composed perhaps in the first century A.D., the triumph of the divine smith Hephaistos over the adulterer Ares and the subsequent rescue of Ares by Poseidon really signifies that the hardness of iron (= Ares) is softened by fire (= Hephaistos), which is stronger than iron, but the fire in turn is extinguished when the glowing mass of iron is dipped into water (= Poseidon).[7] If a traditional chain helped to suggest this interpretation, then Diphilos's chain is perhaps a bawdy form of, or play upon, the conventional one. The gender of the riddlers reflects Greek custom, for Plutarch mentions that during the Agrionia, a festival of Dionysos, women posed riddles and puzzles to one another after they ate, so that the practice of women riddling during certain festivals was customary.[8]

Questions and statements of the superlative certainly belong to the tradition of many peoples, but the Greeks seem to have had a special fascination with them. Kroisos wants to know who is the happiest of men.[9] Plutarch reports a contest in riddling between the kings of Egypt and Ethiopia, in which the former asks the latter what the oldest thing is (answer: time), what the greatest thing is (cosmos), what the wisest thing is (truth), etc.[10] Thales elsewhere declares that the oldest thing is god, the most beautiful thing is the cosmos, the largest thing is space, the strongest thing is necessity, the wisest thing is time, etc.[11] Alexander

the Great asks the gymnosophists of India one superlative question after an-
other.[12] And so on.[13]

A Roman Chain

An indication that chain tales of this sort were also current among the Ro-
mans is found in an anecdote concerning Julius Caesar that is recounted by
Suetonius in his *Life of the Divine Julius*, one of the gossipy imperial biographies
in this author's *Lives of the Emperors*.[14] At one point Suetonius gives a string of
humorous anecdotes and bons mots illustrating Caesar's reputed fondness for
passive homosexual relations. Some of this lore refers to an infamous affair be-
tween Caesar and Nikomedes, king of Bithynia. This was Nikomedes IV
Philopator, who reigned ca. 94–74 B.C. Suetonius reports:

> "Finally, during the triumphal procession following his victory in Gaul, his
> soldiers escorted his chariot while singing various humorous songs, includ-
> ing the notorious one that went:
>
>> 'Caesar subdued Gaul, but Nikomedes subdued Caesar.
>> Behold, this is the triumph of Caesar, who subdued Gaul,
>> But there's no triumph for Nikomedes, who subdued Caesar.' "[15]

Some manuscripts omit the second verse, and a few give the second and third
verses somewhat differently:

> 'And why is there a triumph for Caesar, who subdued Gaul,
> When there's no triumph for Nikomedes, who subdued Caesar?'[16]

A triumph in this sense was a ritual procession of a victorious Roman general
along a prescribed route in Rome to the temple of Jupiter Capitolinus. The pro-
cession included civic officials, the spoils won by the *triumphator*, prominent
captives, sacrificial animals, the general himself in a chariot, and his army. The
song Suetonius cites is therefore an instance of a *carmen triumphale*, a song that
the soldiers sang during a triumph. Triumphal songs might be ribald, like
songs for certain other ritual occasions such as weddings.

The song allegedly devised by Caesar's men cleverly praised and mocked
the general at the same time, linking his military activities, in which he con-
quered, with his sexual activities, in which he was conquered in the sense of his
playing the role of the passive, or penetrated, homosexual. Comparisons be-
tween military and sexual activities were familiar in antiquity, as they are
today, so that one activity was often spoken of in terms of the other.[17]

The chain in the song is Gaul, Caesar, Nikomedes; that is, Gaul is strong,
Caesar is stronger because he subdued Gaul, but Nikomedes is the strongest of
all because he subdued Caesar. It is similar to the three-part chain in Diphilos's
comedy—iron, smith, penis—in that the initial item is something strong (the
substance iron/the country Gaul), the second item is the man who masters it
(the smith/the general), and the third item is, with humorous irony, the mas-
ter's homosexual lover. It appears, then, that this chain was traditional among

both the Greeks and the Romans. Diphilos in fourth-century Greece, and Caesar's soldiers in first-century Rome, adapted it each to their own comic purposes. Even if the licentious Latin song was invented later and only attributed anecdotally to the soldiers at the time when Suetonius wrote, approximately a century after the triumph, the implications are the same regarding the familiarity of the chain to the Romans.

Lit. AT 2031, *Stronger and Strongest*. Köhler 1857. Stiefel 1895. Ohlert 1912:69–70. *RE* 1A:101. Haavio 1929:20, 79–80. Taylor, in Mackensen (1934–40) 2:182–184. Trenkner 1958:144 n. 7. Schwarzbaum 1979:173–174. Ashliman, type 2031.

The Esdras Chain

The story of the Three Bodyguards, which is found in I Esdras 3.1–5.6, is the locus classicus for AT 2031A, *The Esdras Chain: Stronger and Strongest*.[18] The dramatic date of the events is sometime during the reign of Darius (521–485 B.C.), at whose court the events transpire. I Esdras (also called III Ezra) was composed around the second century B.C., probably in Egypt. The Greek apocryphal book, which is primarily Jewish in culture whether it was originally composed in Greek or in a Semitic language, was anciently translated into Latin, Syriac, and Ethiopic.[19]

According to a charming but somewhat confused narration, King Darius of Persia went to his bedroom and fell asleep but then woke up again. Three members of his bodyguard decided that each of them should name the thing which he judged to be the strongest. King Darius would give rich prizes to the man whose answer should prove to be the wisest: he would be clothed in purple, drink from golden cups, sleep on a golden bed, etc., as well as sit next to Darius and be called his kinsman. So each man wrote down his own opinion, sealed it, and placed it under the king's pillow. The plan was to give the statements to the king when he awoke, whereupon he and the three chief men of Persia might judge them. One wrote that wine was strongest, another that the king was strongest, and the third that women were strongest, but truth conquered everything. The king invited the chief men of Persia and Media, before whom the statements were read aloud. Then the king had the young men summoned to explain their statements. The first explained that wine overcame the minds of men; the second, that man was the strongest, but the king was the strongest of men; the third, whose name was Zorobabel, that men including kings were slaves to women, but truth was strongest of all, since it alone did not perish. The third speaker was acclaimed the winner. Darius offered the winner any boon he should like, in addition to the aforementioned prizes, and the youth asked the king to keep the vow he had made to rebuild Jerusalem and to return the vessels taken from it. Darius kissed him and proceeded to act upon his request. The young man went outside, where he praised the King of Heaven, crediting him with the victory and the wisdom. Then he went on to Babylon to inform his brethren (that is, the Jews) that they might rebuild Jerusalem, and persons were selected to go to Jerusalem.[20]

The story of the three guards disturbs the chronology of I Esdras and has no parallel in the sources known to have been employed by the composer of I Es-

dras. For this and other reasons different scholars have held that it is an addition to the text made by the composer, an insertion made by the Greek translator (if the original language of the book was Semitic rather than Greek), or a later insertion worked into the text by an interpolator. Since the story has been recognized as some kind of immigrant into the text, there also has been discussion whether it is culturally Jewish or Greek or Persian. But these questions are not of importance for the present investigation.

There are some oddities in the telling of the story. For one thing, the author gives Darius an awkwardly passive role in the establishment of the contest, although there are internal hints that he played a more active role in different versions of the story. For Darius retires to bed, wakes up again, and . . . is forgotten, while nearby his bodyguards, conversing among themselves, devise a contest for themselves and happily decide on their own that the king will give certain astonishingly lavish prizes to whichever one of them wins the contest. In the meantime and without explanation, Darius is again sleeping, for the guards now file their written statements under his pillow, to be given to him upon his awakening. It would make far better sense for the sleepless Darius to join his guards in conversation, establish the contest himself, and determine the lavish prizes that he himself is to provide. He may then retire once more, and his guards may file their answers at his pillow.[21]

Be that as it may, the chain itself is even odder and has occasioned much discussion. The sequence that all scholars perceive but none accepts is wine, king, women, truth. It is widely agreed that the third guardsman cannot originally have been permitted two answers and that his second answer, "truth," is a later addition to the story. One scholar concludes that there must once have been four guardsmen, each nominating one candidate for the strongest thing, and that a redactor has reduced their number to three, giving the third youth the unexplained and unfair privilege of entering two nominations.[22] But that is not all, for interpreters also agree that there is no coherent connection between the remaining three items in the order in which they are presented in the text (wine, king, women), and that the original sequence must have been rather king, wine, women.[23] Indeed, the first speaker begins by saying that wine overcomes all persons who drink it, including kings, which implies the sequence "king, wine."[24] It is suggested that when the setting of the story was made to be Darius's court, it was necessary to elevate the monarch from the lowest rank in the hierarchy of the world's strongest things, so as not to insult him, as a result of which he rose a step, and "wine" was accordingly demoted.[25]

I do not find this reconstruction convincing, nor am I sure that a reconstruction back to a satisfying sequence is possible. Whether it is or not, the chain "king, wine, women" does not present a logically satisfying gradation. A king is strong, and wine is stronger, since it overcomes even kings, but in what sense are women stronger than wine? Do women not also drink wine? Indeed, the first guardsman states that wine confuses the minds of all persons who drink, not just kings. If his speech argues that wine is stronger than kings, it also argues that wine is stronger than women.

In attempting to understand this text, we must consult not only internal logic but also the international narrative tradition to which the story of the Three Bodyguards belongs.

First, notice that there is a hint of a fifth link in the chain of strong elements. For though the second speaker cites only "king" in his written statement, he mentions both "men" and "king" as the strongest things in his speech. He begins: "Gentlemen, are not men (*hoi anthropoi*) the strongest, inasmuch as they are masters of the land and the sea and everything that is in them? But the king is the strongest, since he rules over them, and whenever he tells them something, they obey him."[26] The third speaker evidently hears these two answers quite clearly, for he names "wine," "men," and "king" at the beginning of his speech in order to refute them. He says: "Is not a king great, are not men numerous, and is not wine strong? But who rules over them? Is it not women? For women gave birth to the king and to all the people who govern the sea and the land, and women have reared the persons who planted the vines that produce the wine"; and he goes on to speak of women in their roles of wives and of lovers.[27] So "men" is not merely a foil to "king" but an answer, apparently half-suppressed, in its own right. This conclusion receives confirmation from the fact that "men, king, women" not only makes a coherent sequence of strong, stronger, and strongest but also corresponds perfectly to the Greco-Roman chain "something strong, master of something strong, master's lover." This gives us the chain "wine, (men,) king, women, truth."

Let us now look at the narrative from another viewpoint. Notice that the dramatic situation of the story is essentially the same as that in Diphilos's story. (a) Three persons compete in a contest of riddling. (b) One of them poses the riddle: What is the strongest thing? (c) Each player offers an answer. (d) Since the third answer is the best, the last player wins.[28] But there is one important difference in procedure between the game played by the Samian girls and that played by the royal bodyguards. The Samian girls each improvise their solution the one after the other, so that the second girl attempts to improve upon the response of the first girl, which she has heard, and the third girl tries to improve upon the response of the second, which she too has heard. The bodyguards play by other rules. They individually write down their solutions in private and seal them. None of them knows the solutions that his comrades have devised until the day on which Darius has the statements unsealed and read aloud in public, one after the other. That being the case, even if their three blind solutions *could* be arranged into a coherent relationship of strong, stronger, strongest, which is not in itself likely (for example, they could have nominated "iron," "wine," and "sky"), there is only a small chance—one in six—that the three statements would then happen to be read in precisely the requisite order. The rules of the bodyguards' game, therefore, are such that the solutions will not emerge in a sequence of increasingly better answers, for the procedure dictates that the three responses will appear in a purely arbitrary order. The advantage to the narrator is that he is thereby freed from the constraint of presenting the guards' answers according to the demands of a strict chain, which means that he can introduce an item or two that might not otherwise fit into a traditional chain. And this must be a privilege he wants for his presentation.

At the same time, however, there is a counterforce that is at least as strong, the artistic requirement that the story be coherent and pleasurably suspenseful in order to be successful as a story. For example, it would hardly do for the first speaker to propose the best solution right off. This constraint dictates that the

responses shall emerge in a logical and approximately suspenseful progression. Although the two principles are opposed to each other, it appears that both are at work in the story.

Answering to arbitrariness, neither "wine" nor "truth" fits into a satisfying progression of strong followed by stronger. "Wine" is followed by "men" or "king," whereas we should rather expect something like: men are strong, and wine is stronger, since it overcomes them, but sleep (as in Rabbi Jehuda's chain, above) is strongest, since it returns to men their strength. Instead, "wine" remains isolated. As for "truth," which follows "women," the concept "truth" does not represent something stronger than women in the same way as lovers are stronger than the men who love them. So neither "wine" nor "truth" gradates coherently with its neighbor. But answering to progressiveness, the internal sequence "men, king, women" shows a coherent gradation, even if its first element is for some reason de-emphasized in the text. Moreover, the entire series concludes climactically with "truth," which is situated at the end of the series, where, for dramatic reasons, the winning answer should be. In sum, we have the chain "men, king, women," which is framed on the one side by "wine" and on the other side by "truth," neither of which gradates coherently with its neighbor.

The solution "truth," which seems to come out of nowhere, serves primarily to elevate the tone of the contest in order to accord with the sequel, in which the youth, a pious Jew as it turns out, turns toward Jerusalem and addresses the King of Heaven, saying that victory and wisdom (that is, the winning answer) came from him. Like Joseph in Egypt, the riddler is a clever and god-fearing youth who finds himself at the court of a foreign monarch, wins the favor of the ruler, and helps his people in a time of need. The composer of the Three Bodyguards evidently had, or created, more answers to the riddle of the strongest than he really had room for in his tale. He loosened the structure by freeing himself from the strict chain as such, but he did not work out his idea consistently and smoothly, since without explanation he allowed his players more than three answers.

The six narratives cited in this discussion fall into one or the other of two basic formats. Either the principal character follows and participates in the chain as a character (so the quests of the ant and the thrush), or the principal character or characters create the chain as an intellectual construction (so all the rest). The Greek and apocryphal Jewish stories share the same structure of a riddling contest featuring three contestants, which implies that this was a feature of the traditional story of the time. And the Greek, Roman, and Jewish stories are all acquainted with the sequence "something strong, master of something strong, master's lover," which implies that this chain formed part of that story. In the Greek and Roman texts the chain is deliberately humorous and obscene, and in the Jewish narrative it is somewhat light and playful before it continues with a more dignified tone. The chains conclude sometimes on a serious and unassailably high note such as "God" (Mexican text) or "truth" (Esdras) and sometimes on a humorously low note such as "a bad wife" (Midrash) or the variously expressed forms of "lover": penis (Diphilos), Nikomedes (Suetonius), and, capping an internal sequence, women (Esdras).[29]

For other contest-tales, often structured as three persons trying to best one another in some activity, see "Wishing Contest" and "Three Lazy Ones."

Lit. AT 2031A, *The Esdras Chain: Stronger and Strongest.* Laqueur 1911:168–172 n. 1. Taylor, in Mackensen (1934–40) 2:184. Neuman 1953:35–59. Zimmerman 1963–64:179–200. Rudolf 1945–48:176–190. Lommatzsch 1961:236–238. Schmid 1964:110–117. In der Smitten 1972:492–495. Dvořák 1978, no. 5317. Crenshaw 1981:74–88. Schürer (1987) 3:708–718.

1. Paredes 1970:192–194, no. 78.
2. Pino-Saavedra 1967:245–246, no. 50.
3. Stiefel 1895:148–149, citing the Midrash Koheleth.
4. See for example Köhler 1857:481–482.
5. 10.451b.
6. Fr. 50 = Kock 2:557. See Ohlert 1912:69–70; *RE* 1A:101; Trenkner 1958:144 n. 7. On chain tales generally, see *EM* 7:1194–1201.
7. Herakleitos *Homeric Questions* 69; schol. E on Homer *Od.* 8.267.
8. Plutarch *Mor.* 717A. Cf. Ohlert 1912:60–82.
9. Herodotos 1.30.2–3.
10. *Mor.* 153A.
11. Plutarch *Mor.* 153C–D.
12. Plutarch *Alexander* 64; *Alexander Romance* 3.5–6.
13. See further *RE* 1A:110–111; Ohlert 1912:107–114; Rudolf 1945–48:178.
14. *Iulius* 49.
15. Gallias Caesar subegit, Nicomedes Caesarem:
 Ecce Caesar nunc triumphat qui subegit Gallias,
 Nicomedes non triumphat qui subegit Caesarem.
16. Et quare triumphat Caesar qui subegit Gallias?
 Nicomedes non triumphat qui subegit Caesarem.
17. For military language used erotically, see Spies 1930; Henderson 1975 (e.g., nos. 47, 50, 58, 65, 339); Adams 1982:155–156, 158–159. The contrary—erotic metaphors in military activity—is also found (e.g., Nagler 1974:44–63).
18. I Esdras 3.1–5.6.
19. I Esdras must be distinguished from the Greek translation of the Hebrew and Aramaic Ezra, which appears as II Esdras in the *Septuagint* and in most English renderings of the *Apocrypha;* however, authors cite I Esdras as III Ezra when they refer to the canonical Ezra as I Ezra, and Nehemiah as II Ezra. See further Schürer (1987) 3:708–718.
20. I Esdras 3.1–5.6.
21. Zimmerman 1963–64:181. Josephos retells the story, with some differences, in his *Antiquities of the Jews* 11.3 (31–69). Among the differences are that Darius, unable to sleep, chats with his guards and establishes the contest. Moreover, the king assigns the topics in advance to each of the three young men, so that their goal in the contest is to present the finest possible speech on the topic (e.g., to speak to the question: Is wine the strongest thing?) rather than to devise the best answer to the general question: What is the strongest thing?
22. Zimmerman 1963–64:198.
23. Laqueur 1911:171; Rudolf 1945–48:179; Neuman 1953:51; Zimmerman 1963–64:197; In der Smitten 1972:493.
24. 3:18–19; see Rudolf 1945–48:179.
25. In der Smitten 1972:493.
26. 4:2–3.
27. 4:14–16.
28. The Greek parallel argues against Zimmerman's conjecture that the three Persian guards are a reduction of an original four (Zimmerman 1963–64:198); rather, the number of guards has remained constant while the number of answers has increased.
29. Plutarch also mentions a couple of humorous chains framed as apothegms, or clever utterances attributed to particular persons. Thus Marcus Cato is said to have declared that women are ruled by men, men by the Romans, and the Romans by their wives (*Mor.* 198d [3], *Cato Maior* 8 [340b]). In this chain the first and last elements are verbally identical, since

the same word means both "women" and "wives." More elaborately, Themistokles is said to have joked that his son was the most powerful of the Greeks, for the Athenians commanded the Greeks, he himself commanded the Athenians, the boy's mother commanded Themistokles, and the boy commanded her (*Mor.* 185d [10], *Themistocles* 18 [121b]). Both chains are variations on the familiar sequence of something ruled, the ruler, and the ruler's lover/wife, which in the case of the second chain features an additional ironic link: the wife's son.

Sunlight Carried in a Bag 🦢 Perdikkes

Persons fill a bag (box, wheelbarrow, etc.) with sunlight and bring it into a windowless building in order to illuminate it.

This numskull tale is AT 1245, *Sunlight Carried in a Bag into the Windowless House.*

In an English tale the stupid inhabitants of Coggeshall built themselves a church but forgot to make windows in it. So they set some hampers outside in the sun to catch the light, shut them up, wheeled them into the church in wheelbarrows, and opened them up in order to release the light.[1]

Perdikkes Collects Light

Although this tale of foolish behavior is not found in ancient literature, worth noticing is a Greek legend in which a character treats light as a substance that can be collected. Herodotos relates that three Argive brothers hired themselves out to do menial work for the king of Macedon. The king's wife noticed that when she baked bread, the loaf intended for the youngest brother, Perdikkes, always doubled in size. She informed the king, who, taking it as an omen portending some major event, ordered the menials to leave his kingdom. The brothers said they would leave after they had been paid. Now, the sun was shining through the smoke hole in the roof onto the floor of the room in which they were talking, and the king, saying he would give them the wages they deserved, pointed to the sun. While the two older brothers stood astonished, Perdikkes told the king that they accepted what he was giving. Taking his knife, Perdikkes drew a line around the patch of light on the floor, three times collected the sun into his lap, and departed with his brothers. When one of the king's attendants remarked on the youth's action, saying that there was a significance in his taking the offered wage, the king became incensed and dispatched horsemen after the youths to kill them. But once the three brothers had crossed a certain sacred river, it rose so high that the pursuers could not follow. The brothers settled elsewhere in Macedonia, on Mount Bermion near the Gardens of Midas, and from there they conquered all of Macedonia.[2]

Herodotos does not explain either the import of the youngest brother's actions or why he is pursued, and it may be that the historian himself does not know. Perhaps Perdikkes symbolically takes possession of the king's hearth and thereby of the king's entire estate, and then calls the sun as witness to his claim.[3] That is, pretending that the stingy monarch generously offers the brothers his entire kingdom as their wages, Perdikkes symbolically accepts the offer on their behalf, the entire transaction playing out in advance the king's even-

tual loss of his kingdom to the three brothers. It is not clear, however, why Perdikkes' act of circumscribing the sunlight on the floor should signify precisely his taking possession of the hearth and why his act of drawing the rays of the sun into the folds of his cloak should signify his calling the sun to witness his claim.

Rather, when the monarch offers him the sun, Perdikkes seems to take it, circumscribing the light on the floor, perhaps thereby establishing a boundary around his property, and collecting (ἀρυσάμενος) sunlight in his cloak. In ordinary usage this verb (ἀρύω) refers to the action of drawing water into a container, so that Perdikkes must be drawing the rays of the sun into the folds of his cloak or to be acting as if he were doing so. Wolf Aly, pointing to the close connection between sunlight and gold in Greek poetry, suggests that Perdikkes departs taking the sunlight with him, for the brothers arrive forthwith at the Gardens of Midas.[4] Whether there is a latent connection here with gold or not, Perdikkes does seem to be taking the sunlight with him, at least symbolically, and it is on the significance of this act that the story must turn. Perhaps the sun signifies not gold but sovereignty.

In important respects this legend is the opposite of *Sunlight Carried in a Bag into the Windowless House*, for the hero is a trickster rather than a simpleton, and he conveys light out of a building rather than into one. For our present purpose the interest of the complex and puzzling story of Perdikkes is not that it is a Greek or Macedonian realization of the much simpler tale of *Sunlight Carried in a Bag*, which it is not, but that it features an unusual motif—catching light in a container and conveying it elsewhere—that is later attested as the principal motif of the folktale.[5]

A similar instance of an apparently foolish idea employed cleverly by a clever man is the tradition that, like a latter-day Aiolos, the philosopher Empedokles once captured the etesian winds in sacks made of donkey skin.[6] According to the biographer Diogenes Laertios, when the etesian winds were blowing so fiercely that they threatened to ruin the crops, Empedokles had some donkeys flayed and bags made of their hides. He stretched these out on hilltops and mountain ridges in order to catch the wind in them, succeeded in stopping the wind, and so earned for himself the nickname "wind-checker."[7] So Empedokles treats the wind the way Perdikkes treats sunlight, as a material thing that can simply be collected and carried away.

These stories should be distinguished from narratives in which a clever man deliberately employs a foolish idea in order to give the false impression that he is a fool, as Odysseus does when he sows a field with salt (see "Sowing of Salt"), an instance of the adaptation of a numskull tale to a trickster who is only playing the fool.

Lit. Cf. AT 1245, *Sunlight Carried in a Bag into the Windowless House.* Aly 1969:196–197. Liungman 1961:278–279. Ashliman, type 1245.

1. Briggs (1970) A2:43.
2. Herodotos 8.137–139.
3. How and Wells 2:283.
4. Aly 1969:197.
5. For an interesting instance of fire as an object (in addition of course to the myth of

Prometheus's theft of fire and the philosophic doctrine of the four elements, according to which air, fire, water, and earth are the four irreducible elements of the universe), see the disquisition of Philostratos (*Vita Apollonii* 3.15) on how the Indian Brahmans extract fire as a material substance from the rays of the sun.

6. Aiolos: Homer *Od.* 10.1–76.

7. Κωλυσανέμας. Diogenes Laertios 8.60. See Page 1972:73–78 for a discussion of ancient and modern magic for controlling the wind.

Three Brothers ✌ Roman Proverb

Since a certain man had three sons and only one house to leave them, he told them to go out into the world and learn a trade, and upon their return he who should put on the best performance would get the house. So they each learned a trade, one to be a farrier, the second to be a barber, and the third to be a fencer. When they returned home to display their skills, the barber shaved a hare as it ran past without cutting the animal, the farrier replaced the shoes of a horse as it raced past drawing a carriage, and the swordsman brandished his sword so skillfully that, though it was raining, no drops reached him. The father awarded the house to the fencer. But as the brothers were fond of one another, they all moved in and lived together, made much money from their skills, and when one died the others grieved so much that they too died, so that all three were laid in a single grave.[1]

This comic tale is classified as AT 654, *The Three Brothers*. It is first found ca. A.D. 1300 in the *Scala Celi* of Johannes Gobii, where one skillful brother can remove the pelt of a running hare without hampering its movement, another can remove the shoes and rider of a galloping horse without causing it to lose speed, and the third can keep in place all the feathers of a featherbed that has been opened up on a windy mountaintop.[2]

A Roman Proverbial Expression

Although the tale is not attested in ancient sources, a proverb employed by a character in Petronius's *Satyrica* shows a familiarity with a motif like that of the skillful barber or perhaps of the amazing farrier, reminding folk-narrative scholars of the present folktale.[3]

Speaking of the craftiness of a certain man, the freedman Echion, whose speech is full of proverbs, remarks: "He could trim the claws of a kite in flight."[4] Trimming the claws of a predatory bird without disturbing its flight is much like shaving a running hare without harming it or, as other texts have it, flaying a running hare. Witty claims of similarly fantastic skills are occasionally found as independent statements in more recent times as well, such as "He could gird a saddle on a nag in full gallop."[5] Since it is impossible to say whether they have been inspired by the oral tale or are old instances of popular wit that have contributed to the formation of the tale, we can only speculate whether *The Three Brothers* or a tall tale like it was known to the Romans.

Other proverbial expressions in Petronius that may allude to folktales in-

clude "If you were anywhere else, you'd say that there were baked pigs walking around here" (see "Schlaraffenland") and "So your friend who once was a frog is now a king" (see "Frog King").

Lit. (AT 654, *The Three Brothers*.) Cf. Motifs F663.1, *Skillful smith shoes running horse;* F664.1, *Skillful flayer skins running rabbit;* and F665.1, *Skillful barber shaves running hare.* BP 3:10–12. Otto 1890:223, no. 1115. Wesselski 1925:213, no. 20. Liungman 1961:188–189. Ashliman, type 654. Hayes 1997:74–88.

1. Grimm 124.
2. BP 3:11–12; Wesselski 1925:61.
3. Otto 1890:223; Crusius 1890:41; Friedländer 1910:533; BP 2:11. Similar motifs are found in AT 513, *The Extraordinary Companions*, which appears in classical tradition as the adventures of the Argonauts, among whom are numbered the sharp-sighted Lynkeus, the singer Orpheus, the transformer Periklymenos, the runner Euphemos, the trickster Autolykos, the winged Boreades, and the boxer Polydeukes (*EM* 1:769). In Greece the story of the extraordinary companions is loosely combined with the story of Jason and Medeia (see "Girl as Helper").
4. Petronius 45.9: *Ille milvo volanti poterat ungues resecare.*
5. BP 2: 11.

Three Joint Depositors 🌿 Demosthenes

Three men deposit a sum of money with another person on the understanding that the money will be delivered only upon the demand of all three. Sometime later, one of the depositors returns and on a false pretext persuades the person to deliver to him the money (or he steals the money). Subsequently the other depositors show up and, when the person is unable to produce the money, sue her (him) in court. The case is about to go against the holder of the money when a clever person, moved by the victim's plight, comes to her (his) aid. He reminds the court of the original understanding, declaring that the defendant has the money and is prepared to deliver it when all the depositors jointly demand it. The defendant is acquitted.

This tale is AT 1591, *The Three Joint Depositors.* Despite the title, the number of the depositors varies in different tellings.

In a Scottish narrative the role of the clever adviser is assigned to a historical personage, George Buchanan (1506–82), author and tutor to James VI of Scotland and hero of many anecdotes.[1] Thus, three men posing as merchants decided to play a trick on an innkeeper, who was a widow. After drinking at her inn, they asked her to keep for them a certain pack and instructed her in front of witnesses not to deliver it to any of them unless they came to ask for it jointly. Some weeks later, two of the men returned and asked for the pack, explaining that the third man had gone to a fair where they all were to meet. Suspecting nothing, the simple woman gave them the pack. But a few days later the third man returned and desired the pack, and when she explained that she had delivered it to the other two men, the third man brought her to court. The

process went on for two years, by which time the cause was about to go against her. The woman had, moreover, exhausted her own funds, and as a consequence her attorney announced he could no longer defend her. The woman went to London in the hope of securing another attorney, but none would help her since she had no money. George Buchanan happened to overhear her plight and promised to send her an attorney at no cost to her. So on the appointed day George dressed himself up as an attorney and went to the court. First he asked the court not to charge the poor widow with court expenses, but the plaintiff's attorney answered that, according to law, he who gains the plea gains his expenses as well. George then reminded the judges that the woman had agreed to keep the pack until all three merchants were present to demand it back; therefore, the woman must not return the pack until the present merchant should locate the other two men. Thereupon the judges ordered the merchant to seek his two companions. But George demanded that the plaintiff pay the woman's expenses first, which he was forced to do. Afterward George returned to London, and many people searched in vain for the unknown advocate from London.[2]

An amusing tale of rascality and cleverness, *The Three Joint Depositors* is found in both the East and the West in literary compilations and in oral tradition. It is unusual for its positive portrayal of depositaries.[3] For greedy depositaries and victimized depositors, see "Children Play At Hog Killing."

Demosthenes' Clever Defense

Valerius Maximus gives the earliest text of the story, placing it in his collection of exempla as a non-Roman story in the section featuring "Clever Utterances and Deeds."

According to Valerius, an old woman was once helped by the astuteness of Demosthenes. She had agreed to hold an amount of money for two visitors on the condition that she return it to them both at the same time. But a while later one of them returned in filthy clothes, pretended that his companion was deceased, and carried away all the money. Subsequently the other man showed up and asked for the deposit. The wretched woman, who had neither money nor a good defense, was thinking of doing away with herself, but at an opportune time Demosthenes appeared as her advocate. Speaking in her defense, he declared that the woman was prepared to return the deposit, but she would be unable to do so unless the plaintiff produced his companion, since, as the plaintiff himself emphasized, the deposit might not be returned to one man without the other.[4]

Valerius makes no further comment on the story other than his introductory remark, which indicates that for him the interest and value of the narrative lies in the cleverness of Demosthenes' defense. Since the narrative features Demosthenes, it presumably derives from Greek tradition.

The exemplum was frequently retold by Renaissance humanists and appeared in different collections of exempla and comic tales in the West, and the story has also been featured in Eastern collections of tales, so that there has probably been much interaction between the literary and the oral traditions.[5]

Lit. AT 1591, *The Three Joint Depositers.* Clouston (1887) 2:1–14. Chauvin (1904) 8:63–64, no. 28. Burton (n.d.) 6:210–211. Penzer (1924) 1:186 n. 1. Pauli (1924) 2:285–286, no. 113. *EM* 5:1274–1276. Ashliman, type 1591.

1. Briggs (1970) A2:102.
2. Briggs (1970) A2:95–97, from the chapbook *The Witty and Entertaining Exploits of George Buchanan* (1703), pp. 27–29.
3. *EM* 2:1275.
4. *Facta et Dicta Memorabilia* 7.3, *externa* 5.
5. West: *EM* 2:1274. East: for example, Artola 1978:24–25.

Three Lazy Ones ⟨ Lazy Debtor and Creditor

Three lazy men engage in a contest to see who is the laziest. Usually the second person proves to be lazier than the first, and the third proves to be the laziest of all.

This comic tale is AT 1950, *The Three Lazy Ones.*

In an English tale about the silly people of Fimber, a gentleman riding through Fimber came upon three of the villagers lying on the grass. When he got little response from them, he offered half of crown to the man who would tell him which of the three was the laziest. The first villager said he would not thank the man for the half-crown unless the man threw it within his reach. The second man said he would not thank the man for the half-crown if the man did not get down from his horse and place the money in his hand. The third said he would not thank him for it unless the man put it in his pocket. So the reader must guess who got the half-crown.[1]

In this tale the extent of each man's laziness is measured by a single standard, which is how much effort he would make to acquire a half-crown. In some versions more than one standard is used. So in an Egyptian folktale collected from a sixty-three-year-old man in 1969, Haroun al-Rasheed once possessed a pitcher made of silver and gold. Summoning three of his courtiers before him, he offered it to the man who proved to be the laziest. The first courtier said that once he was lying beside a wall that began to fall down, but he was too lazy to move. The second explained that once, while he was leaning against a tree, a serpent crawled over him on its way to the top of the tree, and he was too lazy to move out of its path. When the third courtier was asked to tell his story, he did not care even to open his mouth. When Haroun al-Rasheed shouted at him, asking whether he was not going to obey the calif's order, he said he was too lazy. He won the prize.[2] In this narrative, the first two men cite frightening situations that they were too lazy to avoid, whereas the third man is too lazy even to compete in the contest.

The ironic form of the competition, in which a prize is awarded to the laziest man rather than to the most industrious man or best athlete or the like, is a comic inversion of conventional contests, a topsy-turvy competition (see "Topsy-Turvy Land"). It attains its most outrageous form in texts in which a king establishes a contest in laziness in order to determine which of his sons shall succeed him on the throne.[3]

Lazy Creditor and Lazy Debtor

In a little joke found in an ancient Greek jokebook, a lazy man owed a denarius to another lazy man. When they happened to meet, the lender asked for the coin. The borrower told him to untie his handkerchief and take it out. The lender replied: "Oh, never mind. I forgive the debt."[4]

Though this comic tale features only two lazy men rather than three, it is identical in spirit to *The Three Lazy Ones* because of the implicit contest in laziness. The debtor is willing to repay the coin, but he is too lazy to remove it from his napkin, and since the creditor is also too lazy to get it, he cancels the debt. In a sense, both men are equally lazy, since neither can be bothered to untie the cloth in which the coin is being carried, but only the creditor loses thereby.

This brief tale could represent a nascent form of *The Three Lazy Ones*. If so, the tale has been intensified, for the competition has been made explicit, being now framed as a contest, and the number of competitors has been raised to the conventional number of three, as in other contest tales (see "Stronger and Strongest" and "Wishing Contest"). But sometimes an individual instance of laziness that is known from *The Three Lazy Ones* appears as an independent narrative, as in the following English joke. "A young farmer, inspecting his father's concerns in the time of hay-harvest, found a body of the mowers asleep, when they should have been at work. What is this? cried the youth; why, me, you are so indolent, that I would give a crown to know which is the most lazy of you.—I am he, cried the one nearest to him, still stretching himself at his ease. Here then, said the youth, holding out the money. O, Master George, said the fellow, folding his arms, do pray take the trouble of *putting it into my pocket* for me."[5] The joke hints of a contest but features only one instance of laziness, going directly, as it were, to the climactic example of extreme laziness as found in the English comic tale summarized above. Likewise the ancient Greek witticism may be either a nascent form of the more complex comic tale known from later sources, or a biform of the tale, cast in a pithy form in order better to serve as a joke.

Diogenes Suns Himself

Although it involves only one loafer, and not necessarily a lazy man at that, mention must be made of the famous anecdote of the meeting of Diogenes the Cynic and Alexander, king of Macedon. The young Alexander, passing through Greece on his way to conquer Asia, encountered Diogenes lying (or sitting) in the sun in a grove in Corinth (or Athens). When Alexander offered the man anything he wanted, Diogenes bade Alexander move out of his sunlight.[6]

There is no question here of a contest among lazy men lying in the sun, of course, since Diogenes is alone in passing the time sunning himself, and yet it is worth observing that the situation is otherwise identical to that in some tales of *The Three Lazy Ones*. As in the English story summarized above, in which a gentleman who is riding through Fimber sees three villagers lying on the grass, so in the Greek anecdote Alexander as he passes through Corinth

spies a man lazily sunning himself in a public place. And just as the English gentleman gets little response from the loafing villagers, so also Alexander finds that Diogenes is virtually indifferent to his presence. The Englishman proceeds to institute a contest in laziness with a monetary reward, whereupon the three lazies lazily compete in conserving their energy and manifesting their near indifference to the proffered prize. In the same way Alexander offers Diogenes anything he wants, whereupon Diogenes responds *as though* he were in a contest of laziness, conserving his own energy at all cost and demonstrating his near indifference to the monarch's offer. Having only one wish, and therefore an implicit choice between the resources of a king (but having to move if he wanted sun) and not having to move, the loafing philosopher chooses not to have to move, that is, to continue lying lazily in the sun like a dog, which was in fact his nickname (ὁ κύων "the dog," whence κυνικός "doglike," "Cynic"). As the modern texts show, the most frequent way to express laziness in the oral tale is simply to show an unwillingness to move, whether to gain something valuable or to avoid something dangerous.

This, I think, was the point of the original matter of this story.[7] But once it was borrowed from a tale of laziness, perhaps *The Three Lazy Ones*, it was creatively refashioned to emphasize a different aspect of the loafer, his self-sufficiency.[8] The loafer-become-philosopher does not require wealth and power for happiness. Unlike the monarch he can be content with what is at hand. The encounter of the lazy man and the passerby was thus recast in one of antiquity's favorite molds, the confrontation of philosopher and king, as in the encounter of Solon and Kroisos, an encounter in which the philosopher always emerges victorious.

Lit. (AT 1950, *The Three Lazy Ones*.) BP 3:207–213. Wesselski 1925:62, 213–214, no. 21. Liungman 1961:343–344. Tubach 1969, no. 3005. Ashliman, type 1950. Hansen 1997c.

1. Briggs (1970) A2:86.
2. El-Shamy 1980:226–227, no. 62.
3. For example, Grimm 151.
4. *Philogelos* 213. "Handkerchief" renders μάπουλον (from Latin *mappula*), a little cloth in which the man has tied up his coins in order to carry them. In my summary I have labeled the men as borrower and lender in order to distinguish them clearly, but the Greek says only that one man owed the other man a denarius, which of course could have come about otherwise than through borrowing. For other jokes about laziness see *Philogelos* 211–212.
5. Miller 1884:360, no. 1673.
6. Dio Chrysostomos *De Regno* 4:14–15; Plutarch *Alexander* 14; Arrian *Anabasis* 7.2.1–2; Diogenes Laertios 6.38; Cicero *Tusc. Disp.* 5.32; Valerius Maximus 4.3, *ext.* 4. See further Sayre 1938:82–87.
7. Cf. Liungman 1961:344.
8. Hansen 1997c.

Threefold Death ⚘ The Hermaphrodite

Three different prophecies are made concerning the kind of death a person will meet. All three predictions come true.

This tale is AT 934A[1], *Threefold Death*.

The story was popular in mediaeval Ireland. In a text from the eleventh century the king asked his wizards how he would die. The first said he would perish by killing, the second by drowning, and the third by burning; and a number of apparently impossible conditions also had to be fulfilled. Because of the lack of agreement, the king felt secure. Later the hall in which he was feasting was attacked, in the course of which he was wounded with a spear by Aedh the Black, the house was burnt over him, and the king, trying to avoid the flames, crawled into a vat of beer where he drowned.[1]

According to the *Vita Merlini*, Queen Ganieda, wishing to prove that Merlin was a liar, sent a boy three times in different clothing (on the third occasion in woman's attire) to Merlin to ask how he would die. Merlin's three prophecies were that the youth would fall from a rock, die in a tree, and drown in a river. The contradictions appeared to prove that Merlin was not a true seer. But when the boy grew up, he fell from a rock while hunting, caught his foot in a tree, and his head became submerged in the river below.[2]

A modern Slovenian tale relates how the Rojenice (three sisters similar to the classical Fates) determine in advance the way each person will meet his or her death. Concerning a particular child, one said that he would die from a snake, the second that he would fall to his death, and the third that he would drown. When the child grew up, he climbed a tree to pick some fruit where a snake bit him; frightened, he fell from the tree to a cliff and from the cliff to water, where he drowned.[3]

In this folktale the first episode suggests an enigma that the second episode, like the solution to a riddle or the punch line to a joke, solves in an ingenious and unexpected way. Since a person can die only once, three different causes of death appear to be an impossibility. Accordingly, unlike other stories in which it is foretold that a person will die in a certain way, there may be little attempt to avert the predicted fate.[4] But then one day the person dies a strange, threefold death, usually experiencing a chain of linked mishaps any one of which could kill a person. Of course the person really dies not three deaths, but one death for which there are several contributing causes.

It has been cleverly argued that the folktale derives from heroic legends that in turn were inspired by the Indo-European practice of honoring different deities with different kinds of human sacrifice, for example, the old Scandinavian practice of consecrating a man to Odin by hanging him. There is some evidence that among the Germanic peoples different human beings might be ritually sacrificed or executed in honor of different deities by hanging, wounding, and drowning, respectively, and that the corresponding sacrifices among the Celts were hanging, burning, and drowning. There is also some indication, though not very strong, that Germanic peoples performed all three kinds of offering simultaneously in celebration of a military victory, that is, they hanged some victims, stabbed others with a weapon, and drowned a third group.[5]

This theory does not, however, really explain the development of the motif, let alone the story. Even if the ancient Germans and Scandinavians performed all three kinds of sacrifice on some occasions, they did not perform all three on the same person, for each victim died only one death. Consequently there is no obvious reason why this event should have given rise to the narrative motif of a threefold death. Nor do the three deities and three manners of death in the

Petronian poem correlate significantly with one another or reflect the trifunctional scheme that is alleged for Indo-European mythologies. And even if the theory were correct, one would of course still have to explain why the motif continued to appeal to narrators and listeners after its ritual significance was long forgotten.

Death of a Hermaphrodite

In a Latin poem of uncertain date and authorship, the narrator relates in the first person the story of his own birth and death, as follows. The poem has been attributed by different scholars to Gallus (first century B.C.), Petronius (first century A.D.), Bishop Hildebert of Le Mans (twelfth century), and Matthaeus of Vendôme (late twelfth century).[6]

> When my mother was carrying me in her womb, she asked the gods what she would bear. "A male," said Phoebus. "A woman," said Mars. And Juno said, "Neither." So I was born a hermaphrodite. When my mother inquired how I would die, the goddess said, "By arms." Mars said, "On the cross." And Phoebus said, "By water." So each of these modes of death was established. There was a tree giving shade to some water, and I climbed it. The sword I was carrying fell and by chance I slipped onto it. As I hung by my feet from the branches, my head went into the stream. And so I—woman, man, and neither—was drowned, impaled, and crucified.

The poem agrees exactly with the traditional story in that three different manners of death are predicted of the subject, who on some later occasion dies all three ways. The particular forms of death are also among those found in other texts, namely, wounding by a weapon, together with the combination of slipping while in a tree into water, and specifically in the same bizarre form in which we find it in the *Vita Merlini* where the victim, caught in the tree, remains hanging upside down with his head beneath water, rather than falling from the tree into a body of water. The seers in the Latin poem are not the Fates, as one might expect, but three Roman deities, who like the Slovenian Rojenice appear not simply to foresee but actually to determine what will happen. The poet makes no effort to harmonize the individual modes of death with the spheres of influence traditionally associated with the each of the deities, for a death by arms would be more fittingly foreseen by Mars than by Juno, and it is less appropriate for Apollo to foresee a death by water than it would be for Neptune, whom the poet does not introduce into the poem at all.

Unlike the oral tale, the Latin verses deal with the subject's birth as well as his death. Presumably the poet started with the international story of the threefold death and chose to balance it with an account of the beginning of the protagonist's life as well, whom the poet makes a tri-natural being.[7] The idea may have suggested itself to him by a form of the story like that later worked up in the *Vita Merlini*, in which the youth adopts three different disguises, pretending to be three different persons, one of them female. The poet also narrates the whole account in the first person. Accordingly, before the subject's birth and again before his death three gods make three apparently irreconcilable predictions about the protagonist, and contrary to all likelihood all three prove to be correct. With equal improb-

ability, the subject of the story narrates it, even though the narrative includes an account of his own demise. The threefold identity of the protagonist—male, female, and neither—and the threefold death intimate with whimsically dark humor that, in order for the protagonist to die, his several natures must individually perish, so that he must die three deaths. Just as there is no relationship between the mode of death and the deity who predicts it, there is no correlation between the gender of the protagonist and the deity who calls it (Apollo predicts male, Mars predicts female, Juno predicts neither) or between gender and manner of death.

In a somewhat longer Latin poem attributed to Bishop Hildebert of Le Mans or Petrus Riga in the twelfth century, the pregnant wife of Thyresias asked the gods what her child would be. Phoebus said, "A man." Venus said, "A woman." And Neptune said, "Nay, rather a girl-boy." Reality corresponded to the predictions, for she conceived, and a man, woman, and neither were born simultaneously. In time the youth asked the gods how he would die. Venus said, "By a noose." Mars said, "By a weapon." Neptune said, "By water." Each utterance had its own force, for, climbing a tree above a river, the youth fell such that his sword pierced his chest, his foot became caught in the tree, and his head became submerged in the water. Thus a single person perished thrice.[8] Unlike the poem discussed above, this one makes an effort to correlate death and deity. The action is recounted in the third person.

Several other characters in classical narrative die more than one death. Odysseus and his men, having voyaged to the death realm and back, are called by their hostess Kirke "twice mortal" or "twice dying," since they have died a kind of death by virtue of their going to the House of Hades and will later die a physical death.[9] And the wily Sisyphos, who is carried off by Thanatos to the realm of the dead, tricks the Lord of the Dead into allowing him to return to the world of the living to take care of certain business, and then happily stays there until he eventually dies a natural death (see "Smith and the Devil"). These characters die a sort of technical death, defined as their visiting while alive the abode of the human dead, from which there is normally no exit for human beings once they have entered the place, followed years later by their dying a physical death. There is a kind of cosmic pun here on death as a place of residence and death as a state of being. But these legends differ from the story under discussion in that they are not tales of fate, they tell of two rather than three deaths, and of course the deaths do not occur simultaneously.

Lit. AT 934A[1], *Three-Fold Death.* Jackson 1940. Brednich 1964:138–145. Ward 1970. Dvořák 1978, no. 1482*.

1. Jackson 1940:535, no. 1.
2. Jackson 1940:546–547, no. 3.
3. Brednich 1964:142.
4. Brednich 1964:138.
5. Ward 1970. Cf. Ellis 1994.
6. Maurice Rat includes it in his edition of Petronius (Rat 1934:390, no. 33), commenting that it has been attributed by some scholars to Petronius and by others to Gallus,

though Rat says that it was doubtless composed by neither of them (1934:579). The same poem appears as no. 786 in Riese's *Supplementum* to the *Anthologia Latina* (ed. Buecheler and Riese) with the comment in the first edition (1870) that, although it is found among the poems of Bishop Hildebert, a poem of this kind seems not to be one of Hildebert's but rather to be ancient. In the second edition, however, Riese changes his mind and, following Traube, now believes that it is a mediaeval poem composed by Matthaeus Vindocinensis. Two different poems about the threefold death of a hermaphrodite are printed among the verse of Bishop Hildebert in Migne's *Patrologia Latina* (171, no. 1445–1446). One of them, recounted in the first person, is essentially that printed by Riese; the other, recounted in the third person, is very similar in conception but entirely dissimilar in execution (for its contents see below). Traube (1892:317–321) argues that the first-person poem was composed by Matthaeus of Vendôme, and that the longer, third-person poem was composed subsequently by Petrus Riga. The first-person poem is included by Sullivan (1977:177–178, no. 55) in his translation of Petronius, and by Branham and Kinney (1997:168, no. 64) in theirs, though the latter label it as probably spurious.

7. In his commentary on the poem Rat (1934:580) refers to the mythological Hermaphroditos, but there is no indication that the poet intends an allusion to him. Tradition differs about the hermaphroditism of Hermaphroditos, whether he was a hermaphrodite from birth (as in Diodorus 4.6.5) or, born a male child of Hermes and Aphrodite, became a hermaphrodite when the naiad of the pool in which he was bathing took hold of him, after which their bodies fused (as in Ovid *Met.* 4.285–388). See further Roscher 1.2314–2342; Delcourt 1961, 1976; *LIMC* 5.1:268–285.

8. *Patrologia Latina*, ed. Migne, 171:1445–1446, cited by Jackson 1940:535–536, no. 3. On its authorship see Traube 1892:317–321.

9. Homer *Od.* 12.21–22: *disthanees.*

To Sacrifice a Giant Candle ✑ To Sacrifice a Hecatomb

A man in need promises a certain offering to god (a saint) in exchange for help, but reneges when the need passes.

This is the core idea of AT 778, *To Sacrifice a Giant Candle*, which is developed in various ways, sometimes more piously, sometimes more comically.

Two established forms of the type, which we can name after the extravagant vows made by the protagonist, are the Cow and Calf and the Giant Candle. In a text of the Cow and Calf dating to around 1300, a man who was leading a cow and calf to Mont St. Michel during low tide was overtaken by high tide. He called upon St. Michael for help, promising him his calf. When the danger was over, he decided the saint was a fool to think that he would get the calf. But the tide returned, and this time the man anxiously promised the saint both his calf and his cow. When subsequently he also declared this vow void, the tide came a third time and drowned him together with his two animals.[1]

A text of the Giant Candle is given by the Spanish author, Mal Lara, when he glosses the expression "To beseech the saint until the problem is over."[2] "Those who are driven only by the present danger ask to escape from the danger in question, but their prayers do not last any longer than the task. The story is told of a mariner who during a storm promised St. Cristóbal to make an effigy of him in wax, and when the mariner was told by the man standing next to him that he was making a big promise, he replied: 'Quiet. Get me out of this prob-

lem, and later I'll pay him off with a five-cent candle.' "[3] The Spanish text is formulated as a mono-episodic joke with a punch line.

The Hecatomb

The story of the shifty man who makes an extravagant vow while in need, and who subsequently, when the crisis passes, either substitutes a lesser payment or disregards it entirely, was familiar to the ancient Greeks. A comic version appears as a prose fable in the Aesopic corpus as early as the first or second century A.D.

A poor man who was sick promised the gods a hecatomb if they should make him well. Wishing to test him, the gods quickly made him recover. But since he had no real oxen, he fashioned a hundred oxen of dough and burned them on an altar, declaring that he had fulfilled his vow. The gods, wanting to repay the deceit, sent him a dream in which they urged him to go to the beach, where he would fetch a thousand Attic drachmas. He happily ran to the shore, where pirates fell upon him. When they sold him, he fetched a thousand drachmas.[4]

The Greek protagonist makes a promise so great that, as in the story of the Giant Candle, there is no real possibility of its fulfillment. Here the extravagant vow is for a hecatomb, that is, a public sacrifice of many oxen, originally of a hundred oxen, a gesture of epic magnitude for a man of wealth, which of course the impoverished protagonist is not. The story continues with his deceit, in which he executes his obligation in an inexpensive fashion by sacrificing a hundred oxen made of dough. This device for observing the form but not the spirit of an oath was a traditional motif in Greek storytelling, as shown by the similar trick of another cheat, the cunning Kinyras, who promised Agamemnon or Menelaos that he would send fifty ships to Troy. He sent one real ship and launched into the sea forty-nine little clay ships filled with little clay men.[5] The fable of the sick man concludes with countermeasures taken by the gods, who send the man a deceptive dream that takes advantage of two different meanings of the Greek verb εὑρήσειν. The man, happily taking the verb in its usual sense of "find," expects to find an amount of money, whereas the gods, intending it in its less common sense of "bring in" by sale, arrange for the man to be captured and sold as a slave. As in the Cow and Calf tale, heaven triumphs in the end over petty human deceit.

A somewhat similar tale known to ancient authors involves a stingy sick man who decides he would rather remain sick (or even die) than become well and have to pay what he has promised to the doctor (or the gods). Thus, according to a joke in a Greek jokebook, a sick man made an agreement with his doctor whereby he would pay the doctor a certain amount of money if he should get well. When his wife chided him for drinking wine while he had a fever, he replied: "Do you want me to get well and have to pay the doctor?"[6] An epigram of Lucilius describes a certain Hermokrates, who was so miserly that he named himself as his own heir. Lying on his deathbed and considering how much he would have to pay the doctors if he recovered and how much it would cost him to die, he decided it was more profitable to die, and stretched himself out.[7] Formally, if not genetically, the tale of the stingy sick man is a kind of reductio ad absurdum of the tale type, showcasing a character so avaricious that he does not even wish to survive if to do so he must repay a debt.

Minos and the Bull from the Sea

The international type was also productive of noncomic stories in Greek mythology. In the legend of Minos and the bull, the protagonist does not suddenly find himself in need of divine help because of a crisis of nature such as flood or storm, but rather wishes divine aid in order to acquire something that he desires to possess. Like the hero of the tale, however, after he gets what he wishes he neglects to honor his benefactor.

Minos wished to become king of Crete but faced opposition. He said that he had received the kingdom from the gods, and to make his claim credible he said that whatever he prayed for would happen. So he prayed to Poseidon for a bull to appear from the depths of the sea, promising to sacrifice it. Poseidon sent a fine bull, but when Minos saw its beauty, he sent it to his own herds and sacrificed another. Although Minos got the kingship, Poseidon, angry at the deceit, made the bull wild and also made Minos's wife Pasiphae conceive an erotic desire for it.[8]

The legend of Minos and the beautiful bull has an interesting counterpart in that of Atreus and the golden lamb. Like it, the narrative is not an independent story but part of a larger saga. Unlike the poor man's comic promise of a hecatomb, something that is far beyond his resources, the vows of the mythological Atreus and Minos are modest and could easily be fulfilled, and yet they renege.

Atreus and the Golden Lamb

The story of Atreus is known in two slightly divergent versions. In one, Atreus promised to sacrifice to Artemis the most beautiful animal in his flocks, but when a golden lamb was born, he neglected the sacrifice, strangling the lamb and hiding it in a box. Then Thyestes seduced Aerope, and she secretly gave the lamb to her lover, who used it to become king. But after the gods caused a celestial portent on Atreus's behalf, he succeeded to the kingship of Mycenae. Partly because of his deceit, the angry Artemis later caused the winds not to blow for Atreus's son Agamemnon when he wished to sail to Troy (see further "Boastful Deer Slayer"). In the other version, Atreus contested with his brother Thyestes for the throne of Mycenae. With the deliberate intent of causing trouble, Hermes provided a golden lamb, which Atreus proclaimed to be a sign of his right to the kingship. But Thyestes then seduced Atreus's wife, Aerope, and she in turn gave the lamb to Thyestes, who used it to become king, etc.[9]

The idea of the present story appears to be that when Atreus was vying with his younger brother, Thyestes, for the throne of Mycenae, it was agreed that the brother who could exhibit the more impressive portent should rule. Atreus expected to produce the golden lamb, but unbeknownst to him his wife, Aerope, had given it to her lover Thyestes. So Thyestes produced it and initially obtained the throne, but with the help of the gods Atreus produced an even greater portent and so ultimately prevailed.[10] If this is correct, the legends of Atreus and Minos are so parallel in their course of action that they must be different developments of the same basic story. (1) Minos (Atreus) is vying for a vacant throne, but his claim is contested, so that (2) he prays to Poseidon (Artemis) for a bull from the sea (for a beautiful animal). But (3) when a bull

emerges from the sea (a golden lamb is born among his flocks), (4) he neglects his vow, substituting a lesser bull (keeping the lamb for himself). (5) The slighted deity then punishes him, causing his wife to become enamored of the bull (causing the winds not to blow for his son). In addition to the functional correspondence between Pasiphae's infidelity and Agamemnon's windlessness, both being divine punishments for the protagonist's slighting the deity, there is also a formal correspondence in the sexual misbehavior of Minos's wife Pasiphae and Atreus's wife Aerope. Pasiphae becomes enamored of the bull and covertly has sexual intercourse with it, just as Aerope becomes enamored of her husband's rival Thyestes and carries on a secret affair with him.

Hermon of Thasos

A brief Greek narrative in the spirit of *To Sacrifice a Giant Candle* is found on a testimonial tablet in stone from the ruins of Asklepios's incubation sanctuary near Epidauros. The stone is one of several inscribed tablets at the site recording cases of marvelous healing credited to the god.[11]

One of the tablets, dating to the late fourth or the third century B.C. and entitled "Cures of Apollo and Asklepios," relates several miracles, including the story of a certain Hermon of Thasos, as follows. "He healed him from his state of blindness. Afterwards, however, the god made him blind again because he did not pay the thank-offering he owed. But when he came and slept here again, the god made him well."[12] Hermon reneges on his payment to the god, presumably one that he promised to give to Asklepios if the god should cure his blindness. As in the other stories of this sort, the god does not let it pass, but all ends well when Hermon returns, is healed once again, and, we assume, treats the god honestly on the second occasion.

It is uncertain whether the Greek fable of the deceitful sacrifice and the Greek legends of the neglected sacrifice or payment reflect different branches of the same narrative family or are similar but historically unrelated stories in Greek tradition. The narrative matter shared by both branches is not so complex as to force us to posit a common origin, but the fable and legend traditions may represent an ancient bifurcation of the type into a more comic branch and a more serious branch.

Lit. AT 778, *To Sacrifice a Giant Candle.* Pauli (1924) 2:329–330, nos. 304, 305. *EM* 7:1178–1183.

1. *EM* 7:1179, citing *Alphabetum narrationum,* no. 782. On the Cow and Calf tradition see also Tubach 1969, no. 1297.

2. *Rogar al santo hasta pasar el tranco.*

3. Chevalier 1983:87, no. 48, citing Mal Lara, *Filosofía vulgar* 1:289. On the Giant Candle tradition see Motif K231.3.1 *Sailor offers saint a candle as large as a mast;* Tubach 1969, no. 3975; and *EM* 7:1178–1180. A similar tale is AT 1553A*, *The Sailor's Promise.*

4. Perry 28; Hsr 28.

5. Apollodoros *Epit.* 3.9; Eustathios on Homer's *Il.* 11.20 (p. 827); and Frazer (1921) 2:179.

6. *Philogelos* 27. Cf. Thierfelder 1968:210–211.

7. Lucilius *AP* 11.171; see further Burnikel 1980:101–105. Another version is found in the Aesopic corpus (Perry 34, Hsr 34), and Horace (*Sat.* 2.3.142–157) relates a similar tale.

8. Apollodoros *Bibl.* 2.5.7 and 3.1.3–4. See also Diodorus Sic. 4.77.2; Pausanias 1.27.9; Lactantius Placidus *Theb.* 5.431–432.

9. For the former version see schol. on Euripides *Orestes* 995 and 998, and for the latter see Apollodoros *Epit.* 2.10–12 and 3.21–22; schol. on Euripides *Orestes* 811; schol. on Homer *Il.* 2.105. On the legend in general see Frazer (1921) 2:164–167; Gantz 1993:545–550.

10. Frazer (1921) 2:165–166.

11. On the site see Pausanias 2.26–28; Frazer (1898) 3:236–251, 5:570–579; LiDonnici 1995. For another text from the same inscription reflecting a different international story see "Gifts of the Little People."

12. *IG* IV², 1, no. 121–122 (XXII); Edelstein and Edelstein (1945) 1:225, no. 423 (XXII); LiDonnici 1995:100–101, no. B2. "because he did not pay the thank-offering [or doctor's fee] he owed" (τὰ ἴατρα οὐκ ἀπάγοντα).

Topsy-Turvy Land ✍ Mundus Inversus

There is a place where everything is opposite of the usual; for example, terrestrial animals fly (swim), while fish walk (fly), predators are pursued by prey, people cry when a child is born and laugh during funerals. Nonsensical things may happen there; for example, a donkey dances on a rope, cows fly into bird nests and sit on the eggs, on a hot summer day everything is frozen.

This lying tale, AT 1935, *Topsy-Turvy Land*, which may consist of a single idea or of several motifs arranged paratactically, describes a place where (or a time when) relationships are inverted or in which silly, nonsensical things take place. Its loose, motific structure is similar to that of narratives of comic utopias (see "Schlaraffenland"), and indeed motifs that belong conceptually to the idea of a topsy-turvy world are commonly found in descriptions of a comic utopia. The tone is likely to be whimsical, and the medium is often verse, although the idea of topsy-turvydom is found as well in noncomic contexts.

A version of the British ballad entitled "The World Turned Upside Down" relates that if buttercups sought out bees, if boats were on land and churches were at sea, if ponies rode people, if grass ate the cows, if mice chased cats, if mothers sold their babies to gypsies, if summer were spring and vice versa, then the world would be upside down.[1] In an English rhyme written down in 1882, the narrator urges his listener to come with him and he will take the listener to a place where the moon shines in the daytime and the sun at night, where donkeys bark and dogs bray, where the dumb speak and the blind fight.[2] These texts illustrate a number of common themes: inversions of place (boats and buildings in each other's territory), inversions of time (seasons or luminaries in each other's territory), inversions of the relationship of predator and prey (flowers go after bees, mice chase cats, grass eats cows), inversions of the relationship of master and servant (ponies ride people), etc.[3]

Texts may also include images of nonsense unrelated to inversion. Thus, in an anonymous anglophone nonsense verse, at midnight the setting sun is rising in the west, as the rapid rivers run slowly and the frog is in its downy nest, while a goat and a cow hop from bough to bough.[4] This humorous poem mixes inversions (various non-birds behaving like birds in trees) with self-contradictions (a sun that rises in the west at midnight, fast rivers that are slow).

Instances of topsy-turvydom are often found in visual illustration. So an English chapbook of the eighteenth century entitled "The World Turned Upside Down or the Folly of Man Exemplified in Twelve Comical Relations upon Un-

common Subjects, Illustrated with Twelve curious Cuts Truly adapted to each Story" features, as the title promises, woodcuts on the theme such as The Ox Turned Butcher (= ox butchers a man) and Sun, Moon, Stars and Earth Transposed (= earth above, sky below).[5]

Topsy-Turvy Land or Time in Antiquity

Two ancient authors mention in passing that tales of topsy-turvydom were popular with children, being related by nurses to children as bedtime stories and also circulating among the children themselves as playful talk. The second-century orator Aristides says that in order to lull children asleep nurses tell them of a certain sea that is sweet, of river horses, of the sea that flows into the river, and other such soporifics.[6] In the same century Tertullian, criticizing the cosmological views of another author, compares them to the nonsense of children (*puerilia dicibula*) according to which apples grow at sea and fishes grow on a tree.[7] In these brief allusions we find inversions of place (fruit growing in the sea and fishes growing on trees) and of natural phenomena (sweet-water sea that flows into a river). The mention of "river horses" (*hippous potamious*), the Greek term for hippopotami, probably refers both to the exotic Egyptian animal and also, because of the name, to an inversion of place (horses that live in water). Children doubtless found such narratives particularly accessible because of their simple motific structure and their silliness. Inverted relationships of power may also have had a special appeal to children since they themselves enjoyed little power.

If there is no direct evidence for the popularity of whimsical tales of topsy-turvydom among adults, except of course in their role as narrators of such tales to children, there is evidence for the currency of these ideas among adults in other expressive forms such as the visual arts, festivals, and rhetoric. Humorous pictures, mostly Hellenistic and Roman, show scenes of different animals drawn in carts by other animals: a fox by hens, a cricket by a pigeon, a dolphin by a snail. In other scenes a fish walks on land, a stork carries weapons, a mouse outweighs an elephant. Similar illustrations are known in Egyptian and Mesopotamian art.[8] Ancient Greek expressions for topsy-turviness, like ours, tend to emphasize spatial inversion, such as "to make the higher lower and the lower higher."[9]

In the Kronia, an old festival of the god Kronos that for the Athenians fell in the month Hekatombaion, slaves enjoyed the privilege of dining with their masters, an occasion that Plutarch describes as boisterous.[10] But the festival seems to have involved more a suspension of the usual categories rather than an inversion of them, that is, a state of affairs halfway between right side up and upside down. Compare Vergil's eighth *Eclogue*, discussed below, in which a normal state of affairs is followed by a state in which the established categories have no meaning (e.g., predator and prey drink together), which in turn is succeeded by a state in which everything is completely topsy-turvy (e.g., prey pursues predator). Answering to the Greek Kronia was the Roman Saturnalia and other, similar festivals.[11]

The paroemiologist Otto Crusius saw indirect evidence for topsy-turvydom in ancient *adynata*, or proverbial expressions for impossibility, futility, and foolishness, which he contends presuppose comic tales and lying tales of a topsy-

turvy land. Taken together, Crusius suggests, they portray a merrily inverted world. Whoever wants to go to there "rides a doe as a horse" and slips through a door that is as small as "the eye of a needle" or as "a finger ring." There he sees marvelous things. "Clouds of dust come from over the sea," "rivers flow up the mountains," "the mountains give birth to a mouse," "wolves fly through the air," "the donkey plays the lyre," "the cart draws the ox," "the wolf keeps watch over the sheep," "the doe overpowers the lion," "the crab runs faster than the hare," "the lion lets itself be sheared," "frogs drink wine," and so on. The inhabitants of the land are amazingly odd, for "they weep for a stranger's corpse," "braid ropes out of sand," "shear the donkey," "milk the buck," "use their plow as a hunting spear," "carry water in a sieve," "flay an animal before they have slaughtered it," and so on.[12]

Crusius's argument seems to me overconfident. Except for the material from Aristides, discussed earlier, it is impossible to know whether any of these images once were elements of old narratives about a topsy-turvy land, though certainly most of them would be at home in such a narrative. In any case, since whimsical ideas of the sort that appear in *Topsy-Turvy Land* were familiar to adults from children's tales as well as from proverbs, pictures, and festivals, it is likely that they circulated also in the form of entertaining tales or songs for adults. Unfortunately these kinds of expression are not commonly recorded by ancient authors.

We do have however many texts of adults' employing ideas of topsy-turvy-dom in a more serious spirit. These instances all concern some form of cosmic disorder, (1) representing the proposition that, since the old rules or conditions do not seem to apply any more, the whole cosmos is becoming inverted, or (2) illustrating a willful interference with the normal order of nature, or (3) expressing an *adynaton* "impossibility," and forcefully conveying the idea of "never" or "forever" in oaths and other asseverations. For convenience I refer to these three usages respectively as "change of rules," "interference," and "forever/never."

Change of Rules

The motif of rivers running backward, which Aristides mentions as a motif of topsy-turvy tales told to children, is the most frequently employed image of cosmic inversion in classical authors.[13] In Euripides' *Medeia* when Medeia laments the fact that her husband Jason has broken the sacred vow of marriage he made to her, the chorus sings in a famous strophe:

> The waters of the holy rivers are running uphill, and
> The order of things and all else is inverted.
> Men devise deceits, and their vows in the name of the
> gods can no longer be relied upon.[14]

The same imagery can be employed to illustrate the use of interference, as in Ovid's description of a certain old witch, Dipsas:

> She knows the magic arts and Aeaean charms, and
> By her art she turns the fluid waters back to their source.[15]

The earliest attestation of change of rules in classical literature is a fragment of an iambic poem by Archilochos that apparently refers to an eclipse of the sun that occurred in 648 B.C. After Olympian Zeus has made night out of noon by hiding the sun (the poet says), nothing is impossible, and everything is believable. No one should marvel if terrestrial animals trade their pasture with dolphins and come to love the waves more than the hills.[16]

An elaborate instance of this kind of rhetoric is found in a story in the historian Herodotos relating how the Spartans, fearing the growing strength of Athens, proposed to check it by installing Hippias as a tyrant. Sparta's proposed support of tyranny surprised her allies, provoking a certain Sosiklees of Corinth to exclaim: "Surely the sky will be beneath the earth, and the earth will be in the air above the sky; humans will have their dwelling place in the sea, and fishes will have theirs where humans used to dwell now that you Spartans are preparing to abolish democratic governments and introduce tyrannies into cities."[17] Here inversions of place of exactly the same kind as those familiar from tales of *Topsy-Turvy Land* serve to illustrate the speaker's sentiment that the Spartans' proposal, being the opposite of their usual policy, is so contrary to the expected order of things that it will certainly be followed presently by major instances of cosmic inversion.

Similar in spirit is a seriocomic anecdote concerning Diogenes of Sinope. The cynic philosopher was asked how he would prefer to be buried. "Face down," he responded. "Why so?" asked his interrogator. "Because presently everything that is down is going to be up," he answered, referring to the fact that the Macedonians were now prevailing, having gone from being a lowly nation to a lofty one.[18] Diogenes speaks as though the whole world has been turned upside down; accordingly, he wishes to be buried upside down so that when the world is again right-side up, as he expects it will be, he will then be right-side up along with it.

Both Diogenes and Sosiklees draw upon the imagery of inversion of place to convey their distaste for a present or imminent feature of the world, classifying it as contrary to nature. Sosiklees speaks as though he glimpses the first signs of a cosmic upheaval and wishes to head it off, whereas for Diogenes, as one might expect in a cynic, the world has already been overturned, and he is merely waiting for it to be set aright again.

Curiously, several local traditions in nineteenth-century England told how this or that man arranged to be buried, not simply face down, but actually perpendicular and head downward, either because he regarded the world as having turned topsy-turvy and wanted to be right at last, or because he believed that the world would turn over on the Day of Judgment, whereupon he would be in the right position. One such person, a Major Peter Labellière, seems actually to have been so buried in the year 1800. The tradition has been investigated by folklorist Herbert Halpert, who concludes that the English story derives ultimately from the anecdote concerning Diogenes. An intermediary between the story of the cynic philosopher and the fate of the eccentric major was evidently a passage in Jonathan Swift's *Gulliver's Travels*, presumably inspired by the Greek anecdote, in which it is reported that the Lilliputians bury their dead with their heads downward in the belief that in eleven thousand moons they will rise again, at which time the earth will turn upside down so that they themselves will be standing on their feet.[19] But the basic story is found in oral

circulation. Hodja Nasreddin, a Muslim comic figure, grew old and instructed his friends to bury him upside down. When they asked him why, he explained: "Since the world will turn upside down on Judgment Day, I will be in the right position."[20]

In fact persons were sometimes crucified head downward in Rome, and a notion of cosmic inversion expressly underlies the request of the apostle Peter in the apocryphal Acts of Peter to be so crucified, for Peter explains that, according to Christ, one must make the right to be like the left, the bottom to be like the top, and the aft to be like the fore, in order to recognize the Kingdom.[21] Like Diogenes, Peter dislikes the contemporary order and anticipates an imminent shift, but for different reasons. For the philosopher inversion has a negative value, in this case signifying political disorder, but for the apostle it possesses an ironically positive value, expressing as it does a spiritual revolution.

We find similar usage in Roman tradition. A real-life experience that in some ways parallels the legendary experience of Medeia prompts Ovid in his exile to say that the rivers will flow back to their source, the sun will travel backward, the earth will bear the stars, men will plough the sky, water will produce fire, and fire will produce water. Everything will be inverted, everything that the poet once deemed impossible will soon take place. He makes this prophecy because (he says) he has been deceived by the very man from whom he had expected support.[22] Another character who has been deceived in his expectations is the unhappy lover Damon, since the woman he was going to wed married another. After this treachery and this mismatch, what may lovers not expect? Griffins will mate with mares, and presently timid deer will join the hounds in drinking. Let the wolf flee the sheep, let oaks bear apples, let the alder bloom with narcissus, let tamarisks produce amber, let owls contend with swans, let a shepherd be an Orpheus.[23] Here the Roman poet presents a gradation of things moving from normalcy to a leveling of relationships (as in Isaiah's famous vision of peace among the animals) to their inversion.[24] Thus, unnatural matches such as a comradeship between predator and prey, reflecting Damon's view of his lover's marriage as a mismatch, culminate in cosmic inversions of nature in which inter alia prey pursues predator.

Interference

The use of interference is found in association with witchcraft, as in the passage quoted above about Dipsas the witch, and in mythological contexts. It appears first in Homer's *Odyssey*, where the god Helios was outraged that Odysseus's men had slaughtered some of his cattle, which he said he delighted in seeing as he crossed the sky. So he threatened Zeus and the other gods, saying that if he was not compensated, he would go down to Hades' realm and shine among the dead. Zeus told him to continue to shine for immortals and for mortals on the earth: Zeus would soon strike the offenders' ship with a thunderbolt in the midst of the sea.[25] Here the threat of a willful inversion of cosmic order is averted by placating the threatener.

Similarly in Mesopotamian mythological literature a goddess sometimes threatens another deity with cosmic disruption if she does not get what she wants. So in the *Epic of Gilgamesh* Ishtar said she would raise up the dead, who

would then outnumber the living, if Anu did not give her the Bull of Heaven in order that she might strike down Gilgamesh.[26] Like Helios, the goddess got her way.[27] One occasion when all cosmic order really did break down for a while and natural categories became confused was the Great Deluge. Ovid portrays the worldwide flood as a topsy-turvy world: a man now rowed his boat where once he had plowed, another snatched fish from the top of an elm tree, there were seals where there used to be goats, a wolf swam in the water among the sheep.[28]

Forever/Never

The order of the cosmos normally implied stability and unchangeableness. If there was anything that one could rely upon, it was the order of reality. So in a third application of topsy-turvy imagery, the theme of forever/never, one might swear an oath that such and such would be the case so long as the earth should abide.[29] According to Herodotos the Athenians once said that so long as the sun should travel the same course as it now traveled, they would never come to terms with Persia.[30] In an *Eclogue* of Vergil the shepherd Tityrus expresses his adoration for a certain youth by saying that the stags will sooner graze in the air, the sea will sooner deposit its fish to live on the shore, and the Parthians and Germans will sooner exchange their countries with each other, than that the image of that youth will fade from his heart.[31] These conditions are all vivid formulas for time, denoting either "forever" or "never," like the colloquial American *adynaton* "till hell freezes over."[32]

The idea of a topsy-turvy place or time, of a whimsically nonsensical world or of a gravely disordered world, was clearly familiar to Greeks and Romans, young and old.[33] It served the poet, the philosopher, and the public speaker with a vivid rhetoric of order and disorder, of stability and instability. It could give delight, not only in the form of silly tales about a bizarre, nonexistent land, but also in the guise of ethnography, as when Herodotos presents the Egyptians as a kind of topsy-turvy people whose strange customs are the opposite of those of all the rest of mankind, or when Athenian tradition characterizes Amazonian society as the inverse of the Athenian order.[34]

Lit. AT 1935, *Topsy-Turvy Land.* Crusius 1889:38–40. Wendeler 1905:158–164. Bolte 1907:425–432. Wienert 1925:44–46. Coon 1928. Luria 1929. BP 3:254–256, 4:119–120. Dutoit 1936. Curtius 1938:151–158. Ackermann 1944. Haavio 1959. Cocchiara 1963. Smith 1969–70. Kenner 1970. Halpert 1976. Babcock 1978. Rooth 1983:22–34, 123–124. Rammel 1990.

1. Rammel 1990:85.
2. Rammel 1990:82.
3. For a story based upon an inversion of the usual relationship of predator and prey see "Battles of the Pygmies and the Cranes."
4. Rammel 1990:84.
5. Ashton 1882:265–272. See further Wendeler 1905:158–164; Bolte 1907:425–432; Odenius 1954; Grant 1972; Kunzle 1978.
6. *Orations* 48 (2:475–476 Dindorf) = BP 4:44, no. 11. See Dutoit 1936:94.

7. *Adversus Valentianos* 20 = Migne, *Patrologia Lat.* 2.612 = BP 4:46, no. 27.

8. Brunner-Traut 1959; Kenner 1970.

9. Herodotos 3.3.3; Aristophanes *Lysistrata* 772–773, on which see Henderson (1987:168). But Theokritos (1.134) speaks simply of everything becoming different.

10. Plutarch 1098b; Parke 1977:29–30.

11. Kenner 1970:82–95; Shoshan 1993:45. Cf. Auffarth 1991; Shoshan 1993:40–51; Burke 1994:178–204.

12. Crusius 1889:38–39; cf. Kenner 1970:63–64.

13. For additional references see Dutoit 1936:16–18, 168; Page 1952:103; Scheiber 1973:356–358 = Scheiber 1985:294–296. A verse in Psalms in which the Jordan River turns backward (114:3 = *Septuagint* 113:3) resembles the classical image formally but not functionally, since it exemplifies not cosmic inversion but rather how nature rejoices at the exodus of the Israelites from Egypt, and welcomes their passage.

14. Vv. 410–413.

15. *Amores* 1.8.5–6.

16. Archilochos fr. 122. See Dutoit 1936:5–8. Cf. Euripides fr. 688 Nauck; Dutoit 1936:18.

17. Herodotos 5.92.1.

18. Diogenes Laertios 6.31–32; cf. Sayre 1938:82.

19. *Gulliver's Travels*, part 1, chap. 6. Halpert 1976.

20. Başgöz and Boratav 1998:64, no. 97.

21. Crucifixion head downward in Rome: Seneca *De Consolatione ad Marciam* 20. Peter's crucifixion: Acts of Peter 37–38; Smith 1969–1970.

22. *Tristia* 1.8.1–10.

23. Vergil *Eclogue* 8.17–60; cf. Theokritos *Id.* 1.132–136.

24. Isa. 11:6–9 and 65:25.

25. *Od.* 12.374–388.

26. 6.3.

27. For a rendering see Dalley 1989:80. The same threat is made by Ishtar in *The Descent of Ishtar to the Underworld* and by Ereshkigal in *Nergal and Ereshkigal* (Dalley 1989:155, 173). Notice also an anecdote about Aesop recounted in the *Life of Aesop*. When someone posed the problem, "What would cause the most confusion among human beings?" Aesop replied: "For the dead to arise and ask for their property back" (*Vita Aesopi* 47).

28. *Met.* 1.291–310.

29. Dionysios of Halicarnassus 6.95; Herodotos 4.201.2. Cf. Canter 1930:38–39.

30. 8.143.2.

31. 1.59–64. See Dutoit 1936:67–71.

32. Cf. Taylor 1948–49.

33. Many more classical passages are gathered by Coon 1928, who examines the reversal of nature as a rhetorical figure, and Canter 1930 and Dutoit 1936, who consider *adynata* in ancient poetry. See also Kenner 1970, who also deals at length with inversion of gender in story and in reality, and Manzo 1988.

34. Egyptians: Herodotos 2.35–37. Amazons: Tyrrell 1984:40–63.

Tree Trunks Laid Crosswise ᪥ Beam Carried Crosswise

One or more fools struggle with the problem of conveying a beam of wood through a doorway or gateway, which they attempt to do crosswise.

This is AT 1248, *Tree-Trunks Laid Crosswise of the Sledge.*

In an English tale a number of workmen were repairing the roof of the Priory Church in Bridlington, East Riding. Having brought to its western entrance a long beam of timber that had to be taken into the church in order to be hoisted up to the roof, they discovered that the length of the beam was greater than the width of the doorway. While the workmen considered solutions, such as to cut the beam in two, one of them noticed a jackdaw, which was building a nest, fly

into one of the crevices of the steeple with the end of a long straw in its mouth. He exclaimed that the bird took the straw in endwise rather than sideways, and his mates, struck with inspiration, thereupon turned the beam endwise, and got it into the church without difficulty.[1]

In a Danish text collected in the nineteenth century a man borrowed a horse and rode to Tisted, where he bought a twelve-foot piece of timber for an oar for his boat. Having no way to transport it he wanted to ride home with it. Placing it in front of him on the horse, he started to ride out the merchant's gate, which was not wide enough, so that the timber met the gate. Then the merchant's hired hand said: "No, that's not the way you should do it. You should turn the end toward it (*vende enden til*)." Thinking the fellow had said he should run at it (*rende til*), he had his horse dash for the gate, knocking himself off.[2]

A Greek Proverb

Crusius suggests that the Greek proverb "the man carrying the beam" refers to this tale.[3] Aristotle employs "the man carrying the beam" in the course of a discussion about the need for variation in effective oral delivery: "Unless the speaker varies such expressions in his delivery, he becomes 'the man carrying the beam.' "[4] Crusius's suggestion is supported by the Byzantine scholar Photios, who lists several proverbs that refer to persons who keep doing the same thing but accomplish nothing, among them "the man carrying the beam."[5] Photios's testimony that the proverb signifies repeated ineffective behavior is consistent with the image of a fool trying again and again to carry a beam crosswise through a doorway. On this interpretation Aristotle employs the proverb to convey the idea that unvaried repetition produces monotony.

Other interpretations of the proverb have also been offered. The favorite explanation among English-language commentators is that the expression refers to stiffness.[6] For example, Cope says that it means "stiff and awkward, like one that has 'swallowed a poker,' as *our* proverb has it."[7] On this interpretation the image in the proverb is of the stiff and ungraceful demeanor of a man carrying a heavy or lengthy beam, and Aristotle therefore employs it to convey the idea of stiffness in delivery. This image, however, is unrelated to the problem of repetition, with which Aristotle concerns himself in the passage, and is entirely inconsistent with Photios's statement that "the man carrying the beam" is applied to repetitive, ineffectual behavior.

Killeen, who finds fault with this last explanation for making no obvious reference to repetition, cleverly proposes that the proverbial phrase alludes rather to a particular anecdote concerning Diogenes the Cynic.[8] When a man accidentally struck the philosopher with a beam and then said, "Watch out!" Diogenes replied: "Why, are you going to hit me again?"[9] The trouble with this explanation is that the proverb should apply, as Killeen himself says, to "tiresome or pointless repetition," which, however, is not the theme of the anecdote about Diogenes. Although the anecdote does contain the idea of repetition, it is not the same sort of repetition as Aristotle is addressing. Nor does the anecdote illustrate ineffectual behavior, which according to Photios is the point of the proverb.

Crusius's understanding of the proverb, which has been overlooked by com-

mentators on Aristotle, is the only one that makes a good fit with the content of the proverb itself, the context in which Aristotle uses it, and the statement that Photios makes about it.

Lit. (AT 1248, *Tree-Trunks Laid Crosswise of the Sledge.*) Crusius 1889:40. BP 3:297–305, 4:117. Christensen 1939:214. Dvořák 1978, no. 2135. Ashliman, type 1248. EM 8:411–413.

1. Briggs (1970) A2:24–25. This is also the form the tale takes in Germany, where it is said to be quite common (Christensen 1939:214).
2. Christensen 1939:156–157, no. 72. The basic motif also occurs within a larger tale, AT 801, *Master Pfriem*, where it is one of several unusual sights that the protagonist sees in the other world (Clouston 1888:117–118; BP 3:297–305). This more complex tradition goes back at least as far as a Greek legend of ca. A.D. 800, in which St. Arsenios had a vision of, among other strange sights, two men on horseback who were holding a beam crosswise and trying in vain to pass through a doorway (*Acta Sanctorum* Julii 4, 626 E, cap. 3.19, cited by BP 3:302); see further *EM* 1:827–828 and "Carrying Water in a Sieve."
3. Crusius 1889:40 (ὁ τὴν δοκὸν φέρων).
4. *Rhetoric* 3.12.3 = 1413b28.
5. *CPG* 1:168.
6. Killeen 1971:186.
7. Cope 1877:149; so also LSJ.
8. Killeen 1971:186–187.
9. Diogenes Laertios 6.41. Cicero (*De Oratore* 2.69.279) tells the same anecdote of Cato, except that the man is carrying a box (*arca*) rather than a beam; see further McCartney 1931:201.

Trespasser's Defense 🌿 The Lokrians' Oath

Two men (parties) dispute the ownership of a piece of land, each claiming it as his (their) own. The dispute sometimes comes before a judge. One man declares that he will swear that the land is his (theirs). Secretly putting some soil from his own house (property, village) in his shoes (boots) and sometimes also a ladle (comb) under his hat, he proceeds to the other's land where he swears that he is standing on his own soil, calling the Creator (Judge) above him as witness. The perjurer wins the dispute, but he usually suffers thereafter a punishment of supernatural or human origin.

This scheme summarizes one of the principal forms taken by AT 1590, *The Trespasser's Defense*, a story found in many parts of Europe and in lands influenced by Europeans. When the perjurer conceals something under his hat, he does so in order to pun on its name, such as German *Schöpfer* "scoop, ladle" but also "creator," and *Richter*, which in folk speech can mean "comb" (from its etymological signification of "straightener"), though it normally means "judge."[1] The story is told regularly as a legend, that is, as an alleged historical occurrence situated in time and space and attributed to named disputants, rather than as a folktale.

Thus, according to a narrative collected in Sweden, a boundary dispute once arose between the inhabitants of Suntak and those of Valstad. A farmer at Valstad, insisting that their parish extended to Korsli, said he was willing to take an oath at the disputed boundary. After placing some soil from a graveyard at Valstad in his shoes, he swore that he was standing on the soil of his own

parish. But then he sank into the ground. In the 1860s a stone was said to have marked the place.[2]

According to a German tradition, the inhabitants of Neumarkt and the inhabitants of Greith once disputed the possession of a beautiful meadow on Mount Schinder, which lay between the two communities. Since they were unable to agree, the judge at Neumarkt had to decide to whom it belonged. He invited representatives of both parties to meet on the mountain, having declared that the matter would be determined by the swearing of an oath. Two citizens of Neumarkt were prepared to offer the required oath. One said: "The meadow belongs to us as truly as there is a true Creator (*Schöpfer*) above me!" The second swore: "I stand upon my own soil as truly as the ground belongs to us!" Inasmuch as the citizens of Greith were unwilling to swear a similar oath, the judge awarded the disputed meadow to Neumarkt. But an elderly citizen of Greith was so furious that he shouted: "You can have the meadow, but as truly as you have sworn a false oath, so truly will the grass no longer grow where you stand." The place came to be called Oath Meadow, and in fact no grass did grow there because the two men of Neumarkt were really rascals. For the first man had hidden a soup ladle (*Suppenschöpfer*) under his hat, and the second had put soil from his own garden in his shoes. But the judge was the biggest rascal of all, since he was party to the deception, and so his punishment was the most severe. At his death some years later a black figure rushed howling through the air bearing the deceased judge and disappeared into the Wild Hole, which was a gateway to Hell.[3]

The earliest known text of the story is generally acknowledged to be a passage in the Latin *Vita* of St. Egwin, an English bishop who died in 717. After his death, god deigned to work many miracles. A farmer appropriated part of St. Egwin's land, and when the judges ordained that on a certain day the farmer was to come and swear that the land was his own, the man took soil from his own house and filled his shoes with it in order to be able to swear safely that he was standing upon his own soil. But when he stretched out his hand to swear upon the relics of St. Egwin, the sickle he was carrying in his hand struck his head, so that he fell dead to the ground, losing both life and land.[4]

The Lokrians and the Sikels

But the central motifs of the legend if not the legend itself occur already in antiquity. The Greek historian Polybios relates that when the Lokrians first entered the land of the Sikels, the inhabitants received them in fear. So the Lokrians made an agreement with the Sikels, swearing to treat them as friends and to share the land with them so long as they, the Lokrians, trod on this earth and bore their heads upon their shoulders. But before the Lokrians swore this oath they had placed some earth onto the soles of their sandals and had concealed some heads of garlic on their shoulders, and after the oath they removed the earth from their sandals and threw away the heads of garlic. Soon thereafter, when they had the opportunity, they drove the Sikels from the land.[5]

With minor differences the same story is told by Polyainos of Macedon in his collection of military stratagems.[6] According to this author, the Lokrians attacked and massacred the Sikels the day after they swore their deceptive oath.

The Lokrian legend and the modern legend are parallel, though not quite in the same way. (1) In the modern legend two parties dispute the ownership of a piece of land (in the ancient legend two parties occupy the same piece of land, and one party fears the other will take the land). (2) To settle the dispute one party declares it will swear an oath on the boundary (to allay the other's fears one party says it will swear an oath of friendship). (3) But the perjurers secretly conceal some of their own soil in their shoes and a ladle (comb) under their hats (the perjurers secretly conceal soil in their sandals and heads of garlic on their shoulders), and (4) swear an oath at the boundary that they are standing upon their own soil, etc. (swear an oath on the land that so long as they walk on this soil and bear these heads on their shoulders they will be peaceful neighbors). (5) The perjurers thereby succeed dishonestly in gaining the land for themselves (the perjurers, thereby putting the other party off guard, drive them out and gain the land for themselves).

In the ancient Greek legend the dispute over land takes place between natives and newcomers rather than between neighboring villagers, and initially it is somewhat covert. Dissembling their true intent, the newcomers swear a deceptive oath saying, not that they already are the rightful owners of the land, but that they will share it in good faith. The false oath leads to the same outcome as does its modern counterpart, namely, the acquisition of the land in question.

Polybios says that the account of these events comes from Lokrian oral tradition. Presumably the Lokrians viewed the deceit as an instance of the cleverness rather than of the villainy of their ancestors, for unlike the deceitful oath takers in the modern legend the Lokrians do not suffer for their perjury.[7] Indeed, the Lokrians seemed to relish the memory of their trick, for Polybios says everyone knew the story.

The more or less parallel structures of the Lokrian and the modern international legend imply a close affinity. The peculiarities of the ancient legend suggests that it is an adaptation of the international story to established local tradition, such as the incursion of the Lokrians into Sikel territory; alternatively, it could be a developmentally earlier form of *The Trespasser's Defense*. The Lokrian text, as we have it, dwells on the tension between natives and immigrants, whereas most of the modern texts focus upon the insecurity that natives feel concerning boundaries between towns or between individual landholdings, a concern that certainly was present in the Greco-Roman world as well.

Lit. (AT 1590, *The Trespasser's Defense*.) Feilberg (1886–1914) 1:234, s.v. *ed*; 2:45b, s.v. *jord*. Wesselski 1920:96–98. Pfleger 1938. Orend 1958. Liungman 1961:314. Kretzenbacher 1976:125–139. *EM* 3:1142–1150. Ashliman, type 1590.

1. *EM* 3:1142.
2. Kvideland and Sehmsdorf 1988:333.
3. Kretzenbacher 1976:128–129.
4. Kretzenbacher 1976:129–130; *EM* 3:1142.
5. Polybios *Histories* 12.6.
6. *Strategemata* 6.22.

7. The perjurer is not always punished in the modern texts (*EM* 3:1144). Like the Lokrians, he is sometimes regarded as clever rather than villainous.

Twins or Blood Brothers ⬧ Menaechmi

Two twin brothers are born so similar in appearance that no one can tell them apart. Eventually one of them sets out into the world, and before departing he leaves his twin a life token that will serve to indicate whether he is alive or dead (e.g., a plant that will wither or a knife that will rust if he is dead or in trouble). He journeys far, accompanied by animals or weapons with magical properties, until he reaches a foreign city where he wins the hand of the princess and weds her. Shortly after their marriage, a witch, sometimes in the form of an attractive young woman, draws the young prince away from his wife, despite her protests, and entices him into her dwelling. Before he can enjoy her company, she holds him captive, bewitches him, or kills him.

The second twin, who has remained at home, sets out to look for the first twin because the life token indicates that the first twin is in trouble (or for some other reason such as that the first twin has been gone for a long time). Like the first twin, he possesses animals and weapons with special properties. The second twin eventually arrives at the same town, and everyone he meets, including his brother's wife, mistakes him for the first twin. He plays the role, since he hopes thereby to learn something of the fate of his brother. He spends the night with the princess in her bed, laying a sword between them. Despite her protests the second twin departs and encounters the same witch, who approaches him in the same way as she approached his brother before him. More suspicious than he, however, the second twin overcomes the witch, forces her to release (disenchant, revive) the first twin, and then disposes of her. The two twins are reunited and return together happily to the palace.[1]

This complex folktale is AT 303, *The Twins or Blood-Brothers*, often called *The Two Brothers*.[2] It is one of the most frequently told of all international tales. Over two thousand texts have been collected.[3]

The Twins is a bipartite tale with two principal characters, the first of whom enjoys a mixture of success and failure, and the second of whom repeats the same tasks with unmixed success: Twin I goes abroad, wins a wife, and gets into trouble, whereafter Twin II goes to the same city, wins the same woman, eludes the same trouble, and rescues his brother. Since Twin II is nearly identical with Twin I, it is almost as though the tale concerned a single hero who got a second chance at a failed task.

The texts fall into two broad groups, those in which Twin I is said briefly to win his princess in a tournament or the like, and those in which an entire, additional tale is inserted, according to which Twin I wins his bride by rescuing her from a dragon. When it appears, the inserted tale is AT 300, *The Dragon Slayer*, which also circulates as a folktale in its own right (see "Dragon Slayer"). Since the ancient analogue reflects the former, less elaborate redaction of the tale, which makes up about one-third of the known texts, I focus upon it.[4]

According to a Chilean tale a poor fisherman once caught a lovely colored

fish, and a voice from above instructed him to give the water in which he cleaned it to his mare, his dog, and his wife. He did so, after which the bitch bore twin puppies, the woman bore two sons, and the mare bore identical colts. When the boys were eighteen years old, the elder wished to go a-wandering. Telling his brother that if a particular olive tree should wither, he would have found work, he set out on a mare with one of the dogs and a sword. He came to the palace of a king, who invited him in, fetched his two daughters, and let him choose one. He selected the elder, and they wed. Some months later he asked him wife about a green meadow he saw in the distance, but his wife begged him not to go there, for he would never come back. But he rode there and found an old crone with twelve strands of hair. She told him to tie up his animals with the twelve strands of hair and come into the house. He did so, but once inside she threw a handful of dust at him, whereupon he turned to stone, and she did the same to his mare and dog.

The next day the other brother noticed that the olive tree had withered, so that the first brother must have found work. He set out to look for him. Taking the same road and coming to the same palace, he was taken by the same princess for her husband. She gave him a warm welcome, and he realized that she must be his brother's wife. That night he placed a sword between them in bed. The next morning he asked her about the same meadow, and the princess explained again that it was a place from which one did not return. Concluding that his brother must have gone there, he set out and encountered the same old crone, who gave him two strands of hair to tie up his horse and dog. But the lad, who was no fool, merely concealed the strands of hair, entered the house, and recognized his petrified brother. He forced the old woman to disenchant his brother and the animals, and then told the dogs to tear the old woman to pieces, which they did. As the youths were returning to the palace, the second brother explained that he had slept with the first brother's wife. The married brother killed his twin before he could say any more, but upon learning from his wife that they had slept together chastely, he restored him to life. The second brother wed the other princess, and both brothers became rich and powerful men.[5]

The Menaechmi Twins

The story of the Menaechmi twins is known from Plautus's comedy *Menaechmi*, which is assumed in turn to be an adaptation of a Greek original that is no longer extant. The title and author of the original play are unknown.[6]

The beginning of the story is narrated in the prologue, according to which twin brothers, Menaechmus and Sosicles, were born to a merchant and his wife in Syracuse. Neither their mother nor their wet nurse could tell the boys apart. One day Menaechmus went with his father on a voyage to Tarentum. Once there the lad wandered away from his father, and another merchant kidnapped him, taking him to Epidamnus, where the merchant reared him and in time procured for him a dowered wife. Menaechmus inherited the man's wealth and became a well-to-do advocate. As the drama begins, Menaechmus sneaks from his own house and his watchful wife to the house of the courtesan Erotium, where he makes arrangements for enjoying an afternoon of feasting

and sex with her, and then departs for the forum. But he presently encounters one difficulty after another, beginning with a stubborn client who detains him in court, all of which prevent his timely return to the house of the courtesan.

In the meantime, Menaechmus's brother Sosicles, who was long ago renamed Menaechmus after his lost twin, arrives in Epidamnus. He had set out with his slave some six years earlier in the hope of finding his brother or of determining that he had perished. Naturally, everyone whom Menaechmus II encounters in Epidamnus mistakes him for his twin. Menaechmus II astonishingly fails to perceive why the residents of Epidamnus should be mistaking him for someone else of the same name, and soon accepts the role they offer him, indeed plays it vigorously in order to gain access to Erotium's house. There he enjoys the feast and bed that were intended for Menaechmus I, who is being detained unhappily in court. Menaechmus I's comic troubles increase until finally he is rescued from them by Menaechmus II's slave, who reunites the exasperatingly naive twins by explaining to them who they are. The two brothers happily go off to celebrate, deciding to return together to Syracuse.

Now, the Greek writers of New Comedy got their plots in one of two ways. Most of them they made up themselves. The rest they adapted from traditional oral stories, primarily myths and heroic legends with their well-known gods and heroes, but also folktales, a fact that has been mostly overlooked in the scholarly literature. Naturally, they treated all borrowed stories comically, whether the originals were comic or not. Thus, Menander's *Dyskolos* shows an original if also essentially conventional comic plot with no parallel in folk narrative, whereas Plautus's *Amphitruo* is a burlesque treatment of a Greek myth, and his *Miles Gloriosus* is based upon an international comic folktale (see "Underground Passage to Paramour's House"). The story burlesqued in the *Amphitruo* is easily identified as a traditional story because it is familiar from Greek mythology, whereas the story underlying the *Miles Gloriosus* is not readily recognized, since it is a humble folktale rather than a narrative with supposedly historical characters and is not found elsewhere in ancient literature. It is recognizable as a traditional narrative only because of the evidence of international tradition.

There is no obvious analogue to the story of the Menaechmi twins in folk narrative. But there is an unobvious analogue, unobvious because the analogue shows the usual elements of the magic tale, or fairy tale, namely, princes and princesses, witches, magic helpers, magic objects, enchantment, and even death, whereas in Roman comedy we have merchants, farmers, professional men, courtesans, clever slaves, improbable coincidences, and comic troubles. If, however, we allow that the original Greek playwright had sufficient imagination to adapt a noncomic tale to a comic medium, then his starting point was surely a version of *The Two Brothers*, for it is a folktale about identical twins, and its basic story, shorn of fabulous elements, is essentially that of the play. (1) Identical twins are born. (2) One twin sets out on a journey, ending up at a distant town where (3) he weds a princess (dowered lady) and becomes a prince (wealthy advocate). One day, despite her protests, (4) he leaves her to go to the dwelling of a witch (courtesan), (5) whose company he is prevented from enjoying because of serious (comic) restraints. Meanwhile (6) the second twin sets out to find him dead or alive and (7) after a long journey arrives at the same

city. (8) Everyone there mistakes him for his twin, and (9) he exploits the role in order to gain access to the witch (courtesan). (10) When he goes to her dwelling, she approaches him in the same way as she approached his twin before him, but (11) he gets the best of her. (12) The second twin (second twin's helper) rescues the first twin, and (13) the two twins, happily reunited, return home together.

In short, the play is a magic tale without the magic, a folktale converted into a situation comedy. The comic possibilities that were latent in the confusion of the identical twins appealed to the original Greek playwright, such confusions being a favorite source of humor in late comedy, as the *Amphitruo* and the *Miles Gloriosus* illustrate. The tradition continued into Shakespeare, whose *Comedy of Errors* draws in turn upon Plautus's *Menaechmi*.

The parallelism of the *Menaechmi* and the folktale of *The Twins* was pointed out more than a century ago by Zielinski.[7] Although he knew only a single text of the folktale, he argued that the plot of the *Menaechmi* must have been adapted from just such a folktale, pointing out that the absence of fabulous motifs in later comedy need not have prevented the playwrights from borrowing plots from tales that were originally fabulous.[8] The same observation was made independently by Hansen, who was able to draw upon the full-scale study of over six hundred texts of *The Twins or Blood-Brothers* that had been published in the meantime by Ranke.[9]

Lit. (AT 303, *The Twins or Blood-Brothers*.) Zielinski 1886. Ranke 1934. Liungman 1961:49–53. Trenkner 1958:99–108. Hansen 1977a. *EM* 2:912–919. Scherf 1982: 456–463. Rubow 1984. Ashliman, type 303. Brockington 1995.

1. Ranke 1934:109–306.
2. Similarity of name has prompted many scholars to seek a connection between the tale and the ancient Egyptian *Story of Two Brothers* (see "Potiphar's Wife"), but in fact the two narratives have very little in common.
3. *EM* 2:912–914.
4. The figure derives from Ranke 1934:187.
5. Pino-Saavedra 1967:26–31, no. 5. The tale was collected in 1951 from Francisco Coronado.
6. For a recent survey of the basic issues see Gratwick 1993. He does not however discuss the oral analogues to the underlying story.
7. Zielinski 1886; revised and reprinted 1931:140–144.
8. The tale known to Zielinski was collected in Epirus in 1848 and first printed in the pioneering collection of modern Greek folktales published by J. G. von Hahn (1864) 1:166–173, no. 22. It appears in English translation in Megas 1970:37–42, no. 21.
9. Hansen 1977a. Ranke (1934) concluded on the basis of evidence available to him that the folktale probably arose in France in the fourteenth century. If the ancient parallel is accepted, the folktale must have been in circulation already by at least the fourth century B.C.

Underground Passage to Paramour's House 🦢 Miles Gloriosus

One man, A, has a beautiful wife, whom he may keep secluded (in a tower, under lock and key, etc.). Another man, B, desires her. Moving nearby, B secretly constructs an underground tunnel between his house and the woman's room (mov-

ing next door to A's dwelling, B secretly makes a hole in the party wall between his house and the woman's room, or there is a secret or little-used door in B's house that leads to A's house). By means of the secret passage, the woman visits her lover, B, in his house. B may display to A an object (shoe, jewelry, dagger, clock, furniture, utensil, animal, etc.) that has been smuggled from A's house through the passageway. Struck by the resemblance, A rushes home to verify that the object is still in his possession, and finds it in its proper place, since it has been returned in the meantime via the secret passage. Coming as an invited guest (or as an unexpected visitor) to B's house, A sees his own wife, who is represented to him as B's fiancée. A rushes home to confirm that his own wife is at home, which she is, having returned by means of the secret route. The husband may repeat this test until he convinces himself that his neighbor's fiancée is not his own wife. Finally, A participates in B's wedding ceremony, giving his wife away to B. The couple departs. Returning home and finding an empty house, A perceives that he has been duped.

This tale is AT 1419E, *Underground Passage to Paramour's House (Inclusa)*. It is known in the Orient and the Occident both from oral tradition and from literary adaptations. The tale is often called *Inclusa* after the Latin text in the famous collection *The Seven Sages of Rome*, different versions of which are known in most European languages.[1]

Some texts have a different ending according to which the newlyweds remain in the house and eject the husband. A is made drunk at the wedding ceremony, after which B cuts his hair or beard, dresses him in different clothing, and deposits him at a distant place. When A awakens, he believes he is someone else and goes his way. This episode is classified as AT 1419E*, *Husband Cannot Recognize Himself*.

In the tale of The Tanner and his Wife, from the 896th night of the *Thousand and One Nights*, a beautiful woman was married to a tanner but had an officer as her lover. After some time the officer bought a house near that of the woman and constructed an underground tunnel between the two residences. One day, upon her husband's return from a journey, the woman informed him that after a long absence her sister and her sister's husband had returned and were renting the neighboring house, that she and her sister looked exactly alike, and that he should go next door to see for himself. The husband did so and found his own wife sitting next to the officer. Astonished, he rushed back to his own house, where his wife sat at her work, having returned through the tunnel. The incident was repeated several times, until the man was no longer suspicious and accepted an invitation to join their meal. The husband drank himself into drunkenness and fell into a deep sleep, whereupon the officer cut his hair, dressed him as a Turk, and left him in a distant place. When he awoke he was confused, not knowing whether he was a Turk or Ahmed the tanner. Returning home he was put out of his house by his wife. So he hired an animal and journeyed to Ispahan, leaving his wife to the officer.[2]

In the story of *Inclusa*, found in the *Seven Sages of Rome*, a Hungarian knight once dreamed of a beautiful woman, who simultaneously dreamed of him. He set out to find the woman and after long travels came to Hungary, where at a window he saw the woman of his dream, and she also recognized him. She was the wife of a nobleman, who jealously kept her secluded in a tower, for which he always carried the keys. The newcomer now entered the service of the no-

bleman, presently rose in his favor, and was permitted to construct a house nearby, from which he had an underground passageway constructed to the room of the woman. He visited her in her room, and she gave him a costly ring that her husband once had given her. When on a later occasion the nobleman saw it he rushed to his wife and asked to see the ring; but the knight had taken the precaution of returning it. One day the knight informed the nobleman that his beloved had just arrived and that he must return to his own country. He requested the nobleman's presence one last time at his house. The nobleman arrived and was seated next to his own wife; confused and upset, he went back to the tower where he found his wife and concluded that, like rings, there were also beautiful women who looked alike. The knight hired a ship and told the nobleman he wished to return home with his beloved. The nobleman escorted the lovers out to sea, after which he found his tower empty.[3]

A tale in the collection of ribald novelle entitled *Les cent nouvelles nouvelles*, composed in France in the fifteenth century, contains a realization of the tale type that differs in interesting ways from these treatments, since there is no artificial passageway, and the lovers, surprised by the husband, must improvise their strategy. According to this tale, a certain widower lived in a fine house in the town of Valenciennes. On one side of his house there was a little postern door, and opposite this there lived a friend of his who had a young and pretty wife. The widower greatly desired his neighbor's wife, and in order to win her he first cultivated the friendship of his neighbor and then won the love of his wife. The two now awaited an opportunity to be together. One day the husband left on a journey, having instructed his wife to stay within doors; and she in turn informed the widower that their opportunity had come. That evening she entered by the postern door and was received in the master's bedroom, where they bathed and dined and drank wine. At this point the husband returned unexpectedly and knocked on the door of the widower's house. The couple quickly got into the bed, and the woman turned her face to the wall. When the neighbor was admitted into the room, he insisted on seeing the woman. The master of the house refused but allowed him to look at her backside. Upon doing so, the husband exclaimed that she so resembled his own wife that, if he were not certain that his own wife was at home, he would have said that this woman was she. They reprimanded him for his suspicions and insisted that he eat and drink what remained of the meal. When it was time to leave, the neighbor asked to leave by the postern door, but the widower replied that the key was lost and the lock was rusted. So he left by the front gate and reached his house by a long detour, while his wife exited through the postern door and was soon home. When the husband knocked at his own door, she did not at first let him in, accusing him of being someone else and then of only pretending to go on a journey in order to test her. He became very contrite, and after that day she frequently passed through the postern door without her husband's notice.[4]

The Underground Passage to Paramour's House is a lively, ribald novella in which a trickster devises the ruse of a secret passage from house to house in order to gain access to and eventually win another man's wife, who is kept in seclusion. Sometimes the woman is as much the trickster as her lover, or more so. The tale can be compared with *The Golden Ram*, in which the lover, faced

with a similar challenge, employs the ruse of a hollow container and gains access to the secluded princess by smuggling himself into her room inside of it. In both tales the woman herself is receptive to the hero's advances, so that his efforts are spent more on reaching her than on winning her over.

Once the lover has situated himself next door and devised a secret entry to the woman's room, the husband is startled to see in his neighbor's house a woman who appears to be his own wife. Usually the confrontation occurs by the design of the lover, who invites the husband over to meet his beloved, and sometimes it is preceded by the husband's noticing that his neighbor possesses a certain object that greatly resembles one in his own household, an experience that eventually helps to condition the husband to the idea that the world is full of such doubles.[5] But it can also happen that, as in the third text above, the husband just shows up unexpectedly, so that the confrontation takes place by accident and the lovers are forced to improvise a deceit on the spot.

The ultimate irony is attained in those texts that culminate in the marriage of the lovers, for by this time the husband is so convinced that his neighbor's fiancée is not his own wife that he even gives her away to the groom at the ceremony and wishes the new couple well. Less frequently the husband is deprived even of his own identity. After his neighbor persuades him that his wife is not his wife, he also induces him to believe that he is not even himself, so that in the end the duped husband loses his wife, his house, and his self.

Miles Gloriosus

The resemblance of Plautus's comedy, *Miles Gloriosus*, or *The Braggart Soldier*, to the international tale was perceived in the early nineteenth century and first studied at length toward the end of the century by Eduard Zarncke.[6] The *Miles Gloriosus*, first produced around 206 B.C., was based in turn upon a Greek play named *Alazon* (Braggart), which has not survived.[7]

Much of the story of the ancient comedy transpires before the dramatic action begins. In Athens a man named Pleusicles and a courtesan, Philocomasium, were in love. While Pleusicles was away on a mission, however, a soldier named Pyrgopolynices turned up, abducted Philocomasium, and brought her to Ephesus, where they lived together. The slave of the absent Pleusicles, Palaestrio, set out to inform his master of the abduction but was captured by pirates and given as a gift, as it turned out, to the same Pyrgopolynices who had abducted Philocomasium. She, for her part, loved Pleusicles and hated the soldier who had abducted her, and wished to be reunited with her lover. The clever slave Palaestrio managed to inform Pleusicles by letter of their whereabouts, so that Pleusicles came to Ephesus, where he lodged with a friend of his father's, Periplectomenus, a kindly old man who lived next door to the soldier. In order to allow the lovers to meet, the slave Palaestrio cut a hole in the party wall shared by the neighbor's house and the soldier's house, where the girl had a room of her own. The girl now came and went secretly between the two houses, though she was watched closely by the soldier's slave, Sceledrus.

As the play opens, the old neighbor and the clever slave discover that today, after the girl came next door to be with her lover, Sceledrus happened to see, though an opening in the roof, the two lovers kissing. Neighbor and slave form

a plan to convince Sceledrus he did not see what he saw: they will pretend that the girl's identical twin sister and her lover have just arrived from Athens and are lodging at the old man's house, and it was they whom the slave saw making love. They communicate their plan to the girl, who joins the conspiracy. She now returns through the passageway to her own house where she appears outside to Sceledrus to show him that she is in fact at home; then, reentering the house, she goes back through the passageway to the neighbor's house where she appears outside to Sceledrus in the guise of her twin sister Dicea; reentering the neighbor's house she returns through the passageway again to her own room, and the suspicious Sceledrus, going indoors, finds that she is there; she returns once again to the neighbor's house, where Sceledrus goes in and sees her in the guise of Dicea kissing her lover; and finally she goes back quickly to the soldier's house, where Sceledrus again sees her indoors. The clever slave Palaestrio finally convinces the dull-witted Sceledrus that the girl he saw was not Philocomasium but her sister, so that Sceledrus agrees to say nothing of what he saw.

Now Palaestrio forms a plan to help Pleusicles abduct Philocomasium: they will pretend that the old neighbor has a young, attractive wife who is greatly in love with the soldier. The clever slave borrows a ring from the old neighbor that he will represent as a love gift from the wife to the soldier, and two women are retained to play the roles of the wife and her maid. The clever slave gives the alleged token to the vain and lustful soldier, explaining that the woman next door desires him. Since the soldier decides he must rid himself of Philocomasium in order to bring a new woman into his house, the slave suggests that he allow Philocomasium to keep all her jewelry and other possessions and urge her to return home with her mother and twin sister, who have recently arrived in Ephesus. The soldier eagerly does so, giving her the clever slave as a gift. The girl and the clever slave take their leave of the soldier and depart for Athens with the lover, who is disguised as a sailor. The soldier now enters the house next door, expecting to meet his new lover, but instead he is set upon by the old neighbor and his slaves, who drag him outside and beat him. Learning that the girl and the apparent sailor were lovers and that they showed affection to each other once they were out of his sight, he perceives that he has been deceived.

As commonly happens in ancient comedy, the action that precedes the drama is narrated in the prologue and the action that is dramatized is situated outdoors.[8] Thus the scenes in which Philocomasium rushes back and forth from house to house, playing now herself and now her sister, are partly acted in front of the houses and partly reported as taking place indoors, whereas in the folktale they all take place indoors. These are predictable features in the adaptation of a narrative to the ancient comic stage.

No doubt another consequence of the adaptation was the casting of the woman as a courtesan rather than as a married woman, avoiding the problem of attributing in a play unseemly sexual behavior to a properly married woman. As a result, Philocomasium is not married to Pyrgopolynices, the soldier who abducted her from a brothel and kept her as his unwilling lover, nor at the end of the play does she wed Pleusicles, her Athenian lover, who merely abducts her back.

An unexpected change, however, is the way the playwright reassigns much

of the action that in the folktale is regularly associated with the lover and the husband; instead of assigning it to Pleusicles and Pyrgopolynices, Plautus gives it to two slaves, who act out the roles of trickster and dupe on their behalf. The clever slave Palaestrio takes most of the action that one would expect the lover Pleusicles to perform: he devises and carries out the plan to convince the dupe that there are in fact two women rather than one. And the dull-witted slave Sceledrus takes the role that one would have expected the soldier Pyrgopolynices to play: he is astonished at seeing a woman resembling Philocomasium in the neighbor's house and repeatedly checks for her presence at each house in order to confirm or allay his suspicions. When Palaestrio briefly anticipates duping also the soldier, we seem to have a glimpse of the ruse in a form closer to that of the traditional tale.[9]

This transference of roles from the actual adversaries to their representatives is not required by any convention of the ancient comic stage and is probably best explained as being a consequence of the playwright's desire to employ in his play a second ruse against the soldier. The second deception, in which a courtesan is hired to feign amorous interest in the soldier in order that he willingly give up his current lover, is more easily accommodated if the dupe is not in both cases the same man.[10] The latter trick is not a familiar element of *The Underground Passage to Paramour's House*.[11] The second ruse may have been introduced either by the original Greek playwright or by Plautus; if the latter, we may suppose he has drawn for his play upon two Greek models.[12]

I summarize the more important points of contact between the play and the oral tale. (1) Man A secludes his wife (lover), but (2) man B, who is in love with her, (3) moves in next door and (4) constructs a secret passageway between his house and her room, (5) by means of which the woman visits her lover. One day, (6) when the lovers are (unexpectedly) seen together in the neighbor's house, (7) they devise a plan to convince the witness that there are two women of identical appearance. (8) The woman is represented as being the neighbor's fiancée (lover), so that (9) the suspicious witness goes home to see whether the woman is there, and (10) he does find her there, (11) since she has returned via the secret passage. (12) After repeated inspections, he convinces himself that there are two such women. (13) Eventually A facilitates the woman's departure, (14) the lovers leave, and (15) A learns that he has been duped.

Although the conclusion of the play reflects the common conclusion of the oral tale in which the lovers quickly depart before their deception is discovered, it is possible that the play also preserves a hint of the tale *The Husband Cannot Recognize Himself*, an alternative ending found in some texts, especially, as it seems, in Greece.[13] We have seen this episode at the conclusion of the tale of The Tanner and his Wife, above, in which the tanner is made to believe he is a Turk. In an Albanian version of *Underground Passage* the original husband, a priest, is made drunk during the wedding feast, his beard is shaved off, ragged clothes are put on him, a pistol is placed in his belt, and he is dragged outside. When he awakens he finds his beard gone, discovers a fez on his head, ragged clothes on his body, and a pistol in his belt. When he sees five armed men pass-

ing by who inform him that they are robbers, he concludes that he is one, too.[14] Now, in the second act of the comedy, when the girl Philocomasium first adopts the identity of her twin sister, Dicea, she pretends not to recognize the slaves Sceledrus and Palaestrio. As a result they are uncertain who they are and wonder if they have been *transformed into someone else*.[15]

> *Scel.* You don't know us?
>
> *Phil.* Neither of you.
>
> *Scel.* Oh oh, I'm really afraid.
>
> *Pal.* Of what?
>
> *Scel.* That we have lost our identities somewhere (*ne nos nosmet perdiderimus uspiam*). This woman says she doesn't know either of us.
>
> *Pal.* I want to investigate this, Sceledrus, to see whether we are ourselves or somebody else. It may be that someone around here has changed us into other persons without our knowing it.

Here, where the two slaves briefly worry about who they are, the playwright has possibly borrowed a comic situation from *The Husband Cannot Recognize Himself* and adapted it to the present scene early in the play. If so, he must have been acquainted with more than one version of the oral tale, for the two endings of the tale—in which the lovers either depart or rob the husband of his identity—belong to different versions.

For another tale of a ruse by means of which a lover gains access to a secluded woman, see "Golden Ram," and for another tale in which a character does not know who he is, see "Person Does Not Know Himself."

Lit. AT 1419E, *Underground Passage to Paramour's House* (+ AT 1419E*, *Husband Cannot Recognize Himself*). Rehatsek 1880:77–81. Zarncke 1884. Clouston (1887) 2:212–228. Campbell 1907:cix–cxii. Rohde 1960:596 and note 4. Hilka 1917. Kuntze 1925. Krappe 1935. Trenkner 1958:131–133. Perry 1959:11. Small 1976.

1. For another such tale, *Vidua*, see "Matron of Ephesus."
2. Kuntze 1925:719–720.
3. Krappe 1935:213–215.
4. *The Hundred Stories*:21–25, first story.
5. Dawkins 1953:376–377.
6. Zarncke 1884.
7. Schaaf 1977:377. *Miles Gloriosus* vv. 86–87.
8. Narration in prologue: vv. 79–155.
9. Vv. 249–255.
10. Vv. 770 ff.
11. The deception resembles the action of a different folktale, AT 1359B, *Husband Meets the Paramour in the Wife's Place*, in which the husband awaits his wife's lover and beats him. In the present play, the apparent husband of the woman meets her would-be lover in the house where he has been led to believe she awaits him, and beats him. See Trenkner 1958:132.
12. Speculation on this question has a long history. For a discussion see Schaaf 1977.
13. In the entry for AT 1419E*, *Husband Cannot Recognize Himself*, Aarne-Thompson list nine texts, all from Greece.

14. Zarncke 1884:2, citing Gustav Meyer, *Albanische Märchen*, Archiv für Literaturgeschichte, vol. 12, Heft 1, pp. 92–148, no. 12.
15. Vv. 428–432.

Unfinished Tale ≋ "And Then I Woke Up"

The narrator of an "unfinished tale" begins relating an event and then, after arousing the interest of his (her) hearers, abruptly leaves off, uttering one or another exit line.

AT 2250, *Unfinished Tales*, is a structural classification, a catch-all category for unfinished tales of various kinds.

For example, a shepherd tried to pull his drowning sheep out of the water by the animal's tail, but the tail broke off. If the tail had not broken off, this tale would have been longer.[1] This is a version of AT 2251, *The Rabbit's Tail*. In another unfinished tale, a poor boy went to fetch wood during the winter. He was so cold that he thought of building a fire, and as he cleared the ground of snow he found a golden key. Thinking that if there was a key, there should also be a lock, he dug in the ground where he found an iron box. He hoped the key would fit, and finally found a small keyhole. He inserted the key and turned it once, and now we must wait until he has opened the box before we can learn what wonderful things were in it.[2] This text is an example of AT 2260, *The Golden Key*.

Each of these tales begins with a narrative introduction that contains an element of suspense, and concludes with a teasing exit formula. Both the introduction and the conclusion are traditional. A narrator setting out to relate such a tale never intends to tell a whole tale because no whole tale exists.

Unfinished tales of this kind are not found in ancient literature. There is, however, another kind of unfinished tale, which like these has a two-part structure consisting of an initial narrative that is interrupted or closed by a sudden exit formula, but differing from these types in that only the exit formula is traditional. A speaker begins a narrative consisting of any content whatever and then, wishing to discredit it for one reason or another, says: "And then I woke up"—in other words, abruptly claims that the story was merely a dream. The formula "And then I woke up" is a rhetorical device by means of which a speaker whose original intent might have been to relate a whole narrative about an allegedly true occurrence can not only spontaneously exit from the narration at whatever point but also deny the truth of what was said, contrary to his or her original framing of the narrative. This kind of tale can occur within other folktales. In the final episode of AT 1364, *The Blood-Brother's Wife*, a man narrates to his blood brother his erotic adventures with a particular woman. When he suddenly realizes that the woman of whom he speaks is his blood brother's wife, he says, "Just then I woke up," so that no one believes his story. This formula is found in oral stories from India to Europe.[3]

In an extension of this usage, a listener who wishes to mock as untruthful what a narrator is presenting as truthful can interject, "And then I woke up," as

though he were stating the narrator's next line. The event becomes thereby a kind of spontaneously cooperative tale between narrator and auditor. So in Greece today, when a speaker goes on extravagantly, a listener may say ironically, "And then I woke up."[4] The expression is employed similarly by speakers of German and of French.[5]

Dionysos, Herakles, and Xanthias

Precisely this interaction takes place in a conversation between Herakles, Dionysos, and Dionysos's slave Xanthias in Aristophanes' *Frogs*.[6] Dionysos boasts to Herakles that he recently served aboard ship.

> Herakles: And did you engage in battle at sea?
> Dionysos: Yes, indeed. We sank twelve or thirteen of the enemy's ships.
> Herakles: *You* two?
> Dionysos: Yes, by Apollo.
> Xanthias: And then I woke up.

Here the god Dionysos, not known for his martial courage, vaunts to his half-brother Herakles that he recently participated in a victorious sea battle. When Herakles asks incredulously, "*You* two?" Dionysos reaffirms his boast, prompting Xanthias to interject, "And then I woke up."[7]

The scholiastic commentators on the Aristophanic passage explain that the speaker is making fun of Dionysos, saying that the expression means, "I just woke up from a dream; that is, I did these things in a dream." One ancient commentator attributes the line to Dionysos himself, pointing out that persons who tell a lie (or, who tell a lying tale) sometimes add at the end, "And then I woke up."[8] The expression perhaps served the Greek teller of tall tales as a closing formula, acknowledging that the allegedly true experiences the raconteur just described were in fact untrue.

A character in another Greek play probably alludes to the same expression. In Euripides' satyr play *Kyklops*, the satyr Seilenos boastfully complains in the prologue how he has suffered for the sake of Dionysos, having fought alongside the god in the battle against the giants and put a spear through the giant Enkelados. Then he abruptly says: "What, I'm saying what I saw in a dream?" as though he expected the playgoers to say or think, "And then I woke up."[9]

For other tales that can involve both narrator and listener, see "Catch-Tale" and "Wooden Doll."

Lit. AT 2250, *Unfinished Tales*. Motif J1155, *"Then I woke up": man discredits his confession by declaring it all a dream*. Bolte 1905:69–70. BP 2:210, 3:455–456, 4:32. Wesselski 1925:187–188. Köhler (1855) 1:269–270. Taylor, in Mackensen et al. (1934–40) 2:189b–190a. Trenkner 1958:87 n. 9. Ashliman, types 2251, 2260, and 2271.

1. Köhler (1898) 1:269, citing Jacobs, *More Celtic Folk Tales*, no. 46.
2. Grimm 200.
3. Bolte 1905; Wesselski 1925:187–188. Another instance of "And then I woke up" framed within another tale is found in AT 1790, *The Parson and Sexton Steal a Cow*.

4. καὶ μετὰ ξύπνησα. I owe this information to a student of mine, Dr. Dimitris Sagias.
5. Bolte 1905:69 note 1.
6. Vv. 48–51.
7. κἀ ἔγωγ' ἐξηγρόμην.
8. Schol. *Frogs* 51.
9. Vv. 1–8.

White Serpent's Flesh ≷ Melampous the Seer

A man (youth) chances to taste the flesh of a white serpent, which is intended for another man (king, doctor, sorcerer). He finds that he has acquired a magical ability, and his adventures develop differently according to whether he now understands the language of animals or can see through things. In the former case, he hears two birds conversing, in the course of which one bird mentions that a certain house is about to collapse; the man warns the owner of the house, who is his master. Or when he is accused of stealing a piece of jewelry belonging to his master's wife, he overhears two animals talking, in the course of which one tells the other of having accidentally swallowed the object; the man has the animal butchered, whereupon the object is discovered. In the latter case, he uses his special vision to see the causes of mysterious illnesses, whereby he becomes a healer. He heals the king and, winning the king's favor, weds the princess.

This tale is AT 673, *The White Serpent's Flesh*, named from the usual source of the magical gift. We might label particular texts as reflexes of the "aural redaction" or the "visual redaction," depending upon whether the hero acquires extraordinary ability to decode sounds or to see through things.

Thus in a Scottish legend Sir James Ramsay of Bamff was banished from the country, his lands were confiscated, and a price was set upon his head if he should return, on the grounds that he had conspired against the crown. He went to Spain and was poorly off. There he became an apprentice to a doctor, who sent Sir James to acquire the ingredient with which they might make the most wonderful medicine in the world, a certain white serpent. Sir James caught it and killed it, and his master told him to cook it till it turned to oil but not to taste it lest he perish instantly. But Sir James, accidentally spilling some drops on his fingers, licked them without thinking, whereupon he eyes were opened, for he could see through everything. Thus, he could see his master's insides. Since his master would have killed him had he learned that Sir James discovered the secret of the medicine, Sir James said nothing. In time Sir James learned to be a skillful doctor under his master and eventually managed to get away from him. He traveled the world doing wonders, and after a while returned to Scotland unrecognized as a doctor. As it happened, the king was ill, and no man was able to cure him, so that the king proclaimed that he who could cure him would receive the princess as wife. Sir James went to court, saw that there was a ball of hair inside the king, and removed it, freeing the king of illness. Then Sir James revealed his identity, and the king pardoned him, returning his lands and giving him his daughter as wife.[1]

According to the Grimms' tale *The White Snake*, which was collected in 1812 from a twelve-year-old girl, there lived a king long ago who was famous for

knowing everything. He had an unusual habit, which was that every day at noon he ate some food in private. One day a curious servant secretly looked at the food, which was a white snake, and ate a piece of it. Presently he found that he understood the speech of the sparrows outside his window. The snake had given him the power to understand the language of animals. The same day the queen had lost her ring, and this same servant was held responsible. A while later he heard some ducks conversing, and one said that it had swallowed a ring inadvertently. So the servant had the duck butchered, and the ring was found. The king, who wished to make amends for his false accusation, promised the servant a high position at court. The servant went on to have other adventures.[2]

In the Norse legend of the dragon slayer Sigurð, Regin told Sigurð where there was treasure guarded by the dragon Fáfnir, and provided Sigurð with an exceedingly sharp sword. After Sigurð slew the dragon, Regin informed him that the dragon was Regin's brother, but he offered to be reconciled on the condition that Sigurð should take Fáfnir's heart and roast it over a fire. As Regin slept, Sigurð roasted the dragon's heart, and when he thought it was done, he touched it with his finger to check it for tenderness, but the juice burnt him so that he licked his finger. As soon as his tongue had tasted the dragon's blood, Sigurð understood the language of birds. And indeed, overhearing birds speaking nearby, he learned that Regin intended to betray him. So Sigurð killed him, took the gold, and, after receiving additional information from the birds, rode away.[3] So begins the action of the Sigurð legend, employing an episode that is familiar from the present folktale. But it is presently forgotten, and Sigurð's ability to understand the conversation of birds plays no further role in the story.

Melampous the Seer

In antiquity a similar story was told of the legendary Greek seer Melampous, who lived in the generation just before the Trojan War. In the account of the legend given by the mythographer Apollodoros, Melampous dwelled in the countryside near Pylos. After his servants one day killed some snakes that had a lair in a tree in front of his house, he gathered wood and burnt the dead snakes, and reared their young. When the snakes grew up, they cleansed his ears with their tongues as he slept, after which Melampous was able to understand the speech of birds and thereby to foretell future events. Moreover, he once encountered Apollo at the Alpheios River and from him learned how to take auspices.

Melampous's brother, Bias, was one of the suitors for the hand of Pero. Her father, Neleus, said he would give his daughter to the man who should bring him the cattle of Phylakos. These cattle were guarded by a dog that neither humans nor animals were able to approach. Since Bias could not steal the cattle he asked his brother Melampous to help him, and Melampous promised to do so, foretelling however that he would be caught in the attempt, detained for a year, and then get the cattle. He was in fact caught in the act of stealing and detained as a prisoner. After he had been confined for almost a year, he heard some worms in the roof above him conversing. One asked how much of the beam had been gnawed through, and others replied that very little of it was left. Melampous quickly asked to be moved to another building, and presently the original building collapsed.

Phylakos, astonished at Melampous's skill in seercraft, released him and asked him how his childless son Iphiklos might have children. Melampous promised to tell him in return for the cattle. Then the seer learned from a bird that once when Phylakos was gelding rams he lay the bloody knife beside Iphiklos; the child ran away, and the father stuck the knife in a sacred oak tree, which since then surrounded and hid the knife. Phylakos must find the knife, scrape off the rust, mix the rust with wine, and give it to his son to drink for ten days, after which Iphiklos would beget a son. It so happened. Melampous then got the cattle, drove them to Pylos, received Neleus's daughter, and gave her to his brother.

As the legend continues, King Proitos of Argos had three daughters, who, because they offended either Dionysos or Hera, went mad and roamed the regions around Argos. Now Melampous, who had invented the use of drugs and purifications for treating the sick, offered to treat the maidens for a third of Proitos's kingdom, but Proitos refused so high a price. But when other women joined his daughters and the situation worsened, Proitos agreed to the price. Now, however, Melampous said he would treat them at the price of a third of the kingdom for himself and another third for his brother, Bias. Proitos agreed, lest the price rise still higher. With the aid of some young men Melampous chased the women to Sikyon, where he purified and cured them. One of the daughters had perished in the pursuit, but King Proitos gave the other two in marriage to Melampous and Bias.[4]

There are four episodes, or clusters of incidents, in which the ancient legend and the modern tale show similar or identical material. (1) The hero acquires from serpents the gift of understanding the language of animals. The ancient story therefore reflects the aural redaction. As a result, he is able to learn of future events, of past events known to animals but not to humans, or both. This incident sets up the episodes that follow. (2) Using this gift he overhears animals talking about a building that is about to collapse, and so saves himself or his master. (3) Using his gift again, he cures a person of a seemingly hopeless malady. (4) Gaining the favor of a king, he wins the princess in marriage, part of the kingdom, or the like. The close correspondence shows that the Melampous legend and the international folktale must be genetically related stories.

That serpents possessed special powers of prescience and healing was a familiar idea in classical antiquity. A human could obtain a knowledge of miraculous plants by observing how one serpent healed another serpent with herbs, as in the legend of Glaukos and Polyidos the seer.[5] The ability to understand animal languages could be acquired from serpents in two different ways. One method was to eat a particular kind of snake in whole or part, as Pliny relates, explaining that there is a serpent born from the blood of certain birds, and whoever eats this serpent understands the conversations of birds.[6] It was by this means that the ancient Greek sage Apollonios of Tyana acquired his ability to understand the language of animals (see below) and that the mediaeval Northern hero Sigurð learned the speech of birds. This mode, which one might call the culinary method, is preferred by the protagonists of *The White Serpent's Flesh*.

The other way involves not the ingestion of a magic substance but, it seems, the unblocking of the apparatus of perception. Serpents licked a person's ears,

cleansing them, as he slept. Not only Melampous but also Helenos and Kassandra become seers in this way.[7] Unlike eating, this experience was not a willful act for a human being, something one could choose to do, but it might happen to a person if conditions were right. But even the first method is often presented as an unthinking, automatic response—the hero licks the hot liquid from his burning fingers—rather than as a premeditated act. The second method implies that the potential for understanding the conversations of animals resides in humans all the time, but some kind of blockage, concerning which serpents have a special knowledge, prevents us from using it. We find similar ideas of perception elsewhere in Greek sources, especially in early literature. In Homer a god can make himself or another invisible by surrounding him with mist, and were it not for a kind of permanent mist, apparently a regular feature of reality, the heroes at Troy would be able to see the gods who are on the battlefield participating in the fighting.[8] So humans might understand the speech of all creatures and see all things if only there were not something in the way, but, as it is, only gods and certain animals are naturally gifted with unclouded perception, and only a few exceptional human beings acquire the ability in their lifetimes.

Whereas in the international tale, as also in the Sigurð legend, the hero intercepts a magic meal or potion intended for another, either inadvertently or without knowing the special property of the food, in the Greek legend he earns his boon because of a kindness he does to animals. After Melampous's servants destroy some adult snakes, he cremates them and takes care of their young. When the survivors grow up, they gratefully repay their benefactor by cleansing his ears as he sleeps, giving him the gift of understanding the speech of animals, and making him a seer and a healer. According to Hesiod's slightly different account of this episode, Melampous was away from home at the time, lodging with a certain King Polyphontes. An ox was being sacrificed in his honor, and when a serpent crawled upon the sacrificial victim, the king's servants killed it. The king was angry, but Melampous took the serpent, buried it, and reared its young, which later licked his ears and bestowed upon him the gift of prophecy.[9]

The ancient and modern forms of this incident vary more on their surface than in their essential structure. For in both forms, (a) the protagonist and another man (king, doctor, rival, etc.) are preparing food, in the course of which (b) a snake is killed. (c) The hero takes possession of the snake and (d), as an unforeseen result, acquires the gift of understanding the speech of animals. The particular forms that the incident takes serve to characterize the hero of the story. The hero of the more recent texts is often adventurous (he goes off with a stranger), curious (he wonders what the mysterious dish is), and lucky (fortune favors him), whereas Melampous is shown to be kind-hearted (he tends to a dead serpent and rears its offspring, two acts of kindness for which he can realistically expect no reward). This characterization of him as a selfless person is presently restated and confirmed when he undertakes a dangerous task (to rustle cattle) not for himself but for his brother.

Melampous is captured, as he foresaw he would be. He is bound and kept imprisoned in Iphiklos's house, and about a year later he hears the woodworms saying that they have all but finished consuming the beam and the house is about to fall. There are two versions of what happens next. Melampous informs Iphiklos of the forthcoming catastrophe, directly or via an old

maidservant, so that he escapes from the house in time.[10] Or the seer, feigning illness, asks the old man and old woman who watch him to carry his bed outside, which they do, though the house collapses just as they are doing so, killing the old woman. The man informs Phylakos of the event, and he tells his son Iphiklos.[11] As a result, Iphiklos learns that Melampous is a seer and releases him.

Phylakos now agrees to give Melampous the cattle he seeks if the seer can cure his son's childlessness. So the seer performs a sacrifice to Zeus, setting out portions for all the birds, who come except for one vulture. When Melampous, who understands their language, asks them how Iphiklos may get children, they are all at a loss and fetch the vulture, who reveals the cause of the problem and probably also its treatment.[12] Animals are portrayed here as having a society of their own that resembles human society, with their own knowledgeable elders, and the scene conveys the idea that the information sought is a scarce commodity even among creatures who are more knowledgeable than humans.[13]

The actual nature of Iphiklos's problem is obscurely told by the ancient mythographers and commentators, but probably he is impotent rather than sterile, since the childlessness is viewed strictly as Iphiklos's problem, not his wife's; if he were potent, the blame should have fallen upon his wife for infertility.[14] The event that causes Iphiklos's problem seems to be as follows. Once when he was only a young boy, his father Phylakos was gelding rams. The boy misbehaved in some way, and the father tried to frighten him by pursuing him with the knife he was using; he may have even brought it into contact with the boy's genitals. Then he stuck the knife in a tree, where it remained, since the tree eventually enveloped it. To be cured, Phylakos must find the knife, scrape off the rust, mix it with wine, and give it to his son to drink for ten days. The tool that deprived the rams of their manhood did the same for the boy, and by the principle that one can be cured by that which caused the problem, the knife also provides the treatment.[15] Melampous's cure works, and he is given the cattle.

In the final adventure Melampous negotiates with King Proitos, offering to cure his daughters of their madness in exchange for a third of his kingdom. Proitos refuses, but he relents when the plague of female madness spreads, only now Melampous doubles his fee. This time the king agrees, fearing things could become even worse.[16] Melampous's cure is successful, and Proitos gives his daughters in marriage to Melampous and Bias, so that Bias, who presumably has wed Pero, acquires a second wife.

The last two episodes, each telling of a marvelous cure effected by Melampous, are obviously doublets, that is, two forms of essentially the same action. First, Melampous miraculously cures Phylakos's son Iphiklos of his impotence, which leads (through the intermediate step of a trade of cattle) to his gaining the hand of the daughter of King Neleus of Pylos, Pero, whom he gives to his brother Bias. Second, he miraculously cures the mad daughters of King Proitos of Argos on the condition that he receive a third of the kingdom and his brother Bias another third, and after the successful healing the king gives Melampous one princess to wife and Bias the other. Each episode is a slightly different realization of the concluding episode in the international tale, in

which the hero heals a member of the royal family and gains the hand of the princess in marriage.

The legend of Melampous is very old. Homer alludes to it extensively as a story that is already familiar to his audience, though in accord with his usual practice he mentions only the more realistic details of the story.[17] It is recounted by Hesiod more than once.[18] The early mythographer Pherekydes also relates the legend.[19]

Apollonios of Tyana

According to his biographer Apollonios of Tyana, a Neopythagorean sage and wonder-worker of the first century A.D., visited Mesopotamia on his way to India and acquired an understanding of the language of animals. This he did among the Arabs, who were adept at it and, according to Philostratos, commonly listened to birds foretelling the future. One acquired the ability by eating the heart or the liver of serpents.[20] On one occasion Apollonios translated for bystanders the excited conversation of some sparrows who had discovered a supply of food, and on another occasion the lament of a lion into whom the soul of King Amasis of Egypt had transmigrated.[21]

The resemblance between the careers of Melampous and Apollonios extends beyond their learning from serpents the language of animals, for, like Melampous, Apollonios was both a seer and a miraculous healer, though Philostratos does not mention Apollonios's ability to understand the speech of animals when he recounts the sage's prophecies and healings.[22] Nevertheless, just as Melampous foresaw that the building in which he was confined was about to collapse, so also Apollonios once foretold that the ship on which he and his companions were about to embark would presently sink, so that they changed ships, though, again, his prescience is not credited to his knowledge of animal languages.[23] Finally, like Melampous, who won a portion of the kingdom as well as the daughter of King Proitos, Apollonios eventually won great favor with the Emperor Vespasian.[24]

The parallels are scattered throughout the career of Apollonios and are related to one another only in that they are attributed to the same person, whereas in the case of Melampous his powers as a seer, his success as a healer of Iphiklos, and probably his healing of the madwomen are all ultimately connected with his ability to understand the speech of animals. Similarly, the adventures of the folktale hero are opportunities for the exercise of the magic gift that he acquires at the beginning of the tale. So it is uncertain whether the fabulous stories that grew up around Apollonios were conditioned by either the legend of Melampous or the tale of *The White Serpent's Flesh*.

Alexander and His Cook

An incident in the *Alexander Romance* may have been suggested by the introductory episode of the present folktale. In the course of Alexander's travels to the east he came to the area of the Land of the Blessed, reaching a place where the air was fragrant. Feeling hungry he told his cook Andreas to prepare a meal. Andreas took a salt fish and rinsed it in a spring, whereupon it returned

to life and swam away. The cook did not tell Alexander but himself drank some of the water and saved more in a container. Later the cook seduced one of Alexander's daughters by offering her a drink of water from the immortal spring, so that both the cook and the woman became immortal. Alexander sent them away to live with other water spirits, bemoaning the fact that it was not ordained for him to drink from that water that was not denied even his cook.[25]

In this case the wonder-working agent is a spring whose water grants, not special hearing or sight, but immortality to him or her who tastes it. As usual the magic food or liquid intended for the master is consumed by the servant, or, more precisely here, the food that is intended for the master leads the cook by chance to the magic beverage. What is unexpected about this treatment of the events is that the main interest of the story is the unlucky master, whereas in the folktale it is the lucky servant. The narrator's strategy here is to show how very close Alexander, like Gilgamesh, comes to the immortality for which he longs but that he is not fated to acquire.

Lit. AT 673, *The White Serpent's Flesh.* BP 1:131–134. Marx 1889:109–111. Aly 1928:267–268. Frazer (1921) 1:86–87, 2:350–355. Μαρινᾶτος 1953:44–49. Christiansen 1958, type 3030. Liungman 1961:190–191. Ranke (1962) 3:8. Löffler 1963:30–40. Scherf 1982:436–439. Ashliman, type 673.

1. Briggs (1971) B2:578–580.
2. Grimm 17.
3. See "Reginsmál" and "Fáfnismál" in the *Elder Edda*.
4. Apollodoros *Bibl.* 1.9.11–12; 2.2.2.
5. For example, Apollodoros *Bibl.* 3.3.1. See further Frazer (1921) 2:363–370, App. 7; AT 612, *The Three Snake-Leaves*.
6. *NH* 10.137; 29.72.
7. Schol. Homer *Il.* 7.44; cf. Porphyry *De abstinentia* 3.3–3.4. See further Frazer 1888:166–168; Frazer (1921) 1:86–87 n. 2; Röhrich 1991:77–79. According to a scholium on Apollonios of Rhodes, the serpents licked Melampous's ears and *breathed into him* the gift of being a seer (*leichein ta ota kai empneusai autoi ten mantiken*), just as the Muses breathed into Hesiod a divine voice when they made him a bard (Hesiod *Th.* 31–32). In this narration the serpents do not so much liberate a latent power as they "inspire" Melampous with a gift from without. Aristophanes mentions serpents' curing blindness by licking eyelids (*Plutus* 730–741), and Apollodoros (*Bibl.* 3.6.7) reports that the goddess Athene cleansed the ears of Teiresias, after which he understood the speech of birds. Compare also *Vita Aesopi* 7.
8. Mist of invisibility: *Il.* 5.187 (ad hoc); *Il.* 5.127 (permanent).
9. Hesiod fr. 261 M-W.
10. Hesiod fr. 261 M-W; schol. Theokritos 3.43.
11. Schol. Homer *Od.* 11.287; Eustathios on Homer's *Od.* 11.292, p. 1685.
12. Schol. Homer *Od.* 11.287.
13. The scene is familiar from modern folktales. A person summons birds or other animals in order to consult them. Except for one creature they all come, but those present cannot answer the question; finally the missing animal shows up and reveals the information. The incident can occur, for example, in episode 5 of AT 400, *The Man on a Quest for His Lost Wife*. For illustrative texts of the episode see Frazer (1921) 2:354–355; Zielinski 1931:25–26, 55–57. The motif appears not to be listed in Thompson's *Motif-Index* (Thompson 1955–58).
14. Iphiklos as impotent: Frazer (1921) 2:189 n.; Μαρινᾶτοζ 1953:45; Gantz 1993:187. Sterile: Löffler 1963:34; Hoekstra *apud* Heubeck (1989) 2:246.
15. Frazer (1921) 2:189–191, 350–355; cf. Μαρινᾶτοζ 1953 and Hartland (1895) 2:172–174. Notice the Greek proverb, "He who wounded will also heal" (ὁ τρώσαζ καὶ ἰάσεται), sprung from the legend of Telephos, who could only be cured by the spear that had wounded him (*CPG* 2:762–763).
16. The transaction of the doubled fee is also known from other oral stories. In a modern legend a stranger offers for a price to lead away the rats that plague a place, but his services

are declined; when the plague of rats become worse, the stranger is hired, but now his customer must pay twice the original price (Holbek 1985:133). The ancient legend of the purchase of the Sibylline books shows the same structure; see Hansen 1996b:128.

17. *Od.* 11.287–297, 15.226–242; cf. Heubeck 1954:19–22.

18. *Catalogue of Women* fr. 37 M-W; *Megalai Eoiai* fr. 261 M-W; and of course in the *Melampodia*, of which almost nothing survives.

19. *FGH* 3 F 33. Other useful sources, in addition to the account of Apollodoros, summarized above, are Herodotos 9.34; Pausanias 8.18.7–8, 4.36.3–4; schol. Theokritos *Id.* 3.43; Eustathios on Homer *Od.* 11.292 (p. 1685); and Propertius 2.3.51–54. Differences in detail in the various accounts are not great. See further Roscher 2.2567–2573; Gantz 1993:185–188, 312–313.

20. Philostratos *Vita Apollonii* 1.20.

21. *Vita Apollonii* 4.3, 5.42.

22. Apollonios as seer: for example, 5.11–13. Healer: 3.38–40, 4.10, 4.20, 4.45, 6.43.

23. 5.18.

24. 5.36–38.

25. *Alexander Romance* 2.39 and 2.41.

Wisdom of Hidden Old Man Saves Kingdom

During a famine (war) or by order of the ruler (by decision of the younger citizens) or because it is customary practice, all the old people in a community are to be killed. One son, however, spares and conceals his aged father. When the community faces a crisis, the clever old man offers crucial advice (demonstrates his usefulness otherwise). As a result he is honored, and the order to kill the old members of the community is rescinded (the custom of killing the old is abolished).

This story, found sometimes as a folktale and sometimes as an account of an allegedly historical event, is AT 981, *Wisdom of Hidden Old Man Saves Kingdom*. It is attested in much of Europe, in Turkey, and in India and China.

Individual texts differ in the particular reason they give for the execution of the elderly and can be divided broadly into those that present the killings as a one-time event, the result of some special circumstance such as famine, and those that present them as an established custom, something the community has always done. They also differ in the particular service that they attribute to the singular old man, often employing difficult tasks and clever solutions that are known also from other international narratives.

According to a story in the mediaeval *Dolopathos*, one of the early kings of Rome died, leaving his kingdom to his young son. The country suffered a period of disorder and rebellion, and the city underwent a long siege by its enemies. In the course of the siege, everyone suffered from hunger and fear, and the young king was persuaded by his princes, who were his peers in age and wisdom, to decree that all old men and old women should be put to death, on the ground that anyone who consumed food daily while neither defending the city with weapons nor producing food by manual labor was unworthy to live; moreover, anyone who spared his parents was condemned to death. And so Roman sons killed their parents, except that one son in collusion with his wife spared his wise old father and hid him underground. Presently peace returned, but in time the kingdom came more and more to be governed in an arbitrary and unjust manner because of the absence of wise and knowledgeable men in

the young king's council. Now the young man who had preserved his father was a nobleman at court, and he would report to his father all the matters that were raised at court, and his father always provided solutions, which the son brought back to the court. This steady stream of good advice earned the young man a high place in the king's favor and the resentment of the other nobles. Suspecting that the man's father might still be alive but not daring to say as much, they hoped to expose the duo. So they suggested to the king that he hold a ball for his princes, instructing each man to bring along his best friend, his worst enemy, his most excellent jester, and his most faithful servant. The young noble reported this news to his father, who asked him whether anyone felt jealousy toward him, to which the son replied that all his associates envied him. Then the father perceived that the task was a trap to induce the son to bring his father as his best friend, after which he could be charged with ignoring the king's decree. He told his son to be the last to approach the king, bringing his dog, his donkey, his wife, and his little son; and he instructed his son what to say in each case. When the son went to the ball, his donkey brayed at the sound of the musicians. Though his enemies accused him to the king, the monarch asked him what each thing represented. The man replied that the dog exemplified his best friend, since his dog accompanied him wherever he went, staying by him through every danger, and was never happy without him nor ever sad in his company. He brought the donkey (he said) as his best servant, and he enumerated the chores that the donkey willingly performed for meager compensation. His little son he touted as his best jester, and his wife he presented as his worst enemy. Thereupon his wife, angered at being so labeled, yelled at him for his thanklessness, seeing as she had shown so much compassion for his father whom he had not executed but kept hidden underground. Then the youth pointed out to the king how true his characterization had been, since as a result of a mere word his wife had revealed his secret and thereby condemned him to death. And the king marveled at the young man's cleverness, ordering him to fetch his father. When the old man came, the king appointed him Father of the City and Judge of the Land, and in short order the wise man restored law and justice to the country.[1]

Similarly, in an oral text collected in 1930 from an unnamed informant in Tuxpán, State of Jalisco, Mexico, a king once decreed that all old persons should be shot, but one son hid his old father underground and brought him food daily. When finally the son's money ran out, he asked his father what they should do. The old man told him to go to a rich man named Miguel and ask for a loan of a hundred pesos. When the son asked Don Miguel for the loan, Miguel inquired about the purpose of the loan. He answered that it was for his field. Miguel asked: "And your father, where is he?" He replied that they killed him in accordance with the decree. But Miguel decided to pose a difficult problem, and if he could solve the problem, it would show that his father was alive. So Miguel said: "I'll give you the loan, but on the condition that you bring me your friend and your enemy." The son agreed, went away, and told his father, who told him to bring his wife and his dog, to strike each one of them in Miguel's presence, and then to call his dog. The son did so, and his dog came to him again, but when he called his wife, she told Miguel not to lend her husband any money, saying he has kept his father hidden underground. Miguel

admitted that this was what he wanted to know. He gave the son five hundred pesos to take to his father, revealed that there was a plot to overthrow the king, and asked the son to be governor. In time the king was overthrown, the young man became governor, and when he came to power he issued all kinds of guarantees to all the old people, and they all lived very happily.[2]

The setting in this twentieth-century Mexican tale remains a kingdom, though the means of execution of the old persons has been technologically updated to shooting. Another innovation is that it is not the clever father who is eventually honored but rather the dutiful son, who as usual is unnamed.

Both texts illustrate the old man's cleverness by means of his ingenious solution to the strange task of bringing one's best friend, worst enemy, etc. This incident is itself an international narrative that is found as an independent tale (see "Best Friend, Worst Enemy"). Other texts exhibit other problems with other clever solutions.[3] Thus, a king orders the folk to make ropes of sand, to which the clever reply is that they will do so if they are first provided with hinny milk, which is needed to make the rope cohere, or if they are first provided with a sample of such a rope to serve as a model.[4] In short, the old man responds to the impossible task by posing an impossible countertask. Other texts relate how the community lacks seed following a poor harvest, a problem for which the clever solution is to sow the fields with the straw thatch.[5] In still others the challenge is to be the first person to see the sunrise (see below). And so on.

Worth mentioning is also an American comic tradition according to which old persons are deliberately frozen for the winter in order to save on scarce food, and then thawed out in the spring.[6]

An Episode in the History of Tyre

The earliest attestations of the international story are found in works of two Roman epitomizers, Justinus and Festus. Around the third century of our era Justinus made an epitome in Latin of an earlier historical work, now lost, the *Historiae Philippicae* of the Romanized Gaul, Pompeius Trogus.

In his section on the history of Tyre, Justinus recounts how the Tyrians' strength was once diminished by a series of wars they fought with the Persians. The Tyrians' slaves, who were very numerous, took this opportunity to conspire against their masters, killing them along with the entire free population, after which they took over the city, seized their masters' homes, married, and produced children. Of these thousands of slaves, one was a man of gentle temperament who, moved by the plight of his aged master and the latter's young son, compassionately hid them away. Meanwhile the slaves deliberated about what form of government to create and decided to elevate one of their own number to king. The man who was the first to see the rising sun would be so chosen, on the ground that he would be the most pleasing to the gods. This resolution was reported to Straton (for this was the master's name) in his place of hiding. In the middle of the night, then, everyone went to a certain field, and while all the others looked east, Straton's slave alone faced west. At first it seemed folly to look for sunrise in the west, but when day was approaching and the rising sun began to shine in the highest parts of the city, and while the

others tried to catch a glimpse of the sun itself, he was the first to point to the sunshine that was visible on the topmost parts of the city. Now this strategy did not appear to be that of a slave, and when he was asked who devised it he confessed that it had in fact come from his master. Everyone then perceived how superior the intellect of free men was to that of slaves and that slaves excelled more in roguery than in wisdom. So the old man and his son were pardoned, and since the people believed that the two had been kept alive by a deity, they made Straton king. At his death the kingdom descended to his son and after that to his grandsons.[7]

The general sequence of events is the same as in other texts of the type. (1) There is a mass killing of a segment of the population (usually the old, but here the free), except that (2) one old man is saved and hidden. Subsequently (3) a problem arises, which (4) is solved by the advice of the clever old man. When (5) the secret source of the advice is revealed, (6) the old man is honored. Despite the inherent improbability of the plan of awarding the kingship to whoever first spots the sunrise, the tradition is presented unskeptically as a historical event, evidently forming part of the traditional history of the Phoenician city of Tyre. If so, it certainly does not give the Tyrians an exalted pedigree.

Interestingly, the principal opposition in this text is between slave and free rather than between young and old, although we can glimpse a vestige of the more usual opposition in the person of the clever counselor, who is described as an old man (*senis*) just as in texts in which the principal opposition is between youth and old age, revealing that the Tyrian legend is probably a special adaptation of the usual story. Justinus's narrative acts out the proposition that the characteristics of slaves and free persons are not accidents of status but rather features intrinsic to their nature. Slaves are slaves because they are unfit to rule, even to rule themselves, just as free men are born to govern both themselves and others. Consequently, a society constructed contrary to this basic truth is doomed to failure, as in the present instance, which illustrates how slaves are capable of lowly treachery but are pitifully incompetent when they undertake the high offices of government.

The contest of being the first to see the sunrise, which appears in many modern texts of the folktale, is also found as an independent story in international oral tradition, told sometimes of human characters but more often of animals. In the animal tale one animal looks to the east, whereas the other animal looks to the west, sees the rays of the sun striking the crests of the western mountains before the sun itself is visible on the horizon, and so wins a contest or wager.[8] In some texts the object of the contest is to determine who shall rule, as in the Tyrian legend.

Sexagenarians from the Bridge

The other Roman text is owed to the epitomizer Festus, who in the late second century A.D. wrote a summary of the lost *De significatu verborum* (On Word Meanings) of Verrius Flaccus, an erudite scholar of the first century A.D. The materials are arranged in alphabetical order in the manner of a reference work.

According to Festus's account of the proverbial expression *sexagenarios de ponte* "sexagenarians from the bridge," some people say that after Rome was

liberated from the Gauls there was a shortage of food, and persons sixty years of age were thrown into the Tiber. But one such person who was dutifully concealed by his son frequently benefited the state through the agency of his son. When the matter became known, the young man was forgiven, and thereafter sexagenarians were allowed to live.[9]

The Roman legend is obviously a form of the international story, but the narrative is so severely abbreviated that we do not learn the nature of the old man's advice and of the crises that provoke it, though perhaps it had to do with the provision of food. Among the Romans sixty years was often regarded as the period at which old age commenced.[10] The term of sixty years as the normal or enforced boundary of human life is also found elsewhere, for example in Chinese tradition.[11]

Some researchers infer from the motif of the customary killing of the old folk that such a custom must once have been practiced, assuming that the narrative idea can only have arisen from actual practice, and Paudler, arguing along these lines, concludes that the custom must once have existed in ancient Greece.[12] But this conclusion is too drastic, since it assumes that narrative ideas must be simple reflections of reality, a notion that is readily disproved by the existence of tales in which animals and even plants talk. Several Greek authors, however, declare that the custom was practiced in this or that place; for example, Strabo and Aelian describe an alleged custom of Keos according to which, when folk grew very old and were conscious of the fact that they were no longer useful to their society, they assembled for a party in which they wore garlands and drank hemlock.[13]

In any case the motif of the systematic killing of the old people surely gives expression to the resentment that the elderly are unproductive members of society, drones who consume but do not contribute, a sentiment that many persons must have, if only fleetingly or unconsciously. In the context of the present story the motif represents for narrative purposes the proposition that, since the old are useless, the community would be better off without them. But the rest of the story soundly refutes this proposition when the cleverness of the hidden old man proves to be crucial for the survival of the community. The conventional name of the tale, then, is something of a misnomer, since it is cleverness rather than wisdom that the hidden old man displays. The wisdom of the tale lies rather in its moral, which is that the community cannot afford simply to dispose of its elderly population.

Alexander and the Old Man

Although no text of *Wisdom of Hidden Old Man Saves Kingdom* is found in Greek authors, an episode in the Greek novel known as the *Alexander Romance* is so reminiscent of the folktale that it must have been inspired by it.

As Alexander made his way eastward and wished to proceed further to the end of the earth, he selected a group of young soldiers to accompany him, giving orders that no old man should march with them. But one old man persuaded his two sons, who were among Alexander's select troops, to shave his chin, disguise him, and take him along, since in a crisis Alexander would look for an old man. After several days they reached an area of dark-

ness, and the young men advised their leader not to proceed since they might not be able to return if the horses became separated in the darkness. Alexander replied that they had courage but not intelligence, for which an old man was needed. He offered a reward for the man who would be brave enough to ride back to their main camp and bring back an old man. When no one volunteered for the task, the old man's sons revealed to Alexander that they had brought their father along. The old man told Alexander that in order to have any hope of return he must travel with horses, and that he should select mares with foals, leaving the foals there and setting out with the mares, who would be sure to return because of their foals. Alexander followed his advice. During the journey the old man told his sons to gather whatever they found lying on the ground and put it into their saddlebags. When Alexander decided to return, he placed the mares in front and followed them back to their foals. There they found that the saddlebags of the old man's sons were filled with gold and pearls. Alexander and the others thanked the old man for his excellent advice.[14] Here a taboo on the presence of old men replaces the actual killing of old men; otherwise, the episode is quite similar.

In sum, the tale of the hidden old man is already attested in quite varied manifestations in Greek and Latin literature in the early centuries of our era, in sources that are in turn adaptations of earlier materials.

Lit. AT 981, *Wisdom of Hidden Old Man Saves Kingdom.* Köhler 1855. Sartori 1895. Polívka 1898b. Wesselski 1925:237. Vries 1928:220–232. Paudler 1937. Liungman 1961:250–251. *EM* 1:388–395. Scherf (1995) 1:278–280.

1. Wesselski 1925:133–136, no. 48.
2. Wheeler 1943:6–7, no. 3.
3. *EM* 1:392.
4. Polívka 1898b:26–27. See further Zachariae 1907; "Making a Rope of Sand."
5. Polívka 1898b:27–28; Paudler 1937:20–21.
6. Randolph 1993:206–207.
7. *Epitoma Historiarum Philippicarum Pompei Trogi* 18.3.6–16.
8. The story of the contest is classified among the animal tales by Aarne-Thompson: AT 120, *The First to See the Sunrise.* See further Dähnhardt (1910) 3:150–151; Liungman 1961:17–18; *EM* 1:392.
9. Festus *De verborum significatu* pp. 66, 450, 452 Lindsay. On the expression see further Otto 1890:320–321, no. 1638; Néraudau 1978; Guarino 1980.
10. Eyben 1989:232, 237. See also Suder 1978, 1986.
11. Eberhard 1937:115–117.
12. Paudler 1937:30.
13. Strabo 10.5.6; Aelian *VH* 3.37. See further Schmidt 1903; Rohde 1960:230 n. 1; Dumézil 1950.
14. *Alexander Romance* 2.39–41. See further Köhler 1855; Paudler 1937:21–25. Here, too, the old man's cleverness is traditional stuff, for Herodotos relates that a similar strategy was employed by the Indians. Setting out into the desert in quest of gold, the Indians took care to bring along female camels that had recently given birth, for during their return the females, mindful of the offspring they had left behind, showed more determination to reach home than the male camels did (3.102–105). In their comment on the passage, W. W. How and J. Wells add that according to Marco Polo the Tartars ride mares during their raids for the same reason (1:290). The mediaeval Danish author Saxo Grammaticus describes an application of the same principle in reverse. The brothers Frodi and Harald are joint kings in a diarchy, one of them taking charge of the land and the other of the sea in yearly shifts. As

the first sea king, Frodi suffers terrible losses because the men he takes along with him are recently wed and yearn for their wives. When it is Harald's turn as sea king, he selects only unmarried men, so that his expeditions prove to be very successful (*Gesta Danorum* 7.1.1–3).

Wishes. *See* Hospitality Rewarded

Wishing Contest

In this comic tale, several men agree to engage in a contest of wishing, whereupon each man expresses one or more impossible wishes.

The tale is AT 1925, *Wishing Contests*. A more accurate title would be *Contest in Wishing*, since each tale features only one contest.

In a Latin narrative included in the fifteenth-century collection of fables made by the German humanist Hainricus Stainhöwel, three sons inherited three things from their father. Among them was a goat, which was to belong to the son who was able to pray for the largest goat. A judge was to decide the matter. The eldest son prayed that the goat might be so big that when it was thirsty it could drink up all the water beneath the sky and still be less than half full. The next son, confident that he would win, prayed that the goat might be so large that if all the world's linen, hemp, and wool were woven into a single string, the string would not be long enough to encircle the goat's shin. And the youngest son, believing he would win because his prayer would be the longest, prayed that the goat might be so great in height, length, and width that it would extend to every point that would be visible to a great eagle looking down from the heavens upon the four quarters of the earth. The judge declared that neither he nor anyone else could determine which of them wished for the largest goat.[1]

In a tale written down by a Norwegian woman in 1959, three rich whaling men were sitting in a cafe in Tønsberg, each boasting that he was able to wish for riches better than the others could. So one said he wished that all the sackcloth in the world were made into empty sacks, that each of them were filled with thousand-crown bills, and that they all belonged to him. The second wished that all the ink in the world were employed to write nines and that the sum were in his bankbook. The third wished that all the trees in the world were cut down to a yard above the ground and that thousand-crown bills were counted out on the stumps until the stumps were worn down. The three men then turned to Ola Jensen, who was listening at the next table, and asked him if there were not something he would wish for. Yes, Ola wished that the three of them would die and he would be their sole heir.[2]

In these texts, three men linked together in some way agree to compete with one another in a contest of wishing. In each instance the men explicitly decide upon the activity before they engage in it, though in the first case it is a formal

contest for a prize while in the second case it is a casual game. Each man speaks in turn, the second speaker trying to outdo the first, and the third the second. Although we are perhaps expected to imagine that each entry succeeds in surpassing its predecessor, the wishes are all more or less equally good, and in these texts (but not in all such texts) none of the contestants emerges as a clear winner. Indeed, in the second text, the best wish is made by a nonparticipant, who, when asked if he had a wish, dryly asked for the sum of the other wishes. This punch line corresponds to the comment, which I take also to be comic, made by the judge at the conclusion of the Renaissance text. Though appointed the judge of the competition, he said in effect that he had no idea which of the brothers uttered the best wish.

Since the particular wishes in narratives of *Wishing Contests* may differ considerably, the texts may be alike only in their paradigmatic structure, or basic situation. For this reason, tales about contests in wishing, like tales about contests in lying, really constitute a "form type" rather than a "content type."[3] More or less the same can be said of other contest tales such as contests in laziness (see "Three Lazy Ones") and contests in riddling (see "Stronger and Strongest"), as well as a number of other tale types that tend to be tales of the superlative.

A Greek Wishing Contest

Lucian's dialogue, *The Ship, or the Wishes,* is devoted to the theme of what was popularly called by the Greeks *kene makaria,* or "empty bliss," that is, daydreams of wealth and the like.[4] In the first part of the work four male friends walk to the Peiraieus to see a magnificent Egyptian merchant ship, an experience that causes one of their number to fall into a grandiose daydream in which he himself becomes the rich shipowner, busily acquiring a fine house, slaves, and horses, being esteemed all but a king, and sailing on his fine vessel until his daydream is interrupted, forcing him to return to the reality of his poverty (see "Foolish Man Builds Aircastles"). In the continuation of the work, as the friends walk back to Athens, Timolaos suggests that they divide their journey into four parts, in each of which one of them should ask whatever he would like from the gods. It would take their minds off their tiredness, and they would enjoy themselves with pleasurable dreams of their own choosing. Each man would himself determine what boundary to put on his wish, and they would imagine that the gods would grant every wish, however improbable the wishes may be. Best of all, it would show which of them would be best at wishing and using his wealth. Timolaos's proposal is agreeable to the other three men, and they decide the sequence in which each shall speak.

Adeimantos wishes for the ship and everything in it, for a boy he admired, and for the ship's cargo of wheat to be changed to gold coins. He wishes also for a treasure in gold to be found in his courtyard, and he would like a house, all the desirable land in Greece, and golden service for dining. He adds as well purple clothing, an easy life, sweet sleep, friends begging for favors, and two

thousand good-looking slave boys. He will dine on rare foods, give a monthly dole to every citizen, beautify the city, and give heaps of gold to his friends. Simippos's wish is not for money and luxuries but to be the king of a huge army. After conquering Greece he will march east, reaching Babylon, where he will face the king at the head of a million men, kill him in single combat, and become king in his place, whereupon everyone will do him obeisance, and he will found countless cities that he will name after himself. Speaking third, Timolaos wishes for Hermes to give him a number of magic rings—one to make him healthy and invulnerable, another to make him invisible, another to make him as strong as ten thousand men, another to permit him to fly, another to put persons to sleep and to open locked doors, and a final one to make boys, women, and whole peoples fall passionately in love with him, in addition to which he wishes to live for a thousand years, renewing his youth every seventeen years. When it is Lykinos's turn, however, he says he has no need of a wish, and besides their journey is over. It is sufficient for him (he says) to laugh at all that his companions wish for, despite their praise of philosophy.[5]

Lucian's tale parallels oral tales of contests in wishing in that (1) several men agree to engage in a contest of wishing, whereupon, (2) speaking in turn, three participants each make outrageously impossible wishes for themselves. Interestingly, in the Greek text as also in the Renaissance text, the wishes take the form of prayers, and, as it happens, no one is proclaimed the winner, which is likewise true of the other texts here. Finally, (3) the dialogue ends with the comment of a fourth speaker, Lykinos, who, like the judge and like Ola Jensen in the other texts, makes a concluding witty remark. More judgmental of his companions than they of him, Lykinos mocks the inconsistency between their wish for many acquisitions, by means of which they imagine they would become very happy, and their enthusiasm for philosophy, from which one might expect them to aspire rather to self-sufficiency.

So Lucian's narrative corresponds closely to the oral tale. It may also reflect contests in wishing as playful, real-life pastimes. Since oral tales featuring contests in wishing no doubt arose from real-life pastimes rather than the pastimes arising from tales, it is natural to ask whether Lucian drew his inspiration from a tale or from a game. Certainly the give-and-take of the dialogue as well as its considerable length owe more to the diffuseness of life than to the concision of a traditional comic tale. But the author's employment of precisely three fantasts followed by a fourth speaker, a marginal participant who gives comic closure to the competition and to the story as a whole, suggests that Lucian is following the structure of an oral tale in the tradition of *Wishing Contests*. In giving it literary treatment, Lucian preserves the essential form of the folktale while elaborating it in the direction of greater realism.

Lit. AT 1925, *Wishing Contests*. BP 2:515. Holbek (1962) 2:184, no. 132.

1. *Fabulae Extravagantes* 13 = Perry 703. On this text see Sparmberg 1915 and BP 2:515.
2. Henningsen 1965:197.
3. AT 1920, *Contest in Lying*. Henningsen 1965:194–197.

4. Lucian *Navigium* 11.
5. *Navigium* 16–46.

Wooden Doll 🌿 Homo

Several men contribute to the making of a girl, and then each claims her. The question of whom she should belong to is not resolved; instead, the listeners are invited to voice their own opinions on the question.

This narrative is an instance of what folklorists call a *dilemma tale*. The tale itself, *The Wooden Doll*, is found both independently in oral tradition and also (and more commonly) as a tale within the second episode of AT 945, *Luck and Intelligence*, which serves as a frame story.

When *The Wooden Doll* appears as a tale within a tale, it is framed by the tale of the silent princess, in which the hero and his magic helper attempt to make a silent princess speak. On each of several successive nights, the hero's helper recounts a different dilemma tale ending in a question to which various listeners give answers, causing the exasperated princess to break briefly into speech in order to offer her own opinion on the problem posed in the tale. Of this frame tale there is no trace in ancient literature.

In a modern Greek folktale, the princely hero, his magic bird, and the silent princess were closeted together. The hero proposed that the bird tell a tale to pass the time, and the bird told how once there were three brothers who spent a night in a cave, each keeping watch for two hours at a time. The first brother to stay awake was a carpenter, who to pass the time carved a log with his axe into the shape of a woman. The next brother, a tailor, make clothes for it. The third brother, who was a monk, saw the wooden log dressed in clothes, and prayed to God to give it a soul, and God brought it to life. Now, the bird asked, to whom should the woman belong? The prince said she should belong to the man who shaped the wood. The bird itself said she should go to the tailor. And the otherwise silent princess burst out with the view that she should belong to the man whose prayers obtained a soul for her.[1]

In an Egyptian tale recorded in 1969, the hero asked his magic helper to tell a tale to keep them company. According to the tale, a carpenter, a tailor, and a religious savant were traveling together. Spending the night in a lonely area, they divided themselves into three shifts. The carpenter, being on guard first, made a doll out of a piece of wood. When the tailor took over he made it a dress with his sewing machine, and the third man prayed for god to give it a soul, which he did. Then each of the three men said that she was his own. Who, asked the magic helper, should marry her? The boy answered that the religious man should have her, but the girl exclaimed that the carpenter should marry her.[2]

In a Turkish tale collected in 1942, four men participate: a carpenter cut a piece of wood, a tailor clothed it, a goldsmith ornamented it, and a mullah prayed that life be bestowed upon the girl, which happened. When the storyteller asked who had the right to marry the girl, one of the listeners answered that the mullah did, whereupon the king's daughter said that the carpenter did.[3]

A tale collected in Baluchistan can illustrate the narrative as an independent

tale. Four servants of a king were on guard one night. The carpenter, who had the first watch, passed the time by carving a piece of wood into the shape of a beautiful woman. The next watch fell to a Darzi, who sewed clothes for her, and the third watch to a goldsmith, who made jewels for her. The last watch was taken by a Saiyid, who prayed to god to give her breath, which happened. When the day dawned, each of the four men claimed the woman as his own. They took the case to the king, who said she did not belong to the Saiyid, since everyone who was sick got a Saiyid to pray for him, nor did she belong to the carpenter or the goldsmith, who were only practicing their trades; rather, she belonged to the Darzi, for it was the bridegroom who gave clothes to the bride.[4]

Homo

The structure of this tale, in which the matter is referred to an arbiter, exactly parallels a Roman myth. Among the less familiar stories recounted by Hyginus in his Latin collection of mostly Greek myths and legends is an account of the creation of a human being by three deities, Cura ("Care, Worry"), Jove, and Tellus ("Earth").[5]

According to Hyginus, when Cura was crossing a certain stream she saw some chalky clay, picked it up, and began to fashion a human being. While she was thinking about what she had made, Jove came, and when she asked Jove to give it breath, Jove readily agreed to do so. But when Cura wanted to name it after herself, Jove said that it should rather bear his name. And while Cura and Jove were arguing, Tellus stood up and said that it should be named after her inasmuch as she had furnished her own body for it. They took Saturn as their judge, and he made the following judgments. Since Jove contributed breath, . . . would receive his body.[6] Since Cura first fashioned him, she would possess him all his life. As for the dispute concerning his name, he would be called *homo* since he was made *ex humo* (from soil).

The myth tells of the fashioning of the first human being by three deities, Earth providing the material, Care shaping it into the form of a human, and Jupiter giving it breath, that is, life. The creation of a human being by a committee of divine artisans, each of whom contributes something related to his or her own sphere of activity, is of course found elsewhere both in Greek and other mythological traditions. The best-known instance in Greek mythology is the creation of Pandora, the first woman, by several gods. Hesiod describes in one passage how Hephaistos fashioned her from clay after which Athene dressed and ornamented her, and in another context how, at Zeus's order, Hephaistos worked clay and water into the form of a goddess, Athene taught her the art of weaving, Aphrodite and other goddesses ornamented her and gave her charm and sexual attractiveness, and Hermes gave her speech as well as a shameless and deceitful mind.[7] But this is as far as the resemblance goes, for, once the new creature is finished, the deities who make Pandora let her go, whereas each of the gods who create the first person in the present story now proceeds to put forth a claim to the new creation, and this dispute is the issue that Hyginus's story really is about, the relationship of this archetypal human being to its several creators.

The scene is quaintly portrayed as a debate between the three deities. After

Care and Jove make their cases, Earth "stands up" (*surrexit*) to make hers. And when the matter remains unresolved, the three disputants, in good classical fashion, refer the case to an arbiter. But, curiously enough, the question that they ask Saturn to decide is not the question to which he gives most of his attention. They ask whose name the new being should bear, whereas he answers as though they had asked to whom the new creature should *belong*, adding almost as an afterthought and somewhat arbitrarily that it should be named *homo* after the *humus* from which it was made.

Unfortunately, some words have dropped out of Hyginus's text at the point at which Saturn explains to whom she should belong.[8] H. J. Rose, in his edition of the text, makes the plausible suggestion that the sentiment must have been more or less as follows: "Jove, since you contributed breath, [take its soul after death; and let Tellus, since she furnished the substance,] take its body."[9] So Care will possess the creature during its lifetime, and after its death its life-breath will return to Jupiter and its body to Earth.

Since the question in the modern oral versions is always to which of the creators the new creation should belong, and since in the ancient myth Saturn, acting as judge, also responds as though this were the main question, it is hard to escape the conclusion that this really was also the main question of the ancient myth in its oral form, and that the question of naming has been added ostensibly as the primary concern but in the event as a secondary matter. In any case, Saturn actually deals with two dilemmas: to whom should the new creature belong, and after whom should it be named?

In the myth, *homo* belongs in some way to each of the gods, whereas in the folktale the girl is to have a spousal relationship with one of the men and no relationship at all with the others. In this respect the ancient myth is reminiscent of a similar folktale found in India, in which the actions of three or four men restore to life a girl who has died.[10] Answering to the problem of who should have her, each man's action is analogized to some kinship relationship, one of which leads to marriage. Thus, in a tale collected from a thirteen-year-old Indian girl in 1966, one brother stood by her head, another by her side, and a third by her legs during her funeral. When the dead girl revived, she said that the one at her head was her father, the one at her side was her brother, and the one nearest her feet was her husband.[11] The *Vikramacarita*, an Indian text from around the eleventh century, has a tale that in content appears to stand midway between *The Suitors Restore the Maiden to Life* and *The Wooden Doll*. Four men created a woman, one carving her body from wood, another painting her, the third improving her as a woman, and the fourth giving her a soul, after which they disputed about who should possess her. The king asked the opinion of a silent maiden, who replied that the man who made the figure was her father, the one who painted her was her mother, the one who improved her was her spiritual guide, and the one who gave her life was her husband.[12] In Hyginus's story, *homo* has a relationship with all of his creators, belonging at some time to each of them. Care possesses him while he lives; when he dies his soul will belong to the sky god Jupiter and his body to Earth. It may be that these ideas in the Roman and the Indian narratives go back to a common prototype.

Although no frame or comments accompany the myth to clarify its role in ancient storytelling, one could imagine a narrator's recounting it to another

person as an illustration of the inevitability of worries and sorrows in life, in an attempt to reconcile the other to cares as a normal part of living. With its personification of Care, the ancient story has the feel of such other quasi-allegorical and rather intellectual exempla as that of the person (*anthropos*) who opened the jar that originally held all good things, which thereupon flew up to the gods on Olympos (except for Hope, which remained in the jar), as well as its better-known cognate, the myth of Pandora's jar.[13]

Lit. (AT 945, *Luck and Intelligence*: Episode IIb, *The Wooden Doll*.) Motif H621: *Skillful companions create a woman: to whom does she belong?* RE A1:72. BP 3:53–57. EM 3:670–673, 5:1312–1318. Ashliman, type 945. Goldberg 1997:187–189.

1. Dawkins 1953:326–327.
2. El-Shamy 1980:52.
3. Bødker, Hole, and D'Aronco 1963:207.
4. Dames 1892:524–525.
5. *Fab.* 220.
6. The dots indicate a lacuna in the text; see below.
7. *Th.* 570–590; *WD* 60–82.
8. Tu Iouis quoniam spiritum dedisti . . . corpus recipito.
9. Tu Iouis quoniam spiritum dedisti [animam post mortem accipe; Tellus quoniam corpus praebuit] corpus recipito.
10. AT 653B, *The Suitors Restore the Maiden to Life*.
11. Beck et al. 1987:22–23. Cf. Rohde 1960:370 and note 1.
12. BP 3:53–54.
13. Babrius 58.

Youth Who Bathed Himself in Blood ⊗ Achilleus's Heel

A youth slays a dragon and bathes in its blood, acquiring thereby a horny skin that no weapon can penetrate; however, one place on his body is untouched by the creature's blood and so remains vulnerable. The youth eventually perishes from a wound that he receives in his single vulnerable spot.

This is AT 650C, *The Youth Who Bathed Himself in the Blood of a Dragon*, which according to AT has been collected as a folktale in Lithuania.

The story is also attached to various gods and heroes of tradition. According to the mediaeval Austrian epic, *Nibelungenlied*, composed around 1200, the hero Siegfried slew a dragon and bathed in its hot blood, rendering his skin invulnerable except for one place between his shoulder blades where a linden leaf happened to cling while he was bathing. Much later his kinsman Hagen learned of Siegfried's vulnerable spot from the latter's gullible wife Kriemhild, who was even induced to sew a mark on Siegfried's clothing to indicate the spot. Hagen treacherously stabbed him in the back as he drank from a brook.[1] Interestingly, this Germanic story has reentered oral tradition from the epic and been collected as a folktale set in the United States.[2]

Around the same time as the poet of the *Nibelungenlied* was active on the continent, Snorri Sturluson composed his *Prose Edda* in Iceland. In the section entitled *Gylfaginning*, or "Deluding of Gylfi," Snorri relates that when Baldr had some threatening dreams, the other gods decided he needed to be protected. So Frigg

exacted an oath from every kind of animal and object that it would not harm Baldr. After that the gods amused themselves by throwing darts and stones at Baldr, since nothing hurt him. But Loki tricked Frigg into revealing that there was one thing from which she had not bothered to exact an oath, namely, mistletoe. Loki then gave a twig of mistletoe to the blind god Höð, who innocently cast it at Baldr in order to join the other gods in doing him honor. Baldr fell dead.[3]

In this myth, the protagonist's mother (rather than the protagonist himself) takes steps to make him invulnerable, and as in other versions of the story the effort is successful but for one apparently slight exception. The treacherous Loki learns the secret of Baldr's vulnerability from the gullible Frigg, as Hagen does from Kriemhild, and arranges for the fatal wound.

Taking these mediaeval Germanic versions into account, we can say that the international story is comprised minimally of two linked episodes, which may be separated by other events: the *setup*, in which unusual steps are taken to render the hero invulnerable and that succeed in doing so except in one small way, and the *conclusion*, in which an enemy or treacherous companion, taking advantage of his knowledge of the hero's vulnerability, attacks him via the one small window of access, killing him. The two episodes can constitute a succinct story by themselves, or they can serve to frame the action of a larger story.

The hero of the narrative resembles the man whose whole power or life or luck resides in a single place and therefore constitutes his vulnerability in a general sense. In folktales it can be the ogre whose soul (or heart or life) lies hidden in a secret place such as in an egg; when the hero discovers the location of the external soul, he destroys it, thereby killing the ogre.[4] In legend it can be a character such as the Greek Nisos or the Hebrew Samson, whose success is magically bound up in his hair (or the like); cut off his hair, and he is a beaten man.[5] Like Siegfried this character has one great vulnerability, and when his secret is discovered or acted upon, it is his undoing, though in terms of their imagery the two kinds of vulnerability are dissimilar, one being the weak place in the hero's armor, the other being the place where the character's essential being lies concentrated.

When carried to its logical extreme, the idea of a nearly invulnerable man becomes that of a wholly invulnerable man, of whom there are several in Greek mythology.[6] Such a person was Kaineus, who could not be pierced at all. To kill him his enemies had to drive him into the earth.[7] As with the hero of *The Youth Who Bathed Himself in the Blood of a Dragon*, there is some irony in his demise, for the strong hero who appears to be unconquerable is conquerable after all, but Kaineus's death, unlike Siegfried's, is manly rather than ignoble.

In ancient times *The Youth Who Bathed Himself in the Blood of a Dragon* was told of two Greek heroes who were contemporaries in mythological tradition, both being active at the time of the Trojan War: Achilleus (Latin: Achilles), whence of course the modern proverbial phrase, "Achilles' heel," and Aias (Latin: Ajax).

The motif of an Achilles' heel, of having one vulnerable spot, is found commonly in traditional narratives from Europe to India and elsewhere, but the presence of the motif does not always imply also the presence of the full tale of *The Youth Who Bathed Himself in the Blood of a Dragon*.[8] A character may simply be defined as being invulnerable except in one place—or as being invincible except in one way, which of course is not quite the same thing. The story may

then be parallel to the second part of *The Youth Who Bathed Himself in the Blood of a Dragon*. For example, Talos was a brazen man who guarded Crete, running around the island three times a day and pelting intruders with stones or burning them up. A single vein ran from his neck to his ankles, where it was covered by a membrane or plugged by a bronze nail. He met his end when Medeia caused him to graze the membrane against a rock, rupturing the membrane, or tricked him into allowing her to pull out the nail; in either case his ichor (that is, his supernatural blood) spurted out and he died. Or a certain Poias shot him in the ankle with an arrow.[9]

Achilleus

The legend of Achilleus's heel is found only in Latin authors and is not attested with any certainty before the first century A.D. Most of the writers in question merely allude to one or the other of the two linked episodes, so that in their time the story already must have been generally familiar. Thus the poet Statius represents Achilleus's distraught mother, Thetis, as describing threatening visions in which she seemed to take her son down to Tartaros and to dip him again in the Stygian springs; later, as she addresses Achilleus, she refers to the time when she armed him with the water of the Styx, and now wishes she had armed his entire body; and still later Statius mentions the time that Thetis secretly brought her son to the streams of the Styx and made his limbs impervious to iron.[10] Whereas Statius alludes to the first episode, the mythographer Hyginus refers to the concluding episode, saying that Apollo was angry at Achilleus and, taking the form of Paris, shot an arrow at his heel, which was mortal, and so killed him.[11] Hyginus evidently treats "vulnerable" and "mortal" as equivalent and interchangeable qualities, though in fact Greek tradition, or at least Homer, represents both mortals and immortals as vulnerable. The mythographer may have confounded Achilleus's baptism in water with his baptism in fire (see below), the unambiguous purpose of which was to render him immortal.

We first get both episodes in Servius's commentary on the *Aeneid*, according to which Achilleus was dipped by his mother into the Stygian lake and thereby became invulnerable except for the part of his body by which he had been held. Later, when Achilleus went to a temple for a rendezvous with Polyxena, with whom he was in love, he was slain by Paris, who had hidden in ambush behind the cult statue. Paris directed the arrows with Apollo's help.[12] The commentator Lactantius Placidus agrees with this account, explaining that when Thetis learned of Achilleus's fate, she feared for his death and so dipped him in the Stygian pond, rendering his entire body invulnerable except for the place where she had held him. Later when he went to meet his beloved Polyxena in a temple, he was ambushed and slain by Paris, who hid behind the statue.[13] Writing at about the same time, the sixth-century mythographer Fulgentius relates how Thetis dipped Achilleus in the Stygian waters, all except for his heel. As usual this author offers an allegorical interpretation, explaining that the dipping really meant she was hardening him against all kinds of tasks, and pointing out the special significance of the veins of the heel, which according to Fulgentius were connected to various parts of the body all the way up to the thumb.[14]

If we put these accounts together, we get a narrative in which Thetis secretly dipped her infant son into the waters of the Styx, rendering him invulnerable or immortal in all parts of his body except for the part by which she had held him, his heel. Years later during the Trojan War the god Apollo in the form of Paris (or Paris himself or Paris and Apollo together) shot Achilleus in the heel, killing him.[15] As in the Baldr myth, it is the protagonist's divine mother who attempts to render him invulnerable. Since Thetis does so while her son is an infant, an unusually long time intervenes between the initial rite and his terminal wound, so that the episodes completely frame the life of Achilleus. It is surprising that for all its familiarity to us, the story must be pieced together from a number of authorities, none of whom treats it with any fullness.

The matter is even more complicated than this, for there may be a parallel tradition according to which Thetis attempts to make her infant son immortal by burning away his mortal parts. In a scene in the *Argonautica* by Apollonios of Rhodes, composed in the third century B.C., Thetis visited her mortal husband Peleus and then abruptly departed, reminding Peleus painfully of an earlier event in their domestic lives. When their son Achilleus had been an infant, Thetis would secretly burn away his mortal flesh in the hearth fire by night and rub him with ambrosia by day in order that he might become immortal and escape hateful old age. But one night Peleus awoke during this procedure, leapt out of bed, saw his son gasping in the flames, and let out a great cry, whereupon Thetis dropped the screaming baby to the ground and angrily leapt into the sea, after which she never returned till the present occasion.[16]

Burning away the mortal parts of a person by means of fire was an established method in Greek traditional story for making a mortal into an immortal. As early as the *Homeric Hymn to Demeter* the goddess Demeter employs this rite in order to render immortal a mortal infant whose nurse she is, and with the same results. When her secret nocturnal treatment is innocently interrupted by a concerned parent, she instantly leaves off the procedure and departs.[17] This traditional episode has found its way into more than one story.

It would be easy to understand the burning episode and the bathing episode as variant fillers of the same narrative slot: Thetis exposes her infant son Achilleus to water (fire) in order to render him invulnerable (immortal), but the treatment does not quite achieve its end because she fails to treat the part of the body by which she holds him (because she leaves off the treatment when she is interrupted), as a result of which there is a fatal exception to Achilleus's invulnerability (immortality). But it is uncertain whether Apollonios understood the episode as linked with the episode of Achilleus's death in more than a general way. Writing some centuries later, the mythographer Apollodoros perhaps did understand it in this way, since he narrates first Achilleus's immersion in fire and later his death from an arrow in the ankle shot by Paris and Apollo; however, since Apollodoros does not actually qualify Achilleus's ankle as being vulnerable or mortal, we cannot be sure.[18] Nor does Quintus Smyrnaeus single out Achilleus's ankle as being the hero's only vulnerable spot, when in his poem on *The Fall of Troy* he relates how Apollo sent the fatal shaft into Achilleus's ankle.[19] In Greek tradition the site of Achilleus's fatal wound is regularly his ankle (*sphyron*), and if there is a special significance to this site, it is not explained in our sources. So there were different traditions of the death of

Achilleus, the tradition that incorporated the international story of *The Youth Who Bathed Himself in the Blood of a Dragon* being only one of them.

The role of Thetis as the interrupted goddess recurs in an earlier and even stranger story. In a fragment of the lost epic poem *Aigimios*, attributed to Hesiod, Thetis threw each of the children she bore to Peleus into a basin of water in order to see if it was mortal. Many of their children perished in this manner, but Peleus became angry and stopped her before she threw Achilleus into the basin.[20] This test is obviously connected with the fact that the children are the offspring of a mixed marriage between a Nereid and a man, that is, between a divinity of the sea and a terrestrial mortal. What she really wants to discover is whether her offspring have inherited her nature or their father's. If they are wholly human and simply drown in water rather than swim, presumably she has no further interest in them. I shall not pursue this branch of the tradition, which would take us too far from our topic, wishing only to call attention to the bathing, the question of mortality versus immortality, and the active role of the mother.[21] The traditional biography of Achilleus, with its old themes of concern for the shortness of the hero's life, of the wish of the mermaid mother for her sons to be immortal like herself, of her immersing them in water or fire in this connection, and of the hero's eventual death from an unlikely wound, made a good fit with the plot of *The Youth Who Bathed Himself in the Blood of a Dragon*. The international tale was worked into the biography of the hero sometime before Statius alluded to it in the first century A.D. It caught the imagination of Romans more than of Greeks, and no surviving Greek literature mentions it.

A word about the imagery. It is not difficult to accept in a mythological story the fantastic idea that an exotic liquid might harden the skin, making one invulnerable, or that fire might burn away one's mortal component so that only one's immortal component remained, and, as exotic liquids go, the water of the Styx should do as well as dragon's blood. And yet in the context of ancient storytelling it is not obvious why the Styx should have come to play this role.[22] It is, after all, a stream belonging to the death realm and, if anything, might be expected to be baneful, a River of Death. But an ancient epithet of the Styx is "imperishable," both the "imperishable Styx" and the "imperishable water of the Styx"; and if the Styx was traditionally the Imperishable River, it may also have been the River of Imperishability, being both imperishable itself and also conferring imperishability, imparting its own virtue to those who came into contact with it.[23] In any case, the subsequent popularity of the story was doubtless enhanced by its parallelism to the Christian rite of baptism, which developed around the time when the story of Achilleus and the Styx is first mentioned.[24] For the early Christians, baptism meant an immersion into death followed by a resurrection, so that the medium of Christian baptism, like that of the Styx into which Achilleus is immersed, is ironically a water of death that confers life.[25] But there appears to be no direct connection between the two traditions.

Aias

Synthesized from different sources, the story is more or less this. The hero Herakles stayed briefly as a houseguest at the home of Telamon, Aias's father, when Aias was an infant. Wrapping the baby in the invulnerable skin of the

Nemean Lion, which he had acquired during his First Labor, he prayed that the boy might be as invulnerable as the lion's skin. So Aias became invulnerable except in one spot, which by chance the skin had not covered. At Troy many years later, when Aias attempted suicide, he succeeded only after locating his one vulnerable spot and stabbing himself there, since weapons would not penetrate his skin elsewhere.[26]

Aeschylus drew upon the legend in a tragedy, *Threissai*, which has not survived. According to a scholiast who mentions the play, Aias was invulnerable everywhere except for his armpit, for when Herakles had covered him with the lion's skin, this one place remained uncovered because of the quiver Herakles wore. Aeschylus (the scholiast continues) says that Aias's sword bent like a bow when he stabbed himself, since his skin would not yield to it. Eventually a goddess appeared and showed him where to stab himself.[27]

Plato alludes in passing to Aias's being invulnerable to iron, and in his usual obscure manner the poet Lykophron alludes to Aias's having been made invulnerable to weapons except in the place covered by the quiver, to Herakles' holding the child and praying to Zeus, and to Aias's self-slaughter.[28] The author of the *hypothesis* (contextualizing summary) to Sophocles' *Aias* mentions several different accounts of Aias's death, attributing to Pindar a version in which Aias could be wounded only in his ribs, since his body was invulnerable where it had been covered by the lion's skin but vulnerable where it had remained uncovered. And a scholiast on Homer says that Herakles showed up at Telamon's house just after the birth of Telamon's son Aias, picked up the boy, wrapped him in his lion's skin, and prayed that he might be invulnerable; and so he became, except for his neck.[29]

In his scholium on the passage in Lykophron, Tzetzes explains that in Nemea there was a lion that was invulnerable to iron and missiles of any kind. After strangling it, Herakles used its skin as a covering for his body. Herakles was friend to Telamon, who was childless and invited Herakles to visit him and to join him in sacrificing and praying to Herakles' father, Zeus, for offspring. Herakles showed up wearing the lion's skin and prayed that Telamon might have a son. After Aias was born, Herakles returned and covered him with the lion's skin, so that Aias became invulnerable except in one spot that had been covered by the quiver Herakles wore. According to other authors, Tzetzes says, Aias's vulnerable spot was his collarbone. But Tzetzes himself skeptically regards the idea of Aias's being nearly invulnerable as nonsense, saying that the truth is that Aias was an extremely skillful soldier who fought against many men in war but was never himself wounded because he defended himself excellently with his shield. When he took his own life, stabbing himself in the ribs or the throat, the event (Tzetzes believes) was transformed into a fabulous story according to which he was vulnerable only in this or that place.[30] Tzetzes is thinking of the passage in Homer's *Iliad* in which the Greeks fear lest Aias be wounded by Diomedes.[31] Obviously, Homer does not treat Aias as invulnerable.

Although the legend of Aias's near invulnerability is first attested in Aeschylus, it may be much older, for a story suspiciously like it appears in an ode of Pindar. The poet represents Herakles at the house of Telamon, praying that Telamon may have a son with "a body as unbreakable as the hide of the beast

that covers me," and with slight variations this episode was known also to Hesiod.[32] It seems, then, that the episode of Herakles' visit to Telamon was known in two principal forms, one in which Herakles visited the childless Telamon, praying that he might have a son and that the boy might be as invulnerable as the lion's skin Herakles was wearing, and another in which Herakles visited Telamon shortly after the birth of his son, wrapped the boy in his lion's skin, and prayed that he might be as invulnerable as the animal's hide, which, as it turned out, covered most but not all of the child's body. Most authors mention only one or the other; Tzetzes gives them both, one after the other. The first form of the episode could scarcely serve to introduce the story of *The Youth Who Bathed Himself in the Blood of a Dragon*, since there is no provision for a fatal exception, whereas the second form could have little purpose other than to set such a story in motion. Presumably either the former is a rationalization of the more fabulous form or the latter reflects a modification made to accommodate the international story.

In both ancient legends the attempt to make the hero invulnerable is undertaken not by Achilleus or Aias himself but by an interested party (Thetis, Herakles) on his behalf, just as in the Baldr myth Baldr's mother acts on his behalf. In neither case, then, does the legend begin with the hero's slaying a dragon or other beast, as in the Siegfried legend and in the folktale, though a trace of this idea can probably be glimpsed in Herakles' killing and flaying the monstrous Nemean Lion, whose magic skin confers near invulnerability on Aias. If so, the heroic motif of monster slaying is a very old feature of the type, and in this version the feature has been transferred to Herakles, or the preexistence of the feature in the Herakles legend has provided a familiar hook on which to attach the story of the nearly invulnerable hero. Another trait in which both ancient legends agree is that the rite of invulnerability is performed when the protagonist is still an infant. As a result, Aias does not even know where it is that he can be wounded, and ironically he must discover his own secret in order to be his own assailant. The ancient rites of invulnerability do not take the form of bathing in monster's blood, but the imagery is not entirely dissimilar, since one legend involves bathing in a strange liquid and the other features envelopment in a monster's hide.

One could of course imagine that the two stories of near invulnerability grew independently out of earlier themes in each legend, but it is much easier to suppose that narrators incorporated the same international story type into the cluster of narratives already attached to each hero, where it then competed with other versions of the events, especially those concerning the hero's death. Accordingly, the prior existence of related themes in the tradition of each hero served to attract the international story of near invulnerability rather than to provide material out of which the story was invented. Since the story of Achilleus's near invulnerability is known only in Latin authors, and that of Aias only in Greek authors, one may be a Roman development and the other a Greek development, even though both heroes are originally Greek. Though some scholars declare that the story of Aias's invulnerability was borrowed from that of Achilleus, this supposition is arbitrary, and the borrowing can as easily be imagined to have gone the other way—more easily, in fact, since the story of Aias's singular vulnerability is attested many centuries earlier than

that of Achilleus and was given literary treatment by more important authors, even if it is less familiar to us today.[33] But the concept of *The Youth Who Bathed Himself in the Blood of a Dragon* as an international tale type frees us from having to assume that one of the ancient stories must derive from the other or that one or the other of these ancient stories must be the original of the type merely because it is the earliest attestation that we happen to have.

Sardis

The case for a migratory story is confirmed, if confirmation is necessary, by the existence of a third realization of the type.

According to Herodotos, the capture of Sardis happened in the following way. When Meles ruled the Lydians, the Telmessians had declared that if Meles should carry around the city the lion that his concubine had born him, Sardis could never be taken. Meles took this advice, having the lion carried around all of the walls except for one spot where the acropolis seemed unassailable. Later when Kyros, king of the Persians, was besieging Sardis, he promised a reward to the first man to scale the wall. Now a certain Hyroiades determined to make an ascent at this same steep place, where the Lydians had posted no guard because they supposed that an assault there would be impossible. But Hyroiades noticed that a Lydian soldier who had accidentally dropped his helmet down the slope had managed to climb down to retrieve it. So Hyroiades tried climbing it himself, and others followed him, whereupon the city was taken.[34]

Here the plot has been attached not to another hero of tradition but to a city. King Meles of Lydia performs a magical rite to make Sardis impregnable, with of course one fatal loophole. Interestingly, the rite involves magical encirclement by a beast, a lion begotten by the king, suggestive of the lion's skin with similar magical properties in the Aias legend. The slight exception is of the same sort as that in the Baldr myth: one element (mistletoe/precipice) appears to be too insignificant to bother with, and so is deliberately neglected. But years later an enemy soldier discovers the city's one vulnerable spot, by means of which the besiegers penetrate the otherwise invulnerable city, bringing at end to the empire of King Kroisos.

Lit. AT 650C, *The Youth Who Bathed Himself in the Blood of a Dragon.* Sydow 1918:26–34. Thordarson 1972. *EM* 1:59–65. Ashliman, type 650C.

1. Chap. 3, 15–16.
2. Musick 1970:79–106, no. 23.
3. *Gylf.* 49. On the Baldr myth more generally see Lindow 1997.
4. AT 302, *The Ogre's (Devil's) Heart in the Egg.*
5. On Nisos see Gantz 1993:257–258; on Samson, see Judges 13.24–16.31.
6. Berthold 1911.
7. Forbes Irving 1990:155–162.
8. Z311, *Achilles heel*; Rooth 1961:103–106; *EM* 1:59–61.
9. See further Frazer (1921) 1:118–119; Gantz 1993:364–365. The lexicographer Hesykhios glosses Greek ταλώς (*talos*) as ὁ ἥλιος "the sun." Oddly, Latin *talus* signifies "ankle, heel," and is the word employed by the mythographers Hyginus and Fulgentius (3.7) in their accounts of Achilleus's vulnerable heel.

10. *Achilleid* 1.133–134; 1.267–271; 1.480–481.

11. *Fab.* 107.

12. Servius *ad Aen.* 6.57.

13. Lactantius Placidus *ad Achill.* 1.134 and 269.

14. Fulgentius 3.7.

15. The variation is old. In Homer the death of Achilleus by Apollo is foretold by Thetis (*Il.* 21.276–278), and his death by Paris and Apollo is predicted by the dying Hektor (22.359–360).

16. Apollonios of Rhodes 4.865–879. The reason that Thetis leaps into the sea is, of course, that she is a Nereid, a mermaid. For international analogues to the story of the marriage of a mortal and a mermaid, see Frazer (1921) 2:383–388 and Christiansen 1958, type 4080, *The Seal Woman*.

17. *Homeric Hymn to Demeter* 231–281. According to Apollodoros (*Bibl.* 1.5.1), the child perishes in the fire when Demeter is interrupted. Essentially the same story was told of the goddess Isis (Plutarch *Isis et Osiris* 15–16 = *Mor.* 357). A remarkably similar episode is reported from modern German tradition. While a woman in childbed was sleeping, Frau Holle came, took her child, removed its swaddling clothes, cleaned the child, dried its clothing, and lay the child down again. The woman awoke and saw how Frau Holle was sitting with her child next to the fire and drying its clothing. She screamed, whereupon Holle threw the child into the fire and disappeared (Schenkl 1862:195, citing A. Kuhn, *Sagen, Gebräuchen und Märchen aus Westphalen* 2:4, no. 3). More remotely, in a Persian story King Ruzvanshad married the fairy or jinn Princess Sheristání on the condition that he must not reproach her for anything she might do in his presence, however displeased he should be, for if he should upbraid her, they must separate. After a time the princess gave birth to a child, which in the presence of her husband she cast into the fire. He cried out in horror, and she disappeard (Clouston [1887] 1:213–214). See further Frazer (1921) 2:311–317, app. 1: "Putting Children on the Fire"; for a different view, Fehling 1991:72–73.

18. Apollodoros *Bibl.* 3.13.6, *Epit.* 5.3.

19. Quintus Smyrnaeus 3.60–89.

20. Hesiod fr. 300 M-W.

21. On Achilleus's near invulnerability and death, see Roscher 1:23–24; Berthold 1911:35–43; Frazer (1921) 2:68–71 and 212–215; Severyns 1928:254–259; Kakridis 1947; Thordarson 1972; Young 1979; Fehling 1991:72–73; Gantz 1993:625–628. A somewhat similar test is reported of Amphitryon, whose wife Alkmene, having slept with Zeus and shortly after with her husband Amphitryon, bore two sons, Iphikles and Alkaios or Alkides (later called Herakles). In order to determine which, if either, was the child of an immortal, Amphitryon placed snakes in the infants' bed. Iphikles reacted with fear, but the future Herakles strangled them. See Pherekydes (*FGH* 3 F 69); Gantz 1993:377.

22. Young 1979:14.

23. *aphthitos.* Hesiod *Th.* 389, 397, 805; cf. West 1966:377–378.

24. Young 1979:14–17.

25. For example, Romans 6.2–4.

26. On Aias's near invulnerability and suicide see Roscher 1:121–122; Berthold 1911:6–26; Severyns 1928:325–328; Kakridis 1947; Gantz 1993:631–634.

27. Aeschylus fr. 83 Nauck.

28. Plato *Symposium* 219e. Lycophron *Alexandra* 455–466.

29. Schol. Homer *Il.* 23.821.

30. Tzetzes *Scholia on Lycophron* 455–461.

31. Homer *Il.* 23.820–823.

32. Pindar *Isthmian* 6.47. Hesiod fr. 250 MW.

33. Roscher 1:122; Jebb 1887:xviii–xix.

34. Herodotos 1.84.

BIBLIOGRAPHY

Aakjær, Jeppe. 1966. *Jyske Folkeminder*. Edited by Bengt Holbek. Danmarks Folke-minder, no. 76. Copenhagen: Munksgaard.

Aarne, Antti. 1910. *Verzeichnis der Märchentypen*. FFC 3. Helsinki: Suomalaisen Tiedeakatemian Toimituksia.

———. 1913. *Leitfaden der vergleichenden Märchenforschung*. FFC 13. Hamina: Suoma-laisen Tiedeakatemian Kustantama.

———. 1914. *Schwänke über schwerhörige Menschen: Eine vergleichende Untersuchung*. FFC 20. Hamina: Suomalaisen Tiedeakatemian Kustantama.

———. 1918. *Estnische Märchen- und Sagenvarianten*. FFC 25. Hamina: Suomalaisen Tiedeakatemian Kustantama.

———. 1930. *Die magische Flucht: Eine Märchenstudie*. FFC 92. Helsinki: Academia Scien-tiarum Fennica.

Aarne, Antti, and Stith Thompson. 1928. *The Types of the Folk-Tale: A Classification and Bibliography*. FFC 74. Helsinki: Academia Scientiarum Fennica.

———. 1961. *The Types of the Folktale: A Classification and Bibliography*. 2d rev. FFC 184. Helsinki: Academia Scientiarum Fennica.

Abrahams, Roger D. 1970. *Deep Down in the Jungle: Negro Narrative Folklore from the Streets of Philadelphia*. Rev. ed. Chicago: Aldine.

———. 1972. "Folklore and Literature as Performance." *JFI* 8:75–94.

Achelis, T. O. 1917. "Antike Läusefabel." *Berliner Philologische Wochenschrift* 37:61–63.

Ackermann, Elfriede. 1944. "*Das Schlaraffenland* in German Literature and Folksong: Social Aspects of an Earthly Paradise, with an Inquiry into its History in European Literature." Ph.D. diss., University of Chicago.

Ackermann, Hans Christoph, and Jean-Robert Gisler, eds. 1981–97. *Lexicon Icono-graphicum Mythologiae Classicae* (*LIMC*). 8 vols. Zurich: Artemis.

Adams, J. N. 1982. *The Latin Sexual Vocabulary*. Baltimore: Johns Hopkins University Press.

Adolf, Helen. 1950. "The Ass and the Harp." *Speculum* 25:49–57.

Afanas'ev, Alexandr. 1975. *Russian Fairy Tales*. Translated by Norbert Guterman. New York: Pantheon Books.

———. 1998. *Russian Secret Tales: Bawdy Folktales of Old Russia*. Baltimore: Clearfield.

Ἀλεξιάδης, Μηνᾶς Ἀλ. 1982. Οἱ ῾ Ελληνικὲς Παραλλαγὲς γιὰ τὸν Δρακοντοκτόνο ῞Ηρωα (Aarne-Thompson 300, 301A καὶ 301Β). Παραμυθολογικὴ Μελέτη. Diss., University of Ioannina.

Alstrup, Ane. 1967. "Det store Hotel." *Folkeminder* 13:208.

Aly, Wolf. 1928. "Märchen." In *RE* 14:254–281.

———. 1969. *Volksmärchen, Sage und Novelle bei Herodot und seinen Zeitgenossen: Eine Untersuchung über die volkstümlichen Elemente der altgriechischen Prosaerzählung.* 2d ed. Göttingen: Vandenhoeck & Ruprecht.

Amades, Joan. 1950. *Folklore de Catalunya: Rondallística.* Barcelona: Editorial Selecta.

Amalfi, Gaetano. 1896. "Die Kraniche des Ibykus in der Sage." *ZVV* 6:115–129.

Amundsen, Darrel, and Carol Diers. 1969. "The Age of Menarche in Classical Greece and Rome." *Human Biology* 41:125–132.

Andersen, Øivind. 1972. "Odysseus and the Wooden Horse." *Symbolae Osloenses* 52:5–18.

Anderson, J. K. 1970. "The Trojan Horse Again." *Classical Journal* 66:22–25.

Anderson, Walter. 1927–33. *Novelline Popolari Sammarinesi.* 3 vols. Tartu (Dorpat): C. Mattiesen.

———. 1940. "Zu dem estnischen Märchen vom gestohlenen Donnerinstrument." Tartu, 1939. *Acta et Commentationes Universitatis Tartuensis, B: Humaniora,* 45.1.

———. 1955. "Eine neue Monographie über Amor und Psyche." *Hessische Blätter für Volkskunde* 46:118–130.

Apo, Satu. 1986. "Questions Arising in the Comparative Study of Magic Tales." *JFR* 23:177–186.

Arnott, W. G. 1962. "Ocnus, with Reference to a Passage of Apuleius and to a Black-Figure Lekythos in Palermo." *C & M* 23:233–247.

Artola, George. 1978. "The Nature of the *Book of Sindbâd*." In Niedzielski, Runte, and Hendrickson 1978:7–31.

Asadovskij, Mark. 1926. *Eine sibirische Märchenerzählerin.* FFC 68. Helsinki: Suomalainen Tiedeakatemia. English version: Mark Azadovskii, *A Siberian Tale Teller.* Translated by James Dow, *Monograph Series,* no. 2. Austin: Center for Intercultural Studies in Folklore and Ethnomusicology, University of Texas, 1974.

Asbjørnsen, P. Ch., and Jørgen Moe. 1965. *Samlede Eventyr. Norske Kunstneres Billedutgave.* 3 vols. Oslo: Gyldendal Norsk Forlag.

Ashliman, D. L. 1987. *A Guide to Folktales in the English Language. Based on the Aarne-Thompson Classification System.* New York: Greenwood.

Ashton, John. n.d. [original ed. 1882]. *Chapbooks of the Eighteenth Century, with Facsimiles, Notes, and Introduction.* London: Skoob Books.

Auffarth, Christoph. 1991. *Der drohende Untergang: "Schöpfung" in Mythos und Ritual im Alten Orient und in Griechenland am Beispiel der Odyssee und des Ezechielbuches.* Religionsgeschichtliche Versuche und Vorarbeiten, no. 39. Berlin: Walter de Gruyter.

Austin, Norman. 1975. *Archery at the Dark of the Moon: Poetic Problems in Homer's Odyssey.* Berkeley and Los Angeles: University of California Press.

———. 1983. "Odysseus and the Cyclops: Who Is Who." In *Approaches to Homer,* edited by Carl A. Rubino and Cynthia W. Shelmerdine, 3–37. Austin: University of Texas Press.

Austin, R. G. 1959. "Virgil and the Wooden Horse." *Journal of Roman Studies* 49:16–25.

Avanzin, Anton. 1954. "Einige Quellen der lustigen Geschichten von Franz Resl." *Österreichische Zeitschrift für Volkskunde,* n.s., 8:124–136.

Azzolina, David S. 1987. *Tale Type- and Motif-Indexes: An Annotated Bibliography.* Garland Folklore Bibliographies, no. 12. New York: Garland.

Babcock, Barbara A, ed. 1978. *The Reversible World: Symbolic Inversion in Art and Society.* Ithaca, N.Y.: Cornell University Press.

Bächtold-Stäubli, Hans, ed. 1927–42. *Handwörterbuch des deutschen Aberglaubens.* 10 vols. Berlin: Walter de Gruyter.

Baker, Ronald L. 1986. *Jokelore: Humorous Folktales from Indiana.* Bloomington: Indiana University Press.

Baldry, H. C. 1953. "The Idler's Paradise in Attic Comedy." *G & R* 22:49–60.

Ballabriga, A. 1981. "Le malheur des nains: Quelques aspects du combat des grues contre les Pygmées dans la littérature grecque." *Revue des Études Anciennes* 83: 57–74.

Balys, Jonas. 1939. *Griaustinis ir velnias baltoskandijos kraštų tautosakoje: Lyginamoji pasakojamosios tautosakos studija. Donner und Teufel in den Volkserzählungen der baltischen und skandinavischen Völker: Eine vergleichende volkskundliche Studie. Tautosakos Darbai* (Kaunas) 6:1–220.

Barbeau, C. Marius. 1954. "Nos traditions à l'université." *JAF* 67:199–211.

Baring-Gould, Sabine. 1967. *Curious Myths of the Middle Ages*. 1882. Reprint, New Hyde Park: University Books.

Barrett, W. S., ed. 1964. *Euripides: Hippolytos*. Oxford: Clarendon Press.

Bascom, William. 1965. "The Forms of Folklore: Prose Narratives." *JAF* 78:3–20.

——. 1992. *African Folktales in the New World*. Bloomington: Indiana University Press.

Başgöz, İlhan, and Pertev N. Boratav. 1998. *I, Hoca Nasreddin, Never Shall I Die: A Thematic Analysis of Hoca Stories*. Indiana University Turkish Studies Series, no. 18. Bloomington.

Basile, Giambattista. 1932. *The Pentamerone of Giambattista Basile*. Translated by Benedetto Croce. Edited by N. M. Penzer. 2 vols. New York: E. P. Dutton.

Baughman, Ernest. 1966. *Type and Motif-Index of the Folktales of England and North America*. Indiana University Folklore Series, no. 20. The Hague: Mouton.

Bauman, Richard. 1977. *Verbal Art as Performance*. Prospect Heights, Ill.: Waveland.

——. 1986. *Story, Performance, and Event: Contextual Studies of Oral Narrative*. Cambridge Studies in Oral and Literate Culture, no. 10. Cambridge: Cambridge University Press.

Baumgartner, Walter. 1959. "Israelitisch-Griechische Sagenbeziehungen." In *Zum Alten Testament und seiner Umwelt: Ausgewählte Aufsätze*, 147–178. Leiden: E. J. Brill.

Bausinger, Hermann. 1980. *Formen der 'Volkspoesie.'* 2d ed. Berlin: Erich Schmidt Verlag.

Bausinger, Hermann, and Wolfgang Brückner, eds. 1969. *Kontinuität? Geschichtlichkeit und Dauer als volkskundliches Problem*. Berlin: Erich Schmidt Verlag.

Beaton, Roderick. 1986. "The Oral Traditions of Modern Greece: A Survey." *Oral Tradition* 1:110–133.

Bebel, Heinrich. 1907. *Schwänke*. Edited by Albert Wesselski. 2 vols. Munich: Georg Müller.

Beck, Brenda E. F., Peter J. Claus, Praphulladatta Goswami, and Jawaharlal Handoo, eds. 1987. *Folktales of India*. Chicago: University of Chicago Press.

Bédier, Joseph. 1925. *Les fabliaux: Études de littérature populaire et d'histoire littéraire du moyen âge*. 5th ed. Paris: Librarie Ancienne Edouard Champion.

Beekes, Robert S. P. 1986. " 'You Can Get New Children . . . ': Turkish and other Parallels to Ancient Greek Ideas in Herodotus, Thucydides, Sophocles and Euripides." *Mnemosyne* 39:225–239.

Ben-Amos, Dan. 1971. "Toward a Definition of Folklore in Context." *JAF* 84:3–15.

——. 1976. "Talmudic Tall Tales." In Dégh, Glassie, and Oinas 1976:25–43.

Ben-Amos, Dan, and Kenneth S. Goldstein, eds. 1975. *Folklore: Performance and Communication*. The Hague: Mouton.

Benfey, Theodor. 1859. *Pantschatantra: Fünf Bücher indischer Fabeln, Märchen und Erzählungen*. 2 vols. Leipzig: F. A. Brockhaus.

Berendsohn, Walter A. 1921. *Grundformen volkstümlicher Erzählerkunst in den Kinder- und Hausmärchen der Brüder Grimm: Ein stilkritischer Versuch*. Hamburg: Verlag W. Gente.

Bergren, Ann L. T. 1983. "Odyssean Temporality: Many (Re)Turns." In *Approaches to Homer*, edited by Carl A. Rubino and Cynthia W. Shelmerdine, 38–73. Austin: University of Texas Press.

Berthold, Otto. 1911. *Die Unverwundbarkeit in Sage und Aberglauben der Griechen, mit einem Anhang über den Unverwundbarkeitsglauben bei anderen Völkern, besonders den Germanen.* Religionsgeschichtliche Versuche und Vorarbeiten 11, no. 1. Giessen: Verlag von Alfred Töpelmann.

Bertolini, Francesco. 1989. "Dal folclore all'epica: esempli di trasformazione e adattamento." In *Il meraviglioso e il verosimile tra antichità e medioevo,* edited by Diego Lanza and Ottone Longo, 131–152. Biblioteca dell' "Archivum Romanicum," ser. I, vol. 221. Florence: Leo S. Olschki Editore.

Bertolotti, Maurizio. 1979. "Le ossa e la pelle dei buoi: Un mito popolare tra agiografia e stregoneria." *Quaderni storici* 14:470–499.

Bickel, Ernst. 1921. "Gyges und sein Ring." *Neue Jahrbücher für das klassische Altertum* 47:336–358.

Binder, Gerhard, and Reinhold Merkelbach, eds. 1968. *Amor und Psyche.* Wege der Forschungen, no. 126. Darmstadt: Wissenschaftliche Buchgesellschaft.

[Birch, Samuel]. 1843. "The Impatient Widow: A Chinese Tale." *Asiatic Journal,* n.s., 1:607–618.

Bladé, Jean-François. 1885. *Contes populaires de la Gascogne.* 3 vols. Paris: G. P. Maisonneuve & Larose.

Blinkenberg, Christopher. 1987. *The Thunderweapon in Religion and Folklore: A Study in Comparative Archaeology.* New York: Aristide D. Caratzas.

Bloomfield, Maurice. 1923. "Joseph and Potiphar in Hindu Fiction." *TAPA* 54:141–167.

Boberg, Inger M. 1934. *Sagnet om den store Pans død.* Skrifter utgivna av Gustav Adolfs Akademien för Folklivsforskning, no. 2. Uppsala: A.-B. Lundequistska Bokhandeln. With summary in German.

——. 1938. "The Tale of Cupid and Psyche." *C & M* 1:177–216.

——. 1940. "Noch einmal 'die Sage vom Tode des grossen Pan.' " *C & M* 3:119–132.

Bødker, Laurits. 1954. "Den lange løgn." *Danske Studier,* 109–126.

——. 1957. *Indian Animal Tales: A Preliminary Survey.* FFC 170. Helsinki: Academia Scientiarum Fennica.

——. 1959. "Eventyr." In *Kulturhistorisk Leksikon for nordisk Middelalder* (Copenhagen: Rosenkilde and Bagger), 4:71–76.

——. 1965. *Folk Literature (Germanic).* Vol. 2. of *International Dictionary of Regional European Ethnology and Folklore.* Copenhagen: Rosenkilde and Bagger.

Bødker, Laurits, Christina Hole, and G. D'Aronco, eds. 1963. *European Folk Tales.* Copenhagen: Rosenkilde and Bagger.

Boerma, R. E. H. Westendorp. 1982. "Het Weeuwtje van Ephesus (Petron. Satyr. c. 110,6–113,3)." *Hermeneus* 54:94–109.

Boldrini, Sandro. 1989. "Il pasto della vedova: cibo, vino, sesso, da Petronio a J. Amado." *Groningen Colloquia on the Novel* 2:121–131.

Bolte, Johannes. 1905. Untitled Note. *ZVV* 15:69–70.

——. 1907. "Bilderbogen des 16. und 17. Jahrhunderts." *ZVV* 17:425–441.

Bolte, Johannes, and Lutz Mackensen, eds. 1930–40. *Handwörterbuch des deutschen Märchens.* 2 vols. Berlin: Walter de Gruyter.

Bolte, Johannes, and Georg Polívka. 1913–32. *Anmerkungen zu den Kinder-und Hausmärchen der Brüder Grimm.* 5 vols. Leipzig: Dieterich'sche Verlagsbuchhandlung.

Bolte, Johannes, and Willy Scheel, eds. 1901–6. *Georg Wickrams Werke.* 8 vols. Tübingen: Gedruckt für den Litterarischen Verein in Stuttgart.

Bömer, Franz. 1969–86. *P. Ovidius Naso: Metamorphosen. Kommentar.* 7 vols. Heidelberg: Carl Winter, Universitätsverlag.

——. 1986. "Die Witwe von Ephesus. Petron. 111,1 ff. und die 877. in Tausendundeiner Nacht." *Gymnasium* 93:138–140.

Bompaire, J. 1958. *Lucien Écrivain: Imitation et création.* Paris: E. de Boccard.

Bond, Richmond. 1971. *The Tatler: The Making of a Literary Journal*. Cambridge: Harvard University Press.

Bonner, Campbell. 1902. "A Study of the Danaid Myth." *HSCP* 13:129–173.

——. 1910. "Dionysiac Magic and the Greek Land of Cockaigne." *TAPA* 41:175–185.

Borgeaud, Philippe. 1974. "The Open Entrance to the Closed Palace of the King: The Greek Labyrinth in Context." *History of Religions* 14:1–27.

Bottigheimer, Ruth B. 1990. "Marienkind (KHM 3): A Computer-Based Study of Editorial Change and Stylistic Development within Grimm's Tales from 1808 to 1864." *Arv* 46:7–31.

——. 1993. Review of Rosenberg 1991. *JAF* 106:361–362.

——, ed. 1986. *Fairy Tales and Society: Illusion, Allusion, and Paradigm*. Philadelphia: University of Pennsylvania Press.

Bourboulis, Photeine P. 1953. *Studies in the History of Modern Greek Story-Motives*. Ἑλληνικά, παράρτημα 2. Thessalonike.

Braid, Donald. 1993. "The Traveller and the Hare: Meaning, Function, and Form in the Recontextualization of Narrative." *Folklore Forum* 26:3–29.

Brandon, Elizabeth. 1965. "Le sorte d'un conte: AT 1510." *Λαογραφία* 22:37–41.

Branham, R. Bracht, and Daniel Kinney, eds. and trans. 1997. *Petronius: Satyrica*. Berkeley and Los Angeles: University of California Press.

Branky, Franz. 1891. "Volksüberlieferungen aus Österreich." *ZVV* 3:185–186.

Brassloff, Stephan. 1914. "Antike Motive in Volksbrauch und Sage." *Zeitschrift für österreichische Volkskunde* 20:85–89.

Braun, Martin. 1934. *Griechischer Roman und hellenistische Geschichtsschreibung*. Frankfurter Studien zur Religion und Kultur der Antike, no. 6. Frankfurt am Main: Vittorio Klostermann.

——. 1938. *History and Romance in Graeco-Oriental Literature*. Oxford: Basil Blackwell.

Brecht, Franz Josef. 1930. *Motiv- und Typengeschichte des griechischen Spottepigramms*. *Philologus*, Supplementband 22, 2.

Brednich, Rolf. 1964. *Volkserzählungen und Volksglaube von den Schicksalsfrauen*. FFC 193. Helsinki: Academia Scientiarum Fennica.

Brelich, A. 1977. "La metodologia della scuola di Roma." In *Il Mito Greco. Atti del Convegno Internazionale (Urbino 7–12 maggio 1973)*, edited by Bruno Gentili and Giuseppe Paioni, 3–29. Rome: Ateneo & Bizzarri.

Bremmer, Jan N. 1972. "Athena and the Trojan Horse." *Museum Africum* 1:4–7.

——, ed. 1988. *Interpretations of Greek Mythology*. London: Routledge.

Brewster, Paul. 1953. "En gresk Prosa-Analogi til Folkevisen om dei tvo Systar." *Maal og Minne* 49–52.

Brewster, Paul, and Ernest Baughman. 1945. "The Cadaver Arm." *Hoosier Folklore Bulletin* 4:30–32.

Briggs, Katherine M. 1970–71. *A Dictionary of British Folk-Tales in the English Language*. 4 vols. Bloomington: Indiana University Press.

Briggs, Katherine M., and Ruth L. Tongue, eds. 1965. *Folktales of England*. Chicago: University of Chicago Press.

Brockington, Mary. 1995. "The Indic Version of *The Two Brothers* and Its Relationship to the *Rāmāyaṇa*." *Fabula* 36:259–272.

Broholm, H. C. 1966. *Odysseus og Polyphem*. Studier fra Sprog- og Oldtidsforskning, no. 261. Copenhagen: G. E. C. Gads Forlag.

Brommer, Frank. 1955. "Die Königstochter und das Ungeheuer." *Marburger Winckelmann Programm 1955*. Marburg/Lahn. Pp. 3–15.

——. 1986. *Heracles: The Twelve Labors of the Hero in Ancient Art and Literature*. Translated by Shirley J. Schwarz. New Rochelle, N.Y.: Aristide D. Caratzas.

Bronzini, Giovanni Battista. 1993. "Märchen in Italien." In Röth and Kahn 1992:130–146.

Brotherton, Blanche. 1924. "The Plot of the *Miles Gloriosus*." *TAPA* 55:128–136.

Brown, Carolyn S. 1987. *The Tall Tale in American Folklore and Literature*. Knoxville: University of Tennessee Press.

Brown, Mary Ellen, and Bruce A. Rosenberg, eds. 1998. *Encyclopedia of Folklore and Literature*. Santa Barbara: ABC-CLIO.

Bruce, J. Douglas. 1913. "Human Automata in Classical Tradition and Medieval Romance." *Modern Philology* 10:511–526.

Brückner, Annemarie. 1961. "Volkstümliche Erzählstoffe auf Einblattdrucken der Gustav Freytag-Sammlung." *Zeitschrift für Volkskunde* 57:230–238.

Brunner-Traut, Emma. 1959. "Altägyptische Tiergeschichte und Fabel: Gestalt und Strahlkraft." *Saeculum* 10:124–185.

——, trans. and ed. 1965. *Altägyptische Märchen*. 2d ed. Düsseldorf-Köln: Eugen Diederichs Verlag.

Burke, Peter. 1994. *Popular Culture in Early Modern Europe*. Rev. ed. Hants: Scolar Press.

Burkert, Walter. 1979. *Structure and History in Greek Mythology and Ritual*. Berkeley and Los Angeles: University of California Press.

——. 1983. *Homo Necans*. Translated by Peter Bing. Berkeley and Los Angeles: University of California Press.

——. 1984. Review of *Enzyklopädie des Märchens*, vol. 3. *Gnomon* 56:547–548.

——. 1985. *Greek Religion*. Translated by John Raffan. Cambridge: Harvard University Press.

Burlakoff, Nikolai, and Carl Lindahl, eds. 1980. *Folklore on Two Continents: Essays in Honor of Linda Dégh*. Bloomington, Ind.: Trickster.

Burnikel, Walter. 1980. *Untersuchungen zur Struktur des Witzepigramms bei Lukillios und Martial*. Palingenesia, no. 15. Wiesbaden: Franz Steiner.

Burns, Robert. 1965. *The Merry Muses of Caledonia*. Collected by Robert Burns. Edited by G. Legman. New Hyde Park: University Books. Facsimile edition with additional songs from the *Cunningham Manuscript* and other sources.

Burton, Richard. n.d. *A Plain and Literal Translation of the Arabian Nights Entertainments, Now Entituled the Book of the Thousand Nights and a Night, with Introductory Explanatory Notes on the Manners and Customs of Moslem Men and Terminal Essay upon the History of The Nights*. 17 vols. 1885–88. Reprint, N.p.: The Burton Club.

Cabaniss, Allen. 1961. "The Matron of Ephesus Again: An Analysis." *University of Mississippi Studies in English* 2:41–53.

Calame, Claude. 1977a. "La legende du cyclope dans la folklore européen et extra-européen: Un jeu de transformations narratives." *Études de lettres*, ser. 3, 10, no. 2:45–79.

——. 1977b. "Mythe grec et structures narratives: Le mythe des Cyclopes dans l'*Odyssée*." In *Il Mito Greco. Atti del Convegno Internazionale (Urbino 7–12 maggio 1973)*, edited by Bruno Gentili and Giuseppe Paione, 369–392. Roma: Ateneo & Bizzarri.

——. 1990. *Thésée et l'imaginaire athénien: Légende et culte en Grèce antique*. Lausanne: Éditions Payot.

——. 1995. *The Craft of Poetic Speech in Ancient Greece*. Translated by Janice Orion. Ithaca, N.Y.: Cornell University Press.

Calame-Griaule, Geneviève, Veronika Görög-Karady, and Michèle Chiche, eds. 1984. *Le conte, pourquoi? comment? / Folktales, Why and How?* Actes des Journées d'Études en Littérature Orale: Analyze des contes—Problèmes de méthodes, Paris, 23–26 mars 1982. Paris: Éditions du Centre National de la Recherche Scientifique.

Calder, W. M. 1922. "New Light on Ovid's Story of Philemon and Baucis." *Discovery* 3:207–211.

Caldwell, J. R. 1940. "The Origin of the Story of Bothvar-Bjarki." *Arkiv för nordisk filologi* 55:223–275.

Calhoun, G. 1939. "Homer's Gods–Myth and Märchen." *AJP* 60:1–28.

Calvino, Italo. 1979. *Fiabe italiane*. Gli Struzzi, no. 24. 2 vols. 6th ed. Milan: Einaudi.

Cammann, Alfred. 1980. *Turmberg-Geschichten: Ein Beitrag zur westpreussischen Landes- und Volkskunde*. Marburg: N. G. Elwert.

Campbell, Killis. 1907. *The Seven Sages of Rome*. Boston: Ginn & Company.

Canter, H. V. 1930. "The Figure ΑΔΥΝΑΤΟΝ in Greek and Latin Poetry." *AJP* 51:32–41.

Carnoy, Henry. 1889a. "Le conte de Psyché." *La Tradition* 3:4–10, 103–107.

———. 1889b. "La légende de Persée." *La Tradition* 3:353–355.

Carpenter, Rhys. 1946. *Folktale, Fiction, and Saga in the Homeric Epics*. Berkeley and Los Angeles: University of California Press.

Carpenter, Thomas H. 1991. *Art and Myth in Ancient Greece: A Handbook*. London: Thames and Hudson.

Cèbe, Jean-Pierre. 1972–99. *Varron, Satires Ménippéens: Édition, traduction et commentaire*. 13 vols. Rome: École Française de Rome.

Chadwick, John. 1973. *Documents in Mycenaean Greek*. 2d ed. Cambridge: Cambridge University Press.

Charles, R. H. 1913. *The Apocrypha and Pseudoepigrapha of the Old Testament*. Oxford: Clarendon.

Charlesworth, James H., ed. 1983. *Old Testament Pseudepigrapha*. 2 vols. Garden City, N.Y.: Doubleday.

Chase, Richard. 1969. *Quest for Myth*. Westport, Connecticut: Greenwood Press.

Chauvin, Victor. 1892–1922. *Bibliographie des ouvrages arabes ou relatifs aux Arabes publiés dans l'Europe chrétienne de 1810 à 1885*. 12 vols. Liege: H. Vaillant-Carmanne.

Chesnutt, Michael. 1989. "Thor's Goats and the Three Wishes: Contributions to the History of Aarne-Thompson Types 750A–B." *Scandinavian Studies* 61:318–338.

Chevalier, Maxime. 1983. *Cuentos Folklóricos Españoles del Siglo de Oro*. Barcelona: Editorial Crítica.

Child, Francis James, ed. 1956. *The English and Scottish Popular Ballads*. 5 vols. 1882–98. Reprint, Boston: Houghton, Mifflin.

Childs, Brevard S. 1962. *Myth and Reality in the Old Testament*. Studies in Biblical Theology, no. 27. 2d ed. London: SCM.

Christensen, Arthur. 1939. *Molboernes Vise Gerninger*. Danmarks Folkeminder, no. 47. Copenhagen: Det Schønbergske Forlag.

Christiansen, Reidar Th. 1915. "Nogen Iagttagelser over et Par 'Episke Love' indenfor to Eventyrgrupper (Aarnes Märchentypen 332 og 613)." *Danske Studier* pp. 71–89.

———. 1927. "A Gaelic Fairytale in Norway." *Béaloideas* 1:107–114.

———. 1958. *The Migratory Legends: A Proposed List of Types with a Systematic Catalogue of the Norwegian Variants*. FFC 175. Helsinki: Academia Scientiarum Fennica.

———, ed. 1964. *Folktales of Norway*. Chicago: University of Chicago Press.

Cicu, Luciano. 1986. "La Matrona di Efeso di Petronio." *Studi Italiani di Filologia Classica* 79:249–271.

Clark, Raymond J. 1980. "The Returning Husband and the Waiting Wife: Folktale Adaptations in Homer, Tennyson and Pratt." *Folklore* 91:46–62.

Clébert, Jean-Paul, ed. 1986. *Histoires et légendes de la Provence mystérieuse*. Paris: Sand.

Clouston, W. A. 1887. *Popular Tales and Fictions: Their Migrations and Transformations*. 2 vols. Edinburgh: William Blackwood and Sons.

———. 1888. *The Book of Noodles: Stories of Simpletons; or, Fools and their Follies*. London: Elliot Stock.

Clunies Ross, Margaret. 1994–98. *Prolonged Echoes: Old Norse Myths in Medieval Northern Society*. 2 vols. Odense: Odense University Press.

Cocchiara, Giuseppe. 1956. *Il Paese di Cuccagna e altri studi di folklore*. Turin: Einaudi.

———. 1963. *Il mondo alla rovescia*. Turin: Paolo Boringhieri.

———. 1981. *The History of Folklore in Europe*. Translated by John McDaniel. Philadelphia: Institute for the Study of Human Issues.

Cochrane, Timothy. 1987. "The Concept of Ecotype in American Folklore." *JFR* 24:33–55.

Colker, Marvin L. 1963. "A Medieval Rip Van Winkle Story." *JAF* 76:131–133.

Collison-Morley, Lacy. 1912. *Greek and Roman Ghost Stories*. Oxford: B. H. Blackwell.

Colton, Robert. 1975. "The Story of the Widow of Ephesus in Petronius and La Fontaine." *CJ* 71:35–52.

Comhaire, Jean L. 1958. "Oriental Versions of Polyphem's Myth." *Anthropological Quarterly* 31:21–28.

Comparetti, D. 1873. "Die Strafe des Tantalus nach Pindar." *Philologus* 32:227–251.

Connor, W. R. 1988. "Siezed by the Nymphs: Nympholepsy and Symbolic Expression in Classical Greece." *Classical Antiquity* 7:155–189.

Cook, Arthur B. 1964–65. *Zeus: A Study in Ancient Religion*. 3 vols. New York: Biblio and Tannen.

Coon, Raymond H. 1928. *The Reversal of Nature as a Rhetorical Figure*. Indiana University Studies 15, no. 80. Bloomington.

Coote, Mary P. 1978. "Serbocroatian Heroic Songs." In *Heroic Epic and Saga*, edited by Felix J. Oinas, 257–285. Bloomington: Indiana University Press.

——. 1981. "Lying in Passages." *Canadian-American Slavic Studies* 15:5–23.

Cope, Edward M. 1877. *The Rhetoric of Aristotle, with a Commentary*. Revised and edited by John E. Sandys. Vol. 3. Cambridge: Cambridge University Press.

Cosquin, Emmanuel. 1886–87. *Contes populaires de Lorraine, comparés avec les contes des autres provinces de France et des pays étrangers*. 2 vols. Paris: F. Vieweg.

Coulter, C. 1926. "The Great Fish in Ancient and Medieval Story." *TAPA* 57:32–50.

Cox, Marian R. 1893. *Cinderella: Three Hundred and Forty-Five Variants of Cinderella, Catskin, and Cap O'Rushes*. London: David Nutt.

Crane, Thomas F., ed. 1890. *The Exempla or Illustrative Stories from the Sermones Vulgares of Jacques de Vitry*. Publications of the Folk-Lore Society, no. 26. London: Published for the Folk-Lore Society by David Nutt.

Crenshaw, James L. 1981. "The Contest of Darius' Guards." In *Images of Man and God: Old Testament Short Stories in Literary Focus*, edited by Burke O. Long, 74–88. Sheffield: Almond.

Crooke, W. 1898. "The Wooing of Penelope." *Folk-Lore* 9:97–133.

——. 1908. "Some Notes on Homeric Folk-Lore." *Folk-Lore* 19:52–77, 153–189.

Crusius, Otto. 1879. "De Babrii aetate." *Leipziger Studien zur klassischen Philologie* 2:125–248.

——. 1889. "Märchenreminiscenzen im antiken Sprichwort." *Verhandlungen der Versammlungen deutscher Philologen und Schulmänner* 40:31–47.

——. 1891–93. "Epicharm bei den Paroemiographen." *Philologus*, Supplementband 6:281–294.

——. 1895. *Ad Plutarchi de Proverbiis Alexandrinorum Libellum Commentarius*. Tübingen: W. Armbruster & O. Riecker. Reprinted in Leutsch and Schneidewin 1961, IIIb.

Cueva, Edmund P. 1999. "The Art and Myth of *Cupid and Psyche*." In *Veritatis Amicitiaeque Causa: Essays in Honor of Anna Lydia Motto and John R. Clark*, edited by Shannon N. Byrne and Edmund P. Cueva, 53–69. Wauconda: Bolchazy-Carducci.

Curtius, E. R. 1938. "Zur Literarästhetik des Mittelalters, II." *Zeitschrift für romanische Philologie* 58:129–232.

Dacier, B.-J. 1780. "Examen de l'histoire de la Matrone d'Éphèse et des differentes imitations qu'elle a produites." *Mémoires de l'Académie Royale des Inscriptions et Belles Lettres* 41:523–545.

Dähnhardt, Oskar. 1907–12. *Natursagen: Eine Sammlung naturdeutender Sagen, Märchen, Fabeln, und Legenden*. 4 vols. Leipzig: B. G. Teubner

Dale, A. M., ed. 1961. *Euripides: Alcestis*. Oxford: Clarendon.

Dalley, Stephanie, trans. 1989. *Myths from Mesopotamia: Creation, The Flood, Gilgamesh, and others.* Oxford: Oxford University Press.

——. 1991. "Gilgamesh in the Arabian Nights." *Journal of the Royal Asiatic Society of Great Britain and Ireland* 3:1–17.

Dames, M. Longworth. 1892. "Balochi Tales." *Folk-Lore* 3:517–528.

Danaher, Kevin. 1967. *Folktales of the Irish Countryside.* Cork: Mercier.

Dangel, Richard. 1931. "Der Kampf der Kraniche mit den Pygmäen bei den Indianern Nordamerikas." *Studi e Materiali di Storia delle Religioni* 7:128–135.

Dasen, Véronique. 1993. *Dwarfs in Ancient Egypt and Greece.* Oxford: Clarendon.

Dasent, George W. 1970. *East o' the Sun and West o' the Moon: Fifty-nine Norwegian Folk Tales from the collection of Peter Christen Asbjørnsen and Jørgen Moe.* 1888. Reprint, New York: Dover.

Davidson, Hilda E., et al. 1968. *Beowulf and its Analogues.* London: Dent.

Davies, J. K. 1984. "The Reliability of the Oral Tradition." In *The Trojan War: Its Historicity and Context,* edited by Lin Foxhall and John K. Davies, 87–110. *Papers of the First Greenbank Colloquium, Liverpool 1981.* Bristol: Bristol Classical Press.

Dawkins, R. M. 1954. "The Grateful Dead and the Poison Maid." In Προσφορὰ εἰς Στίλπονα Π. Κυριακίδην, Ἑλληνικά, παράρτημα 4:148–167.

——, ed. 1950. *Forty-Five Stories from the Dodekanese.* Cambridge: Cambridge University Press.

——. 1953. *Modern Greek Folktales.* Oxford: Clarendon.

——. 1955. *More Greek Folktales.* Oxford: Clarendon.

Dégh, Linda. 1989. *Folktales and Society: Story-telling in a Hungarian Peasant Community.* Expanded edition. Bloomington: Indiana University Press.

——. 1990. "How Storytellers Interpret the Snakeprince Tale." In *The Telling of Stories: Approaches to a Traditional Craft,* edited by Morten Nøjgaard, et al., 47–62. Odense: Odense University Press.

——. 1995a. *Narratives in Society: A Performer-Centered Study of Narration.* FFC 255. Helsinki: Academia Scientiarum Fennica.

——. 1995b. *Hungarian Folktales: The Art of Zsuzsanna Palkó.* Translated by Vera Kalm. Jackson: University Press of Mississippi.

——. 1996. "What is a Belief Legend?" *Folklore* 107:33–46.

——, ed. 1965. *Folktales of Hungary.* Chicago: University of Chicago Press.

Dégh, Linda, and Andrew Vázsonyi. 1975. "The Hypothesis of Multi-Conduit Transmission in Folklore." In Ben-Amos and Goldstein 1975:207–254. Reprinted in Dégh 1995:173–212.

Dégh, Linda, Henry Glassie, and Felix Oinas, eds. 1976. *Folklore Today: A Festschrift for Richard M. Dorson.* Bloomington: Research Center for Language and Semiotic Studies, Indiana University.

de Jonge, M. 1978. *The Testaments of the Twelve Patriarchs: A Critical Edition of the Greek Text.* Pseudepigrapha Veteris Testamenti Graece 1, part 2. Leiden: E. J. Brill.

Delaney, Carol. 1998. *Abraham on Trial: The Social Legacy of Biblical Myth.* Princeton: Princeton University Press.

Delarue, Paul, and Marie-Louise Tenèze. 1957–85. *Le conte populaire française.* 4 vols. Paris: Éditions Erasme.

Delcourt, Marie. 1961. *Hermaphrodite: Myths and Rites of the Bisexual Figure in Classical Antiquity.* Translated by Jennifer Nicholson. London: Studio Books.

——. 1976. *Hermaphroditea.* Collection Latomus, no. 86. Bruxelles: Latomus.

Demoulin, Hubert. 1901. "Epiménide de Crète." *Bibliothèque de la Faculté de Philosophie & Lettres de l'Université de Liège,* no. 12. Bruxelles: Office de Publicité.

Dermenghem, Emile. 1945. "Le mythe de Psyché dans le folklore nord-africain." *Revue Africaine* 89:41–81.

Des Périers, Bonaventure. 1980. *Nouvelles Récréations et Joyeux Devis I-XC*. Edited by Krystyna Kasprzyk. Paris: Librairie Honoré Champion.

Detter, Ferd. 1892. "Die Hamletsage." *Zeitschrift für deutsches Altertum und deutsche Litteratur* 36:1–25.

Devereux, G. 1973. "The Self-Blinding of Oidipous in Sophokles: *Oidipous Tyrannos*." *JHS* 93:36–49.

Diels, Hermann. 1934–37. *Die Fragmente der Vorsokratiker*. 5th ed. 3 vols. Berlin: Weidmann.

Dieterich, Karl. 1905. "Aus neugriechischen Sagen." *ZVV* 15:380–382.

Dietze, J. 1900. "Zum Märchen vom Amor und Psyche." *Philologus* 59:136–147.

Dijk, Gert-Jan van. 1997. *Αἶνοι, Λόγοι, Μῦθοι: Fables in Archaic, Classical, & Hellenistic Greek Literature. With a Study of the Theory & Terminology of the Genre*. Mnemosyne, Supplementum 166. Leiden: E. J. Brill.

Dijksterhuis, E. J. 1987. *Archimedes*. Translated by C. Dikshoorn. Princeton: Princeton University Press.

Dimitrijevic, P. 1958. "The Origin of Polyphemos Motifs in Our Folklore." *Ziva Antika* 8:155–160. In Serbian with French summary.

Donnini, Mauro. 1981. "Apul. *Met.* X, 2–12: Analogie e varianti di un racconto." *Materiali e Contributi per la Storia della Narrativa Graeco-Latina* 3:145–160.

Doob, Penelope. 1990. *The Idea of the Labyrinth from Classical Antiquity through the Middle Ages*. Ithaca, N.Y.: Cornell University Press.

Dörler, Adolf. 1906. "Märchen und Schwänke aus Nordtirol und Vorarlberg." *ZVV* 16:278–302.

Dorson, Richard M. 1957. "Standards for Collecting and Publishing American Folktales." *JAF* 70:53–57.

——. 1959. *American Folklore*. Chicago: University of Chicago Press.

——. 1964. *Buying the Wind: Regional Folklore in the United States*. Chicago: University of Chicago Press.

——. 1967. *American Negro Folktales*. Greenwich, Conn.: Fawcett Publications.

Dover, K. J. 1974. *Greek Popular Morality in the Time of Plato and Aristotle*. Oxford: Basil Blackwell.

——. 1978. *Greek Homosexuality*. London: Duckworth.

Dracott, Alice E. 1906. *Simla Village Tales or, Folk Tales from the Himalayas*. London: John Murray.

Dumézil, Georges. 1950. "Quelques cas anciens de 'liquidation des vieillards': histoire et survivances." *Revue Internationale des Droits de l'Antiquité* (Mélanges Fernand de Visscher, no. 3) 4:447–454.

Dundes, Alan. 1962a. "From Etic to Emic Units in the Structural Study of Folktales." *JAF* 75:95–105.

——. 1962b. "The Binary Structure of 'Unsuccessful Repetition' in Lithuanian Folk Tales." *WF* 21:165–174.

——. 1964. "Texture, Text, and Context." *Southern Folklore Quarterly* 28:251–265.

——. 1965. "The Study of Folklore in Literature and Culture: Identification and Interpretation." *JAF* 78:136–142.

——. 1969. "The Devolutionary Premise in Folklore." *JFI* 6:5–19.

——. 1984. "The Symbolic Equivalence of Allomotifs: Towards a Method of Analyzing Folktales." In Calame-Griaule, Görög-Karady, and Chiche 1984:187–199.

——. 1997. "The Motif-Index and the Tale Type Index: A Critique." *JFR* 34:195–202.

——. 1998. "New Foreword." In Afanas'ev 1998.

——, ed. 1983. *Cinderella: A Casebook*. New York: Wildman.

——. 1988. *The Flood Myth*. Berkeley and Los Angeles: University of California Press.

——. 1989. *Little Red Riding Hood: A Casebook*. Madison: University of Wisconsin Press.

Dunn, T. F. 1934. *The Facetiae of the Mensa Philosophica.* Washington University Studies, New Series, Language and Literature, no. 5. St. Louis: Washington University

Dupee, F. W. 1984. *"The King of the Cats" and other Remarks on Writers and Writing.* 2d ed. Chicago: University of Chicago Press.

Dutoit, Ernest. 1936. *Le thème de l'adynaton dans la poésie antique.* Paris: Société d'Édition "Les Belles Lettres."

Duval, Yves-Marie. 1973. *Le Livre de Jonas dans la littérature chrétienne grecque et latine: Sources et influence du Commentaire sur Jonas de saint Jérôme.* 2 vols. Paris: Études Augustiniennes.

Dvořák, Karel. 1978. *Soupis Staročeských Exempel. Index Exemplorum Paleobohemicorum.* Acta Universitatis Carolinae, Philosophica et Historica Monographia, no. 72. Prague: Univerzita Karlova.

Eberhard, Wolfram. 1937. *Typen chinesischer Volksmärchen.* FFC 120. Helsinki: Academia Scientiarum Fennica.

———, ed. 1965. *Folktales of China.* Chicago: University of Chicago Press.

Eberhard, Wolfram, and Pertev Boratav. 1953. *Typen türkischer Volksmärchen.* Wiesbaden: Franz Steiner Verlag.

Edelstein, Emma J., and Ludwig Edelstein. 1945. *Asclepius: A Collection and Interpretation of the Testimonies.* 2 vols. Baltimore: Johns Hopkins University Press.

Edmunds, Lowell. 1993. *Myth in Homer: A Handbook.* 2d ed. Highland Park, N.J.: Mill Brook.

———, ed. 1985. *Oedipus: The Ancient Legend and Its Later Analogues.* Baltimore: Johns Hopkins University Press.

———. 1990. *Approaches to Greek Myth.* Baltimore: Johns Hopkins University Press.

Eggan, Dorothy. 1958. "The Personal Use of Myth in Dreams." In *Myth: A Symposium,* edited by Thomas A. Sebeok, 107–121. Bloomington: Indiana University Press.

Eisner, Robert. 1977. "Ariadne in Art, Prehistory to 400 B.C." *Rivista di Studi Classici* 25:165–182.

Eissfeldt, Otto. 1962. "Die Bedeutung der Märchenforschung für die Religionswissenschaft, besonders für die Wissenschaft vom Alten Testament." In *Kleine Schriften,* edited by Rudolf Sellheim and Fritz Maass, 1:23–32. Tübingen: J. C. B. Mohr (Paul Siebeck).

Ejdestam, J. 1946. "Omfärd vid besittningstagande av jordegendom." *Svenska Landsmaal* 69:86–114.

Elderkin, George W. 1924. *Kantharos: Studies in Dionysiac and Kindred Cult.* Princeton: Princeton University Press.

Elish, Karl M. 1946. "Death and the Old Man: A Russian Variant." *New York Folklore Quarterly* 2:59.

Ellis, Bill. 1983. "De Legendis Urbis: Modern Legends in Ancient Rome." *JAF* 96:200–208.

———. 1994. "Multiple Means of Death: Fate or Divinity?" *Dear Mr. Thoms . . .* 34 (May):1–5.

Ellis, Maria DeJ. 1974. "A New Fragment of the Tale of the Poor Man of Nippur." *Journal of Cuneiform Studies* 26:88–89.

El-Shamy, Hasan. 1995. *Folk Traditions of the Arab World: A Guide to Motif Classification.* 2 vols. Bloomington: Indiana University Press.

———. 1999. *Tales Arab Women Tell and the Behavioral Patterns They Portray.* Bloomington: Indiana University Press.

———, ed. and trans. 1980. *Folktales of Egypt.* Chicago: University of Chicago Press.

Engelmann, R. 1904. "Ein neues 'Urtheil Salomonis' und die Friesbilder der Casa Tiberina." *Hermes* 39:146–154.

Enzyklopädie des Märchens: Handwörterbuch zur historischen und vergleichenden Erzählforschung. Edited by Kurt Ranke et al. 1977–. Berlin: Walter de Gruyter.

Espinosa, Aurelio M. 1934. "Las fuentes orientales del cuento de la Matrona de Efeso." *Boletín de la Biblioteca Menéndez y Pelayo* 16:489–502.

——. 1946–47. *Cuentos populares españoles, recogidos de la tradicion oral de España.* 3 vols. 2d ed. Madrid: Consejo Superior de Investigaciones Científicas, Instituto "Antonio de Nebrija" de Filologia.

Eyben, Emiel. 1989. "Old Age in Greco-Roman Antiquity and Early Christianity: An Annotated Select Bibliography." In *Old Age in Greek and Latin Literature*, edited by Thomas M. Falkner and Judith de Luce, 230–251. Albany: State University of New York Press.

Faraone, Christopher. 1992. *Talismans and Trojan Horses: Guardian Statues in Ancient Greek Myth and Ritual.* New York: Oxford University Press.

Faure, M. P. 1965. "Le mythe du Cyclope dans la Crète contemporaine." *REG* 78:xxvii–xxviii.

Faverty, Frederic E. 1931. "The Story of Joseph and Potiphar's Wife in Mediaeval Literature." *Harvard Studies and Notes in Philology and Literature* 13:81–127.

Fehling, Detlev. 1977. *Amor und Psyche: Die Schöpfung des Apuleius und ihre Einwirkung auf das Märchen. Eine Kritik der romantischen Märchentheorie.* Akademie der Wissenschaften und der Literatur (Mainz): Abhandlungen der Geistes-und Sozialwissenschaftlichen Klasse, no. 9. Wiesbaden: Franz Steiner Verlag.

——. 1984. "Die alten Literaturen als Quelle der neuzeitlichen Märchen." In Siegmund 1984:79–92.

——. 1989. *Herodotus and his 'Sources': Citation, Invention and Narrative Art.* Arca Classical and Medieval Texts, Papers and Monographs, no. 21. Leeds: Francis Cairns.

——. 1991. *Die ursprüngliche Geschichte vom Fall Trojas, oder: Interpretationen zur Troja-Geschichte.* Innsbrucker Beiträge zur Kulturwissenschaft, Sonderheft 75. Innsbruck: Institut für Sprachwissenschaft der Universität Innsbruck.

Feilberg, N. F. 1886–1914. *Bidrag til en Ordbog over jyske Almuesmål.* 4 vols. Copenhagen: H. H. Thieles Bogtrykkeri.

Fellmann, Berthold. 1972. *Die antike Darstellungen des Polyphemabenteuers.* Münchener Archäologische Studien, no. 5. Munich: Wilhelm Fink Verlag.

Felton, D. 1999. *Haunted Greece and Rome: Ghost Stories from Classical Antiquity.* Austin: University of Texas Press.

Fine, Elizabeth C. 1984. *The Folklore Text: From Performance to Print.* Bloomington: Indiana University Press.

Fine, Elizabeth C., and Jean Haskell Speer, eds. 1992. *Performance, Culture, and Identity.* Westport, Conn.: Praeger.

Finsler, Georg. 1914. *Homer: Der Dichter und seine Welt.* 2d ed. 2 vols. Leipzig: Verlag von B. G. Teubner.

Fischer, H., and J. Bolte, eds. 1895. *Die Reise der Söhne Giaffers, aus dem Italienischen des Christoforo Armeno übersetzt durch Johann Wetzel, 1583.* Bibliothek des Litterarischen Vereins in Stuttgart, no. 208. Tübingen: Litterarischer Verein in Stuttgart.

Fochi, Adrian. 1972. *Recherches comparées de folklore sud-est-européen.* Études et Documents Concernant le Sud-Est Européen, no. 6. Bucarest: Association Internationale d'Études du Sud-Est Européen.

Foley, John Miles. 1986. "Tradition and the Individual Talent: Oral Epic, Textual Meaning, and Receptionalist Theory." *Cultural Anthropology* 1:203–222.

——. 1990. *Traditional Oral Epic: The* Odyssey, Beowulf, *and the Serbo-Croatian Return Song.* Berkeley and Los Angeles: University of California Press.

Fontenrose, Joseph. 1945. "Philemon, Lot, and Lykaon." *University of California Publications in Classical Philology* 13:93–119.

——. 1948. The Sorrows of Ino and of Procne. *TAPA* 79:125–167.

——. 1959. *Python: A Study of Delphic Myth.* Berkeley and Los Angeles: University of California Press.

——. 1966. *The Ritual Theory of Myth*. Folklore Studies, no. 18. Berkeley and Los Angeles: University of California Press.

——. 1968. "The Hero as Athlete." *California Studies in Classical Antiquity* 1:73–104.

——. 1978. *The Delphic Oracle*. Berkeley and Los Angeles: University of California Press.

——. 1981. *Orion: The Myth of the Hunter and the Huntress*. University of California Publications in Classical Studies, no. 23. Berkeley: University of California Press.

——. 1983. "The Building of the City Walls: Troy and Asgard." *JAF* 96:53–63.

Forbes Irving, P. M. C. 1990. *Metamorphosis in Greek Myths*. Oxford: Clarendon.

Fowler, Murray. 1949. "The Myth of ἘΡΙΧΘΟΝΙΟΣ." *CPh* 38:27–32.

Fraenkel, Eduard, ed. 1950. *Aeschylus: Agamemnon*. 3 vols. Oxford: Clarendon.

Frazer, James George. 1888. "The Language of Animals." *Archaeological Review* 1:81–91, 161–181.

——. 1898. *Pausanias's Description of Greece*. 6 vols. London: Macmillan.

——. 1919. *Folk-Lore in the Old Testament: Studies in Comparative Religion, Legend, and Law*. 3 vols. London: Macmillan.

——, trans. 1921. *Apollodorus: the Library*. 2 vols. London: William Heinemann.

Freeman, Kathleen. 1945. "Vincent, or the Donkey." *G & R* 14:33–41.

Friedländer, Ludwig. 1888–1890. *Darstellungen aus der Sittengeschichte Roms in der Zeit von August bis zum Ausgang der Antonine*. 6th ed. Leipzig: S. Hirzel.

——. 1910. "Das Märchen von Amor und Psyche und andere Volksmärchen im Altertum." In *Darstellungen aus der Sittengeschichte Roms . . .* , 1:527–569. 8th ed. Leipzig: S. Hirzel.

——. 1913. "The Story of Amor and Psyche and other Traces of the Folk-tale in Antiquity." In *Roman Life and Manners under the Early Empire*, 4:88–123. Translated by A. B. Gough. London: George Routledge & Sons.

——. 1921. "Das Märchen von Amor und Psyche und andere Volksmärchen im Altertum." Revised by Otto Weinreich. In *Darstellungen aus der Sittengeschichte Roms in der Zeit von August bis zum Ausgang der Antonine*, edited by Georg Wissowa, 4:89–132. 9th and 10th eds. Leipzig: S. Hirzel.

Fry, Donald K. 1977. "Polyphemus in Iceland." *The Fourteenth Century: Acta* 4:65–86.

Gabrieli, F. 1937. "Un passo di Erodoto e uno del Marzban-nameh." *Revista degli Studi Orientali* 17:111–113.

Gaidoz, H. 1886–87. "Jean de L'Ours." *Mélusine* 3:395–396.

——. 1889. "Le jugement de Salomon." *Mélusine* 4:313–316, 337–341, 366–367, 385–387, 414, 446, 457–460.

Galand, Perrine. 1989. "Le conte de la *Matrone d'Ephèse*: Rhétorique de 'guidage' et reception. Pétrone lu par Fontaine et Saint-Evremond." *Groningen Colloquia on the Novel* 2:109–119.

Gallucci, Ralph F. 1996. "The Trojan Horse and War Machines." *Omnibus* 32:23–25.

Gantz, Timothy. 1993. *Early Greek Myth: A Guide to Literary and Artistic Sources*. Baltimore: Johns Hopkins University Press.

Garvie, A. F., ed. 1994. *Homer: Odyssey, Books 6–8*. Cambridge: Cambridge University Press.

Gaster, Moses. 1880. "Das Gold im Stocke." *Monatsschrift für Geschichte und Wissenschaft des Judentums* 29:316–322.

——. 1928. Review of Krappe 1927. *Folk-Lore* 39:107–109.

Gennep, Arnold van. 1908. *Religions, Mœurs, et Légendes: Essais d'Ethnographie et de Linguistique*. Paris: Société du Mercure de France.

Georges, Robert. 1969. "Towards an Understanding of Story-Telling Events." *JAF* 82:313–328.

——. 1983. "The Universality of the Tale-Type as Concept and Construct." *WF* 42:21–28.

——. 1986. "The Pervasiveness in Contemporary Folklore Studies of Assumptions, Concepts, and Constructs Usually Associated with the Historic-Geographic Method." *JFR* 23:87–103.

Gerhard, G. A. 1915a. "Der Tod des großen Pan." *Sitzungsberichte der Heidelberger Akademie, phil.-hist. Klasse* 5:1–52.

——. 1915b. "Der Tod des großen Pan." *WS* 37:323–352.

——. 1916. "Nochmals zum Tod des großen Pan." *WS* 38:343–376.

Germain, Gabriel. 1954. *Genèse de l'Odyssée: le fantastique et le sacré.* Paris: Presses Universitaires de France.

Gerould, Gordon. 1908. *The Grateful Dead: The History of a Folk Story.* Publications of the Folk-Lore Society, no. 60. London: David Nutt.

Gesemann, Wolfgang. 1972. *Die Entdeckung der unteren Volksschichten durch die russische Literatur.* Wiesbaden: Otto Harrassowitz.

Gibbon, Edward. 1946. *The History of the Decline and Fall of the Roman Empire.* Edited by J. B. Bury. 7 vols. 1776–88. Reprint, N.p.: Limited Edition Club.

Gildemeister, J. 1862. "Zum Asinus Vulgi." *Orient und Occident* 1:733–734.

Gilleland, Brady B. 1978. "The *Dolopathos* of Johannes de Alta Silva: A New Evaluation." In Niedzielski, Runte, and Hendrickson 1978:32–42.

——, trans. 1977. "Three Stories from the *Dolopathos* of Johannes de Alta Silva." *Allegorica* 2:99–117.

Gilliat-Smith, Bernard. 1911–12. "A Fifth Bulgarian Gypsy Folk-Tale." *Journal of the Gypsy Lore Society*, n.s., 5:279–289.

Glassie, Henry H. 1997. *Art and Life in Bangladesh.* Bloomington: Indiana University Press.

——, ed. 1985. *Irish Folktales.* New York: Pantheon Books.

Glenn, Justin. 1971. "The Polyphemus Folktale and Homer's *Kyklôpeia*." *TAPA* 102:133–181.

——. 1978. "The Polyphemus Myth: Its Origin and Interpretation." *G & R* 25:141–155.

Gobius, Johannes. 1480. *Scala Celi.* Typescript copy made by Luella Carter, University of Chicago, 1928.

Gödeke, K. 1862. "Asinus Vulgi." *Orient und Occident* 1:531–560.

Goebel, Franz M. 1932. "Jüdische Motive im märchenhaften Erzählungsgut: Studien zur vergleichenden Motiv-Geschichte." Diss., Universität Greifswald, Gleiwitz.

Goldberg, Christine. 1984. "The Historic-Geographic Method: Past and Future." *JFR* 21:1–18.

——. 1986. "The Construction of Folktales." *JFR* 23:163–176.

——. 1989. "Antti Aarne's Tales with Magic Objects." In *The Old Traditional Way of Life: Essays in Honor of Warren E. Roberts*, edited by Robert E. Walls and George H. Schoemaker, 322–337. Bloomington, Ind.: Trickster.

——. 1992. "The Forgotten Bride (AaTh 313C)." *Fabula* 33:39–54.

——. 1997. "Dilemma Tales in the Tale Type Index: The Theme of Joint Efforts." *JFR* 34:179–193.

Goldman, Shalom. 1995. *The Wiles of Women/The Wiles of Men: Joseph and Potiphar's Wife in Ancient Near Eastern, Jewish, and Islamic Folklore.* Albany: State University of New York Press.

Gomme, George L. 1908. *Folklore as an Historical Science.* London: Methuen.

Gow, A. S. F. 1931. "Μέτρα Θαλάσσης." *CR* 45:10–12.

Grant, Helen F. 1972. "El Mundo al Revés." In *Hispanic Studies in Honour of Joseph Manson*, edited by Dorothy M. Atkinson and Anthony H. Clark, 119–137. Oxford: Dolphin.

Grant, Michael. 1982. *Eros in Pompeii: The Secret Rooms of the National Museum of Naples.* With photographs by Antonia Mulas and a description of the collection by Antonio De Simone and Maria Teresa Merella. New York: Bonanza Books.

Gratwick, A. S., ed. 1993. *Plautus: Menaechmi*. Cambridge Greek and Latin Classics. Cambridge: Cambridge University Press.

Gresseth, Gerald. 1979. "The *Odyssey* and the *Nalopâkhyâna*." *TAPA* 109:63–85.

Greverus, Ina-Maria. 1958. "Die Geschenke des kleinen Volkes. KHM 182 = AT 503. Eine vergleichende Untersuchung." *Fabula* 1:263–279.

Grimal, Pierre, ed. 1963. *Apulei Metamorphoseis (IV, 28–VI, 24) (Le conte d'Amour et Psyché)*. Paris: Presses Universitaires de France.

Grimm, Brüder. 1956. *Deutsche Sagen*. 3d ed. Munich: Winkler-Verlag.

——. 1986. *Kinder- und Hausmärchen, gesammelt durch die Brüder Grimm. Vergrösserter Nachdruck der zweibändigen Erstausgabe von 1812 und 1815 nach dem Handexemplar des Brüder Grimm-Museums Kassel mit sämtlichen handschriftlichen Korrecturen und Nachträgern der Brüder Grimm, sowie einem Ergänzungsheft: Transkriptionen und Kommentare in Verbindung mit Ulrike Marquardt von Heinz Rölleke*. 3 vols. Göttingen: Vandenhoeck & Ruprecht.

Grimm, Jacob. 1864–90. *Kleinere Schriften*. 8 vols. Berlin: Ferd. Dümmler.

——. 1865. "Über Frauennamen aus Blumen." In Grimm (1864–90) 2:366–401.

——. 1966. *Teutonic Mythology*. Translated by James Stallybrass. 4 vols. New York: Dover Publications.

Grimm, Wilhelm. 1857. "Die Sage von Polyphem." *Abhandlungen der Königlichen Akademie der Wissenschaften zu Berlin, phil.-hist. Klasse*, 1–30 = *Kleinere Schriften*. Edited by G. Hinrichs, 4:428–462. Gütersloh: C. Bertelsmann, 1887.

Grisebach, Eduard. 1877. *Die treulöse Witwe: Eine chinesische Novelle und ihre Wanderung durch die Weltlitteratur*. 3d ed. Stuttgart: A. Kröner.

——. 1889. *Die Wanderung der Novelle von der treulosen Wittwe durch die Weltlitteratur*. 2d ed. Berlin: F. & P. Lehmann.

Groome, Francis. 1898. "Tobit and Jack the Giant-Killer." *Folk-Lore* 9:226–244.

Grundtvig, Svend, ed. 1854. *Gamle danske Minder i Folkemunde*. Vol. 1. Copenhagen: Dannebrog.

——. 1958. *Danske Folkeeventyr*. Copenhagen: P. Haase & Søns Forlag.

Grundtvig, Svend, et al., eds. 1853–1976. *Danmarks gamle Folkeviser*. 12 vols. Copenhagen: Samfundet til den danske literaturs fremme.

Guarino, Antonio. 1980. "Depontani senes." *Atti dell'Accademia di Scienze Morali e Politiche della Società Nazionale di Scienze, Lettere e Arti in Napoli* 90 (1979):535–539.

Guidi, Michele. 1990–91. "Greco ΛΑΒΥΡΙΝΘΟΣ: Note di Linguistica Mediterranea." *Minos* 25–26:175–193.

Gunkel, Hermann. 1910. *Genesis, übersetzt und erklärt*. 3d ed. Göttingen: Vandenhoeck & Ruprecht.

——. 1921. *Das Märchen im Alten Testament*. Tübingen: J. C. B. Mohr.

——. 1987. *The Folktale in the Old Testament*. Translated by Michael Rutter. Edited by David Gunn. Sheffield: Almond.

Gurney, O. R. 1972. "The Tale of the Poor Man of Nippur and its Folktale Parallels." *Anatolian Studies* 22:149–158.

Haakh, H. 1958. "Der groβe Pan ist tot." *Altertum* 4:105–110.

Haavio, Martti. 1929. *Kettenmärchen-Studien*. FFC 88. Helsinki: Academia Scientiarum Fennica.

——. 1938. "Der Tod des grossen Pan." *Studia Fennica* 3:113–136.

——. 1959. "The Upside-Down World." In Martti Haavio, *Essais Folkloriques, publiées à l'occasion de son 60e anniversaire*, 209–221. Studia Fennica 8. Porvoo: Werner Söderström Osakeyhtiö.

Hackman, Oskar. 1904. *Die Polyphemsage in der Volksüberlieferung*. Helsingfors: Frenckellska Tryckeri-Aktiebolaget.

Hahn, J. G. von. 1864. *Griechische und albanesische Märchen*. 2 vols. Leipzig: Wilhelm Engelmann.

Hainsworth, J. B. 1984. "The Fallibility of an Oral Heroic Tradition." In *The Trojan War: Its Historicity and Context*, edited by Lin Foxhall and John K. Davies, 111–135. *Papers of the First Greenbank Colloquium, Liverpool 1981*. Bristol: Bristol Classical Press.

Hall, H. R. 1904. "Nitokris-Rhodopis." *JHS* 24:208–213.

Halliday, William R. 1914. "Modern Greek Folk-Tales and Ancient Greek Mythology: Odysseus and Saint Elias." *Folk-Lore* 25:122–123.

——. 1921. "Pygmies and Cranes." *CR* 35:27.

——. 1924. "Perseus and the Kibisis." *Journal of the Gypsy Lore Society* 3:151–158.

——. 1933. *Indo-European Folk-Tales and Greek Legend*. Cambridge: Cambridge University Press.

——. 1963. *Greek and Roman Folklore*. New York: Cooper Square.

——, trans. 1928. *The Greek Questions of Plutarch*. Oxford: Clarendon.

Halpert, Herbert. 1976. " 'The World Will Turn Upside Down': An Unusual Burial Explanation in Folklore and Literature." In Dégh, Glassie, and Oinas 1976:193–207.

Hammer, Severinus. 1923. "De Narrationum Apulei Met. Libro X-mo Insertarum Compositione et Exemplaribus." *Eos* 26:6–26.

Hansen, Terrence L. 1957. *The Types of the Folktale in Cuba, Puerto Rico, the Dominican Republic, and Spanish South America*. University of California Publications: Folklore Studies, no. 8. Berkeley and Los Angeles: University of California Press.

Hansen, William. 1972. *The Conference Sequence: Patterned Narration and Narrative Inconsistency in the Odyssey*. University of California Publications: Classical Studies, no. 8. Berkeley and Los Angeles: University of California Press.

——. 1976. "The Story of the Sailor Who Went Inland." In Dégh, Glassie, and Oinas 1976:221–230.

——. 1977a. "An Oral Source for the *Menaechmi*." *CW* 70:385–390.

——. 1977b. "Odysseus' Last Journey." *Quaderni Urbinati di Cultura Classica* 24:27–48.

——. 1980. "An Ancient Greek Ghost Story." In Burlakoff and Lindahl 1980:71–77.

——. 1982. "The Applied Message in Storytelling." In *Folklorica: Festschrift for Felix Oinas*, edited by Egle Victoria Žygas and Peter Voorheis, 99–109. Indiana University Uralic and Altaic Series, no. 141. Bloomington.

——. 1983a. *Saxo Grammaticus and the Life of Hamlet: A Translation, History, and Commentary*. Lincoln: University of Nebraska Press.

——. 1983b. "Greek Mythology and the Study of the Ancient Greek Oral Story." *JFR* 20:101–112.

——. 1988. "Folklore." In *Civilization of the Ancient Mediterranean: Greece and Rome*, edited by Michael Grant and Rachel Kitzinger, 2:1121–1130. New York: Charles Scribner's Sons.

——. 1989. "Contextualizing the Story of Philinnion." *Midwestern Folklore* 15:101–108.

——. 1990. "Odysseus and the Oar: A Folkloric Approach." In Edmunds 1990:241–272.

——. 1995a. "The Theft of the Thunderweapon: A Greek Myth in Its International Context." *C & M* 46:5–24.

——. 1995b. "Abraham and the Grateful Dead Man." In *Folklore Interpreted: Essays in Honor of Alan Dundes*, edited by Regina Bendix and Rosemary Lévy Zumwalt, 355–365. New York: Garland Publishing.

——. 1996a. "The Protagonist on the Pyre: Herodotean Legend and Modern Folktale." *Fabula* 37:272–285.

——. 1996b. *Phlegon of Tralles' Book of Marvels*. Exeter: University of Exeter Press.

——. 1997a. "Homer and the Folktale." In Morris and Powell 1997:442–462.

——. 1997b. "Mythology and Folktale Typology: Chronicle of a Failed Scholarly Revolution." *JFR* 34:275–280.

——. 1997c. "Idealization as a Process in Ancient Greek Story-Formation," *Symbolae Osloenses* 72:118–123.

——. 2000a. "Foam-Born Aphrodite and the Mythology of Transformation," *AJP* 121:1–19.

——. 2000b. "The Winning of Hippodameia." *TAPA* 130:19–40.

——. 2001. "The Seer and the Computer: On *Philogelos* and Modern Jokes." *Classical Bulletin* 77: 87–102.

——, ed. 1998. *Anthology of Ancient Greek Popular Literature*. Bloomington: Indiana University Press.

Hardy, Clara. 1996. "Nomos and Replaceability in the Story of Intaphrenes and his Wife." *TAPA* 126:101–109.

Hardy, E. 1896. "Jona c. 1 u. Jât. 439." *Zeitschrift der deutschen morganländischen Gesellschaft* 50:153.

Haring, Lee. 1982. *Malagasy Tale Index*. FFC 231. Helsinki: Academia Scientiarum Fennica.

Harrison, Jane E. 1903–4. "Mystica Vannus Iacchi." *JHS* 23:292–324; 24:241–254.

Hartland, Edwin S. 1891. *The Science of Fairy Tales*. London: Walter Scott.

——. 1894–96. *The Legend of Perseus: A Study of Tradition in Story, Custom, and Belief*. 3 vols. London: David Nutt.

——. 1900. *Mythology and Folktales: Their Relation and Interpretation*. Popular Studies in Mythology Romance and Folklore, no. 7. London: David Nutt.

Hartmann, Albert. 1917. *Untersuchungen über die Sagen vom Tod des Odysseus*. Munich: C. H. Beck.

Hatt, Gudmund. 1949. *Asiatic Influences in American Folklore*. Det Kgl. Danske Videnskabernes Selskab, Historisk-filologiske Meddelelser 31, no. 6. Copenhagen: Ejnar Munksgaard.

Hausrath, August, ed. 1959–70. *Corpus Fabularum Aesopicarum*. Vol. 1, fasc. 1–2. 2d ed. Edited by Herbert Hunger. Leipzig: B. G. Teubner.

Hayes, Kevin J. 1997. *Folklore and Book Culture*. Knoxville: University of Tennessee Press.

Hazlitt, W. Carew, ed. 1864. *Shakespeare Jest Books: reprints of the early and very rare jest-books supposed to have been used by Shakespeare*. 3 vols. London: Willis & Sotheran.

Henderson, Jeffrey. 1975. *The Maculate Muse: Obscene Language in Attic Comedy*. New Haven: Yale University Press.

——, ed. 1987. *Aristophanes: Lysistrata*. Oxford: Clarendon.

Hennig, R. 1932. "Der kulturhistorische Hintergrund der Geschichte vom Kampf zwischen Pygmäen und Kranichen." *RhM* 81:20–24.

Henningsen, Gustav. 1963. "Det store Skib or den store Gård: ATT 1960 H og E." *Folkeminder* 9:196–213. With an English summary.

——. 1965. "The Art of Perpendicular Lying: Concerning a Commercial Collection of Norwegian Sailors' Tall Tales." *JFI* 2:180–219.

Henry, R. 1947. *Ctésias: La Perse, l'Inde. Les sommaires de Photius*. Brussels: Office de Publicité.

Hepding, Hugo. 1954. "Ein Märchen aus Syra." In Προσφορὰ εἰς Στίλπονα Π. Κυριακίδην, Ἑλληνικά, παράρτημα 4:267–276.

Herbert, J. A. 1910. *Catalogue of Romances in the Department of Manuscripts in the British Museum*. Vol. 3. London: Longmans.

Herranen, Gun, ed. 1981. *Folkloristikens Aktuella Paradigm*. NIF Publications, no. 10. Åbo: Nordiska Institutet för Folkdiktning.

Herrmann, Léon. 1927. "La matrone d'Éphèse dans Pétrone et dans Phèdre." *Bulletin de l'Association Guillaume Budé* 14:20–57.

Herter, Hans. 1975. "Hippolytos und Phaidra." In *Kleine Schriften*, edited by Ernst Vogt, 119–156. Munich: Wilhelm Fink Verlag.

Herzfeld, Michael. 1982. *Ours Once More: Folklore, Ideology, and the Making of Modern Greece*. Austin: University of Texas Press.

Herzog-Hauser, Gertrud. 1933. "Die Graien." *WS* 51:66–72.

——. 1937. "Märchenmotive in Homers Iliad." *Geistige Arbeit* 21:1–2.

Heubeck, Alfred. 1954. *Der Odyssee-Dichter und die Ilias*. Erlangen: Verlag von Palm & Enke.

Heubeck, Alfred, et al. 1988–92. *A Commentary on Homer's Odyssey*. 3 vols. Oxford: Clarendon.

Hicks, Roger, and Ngakpa Chogyam. 1990. *Great Ocean: An Authorized Biography of the Buddhist Monk Tenzin Gyatso His Holiness the Fourteenth Dalai Lama*. London: Penguin Books.

Hilka, Alfons. 1917. "Die Wanderung der Erzählung von der Inclusa aus dem Volksbuch der Sieben weisen Meister." *Mitteilungen der schlesischen Gesellschaft für Volkskunde* 19:29–72.

Hillers, Delbert R. 1973. "The Bow of Aqhat: The Meaning of a Mythological Theme." In *Orient and Occident: Essays Presented to Cyrus H. Gordon on the Occasion of his Sixty-fifth Birthday*, edited by Harry A. Hoffner, Jr., 71–81. *Alter Orient und Altes Testament* 22. Kevelaer: Verlag Butzon & Bercker.

Hippe, Max. 1888. "Untersuchungen zu der mittelenglischen Romanze von Sir Amadas." *Archiv für das Studium der neueren Sprachen und Litteraturen* 81:141–183.

Hock, Ronald F., and Edward N. O'Neil. 1986. *The Chreia in Ancient Rhetoric*. Vol. 1, The *Progymnasmata*. Atlanta: Scholars.

Hoffmann, Waldemar. 1910. *Ad antiquae Atticae comoediae historiam symbolae*. Berlin: A. Ebering.

Hoffner, Jr., Harry A., trans. 1990. *Hittite Myths*. Edited by Gary M. Beckman. Atlanta: Scholars.

Hofmann, Heinz, ed. 1999. *Latin Fiction: The Latin Novel in Context*. London: Routledge.

Holbek, Bengt. 1962–63. Review of Aarne and Thompson 1961. *Arv* 18–19:408–415.

——. 1964. "Asinus Vulgi: Om Niels Heldvads Oversættele og dens Aner." *Danske Studier* 59:32–53.

——. 1981. "Moderne folkloristik og historisk materiale." In Herranen 1981:129–149.

——. 1983. "Nordic Research in Popular Prose Narrative." In *Trends in Nordic Tradition Research*, edited by Lauri Honko and Pekka Laaksonen, 145–223. Helsinki: Suomalaisen Kirjallisuuden Seura.

——. 1985. "Parallelen zur Rattenfängersage in der dänischen Volksüberlieferung." In *Geschichten und Geschichte: Erzählforschertagung in Hameln, Oktober 1984*, edited by Norbert Humburg, 129–134. Hildesheim: Lax.

——. 1987. *Interpretation of Fairy Tales: Danish Folklore in a European Perspective*. FFC 239. Helsinki: Academia Scientiarum Fennica.

——. 1989a. *Danske Trylleeventyr*. Copenhagen: Nyt Nordisk Forlag Arnold Busck.

——. 1989b. *Tolkning af Trylleeventyr*. Copenhagen: Nyt Nordisk Forlag Arnold Busck.

——. 1990. "Variation and Tale Type." In *D'un conte . . . à l'autre: La variabilité dans la littérature orale*, edited by Veronika Görög-Karady, 471–484. Paris: Éditions du CNRS.

——. 1992a. "On the Comparative Method in Folklore Research. With contributions from Hermann Bausinger, Lauri Honko, and Roger D. Abrahams." *NIF Papers*, no. 3. Turku: Nordic Institute of Folklore.

——. 1992b. "Tendencies in Modern Folk Narrative Research." *NIF Papers*, no. 4. Turku: Nordic Institute of Folklore.

——, ed. 1962. *Æsops Levned og Fabler*. 2 vols. Copenhagen: J. H. Schultz Forlag.

Hollander, H. W., and M. de Jonge. 1985. *The Testaments of the Twelve Patriarchs: A Commentary*. Leiden: E. J. Brill.

Hollander, Lee M. 1912. "The Gautlang Cycle of Sagas. I: The Source of the Polyphemos Episode of the Hrólfssaga Gautrekssonar." *Journal of English and Germanic Philology* 11:61–81.

Hollis, A. S., ed. 1970. *Ovid: Metamorphoses Book VIII*. Oxford: Clarendon.

Hollis, Susan T. 1989. "The Woman in Ancient Examples of the Potiphar's Wife Motif, K2111." In *Gender and Difference in Ancient Israel*, edited by Peggy L. Day, 28–42. Minneapolis: Fortress.

———. 1990. *The Ancient Egyptian "Tale of Two Brothers": The Oldest Fairy Tale in the World*. Norman: University of Oklahoma Press.

Hölscher, Uvo. 1978. "The Transformation from Folk-Tale to Epic." In *Homer: Tradition and Invention*, edited by Bernard Fenik, 51–67. Leiden: E. J. Brill.

———. 1988. *Die Odyssee: Epos zwischen Märchen und Roman*. Munich: C. H. Beck.

Holzberg, Niklas. 1993. "A Lesser Known 'Picaresque' Novel of Greek Origin: The *Aesop Romance* and Its Influence." *Groningen Colloquia on the Novel* 5:1–16.

Honko, Lauri. 1979–80. "Methods in Folk-Narrative Research: Their Status and Future." *Ethnologia Europaea* 11:6–27.

———. 1984. "Folkloristic Studies on Meaning: An Introduction." *Arv* 40:35–56.

———. 1985a. "Zur Quellengeschichte der finnischen Erzählforschung." *Fabula* 26:104–123.

———. 1985b. "Zielsetzung und Methoden der finnischen Erzählforschung." *Fabula* 26:318–335.

———. 1986. "Types of Comparison and Forms of Variation." *JFR* 23:105–124.

Honti, Hans. 1931. *Volksmärchen und Heldensage: Beiträge zur Klärung ihrer Zusammenhänge*. FFC 95. Hamina: Academia Scientiarum Fennica.

Horálek, Karel. 1964. "Ein Beitrag zu dem Studium der afrikanischen Märchen." *Archiv Orientální* 32:501–521.

How, W. W., and J. Wells. 1928. *A Commentary on Herodotos*. 2 vols. Oxford: Clarendon.

Howard, Irene. 1967. "The Folk Origins of 'The Land of Cokaygne.' " *Humanities Association Bulletin* 18:72–79.

Huber, Gerlinde. 1990. *Das Motiv der "Witwe von Ephesus" in lateinischen Texten der Antike und des Mittelalters*. Mannheimer Beiträge zur Sprach-und Literaturwissenschaft, no. 18. Tübingen: Gunter Narr.

Huber, P. Michael. 1910. *Die Wanderlegende von den Siebenschläfern: Eine literargeschichtliche Untersuchung*. Leipzig: Otto Harrassowitz.

Hudson, Arthur Palmer. 1953. "Some Versions of 'The King of the Cats.' " *Southern Folklore Quarterly* 17:225–231.

Huet, G. 1908. "Variante tcheque du tresor de Rampsinite." *RTP* 23:161–163.

———. 1911. "Le 'retour du mari' dans le théatre d'ombres à Java." *RTP* 26:321–326.

———. 1915. "Le Conte du 'Mort Reconnaissant' et le Livre de Tobie." *Revue de l'Histoire des Religions* 71:1–29.

———. 1916. "Le conte du tresor pillé (Le 'Tresor du roi Rhampsinite') dans le roman de Berinus." *RTP* 31:208–217, 261–274.

———. 1917. "Le retour merveilleux du mari." *RTP* 32:97–109, 145–163.

———. 1918a. "Le conte du tresor pillé: les versions africaines." *RTP* 33:1–17.

———. 1918b. "Le conte du tresor pillé: versions diverses." *RTP* 33:109–115, 253–273.

The Hundred Stories. Les Cent Nouvelles Nouvelles. n.d. Translated by Robert B. Douglas. New York: Ace Books.

Imellos, Stephanos. 1984. "Aus dem Kreis der Polyphemsage in Griechenland." In Siegmund 1984:47–52.

In der Smitten, Wilhelm Th. 1972. "Zur Pagenerzählung im 3. Esra (3 Esr. III 1–V 6)." *Vetus Testamentum* 22:492–495.

Jackson, Kenneth. 1940. "The Motive of the Threefold Death in the Story of Suibhne Geilt." In *Essays and Studies Presented to Professor Eoin MacNeill, D.Litt., on the Occasion of his Seventieth Birthday, May 15th, 1938*, edited by John Ryan, 535–550. Dublin: At the Sign of the Three Candles.

Jacoby, Felix. 1923–. *Die Fragmente der griechischen Historiker*. Leiden: E. J. Brill.

Jameson, Michael H. 1990. "Perseus, the Hero of Mykenai." In *Celebrations of Death and*

Divinity in the Bronze Age Argolid: Proceedings of the Sixth International Symposium at the Swedish Institute at Athens, 11–13 June, 1988, edited by Robin Hägg and Gullög C. Nordquist, 213–223. Acta Instituti Atheniensis Regni Sueciae, no. 40. Stockholm: Svenska Institutet i Athen.

Jameson, R. D. 1932. *Three Lectures on Chinese Folklore.* Peking: North China Union Language School.

Jason, Heda. 1970. "The Russian Criticism of the 'Finnish School' in Folktale Scholarship." *Norveg* 14:285–294.

———. 1972. "Structural Analysis and the Concept of the 'Tale-type.' " *Arv* 28:36–54.

———. 1978. "Aspects of the Fabulous in Oral Literature." *Fabula* 19:14–31.

———. 2000. *Motif, Type and Genre: A Manual for Compilation of Indices and a Bibliography of Indices and Indexing.* FFC 273. Helsinki: Academia Scientiarum Fennica.

Jason, Heda, and Aharon Kempinski. 1981. "How Old are Folktales?" *Fabula* 22:1–27.

Jauhiainen, Marjatta. 1998. *The Type and Motif Index of Finnish Belief Legends and Memorates.* FFC 267. Helsinki: Academia Scientiarum Fennica.

Jaunzems, John. 1978. "Structure and Meaning in the *Seven Sages of Rome.*" In Niedzielski, Runte, and Hendrickson 1978:43–62.

Jax, Karl. 1930. "Ein Odysseusmotiv im Volksmärchen der österreichischen Alpenländer." *Wiener Blätter für die Freunde der Antike* 7:64.

Jebb, R. C. 1887. *Sophocles: The Plays and Fragments, with Critical Notes, Commentary, and Translation in English Prose.* Part 7, *The Ajax.* 2d ed. Cambridge: Cambridge University Press.

Jensen, Lisbeth Steenstrup, and Søren Koustrup. 1976. *Udvandrersange.* Copenhagen: Munksgaard.

Joly, A. 1877. *Histoire de deux fables de La Fontaine: Leurs origines et leurs pérégrinations.* Paris: Ernest Thorin.

Jones, Joseph R. 1994. "A Gathering of Nobodies: The Oldest Joke in the World and Its Traces in Cervantes and Hispanic Literatures." *Comparative Literature Studies* 31:128–147.

Jones, Julian W. 1970. "The Trojan Horse: *Timeo Danaos et Dona Ferentis.*" *CJ* 65:241–247.

Just, Roger. 1991. *Women in Athenian Law and Life.* London: Routledge.

Kagan, Zipporah. 1965. "The Jewish Versions of AT 425: Cupid and Psyche (*On the problem of sub-types and oiko-types*)." In *IV. International Congress for Folk-Narrative Research in Athens,* edited by Georgios A. Megas, 209–212. Athens: Ἑλληνικὴ Λαογραφικὴ Ἑταιρεία (= Λαογραφία 22).

Kakridis, Johannes Th. 1928. "Der Fluch des Theseus im 'Hippolytos.' " *RhM* 77:21–33.

———. 1929. *Ἀραί· Μυθολογικὴ Μελέτη.* Athens: P. D. Sakellarios.

———. 1947. "Caeneus." *CR* 61:77–80.

———. 1949. *Homeric Researches.* Lund: C. W. K. Gleerup.

———. 1971. *Homer Revisited.* Lund: C. W. K. Gleerup.

Καλλέργης, Ἡρακλῆς. 1995. "Ἀρχαιοελληνικές ἀπηχήσεις στο νεοελληνικό λαϊκό παραμύθι." In *Λαϊκό Παραμύθι και Παραμυθάδες στην Ελλάδα.* Edited by Β. Δ. Ἀναγνωστόπουλος and Κώστας Λιάπης, 27–39. 2d ed. Athens: Ekdoseis Kastanioti.

Kamenetsky, Christa. 1992. *The Brothers Grimm and Their Critics: Folktales and the Quest for Meaning.* Athens: Ohio University Press.

Karadagli, Triantaphyllia. 1981. *Fabel und Ainos: Studien zur griechischen Fabel.* Beiträge zur klassischen Philologie, no. 135. Königstein/Ts.: Verlag Anton Hain.

Karlinger, Felix. 1986. *Zauberschlaf und Entrückung: Zur Problematik des Motivs der Jenseitszeit in der Volkserzählung.* Raabser Märchen-Reihe, no. 7. Vienna: Im Selbstverlag des österreichischen Museums für Volkskunde.

Kassel, R., and C. Austin, eds. 1983–. *Poetae Comici Graeci*. Berlin: Walter de Gruyter.

Kearns, Emily. 1982. "The Return of Odysseus: A Homeric Theoxeny." *CQ* 32:2–8.

Keene, Donald. 1962. "The Hippolytus Triangle, East and West." In *The Yearbook of Comparative and General Literature* 11, supplement, 162–171.

Kenner, Hedwig. 1970. *Das Phänomen der verkehrten Welt in der griechisch-römischen Antike*. Aus Forschung und Kunst, no. 8. Klagenfurt: Geschichtsverein für Kärnten.

Kenney, E. J. 1990. *Apuleius: Cupid & Psyche*. Cambridge: Cambridge University Press.

Kern, Hermann. 1982. *Labyrinthe: Erscheinungsformen und Deutungen: 5000 Jahre Gegenwart eines Urbilds*. Munich: Prestel.

Keuls, Eva. 1974. *The Water Carriers in Hades: A Study of Catharsis through Toil in Classical Antiquity*. Amsterdam: Adolf M. Hakkert.

Kiefer, Emma. 1947. *Albert Wesselski and Recent Folktale Theories*. Indiana University Publications: Folklore Series, no. 3. Bloomington: Indiana University.

Killeen, J. F. 1971. "Aristotle *Rhet.* 1413b3." *CPh* 66:186–187.

Kirchhof, Hans W. 1980. *Wendunmuth*. Edited by Hermann Oesterley. 5 vols. 1869. Reprint, Hildesheim and New York: Georg Olms Verlag.

Kirk, G. S. 1974. *The Nature of Greek Myths*. Harmondsworth, England: Penguin.

Kirk, G. S., and J. E. Raven. 1957. *The Presocratic Philosophers: A Critical History with a Selection of Texts*. Cambridge: Cambridge University Press.

Kirkpatrick, Patricia G. 1987. *The Old Testament and Folklore Study*. Journal for the Study of the Old Testament Supplement Series, no. 62. Sheffield: Sheffield Academic Press.

Kitchell, Kenneth F., Jr. 1993. "The View from Deucalion's Ark: New Windows on Antiquity." *CJ* 88:341–357.

Kittredge, George Lyman. 1929. *Witchcraft in Old and New England*. New York: Russell & Russell.

Klintberg, Bengt af. 1990. "Do the Legends of Today and Yesterday Belong to the Same Genre?" In Röhrich and Wienker-Piepho 1990:113–123.

Knight, W. F. J. 1930. "The Wooden Horse." *CPh* 25:358–366.

———. 1931. "Epilegomena to the 'Wooden Horse.' " *CPh* 26:412–420.

Knopp, Grace. 1933. "The Motifs of the 'Jason and Medea Myth' in Modern Tradition (A Study of Märchentypus 313)." Ph.D. diss., Stanford University.

Knowles, Rev. J. Hinton. 1893. *Folk-Tales of Kashmir*. 2d ed. London: Kegan Paul, Trench, Trübner.

Knox, Mary. 1979. "Polyphemos and His Near Eastern Relations." *JHS* 99:164–165.

Köchlin, Elisabeth. 1945. *Wesenszüge des deutschen und des französischen Volksmärchen: Eine vergleichende Studie zum Märchentypus "Amor und Psyche" und zum "Tierbraütigam."* Basel: B. Schwabe.

Köhler, Reinhold. 1855. "Eine römische Sage (von der Tötung der Greise)." *Zeitschrift für deutsche Mythologie* 2:110–113.

———. 1857. "Die stärksten Dinge." *Germania* 2:481–485.

———. 1894. *Aufsätze über Märchen und Volkslieder*. Edited by Johannes Bolte and Erich Schmidt. Berlin: Weidmannsche Buchhandlung.

———. 1898–1900. *Kleinere Schriften*. Edited by Johannes Bolte. 3 vols. Weimar: Verlag von Emil Felber.

Korompay, Bertalan. 1978. *Zur Finnischen Methode: Gedanken eines Zeitgenossen*. Helsinki: n.p.

Krappe, Alexander. 1923. "The Story of Phrixos and Modern Folklore." *Folklore* 34:141–147.

———. 1925. "The Story of Iason and Medeia." *Folk-Lore* 36:308–321.

———. 1927. *Balor with the Evil Eye: Studies in Celtic and French Literature*. New York: Institute des Études Françaises, Columbia University.

———. 1933a. "La Légende de Persée." *Neuphilologische Mitteilungen* 34:225–232.

———. 1933b. "Trophonios and Agamedes." *Archiv für Religionswissenschaft* 30:228–241.

———. 1935. "Studies on the *Seven Sages of Rome*." *Archivum Romanicum* 19:213–226.

———. 1964. *The Science of Folklore*. New York: W. W. Norton.

Kretschmer, P. 1917. "Mythische Namen." *Glotta* 8:127.

Kretzenbacher, Leopold. 1957. "Heimkehr von der Pilgerfahrt." *Fabula* 1:214–227.

———. 1976. "Südost-Entsprechungen zur steirischen Rechtslegende vom Meineid durch betrügerische Reservatio Mentalis (AT 1590)." In *Das Recht der kleinen Leute: Beiträge zur Rechtlichen Volkskunde. Festschrift für Karl-Sigismund Kramer zum 60. Geburtstag*, edited by Konrad Köstlin and Kai Detlev Sievers, 125–139. Berlin: Erich Schmidt Verlag.

Kristensen, Evald Tang. 1871–97. *Jyske Folkeminder, især fra Hammerum Herred*. 13 vols. Copenhagen: Karl Schønbergs Boghandel.

———. 1892–1939. *Danske Sagn, som de har lydt i Folkemunde, udelukkende efter utrykte Kilder*. 7 vols. Århus and Silkeborg: Århus Folkeblads Trykkeri; Copenhagen: C. A. Reitzels Forlag.

Kristensen, Johannes Evald Tang. 1949. "Den i Tankerne Rige Mand eller Kone." In *Festskrift til Museumsforstander H. P. Hansen, Herning, på 70–Årsdagen den 2. Oktober 1949*, 270–278. Århus and Copenhagen.

Krohn, Kaarle. 1922. *Skandinavisk Mytologi. Olaus-Petri-Föreläsningar*. Helsingfors: Holger Schildts Förlagsaktiebolag.

———. 1926. *Die folkloristische Arbeitsmethode*. Oslo: Instituttet for sammenlignende kulturforskning. Translated by Roger Welsch under the title *Folklore Methodology, Formulated by Julius Krohn and expanded by Nordic Researchers* (Austin: University of Texas Press, 1971).

———. 1931. *Übersicht über einige Resultate der Märchenforschung*. FFC 96. Helsinki: Suomalainen Tiedeakatemia.

Kronenberg, Andreas. 1955. "The Fountain of the Sun: A Tale Related by Herodotus, Pliny, and the Modern Teda." *Man* 55:74.

Kuntze, Franz. 1925. "Ein plautinisches Lustspielmotiv in der Weltliteratur." *Neue Jahrbücher für Wissenschaft und Jugendbildung* 1:717–728.

Kunzle, David. 1978. "World Upside Down: The Iconography of a European Broadsheet Type." In Babcock 1978:39–94.

Kvideland, Reimund, and Henning K. Sehmsdorf, eds. 1988. *Scandinavian Folk Belief and Legend*. Minneapolis: University of Minnesota Press.

Lacy, Norris J., ed. 1967. *La Femme au Tombeau: Anonymous Fabliau of the Thirteenth Century*. Ph.D. diss.: Indiana University.

Lalande, André. 1968. *Vocabulaire Technique et Critique de la Philosophie*. 2d ed. Paris: Presses Universitaires de France.

Landau, Marcus. 1900–1901. "Die Erdenwanderungen der Himmlischen und die Wünsche der Menschen." *Zeitschrift für vergleichende Litteraturgeschichte* NF 14:1–41.

Lang, Andrew. 1873. "Mythology and Fairy Tales." *Fortnightly Review* 19:618–631.

———. 1910. "Method and Minotaur." *Folklore* 21:132–146.

———. 1970. *Custom and Myth*. 2d ed. Oosterhout N.B., The Netherlands: Anthropological Publications.

Langerbeck, H. 1963. "Die Vorstellung vom Schlaraffenland in der alten attischen Komödie." *ZVV* 59:192–204.

Laqueur, R. 1911. "Ephorus." *Hermes* 46:161–206.

Lassen, Henrik R. 1995. " 'The Improved Product': A Philological Investigation of a Contemporary Legend." *Contemporary Legend* 5:1–37.

Leaf, Walter. 1915. *Homer and History*. London: Macmillan.

Lee, A. C. 1972. *The Decameron: Its Sources and Analogues*. New York: Haskell House.

Lefkowitz, Mary R. 1981. *The Lives of the Greek Poets*. Baltimore: Johns Hopkins University Press.

Legman, G. 1964. *The Horn Book: Studies in Erotic Folklore and Bibliography*. New Hyde Park: University Books.

———. 1971. *Rationale of the Dirty Joke: An Analysis of Sexual Humor*. New York: Grove.

Lerch, P. 1864. "Über eine armenische Bearbeitung der 'sieben weisen Meister.' " *Orient und Occident* 2:369–374.

Lesky, Albin. 1967. "Herakles und das Ketos." *Anzeiger der österreichischen Akademie der Wissenschaften, phil.-hist. Klasse*, 104, no. 1.

Leutsch, E. L., and F. G. Schneidewin, eds. 1958. *Corpus Paroemiographorum Graecorum*. 2 vols. Göttingen: Vandenhoeck & Ruprecht, 1839–51. Reprint, Hildesheim: Georg Olms Verlag.

———. 1961. *Supplementum*. Hildesheim: Georg Olms Verlagbuchhandlung.

Levin, Isidor. 1966. "Etana." *Fabula* 8:1–63.

Lévi-Strauss, Claude. 1978. *The Origin of Table Manners*. Vol. 3 of *Introduction to a Science of Mythology*. Translated by John Weightman and Doreen Weightman. New York: Harper and Row.

Lewy, Heinrich. 1928. "Beiträge zur jüdischen Volkskunde." *ZVV* 37/38:81–89.

Leyen, Friedrich von der. 1899. *Das Märchen in den Göttersagen der Edda*. Berlin: Georg Reimer.

———. 1958. *Das Märchen: Ein Versuch*. 4th ed. Heidelberg: Quelle & Meyer.

LiDonnici, Lynn R. 1995. *The Epidaurian Miracle Inscriptions: Text, Translation and Commentary*. Atlanta: Scholars.

Liebenau, Th. v. 1900. "Der Ring des Gyges in der Schweiz." *SAV* 4:220–221.

Liebrecht, Felix. 1879. *Zur Volkskunde: Alte und Neue Aufsätze*. Heilbronn: Verlag von Gebr. Henninger.

Liljeblad, Sven. 1927. *Die Tobiasgeschichte und andere Märchen mit toten Helfern*. Lund: A.-B. Ph. Lindstedts Univ.-Bokhandel.

———. 1935. "Argonauterna och sagorna om flykten från trollet." *Saga och Sed* 1:29–48.

Limón, J. E., and M. J. Young. 1986. "Frontiers, Settlements, and Developments in Folklore Studies, 1972–1985." *Annual Review of Anthropology* 15:437–460.

Lincoln, Bruce. 1999. *Theorizing Myth: Narrative, Ideology, and Scholarship*. Chicago: University of Chicago Press.

Lindahl, Carl. 1987. *Earnest Games: Folkloric Patterns in the Canterbury Tales*. Bloomington: Indiana University Press.

Lindow, John. 1997. *Murder and Vengeance among the Gods: Baldr in Scandinavian Mythology*. FFC 262. Helsinki: Academia Scientiarum Fennica.

Liungman, Waldemar. 1961. *Die Schwedischen Volksmärchen: Herkunft und Geschichte*. Berlin: Academie-Verlag.

Lloyd, Alan B. 1975–88. *Herodotus, Book II*. 3 vols. Leiden: E. J. Brill.

Löffler, Ingrid. 1963. *Die Melampodie: Versuch einer Rekonstruktion des Inhalts*. Beiträge zur klassischen Philologie, no. 7. Meisenheim am Glan: Verlag Anton Hain.

Lommatzsch, Erhard. 1961. "Die stärksten Dinge." In *Jahrbuch der Akademie der Wissenschaften und der Literatur in Mainz*, 236–238. Wiesbaden: F. Steiner Verlag.

Longo, Stella. 1984. "L'analyse des versions trouvées en Argentine du conte type 313." In Calame-Griaule, Görög-Karady, and Chiche 1984:123–150.

Loorits, Oskar. 1932. "Das Märchen vom gestohlenen Donnerinstrument bei den Esten." In *Sitzungsberichte der Gelehrten Estnischen Gesellschaft, 1930*, 47–121. Tartu: Gelehrte Estnische Gesellschaft.

———. 1937. *Some Notes on the Repertoire of the Estonian Folk-Tale*. Commentationes Archivi Traditionum Popularium Estoniae, no. 6. Tartu: K. Mattieseni trükikoda o.-ü.

———. 1951. *Grundzüge des estnischen Volksglaubens*. Vol. 2. Skrifter utgivna av Kungl. Gustav Adolfs Akademien för Folklivsforskning 18, no. 2. Lund: Carl Bloms Boktryckeri.

———, ed. 1959. *Estnische Volkserzählungen*. Berlin: Walter de Gruyter.

Lord, Albert B. 1962. "Homeric Echoes in Bihac." *Zbornik za narodni zivot i obicaje* 40:313–320.

——. 1965. *The Singer of Tales.* New York: Atheneum.

——. 1969. "The Theme of the Withdrawn Hero in Serbo-Croatian Oral Epic." *Prilozi za knjizevnost, jezik, istoriju i folklor* 35:18–30.

——. 1972. "The Effect of the Turkish Conquest on Balkan Epic Tradition." In *Aspects of the Balkans: Continuity and Change,* edited by Henrik Birnbaum and Speros Vryonis, Jr., 298–318. The Hague: Mouton.

——. 1991. *Epic Singers and Oral Tradition.* Ithaca, N.Y.: Cornell University Press.

Lovejoy, Arthur, and George Boas. 1965. *Primitivism and Related Ideas in Antiquity.* New York: Octagon Books.

Lowenstam, Steven. 1992. "The Uses of Vase-Depictions in Homeric Studies." *TAPA* 122:165–198.

Lucas, Hans. 1903. "Ein Märchen bei Petron." In *Beiträge zur alten Geschichte und griechisch-römischen Alterthumskunde: Festschrift zu Otto Hirschfelds sechzigstem Geburtstage,* 257–269. Berlin: Weidmannsche Buchhandlung.

Lumbroso, Giacomo. 1883. "Sul dipinto pompeiano in cui si è ravvisato il giudizio di Salomone." *Archivio per le tradizioni popolari* 2:569–574.

Lundell, Torborg. 1983. "Folktale Heroines and the Type and Motif Indexes." *Folklore* 94:240–246.

——. 1986. "Gender-Related Biases in the Type and Motif Indexes of Aarne and Thompson." In Bottigheimer 1986:149–163.

Luria, S. 1929. "Die Ersten werden die Letzten sein." *Klio* 22:405–431.

Lüthi, Max. 1961. *Volksmärchen und Volkssage: Zwei Grundformen erzählender Dichtung.* Bern: Francke Verlag.

——. 1964. *Märchen.* 2d ed. Stuttgart: J. B. Metzlersche Verlagsbuchhandlung.

——. 1969. *So Leben Sie Noch Heute: Betrachtungen zum Volksmärchen.* Göttingen: Vandenhoeck & Ruprecht.

——. 1976. *Once upon a Time: On the Nature of Fairy Tales.* Translated by Lee Chadeayne and Paul Gottwald. Bloomington: Indiana University Press.

——. 1984. *The Fairytale as Art Form and Portrait of Man.* Translated by Jon Erickson. Bloomington: Indiana University Press.

——. 1986. *The European Folktale: Form and Nature.* Translated by John D. Niles. Bloomington: Indiana University Press.

Lynn, Loretta, with George Vecsey. 1977. *Coal Miner's Daughter.* New York: Warner Books.

McCartney, Eugene S. 1931. "Ancient Wit and Humor." In *Classical Studies in Honor of John C. Rolfe,* edited by George Depue Hadzsits, 191–211. Philadelphia: University of Pennsylvania Press.

——. 1953a. "Antiphanes' Cold-Weather Story and its Elaborations." *CPh* 48:169–172.

——. 1953b. "Undoing by Night Work Done by Day." In *Studies Presented to David Moore Robinson on his Seventieth Birthday,* edited by George E. Mylonas and Doris Raymond, 2:1249–1253. St. Louis: Washington University.

McCarty, Willard. 1989. "The Shape of the Mirror: Metaphorical Catoptrics in Classical Literature." *Arethusa* 22:161–195.

MacDonald, Dennis R. 1990. *The Acts of Andrew and the Acts of Andrew and Matthias in the City of the Cannibals.* Atlanta: Scholars.

——. 1994. *Christianizing Homer: The Odyssey, Plato, and The Acts of Andrew.* New York: Oxford University Press.

McGlathery, James M., et al. eds. 1991. *The Brothers Grimm and Folktale.* Urbana: University of Illinois Press.

McInnis, Duncan. 1890. *Folk and Hero Tales.* London: The Folk-Lore Society.

Mackensen, Lutz, et al., eds. 1930–40. *Handwörterbuch des deutschen Märchens.* 2 vols. Berlin, Leipzig: Walter de Gruyter.

Malten, Ludolf. 1939. "Motivgeschichtliche Untersuchungen zur Sagenforschung. I. Philemon und Baukis." *Hermes* 74:176–206.

Mannhardt, Wilhelm. 1875–77. *Wald- und Feldkulte*. 2 vols. Berlin: Gebrüder Borntraeger.

Mantero, Teresa. 1970. *La Fabella di Amor et Psyche*. Genoa: Fratelli Bozzi.

Manzo, Antonio. 1988. *L'Adynaton Poetico-Retorico e le sue Implicazioni Dottrinali. Pubblicazione del Dipartimento di Archeologia, Filologia Classica e loro Tradizioni*, n.s., 115. Genova: Università di Genova, Facoltà di Lettere.

Marcovich, M. 1976. "Aelian, *Varia Historia* 13.15." *Živa Antika* 26:49–51.

Μαρινάτος, Σπυρ. Ν. 1953. Ἴφικλος καὶ Μελάμπους. *Λαογραφία* 15:44–49.

Marót, K. 1958. "Zur Entstehungsgeschichte der Odyssee." *L'Antiquité Classique* 27:328–336.

Martin, Richard P. 1989. *The Language of Heroes: Speech and Performance in the Iliad*. Ithaca, N.Y.: Cornell University Press.

Marx, August. 1889. *Griechische Märchen von dankbaren Tieren und Verwandtes*. Stuttgart: W. Kohlhammer.

Marx, Friedrich. 1959. *Plautus, Rudens: Text und Kommentar*. Amsterdam: Verlag Adolf M. Hakkert.

Marzolph, Ulrich. 1987. "Philogelos arabikos: Zum Nachleben der antiken Witzesammlung in der mittelalterlichen arabischen Literatur." *Der Islam* 64:185–230.

Maspero, G. 1885. "Sur une version arabe du conte de Rhampsinite." *Journal asiatique* 6:149–159.

Massaro, Matteo. 1977. "*Aniles fabellae*." *Studi Italiani di Filologia Classica* 49:104–135.

———. 1981. "La redazione fedriana della 'Matrona di Efeso.'" *MCSN* 3:217–237.

Massignon, Geneviève, ed. 1968. *Folktales of France*. Translated by Jacqueline Hyland. Chicago: University of Chicago Press.

Matičetov, Milko. 1972–73. "La fabia di Polifemo a Resia." *SAV* 68/69:407–415.

Matsubara, Hideichi. 1978. "Chinese and Japanese Versions of *Gaza*." In Niedzielski, Runte, and Hendrickson 1978:104–108.

Matthews, Wm. Henry. 1922. *Mazes and Labyrinths: A General Account of Their History and Developments*. London: Longmans, Green.

Mayor, Adrienne. 1992. "Ambiguous Guardians: The 'Omen of the Wolves' (A.D. 402) and the 'Choking Doberman' (1980s)." *JFR* 29:253–268.

———. 1995. "The Nessus Shirt in the New World: Smallpox Blankets in History and Legend." *JAF* 108:54–77.

———. 2000a. "The 'Monster of Troy' Vase: The Earliest Artistic Record of a Vertebrate Fossil Discovery?" *Oxford Journal of Archaeology* 19:57–63.

———. 2000b. *The First Fossil Hunters: Paleontology in Greek and Roman Times*. Princeton: Princeton University Press.

Mayor, John. 1893. "Herodotus II 121.11–17." *Journal of Philology* 21:70.

Megas, Georgios A. 1933. "Die Sage von Danaos und den Danaiden." *Hermes* 68:415–428.

———. 1962. "Märchensammlung und Märchenforschung in Griechenland seit dem Jahre 1864." *Deutsches Jahrbuch für Volkskunde* 8:153–159.

———. 1971. *Das Märchen von Amor und Psyche in der griechischen Volksüberlieferung (Aarne-Thompson 425, 428, & 432)*. Πραγματεῖαι τῆς ᾽Ακαδημίας ᾽Αθηνῶν, 30. Athens: Academy of Athens.

———, ed. 1970. *Folktales of Greece*. Translated by Helen Colaclides. Chicago: University of Chicago Press.

Meraklis, Michael G. 1993. "Märchen in Griechenland." In Röth and Kahn 1992:99–105.

Merivale, Patricia. 1969. *Pan the Goat-God: His Myth in Modern Times*. Cambridge: Harvard University Press.

Merkelbach, Reinhold. 1958. "Eros und Psyche." *Philologus* 102:103–116.

Mesk, Josef. 1925. "Über Phlegons Mirabilia I–III." *Philologus* 80:298–311.

Meslin, Michel. 1980. "Significations rituelles et symboliques du miroir." In *Perennitas: Studi in onore di Angelo Brelich*, 327–341. Rome: Edizioni dell' Ateneo.

Meuli, Karl. 1921. *Odyssee und Argonautika: Untersuchungen zur griechischen Sagengeschichte und zum Epos*. Berlin: Verlag der Weidmannschen Buchhandlung.

Meyer, Gustav. 1885–93. *Essays und Studien zur Sprachgeschichte und Volkskunde*. 2 vols. Strassburg: Verlag von Karl J. Trübner.

Meyer, Maurits de. 1938. "Amor et Psyché: Étude comparée des variantes recueillies en France, en Belgique et en Allemagne." *Folk-liv* 2:197–210.

———. 1942. *Vlaamsche Sprookjesthemas in het Licht der romaansche en germaansche Kultuurstroomingen*. Leuven: De vlaamsche drukkerij.

Miller, Joe. 1884. *Joe Miller's Jest Book: An Immense Collection of the Funniest Jokes, Quaint and Laughable Anecdotes, Mirth Provoking Stories, Brilliant Witticisms, and Queer Sayings, as told by the Original Joe Miller*. 70th ed. Philadelphia: Crawford.

Mondi, Robert. 1983. "The Homeric Cyclopes: Folktale, Tradition, and Theme." *TAPA* 113:17–38.

Moore, Carey A. 1996. *Tobit: A New Translation with Introduction and Commentary*. The Anchor Bible. New York: Doubleday.

Moreau, Alain. 1994. *Le mythe de Jason et Médée: le va-nu-pied et la sorcière*. Paris: Les Belles Lettres.

Moreschini, Claudio. 1999. "Towards a History of the Exegesis of Apuleius: The Case of the 'Tale of Cupid and Psyche.' " In Hofmann 1999:215–228.

Morris, Ian, and Barry Powell, eds. 1997. *A New Companion to Homer*. Leiden: Brill.

Morris, Richard. 1889. "Death's Messengers." *Folk-Lore Journal* 7:179–191.

Morris, Robert. 1931. "Told in Ozarkia." *Folk-Say* 3:94–102.

Moser, Dietz-Rüdiger. 1979. "Die Homerische Frage und das Problem der mündlichen Überlieferung aus volkskundlicher Sicht." *Fabula* 20:116–136.

Müller, Carl Werner. 1980. "Die Witwe von Ephesus—Petrons Novelle und die 'Milesiaka' des Aristeides." *Antike und Abendland* 26:103–121.

Müller, F. Max. 1881. "On the Migration of Fables. A Lecture Delivered at the Royal Institution, on Friday, June 3, 1870." In *Chips from a German Workshop*, 4:139–198. New York: Charles Scribner's Sons.

Mundy, C. S. 1956. "Polyphemus and Tepegöz." *Bulletin of the School of Oriental and African Studies* 18:279–302.

———. 1961. "The Cyclops in Turkish Tradition: A Study in Folktale Transmission." In *Internationaler Kongress der Volkserzählungsforscher in Kiel und Kopenhagen*, 229–234. Berlin: Walter de Gruyter.

———. 1965. "Philogelos, the Nesnas, and Misokolakis." *Λαογραφία* 22:324–327. (= *IV. International Congress for Folk-Narrative Research in Athens*).

Munson, Rosaria V. 1993. "Herodotus' Use of Prospective Sentences and the Story of Rhampsinitus and the Thief in the *Histories*." *AJP* 114:27–44.

Murley, Clyde. 1924. "Pausanias and the Atlas Metope." *CPh* 19:365–368.

Murnaghan, Sheila. 1986. "*Antigone* 904–920 and the Institution of Marriage." *AJP* 107:192–207.

Murray, Gilbert. 1934. *The Rise of the Greek Epic*. 4th edition. London: Oxford University Press.

Musick, Ruth Ann. 1970. *Greens Hills of Magic: West Virginia Folktales from Europe*. Lexington: University Press of Kentucky.

Nagler, Michael N. 1974. *Spontaneity and Tradition: A Study in the Oral Art of Homer*. Berkeley and Los Angeles: University of California Press.

———. 1987. "On Almost Killing Your Friends: Some Thoughts on Violence in Early Cultures." In *Comparative Research on Oral Traditions: A Memorial for Milman Parry*, edited by John Miles Foley, 425–463. Columbus, Ohio: Slavica.

Nagy, Gregory. 1979. *The Best of the Achaeans: Concepts of the Hero in Archaic Greek Poetry.* Baltimore: Johns Hopkins University Press.

Naumann, Hans-Peter. 1979. "Das Polyphem-Abenteuer in der altnordischen Sagaliteratur." *SAV* 75:173–189.

Néraudau, J.-P. 1978. "Sexagenarii de ponte (réflexions sur la genèse d'un proverbe)." *Revue des Études Latines* 56:159–174.

Neuman, Abraham A. 1953. *Landmarks and Goals: Historical Studies and Addresses.* Philadelphia: Dropsie College Press.

Niedzielski, H., H. R. Runte, and W. L. Hendrickson, eds. 1978. *Studies on the Seven Sages of Rome and Other Essays in Medieval Literature, Dedicated to the Memory of Jean Misrahi.* Honolulu: Educational Research Associates.

Nikiforov, A. I. 1975. "Towards a Morphological Study of the Folktale." In *The Study of Russian Folklore,* edited and translated by Felix J. Oinas and Stephen Soudakoff, 155–161. The Hague: Mouton.

Nilsson, Martin P. 1932. *The Mycenaean Origin of Greek Mythology.* Berkeley and Los Angeles: University of California Press.

——. 1952. *A History of Greek Religion.* Translated by F. J. Fielden. 2d ed. Oxford: Clarendon.

——. 1967. *Geschichte der Griechischen Religion.* Munich: C. H. Beck.

——. 1972. *Homer and Mycenae.* Philadelphia: University of Pennsylvania Press.

Nippgen, J. 1914. "Le Cyclope (version albanaise du mythe de Polyphème)." *RTP* 29:49–51.

Nöldeke, Th. 1894. "Zu Herodot 3,119 (Sophokles Antigone 903–913)." *Hermes* 29:155–156.

Noy, Dov, ed. 1963. *Folktales of Israel.* Translated by Gene Baharav. Chicago: University of Chicago Press.

Nyrop, Kr. 1880–82. "Sagnet om Odysseus og Polyphem." *Nordisk Tidskrift for Filologi,* n.s., 5:216–255.

Odenius, Oloph. 1954. "Mundus Inversus: Några inledande bibliografiska anteckningar kring tre mellansvenska bildvarianter." *Arv* 10:142–170.

Oesterley, Hermann, ed. 1872. *Gesta Romanorum.* Berlin: Weidmann.

Ohlert, Konrad. 1912. *Rätsel und Rätselsspiele der alten Griechen.* 2d ed. Berlin: Mayer & Müller.

Oinas, Felix. 1978. "The Transformation of Folklore into Literature." In *American Contributions to the Eighth International Congress of Slavists, Zagreb and Ljubljana, September 3–9, 1978,* edited by Victor Terras, 2:570–604. Columbus, Ohio: Slavica.

——. 1983. "The Sower." *JFR* 20:83–88.

——. 1993. " 'The Sower' in Finnish Folklore Revisited." *Eurasian Studies Yearbook* 65:130–132.

Olrik, Axel. 1892. "Märchen in Saxo Grammaticus." *ZVV* 2:117–123, 252–258, 367–374.

——. 1905. "Tordenguden og hans dreng." *Danske Studier* 2:129–146.

——. 1906. "Tordenguden og hans dreng i lappernes myteverden." *Danske Studier* 3:65–69.

——. 1922. *Ragnarök: Die Sagen vom Weltundergang.* Translated by Wilhelm Ranisch. Berlin: Walter de Gruyter.

——. 1992. *Principles for Oral Narrative Research.* Translated by Kirsten Wolf and Jody Jensen. Bloomington: Indiana University Press.

Opie, Iona, and Peter Opie. 1974. *The Classic Fairy Tales.* London: Oxford University Press.

Orend, Misch. 1958. "Vom Schwur mit Erde in den Schuhen." *Deutsches Jahrbuch für Volkskunde* 4:386–392.

Orso, Ethelyn. 1979. *Modern Greek Humor: A Collection of Jokes and Ribald Tales.* Bloomington: Indiana University Press.

O'Sullivan, James. 1987. "Observations on the Kyklôpeia." *Symbolae Osloenses* 62:5–24.
——. 1990. "Nature and Culture in *Odyssey 9?" Symbolae Osloenses* 65:7–17.
O'Sullivan, Sean, ed. and trans. 1966. *Folktales of Ireland.* Chicago: University of Chicago Press.
Otto, A. 1890. *Die Sprichwörter und sprichwörtichen Redensarten der Römer.* Leipzig: B. G. Teubner.
Page, Denys. 1951. *A New Chapter in the History of Greek Tragedy.* Cambridge: Cambridge University Press.
——. 1955. *The Homeric Odyssey.* Oxford: Clarendon.
——. 1959. *History and the Homeric Iliad.* Berkeley and Los Angeles: University of California Press.
——. 1973. *Folktales in Homer's Odyssey.* Cambridge: Harvard University Press.
——, ed. 1952. *Euripides: Medea.* Oxford: Clarendon.
——. 1962. *Poetae Melici Graeci.* Oxford: Clarendon.
Paksoy, H. B. 1989. *Alpamysh: Central Asian Identity under Russian Rule.* Hartford, Conn.: Association for the Advancement of Central Asian Research.
Panzer, Friedrich. 1910. *Studien zur germanischen Sagengeschichte.* Vol. 1, *Beowulf.* Munich: Oskar Beck.
Parca, Maryline. 1981. "Deux récits milésiens chez Pétrone (*Satyricon,* 85–87 et 111–112): Une étude comparative." *Revue Belge de Philologie et Histoire* 59:91–106.
Paredes, Américo, ed. and trans. 1970. *Folktales of Mexico.* Chicago: University of Chicago Press.
Paredes, Américo, and Richard Bauman, eds. 1972. *Towards New Perspectives in Folklore.* Austin: University of Texas Press.
Paris, Gaston. 1907. "Le conte du tresor du roi Rhampsinite: Étude de mythographie comparée." *Revue de l'histoire des religions* 55:151–187, 267–316.
Parke, H. W. 1977. *Festivals of the Athenians.* Ithaca, N.Y.: Cornell University Press.
Parks, Ward. 1981. "Generic Identity and the Guest-Host Exchange: A Study of Return Songs in the Homeric and Serbo-Croatian Traditions." *Canadian-American Slavic Studies* 15:24–41.
Parry, Milman, and Albert Lord. 1954–. *Serbo-Croatian Heroic Songs.* Cambridge and Belgrade: Harvard University Press and Serbian Academy of Sciences.
Parsons, Elsie Clews. 1917. "Ten Folk-Tales from the Cape Verde Islands." *JAF* 30:230–238.
——. 1923. *Folk-Lore from the Cape Verde Islands.* Memoirs of the American Folk-Lore Society, no. 15, parts 1–2. Cambridge, Mass.: American Folk-Lore Society.
Paudler, Fritz. 1937. *Die Volkserzählungen von der Abschaffung der Altentötung.* FFC 121. Helsinki: Academia Scientiarum Fennica.
Pauli, Johannes. 1924. *Schimpf und Ernst.* Edited by Johannes Bolte. 2 vols. Berlin: Herbert Stubenrauch.
Paulme, Denise. 1963. "Un conte de fées africain: Le garçon travesti ou Joseph en Afrique." *L'homme* 3:5–21.
Pauly, A., and G. Wissowa, eds. 1893–. *Real-Enzyklopädie der classischen Altertumswissenschaft.* Stuttgart: J. B. Metzler.
Pecere, Oronzo. 1975. *Petronio: la novella della matrona di Efeso.* Miscellanea Erudita, no. 27. Padua: Editrice Antenore.
Peeters, Paul. 1914. *Évangiles apocryphes.* Vol. 2. Paris: Auguste Picard.
Pellizer, Ezio. 1988. "Reflections, Echoes and Amorous Reciprocity: On Reading the Narcissus Story." In Bremmer 1988:107–120.
Penzer, N. M. n.d. *The Ḥarêm: An Account of the Institution as it Existed in the Palace of the Turkish Sultans with a History of the Grand Seraglio from its Foundation to the Present Time.* Philadelphia: J. B. Lippincott.

———, ed. and trans. 1924–28. *The Ocean of Story, being C. H. Tawney's Translation of So-madeva's Kathā Sarit Sāgara (or the Ocean of Streams of Story)*. 10 vols. London: Chas. J. Sawyer.

Pepe, Luigi. 1981. "I predicati di base nella 'Matrona de Efeso' petroniana." *MCSN* 3:411–424.

Peradotto, John. 1990. *Man in the Middle Voice: Name and Narration in the* Odyssey. Princeton: Princeton University Press.

Perdrizet, Paul. 1911. "La miraculeuse histoire de Pandare et d'Echédore, suivie de recherches sur la marque dans l'Antiquité." *ARW* 14:52–129.

Perrault, Charles. 1957. *Fairy Tales*. Translated by Geoffrey Brereton. Harmondsworth, England: Penguin Books.

Perry, Ben E. 1952. *Aesopica: A Series of Texts Relating to Aesop or Ascribed to Him or Closely Connected with the Literary Tradition that Bears His Name*. Urbana: University of Illinois Press.

———. 1959. "The Origin of the Book of Sindbad." *Fabula* 3:1–94.

———. 1960. Review of Trenkner 1958. *AJP* 81:442–447.

———. 1962. "Demetrius of Phalerum and the Aesopic Fables." *TAPA* 93:287–346.

———. 1964. *Secundus the Silent Philosopher: The Greek Life of Secundus* Ithaca, N.Y.: American Philological Association.

———. 1967. *The Ancient Romances: A Literary-Historical Account of Their Origins*. Berkeley and Los Angeles: University of California Press.

———. 1981. *Studies in the Text History of the Life and Fables of Aesop*. American Philological Association Monograph Series, no. 7. Chico, Calif.: Scholars.

———, ed. and trans. 1965. *Babrius and Phaedrus*. Cambridge: Harvard University Press.

Pervo, Richard I. 1997. "With Lucian: Who Needs Friends? Friendship in the *Toxaris*." In *Greco-Roman Perspectives on Friendship*, edited by John T. Fitzgerald, 163–180. Atlanta: Scholars.

Peschier, Eugène. 1902. "Zur Polyphemsage." *SAV* 6:154–155.

Petersmann, Hubert. 1981. "Homer und das Märchen." *WS* 94, NF 15:43–68.

Petropoulos, Dimitrios. 1965. "Das Rampsinitos-Märchen in neugriechischen Überlieferungen." *Λαογραφία* 22:343–353.

Petsch, Robert. 1900. *Formelhafte Schlüsse im Volksmärchen*. Berlin: Weidmannsche Buchhandlung.

Pfleger, Alfred. 1938. "Der Schwur beim Schöpfer: Ein kleiner Beitrag zur elsässischen Sagenforschung." *Annuaire de Colmar* 4:75–90.

Pichler, Regina. 1986. *Die Gygesgeschichte in der griechischen Literatur und ihre neuzeitliche Rezeption*. Munich: UNI-Druck.

Pineau, Léon. 1891. "Les Ponts du Diable." *RTP* 6:403.

Pino-Saavedra, Yolando, ed. 1967. *Folktales of Chile*. Translated by Rockwell Gray. Chicago: University of Chicago Press.

Pischel, R. 1893. "Zu Sophokles Antigone 909–912." *Hermes* 28:465–468.

Pitrè, G. 1883. "Il Guidizio di Salomone a Pompei." *Archivio per le Tradizioni Popolari* 2:133–134.

Plath, Margarete. 1901. "Zum Buch Tobit." *Theologische Studien und Kritiken* 74: 377–414.

Platnauer, Maurice, ed. 1938. *Euripides: Iphigeneia in Tauris*. Oxford: Clarendon.

———. 1964. *Aristophanes: Peace*. Oxford: Clarendon.

[Platt, Rutherford]. n.d. *The Lost Books of the Bible and The Forgotten Books of Eden*. n.p.: World Bible. A republication of *The Lost Books of the Bible*, edited by R. H. P., Jr. (N.p.: Alpha House, 1926) and *The Forgotten Books of Eden*, edited by Rutherford H. Platt, Jr. (N.p.: Alpha House, 1927).

Poeschel, Johannes. 1878. "Das Märchen vom Schlaraffenlande." *Beiträge zur Geschichte der deutschen Sprache und Literatur* 5:389–427.

Πολίτης, Νικόλαος. 1904. Μελέται περὶ τοῦ Βίου καὶ τῆς Γλώσσης τοῦ Ἑλληνικοῦ Λαοῦ. Παραδώσεις. 2 vols. Ἀθῆναι: Π. Δ. Σακελλάριος.

Polívka, Georg. 1898a. "Nachträge zur Polyphemsage." *Archiv für Religionswissenschaft* 1:305–336.

———. 1898b. "Seit welcher Zeit werden die Greise nicht mehr getötet? Slawische Parallelen." *ZVV* 8:25–29.

Polle, Friedrich. 1896. *Wie bezeichneten die alten Griechen den Witz? Über Luftschlösserbaukunst. Über Nichts. Drei gemeinverständliche Vorträge nebst einem Anhange von Rätseln.* Leipzig: B. G. Teubner.

Porzig, Walter. 1930. "Illujankas und Typhon." *Kleinasiatische Forschungen* 1:379–386.

Pourrat, Henri. 1954. *A Treasury of French Tales.* Translated by Mary Mian. Boston: Houghton Mifflin.

Prato, Stanislao. 1882. *La Leggenda del Tesoro di Rampsinite nelle Varie Redazioni Italiane e Straniere.* Como: Carlo Franchi.

Preisendanz, Karl, ed. and trans. 1973–74. *Papyri Graecae Magicae: Die Griechischen Zauberpapyri.* 2 vols. Stuttgart: B. G. Teubner.

Preller, Ludwig. 1894–1926. *Griechische Mythologie.* 3 vols. 4th ed., revised by Carl Robert. Berlin: Weidmannsche Buchhandlung.

Preston, Cathy Lynn. 1994. " 'Cinderella' as a Dirty Joke: Gender, Multivocality, and the Polysemic Text." *WF* 53:27–49.

Pritchard, James B., ed. 1955. *Ancient Near Eastern Texts Relating to the Old Testament.* 2d ed. Princeton: Princeton University Press.

Propp, Vladimir. 1968. *Morphology of the Folktale.* 2d ed. Translated by Laurence Scott. Edited by Louis A. Wagner. Austin: University of Texas Press.

———. 1972. "Transformations in Fairy Tales." In *Mythology: Selected Readings,* edited by Pierre Maranda, 139–150. Harmondsworth: Penguin Books.

Rad, Gerhard von. 1972. *Genesis: A Commentary.* Rev. ed. Philadelphia: Westminster.

Radermacher, Ludwig. 1906. "Walfischmythen." *Archiv für Religionswissenschaft* 9:248–252.

———. 1908. "Motiv und Persönlichkeit, II: Die Büsser Vergils." *RhM* 63:531–558.

———. 1909. "Der Knäul Ariadnes." *Wiener Eranos: Festschrift zur 50. Versammlung deutscher Philologen und Schulmänner in Graz 1909,* 285–292. Graz: Hölder.

———. 1911. "Eine aristophanische Reminiszenz?" *RhM* 66:176–182.

———. 1913. "Volkstümliche Schwankmotive bei Aristophanes." *WS* 35:193–196.

———. 1915. *Die Erzählungen der Odyssee.* Sitzungsberichte der kais. Akademie der Wissenschaften in Wien, phil.-hist. Klasse 178, no. 1.

———. 1918. *Beiträge zur Volkskunde aus dem Gebiet der Antike.* Sitzungsberichte der kais. Akademie der Wissenschaften in Wien, phil.-hist. Klasse 187, no. 3.

———. 1921. *Aristophanes' Frösche: Einleitung, Text und Kommentar.* Sitzungsberichte der kais. Akademie der Wissenschaften in Wien, phil.-hist. Klasse 198, no. 4.

———. 1968. *Mythos und Sage bei den Griechen.* 3d ed. Darmstadt: Wissenschaftliche Buchgesellschaft.

Radner, Joan N. 1989. " 'The Woman Who Went to Hell': Coded Values in Irish Folk Narrative." *Midwestern Folklore* 15:109–117.

Rael, Juan B. n.d. *Cuentos Españoles de Colorado y de Nuevo Méjico.* 2 vols. Stanford University.

Rajna, P. 1877. "La Novella Boccaccesca del Saladino e di Messer Torello." *Romania* 6:359–368.

Rammel, Hal. 1990. *Nowhere in America: The Big Rock Candy Mountain and Other Comic Utopias.* Urbana: University of Illinois Press.

Randolph, Vance. 1977. *Pissing in the Snow & Other Ozark Folktales*. Annotations by Frank A. Hoffmann. New York: Bard.

——. 1993. *Stiff as a Poker and Other Ozark Folk Tales*. New York: Barnes & Noble. With notes by Herbert Halpert. Originally published as *The Devil's Pretty Daughter* (New York: Columbia University Press, 1955).

Ranelagh, E. L. 1979. *The Past We Share: The Near Eastern Ancestry of Western Folk Literature*. London: Quartet Books.

Rank, Otto. 1913. " 'Die Matrone von Ephesus': Ein Deutungsversuch der Fabel von der treulosen Witwe." *Internationale Zeitschrift für ärztliche Psychoanalyse* 1: 50–60.

Ranke, Kurt. 1934. *Die zwei Brüder: Eine Studie zur vergleichenden Märchenforschung*. FFC 114. Helsinki: Academia Scientiarum Fennica.

——. 1953. "Der 'Hölzerne Johannes': Eine westeuropäische Redaktion der 'Matrona von Ephesus.' " *Rheinisches Jahrbuch für Volkskunde* 4:90–114.

——, ed. 1955–62. *Schleswig-holsteinische Volksmärchen*. 3 vols. Kiel: Ferdinand Hirt.

——. 1966. *Folktales of Germany*. Translated by Lotte Baumann. Chicago: University of Chicago Press.

——. 1972. *European Anecdotes and Jests*. Translated by Timothy Buck. Copenhagen: Rosenkilde and Bagger.

Raspe, R. E., and others. 1971. *The Adventures of Baron Munchausen*. New York: Meridian Books.

Rastier, Françoise. 1971. "La morale de l'histoire: Notes sur *la Matrone d'Éphèse* (*Satiricon*, CXI–CXII)." *Latomus* 30:1025–1056.

Rat, Maurice, trans. 1934. *Petrone, Le Satiricon, suivi des poesies attribuées à Petrone et des fragments épars*. Paris: Librarie Garnier Frères.

Reckford, Kenneth J. 1987. *Aristophanes' Old-and-New Comedy*. Vol. 1, *Six Essays in Perspective*. Chapel Hill: University of North Carolina Press.

Redford, Donald B. 1970. *A Study of the Biblical Story of Joseph (Genesis 37–50)*. Supplements to *Vetus Testamentum*, vol. 20. Leiden: E. J. Brill.

Rehatsek, E. 1880. "A Few Analogies in the 'Thousand and One Nights' and in Latin Authors." *Journal of the Bombay Branch of the Royal Asiatic Society* 14:74–85.

Reinach, Salomon. 1903. "Sisyphe aux Enfers et quelques autres damnés." *Revue archéologique*, 4th ser., 1:154–200.

——. 1907. "La mort du Grand Pan." *BCH* 31:5–19.

Reinhardt, Karl. 1948. *Von Werken und Formen: Vorträge und Aufsätze*. Godesberg: H. Küpper.

Reitzenstein, Richard. 1912. *Das Märchen von Amor und Psyche bei Apuleius*. Leipzig: B. G. Teubner.

——. 1963. *Hellenistische Wundererzählungen*. 2d ed. Darmstadt: Wissenschaftliche Buchgesellschaft.

Rich, George W. 1971. "Rethinking the 'Star Husbands.' " *JAF* 84:436–441.

Richardson, N. J., ed. 1974. *The Homeric Hymn to Demeter*. Oxford: Clarendon.

Richmond, W. Edson. 1954. "The Textual Transmission of Folklore." *Norveg* 4:173–196.

——, ed. 1957. *Studies in Folklore in Honor of Distinguished Service Professor Stith Thompson*. Bloomington: Indiana University Press.

Richter, Dieter. 1986. "Wie Kinder Schlachtens mit einander gespielt haben (AaTh 2401)." *Fabula* 27:1–11.

Roberts, Leonard W. 1964. *South from Hell-fer-Sartin: Kentucky Mountain Folk Tales*. First Appalachian Heritage Edition. Berea, Kentucky: Council of the Southern Mountains.

Roberts, Warren E. 1958. *The Tale of the Kind and Unkind Girls: Aa-Th 480 and Related Tales*. Berlin: Walter de Gruyter.

——. 1964. *Norwegian Folktale Studies: Some Aspects of Distribution.* Studia Norvegica, no. 13. Oslo: Universitetsforlag.

——. 1965. "Holbek on the *Type Index*: A Rejoinder." *JFI* 2:229–235.

——. 1966a. "The Sheep Herder and the Rabbits." *JFI* 3:43–49.

——. 1966b. "International Folktales among the North American Indians." *Acta Ethnographica Academiae Scientiarum Hungaricae* 15:161–166.

Roberts, Warren E., Richard M. Dorson, and Herbert Halpert. 1957. "The Folktale: A Symposium." *JAF* 70:49–65.

Rocca, R. 1976. "Eliodoro e i due 'Ippoliti' euripidei." *MCSN* 1:25–31.

Rogerson, John W. 1979. *Anthropology and the Old Testament.* Atlanta: John Knox.

Rohde, Erwin. 1876. "Über griechische Novellendichtung und ihren Zusammenhang mit dem Orient." *Verhandlungen der XXX. Philologen-Versammlung zu Rostock 1875* (Leipzig 1876), 55–70 (= Rohde 1960:578–601).

——. 1877a. "Zu den Mirabilia des Phlegon." *RhM* 32:329–339 = *Kl. Schr.* 2:173–185.

——. 1877b. Review of Grisebach 1877, in *Kleine Schriften* (Tübingen: J. C. B. Mohr, 1901), 2:186–192.

——. 1878. "Τέγονε in den Biographien des Suidas." *RhM* 33:161–220 = *Kl. Schr.* 1:114–184.

——. 1880. "Die sardinische Sage von den Neunschläfern." *RhM* 35:157–163 = *Kl. Schr.* 2:197–204.

——. 1882. "Zu der Sage von den Sardinischen Heroën." *RhM* 37:465–468 = *Kl. Schr.* 2:204–208.

——. 1925. *Psyche: The Cult of Souls and Belief in Immortality among the Greeks.* Translated by H. B. Hillis. London: Kegan Paul, Trench, Trubner.

——. 1960. *Der griechische Roman und seine Vorläufer.* 4th ed. Hildesheim: Georg Olms Verlagsbuchhandlung.

Röhrich, Lutz. 1955, 1956, 1957. "Die Märchenforschung seit dem Jahre 1945." *Deutsches Jahrbuch für Volkskunde* 1:279–296; 2:274–319; 3:213–224, 494–514.

——. 1962. "Die mittelalterliche Redaktionen des Polyphem-Märchens (AT 1137) und ihr Verhältnis zur ausserhomerischen Tradition." *Fabula* 5:48–71.

——. 1962–67. *Erzählungen des späten Mittelalters und ihr Weiterleben in Literatur und Volksdichtung bis zur Gegenwart: Sagen, Märchen, Exempel und Schwanke.* 2 vols. Bern: A. Francke Verlag.

——. 1963. "Die Volksballade von 'Herrn Peters Seefahrt' und die Menschenopfer-Sagen." In *Märchen, Mythos, Dichtung: Festschrift zum 90. Geburtstag Friedrich von der Leyens am 19. August 1963*, edited by Hugo Kuhn and Kurt Schier, 177–212.

——. 1979. "Der Froschkönig und seine Wandlungen." *Fabula* 20:170–191.

——. 1984. "Märchen—Mythos—Sage." In Siegmund 1984:11–35.

——. 1991. *Folktales and Reality.* Translated by Peter Tokofsky. Bloomington: Indiana University Press.

Röhrich, Lutz, and Sabine Wienker-Piepho, eds. 1990. *Storytelling in Contemporary Societies.* ScriptOralia, no. 22. Tübingen: Gunter Narr Verlag.

Rölleke, Heinz, ed. 1975. *Die älteste Märchensammlung der Brüder Grimm: Synopse der handschriftlichen Urfassung von 1810 und der Erstdrucke von 1812.* Cologny-Genève: Foundation Martin Bodmer.

Romm, James S. 1992. *The Edges of the Earth in Ancient Thought: Geography, Exploration, and Fiction.* Princeton: Princeton University Press.

Rooth, Anna Birgitta. 1951. *The Cinderella Cycle.* Lund: C. W. K. Gleerup.

——. 1961. *Loki in Scandinavian Mythology.* Lund: C. W. K. Gleerups Förlag.

——. 1983. *Från lögnsaga till paradis.* Studia Ethnologica Upsaliensis, no. 12. Uppsala: Acta Universitatis Upsaliensis.

Roscher, W. H. 1892. "Die Legende vom Tode des grossen Pan." *Jahrbücher für classische Philologie* 145:465–477.

——, ed. 1884–37. *Ausführliches Lexikon der Griechischen und Römischen Mythologie.* 7 vols. Leipzig: B. G. Teubner.

Rose, H. J. 1928. *A Handbook of Greek Mythology.* London: Methuen.

——, ed. 1963. *Hygini Fabulae.* Lugduni Batavorum: In aedibus A. W. Sythoff.

Rosenberg, Bruce. 1991. *Folklore and Literature: Rival Siblings.* Knoxville: University of Tennessee Press.

Röth, Diether, and Walter Kahn, eds. 1993. *Märchen und Märchenforschung in Europa: Ein Handbuch.* Frankfurt am Main: Haag und Herchen.

Rouse, W. H. D. 1904. "A Greek Skipper." *Cambridge Review* 27:414–415.

Rubow, Mette. 1984. "Un essai d'interprétation du conte-type AaTh 303: *Le roi des poissons* ou *La bête à sept têtes.*" *Fabula* 25:18–34.

Rudolf, W. 1945–48. "Der Wettstreit der Leibwächter des Darius 3 Esra 3:1–5:6." *Zeitschrift für die Alttestamentliche Wissenschaft* 61:176–190.

Ruiz Montero, Consuelo. 1982. "Una interpretación del 'estilo KAI' de Jenofonte de Efeso." *Emerita* 50:305–323.

Runeberg, J. 1902. "Le conte de l'île-poisson." *Mémoires de la Société Néo-Philologique à Helsingfors* 3:343–395.

Runte, Hans R. 1978. "The Matron of Ephesus: The Growth of the Story in the *Roman des Sept Sages de Rome.*" In Niedzielski, Runte, and Hendrickson 1978:109–118.

——. 1994. "Variant Widows: On Editing and Reading Vidua." In *Medieval Codicology, Iconography, Literature, and Translation: Studies for Keith Val Sinclair,* edited by Peter Rolfe Monks and D. D. R. Owen, 240–247. Leiden: E. J. Brill.

Ryder, Arthur W., trans. 1956. *The Panchatantra.* Phoenix Books. Chicago: University of Chicago Press.

Ryder, M. L. 1991. "The Last Word on the Golden Fleece Legend?" *Oxford Journal of Archaeology* 10:57–60.

Salles, C. 1981. "Assem para et accipe auream fabulam: Quelques remarques sur la littérature populaire et le répertoire des conteurs publics dans le monde romain." *Latomus* 40:8–16.

Sanders, Irwin T. 1962. *Rainbow in the Rock: The People of Rural Greece.* Cambridge: Harvard University Press.

Sandy, Gerald N. 1999. "The Tale of Cupid and Psyche." In Hofmann 1999:126–138.

Sartori, Paul. 1894. "Der Schuh im Volksglaube." *ZVV* 4:41–54, 148–180, 282–305, 412–427.

——. 1895. "Die Sitte der Alten-und Krankentötung." *Globus* 67:125–131.

Sayre, Farrand. 1938. *Diogenes of Sinope: A Study of Greek Cynicism.* Diss. Baltimore: n.p.

Schaaf, Lothar. 1977. *Der Miles Gloriosus des Plautus und sein griechisches Original: Ein Beitrag zur Kontaminationsfrage.* Studia et Testimonia Antiqua, no. 18. Munich: Wilhelm Fink Verlag.

Schachermeyr, Fritz. 1950. *Poseidon und die Entstehung des griechischen Götterglaubens.* Bern: A. Francke AG. Verlag.

Schaller, Gualterus. 1901. *De Fabula Apuleiana quae est de Psycha et Cupidine.* Leipzig: Hallberg & Buechting.

Scheiber, Alexander. 1963. "Zu den antiken Zusammenhängen der Aggada." *AAASH* 11:149–154 (= Scheiber 1985:234–239).

——. 1969. "Antike Motive in der Aggada." *AAASH* 17:55–59 (= Scheiber 1985: 251–255).

——. 1973. "Beispiele der klassischen Zusammenhänge der Aggada." *AAASH* 21:353–360 (= Scheiber 1985:291–298).

——. 1985. *Essays on Jewish Folklore and Comparative Literature.* Budapest: Akadémiai Kiadó.

Schein, Seth. 1970. "Odysseus and Polyphemus in the *Odyssey.*" *GRBS* 11:73–83.

Schenda, Rudolf. 1965. "Walfisch-Lore und Walfisch-Literatur." *Λαογραφία* 22:431–448.

——. 1970. *Volk ohne Buch: Studien zur Sozialgeschichte der populären Lesestoffe, 1770–1910*. Frankfurt am Main: Vittorio Klostermann.

Schenkl, Karl. 1862. "Griechische und deutsche Sagen." *Germania* 7:193–195.

——. 1866. "Zur deutschen Märchenkunde." *Germania* 11:450–452.

Scherf, Walter. 1982. *Lexikon der Zaubermärchen*. Stuttgart: Alfred Kröner.

——. 1995. *Das Märchenlexikon*. 2 vols. München: C. H. Beck.

Schlam, Carl C. 1976. *Cupid and Psyche: Apuleius and the Monuments*. University Park, Pa.: American Philological Association.

——. 1992. *The Metamorphoses of Apuleius: On Making an Ass of Oneself*. Chapel Hill: University of North Carolina Press.

——. 1993. "Cupid and Psyche: Folktale and Literary Narrative." *Groningen Colloquia on the Novel* 5:63–73.

Schlauch, Margaret. 1934. *Romance in Iceland*. Princeton: Princeton University Press.

Schmid, Ulrich. 1964. *Die Priamel der Werte im Griechischen von Homer bis Paulus*. Wiesbaden: Otto Harrassowitz.

Schmidt, Bernhard. 1903. "Der Selbstmord der Greise von Keos: Ein kulturgeschichtliches Problem." *Neue Jahrbücher für das Klassische Altertum* 11:617–628.

Schmidt, Hans. 1907. *Jona: Eine Untersuchung zur vergleichenden Religionsgeschichte*. Forschungen zur Religion und Literatur des Alten und Neuen Testaments, no. 9. Göttingen: Vandenhoeck und Ruprecht.

Schmidt, Leopold. 1957. "Sichelheld und Drachenzunge." *Fabula* 1:19–25.

——. 1963. *Die Volkserzählung: Märchen, Sage, Legende, Schwank*. Berlin: Erich Schmidt Verlag.

Schneemelcher, Wilhelm, ed. 1991–92. *New Testament Apocrypha*. Rev. ed. Translated by R. McL. Wilson. 2 vols. Louisville: Westminster/John Knox.

Schnorf, Kaspar. 1879. *Der mythische Hintergrund im Gudrunlied und in der Odyssee*. Zurich: Friedrich Schulthess.

Schönberger, Otto. 1967. "Das Verbrechen des Makareus." *Jahresbericht des Wirsberg-Gymnasiums*. Würzburg.

Schreck, Emmy, trans. 1887. *Finnische Märchen*. Weimar: Hermann Böhlau.

Schrempp, Gregory. 1992. *Magical Arrows: The Maori, the Greeks, and the Folklore of the Universe*. Madison: University of Wisconsin Press.

Schröeder, Johan A. 1916. *De Amoris et Psyches Fabella Apuleiana Nova Quadam Ratione Explicata*. Amsterdam: M. J. Portielje.

Schürer, Emil. 1973–87. *The History of the Jewish People in the Age of Jesus Christ (175 B.C.–A.D. 135)*. Rev. ed. 3 vols. Edinburgh: T. & T. Clark.

Schwarzbaum, Haim. 1957. "The Overcrowded Earth." *Numen* 4:59–74.

——. 1963. Review of Aarne and Thompson 1961. *Fabula* 6:182–194.

——. 1968. *Studies in Jewish and World Folklore*. Berlin: Walter de Gruyter.

——. 1979. *The Mishle Shu'alim (Fox Fables) of Rabbi Berechiah Ha-Nakdan: A Study in Comparative Folklore and Fable Lore*. Kiron: Institute for Jewish and Arab Folklore Research.

——. 1982. "Female Fickleness in Jewish Folklore (Aa-Th Narrative *Types* 1350, 1352* and 1510)." In *The Sepharadi and Oriental Jewish Heritage. Proceedings of the 1st International Congress on the Sepharadi and Oriental Jewry*, edited by Issachar Ben-Ami, 589–613. Jerusalem: Magnes Press of the Hebrew University.

Schweitzer, Bernhard. 1922. *Herakles: Aufsätze zur griechischen Religions- und Sagengeschichte*. Tübingen: Verlag von J. C. B. Mohr (Paul Siebeck).

Scobie, Alex. 1975. "The Battle of the Pygmies and the Cranes in Chinese, Arab, and North American Indian Sources." *Folklore* 86:122–132.

——. 1977a. "A Further Note on Pygmies and Cranes in North America." *Folklore* 88:86–87.

———. 1977b. "Some Folktales in Graeco-Roman and Far Eastern Sources." *Philologus* 121:1–23.

———. 1978. "The Structure of Apuleius' *Metamorphoses.*" In *Aspects of Apuleius' Golden Ass,* edited by B. L. Hijmans and R. T. van der Paardt, 43–61. Groningen: Bouma's Boekhuis.

———. 1983. *Apuleius and Folklore: Toward a History of ML 3045, AaTh 567, 449A.* London: The Folklore Society.

Scodel, Ruth. 1984. "Tantalus and Anaxagoras." *HSCP* 88:13–24.

Seaford, Richard, ed. 1988. *Euripides: Cyclops.* Oxford: Clarendon.

Sébillot, Paul. 1891. "Traditions et superstitions des ponts et chaussées." *RTP* 6:279–287.

Sedgwick, W. B. 1947. "Oral Transmission in Ancient Times." *Folk-Lore* 58:288–291.

Seemann, Erich. 1951. "Zum Liedkreis vom 'Heimkehrenden Ehemann.' " In *Beiträge zur Sprachwissenschaft und Volkskunde: Festschrift für Ernst Ochs,* edited by Karl Müller, 168–179. Lahr: Moritz Schauenburg.

———. 1965. "Widerspiegelungen der *Mnesterophonia* der Odyssee in Liedern und Epen der Völker." *Λαογραφία* 22:484–490.

Sega, Giovanni. 1986. "Due Milesie: La Matrona di Efeso e l'Efebo di Pergamo." *MCSN* 4:37–81.

Segal, Charles. 1971. "Croesus on the Pyre: Herodotus and Bacchylides." *WS,* n.s., 5:39–51.

———. 1972. "Curse and Oath in Euripides' Hippolytus." *Ramus* 1:165–180.

Seifert, Edeltraud K. 1952. "Untersuchungen zu Grimm's Märchen 'Das Marienkind.' " Diss., Munich. Typescript.

Seki, Keigo, ed. 1963. *Folktales of Japan.* Translated by Robert Adams. Chicago: University of Chicago Press.

Sellers, Eugénie. 1892. "Three Attic Lekythoi from Eretria." *JHS* 13:1–12.

Sergent, Bernard. 1986. *Homosexuality in Greek Myth.* Translated by Arthur Goldhammer. Boston: Beacon.

Settegast, Franz. 1917. *Das Polyphemmärchen in altfranzösischen Gedichten: Eine folkloristisch-literargeschichtliche Untersuchung.* Leipzig: Otto Harrassowitz.

Severyns, Albert. 1928. *Le cycle épique dans l'école d'Aristarque.* Bibliothèque de la Faculté de Philosophie et Lettres de l'Université de Liége. Liége: H. Vaillant-Carmanne.

Shoshan, Boaz. 1993. *Popular Culture in Medieval Cairo.* Cambridge: Cambridge University Press.

Sicard, Harald v. 1965. "Perseus und Pygmalion in Afrika." *Λαογραφία* 22:498–512.

Sieber, Friedrich. 1957. "Dem Monde kann man kein Kleid machen." *Deutsches Jahrbuch für Volkskunde* 3:366–387.

Siebs, T. 1930–31. "Heck(e)taler." In *Handwörtrbuch des deutschen Aberglaubens,* edited by E. Hoffmann-Krayer and Hanns Bächtold-Stäubli, 1613–1624. Berlin and Leipzig: Walter de Gruyter.

Siegmund, Wolfdietrich, ed. 1984. *Antiker Mythos in unseren Märchen. Veröffentlichungen der Europäischen Märchengesellschaft,* 6. Kassel: Erich Röth Verlag.

Sifakis, G. M. 1998. "Homeric Survivals in the Medieval and Modern Greek Folksong Tradition?" In *Homer,* edited by Ian McAuslan and Peter Walcot, 171–185. Oxford: Oxford University Press.

Siikala, Anna-Leena. 1990. *Interpreting Oral Narrative.* FFC 245. Helsinki: Academia Scientiarum Fennica.

Simeone, William E. 1961. "Italian Folklore Scholars." In *Folklore Research around the World: A North American Point of View,* edited by Richard M. Dorson, 58–67. Indiana University Folklore Series, no. 16. Bloomington: Indiana University Press.

Simonsen, Michèle. 1984. *Le conte populaire.* Paris: Presses Universitaires de France.

Simrock, Karl. 1856. *Der gute Gerhard und die dankbaren Todten: Ein Beitrag zur deutschen Mythologie und Sagenkunde.* Bonn: Adolf Marcus.

Sissa, Giulia. 1990. *Greek Virginity.* Translated by Arthur Goldhammer. Cambridge: Harvard University Press.

Skidmore, Clive. 1996. *Practical Ethics for Roman Gentlemen: The Work of Valerius Maximus.* Exeter: University of Exeter Press.

Skutsch, F. 1900. "Ein Prolog des Diphilos und eine Komödie des Plautus." *RhM* 55:272–285.

Slater, Niall W. 1990. *Reading Petronius.* Baltimore: Johns Hopkins University Press.

Small, Jocelyn. 1976. "Plautus and the Three Princes of Serendip." *Renaissance Quarterly* 29:183–194.

Smith, G. J., and A. J. Smith. 1992. "Jason's Golden Fleece." *Oxford Journal of Archaeology* 11:119–120.

Smith, Jonathan Z. 1969–70. "Birth Upside Down or Right Side Up?" *History of Religions* 9:281–303.

Smith, Kirby F. 1902. "The Tale of Gyges and the King of Lydia." *AJP* 23:261–282, 361–387.

———. 1920. "The Literary Tradition of Gyges and Candaules." *AJP* 41:1–37.

Snodgrass, Anthony. 1998. *Homer and the Artists: Text and Picture in Early Greek Art.* Cambridge: Cambridge University Press.

Snowden, Frank M., Jr. 1970. *Blacks in Antiquity: Ethiopians in the Greco-Roman Experience.* Cambridge: Harvard University Press.

Söderhjelm, W. 1912. "Oculus-Linteus: Zwei Geschichten vom Weiberlist." *Neuphilologische Mitteilungen* 14:57–67.

Soll, William. 1988. "Tobit and Folklore Studies, with Emphasis on Propp's Morphology." In *Society of Biblical Literature 1988 Seminar Papers,* edited by David J. Lull, 39–53. Atlanta: Scholars.

Sourvinou-Inwood, Christiane. 1990. "Myths in Images: Theseus and Medea as a Case Study." In Edmunds 1990:393–445.

Sparmberg, Paul. 1915. "Zu Steinhöwels 13. extravagante." *Zeitschrift für deutsche Philologie* 46:80–83.

Speer, Mary B. 1990. "A Young Wife's Tale: Authority and Subversion in the *Roman des Sept Sages de Rome.*" In *The Ancient Novel: Classical Paradigms and Modern Perspectives,* edited by James Tatum and Gail M. Vernazza, 126. Hanover: Dartmouth College & the National Endowment for the Humanities.

Spies, Alfons. 1930. *Militat Omnis Amans: Ein Beitrag zur Bildersprache der antiken Erotik.* Tübingen: H. Laupp, Jr.

Splettstösser, Willy. 1899. *Der heimkehrende Gatte und sein Weib in der Weltlitteratur.* Diss., Berlin.

Σπυριδάκης, Γ. 1963. "Ὁ Μῦθος τοῦ Πολυφήμου εἰς δημώδεις παραδόσεις περὶ τῶν Τριαμάτηδων." Κρητικὰ Χρονικά 15–16, no. 3:106–116.

Stahl, Sandra Dolby. 1989. *Literary Folkloristics and the Personal Narrative.* Bloomington: Indiana University Press.

Stephens, Susan A., and John J. Winkler, eds. 1995. *Ancient Greek Novels: The Fragments.* Princeton: Princeton University Press.

Sternberg, Meir. 1987. *The Poetics of Biblical Narrative: Ideological Literature and the Drama of Reading.* Bloomington: Indiana University Press.

Stiefel, A. L. 1895. "Die stärksten Dinge." *ZVV* 5:448–450.

Stitt, J. Michael. 1992. *Beowulf and the Bear's Son: Epic, Saga, and Fairytale in Northern Germanic Tradition.* Albert Bates Lord Studies in Oral Tradition, no. 8. New York: Garland.

Stramaglia, Antonio. 1999. *Res Inauditae, Incredulae: Storie di Fantasmi nel Mondo Greco-Latino.* Bari: Levante Editore.

———, ed. 2000. *Ἔρως: Antiche trame greche d'amore.* Bari: Levante Editore.

Straparola, Giovanni. 1906. *The Most Delectable Nights of Straparola of Caravaggio: The First Complete Translation into English of "Le Tredici Piacevolissime Notti de Messer Giovanni Francesco Straparola."* 2 vols. Paris: Charles Carrington.

Strömberg, Reinhold. 1950. "The Aeolus Episode and Greek Wind Magic." *Acta Universitatis Gotoburgensis* 56:73–84.

Stumme, Hans. 1893. *Tunisische Märchen und Gedichte: Eine Sammlung prosaischer und poetischer Stücke im arabischen Dialekte der Stadt Tunis nebst Einleitung und Übersetzung.* 2 vols. Leipzig: J. C. Hinrichs'sche Buchhandlung.

Suder, Wieslaw. 1978. "On Age Classification in Roman Imperial Literature." *CB* 55:5–9.

———. 1986. "L'*Initium Senectutis* nell' Impero Romano e Medio Evo." In *Actes du 110e Congrès National des Sociétés Savants, Montpellier, 1985, Hist. Médiévale,* 1:65–79. Paris: C.T.H.S.

Suggs, M. Jack, Katharine Doob Sakenfeld, and James R. Mueller, eds. 1992. *The Oxford Study Bible.* New York: Oxford University Press.

Sullivan, J. P., trans. 1977. *Petronius: The Satyricon, and Seneca: The Apocolocyntosis.* Harmondsworth, England: Penguin Books.

Sveinsson, Einar Ól. 1929. *Verzeichnis isländischer Märchenvarianten, mit einer einleitenden Untersuchung.* FFC 83. Helsinki: Academia Scientiarum Fennica.

Swahn, Jan-Öjvind. 1955. *The Tale of Cupid and Psyche (Aarne-Thompson 425 & 428).* Lund: C. W. K. Gleerup.

———. 1959. "Jason och Medea i Kråksmåla: En småländsk sagouppteckning med kommentarer." In *Från Småland och Hellas: Studier tillägnade Bror Olsson den 6 Augusti 1959.* Malmö: Allhems Förlag.

———. 1984. "Psychemythos und Psychemärchen." In Siegmund 1984:92–102.

Sydow, C. W. von. 1910. "Tors Färd till Utgård." *Danske Studier,* 65–105.

———. 1918. *Sigurds Strid med Fåvne: En Studie rörande Hjältesagans Förhållande till Folkdiktningen.* Lunds Universitets Årsskrift, n.s., part 1, vol. 14, no. 16.

———. 1935. "Die jetzige Stellung der Märchenforschung: Ziele und Mittel mit besonderer Hinsicht auf organizierte Zusammenarbeit." *Saga och Sed* 1:83–102.

———. 1948. *Selected Papers in Folklore, Published on the Occasion of his 70th Birthday.* Copenhagen: Rosenkilde and Bagger.

Tassy, Ferenc. 1959. "Il Paese di Cuccagna: Contributi alla Letteratura Universale della Tematica." *Acta Litteraria* 2:369–381.

Tatum, James. 1969. "The Tales in Apuleius' *Metamorphoses.*" *TAPA* 100:487–527.

Tawney, C. H. 1883. "Indian Folklore Notes from the Pali Jatakas and the Katha Sarit Sagara." *Journal of Philology* 12:112–126.

Taylor, Archer. 1922a. "Der tote Pan in der Volkssage?" *Schweizer Volkskunde* 12:29.

———. 1922b. "Northern Parallels to the Death of Pan." *Washington University Studies* 10, no. 1 (Humanistic Series):3–102.

———. 1927–28. "Precursors of the Finnish Method of Folk-Lore Study." *Modern Philology* 25:481–491.

———. 1931. "A Theory of Indo-European Märchen." *JAF* 44:54–60.

———. 1933. "Classification of Formula Tales." *JAF* 46:77–88.

———. 1940. "Some Trends and Problems in Studies of the Folk-Tale." *Studies in Philology* 37:1–25.

———. 1948–49. "Locutions for 'Never.' " *Romance Philology* 2:103–134.

Tegethoff, Ernst. 1922. *Studien zum Märchentypus von Amor und Psyche.* Rheinische Beiträge und Hülfsbücher zur germanischen Philologie und Volkskunde, no. 4. Bonn: Kurt Schroeder.

Tenèze, Marie-Louise. 1960. "Jean de Calais (Type 506A) en France: Tradition Écrite, Tradition Orale, Imagerie." In *Humaniora: Essays in Literature, Folklore, Bibliography Honoring Archer Taylor on his Seventieth Birthday,* edited by Wayland Hand and Gustave Arlt, 286–308. Locust Valley, N.Y.: J. J. Augustin.

——. 1979. "Du conte-type et du genre." *Fabula* 20:231–238.

Thiel, Helmut van. 1971. "Sprichwörter in Fabeln." *Antike und Abendland* 17:105–118.

Thierfelder, Andreas, ed. 1968. *Philogelos: Der Lachfreund von Hierokles und Philagrios. Griechisch-deutsch mit Einleitungen und Kommentar.* Munich: Heimeran Verlag.

Thomas, Gerald. 1977. *The Tall Tale and Philippe d'Alcripe: An Analysis of the Tall Tale Genre with Particular Reference to Philippe d'Alcripe's* La Nouvelle Fabrique des Excellents Traits de Vérité *together with an Annotated Translation of the Work.* Memorial University of Newfoundland Folklore and Language Publication Series, Monograph Series, no. 1; Publications of the American Folklore Society, Bibliographical and Special Series, no. 29. St. John's: Department of Folklore, Memorial University of Newfoundland, in association with the American Folklore Society.

Thompson, Stith. 1932. "The Folk-Tale since Basile." In Basile (1932) 2:286–304.

——. 1946. *The Folktale.* New York: Holt, Rinehart and Winston.

——. 1953a. "The Star Husband Tale." *Studia Septentrionalia* 4:93–163.

——. 1955–58. *A Motif-Index of Folk-Literature: A Classification of Narrative Elements in Folktales, Ballads, Myths, Fables, Mediaeval Romances, Exempla, Fabliaux, Jest-Books and Local Legends.* Rev. ed. 6 vols. Bloomington: Indiana University Press.

——. 1958. "Myth and Folktales." In *Myth: A Symposium*, edited by Thomas A. Sebeok, 169–180.

——. 1960. "Fifty Years of Folktale Indexing." In *Humaniora: Essays in Literature, Folklore, Bibliography Honoring Archer Taylor on his Seventieth Birthday*, edited by Wayland Hand and Gustave Arlt, 49–57. Locust Valley, N.Y.: J. J. Augustin.

——. 1974. *One Hundred Favorite Folktales.* Bloomington: Indiana University Press.

——, ed. 1953b. *Four Symposia on Folklore. Held at the Midcentury International Folklore Conference, Indiana University, July 21—August 4, 1950.* Indiana University Publications: Folklore Series, no. 8. Bloomington: Indiana University Press.

Thompson, Stith, and Warren Roberts. 1960. *Types of Indic Oral Tales: India, Pakistan, and Ceylon.* FFC 180. Helsinki: Academia Scientiarum Fennica.

Thomson, J. A. K. 1914. *Studies in the Odyssey.* Oxford: Clarendon.

Thordarson, Fridrik. 1972. "Die Ferse des Achilleus—ein Skythisches Motiv?" *Symbolae Osloenses* 47:109–124.

Tiemann, Ingeborg. 1992. *Die Deutung des Minotauros von den ältesten Quellen bis zum frühen Mittelalter.* Den Haag: Koninklijke Bibliotheek.

Ting, Nai-tung. 1970. "AT Type 301 in China and Some Countries Adjacent to China: A Study of a Regional Group and its Significance in World Tradition." *Fabula* 11:54–125.

——. 1971. "More Chinese Versions of AT 301." *Fabula* 12:65–76.

——. 1974. *The Cinderella Cycle in China and Indo-China.* FFC 213. Helsinki: Academia Scientiarum Fennica.

Toivonen, Y. H. 1937. "Pygmäen und Zugvögel." *Commentationes Instituti Fenno-Ugrici, "Suomen Suku"* 6:87–126 (= *Finnisch-ugrische Forschungen*, no. 24).

Tolstoi, J. 1934. "Einige Märchenparallelen zur Heimkehr des Odysseus." *Philologus* 89:261–274.

Traube, Ludwig. 1892. "O Roma nobilis: Philologische Untersuchungen aus dem Mittelalter." *Abhandlungen der philosophisch-philologischen Classe der Königlich Bayerischen Akademie der Wissenschaften*, 19:297–395. Munich: Verlag der K. Akademie.

Trenkner, Sophie. 1958. *The Greek Novella in the Classical Period.* Cambridge: Cambridge University Press.

Tubach, Frederic C. 1969. *Index Exemplorum: A Handbook of Medieval Religious Tales.* FFC 204. Helsinki: Suomalainen Tiedeakatemia.

Turner, Eric G. 1973. *The Papyrologist at Work.* GRBS Monographs, no. 6. Durham, N.C.: Duke University.

Tyrrell, Wm. Blake. 1984. *Amazons: A Study in Athenian Mythmaking*. Baltimore: Johns Hopkins University Press.

Ure, Peter. 1956. "The Widow of Ephesus: Some Reflections on an International Comic Theme." *Durham University Journal* 49:1–9.

Uther, Hans-Jörg. 1986. "The Encyclopedia of the Folktale." In Bottigheimer 1986: 187–193.

——. 1989. Review of Azzolina 1987. *JAF* 102:479–484.

——. 1996. "Type-and Motif-Indices 1980–1995: An Inventory." *Asian Folklore Studies* 55:299–317.

——. 1997. "Indexing Folktales: A Critical Survey." *JFR* 34:209–220.

Vajda, László. 1953. "A pigmeusok harca a darvakkal" ["The War between the Pygmies and the Cranes"], *Ethnographia* 64:242–256. With a summary in German.

——. 1971. "Zum Polyphem-Abenteuer." *Ethnologische Zeitschrift* 1:245–257.

Vernant, Jean-Pierre. 1972. "Les troupeaux du Soleil et la Table du Soleil (Odyssée XII, 260 sqq.; Hérodote, III, 17–26)." *REG* 85:xiv–xvii.

——. 1989. "Food in the Countries of the Sun." In Marcel Detienne and Jean-Pierre Vernant, *The Cuisine of Sacrifice among the Greeks*, *164–169*. Translated by Paula Wissing. Chicago: University of Chicago Press.

Versnel, H. S. 1988. "Greek Myth and Ritual: The Case of Kronos." In Bremmer 1988:121–152.

Vian, Francis. 1960. "Le mythe de Typhée et le problème de ses origines orientales." In *Éléments orientaux dans la religion grecque ancienne*, edited by Otto Eissfeldt et al., 17–37. Colloque de Strasbourg, 22–24 mai 1958. Paris: Presses Universitaires de France.

Vidossi, G. 1955. *In Margine ad Alcune Avventure di Münchhausen*. FFC 162. Helsinki: Academia Scientiarum Fennica.

Vries, Jan de. 1928. *Die Märchen von klugen Rätsellösern: Eine vergleichende Untersuchung*. FFC 73. Helsinki: Academia Scientiarum Fennica.

——. 1933. *The Problem of Loki*. FFC 110. Helsinki: Societas Scientiarum Fennica.

——. 1954. *Betrachtungen zum Märchen, besonders in seinem Verhältnis zu Heldensage und Mythos*. FFC 150. Helsinki: Academia Scientiarum Fennica.

Waley, Arthur. 1947. "The Chinese Cinderella Story." *Folklore* 58:226–238.

Walker, Henry J. 1994. *Theseus and Athens*. New York: Oxford University Press.

Walsdorff, Friedrich. 1965. "Odysseus bei Polyphem." *Der altsprachliche Unterricht* 8, no. 3:15–39.

Walsh, Peter G. 1970. *The Roman Novel: The 'Satyricon' of Petronius and the 'Metamorphoses' of Apuleius*. Cambridge: Cambridge University Press.

Ward, Anne G., et al. 1970. *The Quest for Theseus*. New York: Praeger.

Ward, Donald. 1970. "The Threefold Death: An Indo-European Trifunctional Sacrifice?" In *Myth and Law among the Indo-Europeans: Studies in Indo-European Comparative Mythology*, edited by Jaan Puhvel, 123–142. Berkeley and Los Angeles: University of California Press.

Waser, Otto. 1898. "Die alten Jungfern im Glauben und Brauch des deutschen Volkes." *SAV* 2:55–58.

Weber, Artur. 1913. "Die Novelle von der Treulosen Witwe in Ungarn." *Ungarische Rundschau für historische und soziale Wissenschaften* 2:455–468.

Webster, T. B. L. 1966. "The Myth of Ariadne from Homer to Catullus." *G & R* 13:22–31.

Wehse, Rainer. 1986. "Past and Present Folkloristic Narrator Research." In Bottigheimer 1986:245–258.

Weinreich, Otto. 1909. *Antike Heilungswunder: Untersuchungen zum Wunderglauben der Griechen und Römer*. Giessen: Verlag von Alfred Töpelmann.

530 *Bibliography*

——. 1910. "Zum Tode des grossen Pan." *ARW* 13:467–473.

——. 1911. *Der Trug des Nektanebos: Wandlungen eines Novellenstoffs.* Leipzig: B. G. Teubner.

——. 1924. Review of Schweitzer 1922. *Berliner philologische Wochenschrift* 44:807–837.

——. 1930. "Eros und Psyche bei den Kabylen." *Archiv für Religionswissenschaft* 28:88–94.

——. 1931. *Fabel, Aretalogie, Novelle: Beiträge zu Phädrus, Petron, Martial und Apuleius.* Sitzungsberichte der Heidelberger Akademie der Wissenschaften, Phil.-hist. Klasse, 1930–31. 7. Abhandlung. Heidelberg.

——. 1942. *Antiphanes und Münchhausen: Das antike Lügenmärchen von den gefrornen Worten und sein Fortleben im Abendland.* Sitzungsberichte der kais. Akademie der Wissenschaften in Wien, phil.-hist. Klasse. 220, 4.

——. 1954. "Zwei Epigramme des Nikarchos und die Volksschwänke über die Schwerhörige." In Προσφορὰ εις Στίλπονα Π. Κυριακίδην, Ἑλληνικά, παράρτημα 4:692–725.

Welcker, Friedrich G. 1857–63. *Griechische Götterlehre.* 3 vols. Göttingen: Verlag der Dieterichschen Buchhandlung.

——. 1883. "Die Kraniche des Ibykos." *RhM* 1:401–410.

Wendeler, Camillus. 1905. "Bildergedichte des 17. Jahrhunderts." *ZVV* 15:27–45, 150–165.

Wendland, Paul. 1911. *De Fabellis Antiquis earumque ad Christianos Propagatione.* Göttingen: Vandenhoeck & Ruprecht.

Wesselski, Albert. 1909. *Mönchslatein: Erzählungen aus geistlichen Schriften des XIII. Jahrhunderts.* Leipzig: Wilhelm Heims.

——. 1911. *Der Hodscha Nasreddin: türkische, arabische, berberische, maltesische, sizilianische, kalabrische, kroatische, serbische und griechische Märlein und Schwänke.* 2 vols. Weimar: Alexander Duncker Verlag.

——. 1925. *Märchen des Mittelalters.* Berlin: Herbert Stubenrauch Verlagsbuchhandlung.

——. 1929a. *Der Knabenkönig und das kluge Mädchen.* Sudetendeutsche Zeitschrift für Volkskunde, Beiheft 1. Prague: J. G. Calve.

——. 1929b. "Der Gott ausser Funktion." *Archiv Orientální* 1:300–311.

——. 1930. "Überlieferungen aus der Zeit Mohammeds, des Propheten." *Archiv Orientální* 2:427–434.

——. 1931. *Versuch einer Theorie des Märchens.* Reichenberg i.B.: Sudetendeutscher Verlag Franz Kraus.

——. 1935. "Narkissos oder das Spiegelbild." *Archiv Orientální* 7:37–63, 328–350.

——, ed. 1920. *Die Begebenheiten der beiden Gonnella.* Weimar: Alexander Duncker Verlag.

West, M. L. 1985. *The Hesiodic Catalogue of Women: Its Nature, Structure, and Origins.* Oxford: Clarendon.

——. 1997. *The East Face of Helicon: West Asiatic Elements in Greek Poetry and Myth.* Oxford: Clarendon.

——, ed. 1966. *Hesiod: Theogony.* Oxford: Clarendon.

Wheeler, Howard T. 1943. *Tales from Jalisco, Mexico.* Memoirs of the American Folk-Lore Society, no. 35. Philadelphia: American Folk-Lore Society.

Wiechers, Anton. 1961. *Aesop in Delphi.* Beiträge zur Klassischen Philologie, no. 2. Meisenheim/Glan: Verlag Anton Hain K. G.

Wiedemann, A. 1894. "Zur Polyphem-Sage." *Am Ur-Quell* 5:85–86.

Wienert, Walter. 1925. *Die Typen der griechisch-römischen Fabel, mit einer Einleitung über das Wesen der Fabel.* FFC 56. Helsinki: Academia Scientiarum Fennica.

Wieringa, Edwin P. 1997. "Humoristic (Obscene) Sudanese and Javanese Versions of the 'The Story of the Three Foolish Wishes' (Mot. J2071)." *Fabula* 38:302–304.

Wilamowitz-Moellendorff, U. von. 1884. *Homerische Untersuchungen*. Berlin: Weidmannsche Buchhandlung.

Williams, R. J. 1956. "The Literary History of a Mesopotamian Fable." *Phoenix* 10:70–77.

Wills, Lawrence M. 1995. *The Jewish Novel in the Ancient World*. Ithaca, N.Y.: Cornell University Press.

Wilson, Ambrose J. 1927. "The Sign of the Prophet Jonah and its Modern Confirmation." *Princeton Theological Review* 25:630–642.

Winkler, Jack. 1980. "Lollianos and the Desperadoes." *JHS* 100:155–181.

——. 1982. "Akko." *CPh* 77:137–138.

Woeller, Waltraud. 1963. "Der Märchentyp von Amor und Psyche und die Gestalt des Tierbräutigams." *Altertum* 9:97–105.

Wolff, Hans Walter. 1986. *Obadiah and Jonah: A Commentary*. Translated by Margaret Kohl. Minneapolis: Augsburg.

Woodward, Jocelyn. 1937. *Perseus: A Study in Greek Art and Legend*. Cambridge: Cambridge University Press.

Wright, James R. G. 1971. "Folk-Tale and Literary Technique in *Cupid and Psyche*." *CQ* 21:273–284.

Wright, Rochelle, and Robert L. Wright. 1983. *Danish Emigrant Ballads and Songs*. Carbondale: Southern Illinois University Press.

Wunderlich, Werner. 1986. "Das Schlaraffenland in der deutschen Sprache und Literatur: Bibliographischer Überblick und Forschungsstand." *Fabula* 27:54–75.

Wünsch, R. 1906. "Was sich das griechische Volk erzählt." *Hessische Blätter für Volkskunde* 5:108–124.

Wünsche, August. 1897. "Zwei Dichtungen von Hans Sachs nach ihren Quellen." *Zeitschrift für vergleichende Literaturgeschichte*, n.s., 11:36–59.

——. 1905. *Der Sagenkreis vom Geprellten Teufel*. Leipzig: Akademischer Verlag.

Wüstenfeld, Ferdinand. 1862. "Die älteste Ägyptische Geschichte nach den Zauber- und Wundererzählungen der Araber." *Orient und Occident* 1:326–340.

Yassif, Eli. 1999. *The Hebrew Folktale: History, Genre, Meaning*. Translated by Jacqueline S. Teitelbaum. Bloomington: Indiana University Press.

Yohannan, John D. 1968. *Joseph and Potiphar's Wife in World Literature: An Anthology of the Story of the Chaste Youth and the Lustful Stepmother*. New York: New Directions.

Young, David C. 1979. "The Diachronic Study of Myth and Achilles' Heel." *Laetaberis: Journal of the California Classical Association, Northern Section* 4:3–34.

Young, Frank. 1970. "A Fifth Analysis of the Star Husband Tale." *Ethnology* 9:389–413.

Zachariae, Theodor. 1899. "Zur 15. Erzählung des Siddhi-Kür." *ZVV* 9:336–337.

——. 1906. "Indische Märchen aus den Lettres édifiantes et curieuses." *ZVV* 16:129–149.

——. 1907. "Zur Geschichte vom wiesen Haikar." *ZVV* 17:172–195.

——. 1923–24. "Niccolao Manucci als Geschichtenerzähler." *ZVV* 33/34:69–81.

Zall, P. M., ed. 1963. *A Hundred Merry Tales and Other English Jest Books of the Fifteenth and Sixteenth Centuries*. Lincoln: University of Nebraska Press.

Zarncke, Eduard. 1884. "Parallelen zur Entführungsgeschichte im Miles Gloriosus." *RhM* 39:1–26.

Zeitz, Heinrich. 1936. "Der Aesoproman und seine Geschichte: Eine Untersuchung im Anschluss an die neugefundenen Papyri." *Aegyptus* 16:225–256.

Zender, Matthias, ed. 1966. *Sagen und Geschichten aus der Westeifel*. Bonn: Ludwig Röhrscheid Verlag.

Zhirmunsky, Victor. 1967. "The Epic of 'Alpamysh' and the Return of Odysseus." *Proceedings of the British Academy* 52:267–286.

Zielinski, Th. 1931. *Die Märchenkomödie in Athen*. *Jahresbericht der deutschen Schulen zu St. Annen. 1885*. Reprint, *Iresione* 1, *Eos*, Suppl. 2, 8–75.

——. 1886. "Quaestiones comicae III: De Menaechmorum paramythio." *Zurnal Minis-terstva Narodnago Prosvieszczenya*, 123–131. 1931. Reprint, *Iresione* 1, *Eos*, Suppl. 2, 140–144.

Zimmerman, Clayton. 1994. *The Pastoral Narcissus: A Study of the First Idyll of Theocri-tus*. Lanham, Md.: Rowman & Littlefield.

Zimmerman, Frank. 1958. *The Book of Tobit: An English Translation with Introduction and Commentary*. New York: Harper.

——. 1963–64. "The Story of the Three Guardsmen." *Jewish Quarterly Review* 54:179–200.

Zingerle, Anton. 1898. *Tirolensia: Beiträge zur Volks- und Landeskunde Tirols*. Innsbruck: Verlag der Wagner'schen Universitäts-Buchhandlung.

Zinserling-Paul, Verena. 1979. "Zum Bild der Medea in der antiken Kunst." *Klio* 61:407–436.

Zipes, Jack, ed. 1993. *The Trials and Tribulations of Little Red Riding Hood*. 2d ed. New York: Routledge.

INDEX OF ANCIENT SOURCES

Achilles Tatius (novelist, 2d cent. A.D.), 2.17: 89n
Acts of Andrew (ca. A.D. 200): 223n; 2.4: 352n
Acts of Paul and Thecla (2d cent. A.D.), 22: 326n
Acts of Peter (2d cent. A.D.), 37–38: 445n
Aelian (sophist, 2d–3d cent. A.D.), Natura Animalium 5.3: 186n; 7.48: 29n; 13.15: 99n; 15.29: 49n; Variae Historiae 3.37: 474n; 5.16: 85n; 7.10: 92n; 8.18: 130n; 12.63: 232n; 13.2: 85n; 13.33: 88n
Aeschylus (tragic poet, 6th–5th cent. B.C.), Agamemnon: 56n; 839: 79n; F 83: 489n; Phorkides F 262: 251n; Prometheus 792–800: 251n; Thressae: 486
Aesopica: Fables (anonymous compilations in Greek prose: Recension I or Collectio Augustana, ca. 2d cent. A.D.; Recension Ia, 3d or 4th cent. A.D.; Recension II or Collectio Vindobonensis, ca. 5th cent. A.D.), Perry 3/Hsr 3: 92n, 187n; Perry 28/Hsr 28: 438n; Perry 34/Hsr 34: 438n; Perry 42/Hsr 42: 29n; Perry 53/Hsr 53: 29n; Perry 55/Hsr 55: 255n; Perry 60/Hsr 60: 316n; Perry 63/Hsr 63: 79n; Perry 133/Hsr 136: 261n; Perry 134/Hsr 137: 246n; Perry 162/Hsr 171: 29n; Perry 173/Hsr 183: 44n; Perry 210/Hsr 226: 404n; Perry 363/Hsr 279: 29n; Proverbs (compilations by different authors, prior to the 11th cent. A.D.) 10: 256n. See also Vita Aesopi
Alexander Romance (different recensions by different unknown authors, all after 4th cent. B.C.), 1: 255n; 1.36: 99n; 2.24–33: 187n; 2.32: 186n; 2.37: 186n; 2.38: 186n; 2.39–41: 469n, 474n; 3.5–6: 423n; 3.17: 186n; 3.21: 186n
Amphis (comic poet, 4th cent. B.C.), Akko: 258
Anacreontea (anonymous poems, 1st–6th cent. A.D.), 14.1–2: 99n

Anthologia Latina, Supplementum (different poets and dates), no. 786: 435n
Anthologia Palatina (different poets and dates), 7.77: 62n; 7.516: 62n; 7.714: 92n; 7.745: 92n; 11.74: 197n; 11.77: 329n; 11.171: 438n; 11.251: 197n
Antipatros of Sidon (epigrammatist, 2d B.C.): 90
Antiphanes of Berge (prose author, 4th cent. B.C.): 146–147
Antoninus Liberalis (mythographer, 2d cent. A.D.), 8: 130n; 17: 190n; 21: 357n
Aphthonios (rhetorician, 4th cent. A.D.), 6: 261n; 35: 261n; 40: 261n
Apion (grammarian, 1st cent. A.D.), Aigyptiaka: 29n; FGH 616 F 23: 190n
Apollodoros (mythographer, 1st–2d cent. A.D.), Bibliotheca 1.4.3: 223n; 1.5.1: 489n; 1.6.3: 186n, 314n; 1.9.1: 165n; 1.9.11–12: 468n; 1.9.16–28: 164n; 2.2.2: 468n; 2.3.1–2: 351n; 2.4.2–3: 251n; 2.4.3: 130n; 2.5.5: 166n; 2.5.7: 438n; 2.5.9: 264n; 2.5.11: 201n; 2.7.2: 166n; 2.7.8: 166n; 3.1.3–4: 438n; 3.3.1: 468n; 3.6.7: 351n; 3.9.2: 165n; 3.13.2–3: 351n; 3.13.6: 489n; 3.13.8: 351n; 3.15.3: 352n; 3.15.6–3.16.2: 165n; 3.16.3: 223n; Epitome 1.1–11: 165n; 1.13–14: 371n; 1.14–15: 166n; 1.18–19: 351n; 2.1: 169n; 2.3–2.9: 62n; 2.4.6–7: 130n; 2.5.9: 130n; 2.6.4: 130n; 2.10–11: 56n; 2.10–12: 439n; 3.1–5.22: 176n; 3.6.7: 468n; 3.7: 415n; 3.9: 438n; 3.13.3: 130n; 3.21–22: 56n, 439n; 3.23–25: 351n; 5.3: 489n; 7.4–9: 300n; 7.34: 378n
Apollonios (paradoxographer, 2d cent. B.C.?), 1: 401n
Apollonios of Rhodes (epic poet, 3d cent. B.C.), Argonautica: 164n; 1.172–173: 166n; 3.66–75: 29n; 3.362–363: 166n. Schol. on Argon. 1.224:

Apollonios of Rhodes (continued)
130n, 351n; 1.172–173: 166n; 2.178: 352n;
3.997: 165n; 4.865–879: 489n

Apostolios (paroemiographer, 15th cent. A.D.),
7.50: 256n; 9.79: 351n; 13.67a: 44n; 14.75:
405n; 17.6: 190n

Appendix Proverbiorum Bodleiana, Vaticana, Cois-
liniana (CPG 1:379–467), 4.57: 130n

Appian (historian, 1st–2d cent. A.D.), Civil War
1.101: 225n

Apuleius (novelist, etc., 2d cent. A.D.), Metamor-
phoses (The Golden Ass) 2.26: 197n; 4.9–11:
371n; 4.27: 113n; 4.28–6.24: 113n; 4.28.1: 28n;
4.33: 114n; 6.25: 113n; 10.2–12: 352n

Archilochos (iambic and elegiac poet, 7th cent.
B.C.), F 122: 445n

Archimedes (geometer, 3d cent. B.C.),
Sand–Reckoner: 98

Aristides (rhetorician, 2d cent. A.D.), Orations
48: 444n

Aristophanes (comic poet, 5th–4th cent. B.C.),
Clouds 555–556: 264n; Frogs 19–32: 67; 48–51:
462n; Lysistrata 723–725: 187n; 772–773: 445n;
784: 28n; Peace 181: 187n; Plutus 730–741:
468n; Thesmophoriazusae 498–501: 227n; Wasps
1182: 28n; 1446–1449: 92n. Schol. on Clouds
1063: 130n, 351n; Frogs 51: 462n

Aristotle (philosopher, 4th cent. B.C.) and
Pseudo–Aristotle, F 556: 352n; History of Ani-
mals 8.12 (597a. 4–9): 49n; Magna Moralia
2.6.20 (1202a.25–29): 119n; Nicomachean Ethics
(Ethica Nichomachea) 7.6.2–3 (1149b.4–20):
119n; Physica 218b.21–26: 401n; Poetics 7
(1451a): 186n; Politics 1259a.9: 145n; Rhetoric
2.21.9: 28n; 3.12.3: 447n; 3.16.5: 66n; 3.16.9:
66n. Schol. on 388a–b: 401n

Arrian (historian and philosopher, 1st–2d cent.
A.D.), Anabasis 7.2.1–2: 431n

Asklepiades of Tragilos (mythographer, 4th
cent. B.C.), FGH 12 F 28: 222n, 351n

Athenaeus (sophist, 2d–3d cent. A.D.), Deip-
nosophistae 1.6f–7a: 40n; 6.267e–270a: 390n;
9.390b: 49n; 10.451b: 423n

Babrius (fabulist, 1st or 2d cent. A.D.), Fabulae
26: 49n; 47: 29n; 58: 481n; 117: 331n; 136: 29n;
179: 261n; Fabulae solutae (BaP) 169: 404n

Catullus (poet, 1st cent. B.C.), 7: 99n; 64: 165n

Charax (historian, 2d cent. A.D.?), FGH 103 F 5:
371n

Cicero (orator and philosopher, 2d–1st cent.
B.C.), Academica 2.16: 242n; 2.48.147: 242n; De
Divinatione 1.27: 62n; 1.49.111: 145n; 2.4.11:
242n; 2.71, 146: 404n; De Oratore 2.67.274:
188n; 2.69.279: 447n; Epistulae ad Familiares
4.5.6: 95n; On Duty (De Officiis) 1.32: 222n;
3.26.97: 415n; On the Nature of the Gods 3.12:
30n; 3.31: 222n; On Old Age (De Senectute) 24:
332n; Tusculan Disputations 5.32: 431n;
5.61–62: 169n

Columella (writer on agriculture, 1st cent. A.D.),
De Re Rustica 10, praef. 4: 257n

Dieukhidas (historian, 4th cent. B.C.), FGH 485 F
10: 130n

Diktys of Crete (novelistic pseudonym, 2d–3d
cent. A.D.), Trojan War 5.9–12: 176n

Dio Chrysostomos (sophist, 1st–2d cent. A.D.),
Orations 35: 391n; De Regno 4.14–15: 431n

Diodorus Siculus (historian, 1st cent. B.C.),
1.64.14: 88n; 1.94.5: 232n; 3.5–7: 117n; 4.6.5:
435n; 4.13.3: 166n; 4.26.4: 201n; 4.27.2: 201n;
4.32: 130n; 4.33.1–4: 166n; 4.40–52: 164n; 4.42:
130n, 264n; 4.43.3–6: 352n; 4.61.1–8: 165n;
4.61.5–6: 166n; 4.62: 351n; 4.77.2: 438n; 5.51.4:
165n, 166n; 5.83.4: 351n

Diogeneianos (paroemiographer, 2d cent. A.D.),
1.25: 351n; 1.35: 92n; 1.90: 151n; 2.4: 260n;
2.27: 99n; 2.86: 301n; 3.31: 351n; 5.56: 99n;
5.88: 79n; 5.97: 142n; 7.1: 79n; 7.27: 75n; 7.30:
42n; 7.33: 42n; 8.40: 190n; 8.75: 42n

Diogenes Laertios (biographer, 3d cent. A.D.),
Lives of the Philosophers 1.26: 145n; 1.109, 112,
115: 401n; 2.108: 242n; 6.27: 79n; 6.31–32:
445n; 6.38: 431n; 6.41: 447n; 8.60: 426n

Dionysios (geographer, 2d cent. A.D.), Descriptio
Graeciae 603–604: 264n

Dionysius of Halicarnassus (rhetorician and
historian, 1st cent. B.C.), Roman Antiquities
2.69: 75n; 4.69.3: 284n; 6.95: 445n

Diphilos (comic poet, 4th–3d cent. B.C.), Theseus
F 50: 423n

Dositheus and Pseudo–Dositheus (fabulist, 2d
cent. A.D.), 40, no. 11: 261n

Epicharmos (comic poet, 5th cent. B.C.), Chytrai
F 136–137: 142n

Epiphanios (ecclesiastical author, 4th cent. A.D.),
Panarion 41.1: 261n

Eratosthenes (philologist, 3d–2d cent. B.C.) and
Eratosthenica, Catasterisms 3–4: 201n; 22:
251n

Etymologicum Magnum (lexicon, 12th cent. A.D.):
260n

Eugammon of Cyrene (epic poet, 6th cent. B.C.),
Telegonia: 371n

Euphorion (epic poet, 3d cent. B.C.), F 101: 223n

Euripides (tragic poet, 5th cent. B.C.), Alcestis
669–672: 316n; Bacchae 141, 704–711: 391n; F
688: 445n; Herakles 394–407: 201n; Hippolytus
337, 351n; 24–28: 351n; 43–46, 887–890,
1315–1324: 222n; Ino: 305n; Iphigenia in Tauris
1–41: 56n; Kyklops: 330n; 1–8: 462n; Medea
410–413: 445n; Orestes 4–10: 169n. Schol. on
Hippolytus 46, 887, 1348: 222n; Orestes 7: 169n;
658: 56n; 811: 439n; 990: 62n; 995, 998: 439n;
Phoenissae 53: 352n

Eusebios (ecclesiastical author, 4th cent. A.D.),
Praeparatio Evangelica 5.17: 136n

Eustathios (commentator, 12th cent. A.D.), Com-
mentary on Homer's Iliad p. 33: 351n;

183.31–184.9: 351n; 484.41–48: 352n; 827: 438n; *Commentary on Homer's Odyssey* p. 1685: 468n, 469n; 1688: 165n; 1875.20: 305n

Festus (scholar, 2d cent. A.D.), Epitome of Verrius Flaccus *De Verborum Significatu*: 474n
Fulgentius (mythographer, 5th–6th cent. A.D.), *Mitologiae* 3.6: 114n; 3.7: 488n, 489n

Galen (medical writer, 2d cent. A.D.), *De Naturalibus Facultatibus* 3.10: 42n; *De Pulsuum Differentia* 2.3: 42n
Gallus, Gaius Cornelius (poet, 1st cent. B.C.): 433
Gellius, Aulus (grammarian, etc., 2d cent. A.D.), *Attic Nights* 5.14: 29n
Gregorios Kyprios (paroemiographer, 13th cent. A.D.), 3.46: 256n

Heliodoros (novelist, 3d cent. A.D.?), *Aethiopica* 1.9–17: 352n; 5.18: 197n; 8.9.9–15: 326n
Hellanikos (historian, 5th cent. B.C.), *FGH* 4 F 26b: 130n, 264n; 164: 165n
Herakleitos (philosopher, 1st cent. A.D.?), *Homeric Questions* 69: 423n
Hermippos (comic poet, 5th cent. B.C.), F 6: 260n
Herodotos (historian, 5th cent. B.C.), 1.6–13: 327n; 1.28–91: 327n; 1.30.2–3: 423n; 1.47.3: 99n, 327n; 1.84: 489n; 1.85.3–4: 327n; 1.86.2: 327n; 1.86.3–4: 327n; 1.87.1: 327n; 1.88.1: 327n; 1.91.6: 327n; 1.107–130: 414n; 1.123–126: 414n; 2.30: 66n; 2.32–33: 49n; 2.35–37: 445n; 2.121: 370n; 2.122: 371n; 2.124–135: 88n; 2.145: 136n; 2.148: 166n; 3.3.3: 445n; 3.17: 391n; 3.40–43: 190n; 3.102: 187n; 3.102–105: 474n; 3.113: 186n; 3.119: 66n; 4.201.2: 445n; 5.92.1: 445n; 6.86: 85n; 8.137–139: 424n; 8.143.2: 445n; 9.34: 469n
Hesiod (epic poet, 8th or 7th cent. B.C.), F 37: 469n; 43(b): 190n; 150: 49n; 208–209: 351n; 209: 130n; 261: 468n, 469n; 274: 28n; 298: 166n; 300: 489n; *Melampodia*: 469n; *Scutum (Shield)* 216–231: 130n; *Theogony* 31–32: 468n; 139–146: 300n; 250: 40n; 270–273: 251n; 280: 130n; 389, 397: 489n; 501–506: 300n; 507–520: 201n; 567: 284n; 570–590: 481n; 805: 489n; 956–962, 992–1002: 164n; *Works and Days* 42–44: 391n; 52: 284n; 60–82: 481n; 109–120: 391n; 166–173: 391n
Hesychios (lexicographer, 5th cent. A.D.), *Lexicon*: 260n; 488n
Hierokles and Philagrios (compilers of jokes, 4th cent. A.D.?): *see Philogelos*
Homer (epic poet, 8th cent. B.C.), *Iliad* 1.38: 62n; 2.104–105: 62n; 2.628–629: 166n; 2.799–801: 99n; 3.1–9: 49n; 5.638–651: 130n; 6.152: 408n; 6.152–202: 351n; 6.158: 245n; 7.452–453: 130n, 264n; 9.385–386: 99n; 9.430–484: 351n; 14.319–320: 130n; 18.375–377: 391n; 20.145–148: 130n; 21.276–278: 489n;

21.441–457: 130n, 264n; 22.359–360: 489n; 23.62–107: 94n; 24.603–617: 169n; *Odyssey*: 210n; 1.55: 211n; 1.74–75: 211n; 4.260–264: 176n; 4.271–289: 176n; 4.561–569: 391n; 5.13–15: 211n; 5.105–108: 211n; 5.127, 187: 468n; 7.36: 211n; 7.201–206: 222n; 7.259–266: 211n; 8.266–366: 279n; 8.492–520: 176n; 8.557–562: 211n; 9–12: 186n; 9.105–542: 300n; 9.107–115: 391n; 9.391–393: 301n; 9.408–411: 301n; 9.515–516: 300n; 10.1–76: 426n; 10.275–309: 29n, 331n; 11.100–103: 378n; 11.115–117: 211n; 11.121–134: 378n; 11.287–297: 469n; 11.321–325: 165n, 166n; 11.362–363: 301n; 11.447–449: 211n; 11.523–532: 176n; 11.582–592: 169n; 12.21–22: 435n; 12.70–72: 164n; 12.260–419: 391n; 12.374–388: 445n; 13.70–125: 211n; 13.86–87: 211n; 15.226–242: 469n; 17.301: 211n; 17.326–327: 211n; 17.481–487: 222n; 18.175–176: 211n; 18.250–270: 211n; 19.518–523: 305n; 19.530–534: 211n; 23.177–230: 232n; 23.248–284: 378n; 23.820–823: 489n; 24.327–344: 211n. Schol. on *Iliad* 1.38: 351n; 1.108: 56n; 1.180: 165n; 2.104: 351n; 2.105: 439n; 2.629: 166n; 4.376: 352n; 7.44: 468n; 9.429: 331n; 9.448: 351n; 23.821: 489n; *Odyssey* 5.121: 223n; 8.267: 423n; 11.122: 378n; 11.128: 378n; 11.130: 378n; 11.287: 468n; 11.322: 165n; 12.69: 352n; 19.518: 305n
Homeric Hymns (authors unknown, 7th cent. B.C. onward): *to Demeter* 231–281: 489n; 302–313: 314n; 303–333: 408n; *to Pan* 33–37: 136n
Horace (poet, 1st cent. B.C.), *Ars Poetica* 340: 30n; *Carmina* 3.11.22–27: 74n; *Epistles* 1.17.52–62: 404n; 2.1.47: 242n; 2.1.199–200: 42n; 2.3.139: 42n; *Epodes* 16.41–66: 391n; *Satires* 2.3.142–157: 438n
Hyginus (mythographer, 2d cent. A.D.?), *Fabulae* 1: 305n; 4: 305n; 12–25: 164n; 19: 352n; 30: 166n, 201n; 41–43: 165n; 47: 351n; 57: 351n; 64: 130n; 82: 169n; 84: 62n; 89: 130n, 264n; 95: 415n; 98: 56n; 107: 489n; 108: 176n; 125: 300n; 185: 165n; 195: 223n; 220: 481n; *Astronomica* 2.2: 351n; 2.3: 201n; 2.12: 251n; 2.16: 89n; 2.18: 351n
Hyperides (orator, 4th cent. B.C.), F 199: 85n

Iliu Persis (epic poem, 7th or 6th cent. B.C.?): 173–174
Inscriptions. Linear B: 166n; *IG* IV2, 1, no. 121–122 (VI–VII): 151n; *IG* IV2, 1, no. 121–122 (XXII): 439n
Irenaeus (ecclesiastical writer, 2d cent. A.D.), *Against Heresies* 2.11: 261n

Joannes Chrysostomos (ecclesiastical writer, 4th–5th cent. A.D.), *De Inani Gloria et de Educandis Liberis*: 30n
Josephos (historian, 1st cent. A.D.), *Antiquitates Judaicae* 2.39–59: 350n; 11.3: 423n; *Bellum Judaicum* 3.9.3: 130n

Julian (philosopher, 4th cent. A.D.), *Orationes* 7:
28n

Justin (scholar, 3d cent. A.D.?), *Epitoma Historiarum Philippicarum Pompei Trogi* 1.4–6: 414n;
18.3.6–16: 474n

Juvenal (satirist, 1st–2d cent. A.D.), *Satires*
6.363–364: 190n; 13.167–170: 49n

Kallimachos (poet, 4th–3d cent. B.C.), *Aitia*
F13–14: 49n; 98–99: 130n; *Hymns* 3.260–263:
56n; 5.75–136: 351n

Konon (historian, 1st cent. B.C.–1st cent. A.D.),
FGH 26 F 1 (24): 260n; (28): 351n; (35): 357n;
(38): 284n

Krates (comic poet, 5th cent. B.C.), F 16: 29n;
16–17: 390n; 25: 29n

Kratinos (comic poet, 5th cent. B.C.), F 63: 29n;
176: 390n

Ktesias (historian and medical writer, 5th–4th
cent. B.C.), *FGH* 688 F 45r: 186n

Kypria (epic poem, 7th–6th cent. B.C.?): 54; 414

Laberius, Decimus (composer of mimes, 2d–1st
cent. B.C.), *Bellonistria*: 352n

Lactantius Placidus, Pseudo– (scholar, 5th or
6th cent. A.D.), *Commentary on Statius's
Achilleis* 192: 165n; 1.93: 415n; 1.134, 269:
489n; *Thebais* 3.27: 223n; 3.516: 164n;
5.431–432: 438n; 7.255–257: 223n; 12.676:
165n

Libanios (rhetorician and sophist, 4th cent.
A.D.), *Orationes* 4.1101: 62n; 31.43: 30n

*Liber Junioris Philosophi in quo continetur Totius
Orbis Descriptio* (geographer, 4th cent. A.D.):
392n

Little Iliad (epic poem, 7th or 6th cent. B.C.?):
173–174

Livy (historian, 1st cent. B.C.–1st cent. A.D.),
Epitome 1.56: 284n; 20: 75n

Lucian (sophist, 2d cent. A.D.) and Pseudo–Lucian, *Adversus Indoctum* 4: 42n; *Contemplantes*
17: 97n; *De Domo* 30: 415n; *De Luctu* 16: 95n;
De Syria Dea 18: 66n; *Dialogues of the Sea Beings* (*Dialogi Marini*) 14: 130n; *Hermotimus* 79:
261n; 84: 99n; *Lover of Lies* (*Philopseudes*)
34–37: 38n; *Navigium* 11: 478n; 11–15: 142n;
16–46: 478n; 22: 142n; 42: 29n; *Quomodo Historia Conscribenda Sit* 23: 42n; *Saturnalia* 7:
390n, 391n; 8: 391n; 20: 390n; *Symposium* 23:
242n; *Toxaris* 61: 66n; *True Stories* (*Verae Historiae*) 1.1–53: 186n; 1.11: 186n; 1.12: 187n;
1.13–16: 187n; 1.16: 186n; 1.30–2.2: 264n;
1.40–42: 186n; 2.3: 187n; 2.3–16: 390n;
2.37–38: 186n; 2.40: 187n; 2.45: 187n

Lucilius (epigrammatist, 2d cent. B.C.): 328,
438n

Lycophron (poet, etc., 4th–3d cent. B.C.), *Alexandra* 31–37: 130n; 455–466: 489n; 468–478:
130n, 264n; 815–819: 415n; 834–841: 264n.
Schol. vetera 232: 351n

Makarios Chrysokephalos (paroemiographer,
14th cent. A.D.), 1.50: 92n; 3.97: 256n; 6.68:
44n

Martial (poet, 1st–2d cent. A.D.), *Epigrams* 13.2:
187n

Maximus of Tyre (sophist, 2d cent. A.D.),
Philosophumena 16.1: 401n

Metagenes (comic poet, 5th cent. B.C.), F 6: 390n

Myrtis (lyric poet, 6th–5th cent. B.C.): 341

New Testament (various authors, 1st cent. A.D.),
Acts 14.8–18: 222n; *1 Timothy* 4.7: 30n; *Romans*
6.2–4: 489n

Nicander (epic poet, 2d cent. B.C.), Schol. on
Nicander *Theriaca* 15: 223n

Nikarchos (epigrammatist, 1st cent. A.D.):
192–193

Nikolaos of Damascus (historian, 1st cent. B.C.),
FGH 90 F 47, 65, 68: 327n

Nikophon (comic poet, 5th–4th cent. B.C.), F 21:
390n

Nonnos (epic poet, 6th cent. A.D.), *Dionysiaca*
1.145–2.712: 314n; 1.427–438: 314n; 9.302–321:
305n; 13.96–103: 223n

Nostoi (epic poem, after 7th cent. B.C.), F 6:
165n; 10: 169n

Old Testament: see Septuagint

Oppian (epic poet, 2d cent. A.D.), *Halieutica*
1.620–625: 49n; 3.15–25: 314n

Ovid (poet, 1st cent. B.C.–1st cent. A.D.), *Amores*
1.8.5–6: 445n; *Ars Amatoria* 1.281–282: 352n;
1.341–342: 352n; 1.527–564: 165n; *Fasti*
5.493–544: 223n; 6.176: 49n; *Heroides* 4: 351n;
6: 164n; 10: 165n; 12: 164n; *Metamorphoses*
1.89–124: 391n; 1.291–310: 445n; 3.339–510:
260n; 4.285–388: 435n; 4.462–463: 74n;
4.663–5.235: 130n; 4.772–781: 251n; 5.220:
130n; 5.446–461: 223n; 7.1–403: 164n;
8.152–182: 165n; 8.174–179: 166n; 8.616–725:
223n; 8.738–878: 190n; 10.560–680: 165n;
11.199–217: 130n; 13.738–897: 40n;
15.479–551: 351n; 15.497–546: 351n; *Tristia*
1.8.1–10: 445n; 3.9: 164n. Schol. on *Ibis* 265,
271: 352n

Palaiphatos (mythographer, 4th cent. B.C.?), *De
Incredibilibus* 5: 223n; 31: 251n

Palatine Anthology: see Anthologia Palatina

Papyri. P. *Oxyrhynchus* 1382: 145n; P.
Oxyrhynchus 2944: 232n

Paraleipomena Jeremiou (author uncertain, 2d
cent. A.D.?), 3–6: 401n

Parthenios (mythographer, 1st cent. B.C.), *Narrationes Amatoriae* 14: 352n

Pausanias (travel writer, 2d cent. A.D.), *Graeciae
Descriptio* 1.2.6: 223n; 1.14.4: 401n; 1.22.1:
351n; 1.22.5: 165n; 1.23.8: 176n; 1.27.9: 438n;
1.41.4–5: 130n; 1.42.7: 130n; 2.26–28: 151n,
439n; 2.27.4: 351n; 2.32.1–4: 351n; 2.35.4:

223n; 4.35.9: 130n; 4.36.3–4: 469n; 5.1.9–10: 166n; 5.3.1: 166n; 5.17.7: 62n; 6.6.7–10: 130n; 6.21.6–11: 62n; 8.14.10–12: 62n; 8.18.7–8: 469n; 8.42: 408n; 8.44.4: 378n; 9.26.7: 130n; 9.31.7: 260n; 9.37.4–7: 371n; 9.39.5: 371n; 10.14.2–3: 351n; 10.29.1–2: 75n; 10.31.9–11: 74n

Persius (satirist, 1st cent. A.D.), *Saturae* 2.37–38: 29n; 6.79–80: 242n. Schol. on 5.116: 261n

Petronius (novelist and poet, 1st cent. A.D.), *Poems* 33 Rat: 434n–435n; *Satirica* 45.4: 390n; 45.9: 427n; 77.6: 145n; 79–80: 232n; 110.6–113.9: 279n; 111.2: 279n

Phaedrus (fabulist, 1st cent. B.C.–1st cent. A.D.), *Appendix Perottina*. 4: 222n; 15: 279n; *Fabulae* 1.4: 261n; 4.24: 42n; 5.6: 151n; 5.7: 234n; *Fabulae solutae* (PhS), Perry 563: 29n

Phainias (philosopher, 4th cent. B.C.), F 13: 40n

Pherekrates (comic poet, 5th cent. B.C.), F 113: 390n; 137: 390n

Pherekydes (historian, 5th cent. B.C.), *FGH* 3 F 11: 251n; 17: 201n; 33: 469n; 37a–b: 62n; 69: 489n; 119: 245n, 408n; 150: 166n

Philiskos (rhetorician, 5th–4th cent. B.C.): 229

Philo Judaeus (philosopher, 1st cent. B.C.–1st cent. A.D.), *De Josepho* 37–79: 350n

Philogelos (attributed to Hierokles and Philagrios, 4th cent. A.D.?), *Facetiae* 2: 241n; 9: 188n; 11: 260n; 12: 266n; 27: 438n; 33: 260n; 49: 243n; 56: 329n; 72: 197n; 96: 138n; 110–127: 266n; 148: 29n; 175: 266n; 206–210: 138n; 211–213: 431n; 222: 266n; 244, 245: 289n

Philostratos (sophist, 2d–3d cent. A.D.), *Vita Apollonii* 1.20: 469n; 3.15: 426n; 3.27: 391n; 3.38–40: 469n; 4.3: 469n; 4.10: 469n; 4.20: 469n; 4.45: 469n; 5.11–13: 469n; 5.18: 469n; 5.36–38: 469n; 5.42: 469n; 6.3: 352n; 6.43: 469n

Philostratos (sophist, 3d cent. A.D.), *Imagines* 1.15: 30n

Phlegon of Tralles (paradoxographer, 2d cent. A.D.), *De Mirabilibus* 1: 397n

Photios (ecclesiastical writer and scholar, 9th cent. A.D.), *Bibliotheca* 166: 147n; *Lexicon*: 28n, 79n, 447n

Physiologus Graecus (author uncertain, 2d–3d cent. A.D.?), 17: 186n

Pindar (lyric poet, 6th–5th cent. B.C.), *Isthmian* 6.47: 489n; *Nemean* 4.54–72: 130n; 4.57–61: 351n; 5.25–39: 351n; *Olympian* 1.23–89: 62n; 1.54–66: 166n; *Pythian* 4.159–162: 351n; 4.244: 264n; 8.95: 79n; 9.46–47: 99n; 10.24–42: 166n; 10.29–43: 391n; 11.17–25: 56n. Schol. on *Nem*. 4.54 (88): 351n; *Pyth*. 4: 164n; 4.162 (288): 351n

Plato (philosopher, 5th–4th cent. B.C.) and Pseudo–Plato, *Axiochus* 371e: 74n; *Euthydemus* 294b: 99n; *Gorgias* 493a–c: 74n; *Laws* 645b: 29n; *Menexenus* 248b–c: 95n; *Philebus* 14a: 29n; *Politicus* 272a–b: 391n; *Republic* 359d–360c: 29n, 327n; 363d: 74n; 377: 30n;

614b2: 301n; 621b: 28n; *Symposium* 219e: 489n; *Theaetetus* 164d: 29n. Schol. on *Gorgias* 497a: 260n; *Laws* 931b: 351n; *Minos* 321a: 165n; *Philebus* 14a: 28n; *Republic* 621b: 28n; *Theaetetus* 164d: 28n

Plautus (comic poet, 3d–2d cent. B.C.), *Menaechmi*: 451; *Miles Gloriosus*: 456; 79–155: 459n; 86–87: 459n; 249–255: 459n; 428–432: 460n; 770 ff.: 459n; *Pseudolus* 100–102: 74n; 369: 74n; *Rudens* 926–937: 142n

Pliny (encyclopedist, 1st cent. A.D.), *Natural History* 7.2.21: 186n; 7.26–27: 49n; 7.154, 175: 401n; 7.202: 176n; 8.21: 29n; 8.142: 92n; 9.2.4: 186n; 9.17.44: 186n; 10.137: 468n; 28.12: 75n; 29.72: 468n; 32.4.10: 186n; 35.129: 415n; 36.19: 166n

Plutarch (biographer and philosopher, 1st–2d cent. A.D.) and Pseudo–Plutarch, *Agesilaus* 36: 42n; *Alexander* 14: 431n; 64: 423n; *Cato Maior* 8: 423n; *De Fluviis* 3.1: 351n; *Demetrios* 27: 232n; *Ekloge* 4: 74n; 8: 74n; 17: 99n; 46: 74n; 50: 74n; *Moralia* 79a: 147n; 151: 99n; 153a: 423n; 153c–d: 423n; 157: 30n; 177a: 29n; 185d (10): 424n; 198d (3): 423n; 300d–f: 351n; 303a: 145n; 314a–b: 351n; 314b: 222n; 357: 489n; 419b–e: 135n; 509f–510a: 92n; 553e–f: 92n; 601c: 243n; 717a: 423n; 848a: 79n; 969c–d: 92n; 1040b: 260n; 1098b: 445n; *Proverbia Alex.* 50: 190n; 65: 260n; *Themistocles* 18: 424n; *Theseus* 17: 165n; 19–20: 166n; 23: 28n

Pollux, Julius (grammarian, 2d cent. A.D.), *Onomasticon* 9.74: 85n; 9.79: 142n

Polyainos (rhetorician, 2d cent. A.D.), *Strategemata* 6.22: 449n

Polybios (historian, 3d–2d cent. B.C.), *Histories* 12.6: 449n

Porphyry (philosopher, 3d cent. A.D.), *De Abstinentia* 3.3–3.4: 468n

Proklos (philosopher, 5th cent. A.D.), *Chrestomathia*: 56n; 176n; *Commentary on Plato's Republic* 2: 397n

Propertius (poet, 1st cent. B.C.), *Elegies* 2.3.51–54: 469n; 4.11: 95n

Pseudo–Kallisthenes: *see Alexander Romance*

Quintilian (rhetorician, 1st cent. A.D.), *Declamationes* 347: 210n

Quintus Smyrnaeus (epic poet, 3d or 4th cent. A.D.), *Posthomerica* 3.60–89: 489n; 12–13: 176n

Rhetorica ad Herennium (rhetorical handbook, 1st cent. B.C.), 1.8.13: 28n

Sappho (lyric poet, 7th–6th cent. B.C.), F 29: 187n

Seneca (philosopher and tragic poet, 1st cent. B.C.–1st cent. A.D.), *De Consolatione ad Marciam* 20: 445n; *Medea*: 164n; *Phaedra*: 351n; 943–949: 222n

Septuagint. *Amos* 9.13–15: 391n; *Deuteronomy* 22.22–27: 350n; 33: 351n; *1 Esdras* 3.1–5.6: 419, 423n; *Exodus* 3.8: 391n; 16.14–36: 391n; *Ezekiel* 47.12: 391n; *Genesis* 2.8–3.24: 391n; 3.12–14: 350n; 6.3: 392n; 13.14–16: 99n; 16: 223n; 17.7: 223n; 18: 331n; 18.1–16: 223n; 19.1–26: 223n; 21.1–4: 223n; 21.6: 223n; 22.15–17: 99n; 39.1–20: 350n; 49: 351n; *Ionas (Jonah)*: 264n; *Isaiah* 11.6–9, 65.25: 391n, 445n; *Joel* 3.17–18: 391n; *Judges* 13.24–16.31: 488n; *3 Kings* 3:16–28: 232n; *4 Kings* 3.21–25: 261n; 6.4–7: 44n; *Psalms* 113.3: 445n; *Tobit*: 62n; 6.1–5: 186n

Servius (grammarian, 4th–5th cent. A.D.), *Commentary on Vergil. Aeneid* 1.535: 223n; 1.550: 130n; 2.15: 176n; 2.81: 415n; 3.74: 165n; 3.209: 352n; 5.30: 130n; 6.14: 165n; 6.57: 489n; 6.445: 351n; 7.761: 351n; 8.157: 130n; 8.299–300: 166n; 10.763: 223n; *Eclogues* 4.34: 164n; *Georgics* 1.222: 165n; 3.7: 62n

Sextus Empiricus (philosopher, 2d–3d cent. A.D.), *Adversus Mathematicos* 1.68, 80: 242n; 3.80: 242n

Simonides (lyric poet, 6th–5th cent. B.C.): 62n

Sophocles (tragic poet, 5th cent. B.C.), *Antigone* 897–915: 66n; 968–980: 352n; *Electra* 563–576: 56n; *Odysseus Mainomenos*: 414; *Phaidra*: 351n; *Philoctetes* 622–625: 245n. Argument to *Aias* (author and date uncertain): 486. Schol. on *Antigone* 981: 352n

Statius, Caecilius (comic poet, 3d–2d cent. B.C.), *Ephebi*: 331–332

Statius, Publius Papinius (poet, 1st cent. A.D.), *Achilleis* 1.333–134, 267–271, 480–481: 489n; *Silvae* 5.3.152–153: 92n

Stephanos of Byzantium (grammarian, 6th cent. A.D.), *Ethnica*: 147n

Stesichoros (lyric poet, 7th–6th cent. B.C.), *Iliou Persis*: 176n

Stobaios (anthologist, 5th cent. A.D.), *Anthologium* 3.28.21: 284n

Strabo (geographer, 1st cent. B.C.–1st cent. A.D.), *Geographica* 1.2.8: 28n; 2.3.5: 147n; 6.1.5: 130n; 7.7.5: 135n; 10.5.6: 474n; 13.1.62–63: 62n; 17.1.33: 88n

Suda (lexicon, 10th cent. A.D.): 79n, 92n, 190n, 351n, 401n

Suetonius Tranquillus (biographer and scholar, 1st–2d cent. A.D.), *Iulius* 49: 423n; *Peri Blasphemion* 194: 260n

Telekleides (comic poet, 5th cent. B.C.), F 1: 390n

Tertullian (ecclesiastical writer, 2d cent. A.D.), *Adversus Valentianos* 2: 30n; 20: 445n

Testamenta XII Patriarcharum (2d cent. B.C.–3d cent. A.D.): 336

Themistios (philosopher and rhetorician, 4th cent. A.D.), *Orationes* 32.359c: 261n

Theognis (elegiac poet, 6th cent. B.C.), *Elegies* 699–718: 245n

Theokritos (bucolic poet, 4th–3d cent. B.C.), 1.132–136: 445n; 1.134: 445n; 2.42–46: 166n; 2.44–46: 165n; 11: 40n; 16.60–63: 99n; 25.54: 166n; 25.85–137: 166n. Schol. on 2.42–46: 166n; 2.45: 165n; 3.43: 468n, 469n

Theophrastos (philosopher, 4th–3d cent. B.C.), *Characters* 14: 194

Theopompos (historian, 4th cent. B.C.), *FGH* 115 F 67–69: 401n; 350: 62n

Tryphiodoros (epic poet, 3d or 5th cent. A.D.), *Halosis Iliou*: 176n

Tzetzes (poet and scholar, 12th cent. A.D.), *Chiliades* 2.278–290: 166n; 6.504–507: 351n; *Posthomerica* 629–723: 176n; *Schol. on Lycophron* 17: 351n; 34: 130n, 264n; 41: 166n; 175: 164n; 183: 56n; 328: 223n; 455–461: 489n; 930: 176n; 1329: 351n

Valerius Flaccus (poet, 1st cent. A.D.), *Argonautica*: 164n; 2.451–549: 264n; 2.451–578: 130n

Valerius Maximus (historian, 1st cent. A.D.), *Facta et Dicta Memorabilia* 1.7 *ext.* 3: 62n; 4.3 *ext.* 4: 431n; 7.3 *ext.* 1: 117n; 7.3 *ext.* 5: 429n; 8.1.5: 75n

Varro (poet, 1st cent. B.C.), *Sexagesis*: 402n

Vergil (poet, 1st cent. B.C.), *Aeneid* 2: 176n; 6.20–30: 165n; 7.761–782: 351n; *Eclogues* 1.59–64: 445n; 4: 391n; 8.17–60: 445n; *Georgics* 1.121–135: 391n

Vita Aesopi (author uncertain, 1st cent. A.D.), 7: 468n; 11–64: 240n; 39–41: 415n; 44–50: 53n; 47: 445n; 69–73: 99n; 101–123: 29n, 240n; 111: 187n; 116: 187n; 129: 279n; 131: 255n; 139: 92n

Vita Secundi (author uncertain, 2d cent. A.D.): 285

Xanthos (historian, 5th cent. B.C.), *FGH* 765: 327n

Xenophanes (philosopher, 6th–5th cent. B.C.), F 22: 28n

Xenophon (historian, 5th–4th cent. B.C.), *Cyropaedia* 1.6.19: 404n; *Oeconomicus* 7.40: 74n

Xenophon of Ephesos (novelist, 2d cent. A.D.?), *Ephesiaca* 2.2–2.10: 352n; 3.12: 352n; 4.2: 326n

Zenobios (paroemiographer, 2d cent. A.D.), 1.37: 92n; 1.53: 260n; 1.80: 99n; 2.1: 151n; 2.6: 75n; 2.33: 79n; 2.55: 351n; 2.60: 232n; 2.87: 351n; 3.92: 391n; 4.58: 99n; 4.92: 164n, 371n; 5.20: 130n; 5.42: 42n; 6.28: 79n

INDEX OF TALE TYPES AND MOTIFS

A. Tale Types

Tale Type		Entry
AT 113A	King of the Cats is Dead	Fairies Send a Message
AT 300	The Dragon Slayer	Dragon Slayer
AT 301A	Quest for a Vanished Princess	Quest for a Vanished Princess
AT 303	The Twins or Blood Brothers	Twins or Blood Brothers
AT 313C	The Girl as Helper in the Hero's Flight	Girl as Helper
AT 325*	Apprentice and Ghost	Apprentice and Ghost
AT 330A	The Smith and the Devil (Death)	Smith and the Devil
AT 335	Death's Messengers	Death's Messengers
AT 440	The Frog King or Iron Henry	Frog King
AT 503	The Gifts of the Little People	Gifts of the Little People
AT 508	The Bride Won in a Tournament	Bride Won in a Tournament
AT 510A	Cinderella	Cinderella
AT 581	The Magic Object and the Trolls	Magic Object and the Trolls
AT 650C	The Youth Who Bathed Himself in the Blood of a Dragon	Youth Who Bathed Himself in Blood
AT 654	The Three Brothers	Three Brothers
AT 673	The White Serpent's Flesh	White Serpent's Flesh
AT 710	Our Lady's Child	Our Lady's Child
AT 729	The Axe Falls into the Stream	Axe Falls into the Stream
AT 745	Hatch-Penny	Hatch-Penny
AT 750A	The Wishes	Hospitality Rewarded
AT 750B	Hospitality Rewarded	Hospitality Rewarded
AT 750*	Hospitality Blessed	Hospitality Rewarded
AT 766	The Seven Sleepers	Seven Sleepers
AT 769	Dead Child's Friendly Return to Parents	Dead Child's Friendly Return
AT 774K	Peter Stung by Bees	Peter Stung by Bees
AT 775*	God and the Emperor of Rome	God and the Emperor of Rome
AT 778	To Sacrifice a Giant Candle	To Sacrifice a Giant Candle
AT 823A*	Mother Dies of Fright When She Learns That She Was About to Commit Incest with Her Son	Mother Dies of Fright

AT 830A	*The Boastful Deer Slayer*	Boastful Deer Slayer
AT 845	*The Old Man and Death*	Old Man and Death
AT 854	*The Golden Ram*	Golden Ram
AT 870C*	*Stepmother Makes Love to Stepson*	Potiphar's Wife
AT 920	*The Son of the King (Solomon) and of the Smith*	Son of the King and of the Smith
AT 921B	*Best Friend, Worst Enemy*	Best Friend, Worst Enemy
AT 926	*Judgment of Solomon*	Judgment of Solomon
AT 928	*Planting for the Next Generation*	Planting for the Next Generation
AT 934A¹	*Threefold Death*	Threefold Death
AT 950	*Rhampsinitos*	Rhampsinitos
AT 960A	*The Cranes of Ibycus*	Cranes of Ibykos
AT 961B	*Money in the Stick*	Money in the Stick
AT 974	*The Homecoming Husband*	Homecoming Husband
AT 980C	*Dragging Old Man Only to Threshold*	Dragging Old Man Only to Threshold
AT 981	*Wisdom of Hidden Old Man Saves Kingdom*	Wisdom of Hidden Old Man Saves Kingdom
AT 985	*Brother Chosen Rather Than Husband or Son*	Brother Chosen Rather Than Husband
AT 1000–1029	*Labor Contract (Anger Bargain)*	Labor Contract
AT 1119	*The Ogre Kills His Own Children*	Ogre Kills His Own Children
AT 1137	*The Ogre Blinded (Polyphemos)*	Ogre Blinded
AT 1148B	*The Ogre Steals the Thunder's Instruments (Pipe, Sack, etc.)*	Ogre Steals the Thunder's Instruments
AT 1172*	*Devil to Count Stars*	Devil to Count Stars
AT 1174	*Making a Rope of Sand*	Making a Rope of Sand
AT 1191	*The Dog on the Bridge*	Dog on the Bridge
AT 1199	*The Lord's Prayer*	Lord's Prayer
AT 1200	*The Sowing of Salt*	Sowing of Salt
AT 1213*	*The Attentive Donkey*	Attentive Donkey
AT 1215	*The Miller, His Son, and the Ass: Trying to Please Everyone*	Carrying Part of the Load
AT 1242	*Loading the Wood*	Loading the Wood
AT 1242A	*Carrying Part of the Load*	Carrying Part of the Load
AT 1245	*Sunlight Carried in a Bag into the Windowless House*	Sunlight Carried in a Bag
AT 1248	*Tree Trunks Laid Crosswise of the Sledge*	Tree Trunks Laid Crosswise
AT 1261	*The Slaughter of the Ox*	Slaughter of the Ox
AT 1282	*House Burned Down to Rid It of Insects*	House Burned Down to Rid It of Insects
AT 1284	*Person Does Not Know Himself*	Person Does Not Know Himself
AT 1293*	*Learn to Swim*	Learn to Swim
Greek Folklore Archives *1298	*The Foolish Fugitives*	Foolish Fugitives
AT 1333	*The Shepherd Who Cried "Wolf!" Too Often*	Shepherd Who Cried "Wolf!"
AT 1334	*The Local Moon*	Local Moon
AT 1336A	*Man Does Not Recognize His Own Reflection in the Water (Mirror)*	Man Does Not Recognize His Own Reflection
AT 1362B*	*Marrying Man of Forty*	Marrying a Man of Forty
AT 1419C	*The Husband's One Good Eye Covered (Treated)*	Husband's One Good Eye Covered
AT 1419E	*Underground Passage to Paramour's House (Inclusa)*	Underground Passage to Paramour's House
AT 1419E*	*Husband Cannot Recognize Himself*	Underground Passage to Paramour's House
AT 1425	*Putting the Devil into Hell*	Maiden's Honor
AT 1464D*	*Nothing to Cook*	Nothing to Cook

AT 1510	*The Matron of Ephesus (Vidua)*	Matron of Ephesus
AT 1530	*Holding up the Rock*	Holding Up the Rock
AT 1542**	*The Maiden's Honor*	Maiden's Honor
AT 1566A*	*Maids Must Rise Even Earlier*	Maids Must Rise Even Earlier
AT 1567C	*Asking the Large Fish*	Asking the Large Fish
AT 1590	*The Trespasser's Defense*	Trespasser's Defense
AT 1591	*The Three Joint Depositors*	Three Joint Depositors
AT 1651A	*Fortune in Salt*	Fortune in Salt
AT 1681*	*Foolish Man Builds Aircastles*	Foolish Man Builds Aircastles
AT 1682	*The Groom Teaches His Horse to Live without Food*	Groom Teaches His Horse to Live without Food
AT 1698A	*Search for the Lost Animal*	Hearing-Impaired Persons
AT 1698F	*The Deaf Man and the Proud Nobleman*	Hearing-Impaired Persons
AT 1698G	*Misunderstood Words Lead to Comic Results*	Hearing-Impaired Persons
AT 1698J	*"Good Day"—"A Woodchopper"*	Hearing-Impaired Persons
AT 1861*	*Keep Your Seats!*	Keep Your Seats!
AT 1889F	*Frozen Words (Music) Thaw*	Frozen Words
AT 1889G	*Man Swallowed by Fish*	Man Swallowed by Fish
AT 1925	*Wishing Contests*	Wishing Contest
AT 1930	*Schlaraffenland*	Schlaraffenland
AT 1935	*Topsy-Turvy Land*	Topsy-Turvy Land
AT 1950	*The Three Lazy Ones*	Three Lazy Ones
AT 1960	*The Great Animal or Great Object*	Great Animal or Object
AT 1960B	*The Great Fish*	Great Animal or Object
AT 1960D	*The Great Vegetable*	Great Animal or Object
AT 1960G	*The Great Tree*	Great Animal or Object
AT 1960H	*The Great Ship*	Great Animal or Object
AT 1960J	*The Great Bird*	Great Animal or Object
AT 1960K	*The Great Loaf of Bread, the Great Cake, etc.*	Great Animal or Object
AT 1960L	*The Great Egg*	Great Animal or Object
AT 1960M	*The Great Insect*	Great Animal or Object
AT 1960Z	*Other Stories of Great Objects and the Like*	Great Animal or Object
AT 2031	*Stronger and Strongest*	Stronger and Strongest
AT 2031A	*The Esdras Chain: Stronger and Strongest*	Stronger and Strongest
AT 2200	*Catch-Tales*	Catch-Tale
AT 2250	*Unfinished Tales*	Unfinished Tale
AT 2401	*The Children Play at Hog Killing*	Children Play at Hog Killing
ML 3020	*Inexperienced Use of the Black Book*	Apprentice and Ghost
ML 6070A	*Fairies Send a Message*	Fairies Send a Message
ML 8005	*Heim til konens bryllup*	Homecoming Husband

B. Selected Motifs

	Motif	*Entry*
F171.6.2	*People in otherworld pour water into tub full of holes*	Carrying Water in a Sieve
F535.5.1	*War of pygmies and cranes*	Battles of the Pygmies and the Cranes
H256	*Test of innocence: apple and gold offered*	Children Play at Hog Killing
H1023.2.1	*Task: carrying water in a leaky vessel*	Carrying Water in a Sieve
H1102	*Task: cleaning Augean stable*	Girl as Helper
H1144.2	*Task: counting the waves*	Devil to Count Stars

J1155	*"Then I woke up": man discredits his confession by declaring it all a dream*	Unfinished Tale
J1761.1	*Whale thought to be island*	Great Animal or Object
J2071	*Three foolish wishes*	Hospitality Rewarded
K602	*"Noman"*	Ogre Blinded
K1082.1	*Missile thrown among enemies causes them to fight one another*	Girl as Helper
K2111	*Potiphar's wife*	Potiphar's Wife
N384.0.1.1	*The cadaver arm*	Rhampsinitos
R121.5	*Ariadne-thread*	Girl as Helper
Z311	*Achilles heel*	Youth Who Bathed Himself in Blood

GENERAL INDEX

Abauchas, 62–66
Abderites, 265
Abimelech, 400
Abraham, 56n, 62n, 98, 116, 218–219, 330
Achikar, 29n, 240n
Achilleus, 93–94, 97, 481–489
active bearer, 4–5
Adeimantos, 138–142
Aedon, 301–305
Aesop, 14, 49–54, 99, 183, 234–240, 251–255, 276, 415, 445n
Agamedes, 357–371
Agamemnon, 54–56
Aias (Ajax), 481–489
aircastles, 138–142
Aithiopians, 261n, 387–388
Akastos, 342
Akko, 257–261
Alcestis, 15
Alexander the Great, 114–117, 180, 430–431, 467–468, 473–474
Alkathous, 119–130
Amor (Eros, Cupid), 100–114
Amyntor, 342–343
Anagyros, 339–340
Androkles and the lion, 16
Andromeda, 119–130, 246–251
anecdote, 223–225, 233–234, 332
anger bargain, 234–240
animal: great, 176–187; resuscitated, 216–219; substituted for human being, 54–56, 114–117
animal tales, 15, 21
Antheus, 344
Antigone, 62–66
Anubis, 333–334
Aphrodite of Dexikreon, 142–145
Apollo, 98, 316–327; of the Vultures, 352–357

Apollonios of Tyana, 467
apothegm, 332
Apsyrtos, 346–347
Aqhat, 219
Archetimos of Erythraie, 279–284
Argonauts, 14, 166n, 427n
Ariadne, 151–166, 337
Aristippos, 347–348
Artemis, 53–56
Ascyltos, 227–232
Astymedousa, 343
Athamas, 340
Atlas, 197–201
Atreus, 437–438
Augean stables, 160–164
Augeias, 368–369
automata, 35–38, 388
axe falls into stream, 42–44

bag of winds, 301n
barber: talkative, 16; mischievous, 327–329
Bata, 333–334
Bear's Son, 300n, 352–357
Bellerophon, 341
Bessos, 91
bird, great, 183
boaster, impious, 54–56
Bokchoris of Egypt, 232
bride won in tournament, 56–62; see also princess: as prize
brother chosen, 62–66
Brutus, Lucius Junius, 279–284, 415
bundle of twigs, 14
buried treasure, 14

Caesar, Julius, 418–419
Camarini, 388–389

Cap of Hades, 248
carrying part of the load, 66–69
catch-tale, 75–79, 460–462
Cato, Marcus, 423n
cautionary tale, 224
chain, 415–424
Cheiron, 98
children play at butchering, 79–85
children's tales, 18
Cinderella, 85–89
clever: advocate, 427–429; judge, 227–232; old man, 469–472; seducer, 453–460; thief, 357–371
clever person: blinds ogre, 289–301; cleans stables with little effort, 160–164; enables lover to escape, 225–227; induces host to give him large fish, 38–40; outwits cruel master, 234–240; steals from the king's treasury, 357–371; substitutes animal for human being, 114–117; tricks Death, 243–246, 405–408
Cockaigne, land of, 378–392
Comminius, 338
comparative method, 24
conduit of transmission, 19, 373
conglomerate, 21, 35
contest: in laziness, 429–431; in riddling, 415–424; in wishing, 475–478
counting sand, stars, waves, 97–99
cranes: battle with Pygmies, 45–49; of Ibykos, 89–92
cumulative tale, 415–424
Cupid, 100–114
Cura, 478–481
curiosity, excessive, 37, 112

Daidalos, 158, 368–369
Damasippe, 339
Damocles' sword, 167
Damon, 443
Danaides, 69–75
Darius of Persia, 62–66
dead child's return, 92–95
deaf person, 190–197; and proud nobleman, 194–195
death: foretold, 14, 431–435; of Pan, 131–136; threefold, 431–435
Death: messengers of, 95–97; and old man, 314–316; outwitted, 243–246
deer slayer, boastful, 54–56
deluge, 11, 219–222
Demades the orator, 75–79
Demainete, 347–348
Demeter, 223n
Demodike, 340
Demosthenes, 75–79
depositor cheated, 279–284
devil (ogre) outwitted, 97–99, 114–117, 243–246
Dexikreon the shipowner, 142–145
diffusion, 2–4, 46
dilemma, 65–66
dilemma tale, 478–481

Diogenes the Cynic, 78, 430–431, 442, 446
Dionysios I of Syracuse, 38–40
Dionysos, 66–69, 460–462
discrimination test, 82–83
disenchanted husband, 100–114, 396
disguised deities, 212
dog: as best friend, 49–54; on the bridge, 114–117; drops his meat for the reflection, 257–261; faithful, 91
donkey, 66–69; attentive, 40–42; as auditor, 106, 110; equal to two mules, 264–266; shadow of, 77–78; wiggles his ears, 40–42
donkey driver, 114–117
donor, 17
dragging old man only to threshold, 117–119
dragon, 178, 199; teeth of, 155, 165n; slayer of, 119–130
dwarves attacked by large birds, 45–49

eagle, 86–88
Echedoros, 147–151
ecotype, 5, 141
Elysian Field, 385–386
Empedokles, 425
Encolpius, 227–232
enemy, worst, 49–54
Epimenides of Crete, 397–401
epimythium: defined, 255
Ereshkigal, 445n
Erysichthon, 189–190
Esdras chain, 419–423
Eteokles, 343
Eukrates, 35–38
Eunostos, 340–341
Eurybatos, 119–130
Euthymos, 119–130
extraordinary companions, 166n, 427n

fable, short, 41
fairies send a message, 131–136
fairy tales, 26n, 106
false hero, 119–130
first to see the sunrise, 472
fish: asking the large, 38–40; great, 178–181, 261–264
fish-island, 180–181
flood: *see* deluge
folktale: distinguished from legend, 2, 9, 25–26n, 157, 173, 274–275, 304, 357n; distinguished from myth, 26n; feminine, 106, 327n; as term, 7
food, great piece of, 184
fool: believes that each town has its own moon, 242–243; builds aircastles, 138–142; burns shirt to rid it of lice, 223–225; counts waves, 98; does not know himself, 327–329, 458–459; does not know how to undo magic spell, 35–38; does not recognize own reflection, 257–261; does not understand sexual intercourse, 251–255; kills the rooster that awakens mistress, 255; lays wood crosswise,

445–447; literal, 52, 237, 240n, 415; mathe-
matical, 264–266; plans to learn how to
swim before entering water, 240–241; pre-
tended, 280–283, 414–415, 425; sows salt,
414–415; trains horse to live without food,
187–188
foolish: fugitives, 136–138; hunter, 403; mistress,
403–404; shepherd, 402–404
forgotten bride, 151–166
formula: introductory, closing, 13
formula tale, 75–79, 415–424, 460–462
fortune in scarce commodity, 142–145
Fountain of Youth, 391n
friend: best friend, worst enemy, 49–54
frog king, 145
frozen words, 146–147

genre, oral, 2–3, 25–26n, 129
genre variance, 8–9, 16
ghost, 56–62, 69–75, 92–95, 392–397
Gidica, 338
gifts of the little people, 147–151
girl as helper, 151–166
Giton, 227–232
Glaukos the child, 14
Glaukos the Spartan, 83–84
golden: lamb, 437–438; ram, 169–176, 455
Golden Age, 378–392
Golden Fleece, 14, 154–157, 165n, 340
Gorgons, 246–251
Graiai, 246–251
Grateful Dead Man, 56–62
great animal or object, 176–187
grief, excessive, 92–95
Gripus, 138–142
Gyges, 13, 316–327

Habrokomes, 346–347
Hades' realm, 69–75, 109, 167–169
hatch-penny, 188–190
hearing-impaired person, 190–197
Hebros, 339
hecatomb promised, 436
Helen, 169–176
Helios, 443
Herakles, 14, 119–130, 151–166, 197–201, 263,
460–462, 485–488
hermaphrodite, 431–435
Hermaphroditos, 435n
Hermes, 217–218, 220, 305–314; and Charon, 96;
as donor, 17; as spokesman for divine justice,
329–331; and the woodcutter, 42–44
Hermon of Thasos, 438
Heros of Temesa, 127–128
Hippodameia, 56–62, 342
Hippolyte, 342
Hippolytos, 332–352
historic-geographic method, 5–6
holding up the rock, 197–201
homecoming husband, 201–211
Homo, 478–481

horse taught to live without food, 187–188
hospitality rewarded, 211–223
house burnt down to rid it of insects, 223–225
husband: cannot recognize himself, 453–460;
has his one good eye covered, 225–227;
homecoming, 201–211
Hyperboreans, 197–201
Hyrieus, 217–218, 369

Ibykos the poet, 89–92
Idaia, 344
identity test, 209–210
Illuyankas, 312–314
Inclusa, 453–460
index: motif-, 20, 30n; type-, 5, 20–23, 30n
independent invention: *see* polygenesis
Indo-European, 3–4, 8
inhospitality punished, 211–223
Ino, 301–305
insect, great, 184–185
Intaphrenes' wife, 62–66
interactive tale, 75–79, 460–462, 478–481
inversions, 439–445
Iphigeneia, 54–56
Ishtar, 443–444
Isis, 489n
Isles of the Blessed, 385–386
Itylos, 301–305

Jason, 151–166, 263
Jesus, 410
Jonah, 261–264
Joppa, capture of, 171–172
Joseph, 332–352
judgment of Solomon, 227–232
Jupiter (Zeus), 220, 478–481

Kadmos (Cadmus), 305–314
Kalasiris, 196–197
Kasandros, 339
Kinyras, 436
Kleoboia, 344
Knemon (Cnemon), 347–348
Koikylion, 99n
Koroibos, 98
Kretheus (Cretheus), 340
Kroisos (Croesus), 316–327
Kronos, 384–386, 440
Kyklops (Cyclops), 289–301, 386
Kyknos (Cygnus), 338
Kyno, 347
Kyros (Cyrus) of Persia, 408–414

labor contract, 234–240
Labyrinth, 157–160
Lamia, 18, 251n
land: of absurd abundance and ease, 378–392;
of dwarves, 45–49; of inversions, 45,
439–445
laziness, contest in, 429–431
learning to swim, 240–241

legend: distinguished from folktale, 2, 25n, 157, 173, 204, 274–275, 304, 350n, 357n; distinguished from myth, 26n, 212–122; relationship to international folktale, 15–16, 60, 85, 129, 211n; transmission of, 134; urban, 85n
loading the wood, 241–242
local moon, 242–243
Locrians, 447–450
Lord's Prayer, 243–246
Lot, 219–222
Lucian, 261–264
lying tale, 15, 21, 146–147, 176–187, 261–264, 378–392, 439–445; *see also* contest: in wishing; tale: tall

Machates, 392–397
magic: chair, 408n; coin, 188–190; flight, 151–166; object and the trolls, 246–251; ring, 13, 327n, 477; table, 390n
magic tale, 6–7, 17–18, 21, 26n; ancient analogues of, 13–15
magician: Pankrates, 35–38; Pases, 188–190
maiden's honor, 251–255
maids must rise even earlier, 255
Makareus the priest, 79–85
man: bitten by ants, 329–331; swallowed by fish, 130n, 261–264
Manto, 346–347
märchen: *see* folktale
marrying a man of forty, 264–266
mathematical humor, 264–266
Matron of Ephesus, 266–279, 287n
Medeia, 151–166
Melampous the seer, 462–469
Meleager, 245n, 301n
Menaechmi twins, 450–453
Menelaos, 169–176
Menestratos, 130n
mermaid, 489n
Mestra, 189–190
Mercury (Hermes), 88, 211–223
messengers, Death's, 95–97
migratory narratives, 4, 11, 168, 202
miles gloriosus, 453–460
miller, his son, and the ass, 66–69
Minos, 157–160, 371n, 437–438
Minotaur, 157–160
miraculous return, 207–209
misogynic tale, 266–279, 284–287
misunderstood words, 192–193
Mnesilochos, 226
Moabites, 257–261
money in the stick, 279–284
monogenesis, 2
monster in the bridal chamber, 62n
Moon asks for clothes, 18
mother dies of fright, 284–287
motif, 20–22, 30
mundus inversus, 439–445
Myrtilos, 56–62, 342

Myself, 295–296
myth, 11–12, 48, 88, 121, 168, 187n, 207, 282; distinguished from folktale and legend, 25–26n; Egyptian, 314n, 333–334, 489n; Hittite, 312–314; Mesopotamian, 443–445; Norse, 308–309, 463, 481–482

Narcissus, 257–261
narrator, 12, 75–79, 106, 110, 112, 226, 253–254, 272–277, 297–299, 327n, 460–462
Nine Heroes of Sardinia, 399–400
Nobody, 295–296
nothing to cook, 287–289
novella, 14–15, 21
numskull tales, 15, 21; *see also* fool

oath, deceptive, 447–450
object, great, 185
obstacle flight, 151–166
Ochne, 340–341
Odysseus: and the oar, 371–378; and Penelope, 201–211; and Polyphemos, 289–301; twice mortal, 434
Oedipus, 15, 343
ogre: blinded, 289–301; kills own children, 301–305; steals thunder instruments, 305–314
ogre's daughter, 151–166
oikotype: *see* ecotype
Oknos, 72–73
old man and Death, 314–316
oracle, 98, 107, 115, 122, 316–327
Orion, 217–218
Our Lady's Child, 316–327

Pan, 305–314; death of, 131–136
Pandaros, 147–151
Pandion, 344
Pankrates, 35–38
paradise, comic, 378–392
Pases the magician, 188–190
passive bearer, 4–5
Patroklos, 93–94
Peleus, 119–130, 342–343
Pelops, 56–62, 342
Penelope, 201–211
Perdikkes, 424–426
Perseus, 119–130, 246–251, 263
personal-experience narrative, 38
Petephres, 335–336
Peter: crucified upside down, 443; stung by bees, 329–331
Philoxenos the poet, 38–40
Phaidra (Phaedra), 332–352
Pharaoh, 86–88
Philemon and Baucis, 219–222
Philinnion, 392–397
Philonome, 338
Phineus, 344
Phobios, 344
Phoinix (Phoenix), 342–343

Phorkides, 246–251
Phrixos, 340
Phthia, 342–343
placating the storm, 264n
planting for the next generation, 331–332
Plexippos, 344
polygenesis, 2–4, 46
Polyidos the seer, 14
Polykrates' ring, 14, 190n
Polyneikes (Polynices), 343
Polyphemos, 289–301
Poseidon, 217–218, 371–378
Potiphar's wife, 332–352
Prince the flautist, 233–234
princess: as prize, 56–62, 119–130; rescued, 62n
Proitos, 341
proverb, 40–42, 69–75, 77–78, 90–91, 98, 139,
 145, 189, 261n, 297, 382, 404, 426–427,
 440–441, 445–447, 472–473
Psyche, 100–114
putting the devil into Hell, 251–255
Pygmies, 45–49, 232

quest: female, 100–114; male, 450–453; for a
 vanished princess, 352–357

rehearsed conversation, 195–197
religious narrative, 21, 54–56, 142–145, 147–151,
 167–169, 211–223, 329–331, 340–341, 352–357,
 371–378, 435–439
rescued princess, 62n
respite from death, 243–246
Rhampsinitos, 357–371
Rhodopis the courtesan, 85–89
riddle, 53n, 65, 415–424
ring, 397n; of Gyges, 13, 327n; magic, 477; of
 Polykrates, 14, 190n
rope of sand, 256–257

sacrifice of a giant candle, 435–439
sailor and the oar, 371–378
Sardis, 481–489
Saturn, 478–481
Schlaraffenland, 294–295, 378–392
seal woman, 489n
search for the lost animal, 191–192
Secundus the philosopher, 284–287
Seilenos, 461
Selene (Moon), 18
service in Hell, 392–397
Seven Sleepers, 397–401
sexagenarians from the bridge, 472–473
shepherd who cried "wolf!" 402–404
ship: great, 182–183; petrified, 301n
shirt burnt to rid it of lice, 223–225
Sibylline books, purchase of, 469n
Simonides the poet, 61
sisters, jealous, 100–114
Sisyphos: in the death realm, 72–73; outwits
 Thanatos, 243–246, 405–408, 434

slaughter of the ox, 404–405
smith and the Devil, 405–408
Solomon, 227–232
son of the king and of the smith, 408–414
sorcerer's apprentice, 35–38
sorites, 241–242, 330
Sosiklees of Corinth, 442
Sostratos, 348–349
sowing of salt, 414–415
Stheneboia, 341
stronger and strongest, 415–424
subtypes, 20, 113n, 128–129
sunlight carried in a bag, 424–426
supernatural: helper, 56–62; spouse, 100–114
sword, wondrous, 125–127
Syrion the mariner, 142–145

Table of the Sun, 387–388
taboo broken, 100–114, 151–166
tale: catch, 75–79, 460–462; cautionary, 224; chil-
 dren's, 18; cumulative, 415–424; dilemma,
 478–481; fairy, 26n, 106; formula, 75–79,
 415–424, 460–462; interactive, 75–79, 460–462,
 478–481; lying, 15, 21, 146–147, 176–187,
 261–264, 378–392, 439–445; tall, 15, 146–147,
 176–187; unfinished, 75–79, 460–462; *see also*
 folktale; magic tale; religious narrative
tale type, 5, 20–25
Tantalos, 167–169
tasks, impossible: carrying water in a sieve,
 69–75, 152; counting sand, stars, waves,
 97–99; making a rope of sand, 256–257; mis-
 cellaneous, 100–114, 151–166
Tellus, 478–481
Tenes, 338
test: of discrimination, 82–83; disguised, 232n;
 of honesty, 42–44; of identity, 209–210; of
 knowledge of sea, 371–378; of motherhood,
 227–232
Thanatos (Death), 243–246, 314–316, 405–408
Themisto, 301–305
Themistokles (Themistocles), 424n
Theseus, 151–166, 215, 337–338
Thetis, 481–489
thief, clever, 357–371
three: bodyguards, 419–423; brothers,
 426–427; joint depositors, 427–429; lazy
 ones, 429–431
threefold death, 431–435
Timasion, 346
Tityrus, 444
Tobias, 179
topsy-turvy land, 439–445
transformation flight, 151–166
treasury: of Augeias, 368–369; of Hyrieus, 369;
 of Rhampsinitos, 357–371
tree: great, 182; planted for next generation,
 331–332
tree trunks laid crosswise, 445–447
trespasser's defense, 447–450

trickster: induces dupe to hold up rock, 197–201; outwits king, 357–371; substitutes clay figurines for real thing, 436; Prometheus as, 199–201; tricks Death, 243–246, 405–408; tricks ogre into killing own children, 301–305
Trojan Horse, 169–176
Trophonios, 357–371
trying to wash black animal white, 261n
Tuccia, 73–75
two brothers, 450–453
type, 20–25; defined, 5
Typhon, 305–314
Tyrians, 469–475

underground passage to paramour's house, 453–460
unfinished tale, 75–79, 460–462
unsuccessful repetition, 44, 149
urban legend, 85n

vegetable, great, 181–182
Venus (Aphrodite), 88, 100–114
vow neglected, 435–439

wait till I am fat enough, 246n
what should I have said (done)? 197n
white serpent's flesh, 462–469
widow, inconstant, 266–279, 284–287
wife as worst enemy, 49–54
wisdom of hidden old man saves kingdom, 469–475
wishes, 212–215; contest in, 475–478; three, 212–215; unwise, 212–215
woman, lustful, 266–279, 287–289, 332–352
wonder tale: *see* magic tale
woodcutter, 42–44
wooden: doll, 478–481; horse, 166–176
Wooden John, 269–270

Xanthias the slave, 66–69, 460–462
Xanthos the philosopher, 49–54, 99, 234–240

youth: calumniated, 332–352; who bathed himself in blood, 481–489

Zeus, 167–169, 217–218, 220, 305–314

MYTH AND POETICS

A SERIES EDITED BY

GREGORY NAGY

After Antiquity: Greek Language, Myth, and Metaphor
by Margaret Alexiou

Helen of Troy and Her Shameless Phantom
by Norman Austin

Poetry in Speech: Orality and Homeric Discourse
by Egbert J. Bakker

The Craft of Poetic Speech in Ancient Greece
by Claude Calame, translated by Janice Orion

Masks of Dionysus
edited by Thomas H. Carpenter and Christopher A. Faraone

The Odyssey *in Athens: Myths of Cultural Origins*
by Erwin F. Cook

The Poetics of Supplication: Homer's Iliad *and* Odyssey
by Kevin Crotty

Poet and Hero in the Persian Book of Kings
by Olga M. Davidson

Gender and Genre in the Folklore of Middle India
by Joyce Burkhalter Flueckiger

The Ravenous Hyenas and the Wounded Sun: Myth and Ritual in Ancient India
by Stephanie W. Jamison

Poetry and Prophecy: The Beginnings of a Literary Tradition
edited by James L. Kugel

The Traffic in Praise: Pindar and the Poetics of Social Economy
by Leslie Kurke

Topographies of Hellenism: Mapping the Homeland
by Artemis Leontis

Mothers in Mourning
by Nicole Loraux, translated by Corinne Pache

Epic Singers and Oral Tradition
by Albert Bates Lord

The Singer Resumes the Tale
 by Albert Bates Lord, edited by Mary Louise Lord

The Language of Heroes: Speech and Performance in the Iliad
 by Richard P. Martin

Heroic Sagas and Ballads
 by Stephen A. Mitchell

The Anger of Achilles: Mênis in Greek Epic
 by Leonard Muellner

Greek Mythology and Poetics
 by Gregory Nagy

Myth and the Polis
 edited by Dora C. Pozzi and John M. Wickersham

Knowing Words: Wisdom and Cunning in the Classical Traditions of China and Greece
 by Lisa Raphals

Heroic Poets, Poetic Heroes: The Ethnography of Performance in an Arabic Oral Epic Tradition by Dwight Fletcher Reynolds

Homer and the Sacred City
 by Stephen Scully

Singers, Heroes, and Gods in the Odyssey by Charles Segal

The Mute Immortals Speak: Pre-Islamic Poetry and the Poetics of Ritual
 by Suzanne Pinckney Stetkevych

Phrasikleia: An Anthropology of Reading in Ancient Greece
 by Jesper Svenbro, translated by Janet E. Lloyd

The Swineherd and the Bow: Representations of Class in the "Odyssey"
 by William G. Thalmann

The Jewish Novel in the Ancient World
 by Lawrence M. Wills